Human Resource M

An Experiential Approach

Fifth Edition

H. JOHN BERNARDIN

Department of Management, International Business, and
Entrepreneurship
Florida Atlantic University

McGraw-Hill
Irwin

Boston   Burr Ridge, IL   Dubuque, IA   New York   San Francisco   St. Louis
Bangkok   Bogotá   Caracas   Kuala Lumpur   Lisbon   London   Madrid   Mexico City
Milan   Montreal   New Delhi   Santiago   Seoul   Singapore   Sydney   Taipei   Toronto

On August 19, 2003, a truck bomb killed United Nations official Sergio Vieira de Mello in Baghdad. As Francis Fukuyama put it, "the ineffectual efforts of American forces to save him were a harbinger of the larger American failure in Iraq." Before he tried to put Iraq back together after "mission accomplished," de Mello had served the U.N. heroically and honorably in postwar Vietnam, Lebanon, Cyprus, Cambodia, Bosnia, Rwanda, Kosovo, and East Timor. To date, not a single one of my students knew de Mello and his lifetime of efforts on behalf of war victims. I hope a few do now.

John Bernardin (November 10, 2008)

The **McGraw·Hill** Companies

HUMAN RESOURCE MANAGEMENT: AN EXPERIENTIAL APPROACH

Published by McGraw-Hill/Irwin, a business unit of The McGraw-Hill Companies, Inc., 1221 Avenue of the Americas, New York, NY, 10020. Copyright © 2010, 2007, 2003, 1998, 1993 by The McGraw-Hill Companies, Inc. All rights reserved. No part of this publication may be reproduced or distributed in any form or by any means, or stored in a database or retrieval system, without the prior written consent of The McGraw-Hill Companies, Inc., including, but not limited to, in any network or other electronic storage or transmission, or broadcast for distance learning.

Some ancillaries, including electronic and print components, may not be available to customers outside the United States.

This book is printed on acid-free paper.

2 3 4 5 6 7 8 9 0 WDQ/WDQ 14 13 12 11 10

ISBN 978-0-07-338143-5
MHID 0-07-338143-8

Vice president and editor-in-chief: *Brent Gordon*
Publisher: *Paul Ducham*
Managing developmental editor: *Laura Hurst Spell*
Editorial assistant: *Jane Beck*
Executive marketing manager: *Rhonda Seelinger*
Project manager: *Dana M. Pauley*
Full service project manager: *Meenakshi Venkat, Aptara®, Inc.*
Senior production supervisor: *Debra R. Sylvester*
Design coordinator: *Joanne Mennemeier*
Media project manager: *Suresh Babu, Hurix Systems Pvt. Ltd.*
Typeface: *10/12 Times Roman*
Compositor: *Aptara®, Inc.*
Printer: *Worldcolor Dubuque Inc.*

Library of Congress Cataloging-in-Publication Data

Bernardin, H. John.
    Human resource management: an experiential approach / H. John Bernardin.—5th ed.
      p. cm.
    Includes index.
    ISBN-13: 978-0-07-338143-5 (alk. paper)
    ISBN-10: 0-07-338143-8 (alk. paper)
    1. Personnel management—United States. I. Title.
HF5549.2.U5B456 2010
658.3—dc22
                                                    2008054848

About the Author

H. John Bernardin is the Stewart Distinguished Professor in the College of Business at Florida Atlantic University in Boca Raton. He earned his Ph.D in industrial/organizational psychology from Bowling Green State University and is the former director of doctoral studies in applied psychology at Virginia Tech. He is past Chair of the Division of Personnel/Human Resources of The Academy of Management. Dr. Bernardin has been editor of *Human Resource Management Review* and has served on the editorial boards of numerous journals, including the *Academy of Management Review, Human Resource Management Journal,* and the *Journal of Organizational Behavior.* He is the author of six books and over 100 articles related to human resource management. His paper on employment discrimination was cited as the best paper of the year by the Society of Human Resource Management. Dr. Bernardin has consulted for many of the most successful companies in the world and he has served as an expert witness in numerous employment discrimination lawsuits. He was denied stardom in the NHL because of that lame "no double runners" rule. A little known but not insignificant accomplishment may have been teaching Nicklas Lidstrom how to poke check.

Preface

The fifth edition of *Human Resource Management* continues with the dual goals of providing theoretical and experiential approaches to the study of human resource management while focusing on the enhancement of student competencies shown to be predictive of a student's ability to obtain and maintain employment. Students are given the conceptual background and content necessary to understand the relevant issues in HRM. In addition, they participate in individual and group exercises that require the application of chapter content to specific problems designed to develop critical personal competencies.

This new edition continues with the basic experiential approach, but changes have been made to improve the text. First, more emphasis is placed on the implications of HRM issues and policies for general managers who apply HRM policy but also who have a profound effect on the success or failure of HRM. Second, more attention is paid to the implications of HRM for small business, where all HRM functions may rest with personnel also performing a myriad of other small business activities and with no formal training in HRM. I continue to point out discrepancies between HRM findings from research and the practice of HRM. I am happy to report that many of these discrepancies are closing as more HR specialists become aware of research on "high-performance work systems" and the growing body of literature linking particular HRM practices to corporate success.

Perhaps the most important improvement in the book is in the writing. An extra effort has been made to simplify and improve the writing and the transitions from chapter to chapter. This text remains the only HR book that attempts to directly link student learning experiences in HRM with assessed competencies judged by experts to be essential for graduating business students. Research on college of business graduates has been critical of the readiness of business graduates for work, noting deficiencies in a number of areas, including communication skills, analytical thinking, decision-making ability, and leadership potential. While other experiential texts are available, this is the first to attempt to provide adequate coverage of the subject matter in each of the vital areas of HRM while preparing the student to "learn by doing." This is also the first attempt among HRM texts to provide a research-based methodology for the assessment of the critical competencies and to provide a process by which students may evaluate the extent to which they have improved their competencies as they progress through the course.

All the experiential exercises in this book were designed to enhance some or all of the critical personal competencies in the context of HRM subject matter. Participation in experiential exercises requires the application of the HRM knowledge expected of practicing managers and HR generalists. The experiential exercises were developed so as to facilitate greater learning through class interaction and projects. There is usually an individual writing component to the exercise followed by group interaction and consensus building. A study by Dr. Richard Light at Harvard University found that this approach to education is superior to other pedagogical options. While it may have something to do with the particular way I lecture, my 30 years of experience in teaching strongly support Dr. Light's research. Successful completion of these field-tested exercises, combined with the assessment processes described in Appendix C, should foster student development in all the areas experts believe to be critical in preparing business students for their first "real jobs."

Studies show that the majority of business graduates will ultimately manage or supervise employees. Research in this area shows that the two areas that prove to be the most challenging for managers are performance management and dealing with an increasingly diverse workforce in the context of equal employment opportunity law. My objective in this book is to emphasize knowledge and direct experience in these areas without compromising treatment of the other domains of HRM.

Procedures are available in this text to require students to evaluate their own performance and that of peer group members after completion of most of the experiential exercises. As discussed in Chapter 7 (Performance Management and Appraisal), this multirater approach provides more valid information about performance and a useful frame of reference for monitoring performance improvements. Research also shows that the more experience a person has had with the performance management process, the more effective that individual is in fulfilling this important managerial responsibility.

Exercises and discussion questions have been incorporated that require the student to consider equal employment opportunity laws in particular HRM contexts. So, unlike the standard HRM text that may cover EEO issues in one chapter, this book compels the student to weigh the EEO implications of HRM activities such as job analysis (Chapter 4), downsizing programs (Chapters 5 and 12), personnel selection processes (Chapter 6), employee training and development (Chapter 8), performance appraisal (Chapter 7), compensation (Chapters 10 and 11), and other major HRM activities.

The most significant and contentious issues of the day are considered head-on in this text. For example, among the controversial topics covered in experiential exercises are ethnic score differences on employee screening devices, affirmative action programs and preferential treatment, the outsourcing of work overseas, binding arbitration agreements, illegal immigration, sexual harassment policies, employment-at-will, random drug testing with no probable cause, smoking in the workplace, CEO and executive compensation, equal pay for work of comparable worth, and labor relations legislation.

Another distinctive feature of this book is that drafts of some chapters were written by experts in the HRM field. Experts were selected on the basis of their experience, knowledge, and research accomplishments in a particular area of HRM and/or their experience with well-tested, experiential exercises that foster learning in a critical HRM content area. Since HRM is strongly influenced by a number of disciplines (e.g., law, economics, psychology, sociology, strategic management), expertise was sought to represent these varied orientations. I believe the finished product represents a broader perspective than a book prepared by an author from only one of those disciplines. I am grateful to Christine Hagan (University of Miami) and Joyce Russell (University of Maryland) for their outstanding chapters.

New "Critical Thinking Applications" (Appendix A) that concern some of the most important and timely issues of the day also have been added. Interwoven in each chapter of the book is an underlying theme of improving quality and increasing competitive advantage with more effective HRM practices compatible with the new research on "high-performance work systems."

A major improvement in this edition is the development of accessory Web-based exercises and critical thinking applications that students can now complete through the Web site for the book. The major benefits of this change are the immediate feedback that students receive once they complete the on-line test or questionnaire and the elimination of erroneous score derivations that seemed to occur at a disturbing rate when students derived their own scores. This innovation will also facilitate the more frequent updating of norms for those tests or questionnaires that require norm-based interpretation.

Acknowledgments

A number of people have made valuable contributions to this book. First, we would like to thank the various editors and staff members with whom we have worked at McGraw-Hill. We also would like to acknowledge the many reviewers from various universities and colleges who provided helpful comments and suggestions: Karen Preston, Harry Schwartz, Barry Axe, Florida Atlantic University; Steven E. Abraham, State University of New York at Oswego; Debra A. Arvanites, Villanova University; Dan Braunstein, Oakland University; Cheryl Head, Central Piedmont Community College; Laura Alderson, University of Memphis; Michelle Alarcon, Hawaii Pacific University; Susan Jespersen, Walden University; Herschel N. Chait, Indiana State University; Joan G. Dahl, California State

University, Northridge; Randy L. DeSimone, Rhode Island College; William L. Eslin, Glassboro State College; John Fielding, Roger Williams University; Robert Figler, University of Akron; Cynthia Fukami, University of Denver; David Gilmore, University of North Carolina–Charlotte; Roger Griffith, Georgia State University; Nancy Johnson, University of Kentucky; John Kammeyer-Mueller, University of Florida; Katherine Karl, Western Michigan University; John F. P. Konarski, Florida International University; Jack Kondrasuk, University of Portland; Jacqueline Landau, Suffolk University; Robert M. Madigan, Virginia Polytechnic Institute; A. Amin Mohamed, Indiana University of Pennsylvania; Herff L. Moore, University of Central Arkansas; Joseph Morrell, Aquinas College; Paul Poppler, Bellvue University; James S. Russell, Lewis and Clark College; Janet Stern Solomon, Towson State University; Lee Stepina, Florida State University; Charles M. Vance, Loyola Marymount University; Susan C. Wajert, College of Mount St. Joseph; Richard A. Wald, Eastern Washington University; Elizabeth C. Wesman, Syracuse University; Kenneth M. York, Oakland University; and Mary D. Zalesny, University of Missouri–St. Louis.

Contributors of chapters or portions of chapters were Stephanic Thomason, Jennifer Robin, David O. Ulrich, Joyce E. A. Russell, Barbara A. Lee, Scott A. Snell, Chris Hagan, Monica Favia, Michael M. Harris, Barbara K. Brown, Joan E. Pynes, P. Christopher Earley, Diana Deadrick, Philip J. Decker, Barry R. Nathan, Jeffrey S. Kane, Sabrine Maetzke, Lee P. Stepina, James R. Harris, Alan Cabelly, E. Brian Peach, M. Ronald Buckley, Nancy Brown Johnson, Joseph G. Clark Jr., Roger L. Cole, Harriette S. McCaul, Fred E. Schuster, Thomas Becker, Susan M. Stewart, and Peter Villanova. Contributors of experiential exercises were Sue A. Dahmus, Jeffrey D. Kudisch, Jennifer Collins, David Herst, Barry Axe, Marilyn A. Perkins, Lori Spina, Jarold Abbott, Mary E. Wilson, Joan E. Pynes, Peter Villanova, M. Ronald Buckley, Robert W. Eder, J. R. Biddle, Patrick Wright, James A. Breaugh, Barbara Hassell, Lee P. Stepina, James R. Harris, Jeffrey S. Kane, Richard Peters, Roger L. Cole, Christine M. Hagan, Scott A. Snell, Ann M. Herd, Larry A. Pace, Caroline C. Wilhelm, Sheila Kennelly-McGinnis, Stephanie D. Myers, Paul Guglielmino, Lucy Guglielmino, Fred E. Schuster, E. Brian Peach, Brenda E. Richey, Steven M. Barnard, Steve Long, Lillian T. Eby, Jennifer Robin, Sharon L. Wagner, Richard G. Moffett III, Catherine M. Westerberry, Esther J. Long, Joseph G. Clark Jr., Susan M. Stewart, Nancy Brown Johnson, Karen Preston, and Renee Bartlett.

Many colleagues have provided assistance on this edition—by contributing their comments on earlier drafts, reviewing exercises, or furnishing extensive reference materials. I appreciate the efforts of Jennifer Robin, Joseph Clark, Stephen H. Gaby, Lynn B. Curtis, Laura A. Davenport, Aaron T. Fausz, David Herst, Jeffrey D. Kudisch, Ann Rigel, and (especially) Christine Hagan, Renee Bartlett, and Stephanie Thomason.

John Bernardin

Brief Table of Contents

Table of Contents

Part 2   Acquiring Human Resource Capability   87

Part 3   Developing Human Resource Capability   217

Chapter 7   Performance Management and Appraisal   219

Chapter 8   Training and Development   245

Chapter 9   Career Development   293

*The test or questionnaire component of these exercises is available online at the
book's Web site (www.mhhe.com/bernardin5e).

*The test or questionnaire component of these exercises is available online at the
book's Web site (www.mhhe.com/bernardin5e).

**The questionnaire for this exercise is available online at
www.mhhe.com/bernardin5e

Part 1

Human Resource Management and the Environment

Chapter

1

Strategic Human Resource Management in a Changing Environment

OBJECTIVES

After reading this chapter, you should be able to

1. Describe the field of human resource management (HRM) and its potential for creating and sustaining competitive advantage.
2. Describe discrepancies between actual HRM practices and recommendations for HRM practice based on scholarly research.
3. Describe the major activities of HRM.
4. Explain important trends relevant to HRM, including the increasing globalization of the economy, changing technology, the role of regulations and lawsuits, the changing demographics of the workforce, and the growing body of research linking particular HRM practices to corporate performance.
5. Emphasize the importance of measurement for effective and strategic HRM.
6. Understand what is meant by competitive advantage, and what the four mechanisms are for offering and maintaining uniqueness.

OVERVIEW

In the 2008 presidential campaign, the *Los Angeles Times* ran an assessment of the two major presidential candidates' fitness for office based on an analysis of their handwriting known as graphology. According to graphologist Paul Sassi, the fluidity of Barack Obama's signature is a sign of high intelligence, while its illegibility shows he is protecting his privacy. "He doesn't want you to know him too well." Another handwriting expert concluded: "The large letters in Obama's signature show that he is ambitious, self-confident, and views himself as a leader. . . . The fluid letter forms reveal that he can form a coalition, be diplomatic, and get along with both sides of the aisle." She added: "He's the type of guy who could tell you to go to hell and you'd enjoy the trip." Another graphologist concluded that John McCain is proud but has a volatile temper, that he is a very accommodating person and will go out of his way to compromise and even yield up his own will, and that he tends to gloss over details and leaves too much to others. The graphologist thought he might sign agreements contrary to American interests.[1]

When I shared theses assessments with undergraduate human resources classes, about 25 percent of students thought the evaluations were "dead on accurate," another 25 percent described the profiles as "mostly accurate," about 20 percent thought they were "completely inaccurate," and about 30 percent had no opinion at all on the accuracy of the profiles. Within the last group, however, about half the students expressed great skepticism about assessing someone's personality, intelligence, motivation, or anything else important using the person's handwriting. It is this group of students who are "dead-on accurate." Research clearly shows that handwriting is not a valid means of assessing anything important (except your handwriting!).

The assessment of presidential candidates is not the only application you will find of such invalid assessment methods. *Inc.* magazine, one of the most popular magazines for U.S. small business, ran a story extolling the benefits of using graphology to hire managers.[2] The article reported that the use of graphology was on the increase and that the method was very effective for selecting managers and salespersons. Sound research in human resource management (HRM) has determined that companies would do just about as well picking names out of a hat to make personnel decisions.

Major HRM responsibilities

Skilled HRM specialists help organizations with all activities related to staffing and maintaining an effective workforce. Major HRM responsibilities include work design and job analysis, training and development, recruiting, compensation, team-building, performance management and appraisal, and worker health and safety issues, as well as identifying and developing valid methods for selecting staff.

Research by academics who study and teach HRM is devoted to identifying the most effective and efficient methods for meeting these HRM responsibilities. A recurring theme of this book is that the most effective HRM programs, policies, and practices are those that are developed in deference to such research in HRM. One theme of this book is that practicing HRM often ignores the sound research about policy, practice, or people that is available to help make decisions. Instead, organizations are apt to adopt an HRM procedure merely because competitors are using it (this was a main theme of the *Inc.* article about graphology).

The author once had a conversation with a business owner who had hired his 145-person sales staff based on graphology reports (at $75 per report) and the answer to a single question posed in an interview. When questioned about the validity of these methods, the business owner described one terrible salesman he had hired out of desperation in a tight labor market despite a graphologist's report that said the "small writing with little slant indicated he may be too introverted for sales work." This one example had stuck in his mind as "proof" of graphology's effectiveness. He lamented, "If only I had listened to the handwriting expert. I wasted a bundle training the guy!" Those of us who teach statistics refer to this type of "research" as a "man who statistic." When you discuss the overwhelming evidence showing that smoking causes cancer, someone might offer the counterargument that "I knew a man who smoked three packs a day and lived to be 90." An article in the *Washington Post* reported that the Pilot Pen Company's CEO Ronald Shaw was a big believer in graphology and would use it for all hiring decisions because the graphologist's profile based on his own handwriting showed he was "sincere and intelligent and had a lot of integrity."[3] While (apparently) flattery will get you somewhere, graphology will not get you accurate or valid assessments of personal characteristics related to job performance. Needless to say, this is not the way to do research on a procedure.

Sound measurement is critical to effective HR

There are good ways to do research and good ways to assess the effects of programs, procedures, and activities of HRM. Sound measurement is a key to effective management. Remember the old adage: if it's not measured, it's not managed. Graphology has been the subject of sound research looking at how well it predicts performance. It doesn't. There are many methods that do accurately predict performance. Effective HRM means decision makers are aware of these methods and use them. Ineffective HRM means management is either unaware of what really works and/or doesn't use them.

Many HRM systems and activities are not subjected to systematic measurement. Many organizations do not assess either the short- or long-term consequences of their HRM programs or activities. A recurring theme of the book is that measurement and accountability are key components to organizational effectiveness and competitive advantage. Good measurement, allied with business strategies, will help organizations select and improve all of their HRM activities and provide a much stronger connection between HRM activities and organizational effectiveness.

Stanford University professor Jeffrey Pfeffer considers measurement to be one of the keys to competitive advantage. His book *Competitive Advantage Through People* cites measurement

The Balanced Scorecard

[handwritten: measurement →]

The Workforce Scorecard

Lagging and leading indicators

The vision of HRM for the 21st century

[handwritten:
1. Responsive to market
2. linked to bus. plans
3. Line+HR man. ownership
4. focus on quality, CS
*   etc.]*

Keep mission in mind

as one of the 16 HRM practices that contribute the most to competitive advantage.[4] Pfeffer's views were echoed and expanded in the popular text *The Balanced Scorecard* by Harvard professor Robert Kaplan and consultant David Norton.[5] Kaplan and Norton stress that "if companies are to survive and prosper in information age competition, they must use measurement and management systems derived from their strategies and capabilities" (p. 21). Their "balanced scorecard" emphasizes much more management attention to "leading indicators" of performance that predict the "lagging" financial performance measures. The "balance" reflects the need to measure short- and long-term objectives, financial and nonfinancial measures, lagging and leading indicators, and internal and external performance perspectives.

In their book *The Workforce Scorecard*, Professors Mark Huselid, Brian Becker, and Dick Beatty extend research on the "balanced scorecard" to a comprehensive management and measurement system to maximize workforce potential.[6] These authors show that the traditional financial performance measures such as return on equity, stock price, and return on investment, the "lagging indicators," can be predicted by the way companies conduct their HR. HR practices are the "leading indicators" that predict subsequent financial performance measures. Unfortunately, research indicates that only a small percentage of HRM programs or activities are subjected to analysis. The good news, however, is that the percentage is at least going up. Measurement is essential for American business in the 21st century!

One prophetic study defined the vision of human resource management for the 21st century. HRM activities must be (1) responsive to a highly competitive marketplace and global business structures, (2) closely linked to business strategic plans, (3) jointly conceived and implemented by line and HR managers, and (4) focused on quality, customer service, productivity, employee involvement, teamwork, and workforce flexibility.[7]

The status of HRM is improving relative to other potential sources of competitive advantage for an organization. Professor Pfeffer notes that "traditional sources of success (e.g., speed to market, financial, technological) can still provide competitive leverage, but to a lesser degree now than in the past, leaving organizational culture and capabilities, derived from how people are managed, as comparatively more vital."[8]

You are likely to manage people at some point in your career. Research shows that the manner in which you conduct the human resource responsibilities of your management job will be a key to your effectiveness. We believe that the knowledge and experiences provided by this book will make you a more effective manager. The thesis of this book is that the most effective HRM programs, policies, and practices are those that keep the organization's mission and strategic plan in mind. All HRM activities should be evaluated in this context, using "leading indicator" performance measures.

WHAT IS HUMAN RESOURCE MANAGEMENT?

The human resources of an organization consist of all people who perform its activities. In a sense, all decisions that affect the workforce concern the organization's HRM function. Human resource management concerns the personnel policies and managerial practices and systems that influence the workforce. Regardless of the size—or existence—of a formal HRM or Personnel Department (many small businesses have no HRM department), the activities involved in HRM are pervasive throughout the organization. Line managers, for example, will spend more than 50 percent of their time involved in human resource activities such as hiring, evaluating, disciplining, and scheduling employees.

Line managers and HRM

The effectiveness with which line management performs HRM functions with the tools, data, and processes provided by HRM specialists is the key to competitive advantage through HRM. This principle generalizes from very small businesses to the very largest global enterprises. Dr. James Spina, former head of executive development at the Tribune Company, really put things in perspective about the role of HRM. He said, "The HRM focus should always be maintaining and, ideally, expanding the customer base while maintaining and, ideally, maximizing profit. HRM has a whole lot to do with this focus regardless of the size of the business, or the products or services you are trying to sell."

Those individuals classified within an HRM functional unit provide important products and services for the organization. These products and services may include the provision of, or recommendation for, systems or processes that facilitate organizational restructuring, job design, personnel planning, recruitment, hiring, evaluating, training, developing, promoting, compensating, and terminating personnel. A major goal of this book is to provide information and experiences that will improve the student's future involvement and effectiveness in HRM activities.

While HR can create and sustain competitive advantage, some would argue that HR as it is practiced is often more a weakness than a strength. A recent survey found that only 40 percent of employees thought their companies were doing a good job retaining high-quality workers and only 41 percent thought performance evaluations were fair. A mere 58 percent of respondents reported their job training as favorable. A majority said they had few opportunities for advancement and they had little idea about how to advance in the first place. Only about half of those surveyed below the managerial level believed their companies took a genuine interest in their well-being.[9]

HRM and Corporate Performance

High-performance work systems

A growing body of research shows that progressive HRM practices can have a significant effect on corporate performance. Studies now document the relationship between specific HR practices and critical outcome measures such as corporate financial performance, productivity, product and service quality, and cost control. Many of the methods characterizing these so-called high-performance work systems (HPWS) have been researched and developed by the HRM academic community. Figure 1-1 presents a summary of this research.

HPWS comprises HR practices or characteristics designed to enhance employees' competencies and productivity so that employees can be a reliable source of competitive advantage. They have been called "coherent practices that enhance the skills of the workforce, participation in decision making, and motivation to put forth discretionary effort." Research shows that "firm competitiveness can be enhanced by high-performance work systems." A summary of this research found that one standard deviation of improved assessment on an HPWS measurement tool increased sales per employee in excess of $15,000, an 8 percent gain in labor productivity.[10]

Validation

Recall the critical remarks earlier about graphology, or handwriting analysis. Validated selection and promotion systems are related to higher productivity and reduced costs (see Figure 1-1). The term *validated* means that the method has actually been shown to predict something important. If you're using a method to select managers or sales personnel, a "validated" method is a method shown to actually predict managerial or sales success. While graphology is no way to assess personality attributes, there are highly valid methods and procedures for predicting future employee performance based on the assessed personal characteristics of job candidates.

Better training and development programs and team-based work configurations improve performance and job satisfaction and decrease employee turnover. Particular incentive and

---

Figure 1-1
Characteristics of High-Performance Work Systems (HPWS)
- Large number of highly qualified applicants for each strategic position.
- The use of validated selection and promotion models/procedures.
- Extensive training and development of new employees.
- The use of formal performance appraisal and management.
- The use of multisource (360 degree) performance appraisal and feedback.
- Linkage of merit increases to formal appraisal processes.
- Above-market compensation for key positions.
- High percentage of entire workforce included in incentive systems.
- High differential in pay between high and low performers.
- High percentage of workforce working in self-managed, project-based work teams.
- Low percentage of employees covered by union contract.
- High percentage of jobs filled from within.

Source: Reprinted by permission of Harvard Business School Press. *The HR Scorecard*, by B. Becker and M. Ulrich (Boston: Harvard Business School Press, 2001). All rights reserved.

compensation systems also translate into higher productivity and performance. The fair treatment of employees results in higher job satisfaction, which in turn facilitates higher performance, lower employee turnover, reduced costs, and a lower likelihood of successful union organizing.

Greater demands are now being made on HRM practitioners to respond to contemporary trends in the business environment. Today, the most effective HRM functions are conceptualized in a business capacity, constantly focusing on the strategy of the organization and the core competencies of the organization. HRM specialists must show how they can make a difference for the company's bottom line. Costs and efficiencies are necessary criteria for evaluating recommendations from research in HRM.

Focus on core competencies

Many corporate strategy specialists maintain that the key to sustained competitive advantage is building and sustaining core competencies within the organization and maintaining flexibility in order to react quickly to the changing global marketplace and the advances in technology. One primary role of HRM practitioners should be to facilitate this process.

DISCREPANCIES BETWEEN ACADEMIC RESEARCH AND HRM PRACTICE

SHRM

While HRM executives and managers are more educated and professional than in the days when they were in charge of personnel, the level of knowledge in practicing HRM is another story. Many companies hire MBAs for HRM jobs when not even a single HRM course is required in the typical curriculum for an MBA. The 190,000-member Society for Human Resource Management (SHRM, see www.SHRM.org), which established the Human Resource Certification Institute, formally recognizes human resource professionals who have demonstrated particular expertise in HR. As of 2009, over 75,000 HR professionals hold the Professional in Human Resources (PHR), the Senior Professional in Human Resources (SPHR), and the Global Professional in Human Resources (GPHR) designation.

HRM practitioners need to pay more attention to academic research. There is a great deal of carefully crafted academic research that is highly relevant to HRM practice. Figure 1-2 presents a few examples of discrepancies between the current state of HR practice and

---

Figure 1-2	Sample of Discrepancies between Academic Research Findings and HRM Practices
Academic Research Findings	**HRM Practice**

RECRUITMENT

Quantitative analysis of recruitment sources using yield ratios can facilitate efficiencies in recruitment.	Less than 15% calculate yield ratios. Less than 28% know how.

STAFFING

Realistic job previews can reduce turnover.	Less than 20% of companies use RJPs in high-turnover jobs.
Weighted application blanks reduce turnover.	Less than 35% know what a WAB is; less than 5% use WABs.
Structured and behavioral interviews are more valid.	40% of companies use structured interviews. Less than 50% use behavioral interviews.
Use actuarial model of prediction with multiple valid measures.	Less than 5% use actuarial model.
Graphology is invalid and should not be used.	Use is on the increase in the United States.

PERFORMANCE APPRAISAL

Do not use traits on rating forms.	More than 70% still use traits.
Train raters (for accuracy, observation bias).	Less than 30% train raters.
Make appraisal process important element of manager's job.	Less than 35% of managers are evaluated on performance appraisal.

COMPENSATION

Merit-based systems should not be tied into a base salary.	More than 75% tie merit pay into base pay.
Gain sharing is an effective PFP system.	Less than 5% of companies use it where they could.

Source: H. J. Bernardin (2009), "A Survey of Human Resource Practices: Discrepancies Between Research and HRM Practice." Paper presented at the annual meeting of Applied Psychologists.

"Knowledge gap"

Actual practice vs. what should happen.

outsourcing

what the academic literature clearly recommends. One study reinforced this "knowledge gap."[11] HR professionals were given a 35-item test that assessed the extent of their HR knowledge. The test was scored on findings from academic research, which would likely be covered in any basic HR course like this one. Items were developed where there was little or no argument on the correct answer within the academic community. The average grade for the nearly 1,000 HR professionals was "D." On numerous items, over 50 percent of the HR professionals got the answer wrong!

Throughout the book, we intend to emphasize the most glaring discrepancies between the way HRM is actually being practiced and what academic research has to say about particular practices. The failure on the part of practicing HRM personnel to either be aware of the research or understand it is a problem that can have a profound effect on an organization's bottom line, such as return on equity, profit, profit growth, and stock price. Although line management plays a critical role in the successful implementation and execution of HRM programs, these programs are typically either developed or purchased by HRM specialists.

Many HR activities such as payroll, recruitment, and pre-employment screening are now outsourced to organizations that specialize in these areas. The number of consulting organizations specializing in HR activities has increased substantially in the last 10 years. There are now Web-based HR products and services in almost every major functional area and full-service HR online department. An organization's HR specialist must have the necessary knowledge and skills to be able to identify the best and most cost-effective of these HR products and services for a particular situation.

HRM professionals should possess up-to-date knowledge about the relative effectiveness of the various programs and activities related to HR planning, training and development, compensation, performance management, selection, information systems, equal employment opportunity/diversity, labor relations, recruitment, and health and safety issues. HRM professionals also should be capable of conducting their own research to evaluate their programs and program alternatives. Unfortunately, recent evidence suggests that HR professionals adopt many programs based either on effective marketing from the plethora of vendors selling HR materials and programs or simply on what other companies are doing. While some consideration may be given to the leading-indicator research described in Figure 1-1, greater weight seems to be given to slick marketing programs and simply what others are doing. When "bottom-line" questions arise later on—as they inevitably do—HR departments are caught off guard because costly and relatively ineffective programs have been adopted. A careful study of programs with evaluative criteria linked to strategic goals might reveal negligible or no impact. Again, if you don't measure it, you can't manage it. A large number of quantitative reviews, known as **meta-analyses**, are now available to help managers make more informed decisions about methods for such critical HR activities as staffing, recruiting, evaluating, and compensating. These studies will be cited throughout the book and often used to make "bottom-line" recommendations for an HR practice or method.

Meta-analyses

Research should drive HRM practice

poorly researched/ implemented test

Many HR professionals are not even trained to ask the right questions and conduct the appropriate study of a given HR program or activity. The author had a conversation with a VP of HR of a Fortune 500 company. He had a Big-Ten MBA and was convinced that one particular test was the best way to hire retail sales personnel. The basis for his position was conversations with other poorly informed HRM MBAs who were using the test. This is no way to evaluate a selection method. Another HR vice president for a retailer adopted an expensive computerized testing program that the publisher claimed would reduce employee turnover by 50 percent. The VP did not request the research that purported to document this effect and later admitted that although he ultimately made the decision to adopt the test, he was unqualified to assess the test's usefulness since he could not even ask fundamental measurement questions that should be the focus of any evaluation of such a product or service. In addition, although the retailer had been using the test for over two years, it apparently never occurred to him to evaluate the extent to which the test actually did reduce turnover in his organization. A Connecticut police department used an intelligence test to screen for officers but eliminated candidates if their scores were too high. Their argument was that highly intelligent officers would get bored and quit. They had no evidence to support their theory and conceded that their leaders (e. g., their Captains, even the Chief of Police) were all selected from within the organization. This kind of theory should be tested first and its unintended consequences carefully examined before implementation!

Buros Mental Measurements Yearbook

One of the great values of academic research is the objective evaluation of activities or programs using well-controlled experimental designs, which allow for unambiguous assessments of effects. For example, *Buros Mental Measurements Yearbook* is a reference source that publishes evaluations of tests written by qualified academics who have no vested interest in the tests themselves. Over 2,000 tests have been reviewed, and the reviews can be downloaded from the Buros Web site for $15 per test (http://buros.unl.edu/buros/jsp/search). Many HRM professionals who adopt tests do not know that this very useful text (and Web site) even exists.

THE DOMAINS OF HUMAN RESOURCE MANAGEMENT

Figure 1-3 presents a listing of some of the most commonly performed activities by HRM professionals. These HRM activities fall under five major **domains**: (1) Organizational Design, (2) Staffing, (3) Performance Management and Appraisal, (4) Employee Training and Organizational Development, and (5) Reward Systems, Benefits, and Compliance.

[handwritten: Main duties performed by HR]

Figure 1-3
Major Activities of Human Resource Management

ORGANIZATIONAL DESIGN
Human resource planning based on strategy
Job analysis/work analysis
Job design
Information systems
Downsizing/restructuring

STAFFING
Recruiting/interviewing/hiring
Affirmative action/diversity/EEO compliance
Promotion/transfer/separation
Outplacement services
Induction/orientation
Employee selection methods

PERFORMANCE MANAGEMENT AND APPRAISAL
Management appraisal/management by objectives/strategy execution
Productivity/enhancement programs
Customer-focused performance appraisal
Multirater systems (360°, 180°)
Rater training programs

EMPLOYEE TRAINING AND ORGANIZATIONAL DEVELOPMENT
Management/supervisory development
Career planning/development
Employee assistance/counseling programs
Attitude surveys
Training delivery options
Diversity programs

REWARD SYSTEMS, BENEFITS, AND COMPLIANCE
Safety programs/OSHA compliance
Health/medical services
Complaint/disciplinary procedures
Compensation administration
Insurance benefits administration
Unemployment compensation administration
Pension/profit-sharing plans
Labor relations/collective bargaining

Although the particular activities subsumed under these five domains are conceptually independent, in practice they are not. Nevertheless, many organizations pursue the various activities in a particular domain as if they had no implications for any of the other domains. For example, many organizations have reduced or eliminated health care benefits without due consideration of the impact of the new compensation package on staffing and employee retention. In addition, all domain activity must be weighed in the context of the new global environment and contemporary legal interpretations.

Organizational design

Acquiring human resource capability should begin with organizational design and analysis. **Organizational design** involves the arrangement of work tasks based on the interaction of people, technology, and the tasks to be performed in the context of the mission, goals, and strategic plan of the organization. HRM activities such as human resources planning, job and work analysis, organizational restructuring, job design, team building, computerization, and worker-machine interfaces also fall under this domain.

Organizational and work design issues are almost always the first ones that should be addressed whenever significant change is necessary because of changing economic conditions, new technologies, new opportunities, potential advantages, or serious internal problems. Design issues usually drive other HR domains such as selection, training, performance management, and compensation. Economic downturns can provide an opportunity for a more serious evaluation of the organization's strategy and its competitive position. But there are clearly effective and ineffective approaches to organizational design.

Corporate downsizing, outsourcing, and reengineering efforts often begin with human resources planning in the context of a strategic plan and an analysis of how the work is performed, how jobs and work units relate to one another, and, of course, cost analysis. These decisions can be critical for the long-term survival of a struggling company. Research shows that layoffs designed to derive a short-term "cost savings" may foster an increase in market value in the short run but that investors often lose all of this value plus considerably more. The issues of HR design, planning, downsizing, and restructuring will be covered in Chapters 4 and 5.

Staffing

After the organization is structured and jobs are clearly defined in terms of the necessary knowledge, skills, and abilities and how jobs and work relate to one another, positions must be staffed. Recruitment, employee orientation, selection, promotion, and termination are among the functions that fit into the **staffing** domain. Of the HR activities within this domain, selection and termination are probably the two most likely affected by the regulation and litigation we discuss in Chapter 3. Chapter 6 will cover the critical area of selection. Termination will be discussed in Chapters 7 and 12.

Performance management

The **performance management** domain includes assessments of individual, unit, or other aggregated levels of performance to measure, and improve, work performance. Chapter 7 will deal with these subjects, which, like selection, are also the focus of numerous lawsuits. A lawsuit can occur if the organization maintains that an employee was terminated, not promoted, or not given a merit raise because of performance, and the employee believes the negative personnel action was because of his or her gender, race, religion, age, disability, or some other personal characteristic. An employee also can claim an unlawful discharge based on an alleged contract or implied contract violation and even make a claim for pre-emptive retaliation. Obviously, merit pay systems require accurate measures of employee performance.

Employee training and development

Employee training and organizational development programs are concerned with establishing, fostering, and maintaining employee skills based on organizational and employee needs. Activities include specialized training for jobs or management functions, career development, and self-directed learning. Chapters 8 and 9 cover these vital areas.

Rewards systems, benefits, and compliance

Reward systems, benefits, and compliance have to do with any type of reward or benefit that may be available to employees. Direct and indirect compensation, merit pay, profit sharing, health care, parental leave programs, vacation leave, and pensions are among the critical areas within this domain. The activities also include the myriad of compliance requirements facing organizations from local, state, and federal agencies. Labor law, health and safety issues, and unemployment policy are three other major areas within this domain. These issues are covered in Chapters 10 and 11.

This domain also concerns managing employment relationships, labor relations law and compliance, and procedures designed to maintain good working relationships between employees and employers. This may include the negotiation of collective bargaining agreements, which require employers to negotiate with unionized workers over the conditions of employment. These areas are covered in Chapters 12 and 13.

Employee health and safety issues are also subsumed under this domain and include compliance with laws and regulations concerned with the work environment and the effects of health and safety policy and practice on workers and the "bottom line." The focus will be health and safety policy as a leading indicator of HR effectiveness. This area is explored in Chapter 14.

TRENDS ENHANCING THE IMPORTANCE OF HRM

As we have said, there is an increasing realization that the manner in which organizations conduct their HR activities will help create and sustain a competitive advantage. The contemporary trends and challenges in the business environment necessitate that even greater attention be given to the human resources of an organization. Let us examine these trends next and relate each to particular HRM activities. Figure 1-4 presents a summary of major current trends.

The most significant trend is the increasing globalization of the economy and a growing competitive work environment with a premium on product and service quality. One of the most important factors affecting globalization and the growth of transnational corporations is the goal of reducing the cost of production, labor costs being the most significant for U.S. companies. But as discussed in Chapter 2, market-seeking behavior is now as important a motivator of globalization as the search for low-cost productivity.

Another major trend is the unpredictable but inevitable power of technology to transform HRM. There is a need to be more flexible today because of the incredible pace of change in markets and technology. HRM can facilitate this flexibility. The growth and proliferation of lawsuits related to HR practice and changes in workforce characteristics also have had a big impact on HRM. So is the fact that many in the workforce are ill-equipped with the necessary knowledge, skills and abilities, and job requirements to do their jobs well.

Trend 1: The Increased Globalization of the Economy

In his bestseller *The World Is Flat: A Brief History of the Twenty-First Century*, Thomas Friedman described the next phase of globalization.[12] An Indian software executive told him how the world's economic playing field is being leveled. So-called barriers to entry are being destroyed. A company (or even an individual) can compete (or collaborate) from almost anywhere in the world. Over 500,000 American tax returns were prepared in India in 2008. Says

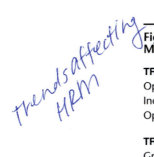

Figure 1-4
Major Trends Affecting HRM

TREND 1: THE INCREASED GLOBALIZATION OF THE ECONOMY
Opportunity for global workforce and labor cost reduction
Increasing global competition for U.S. products and services
Opportunity for expansion that presents global challenges for HR

TREND 2: TECHNOLOGICAL CHANGES, CHALLENGES, AND OPPORTUNITIES
Great opportunities presented by Web-based systems
New threats: privacy, confidentiality, intellectual property

TREND 3: INCREASE IN LITIGATION AND REGULATION RELATED TO HRM
Federal, state, and municipal legislation and lawsuits on the increase
Wrongful discharge; negligent hiring, retention, referral

TREND 4: CHANGING CHARACTERISTICS OF THE WORKFORCE
Growing workforce diversity, which complicates HRM
Labor shortages/aging workforce/Millennials rising

Jerry Rao, Indian entrepreneur, "Any activity where we can digitize and decompose the value chain, and move the work around, will get moved around. Some people will say, 'Yes, but you can't serve me a steak.' True, but I can take the reservation for your table sitting anywhere in the world." Rao's 2009 projects include a partnership with an Israeli company that can transmit MRI and CAT scans through the Internet so Americans can get a second opinion very quickly (and relatively cheaply). When you order a Big Mac at the McDonald's on Route 55 in Cape Girardeau, Missouri, the person taking the order is at a call center in India.

There is no question that the increasing globalization of most of the world's economies will affect HRM. It is predicted that most of the largest U.S. companies soon will employ more workers in countries other than the United States and the growth for most major corporations will derive from off-shore operations. With technological advances, one of the strongest trends is the development of a worldwide labor market for U.S. companies. In their quest for greater efficiencies and reduced costs, American companies can now look globally to get work done. While this opportunity stands to decrease the cost of labor, the process of HRM can be more complicated. Of course, U.S. workers will resist this trend through union and political activity. They haven't been very successful in manufacturing. The United States lost over 4 million manufacturing jobs from May 1998 to May 2008.

The rise in oil prices and the cost of transportation have recently caused a bit of "reverse globalization" in the form of some jobs returning to the United States. In 2000 when oil was $20 a barrel, it cost $3,000 to ship one container of furniture from Shanghai to New York. In 2008, the cost of the same container is $8,000. The long-suffering furniture manufacturing business in North Carolina is making a comeback. DESA, a company that makes heaters to keep football players warm, is moving all of its production back to Kentucky from China. Carrier Battery is coming back to Ohio. "Cheap labor in China doesn't help you when you gotta pay so much to bring the goods over," says economist Jeff Rubin.

Labor cost reductions

Nevertheless, most U. S. companies still see great potential for labor cost reductions by looking overseas, with more emphasis on services these days. But outsourcing can bring many problems along with the cheap labor. It's been over 10 years since some of the biggest companies in the world, because of political and consumer pressure, began their efforts to eliminate the "sweatshop" labor conditions that were pervasive across Asia. Yet, worker abuse is well-documented in many Chinese factories that supply U.S. companies. Chinese companies providing goods and services for Wal-Mart, Disney, and Dell routinely shortchange their employees on wages, withhold health benefits, and expose their workers to dangerous machinery and harmful chemicals like lead and mercury. Wal-Mart, the world's biggest retailer, sourced over $9 billion worth of goods from China in 2007. In 2008, two nongovernmental organizations documented incidents of abuse and labor violations, including child labor, at 15 factories that produce or supply goods for Wal-Mart. "At Wal-Mart, Christmas ornaments are cheap, and so are the lives of the young workers in China who make them," the National Labor Committee report said.

More concern over productivity

Globalization creates greater competition and fosters more concern over productivity and cost control. The fiscal conditions of General Motors and Ford Motor Company are clear illustrations. One important reason for the recent increased interest in HRM is the perceived connection between HRM expertise and productivity. A growing portion of corporate America has come to the realization that competing in an increasingly global environment requires constant vigilance over productivity and customer satisfaction. A smaller but growing percentage of managers recognize the importance of human resources in dealing with these issues. Indeed, a great deal of the recent corporate downsizing can be linked to technological improvement and corresponding estimates of productivity improvements with HR interacting with the technological changes. Bank of America, American Express, Coca-Cola, and General Electric have successfully followed a formula of cutting personnel costs while investing in automated equipment and more efficient facilities. The recent plant closures by Ford and GM are examples of major cost cutting.

U.S. exports now generate about one in six American jobs, an increase of over 20 percent in just 10 years. McDonald's opened its first non-U.S. restaurant in Canada in 1967. By 2009 their total sales outside of the United States contributed over 50 percent of the operating income of the firm. Two-thirds of McDonald's new restaurants are now opened outside the United States each year. While McDonald's has moved more quickly than other U.S. firms, many other U.S. firms are now expanding rapidly in both new countries and new markets. The

[handwritten margin note: globalization – gas prices – moving back to US]

majority of new restaurants opened by Burger King and KFC are now in international markets. The majority of new stores opened by Wal-Mart are now opened outside the United States.

Another response to increasing global competition is restructuring/downsizing, as mentioned earlier. Coca-Cola, Ford, Sears, AT&T, CBS, DuPont, GM, Kodak, Xerox, and IBM are among the many corporate behemoths that have reduced their workforces by more than 10 percent in the last decade. Many HRM specialists are experts in organizational restructuring and change procedures. They have expertise in downsizing and outsourcing options that can reduce labor costs. They may also conduct vocational counseling for those who are displaced or assist in developing new staffing plans as a result of the restructuring.

As described in more detail in later chapters, HRM specialists are also asked to help in legal defenses against allegations of discrimination related to corporate downsizing. Ford recently settled two discrimination lawsuits related to downsizing efforts. In an attempt to compete more effectively against Geico and Progressive, Allstate Insurance converted all of its 15,200-member sales force to independent contractors. To continue as contractors, the agents had to sign a waiver that they would not sue Allstate for discrimination. The result was a costly age discrimination lawsuit brought against Allstate. The law can impose constraints on companies trying to cut costs through changes in labor policies. Recent Supreme Court decisions have increased the likelihood of lawsuits related to downsizing.

Trend 2: Technological Changes, Challenges, and Opportunities

The second trend is the rate of change in technology. More organizations are now evaluating their human resources and labor costs in the context of available technologies, based on the theory that products and services can be delivered more effectively (and efficiently) through an optimal combination of people, software, and equipment, increasing productivity. Instead of speaking to a customer service representative at Bank of America to discuss your account, you can interact with an automated system via the Internet or an automated teller machine (ATM) or through an 800 number. The program is designed to handle almost any problem about which you might inquire. With the automated system, BOA is able to shed customer service representatives, thereby reducing labor costs. As more people use their automated services and ATMs, there is less need for supervision. Customers, as a result, pay less in service charges and may earn more interest on their money. As these automated systems evolve, customers ultimately could be more satisfied with the service, even though they are not dealing with an actual person. HRM specialists participate in the development and execution of user testing programs to assess the design of the automated interface.

Today, with the assistance of HR, more companies are evaluating the role of organizational structure, technology, and human resources with the goal of providing more and higher-quality products and services to the customer at a lower price. This pricing reduction is at least partially achieved by controlling the cost of labor while not losing the focus on meeting customer definitions of quality. Of course, the ultimate goal of for-profit organizations is to maximize profit margins while sustaining (or improving) perceived customer value. HR has a great deal to offer in this endeavor.

35 percent HR involvement in offshoring

While the potential is there, HR specialists are often ignored. Technological advances and offshoring are of course related. A recent survey found that only 35 percent of respondents reported that HR was involved in the offshoring process from an early stage, although HR does typically play a major role in restructuring the organization's workforce as a result of offshoring. Says Jennifer Schramm, manager of workplace trends and forecasting at the Society of Human Resource Management (SHRM.org), "From training HR professionals from offshore sites in the home organization's corporate culture and policies, to developing strong channels of communication between global satellite offices, HR's involvement is crucial in effectively managing cross-border human capital. . . . HR's role in boosting productivity through human capital and workplace culture, even as the scope of the workplace extends across the globe and spans very different cultures, will continue to grow."[13]

Technology is revolutionizing many HRM activities. Most organizations now use software packages to aid all HR domains. Many HR activities and outcome data are tracked electronically, such as recruitment, turnover, performance appraisals, and training. Managers from different departments, states, or even countries can readily access the HR system and update employment files. Software packages are easily customized to fit a specific organization's HR activities.

Technology has also changed the speed with which HR communicates with employees. HR can draft and e-mail a companywide memo to all employees within a single hour. In addition, employees can instantly communicate with Human Resources. Many companies have created intranet sites. These Web sites provide employees with a variety of information, such as health care benefits, personnel policies, and proposed changes.

Technology and privacy

The advent of new technology has created a variety of concerns for management. Employee privacy and intellectual property rights are increasingly cited as major concerns. With computer attacks occurring worldwide, ensuring confidentiality of employee data is a growing concern, and the liability of an organization in the event of security breaches is still unclear.[14]

Protecting intellectual property is vital for all organizations, especially emerging technology and research and development organizations. As a result, organizations are developing electronic communication policies that clearly outline permitted electronic activities, uses of employer systems, and monitoring of employees' files such as e-mail. Many companies have banned cellular cameras and instant messaging because of the increased risk of intellectual property theft.

21st century staffing

Although still rare, the following scenario is already here for some companies: A manager or supervisor gets authorization to hire someone. The manager goes into a "node" on the Internet and completes a job analysis for the new position that establishes critical information regarding the job, including the necessary knowledge, ability, skills, and other critical characteristics. The job description is then used to conduct a "key word" computer search of a potential applicant pool in order to match the requirement of the job with the standardized résumés in the database. Out pops a number of potential candidates for the job. The manager then immediately sends out the job vacancy announcement to all of the potential candidates in the database through electronic mail. Interested candidates respond back via e-mail. The manager then selects the "short list" of candidates to compete for the job based on a quantitative analysis of the resumes.

The same job analysis information could also be used to construct or retrieve job-related tests or questions for an employment interview. The manager might even have a Web camera and could conduct the testing and "face-to-face" interviewing of the candidates as soon as the contact is made (assuming the candidate also has access to a camera-based computer). This process of going from describing the job to actually interviewing candidates could take less than a day. HR is playing a key role in getting these systems up and running.

Some of the most successful high-tech companies today rely on the Internet for fast, convenient, and efficient recruiting of their core personnel. Even the CIA and the FBI do recruiting on the Internet (try www.odci.gov/cia if you'd like to be a spy).

Trend 3: Increase in Litigation and Regulation Related to HRM

In addition to the recent concerns over survival, changes in technology, and increases in global competition, another important trend affecting the status of HRM is the proliferation of regulations and lawsuits related to personnel decisions. As predicted by one cynical statistician, by the year 2010, there will be more lawyers in this country than people. While this is obviously a joke, there is no question that the proliferation and creativity of lawyers have helped to foster our highly litigious society. There is no sign of this activity letting up in the near term. In fact, federal lawsuits charging violations of labor laws have increased faster (up over 125 percent since 1991) than any other area of civil rights legislation. Jury awards have gotten much bigger in recent years. In 2008, 26 percent of judgments against companies related to HR were $1 million or more. In 1994, the percentage of such awards was only 7 percent. The elections of 2008 are likely to increase legislation, regulation and litigation related to HRM.

Civil Rights Act

In general, HRM-related laws and regulations reflect societal responses to economic, social, technical or political issues. For example, the Civil Rights Act of 1964, which prohibits job discrimination on the basis of race, sex, color, religion, or national origin, was passed primarily in response to the great differences in economic outcomes for blacks compared to whites. The 2008 Genetic Information Nondiscrimination Act is designed to address concerns that job seekers or workers could be denied employment opportunities due to a predisposition for a genetic disorder. Other examples are the proliferation of state laws regarding corporate acquisitions and mergers, laws protecting AIDS victims and homosexuals from employment discrimination, and regulations regarding family leave benefits.

Genetic Information Nondiscrimination Act

Organizations are bound by a plethora of federal, state, and local laws, regulations, executive orders, and rules that have an impact on virtually every type of personnel decision.

There are health and safety regulations, laws regarding employee pensions and other compensation programs, plant closures, mergers and acquisitions, new immigration laws, and a growing number of equal opportunity laws and guidelines. Today's HRM professionals and line managers must be familiar with the ADEA, OFCCP, OSHA, EEOC, ADA, FLSA, GINA, NLRA, and ERISA—among many other acronyms. Each represents a major regulatory effort. There is every indication that regulation will increase in the years ahead in the form of new EEO legislation related to fair pay, union organizing, several orientation protection, and especially laws related to work and illegal immigrants. In 2007 alone, 1,562 bills related to

Illegal immigration

illegal immigration were introduced nationwide at the state or local level and 240 were enacted in 46 states.[15] A 2008 federal government plan may force businesses to fire employees whose names don't match the Social Security database. Companies that receive "no match" letters from the Social Security Administration warning of a discrepancy are put on notice and given 90 days to deal with the discrepancy. If employers do not comply, they face stiff penalties.

Organizations spend considerable time and expense in order to comply with labor laws and regulations and/or to defend against allegations regarding violations. Line managers who do not understand the implications of their actions in the context of these laws can cost a company dearly. Line managers may also be personally liable. Employers and managers now face huge fines, the possible loss of business licenses, and even criminal prosecution because of violations of new laws related to employing illegal immigrants.

Sometimes companies learn the hard way about the complexities of labor laws. In 2008,

Examples of HR lawsuits

drivers in FedEx's Ground division claimed to have been improperly classified as independent contractors. IBM recently settled a lawsuit brought on behalf of 32,000 technical and support workers for $65 million who claimed they were entitled to overtime pay. Citigroup/Salomon Smith Barney settled a similar suit for $98 million. Abercrombie and Fitch recently settled a race discrimination lawsuit for $40 million and now conducts its staffing under close court-imposed scrutiny. Texaco and Coca-Cola settled similar lawsuits for over $165 million each. Baker and McKenzie, the largest law firm in the United States, was assessed $3.5 million in punitive damages for sexual harassment committed by one partner at the firm. The EEOC settled a similar suit with Honda of America for $6 million. Westinghouse Electric Corporation agreed to a $35 million settlement in an age discrimination suit involving 4,000 employees affected by the company's reorganization. Ford recently agreed to a $10.6 million settlement in an age discrimination case. Morgan Stanley settled a sex discrimination case for $54 million. Wal-Mart remained mired in a massive sex discrimination lawsuit over pay and promotions as this book went to press.

Trend 4: Changing Characteristics of the Workforce

Several trends regarding the future of the American workforce underscore the challenges to and the importance of the human resource function. Compared to 10 years ago, American workers are more ethnically diverse, more educated, more cynical toward work and organizations, getting older, and, for a growing number, becoming less prepared to handle the challenges of work today. The composition of the workforce is changing drastically, and these changes are affecting HRM policies and practices.

Increasing diversity

Increasing diversity creates the need for more diverse HRM systems and practices and increases the probability of litigation. It is estimated that by 2010 only 15 percent of the U.S. workforce will be native-born white males.[16] A greater proportion of women and minorities have entered the workforce and are beginning to move into previously white male–dominated positions, including managers, lawyers, accountants, medical doctors, and professors. Nearly 90 percent of the growth in the U.S. workforce from 1995 to 2008 came from women, immigrants, African-Americans, and people of Hispanic or Asian origin. In addition, there are more dual-career couples in the labor force. The "typical" U.S. worker in the past was a male—often white—who was a member of a single-earner household. Fewer than 20 percent of today's employees fit this description. In May 2008, an estimated 11.6 percent of the U.S. population was foreign born. The rapid increase in the foreign-born population from 9.6 million in 1970 to 33 million in 2008 reflects the very high rate of international migration. About half of the youngest 100 million Americans are immigrants and their U.S.-born children.[17]

The Millennials
Boomer retirements

Two other trends will surely make HR more challenging: a growing rate of "Baby-Boomer" retirements and a growing rate of Generation Yers (or Millennials) entering the workforce. The retirement of the Boomer generation, those born between 1946 and 1964, is expected to create

15

Millennials' growth

a shortage of skilled workers and perhaps affect economic output. It is estimated that by 2014 there will be almost 63 million Generation Y employees (people born between 1977 and 1994) in the workforce, while the number of Baby Boomers in the workplace will decline to less than 48 million. In one recent survey, a majority of companies already reported intergenerational conflict at work between these two generations. The effects of the economic turmoil that began in 2008 may have a big impact on Baby Boomer retirement plans.

By 2030, American 65 and older will make up about 20 percent of the total population of the country. This could involve horrendous costs in the form of social security and Medicare contributions. Fortunately, some experts predict that enough Baby Boomers will remain in the workforce to make up for any shortfall of workers and hopefully reduce a portion of the staggering projected government unfunded obligations. The economic turmoil that began in 2008 will probably facilitate this. Unfortunately, this might aggravate the generational conflict alluded to earlier. Because of the larger numbers of workers over the age of 40, age discrimination litigation is expected to increase; moreover, a 2008 Supreme Court age discrimination ruling (to be discussed in Chapter 3) changed the burden of proof needed to prove age discrimination and may increase the amount of litigation. Also, the workforce under the age of 40 is expected to acquire more family responsibilities. The Generation Xers, the "sandwich generation," those workers born between the Boomer generation and Generation Y, are be expected to juggle both child care and especially elder care demands as the Boomers live longer. This is a concern HRM must address in the coming years.

As a result of these changes in workforce composition, organizations are having to develop and implement programs on diversity, more flexible work schedules, better training programs, child and elder care arrangements, and career development strategies, so that work and nonwork responsibilities can be more easily integrated. Building and sustaining a quality workforce from this diversity is a great challenge for HR.

Diversity and legal implications

While increasing diversity translates into a greater probability of EEO legal actions, many experts also argue that the diversity of the workforce must match the population demographics or an organization is vulnerable to public criticism that can hurt the business and the society. It is little wonder that most large U.S. companies have as a goal increasing the diversity of their workforce. As discussed in later chapters, the diversity goals of corporations can have an impact on the less diverse but older part of the workforce, particularly in downsizing situations. Such scenarios create difficulties for corporations. But here's some good news: Regarding Generation Y, one recent study concluded that "They combine the teamwork ethic of the Boomers with the can-do attitude of the Veterans and the technological savvy of the Xers. At first glance, and even at second glance, Generation Next may be the ideal workforce—and ideal citizens."[18] The Baby-Boomers should be proud of their parenting!

Millennials are not only more racially and ethnically diverse than Boomers or Xers, they are also more comfortable working in a diverse environment. Although there isn't strong research on this subject to date, it is thus likely that the Millennial generation might help run things a little more smoothly as organizations get more and more diverse. Figure 1-5 presents a summary of the 75-million-strong Millennials.

Summary of Trend Effects

All of these trends are having a profound effect on the way HR is conducted. The changing demographics and cultural diversity of the workforce, the increased number of lawsuits and regulations, and the growing demands on American workers in the context of a paramount need to improve U.S. productivity and establish a competitive edge all create a situation that will challenge HRM professionals and line management. Yet through better coordination with organizational planning and strategy, human resources can be used to create and sustain an organization's advantage in an increasingly competitive and challenging economy.

Being innovative and responsive to changing business environments requires great flexibility. The trend toward the "elastic" company is clearly affecting the HR function, too. As more companies focus on their core competencies—essentially, what they do best and what is the essence of their business—they outsource other work, use temporary or leased employees or independent contractors to perform services or work on specific projects even at the professional level, and replace personnel with new technology. These so-called "modular" companies such as Apple, Nike, and Dell Computers have been successful because

Figure 1-5
Who Are the Millennials? (aka: GenY, GenWHY, Nexers, Boomlets, Netizens, GenNext)

DEMOGRAPHICS
- Born between 1978 and 1995
- Baby Boomer kids
- Largest generation (75 million) after the Boomers
- 38 percent of Millennials identify themselves as "nonwhite"
- Well educated

CHARACTERISTICS
- Techno savvy
- Connected 24/7
- Independent
- Self-reliant
- Global/civic minded
- Green
- Diverse
- Entrepreneurial
- Life-style centered
- Less religious

DEFINING LIFE EXPERIENCES/ EVENTS
- Most "hovered over" generation
- 9/11
- Wars in Iraq, Afganistan
- Corporate scandal and greed
- Emerging nations (China, India, South Korea)
- Immigration issues/growing diversity

AT WORK
- Adaptable/comfortable with change
- Impatient/demanding/efficient
- More interested in corporate social performance and responsibility
- Want to produce something that makes a difference
- Thrive on flexibility and space to explore
- Require an explanation
- Like feedback/guidance

Source: Adapted from Zemke, R., Rainess, C., and Filipezak, B. (2000). *Generations at Work*. (New York: AMACOM).

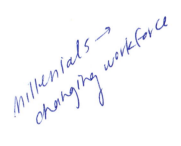

Millenials → changing workforce

they have reliable vendors and suppliers and, most important, hot products. HR consultants have been instrumental in helping companies discover their core competencies and then developing optimal work design and HR strategies. HR departments themselves are not exempt from this trend toward outsourcing. The result has been a proliferation of consulting firms that compete for HR-related projects and programs previously performed within the company. Consulting is now a thriving business for HRM.

HR Outsourcing

Outsourcing trends along with a myriad of Internet, software, and consulting options have reduced the size of many HR departments and have the potential for making them more efficient and more effective. How lean can you get in HR? Nucor, a steel company with 6,000 employees, has an HR staff of four at its headquarters. Most of the HR work is farmed out to HR consultants. Some experts argue that the most efficient and perhaps most effective HRM departments select the best and least costly outside contractors for HRM products and services, make certain these products or services are being used properly, and then evaluate and adapt these products and services to make certain they are working effectively and efficiently.

This trend toward outsourcing some of the personnel function supports the thesis of many experts that the HRM functions must be very lean in structure so that companies can react quickly to the changing world. Many HRM departments now assess the need for any expense, personnel included, in the context of the primary functions of the organization and its competitive strategy. So, if companies can maintain a leaner and more cost-effective structure by outsourcing, where will that leave the HR department in the future? One recent survey found that 94 percent of large companies reported they were outsourcing at least one human resources activity. Most employers indicated that they plan to expand HR outsourcing to include training and development, payroll, recruiting, health care, and global mobility.

94 percent of companies have outsourced one HR activity

outsourced vs. in house HR.

Keith Hammonds, executive editor of *Fast Company,* predicts companies will "farm out pretty much everything HR does. The happy rhetoric from the HR world says this is all for the best: Outsourcing the administrative minutiae, after all, would allow human resources professionals to focus on more important stuff that's central to the business. You know, being strategic partners." Hammonds argues that most HR people are not equipped to take on this more important, strategic responsibility because they don't know enough about the business.

There is no question that intense and growing competition has placed greater pressure on organizations to be more adaptive and to carefully examine all of their costs. Edward Lawler, a prominent management author and consultant, states, "All staff departments are being asked to justify their cost structures on a competitive basis . . . head-count comparisons are being made by corporations to check the ratio of employees to members of the HR department." In *Human Resources Business Process Outsourcing,* Lawler and colleagues illustrate how outsourcing can be a very effective and efficient approach to HR and give HR managers new opportunities to make a more important contribution to a company's bottom-line and overall strategy. They present a template for analyzing an HR department's value, value added, and cost-to-serve.

Whether the organization is facing increasing international competition or simply more intense pressure to improve the bottom line, HR has a great opportunity to meet new and old challenges as a business partner. Lawler sees the most pressing need in the area of corporate strategy. "The HR function must become a partner in developing an organization's strategic plan, for human resources are a key consideration in determining strategies that are both practical and feasible."[19] This HR partnership must evolve out of the major activities of the HR function. A key to this partnership is good, strategic measurement.

THE IMPORTANCE OF HRM MEASUREMENT IN STRATEGY EXECUTION

The Workforce Scorecard

In their excellent book *The Workforce Scorecard: Managing Human Capital to Execute Strategy,* Professors Mark Huselid, Brian Becker, and Dick Beatty argue that of all the controllable factors that can affect organizational performance, a workforce that can execute strategy is the most critical and underperforming asset in most organizations.[20] Measurement is front and center in their prescription for a more effective workforce.

Three challenges

They outline three challenges organizations must take on to maximize workforce potential in order to meet strategic objectives: (1) view the workforce in terms of contribution rather than cost; (2) use measurement as a tool for differentiating contributions to strategic impact; and (3) hold line and HR management responsible for getting the workforce to execute strategy.

Their measurement strategy calls for the development of a "workforce scorecard" that evolves from six general steps an organization needs to take. Figure 1-6 summarizes this process: (1) identify critical and carefully defined outcome measures that really matter; (2) translate the measures into specific actions and accountabilities; (3) give employees detailed descriptions of what is expected and how improvements can be facilitated; (4) identify high and low performing employees and establish differentiated incentive systems; (5) develop supporting HR management and measurement systems; and (6) specify the roles of leadership, the workforce, and HR in strategy execution (go to www.theworkforcescorecard.com for more detail).

Figure 1-6

Steps and Challenges for Developing a Workforce Scorecard

STEPS

1. Identify critical and carefully defined outcome measures related to strategic objectives.
2. Translate the measures into specific actions and accountabilities.
3. Develop and communicate detailed descriptions of what is expected. Determine how (or if) improvements can be facilitated.
4. Identify high and low performing employees. Establish differentiated incentive systems.
5. Develop supporting HR management and measurement systems of selection, formal performance appraisal, promotion, development, and termination practices.
6. Specify the roles of leadership, the workforce, and HR in strategy execution.

CHALLENGES

Perspective challenge—Does management fully understand how workforce behaviors affect strategy execution?

Metrics challenge—Has the organization identified and collected the right measures of success?

Execution challenge—Does management have access to the data and the motivation to use the data in decision making?

Source: Adapted from M. A. Huselid, B. E. Becker, and R. W. Beatty, *The Workforce Scorecard: Managing Human Capital to Execute Strategy* (Boston: Harvard Business School Press, 2005).

Perspective challenge

Metrics challenge
Execution challenge

Huselid, Becker, and Beatty propose three challenges for successful workforce measurement and management (see Figure 1-6). The "perspective" challenge asks whether management fully understands how workforce behaviors affect strategy execution. The "metrics" challenge asks whether they have identified and collected the right measures of success. Finally, the "execution" challenge asks whether managers have the access, capability, and motivation to use the measurement data to communicate strategy and monitor progress.

Human resource activities, practices, and research typically focus on a relatively small number of criteria or outcome measures. These measures can be fine-tuned on the quality of their measurement and the extent to which they are related to customer satisfaction and then long-term profitability and growth. Much of the research in HRM and many of the criteria used to assess management practices focus on employee satisfaction. Figure 1-7 presents a simple model that illustrates why there is (and should be) such a focus. Throughout the book, many studies will be referenced that establish some relationship between an HR practice or HR policy or employee characteristics (e.g., employee job satisfaction) and one or more "bottom-line" criteria such as corporate profit or customer satisfaction. For example, in an excellent study of the relationship between employee attitudes and corporate performance measures in almost 8,000 business units and 36 companies, strong and reliable correlations were found between unit-level employee job satisfaction and job engagement and critical business-unit outcomes, including profit. "Engagement" in this study had to do with, among other things, the level of employee satisfaction regarding working conditions, recognition and encouragement for good work, opportunities to perform well, and commitment to quality. The authors estimated that those business units in the top quartile on the job engagement scale had, on average, from $80,000 to $120,000 higher monthly revenues or sales.

Employee satisfaction and corporate performance

Can HRM practices facilitate higher engagement? Absolutely! It is clear that changes in HRM practices that serve to increase employee satisfaction and engagement can increase critical business-unit outcomes.[21] Many HR experts now say that the emphasis in corporate America is no longer on "happy" workers who will stay with the company forever. Rather, the new mantra is to retain employees who are "productive" and "engaged." Pay and bonuses are thus more driven by performance measures instead of seniority. "It's an, 'If you give, you'll get' model," says David Ulrich, professor at the University of Michigan business school. "That's kind of the productive contract."[22]

Of course, many experts maintain that these simple "this for that" arrangements may have contributed to the trouble and demise of many U.S. corporations in 2008. Countrywide

**Figure 1-7
The Chain of Relationships Linking Management Practices to Employee Satisfaction, Customer Satisfaction, and Long-Term Profitability and Growth**

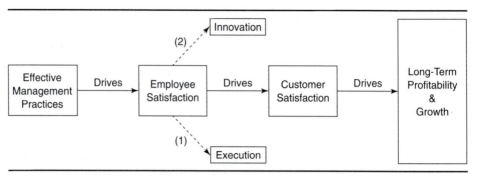

Source: W. Cascio, "From Business Partner to Driving Business Success: The Next Step in the Evolution of HR Management," *Human Resource Management* 44 (2005), p. 162. Reprinted with permission of John Wiley & Sons.

The costs of bad reward systems

Financial rewarded its brokers for closing mortgages with questionable borrowers and its CEO Angelo Mozillo got over $10 million in bonuses in 2007, clearly connected to these bad mortgages. Borrowers began to default on the mortgages in droves in that same year, and the company was eventually swallowed up by Bank of America in 2008. Over 11,000 employees lost their jobs. Unfortunately, Countrywide is but one of many examples of companies rewarding employees for behaviors and outcomes that may be beneficial to these employees and their bosses in the short term but toxic for the company in the not too distant future. Corporate bankrupcies were at record levels in 2008. Some of the most costly (e.g., Lehman Brothers, Washington Mutual) can clearly be linked to deeply flawed "pay for performance" systems.

Employee attitudes, performance, and turnover

We should also be interested in how the various criteria relate to one another. A recent review showed a strong relationship between an employee attitudinal measure known as "organizational commitment" and both job performance and employee turnover. Employees with higher levels of "organizational commitment" were more likely to be better performers and also stay with the company longer. Obviously, managers will want to know how more "committed" or "engaged" employees can be found or developed. The author knows one CEO who was highly critical of academic research because it focused so much attention on variables like "engagement" and "commitment" or even "job satisfaction." He referred to these as "softies" and argued that they were not relevant to the "bottom line." In fact, an abundant literature now exists which documents that such "softies" are indeed strong predictors of bottom-line accounting and financial measures of organizational performance. A key to effective HR policy and practice is measuring such "softies" and understanding how they do relate to critical bottom-line measures like performance, costs, profit, and customer satisfaction.

Organizations should certainly strive to satisfy their employees with good pay, good supervision, and good, stimulating work. But the model presented in Figure 1-7 also helps keep measures of employee job satisfaction in perspective. Employee satisfaction is related to customer satisfaction. So is cost. Customers are particularly impressed with low cost. Wal-Mart does so well not because their employees are happy but because their products are on average 14 percent cheaper than their competitors'. The author would be a lot happier if his university salary was doubled! You'd probably be unhappy if your tuition was raised (again).

Linking measurement to strategic goals

The key is linking measurement to strategic goals. "Thinking strategically means understanding whether the measurement system you are considering will provide you with the kinds of information that will help you manage the HR function strategically."[23] This linkage creates the connection between leading indicators and lagging indicators. Let us turn to illustrations of recent HRM activities directed at these criteria.

Frito-Lay had a problem with job vacancies in key positions, which they believed had a direct effect on sales. They instituted a training and development program through their HRM division to cross-train workers for several jobs in an effort to reduce downtime from employee vacancies and provide more opportunities for employees to move up. The downtime could be operationally defined in terms of dollars, and the training program saved the company $250,000 in the first year.

AMC Theaters developed a battery of applicant tests to identify individuals most likely to perform more effectively and to stay with the company longer. The reduction in turnover saved the company over a half million dollars in five years. Blockbuster Video tried an applicant test that purported to help reduce employee theft and developed a new performance management system for all employees. They estimated savings at $750,000. Owens-Corning Fiberglas trained all of its managers in statistical quality analysis as a part of their total quality management program. Trainees were made accountable for improving the quality at Owens-Corning and the program worked. Reduction of rejected materials saved over a million dollars. John Hancock Insurance installed a new managerial pay-for-performance system in order to increase regional sales and decrease employee turnover. J. Walter Thompson developed a new incentive system to promote creative advertising ideas from its consumer research and accounting units. RJR Nabisco replaced a fixed-rate commission with a new compensation system for its advertisers, which linked ad agency compensation to the success of the campaign. Concerned about the quality of one managerial level, Office Depot developed a managerial assessment center to select their district managers. They then determined the extent to which the quality of management improved as a function of the new screening method.

Turnover is a serious problem for many service industries and especially fastfood. Many consultants just write it off as part of the business. David Brandon, CEO of Domino's Pizza, did a study inside Domino's, the results of which surprised his top management team.[24] He found that the most important factor related to the success (or failure) of any individual store was not marketing, or packaging, or neighborhood demographics. It was the quality of the store manager. Store managers had a great deal to do with employee turnover, and turnover had a great deal to do with store profit. Domino's calculated that it costs the company $2,500 each time an hourly employee quits and $20,000 each time a store manager quits. Mr. Brandon focused on reducing the 158 percent turnover rate among all employees. Domino's implemented a new and more valid test for selecting managers and hourly personnel, installed new computerized systems for tracking and monitoring employee performance and output, and developed a much more focused pay-for-performance system for all managers. As of 2008, the program was a great success by all counts. Turnover was way down, store profit was up, and the stock price was doing well in an otherwise very difficult market. Brandon clearly showed how important HRM is to the bottom line. Attracting and keeping good employees, measuring and monitoring performance, and rewarding strategically important outcomes are all keys. Obviously, all of this has to translate into good (and cheap) pizza. Long-term profitability and growth are driven by customer satisfaction, and that's mainly a function of the quality and cost of the products and services. Research clearly shows HRM practice and employee satisfaction are in the "chain of relationships."

Customer satisfaction and profitability

In the past, HRM interventions were rarely linked to financial measures or cost figures in order to show a reliable financial benefit. This inability to link such HRM practices to the "big picture" might explain why personnel departments in the past have had so little clout. While marketing departments were reporting the bottom-line impact of a new marketing strategy in terms of market share or sales volume, personnel could only show that absenteeism or turnover was reduced by some percentage, rarely assessing the relationship between these reductions and a specific financial benefit. Stanford professor Jeffrey Pfeffer summed it up: "In a world in which financial results are measured, a failure to measure human resource policy and practice implementation dooms this to second-class status, oversight neglect, and potential failure. The feedback from the measurements is essential to refine and further develop implementation ideas as well as to learn how well the practices are actually achieving their intended results."[25]

Management by measurement

Developing clear criteria linked to strategic goals is critical for managerial success and should be a major driver of HR policy. Some experts argue that HR specialists should "quarterback" the development and administration of a "management by measurement" system, ensuring all functional business units are subscribing to the guidelines for sound, strategic measurement. Allowing business units to develop and administer "leading indicator" measures can result in the measurement of criteria more closely linked to making that unit (and particular managers) look good rather than the strategic goals of the unit. By contrast HR can help with sound measurement.

Most effective employees

But what is sound measurement? One HR executive laid the groundwork with this definition: "The most effective employees are those who provide the highest possible quantity and quality of a product or service at the lowest cost and in the most timely fashion, with a maximum of positive impact on co-workers, organizational units, and the client/customer population." This statement of effectiveness also applies to particular HR programs, products, and services and all functional business units. In evaluating an outsourced recruiting effort, an HR VP provided the following criterion for evaluation: "Give me a large pool of highly qualified candidates, give me this list as quickly as possible, and don't charge me much when you're doing it." The details of the measurement system (e.g., the quantity and quality of products/services) must be linked to strategic goals. These measurement details are critical. As stated earlier, many of the problems at companies in crisis in 2008 and 2009 have been attributed to faulty incentive systems that met short-term goals and created long-term disasters.

The most effective organizations get down to specifics about all important criteria, and these are directly linked to key objectives or desired outcomes for the organization. This prescription applies to HR as for any other business function. Wayne Keegan, VP of HR for toymaker ERTL in Dyersville, Iowa, clearly represented the bottom line for HR: "HR managers

Quantify all aspects of HR

should strive to quantify all facets of HR to determine what works and what doesn't."[26]

What works and doesn't work should focus on the "big picture." The most effective organizations are driven by measurement strategies perhaps conceptualized by HR specialists and applied to HR functions but, more important, applied throughout the workforce. HR

Develop key workforce measures

can (and should) help senior management develop and focus on key workforce measures that derive from organizational strategy. The most effective organizations develop a set of "top tier" measurement tools that reflect and integrate the company's strategic goals. As Mark Huselid and his colleagues put it, "There should be no gap between what is measured and what is managed." Linking workforce success at the individual and unit level to the most critical business outcomes is a key to competitive advantage. Linking these outcomes to long-term measures of success is the key to long-term advantage and survival.

COMPETITIVE ADVANTAGE[27]

Competitive advantage refers to the ability of an organization to formulate strategies that place it in a favorable position relative to other companies in the industry. Two major principles describe the extent to which a business has a competitive advantage. These two principles are perceived customer value and uniqueness.

Customer Value

Competitive advantage occurs if customers perceive that they receive more value from their transaction with an organization than from its competitors. Ensuring that customers receive value from transacting with a business requires that all employees be focused on understanding customer needs and expectations. This can occur if customer data are used in the designing of products or service processes and customer value is used as the major criterion of interest. Some companies conduct value chain analysis that is designed to assess the amount of added value produced by each position, program, activity, and unit in the organization. The value chain analysis can be used to refocus the organization on its core competencies and the requirements of the customer base.

customer focus by company

price

Customers not only perceive but actually realize value from Wal-Mart in the form of price. The products and services are available in convenient stores and average prices are 14 percent lower than its competitors. While there are many reasons Wal-Mart can price goods lower than competitors (e.g., economies of scale, price control pressures on suppliers, technology on products bought and sold, cheaper imports), low labor cost is certainly one factor. Sales clerks earn less at Wal-Mart compared to unionized workers doing essentially the same work for competitors. Health care benefits are estimated to be 15 percent less than coverage for workers within the same industry.

Wal-Mart's strategy to be a price leader and its obsession with cost control have the potential for trouble. The company has been mired in various labor-related lawsuits in recent years, all of which may be related to controlling costs. They paid a huge fine in 2005 for contracting with a company that employed illegal aliens, have been sued numerous times for violating labor laws, including firing people for union organizing efforts, and have been found guilty of violating the Fair Labor Standards Act regarding overtime. While they are the largest employer in the United States, the proportional rate of complaints related to their HR practices is high.

Value to Abercrombie and Fitch is related to creating and sustaining an image for its young customers. A&F went for an all-American look and it certainly worked. They are the largest teen retailer in the United States with over 600 stores and over a billion dollars in revenues. Their clothes are certainly not cheaper than competitors'. A&F is clearly promoting image as a part of its definition of value. But just like Wal-Mart's cost control/price strategy, A&F's "image" strategy created big trouble for the company. In a discrimination lawsuit settled for $40 million, A&F was accused of favoring white job applicants and employees. A&F agreed to change some of its marketing strategy as a part of the settlement.

Customer Value and Corporate Social Responsibility (CSR)

The notion of customer value is more complicated than it may seem to the uninitiated. Many customers seek out products and services at least to some extent as a function of the reputation of the organization selling the product or service in matters not directly related to the cost or quality of the particular product or service. One of the reasons companies (and politicians) wrap themselves around the Olympics every four years is they believe that the basic sense of American pride and excellence that goes with the Olympics tends to rub off onto the company. Research in marketing shows that perceptions of product quality are positively affected by affiliation with the Olympics and Olympic heroes such as Michael Phelps. Thus, at least the theory is that customer value is affected by this connection.

Likewise, the reputation of a company's environmental policies affects the decision making of a growing number of consumers. Concerns about global warming, the price of gasoline, and air pollution have prompted many companies to offer incentives to employees to encourage them to buy fuel-efficient vehicles that emit less carbon dioxide. As the companies go "Green," they report improvements in employee retention and increases in job applications, two HR metrics that have been linked to subsequent improvements in the bottom line.

Companies go "Green"

Most companies with a connection to manufacturing facilities abroad are very concerned about pitiful labor conditions and child labor issues at these international facilities. When Kathy Lee Gifford was accused of exploiting child labor in Honduran clothing plants, some consumers avoided her line of clothing. Nike was accused by the chairman of the Made in the USA Foundation of using child labor in Indonesia to make its athletic shoes. Nike's business was affected to the extent that consumers consider these allegations when they buy sneakers. Jesse Jackson launched a boycott against Mitsubishi to "encourage" the company to put more women and minorities in executive positions.

American companies spend millions and hire thousands of foreign plant auditors to inspect off-shore plants, and there is no doubt worker conditions have improved since the 1990s. But many bad factories remain and Asian suppliers regularly outsource to other suppliers, who may in turn outsource to yet another operation, creating a supply chain that is difficult to follow.

Some companies obviously believe that their reputation for corporate social and environmental responsibility figures into the complicated calculation of value. There is evidence that companies are under increasing pressure to behave in a socially responsible manner. While there are a variety of definitions of corporate social/environmental performance (CSP), there is debate over the extent to which (or whether) a positive image of CSP is related to corporate financial performance. Two excellent studies on this subject provide compelling data that **CSP and the "bottom line"** CSP does indeed affect the bottom line and investor behavior. The results suggest that "corporate virtue in the form of social responsibility and, to a lesser extent, environmental responsibility is likely to pay off."[28] Perhaps Wal-Mart already knew this. Have you noticed the many ads on TV informing the public about their many good deeds and how nice they are to their employees and their environment?

CSP has spawned socially responsible investing, or SRI, which enables investors to buy into companies with favorable CSP reputations. Mutual funds such as Calvert World Values,

Handwritten margin notes:
CSR = Corporate Social Resp.
CSP = Corporate Social/Environ. performance
SRI = socially Respons. Investing.

CSP and investment

AXA Enterprise Global, and Henderson GlobalCare Growth invest only in companies that pass CSP muster. It is estimated that one out of every eight dollars invested by professional money managers is invested based on corporate CSP.[29] So, who are these socially responsible companies that dominate SRI? Among the well-known companies most likely to be part of an SRI mutual fund are Canon, Toyota and Sony (Japan), British Petroleum (UK), Nokia (Finland), SAP (Germany), and in the United States, Bank of America, Cisco Systems, Coca-Cola, Johnson & Johnson, Microsoft, and Procter and Gamble.

Corporate "Sustainability"

There is a related and growing "corporate sustainability movement." "Sustainability" has to do with a company's ability to make a profit while not sacrificing the resources of its people, the community, and the planet. Many executives now claim sustainability can improve the company's financial performance. A 2007 survey of executives indicated that the greatest benefits of sustainability programs are improving public opinion, improving customer relations, and attracting and retaining talent. Over 75 percent of the participating executives anticipated more investment in environmental programs.[30]

The Worker's Rights Consortium

Many college students are now involved in tracking the manufacturing process for their school paraphernalia. The United Students Against Sweatshops (USASNET.org) is an organization of students from over 200 universities affiliated with the Worker's Rights Consortium. The WRC conducts investigations of manufacturing plants, issues reports, and initiates boycotts against certain university products such as hats or T-shirts if plants do not meet its standards for wages and safety. This movement is growing and has already had some major successes.

Many consumers use "Newman's Own" products (as in the late actor Paul Newman) not only because they like the products but because all profits are donated to "educational and charitable purposes." (Go to newmansown.com.) Sure, Newman's Sockarooni spaghetti sauce is tasty. But does the taste account for all of the customer value when the sauce typically costs more than other sauces? Customer value can be complicated. Jesse Jackson and Burger King were well aware of this when Burger King agreed to special financing and support for minority-owned franchises. Most people do not live and die for a Whopper. Consumers' knowledge regarding Burger King's policy toward minorities could affect their fast-food decision.

So, an organization's CSR and CSP reputation regarding its corporate ethics, environmental positions, pro-family policies, or affirmative action/diversity practices can go into the "customer value" assessment. For years, Dow Chemical in Midland, Michigan, had a negative reputation on college campuses because of its production of napalm, a chemical agent used in the Vietnam war. Dow had a terrible time recruiting chemists and other vital professionals because of this one product. Dow launched a public relations campaign to enhance its reputation. They focused their advertising on the many agricultural products that they produced and marketed. The result was a profound improvement in Dow's ability to recruit on college campuses. Obviously, Dow's ability to recruit and retain the best chemists was vital to their competitiveness.

Customer value includes "intangibles"

While consumers undoubtedly place greater weight on the quality of the product or service, there is no question that "customer value" can also include intangible variables such as corporate responsibility, environmental impacts, diversity policies, and being on the right side of political issues. Activist consumer groups, by calling attention to corporate greed, may foster more social responsibility by simply affecting the complicated variable of the customer value equation. There is also evidence that Gen Y Americans are more sensitive to CSR and CSP issues, especially environmental concerns, and that this Millennial generation is more likely to buy from (and invest in) companies with strong CSP reputations and more inclined to work for such companies.

"Most admired" companies

One hot issue related to the complicated equation of "customer value" is the way a company treats its employees. The reputation of a company regarding how it treats its employees can also affect the size of the pool of candidates for any job within the organization. Organizations work hard to make the list of the "most admired" companies for which to work because it does help attract more qualified workers. Google, the most admired company on *Fortune* magazine's list in 2008, received almost 800,000 applicants for the 3,100 positions it filled in 2007. Recall that the ratio of the number of qualified applicants to the number of key positions is a "high-performance work system characteristic" and is thus related to corporate financial success (see again Figure 1-1).

At SAS, a North Carolina computer software company with over 10,000 employees, it all started with free M&Ms every Wednesday. The SAS HR strategy is clearly designed to attract the best programmers and to keep the SAS workforce happy. The strategy has worked. They sold over a billion dollars of analytical software to retailers like Victoria's Secret and the U.S. military in 2008 alone. SAS has never had a losing year and has never laid off a single employee! Says Jim Goodnight, the founder of the company, "If employees are happy, they make the customers happy. If they make the customers happy, they make me happy." SAS is always ranked high in *Fortune* magazine's list of best companies to work for (they ranked 29th in 2008; go to Fortune.com or SAS.com for their current rank). SAS offers a myriad of benefits you don't find at many companies. They have a Work/Life Center made up of social workers who help SAS employees solve life's problems like elder care and college selection for SAS kids. They'll even have someone pick up and deliver your dry cleaning! Says Jeff Chambers, director of HR, "We do all

SAS: 5 percent turnover rate

these things because it makes good business sense," saving staff time. SAS claims a turnover rate differential of 5 percent at SAS versus 20 percent at competitors (true even in the heat of the 90s' dot-com craze!). That savings in turnover at SAS is estimated at $60–70 million annually. While some companies treat employees as costs or necessities, Jim Goodnight regards his SAS employees as the best investments he ever made. "Ninety-five percent of my assets drive out the front gate every evening. It's my job to bring them back." Google has adopted this HR philosophy with record-low turnover rates as a consequence.

There is hard and growing evidence that treating employees well will translate into better financial performance. One study found that positive employee relations served as an "intangible and enduring asset and . . . a source of sustained competitive advantage at the

The "Best Companies" and corporate performance

firm level."[31] The study found that companies that made the "100 Best Companies to Work for in America" list had much more positive employee attitudes toward work and a significant financial performance advantage over competitors. The advantage is self-sustaining. Once companies make the list, the quality and quantity of their applicants for key positions go up and thus the quality of their new hires improves! Among the companies that have been on the list for years are Starbucks, Whole Foods, Cisco Systems, JM Family Enterprises, J.M. Smucker, Nordstrom, and Ernst and Young. Perceived customer value is the principle source of competitive advantage. While it mainly derives from the actual product or service, it derives indirectly from an organization's reputation.

Maintaining Uniqueness

The second principle of competitive advantage derives from offering a product or service that your competitor cannot easily imitate or copy. For example, if you open a restaurant and serve hamburgers, and a competitor moves in next to you and also serves hamburgers that taste, cost, and are prepared just like yours, unless you quickly offer something unique in your restaurant, you may lose a large part of your business to your competitor. Your restaurant needs to have something that is unique to continue to attract customers. Competitive advantage comes to a business when it adds value to customers through some form of uniqueness. The author of this book works in Boca Raton, Florida, one of the great resort areas of the world (and a golfer's paradise). This location enables his university to attract (and retain) top faculty from around the world—clearly a competitive (and unique) advantage.

Apple has a great history for being unique. Consider the Apple strategy for the original iPod. Says Apple VP Phillip Schiller, the iPod development was about how many songs it holds, how quickly songs can be transferred, and how good the sound is in the context of the design. These were the essential questions the customer was asking regarding MP3 players. The uniform whiteness, even the headphones, certainly contributed to the product's iconic (and unique) status. But as one devoted iPod owner put it, "If it didn't load up fast, store a lot and, above all, sound good, I probably would have stuck with my Walkman for a while longer." Apple's latest iPhone is even more sensitive to customer demands and projected to be more profitable than any of the other products in the iPod line of music players, even though the price tag is about half of the original iPhone. Because of lower component costs, profit margins for the new iPhone should exceed the 50 percent level achieved by the original Apple iPod and the first iPhone.[32] Apple products have succeeded in maintaining their uniqueness.

Sources of Uniqueness

Financial capability

The key to any business's sustained competitive advantage is to ensure that uniqueness lasts over time. Three traditional mechanisms exist to offer customers uniqueness. A fourth is often a necessary condition to take advantage of one (or more) of the other three. The four mechanisms for offering uniqueness are described below and summarized in Figure 1-8. First, **financial or economic capability** derives from an advantage related to costs; when a business is able to produce or provide a good or service more cheaply than competitiors. If in your hamburger restaurant, you have received a financial gift from family or friends to build the restaurant, without repayment of the gift, you may be able to charge less for your product than a competitor who borrowed money from a bank or financial institution. Your cheaper-priced hamburger would then become a source of uniqueness that customers value. Toyota and Honda do not have anywhere near the "legacy" costs that Ford, GM, and Chrysler have (pension and health care commitments to retirees). This is a huge financial advantage.

The question of what is unique about a product or service is almost always asked and answered in the context of the usually overriding "cost" question. Wal-Mart's source of uniqueness is rather simple: They have what we want and it's cheaper (on average, about 14 percent)! For most people and for almost any product or service, the assessment of the product or service is done in the context of price or cost, at both a relative and an absolute level.

Strategic/product capability

The second source of uniqueness comes from having **strategic or product capability**. That is, a business needs to offer a product or service that differentiates it from other products or services. The iPod is a clear example. One early reviewer of the iPod took a look at the $400 initial price tag and suggested that the name might be an acronym for "Idiots Price Our Devices"! But despite its pricey introduction, the iPod overwhelmed the other MP3

Figure 1-8
The Four Mechanisms for Offering and Maintaining Uniqueness

- FINANCIAL OR ECONOMIC CAPABILITY DERIVES FROM AN ADVANTAGE RELATED TO COSTS

    WHEN A BUSINESS IS ABLE TO PRODUCE OR PROVIDE A GOOD OR SERVICE MORE CHEAPLY THAN COMPETITORS

    EXAMPLES: WAL-MART, BANK OF AMERICA

- STRATEGIC OR PRODUCT CAPABILITY

    A BUSINESS OFFERS A PRODUCT OR SERVICE THAT DIFFERENTIATES IT FROM OTHER PRODUCTS OR SERVICES.

    EXAMPLES: McDONALD'S, APPLE, GOOGLE, ROCKSTAR GAMES

- TECHNOLOGICAL OR OPERATIONAL CAPABILITY

    A DISTINCTIVE WAY OF BUILDING OR DELIVERING A PRODUCT OR SERVICE

    EXAMPLES: GOOGLE, E-BAY, CISCO SYSTEMS, MICROSOFT, MICROPOSITE

- ORGANIZATIONAL CAPABILITY

    ABILITY TO MANAGE ORGANIZATIONAL SYSTEMS AND PEOPLE THAT MATCHES CUSTOMER AND STRATEGIC NEEDS

    EXAMPLES: GOOGLE, SAS, WHOLE FOODS, JM FAMILY ENTERPRISES, PUBLIX SUPER MARKETS

---

players and acquired what pop star Moby referred to as an "insidious revolutionary quality . . . it becomes a part of your life so quickly that you can't remember what it was like beforehand." Apple has had the same success with the iPhone. Now that's uniqueness! In the hamburger wars, fast-food restaurants have attempted to offer unique products and services to attract customers. Salad bars, taco bars, kiddie meals, and $30 breakfasts with giant rodents named Mickey and Minnie are all examples of restaurants attempting to make their product unique and appealing to customers. The possession of a patent for a critical drug is an advantage for a pharmaceutical company.

Technological/operational capability

A third source of uniqueness for a business is a **technological or operational capability**. That is, a business can have a distinctive way of building or delivering its product or service. In the hamburger restaurant, the different methods of preparing the hamburgers may distinguish restaurants from each other (broiled versus flame-grilled). Customers may prefer one technological (cooking) process over another, and thus continue to patronize one restaurant. In more complex businesses, technological capability may include research and development, engineering, computer systems and/or software, and manufacturing facilities. Microsoft has thrived in this area by getting consumers to purchase and get comfortable with one of their products so they are more attracted to future products related to their technological capability. Google is a great example of unique technological and operational capability. Another example is Michigan-based Microposite that introduced a patented, state-of-the-art form of siding in 2008.

Organizational capability

A fourth source of uniqueness aiding a company in seeking competitive advantage is **organizational capability**. Organizational capability represents the business's ability to manage organizational systems and people in order to match customer and strategic needs. In a complex, dynamic, uncertain, and turbulent environment (e.g., changing customers, technology, suppliers, relevant laws and regulations), organizational capability derives from the organization's flexibility, adaptiveness, and responsiveness. In a restaurant, organizational capability may be derived from having employees who ensure that when customers enter the restaurant, their customer requirements, their needs, are better met than when the customers go to a competitor's restaurant. That is, employees will want to ensure that customers are served promptly and pleasantly, and that the food is well prepared.

The implications for human resource management should be clear. HR systems need to be put in place that maximize organizational capability and exploit all other potential sources of uniqueness. Organizations with serious problems on the organizational capability side of the ledger can fail to exploit other potential sources of competitive advantage. The cultural problems after the merger of Chrysler and Daimler-Benz are a good illustration of this interaction. Despite a solid financial situation and unique technological advantages the company never gained synergy as DaimlerChrysler and eventually split up in 2006.

With increased globalization and the need for strategic alliances, organizational capability is a key to sustained competitive advantage as companies expand their businesses around the world. Take McDonald's as one example of a successful global expansion with a need for strategic alliances. McDonald's has restaurants in over 115 countries, and expansion to some areas of the world poses special challenges. Their marketing determined that they could sell the Big Macs in Saudi Arabia. Here's the line-up for the Saudi Big Mac: two all beef patties from Spain, the special sauce from the United States, lettuce from Holland, cheese from New Zealand, pickles from the United States, onions and sesame seeds from Mexico, the bun from Saudi wheat, sugar and oil from Brazil, and the packaging from Germany. Organizational capability enables McDonald's to pull this integration off, and the result is a highly popular and profitable product. Globalization will necessitate more of these challenging arrangements. HR will have a lot to do with success through enhanced organizational capability, as HR systems help determine how smart people are recruited, hired, trained, motivated, treated, evaluated, paid, and integrated into the organization.

Organizational capability and corporate performance

Research shows that organizational capability influenced by particular HR activities is a reliable predictor of corporate financial performance. HR activities and processes such as those characterizing "leading indicator" high-performance work systems illustrate organizational capability as a source of competitive advantage. The ability to attract and retain individuals with the skills to establish and maintain potential sources of uniqueness should be a key metric in any "management by measurement" system.

SUMMARY

Line management is responsible for application of HRM policy

Human resource management is to some extent concerned with any organizational decision that has an impact on the workforce or the potential workforce. The trends described in Chapter 1 underscore the importance of HR to meet the challenges of the 21st century. While there is typically a human resource or personnel department in medium-sized to large corporations, line management is still primarily responsible for the application of HRM policies and practices. There are critical competencies for general management and HRM professionals. An organization needs both competent personnel trained in HRM and motivated managers who recognize the importance of HRM activities and will apply the best procedures in the recommanded manner. HR managers are more likely to convince line managers of the value of HR programs by focusing on "leading indicator" measurements, which can be linked to the lagging financial indicators that are more clearly understood by management. Personnel/HR functions are often perceived by line managers to be out of step with the real bottom-line outcome measures for the organization. Therefore, the

HRM policy and strategic objectives

most effective human resource departments are those in which HRM policy and activities are established and measured in the context of the mission and strategic objectives of the organization. HRM should assist management in the difficult task of integrating and coordinating the interests of the various organizational constituencies, with the ultimate aim being to enhance the organization's competitive position by focusing on meeting or exceeding customer requirements and expanding the customer base.

Competitive advantage is the key to success for most businesses. To attain competitive advantage, businesses need to add (and sustain) value for customers and offer uniqueness. Four capabilities provide a business's uniqueness: financial, strategic or product, technological or operational, and organizational. To sustain competitive advantage, organizational capability should be emphasized, ideally in the context of the other sources of uniqueness. Organizational capability derives from a business's HRM practices.

The view of HRM outlined in this chapter provides a foundation for integrating HRM activities into the organization's mission and goals. HRM professionals should be actively involved in building more competitive organizations through the HRM domains. One necessary competency for both line managers and HRM professionals is an understanding of the growing impact of globalization in HR policy and practice. This critical area is explored in the next chapter.

Discussion Questions

1. Describe the changing status of HRM. What factors have led to these changes?
2. How do productivity concerns influence organizational policies and procedures regarding HRM activities?
3. Describe the major HRM activities conducted in an organization. Provide an example of each from an organization with which you are familiar.
4. What impact should the composition of the workforce have on HRM practices or activities? What future trends do you see that will influence HRM activities? Why is the growing cultural diversity of the workforce a management challenge?
5. Why is the support of line management critical to the effective functioning of HRM practices in an organization? Provide some suggestions to ensure that this support is maintained.
6. Why does the number of qualified applicants for each strategic position relate to corporate effectiveness? How can HRM enhance this applicant pool?
7. What are the sources of uniqueness that can aid a company seeking competitive advantage?
8. Explain how Ford and GM have a competitive disadvantage related to financial capability. How does Wal-Mart have an advantage?

Chapter 2

The Role of Globalization in HR Policy and Practice*

OBJECTIVES

After reading this chapter, you should be able to

1. Describe the different ways companies may engage in international commerce.
2. Explain the different international business strategies.
3. Explain how international human resource management (IHRM) differs from traditional, domestic HRM.
4. Understand the different IHRM strategies.
5. Describe the trends relating to international job assignments.
6. Understand the issues and trends relating to the development of globally competent business leaders.

OVERVIEW

In Chapter 1, we described the importance of aligning human resource (HR) programs with the business strategy. This means that as organizations change, HR policies and programs must adapt as well. One of the major challenges facing businesses today is the increasing globalization of the world economy and competition.

Thomas Friedman's critically acclaimed book on globalization, *The World Is Flat: A Brief History of the Twenty-First Century*, describes the next phase of globalization.[1] Technological and political forces have facilitated a global, Web-based "playing field" that allows for multiple types of collaboration regardless of geography, distance, and even language. Morgan Stanley estimated that from 1995 to 2005, cheap imports from China saved American consumers over $600 billion. Yet some say that the free ride is coming to an end, as rising energy and labor costs have led to inflation in many Asian economies, making exports to the United States more expensive. In the 12 months prior to February 2008, prices in the United States for goods rose by 4 percent.[2] While rising prices for imports have affected U.S. consumers, prices for exports have seemingly decreased for foreign buyers, as the U.S. dollar has declined in value over the past few years relative to other strong currencies, such as the euro of the European Union.

*Contributed by Christine M. Hagan and Stephanie J. Thomason.

Over the past 50 years, world output has increased by more than 600 percent, and world trade by 1,500 percent.[3] In 1948, world merchandise exports totaled $59 billion. In 2006, they were estimated to be over $11.8 trillion. Between 1950 and 2006, world exports increased annually by 6 percent.[4] The World Bank now estimates that global trade accounts for half of all of the world's gross national product (GNP). Six out of 10 firms say they have at least one foreign company among their top five competitors.[5]

The same explosive growth has occurred in foreign direct investment (FDI). Foreign direct investment involves the control of a company through its ownership by a foreign company or foreign individuals. This growth was most dramatic in the last decade.[6] One expert indicates that about 63,000 companies worldwide have FDIs.[7]

Offshore centers

Another strong trend is the creation of offshore professional and operations centers, regardless of where the final work product is ultimately marketed. Many U.S. and European software manufacturers now have facilities in India to take advantage of the high concentration of computer skills in that country and the low cost of labor. Traditionally, business facilities were strategically located in order to be close to suppliers or customers, and/or within trade alliance borders. Today, however, the use of private satellite links, e-mail, fax machines, and the World Wide Web has made workers from all over the world very accessible. Even customer service facilities are being located overseas, particularly when there is a sufficient supply of productive workers who are willing to work for relatively low pay.

Global recruitment

Global recruitment and staffing are now the rage. Technology now even allows a great deal of service work to move offshore where labor costs are less than in the United States. Workers can (and do) telecommute across continents. As a consumer, you may be unaware that your X rays may be read by someone in India, that your software is repaired by specialists in Ireland, that your airline reservations were booked with a customer service rep in Jamaica, or that your insurance claims were processed in the Philippines.

Why are so many organizations today under pressure to expand their business interests beyond their national boundaries? Major reasons include access to additional resources (including skilled workers), lower costs, economies of scale, favorable regulations and tax systems, direct access to new and growing markets, and the ability to customize products to local tastes and styles. In addition, the rise of regional trade alliances (such as NAFTA and the European Union) is another important reason organizations have increasingly internationalized. Later in this chapter, we will describe some of the problems associated with the rise of regional trade alliances, such as the "banana wars" and Mexico's "screwdriver factories."

These trends are not expected to slow over the next several years. Let's take a brief look at a few examples. Founded in 1901 in the United States and headquartered in Livonia, Michigan, TRW Automotive is one of the top 10 automotive suppliers in the industry worldwide, with record sales in 2007 of over $14 billion. The company employs over 66,000 people in 209 facilities in 27 countries, two-thirds of whom are outside of North America in either Europe, South America, or Asia. In 2007, 70 percent of TRW Automotive's sales were from Europe, Asia, or South America.[8]

McDonald's opened its first non-U.S. restaurant in Canada in 1967. By 2005, its sales outside the United States represented 66 percent of their total sales.[9] In fact, every three hours, a new McDonald's opens somewhere on earth.[10] Two-thirds of these new stores are outside of the United States.

Coca-Cola and Wal-Mart are two other great examples of the potential represented by the global economy. With operations in more than 200 countries, Coke derives over 70 percent of its operating income from overseas operations. In 1991, Wal-Mart first ventured offshore in a joint venture in Mexico. Wal-Mart is now the largest retailer in Canada and Mexico and has over 7,350 stores in 14 countries.[11]

This global expansion presents great challenges for HRM. When McDonald's entered into a joint venture with the Moscow city council, the company placed a help-wanted ad and received about 27,000 Russian applicants for its 605 positions. It sent six Russian managers to its Hamburger University outside Chicago, Illinois, for six months of training and another 30 managers for several months of training in Canada and Europe.[12] It also needed to overcome significant problems obtaining high-quality supplies, most of which were perishable. Ultimately, McDonald's opened a $40 million food-processing center about 45 minutes from its first Moscow restaurant.[13]

An estimated 80 percent of Coca-Cola employees are non-U.S. personnel.[14] Coke now has six largely autonomous regional groups (North America, Latin America, Europe, Africa, Asia, and the South Pacific).[15] In addition, they have established a global service staff of 500 people who are trained to go anywhere in the world to offer advice and expertise concerning operational and customer service problems. These team members are paid U.S. wages, even though many of them are not from the United States.

The majority of Fortune 500 companies are now multinational in that some portion of their business (and profits) is derived from overseas operations.[16] Many of our largest, most prestigious companies, including IBM, Exxon, GE and Microsoft, derive more than half of their revenues from overseas business. With the immense market potential overseas, particularly in Asia, this figure is likely to get even higher for many U.S. corporations. It is estimated that by 2020, the six largest world economies will be the United States plus five Asian economies: China, Japan, India, Indonesia, and a united Korea. Along with this success will come great demand for products and services for the new middle classes of these countries. In 2000, about one-third of the sales of Fortune 500 companies came from outside the United States.[17]

Of course, global expansion is not reserved for U.S. companies. Many organizations headquartered in Europe and Asia have expanded their global reach over the last decade or so. In fact, chances are better than ever that you may work for a foreign corporation in your own community. Consider that nearly 80 percent of all Honda and Acura vehicles sold in America are built in one of Honda's six manufacturing facilities in the United States. Today, Honda employs over 25,000 people in all 50 U.S. states.[18] In the last 10 years, more than 200 German businesses established direct investments in North and South Carolina alone. Most Mercedes and BMW cars driven in the United States are now assembled in the United States. Nokia, the cell phone giant with headquarters in Finland, employs 116,000 workers worldwide, 70 percent of whom are outside of Finland.[19] Philips, the electronics multinational, employs 83 percent of its workforce outside its headquarters in the Netherlands. The Roche Group, the Swiss pharmaceutical giant, has 88 percent of its workforce outside Switzerland.[20] Today, an estimated 4.9 million U.S. citizens work in U.S. affiliations of foreign-owned corporations.[21]

In addition, your company is now more likely than ever before to have some type of business partnership with a foreign corporation. Earlier we mentioned that McDonald's opened its first restaurant in Russia through a joint venture with the Moscow city council. Businessland, one of the largest U.S. dealers of personal computers, moved into Japan with the help of Japan's four largest electronics firms. There are estimates that over 80 percent of U.S. businesses could successfully market their products or services overseas provided that they had the required knowledge of foreign markets.[22] Since U.S. markets are regarded as mature or "soft" in many product lines, international markets appear to offer potential for substantial growth. Today, over 95 percent of the world's population lives outside of the United States.[23] That's a lot of Coke, Big Macs, and even Vegamatics!

There is also a higher probability than ever before that you will have an overseas assignment. A 1997 study by the National Foreign Trade Council estimated that there are more than 250,000 Americans on overseas assignments and that that number is expected to increase in the future.[24]

Even if you don't ever work for a foreign-owned firm, or for a U.S. firm with significant foreign investments, experts tell us that all organizations today are affected by the global economy. Even small businesses are using foreign-made materials or equipment, are competing with foreign firms, and are selling their products and services in foreign markets.[25]

As we discussed in Chapter 1, this inevitable globalization of the world's business presents challenges and opportunities for human resources professionals. The purpose of this chapter is to describe and discuss the implications of this increasing globalization for HR activities.

80 percent of Hondas and Acuras are built in the U.S.

Business partnership

31

HOW DO COMPANIES ENGAGE IN
INTERNATIONAL COMMERCE?

Organizations conduct international business in a variety of ways. Each of these forms of international commerce has implications for human resource strategies and tactics. An effective HR professional recognizes the range of choices that each of these international business forms (or combinations of these forms) offers. In this section, we will review the different ways firms may internationalize. Then we will describe some of the ways that HR practices may facilitate and advance these business goals.

When a firm simply wants to sell its products and services in foreign marketplaces, it may choose to **export**. Most companies that export do so in order to increase sales and revenues. For some companies, particularly companies with high research and development costs, exporting is necessary in order to spread these costs over a larger sales volume. Companies may also export in order to relieve excess capacity. Some companies export as a form of diversification because they are concerned that their domestic markets may be maturing. Finally, some companies export because they believe that they lack the necessary knowledge to directly do business effectively on foreign shores. In this case, exporting may be the first step toward a more aggressive international strategy. Baskin-Robbins followed this approach with its entry into Russia. In 1990, it began shipping ice cream to that country from its company-owned plants in Texas and Canada. Over the next five years, the company opened 74 retail outlets with Russian partners, carefully observing the likes and dislikes of local consumers. Finally, in 1995, Baskin-Robbins opened its first, full-service ice cream plant in Moscow.[26] Companies that choose to export may directly sell their products in a foreign market, or they may do business through third parties that specialize in

Intermediaries

facilitating importing and exporting, called **intermediaries**.

There is little risk in exporting: relatively low investment is involved and a decision to withdraw from a market can be made and executed very quickly. Exporting, however, has several disadvantages, including the high cost of transportation and the difficulty of finding good distributors. Tariffs and quotas are also major problems when goods or services enter a country that is part of a regional pact or a free-trade area. For example, products created within the European Union (EU) move from country to country within the Union tariff-free. The same products and services imported from countries outside the Union typically pay tariffs upon entry. This increases the cost of the product and often places "outside" organizations at a competitive disadvantage. The banana trade provides an interesting example. During the 1990s, when Caribbean bananas were exported to EU countries, they were subject to tariffs and quotas. However, bananas grown in Martinique and Guadeloupe were not subject to these tariffs because those particular islands were still provinces of France and, therefore, enjoyed insider status within the EU.[27] The wars were officially ended by treaty in 2001.[28]

Similarly, extensive rules were required in order to regulate so-called "screwdriver" plants in Mexico. Capitalizing on Mexico's membership in the North American Free Trade Agreement (NAFTA), companies in other parts of the world were shipping virtually finished

NAFTA

goods to plants in Mexico where, typically, a screwdriver was the only tool needed to complete the assembly. Then, the exporting country would assert that the product had been "manufactured" in Mexico and, therefore, would qualify for favorable tariff treatment within NAFTA. Since most of these goods ended up in the United States and Canada, these NAFTA members were particularly worried about the loss of tariff revenues and the loss of jobs to non-NAFTA countries whose goods might qualify for treatment as though they had been created within the NAFTA region. As a result, NAFTA contains complex rules of origin that specify how much and what type of assembly qualifies an item as having actually been produced within the NAFTA area. For example, NAFTA's rules of origin specify that for an automobile to qualify as a North American product, 62.5 percent of its value must be created in Canada, Mexico, or the United States. Similarly, to protect textile industry jobs, clothing and other textile products must use North American–produced fibers in order to benefit from NAFTA's preferential tariff treatment.

Licensing

Another means of entering a foreign market is **licensing**. In this approach, one firm, called the *licensor,* leases the right to use its intellectual property to another firm, called the *licensee,* in exchange for a fee. Intellectual property typically includes patents, formulas, patterns, copyrights, trademarks, brand names, methods, and procedures. Licensors are usually required to provide technical information and assistance, and the licensee is obliged to use the rights responsibly and effectively, and to pay the agreed-upon fees. Heineken, for example, is exclusively licensed to manufacture and sell Pepsi-Cola in the Netherlands. To implement this agreement, Pepsi either provides Heineken with its formula or agrees to supply the cola syrup. Heineken then adds carbonated water, packages it in appropriate containers, and sells it in the Netherlands. Under the conditions of the license agreement, Pepsi cannot enter into a similar agreement with another firm to sell Pepsi in the Netherlands, and Heineken cannot alter the product, nor can it begin duplicating other Pepsi products (such as Lays Potato Chips) without a separate agreement.

Franchising

Franchising is a special form of licensing. One of the fastest-growing forms of international business activities today, a franchise agreement allows an independent organization, called the *franchisee,* to operate a business under the name of another, called a *franchisor,* in return for a fee. Franchising typically allows the franchisor more control over the franchisee and provides for more ongoing support from the franchisor to the franchisee than is the case in the typical licensing agreement. For instance, a franchisor may provide ongoing services such as advertising, training, quality assurance programs, and reservation systems (for airline or hotel operations). Fast-food chains such as McDonald's, Dairy Queen, Domino's Pizza, and KFC have franchised restaurants worldwide.

On the plus side, licensees (and franchisees) receive access to a business that has an established product and operating system plus a good reputation. Licensors (and franchisors) get the opportunity to expand internationally with very limited knowledge about local markets. In addition, over time, each party to the agreement learns valuable information from the other: franchisees learn how to operate a successful business; franchisors learn quickly about the marketplace. On the negative side, both parties typically share the revenues, while neither party has full decision-making authority. Disputes about the terms and conditions of the agreement can become a problem. Of course, in some areas of the world, patents and copyrights are not protected, so a particular company could find its intellectual property duplicated and sold everywhere. This has been particularly problematic in the computer software and the music industries in Asia and Eastern Europe. In addition, licensors (and franchisors) must make certain that the required technical skills are available to support the quality of the product or service. McDonald's, for example, spent considerable resources teaching Russian farmers how to grow potatoes that would meet their standards.

Contract manufacturing

Some firms may choose to use a specialized strategy to participate in international business without making direct, long-term investments. Nike engages in **contract manufacturing** when it outsources the creation of its athletic footwear to numerous factories in southeast Asia. This permits Nike to focus its efforts on product design and marketing, rather than production. Contract manufacturing typically means that the organization gives up a major amount of control over the processes, and this may lead to quality problems or other surprises. Nike has suffered considerable negative publicity about the working conditions employed by its contractors in the factories manufacturing its products. (See Appendix A, Critical Thinking Application 2-A.)

Management contracts

Another specialized international business strategy involves **management contracts**. In this form of business, one company sells its management (and sometimes technical) expertise to a company in another area of the world. BAA of Britain, for example, operates the Indianapolis Airport under a 10-year management contract and provides retail services management at the Air Mall in the Pittsburgh Airport.[29] Similarly, major airlines such as Delta, Air France, and KLM often sell their management expertise to small state-owned airlines headquartered in developing countries.[30] Other benefits may become available to organizations that seek managerial partners. For instance, when Sheraton Corporation signs a contract to manage a hotel facility overseas, it usually includes access to and use of its international reservation system.[31]

All of the above approaches enable an organization to internationalize its business interests without actually investing in foreign factories or facilities. Of course, some firms prefer to enter international markets through actual ownership of business. We mentioned earlier that when an organization directly owns part of or an entire business in a foreign

Foreign Direct Investment (FDI)

Alliances

Joint ventures

market, this form of commerce is called **foreign direct investment (FDI)**. Often, FDI follows a period in which an organization seeks to learn about and understand a particular market or region using one of the lower-risk entry alternatives, such as exporting, licensing, franchising, or contracting. Although FDI involves much greater risk, it also means increased managerial and operational control, and it ultimately may mean greater profitability if the venture is successful. One common approach to FDI is to identify an appropriate organization with which to "partner." Such an **alliance** allows an organization to make direct investment very gradually while sharing its risk with a knowledgeable, experienced other party. Sometimes, partners enter into **joint ventures**, which involve creating a new, separate company that is owned jointly by the venture partners. Joint venture partners can be privately owned companies, government agencies, or government-owned companies. For instance, Suzuki Motors Corporation of Japan teamed with the government of India to produce an efficient, small-engine car specifically for the Indian marketplace.[32] Sometimes, organizations enter into joint ventures as defensive moves. Caterpillar (U.S.) and Mitsubishi (Japan) created a joint venture to improve each of their competitive positions against joint rival Komatsu (Japan).[33] General Mills (U.S.) and Nestlé (Switzerland) created Cereal Partners Worldwide (CPW) to combat Kellogg's 50 percent market share of the global cereal industry and, in particular, Kellogg's considerable domination of the European cereal marketplace.[34]

The major disadvantage to joint ventures is the potential for conflict between the partners. This potential is increased considerably when each partner owns 50 percent of the venture. Common areas of conflict include future investments and the sharing of future profits. Joint ventures with local governments also create challenges, particularly when the government's motives and priorities are considerably different from those of its business partner. This situation occurs most often in industries considered to be culturally sensitive or important to national security such as broadcasting, infrastructure projects, and defense.[35]

Strategic alliances

When companies agree to partner with one another, but do not set up a separate entity, they have formed a **strategic alliance**. Such alliances can be set up between an organization and its suppliers, its customers, and its competitors. Strategic alliances share most of the same advantages as joint ventures and some experts regard joint ventures as a form of strategic alliance. Strategic alliances permit organizations to share risk and expenses, particularly related to research and new product development. They also enable each partner to tap into (and, ultimately, benefit from) the strengths of the other. Disadvantages tend to center on the possibility that each is helping to create a future competitor. Thus, organizations are advised to protect their core competencies from the other, which may mean that trust and communication become problematic.[36]

Sole ownership risks

Of course, some organizations prefer the high risk of **sole ownership** of operations in foreign countries in order to ensure that they have full decision-making authority and operational control. In such cases, organizations would rather not audit the practices of franchisees or manage the compromises that shared alliances tend to create. Such businesses may take the form of start-up operations (that is, built from scratch), or they may be carried out through acquisition. Acquisitions involve the purchase of an already up-and-running business with an existing group of suppliers and customers. As a result, growth in foreign markets through acquisitions tends to allow a firm to enter and compete in a new market more quickly than it would if it created a start-up operation. General Electric's 1990 acquisition of Tungsram, a lighting company in Hungary, is an example of this. The acquisition occurred just as communist rule was being eliminated in Eastern Europe. General Electric wanted to learn how to do business in this part of the world. Tungsram was willing to be acquired in order to access Western capitalism and management practices. Some assert that GE's acquisition was a defensive response to the earlier acquisition of Westinghouse's lamp division (GE's traditional rival in its domestic market) by Philips Electronics of Holland. As GE's then–lighting chief, John Opie, indicated, "Suddenly we have bigger, stronger competition. They're invading our market, but we're not in theirs. So, we're immediately put on the defensive."[37]

Within a year of acquiring Tungsram, GE Lighting also acquired Thorn EMI in Great Britain and created a joint venture with Hitachi that would allow entry into the Asian market. As a result of these efforts, GE Lighting's business focus quickly shifted. In 1988, GE Lighting got less than 10 percent of its sales from outside the United States; within five years, more than 40 percent of GE Lighting's sales were coming from abroad. In this case, the speed of GE Lighting's internationalization was facilitated by its use of an acquisition strategy.

Exporting Work

Offshore centers

Earlier we mentioned the recent trend toward businesses creating **offshore professional and operations centers**. Either as a form of sole ownership or as a strategic alliance, these centers involve the exporting of the work itself to places around the globe in order to obtain competitive advantage by leveraging combinations of such factors as workforce skills, cultural similarities, costs, time, and government policies, regardless of where the work product is ultimately marketed. A good case in point is India, which has been the recipient of many U.S. technical and customer service jobs over the past several years. Among developing countries, the Indian workforce is comparatively well educated and speaks English. Upon achieving independence from Great Britain in 1947, India adopted a democratic political system, although its economic system involved significant government planning and intervention. Over the past 10 years, however, the Indian government's regulation of and involvement in private business matters has been steadily declining in order to specifically encourage foreign direct investment. At the same time, the cost of living in India is much lower than in developed countries, which means that the relative cost of labor is extremely attractive for Western companies.

India's programmers ranked number one

When the World Bank surveyed 150 prominent U.S. and European computer hardware and software manufacturers, India's programmers were ranked first out of eight countries, well ahead of Ireland, Israel, Mexico, and Singapore. In fact, one in four software engineers in the world is of Indian origin. With average annual programmer salaries in India of approximately $3,000 per year, no wonder companies such as Hewlett-Packard, IBM, Texas Instruments, Honeywell, and Motorola employ skilled technical workers there.[38] (Of course, this pay could rise significantly and rapidly as the demand for Indian programmers grows and the country continues to develop economically.) In addition to competent workers at advantageous costs, organizations also are benefiting from time advantages by increasingly using international teams of skilled programmers in the United States, Western Europe, and India who pass the work to the next team as each location's workday ends. This permits around-the-clock product development and/or troubleshooting to be done, a huge benefit in industries in which competitive advantage is influenced by "first-to-market" capability.

Call centers

Customer service facilities are also increasingly moving from the United States to India. Customer service representatives at one call center in India are taught to speak English with midwestern accents in order to fend off consumer concern about the use of foreign customer service centers by U.S. companies. Each Indian customer representative is also provided a "U.S. biography" that is used when conversations with customers become personal.[39] The net result of these trends is lower labor costs for American companies, and thus greater profits. Of course, it also means the increased shipment of previously American jobs overseas and the continued stagnation of middle-class wages in this country.

Summary

In summary, then, there are a broad variety of approaches organizations may take to internationalizing their business, ranging in risk and degree of involvement from an export strategy to sole ownership of foreign facilities. Each of these approaches has substantially different implications for human resource professionals. When companies engage in exporting, licensing, or contract manufacturing, the major challenges may be primarily related to operations, marketing, and legal issues. HR issues may be affected only on a secondary basis. For instance, in Chapter 1, we mentioned the increasing importance of a company's reputation for social responsibility and the way this relates both to consumers and to potential (or current) employees. When Nike's or another company's reputation suffers because of the labor conditions used by its contract facilities, HR professionals may find that it is increasingly difficult to attract, retain, and motivate qualified and high-performance employees.

On the other hand, when companies engage in management contracts or franchising, the terms and conditions of the agreement will affect the degree of HR involvement and challenge. Certainly, as McDonald's has franchised foreign restaurants, it has maintained an extremely strong role in the training and development of workers at all levels. However, when McDonald's directly owns and operates a restaurant on foreign shores, the HR challenge increases exponentially to include all the HR domains described in Chapter 1. In general, the HR challenge increases as the degree of an organization's international involvement increases. Thus, sole ownership of foreign subsidiaries presents the highest level of HR involvement and challenge.

The HR challenge also is affected by such things as the degree of cultural similarity among a firm's business holdings and the degree of internationalization of a firm, both of which we will discuss later in this chapter. In the next sections, we will describe the managerial strategies that firms may implement and the way they influence HR issues.

WHAT INFLUENCES THE DECISION TO INVEST IN A PARTICULAR INTERNATIONAL MARKET?

Multinational organizations must also make decisions about the particular markets in which they plan to invest. This decision is typically based on a number of factors. First, issues in a country's general environment make a difference. A country's **general environment** tends to affect all organizations in a similar way. A particular country's economic, legal, political, and sociocultural systems, plus diversity in language and religious beliefs, are all examples of general environment issues. For example, the increasing cultural diversity of the U.S. workforce and the general aging of the population are sociocultural factors that foreign companies would typically consider before they located operations in the United States. U.S. laws on taxation, regulation, free trade agreements, currency valuations, inflation, and unemployment levels are other important factors influencing whether Asian, European, and Latin American companies would open subsidiaries here and what particular business and HR strategy they would implement. Political instability in a particular world region is obviously a major influence on all businesses in the region.

Task environment

A second factor that influences a company's decision to invest in the international market is the company's **task environment**, typically those forces that are directly related to the industry within which a firm operates. Such issues as cost pressures, the intensity of competitive rivalry, the ease with which organizations may enter or leave the industry, and the degree of power over the company maintained by suppliers and customers are all examples of a firm's task environment. Harvard professor Michael Porter argues that such characteristics of an organization's industry are among the most important factors that influence the choice of which international strategy to implement. Porter addresses two types of international industries.[40] In **multilocal industries**, competition in each country, or region, is essentially independent of the competition in other regions. In multilocal industries, business policies and practices can be as centralized or as decentralized as management prefers. In this situation, the organization may choose to manage a portfolio of businesses, each with its own policies and practices. Such multilocal industries include retailing, many consumer food products, wholesaling, life insurance, consumer finance, and caustic chemicals. At the other end of the continuum is the **global industry** in which a firm's competitive position in one country is significantly affected by its position in other countries. Global industries require high integration among units in order to leverage gains and to achieve overall competitive advantage. It is difficult to operate in a decentralized fashion in a global industry because of the high need for coordination. Yet, HR professionals in these organizations must find the appropriate balance between global competitiveness and local responsiveness. Global industries include commercial aircraft, semiconductors, copiers, automobiles, and watches.

A third factor that influences the decision to invest in the international market is the **internal strengths or weaknesses** of the organization. Relevant internal factors include an

General environment

Porter's two international industries

Multilocal

Global

organization's culture, the expertise of its management staff, the sophistication of its information systems, and the ability to detect and respond to consumer trends. In many cases, these are critical assets that add value within the firm. Organizational capability is an important internal strength and, as we indicated in Chapter 1, may be a source of sustainable competitive advantage for an organization, thus influencing its readiness to pursue a particular international strategy.

DOMESTIC VERSUS INTERNATIONAL HRM

How does HRM in an organization that is actively international differ from HRM in a firm that is essentially rooted within the borders of a single nation? HR activities all relate to the procurement, allocation, and utilization of people. Thus, the particular activities themselves may not be all that different regardless of where they are performed or whom they cover. Experts assert that what differentiates domestic HR from international HR is the complexity involved in operating in different countries with different cultures, politics, and laws and regulations.[41]

HRM activities and challenges

Operating in different countries means that individuals must work with different national governments, different legal systems, under widely different economic conditions, with people of diverse cultures and values, and with suppliers and customers over vast geographical distances.[42] Figure 2-1 presents a summary of HRM activities and challenges related to international joint ventures.

In Chapter 3, we will describe the broad array of employment laws that regulate organizations that operate within the United States. But this isn't all there is! Later in the text, you will be introduced to the extensive legal rules governing pay and benefits (Chapter 10), labor relations (Chapter 13), and worker health and safety (Chapter 14). When a foreign firm moves into the United States, it must be expert at understanding and applying legally defensible HR policies and practices. One recent study indicated that the amount of U.S. work-related legislation combined with the litigious orientation of Americans in general places foreign companies at a competitive disadvantage here that they must overcome if they are to be successful.[43] But the reverse is also true. Most developed countries and many emerging economies have a broad framework of work-related legislation. The effective HR professional must understand the implications of such legislation in relevant areas of the world and must have a solid grasp of the costs relating to compliance.

In addition to the legal complexity of operating internationally, other factors affect the level of difficulty involved in operating HR on an international basis.[44] First, the degree of cultural difference influences the complexity of HR and managerial challenges. Culture has been defined as "a system of values and norms that are shared among a group of people and that when taken together constitute a design for living."[45] Studies indicate that culture

Figure 2-1
Unique HRM Challenges in International Joint Ventures

HR Activity	HRM Challenges
Staffing	Host country may demand staffing policies contrary to maximizing profits.
Decision making	Conflicts among diverse constituent groups; complexity of decision processes.
Communication	Interpersonal problems due to geographical dispersion and cultural differences.
Compensation	Perceived and real compensation differences.
Career planning	Perceptions regarding value of overseas assignments; difficulties in reentry.
Performance management	Differences in standards; difficulties in measuring performance across countries.
Training	Special training for functioning in international joint venture (IJV) structure.

Source: Richard J. Klimoski, *Academy of Management Review.* Copyright 1987 by Academy of Management (NY). Reproduced with permission of Academy of Management (NY) in textbook format via Copyright Clearance Center.

affects the policies and practices of HRM and that a major reason that international assignments fail is culture shock, or the expatriate's inability to adjust to a different cultural environment.[46]

Geert Hofstede's five cultural values

A popular study of culture by Geert Hofstede suggests that societies vary in levels of what he calls individualism/collectivism, power distance, uncertainty avoidance, masculinity/femininity, and long-term versus short-term orientations.[47] These represent examples of cultural values that have important implications for multinational organizations, as differences in such values between cultures affect employee and employer preferences in areas such as compensation, training, and recruitment.

Individualism

Individualism is the opposite of collectivism. This dichotomy refers to the degree to which individuals look after themselves or operate in groups. People from highly individualistic societies, such as the United States, Australia, and Great Britain, attach more importance to freedom and challenges in jobs, individual decision making, self-started activities, and individual achievement and initiative than do their counterparts from collectivist societies. Individuals from more collective societies, such as Panama, Ecuador, and Guatemala, may prefer working in groups, team-based pay, and group-based decision making instead of individual-based decision making.

Power distance

Power distance refers to the extent to which less powerful members of society accept and expect that power is distributed unequally. Individuals from societies high in power distance, such as Mexico, Malaysia, and Panama, may prefer centralized decision structures, tall organization pyramids, a wide salary range between the top and bottom of the organization, and a large proportion of supervisory personnel. Individuals from societies low in power distance, such as Austria, Israel, and Denmark, tend to prefer the opposite. With the exceptions of France and Israel, individualist societies tend to be low in power distance, while collectivist societies tend to be high in power distance.

Uncertainty avoidance

Uncertainty avoidance refers to whether members of society feel comfortable in unstructured situations. Individuals from societies with high levels of uncertainty avoidance, such as Greece, Portugal, and Guatemala, tend to have a strong task orientation, prefer flexible work hours, and feel a strong loyalty to their employer. Those from societies with low levels of uncertainty avoidance, such as Singapore, Jamaica, and Denmark, have a strong relationship orientation, find flexible work hours to be unappealing, and feel less loyalty to their employer.

Masculinity/femininity

Masculinity/femininity refers to different expectations about gender roles in society. In highly masculine societies, such as Japan, Austria, and Venezuela, there exists a larger wage gap between the genders, fewer women are bosses, and job applicants oversell themselves. In less masculine societies, such as the Netherlands, Norway, and Sweden, more women are in management, a smaller wage gap exists, and job applicants undersell themselves.

Long-term vs. short-term orientation

Long-term versus short-term orientation refers to the extent to which members of a society accept delayed gratification of their material, social, or emotional needs. Individuals from societies with a long-term orientation, such as China, Hong Kong, and Taiwan, emphasize perseverance, personal adaptability, and relationships ordered by status. Those from societies with a short-term orientation, such as Canada, the Philippines, and Nigeria, expect quick results, and personal steadiness and stability and place less emphasis on status.

Furthermore, regional similarities exist. For example, the Nordic countries of Norway, Sweden, and Denmark tend to cluster together in values. Table 2-1 presents an overview of Hofstede's values for 25 countries. While cultural values vary within countries and may change over time with social, religious, political, and economic developments, understanding societal variations in cultural values may be one useful tool for organizations in effectively managing their human resources.

Experts suggest that a third issue that increases the complexity in managing HR internationally is an organization's degree of foreign investment in relation to its domestic investment. The United States is both the largest national economy and the largest national consumer market in the world. Thus, businesses have had many options concerning growth and expansion (e.g., introducing new products, entering new market segments, finding new uses for existing products, etc.). When U.S. organizations enter foreign markets, they often stumble and fall because they lack experience in effectively operating and managing

Table 2-1
Hofstede's Values for 25 Countries

Country	PDI	UAI	IND	MAS	LTO*
Argentina	49	86	46	56	31
Australia	36	51	90	64	31
Brazil	69	76	38	49	65
Canada	39	48	80	52	23
China	80	30	20	66	118
Denmark	18	23	74	16	46
France	68	86	71	43	39
Germany	35	65	67	66	31
Great Britain	35	35	89	66	25
Hungary	46	82	80	88	50
Indonesia	78	48	14	46	
India	77	40	48	56	61
Israel	13	81	54	47	
Japan	54	92	46	95	80
Mexico	81	82	30	69	
Netherlands	38	53	80	14	44
Panama	95	86	11	44	
Poland	68	93	60	64	32
Russia	93	95	39	36	
Spain	57	86	51	42	19
Sweden	31	29	71	5	33
Thailand	64	64	20	34	56
Turkey	66	85	37	45	
United States	40	46	91	62	29
Vietnam	70	30	20	40	80

PDI = Power distance
UAI = Uncertainty avoidance
IND = Individualism
MAS = Masculinity
LTO = Long-term orientation
* Data not available for some countries.

foreign businesses. Wal-Mart is a great example of a company that has struggled through a number of missteps in its thrust to internationalize. While they are successful in Canada and Mexico now, they started out on very shaky ground. Their problems in Germany persist despite considerable investment.

Organizations headquartered in Switzerland (e.g., Nestlé, ABB, Roche Pharmaceuticals) have tended to plan for growth by internationalizing, since the Swiss domestic market is so small. Such growth, then, is fundamentally based on the organization's ability to effectively manage foreign operations and foreign workers, and organizations tend to plan for this eventuality. In the United States, we have traditionally measured complexity based on size. *Fortune*'s annual Global 500 list identifies the largest 500 international organizations in the world based on total revenues. Using this measure, the United States. headquarters 189 (or 38 percent) of the world's largest international corporations. On the other hand, the United Nations Conference on Trade and Development (UNCTAD), which tracks industrial development around the world, measures the degree of internationality among firms, based not on *how much* an organization directly invests in or derives from its foreign business assets, but rather on the *proportionate share* of an organization's overall business that foreign investment and commerce represent. According to UNCTAD, it is considerably more complex to manage a business and its people when the resources are deployed in various ways all over world than it is to manage just a big organization. The UNCTAD index is based on a composite of three ratios: (1) foreign assets to total assets, (2) foreign sales to total sales, and (3) foreign employment to total employment. Thomson Corporation (Canada), a global media powerhouse, tops the UNCTAD transnationality list with an overall index of 97.2, which means that 97.2 percent of its sales, assets, and employees are based outside of Canada. The Thomson Corporation Web site (www.thomson.com) boasts that its media properties are viewed by over 1 billion people per day!

UNCTAD transnationality index

Figure 2-2
Top 10 Nonfinancial
Organizations Based on
UNCTAD's Transnationality
Index, 2007

Company	Country	Industry
1. Thomson Corporation	Canada	Media
2. Liberty Global Inc.	United States	Telecommunications
3. Roche Group	Switzerland	Pharmaceuticals
4. WPP Group PLC	United Kingdom	Business services
5. Philips Electronics	Netherlands	Electrical and electronic equipment
6. Nestlé SA	Switzerland	Food and beverages
7. Cadbury Schweppes PLC	United Kingdom	Food and beverages
8. Vodaphone Group PLC	United Kingdom	Telecommunications
9. Lafarge SA	France	Nonmetallic mineral products
10. Sabmiller PLC	United Kingdom	Consumer goods/brewers

Source: *World Investment Report 2007.* Available at www.UNCTAD.org/wir.

Ranking second is Liberty Global (United States) with a transnationality index of 96.5 Liberty Global operates broadband communications networks in 15 countries.[48] Figure 2-2 illustrates the top 10 organizations in terms of UNCTAD's transnationality index. Other than that one blockbuster U.S. firm Liberty Global, one can't help but notice the conspicuous absence of any other U.S.-based organization on the top-10 list. In fact, you have to go all the way down to number 26 to find Coca-Cola. Figure 2-3 identifies the 20 "most international" U.S. firms. Thus, the UNCTAD approach to organizational complexity would suggest that, as the degree of a company's internationalization increases, the complexity of the HR challenge increases exponentially.

Recognize differences between domestic and international operations

Another issue (perhaps somewhat related to the above issue) is the attitude of senior management toward international operations. If senior management lacks an international orientation and considers its foreign subsidiaries as nothing more than "outposts" of the home office, the overall importance of internationalization is diminished. Thinking can become very parochial, as managers focus on domestic issues and assume that international issues are identical to those at home. Regardless of the reason, this failure to recognize differences between domestic and international operations frequently creates problems in foreign business units.[49] This failure often limits the problem-solving capacity of the firm and increases the difficulty of successfully operating offshore.

Figure 2-3
The 20 "Most International"
U.S. Companies, 2007

Company	TNI Rank	Industry
1. Liberty Global	2	Telecommunications
2. AES Corporation	15	Electricity, gas, and water
3. Coca-Cola	26	Beverages
4. McDonald's	31	Food and beverages
5. Exxon Mobil	38	Petroleum
6. Chevron Corp.	53	Petroleum
7. Hewlett Packard	54	Electrical and electronic equipment
8. IBM	57	Electrical and electronic equipment
9. United Technologies Corporation	59	Transport equipment
10. Dow Chemical	65	Chemicals
11. Alcoa	66	Metal and metal products
12. Procter and Gamble	67	Diversified
13. Pfizer Inc.	68	Pharmaceuticals
14. Abbott Laboratories	69	Pharmaceuticals
15. General Electric	70	Electrical and electronic equipment
16. Ford Motor	79	Motor vehicles
17. Johnson and Johnson	80	Pharmaceuticals
18. Wyeth	82	Pharmaceuticals
19. General Motors	85	Motor vehicles
20. Altria Group	88	Tobacco

Source: Based on UNCTAD's Transnationality Index—TNI. *World Investment Report 2007.* Available at www.UNCTAD.org/wir.

IHRM is more complex

In summary, then, IHRM is generally more complex than domestic HR because it crosses a number of different systems, including different political systems, economic systems, and legal systems. However, when cultures are very similar, the challenge may not be as difficult as when cultures vary considerably from one another. In addition, when businesses move into the international arena earlier in their history, perhaps because of domestic market size constraints, they build important internal capabilities that may be more difficult to develop later in a firm's experience curve. Finally, when senior managers adopt a multicultural mindset, their international ventures are more likely to be successful.

In the next section, we will turn our attention to the different strategic approaches that may be used when procuring, deploying, and utilizing people on an international basis.

INTERNATIONAL HR STRATEGIES

Ethnocentric approach

International firms choose among four general HR management strategies although many use different strategies for different situations. First, in the **ethnocentric** approach, foreign subsidiaries have little autonomy, operations are typically centralized, and major decisions are made at the corporate headquarters. Although rank-and-file workers are probably locals, key positions in foreign subsidiaries are typically held by management who are moved to the assignment by or from the company headquarters. Individuals who are residents of the organization's home country who are sent offshore on assignment are called **parent-country nationals** (PCNs). Toyota, for example, typically sends a team of Japanese executives to oversee the start-up of a new operation in the United States. Many organizations in the United States manage foreign operations using the same basic format. Research suggests that companies follow this approach because they believe that their management and human resource practices are a critical core competence that provides competitive advantage to the firm.[50] Within this type of strategy, pay for the local workers will tend to be based on the local marketplace. Pay for the management team, particularly if they are PCNs, will tend to be related to the home country. One expert described the traditional mind-set about managing overseas operations of U.S. companies as being related to two questions: "Who's the best U.S. person to handle this job?" and "What will it take to get him or her there?"[51] In ethnocentric situations, training and development efforts will tend to be focused on ensuring that the local workers possess the necessary knowledge, abilities, skills, and other characteristics (KASOCs) to perform effectively.

PCNs

Polycentric philosophy

When organizations adopt a **polycentric** philosophy, they tend to treat each subsidiary as a distinct entity with some level of decision-making authority. This approach suggests that parent-company HR management systems should not be imposed on overseas affiliates since these operations face considerably different legal, social, and cultural conditions.[52] Thus, subsidiaries will be encouraged to craft policies and procedures that will work most effectively based on the particular situation and locale. Within this strategy, subsidiaries are typically led by talented individuals who have proven themselves in the local marketplace. However, there is very little movement of talent from assignment to assignment, and foreign talent is rarely promoted to key positions at headquarters. Individuals who are residents of countries in which a foreign subsidiary is located are called **host-country nationals** (HCNs). During the early stages of internationalization, HCNs tend to fill middle-and lower-level positions. As time progresses, and the organization builds up management experience, it is increasingly common to see HCNs replace PCNs in key management positions. Many organizations specifically target promising HCNs for training and development initiatives. This is at least partly because HCNs are considerably less expensive than PCNs. As with other HR policies, pay in polycentric organizations will tend to be based on local marketplace trends. In polycentric settings, training and development efforts begin to focus on preparing talented locals (HCNs), particularly in developing countries, for future managerial positions and challenges.

Host-country nationals

Geocentric philosophy

When a company chooses to pursue a **geocentric** managerial approach, it strives to integrate its businesses. In these organizations, relationships between headquarters and foreign subsidiaries tend to be extremely collaborative, with each participant contributing important information, perspective, and decision-making factors. Organizations begin considering themselves to have a **global** workforce that can be deployed in a variety of ways, throughout the world. Key positions tend to be filled by the most qualified individual, regardless of national origin. In other words, individual differences in nationality are not as important as individual differences in talent. Geocentric organizations may still rely heavily on HCNs to fill most of their entry-level and operating jobs, but key jobs will tend to be

Third-country nationals

filled by HCNs, PCNs, or **third-country nationals** (TCNs). TCNs are residents of a different country than the parent country or the host country. Thus, when IBM (a U.S. company) transfers an Australian to a position in its Singapore office, they are using a TCN.

Like the staffing patterns, compensation plans in geocentric organizations tend to be based on the concept of a "global marketplace." Pay differences will focus less on an individual's country of origin. Instead, pay will begin to consider the value of this particular work to the organization, at this particular time, in this particular setting, by a person with these particular credentials. Training and development will be especially important in geocentric organizations because of the importance of developing a globally competent group of managers. Investments will be made in sending talented individuals from all corners of the globe to all corners of the organization, including to developmental positions in corporate headquarters.

Regiocentric approach

The **regiocentric** managerial approach may be thought of as a scaled-down version of the geocentric model in that it tends to appoint people to positions within general regions of the world. Thus, European subsidiaries tend to be managed by Europeans, while Asian subsidiaries tend to be managed by Asians. When this approach is used, there is limited movement between corporate headquarters and regions. However, there typically is a strong regional headquarters that is vested with considerable power to manage its operations. Such regional headquarters work very collaboratively and independently with the subsidiaries within the region. Some organizations may use the regiocentric approach as an interim step on their way to a geocentric philosophy. As indicated earlier, Coca-Cola is regionally managed, although it maintains a group of global troubleshooters. In the regiocentric management model, the staffing, compensation, and training strategies also generally relate to regional norms.

What Influences the Choice of IHRM Strategy?

The selection and implementation of an IHRM strategy are very similar to the process used when an organization decides upon its business strategy. A variety of factors must be carefully assessed, including the general environment, the industry environment, and the firm's internal strengths and weaknesses. However, as we described in Chapter 1, the development of an HR strategy also involves careful consideration of the firm's strategy.

For example, a multilocal firm is one that is primarily targeted at local responsiveness. As such, it tends to be a decentralized collection of relatively independent operating organizations. Many such organizations would find a polycentric IHRM strategy to effectively respond to its need for local focus. However, if the firm was anticipating rapid growth in the near future and was concerned about a sufficient supply of local talent to meet the upcoming managerial challenges, a regiocentric strategy might provide an improved opportunity to identify and develop the necessary local talent. If the availability of qualified talent on a regional basis was uncertain, the organization might find that a geocentric or even an ethnocentric strategy could provide an effective transition that would enable a firm to transfer the necessary managerial and operational know-how from talented parent-country or third-country nationals to local-country nationals. The decision concerning which IHRM strategy to implement also may be influenced by the cost pressures within an industry. Firms with high cost pressures may find that the polycentric strategy—with its high level of decentralization—requires so much duplication of functions and services that the strategy is not economically feasible. The key point is that IHRM strategies do not necessarily "match" firm strategies. This is because the particular elements of the firm's environments that indicate what products and services the firm should create do not necessarily consider critical IHRM issues, such as the supply of and demand for labor in a particular area of the world, its relative cost, and its skill level. In Chapter 5, we will describe the HR planning process and the way it relates to both domestic and international businesses.

INTERNATIONAL BUSINESS ASSIGNMENTS

International businesses need international expertise. International job rotation has long been recognized as a key tool for developing such expertise.[53] Yet, foreign job assignments create important HR challenges. In this section, we will describe the use of expatriates and their advantages and disadvantages, and we will note contemporary trends concerning international job assignments.

Expatriates

Employees who are placed in an assignment outside their home country are called **expatriates**. Traditionally, most expatriates have been parent-country nationals (PCNs) assigned by the home office to lead and manage overseas expansions for two reasons.[54] First, top management doubted whether local talent was up to the challenge of managing a business unit. Second, top management wanted to "mold" offshore affiliates into its own culture and practices. Today, organizations report a shift away from using PCNs and increasing their reliance on host-country nationals (HCNs) and third-county nationals (TCNs) to fill their managerial ranks. This is particularly true as multinational organizations move toward a geocentric managerial philosophy. In addition, governments often exert pressure to fill increasing numbers of managerial positions with HCNs.[55]

Goals of International Business Assignments

Today, organizations report using international assignments in order to achieve one or more of the following goals.

First, international assignments are a key element in developing management teams that are globally focused and globally competent. The global leadership challenge is discussed later in this chapter. Second, expatriate assignments encourage high levels of coordination and control among business units. This is especially important when an organization internationalizes by acquiring or creating widely dispersed production and marketing facilities, then integrating them with the rest of the overall business. Expatriates possess knowledge about the way the overall company operates, its long-term goals, and its problem-solving resources that may enable them to identify and capitalize on synergies, while noting duplications of effort.

Third, international business requires high levels of internal communication, both information sharing and information exchange, because of geographical distances, cultural diversity, complex supply and demand conditions, and other similar pressures. Such information sharing is key to effective strategic and tactical decision making. While e-mail and other technological developments facilitate interpersonal contact, global assignments provide the opportunity to work side by side and to develop relationships of collaboration and trust over an extended period of time. Such relationships do not end after the expat "returns home" (or goes on to the next assignment). The continuous exchange of rich information, particularly when people share competitive, marketplace, and technological information, may enable an organization to seize opportunities and respond to challenges more quickly and effectively.

Challenges of International Business Assignments

In spite of their strategic value, managing an effective program of international assignments presents huge challenges.

Assignment Failure

First, there is a high level of expatriate assignment failure. Traditionally, "failed" assignments were those in which the expatriate left the assignment prematurely. It is estimated that 10–20 percent of assignments are failures based on this definition. The most common factors relating to assignment failure are spouse/partner dissatisfaction, inability to adapt, the job doesn't meet expectations, and poor candidate selection.[56] Assignment location also plays a role in assignment failure. When asked for the top three locations for assignment failure, respondents cited China (21 percent), followed by the U.K. (9 percent), and the United States (7 percent).[57] Figure 2-4 reports the results of a survey of Japanese, European, and U.S. firms concerning key problems with international job assignments.

Figure 2-4
Comparative Illustration of HR Challenges

Description of Challenge	U.S. Firms Reporting Challenges	European Firms Reporting Challenges	Japanese Firms Reporting Challenges
Difficulty attracting high-performance managers for offshore assignments	21%	26%	44%
Poor relationships between parent-country nationals (PCNs) and host-country nationals (HCNs)	13%	9%	32%
HCNs reporting frustration about advancement opportunities	8%	4%	21%
High turnover among HCNs	4%	9%	32%
Lack of PCNs skilled in international management	29%	39%	68%
Few PCNs interested in accepting offshore assignments	13%	26%	26%
Reported PCN adjustment problems upon completion of offshore assignment	42%	39%	24%

Source: Adapted from R. Kopp, "International Human Resource Policies and Practices in Japanese, European, and United States Multinationals," *Human Resource Management* 33, no. 4 (Winter 1994), pp. 58–99.

International Compensation

Balance sheet approach

A second challenge relates to the relatively high cost of expatriated executives, as one estimate indicates that the cost of a manager triples as soon as he/she steps into a foreign country. This high cost can be attributed to the traditional method of compensating expatriates based on home-country practices. For example, expatriates from companies based in the United States, Germany, and Japan are typically compensated by a "**balance sheet approach**."[58] The goal of this approach is to ensure that the expatriate maintains the same standard of living in the host country as he/she had in the home country by providing a variety of financial, social, and family benefits. Financial benefits include housing, transportation, and goods and services differentials; company-paid children's education allowances; and tax equalization. Social benefits include a company car and/or driver, rest and relaxation leave, club memberships, domestic staff, language and cross-cultural training, and assistance with locating a new home. Family support benefits include language training, child care providers, locating schools for children, and assistance in locating spousal employment. Factors influencing these benefits include the expatriates' level in the organization, hazardous or difficult host country environments, and market surveys.[59] High-level positions and difficult or hazardous locations require greater premiums and allowances to attract expatriates.

Localization

To mitigate the high costs of the balance sheet approach, many companies have opted to use a second method to compensate their employees: **localization**. Localization, also known as the "going-rate approach," refers to converting expatriates to local standards. For example, an expatriate manager acting as a director for a firm would be paid at the same level as local directors in similar positions are paid, with consideration for performance, work experience, and other inputs. One recent study found that 19 percent of companies localized expatriates immediately, while 7 percent made the transition over a year, 12 percent in two years, and 19 percent in three years.[60] Localization offers another advantage over the balance sheet approach, as local employees may perceive that the pay of their localized counterparts is fair and not based on U.S. pay levels. Localization is not always attractive to expatriates, however, particularly those in developing host countries where pay levels are significantly less than home-country levels.

Cafeteria-style benefit package

A third approach used by firms to reduce costs is to offer expatriates a **cafeteria-style benefit package**, under which expatriates can choose from a variety of benefits, at costs that meet a specified total.[61] This package is less expensive than the balance sheet approach, as certain benefits need not be offered to all expatriates. For example, expatriates with children may choose tuition reimbursement, while those without children may prefer a company car. Certain benefits offer greater appeal, given the country of assignment. As an example, tax equalization is less attractive in Dubai, where employment taxes are not paid, so paying employment taxes may be considered unfair.[62] Tax equalization is a benefit often provided to U.S. expatriates working for U.S. multinationals abroad to offset double taxation: taxation by the U.S. and by the country of assignment. While certain treaties and foreign tax credits from the IRS offset some of these taxes, these offsets may not fully reduce the expatriates' tax liability to that of a single country. Tax equalization is provided to make up the difference.

Recently, as the number of dual-income families has increased in the United States, international HR deals have expanded to include "trailing spouse" benefits. Deals typically include direct assistance in locating a position for the spouse, paying the search firm fee when a position is located, or actually paying the spouse's salary until suitable employment can be located. If no suitable employment can be found, the company often continues to subsidize the spouse for lost wages, which can be costly for organizations. See Chapter 10 for a further discussion on international compensation.

Cross-Cultural Training

Factual information

Cultural orientation

Cultural assimilation

Language training

Sensitivity training

Field experience

A third challenge relates to the necessity of adequate cross-cultural training for expatriates and accompanying families. Organizations invest significant time and resources preparing individuals and their families for international assignments. Such preparation may include cross-cultural training. A classic study by Rosalie Tung suggests that expatriates should be provided with the following forms of cross-cultural training: (1) training on factual information about geography, climate, housing, and schools; (2) cultural orientation training, which provides information related to the cultural institutions and value systems of the host country; (3) cultural assimilation training, which provides brief episodes describing intercultural encounters; (4) language training, (5) sensitivity training, so trainees can develop some attitudinal flexibility; and (6) a field experience, where candidates are sent to the host country or a "microculture" nearby and can undergo some of the stress of living and working with people abroad.[63] Some researchers suggest that pre-departure training is not enough, however, and suggest that "real-time" training, where training is conducted throughout the international assignment, is very useful in reducing problems that occur as the assignment progresses. A newer form of training has also emerged, self-training via the Internet, where trainees teach themselves about cultures by surfing the Web.[64] See Chapter 8 for a further discussion on international training.

Repatriation

Reverse culture shock

A fourth challenge occurs when the expatriates return to the home country. Organizations report increased difficulty in retaining expatriates after completion of an overseas assignment. One study indicates that 27 percent of expatriates leave their organizations within one year and 25 percent leave between the first and second year following repatriation. This rate far exceeds the annual turnover rate for all employees of 13 percent.[65] Consultants add that anecdotal evidence leads them to place an annual expatriate turnover rate closer to 50 percent.[66] Why is there such turnover following an experience that should deliver a clear benefit to both the company and the individual? One reason is a reported lack of concern on the part of organizations about repatriation adjustment. Apparently, most organizations think that "repatriation" means calling the mover and buying the return airline tickets. Yet, "**reverse culture shock**" is a very real problem,[67] and fewer than 20 percent of organizations report even discussing repatriation when an individual agrees to accept an international assignment. Expatriates who live and work in foreign cultures often become immersed in their new cultures and grow to enjoy their new lives. When they return home, they often are surprised to find that everything has changed, from their companies to their communities.[68] If frequent communication between the expatriate and the home office did not exist while on assignment, these changes may seem drastic. In addition, expatriates and repatriates are increasingly reporting frustration with perceived career opportunities when the international assignment is complete. Organizations sometimes fail to take account of the repatriates' international experience and may place them in lateral positions. They may also fail to consider the significant degree of discretion and authority the repatriates had while on assignment when placing them in new positions with greater reporting requirements and more hierarchy.[69]

Recent Trends in Overseas Assignments

Short-term assignments

It is also interesting to note that the length of overseas assignments is declining. In 1996, 32 percent of such assignments lasted more than three years. In 1999, 23 percent of assignments were this long. In 2003, 70 percent of international assignments lasted for one year or less. Cost and family pressures were the major reasons given for the decline in duration. Today, four types of expatriate assignments are identified. **Short-term assignments**, described as "something longer than a business trip," are increasingly popular. Typically,

Developmental assignments

Strategic assignments

Long-term assignments

More international assignments for women

The "typical" expatriate

these are project-oriented assignments with the worker staying in a hotel and the family remaining behind at home. The second type is **developmental assignments** that are increasingly considered to be a necessity for a high-potential fast-tracker in many large international companies. **Strategic assignments** involve persons with special skills who are moved to become a country manager in an unfamiliar area. For example, an individual may be sent to Korea because an organization is planning an expansion and wants a complete immersion in learning the marketplace, in relationship-building, and in understanding the way business is conducted. A **long-term assignment** is similar to the traditional expatriate role. Typically, long-term assignments involve start-ups, or an ongoing managerial presence to resolve major problems, and would typically be taken by a "career expatriate."[70]

These changing trends in international assignments may mean that such assignments become more available to women. Today, although women occupy an estimated 50 percent of the U.S. middle-management labor pool, they represent only 18 percent of the expatriate pool. One study indicated that, when actually offered an international assignment, 80 percent of women accepted the offer, while only 71 percent of men did. Yet, women are rarely offered international assignments. Two surveys have indicated that women were left out because of managerial beliefs that women were not as globally mobile as men and because supervisors were worried about crime overseas as well as cultural biases against women in some areas of the world.[71] Thus far, studies have failed to find a rational foundation for these beliefs. Even though the use of expatriates may be slowing, expatriates continue to occupy a critically important position in organizations' international expansion and management development strategies. One recent survey provided a snapshot of the characteristics of the "typical" expatriate in 2008:[72]

- 11 percent of current expatriates were hired specifically to fill their present international assignment.
- 19 percent of expatriates were women.
- 50 percent of expatriates were between 20 and 39 years old.
- 60 percent of expatriates were married and 83 percent of spouses accompanied their partners on assignment.
- 51 percent of expatriates had children accompanying them.
- 54 percent of spouses were employed before the assignment (but not during); 12 percent were employed on assignment (but not before); and 20 percent were employed both during and before the assignment.

In response to the recent economic climate, more than half (58 percent) of respondents in the same study were reducing expenses. Forty-nine percent were seeking alternatives to long-term assignments, 29 percent reduced policy offerings, 20 percent relied on localization, and 16 percent took more care in selecting candidates. A recent meta-analysis of the expatriate literature revealed some surprising effects.[73] While expatriate adjustment was found to be sensitive to many stressors, some of the most obvious predictors such as previous overseas experience and host country language ability had negligible effects. Spouse—family adjustment, role clarity, and relational skills were potent predictors of assignee adjustment and success.

The United States, China and the United Kingdom are the most active destinations, while China, India, and Russia present the greatest challenges for program managers and expatriates. Chief issues cited—by both expats and program administrators—relate to fluctuating inflation for goods and services, cultural differences, time delays, complex laws, and general inconvenience.

Recommendations for successful international assignments

Figure 2-5 summarizes expert recommendations for successful international assignments. In summary, then, international business assignments provide critical opportunities and resources to organizations as they internationalize. Although the traditional use of expatriates, particularly parent-country nationals, continues to be popular, their costs are increasingly under scrutiny. Firms are investing more resources in third-country nationals and other developmental programs in order to increase the managerial potential of local workers.

**Figure 2-5
Three Steps to Getting
Payback from Expat
Investments**

	Specific Considerations
Step 1: Send people for the right reasons	Specifically what do we want to achieve?
	■ Response to immediate business demands?
	■ Generating new knowledge?
	■ Developing global capability?
	■ Some combination of the above?
Step 2: Send the right people	Technical skills are needed plus
	■ Communication skills
	■ Cultural flexibility
	■ Broad social skills
	■ "Cosmopolitan orientation"
	■ Collaborative negotiation style
Step 3: Finish the assignment the right way	Create straightforward processes to smooth transition
	■ Start planning *early*
	■ Involve the expat in reentry planning
	■ Find suitable job—focus on direct application of new knowledge and skills
	■ Prepare expat for social adjustment realities:
	■ Family's readjustment
	■ Mentors may be gone, reassigned
	■ Transition from "in-charge leader" to "fitting back in" or "starting over again" in new international assignment

Source: Reprinted by permission of *Harvard Business Review*. From "The Right Way to Manage Expats," by J. S. Black and H. B. Gregerson, *Harvard Business Review* 77(2), pp. 52–63. Copyright © 1999 by the Harvard Business School Publishing Corporation, all rights reserved.

GLOBAL LEADERSHIP CHALLENGES

Global management skills are a core competence

As organizations internationalize, there is an increasing sense that managing global operations involves a particular expertise that is separate and distinct from traditional U.S. domestic managerial techniques. Today, organizations are increasingly committed to developing management teams that are globally focused. According to management guru Rosabeth Moss Kanter, global management skills are becoming a major core competence for future business leaders.[74] In some organizations, considerable global experience is recognized as a major strategic imperative. At General Electric, for example, an individual will not advance beyond a particular level without significant experience managing overseas operations. Each of the final candidates in the search for GE CEO Jack Welch's replacement had spent considerable time working outside the United States during the past decade or so. Richard Waggoner was promoted to president and CEO of General Motors after he successfully turned around GM's South American operations. Avon appointed Charles Perrin as CEO largely based on the global business expertise he demonstrated at Duracell. Recently appointed leaders at Campbell's Soup, Ford, Gillette, Tupperware, Goodyear, and General Mills all spent significant time in major offshore assignments.[75] *The Wall Street Journal* reported that, in 1996, 28 percent of executive-level searches required individuals with significant overseas management experience.[76] Yet, progress is slow. A 2001 study reported that only 22 percent of U.S. international firms were led by CEOs with international experience, and that only half that percentage (11 percent) of other top management team members had international experience. The most common international experience was in Canada. In the coming years, however, it is expected that progress will continue and that the nature of the international experience will become more diversified.[77]

Most important HR goal: Develop solid global teams

A Conference Board study of executives in 33 countries indicated that the most important HR goal for the coming years is to develop solid global leadership teams.[78] Some argue that the lack of global management bench strength in many organizations has limited business's ability to implement global growth strategies.[79] In other words, the stage is ready for major expansion, but the supply of effective, well-trained leadership talent is short of the mark.

A Fortune 200 global consumer products company provides a good illustration of the challenge.[80] In the early 1990s, the organization had approximately 60 "globally competent" managers, that is, knowledgeable, effective, well-rounded individuals who could be sent anywhere on the globe to run an operation. Estimates indicated that this was a shortfall of 30–35 people if the company was going to be able to implement its strategic growth plans during the next five years. Why the shortfall? First, the organization had grown faster internationally over the past five years than they anticipated. In the early 1990s, they had opened facilities in 25 new locations, primarily in developing markets, including Eastern Europe, Africa, and Asia. Second, a third of their current globally competent team was nearing retirement age. In addition, the firm was having difficulty maintaining its high-potential employees. As investments were being made in developing global capabilities, individuals were being scooped up by other organizations (including many competitors). Most of these high-potential individuals were part of dual-career, high-potential families who were not particularly interested in expatriate duty, especially in the organization's high-growth areas such as the Ukraine, Nigeria, and Vietnam. In addition, many of the developmental attempts seemed to be "hit or miss" propositions, since the firm had never really articulated exactly what a globally competent leader was. Finally, HR development specialists expressed ongoing frustration because the KASOCs for successful global managers seemed to be changing while developmental efforts were taking place. Review of the popular press would suggest that this organization's experience is not unusual.

What is a globally competent leader?

Exactly what is a globally competent leader? A variety of answers have been offered. One expert describes three key skills relating to globally competent managers and leaders. First, they are integrators who see beyond obvious country and cultural differences. Second, they are diplomats who can resolve conflicts and influence locals to accept world standards or commonalities. Finally, they are cross-fertilizers who recognize the best from various places and adapt it for utilization elsewhere.[81] Another expert cites three knowledges as being critical. First, globally competent managers have an in-depth understanding of world markets, their potentials and their problems. Second, they master all elements of the global supply chains and distribution channels. Finally, they skillfully embrace cultural diversity.[82] In general, it appears that the need for global leadership is clear, but exactly what this is and how it is developed are much less clear.[83]

Understand world markets

Master global supply chains

Embrace cultural diversity

One of the difficulties in agreeing about the attributes of effective global skills may be related to the evolution taking place in the way people think about management roles in global settings in general. One expert asserts that management is currently in the fourth stage of an evolving process of international management philosophy and practices.[84] During early internationalization efforts, companies typically relied on domestic leadership style, at least partly because they didn't see a reason for managing differently. The traditional assumption was that companies achieved competitive advantage by noting and exploiting marketplace discontinuities. For example, if an organization spotted an unfilled need for a particular type of product or service, or noted a rapid improvement in a culture's standard of living, and a dearth of middle-class products, the ability to rush in and produce the desired goods or services could create a windfall for the company. Mostly these were temporary opportunities, however, because other organizations would imitate a successful campaign and drive the price down, and eventually the market would return to a balanced state. This thinking, then, assumed that international success was based on operational capability and marketing savvy, rather than any particular adaptation of managerial style.

During the second stage, international operations began falling short of expectations, and issues of "How should this facility be managed?" arose. Emerging from this thinking was a general consensus that effective management style varied based on the particular situation and setting. Usually referred to as contingency theory, leaders began to examine the applicability of different managerial styles and mindsets, seeking the one that "fit" best, given a specific situation. In the third stage of international managerial development, the spotlight increased its focus on management practices, but thinking shifted away from a pure "it depends on the situation" attitude, and began examining the way managerial roles and styles need to be altered and adjusted to meet the needs of a particular cultural setting. A wealth of cross-cultural managerial literature emerged, including such bestsellers as *Kiss, Bow or Shake Hands* and *Riding the Waves of Culture*.[85] Today, the interest in cross-cultural management and contingency theory continues, but there is an increasing belief that global business leadership needs an overarching managerial philosophy that considers the collection of situations, challenges, and styles as its primary frame of reference.

Competency model of global leadership

A review of the popular literature suggests that the most widespread (and perhaps faddish) approach to global leadership development currently in use is a "competency model." This thinking assumes that effectiveness in global leaders is based on the degree to which individuals possess particular knowledges, abilities, skills, and other characteristics (KASOCs), such as "customer orientation," "building alliances," and "intellectual capacity." However, critics of this approach assert that these competencies are often subjectively derived, poorly defined, and related to an individual's basic traits, rather than learned behavior. In addition, some organizations have too many competencies and they overlap considerably. For example, Chase Manhattan identifies 250 competencies that comprise effective global leadership. Furthermore, little research has been conducted to investigate whether measures of individual competencies can predict actual performance, domestically or internationally. In Chapter 1 we emphasized the need to measure the effects of HR interventions. Competency models are nice. Good measurement is absolutely necessary.

Global mindset

The term *global mindset* is frequently seen these days in the popular press. Global mindset is more a general description of the need for all organizational decision makers to think well beyond domestic issues. One European expert indicates:

> The idea of the global mindset as a roving globetrotter is probably overblown, and clearly, managers possessing, or aspiring to, a global mindset need to come equipped with a globalized database, or some factual knowledge that is different from the domestic mindset. Furthermore, they need to be able to view the world differently. And, finally, their thinking patterns, responses, and cognitive skills differ sharply from a traditional domestic or even multi-domestic mindset.[86]

Figure 2-6 lists the general components of this global mindset according to this expert. In summary, then, developing global leaders and global mindsets will be a continuing challenge faced by HR professionals probably both in the short term as well as over the long term.

Figure 2-6
General Components of a Global Mindset

Component	Description/Illustration
Global data bank	Maintaining relevant, current, "hard" data about countries, regions.
Market knowledge	What are the top 20 markets in our industry?
	What are a key country's defining historic moments?
	What are a key country's defining cultural moments?
	What is the economic system and performance of a key market?
	What is the key country's political system?
	What are the relevant business practices in a key country?
	What are the major geographic features of the key country?
Understanding the global superstructure	Same questions as required for market knowledge, but applied to critical regions.
Global economic system	Appreciation for and knowledge of the "interconnected economy"; that is, the system that connects the world and covers trade and finance, the world capital markets, and the major trade areas.
Cross-cultural skills	Competence in effectively interacting with managers from many countries or cultures.
	Foreign language skills.
	Understanding nonverbal communication commonalities. Appreciation for culture-based nuances in communication techniques.
Cultural roots	Global mindsets require grounding in a home culture for personal balance.
Spirit of generosity, magnanimity	Giving others the opportunity to proceed and to define own directions.

Source: Jean-Pierre Jeannet, *Managing with a Global Mindset*, 1st Edition, © 2000. Electronically reproduced by permission of Pearson Education, Inc., Upper Saddle River, NJ.

SUMMARY

Business and commerce are increasingly crossing national, regional, and continental borders. Some organizations have expanded their marketplaces; some organizations have extended their operations; some organizations operate globally. Even if you never work for an international organization, the global economy affects the marketplaces and the operational environments of most business, even small domestic organizations. In this chapter, we described and discussed the way that this expansion affects human resource practices.

When organizations decide to focus attention outside their national borders, there are a variety of approaches that may be taken. Such choices range in risk and degree of involvement from simply exporting goods and services to sole ownership of foreign facilities. Each of these approaches may present very different HR challenges, ranging from providing technical advice and expertise all the way up to (and including) providing in-depth, comprehensive management services and job-related training to people who live in developing parts of the world.

International organizations tend to choose among four general HR strategies. In ethnocentric organizations, offshore operations have little autonomy, major decisions are made at corporate headquarters, and managers are often moved to assignments from the home country (parent-country nationals). At the other end of the spectrum is the polycentric strategy in which each subsidiary is empowered to make important decisions concerning its own operations and markets. When this approach is adopted, employees tend to have stable assignments and rarely move from location to location. The geocentric HR strategy tends to balance the two philosophies: relationships between headquarters and foreign subsidiaries tend to be collaborative, with each participant contributing important inputs. The partnership found in the geocentric HR strategy often gives rise to a global workforce that can be deployed as needed in various areas throughout the world. A scaled-down version of this philosophy is the regiocentric approach in which the world is viewed as a collection of areas in which people and resources may move fluidly, but cross-regional movement may be the exception rather than the rule. Some organizations use a regiocentric approach as a stepping stone to a global philosophy. In deciding on which international HR management (IHRM) strategy to consider, a company typically considers a variety of factors, including the general environment, an organization's industry characteristics, the business's strategy, and the firm's internal strengths and weakness. In other words, the process of choosing an IHRM philosophy is very similar to the process of deciding which business strategy an organization will choose to pursue.

Traditionally, U.S. organizations have used key management talent and international job rotation as a means for developing and deploying strategic capability during efforts to internationalize business. Yet, such job rotation creates huge cross-cultural challenges, and the record of expatriate success has been increasingly called into question. These challenges include a relatively high expatriate failure rate, the high costs and challenges associated with international compensation, the need for cross-cultural training of expatriates and families, and repatriation. At this time, two trends are emerging: (1) the widespread reliance of U.S. companies on their own expatriate managers to build effective businesses abroad is decreasing and (2) expatriate job rotation is increasingly being used to aid in the development of global capability, rather than primarily as a tool for transplanting specific home-country business, managerial, and HR practices. In other words, international job rotation is increasingly being used as a developmental assignment for an organization's managerial talent, rather than as a way of creating "satellite offices" or "home-country clones."

The development of effective global leadership continues to be a major challenge for organizations. Most international companies view such development as critical to their long-term effectiveness in international marketplaces. There is little question that business leaders everywhere in the world have a great deal to learn about the way to establish, build, and leverage subsidiaries in foreign countries in order to fully deliver strategic capabilities and organizational excellence.

Discussion Questions

1. Why do you think businesses internationalize? Which forces are most influential and which are secondary forces?

2. Think of three or four organizations with which you are familiar. How have they been affected by the globalization of business? Make sure you consider both direct and indirect influences. If they have not been particularly affected, what are some of the reasons for their insulation from the trend?

3. Think about two businesses: (1) a manufacturer of athletic gear and (2) a property and casualty insurance company. How might the internationalization of each of these companies differ from the other? What factors might account for these differences? Choose one company and pretend that you're the HR director. How would you figure out the "right" way to manage this international expansion?

4. How do differences in international HR management (IHRM) strategies affect the relative importance of each of the HR domains?

5. What are the advantages and disadvantages of using home-country, host-country, and third-country nationals? Under what specific circumstances might an organization choose to utilize third-country nationals?

Chapter 3

The Legal Environment of HRM: Equal Employment Opportunity

OBJECTIVES

After reading this chapter, you should be able to

1. Explain the legal issues affecting HRM activity and the various laws related to equal employment opportunity and employment discrimination.
2. Identify potential problems in HRM policy and practice as related to equal employment opportunity laws.
3. Know the importance of judicial interpretation in EEO law.
4. Understand the implications of EEO law in the international context.
5. Describe the future trends related to EEO law and their implications for HRM practice.

OVERVIEW

Chapter 1 briefly summarized the regulatory environment in which HRM is practiced today, and Chapter 2 discussed this environment in the context of the globalization of the economy. Many experts in HRM have noted that the legal environment is a critical component of the external environment for HRM and that legal considerations are a primary force shaping staffing policies and the outsourcing of manufacturing and service jobs. Indeed, legal and regulatory studies related to labor issues and labor costs often cite the regulatory environment as a major reason that some U.S. jobs (and facilities) are moved offshore.

There is a plethora of federal, state, and local laws and regulations that can be the basis of a lawsuit against an employer for actions (or inactions) related to labor relations, workers' compensation, unemployment compensation, wages, health and safety in the workplace, whistleblower's protection, retirement, employee benefits, rights of privacy, and protection against unjust dismissal. The most important of these laws will be considered when the various HRM activities are covered in the chapters to follow.

No other area of the regulatory environment has had such a profound effect on HRM as the laws related to equal employment opportunity (EEO). Surveys of perceived discrimination in the workplace underscore the importance of EEO law for HRM practice. A recent Gallup Poll found that 15 percent of all workers perceived they had been subjected to discrimination.[1] Over 31 percent of Asians reported incidents of discrimination (the largest ethnic group percentage), with 26 percent of African-Americans reporting incidents. Other noteworthy statistics: 22 percent of white women perceived discrimination versus 3 percent of white men; 20 percent of Hispanic men reported discrimination versus 15 percent of Hispanic women.[2]

Such findings, in the context of the increasing diversity of the workforce, translate into a picture of expanding legal activity related to personnel decisions. The focus of discussion in this chapter will be on federal EEO law since most work areas of HRM can be affected by the EEO laws and the regulations about to be discussed. The processes by which employers recruit, hire, place, evaluate, transfer, train, promote, compensate, monitor, lay off, and terminate employees can fall under the close scrutiny of the courts and regulatory agencies based on some form of EEO legislation. There are numerous state and local laws that also affect HRM practice. For example, California has a number of state-specific laws and recently added two major HR laws. Nebraska amended its constitution in 2008 with a civil right initiative.

The purpose of this chapter is to provide an overview of the legal environment with particular emphasis on equal employment opportunity laws and regulations. Descriptions of the most important laws in EEO and the legal interpretations of those laws will be provided. The chapter will conclude with a discussion of the implications of these laws in the global environment and likely future trends related to EEO.

Increasing litigation and regulation

The trend of increasing litigation and regulation has had an impact on virtually all aspects of HRM. Let's start out with some recent cases that represent fairly typical legal actions today. Figure 3-1 presents some examples of cases that reflect this trend.

As discussed in Chapter 1, litigation related to workplace activity is on the rise despite the fact that practicing managers should know more about the legal implications of their behavior than managers did 20 or even 10 years ago.[3] Jury verdicts have grown substantially in recent years with about 25 percent of verdicts resulting in awards of $1 million or more.

One of the reasons for the rise in legal activity is that there are more and more legal options and theories available to someone who feels he or she has been treated unfairly in the workplace. One review summarized the "piecemeal evolution of the U.S. employment law system" as follows:

> [E]mployees are now statutorily protected from workplace discrimination on the basis of race, color, sex, religion, national origin, age, union status, disability, marital status, and in some places, sexual preference, smoking habits, personal appearance, height and weight, political affiliation, arrest and conviction records, and even the method of birth control they choose. Simultaneously, courts have applied long-standing common law to recognize torts of

---

Figure 3-1   **Examples of Recent Litigation**

- A federal judge and the Ninth U.S. Court of Appeals certified a class of 1.6 million women in a Title VII lawsuit against Wal-Mart.
- A federal judge threw out the minimum test score requirement imposed by the NCAA for college athletic eligibility, ruling that the SAT or ACT score requirement had "an unjustified disparate impact against African-Americans."
- Seven Muslim security workers filed a complaint with the EEOC alleging they were fired because they refused to remove their hijabs while at work.
- The EEOC settled a lawsuit for $8.5 million against Ford and the United Auto Workers (UAW) on behalf of African-Americans denied apprenticeships based on a written application test.
- Lockheed Martin Corporation agreed to pay $13 million to settle claims of age discrimination brought by former employees of Martin Marietta.
- Bus drivers in Indianapolis challenged the mandatory retirement age of 55 under the Age Discrimination in Employment Act.
- Target Stores was sued for using a psychological test to screen applicants for security guard positions that the plaintiffs regarded as an invasion of privacy.
- A jury found Circuit City guilty of racial discrimination after plaintiffs' attorneys argued promotion decisions were made under an "excessively subjective" personnel system.
- A California jury awarded a college instructor $2.75 million after San Francisco State University turned him down for tenure because he was white.
- Women working for Home Depot claimed that the company discriminated against women in its selection of supervisors and managers.
- A supervisor was sued by a former employee who claimed the supervisor libeled him in a reference check.
- Ford Motor Company settled a reverse discrimination lawsuit related to their downsizing efforts.
- African-Americans working for Coca-Cola claimed racial discrimination in the manner in which the company promoted people. The case settled for $196 million.
- A terminated employee sued his former employer for disability discrimination, citing his clinical depression as a disability.

wrongful discharge, negligent and intentional infliction of emotional distress, breach of contract, invasions of privacy, fraud, defamation, and negligent hiring, retention, training and supervision. Employment law further affords employees the right to a minimum wage and to overtime pay, the right to a safe and healthful workplace, and the right to benefits of social security, unemployment insurance, worker's compensation, family and medical leave, and proper administration of their pension. Thus, U.S. employment law is a broad patchwork of federal and state statutory rights, common law rights, and administratively created rights that can be implicated by almost any managerial decision that affects employees.[4]

Employment-at-will

The cases listed in Figure 3-1 illustrate the situation. Most Americans work under the **employment-at-will** doctrine that stipulates that both employer and employee can terminate a working relationship at any time and for any reason other than those explicitly covered by law, which as illustrated by the review quoted above have been expanding rapidly.

There are more and more challenges to the employment-at-will doctrine today, and plaintiffs are winning large judgments against employers under creative legal theories related to contract or tort law. For example, courts have ruled that an **implied contract** exists as a consequence of actions or statements of an employer. Statements in employment documents and manuals are often used to define this implied contract. The use of such a theory of violation of the implied contract or other exceptions to the employment-at-will doctrine depends on the particular state. (Employment-at-will is discussed in detail in Chapter 12.)

The trends in litigation related to specific HR practices will be covered when the particular HRM activity is covered. But what you should know at the outset is that the practice of human resources management is a litigious minefield with even more "mines" being planted in the form of new laws and regulations due to the elections of 2008.

A legal "minefield"

This expansion of new legal theories, combined with the changing demographics of the workforce (an aging, more diverse workforce), strongly suggests the likelihood that the legal "minefield" will be more heavily mined in the future. Practicing HRM specialists need to know where the mines are. HRM researchers can shed light on issues related to the legality of certain HRM practices. Let's first enter perhaps the most contentious of the minefields: equal employment opportunity law.

EQUAL EMPLOYMENT OPPORTUNITY LAW

Prior to the civil rights movement of the early 1960s, employment decisions often were made on the basis of an applicant's or worker's race, gender, religion, or other characteristics unrelated to job qualifications or performance. And across racial groups, women earned less than men, even in identical jobs.

The laws we will discuss in this chapter were designed to punish employers that used such criteria as race, gender, disability, or age to exclude certain persons from employment or from certain employment benefits. They also were designed to restore the unfairly treated worker to the position she or he would have held absent the discrimination. Our focus will not be on punishment, however, but on preventing unfair treatment and the legal vulnerability of managers under the civil rights laws.

What Is Employment Discrimination?

Employment discrimination occurs in a variety of ways, and there are a number of methods for seeking redress through the courts. While the legal definition of **discrimination** differs depending on the specific law, it can be broadly defined as *employment decision making or working conditions that are unfairly advantageous (or disadvantageous) to members of one group compared to members of another group.* The decision making can apply to personnel selection, admission to training programs, promotions, work assignments, transfers, compensation, layoffs, punishments, and dismissals. The conditions also can pertain to the work atmosphere itself. For example, a common lawsuit today concerns allegations of sexually harassing behaviors at work that place an individual in an offensive or intimidating environment.

What Are the Major Sources of EEO Redress?

Equal Employment Opportunity Commission (EEOC)

Figure 3-2 presents a summary of illegal discriminatory practices. Of the many sources of redress that are available, the most frequently used sources are federal laws: **Title VII of the 1964 U.S. Civil Rights Act** (CRA), the **Age Discrimination in Employment Act of 1967** (ADEA), and the **Americans with Disabilities Act of 1990** (ADA). (See Figure 3-3 for some excerpts from Title VII.) Most of the states and many municipalities also have their own fair employment laws. Complainants can also use the **equal protection clause** of the U.S. Constitution in lawsuits against the states.

All claims of discrimination under CRA, ADEA, and ADA must first be filed with the EEOC, which received 82,792 charges of discrimination in 2007, an increase of 9 percent from 2006 (check out their Web site at www.eeoc.gov). The highest percentage of claims of discrimination are for race, gender, age, disability, national origin, and religion (in that order).

Figure 3-2   **Discriminatory Practices**

Under Title VII of the Civil Rights Act of 1964, the Americans with Disabilities Act (ADA), and the Age Discrimination in Employment Act (ADEA), it is illegal to discriminate in any aspect of employment, including:

- Hiring and firing
- Compensation, assignment, or classification of employees
- Transfer, promotion, layoff, or recall
- Job advertisements
- Recruitment
- Testing
- Use of company facilities
- Training and apprenticeship programs
- Fringe benefits
- Pay, retirement plans, and disability leave
- Other terms and conditions of employment

Discriminatory practices under these laws also include:

- Harassment on the basis of race, color, religion, sex, national origin, disability, or age.
- Retaliation against an individual for filing a charge of discrimination, participating in an investigation, or opposing discriminatory practices.
- Employment decisions based on stereotypes or assumptions about the abilities, traits, or performance of individuals of a certain sex, race, age, religion, or ethnic group, or individuals with disabilities.
- Denying employment opportunities to a person because of marriage to, or association with, an individual of a particular race, religion, national origin, or an individual with a disability. Title VII also prohibits discrimination because of participation in schools or places of worship associated with a particular racial, ethnic, or religious group.

Employers are required to post notices to all employees advising them of their rights under the laws EEOC enforces and their right to be free from retaliation. Such notices must be accessible, as needed, to persons with visual or other disabilities that affect reading.

Note: Many states and municipalities also have enacted protections against discrimination and harassment based on sexual orientation, status as a parent, marital status and political affiliation. Federal legislation prohibiting discrimination based on sexual orientation passed the U.S. House of Representatives in 2007 and may become law in 2009.

TITLE VII

Title VII prohibits not only intentional discrimination, but also practices that have the effect of discriminating against individuals because of their race, color, national origin, religion, or sex.

Race or Color Discrimination

Equal employment opportunity cannot be denied any person because of his/her racial group or perceived racial group, his/her race-linked characteristics (e.g., hair texture, color, facial features), or because of his/her marriage to or association with someone of a particular race or color.

National Origin Discrimination

- It is illegal to discriminate against an individual because of birthplace, ancestry, culture, or linguistic characteristics common to a specific ethnic group.
- A rule requiring that employees speak only English on the job may violate Title VII unless an employer shows that the requirement is necessary for conducting business. If the employer believes such a rule is necessary, employees must be informed when English is required and the consequences of violating the rule.

The Immigration Reform and Control Act (IRCA) of 1986 requires employers to assure that employees hired are legally authorized to work in the U.S. However, an employer who requests employment verification only for individuals of a particular national origin, or individuals who appear to be or sound foreign, may violate both Title VII and IRCA; verification must be obtained from all applicants and employees. Employers who impose citizenship requirements or give preferences to U.S. citizens in hiring or employment opportunities also may violate IRCA.

Additional information about IRCA may be obtained from the Office of Special Counsel for Immigration-Related Unfair Employment Practices at 1-800-255-7688 (voice), 1-800-237-2515 (TTY for employees/applicants) or 1-800-362-2735 (TTY for employers) or at http://www.usdoj.gov/crt/osc.

(Continued)

Figure 3-2 (*Continued*)

Religious Accommodation

- An employer is required to reasonably accommodate the religious belief of an employee or prospective employee, unless doing so would impose an undue hardship.

Sex Discrimination

Title VII's broad prohibitions against sex discrimination specifically cover:

- Sexual harassment—This includes practices ranging from direct requests for sexual favors to workplace conditions that create a hostile environment for persons of either gender, including same sex harassment. (The "hostile environment" standard also applies to harassment on the bases of race, color, national origin, religion, age, and disability.)
- Pregnancy-based discrimination—Pregnancy, childbirth, and related medical conditions must be treated in the same way as other temporary illnesses or conditions.

Additional rights are available to parents and others under the Family and Medical Leave Act (FMLA), which is enforced by the U.S. Department of Labor. For information on the FMLA, or to file an FMLA complaint, individuals should contact the nearest office of the Wage and Hour Division, Employment Standards Administration, U.S. Department of Labor. The Wage and Hour Division is listed in most telephone directories under U.S. Government, Department of Labor or at http://www.dol.gov/esa/whd_org.htm.

AGE DISCRIMINATION IN EMPLOYMENT ACT

The ADEA's broad ban against age discrimination also specifically prohibits:

- Statements or specifications in job notices or advertisements of age preference and limitations. An age limit may only be specified in the rare circumstance where age has been proven to be a *bona fide* occupational qualification (BFOQ).
- Discrimination on the basis of age by apprenticeship programs, including joint labor-management apprenticeship programs.
- Denial of benefits to older employees. An employer may reduce benefits based on age only if the cost of providing the reduced benefits to older workers is the same as the cost of providing benefits to younger workers.

EQUAL PAY ACT

The Equal Pay Act (EPA) prohibits discrimination on the basis of sex in the payment of wages or benefits, where men and women perform work of similar skill, effort, and responsibility for the same employer under similar working conditions. Note that:

- Employers may not reduce wages of either sex to equalize pay between men and women.
- A violation of the EPA may occur where a different wage was/is paid to a person who worked in the same job before or after an employee of the opposite sex.
- A violation may also occur where a labor union causes the employer to violate the law.

Note: The Paycheck Fairness Act may have amended this law in 2009.

TITLES I AND V OF THE AMERICANS WITH DISABILITIES ACT

The ADA prohibits discrimination on the basis of disability in all employment practices. It is necessary to understand several important ADA definitions to know who is protected by the law and what constitutes illegal discrimination:

Individual with a Disability

An individual with a disability under the ADA is a person who has a physical or mental impairment that substantially limits one or more major life activities, has a record of such an impairment, or is regarded as having such an impairment. Major life activities are activities that an average person can perform with little or no difficulty such as walking, breathing, seeing, hearing, speaking, learning, and working. Note: The 2008 ADA Amendments Act changed the definition of a disability.

Qualified Individual with a Disability

A qualified employee or applicant with a disability is someone who satisfies skill, experience, education, and other job-related requirements of the position held or desired, and who, with or without reasonable accommodation, can perform the essential functions of that position.

Reasonable Accommodation

Reasonable accommodation may include, but is not limited to, making existing facilities used by employees readily accessible to and usable by persons with disabilities; job restructuring; modification of work schedules; providing additional unpaid leave; reassignment to a vacant position; acquiring or modifying equipment or devices; adjusting or modifying examinations, training materials, or policies; and providing qualified readers or interpreters. Reasonable accommodation may be necessary to apply for a job, to perform job functions, or to enjoy the benefits and privileges of employment that are enjoyed by people without disabilities. An employer is not required to lower production standards to make an accommodation. An employer generally is not obligated to provide personal use items such as eyeglasses or hearing aids.

Undue Hardship

An employer is required to make a reasonable accommodation to a qualified individual with a disability unless doing so would impose an undue hardship on the operation of the employer's business. Undue hardship means an action that requires significant difficulty or expense when considered in relation to factors such as a business's size, financial resources, and the nature and structure of its operation.

Prohibited Inquiries and Examinations

Before making an offer of employment, an employer may not ask job applicants about the existence, nature, or severity of a disability. Applicants may be asked about their ability to perform job functions. A job offer may be conditioned on the results of a medical examination, but only if the examination is required for all entering employees in the same job category. Medical examinations of employees must be job-related and consistent with business necessity.

Drug and Alcohol Use

Employees and applicants currently engaging in the illegal use of drugs are not protected by the ADA when an employer acts on the basis of such use. Tests for illegal use of drugs are not considered medical examinations and, therefore, are not subject to the ADA's restrictions on medical examinations. Employers may hold individuals who are illegally using drugs and individuals with alcoholism to the same standards of performance as other employees.

THE CIVIL RIGHTS ACT OF 1991

The Civil Rights Act of 1991 made major changes in the federal laws against employment discrimination enforced by EEOC. Enacted in part to reverse several Supreme Court decisions that limited the rights of persons protected by these laws, the Act also provides additional protections. The Act authorizes compensatory and punitive damages in cases of intentional discrimination and provides for obtaining attorneys' fees and the possibility of jury trials. It also directs the EEOC to expand its technical assistance and outreach activities.

Figure 3-3　　　　　　　　　　**Excerpts from Title VII of the Civil Rights Act of 1964**

SECTION 703

(a) It shall be an unlawful practice for an employer

(1) to fail to hire or to discharge any individual, or otherwise to discriminate against any individual with respect to compensation, terms, conditions, or privileges of employment, because of such individual's race, color, religion, sex, or national origin; or (2) to limit, segregate, or classify employees or applicants for employment in any way which would deprive or tend to deprive any individual of employment opportunities or otherwise adversely affect status as an employee, because of such individual's race, color, religion, sex, or national origin.

(e) Notwithstanding any other provision of this title,

(1) it shall not be an unlawful employment practice for an employer to hire and employ those employees . . . on the basis of religion, sex, or national origin in those certain instances where religion, sex, or national origin is a bona fide occupational qualification reasonably necessary to the normal operation of that particular business or enterprise . . .

(h) Notwithstanding any other provision of this title, it shall not be an unlawful employment practice for an employer to apply different standards of compensation, or different terms, conditions, or privileges of employment pursuant to a bona fide seniority or merit system, or a system which measures earnings by quantity or quality of production or to employees who work in different locations, provided that such differences are not the result of an intention to discriminate because of race, color, religion, sex, or national origin, nor shall it be unlawful employment practice for an employer to give and act upon the results of any professionally developed ability test provided that such test, its administration or action upon the results is not designed, intended, or used to discriminate because of race, color, religion, sex, or national origin . . .

(j) Nothing contained in this title shall be interpreted to require any employer . . . to grant preferential treatment to any individual or to any group because of the race, color, religion, sex, or national origin of such individual or group on account of an imbalance which may exist with respect to the total number or percentage of persons of any race, color, religion, sex, or national origin employed by any employer . . . in comparison with the total number or percentage of persons of such race, color, religion, sex, or national origin in any community, State, section, or other area, or in the available work force in any community, State, section, or other area.

SECTION 704

(a) It shall be an unlawful employment practice for an employer to discriminate against any employees or applicants for employment . . . because the employee or applicant has opposed any practice made an unlawful employment practice by this title, or because he or she has made a charge, testified, assisted, or participated in any matter in an investigation, proceeding, or hearing under this title.

Claims of Title VII discrimination are up

Unfortunately, claims of discrimination are up for all of these areas. National-origin lawsuits represented 11 percent of Title VII claims in 2007 and this includes suits from resident aliens. Aliens who are eligible to work in the United States are covered by Title VII.[5]

The 1991 amendment to Title VII of the Civil Rights Act and the increasing diversity of the workforce have increased the number of lawsuits brought under Title VII. This amendment added compensatory and punitive damages as remediation for violations of the law, thus creating a greater financial incentive for plaintiffs and plaintiffs' attorneys to pursue these cases. Also, Title VII now covers employees of U.S. companies working abroad.

Equal employment laws similar to Title VII exist in 41 states as well as Washington, DC, and Puerto Rico. There are also state and local laws that vary on the legality of certain personnel practices. For example, as of 2008, 10 states, the District of Columbia, and over 165 cities and counties had laws prohibiting employment discrimination based on sexual orientation. Bills are pending and already may have passed in other states (see www.aclu.org for up-to-date data) and there may now be a federal law. Most laws cover actual and perceived sexual orientation. Several state laws include all orientation, including heterosexuals and bisexuals. Some states also provide additional protection beyond the ADA opposing discrimination against people who are HIV positive or are victims of AIDS.

What Is the Cost of Violating EEO Laws?

The costs of violation can be substantial, not only because of direct expenses related to litigation, but also in terms of a company's reputation. In certifying the largest class in an employment discrimination lawsuit, a federal judge concluded that promotion decisions at Wal-Mart were "excessively subjective." Testimony in the case indicated that the company required only a current "above average" performance evaluation and a willingness to relocate as minimal requirements for promotion. The selection of employees for the management training program was a "tap on the shoulder process" with evidence that jobs were posted only on occasion.

Women's total earnings at Wal-Mart were 5 percent to 15 percent less than men's total earnings in similar jobs. About 65 percent of hourly employees are women, but women hold only 33 percent of management positions. Women take 4.38 years from date of hire to be promoted to assistant manager while men take only 2.86 years. Women take 10.12 years to reach the store manager level while men take only 8.64 years. An expert witness also used "external benchmarking" in showing that Wal-Mart lagged far behind the retail industry in rates of women in managerial positions The court concluded that gender was a significant variable in explaining these discrepancies. This conclusion led to the certification of a class of 1.6 million women in the Title VII lawsuit.

Recent EEO cases

Employers are now well aware of how costly violations of EEO laws can be. The EEOC filed and then settled a race discrimination lawsuit against Walgreens for $24 million in 2008. In a much-publicized case, Abercrombie and Fitch settled a Title VII suit for $40 million in 2006. A&F's staffing procedures and outcomes are currently under strict court scrutiny. Morgan Stanley agreed to pay $52 million to end a sex discrimination suit in 2005. The firm was accused by the EEOC of a pattern of discrimination that denied women opportunities for promotions and higher salaries. Another $2 million was set aside for a training program directed at gender-based discrimination. Home Depot settled a class-action lawsuit alleging sex discrimination for $65 million. The federal government is not immune from charges of discrimination. The Department of Justice settled a lawsuit against the Voice of America for $108 million, and the Social Security Administration settled a race discrimination lawsuit for $7.75 million in 2002. The "jury is still out" (so to speak) on the huge class action, sex discrimination lawsuit against Wal-Mart.

With some 25 percent of jury verdicts at $1 million or more, organizations try to be more careful about their personnel practices, with monitoring systems and EEO offices and training programs for personnel decision makers and supervisors. HRM specialists and labor attorneys are active in conducting training and research in areas related to EEO.

One major component of training programs is simply making personnel decision makers aware of EEO laws. Let us follow this approach by introducing you to the major laws that account for most of the regulation and litigation in EEO. The major federal laws are presented in the same order as the frequency with which they are used as a source of redress in employment discrimination claims. Remember that there are many other laws related to HRM practice and policy. These laws will be introduced when relevant to each HRM activity covered in the text.

TITLE VII OF THE CIVIL RIGHTS ACT OF 1964

The Civil Rights Act was signed by President Johnson in 1964, and was amended by the **Equal Employment Opportunity Act** in 1972 and the **Civil Rights Act of 1991.** Title VII deals specifically with discrimination in employment and prohibits discrimination based on race, color, religion, sex, or national origin. Figure 3-3 provides major excerpts from Title VII. The Act covers all employers having more than 15 employees except private clubs, religious organizations, and places of employment connected to an Indian reservation.

What Is the EEOC?

The **U.S. Equal Employment Opportunity Commission (EEOC),** an agency of the U.S. Department of Labor, was created to monitor and enforce compliance with several laws, including Title VII. The EEOC can (and often does) file Title VII suits against organizations for violations of the law. The EEOC also issues interpretive regulations regarding employment practices (see www.eeoc.gov to review these guidelines). Among the many regulatory interpretations issued by the EEOC are the **Uniform Guidelines on Employee Selection Procedures** that provide recommendations for employment staffing, the **Interpretative Guidelines on Sexual Harassment,** and the **Policy Guidance on Reasonable Accommodation Under the Americans with Disabilities Act**. HRM specialists participated in the development of these guidelines. While these guidelines are not law, the courts often use them to evaluate claims in a case.

EEO-1 forms

The EEOC also requires that most employers with 100 or more employees submit an annual **EEO-1** form. Figure 3-4 presents the new 2008 form. Data from these forms are used to identify possible patterns of discrimination in particular organizations or

Figure 3-4   EEO-1 Form

Joint Reporting Committee

- **Equal Employment Opportunity Commission**
- **Office of Federal Contract Compliance Programs (Labor)**

EQUAL EMPLOYMENT OPPORTUNITY

EMPLOYER INFORMATION REPORT EEO—1

Standard Form 100
(Rev. 3/97)

O.M.B. No. 3046-0007
EXPIRES 10/31/99
100-214

Section A—TYPE OF REPORT
Refer to instructions for number and types of reports to be filed.

1. Indicate by marking in the appropriate box the type of reporting unit for which this copy of the form is submitted (MARK ONLY ONE BOX).

    (1) ☐ Single-establishment Employer Report

    Multi-establishment Employer:
    (2) ☐ Consolidated Report (Required)
    (3) ☐ Headquarters Unit Report (Required)
    (4) ☐ Individual Establishment Report (submit one for each establishment with 50 or more employees)
    (5) ☐ Special Report

2. Total number of reports being filed by this Company (Answer on Consolidated Report only) _____

Section B—COMPANY IDENTIFICATION (To be answered by all employers)

	OFFICE USE ONLY

1. Parent Company
    a. Name of parent company (owns or controls establishment in item 2) omit if same as label

    a.

    Address (Number and street)

    b.

City or town	State	ZIP code

    c.

2. Establishment for which this report is filed. (Omit if same as label)
    a. Name of establishment

    d.

Address (Number and street)	City or Town	County	State	ZIP code

    e.

    b. Employer Identification No. (IRS 9-DIGIT TAX NUMBER)

    f.

    c. Was an EEO-1 report filed for this establishment last year? ☐ Yes ☐ No

---

Section C—EMPLOYERS WHO ARE REQUIRED TO FILE (To be answered by all employers)

☐ Yes ☐ No   1. Does the entire company have at least 100 employees in the payroll period for which you are reporting?

☐ Yes ☐ No   2. Is your company affiliated through common ownership and/or centralized management with other entities in an enterprise with a total employment of 100 or more?

☐ Yes ☐ No   3. Does the company or any of its establishments (a) have 50 or more employees AND (b) is not exempt as provided by 41 CFR 60-1.5, AND either (1) is a prime government contractor or first-tier subcontractor, and has a contract, subcontract, or purchase order amounting to $50,000 or more, or (2) serves as a depository of Government funds in any amount or is a financial institution which is an issuing and paying agent for U.S. Savings Bonds and Savings Notes?

If the response to question C-3 is yes, please enter your Dun and Bradstreet identification number (if you have one): ☐☐☐☐☐☐☐☐

NOTE: If the answer is yes to questions 1, 2, or 3, complete the entire form, otherwise skip to Section G.

Employment at this establishment – Report all permanent full- and part-time employees including apprentices and on-the-job trainees unless specifically excluded as set forth in the instructions. Enter the appropriate figures on all lines and in all columns. Blank spaces will be considered as zeros.

Job Categories	Number of Employees (Report employees in only one category)														Total Col A - N
	Race/Ethnicity														
	Hispanic or Latino		Not-Hispanic or Latino												
			Male						Female						
	Male	Female	White	Black or African American	Native Hawaiian or Other Pacific Islander	Asian	American Indian or Alaska Native	Two or more races	White	Black or African American	Native Hawaiian or Other Pacific Islander	Asian	American Indian or Alaska Native	Two or more races	
	A	B	C	D	E	F	G	H	I	J	K	L	M	N	O
Executive/Senior Level Officials and Managers 1.1															
First/Mid-Level Officials and Managers 1.2															
Professionals 2															
Technicians 3															
Sales Workers 4															
Administrative Support Workers 5															
Craft Workers 6															
Operatives 7															
Laborers and Helpers 8															
Service Workers 9															
TOTAL 10															
PREVIOUS YEAR TOTAL 11															

1. Date(s) of payroll period used: _____ (Omit on the Consolidated Report.)

O.M.B. No. 3046-0007
Revised 01/2006
Approval Expires 1/2009

Section E—ESTABLISHMENT INFORMATION *(Omit on the Consolidated Report)*

1. What is the major activity of this establishment? (Be specific, i.e., manufacturing steel castings, retail grocer, wholesale plumbing supplies, title insurance, etc. Include the specific type of product or type of service provided, as well as the principal business or industrial activity.)

OFFICE USE ONLY

g.

Section F—REMARKS
Use this item to give any identification data appearing on last report which differs from that given above, explain major changes in composition of reporting units and other pertinent information.

Section G—CERTIFICATION *(See Instructions G)*

Check one
1 ☐ All reports are accurate and were prepared in accordance with the instructions (check on consolidated only)
2 ☐ This report is accurate and was prepared in accordance with the instructions.

Name of Certifying Official	Title	Signature	Date
Name of person to contact regarding this report (Type or print)	Address (Number and Street)		
Title	City and State	ZIP Code	Telephone Number (Including Area Code)	Extension

All reports and information obtained from individual reports will be kept confidential as required by Section 709(e) of Title VII.
WILLFULLY FALSE STATEMENTS ON THIS REPORT ARE PUNISHABLE BY LAW, U.S. CODE, TITLE 18, SECTION 1001.

segments of the workforce. The EEOC may then take legal action against an organization based on these data.

EEOC mediation program

The EEOC offers a mediation program that is available at no cost to the parties. Mediation is an informal process in which a neutral third party assists the opposing parties to reach a voluntary, negotiated resolution of a charge of discrimination. The decision to mediate is completely voluntary for the charging party and the employer. Mediation gives the parties the opportunity to discuss the issues raised in the charge, clear up misunderstandings, determine the underlying interests or concerns, find areas of agreement, and, ultimately, incorporate those areas of agreements into resolutions. A mediator does not resolve the charge or impose a decision on the parties. Instead, the mediator helps the parties to agree on a mutually acceptable resolution. The mediation process is strictly confidential. In 2005, the EEOC and McDonald's USA signed an agreement to mediate workplace disputes prior to an EEOC investigation or potential litigation when a charge of discrimination is filed with the federal agency in some regions of the United States. This mediation partnership was the 90th such national or regional agreement between the EEOC and a large employer (mainly Fortune 500 companies). The EEOC oversees over 12,000 mediations annually. Under the terms of such agreements, all eligible charges of discrimination filed with the Commission naming McDonald's as the employer will be referred directly to the mediation unit.

What Is Not Prohibited by Title VII?

Title VII does not prohibit discrimination based on seniority systems, veterans' preference rights, national security reasons, or job qualifications based on test scores, backgrounds, or experience, even when the use of such practices may be correlated with the race, gender, color, religion, or national origin. Title VII also does not prohibit **bona fide occupational qualifications (BFOQs)** or discriminatory practices whenever these practices are "reasonably necessary to the normal operation of the organization." For example, a BFOQ that excludes one group (e.g., males or females) from an employment opportunity is permissible if the employer can argue that the **"essence of the business"** requires the exclusion, that is, when business would be significantly affected by not employing members of one group exclusively.

BFOQs

"Essence of the business"

Diaz v. Pan America

What if a company had data showing customers clearly prefer employees with certain protected class characteristics? Pan American Airways tried this argument in *Diaz v. Pan America*. They presented data showing the vast majority of their customers (overwhelmingly male) preferred female flight attendants. The Supreme Court said that customer preference was not a legally defensible reason to discriminate.

In general, the position of the courts regarding BFOQs favors judgments about the performance, abilities, or potential of specific individuals rather than discrimination by class or categories. The court has said that the BFOQ exception to Title VII is a narrow one, limited to policies that are directly related to a worker's ability to do the job and the essence of the business.

How Do You File a Title VII Lawsuit?

If an individual believes that he or she has been a victim of illegal discrimination and wishes to pursue a claim through the legal system, the complaint must first be filed with an office of the EEOC. The EEOC guidelines for filing a charge are presented in Figure 3-5.

What Legal Steps Are Followed in a Title VII Case?

The Supreme Court has established the legal steps to be followed in a Title VII action through the federal court system. Although the plaintiff retains the "burden of proof," a model is used such that the burden of producing evidence shifts from the plaintiff to the defendant and back to the plaintiff. Initially the complainant or plaintiff has the burden to show that a **prima facie** case of discrimination exists. Prima facie means "presumed to be true until proven otherwise"; the plaintiff must show that there is a high likelihood that a violation of EEO law has occurred. After the plaintiff produces sufficient evidence to establish a prima facie case, the burden of producing evidence shifts to the employer

Prima facie evidence

Figure 3-5 **Filing a Charge of Employment Discrimination**

Note: Federal employees or applicants for Federal employment should see Federal Sector Equal Employment Opportunity Complaint Processing.

WHO CAN FILE A CHARGE OF DISCRIMINATION?
- Any individual who believes that his or her employment rights have been violated may file a charge of discrimination with EEOC.
- In addition, an individual, organization, or agency may file a charge on behalf of another person in order to protect the aggrieved person's identity.

HOW IS A CHARGE OF DISCRIMINATION FILED?
- A charge may be filed by mail or in person at the nearest EEOC office.
- Individuals who need an accommodation in order to file a charge (e.g., sign language interpreter, print materials in an accessible format) should inform the EEOC field office so appropriate arrangements can be made.
- Federal employees or applicants for employment should see Federal Sector Equal Employment Opportunity Complaint Processing.

WHAT INFORMATION MUST BE PROVIDED TO FILE A CHARGE?
- The complaining party's name, address, and telephone number.
- The name, address, and telephone number of the respondent employer, employment agency, or union that is alleged to have discriminated, and number of employees (or union members), if known.
- A short description of the alleged violation (the event that caused the complaining party to believe that his or her rights were violated).
- The date(s) of the alleged violation(s).
- Federal employees or applicants for employment should see Federal Sector Equal Employment Opportunity Complaint Processing.

WHAT ARE THE TIME LIMITS FOR FILING A CHARGE OF DISCRIMINATION?
All laws enforced by EEOC, except the Equal Pay Act, require filing a charge with EEOC before a private lawsuit may be filed in court. There are strict time limits within which charges must be filed:
- A charge must be filed with EEOC within 180 days from the date of the alleged violation, in order to protect the charging party's rights.
- This 180-day filing deadline is extended to 300 days if the charge also is covered by a state or local antidiscrimination law. For ADEA charges, only state laws extend the filing limit to 300 days.

Note: The Ledbetter Act may become law in 2009.
- These time limits do not apply to claims under the Equal Pay Act, because under that Act persons do not have to first file a charge with EEOC in order to have the right to go to court. However, since many EPA claims also raise Title VII sex discrimination issues, it may be advisable to file charges under both laws within the time limits indicated.
- To protect legal rights, it is always best to contact EEOC promptly when discrimination is suspected.
- Federal employees or applicants for employment should see Federal Sector Equal Employment Opportunity Complaint Processing.

WHAT AGENCY HANDLES A CHARGE THAT IS ALSO COVERED BY STATE OR LOCAL LAW?
Many states and localities have antidiscrimination laws and agencies responsible for enforcing those laws. EEOC refers to these agencies as "Fair Employment Practices Agencies (FEPAs)." Through the use of "work sharing agreements," EEOC and the FEPAs avoid duplication of effort while at the same time ensuring that a charging party's rights are protected under both federal and state law.
- If a charge is filed with a FEPA and is also covered by federal law, the FEPA "dual files" the charge with EEOC to protect federal rights. The charge usually will be retained by the FEPA for handling.
- If a charge is filed with EEOC and also is covered by state or local law, EEOC "dual files" the charge with the state or local FEPA, but ordinarily retains the charge for handling.

HOW IS A CHARGE FILED FOR DISCRIMINATION OUTSIDE THE UNITED STATES?
U.S.-based companies that employ U.S. citizens outside the United States or its territories are covered under EEO laws, with certain exceptions. An individual alleging an EEO violation outside the U.S. should file a charge with the district office closest to his or her employer's headquarters. However, if you are unsure where to file, you may file a charge with any EEOC office.

For answers to common questions about how EEO laws apply to multinational employers, please see:
- The Equal Employment Opportunity Responsibilities of Multinational Employers
- Employee Rights When Working for Multinational Employers

or defendant, who must provide some proof of a legitimate, nondiscriminatory reason for the employment decision. Finally, the burden of producing evidence shifts back to the plaintiff to either show that the reason given was a pretext for discrimination or that an alternative practice, less discriminatory in its effect, would have achieved the employer's purpose equally well. Title VII cases can be brought under either (or both) of two theories: **disparate treatment** and **disparate impact.** The steps to follow for each are illustrated in Figure 3-6.

What Is Disparate Treatment?

McDonnell Douglas v. Green

Plaintiffs can demonstrate a prima facie case by showing **disparate treatment,** the most frequently used theory of discrimination. According to the procedures established in the 1973 *McDonnell Douglas v. Green* Supreme Court case, plaintiffs must show that an employer treats one or more members of a protected group differently.[6] For example, the use of

Figure 3-6 **Evidence and Proof in Title VII Cases**

Evidence Burden	Disparate Treatment	Disparate Impact
Plaintiff's initial burden (prima facie case)	He or she belongs to the discriminated-against group. He or she applied and was qualified. He or she was rejected. The position remained open to applicants with equal or fewer qualifications.	Unequal impact of the practice(s) in question on different groups (e.g., 80% rule violation)
Defendant's rebuttal burden	Articulate a "legitimate nondiscriminatory reason for the rejection."	Demonstrate that the challenged practice is job-related for the position in question and consistent with business necessity.
Plaintiff's burden in response	Show that the stated reason is a pretext by demonstrating, e.g.: • The employer doesn't apply that reason equally to all. • The employer has treated the plaintiff unfairly before. • The employer engages in other unfair employment practices. OR Show the plaintiff's group membership was a factor in the rejection decision.	Show that a less discriminatory and equally valid alternative practice or method does exist.
Defendant's burden in response	Show that the decision would have been the same even if it had not taken plaintiff's group membership into account.	

Source: From J. Ledvinka, *Federal Regulation of Personnel in Human Resource Management* 1e. © 1982 South-Western, a part of Cengage Learning, Inc. Reproduced by permission.www.cengage.com/permissions.

different criteria for promotion depending on the candidate's sex would constitute disparate treatment. Female applicants who were not hired by a firm might show that the employer asked them questions about their marital status or child care arrangements that were not asked of male applicants. In disparate treatment cases, the Supreme Court established that the burden is on the plaintiff to prove that the employer *intended* to discriminate because of race, sex, color, religion, or national origin.[7]

Title VII and retaliation

One special form of disparate treatment is **retaliation.** Employers cannot retaliate against employees who file EEO charges or parties who testify on behalf of plaintiffs in such cases. Retaliation accounted for 24 percent of Title VII charges in 2007.

What Is Disparate Impact?

Griggs v. Duke Power

Class action lawsuits

According to procedures established in the 1971 Supreme Court ruling in *Griggs v. Duke Power*,[8] plaintiffs can show that an employer's practices had a **disparate impact** on members of a protected group by showing that the employment procedures (e.g., tests, interviews, credentials) had a disproportionately negative effect or "adverse impact"on members of a protected group. Impact cases are often established as **class-action** cases in which a judge can certify a class of people who make similar claims against a company. For example, the plaintiffs in the *Wal-Mart* case were certified as a class before the rest of the case was pursued. Such impact is (usually) considered unintentional but illegal discrimination if the employment practice is not shown to be "job related."

Business necessity

Job relatedness

Whether or not the employer had good intentions or didn't mean to discriminate is irrelevant to the courts in "disparate impact" cases. After the plaintiff shows evidence of adverse or disparate impact, the employer must carry the burden of producing evidence of **"business necessity"** or **"job relatedness"** for the employment practice. Finally, the burden shifts back to the plaintiff, who must then show that an alternative procedure is available that is equal to or more effective than the employer's practice and has less adverse impact.

HRM specialists are very much involved in this important area. The concept of "job relatedness" as defined in *Griggs* is very similar to the concept of validity developed by industrial psychologists. Thus, once evidence is established showing an employment practice has an adverse impact on a protected class, the burden will be on the employer to show the practice is "job related" or a "business necessity."

How Do You Determine Disparate or Adverse Impact?

Four-fifths rule

Adverse impact

"Uniform Guidelines"

Fisher's Exact Test

Race/gender norming outlawed

One common "yardstick" recommended (and used) by the EEOC in the *Uniform Guidelines* and adopted in numerous court cases for determining disparate or adverse impact is the **four-fifths rule** (also known as the 80 percent rule). This rule means that a selection rate (number selected/number considered) for a protected group cannot be less than four-fifths or 80 percent of the selection rate for the group with the highest selection rate. For example, the City of Columbus, Ohio, used a paper-and-pencil, multiple-choice examination to screen applicants for its firefighter positions. While 84 percent of the whites passed the examination, only 27 percent of the blacks did. Using the four-fifths rule, 80 percent of the white selection rate is 67 percent (.8 ×.84). Since the 27 percent selection rate for blacks was less than 67 percent, the Columbus test was determined to have an **adverse impact** on blacks.

The 80 percent or four-fifths rule derives from the EEOC's **Uniform Guidelines on Employee Selection Procedures.** However, it is not the only statistical measure of adverse impact that can be used to establish prima facie evidence of discrimination. The makeup of a workforce can also be compared to population or industry data (e.g., a geographical area is 15 percent Hispanic while only 3 percent of workers for Company X in that same area are Hispanic). In the class-action sex discrimination lawsuit against Wal-Mart, the plaintiffs presented data showing that 58 percent of managers in general merchandising were women while only 32 percent of Wal-Mart's managers were women. Plaintiffs (or the EEOC) can also analyze the extent to which a protected class possesses a particular credential or years of experience versus a majority group.

A superior statistic also used in numerous EEO cases to examine and define "prima facie" evidence of discrimination is the **Fisher's Exact Test** (for a demonstration go to: http://www.langsrud.com/fisher.htm). The Fisher test can be used to test whether there is any relation between two categorical variables (e.g., males and females) and two levels (e.g., promoted/not promoted).

Remember that these statistical data establish only prima facie evidence of discrimination. The employer still has the opportunity to prove "job relatedness" and/or "business necessity" for the practice or procedure. Such statistical analysis can also be used in **disparate treatment** cases to buttress a claim of intentional discrimination and a "pattern and practice" of such discrimination.

The disparate impact theory has been used in a great many cases involving "neutral employment practices" such as tests, entrance requirements, particular credentials, or physical requirements. For example a class of African-Americans who were denied apprenticeships at Ford Motor using the test score requirements applied the 80 percent rule to show that the proportion of African-Americans meeting the minimum requirements was less than 80 percent of the rate for whites.

The Civil Rights Act of 1991 is unclear as to precisely what an employer must demonstrate; it simply says that the employer must demonstrate *"that the challenged practice is job related for the position in question and consistent with business necessity."* There is a great deal of litigation over just what both employees and the organizations they sue must demonstrate under the CRA of 1991.

HRM specialists and academics often find themselves on both sides of a court case, attacking (and defending) the validity evidence and the statistics presented to support or refute a theory of discrimination and claims of "job relatedness."

Prior to 1991, organizations attempted to avoid statistical adverse impact by interpreting test scores based on the ethnicity of the test taker. Called **race norming** and even practiced by the U.S. Department of Labor, the exact raw scores on the same test were interpreted (and converted) depending on whether the test taker was white, Latino, or African-American. The practice of race (and gender) norming was outlawed by the Civil Rights Act of 1991. Title VII now states that "It shall be an unlawful employment practice for a respondent, in connection with the selection or referral of applicants or candidates for employment or promotion, to adjust the scores of, use different cutoff scores for, or otherwise alter the results of, employment related tests on the basis of race, color, religion, sex, or national origin."

How Does an Employer Prove "Job Relatedness"?

Griggs v. Duke Power

There is a large body of case law that provides legal definitions of the term *job related*. The major case in this area is *Griggs v. Duke Power*, in which the Supreme Court struck down the use of an employment test and a high school educational requirement for entry-level personnel selection. Such practices were judged to be discriminatory because they excluded a disproportionate number of blacks from employment and thus had an "adverse impact," and because the employer could not show that the hiring requirements were "job related," or related to performance on the job. As the court noted, if an employment practice cannot be shown to be related to job performance, and that practice causes an "adverse impact" against protected class members, then the practice is prohibited.

Adverse impact

Albemarle v. Moody

Since the *Griggs* decision was rendered in 1971, there have been many cases that have focused on job-relatedness issues. In *Albemarle Paper Company v. Moody* (1975), the Supreme Court clarified the job-relatedness defense, requiring a careful job analysis to identify the specific knowledge, skills, and abilities necessary to perform the job or a study that shows a clear statistical relationship between applicants test scores (or a particular credential) and their job performance.[9]

The Supreme Court declared that the job-relatedness argument must be applied to *all* steps of a multiple-hurdle selection procedure.[10] Winnie Teal had been denied promotion to a supervisory position because of a low score on a written exam that was the first hurdle of the promotion process. When the final promotion decisions were made, the "bottom line" decisions (i.e., who was actually promoted) actually favored African-Americans. But the Supreme Court ruled in *Connecticut v. Teal* (1982) that the "bottom line" is *not* an acceptable legal defense in such a case. Rather, the "job relatedness" argument must be made for any step where "prima facie" evidence is presented. Thus, in *Connecticut v. Teal*, the burden was on the defendant to prove the test was "job related" even though the state had actually promoted a proportional number of African-Americans.

Connecticut v. Teal

Evidence of a significant correlation between test scores and job performance is considered ideal to support an argument of job relatedness. HRM specialists conduct such studies routinely to evaluate the use of a test or selection procedure. Suppose a company is sued based on the disparate impact theory and must establish the "job relatedness" of their test. The company does not have enough data to conduct an internal study. What if a study exists showing that the test being challenged has validity for the same or similar jobs? Could the company "borrow" a validity study based on data collected in several other organizations? Called **validity generalization** (VG) studies and based on meta-analytic research, there are now many studies based on the correct assumption that the mean of several correlational studies is probably a strong basis for concluding that there is a valid relationship between test scores and job performance for similar job situations. However, the most recent review on this issue concludes that the courts have not been that impressed with VG evidence. In order to "borrow" validity in this manner, the organization needs to demonstrate that the job connected to the lawsuit is similar to the jobs under study in the VG study. In addition, the VG study should present sufficient detail on the individual studies that led to the inference that the test was valid.[11] Even with solid VG evidence, however, it is unclear whether the exclusive use of "borrowed" validity in the form of a VG study will meet the "job relatedness" burden for organizations.

Validity generalization

Alternative procedures

Once the defendant has presented acceptable evidence of job relatedness, the case is not necessarily over. Title VII allows that where two or more selection procedures are available which serve the user's "legitimate interest in efficient and trustworthy workmanship," and which are equally valid for a given purpose, the user should use the procedure which has been demonstrated to have the lesser adverse impact. Thus, the plaintiffs could present evidence that an alternative method exists and that its use would result in less (or no) adverse impact. This step in the process could even apply to the use a particular "cutoff" score for a test (e.g., 70 percent is passing).

Watson v. Fort Worth Bank

Another critical case related to "disparate impact" theory is *Watson v. Ft. Worth Bank & Trust* (1988). Clara Watson was denied a promotion based on an interview. The critical question that the Supreme Court addressed here was whether "impact" theory could be used in "subjective" employment practices such as interviews and performance appraisals (the *Griggs* and *Albemarle* cases concerned "neutral employment practices" such as credentials or test scores). In a unanimous decision, the Court allowed "disparate impact"

Dukes v. Wal-Mart

theory for subjective employment practices. This decision is of course critical for many class-action cases, including *Dukes v. Wal-Mart*, where women maintain that the "subjective" method of selecting and promoting managers was discriminatory.

What is Illegal Harassment?

Harassment is another form of employment discrimination that also violates Title VII and other federal laws (the Age Discrimination in Employment Act and the Americans with Disabilities Act). Harassment is unwelcome conduct that is based on race, color, sex, religion, national origin, disability, and/or age. Sexual harassment is one form of such illegal harassment. There were over 27,000 charges of illegal harassment in 2007, not including sexual harassment. In a much-publicized case, the EEOC settled a harassment case in 2008 with *Tavern on the Green*, a landmark restaurant located in Central Park in New York City. The settlement was for over $2 million but also entailed substantial remedial relief and careful court scrutiny in the future. The EEOC alleged that the restaurant's managers and others engaged in severe and pervasive sexual, racial, and national origin harassment of female, black, and Hispanic employees and then retaliated against employees who complained.

Unlawful harassment, two conditions

The harassment becomes unlawful where (1) enduring the offensive conduct becomes a condition of continued employment, or (2) the conduct is severe or pervasive enough to create a work environment that a reasonable person would consider intimidating, hostile, or abusive. Antidiscrimination laws also prohibit harassment against individuals in retaliation for filing a discrimination charge, testifying, or participating in any way in an investigation, proceeding, or lawsuit under these laws; or opposing employment practices that they reasonably believe discriminate against individuals, in violation of these laws.

Petty slights, annoyances, and isolated incidents (unless extremely serious) will not rise to the level of illegality. To be unlawful, the conduct must create a work environment that would be intimidating, hostile, or offensive to reasonable people. The offensive conduct may be offensive jokes, slurs, epithets or name calling, physical assaults or threats, intimidation, ridicule or mockery, insults or put-downs, offensive objects or pictures, and interference with work performance.

Harassment can occur in a variety of circumstances. The harasser can be the victim's supervisor, a supervisor in another area, an agent, client or customer of the employer, a co-worker, or a nonemployee. The victim does not have to be the person harassed, but can be anyone affected by the offensive conduct. The harassment can be illegal even without economic injury to, or discharge of, the victim.

What Constitutes Sexual Harassment under Title VII?

Sexual harassment filings in 2007 totaled 12,510, a 4 percent increase from the prior fiscal year. Under Title VII, sexual harassment, like racial and ethnic harassment, is illegal since it constitutes discrimination with respect to a person's conditions of employment. These conditions can refer to psychological and emotional workplace conditions that are coercive or insulting to an individual. The EEOC has published Guidelines for employers dealing with sexual harassment issues (go to www.eeoc.gov). According to these Guidelines, sexual harassment is defined as follows:

> unwelcome sexual advances, requests for sexual favors, and other verbal or physical conduct of a sexual nature constitute sexual harassment when (1) submission to such conduct is made either explicitly or implicitly a term or condition of an individual's employment, (2) submission to or rejection of such conduct by an individual is used as the basis for employment decisions affecting such individual, or (3) such conduct has the purpose or effect of unreasonably interfering with an individual's work performance or creating an intimidating, hostile, or offensive working environment.

A growing number of sexual harassment complaints are filed by males (16 percent in 2007). However, harassment of an employee because of sexual orientation does not constitute illegal harassment under Title VII (it probably does under applicable state or local laws prohibiting discrimination based on sexual orientation).

Meritor Savings v. Vinson

In 1986, the Supreme Court in *Meritor Savings v. Vinson* stated that it was not necessary for the plaintiff to establish a causal relationship or **quid pro quo** between the rejection of sexual advances and a specific personnel action such as a dismissal or a layoff.[12]

Quid pro quo harassment

Rather, it was necessary for the plaintiff only to establish that the harassment created unfavorable or hostile working conditions for him or her. Any workplace conduct that is "sufficiently severe or pervasive to alter the conditions of employment and create an abusive working environment" constitutes illegal sexual harassment.[13]

The Supreme Court has since provided further clarification on this and other harassment issues. In *Harris v. Forklift* (1993), Theresa Harris was asked to remove coins from her boss's front pocket, was asked to go to the Holiday Inn to "negotiate" her raise, and was exposed to hundreds of other disgusting suggestions and behaviors.[14] A lower court determined that Harris had not suffered emotionally from the harassment and thus a hostile working environment was not created. The Supreme Court disagreed, stating that the psychological effect was unnecessary and that only a "reasonable person" needed to find it hostile or abusive. The Court also provided some guidance for the lower courts in determining a hostile working environment. The frequency of the behavior or verbal abuse, its severity, the extent to which it is threatening or humiliating, and whether the abuse interferes with the employee's work performance all may be considered in making the determination of a hostile working environment.

Harris v. Forklift

Legal outcomes in harassment suits

Research on the judicial outcomes of sexual harassment claims identified the following correlates of favorable legal outcomes for the claimant: (1) when the harassment involved physical contact of a sexual nature, (2) when sexual propositions were linked to threats or promises of a change in the conditions of employment, (3) when the claimant notified management of the problem before filing charges, (4) when the claims were corroborated, and (5) when the organization had no formal policy toward sexual harassment that had been communicated to its employees.[15]

Compensatory and punitive damages

The Civil Rights Act of 1991 provides for compensatory and punitive damages (in addition to back pay) of up to $300,000 for companies with over 500 employees. That's $300,000 per complaint. The price tag for sexual harassment can be even much higher under state laws that may have no ceilings on compensatory or punitive damages.

What Is the Employer's Liability in Harassment Cases?

Two 1998 Supreme Court decisions provided clarification on employer liability for sexual harassment by supervisors. In *Burlington Industries, Inc. v. Ellerth* and in *Faragher v. City of Boca Raton,* the Court said that the employer is always liable when a hostile environment is created by a supervisor that results in a tangible employment action (e.g., termination).[16] However, the employer may not be liable when there is no tangible employment action if it can be shown that the employer exercised "reasonable care" in preventing and correcting the harassing behavior and the plaintiff failed to take advantage of corrective opportunities that were available. This so-called **affirmative defense** clearly indicates that organizations should have sexual harassment policies in place and communicated to all employees. Figure 3-7 presents a summary of employer liability for all forms of harassment by supervisors.

Burlington Industries v. Ellerth

Faragher v. City of Boca Raton

Affirmative defense

Regarding co-workers, the employer will be liable if someone in authority knew or should have known of the harassment and did nothing to stop it. The courts are generally clear that this rule applies to any kind of harassment: racial, ethnic, or religious also. Employers also may be liable for behaviors committed by nonemployees, clients, temporary employees, or outside contractors in the workplace if they knew or should have known about the acts and didn't take appropriate action. Essentially, the courts have made it clear that an organization is liable for sexual harassment when management is aware of the activity yet does not take immediate and appropriate corrective action.

Employer not always liable

Thus, an employer is not always liable for sexual harassment. For example, a company is less likely to be found liable under the following conditions: (1) There is a specific policy on harassment that an employee violated, (2) there is a company grievance procedure that the complainant did not follow, and (3) the grievance procedure allows the complainant to bypass the alleged harasser in filing the violation.

The policy has to be acceptable. A policy that requires that a complaint be made through an immediate supervisor (with no alternatives) is not an acceptable policy. But a good harassment policy (for any type of harassment) can give an employer legal protection.

Figure 3-7 **Employer Liability for Harassment by Supervisors**

1. When does harassment *violate federal law*?

   Harassment violates federal law if it involves discriminatory treatment based on race, color, sex (with or without sexual conduct), religion, national origin, age, disability, or because the employee opposed job discrimination or participated in an investigation or complaint proceeding under the EEO statutes.

   Federal law does not prohibit simple teasing, offhand comments, or isolated incidents that are not extremely serious. The conduct must be sufficiently frequent or severe to create a hostile work environment or result in a "tangible employment action," such as hiring, firing, promotion, or demotion.

2. Does the guidance apply *only to sexual harassment*?

   No, it applies to all types of unlawful harassment.

3. When is an employer legally responsible for harassment by a supervisor?

   An employer is always responsible for harassment by a supervisor that culminated in a tangible employment action. If the harassment did not lead to a tangible employment action, the employer is liable unless it proves that: (1) it exercised reasonable care to prevent and promptly correct any harassment; and (2) the employee unreasonably failed to complain to management or to avoid harm otherwise.

4. Who qualifies as a "*supervisor*" for purposes of employer liability?

   An individual qualifies as an employee's "supervisor" if the individual has the authority to recommend tangible employment decisions affecting the employee or if the individual has the authority to direct the employee's daily work activities.

5. What is a "*tangible employment action*"?

   A "tangible employment action" means a significant change in employment status. Examples include hiring, firing, promotion, demotion, undesirable reassignment, a decision causing a significant change in benefits, compensation decisions, and work assignment.

6. How might harassment culminate in a tangible employment action?

   This might occur if a supervisor fires or demotes a subordinate because she rejects his sexual demands, or promotes her because she submits to his sexual demands.

7. What should employers do to *prevent and correct harassment*?

   Employers should establish, distribute to all employees, and enforce a policy prohibiting harassment and setting out a procedure for making complaints. In most cases, the policy and procedure should be in writing.

   Small businesses may be able to discharge their responsibility to prevent and correct harassment through less formal means. For example, if a business is sufficiently small that the owner maintains regular contact with all employees, the owner can tell the employees at staff meetings that harassment is prohibited, that employees should report such conduct promptly, and that a complaint can be brought "straight to the top." If the business conducts a prompt, thorough, and impartial investigation of any complaint that arises and undertakes swift and appropriate corrective action, it will have fulfilled its responsibility to "effectively prevent and correct harassment."

8. What should an antiharassment *policy* say?

   An employer's antiharassment policy should make clear that the employer will not tolerate harassment based on race, sex, religion, national origin, age, or disability, or harassment based on opposition to discrimination or participation in complaint proceedings.

   The policy should also state that the employer will not tolerate retaliation against anyone who complains of harassment or who participates in an investigation. (Retaliation was the second highest charge category, behind race, in 2007.)

9. What are important *elements of a complaint procedure*?

   The employer should encourage employees to report harassment to management before it becomes severe or pervasive.
   The employer should designate more than one individual to take complaints, and should ensure that these individuals are in accessible locations. The employer also should instruct all of its supervisors to report complaints of harassment to appropriate officials. The employer should assure employees that it will protect the confidentiality of harassment complaints to the extent possible.

10. Is a complaint procedure adequate if employees are instructed to report harassment to their immediate supervisors?

    No, because the supervisor may be the one committing harassment or may not be impartial. It is advisable for an employer to designate at least one official outside an employee's chain of command to take complaints, to assure that the complaint will be handled impartially. A policy that requires that the complaint go through the supervisor is unacceptable.

11. How should an employer *investigate* a harassment complaint?

    An employer should conduct a prompt, thorough, and impartial investigation. The alleged harasser should not have any direct or indirect control over the investigation.

    The investigator should interview the employee who complained of harassment, the alleged harasser, and others who could reasonably be expected to have relevant information. Before completing the investigation, the employer should take steps to make sure that harassment does not continue. If the parties have to be separated, then the separation should not burden the employee who has complained of harassment. An involuntary transfer of the complainant could constitute unlawful retaliation. Other examples of interim measures are making scheduling changes to avoid contact between the parties or placing the alleged harasser on nondisciplinary leave with pay pending the conclusion of the investigation.

(Continued)

12. How should an employer *correct harassment*?

    If an employer determines that harassment occurred, it should take immediate measures to stop the harassment and ensure that it does not recur. Disciplinary measures should be proportional to the seriousness of the offense.

13. Does an employee who is harassed by his or her supervisor have any *responsibilities*?

    Yes. The employee must take reasonable steps to avoid harm from the harassment. Usually, the employee will exercise this responsibility by using the employer's complaint procedure.

14. Is an employer legally responsible for its supervisor's harassment if the *employee failed to use* the employer's complaint procedure?

    No, unless the harassment resulted in a tangible employment action or unless it was reasonable for the employee not to complain to management. An employee's failure to complain would be reasonable, for example, if he or she had a legitimate fear of retaliation. The employer must prove that the employee acted unreasonably.

15. If an employee complains to management about harassment, should he or she wait for management to complete the investigation before *filing a charge* with EEOC?

    It may make sense to wait to see if management corrects the harassment before filing a charge. However, if management does not act promptly to investigate the complaint and undertake corrective action, then it may be appropriate to file a charge. The deadline for filing an EEOC charge is either 180 or 300 days after the last date of alleged harassment, depending on the state in which the allegation arises. This deadline is not extended because of an employer's internal investigation of the complaint.

Farley v. American Cast Iron Pipe

In *Farley v. American Cast Iron Pipe*, the 11th U.S. Circuit Court of Appeals established that once an employer has promulgated an effective antiharassment policy, it is incumbent upon the employees to utilize the procedural mechanisms established by the company specifically to address problems and grievances.

What Steps Should a Company Follow Regarding Sexual Harassment?

Because of the increase in Title VII litigation regarding sexual harassment, the following "affirmative defense" strategies have been recommended for organizations: (1) Develop a written policy against sexual harassment, including a definition of sexual harassment and a strong statement by the CEO that it will not be tolerated (some courts have concluded that an employer without a harassment policy is sanctioning a hostile environment); (2) conduct training to make managers aware of the problem (required in Massachusetts, California, Connecticut, and Maine); (3) inform employees that they should expect a workplace free from harassment, and what actions they can take if their rights are violated; (4) detail the sanctions for violators and protection for those who make any charges; (5) establish a grievance procedure for alleged victims of harassment; (6) investigate claims made by victims; and (7) discipline violators of the policy.[17] On this last point, companies must be careful. Individuals can claim "unlawful termination" and have prevailed in cases where they show that they were not treated fairly in the investigation or the hearing that led to the dismissal. Judgments have been in the millions. The person being accused of sexual harassment deserves as fair a treatment as that which is afforded the accuser. Miller Brewing executive Jerold MacKenzie was awarded over $26 million after he was fired for "sexually harassing" a female employee by describing an episode of the *Seinfeld* show. The sexual harassment policy should stipulate that the policy applies to same-sex harassment as well.

Oncale v. Sundowner offshore services

In *Oncale v. Sundowner Offshore Services,* The Supreme Court ruled unanimously in 1998 that same-sex harassment was illegal under the CRA.[18]

Mandated harassment training

The California law mandating sexual harassment training for all supervisors of employers with 50 or more employees took effect in 2006. The law sets specific standards for the training. The training must be conducted via "classroom or other effective interactive training" and include the following topics: (1) information and practical guidance regarding the federal and state statutory provisions concerning the prohibition against and the prevention of sexual harassment; (2) information about the correction of sexual harassment and the remedies available to victims of sexual harassment in employment; and (3) practical examples aimed at instructing supervisors in the prevention of harassment, discrimination, and retaliation.

What Is Affirmative Action?

Although there is no one generally recognized definition, **affirmative action** has to do with the extent to which employers make an effort through their personnel practices to attract, retain, and upgrade members of the protected classes of the 1964 Civil Rights Act.

Affirmative action may refer to several strategies, including actively recruiting underrepresented groups in a firm, changing management and employee attitudes about various protected groups, eliminating irrelevant employment practices that bar protected groups from employment, and granting preferential treatment to protected groups. The term *affirmative action* is related to corporate *diversity programs* and policies, but the actual HRM activities defining the old affirmative action programs and the new diversity programs are similar. The issue of affirmative action and how it is carried out has been identified as a source of difficulty between HRM professionals and line managers. Whether or not preferential treatment can or should be granted based on protected class characteristics is at the heart of the trouble. *Diversity* is a complex term. The 1990 census included five categories of ethnicity. The 2000 census included 63 categories.

Contractors and subcontractors with more than $50,000 in government business and 50 or more employees not only are prohibited from discriminating, but also must take affirmative action to ensure that applicants and employees are not treated differently as a function of their sex, religion, race, color, and national origin.

Rehabilitation Act

Executive Order 11246

OFCCP

Section 503 of the Rehabilitation Act requires federal contractors to take affirmative action to employ and advance qualified people with disabilities. Under **Executive Order 11246,** contractors and subcontractors are required to develop a written affirmative action plan that is designed to ensure equal employment opportunity. These plans are monitored by the Office of Contract Compliance Programs (OFCCP) in the U.S. Department of Labor (www.dol.gov).

What Is the Legal Status of Affirmative Action?

Federal courts can order involuntary affirmative action programs or organizations can implement voluntary affirmative action without a court mandate. Given the recent personnel changes on the Supreme Court, the legality of such programs is now more questionable than ever. As either part of a judicial decision or the negotiated settlement of a lawsuit, a court also can order targeted quota hiring. For example, as a part of a negotiated settlement with the U.S. Forest Service in 1994, a California federal judge ordered the Forest Service to hire a set number of females over a prescribed period of time. The Forest Service had to submit an annual report on compliance with the quota and was subject to punitive action for failure to comply.

U.S. Steelworkers v. Weber

Voluntary AA programs

In 1979, the Supreme Court in *U.S. Steelworkers v. Weber* approved Kaiser Aluminum's voluntary affirmative action plan because it did not "unnecessarily trammel" the interests of majority employees and it was a temporary measure that would cease when blacks reached parity with their representation in the labor market. Lower courts reviewing subsequent challenges to voluntary affirmative action programs have used the *Weber* test to ascertain their legality.[19]

Johnson v. Santa Clara Transportation

"Manifest imbalance"

"Equally qualified"

It has been argued that affirmative action is appropriate only as a remedy for past discrimination against specific individuals. The Supreme Court had opposed this narrow application in early decisions. The 1987 Supreme Court ruling in *Johnson v. Santa Clara Transportation Agency* provided some clarity to the remedies that have been pursued under affirmative action and equal employment opportunity.[20] According to the court, organizations may adopt voluntary programs to hire and promote qualified minorities and women to correct a "manifest imbalance" in their representation in various job categories, even when there is no evidence of past discrimination. This was the first time that the Supreme Court explicitly ruled that women as well as blacks and other minorities can receive preferential treatment. The decision also affects the most common employment situation in the United States today: work situations where it is difficult or impossible to prove past discrimination, but a statistical disparity exists in the number of females and minorities in certain occupations relative to population statistics. Even that decision emphasized that "manifest imbalance" meant substantial, inexplicable differences in workforce representation. The decision also emphasized that preferential treatment may only be granted when job candidates are judged to be "equally qualified." Thus, race or gender may be considered to essentially break a tie under a condition of "manifest imbalance."

While the majority of the Supreme Court decisions have favored affirmative action and most forms of preferential treatment, there now appear to be some important qualifiers on their appropriateness. These qualifiers include (1) affirmative action plans should be "narrowly tailored" to achieve their ends with a timetable for ending the preferential practice, (2) class-based firing or layoff schemes are too harsh on the innocent and inappropriate in most circumstances, and (3) preferential personnel practices of any kind are appropriate only in employment situations where there is a prior history or indication of past discrimination. Also unclear is the literal meaning of *prior discrimination.* In its earlier decision in *U.S. Steelworkers v. Weber,* the Supreme Court said it was acceptable to use affirmative action programs to remedy "manifest racial imbalance" regardless of whether an employer had been guilty of discriminatory job practices in the past.

In two cases involving the University of Michigan in 2004, the Supreme Court provided some clarity to the issue of affirmative action and college admissions. Both Michigan cases (*Gratz v. Bollinger*; *Grutter v. Bollinger*) addressed the question of whether racial preference programs unconstitutionally discriminate (based on the **Equal Protection Clause** of the U.S. Constitution) against white students.[21]

Gratz v. Bollinger

Grutter v. Bollinger

The Court ruled that race can be a factor in college admissions since a social value may be derived from greater "diversity" in the classroom. However, race cannot be an "overriding" factor in admissions decisions. While these twin decisions only directly applied to public universities, the decisions could have implications for private schools, other governmental decision making, and perhaps the business world. The impact of both decisions is that schools have dropped fixed or rigid, point-based systems for admission. Justice Sandra Day O'Connor, writing for the majority in the law school admissions case (*Grutter*), stated that the Constitution "does not prohibit the law school's narrowly tailoring use of race in admissions decisions to further a compelling interest in obtaining the educational benefits that flow from a diverse student body."[22] Justice O'Connor retired in 2006. The Supreme Court is likely to revisit this issue soon. In reaction to the Supreme Court's decision in *Grutter* favoring a form of affirmative action where race can be a factor in decision making, the state of Michigan amended its Constitution in 2006 with Proposition 2, banning race and gender preferences in public education, employment, and contracting. A similar law amended the Nebraska Constitution in 2008. Thus, at present, California, Michigan, Nebraska and Washington now have amendments to their Constitutions banning race and gender preference.

State constitutional amendments

What Is Required before a Company Embarks on a Voluntary Affirmative Action/Diversity Program?

The courts have clarified criteria for *voluntary* affirmative action plans. For voluntary plans, it has been suggested that they (1) be designed to eradicate old patterns of discrimination, (2) not impose an "absolute bar" to white advancement, (3) be temporary, (4) not "trammel the interests of white employees," (5) be designed to eliminate a "manifest racial imbalance," and (6) show preference only from a pool of equally qualified candidates. For involuntary affirmative action programs, it was suggested that preferential treatment is legal when it (1) is necessary to remedy "pervasive and egregious discrimination"; (2) is used as a flexible benchmark for court monitoring, rather than as a quota; (3) is temporary; and (4) does not "unnecessarily trammel the interests of white employees."

Reverse discrimination claims

U.S. Office of Contract Compliance (OFCCP)

Despite the apparent legal protection for voluntary affirmative action plans, managers must tread very carefully to avoid "reverse discrimination" lawsuits. Race- or gender-conscious employment decisions made in the absence of an AA plan may result in a successful claim of reverse discrimination by a rejected majority applicant or employee. Even when OFCCP-approved AA programs exist, managers must ensure that all individuals meet the stated job requirements and that affirmative action plans are carefully drafted and followed. The most difficult and legally troublesome issue related to AA is when (and if) a protected class characteristic may be considered relative to the qualifications of the job candidates.

Is Affirmative Action Still Necessary?

Some now argue that Barack Obama's election in 2008 supports the argument that AA is now unnecessary because equal employment opportunity already exists. Women and minorities strongly disagree with this argument. A three-year study conducted by a bipartisan federal commission concluded that women and minorities still face barriers to their advancement: the so-called **glass ceiling.** The glass ceiling refers to the lack of women and minorities in top managerial positions. The various diversity programs are designed to break down some of these barriers. Go to www.ilr.cornell.edu for the Glass Ceiling Commission archives.

Glass ceiling effect

There is no question that the general public is opposed to preferential treatment when it is defined as taking a protected class characteristic such as race or gender into account in making staffing or admission decisions. People tend to favor affirmative action in terms of recruitment, training opportunities, and attention to applicant qualifications. They tend to oppose preferential treatment and any form of quota-based decision making. The state of California amended its Constitution in 1996, approving Amendment 209, which explicitly outlaws any preferential treatment by California public agencies. (The language of the amendment is almost identical to Section 703J of the 1964 Civil Rights Act but with less ambiguity.) The states of Washington, Nebraska and Michigan have adopted similar provisions banning preferential treatment by governments within these individual states.

THE AGE DISCRIMINATION IN EMPLOYMENT ACT OF 1967, AMENDED IN 1978 AND 1986

ADEA lawsuits are up

Smith v. Jackson

Meacham v. Atomic Power

The Age Discrimination in Employment Act (ADEA) was designed to prohibit age discrimination in employment decisions (e.g., hiring, job retention, compensation, and other terms and conditions). The law applies to workers over the age of 39. The ADEA applies to employers with 20 or more employees, unions of 25 or more members, employment agencies, and federal, state, and local governments. There were almost 18,000 claims of age discrimination in 2007, up 26 percent from 1999. While it has been difficult for claimants to win ADEA cases, two recent cases will surely benefit the plaintiffs. In 2005 the Supreme Court decision in *Smith v. Jackson* ruled that "disparate impact" theory could be used in ADEA cases. In 2008, the Supreme Court, in *Meacham v. Atomic Power*, ruled that the burden is on the employer to show that action against a worker stems from "reasonable factors other than age."[23]

What Is Required to Establish Prima Facie Evidence of Age Discrimination?

Difficult burden for plaintiffs

Similar to Title VII cases, there are certain requirements for establishing a prima facie case of age discrimination. These include showing that (1) the employee is a member of the protected age group (40 or older); (2) the employee has the ability to perform satisfactorily at some absolute or relative level (e.g., relative to other employees involved in the decision process or at an absolute standard of acceptability); (3) the employee was not hired, promoted, or compensated, or was discharged, laid off, or forced to retire; and (4) the position was filled or maintained by a younger person (just younger, not necessarily under age 40). The second condition is the biggest challenge for the plaintiff and is usually the one where the plaintiff falls short in establishing a prima facie case due to the usual subjectivity in comparing individuals.[24] Expert witnesses are often used who present evidence that the plaintiff is more qualified than the person (or persons) hired (or retained). Of course, a defendent can rebut all such claims based on other data or critiques of the plaintiff's evidence and expert testimony.

Once a prima facie case has been established based on the evidence presented by the plaintiff, the defendant must then present evidence that "reasonable factors" other than age were the basis of the personnel decision. At this point, appearing to be untruthful or incomplete in communications could be costly for employers.

Mastie v. Great Lakes Steel

One of the most common scenarios for litigation under ADEA concerns the termination of an employee because of alleged poor performance. For example, in *Mastie v. Great Lakes Steel Corp.*, the employer maintained that Mr. Mastie had been discharged in reduction-in-force efforts because of his poorer performance relative to other employees.[25] Mr. Mastie presented personnel records reflecting an exemplary performance record and a history of merit-based salary increases. However, the court found for the employer and said

Is age the determinative factor?

that the controlling issue is whether age was a *determinative* factor in the personnel decision, not the "absolute accuracy" or correctness of the personnel decision. Several other courts have established that it is not the role of the court to "second guess" employers in their

ADEA and disparate impact

personnel decisions—that is, did they really discharge the poorest performer or hire the very best person? *A critical question in ADEA litigation is whether age was a "determinative factor" in a personnel decision.* In individual ADEA cases alleging claims of intentional discrimination based on age, it is the plaintiff's burden to establish that age was the determinative factor in the decision, which makes it difficult for plaintiffs to win such individual cases.

In his 2005 majority opinion in *Smith v. Jackson*, Justice John Paul Stevens wrote that employers must show an age-neutral "business necessity" for their actions. The Court thus shifted the burden to employers once evidence is presented, usually statistical, showing "prima facie" discrimination. According to Sheryl J. Willert, a Seattle labor lawyer, the 2008 *Meacham* decision "will make it easier for employees to institute litigation against employers and to get to a jury in their cases." She added that employers will have to be "significantly more vigilant" in evaluating prospects for layoffs and documenting the reasons for choosing particular employees. Thus, as in Title VII cases, the burden of proof rests with the defendant in "disparate impact" ADEA cases.

But as *Fortune* magazine put it so delicately, "there usually is a 'business necessity' for dumping workers over 50." That "business necessity" is cost reduction. A provocation issue is whether a "reasonable factor other than age" is compansation; the organization fired the higher paid employees who just happened to be older.

General Dynamics v. Cline

Is it a violation of the ADEA to eliminate health care benefits for workers who are under the age of 50? The Supreme Court ruled in *General Dynamics Land Systems v. Cline* that the ADEA does not prohibit an employer from practicing "reverse age discrimination" where older workers are favored (they kept their health care) over younger workers (they didn't) who are over 39.

Can Employers Claim Age as a Bona Fide Occupational Qualification (BFOQ)?

Greyhound Bus Lines survived a court challenge to their rule that they would accept no applicants over 40 years of age to drive their buses. The company successfully contended that age was a bona fide occupational qualification (BFOQ) since it was related to the safe conduct of the busline.[26] Other cases have supported the use of age as a BFOQ. *In general, if public safety is relevant and the employee must be in good physical condition, the courts have supported the use of age requirements, both in terms of entry-level positions and, more commonly, mandatory retirement for certain jobs.* Congress specifically exempted public safety personnel, allowing mandatory retirement for police officers and firefighters (usually 55 years of age). The courts have generally recognized age ceilings as legal BFOQs, but only when the employer can demonstrate that (1) physical fitness, and especially good aerobic fitness, is important to the job and (2) the employer applies the same physical fitness standards to employees under 40 as well as to older employees. The EEOC provides the following rules for the imposition of BFOQs: (1) the age limit is reasonably necessary for the business, (2) all or almost all individuals over the age are unable to perform adequately, or (3) some people over the age have a disqualifying characteristic (e.g., health) that cannot be determined independent of age.

One managerial implication is to determine if it is in the employer's best interests to impose an age ceiling or mandatory retirement. A 59-year-old pilot successfully crash landed a 737, saving hundreds of lives. He celebrated his mandatory retirement only a few weeks later. In 2008, the retirement age for commercial pilots was raised to 65, the mandatory age used by the rest of the world.

THE AMERICANS WITH DISABILITIES ACT OF 1990 (ADA)

In 1990, Congress passed the Americans with Disabilities Act, which extends the rights and privileges disabled employees of federal contractors have under the Rehabilitation Act of 1973 to virtually all employees. Figure 3-8 presents a summary of the ADA, some excerpts from the law, and a list of the EEOC ADA Enforcement Guidelines and Policy Documents. You can retrieve these documents at eeoc.gov. Keep in mind, however, that EEOC Guidelines are only guidelines and are subject to judicial interpretation. For example, in 2002, the

2008 ADA Amendment Act

EEOC had to amend its guidelines on "reasonable accommodation" based on a Supreme Court ruling. The EEOC also issues new regulations, so be sure to monitor the EEOC Web site for changes. The EEOC received almost 18,000 charges of disability discrimination in fiscal year 2007. They resolved almost 16,000 charges and recovered over $54 million in monetary benefits for charging parties (not including benefits derived through litigation). ADA complaints and litigation are likely to increase due to passage of the 2008 ADA Amendments Act.

Figure 3-8   **A Summary of the ADA and the 2008 Amendments Act; Excerpts from the ADA; Guidelines Available at eeoc.gov**

DISABILITY DISCRIMINATION

Title I of the Americans with Disabilities Act of 1990 prohibits private employers, state and local governments, employment agencies and labor unions from discriminating against qualified individuals with disabilities in job application procedures, hiring, firing, advancement, compensation, job training, and other terms, conditions, and privileges of employment. The ADA covers employers with 15 or more employees, including state and local governments. It also applies to employment agencies and to labor organizations. The ADA's nondiscrimination standards also apply to federal sector employees under section 501 of the Rehabilitation Act, as amended, and its implementing rules.

An individual with a disability is a person who:

• Has a physical or mental impairment that substantially limits one or more major life activities (2008 Amendment expands the definition of "major life activities").

• Has a record of such an impairment.

• Is regarded as having such an impairment.

A qualified employee or applicant with a disability is an individual who, with or without reasonable accommodation, can perform the essential functions of the job in question. Reasonable accommodation may include, but is not limited to:

• Making existing facilities used by employees readily accessible to and usable by persons with disabilities.

• Job restructuring, modifying work schedules, reassignment to a vacant position.

• Acquiring or modifying equipment or devices, adjusting or modifying examinations, training materials, or policies, and providing qualified readers or interpreters.

An employer is required to make a reasonable accommodation to the known disability of a qualified applicant or employee if it would not impose an "undue hardship" on the operation of the employer's business. Undue hardship is defined as an action requiring significant difficulty or expense when considered in light of factors such as an employer's size, financial resources, and the nature and structure of its operation.

An employer is not required to lower quality or production standards to make an accommodation; nor is an employer obligated to provide personal use items such as glasses or hearing aids.

Title I of the ADA also covers:

• *Medical examinations and inquiries*—Employers may not ask job applicants about the existence, nature, or severity of a disability. Applicants may be asked about their ability to perform specific job functions. A job offer may be conditioned on the results of a medical examination, but only if the examination is required for all entering employees in similar jobs. Medical examinations of employees must be job related and consistent with the employer's business needs.

• *Drug and alcohol abuse*—Employees and applicants currently engaging in the illegal use of drugs are not covered by the ADA when an employer acts on the basis of such use. Tests for illegal drugs are not subject to the ADA's restrictions on medical examinations. Employers may hold illegal drug users and alcoholics to the same performance standards as other employees.

• *Retaliation*—It is also unlawful to retaliate against an individual for opposing employment practices that discriminate based on disability or for filing a discrimination charge, testifying, or participating in any way in an investigation, proceeding, or litigation under the ADA.

Need More Information?

The law:

• Titles I and V of the ADA

The regulations:

• 29 C.F.R Part 1630

• 29 C.F.R Part 1640

• 29 C.F.R Part 1641

EEOC Enforcement Guidances and Policy Documents:

• Veterans with Services-Connected Disabilities in the Workplace and the ADA

• The Family and Medical Leave Act, the ADA, and Title VII of the Civil Rights Act of 1964

• The ADA: A Primer for Small Business

• Your Responsibilities as an Employer

• Your Employment Rights as an Individual with a Disability

• Job Applicants and the ADA

• Small Employers and Reasonable Accommodation

• Work at Home/Telework as a Reasonable Accommodation

• The ADA: Applying Performance and Conduct Standards to Employees with Disabilities

(Continued)

- Obtaining and Using Employee Medical Information as Part of Emergency Evacuation Procedures
- How to Comply with the Americans with Disabilities Act: A Guide for Restaurants and Other Food Service Employers
- Questions and Answers about:
  - Diabetes in the Workplace and the ADA
  - Epilepsy in the Workplace and the ADA
  - Persons with Intellectual Disabilities in the Workplace and the ADA

EXCERPTS FROM ADA

(a) General Rule. No covered entity shall discriminate against a qualified individual with a disability because of the disability of such individual.

(b) Construction. As used in subsection (a), the term "discrimination" includes:

    (1) limiting, segregating, or classifying a job applicant or employee in a way that adversely affects the opportunities or status of such applicant or employee because of . . . disability . . .

    (2) participating in a contractual or other arrangement or relationship that has the effect of subjecting a qualified applicant or employee with a disability to the discrimination prohibited by this title . . .

    (5) not making reasonable accommodations to the known physical or mental limitations of a qualified individual who is an applicant or employee, unless such covered entity can demonstrate that the accommodation would impose an undue hardship on the operation of the business of such covered entity, and

    (7) using employment tests or other selection criteria that screen out or tend to screen out an individual with a disability or a class of individuals with disabilities unless the test or other selection criteria, as used by the covered entity, is shown to be job-related for the position in question and is consistent with business necessity.

(c) Medical Examinations and Inquiries.

    (1) In general. The prohibition against discrimination as referred to in subsection (a) shall include medical examinations and inquiries.

Definitions

    (2) Disability. The term "disability" means, with respect to an individual:

    (A) a physical or mental impairment that substantially limits one or more of the major life activities of such individual (The 2008 Amendments Act expands the definition of "major life activities")

    (B) a record of such an impairment, or

    (C) being regarded as having such an impairment.

    (D) mitigating measures shall not be considered in assessing whether an individual has a disability.

Definitions

(7) Qualified Individual with a Disability. The term "qualified individual with a disability" means an individual with a disability who, with or without reasonable accommodation, can perform the essential functions of the employment position that such individual holds or desires.

(8) Reasonable Accommodation. The term "reasonable accommodation" may include:

    (A) making existing facilities used by employees readily accessible to and usable by individuals with disabilities, and

    (B) job restructuring, part-time or modified work schedules, reassignment to a vacant position, acquisition or modification of equipment or devices, appropriate adjustment or modifications of examinations, training materials or policies, the provision of qualified readers or interpreters, and other similar accommodations for individuals with disabilities.

(9) (A) In general. The term "undue hardship" means an action requiring significant difficulty or expense.

    (B) Determination. In determining whether an accommodation would impose an undue hardship on a covered entity, factors to be considered include:

        (i) the overall size of the business;

        (ii) the type of operation; and

        (iii) the nature and cost of the accommodation.

Defenses

(b) Qualification Standards. The term "qualification standards" may include a requirement that an individual with a currently contagious disease or infection shall not pose a direct threat to the health or safety of other individuals in the workplace.

Illegal Drugs and Alcohol

(a) Qualified Individual with a Disability. For purposes of this title, the term "qualified individual with a disability" shall not include any employee or applicant who is a current user of illegal drugs . . .

(b) Authority of Covered Entity. A covered entity:

    (1) may prohibit the use of alcohol or illegal drugs at the workplace by all employees;

    (2) may require that employees shall not be under the influence of alcohol or illegal drugs at the workplace;

    (3) may require that employees behave in conformance with the requirements established under "The Drug-Free Workplace Act" (41 U.S.C. 701 et seq.) [See Chapter 14.];

    (4) may hold an employee who is a drug user or alcoholic to the same qualification standards for employment or job performance and behavior that such entity holds other employees . . .

(c) Drug Testing.

    (1) In general. For purposes of this title, a test to determine the use of illegal drugs shall not be considered a medical examination.

Essential functions

The ADA provides that qualified individuals with disabilities may not be discriminated against by a private-sector organization or a department or agency of a state or local government employing 15 or more employees, *if the individual can perform the essential functions of the job with or without reasonable accommodation.* Reasonable accommodations are determined on a case-by-case basis and may include reassignment, part-time work, and flexible schedules. They also may include providing readers, interpreters, assistants, or attendants. No accommodation is required if an individual is not otherwise qualified for the position. The EEOC *Policy Guidance on Reasonable Accommodation Under ADA* suggests the following process for assessing "reasonable accommodation":

EEOC guidelines

1. Look at the particular job involved; determine its purpose and its essential functions.

2. Consult with the individual with the disability to identify potential accommodations.

3. If several accommodations are available, preference should be given to the individual's preferences.

Public facilities such as restaurants, doctor's offices, pharmacies, grocery stores, shopping centers, and hotels must be made accessible to the disabled unless undue hardship would occur for the business. It is not clear, however, how exactly organizations will show "undue hardship," although the law suggests that a reviewing court compare the cost of the accommodation with the employer's operating budget.

Common areas of disability claims

The three areas of disability that are the most common for ADA claims as of 2009 are various mental difficulties (e.g., depression), headaches, and backaches. The most common personnel action has been termination. While some claims of mental duress and headaches are undoubtedly legitimate, there is no question that some people have taken advantage of the ambiguity in the law to make costly and unwarranted claims.

What Is Legal and Illegal under ADA?

The EEOC approved enforcement guidelines on preemployment disability-related inquiries, and medical exams under ADA. The guidelines state that "the guiding principle is that while employers may ask applicants about the ability to perform job functions, employers may not ask about disability." For example, a lawful question would be: "Can you perform the functions of this job with or without reasonable accommodation?" But it is unlawful for an employer to ask questions related to a disability, such as "Have you ever filed for worker's compensation?" or "What prescription drugs do you take?" or "Have you ever been treated for mental illness?"

After an employer has made an offer and an applicant requests accommodation, the employer may "require documentation of the individual's need for, and entitlement to, reasonable accommodations."

There has been a great deal of litigation under ADA since the law took effect for most employers, and the Supreme Court has been very much involved in attempting to clarify the law and its implications. Perhaps the most important issue is what constitutes a disability under ADA.

Bonnie Cook was a 300-pound Rhode Island woman who was rejected for an attendant's job at a school for the mentally retarded. She sued claiming her obesity was a disability under ADA. The EEOC has taken the position that only severely obese people are covered by ADA (weight in excess of 100 percent of the norm for a particular height) or if their weight can be linked to a medical disorder. The courts have deferred to the EEOC's position on this matter.

Toyota v. Williams

Two Supreme Court rulings established that courts can consider remedial aids, such as eyeglasses for poor eyesight or medication for high blood pressure, to mitigate impairments when determining whether an individual has a disability under the ADA. A third case, *Toyota v. Williams* (2002), considered the degree that impairments can be considered to "substantially" interfere with a person's daily activities, and therefore require coverage under the ADA. In *Toyota*, the Court held the plaintiff was limited by carpal tunnel syndrome only in certain activities that were not considered major life activities, as the plaintiff was able to perform other nonmanual work duties.[27]

ADA Amendments Act of 2008

The Americans with Disabilities Act Amendments Act of 2008 makes important changes to the definition of the term "disability" by rejecting the holdings of these Supreme Court decisions. While retaining the basic definition of "disability" as an impairment that substantially limits one or more major life activities, a record of such an impairment, or being regarded as having such an impairment, the new law changes the way that these terms should be interpreted. In addition to directing the EEOC to revise its regulations defining the term "substantially limits," the 2008 Amendment emphasizes that the definition of "disability" should be interpreted broadly. (go to EEOC.gov for new information on ADA-related action pursuant to this new law).

Major life activities

The ADA Amendments Act expands the definition of "major life activities" by including those activities that the EEOC had recognized (e.g., walking) and adding other activities that EEOC had not specifically recognized (e.g., reading, bending, and communicating). In addition, a second list is stipulated in the amendment that includes major bodily functions (e.g., "functions of the immune system, normal cell growth, digestive, bowel, bladder, neurological, brain, respiratory, circulatory, endocrine, and reproductive functions").

Mitigating measures

The ADA Amendment also states that mitigating measures other than "ordinary eyeglasses or contact lenses" shall not be considered in assessing whether an individual has a disability and that an impairment that is episodic or in remission is a disability if it would substantially limit a major life activity when active.[28]

GENETIC INFORMATION NONDISCRIMINATION ACT (GINA)

The Genetic Information Nondiscrimination Act (GINA) became law in 2008.[29] The legislation is designed to address concerns that workers could be denied employment or job benefits due to a predisposition for a genetic disorder. GINA has the following major provisions:

1. GINA prohibits insurers from denying coverage to patients; and

2. GINA prohibits employers from making hiring, firing, or promotional decisions based on genetic test results.

DNA testing

Figure 3-9 presents a summary of GINA protections, exceptions, and remedies. Supporters of the new law, which evolved over 13 years of legislative work, proclaim that GINA will help usher in an age of genetic medicine where DNA tests will help predict if a person is at risk for a particular disease so as to take action in order to prevent it.

Figure 3-9   **Genetic Information Nondiscrimination ACT of 2008 (GINA)**

Nondiscrimination in Employment—GINA prohibits an employer from discriminating against an individual in the hiring, firing, compensation, terms, or privileges of employment on the basis of genetic information of the individual or family member of the individual. An employer would also be prohibited from limiting, segregating, or classifying an employee in any fashion that would deprive the employee of any employment opportunities or adversely affect the status of the employee because of the employee's genetic information (or the genetic information of the family member of the individual).

Health Care Coverage Protections—GINA prohibits an insured or self-insured health care plan from denying eligibility to enroll for health care coverage or from adjusting premium or contribution rates under a plan based on an individual or family member's genetic information. Health care plans cannot require an individual or a family of a plan participant to undergo a genetic test to be eligible for coverage under a health care plan or maintain enrollment restrictions based on the need for genetic services.

Exceptions for Genetic Testing for Health Care Treatment—GINA allows a health care professional to request that a patient undergo a genetic test or advise a patient on the provision of genetic tests or services through a wellness program.

Remedies for Violations of the Health Care Coverage Provisions—GINA allows plan participants to receive injunctive relief under the Employee Retirement Income Security Act (ERISA) and to have health care coverage reinstated back to the date of loss of coverage. Plan administrators could be personally liable for discriminating in coverage decisions and be assessed a penalty of $100 per day for the period of noncompliance. Plans could be fined a minimum penalty of $2,500 to $15,000 for violations up to a total of $500,000 for multiple violations.

Confidentiality of Genetic Health Care Information—GINA provides that the disclosure of protected genetic health care information is governed by the medical privacy requirements of the Health Insurance Portability and Accountability Act of 1996 (HIPAA). GINA allows injunctive relief for violations of the confidentiality provisions of the bill. For violations of the privacy provisions of the bill, civil monetary penalties of $100 per day up to $250,000 and 10 years in prison for egregious violations.

State Genetic Law Preemption—GINA allows state laws that are more stringent in the requirements, standards, or implementations then those contained in GINA to supersede the federal act. Most states have genetic testing laws.

(Continued)

Definition of Family Member—GINA defines a family member as the:

(1) spouse of the individual;

(2) a dependent child of the individual, including a child who is born to or placed for adoption with the individual; or

(3) parent, grandparent, or great-grandparent.

Restrictions on Collecting Genetic Information—GINA forbids an employer from requesting, requiring, or purchasing genetic information of the individual or family member except

(1) where the employer inadvertently requests or requires the information,

(2) for genetic services offered by the employer (including wellness programs),

(3) for purposes of complying with the Family and Medical Leave Act, and

(4) where the employer purchases documents that are commercially available. GINA also limits or expand the protections, rights, or obligations of employees or employers under workers' compensation laws.

Genetic Monitoring in the Workplace Exception—GINA allows for genetic monitoring of biological effects of toxic substances in the workplace, but only if

(1) the employer provides written notice of the monitoring to the employee;

(2) the employee agrees to the monitoring in writing or the monitoring is required by federal, state, or local law;

(3) the employee is informed of the results of the test;

(4) the monitoring conforms to any federal or state law, including rules promulgated by OSHA; and

(5) the employer receives the results of the tests in aggregate terms. Employers also may offer genetic services to the employee, but only if the services are voluntary and shared only with the employee or family member of the employees.

PREGNANCY DISCRIMINATION ACT OF 1978

Claims up 14 percent in 2007

In 2007, pregnancy complaints filed with the EEOC surged to a record high level of 5,587, up 14 percent from the prior fiscal year. The Pregnancy Discrimination Act (PDA) prohibits employment practices that discriminate on the basis of pregnancy, childbirth, or related medical conditions (e.g., abortion). This means that a woman is protected from being fired or refused a job or promotion simply because she is pregnant or has had an abortion. She also cannot be forced to take a leave of absence as long as she is able to work. What about refusing to hire a woman because she may become pregnant soon? Can't do that either. An employer may not use potential pregnancy as a basis for a decision. Pregnant women must be treated in the same manner as other applicants (or employees) with similar abilities. Like the ADA, the PDA stipulates that an employer cannot refuse to hire a pregnant woman if she can perform the essential functions of the job. What about a pregnant woman who freely admits that she plans to take a leave three months after her starting date? Surely this is a "job-related" reason to not hire her? While this may be costly to the employer, in fact the employer cannot consider either her pregnancy or her impending leave in a hiring decision.

Under the law, women are not guaranteed the same job or, indeed, any job when they return from their pregnancy leave. However, most U.S. companies have adopted either a "same job," "comparable job," or "some job" policy for women who wish to return to work. The employer must adopt such a policy with consideration to the disparate treatment theory of Title VII, and pregnancy should be treated like any other disability. In other words, if other employees on disability leave are entitled to return to their jobs when they are able to work again, then so should women who have been unable to work due to pregnancy.

Benefit coverage

The Act also requires that employers must provide benefit coverage for pregnancy as fully as for other medical conditions. In other words, a woman unable to work for pregnancy-related reasons is entitled to disability benefits or sick leave on the same basis as other employees unable to work for medical reasons.

The PDA does not prohibit states from requiring additional benefits for pregnant employees. The Supreme Court, for example, upheld a California law that required employers to provide up to four months' unpaid pregnancy disability leave with guaranteed reinstatement, even though disabled males were not entitled to the same benefit. The **Family and Medical Leave Act,** discussed in Chapter 10, provides additional protection related to pregnancy. Figure 3-10 presents a summary of the PDA.

Family and Medical Leave Act

Figure 3-10   **Pregnancy Discrimination**

The Pregnancy Discrimination Act is an amendment to Title VII of the Civil Rights Act of 1964. Discrimination on the basis of pregnancy, childbirth, or related medical conditions constitutes unlawful sex discrimination under Title VII, which covers employers with 15 or more employees, including state and local governments. Title VII also applies to employment agencies and to labor organizations, as well as to the federal government. Women who are pregnant or affected by related conditions must be treated in the same manner as other applicants or employees with similar abilities or limitations.

Title VII's pregnancy-related protections include:

• *Hiring*—An employer cannot refuse to hire a pregnant woman because of her pregnancy, because of a pregnancy-related condition, or because of the prejudices of co-workers, clients, or customers.

• *Pregnancy and maternity leave*—An employer may not single out pregnancy-related conditions for special procedures to determine an employee's ability to work. However, if an employer requires its employees to submit a doctor's statement concerning their inability to work before granting leave or paying sick benefits, the employer may require employees affected by pregnancy-related conditions to submit such statements.

    If an employee is temporarily unable to perform her job due to pregnancy, the employer must treat her the same as any other temporarily disabled employee. For example, if the employer allows temporarily disabled employees to modify tasks, perform alternative assignments, or take disability leave or leave without pay, the employer also must allow an employee who is temporarily disabled due to pregnancy to do the same.

    Pregnant employees must be permitted to work as long as they are able to perform their jobs. If an employee has been absent from work as a result of a pregnancy-related condition and recovers, her employer may not require her to remain on leave until the baby's birth. An employer also may not have a rule that prohibits an employee from returning to work for a predetermined length of time after childbirth.

    Employers must hold open a job for a pregnancy-related absence the same length of time jobs are held open for employees on sick or disability leave.

• *Health insurance*—Any health insurance provided by an employer must cover expenses for pregnancy-related conditions on the same basis as costs for other medical conditions. Health insurance for expenses arising from abortion is not required, except where the life of the mother is endangered.

    Pregnancy-related expenses should be reimbursed exactly as those incurred for other medical conditions, whether payment is on a fixed basis or a percentage of reasonable-and-customary-charge basis.

    The amounts payable by the insurance provider can be limited only to the same extent as amounts payable for other conditions. No additional, increased, or larger deductible can be imposed.

    Employers must provide the same level of health benefits for spouses of male employees as they do for spouses of female employees.

• *Fringe Benefits*—Pregnancy-related benefits cannot be limited to married employees. In an all-female workforce or job classification, benefits must be provided for pregnancy-related conditions if benefits are provided for other medical conditions.

    If an employer provides any benefits to workers on leave, the employer must provide the same benefits for those on leave for pregnancy-related conditions.

    Employees with pregnancy-related disabilities must be treated the same as other temporarily disabled employees for accrual and crediting of seniority, vacation calculation, pay increases, and temporary disability benefits.

    It is also unlawful to retaliate against an individual for opposing employment practices that discriminate based on pregnancy or for filing a discrimination charge, testifying, or participating in any way in an investigation, proceeding, or litigation under Title VII.

Need More Information?

The law:

• Title VII of the Civil Rights Act

The regulations:

• 29 C.F.R Part 1604

The EEOC has also issued guidance on:

• The Family and Medical Leave Act, the Americans with Disabilities Act, and Title VII of the Civil Rights Act of 1964

ARE EXPATRIATES COVERED BY FEDERAL EEO LAWS WHEN THEY ARE ASSIGNED TO COUNTRIES OTHER THAN THE UNITED STATES?

Extraterritoriality

Figure 3-11 presents guidelines to help multinational employers determine their obligations under EEO laws. In general, the Civil Rights Act, the ADEA, and the ADA all have **extraterritoriality.** This means that an American working for an American corporation on foreign soil is covered by these laws. With some exceptions, the laws also apply to resident aliens working for foreign companies on U.S. soil.

Many U.S. companies have branches, subsidiaries, or joint venture partners in Western Europe (and, increasingly, in Eastern Europe as well). U.S. multinationals have considerable experience with the various regulatory systems of Western European countries, some of which require national-level collective bargaining and others of which have relatively little labor regulation. The situation was simplified in 2003 when the European Union adopted standards regarding most labor issues.

Figure 3-11 **The Equal Employment Opportunity Responsibilities of Multinational Employers**

The globalization of business activity has resulted in employers from around the world assigning increasing numbers of personnel internationally. The following general guidance is intended to help multinational employers determine their obligations under U.S. equal employment opportunity laws (EEO laws).

OPERATIONS IN THE UNITED STATES OR U.S. TERRITORIES
Multinational employers that operate in the United States or its territories—American Samoa, Guam, the Commonwealth of the Northern Mariana Islands, Puerto Rico, and the U.S. Virgin Islands—are subject to EEO laws to the same extent as U.S. employers, unless the employer is covered by a treaty or other binding international agreement that limits the full applicability of U.S. antidiscrimination laws, such as one that permits the company to prefer its own nationals for certain positions.

OPERATIONS OUTSIDE THE UNITED STATES AND U.S. TERRITORIES
Companies Based in the U.S.
Employers that are incorporated or based in the U.S. or are controlled by U.S. companies and that employ U.S. citizens outside the United States or its territories are subject to Title VII, the ADEA, and the ADA with respect to those employees. U.S. EEO laws do not apply to non-U.S. citizens outside the U.S. or its territories.

How to Determine Who Is a U.S. Employer
An employer will be considered to be a U.S. employer if it is incorporated or based in the United States or if it has sufficient connections with the United States. This is an individualized factual determination that will be based on the following relevant factors:

• The employer's principal place of business, i.e., the primary place where factories, offices, and other facilities are located.
• The nationality of dominant shareholders and/or those holding voting control.
• The nationality and location of management (the officers and directors of the company).

How to Determine Whether a Company Is "Controlled" by a U.S. Employer
Employers operating outside the United States are covered by Title VII, the ADEA, and the ADA only if they are controlled by a U.S. employer. Whether a company is controlled by a U.S. employer is also an individualized determination, which will be based on the following relevant factors:

• Whether the operations of the employers are interrelated.
• Whether there is common management.
• Whether there is centralized control of labor relations.
• Whether there is common ownership or financial control.

Foreign Laws Defense
U.S. employers are not required to comply with the requirements of Title VII, the ADEA, or the ADA, if adherence to that requirement would violate a law of the country where the workplace is located. For example, an employer would have a "Foreign Laws Defense" for a mandatory retirement policy if the law of the country in which the company is located requires mandatory retirement.

A U.S. employer may not transfer an employee to another country in order to disadvantage the employee because of his/her race, color, sex, religion, national origin, age, or disability. For example, an employer may not transfer an older worker to a country with a mandatory retirement age for the purpose of forcing the employee's retirement.

WHAT U.S. EEO LAWS COVER
The federal EEO laws enforced by the EEOC are Title VII of the Civil Rights Act of 1964 (Title VII), the Age Discrimination in Employment Act (ADEA), the Americans with Disabilities Act (ADA), and the Equal Pay Act (EPA). These laws prohibit covered employers from discriminating on the bases of race, color, sex, national origin, religion, age, and disability. Examples of conduct prohibited include:

• *Discriminatory employment decisions*—Title VII, the ADEA, and the ADA prohibit discrimination in all aspects of the employment relationship including recruitment, hiring, assignment, transfer, firing, layoffs, and other conditions or privileges of employment.
• *Discrimination in compensation and benefits*—Title VII, the ADEA, and the ADA prohibit discrimination in compensation based on race, color, sex, national origin, religion, age, and disability. In addition, the EPA prohibits pay discrimination between men and women who are performing substantially equal work. Although the EPA does not apply outside the United States, such claims are covered by Title VII, which also prohibits discrimination in compensation on the basis of sex.
• *Harassment*—Title VII, the ADEA, and the ADA also prohibit offensive conduct that creates a hostile work environment based on race, color, sex, national origin, religion, age, and disability. Employers are required to take appropriate steps to prevent and correct unlawful harassment and employees are responsible for reporting harassment at an early stage to prevent its escalation.
• *Retaliation*—Title VII, the ADEA, the ADA, and the EPA prohibit employers from retaliating against employees because they have opposed unlawful discrimination or participated in a discrimination-related proceeding.

Need More Information?
For more detailed information, including a comprehensive discussion of these and other issues, please see:

• EEOC's Web site at www.eeoc.gov for detailed information on EEO laws. Go to "Laws, Regulations and Policy Guidance" for Compliance Manual Sections and Enforcement Guidance.
• EEOC Enforcement Guidance, "Application of Title VII and the Americans with Disabilities Act to Conduct Overseas and to Foreign Employers Discriminating in the United States" (1993).
• EEOC Policy Guidance, "Application of the Age Discrimination in Employment Act of 1967 and the Equal Pay Act of 1963 to American Firms Overseas, Their Overseas Subsidiaries, and Foreign Firms" (1989).
• EEOC Policy Guidance, "Analysis of the sec. 4(f)(1) 'foreign laws' defense of the Age Discrimination in Employment Act of 1967."

To be automatically connected to an EEOC field office, call 1-800-669-4000 or TTY 1-800-669-6820. For more information on EEO law in other countries, see:

• Directorate General for Employment and Social Affairs for the European Union, http://www.europa.eu.int/comm/employment_social/ fundamental_rights/index_en.htm
• Canadian Human Rights Commission http://www.chrc-ccdp.ca
• UK Equal Opportunities Commission http://www.eoc.org.uk
• UK Disability Rights Commission, http://www.drc-gb.org
• UK Commission on Racial Equality, http://www.cre.gov.uk
• Hong Kong Equal Opportunity Commission http://www.eoc.org.hk

What Are Employee Rights When Working for Multinational Employers?

What EEO laws apply to an American working for a foreign company operating in the United States or in another country? Figure 3-12 presents a summary of these rights. In general, all three laws apply to the American company and protect the American worker. However, an American working for a foreign company on foreign soil is not protected. HRM specialists working in these various contexts must be well aware of the various laws and their applications. A great resource is the global forum of the Society of Human Resource Management (www.SHRMglobal.org).

American women have equal opportunity legal protection regarding expatriate assignments. While things are clearly improving, the so-called "glass-border" still exists where women are victims of discrimination for important overseas assignments.[30]

Figure 3-12   **Employee Rights When Working for Multinational Employers**

As the workplace grows more global and mobile, increased numbers of employers have international operations, resulting in more international assignments of their employees. The following provides general guidance concerning employees' rights under the United States' equal employment opportunity laws (U.S. EEO laws) when working for multinational employers.

WORK IN THE UNITED STATES AND U.S. TERRITORIES
All employees who work in the U.S. or its territories—American Samoa, Guam, the Commonwealth of the Northern Mariana Islands, Puerto Rico, and the U.S. Virgin Islands—for covered employers are protected by EEO laws, regardless of their citizenship or work authorization status. Employees who work in the U.S. or its territories are protected whether they work for a U.S. or foreign employer.

Example:

Kim is a Chinese citizen working in the Commonwealth of the Northern Mariana Islands for a Chinese manufacturer of women's attire. Kim's manager threatens Kim with losing her job if she does not comply with his sexual demands. Kim is protected by U.S. EEO laws because she works in a U.S. territory. The employer can be held liable for sexual harassment.

WORKING FOR NON-U.S. EMPLOYERS IN THE U.S.
The only exception to the rule that employees working in the U.S. are covered by federal EEO laws occurs when the employer is not a U.S. employer and is subject to a treaty or other binding international agreement that permits the company to prefer its own nationals for certain positions.

Example:

ABC Communications is an Egyptian company doing business in the U.S. Under a "friendship, commerce and navigation treaty" ("FCN") between the U.S. and Egypt, Egyptian companies operating in the U.S. are authorized to hire Egyptian citizens for executive positions. Thomas, a U.S. citizen, alleges that he was subjected to national origin discrimination when he was denied a position as Vice President of Legislative Affairs in favor of Menkure, who is an Egyptian citizen. ABC Communications admits that it favored Menkure because he is an Egyptian citizen and can successfully assert the FCN treaty as a defense.

However, if Menkure were not an Egyptian citizen but a citizen of the U.S. or a third country, ABC would not have the treaty as a defense because the treaty authorizes a preference only for Egyptian citizens.

WORK OUTSIDE THE UNITED STATES
Individuals who are not U.S. citizens are not protected by U.S. EEO laws when employed outside the U.S. or its territories. Consult your embassy to determine whether EEO laws for other countries exist and whether they apply to your situation.

U.S. citizens who are employed outside the U.S. by a U.S. employer—or a foreign company controlled by an U.S. employer—are protected by Title VII, the ADEA, and the ADA.

Example:

Isaac is an African-American U.S. citizen working in Africa for a U.S. employer as a customer service manager. Isaac alleges race discrimination after he was transferred to a less desirable and less public position. The new position involved a loss of pay and lack of upward career mobility opportunities. The employer admitted that it transferred Isaac because its predominantly white customers did not want to deal directly with nonwhites. Customer preference is never a defense to violations of U.S. EEO law. The transfer violates Title VII.

Whether a Company Is a U.S. Employer or Controlled by a U.S. Employer
An employer will be considered a U.S. employer if it is incorporated or based in the United States or if it has sufficient connections with the United States. Several factors help determine whether a company has sufficient connections with the U.S., including the company's principal place of business and the nationality of its dominant shareholders and management. Whether a foreign company is controlled by a U.S. employer will depend on the interrelation of operations, common management, centralized control of labor relations, and common ownership or financial control of the two entities. For more information, see http://www.eeoc.gov/docs/threshold.html#2-III-B-3-c.

Foreign Laws Defense
U.S. employers are not required to comply with the requirements of Title VII, the ADEA, or the ADA if adherence to that requirement would violate a law of the country where the workplace is located.

Example:

Sarah is a U.S. citizen. She works as an assistant manager for a U.S. employer located in a Middle Eastern Country. Sarah applies for the branch manager position. Although Sarah is the most qualified person for the position, the employer informs her that it cannot promote her because that country's laws forbid women from supervising men. Sarah files a charge alleging sex discrimination. The employer would have a "Foreign Laws" defense for its actions if the law does contain that prohibition.

An American employer cannot transfer an employee to another country in order to disadvantage the employee because of race, color, sex, religion, national origin, age, or disability. For example, an employer may not transfer an older worker to a country with a mandatory retirement age for the purpose of forcing the employee's retirement.

(Continued)

WHAT U.S. EEO LAWS COVER

The federal EEO laws enforced by the EEOC are Title VII of the Civil Rights Act of 1964 (Title VII), the Age Discrimination in Employment Act (ADEA), the Americans with Disabilities Act (ADA), and the Equal Pay Act (EPA). These laws prohibit covered employers from discriminating on the bases of race, color, sex, national origin, religion, age, and disability. Examples of conduct prohibited include:

- *Discriminatory employment decisions*—Title VII, the ADEA, and the ADA prohibit discrimination in all aspects of the employment relationship, including recruitment, hiring, assignment, transfer, firing, layoffs, and other conditions or privileges of employment.
- *Discrimination in compensation and benefits*—Title VII, the ADEA, and the ADA prohibit discrimination in compensation based on race, color, sex, national origin, religion, age, and disability. In addition, the EPA prohibits pay discrimination between men and women who are performing substantially equal work. Although the EPA does not apply outside the United States, such claims are covered by Title VII, which also prohibits discrimination in compensation on the basis of sex.
- *Harassment*—Title VII, the ADEA, and the ADA also prohibit offensive conduct that creates a hostile work environment based on race, color, sex, national origin, religion, age, and disability. Employers are required to take appropriate steps to prevent and correct unlawful harassment and employees are responsible for reporting harassment at an early stage to prevent its escalation.
- *Retaliation*—Title VII, the ADEA, the ADA, and the EPA prohibit employers from retaliating against employees because they have opposed unlawful discrimination or participated in a discrimination related proceeding.

FILING A CHARGE

If you believe that you have been discriminated against, you may file a charge with the EEOC. An individual alleging an EEO violation outside the U.S. should file a charge with the district office closest to his or her employer's headquarters. However, if you are unsure where to file, you may file a charge with any EEOC office. For information on filing a charge of discrimination see *How to File a Charge of Employment Discrimination*. Charges may be filed in person, or by phone, mail, or facsimile.

Example:

Isaiah is a U.S. citizen working in Canada for a U.S. employer that is headquartered in New York and has an office in Detroit, Michigan. Isaiah alleges a failure to accommodate his religious beliefs. Although the charge will be processed by the New York District Office because it is closest to his employer's headquarters, Isaiah may file the charge in any convenient EEOC office.

FUTURE TRENDS IN EEO

Given the election results of 2008, more legislation is likely and may already be the law as you read this. The issue of affirmative action will be at the forefront of litigation and legislation. With the plaintiffs' recent successes in much-publicized cases and the huge jury verdicts and settlements, an increasing number of class-action lawsuits are likely. The number of ADEA cases also is expected to increase because of the recent Supreme Court rulings in *Smith v. Jackson* and *Meacham v. Atomic Power* allowing "disparate impact" theory and putting the burden of proof on the employer in "disparate impact" cases, and the increasing proportion of workers who are over 39 and therefore eligible to sue.

Employment practices liability insurance should become more common in the years ahead although premiums already have increased substantially because of the increased risk of large jury verdicts. A growing area of business-related insurance, some policies make stipulations about how HRM should be practiced as a condition of coverage. Providing training in EEO laws is often one such condition. Requiring alternative dispute resolution as a condition of employment is another recommended HRM policy that has gained in popularity.

Alternative Dispute Resolution: An Employer Reaction to Increased Litigation

Mandatory and binding arbitration

One trend with regard to management reaction to increased legislation and litigation is in the area of **alternative dispute resolution**. As discussed earlier, many large employers have entered mediation agreements with the EEOC in an effort to expedite the resolution of employment disputes. A growing number of companies have adopted **mandatory arbitration** to settle all claims related to employment. They cite the provisions of the Civil Rights Act of 1991 that allow alternative dispute resolution as an alternative to litigation. Although mandatory arbitration is controversial, and is opposed by the EEOC, many companies have nevertheless adopted this policy. The policy is almost always imposed after a process of mediation.

Mandatory arbitration requires employees and job applicants to sign a contract in which they agree to binding arbitration in order to resolve virtually any dispute related to their employment. With mandatory arbitration, the employees forfeits the right to litigate the complaint. So, let's say you feel you were a victim of gender discrimination. With the mandatory arbitration policy, the complaint must be submitted to an arbitration association such as the **American Arbitration Association** for a hearing and binding decision. If you refused to sign an arbitration agreement, a company could decide to not hire you and, in most states, could fire you if you refused to sign a newly imposed policy.

American Arbitration Association

The courts have in general supported arbitration as an alternative to litigation in settling employment disputes. Given the likely increases in most forms of EEO litigation, mediation followed by arbitration may prove to be advantageous to all concerned.

As a presidential candidate, Barack Obama supported three pieces of EEO legislation that may already be the law of the land. The **"Fair Pay Act"** expands the time for and the rules for filing claims for discriminatory pay practices. The **"Employment Non-Discrimination Act"** prohibits employers from discriminating against any employee with respect to the conditions and privileges of employment based on the employee's actual or perceived sexual orientation. The **"Paycheck Fairness Act"** gives employees new ways to seek damages for gender-based wage discrimination.

SUMMARY

Despite the confusing array of laws and regulations on EEO, the underlying principle is clear. EEO simply means individuals should be given an equal opportunity in employment decisions. EEO does not mean preferential treatment for one individual over another because of race, color, sex, religion, national origin, age, or disability. For instance, white males have won racial and sex discrimination suits against organizations that have violated Title VII by hiring less-qualified minorities or women. The EEO laws clearly state that treatment at work and opportunity for work should be unrelated to the race, sex, and other personal characteristics of individual workers.

Remember that this chapter discussed only federal EEO law and that there are numerous other federal, state, and local laws and labor regulations that can be the basis of a lawsuit. In fact, the trend is toward more state and local laws that regulate the workplace. In the applicable chapters, other laws will be discussed that affect labor and collective bargaining law, workers' compensation, unemployment compensation, wages, health and safety legislation, whistleblower's protection, retirement, employee benefits, rights of privacy, protection against unjust dismissal, and other issues related to the workplace. The election results of 2008 are likely to increase the legislation and regulation related to employment.

One Implication of Increased Litigation: Better HRM Practices

While the trend of increasing litigation can create competitive problems for U.S. employers in a global economy, many of the regulations and guidelines for HR practice, particularly EEO laws, actually encourage more effective HRM practices and underscore the need for HRM expertise. One large retailer specified that applicants for a district manager job for *certain* regions had to have a minimum of five years' experience as a district manager from some other retailer. This job specification created a disadvantage for women and minorities who may have been denied opportunities throughout the retail industry and thus could not

Glass-ceiling effect

have accumulated the required experience. This is an illustration of the "glass-ceiling effect," which refers to invisible barriers for women that serve as obstacles to moving up the corporate ladder. In addition, an internal study showed that years of previous experience was unrelated to performance as a district manager. The company was thus vulnerable to a lawsuit and, based on their own study, would have great difficulty proving the five-year specification was related to job success. The specification also forced the company to compensate the district manager job at a higher rate and made it much more difficult to recruit. This combination of facts seems to lead to a simple conclusion: change the job specification and reduce the number of years of experience required to be considered for the job. Many times, EEO laws and regulations and effective HR practices go hand in hand.

Legal HR practices are often the most effective and valid

The point is that the legality of human resource practices is often related to the effectiveness of human resource practices as well. Remember the discussion of "validated" selection procedures as characteristic of **"high-performance work systems."** *Validated* means the procedures actually predict what the employer intends for them to predict. This is essentially what EEO law requires regarding the burden on an organization after adverse impact is established.

Organizations thus would do well to evaluate all of their HR policies and practices in the context of the laws and case law and adjust those practices accordingly after their internal assessment. The result just might be more legally defensible and more effective HR policies. The old adage, an ounce of prevention is worth a pound of cure, really applies to the legal issues related to HR.

While the implications of HR-related litigation may be confusing, there can be no question that managers will be on relatively safer ground if they adhere to the following strategy with regard to employment practices: (1) monitor personnel decisions to ensure there is no evidence of disparate treatment or adverse impact caused by particular personnel practices; (2) if there are disparities, determine whether the practices causing the disparity are essential for the business and/or are job related; and (3) eliminate the practices if they are not job related or replace them with practices that do not cause such a disparity or less of a disparity. Not only will such a strategy protect managers from EEO claims, it also will lead to better and more cost-effective personnel decisions. HRM specialists have the expertise to assist organizations to pursue these strategies.

EEO laws have fostered a fairer system

In general, most would agree that EEO legislation has had positive effects on the occupational status of minorities and females. An additional benefit is that EEO laws and the threat of EEO litigation have helped to get managers to "clean up their act" with regard to personnel policy and practice. While the paperwork may be voluminous and the compliance requirements may seem ominous, there can be little question that EEO laws and regulations have fostered a fairer system of employment opportunity and a more systematic and valid process for personnel decisions. The efforts of managers in this regard are critical to organizational effectiveness and their mistakes can be extremely costly. Personnel practices may be the most heavily regulated area of organizational life today. HRM specialists in staffing issues cannot learn too much about this vital area.

In the following chapters, there will be much more to say about labor legislation and employment practices. The importance of EEO issues for virtually all HRM activities cannot be overstated. Students should consider the implications of the Civil Rights Act, GINA, the ADEA, the PDA, the ADA, and the myriad of other federal, state, and local laws when specific HR functions are covered such as job analysis and design (Chapter 4), planning and recruitment (Chapter 5), personnel selection (Chapter 6), performance appraisal (Chapter 7), training and development (Chapter 8), and compensation (Chapter 10).

The content of this chapter is more likely to go out of date faster than any of the others in this book (there were several pieces of legislation pending in Congress in 2008). In the volatile area of EEO, current, state-of-the-art knowledge is a competitive advantage for any organization. Make sure your knowledge in this area is indeed current.

Discussion Questions

1. In terms of EEO, how can customer requirements or preferences be used in the process of hiring people?

2. Given the great economic incentives for plaintiffs' attorneys today, why is the EEOC even necessary? Why can't a person simply be allowed to sue without the involvement of the EEOC?

3. Describe the procedures required to file a discrimination lawsuit under the disparate impact and disparate treatment theories. How is adverse impact determined? Provide a scenario illustrating evidence of adverse impact in an employment decision.

4. Based on your reading of the major EEO laws, what information should an employer include in a personnel policies and procedures manual given to all employees?

5. What will be the impact of the 2008 ADA Amendments Act? Explain your answer.

6. What steps would you take to prevent ADEA cases after a major restructuring or reduction in workforce?

7. Would you be less likely to join an organization that required you to agree to binding arbitration regarding labor disputes and to waive your right to a jury trial?

8. Should Title VII of the Civil Rights Act be amended to include sexual orientation? Justify your position.

Part 2

Acquiring Human Resource Capability

Chapter

4

Work Analysis and Design

After reading this chapter, you should be able to

1. Understand what work analysis is and what its major products are.
2. Explain the purposes of and uses for work analysis data.
3. Compare and contrast methods for collecting data.
4. Describe commonly used and newer methods for conducting work analysis, including O*NET.
5. Explain how work analysis information is applied to job design efforts.
6. Understand that different procedures emphasize different kinds of information that may be more or less useful for different HRM functions.
7. Conduct and prepare a work analysis report.

OVERVIEW

Among the HR prescriptions cited in Chapter 1 as predictive of corporate performance was the use of "validated" selection procedures, the use of formal performance appraisal, and the percentage of the workforce working in self-managed work teams. These prescriptions require some form of work or job analysis. An analysis of work is considered a building block for most HR systems in organizations. Corporate restructuring processes, quality improvement programs, human resource planning, job design, recruitment strategies, training programs, succession planning, and compensation systems are among the other HR activities that are based on work analysis. Let us not forget the importance of job analysis in the legal context discussed in Chapter 3.

Work analysis for organizational capability

    Work analysis, a term within which is included traditional job analysis and job design, provides the basic information that leads to specific products used or actions taken by management to create and sustain **organizational capability.** While sometimes a highly formal system involving trained analysts and standardized instruments and other times a more informal process, work analysis should be the first step for actions within most of the functional areas of HR. Consider the following scenarios:

- General Cinema is interested in the development of a screening test for theater manager positions. They want to be certain that the test is legally defensible and "job related" and emphasizes the most important elements of the job. Having also read the previous chapter in this book on equal employment opportunity (EEO), the consultant recommends two methods of work analysis to gather information. Why two methods?

■ The State of Virginia passed a law mandating that state employee pay be based on performance. However, there was a need for the development of a new performance appraisal system. The first step in the development of the appraisal system was the use of the critical incident method to identify the critical outcomes and behaviors for each position to be evaluated. Why?

■ Two laboratory technicians have similar job experience and education, but are employed at different local hospitals. One technician makes $5,000 more per year than the other. The lower-paid employee asks her HR department to review her pay based on the external compensation market. What information will the hospital need in order to establish fair compensation?

■ O*NET, the federal government's online database for work analysis, proves to be very valuable for military personnel leaving the service and their families. Veterans are using the O*NET to help with relocating or transitioning from military to civilian careers and for vocational guidance. Based on the O*NET database, the Military to Civilian Occupation Translator was developed to help service members match military skills and experience to civilian occupations. The database is also useful for disabled vets because job requirements and particular disabilities can be matched. The Military Spouse Resource Center, also known as MilSpouse.org (www.milspouse.org), is designed to help spouses and their families with career and job decisions. O*NET is a critical component of this comprehensive service. How was the Military to Civilian Occupation Translator developed?

■ The Monsanto Corporation has many jobs that stipulate specific physical requirements (e.g., must be able to lift 75 lbs.). The company is concerned that some of the requirements are unnecessary and may be in violation of the Civil Rights Act or the Americans with Disabilities Act. Will a work analysis help?

■ A division of Ford Motor Company decided to adopt autonomous work groups (AWGs) to reconfigure a factory floor. Teams rather than individuals would be assigned specific tasks. The teams would divide up the work, which was as clearly defined and standardized as in typical American factories, but all team members would be expected to be able to perform any of the work tasks. What information did the HR department at Ford need in order to help redesign jobs into these AWGs?

■ The James River Corporation uses a standardized job analysis questionnaire known as the *Position Analysis Questionnaire (PAQ)* to identify the best written tests to determine admission to their pipe fitter and millwright apprenticeship programs. Based on their understanding of *Griggs v. Duke Power* on the use of tests for hiring purposes, they attempt to establish the "job relatedness" of the tests based on the results from the PAQ. Will the PAQ results establish the "job relatedness" and thus the legal defensibility of the test?

■ Pratt and Whitney, the jet engine division of United Technologies, seeks to improve its competitiveness through the elimination of activities no longer essential to the business and the improvement of existing job functions in the context of customer requirements. Can work analysis help them?

■ The State of Maryland asked the consulting firm of Booz, Allen, and Hamilton to determine the necessary knowledge, skills, and abilities required to perform certain social work positions for the state. The study led to the reclassification of many positions, stipulating that only a Bachelor's degree should be required to do the work rather than a Master's in Social Work. Could the reclassification save the state money?

■ The city of Ft. Lauderdale, Florida, updates all of its job descriptions by identifying the "essential functions" of each job according to the Americans with Disabilities Act and incorporating this language into new job descriptions. How does this serve them?

■ The city of Chicago loses a lawsuit because it cannot justify a particular passing score on a test used to screen firefighter applicants. Could it have avoided this?

Work analysis information is needed for each of these situations to assist organizations in achieving certain objectives. Job descriptions and job specifications are needed to attract and select qualified (but not overqualified) employees and evaluate compensation systems. Job standards and performance criteria are used to evaluate employee and/or unit performance; job factors are needed to group jobs to assess wage and salary systems; and tasks and context factors are examined to redesign and evaluate jobs, restructure organizations, develop succession planning, and stay on the right side of the law. Almost all programs of interest to human resource specialists and other practitioners whose work pertains to organizational personnel depend on work analysis results.[1]

This chapter describes the importance of work analysis for the field of HRM. Discussion will center on the purposes for work analysis as well as the major approaches for collecting data. The nature of work is changing, and traditional work arrangements exist alongside contingent workers, independent contractors, outsourced activities, and work teams. But while the world of work may be changing, the basics of work analysis can (and should) be the cornerstone of HR activities. Good work analysis increases the probability that the "deliverables" from the HR suppliers will meet the requirements of their customers' both, internal and external. This applies even though jobs are becoming more elastic and less static and even if we don't call them jobs anymore but rather projects or roles.

WHAT IS WORK ANALYSIS?

Work analysis is a systematic process of gathering information about work, jobs, and the relationships among jobs.[2] Figure 4-1 presents a chronology of the steps to be undertaken in a comprehensive (and effective) work analysis. Please note that this approach should focus on (and begin with) customer requirements and meeting customer demands. Thus, the focus is on internal and especially external customers to first identify the critical products, services, or performance outcomes that are required of the supplier. This list of carefully defined products and services should then be the frame of reference for the rest of the steps in the analysis of that supplier's job, starting with the major tasks or activities necessary to achieve the required outcomes defined by the customers. The required outcomes as defined by customers are derived from the strategic planning of the organization.

General Cinema, for example, in one of the scenarios described above, required a cost-effective and job-related test that would help identify persons most likely to be effective theater managers. The product to be delivered by HR was the test, and the internal customers were managers who would have to make the hiring decisions. Of course, the main frame of reference for these managers must be the external customer, the theater goers.

Work analysis to identify essential functions

Once the products are defined and the tasks and activities have been identified, the relative importance, relative frequency, or essentiality with which the various tasks are performed can be assessed. Remember that word *essentiality*. Many methods now require the determination of *essential functions* for jobs because of the language of the Americans with Disabilities Act (see Chapter 3 discussion).

Figure 4-1
The Chronological Steps in Effective Work Analysis

Step	Critical Questions
1	What are the required outcomes/measures for assessing strategy execution (e.g., customer requirements for products/services)?
2	What are the essential tasks, activities, behaviors required to meet or exceed the requirements established at step 1? What is the relative importance, frequency, and essentiality of these tasks for achieving measures at step 1?
3	What are the necessary knowledges, skills, abilities, and other characteristics or competencies required to perform the activities at step 2?
4	How should jobs/work be defined? Where does the work get done to maximize efficiency/effectiveness? Do we use individual jobs, work teams, independent contractors, full-time/part-time? Do we outsource?

Knowledges, abilities, skills, and other characteristics (KASOCs)

Next, the critical **knowledges, abilities, skills, and other characteristics** (or **KASOCs**) necessary to perform the tasks must be identified. KASOCs are also called "competencies." This step is roughly equivalent to **competency modeling,** which is discussed later. **Knowledge** refers to an organized body of information, usually of a factual or procedural nature applied directly to the performance of a function. For example, computer programmers may need knowledge of specific languages such as Java. Your instructor in this class should obviously have knowledge of research and practice in human resource management.

An **ability** refers to a demonstrated competence to perform an observable behavior or a behavior that results in an observable product. Police officers, for example, are required to possess the physical ability to apprehend and detain a suspect and the cognitive ability to understand and complete arrest forms. Vigilance also may be such an ability. For example, while the ability to perform as an airport baggage checker may not require high levels of cognitive ability, the ability to be vigilant in a fairly boring task may be a critical ability NFL quarterbacks should possess high levels of cognitive ability to be able to read (and react quickly) to defense formations.

A **skill** is a competence to perform a learned, psychomotor act, and may include a manual, verbal, or mental manipulation of data, people, or things. So, in the case of a police officer, she or he must demonstrate an acceptable level of driving skill and skill in operating and maintaining a weapon, among many others.

Finally, **other personal characteristics** include various personality characteristics, attitudes, or physical or mental competencies needed to perform the job. Even something as obvious as being courteous to civilians plays an important role in determining how well officers perform their jobs. When officers are unable to empathize with crime victims, are callous in treating witnesses, or are impulsive and destroy evidence at a crime scene, they demonstrate some shortcoming on personal characteristics that affects their job performance. Being able to tolerate the belligerence of customers and control one's temper may be critical in certain circumstances. Being able to work in teams is another example of a critical characteristic for many jobs today. An analysis could conclude, for example, that armed security guards must not have a history indicating psychiatric problems.

As you can tell from these examples, the *products* of competencies or KASOCs are typically easy to observe and ultimately serve as the basic units of observation for analysis.[3] For example, the customer of the computer programmer requires a Java program that meets certain specifications. Knowledge of a computer language such as Java can be determined from an interview, responses to a written test, the possession of a certain license, or graduation from a certain class or by observing an individual attempt to program. The knowledge required to teach a class in human resource management can be determined based on the possession of certain credentials (e.g., Ph.D. in human resource management or industrial/organizational psychology) or through an interview or test.

Establishing that someone requires driving skill to perform a job is one thing, and ascertaining that an individual has this skill is another. It would be difficult in an interview or written test to measure the latter, as they do not afford an opportunity to observe the series of behaviors that demonstrate the application of this knowledge domain in the job environment. This would seem to require observations of actual motor vehicle operation. To establish that driving skill is a requirement in the first place depends on observation in the field and a work analysis.

What Are the Major Goals for Work Analysis?

As you've probably gathered by now, much of the success (i.e., validity) of work analysis efforts is a function of the accuracy of the inferences drawn about the job from observations, interviews, and/or questionnaire data gathered through the work analysis. One underlying objective of work analysis is to minimize the inferential leaps required to arrive at a conclusion. The context for work analysis should always be critical outcome measures that define strategy. Toward this end, the following are offered as goals one should strive for in the course of work analysis:[4]

Focus on observables

1. *Work analysis should be the description of observables.* Often the behavior or competency necessary for performing the job is not observable but the products or outcomes, kinds of materials or work aids used, and the people included in the decision process can be reported. Work analysis should focus on observable behaviors and work outcomes. A *job description* is the usual product of this analysis.

Describe work not persons doing work

2. *Work analysis should describe work behavior independent of the personal characteristics of particular people who perform the job.* Quite simply, work analysis describes how a job is performed and focuses on the position, not the person doing the work. **Performance appraisal** is used to describe how well individuals perform their jobs. The actual performance appraisal instrument may have been developed from work analysis and should be linked to the job description.

Data must be reliable

3. *Work analysis data must be verifiable and reliable.* The organization should maintain records of the data, document all decisions that are data-based, and be able to justify work analysis products. The data must be reliable, indicating that different sources agreed on judgments about the work. Recall the importance of job analysis in EEO litigation and, in particular, in establishing **job relatedness**. The City of Chicago lost a lawsuit because the particular passing score on a hiring test (which caused adverse impact against African-Americans) could not be legally justified by job analysis results.[5]

Do We Really Need All the Specificity in Formal Job Analysis?

Most American workers have a detailed job description that describes their work. This approach is not without critics. In Japan, for example, new employees are typically hired without a job description or specifications. Japan places much greater reliance on in-house training and job rotation to foster a versatility in the skills of each new employee. Japanese managers think job descriptions can be harmful to their team-building approach to management. Many experts in job design and organizational restructuring embrace this view and believe job descriptions should be written for units or teams with all team members responsible for (or at least qualified to perform) all unit functions or activities. Individual job descriptions are thought to be detrimental to work group effectiveness. However, as discussed in Chapter 3, job descriptions may be needed for legal reasons and can be written in such a way as to facilitate a team-oriented approach to work processes.

Highly detailed job descriptions are very common in Europe, where they are frequently required by regulation or union agreement. Every employee at the Volvo plants in Sweden, for example, has a detailed job description based on a quantitative job analysis even though the assembly process at Volvo is team-based rather than the traditional assembly line.

While work analysis is often used to derive specific information about particular jobs, the data can be aggregated to the unit or function level so that the end products such as job descriptions or job specifications are defined at the team level rather than for particular positions. Often this approach to defining the job in terms of team member competencies is coupled with skill-based pay systems where individuals are compensated on their potential to perform multiple tasks as opposed to a limited set of tasks specific to a job. So, a team member may be expected to perform the tasks of another who is absent, rotate task assignments with others as needed, and provide additional expert opinion on task processes or products. In this way, the team member is cross-trained to perform a number of different tasks, perhaps even all of those involved in a specific work process. In other words, no one has a monopoly on a set of tasks, as the responsibility for performance of these tasks is shared by team members.

Need for specificity depends on purpose for work analysis

So what's the answer to the question about the value of specificity? Unfortunately for those seeking "specificity" in this answer, it really depends on the context! While in many situations organizations can retrieve general job descriptions right off the Internet through O*NET or other sources, there are other situations where great detail in the job description and job specifications may be required. For example, had a job analysis existed with greater specificity in the Chicago lawsuit mentioned above regarding a particular passing score that caused adverse impact, it might have helped the city in its defense.

What Is the Legal Significance of Work Analysis?

Job relatedness

See "Uniform Guidelines" at eeoc.gov

There has been strong interest in job analysis since passage of the Civil Rights Act, the ADA, and subsequent court rulings and government guidelines. As discussed in Chapter 3, the "Uniform Guidelines on Employee Selection Procedures" (see eeoc.gov) and the Supreme Court decisions in *Griggs v. Duke Power* and *Albemarle Paper Company v. Moody* have emphasized the importance of demonstrating the **job relatedness** of employer selection systems. One way to do this is by conducting a thorough work analysis to justify personnel job specifications such as passing scores on tests or particular credentials for the job.

There are a great number of court cases that focus on the results of (or the nonexistence of) a job analysis. For example, many women have filed lawsuits contesting the physical ability tests (e.g., push-ups, sit-ups) mandated for entry into police or firefighters' academies. They often claim "adverse impact" since a greater proportion of women than men are disqualified as a result of such tests. As in the Chicago case that focused on a particular passing score on a written test that caused adverse impact, the outcomes of such cases may turn on the quality of any work analysis that formed the basis of a test and a particular passing score on a physical or mental ability test.

There also have been a number of lawsuits filed on behalf of older workers who lost their jobs because of a mandatory retirement age. For example, an Indianapolis bus driver used the ADEA to challenge the mandatory retirement age of 55 (he lost). In this case, job analysis data were successfully introduced at trial to support the age limit. On the other hand, the American Association of Retired Persons has been active in challenging mandatory retirement ages using job analysis data. The Federal Aviation Administration raised the mandatory retirement age to 65 based on work analysis data.

As discussed in Chapter 3, statistics can be used to establish prima facie evidence of discrimination under the disparate impact theory of Title VII. The burden of proof then rests with the employer to show that the selection device or job specification (e.g., the test, test score, specified years of experience, educational requirement) is "job related" or a "business necessity." In a 2005 lawsuit against the city of Chicago, African-Americans established the adverse impact of an entrance exam and questioned the use of a cutoff score to screen applicants. The court ruled that the City of Chicago had not provided sufficient evidence for the job-relatedness of the test and the particular cutoff score. Had certain job analysis methods been used, results could have justified the use of the test and cutoff score.

May need work analysis to justify cut-off scores

Firefighter candidates in Dallas, Texas, were required to scale a fence six feet high in a prescribed amount of time. Since a higher percentage of women were unable to scale the fence than men, the court asked the city to show how scaling a fence six feet in height was job-related. The city presented data that demonstrated that the average fence in the jurisdiction was six feet high and that scaling fences was a frequent activity that must be performed by competent firefighters.

Legal challenges to job specifications involving physical attributes (e.g., strength, speed) and mental attributes have increased since the Americans with Disabilities Act took effect in 1990. The ADA specifies that employers must make "reasonable accommodations" that would allow qualified disabled workers to perform the "essential functions" of the job. According to the EEOC, these accommodations may include physical renovations to the job and the workplace.

What Are the Major Work Analysis Products?

Job descriptions

There are numerous products that can be derived from work analysis. The most frequently and commonly used products include "job descriptions" and "job specifications." **Job descriptions** define the job in terms of its content and scope. Although the format can vary, the job description may include information on job duties, tasks, activities, behaviors, and/or responsibilities. An identification of critical internal and external customers, equipment to be used on the job, working conditions, relationships with co-workers, and the extent of supervision required is also typical in a job description. Figure 4-2 presents an example of a job *description* for a compensation manager. In a sense, you can think of a job description as being a report of the job situation. Job descriptions are often summarized in classified employment ads and, more recently, available on the Internet through various job placement services. Go to www.online.onetcenter.org for over 1,000 job descriptions.

Figure 4-2 **Job Description and Job Specifications for a Compensation Manager**

Job Title: Compensation Manager DOT Code: 166.167–022

Reports to:

Job Description

Responsible for the design and administration of employee compensation programs. Ensures proper consideration of the relationship of salary to performance of each employee and provides consultation on salary administration to managers and supervisors.

Principal Duties and Responsibilities:

1. Ensures the preparation and maintenance of job descriptions for each current and projected position. Prepares all job descriptions, authorizing final drafts. Coordinates periodic review of all job descriptions, making revisions as necessary. Educates employees and supervisors on job description use and their intent by participation in formal training programs and by responding to their questions. Maintains accurate file of all current job descriptions. Distributes revised job descriptions to appropriate individuals.

2. Ensures the proper evaluation of job descriptions. Serves as chair of Job Evaluation Committee, coordinating its activities. Resolves disputes over proper evaluation of jobs. Assigns jobs to pay ranges and reevaluates jobs periodically through the Committee process. Conducts initial evaluation of new positions prior to hiring. Ensures integrity of job evaluation process.

3. Ensures that Company compensation rates are in accordance with the Company philosophy. Maintains current information concerning applicable salary movements taking place in comparable organizations. Obtains or conducts salary surveys as necessary. Conducts analysis of salary changes among competitors and presents recommendations on salary movements on an annual basis.

4. Ensures proper consideration of the relationship of salary to the performance of each employee. Inspects all performance appraisals and salary reviews, authorizing all pay adjustments.

5. Develops and administers the performance appraisal program. Develops and updates performance appraisal instruments. Assists in the development of training programs to educate supervisors on using the performance appraisal system. Monitors the use of the performance appraisal instruments to ensure the integrity of the system and proper use.

6. Assists in the development and oversees the administration of all bonus payments up through the Officer level.

7. Researches and provides recommendations on executive compensation issues.

8. Coordinates the development of an integrated HR information system. Assists in identifying needs; interfaces with the Management Information Systems Department to achieve departmental goals for information needs.

9. Performs related duties as assigned or as the situation dictates.

Job Specifications

Required Knowledges, Skills, and Abilities:

1. Knowledge of compensation and HRM practices and principles.
2. Knowledge of job analysis procedures.
3. Knowledge of survey development and interpretation practices.
4. Knowledge of current performance appraisal issues for designing, implementing, and maintaining systems.
5. Skill in conducting job analysis interviews.
6. Skill in writing job descriptions, memorandums, letters, and proposals.
7. Skill in making group presentations, conducting job analysis interviews, and explaining policies and practices to employees and supervisors.
8. Skill in performing statistical computations including regression, correlation, and basic descriptive statistics.
9. Ability to conduct meetings.
10. Ability to plan and prioritize work.

Education and Experience Requirements:

This position requires the equivalent of a college degree in personnel, human resources, industrial psychology, or a related degree, plus 3–5 years' experience in Personnel, 2–3 of which should include compensation administration experience. An advanced degree in Industrial Psychology, Business Administration, or Personnel Management is preferred.

Work Orientation Factors:

This position may require up to 15 percent travel.

Job specifications

Job specifications consist of the KASOCs needed to carry out the job tasks and duties. Specific educational requirements (e.g., Ph.D., MD, MBA, Ed.D., MSW), certifications or licenses (e.g., CPA, CFP), or other qualifications (e.g., years of experience) are often stipulated as job specifications. Cutoff scores on tests are also job specifications. Figure 4-2 also presents an example of the job *specifications* for a compensation manager. You will note that a college degree in personnel, human resources, industrial psychology, or a related field is required for the compensation manager job. Job specifications detail the specific KASOCs or competencies required. Work analysis should be the basis of each specification.

Job specifications often are contested in court because they have adverse impact against groups protected by EEO laws. Certainly job specifications that result in adverse impact against groups covered by EEO legislation should be validated with a thorough analysis. Where data are available in company records that shed light on the relationship between a given job specification and some measure of effectiveness, these data should certainly be used. A regional manager of a 500-store clothing retailer proposed that all assistant managers

Validate job specifications using company records

Adverse impact

in his region should have college degrees. However, research from the HR Department indicated there was no correlation between having or not having a college degree and performance as an assistant store manager. In addition, HR determined the College degree specification caused costly recruiting problems and **adverse impact** against minorities. The manager was persuaded to change his mind about requiring the degree for the job.

Unnecessary job specifications can also translate into higher labor costs. The State of Maryland, as mentioned in the chapter opening, was concerned about the number of state positions that required a Master's in Social Work (MSW), a requirement that necessitated a higher starting salary. The consulting firm of Booz, Allen, and Hamilton conducted work analysis of these jobs and determined the extent to which the knowledge acquired by the MSW was essential for these jobs. In addition, since many positions had some MSW-trained occupants and others doing the same work with only a Bachelor's degree, the consultant firm also could study whether the more advanced degree was related to better performance on the job (it wasn't). Booz, Allen also found the MSW requirement hindered the state's ability to meet its diversity goals and caused adverse impact against minorities. They recommended that the MSW job specification be dropped for these positions. The state saved millions of dollars by dropping the higher degree requirement and was able to recruit from a much larger pool of potential candidates.

Many business schools now stipulate that a Ph.D. is required for any faculty position although it is conceivable that a candidate with an MBA would be less costly and perhaps as (or more) effective as an instructor of undergraduate students. Job specifications such as reading level, formal education requirements, and the like must be established at a level that reflects the minimum necessary for job entry. Establishing specifications at too high a level often results in adverse impact and can hinder diversity and affirmative action goals.

Glass-ceiling effect

For this reason, such practices are closely scrutinized by the courts. The so-called **glass-ceiling effect** in certain industries may to some extent be caused by job specifications that block women from many key positions because they lack certain credentials or experience.

For example, requiring an advanced degree and a minimum number of years of previous experience are examples of job specifications that could hinder the ability of women or minorities to even compete for a job—and those specifications may have been set arbitrarily. It is in an organization's best interest to determine whether a particular job specification is really necessary for success on a job. After all, more education or more years of experience almost always translate into higher salaries and more difficulty recruiting. Organizations should constantly monitor their specifications. Larger companies often have the data available to be able to assess the correlation between job specifications and important outcomes like performance. If the data are available, they really need to test the validity of job specifications. Should an employment discrimination lawsuit ensue, the plaintiffs will surely examine these data very carefully and perhaps use their own analysis to support their theory of discrimination.

In addition to job descriptions and job specifications, work analysis is used for a variety of purposes and products for both the private and the public sector, particularly in larger organizations (see Figure 4-3). Many products are related to employee compensation. Smaller businesses are less likely to use formal approaches for conducting job analyses and less likely to even use formal job descriptions. In larger organizations, including state and federal government agencies, personnel are hired, trained, and classified as job analysts. In these positions, their primary duty is to perform work analyses for **job classification** and **job evaluation** (See Figure 4-3). A great deal of their work today concerns legal compliance and, in particular, compliance with the Americans with Disabilities Act (ADA). For example, as mentioned at the start of the chapter, job analysts employed by the city of Fort Lauderdale, Florida, developed a new job analysis method that incorporated ADA language regarding "essential functions."

Work analysis also is used for recruitment and selection purposes by many companies. For example, General Cinema developed a test and a structured interview using the *Management Position Description Questionnaire,* a standardized job analysis instrument, and the **critical incident technique.** Exxon Corporation and AT&T employ a standardized questionnaire to analyze their jobs in order to develop or identify personnel selection tests for their entry-level employees. The City of New York and the Monsanto Corporation also use a quantitative job analysis method to establish very specific physical requirements for certain jobs.

Figure 4-3   **Products of Job Analysis Information**

Job Description. A complete job description should contain job identification information, a job summary, the job duties, accountabilities, and job specification or employment standards information.

Job Classification. Job classification is the arrangement of jobs into classes, groups, or families according to some systematic schema. Traditional classification schemes have been based on organizational lines of authority, technology-based job/task content, and human behavior–based job content.

Job Evaluation. Job evaluation is a procedure for classifying jobs in terms of their relative worth both within an organization and within the related labor market. Job evaluation is used to determine compensation.

Job Design/Restructuring. Job design deals with the allocation and arrangement of organizational work activities and tasks into sets where a singular set of activities constitutes a "job" and is performed by the job incumbent. Job restructuring or redesign consists of reallocation or rearrangement of the work activities into different sets.

Job Specifications. Personnel requirements and specifications for a particular job are the personal knowledge, skills, aptitudes, attributes, and traits that are required for successful performance. Job specifications may be identified as minimum qualifications, as essential characteristics, or as desirable specifications. Cutoff scores on tests, credentials, licenses, degrees, and previous experience are all job specifications.

Performance Appraisal. Performance appraisal is a **systematic** evaluation of employees' job performance by their supervisors or others who are familiar with their performance. Job analysis is used to develop the criteria or standards for the appraisal.

Worker Training. Training is a systematic, intentional process of developing specific skills and influencing behavior of organizational members such that their resultant behavior contributes to organizational effectiveness.

Worker Mobility/Succession Planning. Worker mobility (career development and pathing) is the movement of individuals into and out of positions, jobs, and occupations. From the perspective of the individual, both self-concepts and social situations change, making the process of job/occupational choice continuous due to growth, exploration, establishment, maintenance, and decline.

Efficiency. Improving efficiency in jobs involves the development of optimal work processes and design of equipment and other physical facilities with particular reference to work activities of people, including work procedures, work layout, and work standards.

Safety. Similar to efficiency, improving safety in jobs involves the development of optimal work processes and safe design of equipment and physical facilities. However, the focus is on identifying and eliminating unsafe work behaviors, physical conditions, and environmental conditions.

Human Resource Planning. Human resource planning consists of anticipatory and reactive activities by which an organization ensures that it has and will continue to have the right number and kind of people at the right places, at the right times, performing jobs that maximize both the service objectives and/or profit of the organization. It includes the activities by which an organization enhances the self-actualization and growth needs of its people and allows for the maximum utilization of their skills and talents.

Legal/Quasi-Legal Requirements. Laws, regulations, and guidelines established by government agencies (e.g., EEOC, OFCCP, OSHA) have set forth requirements related to one or more of the job analysis products or purposes listed above.

Source: Adapted from R. A. Ash, "Job Analysis Questionnaire (PAQ)," in *The Job Analysis Handbook for Business, Industry and Government*, ed. S. Gael, vol. II, pp. 826–827. Reprinted with permission.

Job design

Work analysis is also used to **redesign jobs** and to determine how jobs relate to one another. Pratt and Whitney, a division of United Technologies, conducted work analysis as a part of a corporatewide restructuring effort. Motorola Corporation and Ford used a standardized, task-based instrument known as the *Job Diagnostic Survey* to collect information related to the development of work teams. Numerous organizations also use work analysis to develop training curricula.

Performance appraisal

Work analysis is often used to develop **performance appraisal** systems. Office Depot conducted work analysis using **competency modeling** in order to develop a multi-rater assessment program that would be used for feedback and development for its store managers and as a possible source of data to be used for determining managerial potential for higher level management. Your author led groups of district managers and HR specialists in a process of refining the company's mission/vision statement followed by the development of "core competencies" to meet new strategic business goals. This step was followed by a refinement of the competency definitions and the development of **behaviorally anchored rating scales** to be used by peers, subordinates, supervisors and customers in the assessment of managers.

What Are the Major Methods of Work Analysis?

There are a variety of methods used to collect information about jobs, including observation of the job, actual performance of the job, interviews, identifying critical incidents, diaries, and organization records, including customer complaints and questionnaires. Figure 4-4 presents a list of the various data collection methods available along with some of their relative advantages and disadvantages. As noted, an analyst, often the supervisor for the position under study, can simply observe the job and record his or her observations. The analyst also can actually perform the job. Many corporations now require high-level managers to spend

Figure 4-4   **Common Work Analysis Data Collection Methods**

Collection Method	Advantages	Disadvantages
Observation: Direct observation of job duties, work sampling or observation of segments of job performance, and indirect recording of activities (e.g., film).	Allows for a deeper understanding of job duties than relying on incumbents' descriptions.	Unable to observe mental aspects of jobs (e.g., decision making of managers, creativity of scientists); may not sample all important aspects of the job, especially important yet infrequently performed activities (e.g., use of weapons by police officers).
Performing the Job: Actual performance of job duties by the analyst.	Analyst receives firsthand experience of contextual factors on the job, including physical hazards, social demands, emotional stressors, and mental requirements; useful for jobs that can be easily learned.	May be dangerous for hazardous jobs (e.g., firefighters, patrol officers) or unethical/illegal for jobs requiring licensing or extensive training (e.g., medical doctor, psychologist, pharmacist); analyst may be exposed only to frequently performed activities.
Interviews: Individual and group interviews with job incumbents, supervisors, subordinates, clients, or other knowledgeable sources.	Information on infrequently performed activities, and physical and mental activities can be collected; use of multiple sources instead of one source can provide a more comprehensive, unbiased view of the job.	Value of the data is dependent on the interviewers' skills and may be faulty if they ask ambiguous questions; interviewees may be suspicious about the motives for the job analysis (e.g., fearful it will alter their compensation) and distort the information they provide.
Critical Incidents: Descriptions of behavioral examples of exceptionally poor or good performance, and context and consequences in which they occur.	Since observable and measurable behaviors are described, the information can be readily used for performance appraisal and training purposes; may provide insights into job expectations as defined by incumbents.	Descriptions of average or typical behavior are typically not collected so the data may be less inclusive of the entire job domain; time-consuming to gather the incidents.
Diaries: Descriptions of daily work activities by incumbents.	Written in terms familiar to incumbents and supervisors so the data may be easier to use (e.g., in developing performance appraisal measures); may provide insights into the reasons for job activities.	Time-consuming to document; may be biased accounts; may not include mental activities (e.g., innovativeness) or a representative account of all activities.
Background Records: Data mining review and analysis of relevant materials and data including: organizational charts, O*NET, company training manuals, organizational policies and procedures manuals, existing job descriptions, correlational studies relating work variables (e.g., job specifications) to important outcomes.	Provide analyst with job information that assists in developing interview questions or questionnaires; validating job specifications; is relatively easy to collect/ and analyze; can help determine the value of job specifications; necessary in legal context	May not provide complete information and generally needs to be supplemented with data collected using other methods; may be outdated materials; usually provide limited information on specific KASOCs required as well as importance ratings of tasks.
Questionnaires: Structured forms and activity checklists (PAQ, JDS, WDQ, MPDQ, JCQ) as well as open-ended or unstructured questions (see www. onetcenter.org/questionnaires.html for downloadable questionnaires on abilities, background, education and training, knowledge, skills, work context, and work style).	Commercially available questionnaires are generally less expensive and quicker to use than other methods; can reach a large sample of incumbents or sources, which allows for a greater coverage of informed individuals; responses often can be quantified and analyzed in a variety of meaningful ways (e.g., comparisons can be made across jobs or departments for compensation or selection purposes); can be integrated with O*NET database.	Questions may be interpreted incorrectly; difficult to assess how respondents interpreted questions; response rate may be low, making the results less generalizable; often expensive and time-consuming to develop, score, or analyze; open-ended questions are difficult to quantify and require content analysis that is time-consuming.

time performing jobs where there is personal contact with the customer. Blockbuster Video, for example, makes their managers work the cash register on weekends and Xerox Corporation sends its top managers on sales calls. The basic idea is to better understand the customer's perspective on the busness. Individual or group interviews can be conducted with clients or customers incumbents, supervisors, or subordinates for the position under study. Incumbents or observers can be asked to maintain a diary or to record critical incidents regarding their performance or behavior on the job. Available records of work activities or other relevant information such as job descriptions, an organizational chart, and policies and procedures manuals can be reviewed by the analyst to gain background data on the job. Relevant job descriptions can also be retrieved from the Internet through O*NET, a product of the United States Department of Labor.[6]

Questionnaires or checklists also can be completed by incumbents, supervisors, clients, or subordinates. Respondents can be asked to list the major tasks they perform as well as to rate the importance, frequency, time spent, or "essential" nature of each task. Respondents also can indicate how important a specific knowledge, skill, or ability is for completing the tasks. Methods are available for determining the importance of job tasks. A variety of standardized questionnaires exist for conducting job analyses and some of the more commonly used instruments are described in a later section. Questionnaires are also available through O*NET. Go to www.onetcenter.org/questionnaires.html for downloadable instruments in English and Spanish.

Background records

Background records should almost always be used with organizational data directly relevant to the purposes for doing the work analysis when such data are available. For example, in the State of Maryland study of social workers described earlier, one of the primary purposes of the study was to determine whether a graduate degree was really essential for the actual work being done. Some past and present social workers for the state had graduate degrees while others did not. Fortunately, the State of Maryland had performance data on social workers and could thus conduct an empirical study correlating educational level (e.g., MSW or not) with job performance. This correlational analysis was the primary basis for recommending that the MSW should be dropped as a required credential for employment (the correlation between the degree and job performance was near zero) of course, such recommendations must be made with deference to critical licensing, certification or accreditation standards.

Correlating specifications with performance

What Are the Dimensions on Which Work Analysis May Vary?

Work analysis methods can vary along several dimensions, including (1) the types of information provided, (2) the forms in which job information is illustrated, (3) the standardization of the analysis, and (4) the sources of job information.[7] Each of these dimensions is described below.

Types of Information

Work analysis methods can solicit a variety of types of information. Some approaches are called **task-** or **job-oriented** methods since they indicate the tasks or duties required to perform the job. For example, "performing cardiopulmonary resuscitation" is considered an important task for a nurse. Similarly, "study and evaluate state-of-the-art techniques to remain competitive and/or lead the field" may be considered an essential task for a member of the management information systems (MIS) staff. Task/job-oriented approaches can be distinguished from the other two approaches we will discuss by their identification or, at least, implication of an end-product. That is, task/job-oriented approaches tend to stress "what gets done on the job." These approaches typically produce quite detailed descriptions of the objectives for each job. As a result, they are very good for fine-grained analysis of jobs but often are too specific to allow for useful comparisons across jobs.

Position Analysis Questionnaire

Other methods such as the **Position Analysis Questionnaire** (PAQ) are considered to be **person-** or **worker-oriented** approaches since information is more focused on the KASOCs or behaviors (e.g., decision making, communicating) needed to perform the tasks satisfactorily. In the nurse example, a person-oriented analysis may determine that "knowledge of disorders of the circulatory system" is critical for competent nursing. These approaches provide less detailed information than the job/task-oriented approach but tend to provide better information for the purpose of comparing jobs and identifying job specifications.

Threshold traits analysis

Finally, **trait-oriented** approaches such as **threshold traits analysis** focus more on the latent traits (physical and mental abilities and sometimes personality or temperament) a worker must possess in order to perform the required behaviors that lead to specific ends. These approaches detail the job specifications necessary for job success. In a sense they generate a prototype of the ideal job incumbent. They ask, "Who can perform these behaviors?" Oftentimes several approaches are combined into a more comprehensive analysis. As you can imagine, it makes little sense to ask "Who can perform these behaviors?" without first answering the questions: "What behaviors are performed?" and "For what ends?" In fact, some courts have ruled that detailed task analysis must precede any attempt to identify critical competencies or job specifications.[8]

Almost all systematic work analysis methods collect data on the machines, tools, and work aids used. More complete analyses also include records of contextual factors of the job (e.g., physical working conditions, environmental hazards, contact with co-workers).

Figure 4-5 Job Analysis Approach and HR Function Matrix

Job Analysis Method	Human Resource Function				
	Job Redesign	Personnel Selection	Compensation	Training	Performance Appraisal
Job/task	+	0	+	+	+
Person/worker	0	+	+	+	+
Trait/competency-based	0	+	0	0	−

+ = The approach is well-suited for meeting the information requirements of this function.

0 = The approach provides useful information for this function but should not be used in isolation.

− = The approach defeats the aims of this function by providing largely useless information.

Use different work analysis methods for different HR functions/purposes

Some methods also provide information on work performance standards (e.g., quality and quantity standards, error analysis) and specific customer requirements. These latter pieces of information are essential to support personnel decisions based on performance appraisal such as terminations, assignment to training, or promotion.

The last paragraph has probably already clued you into the fact that different approaches to work analysis are better suited to supporting different HRM functions and providing necessary products and that the wisest strategy is to support one approach through the use of at least a second, somewhat different approach. Figure 4-5 provides a convenient approach and HRM function matrix to better illustrate this idea. As you can tell from this figure, trait- or competency-oriented approaches are well-suited for identifying KASOCs for personnel selection purposes. Also, trait-oriented approaches are useful for identifying skill requirements for skill-based job evaluation plans. Note that job/task-oriented approaches are the best method for job redesign efforts whereas both job/task- and person/worker-oriented approaches are better suited for performance appraisal development than is the trait approach. In fact, in Figure 4-5 the trait approach receives a "−" for this function as it is uniquely tailored to invite employee grievance and subsequent employer liability for personnel decisions based on trait appraisal.

The Form of Job Information

Work analysis information can be presented in qualitative or quantitative form depending on the method used. Most methods are **qualitative** in the sense that the job is described in a narrative, nonnumerical manner and results in verbal or narrative descriptions of job information. The critical incident technique (CIT), discussed later, is an example of a qualitative method. Other methods such as the O*NET questionnaires, PAQ, the JCQ, the MPDQ, and empirical analysis of background data and performance relationships are **quantitative** and provide descriptive information in numerical form. Common examples include a listing of tasks and ratings of the relative frequency, essentiality, or importance with which they are performed and descriptions of the production or error rates per time period. In most cases, work analyses include both quantitative and qualitative information.

The Standardization of the Work Analysis Content

Many HRM professionals have created a uniform or consistent method for work analysis. Some methods, for example, have a set number of questions or items to which responses are required. The job analyst may be asked to write the major objectives of the position, the most important or essential tasks or functions to be performed, the KASOCs that an occupant should have for the position, the major work products or outcomes, and the critical internal or external customers for the products or services. The quantitative approaches are more standardized. The PAQ, for example, has standard content for all the jobs that are under study. Other methods have a standardized content (listing of tasks) for a group of similar jobs, but another list may be used for a different set of jobs.

Another component of the standardization process is the response format. Many methods are completed using computer sheets, direct entry through a computer diskette, or, for many approaches now, through the Internet. Many questionnaires can be completed online with near instant results for the job analyst.

Recall the discussion of the elasticity of work itself and how jobs change so rapidly. So, the recommendation here is not to have too much faith in an already standardized measure since many jobs, their duties, and necessary worker competencies can change dramatically. Who would have envisioned just 15 years ago that clerical workers would have so much of their job activity centered on the computer or that automobile assembly plants would require computer competencies to the extent they do today? As a more vivid example for you, think about how the role of human resource assistant has changed from the days when most jobs in the personnel office were largely clerical and centered around payroll issues.

Sources of Job Information

There are a number of potential sources for information about a job. Cameras can be used to observe tasks and a variety of recording devices can be used to assess employees' physiological reactions. The most common source for information is job incumbents and supervisors for the job under study. Other possibilities include job analysts or specialists trained to conduct job analyses, outside observers or consultants, subordinates to the job under study, clients or customers, or persons simply in a good position to observe the job as it is performed. Most agencies of the federal government have job analyst positions whose major responsibility is analysis of other agency jobs. Obviously, more sources of information will probably more fully capture a job on a project.

WHAT ARE THE MOST USEFUL FORMAL APPROACHES TO WORK ANALYSIS?

There are a great number of formal approaches available today. One of the best sources of information on traditional job analysis is the two-volume *Job Analysis Handbook for Business, Industry, and Government.* The handbook describes 18 different job analysis methods in use today.[9] A very readable text for novices is *Everything You Always Wanted to Know about Job Analysis,* authored by one of the leading authorities in the field.[10] This chapter will concentrate discussion on methods that have been used to accomplish a specific purpose.

Position Analysis Questionnaire (PAQ)

The **Position Analysis Questionnaire (PAQ)** is a standardized questionnaire that assesses activities using 187 items in six categories.[11] These are

Six categories of activities

1. *Information input*—where and how does the worker obtain the information needed to perform the job (e.g., use of visual or sensory input)?
2. *Mental processes*—what reasoning, planning, decision-making, or information-processing activities are necessary to perform the activities?
3. *Work output*—what physical activities are performed, and what tools are used?
4. *Relationships with other people*—what relationships with other people are required to perform the job (e.g., negotiating, performing supervisory activities)?
5. *Job context*—in what physical and social contexts is the work performed (e.g., hazards, stress)?
6. *Other job characteristics*—what other activities or characteristics are relevant to the job (e.g., apparel required, work schedule, salary basis)?

Sample items for each of the six PAQ categories are presented in Figure 4-6. Items on the PAQ are rated using several different scales, including importance, amount of time required, extent of use, possibility of occurrence, applicability, and difficulty.[12] The PAQ can be completed in about two-and-one-half hours. An online scoring form is now available (www.paq.com). Each job is scored on 32 dimensions, and a profile is constructed for the job. Norms are provided so that the job profile can be compared to profiles of benchmark jobs. PAQ results are provided based on the user's purpose(s) for conducting the work analysis. For example, a user may request "test predictions" where the PAQ results identify particular tests with estimated validities for the job under study. Or, job evaluation points could

PAQ results can identify useful tests

Figure 4-6   **Sample Items from the PAQ**

POSITION ANALYSIS QUESTIONNAIRE (PAQ)

1 INFORMATION INPUT

1.1 Sources of Job Information

Rate each of the following items in terms of the extent to which it is used by the worker as a source of information in performing the job.

Code	Extent of Use (U)
N	Does not apply
1	Nominal, very infrequent
2	Occasional
3	Moderate
4	Considerable
5	Very substantial

1.1.1 Visual Sources of Job Information

1 |U_ Written materials (books, reports, office notes, articles, job instructions, signs, etc.)

2 |U_ Quantitative materials (materials that deal with quantities or amounts, such as graphs, accounts, specifications, tables of numbers, etc.)

3 |U_ Pictorial materials (pictures or picturelike materials used as *sources* of information, for example, drawings, blueprints, diagrams, maps, tracings, photographic films, x-ray films, TV pictures, etc.)

2 MENTAL PROCESSES

2.2 Information Processing Activities

In this section are various human operations involving the "processing" of information or data. Rate each of the following items in terms of how important the activity is to the completion of the job.

Code	Importance to This Job (I)
N	Does not apply
1	Very minor
2	Low
3	Average
4	High
5	Extreme

39 |I_ Combining information (*combining,* synthesizing, or integrating information or data from two or more sources to establish new facts, hypotheses, theories, or a more complete body of *related* information, for example, an economist using information from various sources to predict future economic conditions, a pilot flying aircraft, a judge trying a case, etc.)

40 |I_ Analyzing information or data (for the purpose of identifying *underlying* principles or facts by *breaking down* information into component parts, for example, interpreting financial reports, diagnosing mechanical disorders or medical symptoms, etc.)

49 |S_ Using mathematics (indicate, using the code below, the highest level of mathematics that the individual must understand as required by the job)

Code	Level of Mathematics
N	Does not apply.
1	Simple basic (counting, addition and subtraction of 2-digit numbers or less)
2	Basic (addition and subtraction of numbers of 3 digits or more, multiplication, division, etc.)
3	Intermediate (calculations and concepts involving fractions, decimals, percentages, etc.)
4	Advanced (algebraic, geometric, trigonometric, and statistical concepts, techniques, and procedures usually applied in standard practical situations)
5	Very advanced (advanced mathematical and statistical theory, concepts, and techniques, for example, calculus, topology, vector analysis, factor analysis, probability theory, etc.)

3 WORK OUTPUT

3.6 Manipulation/Coordination Activities

Rate the following items in terms of how important the activity is to completion of the job.

Code	Importance to This Job (I)
N	Does not apply
1	Very minor
2	Low
3	Average
4	High
5	Extreme

93 |I_ Finger manipulation (making careful finger movements in various types of activities, for example, fine assembly, use of precision tools, repairing watches, use of writing and drawing instruments, hand painting of china, etc., usually the hand and arm are *not* involved to any great extent).

94 |I_ Hand-arm manipulation (the manual control or manipulation of objects through hand and/or arm movements, which may or may not require continuous visual control, for example, repairing automobiles, packaging products, etc.)

(continued)

Figure 4-6 *(Continued)*

RELATIONSHIPS WITH OTHER PERSONS

4 RELATIONSHIPS WITH OTHER PERSONS

This section deals with different aspects
of interaction between people involved
in various kinds of work.

Code	Importance to This Job (I)
N	Does not apply
1	Very minor
2	Low
3	Average
4	High
5	Extreme

4.1 Communications

Rate the following in terms of how important the *activity* is to the completion of the job.
Some jobs may involve several or all of the items in this section.

4.1.1 Oral (communicating by speaking)

99 | I   Advising (dealing with individuals in order to counsel and/or guide them with regard to problems that may be resolved by legal, financial, scientific, technical, clinical, spiritual, and/or other professional principles)

100 | I   Negotiating (dealing with others in order to reach an agreement or solution, for example, labor bargaining, diplomatic relations, etc.)

4.3 Amount of Job-Required Personal Contact

112 | S   Job-required personal contact (Indicate, using the code below, the extent of job-required contact with others, individually or in groups, for example, contact with customers, patients, students, the public, superiors, subordinates, fellow employees, official visitors, etc.; consider *only* personal contact which is definitely *part* of the job).

Code   Extent of Required Personal Contact
1   Very infrequent (almost no contact with others is required)
2   Infrequent (limited contact with others is required)
3   Occasional (moderate contact with others is required)
4   Frequent (considerable contact with others is required)
5   Very frequent (almost continual contact with others is required)

5 JOB CONTEXT

5.1 Physical Working Conditions

This section lists various working conditions. Rate
the average amount of time the worker is exposed
to each condition during a *typical* work period.

Code	Amount of Time (T)
N	Does not apply (or is very incidental)
1	Under 1/10 of the time
2	Between 1/10 and 1/3 of the time
3	Between 1/3 and 2/3 of the time
4	Over 2/3 of the time
5	Almost continually

5.1.1 Outdoor environment

135 | T   Out-of-door environment (subject to changing weather conditions).

6 OTHER JOB CHARACTERISTICS

6.4 Job Demands (cont.)

172 | I   Following set procedures (need to follow specific set procedures or routines in order to obtain satisfactory outcomes, for example, following check-out lists to inspect equipment or vehicles, following procedures for changing a tire, performing specified laboratory tests, etc.)

173 | I   Time pressure of situation (rush hours in a restaurant, urgent time deadlines, rush jobs, etc.)

Source: E. J. McCormick and P. R. Jeanneret, "Position Analysis Questionnaire (PAQ)," in *The Job Analysis Handbook for Business, Industry and Government,* ed. S. Gael, vol. II, pp. 826–827. Reprinted with permission.

Figure 4-7
Option 4A: Job Profile—Part I

IDENTIFICATION INFORMATION

PAQ Number: 002335 Organization Number: 1
Organization: DOTPAQ Group #: 2335 Record #: 0001
Job Title: JOB ANALYST NUMBER OF ANALYSTS / TYPE
Dept/Unit: ADMIN SPEC Incumbents: Analysis:
Analyst(s): AVERAGE/DB Supervisors: Unknown:
Completed: 01/91 WORKFORCE ANALYSTS (optional)
Dot Number: 166267018 N Number of Job Incumbents: 39
Dot Coded By: ORGANIZATION % FM: % WH: %BL:
Processed: 08/20/08 % HS: % TO:

JOB EVALUATION, FLSA EXEMPTION AND JOB PRESTIGE PREDICTIONS

Equation(s) Used to Calculate Job Evaluation Points
(2)
Job Evaluation Points: 816
Reported Median Monthly Compensation:
Probability this Job is EXEMPT from the Fair Labor Standards Act: 1.000
Job Prestige Score: 55.1

TEST PREDICTIONS

GATB TESTS* *General Aptitude Test Battery	Predicted Score Range Low Avg High	Prob. of Use	Predictive Validity Coefficient	SIMILAR TESTS	Predicted Score Range Low Avg High
G-Intelligence	102 115 128	.93	(.33) –	Adaptability	17 20 25
				Learning Abilt	37 43 49
				Wonderlic P.T	19 26 33
V-Verbal Aptitude	99 113 127	.37	.27 –	EAS-Verbal	13 18 22
				PTI-Verbal	24 33 40
				SET-Verbal	24 37 46
				DAT-Verbal Rsn	. . .
				DAT-LU Sentenc	. . .
				DAT-LU Spelling	. . .
N-Numerical Apt.	100 113 127	.60	.28 –	Arith Fundmntl	31 36 40
				Arithmtc Index	40 47 53
				EAS-Numerical	25 34 43
				FIT-Arithmetic	28 34 39
				PTI-Numerical	14 20 24
				SET-Numerical	28 40 50
				DAT-Numrcl Abil	. . .
S-Spatial Apt.	92 109 126	.16	.18 –	EAS-Spatial	17 27 34
				FIT-Assembly	8 11 14
				Mn Ppr Frm Brd	42 50 57
				DAT-Space Rltn	. . .
P-Form Percept.	94 111 128	.19	.18 –	None	
Q-Clerical Percept.	101 116 131	.50	.23 –	EAS-Visual Spd	83 96 111
				Mn Clrcl-Names	113 136 165
				SET-Clerical	28 34 42
				DAT-Clercl Spd	. . .
K-Motor Coord.	95 112 129	.20	.17 –	None	
F-Finger Dexterity	81 101 120	.01	.15 –	None	
M-Manual Dexterity	83 104 124	.07	.14 –	None	

MYERS-BRIGGS TYPE INDICATOR (MBTI) (est. % of incumbents with high score on):

| Extraversion | 54 | Sensing | 52 | Thinking | 50 | Judgment | 62 |
| Introversion | 46 | Intuitive | 48 | Feeling | 50 | Perception | 38 |

be provided for compensation purposes. Figure 4-7 presents a printout from a PAQ analysis of a job analyst's job. This printout identifies "G" or general intelligence as the most valid factor underlying job performance as a job analyst and even recommends particular tests (e.g., Wonderlic) that can be used to measure "G" intelligence. The .33 "Predictive Validity Coefficient" is the estimated correlation between scores on a general intelligence or cognitive ability test and job performance. This correlation indicates that the construct of general intelligence and the tests that measure it are valid predictors for this job (and the most valid of those considered) based on a comparison of the PAQ responses for the job under study with the PAQ database.

The extensive research that has been conducted with the PAQ makes it one of the most useful of the standardized job analysis instruments, particularly for selection and compensation purposes. For example, PAQ results were used to first select a particular test and then to successfully support an argument of **job relatedness** in a Title VII case involving a cognitive ability test that had caused adverse impact at the James River Corporation.[13] The approach is also excellent for small businesses with little or no expertise in human resources. Considerable research supports the use of the PAQ. However, the PAQ must usually be completed by a trained job analyst rather than incumbents since the language in the questionnaire is difficult and at a fairly high reading level. The instrument also lacks the specificity that can be gained by a questionnaire developed within the company for one or more

PAQ results and job relatedness

Taylor v. James River

Technical feasibility

particular positions or one adapted from the O*NET. While in *Taylor v. James River* the company was able to successfully defend a test that caused adverse impact, the safest approach would be to use PAQ results to recommend particular tests for hiring, but as soon as it is "technically feasible," an emprical study relating test scores to job performance should be done. ("technical feasibility" means at least 100 pairs of scores).

As with almost all questionnaires, results must be interpreted with caution and with consideration of the "hidden agendas" of the source of the data. The PAQ was administered to a graphic artist of a specialty mail-order firm. The graphic artist job was part-time and paid about 50 cents per hour above minimum wage. The job entailed creating original stencils for use in casting and dying. The current incumbent had approximately six months' experience at the job and was taking courses part-time at a local community college. PAQ analysis of the job revealed that the job required a Ph.D. in art history or related areas and that compensation appropriate for the work was $55,000 per year! This result can be explained in large part by two factors. First, in the course of the analysis, answers were recorded just as the incumbent provided them to the analyst despite observations of the work performed that indicated the incumbent was grossly exaggerating the behavioral requirements of the job. And perhaps more importantly, there had been a rumor in this organization that the job analyses were to be used to revise current compensation practices. The lesson here is that the organizational context can strongly influence the validity of work analysis.

Management Position Description Questionnaire (MPDQ)

Although the PAQ has been and can used to study managerial positions, other instruments are more suitable for executive and managerial jobs. The most heavily researched of such instruments is the **Management Position Description Questionnaire (MPDQ)**, a standardized instrument designed specifically for use in analyzing managerial jobs. The 274-item questionnaire contains 15 sections, one of which is presented in Figure 4-8.[14]

Two and one-half hours are required to complete the entire MPDQ. In most sections, respondents (usually the managers above the position under study) are asked to indicate how significant each item is to the position. For example, they may state that "marketing decisions" are of substantial significance to the position. A computer program generates eight reports, including a management position description, a position-tailored performance appraisal form, and a group comparison report, among others.[15] The data provided by this report are particularly valuable for determining areas of emphasis in hiring, training, and staff development. For example, Office Depot relied on the MPDQ results to develop testing materials to be used in hiring its district managers. Figure 4-8 also presents a portion of their results. General Cinema relied on the MPDQ to construct a job-related, behavioral interview and a test for theater managers.

MPDQ results, however, will not tell you whether a particular job specification is necessary for any given position. For example, Office Depot dropped their new requirement that associate store managers have college degrees not based an MPDQ results but rather a study showing no statistical relationship or correlation between having a graduate college degree and managers performance.

Competency Modeling

Although the term is confusing and, some would argue, describes a process similar to job analysis, most experts contend that **competency modeling** is focused more on how objectives are accomplished than on what is accomplished. In addition, the process of competency modeling is usually concentrated on managerial positions and should be more closely linked to business goals and strategies. Competency modeling attempts to identify and define the individual competencies that are common or core for an occupational group or the organization as a whole. By contrast, job analysis methods such as the PAQ and the MPDQ attempt to draw distinctions across jobs. The most common purpose for competency modeling is to derive performance management and training programs.

Software, now available for competency modeling through PeopleSoft, SAP, and Oracle, is very popular as the starting point for comprehensive enterprisewide resource planning systems. Try www.Haygroup.com for a popular competency modeling approach.

The focus on core competencies to drive HR systems and applications is very popular today despite the general lack of rigor in the derivation of the so-called competencies.

Figure 4-8   Sample Portion of

MANAGEMENT POSITION
DESCRIPTION QUESTIONNAIRE (MPDQ) and results

NAME:	B. B. BARKER	ORGANIZATION:	CDBA
EMPLOYEE I.D.:	222	SUPERVISOR:	D. D. DUNCAN
POSITION TITLE:	MANAGER	SUPERVISOR'S TITLE:	MANAGER
FUNCTIONAL AREA:	HUMAN RESOURCES	% OF JOB DESCRIBED:	90%
SUPERVISORY LEVEL:	SUPERVISOR	DATE COMPLETED:	9/11/84

I. GENERAL INFORMATION

A. HUMAN RESOURCE RESPONSIBILITIES

—Management responsibility for **7** employees: **5 (71%)** Full Time—Salaried Exempt

2 (28%) Part Time—Salaried Nonexempt

—**7** report directly and **0** report on a dotted line basis.

—Highest direct subordinate: **SR. PROGRAMMER**

—**No** geographically separate facilities managed directly.

B. FINANCIAL RESPONSIBILITIES

—No annual operating budget.	
—Sales for last fiscal year:	**$ 78,000.**
—Sales objective for current fiscal year:	**$ 220,000.**
—Revenue for last fiscal year.	**$ 275,000.**
—Revenue objective for current fiscal year:	**$ 230,000.**

II. POSITION ACTIVITIES

A. DECISION MAKING

Decision Making: **5%** of jobholder's time is spent on this function and it is **VERY IMPORTANT** to this position.

—Related activities and their significance:

Significance	Item No.	Activity
CRUCIAL	5	Consider the long-range implications of decisions.
CRUCIAL	8	Make decisions in new/unusual situations without clear guidelines on basis of precedent/experience.
CRUCIAL	11	Make critical decisions under time pressure.
CRUCIAL	18	Process and evaluate a variety of information before making a decision.
CRUCIAL	21	Make decisions that significantly affect customers/clients.
SUBSTANTIAL	4	Make decisions concerning the future direction of operations.
SUBSTANTIAL	7	Consider legal or ethical constraints, as well as company policy or goals, when making decisions.
SUBSTANTIAL	12	Make major product/program/technology/marketing decisions in implementing strategic business plan.
SUBSTANTIAL	14	Make decisions without hesitation when required.
MODERATE	1	Evaluate the costs/benefits of alternative solutions to problems before making decisions.

SIGNIFICANCE

THE DUTIES OF THIS POSITION REQUIRE YOU TO:

—— 1. Define areas of responsibility for supervisory/managerial personnel.

—— 2. Schedule activities of subordinates on a day-to-day basis to maintain steady work flow.

—— 3. Interact face-to-face with subordinates on an almost daily basis.

—— 4. Delegate work and assign responsibility to subordinates.

—— 5. Facilitate the completion of assignments when subordinates are unable to meet commitments.

Figure 4-8 *(MPDQ Continued)*

——— 6. Provide detailed instructions to subordinates when making assignments.

——— 7. Coach subordinates on technical aspects of the job.

——— 8. Provide on-the-job training for employees.

——— 9. Frequently review and provide feedback concerning the accuracy and efficiency of subordinates' work.

——— 10. Motivate employees through interpersonal interactions rather than through external incentives (e.g., pay, promotion, status, etc.).

——— 11. Motivate subordinates to improve performance through a process of goal setting and positive reinforcement (i.e., incentives).

——— 12. Work with subordinates to identify and correct weaknesses in performance.

——— 13. Conduct formal performance appraisals with subordinates.

——— 14. Develop executive-level management talent.

——— 15. Establish formal career development plans with employees.

——— 16. Implement career development and management succession plans.

——— 17. Identify the training needed for employees to acquire the skills/knowledge necessary for advancement and ensure that the appropriate training is obtained.

——— 18. Work with employees in highly emotional situations concerning personal or career problems.

——— 19. Arbitrate conflicts between supervisors and employees.

——— 20. Investigate and/or settle employee grievances/complaints.

——— 21. Take necessary action to prevent and/or resolve alleged discriminatory practices.

——— 22. Interpret, administer, and enforce personnel policies and practices (e.g., employee benefits, training or education reimbursement, affirmative action).

——— 23. Interpret and administer union contract agreements in the supervision of subordinates.

——— 24. Interview and hire individuals for approved positions.

The integration of the measurement rigor of methods such as the PAQ and the MPDQ with this focus on core competencies for HR applications should make competency modeling a more effective method for whatever purpose the data are collected.

What is a competency?

Competency modeling is a popular form of work analysis today. A competency has been defined as an "underlying characteristic of a person which results in effective and/or superior performance on the job" or as a "cluster of related knowledge, skills and attitudes that affects a major part of one's job (role or responsibility), that correlates with performance on the job, and that can be measured against well-accepted standards."[16] Competencies are essentially no different than KASOCs but competency modeling tends to stay more focused on organizational strategy goals and important outcomes measures.

The use of competencies as a fundamental building block of organizations and the people they employ is increasingly popular. It is estimated that over 75 percent of companies have some form of competency-based application. This competency modeling has exploded onto the field of human resources.[17] One study reported that over 500 articles were published on the topic between 1995 and 2003. It is estimated that firms spend $100 million per year developing, implementing, and revising competency models. One popular, two-level competency model distinguishes "can-do competencies" (skills and knowledge derived from education and experience) from "will-do competencies" (personality and attitudinal characteristics that reflect an individual's willingness to perform).[18]

In one recent study of retail management, competencies were defined as clusters of measurable and relevant behaviorally based characteristics or capabilities of people.[19] The capabilities were described as descriptors reflecting abilities to perform specific work activities and included specific skills or specific knowledge. The goal was to define all competencies with specific, observable, and verifiable descriptors that were reliably and logically classified together. The researchers used a variety of methods and data to derive competencies for assessment. First, they used the **Critical Incident Technique** for

Critical incidents

associate and store manager jobs. They also reviewed company records and performance assessment criteria, and conducted correlational studies of the relationship between store managers' characteristics (KASOCs). Next, they interviewed subject matter experts (SMEs) and administered a questionnaire that derived ratings of the importance of various managerial tasks, activities, behaviors, knowledge, skills, and abilities for retail management positions within the company.

Four groups of SMEs, who participated in the refinement of the company's mission/ vision statement, the derivation of a competitive strategy, and the initial development of core competencies to meet strategic business goals, drafted and refined a list of competencies based on both the strategic business goals for the company and the questionnaire results. The descriptor content for each competency was then refined into the list of competencies. A different group of SMEs was then asked to evaluate the "relative importance" weights for each competency and "relative predictive" weights for each competency. Seven competencies were identified as "core" or "generalizable" competencies such that each was judged to be a critical and independent underlying competency for successful performance at two levels of management. These categories were: Technical knowledge, Oral presentation/ Communication, Written communication, Interpersonal skills, Planning and Organizing, Decision making, and Leadership. These competencies were judged to be important for and representative of relatively stable and important work activities for three layers of retail management jobs within the organization. Figure 4-9 presents the "Planning and Organizing" competency. The core competencies and their descriptors formed the basis for the development of tools for assessing job candidates for managerial positions.

While competency modeling is popular and there are a number of so-called validated models available for managerial jobs, this approach usually does not help determine what *specific* job specifications to require for a particular job or assignment. For example, the typical competency modeling process would require an inferential leap to determine how particular educational credentials or the number of years of experience, the types of specifications most often written into want ads and provided to recruiters for searches. In general, much like the discussion in Chapter 3 regarding validation and job-relatedness, the recommendation

Core competencies

Figure 4-9 **Behavioral Expectation Scale for Planning and Organizing Competency**

Based on what you know of _____'s knowledge, skills, and abilities, plus his (her) relevant performance on the job, indicate what level of competence you would expect for this person at the store manager level.

This manager could be expected to:

7- create a *detailed* plan for achieving all strategic results with a level of precision that facilitates the setting and meeting of *very clear, appropriate and attainable* objectives.

6-

5-

4- establish clear strategies that are tied to specific objectives for all occasions in which such strategies are needed with a level of precision that facilitates the setting and meeting of *mostly clear, appropriate and attainable* objectives.

3-

2-

1- create an *ambiguous plan (or no plan at all)* for achieving the most important strategic results. The level of precision would *probably be as much of a hindrance* as a help to the setting and meeting of *clear, appropriate and attainable* objectives.

Source: C. H. Hagan, R. Konopaske, H. J. Bernardin, and C. L. Tyler, 2006. "The Criterion-Related Validity of 360-Degree, Top Down and Customer-Based Competency Assessments Using Assessment Center Performance as the Criterion: A Competency Modeling Approach," *Human Resource Management,* 45, p. 366.

here would be to use whatever data you have to assess particular job specifications. If it's possible to correlate a particular job specification with job performance (if you have the data available), do the study. If EEO difficulties (e.g., prima facie evidence) should arise because of a particular job specification that has been used to screen job candidates, the plaintiffs will make every attempt to obtain data and conduct such a study.

Competencies vs. Traits

Driven by the availability of vendor software, many companies use competency modeling to evaluate the performance of their managers. The performance appraisals are then used to make important decisions about these managers. The problem here is the difficulty in distinguishing between competencies and psychological traits. For example, the managerial competencies utilized by the American Management Association include self-confidence, positive regard, self-control, spontaneity, stamina, and adaptability. Jaguar Cars reported complaints from managers who received low performance ratings on the "integrity" competency as a part of the performance appraisal process. Office Depot evaluates its store managers on their "personal maturity." Store managers often disagreed with ratings indicating they needed to work on their personal maturity. Ratings on these types of competencies can cause the legal difficulties covered in Chapter 3 when ratings are used to make important personnel decisions about people such as promotions, terminations, or raises. Assessments of competencies should be clearly distinguished from measures of performance on any given job.

O*NET

The Occupational Information Network or O*NET provides an automated database for collecting, describing, and presenting reliable and valid occupational information. O*NET is now the federal government's primary source of information about occupations (see Figure 4-10 for a summary of what O*NET can do). O*NET uses multiple descriptors to

---

Figure 4-10 **What Is O*NET?**

O*NET, the Occupational Information Network, is a comprehensive database of worker attributes and job characteristics. As the replacement for the *Dictionary of Occupational Titles (DOT)*, O*NET will be the nation's primary source of occupational information.

O*NET is being developed as a timely, easy-to-use resource that supports public and private sector efforts to identify and develop the skills of the American workforce. It provides a common language for defining and describing occupations. Its flexible design also captures rapidly changing job requirements. In addition, O*NET moves occupational information into the technological age.

As the basis for enhanced product development, the O*NET database can serve as the engine that drives value-added applications designed around core information. It provides the essential foundation for facilitating career counseling, education, employment, and training activities. The database contains information about knowledges, skills, abilities (KSAs), interests, general work activities (GWAs), and work context. O*NET data and structure will also link related occupational, educational, and labor market information databases to the system.

O*NET may be used to:

- Align educational and job training curricula with current workplace needs.
- Create occupational clusters based on KSA information.
- Develop job descriptions or specifications, job orders, and resumes.
- Facilitate employee training and development initiatives.
- Develop and supplement assessment tools to identify worker attributes.
- Structure compensation and reward systems.
- Evaluate and forecast human resource requirements.
- Design and implement organizational development initiatives.

(continued)

Figure 4-10 *(Continued)*

- Identify criteria to establish performance appraisal and management systems.
- Identify criteria to guide selection and placement decisions.
- Create skills-match profiles.
- Explore career options that capitalize on individual KSA profiles.
- Target recruitment efforts to maximize person-job-organizational fit.
- Improve vocational and career counseling efforts.

WHAT IS THE FOUNDATION OF O*NET?

Common Language

O*NET offers a common language for communication across the economy and among workforce development efforts. It provides definitions and concepts for describing worker attributes and workplace requirements that can be broadly understood and easily accepted. Using comprehensive terms to describe the KSAs, interests, content, and context of work, O*NET provides a common frame of reference for understanding what is involved in effective job performance.

The goal of O*NET's common language is straightforward: "improve the quality of dialogue among people who communicate about jobs in the economy, generate employment statistics, and develop education and training programs." It provides the shared foundation of language upon which to build private and public sector workforce development efforts. Employer hiring requirements will have the same meaning for human resource practitioners, workers, education and training developers, program planners, and students.

Conceptual Framework

The conceptual foundation of O*NET is called the Content Model. The Content Model provides a framework for classifying, organizing, and structuring O*NET data.

reveal "multiple windows" on the world of work that can be used to address different uses for the information.

O*NET has more than 275 standardized descriptors of skills, knowledges, tasks, occupation requirements, and worker abilities, interests, and values to assist managers in the building of accurate job descriptions. Companies can also use the *O*NET Questionnaires* for free to apply O*NET descriptors to their own particular work situation. O*NET information and tools can be used to identify important elements of a job for developing or choosing training materials, to identify skill requirements to align job needs with more qualified applicants, and to define success factors for promotion and advancement.

O*NET uses "generalized work activities," which are broader than traditional task statements so that the same descriptors can be used across jobs. Because of the many intended uses for O*NET, the descriptors for each job include tasks, behaviors, abilities, skills, knowledge, styles, and work context. O*NET is based on a six-domain content model that attempts to provide a descriptive framework for describing jobs in greater detail. Figure 4-11 presents the content model and major categories within each of the six domains of the model. All of the questionnaires used to describe work using the O*NET model can be completed by job incumbents, which will be the primary source of information about work. Unlike many popular methods (e.g., PAQ), the reading level for the questionnaires allows for most incumbents to participate. All questionnaires can be downloaded from the O*NET Web site (onetcenter.org).

O*NET useful for developing hiring procedures

One of the many unique features of O*NET is that it classifies jobs according to worker personality and dispositional styles. Jobs are classified according to seven general style categories and 17 subcategories. The seven style categories are achievement orientation, social influence, interpersonal orientation, adjustment, conscientiousness, independence, and practical intelligence. This information can be useful for the development of selection procedures for hiring employees and for vocational counseling.

O*NET is the most comprehensive methodology for describing occupations and workers. Preliminary work and research with O*NET have been positive. One study showed O*NET data can help practitioners identify useful tests for employee selection.[20] Many companies now use O*NET to download basic job descriptions (there are over 1,000 job

FIGURE 4-11
O*NET Content Model

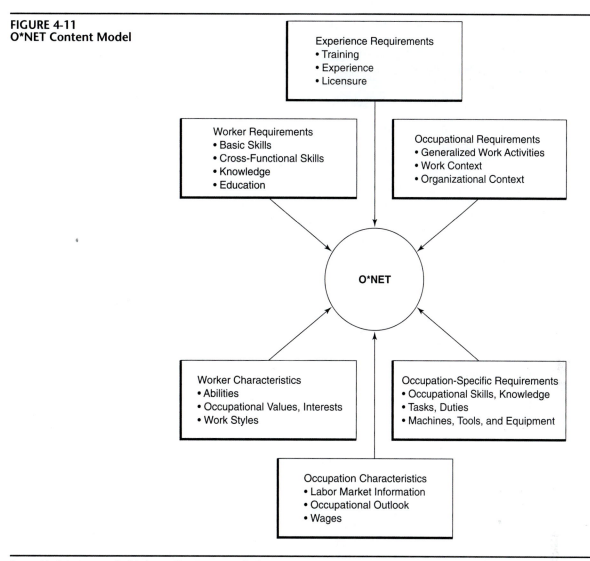

Source: N. G. Peterson et al., "Understanding Occupational Information Network (ONET): Implications for Practice and Research," *Personnel Psychology* 54 (2001), p. 58. Reprinted by permission of Blackwell Publishing.

Download job descriptions from O*NET

descriptions). Figure 4-12 presents a portion of the job description for human resources managers retrieved from O*NET. Occupational data, including salary information, are also available. The information is obviously a great start on a detailed job description for any HRM job. Completion of the work context questions will add useful detail. The O*NET database also provides very useful (and accurate) compensation data (see Figure 4-12).

Critical Incident Technique (CIT)

The **critical incident technique** is a qualitative approach for obtaining specific, behaviorally focused descriptions of work or other activities. The technique originally was developed as a training needs assessment and performance appraisal tool.[21] In this regard, individuals recalled and reported specific behavioral examples of incidents that reflected exceptionally good or exceptionally poor performance.

Four characteristics of a good critical incident

A critical incident should possess four characteristics. It should be *specific,* focus on *observable* behaviors that have been exhibited on the job, describe the *context* in which the behavior occurred, and indicate the *consequences,* outcomes, or products of the behavior. A critical incident also must be sufficiently detailed so that knowledgeable people will

111

Figure 4-12 **Job Description from O*NET**

Occupational Information Network

O*NET OnLine

Related Links | OnLine Help | Home   Occupation Quick Search: [   ] [Go]

SUMMARY REPORT FOR: 11-3040.00—HUMAN RESOURCES MANAGERS

Plan, direct, and coordinate human resource management activities of an organization to maximize the strategic use of human resources and maintain functions such as employee compensation, recruitment, personnel policies, and regulatory compliance.

Sample of reported job titles: Human Resources Manager, Director of Human Resources, HR Director (Human Resources Director), Employee Benefits Manager, Employee Relations Manager.

View report: [Summary]   [Details]   [Custom]

Tasks | Knowledge | Skills | Abilities | Work Activities | Work Context | Job Zone | Interests | Work Styles | Work Values | Related Occupations | Wages & Employment

Tasks

- Administer compensation, benefits and performance management systems, and safety and recreation programs.
- Identify staff vacancies and recruit, interview and select applicants.
- Allocate human resources, ensuring appropriate matches between personnel.
- Provide current and prospective employees with information about policies, job duties, working conditions, wages, opportunities for promotion and employee benefits.
- Perform difficult staffing duties, including dealing with understaffing, refereeing disputes, firing employees, and administering disciplinary procedures.
- Advise managers on organizational policy matters such as equal employment opportunity and sexual harassment, and recommend needed changes.
- Analyze and modify compensation and benefits policies to establish competitive programs and ensure compliance with legal requirements.
- Plan and conduct new employee orientation to foster positive attitude toward organizational objectives.
- Serve as a link between management and employees by handling questions, interpreting and administering contracts and helping resolve work-related problems.
- Plan, direct, supervise, and coordinate work activities of subordinates and staff relating to employment, compensation, labor relations, and employee relations.

Knowledge

Personnel and Human Resources—Knowledge of principles and procedures for personnel recruitment, selection, training, compensation and benefits, labor relations and negotiation, and personnel information systems.

English Language—Knowledge of the structure and content of the English language including the meaning and spelling of words, rules of composition, and grammar.

Customer and Personal Service—Knowledge of principles and processes for providing customer and personal services. This includes customer needs assessment, meeting quality standards for services, and evaluation of customer satisfaction.

Administration and Management—Knowledge of business and management principles involved in strategic planning, resource allocation, human resources modeling, leadership technique, production methods, and coordination of people and resources.

Law and Government—Knowledge of laws, legal codes, court procedures, precedents, government regulations, executive orders, agency rules, and the democratic political process.

Clerical—Knowledge of administrative and clerical procedures and systems such as word processing, managing files and records, stenography and transcription, designing forms, and other office procedures and terminology.

Education and Training—Knowledge of principles and methods for curriculum and training design, teaching and instruction for individuals and groups, and the measurement of training effects.

Economics and Accounting—Knowledge of economic and accounting principles and practices, the financial markets, banking and the analysis and reporting of financial data.

Psychology—Knowledge of human behavior and performance; individual differences in ability, personality, and interests; learning and motivation; psychological research methods; and the assessment and treatment of behavioral and affective disorders.

Mathematics—Knowledge of arithmetic, algebra, geometry, calculus, statistics, and their applications.

Skills

Active Listening—Giving full attention to what other people are saying, taking time to understand the points being made, asking questions as appropriate, and not interrupting at inappropriate times.

Figure 4-12 *(Continued)*

Management of Personnel Resources—Motivating, developing, and directing people as they work, identifying the best people for the job.

Reading Comprehension—Understanding written sentences and paragraphs in work related documents.

Writing—Communicating effectively in writing as appropriate for the needs of the audience.

Speaking—Talking to others to convey information effectively.

Negotiation—Bringing others together and trying to reconcile differences.

Time Management—Managing one's own time and the time of others.

Social Perceptiveness—Being aware of others' reactions and understanding why they react as they do.

Critical Thinking—Using logic and reasoning to identify the strengths and weaknesses of alternative solutions, conclusions or approaches to problems.

Monitoring—Monitoring/assessing performance of yourself, other individuals, or organizations to make improvements or take corrective action.

Abilities

Oral Comprehension—The ability to listen to and understand information and ideas presented through spoken words and sentences.

Oral Expression—The ability to communicate information and ideas in speaking so others will understand.

Written Comprehension—The ability to read and understand information and ideas presented in writing.

Written Expression—The ability to communicate information and ideas in writing so others will understand.

Speech Recognition—The ability to identify and understand the speech of another person.

Speech Clarity—The ability to speak clearly so others can understand you.

Problem Sensitivity—The ability to tell when something is wrong or is likely to go wrong. It does not involve solving the problem, only recognizing there is a problem.

Deductive Reasoning—The ability to apply general rules to specific problems to produce answers that make sense.

Inductive Reasoning—The ability to combine pieces of information to form general rules or conclusions (includes finding a relationship among seemingly unrelated events).

Originality—The ability to come up with unusual or clever ideas about a given topic or situation, or to develop creative ways to solve a problem.

Work Activities

Establishing and Maintaining Interpersonal Relationships—Developing constructive and cooperative working relationships with others, and maintaining them over time.

Communicating with Supervisors, Peers, or Subordinates—Providing information to supervisors, co-workers, and subordinates by telephone, in written form, e-mail, or in person.

Making Decisions and Solving Problems—Analyzing information and evaluating results to choose the best solution and solve problems.

Staffing Organizational Units—Recruiting, interviewing, selecting, hiring, and promoting employees in an organization.

Getting Information—Observing, receiving, and otherwise obtaining information from all relevant sources.

Judging the Qualities of Things, Services, or People—Assessing the value, importance, or quality of things or people.

Resolving Conflicts and Negotiating with Others—Handling complaints, settling disputes, and resolving grievances and conflicts, or otherwise negotiating with others.

Guiding, Directing, and Motivating Subordinates—Providing guidance and direction to subordinates, including setting performance standards and monitoring performance.

Evaluating Information to Determine Compliance with Standards—Using relevant information and individual judgment to determine whether events or processes comply with laws, regulations, or standards.

Coaching and Developing Others—Identifying the developmental needs of others and coaching, mentoring, or otherwise helping others to improve their knowledge or skills.

Work Context

Telephone—How often do you have telephone conversations in this job?

Indoors, Environmentally Controlled—How often does this job require working indoors in environmentally controlled conditions?

Structured versus Unstructured Work—To what extent is this job structured for the worker, rather than allowing the worker to determine tasks, priorities, and goals?

Contact With Others—How much does this job require the worker to be in contact with others (face-to-face, by telephone, or otherwise) in order to perform it?

Electronic Mail—How often do you use electronic mail in this job?

Spend Time Sitting—How much does this job require sitting?

Freedom to Make Decisions—How much decision making freedom, without supervision, does the job offer?

Importance of Being Exact or Accurate—How important is being very exact or highly accurate in performing this job?

Face-to-Face Discussions—How often do you have to have face-to-face discussions with individuals or teams in this job?

Letters and Memos—How often does the job require written letters and memos?

(continued)

Figure 4-12   *(Continued)*

Job Zone Title	Job Zone Four: Considerable Preparation Needed
Overall experience	A minimum of two to four years of work-related skill, knowledge, or experience is needed for these occupations. For example, an accountant must complete four years of college and work for several years in accounting to be considered qualified.
Job training	Employees in these occupations usually need several years of work-related experience, on-the-job training, and/or vocational training.
Job zone	Many of these occupations involve coordinating, supervising.
Examples	Managing, or training others. Examples include accountants, chefs and head cooks, computer programmers, historians, pharmacists, and police detectives.
SVP range	(7.0 to < 8.0)
Education	Most of these occupations require a four-year bachelor's degree, but some do not.

Interests

Enterprising—Enterprising occupations frequently involve starting up and carrying out projects. These occupations can involve leading people and making many decisions. Sometimes they require risk taking and often deal with business.

Social—Social occupations frequently involve working with, communicating with, and teaching people. These occupations often involve helping or providing service to others.

Conventional—Conventional occupations frequently involve following set procedures and routines. These occupations can include working with data and details more than with ideas. Usually there is a clear line of authority to follow.

Work Styles

Concern for Others—Job requires being sensitive to others' needs and feelings and being understanding and helpful on the job.

Attention to Detail—Job requires being careful about detail and thorough in completing work tasks.

Integrity—Job requires being honest and ethical.

Initiative—Job requires a willingness to take on responsibilities and challenges.

Independence—Job requires developing one's own ways of doing things, guiding oneself with little or no supervision, and depending on oneself to get things done.

Persistence—Job requires persistence in the face of obstacles.

Dependability—Job requires being reliable, responsible, and dependable, and fulfilling obligations.

Stress Tolerance—Job requires accepting criticism and dealing calmly and effectively with high stress situations.

Leadership—Job requires a willingness to lead, take charge, and offer opinions and direction.

Self Control—Job requires maintaining composure, keeping emotions in check, controlling anger, and avoiding aggressive behavior, even in very difficult situations.

Work Values

Achievement—Occupations that satisfy this work value are results oriented and allow employees to use their strongest abilities, giving them a feeling of accomplishment. Corresponding needs are Ability Utilization and Achievement.

Independence—Occupations that satisfy this work value allow employs to work on their own and make decisions. Corresponding needs are Creativity, Responsibility and Autonomy.

Related Occupations

11-3011.00	Administrative Services Managers
11-9111.00	Medical and Health Services Managers
11-9131.00	Postmasters and Mail Superintendents
13-1073.00	Training and Development Specialists

Wages and Employment

State and National Wages

Location	Pay Period	2007 10%	25%	Median	75%	90%
United States	Hourly	$26.08	$34.06	$44.57	$58.16	$70.01+
	Yearly	$54,200	$70,800	$92,700	$121,000	$145,600+
Florida	Hourly	$23.55	$31.63	$41.55	$51.27	$61.69
	Yearly	$49,000	$65,800	$86,400	$106,600	$128,300

Figure 4-12 *(continued)*

State and National Trends

Human resources managers, which includes **Compensation and Benefits Managers; Human Resources Managers, All Other; Training and Development Managers.**

United States	Employment		Percent Change	Job Openings[1]
	2006	2016		
Human resources managers, all other	58,200	64,800	+11%	1,760

Florida	Employment		Percent Change	Job Openings[1]
	2004	2014		
Human resources managers, all other	1,730	2,210	+27%	80

[1]Job Openings refers to the average annual job openings due to growth and net replacement.
Source: Bureau of Labor Statistics, Occupational Employment Statistics Survey; Florida Agency for Workforce Innovation.

picture the same incident as it was experienced by the individual.[22] One vivid example of a critical incident characterizing extremely poor performance was provided by a police officer in describing an ex-partner. He wrote, "while on duty, this officer went out of his assigned duty area, went into a bar, got drunk, and had his gun stolen."

A critical incident report references actual behavior in a specific situation with no mention of traits or judgmental inferences. The following is an example of a well-written critical incident. "I observed an employee looking through the scrap tub. Shortly later, she came to me stating that someone had thrown a large piece of cast iron piston into the scrap tub. We salvaged this piston and, a short time later, used this piece to make a pulley for a very urgently needed job." The following example does *not* qualify as a well-written critical incident: "The employee completely lacked initiative in getting the job done. While there was plenty of opportunity, I couldn't count on her to deliver." This incident mentions a trait (initiative), does not describe either the situation or the employee's behavior in any detail, and is judgmental in nature.

The critical incident technique has been used to study a variety of jobs such as those of airline pilots, air traffic controllers, research scientists, dentists, industrial foremen, life insurance agents, sales clerks, retail managers, and college professors. One major purpose of the use of CIT is to develop performance appraisal systems. CIT is also an excellent approach for the development of customer satisfaction instruments. Customers provide the examples of effective and ineffective customer service that are then used to develop a standardized customer service evaluation instrument. Burger King, Office Depot, and Continental Bank used the critical incident method to develop a performance appraisal instrument used by "professional customers" to assess compliance with company regulations regarding customer service. The CIT is also very useful for developing highly detailed selection procedures such as assessment centers or behavioral interviews. Office Depot developed their district manager assessment methods using both MPDQ and critical incident results.

CIT is excellent for performance appraisal development

Job Compatibility Questionnaire (JCQ)

The **Job Compatibility Questionnaire (JCQ)** was designed as a work analysis method to be used in the development of personnel selection instruments and intervention strategies.[23] Unlike other work analysis methods, the JCQ gathers information on all aspects of the work experience that are thought to be related to employee performance, absences, turnover, and job satisfaction. The underlying assumption of the JCQ is that the greater the compatibility between a job applicant's preferences for work characteristics and the characteristics of a job as perceived by job incumbents, the more likely that the applicant will stay in the job longer and be more effective. The primary goal of the JCQ methodology is to derive perceptions of job characteristics from incumbents' perspectives and to develop

Work analysis with JCQ generates a selection tool

selection instruments capable of assessing the extent to which job applicants' preferences are compatible with these perspectives. The selection instrument derived from the JCQ is designed to predict and ultimately increase the level of employee effectiveness. In addition, the instrument can be used to redesign jobs to increase group effectiveness and decrease absences and turnover.

The JCQ is a 200-item instrument that measures job factors that have been shown by previous research to be related to one or more effectiveness criteria (e.g., performance, turnover, absenteeism, job satisfaction). Items cover the following job factors: task requirements, physical environment, customer characteristics, co-worker characteristics, leader characteristics, worker compensation preferences, dispositional factors, task variety, job autonomy, physical demands, and work schedule.

The JCQ is administered to job incumbents, who are asked to indicate the extent to which each JCQ item is descriptive of the job. Thus, an incumbent is asked to indicate on a five-point scale how descriptive each item is of his/her job. A sample list of characteristics is presented below:

Working alone all day.

Having different projects that challenge the intellect.

Staying physically active all day.

Working at my own pace.

Being able to choose the order of my work tasks.

Working under the constant threat of danger.

Having to copy or post numerical data all day.

Having to make public speeches.

Working under extreme time pressure.

Having an opportunity to be creative at work.

The average time required to complete the JCQ is 30 minutes and can be reduced by removing items and factors that clearly do not apply to the job under study. There is also a provision for adding important characteristics that are not covered on the JCQ such as those that may characterize organizational culture or climate.

Responses from incumbents on the JCQ are used to derive a selection instrument with a scoring key. The selection instrument items come directly from the items on the JCQ. Figure 4-13 provides some sample items that were derived from the JCQ approach to work analysis. This is part of a 35-item JCQ-based test that was developed for security guard jobs for one of the largest

---

**FIGURE 4-13
Sample Test Items from the Job Compatibility Questionnaire**

From each pair of statements select the one that you consider to be the most undesirable in a job you might have:

1 a. Having frequent face-to-face discussions with people?
   b. Having to be very punctual at work?*
2 a. Having to make frequent speeches?
   b. Having to wear a uniform at work?*
3 a. Having to provide information and ideas in writing?
   b. Having the same routine every day at work?*
4 a. Having constant interactions with customers?
   b. Spending most of my time at work alone?*
5. a. Having to write a lot of reports?
   b. Working on a boring job?*
6. a. Dealing with people who complain a lot?*
   b. Selling a product that is not very good?
7. a. Having to closely monitor the behavior of others?*
   b. Having to frequently and quickly do math at work?
8. a. Having to work outdoors in hot or cold weather?*
   b. Having to work indoors with poor ventilation?

Note: * indicates characteristics that are "very descriptive" of the job being tested for.

security guard companies in the world. The items in Figure 4-13 from within each pair with an * are the job characteristics identified as "very descriptive" of the job for which the test will be used for hiring purposes. The details of this process are discussed in Chapter 6.

Research indicates that the tests that evolve from the JCQ do a good job in predicting retention for low-wage jobs such as customer service representatives, theater personnel, security guards, telephone interviewers, and counter personnel.[24] The JCQ is usually nested within a comprehensive test that also assesses applicants on their job-related competencies. The JCQ has not been validated (or used) for higher-level jobs (e.g., managerial) and is not recommended for such positions.

The JCQ also can be used to identify those characteristics of a particular job that are most highly correlated with important outcomes such as employee turnover and job performance. JCQ results are then used to re-design jobs. For example, at Tenneco Corporation, responses to the JCQ indicated strong preferences for a pay-for-performance system and a more stable work schedule. These work characteristics, shown to be related to employee turnover, were changed at relatively little cost and turnover was reduced by 14 percent, saving Tenneco over $2 million over three years.

Work Analysis for Job Design

One of the direct applications of work analysis has been for job design and redesign efforts. This has been particularly true in recent years with the increasing interest in the quality of employees' work life, the team-oriented concept, and the principle of worker "empowerment." In general, most of these efforts have focused on redesigning jobs by "enriching" them. Such enrichment entails providing more meaningful work, greater responsibility, and greater worker autonomy. One review found that work design had a great impact on worker satisfaction and job performance, explaining an average of 43 percent of the variability in these outcomes.[25]

Job Diagnostic Survey

The most well-known and well-researched job enrichment approach is the **Job Characteristics Model,** which uses the **Job Diagnostic Survey (JDS)** to measure work characteristics.[26] Over 200 studies have investigated the validity and utility of this approach.[27] The Job Characteristics Model emphasizes enhancing the intrinsic aspects of an employee's work to increase satisfaction and performance. The model states that workers will be more motivated and satisfied, produce better quality work, and have less absenteeism and turnover to the extent that they experience three psychological states: (1) they believe their *work is meaningful,* (2) they have *responsibility for the outcomes* of their work, and (3) they *receive feedback on the results* of their work.

Work Design Questionnaire is recommended over the JDS.

There has been much criticism of the JDS and the Job Characteristics Model and the resultant research. A new and superior instrument is the **"Work Design Questionnaire"** (WDQ), which expands knowledge of work design.[28] The WDQ has been used to study the relationship between work design variables and important work outcomes such as job satisfaction and performance outcomes. Figure 4-14 presents the list of the 18 work characteristics and sample items representing each of the characteristics measured using the WDQ.

Predictors of job satisfaction: autonomy and social support

Research with the WDQ indicates that the two best predictors of job satisfaction are autonomy (i.e., the extent to which a job allows freedom, independence, and discretion to schedule work, make decisions, and choose the methods used to perform tasks) and social support (the degree to which a job provides opportunities for advice and assistance from others). Thus, if an organization has an interest in improving job satisfaction, it could work on expanding job autonomy or improving the social support for the work. However, changing a job so as to increase autonomy can also increase demands for more compensation and training while increasing social support does not have these negative trade-offs.[29]

What Is Strategic Job Analysis?

Before closing this section on work and design methods, let's review how job analyses can be conducted in situations where jobs don't already exist, such as when a new small business is started or where jobs are changing dramatically as might result from restructuring or workplace reengineering.

In instances where a job is being created or where an organization is undergoing significant strategy evaluation, work analysis takes on a rather predictive bent in that the idea is to describe a job through the anticipated tasks that need to be performed in order to meet

Figure 4-14   **Sample Items from the Work Design Questionnaire**

Please respond to each item indicating your level of agreement that each statement describes the job you are analyzing:

1 = Strongly Disagree;   2 = Disagree;   3 = Undecided;   4 = Agree;   5 = Strongly Agree

Task Characteristics

Autonomy: Extent to which a job allows freedom, independence,
and discretion to schedule work

Work Scheduling Autonomy

The job allows me to make my own decisions about how to schedule my work.

Decision-Making Autonomy

The job gives me a chance to use my personal initiative or judgment in carrying out the work.

Work Methods Autonomy

The job allows me to make decisions about what methods I use to complete my work.

Task Variety: Degree to which a job requires employees to perform
a wide range of tasks

The job involves doing a number of different things.

Task Significance: Degree to which a job influences
the lives or work of others

The results of my work are likely to significantly affect the lives of other people.

Task Identity: Degree to which a job involves a whole piece of work,
the results of which can be easily Identified.

The job involves completing a piece of work that has an obvious beginning and end.

Feedback from Job: Degree to which the job provides direct and clear
information about the effectiveness of task performance

The work activities themselves provide direct and clear information about the effectiveness (e.g., quality and quantity) of my job performance.

Knowledge Characteristics

Reflects the kinds of knowledge, skill, and ability demands that are placed on an individual as a function of what is done on the job.

The job provides the opportunity to learn

Job Complexity: Extent to which the tasks on a job are
complex and difficult to perform

The job requires that I only do one task or activity at a time (reverse scored).

Information Processing: Degree to which a job requires
attending to and processing data or other information

The job requires me to monitor a great deal of information.

Problem Solving: Degree to which a job requires unique
ideas or solutions and reflects the more active
cognitive processing requirements of a job

The job involves solving problems that have no obvious correct answer.

Skill Variety: Extent to which a job requires an individual
to use a variety of different skills to complete the work

The job requires a variety of skills.

Specialization: Extent to which a job involves
performing specialized tasks or possessing
specialized knowledge and skill

The job is highly specialized in terms of purpose, tasks, or activities.

Social Characteristics

Social Support: Social support reflects the degree
to which a job provides opportunities
for advice and assistance from others.

I have the opportunity to develop close friendships in my job.

My supervisor is concerned about the welfare of the people that work for him/her.

Interdependence: Reflects the degree to which
the job depends on others and others
depend on it to complete the work.

Initiated Interdependence: The extent to which work flows
from one job to other jobs (initiated interdependence)

The job requires me to accomplish my job before others complete their job.

Figure 4-14 *(WDQ Continued)*

*Received Interdependence: The extent to which a job
is affected by work from other jobs*

The job activities are greatly affected by the work of other people.

*Interaction Outside Organization: Extent to which the job
requires employees to interact and communicate with
individuals external to the organization*

The job requires spending a great deal of time with people outside my organization.

*Feedback From Others: Degree to which
others in the organization provide
information about performance*

I receive a great deal of information from my manager about my job performance.

Work Context

*Ergonomics: Degree to which a job allows correct
or appropriate posture and movement*

The seating arrangements on the job are adequate (e.g., ample opportunities to sit, comfortable chairs, good postural support).

*Physical Demands: Level of physical activity or effort required
in the job, focus on the physical strength, endurance, effort,
and activity aspects of the job*

The job requires a great deal of muscular endurance.

*Work Conditions: The environment within which a job is performed,
the presence of health hazards, noise, temperature,
and cleanliness of the working environment*

The workplace is free from excessive noise.
The job takes place in an environment free from health hazards (e.g., chemicals, fumes, etc.).

*Equipment Use: Reflects the variety and complexity
of the technology and equipment used in a job*

The job involves the use of a variety of different equipment.

Adapted from: F.P. Morgeson and S. E. Humphrey). "The Work Design Questionnaire (WDQ): Developing and Validating a Comprehensive Measure for Assessing Job Design and the Nature of Work," *Journal of Applied Psychology, (2006),* 91, pp. 1321–1339.

organizational goals. This approach has been termed **strategic job analysis** as it's purpose is to forecast what a job may be like in a new environment with new strategic goals, new technologies, increased customer contact, or expanded duties. Briefly, conducting a strategic job analysis involves the following steps:[30]

1. If the job currently exists, then a conventional job analysis procedure is used to describe it in detail. If the job isn't in existence yet, then subject matter experts (SMEs) and primary customers of the job's intended services are brought together to identify the tasks that constitute the job based on the new strategic plan. O*NET can be consulted to identify any existing jobs that are similar and can further inform job design.

2. Incumbents and/or SMEs discuss how changes to the job such as new technology or increased contact with external customers will change the tasks making up the job and how the job is performed.

3. Detailed descriptions of the job's tasks and the required KASOCs necessary for successful performance are generated by SMEs and others familiar with the job and the expected changes.

4. The results of the analysis of the projected job are compared to those of the current job to identify differences in tasks and KASOCs.

5. The comparison provides information relevant to developing performance standards, training content, KASOCs for personnel selection, the need for supervision and management, and the relationship between jobs (internal customers and suppliers).

Strategic job analysis requires extensive organizational involvement

The utility of this approach depends on how accurately the SMEs and other participants anticipate changes in the job or in anticipating what a job created from scratch may be like when actually performed by someone. This approach requires widespread involvement from organizational members, often from different functional areas. In addition, when the job change issue is one of introducing new technology, it may be necessary to involve the hardware or software manufacturer in the analysis of job changes. While more focused on tasks, this approach is similar to *competency modeling.*

AUTONOMOUS WORK GROUPS (AWG) OR SELF-MANAGING TEAMS

AWGs: An example of job design

Autonomous work groups (also known as self-managing work teams) are employee groups given a high degree of decision-making responsibility and behavioral control for completing their work.[31] Usually, the team is empowered or given the responsibility for producing (or providing) the entire product or service. A team essentially replaces the boss by taking over responsibilities for scheduling, hiring, ordering, and firing. AWGs are an example of a restructuring or job design work analysis.[32]

Procter and Gamble and Corning are examples of major manufacturing facilities with work teams. At the Procter and Gamble plant in Lima, Ohio, which makes Liquid Tide, Downy fabric softener, and Biz bleach, teams are responsible for their own safety, production targets, quality goals, and improvements in customer service. Team meetings occur at every shift change, and the teams reorganize themselves as they deem necessary.

AWGs are also catching on in the services sector. Using a service quality audit, managers and quality-improvement teams at Ritz-Carlton Hotels identify errors and determine their frequency, assign costs of fixing (or not fixing) the errors, and identify steps to prevent them.

AWGs usually elect an internal leader. Management may appoint an external leader or coordinator as well. The external leader serves primarily as a facilitator rather than as a supervisor and, where the organization is converting to AWGs, may facilitate relationships among AWGs. He or she may assist the group members in receiving feedback on the quality and quantity of their performance as well as make any structural changes in the team design. The coordinator is also responsible for helping the team acquire needed resources (e.g., equipment) and technical assistance.

Self-managing teams may be involved in a number of different activities, including

- Recording quality control statistics.
- Making scheduling assignments.
- Solving technical problems.
- Setting group or team goals.
- Resolving internal conflicts.
- Assessing group or team performance.
- Making task assignments to group or team members.
- Preparing a budget.
- Training team members.
- Selecting new members.
- Allocating pay raises for members.

Suggestions for Using AWGs or Self-Managing Work Teams

For AWGs or self-managing work teams to be effective, training is critical. Training is necessary for team members on a variety of human relations skills, such as problem solving, group dynamics, conflict resolution, cooperation and participation, and technical skills such as statistical quality control and budget preparation. Training is also necessary for managers in their new roles as facilitators.

The Effectiveness of AWGs or Self-Managing Work Teams

The overall effects of AWGs on productivity have been mixed.[33] It often takes up to two years for some of the positive effects of AWGs to materialize. Managers need to be patient in expecting results and should guarantee job security to enable employees to feel comfortable taking risks and being creative and innovative.

There are many success stories. Based on the way in which the plant was reorganized into only three levels (one plant manager, 10 managers, and about 350 technicians working in teams), the Ohio Procter and Gamble plant was 30 percent more productive. At Pacific Bell, employees on craft, clerical, and engineering self-managed teams reported higher productivity and performance and satisfaction with their jobs, work units, and growth potential as compared to similar traditional work groups. At Ritz-Carlton, the quality audit found that the most common error at the front desk at one hotel was not posting late charges on a guest's bill, which cost the hotel an estimated $250,000 per year.

Employees report that team membership provides them with more autonomy, flexibility, skill variety, training opportunities, and financial benefits (e.g., group-based bonuses). It is not surprising then that firms have found that members of AWGs experience higher job satisfaction and morale and lower levels of turnover.

AWGs can lead to higher job satisfaction

ARE THERE BIAS AND INACCURACY IN WORK ANALYSIS DATA?

There has been considerable research on the extent to which work analysis data are subject to inaccuracy or bias.[34] Most of this research has focused on potential sex biases in job evaluation for setting pay rates.[35] Job evaluation is a product of job analysis that can either create considerable trouble for a company or result in a rational and reasonable pay system. Briefly, the research to date indicates that work analysis is generally free of gender and racial bias.[36] In other words, the race or gender of the job analyst or the source for job analysis data doesn't seem to matter in terms of results. However, courts have been critical of the racial/sexual composition of committees responsible for conducting work analysis and deriving job specifications. A job specification stipulated by an all-white-male panel of job experts that ultimately resulted in adverse impact could be subject to a more problematic legal challenge because of the composition of the panel. A more diverse panel of subject matter experts is strongly recommended by the EEOC and experts familiar with EEO law.

Gender and racial bias

Use diverse panel

There also has been some research investigating whether the source of the job information influences the nature of the data collected. In general, incumbents tend to assign more importance to their jobs than do supervisors or trained analysts.[37] There is evidence that incumbents and supervisors agree more about the tasks performed than they do about the attributes that are required to perform the job well.[38] There is also evidence that those who know more about a job tend to make more reliable and accurate judgments.[39] Less knowledgeable raters do not provide work analysis data equivalent to the information provided by experts at the job.[40] However, there is no support for the view that incumbents who are more effective at their jobs provide different information about their jobs than do low performers. Surprisingly, there is no research comparing customer perspectives with those of incumbents or supervisors.

One study found that ratings on the frequency of tasks performed and the importance of tasks performed provided the most reliable data across different types of raters (e.g., incumbents, experts).[41] Another study found that expert ratings of job specifications in the form of specific KASOCs may be more transportable across organizations and that the idiosyncrasies of particular raters contributed the most to unreliability in the ratings.[42] Another study found that Hispanics perceived bilingual language skills as significantly more important than non-Hispanics and that the Hispanic point of view was more compatible with the view of actual customers.[43] Bottom line: Get more experts for more reliable assessments of job specifications and/or competencies and how these assessments relate to strategy execution. And strive for customers' views too.

More research is needed to explore possible sources of bias in work analysis data and the processes involved in deriving work analysis. Such research may reveal better methods for gathering and integrating work analyses to enhance their accuracy and usefulness.

HOW DO YOU CHOOSE THE BEST WORK ANALYSIS METHOD?

PAQ best for job evaluation and test identification

CIT best for performance appraisal development

Mine data to validate job specifications

A number of studies have examined the relative effectiveness of specific work analysis methods. For example, one study asked experienced job analysts to indicate the extent to which four methods accomplished the various purposes for job analysis.[44] In addition, they were asked to evaluate the amount of training required to use the method, the sample sizes required for deriving reliable results, and the cost to administer and score the method. The results indicated that, of the methods evaluated, if the purpose is to generate a job description or to do job classification or job design, a good method is the PAQ. CIT is probably not as good for job classification purposes. The best method for job evaluation is the PAQ. The PAQ was also the best method for identifying specific tests to use for hiring. If the purpose of the analysis is to develop a performance appraisal instrument, detailed and job-related interview questions, or training programs, the recommended method is CIT. No method is ideal in terms of legal compliance, including ADA compliance. For companies in need of highly detailed information about a job, the development of their own job analysis method is probably preferable to an "off-the-shelf" type such as the PAQ, which would not give you the level of detail in describing the job, perhaps a critical issue if you are developing a training program.

Experts agree that organizations should "mine" their own data whenever possible to determine whether particular job specifications (e.g., a particular level of education or experience) are related to critical criteria such as job performance. This is particularly true if job specifications cause adverse impact or if there is a need to determine if a specification could cause adverse impact.

O*NET has a wealth of information that can be used effectively by organizations to accomplish most of the major purposes for which you do work analysis. The job descriptions you can retrieve from the Web site are a great start on a number of the work analysis products discussed in this chapter (if not finished products) and you can even retrieve up-to-date salary information for your particular jobs and geographical areas. And it's all free! You can also download detailed questionnaires that can be adapted for whatever purposes you have in mind.

Choice of work analysis depends on purpose

Experts also agree that the choice of work analysis method depends upon the purposes to be served by the data and the desired product. There is no "one best way" to conduct work analysis. The purposes for the data and the practicality of the various methods for particular organizations must be considered. The most definitive finding from the research on the relative effectiveness of the various methods is that multiple methods of analysis should be used whenever possible. For example, a quantitative approach such as the PAQ should probably be augmented by a qualitative approach such as the CIT, which can provide more specific information about jobs than what can typically be derived from the quantitative methods.

SUMMARY

Jobs are important to people because they have surplus meaning beyond just providing a paycheck necessary to sustain their economic survival. People ask a lot of their jobs, as they become better educated and develop rising expectations about what jobs should supply. As a result of technology and the flattening of organizational structures, jobs are no longer the static entities they once were thought to be. Work has become more dynamic and the lines distinguishing the responsibilities of one job from another continue to blur. Recent research on job performance has shown that there are some generic dimensions of work behavior that apply across a broad spectrum of jobs while others that are more task-based are very specific to a limited set of jobs. Generic work behaviors influence the performance of virtually any job,[45] such as honesty and integrity, goal attendance, treating co-workers with respect, and maintaining good personal hygiene. The idea of generic work behaviors opens the possibility for more direct comparisons of employee performance regardless of the specific tasks for which employees are responsible. It also challenges the traditional idea that jobs and job performance can be neatly compartmentalized.

Yet one of the aims of work analysis is to identify differences between jobs so that selection tests, levels of compensation, training and development efforts, and performance standards are demonstrably relevant to job success. An increasing burden on work analysis today is to describe jobs in sufficient detail so that differences between them are recognized and appropriate criteria for personnel decisions result. At the same time, work analysis should be flexible enough to be applied to the study of jobs as they change in response to technological demands and the organization of projects and work. A detailed work analysis product is also considered to be a critical element of any possible outsourcing effort. Research on successful and unsuccessful outsourcing projects shows that one key variable is the specificity in the job description and the determination of the key outcomes from the customer perspective.[46]

Work analysis and outsourcing

The once traditional idea of "the job" is under challenge as more organizations adopt project-based work assignments. Work analysis remains an essential tool for HR professionals despite contemporary changes in the world of work and the new "team" orientation within many companies. There has been much discussion in the popular press about the "de-jobbing" of organizations.[47] In fact, formal work analysis may be even more significant in the context of a turbulent work environment and need for a more comprehensive work analysis. Regardless of the elasticity of the job, projects, and tasks, work analysis should be a starting point in the design of most HR systems, including restructuring, human resource planning, reengineering of recruitment strategies, selection processes, training and career development programs, performance appraisal systems, customer-based appraisal, job design efforts, compensation plans, and health and safety compliance and improvements. Even project-based employment requires hiring, training, compensation, and performance appraisal functions. The need to describe the work a prospective employee or contractor will perform before hiring still presupposes an inventory of the likely situational demands and worker competencies required to fulfill this broader mission. Work analysis helps to ensure that HR systems will be professionally sound. As noted in Chapter 3, HR systems that involve personnel decisions such as selection, pay, promotion, and terminations should be based on a determination of the important job duties and KASOCs necessary for successful job performance. Even if the legal mandate did not exist, effective HR practice dictates the linkage between these HR activities and work analysis.

"De-jobbing"

While many contemporary management gurus preach that job descriptions promote individualism to the detriment of unit effectiveness, work analysis can facilitate more effective group and unit effectiveness through clearer definitions of responsibilities and a determination of the relative importance of tasks and working relationships between positions and individuals and how all are related to customer requirements. Job descriptions do not have to say, and they rarely ever say, that the incumbent will perform only those tasks defined on the description regardless of circumstances. To the extent that job descriptions foster an "it's not my job" philosophy of work and a deviation in attention away from customer requirements, the gurus are right. The trick is to develop and use work analysis with customer requirements as the focus.

Work analysis with a customer focus

Although static unchanging jobs may be obsolete, work analysis as a tool for understanding and describing work activities will remain an essential HR competency for the foreseeable future. As the various HR functional areas are covered in the chapters to follow, more detail will be provided on how work analysis is used to supply internal and external customers with the most effective HR products.

Discussion Questions

1. What is meant by conducting a work analysis? How might you convince top managers of the importance of conducting work analysis?

2. Do you believe having highly detailed job descriptions for every position can interfere with group effectiveness? If so, is there anything that can be done to avoid this?

3. For each of the following HR systems, what type of analysis is needed to develop a professional and legally defensible system?

   a. Training program for new employees.

   b. Selection system.

   c. Performance appraisal system.

   d. Compensation system.

   e. Job design.

4. Describe the advantages and disadvantages of using interviews, observation, and questionnaires for collecting work analysis data.

5. How might you involve customers in the development of job descriptions and job specifications? Are there any constraints on what customers can stipulate in job specifications?

6. Do PAQ data provide sufficient argument for "job relatedness"? Explain.

7. How would you use O*NET for developing job descriptions and specifications?

8. A fast-growing small business decides to hire a human resources manager for the first time. What steps should be taken next?

Chapter	Human Resource Planning
5	and Recruitment

OBJECTIVES

After reading this chapter, you should be able to

1. Understand the importance of Human Resource Planning (HRP) to the organization.

2. Identify the six steps in the HRP process.

3. Explain the methods by which an organization can develop forecasts of anticipated personnel demand and understand labor markets.

4. Understand how an organization can stay apprised of and evaluate its personnel supply and, if necessary, implement a downsizing program.

5. Determine which recruitment methods are best for given situations, including the role of the Internet.

6. Understand the pros and cons of internal versus external recruiting.

7. Know the most important features of recruitment advertising.

8. Know the legal implications of recruitment and planning.

OVERVIEW

Kathryn Connors, the vice president of human resources at Liz Claiborne, described the ideal role for HR in strategic planning: "Human resources is part of the strategic planning process. It's part of policy development, line extension planning and the merger and acquisition process. Little is done in the company that doesn't involve us in the planning, policy or finalization stages of any deal."[1] Unfortunately, as discussed in Chapter 1, the extent of involvement of human resources in strategic planning as practiced by Liz Claiborne is still rather unusual. While more companies now link HR planning to strategic planning, the linkage is usually focused mainly on the reduction of labor costs with limited consideration of other elements related to HR.[2] The typical practice is for an HRM unit to receive forecasting plans to reduce overhead by reducing labor costs. The role of HR is to devise the HR strategy for implementing the plan. HR planners have been busy lately with forecasting that 37 percent of U.S. companies planned major layoffs in 2008. Since the job market peaked in December 2007, U.S. businesses gave out over half a million "pink slips" up to 2009 (mostly in banking, housing, retail, manufacturing, and temporary employment). Among the Fortune 500 companies that laid off over 1,000 workers in 2008 alone are Bear Stearns, Chrysler, Citigroup, Ford, GM, Indy Mac, Sprint Nextel, and possibly every major airline except Southwest. Given the size of these layoffs, one has to wonder to what extent many of these companies did effective forecasting and HR forecasting before 2008. Amazon.com's layoffs may be an example of more strategic HR planning involving business forecasting, customer demand, and labor force needs and options. They laid off 1,800 workers based on a thorough study of projected sales. Another company with great HR planning processes is Southwest Airlines. While other airlines continue laying people off, Southwest transferred people, cut overtime, and changed some assignments. Not a single Southwest employee was laid off. This was still true in 2008.

IBM also does systematic HR planning tied to its strategic objectives. Their planning includes the identification of the skills most likely to be in demand over the next three years (updated yearly). The 2009 "hot" skills list includes expertise in the life sciences, wireless networks, digital media databases, and Linux programming. IBM then spends $400 million a year training its workers in these skills that the company is betting it will need soon.

IBM's "hot" skills list

In terms of competitive advantage in the global economy, however, the "good" news is that most foreign competitors also conduct their HR planning and recruitment in a more reactive manner rather than as a fully integrated system. Particularly, given the greater HR constraints in reacting to business problems placed on some foreign competitors, especially European, there is opportunity for HR-based competitive advantage for U.S. companies.

Opportunity for competitive advantage

HR planning (HRP) should be an integral part of competitive strategy. The most effective approach to staffing, whether adding workers or eliminating them, is to assess staffing needs with a focus on meeting customer requirements and expanding the customer base.

One important element of HR planning today is a consideration of outsourcing to reduce costs. As exposed in a recent survey, HR should be much more involved in assessing outsourcing and offshoring options. Says Jennifer Schramm, manager of workplace trends and forecasting at the **Society of Human Resource Management** (SHRM.org), "The participation of HR professionals in offshoring is necessary from the beginning stages of exploring the idea of offshoring as a viable option to the implementation stage. . . . HR should be involved in spearheading the country selection process—investigating the most viable offshore labor force—and then in orchestrating the recruitment of qualified staff."[3] The survey shows limited HR involvement in this process.

Limited HR involvement in outsourcing

The goal for organizations of all sizes is quite simple: Keep the cost of labor as low as possible while meeting (or exceeding) customer demand and, if this is a part of the strategic plan, expanding the customer base. The realization of this goal for HR practice is obviously much more difficult. The goal also can be applied to the internal customers who require products or services from internal suppliers, including HRM staff. For example, an internal customer could be a district manager in retail who must hire a store manager for one of the stores in the district. One option could be to use an external headhunter group that specializes in retail, or perhaps the company relies on internal recruiters to compile a list of qualified candidates. Obviously, the company is very interested in the cost of the recruiting effort and the district manager may be particularly interested in filling the position quickly with someone who requires little or no training.

Planning

Two of the most important aspects of staffing are HRM planning and recruitment. Planning is the forecasting of HR needs in the context of strategic business planning. The human resource planning process of the past was typically reactive, with business needs defining personnel needs. However, with major changes in the business environment and increasing uncertainty, many organizations have adopted a longer-term perspective, integrating human resource planning with strategic business planning centered on a consideration of core business competencies.

Recruitment

Recruitment is the process of attracting applicants for the positions needed. As discussed in Chapter 1, recruiting Generation "Y" employees or the so-called "Millennials" poses some special planning and recruiting problems and opportunities for employers. Clearly, employers must do a little more than put ads in the paper these days to attract top talent.

This process *should* be fully integrated with the HR planning process and other HR activities, especially the selection process. Recruitment and other HRM activities are interdependent. For example, a change in a compensation or benefit package can have a profound effect on recruitment and retention. In the 2008 debate over a new G.I. education bill for returning vets, the Congressional Budget Office (CBO) projected that the better benefits offered in the legislation would decrease re-enlistments by 16 percent. At a time when the ability of the Army to recruit and retain good soldiers during wartime was hindered, a 16 percent reduction in "re-ups" would be a serious problem. But the CBO also predicted that the new benefit would increase the number of new recruits by 16 percent. The program could be a strong positive if the motivation to not re-up was offset by more incentives to re-enlist. HR planning and recruitment should be carefully integrated.

This chapter provides an overview of the planning and recruitment process. The relationships among the various HR functions will be discussed; the process of downsizing and reengineering or restructuring; the various sources available for recruiting and their relative effectiveness; the advantages and disadvantages of internal and external recruiting; and the role of equal employment opportunity law and regulations in the planning and recruitment process.

EFFECTIVE HUMAN RESOURCE PLANNING

Organizations that integrate strategy with HR planning and recruitment have an HR competitive advantage. Recruitment planning should flow directly from HR planning. Figure 5-1 presents a model of this relationship. Effective HRP closes the gap from the current

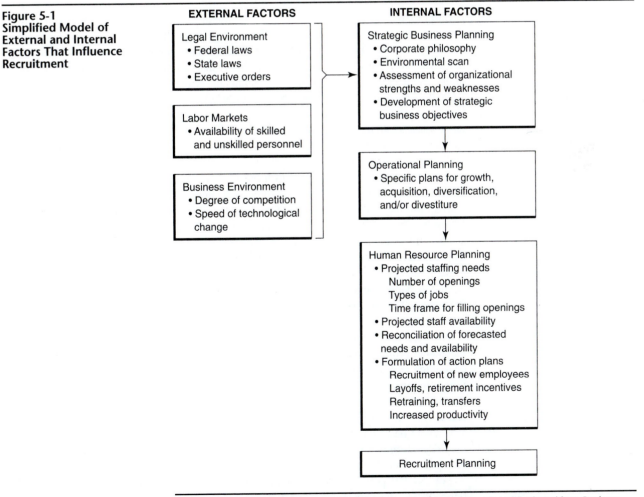

**Figure 5-1
Simplified Model of External and Internal Factors That Influence Recruitment**

EXTERNAL FACTORS

Legal Environment
• Federal laws
• State laws
• Executive orders

Labor Markets
• Availability of skilled and unskilled personnel

Business Environment
• Degree of competition
• Speed of technological change

INTERNAL FACTORS

Strategic Business Planning
• Corporate philosophy
• Environmental scan
• Assessment of organizational strengths and weaknesses
• Development of strategic business objectives

Operational Planning
• Specific plans for growth, acquisition, diversification, and/or divestiture

Human Resource Planning
• Projected staffing needs
   Number of openings
   Types of jobs
   Time frame for filling openings
• Projected staff availability
• Reconciliation of forecasted needs and availability
• Formulation of action plans
   Recruitment of new employees
   Layoffs, retirement incentives
   Retraining, transfers
   Increased productivity

Recruitment Planning

Source: "Simplified Model of External and Internal Factors That Influence Recruitment." Adapted from *Employee Recruitment: Science and Practice* by James Breaugh. Reprinted by permission of the author.

Figure 5-2   **Steps for Effective HR Planning**

1. **Environmental scanning.** Identify and anticipate sources of threats and opportunities, scanning the external environment (competitors, regulation) and internal environment (strategy, technology, culture).
2. **Labor demand forecast.** Project how business needs will affect HR needs, using qualitative methods (e.g., Delphi, nominal) and quantitative methods (trend analysis, simple and multiple linear regression analysis).
3. **Labor supply forecast.** Project resource availability from internal and external sources.
4. **Gap analysis.** Reconcile the forecast of labor supply and demand.
5. **Action programming.** Implement the recommended solution from step 4.
6. **Control and evaluation.** Monitor the effects of the HRP by defining and measuring critical criteria (e.g., turnover costs, break-even costs of new hires, recruitment costs, performance outcomes).

situation to a desired state of affairs in the context of the organization's strategy. The process for determining this match is outlined in Figure 5-2. Effective HRP should involve (1) environmental scanning, (2) labor analysis, (3) supply analysis, (4) gap analysis, (5) action programming, and (6) evaluation. We examine each of these below.

Step One: Environmental Scanning

Environmental scanning helps HR planners identify and anticipate sources of problems, threats, and opportunities that should drive the organization's strategic planning. Scanning provides a better understanding of the context in which HR decisions are/will be made. Both an external and an internal environmental scan are critical for effective planning.

While there can be (and often are) situations with ambiguous problems, threats, and opportunities, the probability of reducing or eliminating the ambiguity is increased by a more thorough environmental scan. The idea here is to at least attempt to turn a threat into an opportunity with information. In general, the greater the amount of relevant information that managers have about a problem, the more likely that problem can be turned into an opportunity. Both external and internal environmental scans are critical for this information. Amazon is a good example here. They closed a large and costly customer service center in Seattle despite projections of 20 to 30 percent sales growth because their study of global labor options told them they could meet their sales growth projections with a far less costly customer service center in India. Numerous other companies have turned to offshoring and outsourcing to save money.

Frame of reference should be strategic goals

Environmental scanning pursued for the purposes of HR planning should not lose sight of the fact that the frame of reference for such scanning should always be on strategic goals with a customer focus. A large law firm in Atlanta was losing young associates, many of whom in exit interviews complained about "burnout" and conflicts with partners and more senior associates. The turnover rate spiked coincidental with the loss of two major clients and almost 400 billable hours a week. While the loss of the associates was obviously important, the customer/client problem was more important. It turned out that the two were related in that partners were sending more work to associates. The clients were increasingly unhappy with work products, and were then complaining, before finally firing the law firm altogether.

Another law firm noted the higher turnover among female associates and the increasing proportion of females the firm was recruiting from top law schools. The firm conducted exit interviews, gathered information, and set a goal to be a leading firm for female attorneys. They installed many pro-family programs such as 90 days of paid maternity leave, coverage of fertility treatments, and concierge services. The firm, Alston and Bird, is now a perennial Fortune "Best company to work for" (#31 in 2008) and a top-ranked best company for working moms. Most importantly, they now claim one of the lowest turnover rates among associates and report improved recruiting success since they put in the programs.

Keep the "big picture" in mind. (i.e. customer issues)

For any HR problem, an environmental scan should always keep the "big picture" in mind. While the "big picture" will mean different things to different organizations, it almost always focuses on meeting or exceeding customer or client requirements. Thus, the scan should never lose this focus. If customers have expressed concerns about a product or service, what specifically are the customer complaints? Can we fix a systemic problem that may be causing customer problems, problems that translate into an HR problem like a need for more employees to hear and respond to the complaints, or a related high employee turnover rate because jobs where employees must deal with customer complaints are almost always high turnover jobs. Reducing customer complaints may take care of the HR problem or sharply reduce it. Military recruiting problems in 2006 were probably not so much related to recruiting procedures or style, pay, benefits, etc. It was probably more of a "big picture" issue. Violence was down significantly in Iraq in 2008. Recruiting for the Army has been more successful recently, probably not a coincidence.

Understanding the Labor Market for HR Planning

One critical component of environmental scanning for HR planning and recruitment is an understanding of the relevant labor market. Labor market conditions influence HR planning in terms of both the number and types of available employees. In a loose **labor market,** qualified recruits are abundant. However, many labor markets are extremely tight. For example, there are shortages in numerous cutting-edge technologies such as optics and laser technology as well as shortages in unskilled labor areas such as child care, security work, and nursing home assistance. Tight markets limit the availability of labor, drive up the costs for those employees who are selected, and even limit the extent to which the organization can be selective in its hiring procedures. Most private security guard companies use psychological tests for screening mainly because of fears of negligent hiring lawsuits. In fact, because of the level of competition in this area, the demand for services, and the tight labor market for largely unskilled labor, these companies cannot be very selective in hiring people despite what the tests may predict. The relevant labor market for an employer is defined by occupation, geography, and employer competition. Obviously, the job and the skills or job specifications play the greatest role in the definition of the relevant labor market and the ease (or difficulty) with which positions can be filled. The labor market is affected by geography but, because of technology, not nearly as much as in the past. Offshoring is having a significant impact on the definition of a labor market. Competing employers are the third factor defining the labor market. The number and type of employers seeking similarly qualified personnel or offering similar compensation in the same location also can serve to define the labor market. Google and Microsoft are now rivals. They compete for the same rare talent and try hard to recruit employees directly from their rivals.

The Global Labor Market/Offshoring

"Globalization has collapsed time and distance"

The technological and communications revolution has truly changed the relationship between geography and labor supply. Says Thomas L. Friedman, author of *The World Is Flat,* "Globalization has collapsed time and distance and raised the notion that someone anywhere on earth can do your job, more cheaply."[4] As discussed in Chapter 2, an international division of labor has emerged. The world is now the labor market for many skilled and unskilled jobs. The outsourcing of the manufacturing/assembly process to a foreign location is now commonplace in most industries although there is some indication that the cost of shipping could slow or even reverse this trend. The chances are also much greater now than just a few years ago that the customer service representative you speak with over the phone or who processes your Internet order is sitting a long way from U.S. soil. According the National Association of Software and Service Companies in India, customer service business is expected to increase to 200,000 employees and $5 billion by 2008. One call center in Bangalore, 247customer.com, founded in 2000, includes several Fortune 500 companies and a major telecommunications company. General Electric and British Airways have large phone banks in India and are expanding this function because of the low cost and low turnover of personnel and the quality of the work. As of 2008, entry-level customer service representatives in India earn between $3,500 and $4,500 per year, a good salary by India's standards, which probably explains the low turnover. The total savings estimates for U.S. companies for this critical work is between 20 and 35 percent.

Offshoring skilled labor

What also is becoming more common is that *skilled* labor is being "offshored" to lower-paid, overseas workers as well. Companies are now offshoring a wide range of service functions, including IT, payroll, finance and accounting, and logistics. Dallas-based software company I2 Technologies runs software centers in Bombay and Bangalore. The programming costs are estimated to be about one-third of the cost of an American programmer. However, this difference could change rapidly as the demand for Indian programmers grows. The consulting firm McKinsey and Company reports that by 2009, new jobs in accounting, software development, and transcribing will have generated 800,000 new jobs and $17 billion in revenue for India.

Most attractive companies for offshoring

India is by no means the only attractive offshoring destination. Figure 5-3 presents the results of a study conducted by A. T. Kearney that derived an index of the most attractive countries for offshoring based on financial attractiveness, the business environment, and

Figure 5-3   **A.T. Kearney Global Services Location Index, 2007**

Rank	Country	Financial attractiveness	People and skills availability	Business environment	Total score
1	India	3.22	2.34	1.44	7.00
2	China	2.93	2.25	1.38	6.56
3	Malaysia	2.84	1.26	2.02	6.12
4	Thailand	3.19	1.21	1.62	6.02
5	Brazil	2.64	1.78	1.47	5.89
6	Indonesia	3.29	1.47	1.06	5.82
7	Chile	2.65	1.18	1.93	5.76
8	Philippines	3.26	1.23	1.26	5.75
9	Bulgaria	3.16	1.04	1.56	5.75
10	Mexico	2.63	1.49	1.61	5.73
11	Singapore	1.65	1.51	2.53	5.68
12	Slovakia	2.79	1.04	1.79	5.62
13	Egypt	3.22	1.14	1.25	5.61
14	Jordan	3.09	0.98	1.54	5.60
15	Estonia	2.44	0.96	2.20	5.60
16	Czech Republic	2.43	1.10	2.05	5.57
17	Latvia	2.64	0.91	2.00	5.56
18	Poland	2.59	1.17	1.79	5.54
19	Vietnam	3.33	0.99	1.22	5.54
20	United Arab Emirates	2.73	0.86	1.92	5.51
21	United States (tier two)	0.48	2.74	2.29	5.51
22	Uruguay	2.95	0.98	1.54	5.47
23	Argentina	2.91	1.30	1.26	5.47
24	Hungary	2.54	0.95	1.98	5.47
25	Mauritius	2.84	1.04	1.56	5.44
26	Tunisia	3.03	0.90	1.50	5.43
27	Ghana	3.27	0.90	1.25	5.42
28	Lithuania	2.60	0.83	1.98	5.42
29	Sri Lanka	3.18	0.96	1.22	5.36
30	Pakistan	3.23	1.00	1.11	5.34
31	South Africa	2.52	1.18	1.60	5.30
32	Jamaica	2.83	0.96	1.49	5.29
33	Romania	2.88	0.87	1.53	5.28
34	Costa Rica	3.00	0.86	1.36	5.22
35	Canada	0.77	2.09	2.30	5.16
36	Morocco	2.92	0.90	1.33	5.14
37	Russia	2.61	1.38	1.16	5.14
38	Israel	1.97	1.27	1.86	5.10
39	Senegal	3.19	0.82	1.05	5.06
40	Germany (tier two)	0.46	2.19	2.40	5.05
41	Panama	2.88	0.75	1.40	5.02
42	United Kingdom (tier two)	0.50	2.16	2.35	5.01
43	Spain	1.18	1.71	2.06	4.95
44	New Zealand	1.53	1.12	2.25	4.91
45	Australia	0.89	1.69	2.31	4.89
46	Portugal	1.59	1.14	2.11	4.84
47	Ukraine	2.76	0.98	1.09	4.83
48	France (tier two)	0.45	2.07	2.27	4.79
49	Turkey	2.06	1.31	1.41	4.78
50	Ireland	0.40	1.54	2.29	4.18

Note: The weight distribution for the three categories is 40:30:30. Financial attractiveness is rated on a scale of 0 to 4, and the categories for people and skills availability, and business environment are on a scale of 0 to 3.
Source; A.T. Kearney.

each country's "people and skills availability." A more recent survey on offshoring options by the *Economist* magazine also ranked India at the top, followed closely by China, the Czech Republic, Singapore, Poland, and Canada (the United States finished 20th in this survey of worldwide CEOs). Asian companies dominated the rankings with six of the top 10 desired locations.[5]

E-mail, fax machines, private satellite links, and the World Wide Web have made workers from all over the world accessible and have expanded the labor market for U.S. companies. The result is lower labor costs for American companies and (usually) greater profits; the shipment of more American jobs overseas; and the continued stagnation of middle-class wages in this country. Rick Younts, executive vice president for international operations at Motorola, claims more than lower wages as the reason Motorola hires Asian programmers. U.S.-based programmers can work on a project during the day and then e-mail their work to Asian counterparts who can work on it while the U.S.-based programmers are sleeping. Younts estimates a 40 percent reduction in time to completion because of this work schedule. Companies that do not take advantage of the global labor market for labor will be at a competitive disadvantage as long as consumers do not place a heavy weight on the extent to which a product or service involves American workers.

Elance: An outsourcing model

One of the leading worldwide outsourcing firms is California-based Elance, which charges a fee for vendors to compete on "Requests for Proposals" submitted through their Web site. Elance claims over 60,000 registered and qualified professionals in more than 150 categories of work (e.g., software design, writing, Web site design, sales and marketing, management and finance, training and development, legal) are ready to bid on a project proposal which is submitted to www.Elance.com. With bids, you also receive credentials, work samples, and a performance assessment on previous projects. Elance claims that companies have saved "over 60%" by outsourcing their projects through Elance. The service is free to outsourcing organizations.

Lexadigm Solutions: offshore legal work

U.S. companies are now outsourcing their legal work offshore. The leading firm in this area is Michigan-based Lexadigm Solutions that offers legal research conducted by Indian lawyers at substantially lower fees (see www.lexadigm.com). The Lexidigm Web site states that "by hiring India-based attorneys, we are able to take advantage of the large wage disparity between Indian attorneys and their U.S. counterparts, and our rates reflect this cost advantage. We are also able to be extremely selective in our hiring practices. Each of our India-based Research Specialists has graduated from one of the top five law schools in India, practiced law for at least three years, received extensive legal training from U.S. attorneys, and passed Lexadigm's rigorous legal research and writing exam. In addition, a large percentage of our India-based attorneys have legal degrees from reputable U.S. law schools."

Since labor can constitute as much as 80 percent of operating expenses, and since most businesses compete at least partly on a price/cost basis, managing the labor market and the cost of labor is a crucial HR activity (the great increase in the proportion of adjunct professors at most universities is a good example of this). Companies usually look at labor first when their corporate performance measures do not meet expectations. Recall the discussion in Chapter 1 about the need to be flexible in this dynamic and more global economy. Compared to European countries, flexibility regarding labor reductions and cost cutting is relatively common in the United States. American companies certainly have a competitive advantage over European countries as they compete on price.

The trend line for offshoring American jobs is clearly up and for a growing number of professional service jobs as well. A. T. Kearney, a financial services company, estimates that they will move over a half million jobs offshore by 2009. These jobs include high-level financial analyst positions. Some experts predict that the greatest growth in offshoring will be for services requiring higher skill levels.

The differences in compensation between U.S. workers and offshored options are, at least for now, considerable. Over 4 million U.S. manufacturing jobs have been lost since 2000. General Motors has had a string of bad years with things getting far worse as of 2009. Over 75,000 jobs were lost (29 percent American) from 2006 to 2008 alone. Every time a car comes off a U.S. assembly line, GM loses $1,100. Said CEO Rick Wagoner at a GM board meeting, "We're reenergizing our global sourcing efforts . . . our move to a global product development system, accompanied by the emergence of excellent supply capabilities in lower cost markets, provide us with some real cost savings opportunities." GM is clearly looking to China, where labor costs are much lower (the average hourly rate for a U.S. GM factory worker is $54 per hour versus $5.80 for a Chinese autoworker; the average worker in China makes about $120 per month).

Of course, there should be more to outsourcing than saving on labor costs. A report by DiamondCluster International, a global management consulting firm, found that 51 percent of U.S. buyers of outsourcing services are dissatisfied with the service providers and terminating contracts early. "The blame cannot be heaped solely on the shoulders of providers," said Tom Weakland, who heads up an outsourcing advisory consulting practice. "Many buyers are now several years into at least one outsourcing relationship, but they still lack effective measures to gauge the success of their outsourcing initiatives, which are critical for knowing and getting what you want." Many companies report that because of quality problems, "companies are learning that the tremendous cost-savings outsourcers have been promising are actually difficult to achieve. And they are learning more about the cost of losing good people and the value of their institutional knowledge." Outsourcing buyers report that the greatest risks of outsourcing include the increased complexity of managing relationships, reduced operational effectiveness, and lower quality of output from their outsourcing providers.

Over 50 percent of outsourcing contracts are terminated early

Affirmative Action/ Diversity Programs and the Law: A Problem, Threat, or Opportunity?

As discussed in Chapter 3, **government regulations** also influence HR planning and must be considered in any environmental scan. Equal employment opportunity legislation such as Title VII of the Civil Rights Act, the 1991 Civil Rights Act, the Age Discrimination in Employment Act, the 1990 Americans with Disabilities Act, and Executive Order 11246 require that companies pay close attention to the manner in which they treat protected class individuals.

Executive Order 11246

Executive Order 11246 requires federal contractors and subcontractors ($10,000 or more) to take affirmative action to ensure that all individuals have an equal opportunity for employment, without regard to race, color, religion, sex, national origin, disability, or status as a Vietnam era or special disabled veteran. Through the **Office of Contract Compliance (OFCCP)**, 11246 requires a contractor, as a condition of having a federal contract, to engage in a self-analysis for the purpose of discovering any barriers to equal employment opportunity.

OFCCP

Section 706(G) of the Civil Rights Act allows a judge to order an affirmative action program if the employer is found guilty of intentional discrimination (the judge overseeing the Abercrombie and Fitch settlement used this order to craft the out-of-court settlement; A&F continues on this court-imposed and court-monitored affirmative action program). Let's return to this issue since diversity goals are an important part of HR planning and recruitment for most large U.S. corporations and government in general.

Hiring to promote a diverse workforce will probably remain a complicated issue because of the confusing state of the EEO case law, particularly in situations in which organizations embark on some form of preferential treatment as a part of a voluntary diversity or affirmative action program. The most contentious situation is one in which the employer shows some form of preferential treatment toward members of one group when there is no proven history of discrimination, and no court-ordered requirement. What organizations can and cannot do under a voluntary affirmative action or diversity program is unclear.

Diversity goals and preferential treat

The ambiguity and potential illegality seem to occur when preferential treatment is shown toward members of groups by placing at least some weight on a job candidate's gender or ethnicity. The controversy lies in whether such a characteristic should ever be considered and, if so, to what extent. The safest strategy for an organization today is to meet diversity goals by increasing the recruitment effort to attract women and minorities and, once the pool of candidates is established, ignore the gender or ethnicity of members of the pool and concentrate on only the job-related credentials of the candidates. The issue of diversity and affirmative action also comes up when companies are downsizing.

Recent out-of-court settlements with Abercrombie and Fitch, Texaco, Coca-Cola, Home Depot, Office Depot, and Circuit City have included provisions where managers would be accountable for meeting diversity goals. Yet these goals can be problematic when companies entertain downsizing options and consider maintaining the diversity goals they had attained when they conceptualized the downsizing steps. This was clearly illustrated in an age discrimination and Title VII lawsuit against the Ford Motor Company. The plaintiffs maintained preferences were shown to women and minorities during the downsizing. There are also many rules and regulations that affect hiring for government agencies. For example, civil service rules for most governments, the federal government included, prohibit the consideration of political affiliation for civil service appointments. (The Department of Justice was reprimanded for such hiring practices in 2008.)

Despite the legal confusion regarding EEO, organizations are continuing their efforts to promote diversity in their workforces. Walt Disney, for example, has minority hiring targets "at every level," according to Marc Pacala, Disney's general manager. Kentucky Fried Chicken maintains separate lists of minority candidates for its executive positions. Xerox continues with its "balanced workforce" program, which has measurable diversity hiring goals for all levels of management. In 2005, Wal-Mart began a diversity program that holds managers responsible (and pays them) for meeting "diversity" goals.

70 percent of Fortune 500 companies engage in race-based hiring

Despite the legal controversy, one survey found that 70 percent of Fortune 500 companies engage in race-based hiring while only 14 percent said they hired by merit alone.[6] The diversity issue is here to stay. Figure 5-4 presents some data and projections that illustrate trends in the U.S. workforce and U.S. businesses. Figure 5-5 presents a summary of research and implications for diversity initiatives. Specific recommendations are made to make diversity programs more effective.

The United States Office of Contract Compliance's Revised Order #4 (see www. OFCCP.gov) describes affirmative action activities and several actions an employer may take to "improve recruitment and increase the flow of minority or female applicants." One recommendation is to contact sources such as the Urban League, the Job Corp, and colleges with high minority enrollment. For example, most major U.S. corporations actively recruit at Florida A&M in Tallahassee, Florida, a predominantly African-American university with an excellent business school.

Step Two: Labor Demand Forecast

In a survey taken when the U.S. economy was growing at a nice clip, 24 percent of small businesses indicated that the "lack of qualified workers" posed a serious threat to their survival.[7] Many entrepreneurs in the survey indicated that labor shortages were preventing them from expanding their businesses and that such shortages made any type of planning more difficult. Over half of the respondents who had labor shortages had stepped up recruitment efforts and sought assistance from temporary employment agencies just to meet current demand for products or services. In the same year, over 30 percent of the largest U.S. companies actually reduced the size of their workforce despite a strong economy and, for many companies, record profits.

Figure 5-4
The Growing Diversity of the U.S. Workforce and U.S. Work

- The fastest-growing labor force age group is 55 and older.
- Workers aged 25–34 will decline by almost 3 million by 2009.
- As of 2009, over 50 percent of the U.S. workforce consisted of women, nonwhites, ethnic minorities, and immigrants.
- Women will constitute 47 percent of the labor force by 2016.
- Hispanics as a percentage of the U.S. workforce will be 16 percent by 2016 (estimated to be almost 27 million by 2016).
- African-Americans as a percentage of the U.S. workforce will hold steady at 12 percent by 2016.
- Asians, Native Americans, Alaska Natives, and Pacific Islanders will constitute 5.3 percent of the U.S. workforce by 2016.
- In 2000, women held 43 percent of executive, managerial, and administrative jobs.
- As of 2000, Hispanics owned 1.2 million businesses and employed more than 1.3 million people.
- As of 2000, women made up 38 percent of U.S. business owners.
- As of 2000, African-Americans owned over 800,000 businesses.
- Service jobs will constitute 88 percent of U.S. jobs by 2016.

Source: U.S. Bureau of Labor Statistics, "Employment Projections, 1996–2016."

Figure 5-5
Research and Implications for Diversity

Gaps between Diversity Rhetoric and Research

1. Increased diversity does not necessarily improve the talent pool.
2. Increased diversity does not necessarily build commitment, improve motivation, or reduce conflict.
3. Increased group-level diversity does not necessarily lead to improved performance.
4. Increased diversity does not necessarily improve organizational performance.

Implications of Research and Theory

1. Benefits of diversity are contingent on the situation.
2. Successful diversity programs are based on meeting specific goals.
3. Diversity initiatives should be framed as strengths and opportunities with individual merit emphasized over numerical measures.
4. Diversity programs are more likely to be successful when employees identify with their work teams and organizations rather than with whichever diverse social groups they are drawn from.

Actions Organizations Can Take to Manage Diversity Effectively

1. Build senior management commitment and accountability.
2. Conduct a thorough needs assessment of people, jobs, and the organization.
3. Develop a well-defined diversity strategy tied to business results.
4. Emphasize team building and group-process training.
5. Establish metrics and evaluate the effectiveness of diversity initiatives.

Source: Adapted from M. E. A. Jayne and R. L. Dipboye, "Leveraging Diversity to Improve Business Performance: Research Findings and Recommendations for Organizations," *Human Resource Management,* 43 (2004), pp. 409–424.

A forecast of labor demand derives from a projection of how business needs will affect HR. Each of the environmental forces discussed above is likely to exert pressure on HR demand—both in terms of the number and the types of employees required, as well as the number and types of jobs utilized. The HR planner must anticipate these needs, add focus to an otherwise confusing array of possibilities, and set priorities for conflicting goals. Labor demand forecasting methods fall into two categories: qualitative and quantitative. As each category embraces certain assumptions, a combination of the two is preferred. Figure 5-6 presents a summary of the most common methods.

Figure 5-6   **Advantages and Disadvantages of Labor Demand Forecasting Methods**

Method	Advantages	Disadvantages
QUALITATIVE		
Delphi • Experts go through several rounds of estimates • No face-to-face meetings	• More futuristic • Incorporates future plans	• May ignore data • Subjective • Time consuming
Nominal • Face-to-face discussion	• Group exchanges facilitate plans	• May ignore data • Subjective
QUANTITATIVE		
Markov • Incorporates past data for time period	• Data-driven	• Need adequate historical data
Regression • Regress staffing needs onto key variables	• Data-driven • Actuarial • Learning curve	• Large and representative sample needed • Difficult to understand
Trend analysis • Required staffing matched to desired outcomes	• Futuristic • Actuarial • Use business	• Many assumptions • Required factors

Qualitative Methods

Centralized approach for projecting labor needs

Decentralized approach

The simplest method for projecting labor demand is a **centralized** approach in which the HR department examines the current business situation and determines staffing requirements for the rest of the firm. While this approach is simple, it can be inaccurate. A top-down approach assumes that the central HR office has an accurate understanding of the business as well as the needs of each unit or function. In large complex firms, these assumptions typically do not hold. A more preferred method involves a **decentralized** process wherein each unit or functional manager subjectively derives his/her own staffing needs. These projections are aggregated to create an overall composite forecast for the company.

At jet engine maker Pratt & Whitney, for example, top management set a goal of 30 percent cost reduction for each functional unit after a study of competitors' overhead. Unit managers were asked to conduct job analysis of each job under their jurisdiction and, after analysis, to submit proposals for workload reduction and other cost-reduction options. A procedure was established to present the various reduction options, including a method for the presentation of a rationale if the manager failed to make the 30 percent target reduction.

Delphi technique

Other firms have experimented with formalized problem-solving methods such as the **Delphi technique** to minimize interpersonal and jurisdictional conflicts.[8] The Delphi technique avoids face-to-face group discussion by the use of an intermediary. Experts take turns at presenting a forecast statement and assumptions. The intermediary passes on the forecasts and assumptions to the others. Revisions are then made independently and anonymously by the experts. The intermediary then pools and summarizes the judgments and gives them to the experts. This process is continued until a consensus forecast emerges or until the intermediary concludes that more than one perspective must be presented. In comparison with linear regression analysis (discussed below), the Delphi technique has been shown to produce better one-year forecasts, but there can be difficulties in reaching consensus on complex problems.[9]

The full Delphi process can take considerable time. For example, The Gap, a clothing retailer, took over four months to forecast the number of buyers needed for the next year using a Delphi method. The use of networked computers can do much to reduce the time for Delphi forecasting.

Nominal group technique

The **nominal group technique** is similar to the Delphi method. However, experts join at a conference table and independently list their ideas in writing.[10] The experts then share their ideas with the group in turn. As the ideas are presented, a master list of the ideas is compiled so that everyone can refer back to them. The ideas are discussed and ranked by member vote.

Quantitative Methods

Trend analysis

Quantitative methods are based on the assumption that the future is an extrapolation from the past. **Trend analysis** incorporates certain business factors (e.g., units produced, revenues) and a productivity ratio (e.g., employees per unit produced). For example, Pratt & Whitney calculated 16 jet engines per factory worker and almost 20 support, marketing, and management personnel for every 100 factory workers. Their external environmental scanning data indicated more favorable ratios for General Electric, Pratt's chief competitor. By projecting changes in the business factor and/or the productivity ratio, we can forecast changes in the labor demand. There are six steps in trend analysis:

1. Find the appropriate business factor that relates to the size of the workforce.
2. Plot the historical record of that factor in relation to the size of the workforce.
3. Compute the productivity ratio (average output per worker per year).
4. Determine the trend.
5. Make necessary adjustments in the trend, past and future.
6. Project to the target year.[11]

Selection of appropriate business factor

The use of the appropriate business factor is critical to the success of trend analysis.[12] Learning curves assume that the average number of units produced per employee will increase as more units are produced. Such an increase is expected because workers learn to perform their tasks more efficiently over time. Learning curves are evident in virtually all industries. For example, in the automotive industry, learning curves for new models improve by over 50 percent through the life of the model. At Pratt, the learning curve for one particular engine exceeded 60 percent from startup to the final production year. The business factor, of course, should be directly related to the essential purpose for the business. Universities typically use student enrollment by discipline, hospitals use patient-days, manufacturers typically use output needs, and retailers use sales adjusted by inventory.

Regression analysis

Regression analysis uses information from the past relationship between the organization's employment level and some important success criterion known to be related to employment. For example, companies can establish a statistical relationship between sales or work output and level of employment. Such a relationship, however, also is influenced by the learning curve. Learning curves can be studied and used to make more accurate projections of future employment levels. More complicated quantitative methods can improve accuracy by incorporating operational constraints (e.g., budgets, mix of labor) into the models. Through this elaboration, it is possible to forecast demand under varying business scenarios. While our discussion of labor demand may suggest that planners attempt to establish a singular forecast, the outcome of this process is typically a set of potential scenarios. A scenario is a multifaceted portrayal of the mix of business factors in conjunction with the array of HR needs. As such, each scenario/forecast is an elaborate set of "if–then" statements; that is, "if" the business context presents us with scenario A, "then" our labor demand forecast would be B. Ideally, HR planning is as comprehensive as possible to provide leeway for a wide variety of business activities. Next, we discuss labor supply forecasts that reveal some of the constraints placed on business planning.

Step Three: Labor Supply Forecast

Whereas the labor demand forecast projects HR needs, the labor supply forecast projects resource availability. This step of HR planning is vital in that it conveys an inventory of the firm's current and projected competencies. This skill base sets an upper limit on the commitments and challenges the firm can undertake (all else being equal). From a problem-solving perspective, labor supply represents the "raw materials" available to address problems, threats, and opportunities. Supply forecasts are typically broken down into two categories: **external supply** and **internal supply**.

Internal Supply

Internal labor supply consists of those individuals and jobs currently available within the firm. Information on personnel is maintained in Human Resource Information Systems (HRIS). Although many systems are available, the new Workday HRIS, developed by the creator of Peoplesoft, is gaining considerable attention. Both Workday (go to Workday.com) and Peoplesoft offer a human capital management, Web-based HRIS system that includes a competency or skill inventory, a comprehensive recruiting system, and an elaborate performance management and development system. Data from these systems can be used to make projections into the future based on current trends. These trends include not only the number and kinds of individuals in each job, but also the flow of employees in, through, and out of the organization. Specifically, a skills or competency inventory includes an assessment of the knowledge, skills, abilities, experience, and career aspirations of each of the present workers. This record should be updated frequently and should include changes such as new competencies, degree completions, and changed job duties.

These inventories also aid in the internal recruitment process. If these inventories are not updated, present employees may be overlooked for job openings within the organization.[13] This may result in increased search costs in addition to dissatisfaction among employees who were overlooked. Accordingly, internal supply forecasts must take into account the company's current practices pertaining to hiring, firing, transfer, promotion, development, and attrition. The best HRISs, Workday being one example, provide great flexibility for managing a global workforce for the process of recruiting, applicant tracking, hiring/placement, and even termination. Requisite components should have the following:

1. Applicant tracking for comparing the pool across the organization, job families, job profiles, and positions.

2. Managing the transition from applicant to employee (including temps).

3. Employee tracking with full worker histories, performance appraisals, and compensation, benefits, and Paid Time OFF (PTO)/leave history.

4. Employee movement system for tracking within the organization to aid in succession planning and internal staffing.

5. Managing the transition from working status to retirement and/or termination.

Succession planning and replacement charts also are used by some companies to identify individuals to fill a given slot if an incumbent should leave. These techniques are most useful for individual-level problems with short-term planning time horizons. There are over 300 computerized HRISs, now available, many of which include skills inventories. The General Electric Company and Dunn and Bradstreet, for example, have used electronic data files on their employees for years as an aid for internal promotions and for required EEO reports. Pratt used an HRIS system to project successions, early retirements, future openings, and overstaffing problems.

Two of the most important concerns regarding the use of electronic databases for personnel are privacy rights and security problems. The latter issues can be handled with the right systems and software provisions. The privacy issue is much more difficult. Many states and many countries have privacy laws and regulations that may pertain to the use, content, and access of the HRIS.

Markov analysis

More complicated transition models such as **Markov analysis** are used for long-range forecasts in large organizations. Markov analysis uses historical information from personnel movements of the internal labor supply to predict what will happen in the future. An estimate is made of the likelihood that persons in a particular job will remain in that job or be transferred, promoted, demoted, terminated, or retired using data collected over a number of years. Probabilities are used to represent the historical flow of personnel through the organization, a "transition matrix" is formed from these probabilities, and future personnel flows are estimated from this matrix.[14] Figure 5-7 presents Markov data from one division of Progressive Tool and Industries, one of the largest tool companies serving the automotive industry (Progressive designs and manufactures the tooling for assembly lines). The transition probability matrix presents percentages or probabilities of employee movement through four positions within the division. These data were retrieved from personnel records and averaged over a five-year period. The matrix shows that 70 percent of the assemblers remain in the position after one year with a turnover (quit or fired) rate of 20 percent. The matrix also shows that 80 percent of the more skilled machinist jobs are retained after one year with only a 5 percent turnover rate. These data were used by Progressive to plan their recruiting strategy based on their projected contracts. The data indicated a strong need to evaluate the assembler job to determine the causes of the high turnover rate and the need to concentrate recruiting at that level in anticipation of shortages of assemblers in the coming year when contracts were expected to expand.

Figure 5-7
Markov Analysis at
Progressive Industries

		A	M	F	S	Exit
Assemblers (A)		.70	.10			.20
Machinists (M)		.05	.80	.10		.05
Foremen (F)			.10	.75	.05	.10
Supervision (S)				.05	.90	.05

	Staffing Levels	A	M	F	S	Exit
Assemblers (A)	250	175	25			50
Machinists (M)	120	6	96	12		6
Foremen (F)	40		4	30	2	4
Supervision (S)	20			1	18	1
Forecast		181	125	43	20	61

Both Eaton Corporation[15] and Weyerhaeuser[16] have used Markov analysis successfully in their forecasts. However, two attempts at Corning Glass proved unsuccessful because the transition probabilities were unreliable.[17] A minimum of 50 people in each job of the transition matrix is recommended to ensure adequate reliability in forecasting. At Progressive, for example, projections for oversupplies of foremen were based on small numbers and proved to be relatively inaccurate. More research is needed on Markov analysis to determine the key variables affecting its accuracy. Variables such as unemployment rate, changes in competitor status, and business plans or customer demand that differ significantly from the situation when the probabilities were established will have a profound effect on the usefulness of the Markov projections for the future.

External Supply

External supply consists of those individuals in the labor force who are potential recruits of the firm (including those working for another firm). The skill levels being sought determine the relevant labor market. The entire country (or world) may be the relevant labor market for highly skilled jobs whereas for unskilled jobs, the relevant labor market is usually (but not always) the local community. Determining the relevant labor market also will determine what type of recruiting approach should be used. Several governmental and industrial reports (e.g., Bureau of Labor Statistics, Public Health Service, Northwestern Endicott Lindquist Report) regularly forecast the supply of labor and make estimates of available workers in general job and demographic categories. These forecasts are also extrapolations into the future based on current trends.

IRCA

What Is the Immigration Reform and Control Act (IRCA) of 1986? The labor pool should be a legal pool. While there is a global market for many jobs today, some jobs just have to be done in person (i.e., the worker is in the United States). The IRCA requires that every U.S. employer, no matter how small, not hire or continue to employ aliens who are not legally authorized to work here. The wave of immigrants entering the U.S. slowed in 2008 as the economy faltered and governments stepped up enforcement of immigration and employment eligibility laws. Employers are supposed to verify the identity and work authorization of every new employee and to sign an I-9 form attesting to the legal status of each worker. Financial penalties for noncompliance can be harsh (from $100 to $1,000 per employee) and criminal penalties are possible. Starting in 2008, Immigration and Customs Enforcement (ICE) and the U.S. Attorney's Office have made individuals who work for companies that employ illegal aliens the targets of criminal prosecutions. This is a change in tactics. HR people and line managers are now doing time for conspiracy and harboring illegal aliens.

I-9 form requirements

The use of illegals is rampant in some American industries as enforcement of the law is limited and criminal penalties are still enforced on a limited basis. Law-abiding companies in some industries such as construction can have difficulty competing on price against the cheaters. One roofing-business owner in Florida reported that he couldn't adequately staff his business without illegals and that he certainly couldn't compete in bidding jobs without low-wage illegals. In addition, he reported that he "saves a ton" on worker's compensation and social security expenses when he uses "illegals."

State laws aim to curb illegal immigration

State lawmakers, in response to Congressional inaction on immigration law, are giving local authorities a wider berth. In 2007, 1,562 bills related to illegal immigration were introduced nationwide and 240 were enacted in 46 states, triple the number that passed in 2006, according to the National Conference of State Legislatures. A new law in Mississippi makes it a felony for an illegal immigrant to hold a job. In Oklahoma, sheltering or transporting illegal immigrants is also a felony. In Arizona, a business can be shut down if it is caught using illegal labor.

E-Verify to determine eligibility

In 2008, the federal government supported the voluntary use of E-Verify, a voluntary program in which employers can check workers' names against databases kept by the Social Security Administration and the Department of Homeland Security. Over 65,000 employers had signed up by June 2008. Legislation has been introduced to require all 7 million-plus employers in the United States to participate in E-Verify and to fire employees who cannot prove that they have the right to work. The Department of Homeland Security also designated E-Verify as the electronic employment eligibility verification system that all federal contractors must use.

Arizona enacted a law in 2008 requiring all employers in the state to use the E-Verify system. Colorado, Georgia, and Minnesota also require some employers to use the system. Many other states have similar proposals pending. Some groups oppose the use of the E-Verify program because it is error-prone. The patchwork of state laws could prove problematic for employers that operate in several states.

H-1B visas

What Are the Immigration Options for U.S. Employers? Another employment option for U.S. employers is legally importing workers through work visas. The H-1B visa program allows employers to hire highly skilled or specialized foreign workers for temporary jobs in the United States. The program is designed for skilled workers in high demand and was capped at 65,000 for 2009 plus 20,000 additional slots with advanced and specified college degrees. An employer must file a labor condition application with the Department of Labor attesting to several items, including payment of prevailing wages for the position and the working conditions offered. Under current law, an alien can only be on H-1B status for six years at a time (go to http://uscis.gov for more detail). The legal limit of H-1B visas was reached for 2008 before the fiscal year even began.

L-1 classifications

Employers can also hire foreign workers to temporarily work in the United States or to receive training. Employers must file a petition for temporary foreign employees. There are many categories of temporary workers, and the categories vary by the maximum time such an employee may stay. One controversial program for temporary employees is the Intracompany Transferee **L-1 classification.** The purpose of these visas is to allow foreign companies to transfer employees into the United States. The number of these visas has risen in recent years. Unlike the H-1B visa, employers do not have to pay L-1 workers prevailing wages. Aliens with "specialized knowledge" or managerial responsibilities who are transferred to the United States by a foreign employer to work for the parent company in the United States qualify for L-1 visa status.

While the United States Citizenship and Immigration Service has specific definitions for "specialized knowledge," "managerial," and "executive" classes, there are accusations that the L-1 program has been abused to the detriment of the American worker. (There may have been changes in this law since publication of this book.) At present, L-1 workers can stay in the United States for a maximum of seven years. Critics charge that L-1 visas are now used by foreign companies to bring workers into the United States who then do contract work for American companies, at times to replace American workers. There have even been accusations that American workers trained the L-1 contract workers before the Americans were fired. In 2008 there were 155,000 L-1 visa holders in the United States. However, there is little research on whether American workers really lost jobs because of the program.

Step Four: Gap Analysis

Gap analysis is used to reconcile the forecasts of labor demand and supply. At a minimum, this process identifies potential shortages or surpluses of employees, skills, and competencies. In addition, however, planners can review several environmental forecasts with alternative supply and demand forecasts in order to determine the firm's preparedness for different business scenarios in the context of business objectives. From a problem-solving perspective, gap analysis is used to match potential strengths and opportunities with solutions in order to evaluate how the firm might attack the future. This decision-making process involves (1) search for alternative solutions, (2) evaluation of alternatives, and (3) choice of solutions.

Is There an Optimal Way to Downsize or Restructure?

This type of gap analysis has been used in employee downsizing or reengineering programs for a majority of the Fortune 1000, even some of the most successful and profitable. More than 75 percent of the Fortune 1000 firms have implemented downsizing programs since 2000.[18] The evidence on the effects of downsizing is mixed. Strategic downsizing and restructuring can clearly be effective in improving a firm's position, but strategic downsizing is more than just "cost reduction." Figure 5-8 presents a summary of the research evidence.

One expert echoes the latest research showing that restructuring by downsizing does not necessarily make a company more profitable. In an excellent book entitled *Responsible Restructuring*, Professor Wayne Cascio presents a strategy for optimal restructuring.[19]

Figure 5-8   **Summary of Research on Downsizing and Outcome Variables**

1. No consistent relationship between downsizing and post-downsizing financial performance.
2. Other cost-saving measures may be more effective (e.g., attrition).
3. Even when payroll is reduced, restructuring charges may offset benefit.
4. Costs to replace downsized employees can be high and wipe out temporary reduction in payroll.
5. Costs connected with negative effect on survivors should be incorporated into calculation of effects.
6. Net effect of downsizing on dollar costs is uncertain.
7. Layoffs may depress post-layoff accounting returns.
8. Large sample studies indicate a general negative effect of layoff announcements on market-adjusted equity values.
9. Reductions framed as restructuring or consolidation tend to realize positive response in equity value.
10. Early retirement programs tend to realize positive response.

Source: W. McKinley, J. Zhao, and K. G. Rust, "A Sociocognitive Interpretation of Organizational Downsizing," *Academy of Management Review* 25 (2000), pp. 227–243.

Figure 5-9 presents Dr. Cascio's prescriptions for enhancing the effectiveness of restructuring and downsizing. He makes a convincing argument that his approach can be an opportunity to focus on the most important elements (and people) of the organization where it has (or could have) a sustained competitive advantage.[20]

Most companies implement downsizing as a reaction to loss of market share, increased competition, or lower productivity. GM and Ford are examples here. Most also look at downsizing as simply a workforce reduction process rather than a restructuring or reengineering of jobs in the context of corporate strategy or planning. As one CEO put it, "We lost the organization in the process . . . we basically fired people and called it re-engineering . . . we jumped on the re-engineering bandwagon without understanding its destination." Another CEO was even more disillusioned with job cutting posing as reengineering. "We cut costs, ruined quality and eliminated more customers than employees. . . . Re-engineering has replaced strategic thinking around here."

Reengineering should focus on core competencies

The most effective reengineering efforts are an opportunity to create or improve the company's competitive advantage through restructuring, overhead reduction, and more effective performance management with a constant focus on the core competencies of the organization and the current and/or future customer base. The process can create a frame of mind that could be sustained after the major downsizing effort is complete. The idea is to create and maintain a "lean and mean" mentality in management that would be sustained long after the specific downsizing goals were met and always in the context of meeting (or exceeding) customer requirements with measurement criteria that best define this customer focus. Reengineering that focuses on the core competencies of the organization and the core business and its customers can help support a clear and compelling organizational strategy. But as strategy expert Darrell Rigby puts it, "Cutting people whose experience is vital to the creation of customer value will never create superior results."

Figure 5-9   **Enhancing the Effectiveness of Employment Restructuring and Downsizing**

1. Carefully consider the rationale behind employment downsizing.
2. Consider the virtues of stability.
3. Before making any final decisions about downsizing, executives should make their concerns known to employees and seek their input.
4. Top management should lead by example, and use downsizing as a last resort.
5. If employment downsizing is unavoidable, be sure that employees perceive the process as fair, and make decisions in a consistent manner.
6. Communicate regularly and in a variety of ways in order to keep everyone abreast of new developments and information.
7. Give survivors a reason to stay and prospective new hires a reason to join.
8. Train employees and their managers in the new ways of operating.
9. Examine carefully all management systems in light of the change of strategy or environment facing the firm.

Source: Adapted from W. F. Cascio and P. Wynn, "Managing a Downsizing Process," *Human Resource Management* 43 (2004), pp. 425–436.

Over 130,000 IBM employees have taken early retirement since their first major downsizing effort in 1988. While the program helped IBM maintain its company policy of never laying off a single full-time employee, IBM lost some of its best employees who opted for one of the attractive termination programs. One major downsizing program focused on offering early retirement to only noncritical employees, terminating marginal employees for cause, and offering less attractive transfer options to those who were not needed in their current jobs. One of their biggest problems in achieving their early downsizing goals, however, was their performance appraisal system, which did not provide enough useful data to take performance-based actions. It does now, and IBM is doing fine.

Selection from a pool of current employees

There are many approaches to downsizing and some may be required due to union agreements. AT&T "selected" current employees for the new positions based on new job descriptions created by the overhaul of their divisions. The skilled-based résumés and the performance appraisals of the "applicants" for the new jobs were assessed in the context of the labor demands projected based on the new corporate strategy. Voluntary buyouts were one part of the options AT&T used to close the gap in their supply and demand for labor.

One survey of 1,600 chief executives and senior managers by Bain and Company, a Boston-based strategy firm, found that executives viewed a customer focus as the framework for downsizing.[21] This focus included increasing their understanding of customer needs, increasing the customer base, and increasing product and service quality. Of course, the relationship between labor costs and pricing is almost always on the top of the list in terms of customer focus. But the list must be longer than just cutting payroll to save money.

Downsizing that is not done in the context of this customer focus will merely exchange old problems for new ones. Many firms that have gone through radical downsizing in recent years have come to realize how important the connection is between customer needs and any form of organizational restructuring, including downsizing.

Outplacement

As indicated in Figure 5-9, some of the problems associated with downsizing (or "rightsizing") can be minimized with good planning and strategy. In addition to examining performance data and redeployment options, such planning may include *outplacement* services for employees who have lost their jobs. Outplacement can involve job coaching, résumé preparation, placement services, and interview training. Every AT&T employee who was not selected for the restructured company was given access to a resource center that provided job counseling and access to job postings within the company and at other companies. Such outplacement services are now available in Europe and even in Japan, where Japanese companies are faced with a need to downsize as well. It is generally believed that offering outplacement services to employees who have lost their jobs will reduce the probability of a lawsuit, such as a claim of age discrimination. (There is actually no definitive study on the subject.)

Virtue in stability

Professor Cascio asks, "Could it be that there is virtue in stability?" He reports that 80 of the 100 companies that made *Fortune*'s 2002 list of the "100 Best Companies to Work For" avoided layoffs in 2001; 47 of them had some form of policy barring layoffs. And remember there is a relationship between that list of the "best companies" to work for and actual corporate financial performance.[22]

These prescriptions for effective (and limited) downsizing do not necessarily rule out strategic termination. A strong argument can be made that having the very best people in the most important strategic positions is a key to strategy execution. Former GE CEO Jack Welsh often talks about having "A" players in the strategic "A" positions and that having "C" players in such positions can kill strategic execution. HR planning should emphasize the placement of the most qualified individuals in the most important positions. Strategic planning may also include a careful look at and action regarding those employees who could be replaced with more effective individuals.

What Are Some Alternative or Additional Solutions?

As discussed above, in HRP there are likely to be multiple scenarios that are worthy of consideration. Environmental scanning and labor forecasts identify a range of possible options. At this stage, the range of possibilities can be increased by seeking input from executives, line managers, employees, customers, and consultants in a "brainstorming" process. A qualitative approach such as *Delphi* can be used at this point as well.

As part of their HR planning process and after a thorough job analysis, pharmaceutical giant Upjohn asked line managers to answer four basic questions:

1. How does each job relate to the strategic plan of the work unit?

2. Are there alternatives to a full-time job that should be considered to accomplish the same objectives (e.g., temporary workers, part-time employees, independent contractors, job sharing, telecommuting, employee leasing, consultants, overtime)?

3. What are the projected costs of each job?

4. What specific impact will the job have on critical and clearly defined effectiveness criteria?

What Is the Role of Temporary Employment?

More and more companies have been asking similar questions regarding their workforce and coming up with rather creative answers. One of the strongest trends in this country is the use of creative labor arrangements. Temporary employment, part-time workers, telecommuters, job sharing, and employee leasing are among the most popular solutions to labor cost control and fluctuating demand. With employee leasing, a leasing company assumes complete responsibility for the employee, including pay and benefits. The major disadvantage for the employer is a loss in some control over the employee. This loss of control, of course, could affect the effectiveness of employees' performance, which could have a direct impact on the customer. There are few studies that compare the performance, productivity, absence rates, or any other criteria of permanent versus leased employees.

Part-time employment

Another significant trend in creative HR planning is the use of permanent part-time employees.[23] For years, IBM's policy of maintaining a 10 percent part-time workforce enabled the company to maintain a labor pool in line with the business cycle and to preserve their sacrosanct policy of no layoffs. They have now increased the percentage to 20 percent and outsourced many functions, including a large share of their HRM functions. Many other companies, particularly in service, are now following suit. Ryder Trucks, UPS, and Wal-Mart are among the major companies now maintaining a sizable percentage of their workforce with part-time status. According to the Bureau of Labor Statistics, 38 percent of the U.S. workforce worked part-time in 2008. Two-thirds of this group were women.

More employers are hiring temporary help in clerical data processing and industrial jobs. The National Association of Temporary Services has reported a growth rate in temporary employment in excess of 30 percent. While employers generally report that temporaries are typically hired for emergencies, an increasing number of companies report considerable cost savings as well with "temps" judged to be as productive as permanent employees.[24]

Independent contractors

A growing number of workers are classified as "independent contractors." Such non-staff workers are becoming more and more common, particularly in some industries such as media, Internet, and other knowledge-based jobs that now power the U.S. economy. A growing percentage of college courses are now being taught by part-time instructors who are hired to teach one or more courses and paid for only this specific work.

While working parents consider the part-time employment option a good thing, women's groups such as the National Organization for Women (NOW.org) decry the trend as fostering a marginal employment policy characterized by low wages and no benefits. But companies that have adopted policies of permanent part-time staff and nonstaff "independent contractors" for many job classifications report substantial cost savings and relatively little difficulty in recruiting and retaining a capable staff.

What Is Job Sharing?

According to a survey conducted in 2000 by Hewitt Associates, 28 percent of employers offered some form of job sharing, in which two employees share the responsibilities, accountability, and compensation of one full-time job. Job sharing is probably more common among small employers.

Management support appears to be the key to the success of these programs. Many managers and supervisors express fear that job sharing will translate into extra work for management and extra expense for the employer. However, the limited research on the subject indicates that any additional compensation is offset by higher productivity and longer tenure. Job sharing has the potential to help with work flow, reduce turnover, and save on recruiting costs. The approach is responsive to employees' needs to balance work and family or other personal issues.

The success of job sharing depends on a good partnership. Among the key questions the partners and management must answer are the following: 1. How will the work schedule be divided?; 2. How will the partners handle critical meetings, deadlines, etc?; 3. How will the partners divide salary and benefits?; 4. How will the work team communicate? (Formal systems are better); and 5. How will performance evaluations be conducted? (individual appraisals are usually more effective).

Technology has facilitated job sharing. Projects no longer have to stop at the end of the American workday. This is especially evident in the IT industry. Americans finish their workday and then turn over a project to computer programmers in India or Dubai who work while the Americans sleep. Needless to say, this 24-hour attention helps companies hit deadlines.

What Is Telecommuting?

Technology enables work to be done from almost anywhere. It is estimated that over 25 million workers telecommuted in 2008.[25] The number is surely much higher today as traffic becomes more problematic, the cost of gas continues to rise, and telecommunications technology improves. Telecommuting is an alternative work arrangement allowing workers to work at home or in some other location other than the employer's physical premises.

Strong supportive evidence

When it is properly implemented, the evidence of its effectiveness and efficiency is quite strong. Companies are able to attract and retain effective workers with considerable cost savings. A disadvantage may be loss of interaction in the workplace.

Is There a Conflict between Downsizing and Diversity Goals?

One of the more complicated issues regarding a major downsizing is the potential conflict between downsizing efforts and programs aimed at promoting workforce diversity. Ciba-Geigy, the pharmaceutical company, had a diversity challenge as a part their retention process. In the assessment of employee performance, managers were asked to value a diverse organization by "proactively considering diversity in this process." After the initial retention decisions were made, "HR challengers will review retention decisions with respect to diversity . . . and to test for adverse impact." HR compared diversity data after the initial retention decisions to pre-downsizing data. According to documents in a lawsuit, "the result of this analysis may lead to a possible further challenge." Several older Ciba-Geigy employees who were fired maintained that the "diversity challenges" resulted in discrimination against older workers since they were not a part of the diversity programs. Given the current state of EEO law regarding preferential treatment, if the plaintiffs could show that race or gender was actually considered in the retention process and that this consideration affected the status of older workers, would the older workers prevail in an ADEA case? This is a tough call and probably would depend on the process that was followed after the internal audit. If the plaintiff could show that performance ratings were simply changed because of statistical adverse impact and changed in such a way as to avoid the adverse impact and that this process changed the status of some workers over the age of 39, the older workers probably would prevail.

Avoid preferential treatment

Organizations that undergo downsizing while attempting to maintain any diversity or affirmative action accomplishments should try to avoid showing preferential treatment on the basis of any protected class characteristic. It is possible (and advisable) to actually evaluate past performance or even potential performance without even considering a protected class characteristic. While conducting adverse impact analysis such as hypothetical violations of the 80 percent rule is certainly recommended, violations of the guidelines should lead to a serious evaluation of the job relatedness of each step of the decision-making system, not the simple adjustment in ratings as a consequence of a protected class characteristic in order to avoid a violation of the 80 percent rule.

Step Five: Action Programming

Action programming is the final step of HRP that takes the adopted solution and lays out the sequence of events that need to be executed to realize the plan. In the previous four steps of HR planning, the task was to derive a solution that best addresses the issues identified through environmental scanning and labor forecasts in the context of the strategic plan. The purpose of action programming is to make certain that those decisions become reality. In general, there are two aspects of programming: internal and external.

Internal Programming

Many of the solutions in HRP rest on actions inside the firm with the current workforce. For routine issues, in particular, bureaucratic adjustments in HR practices can be easily programmed internally (e.g., job design/assignments). GM's action regarding its engineers is one such example. In addition, for some uncertain areas, adaptive adjustments such as training, career planning, promotions, and compensation design can be made internally.

These are the adaptive requirements many companies follow because of labor shortages in key areas. Taking a closer look at **organizational design** around changing technologies is one such example. IBM's "hot skills" program is a great illustration of the effective linking of corporate strategic planning with HR planning and HR recruitment.

External Programming

Other solutions in HRP require going outside the firm to interact with constituencies in the environment (e.g., labor unions, competitors, etc.). In particular, when plans require drastically different competencies from what employees currently possess and/or the time frame for change is quite short, the firm likely will need to recruit from the outside labor market. Motorola's experience with the coordinated efforts of U.S. and Indian programmers is one example of reacting to new time frames.

Step Six: Control and Evaluation

Control and evaluation monitor the effectiveness of human resource plans over time. Deviations from the plans are identified and actions are taken. The extent to which human resource objectives have been met is measured by the feedback from various outcomes. It has been suggested that, essentially, long-range planning activities require the attainment of short-run objectives. Examples include performance or productivity data, turnover costs, workforce reduction effects from early retirement programs, break-even costs of new hires, and analysis of costs of recruits compared to the training and development costs of existing employees. Obviously, actual staffing levels compared to projected levels should be evaluated for accuracy. Doing evaluations such as cost–benefit analysis makes it easier to determine whether long-run planning objectives will be met.

The issue of evaluation of planning can be considered along with the evaluation of recruitment efforts since the criteria used for the evaluations are often the same. This will be discussed later in the chapter. The critical consideration here should be the identification of the vital measurement criteria, which will provide for an assessment of the HR planning implementation in the context of the business strategy. Regarding outsourcing and alternative work arrangements, the most fundamental criterion should be cost savings but always in the context of meeting customer requirements.

When HR planning involves adding to the labor force, the organization must rely on the recruitment function to meet its employment needs. The whole point of the planning exercise is to accurately determine the optimal number of employees to meet internal and external customer requirements. If the gap analysis determines that employees are needed, that is where recruitment comes in. Discussion of this vital HR function is next.

THE RECRUITMENT FUNCTION: PUTTING HRP INTO ACTION

Moving from HRP to recruitment is essentially a process of translating broad strategies into operational tasks. The major responsibility for this process typically rests within the HRM department, although most tasks are shared with line managers. While HR managers are responsible for determining recruitment policy, ensuring EEO compliance, training, and evaluating the recruiters, many organizations such as Oracle, IBM, and Procter and Gamble actively involve line managers and employees as recruiters. As mentioned above, conflict between HR and line managers can occur when their priorities diverge. For example, line

Figure 5-10   **A Model of the Organizational Recruitment Process**

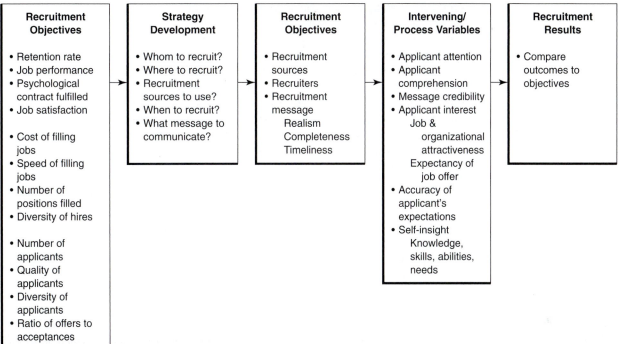

Source: J. Breaugh and B. Starke. "Research on Employee Recruitment: So Many Studies, So Many Questions," *Journal of Management,* Vol. 26, p. 408. Copyright (2000) by Sage Publications, Reprinted by permission.

managers may be more concerned about filling a position quickly (i.e., when the new employee is needed) while HR managers may be more concerned about affirmative action guidelines or complying with EEO regulations. Their goals should be the same: hiring the most qualified person(s) when needed and without violating any laws or regulations. Figure 5-10 presents a model of the organizational recruitment process.

Recruitment, Other HR Activities, and Organizational Attractiveness

Recall the statement earlier about the interdependent nature of recruiting with other HR activities and the reputation of the organization. Decisions regarding employee testing, work policies and programs, compensation, benefits, and corporate image all can have an impact on recruiting. One large retailer required high-level managerial candidates to travel to the company headquarters (for some, over 2,000 miles) to go through a two-day assessment center that was only offered at headquarters. Because of these requirements, many experienced managers who were working for other companies dropped out of the pool of candidates because they didn't have the time to commit to a two-day assessment center with two additional days of travel to the national headquarters. As another example, the 2,900-room Opryland Hotel in Nashville had difficulty attracting housekeepers, kitchen helpers, and laundry workers. They put in a seven-day-a-week child care center and a bus service to transport workers. The two new employee benefits increased the number of applicants by 35 percent.

A company institutes a comprehensive drug-testing program that includes random drug testing with no probable cause for all employees. The company does not consider how the broader pool of candidates might view this and merely assumes that the policy will have an impact only by deterring applicants who would be most likely to use drugs. Another company installs a binding arbitration policy for all employee–employer disputes. A new employee must sign off on the policy as a condition of employment. Once again, the company does not consider the effect of this new policy on the ability to recruit and retain the most qualified applicants. Another company decides to reduce indirect compensation by reducing health benefits for new employees and increasing the premium. They have no idea what the change in policy will do to their ability to recruit. They find out later that recruitment costs have gone up along with the rate of offer rejections. They finally conduct an actual cost–benefit study of their change in policy and discover that in fact the company lost money because of the interactive effect of the policy on staffing and the retention of valuable employees. Recruitment, selection, and personnel policies are indeed interdependent.

Of course, recruitment and human resource planning should be done with the assumption that consideration will be given to where the work is performed. Technology now allows employers to consider many more options for getting the job done. As discussed earlier, along with telecommuting, more companies are now turning to offshoring and the outsourcing of work, particularly work that is strategically less important, can be done for less, and when shipping and the cost of oil do not wipe out the gain from lower labor costs.

"Geography is history" "Geography is history," says Raman Roy, chairman of Wipro Spectramind, one of India's fast-growing customer service companies.[26] Over 500,000 American tax returns were prepared in India in 2008, most of them by SurePrep, headquartered in Bangalore. Tax preparers in India are paid between $350 and $450 per month versus $3,000 to $4,000 per month in the United States. In 2008, SurePrep did work for more than 165 American accounting firms. Morgan Stanley now has Indian stock analysts and Dell sends customer calls to India (estimated savings of around 50 percent on compensation). IBM employs about 330,000 people worldwide and only about 40 percent of them are in the United States. Even SAS, the North Carolina company discussed in Chapter 1 with the incredible employee benefits, now employs a growing percentage of computer tech specialists who live and work in India. Says Jerry Rao, Indian entrepreneur, "Any activity where we can digitize and decompose the value chain, and move the work around, will get moved around." Even when you place an order at the window of a McDonald's today, you may be interacting with an Indian in Bangalore. It is estimated that 650,000 American jobs went to China, Russia, and India between 2001 and 2008. See again Figure 5-3 for offshoring "attractiveness" scores by country.

While "geography may be history" regarding knowledge-based service work that does not require face-to-face contact with customers or clients, geography is not history with regard to manufacturing or any work involving expensive shipping. Because of the increased cost of shipping mainly due to the price of oil, some manufacturing is actually returning to the United States. "Cheap labor in China doesn't help you when you gotta pay so much to bring the goods over," says economist Jeff Rubin. "Made in the USA" now makes more sense for some companies. DESA, the company that makes the giant heaters you see behind the benches at NFL games, relocated back to the United States from China **Reverse globalization** in 2008. Among the other companies practicing this "reverse globalization" in 2008 were Crown Battery (from Mexico to Ohio) and Larouk Systems (1,000 jobs from China to Houston). "It's not just about labor costs anymore," says economist Rubin. "Distance costs money, and when you have to shift iron ore from Brazil to China and then ship it back to Pittsburgh, Pittsburgh is looking pretty good at 40 bucks an hour."[27] Recent developments in China, particularly when combined with added costs because of the price of oil, could contribute to this momentum. Chinese factory workers are demanding and getting better wages, working conditions, and benefits. Minimum wages have climbed 25 percent since 2004 (the average is from $58 to $74 a month, excluding benefits) in Shenzhen, Beijing, and Shanghai. Wages at the largest factories operated by many American multinationals, paying between $100 and $200 a month in 2004, are now also rising. China's progress could bode well for workers in places like Cambodia, Bangladesh, and Madagascar, but the shipping costs might still direct the multinationals back to the United States at least for products sold mainly here. Factory owners may be complaining that they can't find workers in China, but that means they will do what they have always done in such cases: look for cheap labor elsewhere and more efficient logistics. Foreign auto companies employed 113,000 people in the United States in 2007, a figure projected to increase 50 percent by 2011.

For jobs with high turnover rates, as stated earlier, consideration should also be given to telecommuting where a customer call "center" isn't a center at all. When you call JetBlue to make a reservation, you're probably talking to a Utah housewife working from her home. American Airlines is following the JetBlue lead with a growing number of their CSRs sitting in their homes throughout the United States. There is growing evidence that turnover rates and overall costs can be sharply reduced with this approach to work. Job applicants tend to like the approach, the pool of qualified job candidates grows, performance is on a par (or better) than "on premises" workers and the voluntary turnover rate is significantly lower compared to the "on premises" folks. With the cost of gasoline climbing in 2008, telecommuting is looking better and better to corporate America and to working America.

Recruitment can clearly be made harder or easier by a whole host of factors. The state of the economy, the supply and demand for particular KASOCs or competencies, and HR policies and practices are all important. Of course, the attractiveness of the organization from the perspective of potential job candidates is also critical. This attractiveness factor is related to many factors that go into an organization's reputation. As discussed in Chapter 1, an organization's reputation in terms of its effectiveness or as a "socially responsible" employer can clearly affect recruitment. Google may now be the leader in IT applications because of their reputation. Even Microsoft is losing employees to Google perhaps because of their upstart rival's recent accomplishments (and stock price!). No doubt an organization's reputation as a great place to work with an optimistic outlook and a stable history, as a company with great potential for growth, or as a socially responsible company will make a recruiter's job a whole lot easier. Have you noticed how many ads are on television now extolling the virtues of Wal-Mart as a great place to work and how much Wal-Mart is doing for the local community? This PR campaign is probably to some extent a response to the negative news about Wal-Mart in these same areas. Obviously, Wal-Mart wants its reputation to attract and keep good workers and, of course, loyal and a growing number of customers.

The Three Essential Steps for Recruitment Planning

Based on the gap analysis, an organization should have a fairly good idea of its overall recruitment or downsizing needs. This information must be operationalized and communicated to those who will be taking the action. Three essential steps for translating future needs into specific operational terms are (1) work analysis, (2) time lapse data, and (3) yield ratio analysis.

Work Analysis

Recruiters and HR planners rely on two aspects of work analysis information to identify the critical skills for which they will recruit. First, **job descriptions** provide an outline of the responsibilities, duties, and tasks to be performed by the potential employee. Second, the **job specifications** outline the knowledge, skills, and abilities required of the applicant. In general, the more specific the recruitment design, especially in terms of job specifications, the more efficient and effective it is, assuming of course that the specificity is important for the job. Poorly designed recruiting is more expensive and takes longer.

For example, job specifications are sometimes written that are not essential for the job and are sometimes unnecessary and costly. One retailer stipulated three years' experience as a store manager in order to be eligible for consideration as a store manager for the company. The VP of operations drew up specifications unilaterally and based on his "sense" of what was required in the job. The result was a small pool of applicants, higher advertising costs, and fewer females and minorities who were eligible for consideration.

Work analysis information that accurately reflects the requirements needed for the job can have a direct impact on the effectiveness of any recruitment and planning effort. Work analysis information can also be used in a downsizing effort as jobs are restructured based on the new organizational structure or individuals are repositioned based on a new strategy. As discussed in Chapter 4, specific work analysis strategies are available for writing job descriptions and specifications based on an organization's competitive strategy.

Work analysis can also determine where work should be done for maximum efficiency. Office Depot cut 900 call center jobs and then contracted with Willow CSN Corp. in Miramar, Florida, to provide the "home-based" service to customers. Technology now allows for telecommuting where most (or all) work is performed at home. Alston and Byrd, an Atlanta-based law firm, allows lawyers considerable latitude in determining when to go into the office and when to stay home and work. With their entire law library now online and many other communication vehicles available, lawyers don't miss a beat on productivity and they avoid the horrendous Atlanta traffic.

The need for accurate job descriptions and job specifications is particularly critical for Web-based recruiting of any kind. There are numerous examples of Internet recruiting that can quickly get you an overwhelming number of résumés, the vast majority of which are irrelevant to the jobs you are trying to fill.

While HRP provides the number of jobs needed and job analysis provides the requirements of the jobs, management must know when to start a recruiting process and how extensive the search should be. This is where time lapse data and yield ratios come in.

Time Lapse Data

Time lapse data (TLD) provide the average time that elapses between points of decision making in recruiting. For example, if the recruitment plan calls for newspaper advertisements, records may reflect that the job is ultimately filled an average of two months after publication of the ad. Thus, the ad should be placed at least two months before the job has to be filled. Data also may be available on the time lapse between interviews and offers, and offers and acceptances. When combined with yield ratios, the TLD can provide useful information for planning a recruitment effort.

Time lapses have been reduced for some companies taking advantage of the automated recruiting options available through the World Wide Web. Most of the country's largest newspapers now have job listings services on the Internet. Careerjournal.com is an online job board that allows employers to post positions on multiple Web sites. Currently, there are over 150 sites that "partner" to cover many job specialties.

Yield Ratio or Percentage

A **yield ratio** for any recruiting step reflects the number of candidates available at a step compared to a previous step. For example, a series of newspaper ads may result in 1,000 applications for employment. Of these 1,000 applications, 100 are judged to meet some minimum qualifications (to be in the "ball game" so to speak). Thus, the yield ratio at this initial stage is 10 percent. Of the group of 100 candidates, 50 accepted invitations to be interviewed (yield ratio is 50 percent for this stage); of the 50, 10 were given job offers (20 percent yield ratio).

Yield ratios for future planning

Assuming the labor market has not changed dramatically from when the yield ratios were derived and that similar methods of recruiting are to be used (e.g., advertising in the same papers, using a Web service or a headhunter), the ratios can be used as the basis for planning future recruitment efforts. By going backward from the calculated yield ratios, the recruiter can estimate how many applicants will be necessary in order to fill a certain number of positions. The recruiter then can adjust the recruiting effort accordingly with more (or less) advertising, more (or fewer) trips to college campuses, more "Monster" ads, and so on.

Discrepancy between academic research and typical recruiting

The use of time lapse data and yield ratios is another area where there is a wide gap between what academic texts and scholarly research recommend and the extent to which such data are collected in organizations to drive future recruitment planning. While almost every scholar on the subject recommends a recruitment evaluation process that includes yield ratios to assist decision makers in efficient recruitment planning, few companies actually collect these data as a part of a recruitment evaluation.

Recruitment is a never-ending process for many jobs where there are critical shortages of highly specialized skills. As discussed above, there are tight labor markets for many occupations and indications that markets will get even tighter, particularly for knowledge-intensive jobs. Many hospitals recruit for nurses on a continuous basis because they are constantly understaffed. Advertisements for nurses today often promise not only high pay, but more of a say in their jobs and hospital management, bonuses of $3,000 or more for signing up, bonuses for staying on the job a certain length of time, flexible work schedules, child care, and free tuition for advanced courses. Some employers even offer maid service and free housing for nurses who are willing to work at various locations based on demand. Many high-tech manufacturing firms recruit for engineers and computer programmers year round as well.

Some companies have difficulty filling even the unskilled positions. The fast-food industry, for example, beset by turnover rates in excess of 200 percent (two incumbents for every job in one year), often advertises and takes applications for counter personnel throughout the year for many locations. Many companies have mobile recruiting units that visit high schools and shopping malls to solicit applications. McDonald's cooperates with the American Association of Retired Persons to attract senior citizens for hard-to-fill counter-personnel positions. Burger King offered a $6,000 signing bonus in 2005 to attract workers back to New Orleans after Hurricane Katrina. AMC theaters also concentrates on senior citizens for its ticket takers and counter personnel. Chemical Bank in New York must interview 50 applicants to find one who can be successfully trained as a teller. In general, the changing demographics of our workforce and the changing nature of the demands of work indicate that recruitment will be more challenging once the U.S. pulls out of the recession. Many companies still reported difficulties in recruiting unskilled workers in many geographical areas.

The Two Sources of Recruiting: Internal and External

There are two general sources of recruiting: internal and external. Internal recruiting seeks applicants for positions from among the ranks of those currently employed. With the exception of entry-level positions, most organizations try to fill positions with current employees. Figure 5-11 summarizes the advantages and disadvantages of each source of recruiting.

Advantages and Disadvantages of Internal and External Recruitment

There are several major advantages of internal recruiting. First of all, it is considerably less costly than external recruiting. Second, organizations typically have a better knowledge of internal applicants' skills and abilities than that which can be acquired of candidates in an external recruiting effort. Through performance and competency assessment, decision makers typically will have much more extensive knowledge of internal candidates and thus make more valid selection decisions. The third advantage to internal recruiting is that an organizational policy of promoting from within can enhance organizational commitment and job satisfaction. These variables have been shown to be correlated with lower employee turnover rates and higher productivity. A policy of internal recruiting is one component of **high-performance work systems (HPWS),** which were discussed in Chapter 1. Companies that practice internal recruiting are more likely to be successful financially than companies that rely on external recuiting for top talent. Ted LeVino, senior vice president at GE, argues that their internal recruiting policy has fostered stability and continuity in the managerial ranks of the company. Bank of America has a policy in which newly hired college grads receive a career planning guide that describes the typical timetable for progression within the company for their best employees and steps to take in order to get there.

Internal recruiting: A HPWS characteristic

One of the great advantages of detailed work analysis is that succession planning programs can be developed so that management (and employees) can have a good idea of the sources for internal recruiting. At Ford, for example, associates complete a competency-based job analysis describing their current knowledge and skills required for their present job and what knowledge or skills they would like to acquire. These responses are then

Figure 5-11
Advantages and Disadvantages of Internal versus External Recruiting

Recruitment	Advantages	Disadvantages
Internal	Better assessment of candidates	Creates vacancies
	Reduces training time	Can stifle politics diversity
	Faster	Insufficient supply of candidates
	Cheaper	
	Motivates current employees	
External	Increases diversity	Expensive
	Facilitates growth	Slower
	Can save training time	Less valid data about candidates
	New/novel problem solving	Stifles upward movement of personnel

linked to particular vacancies within the company, descriptions of which already have been completed by managers of the these positions.

There may be disadvantages to internal recruiting. Continuity is not always such a good thing. If the organization has decided to change its business strategy, for example, entrenched managers are probably not the "change masters" you want. One theory of internal recruiting is that it promulgates the old ways of doing things, that creative problem solving may be hindered by the lack of "new blood" or a sort of "managerial inbreeding." However, there is no solid research that supports this belief that internal recruiting impedes creativity and innovative thinking, and one recent study at a Fortune 500 company found just the opposite.

Escalation bias

One well-documented managerial blunder is to irrationally stay committed to an initial course of action, particularly if you initiated the action. This misdirected persistence, or **escalation bias** is more likely when internal versus external recruiting is emphasized, especially if the internal candidates were personally involved in a particular course of action.[28] For example, one U.S. company faced new competition to an established product line from a foreign competitor. The senior managers, all of whom had been at the company for at least 15 years and had great ownership in the product and how it was marketed, agreed to deal with the new competition as they had always dealt with competition— by competing on price. This manner was unfortunately out of step with the upstart competitor's strategy, which included competing on price. The result was a disaster for the company with over 30 percent of their workforce laid off because of a loss of market share. A new manager might have been better able to conduct a more rational analysis of the situation.

Entrenched managers sometimes have difficulty understanding that time and money already invested are "sunk costs" and should therefore not be considered in future planning. Managers who had something to do with a present course of action seem to have more difficulty in understanding this.

Unit raiding

Some organizations complain of unit raiding where divisions may compete for the same people. GM, for example, reported raiding of the best design engineers from one division by another despite an agreement that such recruiting was not in the best interests of the company. Raiding is quite common in universities for clerical positions where position descriptions can be written in such a way that a secretary can move to another department because the new position pays more.

Politics

A third possible disadvantage of internal recruiting is that politics probably have a greater impact on internal recruiting and selection than does external recruiting. Thus, while more job-related information may be known about internal candidates, personnel decisions involving internal candidates are more likely to be affected by the political agendas of the decision makers and are also more likely to be contested legally than external staffing decisions.

"Peter Principle"

One survey of high-level federal government managers revealed that the easiest perceived way to get rid of a troublesome employee was to evaluate that employee so positively that the employee would be more likely to get an employment opportunity out of the unit (either within or outside of the same agency). The **"Peter Principle"** states that we rise to our level of incompetence. This survey found that, at least in the federal government, once we reach our level of incompetence, our boss may actually try to get us moved up a notch above our level of incompetence in order to get rid of us with the least amount of paperwork. In other words, things may be even worse than the "Peter Principle."[29] HR managers must constantly monitor very precisely defined job descriptions or job specifications. While this may constitute well-focused recruiting based on precisely what the organization requires, it also can mean that a position has been "wired" for an internal candidate. An effective HR manager should be capable of making the distinction. The manager writing the job description and job specifications should be required to stipulate why highly specific credentials or areas of expertise are required in the context of the organization's or unit's strategic plan.

Internal recruiting programs should be carefully integrated with other HR functions. Effective HR succession planning, job analysis, personnel selection, and performance appraisal are all important for an effective system that can fill required positions with the most qualified personnel in the shortest amount of time. Administrators of such programs should be knowledgeable about EEO legislation and litigation as numerous lawsuits have been filed related to internal recruiting and placement decisions. (Recall the huge Wal-Mart sex discrimination case.)

Job posting

While most large companies have formal succession plans at the managerial level, a much lower percentage of small to medium-size firms have formal systems.[30] A **job-posting** system can enhance the effectiveness of internal recruiting. Job posting is a process where announcements of positions are made available to all current employees through company newsletters, bulletin boards, and so on. Surprisingly, only about 20 percent of organizations have formal systems of job posting for vacant positions within the organization.[31] When properly implemented, job-posting systems can substantially improve the quality of the job placements that are made within an organization and protect the organization from EEO problems (this issue is related to Wal-Mart's problems). The most effective job-posting systems take advantage of a corporate intranet where employees can access information about job openings through their connected computers. Many sophisticated human resource information systems (HRIS) are now available with competency-based, succession planning data and job-posting provisions.

External Recruitment Sources

External recruiting concerns recruitment from outside the organization. Most scholars argue that one of the biggest advantages of external recruiting is that the approach can facilitate the introduction of new ideas and thinking into corporate decision making. The "new blood" comes with no ownership of past strategies that can hinder an objective assessment of future strategy. A major disadvantage of external recruiting is that the introduction of new personnel may have a negative impact on work group cohesion and morale. Also, new personnel from outside the organization typically take longer to learn the ropes of the job and the organization. Another possible disadvantage is that external recruiting can be very costly. For example, companies have paid in excess of $150,000 to executive search firms for locating a single, high-level manager. Figure 5-12 presents some examples of ads for professional and executive global positions.

The Internet has had a profound impact on the cost and the time involved in recruiting personnel, including that of managers. Most Fortune 1000 companies now post available jobs on their Web sites and more and more skilled employees are applying for these jobs through these sites. A formal job posting system for both internal and external recruiting can also give an employer some protection against legal claims based on simple "progression" statistics (e.g., nonsupervisory positions vs. supervisory positions by race or gender).

The final disadvantage of external recruiting is that you typically have less information about external candidates. There is thus a need for good assessment procedures that can be used instead of reliable performance data on the external candidate. Good assessment procedures can be costly and bad assessment procedures and references can be downright deceptive or ineffective. Remember the survey of federal managers regarding using positive evaluations to get rid of incompetent employees. Inflated letters of recommendation or confidential interviews may be intended to land a troublesome employee in a job outside of the organization. (This is probably one reason that letters of reference have low validity; there may actually be an incentive on the part of evaluators to inflate references in order to move a job candidate out of an organization.)

What Methods Are Available for External Recruiting?

There are several methods available for external recruitment

Walk-ins/Unsolicited Applicant Files: The most common and least expensive approach is to make use of direct applications where job seekers submit unsolicited material (e.g., a résumé) or simply show up in person seeking employment. Direct applications can provide a pool of potential employees to meet future needs. While direct applications are particularly effective in filling entry-level and unskilled positions, some organizations, because of their reputations or because of their geographical locations, succeed in compiling excellent pools of potential employees from direct applications for skilled positions.

The **Riley Guide** (www.rileyguide.com) presents an excellent overview for on-line recruiters with links to most major job banks and specialty job sites. Careerbuilder.com is an effective online source for small business. For $450, a company can post one position and access, so the Web site claims, 25 million "candidates."

Figure 5-12 **Ads for Global Executive and Professional Positions**

INTERNATIONAL PROFESSIONALS

In today's dynamic global environment, there are exceptional opportunities for individuals whose experience and skills equip them to live and work overseas. There are currently positions available to men and women throughout a wide spectrum of professional fields, including the sciences, engineering, information and computer systems, economics/finance, education, marketing, business, or management. If you have worked abroad in any of these areas, you have a definite advantage in securing an exciting new overseas career.

These worldwide positions are being offered to people who are already confident and at home in foreign locations. You must be self-reliant and have the integrity to work without direct supervision. Reporting will require excellent verbal and written communications skills, and you must be conversant in at least one foreign language. Advanced degrees are preferred; a bachelor's degree in an appropriate area is a minimum requirement for consideration.

We represent international employers who will pay all fees associated with your selection process. They require that all applicants be U.S. citizens (Legal Permanent Residents also may apply). These positions are open to individuals of all racial and ethnic backgrounds. Compensation and benefits are commensurate with your demonstrated qualifications. For consideration under strict confidentiality, send your résumé and a letter describing your credentials. As we are a third party and not an employer, no phone calls from applicants will be accepted. We will respond only to those applicants who are of interest to our clients.

CAREER SYSTEMS INTERNATIONAL
P.O. Box, Dept. IP-
Philadelphia, PA 19103
Representing equal opportunity employers.

Manager-Expatriate Programs

Philips Electronics North America Corp., a global consumer and electronic business with a significant number of employees on worldwide expatriate assignments, has an excellent career opportunity in Manhattan for a pro-active professional with 5–8 years' human resources expertise to design, develop, implement, and manage the expatriate program. This fundamental position will advise personnel on expatriate and immigration policies/procedures; develop worldwide compensation programs; implement program changes; and serve as an international liaison.

To qualify, you must have 4+ years' immigration/expatriate and supervisory experience, plus a B.A. in business, human resources, or related discipline is highly beneficial. Top-notch organizational, technical, business, interpersonal, and communication skills are essential.

We offer a competitive salary/benefits package and a stimulating work environment. For confidential consideration, please send résumé to: **Human Resources/JM, Philips Electronics North America Corp., 100 East 42nd Street, New York, NY 10017. FAX:**
EOE M/F/D/V. Principals only.

PHILIPS

The reputation of the company has a great deal to do with the usefulness and size of the pool of unsolicited applicants and résumés. Organizations such as Google, Coca-Cola, SAS, Microsoft, GE, IBM, the *New York Times,* and Harvard University receive thousands of unsolicited applications every year. Many excellent candidates can be found in this pool. One of the reasons that companies actively campaign to make one or more of the many top 10 lists of the "best companies to work for" is because the rate of unsolicited résumés is directly related to this honor.

Not only do unsolicited résumés reduce the cost of recruiting, they also increase the probability of hiring the very best employees. The *New York Times* has led the world in Pulitzer Prize winners for years. They spend very little time recruiting the future Pulitzer winners; the best writers just know where to work.

Many companies now scan résumés or applications and then conduct key-word computer searches to quickly get to a reasonable short list of candidates when positions become available. Software now exists to match fairly detailed job specifications with résumé information. The result is usually a much more efficient (and faster) recruiting effort. Monster's "TARGET Reach" filters résumés by a company's criteria (e.g., experience, location, education).

Monster's TARGET Reach

Referrals: Some organizations have formal systems of employee referral for occupations with great demand. Pratt & Whitney, for example, pays current employees a $2,000 bonus if electrical engineers who are referred are ultimately hired and work for the company for at least one year. While formal systems of referral are more effective in attracting interested applicants, there is also some evidence that the quality of the applicants is less than that which results from an informal system of referrals. Microsoft is presently offering referral incentives to its employees for Internet experts of all shapes and sizes.

Referrals increase job tenure

Referrals by friends and family have been found to increase job tenure (and decrease voluntary job turnover) even for jobs with high turnover rates. The "referred" job candidates tend to have a more realistic understanding of the job when they take it and thus have more accurate expectations about the job and the organization. But before we get too excited about an employee referral program, let's not forget about Abercrombie and Fitch. A&F encouraged its mostly beautiful but also mostly white sales staff to recruit its beautiful customers and friends to become sales personnel. The result was a Title VII race discrimination lawsuit that A&F settled for $40 million.

EEOC v. Detroit Edison

The extensive use of employee referrals can thus cause EEO problems. In *EEOC v. Detroit Edison,* the court concluded that "the practice of relying on referrals by a predominantly white workforce rather than seeking new employees in the marketplace for jobs was discriminatory."[32] Of course, this may not be a problem if the workforce is diverse to begin with, if the organization relies on other methods of recruiting as well, or if the organization offers a referral program that specifically targets minorities and women. Coca-Cola and Disney are among the many large corporations that offer targeted referral programs, another of the recommendations from the OFCCP Revised Order #4. Coca-Cola agreed to target African-Americans in recruiting as a part of their out-of-court race discrimination settlement.

OFCCP Order #4

Advertising: A third common method for recruiting is advertising. Advertising can range from a simple classified ad to an elaborate media campaign through radio or television to attract applicants. The approach can be quite versatile in its ability to provide information about job opportunities while targeting specific labor markets in particular geographical areas. While the majority of advertising is in newspapers, many organizations go beyond the typical newspaper ads for tight labor markets. You have undoubtedly seen one of the commercials extolling the virtues of "starting your career" in our armed forces. Comcast, GTE, and Dow Chemical are also among the companies that use television to attract applicants for hard-to-fill positions.[33] Some budgets for classified print ads have been cut because of the Internet. Diane Schlageter, director of employment for Adobe Systems in San Jose, says Adobe has dropped its ad budget by 60 to 70 percent in favor of Internet . "A half-page ad in the San Jose *Mercury News* may be $15,000 to $18,000. You can do a lot of stuff online for that amount of money," says Schlageter.[34] As discussed below, employer advertising on the Web is now the norm.

Required information for advertising

Most experts agree that advertising through any media (including the Internet) should contain the following information:

1. The job content (primary tasks and responsibilities).

2. A realistic description of working conditions, particularly if they are unusual.

3. The location of the job.

4. The compensation, including the fringe benefits.

5. Job specifications (e.g., education, experience).

6. To whom one applies.[35]

Figure 5-13   **Advantages and Disadvantages of Recruitment Media**

Medium	Advantages	Disadvantages
Internet	Global reach	Many unmotivated applicants
	Fast processing	EEO/Diversity problems
	Relatively inexpensive	Not effective for low-skilled jobs
	Appeals to youth	Spam class (if e-mail)
	Technologically savvy	
	More information about job	
Newspapers/Magazines	Local audience	Often ignored/not seen
	Tailored to audience	Expensive
	Specialty outlets	Long lead time
	Good circulation	
	Good yield ratios for low-skilled jobs	
Direct Mail	Can be well targeted with good list	Expensive (for better mailing lists)
		Very long lead time
Televison/Radio	Targeted locally	Very expensive
	More attention to ad	Longest lead time
	Can attract people not seeking a job	Less information regarding jobs

Source: Adapted from "Planning for Recruitment Advertising: Part II," by B. S. Hodes, copyright 1983.

Since advertising can be very expensive, **yield ratios** on the successes of the various media sources can help to identify the approaches with the biggest potential payoff for future recruiting. Figure 5-13 presents a summary of some of the advantages and disadvantages of the various media options. A section to follow will examine online recruiting in particular.

EEO considerations are also critical for advertising.[36] A men's clothing retailer decided to target younger men with their new fall line. As part of that effort, they advertised for "young, energetic" assistant managers at the same time they were firing a 48-year-old man who had been with the company for 10 years. An ADEA lawsuit resulted in an out-of-court settlement in excess of $100,000. Obviously, a person knowledgeable about EEO laws should review all ad copy for potential legal problems.

There are several excellent outlets for targeted advertising to minorities and women. Monster.com allows job seekers to search for positions using diversity organizations as a search criterion (see http://diversity.monster.com). Most highly regarded African-American universities have Web sites that post résumés of new graduates. Many universities place their ads in a newspaper known as *Black Issues* in an effort to attract more minority applicants.

Employment Agencies: Employment agencies are used by many companies for identifying potential workers. There are publicly funded agencies that provide free placement services and private agencies that charge either the employee or the employer for a placement or referral. The major functions of these agencies are to increase the pool of possible applicants and to do preliminary screening. Private agencies are most effective when (1) the organization has had difficulty in building a pool of qualified applicants, (2) the organization is not equipped to develop a sophisticated recruitment effort, (3) there is a need to fill a position quickly, (4) the organization is explicitly recruiting minorities or females, and (5) the organization is attempting to recruit individuals who are not actively seeking employment.[37]

Persons seeking unemployment compensation must register with a state-run employment agency with some funding from the U.S. Department of Labor. All persons drawing unemployment compensation must apply through one of these agencies. The most recent approach to job placement is to attempt a matching of applicants' aptitudes and interests with the requirements of the job. In general, neither employers nor employees are satisfied with the service that is offered, but efforts are being made to improve the service.[38]

EPOs and RPOs

Search Firms: Search firms are private companies that help employers find and hire employees. These firms used to specialize in executive recruiting and placement, but there are now many specialized firms for specific occupations (e.g., IT, nursing, psychologists) and full-service companies that handle all aspects of recruiting. A growing number of companies now use employment process outsourcing (EPO), also known as recruitment process outsourcing (RPO). These are search and recruiting firms that can handle all or a part of a company's recruiting. EPOs are the fourth-largest component of HR being outsourced and the fastest growing, according to Allan Schweyer, executive director of the Human Capital Institute (HCI). InSearch Worldwide Corp. surveyed 300 HR executives about professional-level EPO and found that more than 30 percent of companies are doing at least some recruitment outsourcing.

Recommendations for selecting search firms

In selecting a search firm, experts recommend the following criteria:

1. The firm should recruit in a specific industry.

2. The firm pays its sales personnel based on the completion of an assignment.

3. The firm uses primary data sources rather than secondary sources such as computerized lists of potential candidates and association directories.

4. Firms that also do outplacement services are not recommended (outplacement is professional services for terminated employees that may include placement in another job). Many socially responsible organizations are turning to outplacement programs to assist terminated employees, especially after major downsizing actions.

5. Ensure the firm provides a placement guarantee, typically 30, 60, or 90 days. This gives the organization a specified amount of time to review the employee on the job and receive a refund if a candidate's skills do not meet the requirements of the organization.

6. The firm should also have a recruitment strategy in writing. You would not allow a contractor to build your house without a blueprint, so why would you allow a search firm to staff your organization without a specific plan? This defined process also ties back to your placement guarantee.[39]

7. The firm should not charge a fee to candidates. Charging a fee to candidates limits the number of qualified candidates the search firm can draw on, thereby dramatically limiting the pool of qualified candidates.

8. The firm should be able to provide references from both clients and candidates who have used their services in the past.

"Targeted" recruiters

Many search firms now specialize in "targeted" recruiting for many jobs.[40] Recruitment in a specific industry helps ensure the search firm understands the specific needs of the organization and industry, thereby increasing the probability the candidate placement will be a success. One of the largest firms is DHR International, which for one fee provides a list of candidates whose credentials match job specifications and, for an additional fee, completes the search process. AON Consulting specializes in human resource management practices in Russia, including job recruiting and job placement.

A good source for identifying a qualified search firm is Recruiterlink.com. This Web site helps managers who are responsible for identifying qualified search firms which specialize in over 50 areas such as CEO search, financial services, consumer products, information technology, marketing, and telecommunications. Recruiterlink.com has a database of over 400 executive headhunters, from some of largest firms such as Korn/Ferry to so-called "boutique" recruiters. These recruiters specialize in jobs starting at annual salaries of $125,000. Recruiters pay a $500-a-year fee to be included in the database.

At this Web site, an organization's representative identifies a specialty area, provides geographic specifications (including international), the average salary handled, and other criteria. A list of potential recruiters is then provided with fees and recent experiences/assignments. This is all free to the "searcher" of the search firm.

In addition to negotiating fees, many organizations are developing partnerships with a select group of search firms, known as preferred vendors. The goal of the preferred vendor relationship is that the search firm is better able to match candidates not only on job

155

specifications but also on fit to the organization's culture. In addition, the partnership allows organizations to maintain control over how the organization's open positions are marketed since the search firm has intimate knowledge of the company. The partnership relationship is often mutually beneficial to both parties since the company receives highly qualified candidates and the recruiter has inside knowledge of the "unwritten" needs of the organization.

Search firm fees are high

The fees for search firms can be very high, with estimates ranging from 20 to 50 percent of the first-year salaries of the individuals placed. The reviews on the effectiveness of search firms are mixed. According to one review, 50 percent of the fulfilled job searches take twice as long to fill as promised. Less than 50 percent of contracts to fill positions are ever fulfilled.[41] More search firms are now charging a flat rate rather than a percentage of salary. Says one recruiter, "By charging a flat rate, we are able to remain objective in presenting candidates to the client. We do not show only the high-priced candidates; we show the most qualified." Many companies have begun to demand the flat-fee approach because of the tendency of percentage-based recruiters to recommend high-priced candidates.[42] A sliding scale fee structure can be negotiated so that as the total number of placements increases the fee percentage decreases.

Campus Visits: One major source of recruiting for professional and managerial positions is the college campus.[43] Numerous organizations, and, in particular, the larger organizations, send recruiters to campuses once or twice a year to inform graduates and future graduates about career opportunities. One survey found that 59 percent of all managers and professionals with less than three years' experience were hired through college recruiting.[44] There is no question that college recruiting is successful at filling vacancies. There is a question as to the extent to which the vacancies are filled with people most likely to be successful within the organization. Some companies report turnover rates in excess of 50 percent for new college graduates after only one year.

College recruiting costs are high

The cost of college recruiting can be enormous. Estimates now run as high as $6,000 per hired graduate.[45] Despite this substantial cost, program evaluation is rarely done and little attention is placed on recruiting processes. When evaluation has been done, the criterion for evaluation was simply filled vacancies or number of offers accepted rather than a measure of the quality of those who are recruited or retention rates. Recruiters often receive little guidance on interviewing procedures, despite evidence that the interviewing format is important for the accuracy of the predictions that are made.

The recruiting process should commence long before there are any visits to the campus. Recruiters should get familiar with the university and university personnel before their visit. Job descriptions and specifications should be mailed to the campus before the recruiter arrives.

Internships

Another good strategy is to set up internship programs through the university. In general, the most effective college recruiting efforts are those that facilitate a long-term relationship with the college through a variety of cooperative programs between the school and the organization. Again, record keeping on past experience will be very helpful in planning future campus recruiting. **Campus.monster.com** and **internshipprogram.com** are great sources for internships. Both sites help students locate internships by geography, industry, and salary.

Videoconferencing

Some companies use videoconferencing at college campuses. This allows for interviewing that is much more cost effective than traditional face-to-face interviewing. The extent to which videoconferencing is an effective approach to recruiting is another empirical question. There is now a need to compare the effects (and costs) of campus visits with recruiting (and interviewing) through the Internet. Most college graduates are now capable of going online and may not be adversely affected by highly efficient, computerized recruiting and interviewing.[46]

One of the largest recruiters of college graduates is the federal government. Research on the ability of the government to attract the most qualified graduates is not encouraging. One survey found only 38 percent of graduates interested in careers with the federal government. The private sector was viewed as offering more prestige and power than the public sector.[47] The research also indicated that the government could do a much better job recruiting graduates by more on-campus visits and a concerted effort at dissolving the negative public image.

Two other sources for recruiting that should be mentioned are professional associations and computerized services. The first is professional societies or associations within specialized areas. College faculty for management departments, for example, are often recruited through the Academy of Management (www.aomonline.org) and other academic associations. The Society of Human Resource Management has a placement service available for jobs in all aspects of HR (SHRM.org).

Newly minted MBAs and companies seeking project-related help should consult mbaglobalnet.com. As of 2008, this site charged the employer to post a job for 60 days on the career center. The site then e-mails members new jobs every Tuesday. In addition, the site provides a project worker hiring service and charges 15 percent of the contract. MBAs register on the site for free.

Electronic Recruiting on the World Wide Web

The Conference Board, a business research organization, estimated that 4,833,700 job vacancies were posted online in August 2008.[48] Electronic job descriptions and résumés are now retrievable from numerous recruitment Web sites. The big three sites are **Monster.com, careerBuilder.com** and **Yahoo Hot Jobs.com,** but there are an estimated 5,000 job boards on the Web. Figure 5-14 presents a list of some of the major sites and the costs to the employer. Of course, Craiglist.org is free to all (and quite effective).

The most popular job site is Monster.com, which claims to have more than 500,000 jobs in its databank. *Forbes* magazine named Monster the best job hunting site on the Web based on its design, navigation, content, speed, and customization. As of May 2008, Monster had over 75 million searchable résumés, with an average of 27,000 résumés being added daily and over 1.9 million job postings. Job seekers conduct 4.1 million job searches *daily* at Monster. There are many niche sites on the Web too. Computer-related specialists should check out techies.com or dice.com. There are specialty sites for doctors, pharmacists, toxicologists, and even highly paid executives. (check out The Ladders.com). Those seeking nonprofit work should check out Idealist.org.

Nearly 100 percent of global 500 companies are now posting jobs on their own Web sites. Some companies accept only online applications. When Hewlett-Packard (HP) was looking for an engineer with specific programming skills and five years' experience who could speak Spanish, the software screened the résumés and identified three applicants who met these specifications. While the efficiency of this approach should be obvious, some problems with the software as it reads the résumés can create errors in the search and eliminate applicants who otherwise would have survived at least the initial screening. For example, if you misspell a key word, you could be out of luck.

Excellent software tracking is now available. **Resumix Inc.,** for example, contains 10 million terms related to various industries, including terms such as *application design* and *general ledger* for specialized programmer and accounting applications. Some companies report substantial savings in recruiting and advertising due to this type of software tracking system. HP claims to have over 330,000 résumés in its database. Needless to say, they avoid a paperwork nightmare with the "virtual recruiter" system. They recently received over 100,000 résumés in the staffing of 1,400 new hires.

"Virtual" recruiter system

Recruiting in the very near future may go something like this for most large companies:

1. A line manager completes a standardized job analysis questionnaire on the Internet identifying employment needs for the unit; the questionnaire may include job location and other details of the job in addition to the critical job specifications.

2. The completed questionnaire is then automatically converted into a job posting on the Internet and matched with a current database of "candidates" whose credentials are entered using the same terminology as the job analysis.

3. A list of candidates is identified based on the match of job specifications with job credentials.

4. Almost instantaneously, the line manager has a list of minimally qualified candidates with whom s/he can interact.

5. A testing and interview format (with job-related questions), in compliance with all EEO guidelines, is derived from the same job analysis information completed at step 1.

6. Using the testing/interview material, additional data are collected on the candidates through e-mail and/or Web camera and a list of top candidates is compiled.

157

Figure 5-14 **Recruitment Web Site Comparisons**

Web Sites	Search Options	Job Search Database	Ease of Use for Searcher	Costs for One-Time Posting	Employer Benefits
Monster.com	Location Industry/Job Keyword Employer	**Position/Title**—click and view job description **Company**—search by company name to see all job postings **Posted date**—sorted by most recent; can limit date range **Salary**—not searchable; must click job description to view	• Site easy to use • Can search by company from basic search	1 job/60 days/ $385 on average (differs by state)	• Online database search • Track statistics of each job posting • Search agents (automatically generated list of potential candidates) • International postings available • Company profiles • Diversity section • Likely one of the most recognized job boards by job seekers
Hotjobs.yahoo.com	Location Industry/Job Keyword Employer	**Position/Title**—click and view job description **Company**—click and view all job postings from specific company **Posted date**—sorted by most recent; can limit date range **Salary**—searchable in advanced search; must click job description to view	• Site easy to use • Can search by company; requires change in search option • Search by industry/job was easy to use since further specified state and city	1 job/30 days/ $349	• Online database search • Unlimited job posting changes permitted • Track statistics on each job posting • E-mail potential candidates • Jobs can be posted in U.S. and Canada • Company profile
Careerbuilder.com	Location Industry/Job Keyword Employer	**Position/Title**—click and view job description **Company**—click and view all job postings (must conduct a search first) **Posted date**—sorted by most recent; can limit date range **Salary**—searchable in advanced search; listed on search results page	• Site easy to use • Can search by company; requires change in search option • Site moderately easy to navigate • Cannot search for positions from home page	1 job/30 days/ $419	• Online database search • Additional services such as prescreened candidates, background checks, career fairs • International postings available • Company profile
Employmentguide.com	Location Industry/Job Keyword Employer	**Position/Title**—click and view position **Company**—click and view all positions by employer (sorted alphabetically) **Posted date**—sorted by most recent; cannot limit date **Salary**—not searchable or provided separately	• Site moderately easy to navigate • Cannot search for positions from home page	1 job/30 days/ $350	• Online database search • Entry level to middle management positions (hourly and nonexempt positions)

(continued)

Figure 5-14 *(Continued)*

Web Sites	Search Options	Job Search Database	Ease of Use for Searcher	Costs for One-Time Posting	Employer Benefits
Careerjournal.com	Location Industry/Job Keyword Employer	**Position/Title**—click and view position **Company**—click and view all job postings **Posted date**—sorted by most recent; cannot limit date **Salary**—not searchable or provided separately	• Site moderately easy to navigate • Cannot search for positions from home page	1 job/30 days/ $325	• Online database search (300,000+ résumés) • Diversity career fairs • Brief company overview (Briefing Book) • Partnership with 150+ media sources so positions are posted to additional sites • International job postings
Flipdog.com	Location Industry/Job Keyword Employer	**Position/Title**—click and view position **Company**—click and view all job postings **Posted date**—sorted by most recent; cannot limit date **Salary**—does not include a separate section listing salary	• Site moderately easy to navigate • Advanced search method is interactive and may be confusing for novice job board users	1 job/30 days/ $125	• Online database search • International job postings
Idealist.org (www.idealist.org)	Location Sector/Job Keyword	**Position/Title**—click and view job description **Organization**—click and view all positions by employer (once original search has been completed) **Posted date**—sorted by most recent **Salary**—not searchable but is listed in the search results	• Site easy to navigate	Free	• Online database search • International postings • Non-profiles provided

Source: Contributed by Renee Bartlett.

"Cyber" recruiter

Note that the word *candidates* is used first rather than *applicants* because résumés of qualified persons may be retrieved from Web databases and personnel Web sites and these potential candidates may or may not be interested in a particular job opportunity. They are simply alerted to the new job and then decide whether they wish to become applicants. A new and hot HR position today is "Internet" or "cyber" recruiter. These folks are specialists in locating and placing people off job Web sites. Many also coordinate all Web recruiting activities for companies. There are already 20,000 members of the **Association of Internet Recruiters** (see Recruitersnetwork. com). One of these cyber recruiters boasts that he can access the résumé of every IBM employee.

It is clear that the Internet has great potential for expediting the recruiting process. The scenario above should be contrasted with the more traditional methods of recruiting we have described. Of course, the Internet approach depends on potential job applicants being aware of this convenient method and amenable to the process. A great place to start for both employers and job seekers is **the Riley Guide** which provides loads of free information and links to numerous recruitment sites.

A great Web site for college students is www.campus.monster.com. The site has internships, résumé services, and job listings for students and partnerships with over 1,000 universities. Monster's site is a comprehensive source for first-time job seekers with excellent information on valuable internships.

A major concern for organizations is reaching diversity candidates online. The digital divide between white users and minorities has been a concern of many HR practitioners. There is recent evidence that the differences in Internet access are closing fast. According to the Pew Internet & American Life Project, 75 percent of whites have access to the Internet, while 64 percent of African-Americans and 68 percent of Hispanics have Internet access. Yet, the yearly Internet adoption rate is growing rapidly in African-American and Hispanic households.

What Methods of Recruiting Are Most Effective?

There have been few studies that have compared the effects of different methods for recruitment. The criteria that have been used in these studies also differ and include cost per hire, number of résumés, time lapse from recruiting to filling the vacancy, interview/invitation ratio, applicant performance on the job, and job tenure or turnover. One critical question is obviously how people are findings jobs these days. A 2007 study (conducted by an Internet consulting firm) found that new employees were first linked to the hiring organization through (in this order):

Best "new hire" links to employer

1. Online job boards;
2. Staffing and executive search firms;
3. Tips from friends and family members;
4. Networking in a business context;
5. Career/job fairs;
6. Newspapers.

This order does change as a function of the particular industry, the particular company, and the particular job. In general, the above are the best sources for effective recruiting from the perspective of the job seeker. What are the worst? According to those seeking employment, here are the top five *least* helpful sources for employment opportunities:

Least helpful employment sources

1. Networking at a social event (least effective);
2. Answering an ad in a publication of a professional association;
3. Using a social networking site;
4. Sending a résumé directly to an employer;
5. Responding to a notice posted in a store.[49]

EEOC definition of an "applicant"

A recent emphasis also has been placed on understanding minority hiring patterns as a function of the recruiting effort and relative to population statistics and census data on potential employees. These comparisons may be critical if EEO litigation is pending. The EEOC has stated that the definition of an "applicant" depends upon the user's recruitment and selection procedures. The concept of an applicant is that of a person who has indicated an interest in being considered for hiring, promotion, or other employment opportunities. This interest might be expressed by completing an application form, or might be expressed orally, depending on the employer's practice, or through the Internet and related electronic technologies only. According to the EEOC, in order for an individual to be an applicant in the context of the Internet and related electronic data-processing technologies, the following must have occurred: (1) the employer has acted to fill a particular position; (2) the individual has followed the employer's standard procedures for submitting applications; and (3) the individual has indicated an interest in the particular position.

Attraction outcomes

Figure 5-15 presents a list of some of the most important criteria that could be used to evaluate different approaches to recruiting and the extent to which companies collect such data. One excellent study emphasizes the importance of "attraction outcomes" as a recruitment outcome that should be emphasized when evaluating recruitment practices. Attraction outcomes emphasize (and measure) the quality of the applicant pool as a function of the recruitment source. The authors argue that "adopting methods for evaluating attraction outcomes may be the single most valuable step organizations can take toward improving recruitment effectiveness."[50] They emphasize a more systematic measurement process that includes detail on the methods used to screen candidates. Figure 5-16 presents their

Figure 5-15 **Criteria for Evaluating Recruitment Activities and the Extent to Which They Are Measured**

Most Frequently Used Measures for Evaluating Recruiting Program Effectiveness

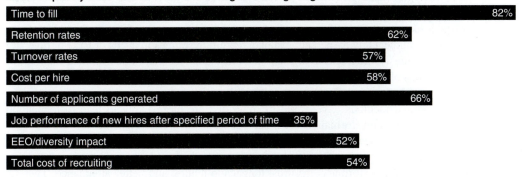

Time to fill	82%
Retention rates	62%
Turnover rates	57%
Cost per hire	58%
Number of applicants generated	66%
Job performance of new hires after specified period of time	35%
EEO/diversity impact	52%
Total cost of recruiting	54%

Source: H. J. Bernardin, "A Survey of SHRM Member Recruiting Practices and Criteria for Evaluation," 2009. Manuscript under review.

Calculate yield ratios for each recruiting source

seven-step plan for assessing attraction outcomes. Their plan includes estimates of the economic yield or utility from each source. Yield ratios are important but there should be close scrutiny of the criteria used to qualify candidates from one recruitment step to the next. Obviously, a recruitment source that yields a high proportion of "qualified" candidates is important but a more fine-tuned analysis will provide more useful definitions of "qualified" that include comparative "scores" on these qualified candidates.

Figure 5-16 **Assessing Attraction Outcomes: A Step-by-Step Overview**

STEP 1: IDENTIFY POSITIONS TO ASSESS

Description: Organizations may choose not to develop scores to evaluate recruitment outcomes for all positions. Those positions where assessment of attraction outcomes is likely to be of greatest value are jobs that generate several new hires and attract large numbers of applicants. Calculate yield ratios for each recruitment source.

STEP 2: IDENTIFY CURRENT SCREENING METHOD AND DETERMINE CURRENT PROPERTIES

Description: Organizations need to identify the current selection methods used at each step in the recruitment process.

STEP 3: DETERMINE STRATEGY FOR ADAPTING CURRENT SCREENING METHOD TO PRODUCE SCORES FOR EACH APPLICANT AND ADAPT CHANGES

Description: Depending on what screening method is currently used, the amount of deviation between current recommended practices and the development of comparable scores for each candidate should be determined.

STEP 4: ASSESS ATTRACTION OUTCOMES

Description: Assess each applicant using the device developed in Step 3. Scores for all applicants in the applicant pool should be evaluated, including those that have left the pool by withdrawing themselves from consideration or because they were hired during the appropriate time period (defined by the organization).

STEP 5: MATCH RECRUITMENT ACTIVITIES TO RECRUITMENT PHASES AND ESTIMATE RECRUITMENT COSTS

Description: In order to evaluate the cost effectiveness of various recruitment practices, recruitment costs must be identified and mapped to the appropriate phase of recruitment (i.e., attraction, status maintenance, gaining job acceptance). Estimate costs of attraction by identifying all activities primarily designed to influence the attraction of applicants to this position.

STEP 6: ESTIMATE INPUT VALUES AND COMPLETE UTILITY ESTIMATES (THIS IS REQUIRED TO COMPLETE EVALUATIONS THAT INCORPORATE BOTH COST AND BENEFIT CONSIDERATIONS)

Description: To be able to use utility analysis to convert differences in quality scores to dollars, several values need to be estimated. These include the validity of screening devices, the standard deviation of performance in dollars for the job in question, the number of individuals to be selected or the subset of candidates to be evaluated, and the average expected tenure of candidates in their positions once hired.

STEP 7: EVALUATE THE ADEQUACY OF CURRENT SCREENING DEVICES

Description: Organizations may decide that alternative screening devices may be more appropriate due to their cost, validity, adverse impact rate, or other properties of the scores they generate.

Source: Adapted from K. D. Carlson, M. L. Connerley, and R. L. Mecham, "Recruitment Evaluation: The Case for Assessing the Quality of Applicants Attracted," *Personnel Psychology* 55 (2002), pp. 461–490.

The Discrepancy between Research and Practice

Unfortunately, there is little systematic research on the effects of recruiting options using any of these criteria. Despite calls for systematic research on the effects of various approaches to recruiting, using yield ratios and performance-based criteria, few companies have strategic measurement criteria for evaluating recruitment and recruitment sources. One survey found that only 53 percent of companies even had a formal system for evaluating their recruiting. Only 35 percent look at the job performance of new hires relative to recruitment source. Only 52 percent evaluate recruiting sources in terms of EEO or diversity issues. Obviously, the tracking of such vital criteria is essential in determining the relative effectiveness of the various recruiting options.

Academics recommend yield ratios

Informal methods related to longer tenure

In general, the limited comparative studies on recruitment methods suggest that the more informal methods (e.g., walk-ins, referrals) are more likely to lead to longer job tenure than the more formal sources, such as newspaper ads. The Internet now exceeds newspaper ads in generating a large number of applicants for a position compared to the other methods. Another study found that people who had worked for the organization earlier had superior performance records, longer job tenure, and better attendance. There is also evidence that recruiting Generation Y job candidates requires emphasis on unique strategies that can increase success.[51]

Many problems in recruiting may be a consequence of the way in which recruiters are rewarded. You may recall the Army recruiting scandals. One recruiter in Colorado, working under a specific "head count" quota, produced a "Faith Hill High School" diploma for a dropout who was actually not eligible. Research has shown that those criteria that pertain to direct costs of recruiting to the organization are the ones on which recruiters are typically evaluated.[52]

For example, recruiters for a large manufacturing company in the South are compensated in relation to a "cost per hire" measure or what one staff member refers to as the "warm body" phenomenon. This emphasis on cost figures may explain the general lack of systematic research relating recruiting methods to higher-level criteria such as work quality. In the context of affirmative action, those persons assigned to meet specific EEO goals or timetables often are evaluated on the extent to which they meet the goals or timetables and not the extent to which the positions have been filled with qualified personnel or whether those individuals are successfully retained. The conflicting incentives of recruiters and line management can cause problems when the time comes to make job offers.

The ideal recruiter

The effectiveness of the various methods of recruiting also has been shown to vary as a function of particular method characteristics. In general, research allows us to construct an ideal recruiter: strong interpersonal skills, extensive knowledge of the organization, and enthusiasm for the organization, the job, and the candidates. College recruiting is apparently enhanced when the recruiter is between the ages of 30 and 55, is perceived to have stature in the company (line managers are preferred to professional recruiters), and is verbally fluent with good interpersonal skills and an extensive knowledge of the company and the particular job.[53] The success of any recruiting effort, however, is more dependent on the job (and offer) characteristics themselves. College students place the greatest weight on pay, fringe benefits, and the type of work. Recruiters often underestimate the importance of such factors relative to others.[54]

Figure 5-17 presents a summary of the latest research findings on recruitment and practical applications. Figure 5-18 summarizes the sparse research on recruiting the Millennial generation.

What Are the Effects of the Internet?

Despite its great potential, the Internet is not necessarily a panacea for all organizations and all jobs. The track record to date is not all that impressive.[55] One CEO of a marketing development company said, "Unless you're looking for programmers in some cutting-edge technology, you're kind of out of luck." While others would certainly disagree with such a sweeping conclusion, there is limited empirical evidence showing Web-based recruiting to be superior to other recruiting options for the most important criteria for assessing the recruitment effort. While the 2007 survey alluded to earlier found favorable results for online recruiting, other research is not as strong (the 2007 survey was conducted by an Internet recruiting company). A 2005 survey found that most small computer-related businesses regarded Internet recruiting as "useful." Less than 50 percent of respondents from all other sectors regarded it as useful.[56]

The Internet will certainly give you a lot of résumés and fast. But whether the Internet facilitates the faster hiring of better people at relatively lower cost has not yet been

Figure 5-17 **Recruitment Research and Practical Applications**

Research Finding	Practical Applications
Recruitment sources affect the characteristics of applicants attracted.	Use sources such as referrals (e.g., from current employees) that yield applicants less prone to turnover and more likely to be better performers.
Recruitment materials have a more positive impact if they contain more specific information.	Provide applicants with information on aspects of the job that are important to them, such as salary, location, and diversity.
Organizational image influences applicants' initial reactions to employers.	Ensure all communications regarding an organization provide a positive message regarding the corporate image and the attractiveness of the organization as a place to work.
Applicants with a greater number of job opportunities are more attentive to and more influenced by early recruitment activities than those with fewer opportunities (i.e., less marketable individuals).	Ensure initial recruitment activities (e.g., Web site, brochure, on-campus recruiting) are as attractive to candidates as later activities.
Recruiter demographics have a relatively small effect on applicants' attraction to the organization.	Worry less about matching recruiter/applicant demographics and more about the content of recruiting messages and the organization's overall image in terms of diversity.
Realistic job previews (e.g., brochures, videos, group discussions that highlight both the advantages and the disadvantages of the job) reduce subsequent turnover.	Provide applicants with a realistic picture of the job and organization, not just the positives.
Applicants will infer job and organizational information based on the organizational image projected and their early interactions with the organization if the information is not clearly provided by the organization.	Provide clear, specific, and complete information in recruitment materials so that applicants do not make erroneous inferences about the nature of the job or the organization as an employer.
Recruiter warmth has a large and positive effect on applicants' decisions to accept a job.	Individuals who have contact with applicants should be chosen for their interpersonal skills.
Applicants' beliefs in a "good fit" between their values and the organization's influence their job-choice decisions.	Provide applicants with accurate information about what the organization is like so that they can make accurate fit assessments.

Source: Adapted from A. M. Ryan and N. T. Tippins, "Attracting and Selecting: What Psychological Research Tells Us," *Human Resource Management* 43 (2004), p. 311. Reprinted with permission of John Wiley & Sons.

determined except with isolated case studies, usually involving technological jobs. Darlene Chapin, recruiting director for Cheetah Technologies in Florida, claims Internet recruiting for programmers has made the process much more efficient. Even so, she says, Web-based staffing should be a supplement not a replacement for traditional recruiting such as newspaper ads, college outreach, job fairs, and headhunters.

Figure 5-18 **Strategies for Recruiting the Millennials**

1. Put More Emphasis on Employee Referrals

While this strategy works for all generations, some headhunters argue that Yers are particularly deferential to company referrals. Millennials are active internal recruiters because they like an active role in picking their peers.

2. Offer Job Internships and Job Tryouts

Paid summer internships (often between junior and senior years of college) are becoming more common. The interns are given many work sample tryouts. Says one prominent headhunter, "The key to retaining young guns is to give them different opportunities throughout the business."

3. "TLK 2 Them"

Millennials are impressed with and attracted to companies with "high tech" recruitment. Electronic communications (videos about the organization, executive blogs) are important elements of recruitment and more valued by the Millennials.

4. Offer Flexible Work Arrangements

Options such as telecommuting or remote working arrangements are more valued by this generation as they tend to question why actual "face" time is really necessary when Internet-based communication is more efficient and, as one Yer put it, "I can do it in my underwear without spending time or gas money."

5. Offer Sabbaticals and Time Off for Community/Volunteer Service

Millennials are more attracted to "green" companies and jobs that offer time off for community service and volunteer work. They are more attracted to companies regarded as "socially responsible."

6. Offer Pay Packages with More Pay at Risk and a Closer Link with Performance and Productivity

Millennials like a closer link between their work products and their pay through pay-for-performance systems. In some segments (e.g., technology), they particularly like stock options as a part of the pay package.

Resume overload

One of the major problems reported with Internet recruiting is the volume of résumés received, the so-called résumé overload. Many recruiters simply download all the "applications." While this type of recruiting will surely get you more applications and faster, the process can be quite inefficient without a strategy for classifying, rating, or ranking résumés based on a matching process between job specifications and candidates' KASOCs or competencies.

"Artificial intelligence" for scoring

More companies are now using online structured approaches to screening that require applicants to submit biographical information according to a specific format. The format allows for an automatic "scoring" of biographical and other information and thus a classification scheme for candidates. This "artificial intelligence" approach allows for greater control over information gathering and storage and has the potential for better decision making. One discrepancy between academic research and personnel practice is the clear finding in research that statistical or actuarial decision making based on the valid weighting of different sources of information about job candidates results in more effective staffing decisions compared to the way personnel decisions are normally made where an evaluator forms a general impression based on an overall evaluation of the information about candidates.

When done properly, "artificial intelligence" can lead to more intelligent decision making. One study reported a 270 percent increase in productivity using an automated résumé scoring system. One expert recommends the following strategies for processing résumés: (1) optimize the e-mail system by pushing candidates to particular job folders; (2) use auto-response e-mails with valid, prequalifying questions or conditions (certain required job specifications); (3) drive candidates to apply online at your Web site so valid scores can be derived based on relevant biographical, competency-based information; and (4) use an outsourced staffing or résumé screening service.[57] This expert is also the co-founder of a company called PeopleBonus that offers this very service (check out their Web site). There is

Millennials more receptive to on-line recruiting

no question that the Millennial generation is more receptive to Internet recruiting, online applications, and even online "interviews." Figure 5-18 presents a summary of the unique elements to Gen Y recruiting.

Two Philosophies of Recruiting: Flypaper versus Matching

The traditional philosophy of recruiting has been to get as many people to apply for a job as possible. The idea is based on trying to obtain the lowest possible selection ratio given a fixed recruiting cost. A **selection ratio (SR)** is the proportion of job openings to applicants. An SR of .10 means there are 10 applicants for every job opening. A lower selection ratio is generally more desirable because it enables the organization to choose job candidates from a larger pool of qualified candidates, thereby increasing selectivity. Research

Lower SRs are characteristic of HPWS

on **High-Performance Work Systems,** first introduced in Chapter 1, clearly shows that more successful firms have significantly lower selection ratios than less successful firms for key positions.

This assumption holds true as long as the cost of recruiting and subsequent screening is not exorbitant and applicants for the job are at least minimally qualified. In general, selection ratios go down when companies are admired by the working public. For example, the number of job applicants is up for most of *Fortune* magazine's "2008 Best Companies" (e.g., Google, Starbucks, Cisco Systems, JM Family Enterprises, SAS, Southwest Airlines) relative to competitors that did not make the list.

Unfortunately, the wars in Iraq and Afghanistan have had a negative effect on military recruiting. However, the projections were more favorable for all branches for 2009 because of the decrease of violence in Iraq, the improved educational benefits now offered to vets, and the high unemployment rate. The percentage of new Army recruits who are black has fallen significantly since the Iraq war. Army research has determined that some of the decline is due to the unpopularity of the war in Iraq among blacks. Projections of black recruitment for 2009 on are more favorable.

Of course, what is critical is that the increases in the applicant pool reflect at least minimally qualified applicants. Many companies express disappointment with Web-based recruiting because of the labor involved in processing a larger collection of résumés, many of which are not really a close match to the requirements of the job. In circumstances where the "quality" of the candidates is most important, along with the attraction of people who are more likely to stay longer, the "matching" philosophy of recruitment may be more efficient.[58] A persuasive argument can be made that matching the needs of the organization to the needs of the applicant will enhance the recruitment process. The result will be a workforce that is more likely to stay with the organization longer and perform at a higher level of effectiveness for a longer period of time. In the context of this matching philosophy, a process of realistic recruitment is recommended. An important component of realistic recruiting is a **realistic job preview (RJP).** RJPs provide the characteristics of the job to applicants so they can evaluate the compatibility of this realistic presentation of the job with their own work preferences. St. Petersburg, Florida, police recruits are shown a video depicting the realistic life of a St. Petersburg police officer. Recruits are told that each arrest they make entails hours of paperwork. RJPs can result in a self-selection process that screens out people most likely to have difficulty on the job. Those applicants who are hired after being exposed to an RJP are also better able to cope because of more realistic expectations about the job.[59] It is said that RJPs "vaccinate" applicants by lowering their unrealistic expectations and bringing them more in line with actual work conditions.

Many companies doing international work provide extensive RJPs for potential expatriates and their families. Bechtel, the giant construction company, provides a 60-minute video of life in Saudi Arabia that engineers and their spouses view before they make a commitment for a one-year assignment. Research on realistic recruiting shows lower rates of employee turnover for employees recruited with RJPs, particularly for more complex jobs, and higher levels of job satisfaction and performance at the initial stages of employment. RJPs are more beneficial for organizations hiring at the entry level, when there are low selection ratios (i.e., many applicants per position), and under conditions of relatively low unemployment (i.e., where people have more job options). Otherwise, the approach may increase the cost of recruiting by increasing the average time it takes to fill each position.[60] RJPs are developed using job analysis information. The critical incident technique is particularly effective for developing RJPs. RJPs also could be incorporated in job postings on the Internet to facilitate the self-selection process.

Another approach to staffing that fits into the matching philosophy is the use of the **Job Compatibility Questionnaire (JCQ)** discussed in Chapter 4.[61] The JCQ provides a quantitative match between job applicant preferences and the actual characteristics of a job, including compensation system characteristics, benefits, work schedule, and, of course, the characteristics of the actual work to be performed. The JCQ results have also been used to construct a realistic job preview and to redesign high-turnover jobs. A study of customer service representatives at one Tribune Company newspaper found that the combination of JCQ as a selection device plus the RJP after the job offer was conveyed reduced voluntary turnover by 35 percent and increased the job satisfaction of the workforce.[62] An instrument such as the JCQ also could be incorporated into a standardized job analysis method for downloading from the Internet. Since the JCQ and the RJP will reduce the pool of potential qualified candidates, these approaches should be used in conjunction with a stronger recruitment effort in order to increase the pool of potential candidates.

Understanding the Recruits

Effective recruiting requires that the organization know what potential applicants are thinking and what their needs and desires are regarding all major characteristics of the job. For example, how important are the various elements of the fringe benefit package? Are applicants interested in special work schedules, child care, particular work locations? Organizations also need to be keenly aware of how candidates search for jobs. What outlets do they rely on for job information? To what extent do they rely on outside referral agencies for job placement? Should recruitment be restricted to specific geographical areas based on the search behavior of potential candidates? At least some answers to these questions can be gathered over time based on the past recruiting successes and failures of the organization. Recruitment is one area of HRM where a computerized system of detailed record keeping would be most beneficial for recruiting efforts in the future.

Realistic job preview

Job Compatibility Questionnaire

Unfortunately, most organizations rely on recruiter "hunches" to make decisions and do little to organize their past recruiting efforts in such a way that systematic research could help to determine their future strategies. Research indicates that these "hunches" are not particularly accurate. A better strategy is to rely on the research that is summarized in Figures 5-17 and 5-18 and to understand that whom you are recruiting has a lot to do with the success of any given strategy.[63]

Human Resource Planning and Recruitment for Multinational Corporations*

The majority of Fortune 500 companies are now multinational in nature and a sizable portion of their business (and profits) is derived from overseas operations. As discussed in Chapter 2, some of our largest, most prestigious companies (e.g., Microsoft, IBM, GE, McDonald's, Coca-Cola) derive close to (or over) 50 percent of their revenues from overseas business. Unfortunately, with few exceptions, the relationship between HR planning and strategic planning for international ventures is even weaker than for U.S. operations despite the fact that many experts regard human resource issues as even more important to the success of an overseas operation than of a domestic operation. Efforts are being made to enhance the recruiting and success of expatriates. As illustrated in Figure 5-19, some companies are responding by consolidating the external hiring requirements and gaining expertise in overseas staffing needs.

As discussed in Chapter 2, international HRM is more complicated than domestic HRM. All of the planning and recruitment are more unpredictable because of potentially volatile environmental and political issues in the host country that can affect the overseas operations. For example, after considerable success penetrating the Japanese market, Milwaukee-based Harley-Davidson has had to respond to considerable political pressure directed at restricting their growth in Japan. The pressure is affecting their forecasts of market penetration in Japan.

Terrorism is something taken seriously all over the world. Before September 11, 2001, terrorism was a concern for Americans with regard to overseas assignments. Needless to say (and unfortunately), the concern Americans feel when they ponder overseas assignments regarding potential problems may now be shared by workers of other nations who are considering assignments to U.S. cities.

The implications of the European Community remain unclear in terms of many HRM activities. With few exceptions (e.g., Poland, Yugoslavia), the current state of the economies of most east European nations makes planning and market forecasting for these markets extremely tenuous.

Almost all other HRM activities (e.g., staffing, performance management, reward systems and compliance, and employee development) are more difficult and unpredictable in overseas operations not only because of environmental volatility but because many of the methods within each of these domains that have proven effective in U.S. settings do not necessarily work for international staffing, performance management, and the other domains. The U.S. insurance industry, for example, puts considerable weight on biographical information in the selection of insurance agents. The validity of the method for predicting sales success, discussed in Chapter 6, has never been studied for overseas sales and thus may not apply in the hiring of expatriate Americans, host-country nationals, or third-country nationals.

Within the rewards/compliance domain of HRM activities, issues related to family, housing, dependent care and schooling, spouse employment, taxation, and health care all tend to complicate the international HRM function. These issues also make the economic and psychological implications of errors in international HRM relatively greater than for domestic assignments.[64]

Critical issues for international planning and recruitment

One study identified the critical issues affecting planning and recruitment aspects of international HRM.[65] The major challenges were:

1. Identifying top managerial talent early in the process.

2. Identifying criteria for success in overseas assignments.

3. Motivating employees to take overseas assignments.

4. Establishing a stronger connection between the strategic plan of the company and HR planning.

*This section was contributed by Stephanie Thomason.

Figure 5-19   **International HR Jobs**

Director, Global eRecruiting International, Munich, Germany

Allianz AG, a global leader in the financial services arena, seeks a highly motivated individual to lead an international team responsible for creating and implementing a comprehensive eRecruiting and employment branding plan and incorporating multiple segmented lead generation tactics that ensure a consistent candidate experience with Allianz and its affiliates.

Requirements:

At least 8 years of Marketing and/or branding experience (project management) in financial services or insurance fields. Recruiting-related marketing experience preferred.

Significant project management experience.

Demonstrated leadership and relationship management abilities.

Sourcing strategist who has developed a total approach to generating leads in a similar environment desired.

Proficient in Internet utilization and Web analysis.

Ability to conduct and report on relevant research.

Bachelor's Degree and/or MBA (e.g., business, economics, marketing) or equivalent.

Work experience abroad (6-month minimum).

HR Director International, Riyadh, Saudi Arabia

New position reporting to COO for one of the world's largest jewelry manufacturing facilities located in Riyadh, SA. Approximately 3,000 employees in seven (7) locations throughout Saudi Arabia. Will be responsible for the development of an effective HR program, building all systems including core competencies and organizational values. Ideal candidate will be fluid in the language, culture, and customs/laws of Middle Eastern manufacturing operations. Excellent salary and benefits package to include housing allowance and relocation. Submit résumé to:

HR Director International, Toronto, Canada

We are one of *Forbes'* 200 Best Small Companies (www.edumgt.com) for the third year in a row. With proprietary colleges throughout the U.S., we have recently acquired three post-secondary institutions specializing in information technology, located in Halifax, Toronto, and Vancouver. We seek a Director of Human Resources for the three locations, to be based in Toronto headquarters.

The Director of Human Resources is a position of leadership within our organization. We seek a seasoned generalist who is familiar with start-ups or acquisitions, and who is able to successfully guide employees through change. The incumbent will possess the ability to integrate HR into key business operations, and to assist senior executives in building an infrastructure with all levels of management, staff, and faculty. Particular emphasis will be placed on organizational development, staffing, compensation, benefits, employee relations, training, and knowledge of provincial employment laws within a tri-site environment.

The successful candidate will possess a broad understanding of HR practices and policies, a minimum Bachelors degree in business, human resources management, or related field and at least seven (7) years of parallel experience in HR management. Some travel will be necessary in order to serve each of the locations.

The environment is challenging and very fast-paced, as well as student and employee-centered. We offer a competitive salary and benefits, with enormous opportunities for advancement. For immediate consideration, your résumé and salary history may be sent via e-mail attachment to:

Identifying top managerial talent in the home and host countries is a recurring problem in international HRM, as noted by the Global Relocation Trends survey (2008). In this survey, 21 percent of respondents cited "finding suitable candidates" as their most significant challenge. Identifying criteria for success, the second challenge listed above, is a complex issue, as performance appraisals and criteria vary as a function of cultural values and norms of the country of assignment. Few experts would argue with the contention that these challenges are more difficult with international planning and recruitment. The third challenge, motivating employees to take overseas assignments, often proves easier to meet, as many executives seeking upward advancement[66] and executives who are open to change and have an adventurous spirit may relish the overseas experience and the immersion into a new culture. Furthermore, the extensive benefit package often provided to expatriates under the commonly used balance sheet approach makes the overseas stay quite comfortable. This package may afford many expatriates the ability to save more while overseas than in the home country. Despite such benefits, some executives refuse to take international assignments.

Family issues a major concern   One study found that "family concerns" was the most common reason for assignment refusal (89 percent), followed by spouse career concerns (62 percent).[67] Family issues remain a challenge throughout the international assignment, as 28 percent of respondents from the same study cited family concerns as their reason for early return. Executives may also refuse the assignment due to the inherent difficulties perceived in the country of assignment. As noted in Chapter 2, the emerging societies of China, India, and Russia present significant cultural and legal problems with which program managers and expatriates must deal.

Repatriation problems   Repatriation policies often are not adequate to meet the needs of returning expatriates. Lawrence Buckley, personnel manager for GE, for example, says the "re-entry process isn't as smooth as we would like it to be." He states that GE is making progress in this area but that it is "still a problem for us and U.S. industry in general."[68] One problem occurs when organizations fail to establish a career development plan for expatriates that takes into account the international experience and knowledge they acquired overseas. This failure may propel expatriates to seek other job alternatives that capitalize on their experience. A second problem occurs when expatriates are placed in lateral positions with less autonomy and freedom than they had enjoyed overseas. Extensive reporting requirements and greater bureaucracy may pose difficulties for executives accustomed to making decisions on their own.[69] A third problem occurs when foreign-service premiums, cost of living allowances, and other benefits and perquisites provided to expatriates while abroad are abruptly terminated. Expatriates, spouses, and children who have grown accustomed to extensive benefits overseas may feel that an abrupt change in lifestyle is unfair, given the expatriates' additional tenure within the company.

Whereas many managers still perceive overseas assignments as a banishment of sorts, corporations now place more and considerable weight on overseas experience as a requirement for high-level executive assignments. For example, Honeywell, Allied-Signal, and Rohm & Haas all require overseas assignments prior to senior management placement. With the increased sophistication of international communications and the growing importance of international operations for corporate strategy, studies showing managers perceiving a loss of visibility at headquarters due to overseas assignments probably apply less today than only a few years ago.

Underlying all HRM challenges is the strategic position of the multinational corporation regarding the relationship of the overseas operation to the parent company.[70] The recruitment strategy for overseas assignments is directly tied to this strategic position. U.S. companies may recruit and select from one (or more) of three sources:

1. The pool of U.S. personnel who would be expatriated to the foreign assignment.

2. The pool of candidates from the country of the overseas operations.

3. Candidates from all nationalities.

Ethnocentrism

Ethnocentrism, the policy of using *only* home-country executives for overseas assignments, really only makes sense either financially or strategically when the company is just starting the operation. Otherwise, the disadvantages of this approach outweigh the advantages. Japanese companies with this philosophy applied to U.S. operations have encountered a number of problems, including a proliferation of equal employment opportunity lawsuits and, in particular, age discrimination cases as Japanese companies replace American managers over the age of 40 with sometimes younger and very often Japanese managers. The use of host-country nationals in overseas operations can reduce language and cultural problems, the need for expensive training programs, and, of course, the tremendous cost of placing expatriates and their families in overseas assignments. This is becoming more common for American companies.[71]

Japanese women may be one major pool of highly skilled workers that American companies could tap for penetration into Japanese markets. Japanese females are still subjected to considerable employment discrimination in their own country and are attracted to U.S. corporations for this reason.

Geocentric policy

The **geocentric policy** of hiring the best person regardless of nationality is the formal policy of choice for most large U.S. corporations but is certainly not without its problems since such a management team may have more difficulties communicating with each other and understanding the subtle implications of cultural differences.

For corporations maintaining a close strategic relationship to the overseas division (as opposed to a philosophy of autonomous operations), the most common strategy for managerial recruitment and job placement for U.S. companies is a balance between expatriates and host- or third-country nationals. Sales and production personnel are typically recruited from the national pool. Companies that have a "hands-off" managerial philosophy toward autonomous foreign operations they may have acquired or developed typically use expatriates in coordination with nationals until the parent company is comfortable with the operation and the profits of the foreign division are acceptable. Most of the expatriates may then be recalled to reduce the overhead of the operation.

SUMMARY

Human resource planning (HRP) seeks to place the right employees in the right jobs at the right time and at the lowest possible cost, thereby providing the means for the organization to pursue its competitive strategy and fulfill its mission. Planning improves the organization's ability to create and sustain competitive advantage and to cope with problems, threats, and opportunities arising from change—technological, social, political, and environmental. HRP and all of its derivatives should always keep the future customer in focus. Reengineering or downsizing programs that lose this focus ultimately may have a negative impact on the organization. HRP systematically attempts to forecast personnel demand, assess supply, and reconcile the two.

Personnel demand can be assessed using qualitative methods such as the Delphi technique and quantitative methods. Internal supply may be forecast by using human resources information systems (HRIS), replacement charts, and Markov analysis. Internal shortages are resolved through training and/or recruitment. This information is used in action planning to develop human resource strategy. HRP is an ongoing process where control and evaluation procedures are necessary to guide HRP activities. Deviations from the plan and their causes must be identified in order to assess whether the plan should be revised. Most labor market analysis should now be done with a global context and keeping in mind the possibility that work can now be done almost anywhere.[72] Remember the quote regarding the labor market: Geography is history!

Recruitment is the process of finding and attracting applicants who are interested in and qualified for position vacancies. The Internet has had an increasingly profound impact on this HR function. Recruitment should encompass both the attraction and the selection of the most qualified personnel. The ideal recruitment program is one in which a sufficient number of qualified applicants are attracted to and ultimately accept the positions in an efficient manner. Unfortunately, the typical assessment of recruitment policies, programs, and personnel in the past has focused on simply whether positions were filled and the cost and speed of filling positions rather than evaluating the quality of the personnel who were hired and placed.

The most recent writing on recruitment, however, has placed a greater emphasis on the quality dimension of the recruiting effort. There is increasing evidence that the various approaches to recruiting result in different outcomes for the organization and that the success of any strategy depends on who is being recruited. The evaluation of recruiting programs in the future is thus more likely to focus on the quality dimension of the people who are hired in addition to the "body count" criteria that are more typically used. The quality criterion has been emphasized in this chapter and the need to establish a match between job seekers' needs and desires for certain job characteristics and those which the organization can offer.

Discussion Questions

1. How should HR planning involve a comparison to competitors? What critical data are required?

2. Why is planning an important activity? What are some of the advantages of effective planning?

3. Some organizations do thorough job analysis first and then human resource planning as part of a restructuring process. What approach makes more sense to you?

4. Discuss the possible pros and cons of the two qualitative methods for forecasting labor demand.

5. If actual performance of the human resource plan differs from desired performance, what remedial steps might you use?

6. Employee referral is a popular method of recruiting candidates. What are its advantages and disadvantages?

7. What are the advantages and disadvantages of the various external recruitment sources described in the chapter?

8. How do human resource planning and recruitment complement each other?

9. Suppose a key employee has just resigned and you are the department manager. After you have sent your request to personnel for a replacement, how could you help the recruiter find the best replacement?

10. Discuss the advantages and disadvantages of using Web-based recruitment.

Chapter

6

Personnel Selection

OBJECTIVES

After reading this chapter, you should be able to

1. Understand the concepts of reliability, validity, and utility.
2. Understand the validity evidence for various selection methods.
3. Discuss approaches to the more effective use for application blanks, reference checks, biographical data, and testing programs in order to increase the validity and legal defensibility of each.
4. Discuss the approaches available for drug testing.
5. Describe the validity of different approaches to interviewing.
6. Explain how the various types of job candidate information should be integrated and evaluated.

OVERVIEW

It sounds simple: Match employees with jobs. Researchers have made this task easier by developing selection methods that successfully predict employee effectiveness. Still, there is a void between what research indicates and how organizations actually do personnel selection. Real-world personnel selection is replete with examples of methods that have been proven to be ineffective or inferior.

Personnel selection (and retention) is key to organizational effectiveness. The most successful firms use methods that accurately predict future performance. The use of validated selection models is another of the **High-Performance Work System** characteristics linking this HR process to corporate financial performance. Organizations are or should be interested in selecting employees who not only will be effective but will work as long as the organization needs them, and will not engage in counterproductive behavior such as violence, substance abuse, avoidable accidents, and employee theft.

Use of validated selection models: A HPWS characteristic

A multiple-hurdle process involving an application, reference and background checks, various forms of standardized testing, and some form of interview is the typical chronology of events for selection, particularly for external hiring decisions. Internal decisions, such as promotions, are typically done with less formality. **Personnel selection** is the *process of gathering and assessing information about job candidates in order to make decisions about personnel.* The process applies to entry-level personnel and promotions, transfers, and even job retention in the context of corporate downsizing efforts. This chapter will

171

introduce you to personnel selection, describe some of the most popular types of screening procedures, review the research evidence on each, and discuss the social and legal implications of the various options.

The chapter begins with an overview of measurement issues related to selection and the typical steps employed in the process. Next, an introduction to the various selection methods will be introduced in their usual order of use. Application blanks, background checks, and reference checks will first be discussed. Then, the various forms of standardized tests that purport to assess applicants' suitability or KASOCs will be reviewed. The use, validity, and possible adverse impact of general mental ability tests and personality tests will be considered. The final sections of the chapter will discuss employment interviews and methods that have been shown to increase their validity, the use of more sophisticated selection procedures such as assessment centers, performance testing and work samples, and drug and medical tests in the preemployment selection process. The context of the discussion will be the legal implications of the various personnel practices and pointing out where there are clear discrepancies between what typically happens in practice and what academic research indicates should happen. This is one chapter where the distance between academic research findings and recommendations and actual selection practices is great. The good news is that the gap is closing.

A Personnel Selection Problem

Wackenhut Security had its share of selection challenges. Although recruitment efforts and a sluggish economy attracted a large number of applicants for its entry-level armed and unarmed security guard positions, there was concern about the quality of those hired and high employee turnover. The turnover rate for some positions exceeded 100 percent—meaning that the quit rate in one year exceeded the number of available positions. Wackenhut Security also was dissatisfied with the quality of its supervisory personnel.

The company contracted with BA&C (Behavioral Analysts and Consultants), a Florida psychological consulting firm that specializes in staffing problems and personnel selection. Wackenhut asked BA&C to develop a new personnel selection system for entry-level guards and supervisors. Underlying this request was a need for Wackenhut to improve its competitive position in this highly competitive industry by increasing sales and contracts, decreasing costs, and, perhaps most important, making certain their security personnel could measure up.

The company, which already compensated its guards and supervisors more than others in the industry, wanted to avoid any increase in compensation. The company estimated that the cost of training a new armed guard was about $1,800. With several hundred guards quitting in less than a year, the company often failed to even recover training costs in sales. Wackenhut needed new selection methods that could increase the effectiveness of the guards and supervisors and identify guard applicants most likely to stay with the company.

Identify KASOCs through work analysis

You will recall from Chapter 4 that work analysis should identify the knowledge, abilities, skills, and other characteristics (KASOCs) or competencies that are necessary for successful performance and retention on the job. In this case, BA&C first conducted a job analysis of the various guard jobs to get better information on the KASOCs required for the work. After identifying the critical KASOCs, BA&C developed a reliable, valid, and **job-related** weighted application blank, screening test, and interview format.

The process of selection varies substantially within this industry. While Wackenhut initially used only a high school diploma as a job specification, an application blank, a background check, and an interview by someone in personnel, competitors have used more complex methods to select employees. American Protective Services, for example, the company that handled security for the Atlanta Olympics, used a battery of psychological and aptitude tests along with a structured interview.

As with the job analysis and the recruitment process, personnel selection should be directly linked to the HR planning function and the strategic objectives of the company. The mission of the Marriott Corporation is to be the hotel chain of choice of frequent travelers. As part of this strategy, the company developed a successful selection system to identify people who could be particularly attentive to customer demands. Wackenhut Security also had a major marketing strategy aimed at new contracts for armed security guards who would be extremely vigilant. They needed a legal selection system that could identify people most likely to perform well in this capacity.

Figure 6-1
Steps in the Development and Evaluation of a Selection Procedure

JOB ANALYSIS/HUMAN RESOURCE PLANNING
Identify knowledge, abilities, skills, and other characteristics (KASOCs) (aka: competencies).
Use a competency model tied to strategy orientation.

RECRUITMENT STRATEGY: SELECT/DEVELOP SELECTION PROCEDURES
Review options for assessing applicants on each of the KASOCs:
Standardized tests (cognitive, personality, motivational, psychomotor).
Application blanks, biographical data, background, reference checks, accomplishment record.
Performance tests, assessment centers, interviews.

DETERMINE VALIDITY FOR SELECTION METHODS
Criterion-related validation.
Expert judgment (content validity).
Validity generalization (meta-analysis)

DETERMINE WEIGHTING SYSTEM FOR SELECTION METHODS AND RESULTANT DATA

Figure 6-1 presents a chronology of the selection process and the major options available for personnel selection. The previous chapters on work analysis, planning, and recruitment have gotten us to the point of selecting job candidates based on information from one or more selection methods. Each of these methods will be reviewed in this chapter. But keep in mind the focus should be on selecting or developing tools that will provide valid assessments on the critical KASOCs, competencies, or job specifications most important for strategy execution. So, the work analysis should identify the strategically important KASOCs or competencies from which the *job specifications* will be derived. Then, particular selection methods (selection tools) should be adopted to assess people in terms of these job specifications.

SELECTION METHODS: ARE THEY EFFECTIVE?

This review includes a summary of the validity of each major approach to selection and an assessment of the relative cost to develop and administer each method. Three key terms related to effectiveness are **reliability, validity,** and **utility.** While these terms are strongly related to one another, the most important criterion for a selection method is *validity.* Remember the discussion of the research on **High-Performance Work Systems.** One of the HR practices shown to be related to corporate financial performance was the percentage of employees hired using "validated selection methods."[1] The essence of the term **validity is the extent to which scores on a selection method predict one or more important criteria.** While the most typical criterion of interest to selection and staffing specialists is job performance, companies also may be interested in other criteria such as how long an employee may stay on the job or whether the employee will steal, be violent, or be involved in accidents. But before addressing the validity of a method, let's look at one of the necessary conditions for validity: the *reliability* of measurement.

What Is Reliability?

A necessary condition for a selection method to be valid is that it first be **reliable. Reliability concerns the consistency of measurement.** This consistency applies to the scores that derive from the selection method. These scores can come from a paper-and-pencil test, a job interview, a performance appraisal, or any other method that is used to make decisions about people. The CIA uses a very long multiple-choice test as an initial screening device for job applicants to be agents. If applicants were to take the test twice three weeks apart, their scores on the test would stay pretty much the same (the same thing can be said for SAT scores). These tests can be considered reliable. The level of reliability can be represented by a correlation coefficient. Correlations from 0 to 1.0 show the extent of the reliability. Generally, reliable methods have reliability coefficients that are .8 or higher, indicating a high degree of consistency in scores. No selection method achieves perfect reliability, but

Good reliability: .8 or higher

the goal should be to reduce error in measurement as much as possible and achieve high reliability. If raters are a part of the selection method, such as job interviewers or on-the-job performance evaluators, the extent to which different raters agree also can represent the reliability (or unreliability) of the method.

Remember the criticism about the use of graphology (or handwriting analysis) discussed in Chapter 1? Handwriting analysis is used by some U.S. companies and even more European firms as an method of selection. But this method is first of all not even reliable, much less valid. If the same handwriting sample were given to two graphologists, they would not necessarily agree on the levels or scores on various employment-related attributes (e.g., drive, creativity, intelligence) supposedly measured based on a handwriting sample. Thus, the method has *low reliability* as an assessment of these attributes. (But even if they did agree, this would not necessarily mean that their assessments are valid.)

Reliable methods tend to be long. One of the reasons the SAT, the GRE, the GMAT, and the LSAT seem to take forever to complete is so these tests will have very high levels of reliability (and they do). But while high reliability is a necessary condition for high validity, high reliability does not ensure that a method is *valid*. The SAT may be highly reliable, but do scores on the SAT predict anything important, such as how well you actually will perform in college? This question addresses the *validity* of the method.

What Is Validity?

Validity is close in meaning to "job relatedness"

Criterion-related validity

The objective of the Wackenhut Security consultants was to develop a reliable, *valid,* legally defensible, user-friendly, and inexpensive test that could predict both job performance and long job tenure for security guards. The extent to which the test was able to predict an important criterion such as performance was an indication of the test's **validity.** The term *validity* is close in meaning but not synonymous with the critical legal term *job relatedness*, which was discussed in Chapters 3 and 4. **Empirical** or **criterion-related validity** involves the statistical relationship between scores on some predictor or selection method (e.g., a test or an interview) and performance on some criterion measure such as on-the-job effectiveness (e.g., sales, supervisory ratings, job turnover, employee theft). At Wackenhut, a study was conducted in which scores on their proposed screening test were correlated with job performance and job tenure. Given certain results, such a study would strongly support a legal argument of job relatedness.

The statistical relationship is usually reported as a **correlation coefficient**. This describes the relationship between scores on the predictor and measures of effectiveness (also called criteria). Correlations from -1 to $+1$ show the direction and strength of the relationship. Higher correlations indicate stronger validity. Assuming that the study was conducted properly, a significant correlation between a method's scores and some important criterion could be offered as a strong argument for the **job relatedness** of the method if the method was alleged to have resulted in adverse impact against a protected class. Figure 6-2 presents a summary of the correlations of validity for the various (and most popular) selection tools, plus the cost of their development and administration.

Content validity

Content validity assesses the degree to which the contents of a selection method (i.e., the actual test items) represent (or assess) the requirements of the job. A knowledge-based test for "Certified Public Accountant" could be considered to have content validity for an accounting job. Subject matter experts are typically used to evaluate the compatibility of the content of a test with the actual requirements of a job (e.g., is the knowledge or skill assessed on the test compatible with the knowledge or skill required on the actual job?). Such a study or evaluation by experts also can be offered as evidence of job relatedness, but the study should follow the directions provided by the Supreme Court in *Albemarle v. Moody* (see Chapter 3) and, just to be safe, comply with the *Uniform Guidelines on Employee Selection Procedures* (UGESP). (See www.eeoc.gov for details on the UGESP.) **Validity generalization**

Validity generalization

tion invokes evidence from past studies on a selection method that is then applied to the same or similar jobs and settings. Meta-analysis determines the average validity of a method.

What Is Utility?

The validity correlation coefficient can also be used to calculate the financial value of a selection method, using a utility formula, which can convert correlations into dollar savings or profits that can be credited to a particular selection method. A method's *utility* depends

Figure 6-2   Selection Tools, Validity, Cost for Development and Administration

Tool	Validity[a]	Costs (Development/ Administration)[b]
Cognitive ability tests (or GMA) measure mental abilities such as reading comprehension, verbal or math skills.	.51	Low/low
Structured interviews measure a variety of skills and abilities using a standard set of questions.	.43	High/high
Unstructured interviews measure a variety of skills using questions that vary from candidate to candidate and interviewer to interviewer.	.31	Low/high
Work samples/ performance tests measure job skills using the actual performance of tasks as on job.	.33	High/high
Job knowledge tests measure bodies of knowledge required by a job.	.48	High/low
"Conscientiousness" measures this "Five Factor Model" personality trait typically with self-report inventories.	.31	Low/low
Biographical information measures a variety of skills and personal characteristics through questions about education, training, work experience, and interests.	.35	High/low
Situational judgment tests measure a variety of skills with short scenarios (either in written or video format) asking test takers what would be their most likely response.	.34	High/low
Integrity tests measure attitudes and experiences related to a person's honesty, dependability, and trustworthiness.	.41	Low/low
Assessment centers measure KASOCs through a series of work samples/exercises with trained assessors (may include GMA and other tests).	.46	High/high
Reference checks provide information about an applicant's past performance or measure the accuracy of applicants' statements on their résumés.	.26	Low/low

[a]Validity values range from 0 to 1.0, with higher numbers indicating better prediction of job performance.
[b]The labels "high" and "low" are costs relative to other tools rather than to some standard specific expense level.
Source: Adapted from A. M. Ryan and N. T. Tippins, "Attracting and Selecting: What Psychological Research Tells Us," *Human Resource Management* 43 (2004), pp. 307–308. Reprinted with permission of John Wiley & Sons.

Low SR is needed for high utility

on its validity but on other issues as well. For example, recall the discussion of **selection ratio** in Chapter 5. Selection ratio is the number of positions divided by the number of applicants for those positions. A test with perfect validity will have no utility if the selection ratio is 1.0 (one applicant per position). This is why an organization's reputation, its recruitment programs, and other HR issues such as compensation are so important for personnel selection. Valid selection methods have great utility for an organization only when that organization can be selective based on the scores on that method.

Utility (U) or expected return based on using a particular selection method is typically derived based on the formula where $U = N_s r_{xy} SD_y Z_x - N_T(C)$ where N_s = number of job applicants selected; r_{xy} = the validity coefficient for the method; SD_y = standard deviation of job performance in dollars and Z_x = average score on the selection method for hired (a measure of the quality of recruitment); N_T = number of applicants assessed with the selection method and C = cost of assessing each job candidate with the selection method.

Selection methods with high validity but that cost relatively little are the ideal in terms of utility. Before contracting with BA&C, Wackenhut Security had studied the options and was not impressed with the validity or utility evidence reported by the test publishers, particularly in the context of the $10–$15 cost per applicant. This was the main reason Wackenhut decided to develop its own selection battery.

BA&C investigated the validity of its proposed new selection systems using both criterion-related and content-validation procedures. This dual approach to validation provides stronger evidence for job relatedness and is more compatible with the Uniform Guidelines issued by the EEOC. The BA&C study recommended that new methods of personnel selection should be used if the company hoped to increase its sales and decrease the costly employee turnover. The resulting analysis showed substantial financial benefit to the company if it adopted the new methods for use in lieu of the old ineffective procedures. The first method BA&C considered was the *application blank*.

APPLICATION BLANKS AND BIOGRAPHICAL DATA

Like most companies, Wackenhut first required an application blank requesting standard information about the applicant to be completed, such as his or her previous employment history, experience, and education. Often used as an initial screening method, the application blank, when properly used, can provide much more than a first cut. However, application blanks, as with any other selection procedure used for screening people, fall under the scrutiny of the courts and state regulatory agencies for possible EEO violations. HR managers should be cautious about using information on an application blank that disproportionately screens out protected class members, and they must be careful not to ask illegal questions. The **Americans with Disabilities Act (ADA)** stipulates that application blanks should not include questions about an applicant's health, disabilities, and worker's compensation history.

Application blanks obviously can yield information relevant to an employment decision. Yet, it is often the weight—or lack of weight—assigned to specific information by particular decision makers that can undermine their usefulness. Decision makers often disagree about the relative importance of information on application blanks. For instance, they might disagree about the amount of education or experience required. Wackenhut required a bachelor's degree in business or a related discipline for the supervisory job. This criterion alone, however, should not carry all the weight. Wackenhut's personnel staff made no effort to develop a uniform practice of evaluating the information on the forms. They did not take into consideration indicators such as the distance an applicant lived from the workplace. A great distance might indicate that, relative to other responses, the candidate is more likely to quit as soon as another job comes along that is closer to home.

A Discrepancy between Research and Practice: The Use of Application and Biographical Data

Weighted application blanks

What companies do to evaluate application blank data and biographical information and what research suggests they should do are worlds apart. Scholarly research shows that when adequate data are available, the best way to use and interpret application blank information is to derive an objective scoring system for responses to application blank questions.[2] The system is based on a criterion-related validation study, resulting in a **weighted application blank (WAB),** with the weights derived from the results of the research. A criterion-related validation study means the responses from the application blanks are statistically related to one or more important criteria (e.g. job tenure or turnover) such that the critical predictive relationships between WAB responses and criterion outcomes (e.g., performance, turnover) can be identified. For example, BA&C was able to show that where a security guard lived relative to his assigned duties was indeed a significant predictor of job turnover. Another useful predictor was the number of jobs held by the applicant during the past three years. Figure 6-3 shows some examples from a WAB. The number and sign in parentheses is the predictive weight for a response. For example, you would lose five points if you had to travel 21 or more miles to work (see #2).

The process of statistically weighting the information on an application blank enhances use of the application blank's information and improves the validity of the whole process. The WAB is simply an application blank that has a multiple-choice format and is scored—similar to a paper-and-pencil test. A WAB provides a predictive score for each job candidate and makes it possible to compare the score with that of other candidates. For example, the numbers in parentheses for the WAB examples in Figure 6-3 were derived from an actual study showing that particular responses were related to job tenure (i.e., coded as either stayed with the company for over one year or not). Thus, applicants who had only one job in the last five years (#1 in Figure 6.3) were more likely to stay over a year while applicants who indicated that they had had over five jobs in the last five years were much less likely to remain on the job for a year or longer.

Biographical information blanks

Biographical information blanks (BIB) are similar to WABs except the items of a BIB tend to be more personal with questions about personal background and life experiences. Figure 6-3 shows examples of items from a BIB for the U.S. Navy. BIB research has shown the method can be an effective tool in the prediction of job turnover,

Figure 6-3
Examples of WAB and BIB

WAB EXAMPLES

1. How many jobs have you held in the last five years? (*a*) none (0); (*b*) 1 (+5); (*c*) 2–3 (+1); (*d*) 4–5 (−3); (*e*) over 5 (−5)

2. What distance must you travel from your home to work? (*a*) less than 1 mile (+5); (*b*) 1–5 miles (+3); (*c*) 6–10 miles (0); (*d*) 11–20 miles (−3); and (*e*) 21 or more miles (−5)

BIB EXAMPLES

How often have you made speeches in front of a group of adults?

How many close friends did you have in your last year of formal education? A. None that I would call "close." (−0.5); B. 1 or 2. (−0.2); C. 3 or 4. (0); D. 5 or 6. (0.2); E. 7 or 8 (0.5); F. 9 or 10 (0.7); G. More than 10 (1.0)

How often have you set long-term goals or objectives for yourself?

How often have other students come to you for advice? How often have you had to persuade someone to do what you wanted?

How often have you felt that you were an unimportant member of a group?

How often have you felt awkward about asking for help on something?

How often do you work in "study groups" with other students?

How often have you had difficulties in maintaining your priorities?

How often have you felt "burnt out" after working hard on a task?

How often have you felt pressured to do something when you thought it was wrong?

Source: Adapted from C. J. Russell, J. Matson, S. E. Devlin, and D. Atwater, "Predictive Validity of Biodata Items Generated from Retrospective Life Experience Essays," *Journal of Applied Psychology* 75 (1990), pp. 569–580. Copyright © 1990 by the American Psychological Association. Reproduced with permission.

job choice, and job performance. In one excellent study conducted at the Naval Academy, biographical information was derived from life-history essays, reflecting life experiences that were then written in multiple-choice format (see Figure 6-3).[3] BIB scoring is also derived from a study of how responses relate to important criteria such as job performance.

WABs and BIBs have been used in a variety of settings for many types of jobs. WABs are used primarily for clerical and sales jobs. BIBs have been used successfully in the military and the insurance industry with an average validity of .35. Many insurance companies, for example, use a very lengthy BIB to screen their applicants. Check out www.e-Selex.com for an online biodata testing service.

Accomplishment record

The **accomplishment record** is an approach similar to a BIB. Job candidates are asked to write examples of their actual accomplishments, illustrating how they had mastered job-related problems or challenges. Obviously, the problems or challenges should be compatible with the problems or challenges facing the organization. The applicant writes these accomplishments for each of the major components of the job. For example, in a search for a new business school dean, applicants were asked to cite a fund-raising project they had successfully organized. HRM specialists evaluate these accomplishments for their predictive value or importance for the job to be filled. Accomplishment records are particularly effective for managerial, professional, and executive jobs.[4] In general, research indicates that methods such as BIBs and accomplishment records are more valid as predictors of future success than credentials or crude measures of job experience. For example, having an MBA versus only a Bachelor's degree is not a particularly valid predictor of successful management performance. What an applicant has accomplished in past jobs or assignments is a more valid approach to assessing managerial potential.

How Do You Derive WAB or BIB or Accomplishment Record Weights?

To derive the weights for WABs or BIBs, you ideally need a large (at least 100) representative sample of application or biographical data and criterion data (e.g., job tenure and/or performance) of the employees who have occupied the position under study. You then can correlate responses to individual parts of the instrument with the criterion data. If effective and ineffective (or long-tenure versus short-tenure) employees responded to an item differently, responses to this item would then be given different weights, depending on the magnitude of the relationship. Weights for the accomplishment record are usually derived by expert judgment for various problems or challenges.

Research supports the use of WABs, BIBs, and the accomplishment record in selection. The development of the scoring system requires sufficient data and some research expertise, but it is worthwhile because the resulting decisions are often superior to those typically made based on a subjective interpretation of application blank information. What if you can't do the empirical validation study? Might you still get better results using a uniform weighted system, in which the weights are based on expert judgment? Yes. This approach is superior to one in which there is no uniform weighting system and each application blank or résumé is evaluated in a more holistic manner by whoever is evaluating it.

REFERENCE CHECKS AND BACKGROUND CHECKS

Most companies use some form of reference or background checking. The goal is to gain insight about the potential employee from people who have had previous experience with him or her. An important role of the background check is to simply verify the information provided by the applicant regarding previous employment and experience. This is a good practice, considering research indicates that between 20 and 25 percent of job applications include at least one fabrication.[5]

Many organizations are now "Googling" applicants' names and searching Facebook and MySpace for information about job candidates as part of a preliminary background check. In some states, teacher hiring administrators routinely search the Web for potentially embarrassing (or worse) material. In some states, teachers have been removed for risqué Web pages and videos. "I know for a fact that when a superintendent in Missouri was interviewing potential teachers last year, he would ask, 'Do you have a Facebook or MySpace page?'" said Todd Fuller, a spokesman for the Missouri State Teachers Association. The Association is now warning its members to audit their Web pages. "If the candidate said yes, then the superintendent would say, 'I've got my computer up right now. Let's take a look.'" Web-based background checks are likely to increase in the years ahead.

Negligent hiring

Fear of **negligent hiring** lawsuits is a related reason employers do reference and background checks. A negligent hiring lawsuit is directed at an organization accused of hiring incompetent (or dangerous) employees. One health management organization was sued for $10 million when a patient under the care of a psychologist was committed to a psychiatric institution and it was later revealed that the psychologist was unlicensed and had lied about his previous experience.

Organizations conduct reference checks to assess the potential success of the candidate for the new job. Reference checks provide information about a candidate's past performance and are also used to assess the accuracy of information provided by candidates. However, HR professionals should be warned: a proliferation of lawsuits has engendered a great reluctance on the part of evaluators to provide anything other than a statement as to when a person was employed and in what capacity. These lawsuits have been directed at previous employers for defamation of character, fraud, and intentional infliction of emotional distress. This legal hurdle has prompted many organizations to stop employees from providing any information about former employees other than dates of employment and jobs. Turnaround is fair play—at least litigiously. Organizations are being sued and held liable if they do not give accurate information about a former employee when another company makes such a request. The bottom line appears simple: Tell the truth about former employees. There are laws in several states that provide protection for employers and former managers who provide candid and valid evaluations of former employees.

What Is the Validity of Reference Checks?

One of the problems with letters of reference is that they are almost always very positive. While there is some validity, it is low in general (.26). One approach to getting more useful (and valid) distinctions among applicants is to construct a "letter of reference" or recommendation that is essentially a performance appraisal form.[6] One can construct a rating form and request that the evaluator indicate the extent to which the candidate was effective in performing a list of job tasks. This approach offers the added advantage of deriving comparable data for both internal and external job candidates, since the performance appraisal, or reference data, can be completed for both internal and external candidates. One study also found that reference checks significantly predicted supervisory ratings (0.36) when they were conducted in a structured and telephone-based format.[7]

With this approach, both internal and external evaluators must evaluate performances on the tasks that are most important for the position to be filled. An alternative approach asks the evaluator to rate the extent of job-related knowledge, skill, ability, or competencies of a candidate. These ratings can then be weighted by experts based on the relative importance of the KASOCs or competencies for the position to be filled. This approach makes good sense whenever past performance is a strong predictor of future performance. For example, when selecting a manager from a pool of current or former managers, a candidate's past performance as a manager is important. Performance appraisals or promotability ratings, particularly those provided by peers, are a valid source of information about job candidates. However, promotability ratings made by managers are not as valid as other potential sources of information about candidates, such as performance tests and assessment centers.

Employers should do their utmost to obtain accurate reference information about external candidates despite the difficulties. If for no other reason, a good-faith effort to obtain verification of employment history can make it possible for a company to avoid (or win) negligent hiring lawsuits.

What Are the Legal Implications of Doing Background Checks on Job Candidates?

The Fair Credit Reporting Act

Callout BGC steps.

Cost vs. Benefit.

Employers often request consumer reports or more detailed "investigative consumer reports" (ICVs) from a consumer credit service as a part of the background check. If they do this, employers need to be aware of state laws related to background checks and **The Fair Credit Reporting Act (FCRA),** amended in 2005, a federal law that regulates how such agencies provide information about consumers. State laws vary considerably on background checks. Experts maintain that it is legally safest to comply with the laws of the states where the job candidate resides, where the reporting agency is incorporated, and the employer has its principal place of business. In general, in order to abide by the FCRA or state law, four steps must be followed by the employer: (1) Give the job candidate investigated a notice in writing that you may request an investigative report, and obtain a signed consent form; (2) provide a summary of rights under federal law (individuals must request a copy); (3) certify to the investigation company that you will comply with federal and state laws by signing a form they should provide; and (4) provide a copy of the report in a letter to the person investigated if a copy has been requested or if an adverse action is taken based on information in the report.

White-collar crime, including employee theft and fraud, is an increasingly serious and costly problem for organizations. One bad hire could wipe out a small business. Enter Ken Springer, a former FBI agent, and now the president of Corporate Resolutions, a fast-growing personnel investigation company with offices in New York, London, Boston, Miami, and Hong Kong. Many of Springer's clients are private equity firms that request management background checks at companies the equity firms are evaluating for possible purchase. Springer also does prescreening for management and executive positions.

Springer's major recommendation is to carefully screen all potential employees (because even entry-level employees can do major damage to an organization), and to carefully research and verify all information on the résumés. He believes that if a single lie is detected, the applicant should be rejected. In addition, Springer says to be wary of claims that are difficult to verify, to carefully research all gaps in applicants' employment histories and vague descriptions of what they did, and to require and contact at least three references to verify as much information as possible. Springer also recommends that that after verifying all facts in a job candidate's résumé, a thorough background check should be done.

Among other companies doing basic job candidate screening, with prices ranging from $100 to $400, are Automatic Data Processing, HireRight, and National Applicant Screening. Google "employment screening" and you'll find numerous other companies doing pre-employment screening and background checks for employers.

PERSONNEL TESTING

GMA tests are valid for virtually all jobs

Many organizations use general mental ability (GMA) (also known as cognitive ability tests) to screen applicants, bolstered by considerable research indicating that GMA tests are valid for virtually all jobs in the U.S. economy. The dilemma facing organizations is this: While GMA tests have been shown to be valid predictors of job performance, they can create legal problems because minorities tend to score lower. GMA tests are ideal for jobs if considerable learning or training on the job is required and where a more "job-related" knowledge-based test is inappropriate or unavailable.[8]

Corporate America also is increasing its use of various forms of personality or motivational testing—in part due to the body of evidence supporting the use of certain methods, concern over employee theft, the outlawing of the polygraph test, and potential corporate liability for the behavior of its employees. Lawsuits for negligent hiring and negligent retention, for example, attempt to hold an organization responsible for the behavior of employees when there is little or no attempt to assess critical characteristics of those who are hired. Domino's Pizza settled a lawsuit in which one of its delivery personnel was involved in a fatal accident. The driver had a long and disturbing psychiatric history and terrible driving record before he was hired.

The paper-and-pencil and online tests most frequently used today for employment purposes are GMA tests. These tests attempt to measure mental, clerical, mechanical, or sensory capabilities in job applicants. You are probably familiar with these cognitive ability tests: the Scholastic Aptitude Test (SAT), the American College Test (ACT), and the General Mental Ability Test (GMAT). Cognitive ability tests, most of which are administered in a paper-and-pencil or computerized format under standardized conditions of test administration, are controversial. On average, African-Americans and Hispanics score lower than whites on virtually all of these tests; thus, use of these tests for selection purposes can cause difficulties for on organization seeking greater diversity in its workforce.

The critical issue of test score differences as a function of ethnicity will be discussed later in the chapter. Let's begin with a definition of GMA and provide brief descriptions of some of the most popular tests. Next, the validity evidence for these tests will be reviewed with a focus on the legal aspects of such testing.

What Is a Cognitive (or General Mental) Ability Test?

Achievement tests

Knowledge-based tests

Cognitive ability tests measure one's aptitude or mental capacity to acquire knowledge based on the accumulation of learning from all possible sources. Such tests are often distinguished from **achievement tests,** which attempt to measure the effects of knowledge obtained in a standardized environment (e.g., your final exam in this course could be considered a form of achievement test). Cognitive ability or GMA tests are typically used to predict future performance. The SAT and ACT, for example, were developed to measure ability to master college-level material. Having made this distinction between achievement tests and cognitive ability tests, however, in practice there isn't a clear distinction between these two classes of tests. Achievement tests can be used to predict future behavior, and all tests measure some degree of accumulated knowledge. **Knowledge-based tests** assess a sample of what is required on the job. If you are hiring a computer programmer, a cognitive ability test score might predict who will learn to be a computer programmer; but, a better approach is an assessment of actual programming knowledge. Knowledge-based tests are easier to defend in terms of job relatedness and are quite valid (.48) and recommended for identifying those job candidates who can be highly effective the very first day of work (i.e., no training on the critical knowledge of the job required). However, knowledge tests can be expensive to develop.

There are hundreds of GMA or cognitive ability tests available. Some of the most frequently used and highly regarded tests are the **Wechsler Adult Intelligence Scale, the Wonderlic Personnel Test, and the Armed Services Vocational Aptitude Battery.** In addition, many of the largest U.S. companies have developed their own battery of cognitive ability tests. AT&T evaluates applicants for any of its nonsupervisory positions on the basis of scores on one or more of its 16 mental ability subtests, for which the weights given to a particular test depend on the particular job based on criterion-related validation evidence. McClachy, the communications giant, has a battery of 10 ability tests, some of which are even used to select newspaper carriers.

The **Wechsler Adult Intelligence Scale** is one of the most valid and heavily researched of all tests. A valid and more practical test is the **Wonderlic Personnel Test.** The publisher of this test, first copyrighted in 1938, has data from more than 3 million applicants. The Wonderlic consists of 50 questions covering a variety of areas, including mathematics, vocabulary, spatial relations, perceptual speed, analogies, and miscellaneous topics. Here is an example of a typical mathematics question: "A watch lost 1 minute 18 seconds in 39 days. How many seconds did it lose per day?" A typical vocabulary question might be phrased as follows: "Usual is the opposite of: a. rare, b. habitual, c. regular, d. stanch, e. always." An item that assesses ability in spatial relations would require the test taker to choose among five figures to form depicted shapes. Applicants have 12 minutes to complete the 50 items. The Wonderlic will cost an employer from $1.50 to $3.50 per applicant depending on whether the employer scores the test. The Wonderlic is used by the National Football League to provide data for potential draft picks (the average score of draftees is one point below the national population).[9]

The Wonderlic and the NFL

You may remember the Wonderlic from the discussion of the Supreme Court rulings in *Griggs v. Duke Power* (discussed in Chapter 3) and *Albemarle v. Moody.* In *Griggs,* scores on the Wonderlic had an adverse impact against African-Americans (a greater proportion of African-Americans failed the test than did whites); and *Duke Power* did not show that the test was job related. Despite early courtroom setbacks and a decrease in use following the *Griggs* decision, according to the test's publisher, the use of the Wonderlic has increased in recent years.

What Are Tests of Specific Abilities?

A variety of tests have also been developed to measure specific abilities, including specific cognitive abilities or aptitudes such as verbal comprehension, numerical reasoning, and verbal fluency, as well as tests assessing mechanical and clerical ability and physical or psychomotor ability, including coordination and sensory skills. The most widely used mechanical ability test is the **Bennett Mechanical Comprehension Test (BMCT).** First developed in the 1940s, the BMCT consists mainly of pictures depicting mechanical situations with questions pertaining to the situations. The respondent describes relationships between physical forces and mechanical issues. The BMCT is particularly effective in the prediction of success in mechanically oriented jobs.

While there are several tests available for the assessment of clerical ability, the most popular is the **Minnesota Clerical Test (MCT).** The MCT requires test takers to quickly compare either names or numbers and to indicate pairs that are the same. The name comparison part of the test has been shown to be related to reading speed and spelling accuracy, while the number comparison is related to arithmetic ability.

Research on the use of specific abilities versus GMA favors the use of the GMA in the prediction of job performance and training. A recent meta-analysis concluded that "weighted combinations of specific aptitudes tests, including those that give greater weight to certain tests because they seem more relevant to the training at hand, are unnecessary at best. At worst, the use of such tailored tests may lead to a reduction in validity."[10]

Physical, psychomotor, and sensory/perceptual are classifications of ability tests used when the job requires particular abilities. Physical ability tests are designed to assess a candidate's muscular strength, movement quality, and cardiovascular endurance. Scores on physical ability tests have been linked to accidents and injuries. One study found that railroad workers who failed a physical ability test were much more likely to suffer an injury at work. Psychomotor tests assess processes such as eye-hand coordination, arm-hand steadiness, and manual dexterity. Sensory/perceptual tests are designed to assess the extent to which an applicant can detect and recognize differences in environmental stimuli. These tests are ideal for jobs that require workers to edit or enter data at a high rate of speed.

As discussed in Chapter 3, the validity of physical ability tests has been under close scrutiny lately, particularly with regard to their use for public safety jobs. Many lawsuits have been filed on behalf of female applicants applying for police and firefighter jobs who had failed some type of physical ability test, such as push-ups, sit-ups, or chin-ups. In fact, the probability is high for adverse impact against women when a physical ability test is used to make selection decisions. Sensory ability testing concentrates on the measurement of hearing and sight acuity, reaction time, and psychomotor skills, such as eye and hand coordination. Such tests have been shown to be related to quantity and quality of work output and accident rates.

Are There Racial Differences in Test Performance?

Many organizations discontinued the use of cognitive ability tests because of the Supreme Court ruling in *Griggs*. Despite fairly strong evidence that the tests are valid and their increased use by U.S. businesses, the details of the *Griggs* case illustrate the continuing problem with the use of such tests. The Duke Power Company required new employees either to have a high school diploma or to pass the Wonderlic Personnel Test and the Bennett Mechanical Comprehension Test. Fifty-eight percent of whites who took the tests passed, while only 6 percent of African-Americans passed. According to the Supreme Court, the Duke Power Company was unable to provide sufficient evidence to support the job relatedness of the tests or the business necessity for their use. Accordingly, based on the "disparate impact" theory of discrimination, the Supreme Court ruled that the company had discriminated against African-Americans under Title VII of the 1964 Civil Rights Act. As we discussed in Chapter 3, the rationale for the Supreme Court's decision gave rise to the theory of disparate impact.

Griggs v. Duke

The statistical data presented in the *Griggs* case are not unusual. African-Americans, on average, score significantly lower than whites on cognitive ability tests; Hispanics, on average, fall about midway between average African-American and white scores.[11] Thus, under the disparate impact theory of discrimination, plaintiffs are likely to establish adverse impact based on the proportion of African-Americans versus whites who pass such tests. If the *Griggs* case wasn't enough, the 1975 Supreme Court ruling in *Albemarle Paper Company v. Moody* probably convinced many organizations that the use of cognitive ability tests was too risky. In *Albemarle*, the Court applied detailed guidelines to which the defendant had to conform in order to establish the job relatedness of any selection procedure (or job specification) that caused adverse impact in staffing decisions. The *Uniform Guidelines in Employee Selection Procedures*, as issued by the Equal Employment Opportunity Commission, also established rigorous and potentially costly methods to be followed by an organization to support the job relatedness of a test if adverse impact should result.

Current interest in cognitive ability tests was spurred by the research on **validity generalization**, which strongly supported the validity of these tests for virtually all jobs and projected substantial increases in utility for organizations that use the tests. The average validity of such tests was reported to be .51.[12] (See again Figure 6-2.)

Some major questions remain regarding the validity generalization results for cognitive ability tests: Are these tests the most valid method of personnel selection across all job situations or are other methods, such as biographical data and personality tests, more valid for some jobs that were not the focus of previous research? Are there procedures that can make more accurate predictions than cognitive ability tests for some job situations? Are cognitive ability tests the best predictors of sales success, for example? (Remember the Unabomber? He had a Ph.D. in math from the University of Michigan. How would he do in sales?) Another issue is the extent to which validity can be inferred for jobs involving bilingual skills. Would the Wonderlic administered in English have strong validity for a job, such as a customs agent, requiring the worker to speak in two or more languages? Bilingual job specifications are increasing in the United States. Invoking the "validity generalization" argument for this type of job based on research involving only the use of English is somewhat dubious. The validity of such tests to predict performance for these jobs is probably not as strong as .5.

Another issue concerns the extent to which other measures can enhance predictions beyond what cognitive ability tests can predict. Generally, human performance is thought to be a function of a person's ability, motivation, and personality. The highest estimate of the validity of cognitive ability tests is about .50. This means that 25 percent of the variability in the criterion measure (e.g., performance) can be accounted for by the predictor, or the test. That leaves 75 percent unaccounted for. Industrial psychologists think the answer lies in measures of one's motivation to perform, personality, or the compatibility of a person's job preferences with actual job characteristics.

Would a combination of methods—perhaps a cognitive ability test and a personality or motivational test—result in significantly better prediction than the GMA test alone? Research indicates that a combination of cognitive and motivational or personality tests may lead to a more comprehensive assessment of an individual and higher validity than any method by itself.[13] Motivational or personality tests or assessments through interviews add what is known as **incremental validity** in the prediction of job performance. In general, GMA or cognitive ability and job knowledge tests are valid but additional (and valid) tools can add validity to the prediction and have the potential to reduce adverse impact. A recent study in retail showed the use of a personality test and an interview provided incremental validity to the strong validity of a GMA and reduced the level of adverse impact for the selection of managerial trainees and in the prediction of subsequent job performance. Accordingly, the use of other tests that address the motivational components of human performance, in addition to a GMA/cognitive ability or knowledge-based test, can help an organization make better decisions. These measures will be discussed shortly.

Incremental validity

Why Do Minorities Score Lower Than Whites on Cognitive Ability Tests?

This question has interested researchers for years; yet there appears to be no clear answer. Most HRM experts now generally take the view that these differences are not created by the tests, but are most related to inferior educational experiences. But the problem is not a defect or deficiency in the tests per se. The critical issue for HRM experts is not how to modify the test itself, but how to use the test in the most effective way. A panel of the **National Academy of Sciences** concluded that cognitive ability tests have limited but real ability to predict how well job applicants will perform, and these tests predict minority group performance as well as they predict the future performance of nonminorities. In other words, the tests themselves are not to blame for differences in scores. Obviously, the dilemma for organizations is the potential conflict in promoting diversity while at the same time using valid selection methods that have the potential for causing adverse impact.[14]

How Do Organizations Deal with Race Differences on Cognitive Ability Tests?

The use of top-down selection decisions based strictly on scores on cognitive ability tests is likely to result in adverse impact against minorities. One solution to this problem is to set a cutoff score on the test so as not to violate the 80 percent rule, which defines adverse impact. Scores above the cutoff score are then ignored and selection decisions are made on some other basis. The major disadvantage of this approach is that there will be a significant decline in the utility of a valid test because people could be hired who are at the lower end of the scoring continuum, making them less qualified than people at the upper end of the continuum who may not be selected. Virtually all of the research on cognitive ability test validity indicates that the relationship between test scores and job performance is **linear;** that is, *higher test scores go with higher performance and lower scores go with lower performance.* Thus, setting a low cutoff score and ignoring score differences above this point can result in the hiring of people who are less qualified. So, while use of a low cutoff score may enable an organization to comply with the 80 percent adverse impact rule, the test will lose considerable utility.

GMA has a linear relationship with performance

Another approach to dealing with potential adverse impact is to use a **banding** procedure that groups test scores based on data indicating that the bands of scores are not significantly different from one another. The decision maker then may select anyone from within this band of scores. Unfortunately, research shows that banding procedures have a big effect on adverse impact only when minority preference within a band is used for selection. This approach is controversial and may be illegal.[15]

Banding

The use of cognitive ability tests obviously presents a dilemma for organizations. Evidence indicates that such tests are valid predictors of job performance and academic performance and that validity is higher for jobs that are more complex (see again Figure 6-2). Employers who use such tests enjoy economic utility with greater productivity and considerable cost savings. However, selection decisions that are based solely on the scores of such tests will result in adverse impact against African-Americans and Hispanics. Such adverse impact could entangle the organization in costly litigation and result in considerable public relations problems. If the organization chooses to avoid adverse impact, the question becomes one of either throwing out a test that has been shown to be useful in predicting job performance or keeping the test and somehow reducing or eliminating the level of adverse impact. But does such a policy leave a company open to reverse discrimination lawsuits by whites who were not selected for employment since their raw scores on the test were higher than scores obtained by some minorities who were hired? Many organizations, particularly in the public sector, have abandoned the use of cognitive ability tests in favor of other methods, such as interviews or performance tests, which result in less adverse impact and are more defensible in court.

However, many other cities and municipalities have opted to keep such tests and then have employed some form of banding in the selection of their police and firefighters primarily in order to make personnel decisions that do not result in statistical adverse impact.

Researchers and practitioners are very interested in how to select the most effective candidates while meeting diversity goals and minimizing (or eliminating) adverse impact. There have been some criticisms of the tests themselves with suggestions to remove the "culturally biased" questions. However, research does not support this recommendation. Figure 6-4 presents a summary of common practices used to reduce adverse impact, the degree of support in research, and the research findings.

What Is Personality/ Motivational/ Dispositional Testing?

While research supports the use of cognitive ability tests for personnel selection, virtually all HRM professionals regard performance as a function of both ability and motivation. Scores on GMA or other ability or knowledge-based tests say little or nothing about a person's motivation to do the job. We can all think of examples of very intelligent individuals who were unsuccessful in many situations (we're back to the Unabomber or perhaps you remember Bobby Fisher, the great but troubled chess player!). Most of us can remember a classmate who was very bright but received poor grades due to low motivation. The validity of GMA tests for predicting sales success is significant but low and we can definitely improve on prediction by using other assessment tools in addition to a GMA test.

Most personnel selection programs attempt an informal or formal assessment of an applicant's personality, motivation, attitudes, or disposition through psychological testing, reference checks, or a job interview. Some of these so-called "noncognitive" assessments are based on scores from standardized tests, performance testing such as job simulations, or assessment centers. Others are more informal, derived from an interviewer's gut reaction or intuition. This section will review the abundant literature on the measurement and prediction of motivation, disposition, and personality using various forms of testing. Without question, some approaches are more valid than others and some are not valid at all for use in staffing decisions.

There is an increased use of various types and formats for personality or motivational testing, including paper-and-pencil types, video and telephone testing, and, most recently, online testing. There is also increasing evidence that many of these methods are valid predictors of job performance and other important criteria such as job tenure or turnover and **counterproductive work behavior (CWB)** such as employee theft, aberrant or disruptive behaviors, and interpersonal and organizational deviance.

Predicting counterproductive behavior

Some organizations place great weight on personality testing for employment decisions. BA&C, the company working with Wackenhut Security, does psychological screening for hundreds of companies using specialized reports based on the **five-factor model (FFM)** of personality. Although the criterion-related validity evidence made available to the public is rather limited, one of the most popular personality assessment tools is the **"Caliper Profile,"** developed by the Caliper Corporation (www.calipercorp.com). Their Web site claims 25,000 clients. BMW, Avis, and GMAC are among the companies that use the Caliper Profile to hire salespeople. The Profile has also been used by numerous sports teams for player personnel issues such as potential trades and drafts. The Chicago Cubs, the Detroit Pistons, and the New York Islanders are among the sports teams that have used the Profile for drafting and trade considerations.

Caliper Profile

Figure 6-4   **Practices Used to Reduce Adverse Impact**

Common Practices to Reduce Adverse Impact	Degree of Support for Practice in Literature	Research Findings and Implications
Target recruitment strategies toward qualified minorities.	+	Characteristics of the applicant pool (e.g., proportion of minorities, average score levels of minorities) have the greatest effect on rates of adverse impact; changing these characteristics through targeted recruitment should help reduce adverse impact. However, simply increasing numbers of minorities in the pool will not help unless one is increasing numbers of qualified recruits.
Use a selection system that focuses on predicting performance in areas such as helping coworkers, dedication, and reliability, in addition to task performance.	+	If the overall performance measure weights contextual performance (e.g., helping, reliability) more than task performance and the tests in a battery are uncorrelated, a test battery designed to predict this definition of overall performance will have smaller levels of adverse impact. Weighting task performance less than contextual performance in the overall performance measure will make cognitive ability less important in hiring and will lead to less adverse impact.
Use a tool with high adverse impact and good validity in combination with a tool with low adverse impact to reduce the overall adverse impact of the system.	0	The degree to which adverse impact is reduced by combining tools with lower adverse impact is overestimated; reductions are small but validity is increased.
Provide orientation and preparation programs to candidates.	0	Coaching and orientation programs have little effect on size of group differences but are well received by examinees.
Remove cognitive ability testing from the selection process.	+/0	Using only noncognitive predictors (e.g., interview, conscientiousness, biodata) will lead to significantly reduced adverse impact, but significant black/white differences will remain. Also, cognitive ability tests are among the most valid predictors of job performance, and their removal may result in a selection system that is less valid.
Use banding of test scores.	0	The use of banding has less effect on adverse impact than the characteristics of the applicant pool. Substantial reduction of adverse impact through banding only occurs when minority preference within a band is used for selection (i.e., preferential selection is employed). This practice is probably illegal.
Use tools with less adverse impact as screening devices early in the selection process and those with greater adverse impact as later hurdles in the process.	+/0	Using tools with less adverse impact as screening devices early in the process and those with greater adverse impact later in the process will aid minority hiring if the selection ratio is low, but will not have much effect if the selection ratio is high (i.e., few applicants per position).
Change the more negative test taking perceptions of minority test takers about test validity, thereby increasing motivation and performance.	0	May provide a very small reduction in adverse impact.
Identify and remove culturally biased test items.	0	Research suggests that clear patterns regarding what items favor one group or another do not exist and that removal of such items has little effect on test scores; however, item content should not be unfamiliar to those of a particular culture and should not be more verbally complex than warranted by job requirements.
Use other modes of presenting test stimuli than multiple-choice, paper-and-pencil testing (e.g., video).	0	Changes in format often result in changes in what is actually measured and can be problematic; in cases where a format change was simply that (e.g., changed format without affecting what was measured), there was no strong reduction in group differences.
Use portfolios, accomplishment records, and performance assessments (work samples) instead of paper-and-pencil measures.	+/0	Evidence suggests group differences may not be reduced by realistic assessments, and reliable scoring of these methods may be problematic. Well-developed work samples may have good validity and less adverse impact than cognitive ability tests.
Relax time limits on timed tools.	0	Research indicates that longer time limits do not reduce subgroup differences, and may actually increase them.

Source: A. M. Ryan and N. T. Tippins, "Attracting and Selecting: What Psychological Research Tells Us," *Human Resource Management* 43 (2004), pp. 312–313. Reprinted with permission of John Wiley & Sons.

Figure 6-5   **Some Examples of Personality/Dispositional/Motivational Tests**

PROJECTIVE TECHNIQUES AND INSTRUMENTS
Thematic Apperception Test (TAT)
Miner Sentence Completion Scale (MSCS)
Graphology (handwriting analysis)
Rorschach Inkblot Test

SELF-REPORT INVENTORIES—EXAMPLES
The NEO-PI-R Personality Inventory (measures FFM and facets of each)
Personal Characteristics Inventory
Gordon Personal Preference Inventory
Myers-Briggs Type Indicator
Minnesota Multiphasic Personality Inventory (MMPI)
California Personality Inventory (CPI)
Sixteen Personality Factors Questionnaire (16 PF)
Hogan Personality Inventory
Job Compatibility Questionnaire (JCQ)
Emotional Intelligence (e.g., EI Scale)
Core Self-Evaluation Scale (CSES)
Caliper Profile

Sears, Roebuck and Company, IBM, and AT&T have used personality tests for years to select, place, and even promote employees. More companies today use some form of personality test to screen applicants for risk factors related to possible counterproductive behavior. There are literally thousands of personality tests and questionnaires available that purport to measure hundreds of different traits or characteristics. (Go to www.unl.edu/buros/ for a sample.) The basic categories of personality testing will be reviewed next. Figure 6-5 presents a list of some of the most popular tests and methods.

Let's start with a definition of personality and provide brief descriptions of some of the more popular personality tests. The validity of the major personality tests will be reviewed along with an overview of relevant legal and ethical issues. The section will conclude with a description of some relatively new "noncognitive" tests that have shown potential as selection and placement devices.

What Is Personality?

While personality has been defined in many ways, the most widely accepted definition is that **personality** refers to an individual's consistent pattern of behavior. This consistent pattern is composed of psychological traits. While a plethora of traits have been labeled and defined, most academic researchers subscribe to a five-factor model (FFM) to describe personality.[16] These so-called "Big Five" personality factors are as follows: (1) **neuroticism** (or emotional stability); (2) **extraversion/introversion** (outgoing, sociable); (3) **openness to experience** (imaginative, curious, experimenting); (4) **agreeableness/likability** (friendliness, cooperative vs. dominant); and (5) **conscientiousness** (dependability, carefulness). There are several questionnaires or inventories that measure the FFM. (Try http://users.wmin.ac./UK/~buchant/ for a free online "Big Five" test.) There is substantial research supporting the validity of the FFM in the prediction of a number of criteria (e.g., performance, sales, counterproductive behaviors) for a variety of jobs. This validity evidence will be reviewed in a later section.

The "Big Five" or FFM

Emotional Intelligence

Two relatively new characterizations of personality are **Emotional Intelligence** (EI) and **Core Self-Evaluations** (CSE). EI is considered to be a multidimensional form or subset of social intelligence or a form of social literacy. EI has been the object of criticism because of differences in definitions of the contruct and the claims of validity and incremental validity. One definition is that EI is a set of abilities that enable individuals to recognize and understand their own emotions and those of others in order to guide their thinking and behavior to help them cope with the environment. The most recent review concluded that "we are still far from being at the point of rendering a decision as to the incremental value of EI for selection purposes."[17]

CSE is a broad and general personality trait composed of four heavily researched traits: (1) self-esteem (the overall value that one places on oneself as an individual); (2) self-efficacy (an evaluation of how well one can perform across situations); (3) neuroticism (the tendency to focus on the negative); and (4) locus of control (the extent to which one believes s/he has control over life's events). The core self-evaluation is a basic assessment of one's capability and potential.

There is some research that investigated the extent to which these new measures add predictive value (or incremental validity) beyond the Big Five or other selection tools. In general, this research indicates useful incremental validity for these measures beyond the Big Five and other selection models or tools. For example, research with a new instrument that purports to measure (CSE) shows scores on the scale are correlated with job performance and that CSE has incremental validity over the five-factor model.[18]

Incremental validity

How Do We Measure Personality?

Projective Tests

Personality tests can be sorted into two broad categories: projective tests and self-report inventories. Of course, we also can use the interview and data from other sources such as performance appraisals or references as a means for assessing personality characteristics or competencies as well. **Projective tests** have many common characteristics, the most significant of which is that the purpose and scoring procedure of the tests are disguised from the test taker.

Much concern has been expressed about the ability of job candidates to fake a self-report personality inventory in order to provide a more favorable impression to an employer. Projective tests make it very difficult to fake responses since the test-taker has little or no idea what a favorable response is. One of the most famous projective tests is the **Rorschach Inkblot Test,** which presents a series of inkblots to respondents who must then record what they see in each one.

MSCS

While numerous projective tests exist, the **Miner Sentence Completion Scale (MSCS)** is one of the few such tests specifically designed for use in the employment setting and with some validity evidence to back its use. Its aim is to measure managers' motivation to manage others.[19] The test appears to work. The test consists of 40 incomplete sentences, such as "My family doctor . . . ," "Playing golf . . . ," and "Dictating letters. . . ." The test taker is instructed to complete each sentence. According to the developer of these tests, the way in which an applicant completes the sentences reflects his or her motivation along seven areas. These areas are capacity to deal with authority figures, dealing with competitive games, handling competitive situations, assertiveness, motivation to direct others, motivation to stand out in a group, and desire to perform day-to-day administrative tasks. On the downside, the MSCS is expensive and there isn't a great deal of validity evidence to support its use.

TAT

Another projective test that has been used occasionally for employment purposes is the **Thematic Apperception Test,** or **TAT,** a test that typically consists of 31 pictures that depict a variety of social and interpersonal situations. The subject is asked to tell a story about each picture to the examiner. Of the 31 pictures, 10 are gender-specific while 21 others can be used with adults of either sex. Test takers are asked to describe who the people are in each picture and what is happening in the situation, which is clearly open to interpretation. The test taker then "projects" the outcome of the situation. Although a variety of scoring systems have been developed for interpreting a test taker's responses, one of the most popular approaches involves rating the responses with regard to the test taker's need for power (i.e., the need to control and influence others), achievement (i.e., need to be successful), and affiliation (i.e., the need for emotional relationships). Like the MSCS, the TAT has been used for managerial selection and the limited research indicates some validity as a predictor of managerial and entrepreneurial success. AT&T has been using the TAT for years as a part of their assessment center to identify high-potential managerial talent.

Graphology

One form of projective test (discussed earlier) that has received considerable attention recently is **graphology,** or handwriting analysis. With this approach, a sample of your handwriting is mailed to a graphologist who (for anywhere from $10 to $50) provides an assessment of your intelligence, creativity, emotional stability, negotiation skills, problem-solving skills, and numerous other personal attributes. According to some writers, graphology is used extensively in Europe as a hiring tool. *The Wall Street Journal* and *Inc.* magazine have reported an increase in the use of the method in the United States since 1989. As described in *The Wall Street Journal,* "With the government pulling the plug on the polygraph, and employers clamming up on job references and liabilities from negligent hiring, it is one alternative managers are exploring in an effort to know whom they are hiring." While the use of the method may be increasing, there is no compelling evidence that the method does anything but provide an assessment of penmanship. The only peer-reviewed and published studies on the validity of graphology have found no validity for the approach.[20]

Self-Report Personality Inventories

Self-report inventories, which purport to measure personality or motivation with the respondent knowing the purpose and/or the scoring procedure of the test, are much more common than projective techniques. Some instruments screen applicants for aberrant or deviant behavior (e.g., the MMPI), others attempt to identify potentially high performers, and others, particularly more recently developed tests, are directed at specific criteria such as employee theft, job tenure/turnover, accident proneness, or customer orientation.[21]

Self-report inventories typically consist of a series of short statements concerning one's behavior, thoughts, emotions, attitudes, past experiences, preferences, or characteristics. The test taker responds to each statement using a standardized rating scale. During the testing, respondents may be asked to indicate the extent to which they are "happy" or "sad," "like to work in groups," "prefer working alone," and so forth.

MMPI

One of the most popular and respected personality tests is the **Minnesota Multiphasic Personality Inventory (MMPI).** The MMPI is used extensively for jobs that concern the public safety or welfare, including positions in law enforcement, security, and nuclear power plants. The MMPI is designed to identify pathological problems in respondents, not to predict job effectiveness. The revised version of the MMPI consists of 566 statements (e.g., "I am fearful of going crazy"; "I am shy"; "Sometimes evil spirits control my actions"; "In walking, I am very careful to step over sidewalk cracks"; "Much of the time, my head seems to hurt all over"). Respondents indicate whether such statements are true, false, or they cannot say. The MMPI reveals scores on 10 clinical scales, including depression, hysteria, paranoia, and schizophrenia, as well as four "validity" scales, which enable the interpreter to assess the credibility or truthfulness of the answers. Millions of people from at least 46 different countries, from psychotics to Russian cosmonauts, have struggled through the strange questions.

Litigation related to **negligent hiring** often focuses on whether an organization properly screened job applicants. For example, failure to use the MMPI (or ignoring MMPI results) in filling public-safety jobs has been cited in legal arguments as an indication of negligent hiring—although not always persuasively. Unfortunately, some companies are damned if they do and damned if they don't. Target stores negotiated an out-of-court settlement based on a claim of invasion of privacy made by a California job candidate who objected to a few questions on the MMPI being used to hire armed guards. Had one of the armed guards who was hired used his or her weapon inappropriately (and Target had not used the MMPI), Target could have been slapped with a negligent hiring lawsuit.

16PF

Another popular instrument is the **16 Personality Factors Questionnaire (16PF),** which provides scores on the factors of the FFM, plus others. In addition to predicting performance, the test is used to screen applicants for counterproductive work behavior, such as potential substance abuse or employee theft. AMC Theaters, C&S Corporation of Georgia, and the U.S. State Department are among the many organizations that use the 16PF to screen job candidates. An advantage of the 16PF over other self-report inventories is that one of the 16PF factors reveals a reliable and valid measure of GMA as well as scores on the Big Five factors and "Big-Five subfactors" (to be discussed later).

NEO-PI-R (FFM)

Although there are many instruments available, the NEO Personality Inventory is one of the most reliable and valid measures of the FFM.[22] Another very popular instrument for employee development but one that is not considered a good selection instrument is the Myers-

MBTI

Briggs Type Indicator (MBTI).[23]

What Is the Validity of Personality Tests?

MSCS validity = .35

Conscientiousness and emotional stability have validity for all jobs

Extraversion has validity for managerial jobs

Use FFM subfactors to increase validity

Potentially useful personality tests exist among a great number of bad ones, making it difficult to derive general comments regarding their validity. Some instruments have shown adequate (and useful) validity while others show little or no validity for employment decisions. In general, the validity is lower for personality inventories than for cognitive ability tests.

The one projective instrument with a reliable track record for selecting managers is the MSCS. A review of 26 studies involving the MSCS found an average validity coefficient of .35.[24] However, almost all of this research was conducted by the test publisher and not published in peer-reviewed journals.

The latest reviews of the FFM found that **Conscientiousness** and **Emotional Stability** had useful predictive validity across all jobs but that Conscientiousness had the highest validity (.31). **Extraversion, Agreeableness, and Openness to Experience** had useful predictive validity but for only certain types of jobs.[25] For example, extraverted workers are more effective in jobs with a strong social component, such as sales and management. Extraversion is not a predictor of job success for jobs that do not have a strong social component (e.g., technical or quantitative work). More Agreeable workers are more effective team members. People with high scores on Openness to Experience are more receptive to new training and do well in fast-changing jobs that require innovative or creative thinking. Research also supports the use of the FFM in an effort to reduce absenteeism among workers.

A particular combination of FFM factors can also predict important criteria more successfully than the factors in isolation. For example, the combination of Emotional Stability (neuroticism) and Extraversion, describing a "happy" person, is a better predictor of job performance in health care than either trait in isolation.[26] Another study found that the combination of highly Agreeable and low to moderately Conscientious managers were the least effective managers for evaluating and developing employees.[27] Research involving the FFM and managerial performance shows that Conscientiousness (.28), Extraversion (.21), and Emotional Stability (.19) are useful predictors of managerial success and that scores on these three factors should be used to select managers.[28]

Recent research also suggests that we might do a better job predicting performance with more narrowly defined traits or subfactors that define a broader trait such as one from the FFM. A meta-analysis found that narrow traits underlying the Conscientiousness (C) factor from the FFM provided incremental predictive validity above and beyond the global Conscientiousness measure. Thus, the subfactors of C (achievement, dependability, order, cautiousness) helped improve the prediction of job performance. There is also evidence that underlying narrow traits of Extraversion might help enhance prediction for certain criterion measures for sales jobs. However, the degree to which the subfactors contribute to prediction depends on the particular performance criterion and the particular occupation under study. For example, in the meta-analysis **potency** was a more valid predictor of overall job proficiency, sales effectiveness, and irresponsible work behavior, while **affiliation** was a stronger predictor of technical proficiency.[29]

Why is the validity of personality inventories low (relative to measures of GMA)? Most people think an employee's motivation or personality or emotional "intelligence" is much more important for job performance than is the employee's GMA or cognitive ability. So, why is the validity of GMA so much stronger than the validities for the noncognitive types of inventories? Experts have given a number of explanations for the low (but useful) validity of personality and motivational tests in the employment context. First, and most obvious, applicants can "fake" personality tests so their personality as reflected on the tests is compatible with the requirements of the job. In essence, in an earnest effort to gain employment, many applicants will try to make responses on a self-report personality inventory that they at least think will make them look as favorable as possible to the prospective employer. (One cannot fake the SATs or the GMATs.) There is no question that applicant faking on most noncognitive measures occurs, but what is not clear is the extent to which faking reduces the validity of personality tests. Most researchers believe that the decrease in the predictive validity of personality measures due to faking is modest. Faking is apparently more problematic for self-report personality inventories (e.g., NEO Inventory) than for some alternative methods of assessing personality (i.e., structured interviews and assessment centers).[30]

Second, experts have been critical of the research designs in validation work and contend that more carefully designed research (with larger sample sizes) would demonstrate higher validity for personality tests. While validities still lag behind that of GMA and other cognitive measures, the improved designs have shown practically useful (but still relatively low) validities for many noncognitive measures and particularly as "add-ons" to GMA or knowledge-based tests for incremental validity. Research shows the weight given to particular personality factors (or combinations of factors) should derive from a careful job analysis or from criterion-related validation research.

Another possible explanation is that behavior is to a great extent determined situationally, making stable personality traits unpredictable for criteria such as job performance or employee turnover. Recall some of the examples of items from personality tests listed earlier in this chapter. Note that most of the examples are not specific to the workplace; in fact, most of them are quite general. Research in other areas has found that behavior is dependent on the situation. A person who is friendly in outside work might be less sociable in the work setting. In order to enhance predictability, some research indicates personality assessment should involve "contexualizing" the frame of reference for completing a personality instrument for selection purposes. The use of a job-related frame of reference (e.g., "I pay close attention to details at work") has been found to show potential for the criterion-related validity of personality scales.[31]

Frame of reference personality assessment

Most experts recommend the use of more than one method (e.g., inventories plus interviews) and more effort to link particular traits (or subtraits) with particular work criteria. Personality assessment could be more specific to the workplace and target particular criterion measures of interest, such as job retention/turnover, CWBs such as employee theft, attendance, or particular and important functions of a job (e.g., driving behavior, customer service). One study proposes that job performance can be broken down into three general domains: task performance (the essence of the job), citizenship performance (a good organizational co-worker), and counterproductive work behavior (theft, deviance). Cognitively loaded predictors such as GMA and knowledge-based tests are the strongest predictors of task performance while noncognitive predictors are the best predictors in the citizenship and counterproductive domains.[32] Let's examine some newer approaches next.

Approaches to the Prediction of Particular Criteria

There is growing evidence that the use of "compound" traits that are more tied to particular work situations and particular criteria can enhance prediction above what can be derived from the traditional FFM instruments. Many forms of personality, dispositional, or motivation assessment attempt to focus on either particular problems or criteria characteristic of the workplace. Examples are the prediction of voluntary turnover and the prediction of employee theft. One instrument attempts to measure job compatibility in order to predict turnover. Other new instruments are designed to address particular employment issues or situations, such as customer service, violence, or accident proneness.

Predicting (and Reducing) Voluntary Turnover

Employee turnover can be a serious and costly problem for organizations. You may recall the discussion of Domino's Pizza. They found that the cost of turnover was $2,500 each time an hourly employee quit and $20,000 each time a store manager quit. Among other things, Domino's implemented a new and more valid test for selecting managers and hourly personnel that was aimed at predicting both job performance and voluntary turnover. As of 2008, the program was a success on all counts. Turnover was down, store profits were up, and the stock was doing well in an otherwise terrible market. Attracting and keeping good employees was a key factor in their turnaround. There are numerous other examples of companies that have expensive and preventable high levels of turnover that can be reduced with better HR policy and practice. Recall the discussion of SAS, the North Carolina software company. Even at the height of the so-called "high-tech" bubble in the late 1990s, SAS had turnover rates that were well below the industry average. Attracting and keeping good employees is considered a key to the SAS success story. As of 2008, SAS remained one of Fortune's "Best Companies to Work For" and reported their usual very low turnover rate among its core personnel.

Figure 6-6   **Predictors of Voluntary Turnover and How to Avoid It**

1. *Rely on employee referrals*

   Voluntary turnover is less likely if a job candidate is referred by a current employee or has friends or family working at the organization.

   Candidates with more contacts within the organization are apt to better understand the nature of the job and the organization.

   Having friends or family within the organization prior to hire is likely to strengthen the employee's commitment to the firm and reduce the likelihood that he or she will leave.

2. *Put weight on tenure in previous jobs*

   A past habitual practice of seeking out short-term employment predicts future short-term employment.

   Short-term employment may reflect a poor work ethic, which is correlated with lack of organizational commitment and turnover.

3. *Measure intent to quit*

   Intention to quit is one of the best (if not the best) predictors of turnover.

   Despite their transparency, expressions of intentions to stay or quit before a person starts a new position are an effective predictor of subsequent turnover (e.g., how long do you plan to work for the company?).

4. *Measure the applicant's desires/motivations and job compatibility for the position*

   New employees with a strong desire for employment will require less time to be assimilated into the organization's culture.

   Job compatibility is correlated with job tenure.

5. *Use disguised-purpose dispositional measures*

   Persons with high self-confidence should respond more favorably to the challenges of a new environment.

   Employees with higher confidence in their abilities are less likely to quit than those who attribute their past performance to luck.

   Decisive individuals are likely to be more thoughtful about their decisions, more committed to the decisions they make, and less likely to leave the organization.

   Decisiveness is a component of the personality trait of Conscientiousness from the five-factor model.

   Decisiveness affects organizational commitment and, indirectly, turnover.

Source: Adapted from M. R. Barrick and R. D. Zimmerman, "Reducing Voluntary, Avoidable Turnover through Selection," *Journal of Applied Psychology* 90 (2005), pp. 159–166.

Employee referrals reduce turnover

One study revealed guidelines regarding methods that have been shown to be effective at reducing voluntary turnover.[33] A summary of the findings merged with previous research on turnover is presented in Figure 6-6. This most recent research drew several conclusions. First, voluntary turnover is less likely if a job candidate is referred by a current employee or has friends or family working at the organization. Candidates with more contacts within the organization are apt to better understand the nature of the job and the organization. Such candidates probably have a more realistic view of the job that may provide a "vaccination effect" that lowers expectations, thereby preventing job dissatisfaction and turnover (realistic job previews can also do this). Also, current job holders are less likely to refer job candidates who they feel are less capable or those who (they feel) would not fit in well with the organization's culture.

Another argument for an employee referral system is that having acquaintances within the organization is also likely to strengthen an employee's commitment to the firm and thus reduce the probability that he or she will leave. Of course, this argument also applies to the employee who made the referral.

Another reliable predictor of voluntary turnover is tenure in previous jobs. In general, if a person has a history of short-term employment, that person is likely to quit again. This tendency may also reflect a lower work ethic (lower Conscientiousness), which is correlated with organizational commitment and turnover. As discussed earlier, tenure in previous jobs, measured in a systematic manner as a part of a **weighted application blank** (WAB), is predictive of turnover. Intention to quit is also a solid predictor of, and perhaps the best predictor of, quitting. Believe it or not, questions on an application form such as "How long do you think you'll be working for this company?" are quite predictive of voluntary turnover. Prehire dispositions or behavioral intentions, derived from questions such as this one or from interview questions, work quite well.

Use WABs to lower turnover for entry-level jobs

Measures of the extent of an applicant's desire to work for the organization also predict subsequent turnover. However, almost all of the research on WABs has involved entry-level and nonmanagerial positions, so applicability to managerial positions is questionable. This is not true for biodata (or BIBs). **Disguised-purpose attitudinal** scales, where the scoring key is hidden, measuring self-confidence and decisiveness have been shown to predict turnover for higher-level positions as well, including managerial positions. Answers to questions such as "How confident are you that you can do this job well?" or responses to statements like "When I make a decision, I tend to stick to it" also predict turnover quite well. In addition, there is little evidence of adverse impact against protected classes using these measures. This research also revealed that disguised-purpose measures added incremental validity to the prediction of turnover beyond what could be predicted by biodata alone.

Job Compatibility Questionnaire (JCQ)

Another example of a disguised-purpose dispositional measure is the **Job Compatibility Questionnaire** (JCQ). As discussed in Chapters 4 and 5, the JCQ was developed to determine whether an applicant's preferences for work characteristics matched the actual characteristics of the job.[34] One theory is that the compatibility or preference for certain job characteristics will predict job tenure and performance. Test takers are presented groups of items and are instructed to indicate which item is most desirable and which is least desirable. As discussed in Chapter 4, the items are grouped based on a job analysis that identifies those characteristics that are descriptive of the job(s) to be filled. Here is an example of a sample group: (a) being able to choose the order of my work tasks, (b) having different and challenging projects, (c) staying physically active on the job, (d) clearly seeing the effects of my hard work.

The items are grouped together in such a way that the scoring key is hidden from the respondent, reducing the chance for faking. Studies involving customer service representatives, security guards, and theater personnel indicate that the JCQ can successfully predict employee turnover for low-skilled jobs. In addition, no evidence of adverse impact has been found. BA&C incorporated the JCQ in their test for security guards. The JCQ has never been used or validated for managerial positions and is not recommended for the selection of managers.

Can We Predict Employee Theft?

It is estimated that employee theft exceeds $400 billion annually. In response to this huge problem and in addition to more detailed background and reference checks, more than 4 million job applicants took some form of honesty or integrity test in 2008. These tests are typically used for jobs in which workers have access to money, such as retail stores, fast-food chains, and banks. Integrity or honesty tests have become more popular since the polygraph, or lie detector, test was banned in 1988 by the **Employee Polygraph Protection Act.** This federal law outlawed the use of the polygraph for selection and greatly restricts the use of the test for other employment situations. There are some employment exemptions to the law, such as those involving security services, businesses involving controlled substances, and government employers.

Honesty/integrity tests

Integrity/honesty tests are designed to measure attitudes toward theft and may include questions concerning beliefs about how often theft on the job occurs, judgments of the punishments for different degrees of theft, the perceived ease of theft, support for excuses for stealing from an employer, and assessments of one's own honesty. Most inventories also ask the respondent to report his/her own history of theft and other various counter productive work behaviors (CWBs).

Sample items typically cover beliefs about the amount of theft that takes place, asking test takers questions such as the following: "What percentage of people take more than $1.00 per week from their employer?" The test also questions punitiveness toward theft: "Should a person be fired if caught stealing $5.00?" The test takers answer questions reflecting their thoughts about stealing: "Have you ever thought about taking company merchandise without actually taking any?" Other honesty tests include items that have been found to correlate with theft: "You freely admit your mistakes." "You like to do things that shock people." "You have had a lot of disagreements with your parents."

Strong validity but few studies predict actual theft

The validity evidence for integrity tests is fairly strong, with little adverse impact. Still, critics point to a number of problems with the validity studies. First, most of the validity studies have been conducted by the test publishers themselves; there have been very few independent validation studies. Second, few of the criterion-related validity studies use employee theft as the criterion. A report by the American Psychological Association concluded that the evidence supports the validity of some of the most carefully developed and validated honesty tests. The most recent studies on integrity tests support their use.[35-] Although designed to predict CWBs, especially employee theft, integrity tests have also

Highest incremental validity with GMA

been found to predict job performance. One major study found that integrity tests had the highest incremental validity (of all other tests) in the prediction of job performance over GMA.[36] Scores on integrity tests are also related to Conscientiousness, Emotional Stability, and Agreeableness of the FFM. It has been proposed that a trait represented on integrity tests is not well represented by the FFM. "Honesty-Humility (H-H)" has been proposed as the sixth factor defined as "sincerity, fairness, lack of conceit, and lack of greed." There is evidence that this sixth factor can enhance the prediction of CWBs or workplace delinquency.[37]

Can We Identify Applicants Who Will Provide Good Customer Service?

SOI

Considerable research demonstrates that employees' customer orientation is a good predictor of customer-related outcomes such as customer- and supervisory-ratings of service performance, customer-focused organizational citizenship behaviors, and customer satisfaction. Thus, identifying employees who would have such an orientation would be advantageous for organizations with a strong customer-focused strategy. The **Service Orientation Index (SOI)** was initially developed as a means of predicting the helpfulness of nurses' aides in large, inner-city hospitals.[38] The test items were selected from three main dimensions: patient service, assisting other personnel, and communication. Here are some examples of SOI items: "I always notice when people are upset" and "I never resent it when I don't get my way." Several other studies of the SOI involving clerical employees and truck drivers have reported positive results as well. The **Job Compatibility Questionnaire** has also been used to predict effective customer service.

Can We Identify Bad and Risky (and Costly) Drivers?

Driving accidents by employees can be a very costly expense for employers where driving to and from jobs is an essential function of the job. Think cable companies, UPS, FedEx, and exterminators for a few examples of companies that should pay careful attention to the "accident proneness" of the drivers they hire. In addition, employers are often held responsible for the driving behavior of their employees when they are on the job. A plethora of **negligent hiring** lawsuits have looked at what screening procedures were used to hire the guy who committed a driving infraction while on the job and caused a serious accident.

So, first off, is there such a thing as "accident proneness," and if so, can we predict it in job applicants? The answers to these two key questions are in fact "yes" and "yes." Research shows that a person's previous driving record is the single best predictor of the on-the-job record and an essential screening tool. But personality is a correlate of risky driving behavior and future traffic violations and accidents. For young drivers (18–25), one study found that a high level of "thrill-seeking" and aggression, combined with a low level of empathy, was a predictor of subsequent risky driving and speeding violations. The researchers measured these subfactors from the "Big-Five" traits. The subfactors derived from the Emotional Stability (anger/aggression), Extraversion ("thrill-seeking"), and Agreeableness (low empathy) components of the FFM.[39]

Driving record is a strong predictor

Personality predicts risky driving

Other research also shows that personality factors are an important influence on risk perceptions and driving behavior. Traits labeled as "sensation seeking," "impulsiveness," and "boredom proneness" have also been shown to predict of aggressive and risky driving using the **"Driving Anger Scale."**[40]

Accident-proneness can be predicted

Another test developed to predict (and prevent) accidents is the **Safety Locus of Control Scale (SLC)**, which is a paper-and-pencil test containing 17 items assessing attitudes toward safety. A sample item is as follows: "Avoiding accidents is a matter of luck." Validity data looks encouraging across several different industries, including transportation, hotels, and aviation. In addition, these investigations indicate no adverse impact against minorities and women.[41]

Results with older drivers also suggests that a "sensation-seeking" personality and low levels of emotional stability are related to risky driving among older drivers in addition to cognitive and motor abilities.[42] The perception of reckless driving as acceptable and desirable or as negative and threatening and the risk assessment related to cell phone usage are other predictors of driving behavior and accidents. There apparently is such a thing as "accident prone" in the sense that the people most "prone" to be involved in accidents can be identified with a background check and a personality inventory.

Not relevant to current work

How Do You Establish a Testing Program?

Establishing a psychological testing program is a difficult undertaking—one that should ideally involve the advice of an industrial psychologist. HR professionals should follow these guidelines before using psychological tests:

1. Most reputable testing publishers provide a test manual. Study the manual carefully, particularly the adverse impact and validity evidence. Has the test been shown to predict success in jobs similar to the jobs you're trying to fill? Have adverse impact studies been performed? What are the findings? Are there positive, independent research studies in scholarly journals? Have qualified experts with advanced degrees in psychology or related fields been involved in the research?

2. Check to see if the test has been reviewed in *Mental Measurements Yearbook (MMY)*. Published by the Buros Institute of the University of Nebraska, the MMY publishes scholarly reviews of tests by qualified academics who have no vested interest in the tests they are reviewing. You can also download Buros test reviews online at http://buros.unl.edu/buros/jsp/search.jsp. You can retrieve reviews by test name or by category (e.g., achievement, intelligence, personality).

3. Ask the test publishers for the names of several companies that have used the test. Call a sample of them and determine if they have conducted any adverse impact and validity studies. Determine if legal actions have been taken related to the test; if so, what are the implications for your situation?

4. Obtain a copy of the test from the publisher and carefully examine all of the test items. Consider each item in the context of ethical, legal, and privacy ramifications. Organizations have lost court cases because of specific items on a test.

Proceed cautiously in the selection and adoption of psychological tests. Don't be wowed by a slick test brochure; take a step back and evaluate the product in the same manner you would evaluate any product before buying it. Be particularly critical of vendors' claims and remember that you can assess personality and motivation using an interview. If you decide to adopt a test, maintain the data so that you can evaluate whether the test is working. In general, it is always advisable to contact someone who can give you an objective, expert appraisal.

DRUG TESTING

Drug abuse is one of the most serious problems in the United States today, with productivity costs in the billions of dollars and on the rise. Drug abuse in the workplace also has been linked to employee theft, accidents, absences, use of sick time, and other counterproductive behavior. Detected amphetamine use tripled between 2000 and 2008. Methamphetamine is the most commonly used form of amphetamine today. According to the 2008 National Survey on Drug Use and Health, over 12 million Americans had tried methamphetamine at least once in their lifetimes (over 5 percent of the population). To combat this growing problem, many organizations are turning to drug testing for job applicants and incumbents.

One survey found 87 percent of major U.S. corporations now use some form of drug testing.[43] While some of the tests are in the form of paper-and-pencil examinations, the vast majority of tests conducted are clinical tests of urine or hair samples. Ninety-six percent of firms refuse to hire applicants who test positive for illegal drug use, methamphetamines, and some prescription drugs (e.g., OxyContin). While the most common practice is to test job applicants, drug testing of job incumbents, either through a randomized procedure or based on probable cause, is also on the increase.

Immunoassay test

The most common form of urinalysis testing is the immunoassay test, which applies an enzyme solution to a urine sample and measures change in the density of the sample. The drawback of the $20 (per applicant) immunoassay test is that it is sensitive to some legal drugs as well as illegal drugs. Because of this, it is recommended that a positive immunoassay test be followed by a more reliable confirmatory test, such as gas chromatography. The only errors in testing that can occur with the confirmatory tests are due to two causes: positive results from passive inhalation, a rare event (caused by involuntarily inhaling marijuana), and laboratory blunders (e.g., mixing urine samples). Hair analysis is a more expensive but also more reliable and less invasive form of drug testing. Testing for methamphetamine use is difficult since the ingredients pass through the body quickly.

Positive test results say little regarding one's ability to perform the job, and most testing gives little or no information about the amount of the drug that was used, when it was used, how frequently it was used, and whether the applicant or candidate will be (or is) less effective on the job.

Drug testing is legal in all 50 states

The legal implications of drug testing are evolving. Currently, drug testing is legal in all 50 states for pre-employment screening and on-the-job assessment; however, employees in some states have successfully challenged dismissals based solely on a random drug test. For those employment situations in which a collective-bargaining agreement has allowed drug testing, the punitive action based on the results is subject to arbitration. One study found that the majority of dismissals based on drug tests were overturned by arbitrators.[44] Among the arguments against drug testing are that it is an invasion of privacy, it is an unreasonable search and seizure, and it violates the right of due process. Most experts agree that all three of these arguments may apply to public employers, such as governments, but do not apply to private industry. State law is relevant here since some drug testing programs have been challenged under privacy provisions of state constitutions. With regard to public employment, the Supreme Court has ruled that drug testing is legal if the employer can show a "special need" (e.g., public safety). Drug testing will be covered in more detail in Chapter 14.

Is Some Testing an Invasion of Privacy?

Politically-oriented questions are illegal in some states

The widespread use of various employment tests has been criticized on the grounds that these procedures may be an invasion of individuals' privacy and unnecessarily reveal information that will affect individuals' employment opportunities. Selection methods that seem to provoke these concerns are drug tests, personality tests and honesty/integrity tests. Questions on tests or interviews that are political in tone are illegal in some states. Experts in the field of employment testing who support testing have responded to this challenge in a number of ways. First, various professional standards and guidelines have been devised to protect the confidentiality of test results. Second, since almost any interpersonal interaction, whether it be an interview or an informal discussion with an employer over lunch, involves the exchange of information, advocates of employment testing contend that every selection procedure compromises applicants' privacy to some degree. Finally, in the interests of high productivity, and staying within the law, they assert, organizations may need to violate individuals' privacy to a certain extent. Companies with government contracts are among those that are obliged to maintain a safe work environment and may need to require drug testing and extensive background checks of employees.

Concerns will continue to be voiced over the confidentiality and ethics of employment testing, particularly as computer-based databases expand in scope and availability to organizations. It is also likely that there will be increasing calls for more legislation at federal, state, and local levels to restrict company access to and use of employment-related information.

PERFORMANCE TESTING/WORK SAMPLES

Despite making valuable contributions to employee selection, paper-and-pencil tests have their problems and limitations. The validity of cognitive ability tests is proven and clear. Unfortunately, the potential legal implications of their use are considerable. Unfortunately, the validity of paper-and-pencil measures of applicant motivation or personality is not nearly as impressive. Many experts suggest that the prediction of job performance can be enhanced through **performance testing** which is the sampling of simulated job tasks and/or behaviors. There is also evidence that the use of such tests can result in less adverse impact than cognitive ability tests and that test takers perceive such tests as more accurate and fair.[45]

Performance tests and work samples have good validity

Performance tests measure KASOCs or competencies (e.g., application of knowledge or a skill in a simulated setting). Like work samples, performance tests involve actual "doing" rather than "knowing how." Thus, a performance test may require a job candidate to demonstrate a skill such as written communication or analytical ability. Applicants may also be required to prepare something for a live demonstration. Thus, preparing a lesson plan for a unit of instruction could be the first step before a simulated class is conducted.

Work sample tests are exercises that reflect actual job responsibilities and tasks. Applicants are placed in a job situation and are required to handle tasks, activities, or problems that match those found on the job. The purpose of a simulation or work sample test is to allow applicants to demonstrate their job-related competencies in as realistic a situation as possible.

Work samples can duplicate a real-life event but eliminate the risks of danger or damage such as substituting safe substances or chemicals to test the correct handling of dangerous materials or using driving or flight simulators. Like performance tests, work samples are conducted under controlled conditions for the purposes of consistency and fairness and can be developed using a number of different formats.

To ensure that performance tests and work samples are tailored to match the important activities of the job, HR professionals should develop the methods from the tasks, behaviors, and responsibilities identified in a job analysis (see Chapter 4).

One form of performance testing is the **Situational Judgment Test (SJT).** This test consists of a number of job-related situations presented in written, verbal, or visual (video) form. Unlike a typical work sample, SJTs present hypothetical situations and ask respondents how they would respond. Here's an example of an SJT question:[46]

> A customer asks for a specific brand of merchandise the store doesn't carry. How would you respond?
> A. Tell the customer which stores carry that brand, but point out that your brand is similar.
> B. Ask the customer more questions so you can suggest something else.
> C. Tell the customer that the store carries the best merchandise available.
> D. Ask another associate to help.
> E. Tell the customer which stores carry the brand.
> Questions:
> 1. Which of the options above do you believe is the best under the circumstances?
> 2. Which of the options above do you believe is the worst under the circumstances?

SJTs have incremental validity

Research on SJTs is quite positive. (See Figure 6-2 for validity data.) A recent review showed that SJTs showed incremental validity above cognitive ability, personality (using the Five-Factor Model), and job/training experiences measures.[47]

The performance testing process should be standardized as much as possible with consistent and precise instructions, testing material, conditions, and equipment. All of the candidates must have the same time allotment to complete tests, and there must be a specific standard of performance by which to compare the applicants' efforts. To illustrate the point, a minimum passing score for a typing exam might be set at 40 words a minute with two errors. This standard would apply to all the applicants. Today, performance tests are available through the Internet. One large retailer had candidates for its district manager position complete a performance test over a Web site. Once responses are made through the Web site, trained assessors conduct interviews that focus on the candidates' responses.

Web-based testing

Although the research is limited, that which exists tends to support proctored, Web-based testing.[48] Studies involving SJTs, biodata, and personality measurement using the Five-Factor Model indicate that proctored, Web-based testing has positive benefits relative to paper-and-pencil measures.

What Is an Assessment Center?

An **assessment center** is a collection of many of the selection tools already discussed. The use of multiple techniques and a standardized process of data collection certainly contributes to the validity of the method (see Figure 6-2; .46 validity for managerial jobs). Unlike most of the research on cognitive ability tests, most of the validity evidence on assessment centers is from studies of management positions. These "centers" use trained observers and a variety of techniques to make judgments about behavior, in part, from specially developed assessment simulations. **Assessors typically test job candidates with a collection of performance tests that simulate the work environment.** Some centers also use paper-and-pencil tests including GMA and personality tests, as part of the assessment process. At the Center for Creative Leadership in Greensboro, North Carolina, managers complete a battery of cognitive and personality tests and receive subordinate and peer assessments prior to their participation in the two-day assessment center which includes five performance tests.

Private sector organizations, educational institutions, military organizations, public safety, and other governmental agencies have used the assessment center method to identify candidates for selection, placement, and promotion. Because of the cost, most organizations use assessment centers for supervisory or managerial selection. There have been some applications of the method for nonadministrative positions such as sales personnel, vocational rehabilitation counselors, planning analysts, social workers, personnel specialists, research analysts, firefighters, and police officers.

Allows for direct comparisons among internal and external candidates

One of the advantages of the assessment center approach for managerial selection is that internal and external candidates can go through the assessment center to provide a direct comparison of the candidates, as they participate (and compete) in the collection of performance tests. Candidates are assessed and compared by trained assessors. Among the numerous organizations that use the assessment center method for selection are the FBI, AT&T, IBM, Ford, Office Depot, Xerox, Procter and Gamble, the Department of Defense, the CIA, and the Federal Aviation Administration. Assessment centers are expensive, with costs ranging from a low of about $300 for each candidate to as much as $8,000 for upper-level managerial selection.

Features trained assessors and multiple performance tests

With the typical assessment center method, information about an employee's strengths and weaknesses is provided through a combination of performance tests that are designed to simulate the type of work to which the candidate will be exposed. A team of trained assessors observes and evaluates performance in the simulations. The assessors compile and integrate their judgments on each exercise to form a summary rating for each candidate being assessed.

Assessment centers tend to vary in terms of length of the assessment process (one day to one week), the ratio of assessors to those being assessed, the extent of assessor training, and the number and type of assessment instruments and exercises that are used to assess candidates.[49]

Assess job dimensions or competencies

All assessment centers call for an assessment of job *dimensions* or competencies. United Technology evaluates managers on the following dimensions: oral presentation, initiative, leadership, planning and organization, written communication, decision making, and interpersonal skills. **Dimensions are clusters of behaviors that are specific, observable, and verifiable and can be reliably and logically classified together.** The dimension "written communication" was defined by United Technology as the following: "clear expression of ideas in writing and in good grammatical form." United Technology breaks down behavioral examples of written communication as: "Exchanges information/reports with superior regarding the day's activities. Completes all written reports and required forms in a manner that ensures the inclusion of all data necessary to meet the needs of the personnel using the information. Uses appropriate vocabulary and avoids excessive technical jargon in required correspondence." **Figure 6-7** presents a set of dimensions and their definitions as used in an assessment center for selecting supervisors. There are essentially no differences between "competencies" and dimensions as they are typically defined.

The assessment dimensions and performance tests or exercises are developed from the results of a job analysis. The exercises allow assessors to observe, record, classify, and evaluate relevant job behaviors. Some of the most common assessment exercises are **in-baskets, leaderless group discussions, oral presentations, and role-playing.** Descriptions of these methods follow.

Figure 6-7   **Assessment Center Dimensions: An Example**

Leadership: To direct, coordinate, and guide the activities of others; to monitor, instruct, and motivate others in the performance of their tasks; to assign duties and responsibilities and to follow up on assignments; to utilize available human and technical resources in accomplishing tasks and in achieving solutions to problems; to follow through within organizational guidelines.

Interpersonal: To be sensitive to the needs and feelings of others; to respond empathetically; to consistently display courtesy in interpersonal contacts; to develop rapport with others; to be cognizant of and respect the need in others for self-esteem.

Organizing and Planning: To create strategies for self and others to accomplish specific results; to utilize prescribed strategies; to fix schedules and priorities so as to meet objectivies; to coordinate personnel and other resources; to establish and utilize follow-up procedures.

Perception and Analysis: To identify, assimilate, and comprehend the critical elements of a situation; to identify alternative courses of action; to be aware of situational or data discrepancies; to evaluate salient factors and elements essential to resolution of problems.

Decision Making: To use logical and sound judgment in use of resources; to adequately assess a situation and make a sound and logical determination of an appropriate course of action based on the facts available, including established procedures and guidelines; to select solutions to problems by weighing the ramifications of alternative courses of action.

Oral and Nonverbal Communication: To present information to others concisely and without ambiguity; to articulate clearly; to use appropriate voice inflection, grammar, and vocabulary; to maintain appropriate eye contact; to display congruent nonverbal behavior.

Adaptability: To modify courses of action to accommodate situational changes; to vary behavior in accordance with changes in human and interpersonal factors; to withstand stress.

Decisiveness: To make frequent decisions; to make decisions spanning many different areas; to render judgments, take action, and make commitments; to react quickly to situational changes; to make determinations based on available evidence; to defend actions when challenged by others.

Written Communications: To present and express information in writing, employing unambiguous, concise, and effective language. To use correct grammar, punctuation, and sentence structure; to adjust writing style to the demands of the communication.

In-Basket

The *in-basket* consists of a variety of materials of varying importance and priority that typically would be handled by a manager the organization is trying to hire. Candidates are asked to imagine that they are placed in the position and must deal with a number of memos and items accumulated in their in-baskets. Assessors give them background information about the unit they are managing, and they must deal with the in-basket materials in a limited amount of time. After writing their responses to the memos, the candidates are interviewed by trained assessors who review the "out-basket" and question the actions taken. In-baskets are typically designed to measure oral and written communication skills, planning, decisiveness, initiative, and organization skills.

Leaderless Group Discussion

Candidates assemble in groups of three to six people after individually considering an issue or problem and making specific recommendations. While a leader is not designated for the group, one usually emerges in the course of the group interaction. Two or more assessors observe the interaction as the group attempts to reach consensus on the issue. Assessors typically use the leaderless group discussion to determine oral communication, stress tolerance, adaptability, leadership, and persuasiveness. Some graduate schools now use the leaderless group discussion to select doctoral students for their business and other graduate programs.

Oral Presentation

In the brief time allowed, candidates plan, organize, and prepare a presentation on an assigned topic. An assessment center developed by IBM requires candidates for sales management positions to prepare and deliver a five-minute oral presentation in which they present one of their hypothetical staff members for promotion, and then defend the staff member in a group discussion. IBM uses this exercise to evaluate assertiveness, selling ability, self-confidence, resistance, and interpersonal contact.[50]

Role-Playing

For this common assessment center exercise, candidates assume the role of the incumbent and must deal with a subordinate about a performance problem. The subordinate is a trained role-player. Another example is to have candidates interact with clients or individuals external to the organization, requiring them to obtain information or alleviate a problem. Vocational rehabilitation counselor candidates who apply for jobs with the Massachusetts Rehabilitation Commission assume the role of a counselor who is meeting a client for the first time. The candidate has the responsibility of gaining information on the client's case and establishing rapport with the client. **Figure 6-8** presents summary descriptions of four exercises used in an assessment center to select store managers in a retail environment.

Figure 6-8   **Description of Assessment Center Exercises for Retail Managers**

Customer Situation: A large equipment user (a select national account) has been experiencing recent problems involving a particular piece of equipment, culminating in a systems down situation. Problems with the equipment could include software, and parts received to fix the equipment are damaged.

 The participant will be required to review information about the problem for 30 minutes and generate potential courses of action. Participants will then meet in groups to devise a consensus strategy for dealing with the problem. Assessors should expect a plan of action from the participants and may probe the participants for additional contingency plans. The participants will have 45 minutes to discuss the customer problem and develop a strategy.

Employee Discussion: In this exercise the participant must develop a strategy for counseling a subordinate (a senior customer service engineer) who has been experiencing recent performance problems. The participant will have 30 minutes to review information regarding the technician's declining performance over the last few months.

 The participant will then have 15 minutes to prepare a brief report on the individual with recommendations for submission to the district manager. The participant will then meet with two assessors to discuss the strategy.

In-Basket: In this exercise, the participant will assume the role of a newly transferred branch manager. The participant will have 90 minutes to review information related to various issues (technical developments, equipment maintenance specifications, customer information, etc.). The participant will be instructed to spend this time identifying priorities and grouping related issues, as well as indicating courses of action to be taken. The participant will then take part in a 15-minute interview with an assessor to clarify the actions taken and logic behind decisions made.

Problem Analysis: In this exercise the participant will be required to review information on three candidates and provide a recommendation on which of the three should be promoted to a branch manager position. The participant will have 90 minutes to review information and prepare a written recommendation. The participants will then meet in groups to derive a consensus recommendation for the district manager.

How Are Assessments Done?

Assessors who have received extensive training on assessment center methodology evaluate all of the candidates in an assessment center—usually 6 to 12 people—as they perform the same tasks. Assessors are trained to recognize designated behaviors, which are clearly defined prior to each assessment.

 Assessors are often representatives from the organization who are at higher levels than the candidates being assessed. This is done to diminish the potential for contamination, which may result from an assessor allowing prior association with a candidate to interfere with making an objective evaluation. Some assessment centers use outside consultants and psychologists as assessors and there is some evidence that this will increase validity.

 Different assessors observe assessment center candidates in each exercise. The assessors are responsible for observing the actual behavior of the candidate during each exercise and documenting how each candidate performed.

 After the participants complete all of the exercises, the assessors typically assemble at a team meeting to pool their impressions, arrive at an overall consensus rating for each candidate on each dimension, and derive an overall assessment rating.

 There is recent evidence that assessment centers can be broken down to make them less costly and more efficient. Research shows that you probably do not have to assemble candidates together at a "center"; performance tests completed online and follow-up interviews by trained assessors reveal essentially the same results as the more typical assessment centers.

What Is the Validity and Adverse Impact of Assessment Centers and Other Performance Tests?

Strong validity for managerial positions

More defensible in court (less AI than GMA)

There is a scarcity of well-done, criterion-related validity studies on assessment centers. With a few exceptions, assessment center validity studies focus on administrative positions such as managers and supervisors with strong positive correlations.[51] The method also has proved to be valid for law enforcement personnel.[52] In general, the validity of assessment centers is strong[53] (see Figure 6-2), particularly for managerial positions. Recent research indicates higher criterion-related validity can be obtained when fewer dimensions are used and when assessors are psychologists.[54]

 While the validities reported for assessment centers are similar to those reported for cognitive ability tests, decisions made from assessment centers are more defensible in court and result in less adverse impact than cognitive ability tests. **The method is ideal when an organization has both internal and external candidates.** Most companies use assessment centers as one of the last steps in a selection process where both internal and external candidates are being considered. People who are assessed by the assessment center method or performance tests perceive the procedure to be fair and job related, making them less likely to take legal action.

Performance Appraisals/ Competency Assessment

The use of competencies as a fundamental building block of organizations and the people they employ is increasingly popular and is often used as the basis for personnel decisions within an organization. Remember that a policy of promotion from within the organization (based to some extent on past performance in other jobs) is a **High-Performance Work System Characteristic.** But there is little research on the validity of performance-based competency assessment or performance appraisal in general for predicting performance at a higher level. Does high performance in Job A, for example (at least as rated by supervisors, co-workers, or others), predict performance in Job B? Many organizations now use some form of a multirater or 360-degree assessment process to measure competencies. (Remember that 360-degree appraisal is also classified as a High-Performance Work System Characteristic.) Appraisal data can often be found in human resource information systems (HRIS) and used for succession planning. PeopleSoft's most popular HRIS, for example, includes a Web-based competency-appraisal system, the data of which is maintained on each employee and helps companies do succession and career planning.

But how does 360-degree appraisal or, for that matter, appraisal from any rating source compare on its ability to predict later performance relative to some of these other tools just described? Is 360-degree appraisal data, or peer assessment, or supervisory assessment as good as (or better than) assessment centers or testing, for example? One study in a retail environment addressed this issue comparing the levels of criterion-related validity and the extent of statistical adverse impact against minorities with three popular methods.[55] Data based on top-down (supervisory) performance appraisals, a 360-degree competency-based appraisal system, and a traditional assessment center were correlated with subsequent job performance of retail store managers. The assessment center and 360-degree systems had the highest levels of predictive validity while the "top-down" managerial assessment was significantly lower (.46 for ACs, .37 for 360-degree versus .19 for "top-down"). The 360-degree data and the assessment center also resulted in less adverse impact than the "top-down" method.

360-degree PA had higher validity than "top-down" appraisal

Incremental validity for 360 appraisal with AC data

Evidence for the incremental validity of 360-degree appraisal data above the AC data was also found, indicating more accurate prediction with the combination of AC and 360-degree data. While this one study showed practical usefulness for the 360-degree appraisal as a source of data for personnel decisions, these data are obviously problematic if both internal and external candidates are being considered, since no 360-degree data would be available for the external candidates. However, you should not ignore useful (and valid) information because some candidates do not have it. Use whatever *valid* data you have but, if possible, try to obtain the full complement of data on all candidates. This is one advantage of assessment centers for higher-level staffing decisions. When you have external candidates competing against internal candidates for managerial positions, assessment centers create a "level playing field" of valid sources of information about the candidates.

INTERVIEWS

While the use of paper-and-pencil tests and performance tests has increased, the employment interview continues to be the most common personnel selection tool. Primarily due to its expense, the interview is typically one of the last selection hurdles used after other methods have reduced the number of potential candidates. The manner in which interviews are conducted is not typically conducive to high validity for the method. But there is clear evidence that interviews, when done properly, can be quite valid.

 One of the bigger discrepancies between HRM research and practice is in the area of interviewing. Research provides clear prescriptions for interviewing the right way and this way is clearly at odds with the way it is typically done. **Figure 6-9** presents the most important discrepancies between research and practice as related to interviewing based on a recent survey conducted of 105 HR managers working for organizations with 100 or more employees. The good news is that the results reported in Figure 6-9 are an improvement on previous survey results. Even academic institutions, from which the vast majority of this research is derived, do not usually practice what they preach when it comes to selecting a new faculty member or administrator.

Figure 6-9   Discrepancies between Research and Practice for Employment Interviews

What Does Research Say?	What Is the Practice?
Use job analysis to derive questions	18% of companies use formal job analysis
Monitor interview data for adverse impact	21% of companies do
Validate interview format/content	14% of companies do
Train interviewers	29% do
Formally weight hiring factors based on job analysis	4% do
Use a structured interview format	12% do
Use "situational" interview questions	29% do
Use "behavioral" interview questions	22% do
Use a formal interview rating system	25% do
Use more than one interviewer	45% do
Use statistical model to combine data from other sources (tests, bio-data, etc.)	2% use actuarial or statistical model

Source: H. J. Bernardin, "The Frequency of Use and Perceived Validity of Staffing Method Options," 2009. Unpublished manuscript (under review).

Almost every student eventually will take part in a job interview. Nearly 100 percent of organizations use the employment interview as one basis for personnel selection. Even some universities now use interviews to select students for graduate programs. Dartmouth, Carnegie-Mellon, and The Wharton School at the University of Pennsylvania routinely interview applicants for their prestigious MBA programs. Many companies now provide extensive training programs and specific guidelines for interviewers. As Tom Newman, director of training at S. C. Johnson & Son, Inc., said, interviewing is now "much more of a science." This "science" clearly pays off as research shows greater validity for more systematic interviewing. Mobil Oil, Radisson Hotels International, the Marriott Corporation, and Sun Bank are among the many companies with extensive programs to prepare their interviewers.

What Factors Affect the Employment Interview?

A veritable plethora of research has been devoted to the employment interview.[56] This research has focused on the attributes of the applicant, the attributes of the interviewer, extraneous variables that affect interview results, interview formats, and, of course, the validity of interviews related to all of these things.

In the context of the interview, the attributes of the applicant refer to characteristics that influence an interviewer's attention to and impression of the applicant. Voice modulation, body language, posture, interviewee anxiety, and visible characteristics such as sex, weight, ethnicity, and physical attractiveness are among the factors that might influence the interviewer's judgments about a job applicant. A common phenomenon here is "stereotyping," in which an impression about an individual is formed due to his/her group membership rather than any individual attributes. **Stereotyping** involves categorizing groups according to general traits and then attributing those traits to a particular individual once the group membership is known. Although stereotypes are a common and convenient means of efficiently processing information, they can be a source of bias when people attribute traits they believe to be true for an entire group to one member—without considering that person as an individual. Expert witnesses in EEO litigation often cite "stereotyping" as an error more likely to occur when the selection process is **"excessively subjective"** such as an informal, unstructured interview conducted by a single white male. This testimony is featured in the Wal-Mart sex discrimination lawsuit.

Excessive subjectivity

The interviewer's personal characteristics also can influence his/her judgment in other way resulting in interviews that can be characterized as "excessively subjective." Personal values and previously learned associations between certain information cues and decision responses might influence an interviewer's decision-making process. One type of subjective perceptual influence is a "similar-to-me" attribution, meaning the interviewer forms an impression of perceived similarity between an applicant and himself/herself based on the interviewer's attitudes, interests, or group membership, causing certain information, or

"Similar-to-me"

individuals, to be placed in a more favorable light than others. The danger is that these judgments on the basis of similarity can cause rating errors and bias; the perceived advantages might not be relevant to the particular job for which the interview is being conducted.

Factors related to attention to information

Factors such as stress, background noise, interruptions, time pressures, decision accountability, and other conditions surrounding the interview also can influence interviewers' attention to information. An important factor is the amount of information about the job the interviewer has prior to the actual interview session. Little background information about the job may cause distortion in the decision-making process because of resulting irrelevant or erroneous assumptions about job requirements. This lack of job information causes the interviewer to rely on his/her assumptions about what the job requires. These can be inconsistent across different interviewers or across different interview sessions. Rating errors occur because interviewers collect non-job-related information and use the information to make decisions.

Applicant, interviewer, and situational attributes can bias interviews

Thus applicant, interviewer, and situation attributes can potentially bias the decision-making process and result in erroneous evaluations during the interview. In response to these problems, as well as the high cost of face-to-face interviews, many companies conduct computer interviews to screen applicants. The next time you're in a Blockbuster Video, check out the "Employment Center," a computer workstation where you complete a job application online and take an employment test. Telecomputing Interviewing Services in San Francisco lists more than 1,500 clients that conduct computer interviews for mostly entry-level jobs. Bloomingdale's hired all of its personnel for its Miami store using computer interviewing that questions applicants about work attitudes, substance abuse, and employee theft. As Ellen Pollin, personnel manager at Bloomingdale's, puts it, "The machine never forgets to ask a question and asks each question in the same way." Other companies are using video-conferencing to interview employees, particularly managerial prospects. Texas Instruments claims, considerable cost savings with no loss in validity using videoconferences.

Citizens Bank of Maryland reduced interviewer involvement by combining a short, structured interview with a video developed especially for tellers and customer service representatives. The video provides a **realistic job preview** that describes the positive and negative features of the job and then tests applicants on job-related verbal, quantitative, and interpersonal skills. The test is completed on a computer and is scored for $32. Citizens Bank reported higher validity and a significant drop in turnover with this method compared to turnover rates when hiring decisions were based on an unstructured interview (i.e., one in which interviewers have no formal set of questions to ask).

Structured and standardized interviewing is growing in popularity. Perhaps the biggest company in this business is the **Gallup Organization** (visit gallup.com and find "talent-based hiring" for a description). Gallup conducted a huge study of management behavior, described in the best seller *Now, Discover Your Strengths*.[57] Gallup associates conducted over 1.7 million interviews at 101 companies from 63 countries. One result of this research was a structured interview that is administered by telephone and then scored based on the taped transcript using a standardized rating form. This talent assessment tool is now used by, among many others, Disney, Toyota, Marriott, and Best Buy to help select managers and sales personnel. This nontraditional way to conduct an interview nonetheless resulted in the same level of validity as the more traditional approach.[58]

What Is the Validity of Employment Interviews?

The information obtained from the interview provides a basis for subsequent selection and placement decisions, whose overall quality depends on the interview. How reliable is the interview information? How valid is that information for predictive purposes? That is, to what extent do interview judgments predict subsequent job performance and other important criteria?

The validity of the employment interview often has been impaired by underlying perceptual bias owing to factors such as first impressions, stereotypes, different information utilization, different questioning content, and lack of interviewer knowledge regarding the requirements of the job to be filled. However, as a result of recent efforts to improve interview effectiveness, research indicates that certain types of interviews are more reliable and valid than the typical, unstructured format. For instance, interview questions based on

Structured interviews have strong validity

a job analysis (see Chapter 4), as opposed to psychological or trait information, increase the validity of the interview procedure.[59] **Structured interviews,** which represent a standardized approach to systematically collecting and rating applicant information, have yielded higher reliability and validity results than unstructured interviews (.51 versus .31; see again Figure 6-2). Research findings also suggest that the effectiveness of interview decisions can be improved by carefully defining what information is to be evaluated, by systematically evaluating that information using consistent rating standards, and by focusing the interview (and interview questions) on past behaviors and accomplishments in job-related situations.

There perhaps is a way to high validity, however, without the benefit (and cost) of structured, behavioral interviews based on a through job analysis. One study showed averaging across three or four independent, unstructured interviews is equivalent in validity to a structured interview done by one interviewer.[60]

Legally, the interview is a test

With potential bias affecting employment interviews comes potential litigation. Many cases have involved the questions that are asked at the interviews. The employment interview is in essence a "test" and is thus subject to the same laws and guidelines prohibiting discrimination on the basis of age, race, sex, religion, national origin, or disability. Furthermore, the interview process is similar to the subjective nature of the performance appraisal process; hence, many of the court decisions concerning the use of performance appraisals also apply to the interview. Judges have not been kind to employers using vague, inadequate hiring standards, "excessive subjectivity," idiosyncratic interview evaluation criteria, or biased questions unrelated to the job. The courts also have criticized employers for inadequate interviewer training and irrelevant interview questions. In general, the courts have focused on two basic issues for determining interview discrimination: the content of the interview and the impact of those decisions.

Discriminatory intent

The first issue involves **discriminatory intent:** Do certain questions convey an impression of underlying discriminatory attitudes? Discrimination is most likely to occur when interviewers ask non-job-related questions of only one protected group of job candidates and not of others. Women applying for work as truck drivers at Spokane Concrete Products were questioned about child care options and other issues not asked of male applicants. The court found disparate treatment against females and a violation of Title VII. An interviewer extensively questioned a female applicant of a bank about what she would do if her six-year-old got sick. The same interviewer did not ask that question of the male applicants. The applicant didn't get the job but did get a lawyer. The court concluded that this line of questioning constitutes sex discrimination.

Discriminatory impact

The second issue pertains to *discriminatory impact:* Does the interview inquiry result in a differential, or adverse, impact on protected groups? If so, are the interview questions valid and job related? Discriminatory impact occurs when the questions asked of all job candidates implicitly screen out a majority of protected group members. Questions about arrests can have a discriminating impact on minorities. The Detroit Edison Company provided no training, job analysis information, or specific questions for its all-white staff of interviewers. The process could not be defended in light of the adverse impact that resulted from interview decisions.

Watson v. Ft. Worth Bank

Take note that the Supreme Court ruled in *Watson v. Ft. Worth Bank* that "disparate impact" theory may be used for evaluating employment interviews that are used for decision making. An informal, unstructured, and therefore "excessively subjective" interview conducted by "stereotyping" white males will be difficult to defend in the context of evidence of adverse impact in the decisions.

In summary, the inherent bias in the interview and the relatively poor validity reported for unstructured interview decisions make this selection tool vulnerable to charges of both intentional "treatment" and "impact" discrimination. Employers need to quantify, standardize, and document interview judgments. Furthermore, employers should train interviewers, continuously evaluate the reliability and validity of interview decisions, and monitor interviewer decisions for any discriminatory effects. Many companies such as S. C. Johnson, Radisson Hotels, and ExxonMobil now have extensive training programs for interviewers. This training covers interviewing procedures, potential discriminatory areas, rating procedures, and role-plays.

Evidence of Discrimination Based on the Interview

Sex Discrimination

Although early research studies indicated that female applicants generally receive lower interview evaluations than do male applicants, more detailed analyses suggest that this effect is largely dependent on the type of job in question, the amount of job information available to the interviewer, and the qualifications of the candidate. In fact, recent research suggests that females typically do not receive lower ratings in the selection interview; in some studies, females scored higher ratings than male applicants. Of course, this research can be (and has been) used in litigation against an organization where there is evidence of disparate impact against women based on interview decisions.

Race Discrimination

There is mixed evidence for racial bias in interviewer evaluations. Positive and negative results have been reported in the relatively few studies that have investigated race discrimination. There is some indication that African-American interviewers rate African-American applicants more favorably while white interviewers rate all applicants more favorably. One study of panel (three or more interviewers) interviews found the effects of rater race and applicant race were small but that the racial composition of the panel had important practical implications in that over 20 percent of decisions would change depending on the racial composition of the interview panel. Black raters evaluated black applicants more favorably than white applicants only when they were on a predominantly black panel.[61]

Age Discrimination

Although the research indicates that older applicants generally receive lower evaluations than do younger applicants, this effect is influenced by the type of job in question, interviewer characteristics, and the content of the interview questions (i.e., traits versus qualifications). The evidence for age bias is mixed and suggests that, as in gender bias, age bias might be largely determined by the type of job under study.

Disability Discrimination

Few studies have examined bias against disabled applicants. The evidence that exists suggests that some disabled applicants receive lower hiring evaluations but higher attribute ratings for personal factors such as motivation. Before any conclusions about disability bias can be made, more research needs to be conducted that examines the nature of the disability and the impact of situational factors, such as the nature of the job. (See Chapter 3 for a discussion of the ADA.)

How Can We Improve the Validity of Interviews?

Some interviewers, no doubt, are guilty of one or more of the discriminatory biases described above. Employers should examine their interview process for discriminatory bias, train interviewers about ways to prevent biased inquiries, provide interviewers with thorough and specific job specifications, structure the interview around a thorough and up-to-date job analysis, and monitor the activities and assessments of individual interviewers.

Use expat managers to develop and conduct expat interviews

Many multinational corporations use successful overseas managers to develop and conduct interviews for the selection of managers for international assignments. These managers tend to understand the major requirements of such jobs better than managers who have no overseas experience. Many U.S. companies, including Ford, Nestlé, Procter & Gamble, Texaco, and Philip Morris, credit improvements in their expatriate placements to their interviewing processes, which involve experienced and successful expatriates who have had experience in the same jobs to be filled.

The **physical environment** for the interviews should be maintained consistently by providing a standardized setting for the interviews. The conditions surrounding the interview might influence the decision-making process; therefore, extraneous factors such as noise, temperature, and interruptions should be controlled. Some companies use computer interviewing to standardize the interview process and reduce costs.

There is a great need for interviewer training. The previous discussion about the decision-making process indicates that interviewers need to be trained regarding how to evaluate job candidates, what criteria to use in the evaluation, how to use evaluation instruments, and how to avoid common biases and potentially illegal questions.

Johnson's Wax found that most interviewers had made their decisions about applicants after only five minutes. They trained their people to withhold judgment and gather information free of **first-impression bias.** Companies should use workshops and group discussions to train interviewers how to do the following:

1. *Use job information*: understand job requirements and relate these requirements to the questioning content and strategy.

2. *Reduce rating bias*: practice interviewing and provide feedback and group discussion about rating errors.

3. *Communicate effectively*: develop a rapport with applicants, "actively listen," and recognize differences in semantics.

The training should focus on the following:

1. Use of interview guides and outlines that structure the interview content and quantitatively rate applicant responses.

2. Exchange of information that focuses on relevant applicant information and provides applicants with adequate and timely information about the job and company.

Interview content

The content of the interview determines what specific factors are to be evaluated by the interviewers. The following are general suggestions based on legal and practical concerns; more specific content guidelines should be based on the specific organization and the relevant state and local laws.

1. Exclude traits that can be measured by more valid employment tests: for example, intelligence, job aptitude or ability, job skills, or knowledge.

2. Assess personality, motivational, and interpersonal factors that are required for effective job performance. These areas seem to have the most potential for incremental validity after GMA or knowledge-based tests. Use interview assessment in conjunction with standardized inventories such as a FFM instrument or the 16PF to assess relevant traits (e.g., Extraversion, Emotional Stability, and Conscientiousness for managerial jobs). Interviewers should assess only those factors that are specifically exhibited in the behavior of the applicant during the interview and that are critical for performance on the job to be filled. Don't place too much weight on interviewee anxiety.

3. Match interview questions (content areas) with the job analysis data for the job to be filled and the strategic goals of the organization.

4. Avoid biased language or jokes that may detract from the formality of the interview, and avoid inquiries that are not relevant to the job in question.

5. Limit the amount of preinterview information to information about the applicants' qualifications and clear up any ambiguous data. While knowledge of test results, letters of reference, and other sources of information can bias an interview, it is a good strategy to seek additional information relevant to applicants' levels of KASOCs.

6. Encourage note taking; it enhances recall accuracy.

7. Be aware of candidate impression management behaviors.

What Are the Major Types of Interviews?

Use formal rating forms

The format suggestions deal with how the interview content is structured and evaluated. These suggestions describe different types of interview procedures and rating forms for standardizing and documenting interviewer evaluations.

Interview questions are intended to elicit evaluation information; therefore, rating forms are recommended in order to provide a systematic scoring system for interpreting and evaluating information obtained from applicants. Based on the job analysis, the specified content of the interview, and the degree of structure for the procedure, rating forms should be constructed with the following features. First, the ratings should be behaviorally specific and based on possible applicant responses exhibited during the interview. Second, the ratings should reflect the relevant dimensions of job success and provide a focused evaluation of only the factors required for job performance. Third, the ratings should be based on quantitative rating scales that provide a continuum of possible responses. These anchors

Figure 6-10   **Sample Situational Interview Questions**

1. A customer comes into the store to pick up a watch he had left for repair. The repair was supposed to have been completed a week ago, but the watch is not back yet from the repair shop. The customer is very angry. How would you handle the situation?

1 (low)	Tell the customer the watch is not back yet and ask him to check back with you later.
3 (average)	Apologize, and tell the customer that you will check into the problem and call him or her back later.
5 (high)	Put the customer at ease and call the repair shop while the customer waits.[a]

2. For the past week you have been consistently getting the jobs that are the most time consuming (e.g., poor handwriting, complex statistical work). You know it's nobody's fault because you have been taking the jobs in priority order. You have just picked your fourth job of the day and it's another "loser." What would you do?

1 (low)	Thumb through the pile and take another job.
2 (average)	Complain to the coordinator, but do the job.
3 (high)	Take the job without complaining and do it.[b]

[a]Source: Jeff A. Weekley and Joseph A. Gier, "Reliability and Validity of the Situational Interview for a Sales Position," *Journal of Applied Psychology* 3 (1987), pp. 484–487. American Psychological Association. Reprinted with permission.

[b]Source: Gary P. Latham and Lise M. Saari, "Do People Do What They Say? Further Studies on the Situational Interview," *Journal of Applied Psychology* 4 (1984), pp. 569–573.

provide examples of good, average, and poor applicant responses for each interview question. The use of anchored rating forms reduces rater error and increases rater accuracy. This approach, using specific, multiple ratings for each content area of the interview, is preferred to using an overall, subjective suitability rating that is not explicitly relevant to the job. **Figure 6-10** presents an example of an actual rating form.

Interview formats

A variety of interview formats are used today, but most interviews are not standardized. While this lack of standardization has contributed to low reliability and validity of both overall interview decisions and the decisions of individual interviewers, improvements in the effectiveness of the procedure have been made based on the following types of interview formats.

Structured interviews

    Structured interviews range from highly structured procedures to semistructured inquiries. A highly structured interview is a procedure whereby interviewers ask the same questions of all candidates in the same order. The questions are based on a job analysis and are reviewed for relevance, accuracy, ambiguity, and bias. A semistructured interview provides general guidelines, such as an outline of either mandatory or suggested questions and recording forms for note taking and summary ratings. In contrast, the traditional, unstructured interview is characterized by open-ended questions that are not necessarily based on or related to the job to be filled. Interviewers who use either of the structured interview procedures standardize the content and process of the interview, thus improving the reliability and validity of the subsequent judgments. Structured interviews are typically behavioral or situational (or both).

Group/panel interviews

    Group/panel interviews consist of multiple interviewers who independently record and rate applicant responses during the interview session. With panel interviews, multiple ratings are combined usually by averaging across raters. The panel typically includes the job supervisor and a personnel representative or other job expert who helped develop the interview questions. As part of the interview process, the panel reviews job specifications, interview guides, and ways to avoid rating errors prior to each interview session. Procter & Gamble uses a minimum of four interviews for each position to be filled. The CIA uses a minimum of three interviews for each job candidate. The use of a panel interview reduces the impact of idiosyncratic biases that single interviewers might introduce, and the approach appears to increase interview reliability and validity. Many team-based production operations use team interviews to add new members and select team leaders. In general, there is greater validity in interviews that involve more than one interviewer for each job applicant. Two approaches to interviewing with excellent track records when they make up a structured interview are situational and behavioral interviews.

Situational interviews

    Situational interviews require applicants to describe how they would behave in specific situations. The interview questions are based on the critical incident method of job analysis, which calls for examples of unusually effective or ineffective job behaviors for a particular job (see Chapter 4). For situational interviews, incidents are converted into interview questions that require job applicants to describe how they would handle a given situation. Each question is accompanied with a rating scale, and interviewers evaluate applicants according to the effectiveness or ineffectiveness of their responses.

The Palm Beach County, Florida, school board asked the following question of all applicants for the job of high school principal: "Members of the PTA have complained about what they regard as overly harsh punishment imposed by one teacher regarding cheating on an exam. How would you handle the entire matter?" Another question had to do with a teacher who was not complying with regulations for administering standardized tests. The candidate was asked to provide a sequence of actions to be taken regarding the situation. The situational approach may be highly structured and may include an interview panel. In the case of Palm Beach County, three principals trained in situational interviewing listened to applicants' responses, asked questions, and then made independent evaluations of each response. The underlying assumption is that applicants' responses to the hypothetical job situations are predictive of what they would actually do on the job. This technique improves interviewer reliability and validity.

Behavioral interviews

Behavioral interviews ask candidates to describe actual experiences they have had in dealing with specific, job-related issues or challenges. Behavioral interviewing may involve probing beyond the initial answer. At GM's Saturn plant, employees are first asked to describe a project in which they participated as group or team members. Probing may involve work assignments, examples of good and bad teamwork, difficulties in completing the project, and other related projects.

For example, to test analytical skills, some possible behavioral questions are:

1. Give me a specific example of a time when you used good judgment and logic in solving a problem.

2. Give me an example of a time when you used your fact-finding skills to solve a problem.

3. Describe a time when you anticipated potential problems and developed preventive measures.

4. What steps do you usually follow to study a problem before making a decision?

The "Bottom Line" on Interview Validity

Behavioral interviews have higher validity than situational interviews

The "high-validity" interview

While situational interviews are valid, the behavioral interviewing approach where candidates describe actual experiences or accomplishments with important job-related situations has been shown to be reliably more valid, particularly when reported achievements or accomplishments are verified or validated.[62] *So, a "high-validity" interview should be structured with behavioral questions derived from a job analysis and involving more than one trained interviewer using a structured interview rating form.* If this cannot be done, the use of three and preferably more independent interviewers will probably get you comparable validity to the "high validity" just described.

Interview data should not be overemphasized but appropriately weighed with other valid information. When done as recommended, interviews can contribute to the prediction of job performance over and above tests of cognitive abilities, personality tests and other measures of personal characteristics and accomplishments.

COMBINING DATA FROM VARIOUS SELECTION METHODS

A number of valid selection procedures have been described in this chapter. BA&C, the consulting firm working with Wackenhut Security, recommended an accomplishment record for its supervisory jobs, which could be completed online, followed by reference checks and a background check. Applicants also could complete an online "in-basket" performance test. The next step involved Web-camera interviews between assessors and candidates, followed by a detailed behavioral interview.

But how should the data from the different selection methods be combined so that a final decision can be made regarding the applicants to be selected? As discussed earlier, most decisions are based on a "clinical" or "holistic" analysis about each candidate without any formal method of weighing scores on the various selection methods. Another way is to weigh scores from each approach equally after standardizing the data (standardizing each score as a deviation from the mean on any given instrument). Each applicant would receive a standard score on each predictor, the standard scores would be summed, and candidates would then be ranked according to the summed scores. A better approach calls for rank ordering candidates on each method and then averaging the ranks for each candidate (the top candidate would have the lowest average rank). Another useful approach, which can be

Weigh data based on validity of method

combined with the standardizing and rank ordering, is to weigh scores based on their empirical validity; that is, the extent to which each method is correlated with the criterion of interest (e.g., sales, performance, turnover). An alternative approach to the use of reported validities is to rely on expert judgment regarding the weight that should be given to each selection method. Experts could review the content and procedures of each of the methods and give each a relative predictive weight that is then applied to applicant scores.

One of the "discrepancies" between research and practice is the clear academic finding that **"actuarial"** or "statistical" decision making is superior to "clinical" or "holistic" pre-

Use "actuarial" prediction not "holistic"

diction. That means you should derive a formula based on the relative validity of different sources of information. This approach is superior to studying a lot of information and then making an overall "clinical" assessment (or prediction). If you can't use validity coefficients, using an average rank ordering process (across methods) is recommended and is superior to "clinical" judgment.[63]

BA&C conducted a criterion-related validity study and derived weights based on the validity of each of the data sources. Structured, behavioral interviewing for only the top candidates was recommended based on the number of positions they had to fill. This multiple-step process saved time and money. Most companies that use a variety of different instruments follow a similar procedure by initially using the least expensive procedure (e.g., paper-and-pencil tests, biodata), and then using a set of procedures, such as performance tests, for those who do well in the first round. These companies perform interviews only on the top scorers from the second phase of testing. The CIA, the FBI, numerous insurance companies, and a number of the most prestigious graduate business schools follow a similar procedure. The Wharton School at the University of Pennsylvania does initial screening on the basis of the GMAT and undergraduate performance. The school then requests answers to lengthy essay test questions. If the student survives this hurdle, several faculty members conduct interviews with the student.

Interviewing, especially in this context, is perhaps the most important of the selection options for assessing the person–organization fit. Google, for example, interviews job applicants several times by as many as 20 interviewers. Toyota (USA) conducts a formal interview for its Georgetown, Kentucky, factory jobs. The interview results are combined with assessment center data, a work sample, and an aptitude test. The most effective selection systems integrate the data from the interview with other sources and weigh the information using the person–organizational fit model. Take note also that self-report personality measures are more prone to faking than structured interviews designed to measure the same (and job-related) personality traits factors.

Connecticut v. Teal

What are the legal implications of this multiple-step process? In the *Connecticut v. Teal* case (Chapter 3), Ms. Teal was eliminated from further consideration at the first step of a multiple-step selection process and claimed she was a victim of Title VII discrimination. The Supreme Court said that even if the company actually hired a disproportionately greater number of minorities after the entire selection process, the **job relatedness** of that *first step* must be determined because this was where Ms. Teal was eliminated.

One excellent example of the effectiveness of using multiple measures to predict is a study that focused on predicting college student performance.[64] Scores from a biographical instrument and a situational judgment inventory (SJI) provided incremental validity when considered in combination with standardized college-entrance tests (i.e., SAT/ACT) and a measure of big-five personality constructs. Also, racial subgroup mean differences were much smaller on the biodata and SJI measures than on the standardized tests and college grade point average. Female students outperformed male students on most predictors and outcomes with the exception of the SAT/ACT. The biodata and SJI measures clearly showed promise for selecting students with reduced adverse impact against minorities.

What Is Individual Assessment?

Individual assessment (IA) is a very popular approach for selecting managers although there has been little research to determine validity. This approach is almost always based on an overall assessment provided by one or more psychologists. The IA is based on information from several sources discussed in this chapter. A lengthy interview and psychological testing, often using projective measures, are almost always involved. The Tribune Company, for example, often uses the services of a company that (for $3,000 per candidate) provides a psychological report on the candidate's prospects based on scores on the 16PF personality test (which measures the Big-Five factors and sub-Factors), a cognitive ability test, and a long interview with a psychologist who is basing the assessment on some prototype of the "ideal" manager. While the psychologist for this company could have used some statistical model for the final assessment based on the relative validity of the various sources of information about the candidates, like almost all IA, the report is based on a "holistic" or clinical assessment of the candidate as a "whole" where the psychologist studies all the information and then writes the report based on his or her own impression.

"Holistic" approach not recommended

This is another example of the discrepancy between research and practice. The research shows to use a statistical model based on the relative validity of the various sources of information. An excellent review of this approach to assessment was very critical of the method and concluded "the holistic approach to judgment and prediction has not held up to scientific scrutiny."[65]

Setting cut-off scores

Another issue is where you set the cutoff score in a multiple-cutoff system such as that recommended by BA&C. Where, for example, do you set the cutoff score for the paper-and-pencil tests in order to identify those eligible for further testing? Unfortunately, there is no clear answer to this important question. If data are available, cutoff scores for any step in the process generally should be set to ensure a *minimum* predicted standard of job performance is met. If data are not available, cutoff scores should be set based on a consideration of the cost of subsequent selection procedures per candidate, the legal defensibility of each step in the process (i.e., job relatedness), and the adverse impact of possible scores at each step. As discussed in Chapters 3 and 4, cutoff scores can be at the center of litigation if a particular cutoff score causes adverse impact. As discussed earlier, the city of Chicago lost a Title VII lawsuit in 2005 because the particular cutoff score used for the firefighters exam caused adverse impact and was not shown to be "job related." [66] Recall the discussion in Chapter 3 about the plaintiff's opportunity to present evidence and testimony for an alternative method with comparable validity and less adverse impact. The lower cutoff score has been offered successfully as the alternative method.

Where the hiring of people who turn out to be ineffective is unacceptable, as, for example, in armed security positions at airports, the setting of a higher (more rigorous) cutoff score is clearly necessary.

PERSONNEL SELECTION FOR OVERSEAS ASSIGNMENTS*

One expert on expatriate assignments tells the story of a major U.S. food manufacturer who selected the new head of the marketing division in Japan. The assumption made in the selection process was that the management skills required for successful performance in the United States were identical to the requirements for an overseas assignment. The new director was selected primarily because of his superior marketing skills. Within 18 months, his company lost 89 percent of its existing market share.[67]

What went wrong? The problem may have been the criteria that were used in the selection process. The selection criteria used to hire a manager for an overseas position must focus on more facets of a manager than the selection of someone for a domestic position. The weight given to the various criteria also may be different for overseas assignments. Besides

* Stephanie Thomason assisted in the preparation of this section.

succeeding in a job, an effective expatriate must adjust to a variety of factors: differing job responsibilities even though the same job title is used, language and cultural barriers that make the training of local personnel difficult, family matters such as spouse employment and family readjustment, simple routine activities that are frustrating in the new culture, and the lack of traditional support systems, such as religious institutions or social clubs. The marketing head in Japan, for example, spent considerable time during the first six months of his assignment simply trying to deal with family problems and to adjust to the new environment. This experience is hardly unique. As discussed in Chapter 2, expatriate selection is a real challenge, often cited by senior human resource managers as one of the most likely causes of expatriate assignment failure.[68] One survey of 80 U.S. multinational corporations found that over 50 percent of the companies had expatriate failure rates of 20 percent or more.[69] The reasons cited for the high failure rate were as follows (presented in order of importance): (1) inability of the manager's spouse to adjust to the new environment, (2) the manager's inability to adapt to a new culture and environment, (3) the manager's personality or emotional immaturity, (4) the manager's inability to cope with new overseas responsibilities, (5) the manager's lack of technical competence, and (6) the manager's lack of motivation to work overseas. Obviously, some of these problems have to do with training and career issues. **Figure 6-11** presents an often-cited model of expatriate selection, which identifies job and personal categories of attributes of expatriate success.

Expatriate failures related to selection

Several of the factors listed above concern the process of selecting personnel for such assignments. The food manufacturer placed almost all the decision weight on the technical competence of the individual, apparently figuring that he and his family could adjust or adapt to almost anything. In fact, we now know that adjustment can be predicted to some extent, and that selection systems should place emphasis on adaptability along with the ability to interact well with a diverse group of clients, customers, and business associates. Surprisingly, few organizations place emphasis on so-called relational abilities in the selection of expatriates. One recent review found that despite the existence of useful tests and questionnaires, "many global organizations do not use them extensively because they can be viewed as overly intrusive."[70] Studies involving the **Big Five** or FFM show better cross-cultural adjustment with higher scores in "Openness to Experience" and stronger performance with high "Conscientiousness" scores.[71] One recent meta-analysis of 30 studies and over 4,000 respondents found that in addition to conscientiousness, extroversion, emotional stability, and agreeableness predict expatriate job performance. While openness to experience did not predict job performance, additional factors such as cultural sensitivity and local language ability did.[72]

Relational ability

The FFM and expatriate success

Of course, one critical question that must first be addressed is whether a corporation would be better off hiring someone from within the host country. **Figure 6-12** presents a decision model that addresses this option. If the answer to this question is no, the model provides a chronology of the questions to be answered in the selection of an expatriate. If the answer is yes, the decision makers must be aware of any applicable host laws regarding personnel selection. In Poland and Sweden, for example, prospective employees must have

---

Figure 6-11 **Categories of Attributes of Expatriate Success**

Job Factors	Relational Dimensions	Motivational State	Family Situation	Language Skills
Technical skills	Tolerance for ambiguity	Belief in the mission	Willingness of spouse to live abroad	Host country language
Familiarity with host country and HQ operations	Behavioral flexibility	Congruence with career path	Adaptive and supportive spouse	Nonverbal communication
Managerial skills	Nonjudgmentalism	Interest in overseas experience	Stable marriage	
Administrative competence	Cultural empathy and low ethnocentrism	Interest in specific host country culture		
	Interpersonal skills	Willingness to acquire new patterns of behavior and attitudes		

Source: S. Ronen, *Training the International Assignee: Training and Career Development,* 1st ed. (San Francisco: Goldstein, 1989). See also J. Chew, "Managing MNC Expatriates through Crises: A Challenge for International Human Resource Management," *Research and Practice in Human Resource Management,* 12 (2) (2004), pp. 1–30.

**Figure 6-12
Model of the Selection
Process for Overseas
Assignments**

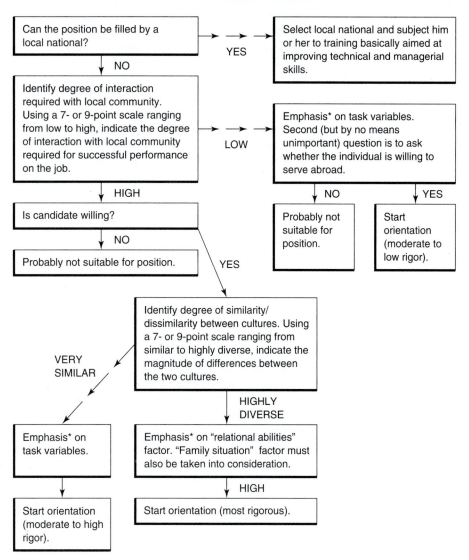

* "Emphasis" does not mean ignoring the other factors. It only means that it should be the dominant factor.

Source: Reprinted from R. L. Tung, "Selection and Training for Overseas Assignments," *Columbia Journal of World Business* 16 (1981), pp. 68–78. Reprinted with permission from Elsevier.

prior knowledge of any testing and can prohibit the release of testing data to the company. Many European countries require union participation in all selection decisions for host nationals. Thus, companies may find that hiring host nationals is more problematic than going the expatriate route. Assuming that the host option is rejected, what steps should be followed to make better selection decisions about expatriates? Let us examine some organizations that select large numbers of expatriates successfully.

The Peace Corps has only about a 12 percent turnover rate (i.e., people who prematurely end their assignments). Of the 12 percent, only 3 to 4 percent are attributed to selection errors. The Peace Corps receives an average of 5,000 applications per month. The selection process begins with an elaborate application and biographical data form that provides information on background, education, vocational preferences, and volunteer activity in the past. Second, the applicant must take a placement test to assess GMA and language aptitude. Third, college or high school transcripts are used for placement rather than screening. The fourth step requires up to 15 references from a variety of sources. Although the general tendency among references is to provide positive views of candidates, one study found that for sensitive positions such as the Peace Corps volunteer, references often provide candid comments about applicants. The final step is an interview with several Peace Corp representatives. During the interview process, the candidate is asked about preferred site locations and specific skills as well as how he or she would deal with hypothetical overseas problems. An ideal candidate must be flexible and tolerant of others and must indicate a capacity to get work done under adverse conditions. The interviews also provide Peace Corps staff with details concerning the candidate's background and preferences so that appropriate work assignments may be determined.

Based on the above four sources of information, the screeners assess a candidate using the following questions: (1) Does the applicant have a skill that is needed overseas, or a background that indicates he or she may be able to develop such a skill within a three-month training period? This question is designed to match the candidate with a job required by a foreign government, such as botanist, small business consultant, or medical worker. (2) Is the applicant personally suited for the assignment? This question focuses on personality traits such as adaptability, conscientiousness, and emotional stability.

Weights for Expatriate Selection

Structure reproducer selection

The weight to be given to expatriate selection factors differs as a function of the position to be filled. For example, a position that has an operational element requiring an individual to perform in a preexisting structure does not require strong interpersonal skills. However, a "structure reproducer," an individual who builds a unit or department, does need strong interpersonal skills. Thus, the selection system should focus on the cultural environment, job elements, and individual talents. The weights given to the various criteria should be determined by the individual job. A job analysis would be helpful in this regard. This system is exemplified by Texas Instruments (TI), a manufacturer of electronics and high-technology equipment based in Dallas. In seeking expatriates for start-up ventures, the company focuses on such issues as an individual's familiarity with the region and culture (environment), specific job knowledge for the venture (job elements), knowledge of the language spoken in the region, and interpersonal skills. TI uses several methods to make assessments on these dimensions, including the Five-Factor Model.

Many companies emphasize the "manager as ambassador" approach since the expatriate may act as the sole representative of the home office. IBM and GE, for example, select people who best symbolize the esprit de corps of the company and who recognize the importance of overseas assignments for the company.

Use a realistic job preview for expatriate assignments

A review of the most successful systems for selecting expatriates provides a set of recommendations for a selection system. First, potential expatriates are identified through posted announcements, peer and/or superior nominations, or performance appraisal data. Second, promising candidates are contacted and presented with an overview of the work assignment. A **realistic job preview** would be ideal at this stage. Third, applicants are examined using a number of selection methods, including paper-and-pencil and performance tests. A growing number of companies now use standardized instruments to assess personality traits. The 16PF, for example, has been used for years to select overseas personnel for the U.S. Department of State and is used by some U.S. companies and executive search companies that specialize in expatriate assignments. Although **relational ability** is considered to be a major predictor of expatriate success, the one available survey on the subject found that only 5 percent of companies were assessing this ability through a formal process (e.g., paper-and-pencil tests, performance appraisals).

Successful expats are ideal interviewers

After a small pool of qualified candidates is identified, candidates are interviewed and the best matches are selected for the assignment. Successful expatriates are ideal as interviewers. Our coverage of employment interviews provides recommendations for enhancing the validity of these interview decisions. Do the more rigorous selection systems result in a higher rate of expatriate success? The answer is clearly "yes."

Two tests that have been shown to be useful (and valid) are the **Global Assignment Preparedness Survey,** which assesses candidates on six dimensions, including cultural flexibility, and the **Cross-Cultural Adaptability Inventory,** which focuses on the ability to adapt to new situations and interact with people different from oneself.[73]

SELECTION IN OTHER COUNTRIES

The use of employment tests in other countries of the world varies considerably as do the government regulations regarding the use of tests. Turning first to Asian countries, Korean employers report the use of employment tests extensively and more than any other country.[74] These tests tend to be written examinations covering English language skills, common sense, and knowledge of specific disciplines. A smaller percentage of Japanese companies use employment tests. Some Japanese companies use the **Foreign Assignment Selection Test** (FAST) to identify Japanese who are more likely to be successful expatriates in the United States. The FAST assesses cultural flexibility, sociability, conflict resolution style, and leadership style. Within Japan, however, most people are hired directly from the universities, and the prestige of the university attended is a major criterion for selection purposes. A survey of companies in Hong Kong and Singapore revealed little use of employment tests, but there are a growing number of U.S. companies that have opened offices in Hong Kong. Aside from some use of clerical and office tests (e.g., typing), only two companies from these countries indicated use of any personality, cognitive ability, or related tests. Finally, recent evidence indicates China makes extensive use of employment testing, contrary to previous research.[75]

European countries have more controls on the use of tests for selection, but there is considerable variability in usage. Due to the power of unions in most European countries, employers have more restrictions on the use of tests for employment decisions, compared to the United States. A wide variety of employment tests appear to be used in Switzerland, including graphology, but in Italy selection tests are heavily regulated. In Holland, Sweden, and Poland, job applicants have access to all psychological test results and can choose to not allow the results to be divulged to an employer.[76]

Several surveys have given us clues about selection methods in England. One survey found that more than 80 percent of companies in England do some type of reference check and another found almost 40 percent had used personality tests and 25 percent had used cognitive ability tests to assess managerial candidates.[77] About 8 percent of the surveyed firms in England reported using cognitive ability tests to select managers.

In general, there is wide variation in the use of employment tests outside the United States. While some countries have restricted the use of tests (e.g., Italy), their use appears to be far more extensive in others (e.g., China, Korea). The United States and England appear to be major centers for research and development of employment tests. Japanese companies make extensive use of testing for their U.S. plants as well as for their expatriates.[78] Their Nissan plant in Tennessee relies on team assessment using a structured interview and a battery of cognitive ability tests to select new team members.

U.S. HRM specialists considering the use of tests outside of the United States to hire employees must be very familiar with laws and regulations within the country where the testing is being considered. These laws, regulations, and collective bargaining issues are very different across countries.

THE BOTTOM LINE ON STAFFING

Figure 6-13 presents a chronology of steps that should be followed based on solid research and legal considerations. You should note that effective selection requires effective recruiting. That recruiting should be done only when the organization has determined which KASOCs or competencies are required to execute strategic goals.[79]

Figure 6-13   **The Bottom-Line Chronology on Staffing**

1. DEFINE THE JOB WITH A FOCUS ON JOB SPECIFICATIONS (COMPETENCIES) COMPATIBLE WITH STRATEGIC GOALS AND EXECUTING THOSE GOALS

Action: Re-do job descriptions/specifications or competencies.

        Define critical KASOCs/competencies.

2. RECRUIT FROM A BROAD POOL OF CANDIDATES

Action: Lower selection ratio (increase number of qualified applicants for key positions) through better and more focused recruiting; for managerial positions, emphasize internal talent.

        Increase pool of qualified minorities.

3. USE VALID INITIAL SCREENING DEVICES

Action: Develop or purchase most valid and most practical screening devices with the least adverse impact.

        Refer to Mental Measurements Yearbook (www.unl.edu/Buros) for test reviews.

        If using Validity Generalization (VG) research to validate, make certain the VG study has sufficient detail to show similar jobs were studied.

        Where more than one valid selection procedure is available, equally valid for a given purpose, use the procedure which has been demonstrated to have the lesser adverse impact.

        Use more than one method to assess job-related traits/competencies (e.g., self-reported inventories and interviews).

        Develop weighting scheme (an actuarial predictive model) for competencies and the information sources that purport to measure them (including interview data).

4. DO BACKGROUND/REFERENCE CHECKS

Action: Develop performance-based reference checking focused on KASOCs/competencies.

5. USE BEHAVIORAL INTERVIEWING TECHNIQUE WITH STRUCTURED FORMAT OR INDEPENDENT MULTIPLE INTERVIEWERS ASKING BEHAVIORAL QUESTIONS

Action: Develop questions to assess KASOCs/competencies.

        Train interviewers on valid interviewing and legal issues.

        Derive a scoring system for interviews regardless of format.

6. USE WEIGHTING SCHEME FOR INFORMATION

Action: Derive weighting scheme based on relative importance of KASOCs/competencies and/or relative validity of the sources of information on each critical KASOC/competency.

        Use "actuarial" not clinical or holistic method for ranking candidates.

7. EXTEND AN OFFER

Action: Offer should be in writing with the facts of the offer; train employees to avoid statements regarding future promotions, promises of long-term employment, etc.

Adapted from: W. F. Cascio and H. Aguinis, "Test Development and Use: New Twists on Old Questions", *Human Resource Management,* 44 (2005), pp. 219–236.

SUMMARY

Personnel selection continues to be a critical HRM responsibility. A number of commonly used tests and other assessment methods have been reviewed. While GMA or cognitive ability tests are among the most valid measures, they also frequently result in adverse impact against minority groups. Conversely, many personality tests are safe from legal problems because they typically have no adverse impact, yet are less valid. These noncognitive measures are clearly less valid than GMA in the prediction of overall job performance. It is clear that job-related personality/motivational constructs should be assessed but that multiple approaches to their measurement should be used (e.g., an inventory and an interview) for greater reliability and validity in the measurement of these constructs. The use of compound traits (more job-related, targeted noncognitive measures) will probably increase validity.

Many companies also use pre-employment drug tests. These tests are generally legal to use, but there are differences from state to state. There is evidence that drug tests will screen out less-effective employees. Reference checks may not be a particularly valid selection device; still, court decisions regarding negligent hiring lawsuits indicate that employers should do their best to check applicant references. Many companies now use integrity tests because of the restrictions on polygraph testing. Despite some political activity to amend the polygraph law by including a federal ban on these tests as well, research on these tests seems to support their use.

Assessment centers ideal for managerial selection

Use behavioral interviewing

Assessment center and performance testing results are valid, job related, more legally defensible, but certainly more expensive than other selection techniques, including the employment interview. Assessment centers are ideal for managerial jobs with both internal and external candidates. There is evidence that structured, behavioral interviewing conducted by more than one interviewer (the "high-validity" interview) can increase the validity of interviews unless unstructured interviews are conducted independently by three or more interviewers. Most companies use a variety of selection procedures, proceeding through the process in the order described in the model in Figure 6-1. But few organizations combine the information using an actuarial or statistical model or expert weighting model, which enhances the accuracy of decision making. Unfortunately, most companies gather information from several sources (e.g., application blanks, cognitive, and personality tests) and apply a subjective and unreliable weighting system to determine the rank of candidates for the positions to be filled. Almost all companies use an employment interview at some point in the selection process. These companies also tend to place entirely too much weight on the results of an unstructured interview that does not approach the characteristics of a "high-validity" interview.

Use actuarial model

The accuracy of interview decisions is limited by the information-processing capabilities of interviewers. Factors such as the characteristics of the applicant, the interviewer, and the situation can influence and distort the decision-making process, resulting in less-than-optimal interview decisions. Because employment interviews entail complex decision-making activities, interviewers often try to simplify that process and, in doing so, bias their decisions. This inherent bias poses both legal and practical implications for management. Overall organization performance can be affected because interviewer bias reduces the probability of selecting the highest-performing candidates.

The administrative guidelines described in this chapter help ensure that the validity of the interview is maximized while interviewer bias is minimized. In turn, the procedural guidelines define both the content and the method of the interview inquiry, providing a means of improving the overall effectiveness of the interview procedure. A final dilemma facing organizations that use the interview as a selection tool continues to be the issue of **"functional utility":** What is the unique contribution of the interview in the employment decision? This is a practical assessment of the usefulness of the interview based on a determination of which information is best collected through the interview process and whether interviewer decisions based on that information are consistent and accurate. In order to achieve any functional utility from the interview, organizations must evaluate their overall selection procedures and determine (1) what factors are best and most consistently evaluated during the interview and (2) whether other selection procedures can measure those identified factors as well as or better than the interview. Organizations also should focus on the purpose of selection interview. Interviews that attempt to assess candidate "fit" while simultaneously recruiting the candidate usually fail at both.

Functional utility

Try to match the person with the job

The most effective personnel selection systems place a great emphasis on the interaction of the person and the organization in the prediction of effectiveness. The "matching" model presented in Chapter 5, for example, calls for an assessment of the applicant in the context of both job and organizational characteristics and a realistic assessment of the organization and the job by the applicant. This "matching" model is particularly effective in "high-involvement organizations" where employees have more latitude in the workplace. As stated at the outset of this chapter, the tools used for selection should ideally be the most valid for the particular KASOCs or competencies most important for strategic execution. This is the optimal "matching" model.

The "fairness factor"

Labor attorney Rita Risser recommends that the "fairness factor" be kept in mind by line managers making hiring decisions.[80] The "fairness factor" is expressed in five questions that should be asked in every hiring decision: (1) Am I basing decisions solely on job-related criteria? (2) Am I treating people consistently? (3) Am I following organizational policy? (4) Am I communicating accurately and honestly? and (5) Should I consult with an HR specialist or a legal expert? Ms. Risser maintains managers who follow the "fairness factor" are more likely to make selection decisions that are free from bias or the perception of bias. Of course, the answers to the first four fairness questions should be "yes" and the importance of the answer to the fifth question about consulting an expert really depends on how knowledgeable the decision maker is about the legal implications of the action. At the most basic level, managers should know that it is either unlawful or potentially unlawful to do any of the following:

1. Base decisions on characteristics such as disability, medical records, pregnancy, parental status, religion, race, sex, age, or national origin. Some states and municipalities also offer protection for sexual orientation, marital status, and other characteristics.

2. Show prejudice in recruiting or advertising for or against persons with particular protected class characteristics.

3. Request information regarding mental and physical disabilities during the interview.

4. Use methods that cannot be shown to be job related or a business necessity and that cause adverse impact.

5. Make inquiries that reveal protected class characteristics. Questions dealing with place of birth, religious affiliations, citizenship of parents, attitudes toward or histories regarding labor unions, and political views are examples of potentially troubling inquiries.

Discussion Questions

1. Are GMA or cognitive ability tests more trouble than they are worth? Given that minorities are more likely to score lower on such tests, would it not be advisable to find some other method for predicting job success?

2. Why do you need tests of clerical ability? Couldn't you just rely on a typing test and recommendations from previous employers?

3. Under what circumstances would GMA or cognitive ability tests be appropriate for promotion decisions? Are there other methods that might be more valid?

4. If you were given a personality test as part of an employment application process, would you answer the questions honestly or would you attempt to answer the questions based on your image of the "correct" way to answer? What implications does your response have for the validity of personality testing? What does the evidence on faking show?

5. Discuss the advantages and disadvantages of performance testing and work samples. Under what circumstances would such tests be most appropriate?

6. Given that the validity of assessment centers and work samples are not substantially different than that reported for cognitive ability tests, why would an organization choose the far more costly approaches?

7. It has been proposed that students be assessed with work simulations similar to those used in managerial assessment centers. Assessments are then made on a student's competencies in decision making, leadership, oral communication, planning and organizing, written communication, and self-objectivity. What other methods could be used to assess student competencies in these areas?

8. What is stereotyping? Give examples of legal and illegal stereotypes.

9. Describe how an organization might improve the reliability and validity of the interview.

10. Contrast an unstructured interview with a situational or behavioral interview.

11. "The most efficient solution to the problem of interview validity is to do away with the interview and substitute paper-and-pencil measures." Do you agree or disagree? Explain.

12. Explain the difference between "actuarial" or statistical and "clinical" or "holistic" prediction.

Part 3

Developing Human Resource Capability

Chapter 7

Performance Management and Appraisal

After reading this chapter, you should be able to

1. Understand the value and uses of performance appraisals in organizations and the prescriptions for effective appraisal.

2. Present a definition of performance and apply the definition to various job functions.

3. Discuss the legal implications of performance appraisal.

4. Explain the various errors in ratings and proven methods to reduce them.

5. Describe the necessary steps for implementing an effective appraisal feedback system.

OVERVIEW

As one review concluded, "the appraisal of performance appraisal is not good."[1] While most organizations report the use of formal systems of performance management and appraisal, the majority of those express considerable dissatisfaction with them.[2] Raters, ratees, and administrators have all expressed dissatisfaction with their appraisal systems. The good news is that things are getting better!

All of the attention paid to performance appraisal is testimony to its potentially pivotal role in influencing organizational performance and effectiveness. Indeed, formal performance appraisal and multirater systems are components of **high-performance work systems** and have been linked to corporate financial performance.[3] Central to this linkage is the view that the most effective PM systems recognize that appraisal is not an end in itself; rather it is a critical component of a much broader set of human resource practices that are linked to business objectives, personal and organizational development, and corporate strategy.

Organizations are constantly searching for better ways to appraise performance. Microsoft dropped their controversial forced-distribution system after a flood of complaints from supervisors and their subordinates. Pratt & Whitney, the jet engine division of United Technologies, and Blockbuster Video both made significant changes in their performance appraisal and management systems in three consecutive years. Ford installed a new and highly controversial system as part of a major restructuring effort because their old system resulted in such uniformly high ratings that few performance distinctions could be made among the workers and the data indicated that there were almost no ineffective workers.

Meacham v. Knolls Atomic Power

The critical role of performance appraisal in EEO and other work-related litigation should also be emphasized. **Performance appraisal is the most heavily litigated personnel practice today.** Since the legal grounds for challenging appraisal systems are expanding, litigation can be expected to increase. For example, a 2008 Supreme Court ruling in an age discrimination case has placed a greater burden on employers to justify their performance appraisal decisions and practices.[4]

The growing diversity of the workforce increases the probability of legal and work-related difficulties. With greater proportions of women, members of minority groups, people of varying sexual orientation, employees with disabilities, and older workers in the labor force, unfairness and biases already present in appraisal systems, either real or perceived, may be magnified by greater diversity among those who evaluate performance and those who are evaluated. Consequently, organizations will need to be increasingly conscientious about facilitating fairness and objectivity in appraisal practices and personnel decisions and eliminating as much subjectivity in the process as is possible.

Major discrepancies

The overall objective of this chapter is to provide recommendations for improving the effectiveness of performance management and appraisal in organizations. **There are major discrepancies between the way in which appraisal is *practiced* and the way in which experts say it *should* be done.** These discrepancies will be emphasized throughout the chapter.

There is hope for performance management and appraisal. Reviews of research, practice, and litigation related to appraisal have led to the recognition that there are some prescriptions that should be followed in order to improve the effectiveness of appraisal systems.[5] The effects of performance appraisal (PA) and performance management (PM) systems will be more positive if and when these prescriptions are followed that have generally *not* been heeded by most practitioners. The major prescriptions are:

1. Precision in the definition and measurement of performance is a key element of effective appraisal.

2. The content and measurement of performance should derive from internal and external customers.

3. The PM system should incorporate a formal process for investigating and correcting the effects of situational constraints on performance.

Figure 7-1 presents an elaboration of these prescriptions, including specific recommendations subsumed under each of them.

As discussed in Chapter 1, research shows that performance management, when done correctly, can (and does) affect corporate performance and the bottom line. In Chapter 4, the role of performance measurement as a focus in work and job design and analysis was discussed. In Chapter 5, an emphasis was placed on the role of PA for succession planning and recruitment. In Chapter 6, the role of PA for promotion systems was emphasized. The identification and measurement of critical performance criteria are vital for improving an organization's competitive advantage through better products and services and greater responsiveness to customer requirements.

Performance management and appraisal practice have improved in recent years but still have a long way to go. Figure 7-2 presents a summary of findings concerning discrepancies between research and practice.

Figure 7-1
Prescriptions for Effective Performance Management

1. Strive for as much precision in defining and measuring performance dimensions as is feasible.
   - Define performance with a focus on valued outcomes tied to strategic goals.
   - Define outcome measures in terms of relative frequencies of outcomes (e.g., 0 to 100% of all opportunities).
   - Define performance dimensions by combining functions with aspects of value (e.g., quantity, quality, timeliness, effects on constituents, cost).
2. Link performance dimensions to meeting internal and external customer requirements.
   - Internal customer definitions of performance should be linked to external customer satisfaction.
3. Incorporate the measurement of situational constraints.
   - Focus attention and training on perceived constraints on performance.

Source: Adapted from H. J. Bernardin, C. Hagan, J. S. Kane, and P. Villanova, "Effective Performance Management: Precision in Measurement with a Focus on Customers and Situational Constraints," in *Performance Appraisal: State-of-the-Art Methods for Performance Management,* ed. J. Smither (San Francisco: Jossey-Bass, 1998).

Figure 7-2   **Performance Management: Discrepancies between Research and Practice**

Rating Content

Finding: Do not evaluate people on traits in performance appraisal.

Practice: 58% of surveyed employers still use traits as criteria.

Finding: Performance dimensions or criteria should be linked to job descriptions.

Practice: 60% of employers report strong linkage; 22% actually evaluate the linkage.

Finding: Setting precise, challenging goals results in higher performance.

Practice: 26% of managerial appraisal goals/objectives are precise.

Finding: Clearly distinguish among aspects of performance (e.g., quality, quantity).

Practice: 14% of employers distinguish aspects of value by job function or goal.

Finding: Link individual performance dimensions to specific strategic goals.

Practice: 9% actually do this; 55% make the claim.

Rating Process

Finding: Employee participation in goal setting increases motivation, commitment, and performance.

Practice: 18% of nonmanagement positions set goals; 58% of management positions allow participation.

Finding: Specific feedback focuses attention on goals.

Practice: 37% of employees indicate they received detailed feedback.

Finding: Establish tight link between goal attainment and rewards.

Practice: 41% of employees perceive a "close link" of goal attainment to rewards.

Finding: Train raters for common frame of reference (FOR).

Practice: 8% of employers use FOR; only 21% know what FOR training is.

Finding: Train raters on giving negative feedback.

Practice: 27% of employers provide such training.

Finding: Avoid training on rater error distributions—it can create other errors.

Practice: 41% of employers use rater error training.

Finding: Structured diary keeping increases reliability in rating.

Practice: 5% of companies require diary keeping by supervisors.

Finding: Train raters on cognitive errors like actor/observer bias.

Practice: 8% of employers know what this error is; 3% train on it.

Finding: Distinguish between ratings of person's characteristics and performance outcomes.

Practice: 46% of employers now rate on competencies and don't clearly distinguish between performance and ratee potential, KASOCs, or competencies.

Administrative Uses

Finding: 360-degree (or, multirater) appraisal data can reduce adverse impact in promotions.

Practice: 16% of companies that use 360-degree appraisal use it for decision making; 84% of companies rely on "top-down" appraisal for promotions.

Finding: Multirater appraisal has higher validity than "top down appraisal."

Practice: Less than 5 percent of companies use multirater appraisal for decision making.

Rating Results

Finding: Audit data for adverse impact against protected classes (including age).

Practice: 24% of companies do this annually; 63% have never done it.

Finding: Evaluate particular rater tendencies (e.g., ratings by ethnicity, gender, age, leniency, other rating errors).

Practice: 15% of companies calculate rating data by rater.

Finding: Reward raters for rating process adherence (e.g., precise criteria, good differentiation).

Practice: 27% of companies include performance management practices as critical component of managers' jobs.

Finding: Assess individual performance levels as related to aggregated, strategic goals.

Practice: 24% actually do this in any way; 58% make the claim.

Source: Adapted from H. J. Bernardin, "Survey of HR Practice: More Evidence on Discrepancies between Research and Practice," Paper presented at the Annual Meeting of the Academy of Management, 2007. See also M. London, E. M. Mone, and J. C. Scott, "Performance Management and Assessment: Methods for Improved Rater Accuracy and Employee Goal Setting," *Human Resource Management* 43 (2004), pp. 319–336.

HOW DO WE DEFINE PERFORMANCE AND WHY DO WE MEASURE IT?

Despite the importance of performance appraisal (PA), few organizations clearly define what it is they are trying to measure. In order to design a system for appraising performance, it is important to first define what is meant by the term **work performance.** Although a person's job performance depends on some combination of ability (or competency), effort, and opportunity, it should be measured in terms of outcomes or results produced. *Performance is defined here as the record of outcomes produced on specified job functions or activities during a specified time period.* For example, a trainer working for the World Bank was evaluated on her "organization of presentations," which was defined as "the presentation of training material in a logical and methodical order." The extent to which she was able to make such "methodical" presentations would be one measure of outcomes related to that function. Those outcomes were evaluated by the clients who received the training.

Obviously a sales representative would have some measure of actual sales as an outcome for the primary function of that job (i.e., sales). Customer service is a likely candidate as another important function that would have very different outcome measures for defining performance. College professors are typically evaluated on three general work functions: teaching, research, and service. Performance in each of these three areas is defined with different outcome measures. Students are obviously one source of data to evaluate the quality of the teaching.

Performance on the job as a whole would be equal to the sum (or average) of performance on the major job functions or activities. For example, the World Bank identified eight job functions for their trainers (e.g., use of relevant examples, participant involvement, evaluation procedures). The functions have to do with the work that is performed and *not* the characteristics of the person performing. Unfortunately, many performance appraisal systems confuse measures of performance with the traits, or competencies of the person.

Let us emphasize this again: The definition of performance refers to a set of outcomes produced during a certain period of time, and does *not* refer to the traits, personal characteristics, or competencies of the performer. (See Critical Thinking Application 7-A.) There is a place for the assessment of competencies or other personal characteristics of the performer. Indeed, there is an important place! However, there should be a clear distinction between the measurement of the person and his or her competencies or knowledge or potentiality and that person's performance. Competencies and performance are surely correlated but they are not the same thing. The measurement of competencies should be viewed as diagnostic and can clearly be used to assess the **potential** to perform. But potential and actual performance are very different things.

What Are the Uses of Performance Data?

The information collected from performance measurement is typically used for compensation, performance improvement or management (e.g., personnel decision making), and documentation. As discussed in Chapter 6, performance data are often used for staffing decisions (e.g., promotion, transfer, discharge, layoffs), and this is where the entire PM system may fall under the scrutiny of the courts. PA is also used for training needs analysis, employee development, and research and program evaluation (e.g., validation research for selection methods).

Performance Management and Compensation

Performance appraisal information is often used by supervisors to manage the performance of their employees. Appraisal data can reveal employees' performance weaknesses, which managers can refer to when setting goals or target levels for improvements. A performance management system should include a diagnostic component where an evaluator attempts to explain a performance level based on a performer's traits, competencies, abilities, or motivations. But an effective PM system should first measure the performance level as accurately as possible and then attempt to explain the obtained level based on a performer's characteristics (competencies, KASOCs). One of the strongest trends in this country is toward some form of pay-for-performance (PFP) system. Chapter 11 will cover the important area of pay-for-performance, a critical component for effective compensation and, as evidenced by the economic meltdown of 2008, an HR function with the potential to destroy an otherwise effective corporation.

Internal Staffing

Performance appraisal information is also used to make staffing decisions. As discussed in Chapters 5 and 6, many organizations rely on performance appraisal data to decide which employees to move upward (promote) to fill openings and which employees to retain as a part of "rightsizing" (or downsizing) efforts. Performance appraisals should also be the basis of terminations when the organization concludes performance fails to meet a minimum or acceptable standard or, perhaps, the organization could do better without an employee (or with an alternative employee or work source).

One problem with relying on performance appraisal information to make decisions about job movements is that employee performance is typically measured only for the *current* job. If the job at the higher, lateral, or lower level is different from the employee's current job, then it may be difficult to estimate how the employee will perform on the new job if that new job requires significantly different competencies (or KASOCs). Assessments of these competencies can be done in a variety of ways, including judgments by supervisors, peers, and even subordinates. Of course, many organizations use assessment tools such as those described in Chapter 6.

Assessments of competencies or other worker characteristics using ratings by qualified rating sources such as supervisors and peers is a perfectly acceptable approach for internal staffing decisions and, in many cases, more valid than other approaches to assessment discussed in Chapter 6. However, such assessments should be distinguished from the measurement of performance.

"Predictive weights" for PA data

It is possible to apply "predictive weights" to performance appraisal data to use the data for promotional decisions. If a study establishes a linkage between effective performance on certain job dimensions of Job A with effective performance in Job B, then ratings on those dimensions could be given predictive weights depending on their relative ability to predict performance. But it is not advisable to rely only on performance appraisal data to make promotional decisions since the jobs are undoubtedly different in some way and thus require somewhat different KASOCs or competencies.

Training Needs Analysis

Most firms use appraisal data to determine employees' needs for training or development. Hundreds of companies, including Microsoft, IBM, and Merck, now use 360-degree or multisource appraisal (e.g., subordinates, peers, clients) as feedback for their supervisors or managers.[6] The results are revealed to each manager with suggestions for specific training and development (if needed). Honeywell, for example, has specific training modules based on 360-degree appraisal ratings on several job functions.

Research and Evaluation

Appraisal data can also be used to determine whether various human resource programs (e.g., selection, training, recruitment) are effective. For example, when Toledo, Ohio, wanted to know whether their police officer selection test was valid, they collected performance appraisal data on officers who had taken the test when they were hired so that test scores could be correlated with job performance ratings.

LEGAL ISSUES ASSOCIATED WITH PERFORMANCE APPRAISALS

Since performance appraisal data are used to make many important personnel decisions (e.g., pay, promotion, selection, termination), it is understandable that appraisal is a major target of legal disputes involving employee charges of unfairness and bias.[7] There are several legal avenues a person may pursue to obtain relief from discriminatory performance appraisals. As discussed in Chapter 3, the most widely used federal laws are Title VII of the Civil Rights Act and the Age Discrimination in Employment Act. However, there are numerous other possible sources of redress.

Figure 7-3 **Employer Prescriptions for Winning Legal Challenges Regarding Performance Appraisal***

Did the Employer:

1. Audit personnel decisions stemming from PA data to make certain there is not prima facie evidence of discrimination (e.g., 80 percent rule violations)?
2. Use procedures for performance appraisal that do not differ as a function of the race, sex, national origin, religion, disability, or age of those affected by such decisions?
3. Use objective or countable (nonrated) performance outcome data?
4. Have a formal system of review and appeal for situations in which the rated individual disagrees with a rating?
5. Use more than one independent evaluator of performance?
6. Use a formal, standardized system for the personnel decision?
7. Document that relevant evaluators have had ample opportunity to observe rated performance or to review work products (if ratings must be made)?
8. Rate behavior or outcomes and avoid ratings on traits such as dependability, judgment, drive, flexibility, aptitude, innovativeness, or attitude?
9. Validate/corroborate the performance appraisal data with other data?
10. Communicate precise and specific performance standards to employee?
11. Provide written instructions to raters on how to complete the performance evaluations?
12. Evaluate employees on specific work dimensions rather than a single overall or global measure of performance or promotability?
13. Require a consistent policy of documentation for extreme ratings (e.g., critical incidents)?
14. Provide employees with an opportunity to review their appraisals?
15. Train personnel decision makers on performance appraisal, rating errors, and laws regarding discrimination?

---

*These prescriptions are in their approximate order of predictive importance. Thus, assuming no 80 percent rule violations (item #1), employers with PA systems that meet these prescriptions are more likely to prevail in court challenges.

Source: H. J. Bernardin, "Legal Prescriptions Based on Expert Judgments of PA System Characteristics," 2009. Manuscript under review.

15 Predictors of the outcomes of court cases

There are several recommendations to assist employers in conducting fair performance appraisals and avoiding legal suits. Figure 7-3 presents a summary of these recommendations based on a recent study and reviews of court cases related to appraisal. The figure lists 15 PA characteristics related to the content, process, and results of PA. They are presented in their approximate order of importance in the prediction of the outcomes of court cases involving PA. For example, a violation of the 80 percent rule using PA to make personnel decisions was found to be the most important predictor of the outcome of cases such that a violation increases the probability that the plaintiff (or protected class of plaintiffs) would prevail in the lawsuit. Many allegations of discrimination in EEO cases involving performance appraisal focus on the level of "subjectivity" in the PA process. For example, expert testimony on behalf of the plaintiffs in the Wal-Mart gender discrimination case emphasized the **"excessive subjectivity"** of the performance appraisal process where statistical prima facie evidence of discrimination was presented, and very few of the prescriptions in Figure 7-3 characterized the Wal-Mart PA systems.

80 percent rule can be used in PA cases

Recall the discussion in Chapter 3 about adverse impact related to personnel decisions and court rulings regarding the **"disparate impact"** theory of discrimination and performance appraisal. The Supreme Court has ruled that adverse impact statistics such as the 80 percent rule can be used in Title VII and ADEA cases where performance appraisal was used to make decisions regarding who gets promoted (consider Wal-Mart's huge sex discrimination lawsuit), who gets terminated (think of Ford's 2001 age and race discrimination case related to its downsizing; see Critical Thinking Application 7-C), who gets merit raises (back to Wal-Mart), and any other important personnel decisions.

Organizations should audit their appraisal data to test for possible adverse impact effects long before they get sued. They might even avoid getting sued. Adverse impact statistics have also been used successfully in **"disparate treatment"** cases to support an individual's claim of race or gender discrimination. Plaintiffs have used such data to augment claims of "disparate treatment" discrimination indicating a "pattern or practice" of discrimination and to buttress a motion for "class certification" that resulted from the "extreme subjectivity" of a bad performance appraisal system.

Such data can be used by the employer to rebut such a claim if in fact there is no evidence of adverse impact related to a particular protected class. Bottom line for organizations: An organization is in trouble if it gets sued, and there is a certified class of alleged victims (e.g., a class of females, minority, or older workers), and the organization has violated the 80 percent rule in its decisions (e.g., promotions, terminations) based on the use of a flawed appraisal system that adheres to few (or none) of the recommendations in Figure 7-3. Prima facie evidence such as the 80 percent rule is considered to be the single best predictor of the outcome of cases involving PA.

80 percent rule violations— best predictor of case outcomes

DESIGNING AN APPRAISAL SYSTEM

The process of designing an appraisal system should involve managers, employees, HR professionals, and, most important, internal and external customers in making decisions about each of the following issues:

- Measurement content.
- Measurement process.
- Control of rating errors.
- Defining the rater (i.e., who should rate performance).
- Defining the ratee (i.e., the level of performance to rate).
- Administrative characteristics.

It is a challenge to make the correct decisions since no single set of choices is optimal in all situations. The starting point should be the strategic plan and objectives of the organization. The details of the plan should be reviewed in order to design an appraisal system consistent with the overall goals of the firm. This is particularly true with regard to measurement content and the outcomes to be emphasized.

Measurement Content

Appraisal is often person-oriented (focusing on the person who performed the behavior), but should be work-oriented (focusing on the **record of outcomes** that the person achieved on the job). Effective *performance* appraisal focuses on the record of outcomes and, in particular, outcomes directly linked to an organization's mission and objectives. Some Sheraton Hotels offer 25-minute room service or the meal is free. Sheraton employees who are directly connected to room service are appraised on the record of outcomes specifically related to this service guarantee. Lenscrafters guarantees new glasses in 60 minutes or they're free. Individual and unit performance are measured by the average time taken to get the new glasses in the customer's hands. These are outcomes. *In general, personal traits or characteristics (e.g., dependability, integrity, perseverance, knowledge, attitude, loyalty) should not be used when evaluating past performance since they are not measures of actual performance.* As personal characteristics of a performer, they may be correlates or predictors of performance, but they are *not* measures of actual performance.

Traits or competencies are correlates of performance—*not* performance

There are six categories of outcomes by which the value of performance in any work activity or work function may be assessed. These six criteria are listed and defined in Figure 7-4. Although all of these criteria may not be relevant to every job activity or job function, a subset of them will be. It is also important for organizations to recognize the relationships among the criteria. For example, sometimes managers encourage employees to push for quantity, without recognizing that quality may suffer or that co-workers might be affected. Likewise, they may focus on quality without emphasizing timeliness, cost effectiveness, quality, or interpersonal impact.

Contextual performance

The interpersonal criterion includes **"contextual or citizenship performance"** as discussed in the literature. A good "organizational citizen" is an employee who contributes beyond the formal role expectations of a job as might be detailed in a job description. Such employees are positively disposed to take on alternative job assignments, respond cheerfully to requests for assistance from others, are interpersonally tactful, arrive to work on time, and

Figure 7-4   **The Six Primary Criteria on Which the Value of Performance May Be Assessed**

1. *Quality:* The degree to which the process or result of carrying out an activity approaches perfection, in terms of either conforming to some ideal way of performing the activity or fulfilling the activity's intended purpose.

2. *Quantity:* The amount produced, expressed in such terms as dollar value, number of units, or number of completed activity cycles.

3. *Timeliness:* The degree to which an activity is completed, or a result produced, at the earliest time desirable from the standpoints of both coordinating with the outputs of others and maximizing the time available for other activities.

4. *Cost-effectiveness:* The degree to which the use of the organization's resources (e.g., human, monetary, technological, material) is maximized in the sense of getting the highest gain or reduction in loss from each unit or instance of use of a resource.

5. *Need for supervision:* The degree to which a performer can carry out a job function without either having to request supervisory assistance or requiring supervisory intervention to prevent an adverse outcome.

6. *Interpersonal impact/contextual performance:* The degree to which a performer promotes feelings of self-esteem, goodwill, and cooperation among co-workers and subordinates.

often may stay later than required to complete a task. Contextual performance operates to either support or inhibit technical production and can facilitate individual-, group-, and system-level outcomes.

Contextual performance contributions such as mentoring, facilitating a pleasant work environment, and compliance with organizational and subunit policies and procedures may have implications for several of the other outcome categories as well. If performance is defined at a more specific task or activity level, contextual performance also could be represented in the description of the function itself and combined with one or more of the value criteria (e.g., quality, quantity). For example, one model of "citizenship performance" includes "personal support" as a dimension and defines it by such behaviors as "helping others by offering suggestions, teaching useful knowledge or skills, and providing emotional support for their personal problems." We could certainly define outcomes in these areas according to quantity and quality values (e.g., how often is emotional support offered; how good was it?).

Measuring Overall Performance

While an overall rating approach where the rater is not asked to distinguish among the criteria is surely faster than making assessments on separate criteria, the major drawback is that it requires raters to simultaneously consider perhaps as many as six different aspects of value and to mentally compute their average. The probable result of all this subjective reasoning may be less accurate ratings than those done on each relevant criterion for each job activity and less specific feedback to the performer. *In general, the greater the specificity and precision in the content of the appraisal, assuming the content is compatible with the strategic goals of the organization, the more effective the appraisal system regardless of the purpose for the appraisal system* (see Figure 7-1 again).

The Measurement Process

There are three basic ways in which raters can make performance assessments: (1) they can make comparisons of ratees' performances, (2) they can make comparisons *among* anchors or standards and select one most descriptive of the person being appraised, and (3) they can make comparisons of individuals' performance *to* anchors or standards. These are shown in simplified form in Figure 7-5. Some of the most popular or promising rating instruments representing each of these three ways are described next.

Rating Instruments: Comparisons among Ratees' Performances

Paired comparisons, straight ranking, and forced distribution are appraisal systems that require raters to make comparisons among ratees according to some measure of effectiveness or simply overall effectiveness. Although controversial, employee comparison systems are growing in popularity to some extent because Jack Welch, GE's famous retired CEO, has been a strong advocate of the approach for many years.

Paired comparisons require the rater to compare all possible pairs of ratees on "overall performance" or some other, usually vaguely defined, standard. This task can become

**Figure 7-5
Rating Format Options**

COMPARISONS AMONG PERFORMANCES

Compare the performances of all ratees to each anchor (or standard) for each job activity, function, or overall performance. Rater judgments may be made in one of the following ways:

- Indicate which ratee in each possible pair of ratees performed closest to the performance level described by the anchor or attained the highest level of overall performance. (Illustrative method: paired comparison)
- Indicate how the ratees ranked in terms of closeness to the performance level described by the anchor or standard. (Illustrative method: straight ranking)
- Identify a predetermined percentage of employees as ineffective and highly effective. (Illustrative method: forced distribution)

COMPARISONS AMONG ANCHORS

Compare all the anchors for each job activity or function and select the one (or more) that best describes the ratee's performance level. Rater judgments are made in the following way:

- Indicate which of the anchors fit the ratee's performance best (and/or worst). (Illustrative method: CARS, forced choice)

COMPARISONS TO ANCHORS

Compare each ratee's performance to each anchor for each job activity or function. Rater judgments are made in one of the following ways:

- Whether or not the ratee's performance matches the anchor. (Illustrative methods: graphic rating scales such as BARS; MBO)
- The frequency with which the ratee's performance matches the anchor. (Illustrative methods: all summated rating scales such as BOS and PDA methods)
- Whether the ratee's performance was better than, equal to, or worse than that described by the anchor. (Illustrative method: mixed standard scales)

cumbersome for the rater as the number of employees increases and more comparisons are needed. The formula for the number of possible pairs of employees is $n(n-1)/2$, where n = the number of employees. **Straight ranking,** or rank ordering, asks the rater to simply identify the "best" employee, the "second best," and so forth, until the rater has identified the worst employee. For example, some NCAA rankings in football and basketball are based on a rank ordering of the teams by coaches and the press. Ranking systems are popular in research labs such as Sandia and Lawrence Livermore. Managers are forced to rank their subordinates in a 1 to N order based on performance.

Forced distribution usually presents the rater with a limited number of categories (usually three to seven) and requires (or "forces") the rater to place a designated portion of the ratees into each category. A forced distribution usually places the majority of employees in the middle category (i.e., with average ratings or raises) while fewer employees are placed in higher and lower categories.

Some organizations use forced distribution to ensure that raters do not assign all (or nearly all) of their employees the most extreme (e.g., highest) possible ratings. Ford adopted a forced letter grade system for each supervisor. Thus, only 10 percent of employees could receive an A grade while first 10 percent (and later 5 percent) had to receive a C grade. Employees who received Cs were not eligible for a raise or a bonus, and two C grades in a row could result in demotion and termination. A lawsuit was filed (and settled) with Ford in 2002 alleging that age and reverse race discrimination were a result of the forced-distribution system.

In addressing GE shareholders former CEO Jack Welch stated, "A company that bets its future on its people must remove that lower 10 percent, and keep removing it every year—always raising the bar of performance and increasing the quality of its leadership."[8] Research on forced distribution is not favorable. Enron had a GE-like system in place when the company collapsed and Microsoft dumped their system in 2008. Companies using forced distribution found improved variability among ratees, a primary purpose of the approach, but a lower overall evaluation of the appraisal system compared to other approaches. Supervisors and managers are often offended that no matter how effective they are as managers they must comply with the required forced distribution.[9]

Research on forced discrimination is not favorable

Rating Instruments: Comparisons among Performance-Level Anchors

Computerized adaptive rating scales (CARS)

Computerized adaptive rating scales (CARS) is a promising rating method that presents raters with pairs of behavioral statements reflecting different levels of performance on the same performance dimension.[10] For example, for the performance dimension entitled "Personal Support," raters could be asked to select one of the following two statements as most descriptive of a particular ratee:

1. Refuses to take the time to help others when they ask for assistance with work-related problems.

2. Occasionally takes the time to help others when they ask for assistance with work-related problems.

Based on the statement selected, additional statements are then paired through a computer program for subsequent rating. The new pair of behavioral statements would then be selected, one of which was scaled by experts to be somewhat higher in effectiveness than the one first selected and the other of which was scaled to be somewhat below the level of effectiveness represented by the first statement selected. A rater's selection from this next pair of statements would then revise the estimate of the ratee's performance effectiveness level. Based on this new estimate, two new statements are selected by the computer program until the performance level can be measured reliably.

Laboratory research with CARS supported this method when compared to behaviorally anchored rating scales (BARS) and simple graphic rating scales.

Forced choice designed to reduce intentional bias

Forced choice is another PA method that requires the rater to compare performance statements and select one (or more) as most descriptive. Unlike the CARS method, the forced choice method is specifically designed to reduce (or eliminate) intentional rating bias where the rater deliberately attempts to rate individuals high (or low) irrespective of their performance. The rationale underlying forced choice is that statements are grouped in such a way that the scoring key is not known to the rater (i.e., the way to rate higher or lower is not apparent). The rater is unaware of which statements (if selected) will result in higher (or lower) ratings for the ratee because all statements appear equally desirable or undesirable. For example, if you were asked to select the two statements that are most descriptive of your instructor for this class, which two would you select?

1. Is patient with slow learners.

2. Lectures with confidence.

3. Keeps the interest and attention of the class.

4. Presents objectives before each class session.

Deliberate bias can be reduced with forced choice

The statements are chosen to be equal in desirability in order to make it more difficult for the rater to pick out the ones that will give the ratee the highest or lowest ratings based on personal bias. However, only two of the items actually distinguish highly effective from ineffective performers. For the present case, items 1 and 3 have been shown to discriminate between the most effective and the least effective college professors. Items 2 and 4 did not generally discriminate between effective and ineffective performers. If you selected statements 1 and 3 as most descriptive of your instructor, then he or she would be awarded two points. This procedure would be used with each of the 20 to 40 groups of statements to determine the total score for each ratee. Raters are not given the scoring scheme, so they are unable to intentionally give performers high or low ratings. Research with forced choice is limited, but there is some evidence that deliberate bias can be reduced with this method. Unfortunately, raters do not like this method specifically because the scoring key is hidden.[11]

Rating Instruments: Comparisons to Performance-Level Anchors

Methods that require the rater to make comparisons of the employee's performance to specified anchors or standards include graphic rating scales, behaviorally anchored rating scales (BARS), management by objectives (MBO), summated scales (e.g., behavioral) observation scales (BOS), and performance distribution assessment (PDA). *Graphic rating scales* are the most widely used type of rating format. Figure 7-6 presents some examples of graphic scales. Generally, graphic rating scales use adjectives or numbers as anchors, but the descriptive detail of the anchors differs widely.

Figure 7-6
Examples of Graphic
Rating Scales

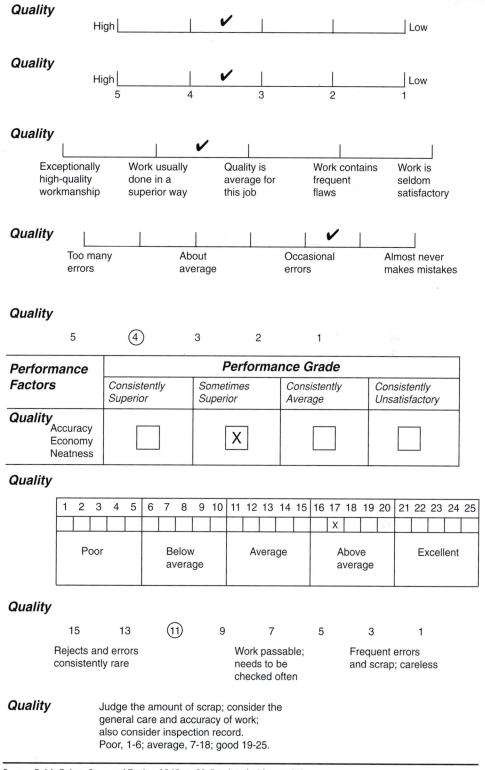

Source: R. M. Guion, *Personnel Testing,* 1965, p. 98. Reprinted with permission.

BARS

One of the most heavily researched types of graphic scales is **behaviorally anchored rating scales (BARS).** As shown in Figure 7-7, BARS are graphic scales with specific behavioral descriptions defining various points along the scale for each dimension. The recommended rating method for BARS asks raters to record specific observations or critical incidents of the employee's performance relevant to the dimension on the scale.[12] In

**Figure 7-7
An Example of a
Behaviorally Anchored
Rating Scale**

Organizational skills: A good constructional order of material slides smoothly from one topic to another; design of course optimizes interest; students can easily follow organizational strategy; course outline followed.

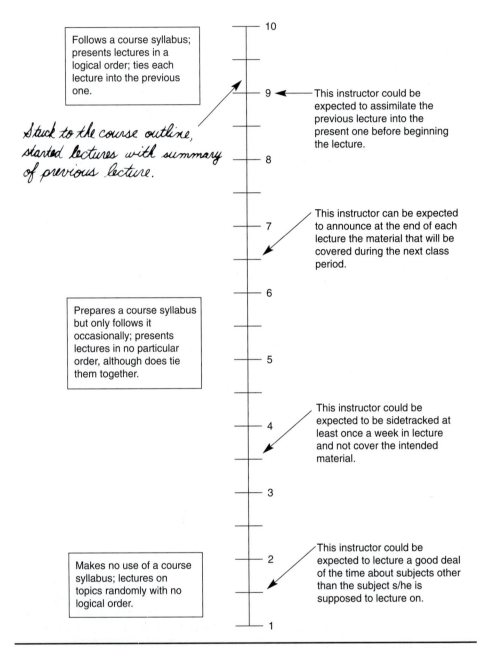

Source: From *Performance Appraisal: Assessing Human Behavior at Work* by H. John Bernardin and Richard W. Beatty, © 1984. Reprinted with permission of South-Western, a division of Thompson Learning: www.thomsonrights.com. Fax 800 730-2215.

Figure 7-7, the rater has written in "Stuck to the course outline, . . ." between points 9 and 10 on the left side of the scale. The rater would then select that point along the right side of the scale that best represents the ratee's overall performance on that function. That point is selected by comparing the ratee's actual observed performances to the behavioral expectations that are provided as "anchors" on the scale. The rationale behind writing in observations on the scale prior to selecting an overall anchor point is to ensure that raters are basing their ratings of expectations on actual observations of performance. In addition, the observations can be given to ratees as feedback on their performance. Research shows this

BARS method improves performance

form of feedback, with all recorded observations or critical incidents, is effective at improving performance and that this particular BARS approach is more effective than other formats at improving performance.

The method of **summated scales** is one of the oldest formats and remains one of the most popular for the appraisal of job performance. One version of summated scales is

BOS

behavioral observation scales (or BOS).[13] An example of a summated scale is presented in **Figure 7-8.** For this scale, the rater is asked to indicate how frequently the ratee has performed each of the listed behaviors. The ratings are then averaged or totaled for each person rated.

Performance distribution assessment (PDA) is a more complicated rating method based on the theory that ratings should be made in the context of opportunities to perform at a certain level.[14] PDA is the only method that statistically incorporates constraints on perfor-

PDA measures constraints

mance as a formal part of the measurement process. For example, in evaluating managers on the quality of their performance "monitoring" at Tiffany's of New York, their managers are asked to consider how many opportunities the manager had to "furnish information in response to an inquiry that was completely accurate with respect to central questions posed

---

**Figure 7-8
A Summated Rating Scale**

Directions: Rate your manager on the way he or she has conducted performance appraisal interviews. Use the following scale to make your ratings:

1 Always
2 Often
3 Occasionally
4 Seldom
5 Never

1. Effectively used information about the subordinate in the discussion.
2. Skillfully guided the discussion through the problem areas.
3. Maintained control over the interview.
4. Appeared to be prepared for the interview.
5. Let the subordinate control the interview.
6. Adhered to a discussion about the subordinate's problems.
7. Seemed concerned about the subordinate's perspective of the problems.
8. Probed deeply into sensitive areas in order to gain sufficient knowledge.
9. Made the subordinate feel comfortable during discussions of sensitive topics.
10. Projected sincerity during the interview.
11. Maintained the appropriate climate for an appraisal interview.
12. Displayed insensitivity to the subordinate's problems.
13. Displayed an organized approach to the interview.
14. Asked the appropriate questions.
15. Failed to follow up with questions when they appeared to be necessary.
16. Asked general questions about the subordinate's problems.
17. Asked only superficial questions that failed to confront the issues.
18. Displayed considerable interest in the subordinate's professional growth.
19. Provided general suggestions to aid in the subordinate's professional growth.
20. Provided poor advice regarding the subordinate's growth.
21. Made specific suggestions for helping the subordinate develop professionally.
22. Remained calm during the subordinate's outbursts.
23. Responded to the subordinate's outbursts in a rational manner.
24. Appeared to be defensive in reaction to the subordinate's complaints.
25. Backed down inappropriately when confronted.
26. Made realistic commitments to help the subordinate get along better with others.
27. Seemed unconcerned about the subordinate's problems.
28. Provided poor advice about the subordinate's relationships with others.
29. Provided good advice about resolving conflict.
30. When discussing the subordinate's future with the company, encouraged him/her to stay on.
31. Used appropriate compliments regarding the subordinate's technical expertise.
32. Motivated the subordinate to perform the job well.
33. Seemed to ignore the subordinate's excellent performance record.
34. Made inappropriate ultimatums to the subordinate about improving performance.

by the inquiry" and then to rate how frequently the manager achieved that level of performance. Although raters report some difficulty with the rating process, PDA provides detailed documentation of constraints on performance and thus has the potential to remove those constraints over time. A Web-based PDA system is now available.

MBO

Management by objectives (MBO) is a performance management and appraisal system that calls for a comparison between specific, quantifiable target goals and the actual results achieved by an employee. MBO is the most popular method of managerial appraisal.[15]

With MBO, the measurable, quantitative goals are usually mutually agreed upon by the employee and supervisor at the beginning of an appraisal period. During the review period, progress towards the goals is monitored. At the end of the review period, the employee and supervisor meet to evaluate whether the goals were achieved and to decide on new goals. The goals or objectives are usually set for individual employees or units and usually differ across employees (or units) depending on the circumstances of the job. For this reason, MBO has been shown to be useful for defining "individual" or unit performance in the context of strategic plans. As a motivational technique, as long as the objectives that are set are defined in specific terms using carefully defined criteria as listed in Figure 7-4, attainable as perceived by the performer while still being difficult, MBO is an effective approach to

MBO: Effective for improving performance

improving performance and motivating employees. Thus, precise definitions of quality and quantity, specifically linked to unit strategic goals, can make MBO a very effective PM system. But the criteria must be defined (and ultimately evaluated) with strategic goals in mind. MBO is not recommended as a method for comparing people or units unless the objectives that are set can be judged to be equally attainable in the context of potential situational constraints on performance, as discussed in a later section.

What is the "Bottom Line" on what it is we should be measuring?

You'll note if you look back at Figure 7-1 that one of the recommendations nested under "strive for as much precision in defining and measuring performance as is feasible" is to assess performance using ratings of **relative frequencies.** There are many options for rating behavior or performance outcomes. First of all, performance appraisal should focus on the *record of outcomes.* Let's pick on your instructor for a bit. Certainly "instruction" is a critical component (i.e., function) of his or her job. You are a type of "customer" who should be evaluating performance on that function (note prescription no. 2 in Figure 7-1 too). The most important criterion to define the "quality" of instruction is probably how much you actually learn from the instruction. Perfection would then be a perfect score on some test of the knowledge you were supposed to acquire from this instruction. For a number of reasons, scores on such a test may not be a practical source of data and such data, with some exceptions, probably does not allow for comparisons on instructors for decision-making purposes. Another way of getting at the "quality" of instruction is to have you (the customer) define levels of performance and then have you rate the extent to which the instructor meets or exceeds these levels of performance. Research says when you do these ratings, your focus should be on how *frequently* (e.g., sometimes, 100 percent of the time, never) the instructor achieved this level of performance in the context of all the times the instruc-

Ratings of relative frequency are superior to other formats

tor had the opportunity to achieve at this level. Ratings of frequency are better than ratings of "intensity" (e.g., strongly agree/disagree) or satisfactoriness (e.g., how satisfied you are with your instructor), primarily because those who are rated regard "frequency" feedback as more accurate and helpful.

Here's an example of "perfection" as defined by students to evaluate "instruction": "Every time a lecture was given, I had a clear, unambiguous understanding of what it was s/he was trying to teach; no questions were needed to clarify the material presented." Let's say this defines the "perfection" level of performance for "instruction." Raters would make ratings of relative frequency on the "quality of instruction" dimension by rating how often the instructor hit this level of performance out of all the times s/he gave lectures (or did instruction). So, you might give your instructor 100 percent on this dimension level; that is, every time a lecture was given, you had a "clear, unambiguous understanding." Obviously, it is also possible that the rating here could be 0 percent! That's why we also need to define at least one other level of performance for "quality of instruction." Raters would then rate how frequently the instructor achieved this level of performance. Research on rating formats shows that ratings of relative frequency result in higher levels of reliability in ratings (across raters rating the same person) and that the people who receive feedback on their performance actually prefer frequency ratings to other feedback options. The PDA system is most compatible with this approach to appraisal although BOS also calls for frequency ratings.

Whatever is measured should obviously be vital to the strategic goals of the organization. Formal performance appraisal should clearly concentrate on reliable and valid measurement of outcomes that are directly linked to strategic goals and outcomes. One would hope that a strategic goal of your institution is superior instruction in every class. Sometimes the linkage between individual performance appraisal and the strategic objectives of the organization is very clear (a 100 percent score on "instruction" would be nice). In general, **the more precision in measurement, the better the performance management and appraisal system regardless of its purpose.** At the individual performer level, having performance dimensions that are derived from that performer's job description (or actually a part of it) makes a whole lot of sense. While some supervisors tend to ignore job descriptions, workers tend to look at job descriptions as contracts (i.e., this is why you're paying me).[16]

Control of Rating Errors

Performance ratings are subject to a wide variety of inaccuracies and biases referred to as rating errors. These errors occur in rater judgment and information processing and can seriously affect performance appraisal results. Unfortunately, many of these errors cannot be eradicated easily. The most common rating errors are leniency/severity, halo/horns effect, central tendency, fundamental attribution errors, representativeness, availability, and anchoring.

Leniency/Severity

Leniency occurs when ratings for employees are generally at the high end of the rating scale regardless of the actual performance of ratees. This error is considered deliberate. Surveys have identified leniency as the most serious problem with appraisals whenever they are linked to important decisions such as compensation, promotions, or terminations.

Research shows leniency (or severity) in ratings is related to the characteristics of the *rater*.[17] The Five-Factor Model discussed in Chapter 6 applies here. Raters who are low on "Conscientiousness" and high on "Agreeableness" tend to be more lenient. Raters high on "Conscientiousness" are the most accurate rates.

Leniency is probably the primary reason companies have turned to forced distribution systems such as the GE "A, B, C" system where managers have to put a certain percentage of subordinates into the "C" category. Jack Welch and others argue that differentiation of employees by performance and making certain the most important positions in the organization (the "A" positions) are occupied by "A" players is a key contributor to competitive advantage. You do not want "C" or even "B" players in vital positions. Obviously, leniency error precludes an organization's ability to differentiate among employees and take action to reward the "A" players, move "C" performers out of key positions as soon as possible, and try to develop the "B" players into "A" players. While forced distribution eliminates leniency, it creates other serious problems.

Self-efficacy training reduces leniency

One study showed promise for **"self-efficacy training for raters."** Raters who were trained in giving negative feedback produced less lenient ratings than a control group. This training involved observing a successful rater, a simulated appraisal session with a "problem" employee, feedback on performance, and then coaching on how to conduct an appraisal discussion. Research shows that this approach to appraisal and training results in more effective appraisals, higher perceptions of procedural fairness, more agreement between raters and performers, and, most important, higher unit performance.[18]

Halo/Horns Effect

"Halo or horns" effect occurs when a rater allows a rating on one dimension (or an overall impression) for an employee to influence the ratings he or she assigns to other dimensions for that employee. That is, the rater inappropriately assesses ratee performance similarly across different job functions, projects criteria, or performance dimensions. This error is not deliberate.

Central Tendency

Central tendency occurs when ratings for employees tend to be toward the center (midpoint) of the scale regardless of the actual performance of ratees. This is a deliberate error although much less common than leniency.

Fundamental Attribution Error/Actor-Observer Bias

The fundamental attribution error refers to the tendency to attribute observed behaviors or outcomes to the disposition of the person being observed while underestimating the causal role of factors beyond the control of the performer.[19] This is related to the **actor-observer bias** where people tend to make the exact opposite attributions for their *own* behavior: they tend to attribute their successes to their own competence and their failures to the influence of external factors beyond their control. **The actor-observer bias is thus the tendency of observers to underestimate the effects of external factors and for performers to overestimate the effects of external factors on less than perfect performance.** Rating systems such as **PDA** that ask the rater to formally consider the possible constraints on performance have been shown to reduce the actor-observer bias and decrease differences between self and supervisory appraisals.

Actor-observer bias is one of the major factors that cause perceptions of unfairness in appraisal decisions. Any student who has been graded on a group project may have experienced this problem in individual appraisal. Many conditions present in the job situation or work assignment can hold a person back from performing as well as he or she could. Some of these constraints include inadequate tools, lack of supplies, not enough money, too little time, lack of information, breakdowns in equipment, ineffective management, and not enough help from others. For example, truck inspectors may be limited in the number of trucks they can check for defects if they spend a considerable portion of their workday in court presenting testimony against offenders. They still may be held accountable, however, for inspecting a certain number of trucks despite these other job duties. If in a group project, one of your team members fails to retrieve vital information, the constraint could seriously hamper your ability to do your tasks. Situational factors that hinder an employee's job performance are called **situational constraints** and are described in Figure 7-9.[20]

Rater training should focus on actor/observer bias

An appraisal system should consider the effects of situational constraints so that ratees are not unfairly downgraded for these uncontrollable factors. Rater training programs also should focus on making raters aware of potential constraints on employee performances and the tendency on the part of raters to commit this attributional error. Research shows training on the actor-observer bias can reduce the error and promote more agreement between the rater (observer) and the ratee (the actor).

**Figure 7-9
Possible Situational
Constraints on Performance**

1. Absenteeism or turnover of key personnel.
2. Slowness of procedures for action approval.
3. Inadequate clerical support.
4. Shortages of supplies and/or raw materials.
5. Excessive restrictions on operating expenses.
6. Inadequate physical working conditions.
7. Inability to hire needed staff.
8. Inadequate performance of co-workers or personnel in other units on whom an individual's work depends.
9. Inadequate performance of subordinates.
10. Inadequate performance of managers.
11. Inefficient or unclear organizational structure or reporting relationships.
12. Excessive reporting requirements and administrative paperwork.
13. Unpredictable workloads.
14. Excessive workloads.
15. Changes in administrative policies, procedures, and/or regulations.
16. Pressures from co-workers to limit an individual's performance.
17. Unpredictable changes or additions to the types of work assigned.
18. Lack of proper equipment.
19. Inadequate communication within the organization.
20. The quality of raw materials.
21. Economic conditions (e.g., interest rates, labor availability, and costs of basic goods and services).
22. Inadequate training.

Figure 7-10   A Performance/Constraint Matrix (R&D) Director

Constraints	Performance Dimensions			
	Assisting Center Researchers	Generating Research Grants	Organizing and Conducting Seminars	Conducting Research
Absenteeism/turnover		a		
Slow procedures				
Clerical support		b		b
Supply shortage				
Excessive restrictions	c	d		
Working conditions				
Poor co-worker performance				
Poor subordinate performance			e	f
Poor manager performance				
Inefficient structure				
Excessive reporting requirements				
Workloads				
Change in administrative policy				
Co-worker pressure				
Change in work assignment	k, h	k, h	k, h	
Lack of equipment				
Inadequate communication			i	
Raw material problem				
Economic conditions				j
Lack of (or poor) training				

Constraints

a. Loss of departmental secretary precluded proposal writing for two months

b. Secretary worked on unrelated project for two months

c. Grant support lifted from four recipients due to lack of funds

d. No money allotted for hiring grantsperson as promised

e. Staff rarely attended seminars although they were scheduled on payday

f. Staff member failed to do literature review in a collaborative research project

h. Given new responsibility for compensation policy and computer records (not on original job description)

i. Failure of management to provide written charge for compensation project resulted in time being wasted in clarification with divisions

j. Severe reduction in research budget has precluded three pilot projects that had great potential for external funding

k. Asked to conduct seminar at last moment due to funding problem; took 15 percent of my time away from all assignments

Goals

a. Proposed backup clerical support for excessive workloads; have plan by 3/1

b. Develop more detailed job description and chain of command for secretaries, that is, only one boss; submit plan by 3/1

c. Review committee will be made aware of total funds available

d. Conduct search to determine if part-time person can be identified; write announcement by 2/15

e. Send memo to staff encouraging attendance

h. Provide written charge in the future

i. Get commitment from management to attend all executive-level meetings

j. More active search for external dollars. Will review foundation interests; submit report by 4/1

k. Will do survey to determine what time would be most favorable; report attendance to director (will submit report in two months)

A goal-based PA that documents constraints

Figure 7-10 presents an example of an MBO-type system that considers the potential for this common error. With this method, raters and ratees must independently complete a performance dimension/constraint matrix. This approach places the focus squarely on discrepancies in perceptions of the effects of particular constraints. In Figure 7-10, the list of constraints was recorded by the ratee (performer) who felt the constraint had a significant impact on her performance for a particular performance dimension. For example, this head of a Research and Development unit indicated that staff attendance at meetings was an indication of poor subordinate performance and that this constraint impeded performance on "Organizing and Conducting Seminars." After the supervisor has reviewed the constraints and recorded his/her own assessment of the effects of the constraints, specific goals are set where the supervisor agrees to attend to some (or all) of the perceived constraints (e.g., supervisor will send out a memo strongly encouraging seminar attendance).

Representativeness Error

This error refers to the tendency to make judgments about people (or their performance) on the basis of their similarity to people who exhibited prominent or memorable levels on the attribute being judged, even though the similarity may have no causal connection to the attribute. For example, popular stereotypes may have given the rater an image that attractive people are more effective in groups.

When confronted with the task of rating someone on factors related to his or her group effectiveness, to the extent that the ratee possesses the *representative* trait (e.g., is attractive), the rater will tend to rate in accordance with this preconception rather than in accordance with actual observations.

The problem with this type of thinking is that it ignores the fact that although some prominent examples of people who performed at the upper or lower extremes of effectiveness may have possessed a certain characteristic, such as attractiveness, most of the people who possess such a characteristic do not so distinguish themselves and in fact the characteristic has no causative connection to actual performance.

This is a difficult tendency to overcome. Perhaps the best means of suppressing it is to use rating scales that are anchored with detailed descriptions of behaviors or outcomes.

Availability Bias

People tend to mistake the ease with which a category of outcomes can be recalled as an indication of its frequency of occurrence relative to other categories. This becomes almost a rule of thumb that some people use in judging the relative frequency of outcomes. The relevance to performance appraisal judgments should be obvious: since more extreme outcomes tend to be more memorable, raters will tend to attribute greater frequency to them than was actually the case. This results in such outcomes being given excessive weight in the formation of appraisal judgments. It has been found that negative events—instances of ineffective performance—seem to have the greatest availability in memory.

There is no easy solution to the availability problem. It is possible that merely making raters aware of their proneness to this type of error will cause them to make efforts to compensate for this tendency. However, there is no research to substantiate this possibility.

Anchoring Error

This error refers to the tendency to insufficiently alter a judgment away from some starting point when new information is received. Most of us start with some initial impression of any situation we encounter, or we form one very quickly after our initial immersion in a situation. This is very true of observations of other people's behavior or performances. Either from past experience, stereotyping, information available, interpersonal affect, or reputation, we generally start off prior to observing another's performance with some initial impression or we form one very quickly. The problem that arises is that once an initial starting point, or **anchor,** is selected, we tend to resist being moved from this point by subsequent information that warrants movement. As a consequence, our final judgments will be much nearer to our "starting point" than they should be. This is a source of unfairness in appraisals. A person's reputation, or even his/her past performance, should not be a factor in how his/her performance during the period under consideration is judged.

Anchoring is a potent error. For example, if a person whom I regard as unreliable and untrustworthy told me that the performance of a new hire had been terrible on his/her last job, even though I had other sources of credible information, I could be affected by that person's opinion in evaluating the new hire and even in subsequent evaluations of the new hire.

This **anchoring** effect also applies to multirater systems. Supervisors, for example, can be inappropriately affected by the level of subordinates' initial self-ratings, particularly if the supervisor has not anchored future judgments with his/her own prior judgments. Supervisors should make assessments before they review (and consider) self-ratings and be wary of their own preconceived notions also.

The origin of this problem again seems to be the holistic consideration of a person's performance on each rating factor rather than attending to the specific behaviors or outcomes that were exhibited. If rating scales are used that don't call for an overall judgment but rather elicit estimates of the frequencies with which the behaviors or outcomes anchoring each level occurred, we might overcome (or reduce) the problem of anchoring.

Rater Training

All of these errors can arise in two different ways: as the result of *unintentional* errors in the way people observe, store, recall, and report events or as the result of *intentional* efforts to assign inaccurate ratings. If rating errors are *unintentional,* raters may commit them because they do not have the necessary skills to make accurate ratings or the content of the appraisal is not carefully defined. Rater training can help.

Frame of reference training increases accuracy

Attempts to control unconscious, unintentional errors most often focus on rater training. Training to improve the rater's observational and categorization skills (called **frame-of-reference training**) has been shown to increase rater accuracy and consistency.[21] This training consists of creating a common frame of reference among raters in the observation process. Raters are familiarized with the rating scales and are given opportunities to practice making ratings. Following this, they are given feedback on their practice ratings. They are also given descriptions of critical incidents of performance that illustrate outstanding, average, and unsatisfactory levels of performance on each dimension. This is done so they will know what behaviors or outcomes to consider when making their ratings.

Intentional bias

Raters may commit rating errors *intentionally* for political reasons or to provide certain outcomes to their employees or themselves. For example, one of the most common intentional rating errors in organizations is leniency. Managers may assign higher ratings than an employee deserves to avoid a confrontation with the employee, to protect an employee suffering from personal problems, to acquire more recognition for the department or themselves, or to be able to reward the employee with a bonus or promotion. Although less common, managers may also intentionally assign more severe ratings than an employee deserves to motivate him or her to work harder, to teach the employee a lesson, or to build a case for firing the employee. There is evidence that the error of leniency can be reduced by training raters on how to provide negative feedback and by holding raters more accountable for their rating tendencies.[22]

Other attempts to control intentional rating errors include hiding scoring keys such as through forced choice, forced distribution or other forms of ratee comparison systems, requiring cross-checks or reviews of ratings by other people, using multirater systems, training raters on how to provide negative evaluations, and reducing the rater's motivation to assign inaccurate ratings. Unfortunately, none of these methods has proven to be reliably effective for controlling deliberate errors and biases.[23]

There are a wide variety of PA training programs available for purchase, some on the Internet. One of the more effective programs for supervisors is "Legal and Effective Performance Appraisals," which takes the supervisors from PA preparation through the post-PA interview process. The highlights of this program, which should be covered in any comprehensive PA training program, are summarized in **Figure 7-11.** Remember that rater training is among the precriptions employers should follow to increase their chances of winning legal challenges related to performance-based decisions.

Hold raters accountable

Most experts contend that the best ways to control for deliberate bias on the part of an individual rater are to hold raters more accountable for their ratings and to use more than one rater. In general, the mean rating compiled from ratings across all (or a sample) of qualified raters will result in less bias and more validity for the performance appraisal system. A "qualified" rater can be defined as any internal or external customer who is the recipient of the performers' products or services.[24] The next section describes multirater (or 360-degree) appraisal systems.

Figure 7- 11   **Legal and Effective Performance Appraisals: A Training Program for Supervisors**

SAFEGUARDS AGAINST BIAS
1. Clearly communicate performance standards

   Avoid subjective judgment-trait language on forms and in feedback

   Expectations should be clearly understood with measurement precision

   Standards should be fair and equitable (think disparate treatment discrimination)

2. Knowledge of PA procedures

   Review evaluations with supervisor(s) before meeting

   Allow employees to read, review, and sign off on performance appraisals

   Have an appeal process—allow procedure for re-evaluation.

3. Linking PAs to job description detail is a key to effective PA

   Good, up-to-date job descriptions facilitate clear understanding of tasks, responsibilities; they further long-term strategic goals of organization

   Write accurate, up-to-date job descriptions

   Set clear standards for rating job performance

   Get job occupant input on job description and standards and sign-off

STEPS IN THE PA PROCESS
1. Preparation—How does the supervisor prepare?

   1. Gather documentation

   2. Review performance log/diary, incident reports, important information

   3. Review attendance records

   4. Review goals/expectations

   5. Review PA form

2. Encourage self-evaluation (remember anchoring!)

   Review self-evaluation after your initial appraisal

3. Set convenient time and place for uninterrupted meeting

4. Rate performance—typical performance level

   Use behavioral/results/outcomes as criteria

   Beware of rating errors (e.g., halo/horns; recency; leniency effects; actor/observer bias)

5. Evaluate yourself as a manager and facilitator of performance

   Consider constraints beyond performer's control

CONDUCTING THE PA INTERVIEW
1. Put employee at ease

   Intention—collaborative, horizontal communication

   Avoid negativity as much as possible

   Attention to: Job-related, objective behaviors and countable results/outcomes/work products

      Not personality traits or the person's characteristics

      Remember: the focus is on *performance* (not traits)

2. Reach agreement on solutions and methods for improvement

   Feedback should be behavioral/outcome/results-based (e.g. Don't say someone is "unreliable"; comment on the specific behavior or outcomes with as much precision as possible (define "unreliable")

   Key to effective feedback is presenting the information in a way that prevents or lowers the probability of emotional reaction

   Concentrate on observed behavior/results/the record of performance outcomes

3. Set goals for next PA period

   Employees should have a say in setting their goals

   GOALS SHOULD BE:

   1. Realistic (attainable)

   2. Motivating

   3. Contribute to productivity and compatible with strategic goals

POST-PA MEETING
   Do final evaluation after considering new information and self-evaluation

   Employee should sign and date form; provide opportunity to comment

EFFECTIVE APPRAISALS ARE AN ONGOING PROCESS—EMPLOYERS AND EMPLOYEES NEED REGULAR COMMUNICATION AND FEEDBACK TO DEVELOP TRUST AND SHARED COMMITMENT

Source: "Legal and Effective Performance Appraisals." Available from Coastal Technologies (http://econ.coastal.com).

Defining the Rater

Multi-rater systems are a high-performance work system characteristic

Ratings can be provided by ratees, supervisors, peers, clients or customers, or high-level managers. While most companies still give the supervisor the sole responsibility for the employee's appraisal, formal multirater systems are becoming quite popular.[25] A growing number of companies use formal self-assessments. The purpose is to encourage employees to take an active role in their own development. Upward appraisals (ratings by subordinates) are also on the increase.

With increasing frequency, organizations are concluding that multiple rater types are beneficial for use in their appraisal systems.[26] Ratings collected from several raters, also known as **360-degree appraisal** systems, are thought to be more accurate and have fewer biases, are perceived to be more fair, and are less often the targets of lawsuits.[27] The use of 360-degree appraisal systems is one of the characteristics of **high-performance work systems,** which have been linked to superior corporate financial performance. There are numerous Web-based systems of 360-degree appraisal, some based on competency-based models of HR strategy.

The probable reason multirater appraisal is successful is that many of the rater types used (e.g., customers, peers) have direct and unique knowledge of at least some aspects of the ratee's job performance and can provide reliable and valid performance information on some job activities. In fact, the use of raters who represent all critical internal and external customers contributes to the accuracy and relevance of the appraisal system.[28]

Many organizations use self-, subordinate, peer, and superior ratings as a comprehensive appraisal prior to a training program. The Center for Creative Leadership in Greensboro, North Carolina, requires all participants in its one-week assessment center program to first submit evaluations from superiors, peers, and subordinates. The data are tabulated by the Center, and the feedback is reported to participants on the first day of the assessment center program. Participants consider this feedback to be among the most valuable they receive.

Mystery shoppers

Many companies now use external customers as an important source of information about employee and unit performance and for reward systems. The Marriott Corporation places considerable weight on its customer survey data in the evaluation of each hotel as well as work units within the hotels. Burger King, McDonald's, Domino's Pizza, and Taco Bell are among the companies that hire professional "customers" or "mystery shoppers" to visit specific installations to provide detailed appraisals of several performance functions.[29] Critical Thinking Application 7-B focuses on this approach to appraisal.

Figure 7-12 presents a summary of recommendations for implementing a multirater/360-degree appraisal system.

Defining the "Ratee"

Many people assume that appraisals always focus on an *individual* level of performance. There are alternatives to using the individual as the ratee that are becoming more common in organizations as more firms (e.g., General Foods Corporation, Rohm & Haas, General Motors, Saturn, Westinghouse) shift to using more **self-managed teams.** Specifically, the ratee may be defined at the individual, work group, division, or organizationwide level. It is also possible to define the ratee at multiple levels. For example, for some performance dimensions, it may be desirable to appraise performance at the work group level for merit pay purposes and additionally at the individual level to identify developmental needs. Burger King, for example, awards cash bonuses to branch stores based on a customer-based evaluation process while maintaining an individual appraisal system within each store. Delta Airlines assesses customer service at the unit level only, while other job activities are assessed at the individual employee level.

Team PAs for high work group cohesiveness difficulty measuring individual performance

Two conditions that make it desirable to assess performance at a higher aggregation level than the individual level are high work group cohesiveness and difficulty in measuring individual contributions. **High work group cohesiveness** refers to the shared feeling among work group members that they form a team. Such an orientation promotes high degrees of cooperation among group members for highly interdependent tasks. Appraisals focused on individual performance may undermine the cooperative orientation needed to maintain this cohesiveness and tend to promote individualistic or even disruptive competitive environments. In some cases, workers are so **interdependent** (their individual performance outcomes cannot be clearly determined) that there is no choice but to focus their appraisals on the performance of their work group only.

Figure 7-12   **Recommendations for Implementing a 360-Degree Appraisal System**

INSTRUMENT ISSUES
- Items should be directly linked to effectiveness on the job.
- Items should focus on specific, observable behaviors and/or outcomes (not traits, competencies).
- Items should be worded in positive terms, rather than negative terms. Raters, particularly employees, may be less likely to respond honestly to negative items about their boss.
- Raters should be asked only about issues for which they have firsthand knowledge (i.e., ask subordinates about whether the boss delegates work to them; don't ask peers since they may not know).

ADMINISTRATION ISSUES
- Select raters carefully by using a representative sample of people most critical to the ratee (and the work unit) and who have had the greatest opportunity to observe his or her performance.
- Use an adequate number of raters to ensure adequate sampling and to protect the confidentiality of respondents (at least three per source; except supervisor). An alternative strategy is to solicit ratings from all possible qualified raters.
- Instruct respondents on how the data will be used and ensure confidentiality.
- To maintain confidentiality, raters should not indicate their names or other identifying characteristics and surveys should be returned in a manner so as to maintain confidentiality.
- Alert and train raters regarding rating errors (e.g., halo, leniency, severity, attributional bias).

FEEDBACK REPORT
- Separate the results from the various sources. The ratee should see the average, aggregated results from peers, subordinates, higher-level managers, customers, or other sources that may be used.
- Show the ratee's self-ratings as compared to ratings by others. This enables the ratee to see how his or her self-perceptions are similar to or different from others' perceptions.
- Compare the ratee's ratings with other norm groups. For example, a manager's ratings can be compared to other managers (as a group) in the firm.
- Provide feedback on items as well as scales so ratees can see how to improve.

FEEDBACK SESSION
- Use a trained facilitator to provide feedback to ratees.
- Involve the ratee in interpreting his or her own results.
- Provide an overview of the individual's strengths and areas for improvement.
- Provide feedback on recommendations and help him or her to develop an action plan.

FOLLOW-UP ACTIVITIES
- Provide opportunities for skill training in how to improve his or her behaviors.
- Provide support and coaching to help him or her apply what has been learned.
- Over time, evaluate the degree to which the ratee has changed behaviors.

Source: Modified from G. Yukl and R. Lepsinger, "360 Feedback," *Training*, December 1995, pp. 45–48, 50.

Many companies rely on aggregated data to assess unit performance. *Benchmarking* is one example of a process whereby a particular unit can evaluate its performance relative to some other comparable unit, either inside or outside the organization.

Benchmarking—Aggregating the Ratee to the Unit or Firm

Benchmarking is the process of gauging the internal practices and activities within a firm to an external reference or standard. It is a continuous process of measuring one's own products, services, systems, and practices against the world's toughest competitors to identify areas for improvement.

An estimated 70 percent of the Fortune 500 companies use benchmarking on a regular basis. For example, Ford Motor Company benchmarked its accounts payable function against Mazda Motor Corporation. Ford found that it had about five times as many employees as it needed. The automaker redesigned the system for tracking orders, deliveries, and invoices and thereby helped employees to perform the same tasks more efficiently. As a result, Ford was able to simplify the process, reduce the number of employees, and reduce errors. Goodyear Tire and Rubber changed its compensation practices by benchmarking what several Fortune 100 firms were doing in compensation. It developed a system to link employee performance to the firm's financial gains. AT&T examined the role of chief financial officers to redesign the job duties and functions of their CFO to be more in line with what world-class CFOs were doing.

Studies on the effectiveness of benchmarking have found that it is critical to have top management support and commitment to the process, including the "benchmarked" companies. In addition, when it results in setting moderately difficult goals that employees believe are attainable, it seems to work. But when poorer-performing companies receive benchmarking data that their practices are significantly different from the "best practices," and their managers set radical, unrealistically high goals, employees have difficulty embracing the changes and may resist them. As a result, performance actually may decline.

Needs top management support

These findings should not discourage managers from benchmarking their practices. Instead, managers should be alerted to the types of goals they should set after receiving benchmarking data. Perhaps setting more realistic goals and gradually increasing the difficulty of the goals would encourage employees. This is known as **shaping,** which is a behavioral change technique that promotes gradual improvement from a known, initial behavior to a desired goal, or, in this case, the benchmark. For example, if an organization wants to meet the best practice of having 1 percent defects in its industry, and their initial performance is at 20 percent defects, the company may need to first use 15 percent defects as a goal. Once workers master that goal and are rewarded, then the company can change the goal to 10 percent defects and so on. In this way, the company is continually moving toward the benchmark goal and employees are less resistant than if they were initially assigned the goal of 1 percent defects, which they may have felt was unattainable. To use shaping effectively in benchmarking practices, the following tips are offered:

1. Identify what is to be benchmarked (a process, product, service, etc.).

2. Identify comparable companies.

3. Collect data to precisely define the target goal (benchmark).

4. Collect data to determine the organization's current performance level against the benchmark.

5. Reduce the target to discrete, measurable, smaller steps or goals.

6. Train, as needed, any employees so that they can meet the smaller goals (subgoals).

7. Periodically provide feedback and use appropriate, valued reinforcers for meeting the subgoals.

8. Increase the subgoals so that they are getting closer to the target goal.

9. Recalibrate benchmarks periodically.

The recalibration is important so that the organization continually monitors the benchmark or target goal because it may change. Successes by companies may lead to new standards.

Benchmarking should be considered one form of performance measurement that provides a basis of comparison to competitors and other outside sources. While this is a useful approach to measurement, the importance attached to any measurement should derive from the extent to which the measurement is related to the strategic goals of the organization.

Administrative Characteristics

Figure 7-13 presents a summary of the many issues to consider regarding the administrative characteristics of a performance management and appraisal system. Among the most important are the extent to which computers are used to make and maintain ratings and the methods of delivering feedback.

Almost all appraisal systems discussed above are computer adaptive and some absolutely require strong computer adaptation (e.g., CARS, PDA). There are now several online systems of 360-degree appraisal that are used by many of the most successful companies of the world. The reader should consult one of the following Web sites to sample online 360-degree systems: PersonnelDecisions.com, 360-degreefeedback.com, performaworks.com, acumen.com, cwginc.com, or fullcirclefeedback.com.

Performance Monitoring

One administrative issue is the possible automation of performance measurement. Can we eliminate those pesky raters altogether? The practice of monitoring employees while they perform their jobs through the use of surveillance cameras, telephone monitoring, or computer monitoring is growing in popularity. Remember the discussion of the JetBlue at-home (in Utah) reservationists? Do you think they can slip away from their workstations and catch "All My Children" or do a little eBaying? Not a chance. JetBlue has an elaborate performance monitoring system that records everything important about each reservationist's performance during their on-duty time. An automated system even tells the employee when to take breaks. More companies are turning to some form of monitoring regarding workers' online behavior. They probably should. The reported rates of on-the-clock, online cruising are rather alarming.

Figure 7-13
Major Administrative Issues to Consider in Performance Management

1. Frequency and timing of formal appraisals
   - Number of times per year (e.g., one per year, every six months, quarterly?)
   - Time period (e.g., anniversary of hire, after project completion)
2. Rating/data collection medium
   - Computerized data collection/data tabulation/integration into database
   - Hard copy for personnel file and sign off?
   - Use of technology for performance data collection and monitoring
   - Computer programs that can monitor rater rating tendencies
3. Training programs
   - For raters (supervisors), ratees, administrators
   - Scheduling/assessment/follow-up
   - Frame of Reference (FOR)/self-efficacy training
4. Method of feedback
   - Feedback via computer versus scheduled sessions
   - Feedback based on comparisons to other employees/companies
   - Formal feedback sessions with supervisors, team, consultants, coaches

Most companies maintain that such performance monitoring is an acceptable and ethical means for gathering information about performance and other aspects of work. Information from electronic monitoring should be incorporated into the full performance management system.

Employees don't like most electronic monitoring. Offering those who are to be monitored input into the monitoring process reduced invasion of privacy concerns and that team leaders are more likely to monitor performance in secret when there is a low level of trust in a work group. In addition, team leaders tend to increase their level of electronic monitoring over time.[30]

Methods of Delivering Performance Feedback

Raters should communicate appraisal results to ratees through a formal feedback meeting held between the supervisor and the employee.[31] Feedback serves an important role both for motivational and informational purposes and for improved rater–ratee communications.[32] For example, **supportive feedback can lead to greater motivation,** and feedback discussions about pay and advancement can lead to greater employee satisfaction with the process. Detailed and specific feedback (e.g., "this book uses too many rambling sentences and big words") is recommended instead of general feedback ("I hate the writing") since **more precision is more likely to improve performance.**

Provide specific and timely feedback

The biggest hazard for the rater in providing performance feedback may be ratee reactions to the feedback. Generally, ratees believe that they performed at higher levels than do observers of that performance. This is especially true at the lower performance levels where there is more room for disagreement and a greater motive on the part of ratees to engage in ego-defensive behavior. Let's not forget about the **actor-observer bias** factor either. It is no wonder that raters are often hesitant about confronting poor performers with negative appraisal feedback and may be lenient when they do. Although pressure on managers to give accurate feedback and to effect change may override a reluctance to give negative feedback, the pressure doesn't make the experience any more pleasant. In addition, feedback to inform poor performers of performance deficiencies and to encourage improvement doesn't always lead to performance improvements.[33]

Accurate feedback doesn't always help

Recommendations

To create a supportive atmosphere for the feedback meeting between the employee and supervisor, several recommendations exist. The rater should avoid being disturbed, and take sufficient time in the meeting. They should keep notes on effective and ineffective behavior as it occurs so that they will have some notes to refer to when conducting the feedback session (review the legal prescriptions presented earlier). Raters should be informal and relaxed and allow the employee the opportunity to share his or her insights. Topics that should be addressed include praise for special assignments, the employee's own assessment of his or her performance, the supervisor's response to the employee's assessment, action plans to improve the subordinate's performance, perceived constraints on performance that require subordinate or supervisory attention, and employee career aspirations, ambitions, and developmental goals. In sum, raters should provide feedback that is clear, specific, descriptive, job related, constructive, frequent, and timely.

SUMMARY

Performance appraisals have become an increasingly important tool for organizations to manage and improve the performance of employees, to make more valid staffing decisions, and to enhance the overall effectiveness of the firm's services and products. The design, development, and implementation of appraisal systems are not endeavors that can be effectively handled by following the latest fad or even by copying other organizations' systems. Instead, a new appraisal system must be considered a major organizational change effort that should be pursued in the context of improving the organization's competitive advantage. This means, like any such change effort, there will be vested interests in preserving the status quo that will resist change, no matter how beneficial it may be for the organization. These sources of resistance to the change have to be identified and managed to build incentives for using a new appraisal system. Once a well-designed system has been implemented, the work is still not done. An appraisal system has to be maintained by monitoring its operation through periodic evaluations. Only keeping an appraisal system finely tuned will enable managers to have a rational basis for making sound personnel decisions to achieve the kinds of gains in productivity that are so critically needed in today's times. Performance management and appraisal should be an integral part of the strategic HR system. Data from this system should be a critical component at internal staffing decisions (promotion, retention, and termination).

Among the personnel decisions, some of the most important concern the organization's compensation system. The prescriptions presented in Figure 7-1, the findings discussed in Figure 7-2, and the training outline presented in Figure 7-11 should be helpful guidelines for improving most appraisal systems. Effective performance appraisal also must be carefully integrated with other human resource domains, particularly compensation systems with a pay-for-performance component. Accurate appraisals also are critical for determining training needs, one of the subjects of the next chapter.

Discussion Questions

1. Why has performance appraisal taken on increased significance in recent years?

2. As the workforce becomes more diverse, why does performance appraisal become a more difficult process?

3. Ford was accused of age discrimination based on the use of their forced-distribution rating system. What evidence would you investigate to test this allegation?

4. Many managers describe performance appraisal as the responsibility that they like the least. Why is this so? What could be done to improve the situation?

5. Describe several advantages and disadvantages to using rating instruments that are based on comparisons among ratees' performance, comparisons among anchors, and comparisons to anchors.

6. What steps would you take if your performance appraisal system resulted in disparate or adverse impact?

7. Under what circumstances would you use customer or client evaluation as one basis for appraising employees?

8. Why are so many companies using 360-degree feedback systems? What are the benefits of such systems?

9. Why should managers provide ongoing and frequent feedback to employees about their performance?

10. As a supervisor, how would you react to a forced-distribution rating system?

Chapter 8

Training and Development*

OBJECTIVES

After reading this chapter, you should be able to

1. Define what is meant by training and explain why it is a critical function for corporations today.
2. Explain how to conduct a needs assessment, including performing organizational, task, and person analyses and deriving instructional objectives for a training program.
3. Know how to design a training program to facilitate learning.
4. Identify the critical elements related to transfer of training.
5. Compare and contrast the various techniques available for training, including their relative advantages and disadvantages, with particular emphasis on e-learning.
6. Identify criteria to use to evaluate training effectiveness.
7. Understand different experimental designs that can be used for evaluating training programs.
8. Understand the components of training programs for employee orientation and onboarding, teamwork, generational issues, diversity awareness, sexual harassment, creativity, and international assignments.

OVERVIEW

Throughout this book we have referred to the empirical research linking particular human resource practices to corporate financial performance. The last chapter emphasized the critical role of performance measurement and management as characteristics of "high-performance work systems."[1] This same body of research also points to the importance of training and development as contributors to the "bottom line" of corporate performance. Training has evolved substantially in recent years with evidence indicating more organizational investment in training and development. Those leaders who understand how to drive business results in an increasingly competitive, global environment recognize that a better-trained workforce improves performance and investing in employee learning and development is critical to

*Contributed by Joyce E. A. Russell.

245

Figure 8-1
Trends in the Workplace

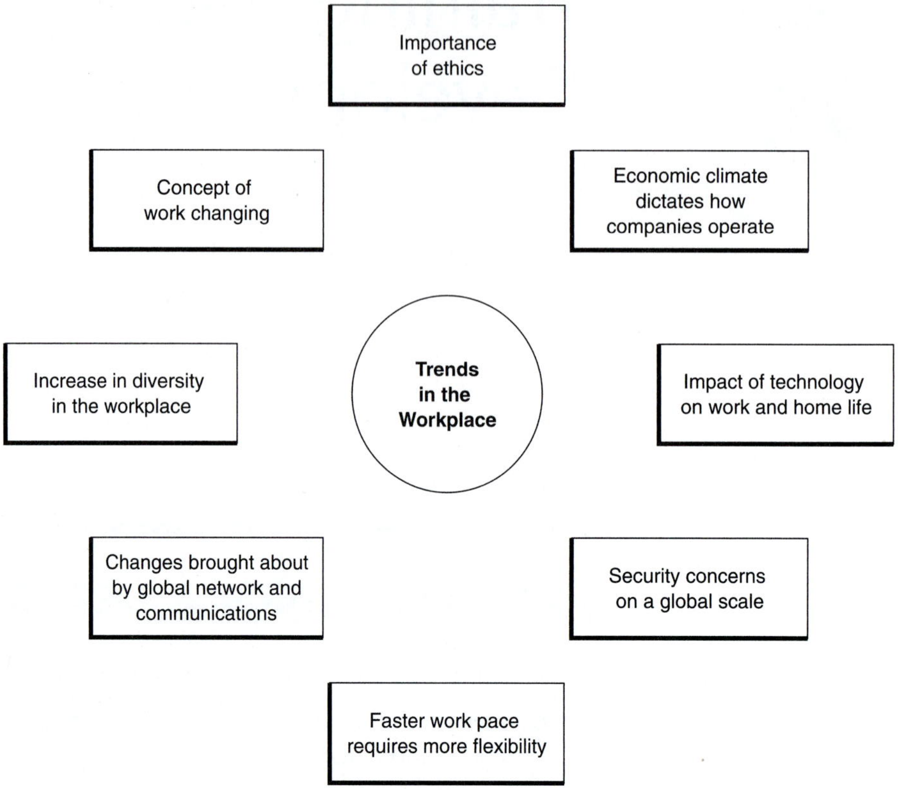

achieving success.[2] See Figure 8-1 for current trends in the workplace shaping **human resource development** (HRD) systems. Given the intense pressure to compete, improve quality and customer service, and lower costs, leading American companies have come to view training as a key to organizational survival and success. One review found that "many organizations are more likely to include training solutions as part of a systemwide change to gain competitive advantage"[3] Caterpillar's companywide training mission is ambitious—to be the best continual learning organization in the world. They are working hard to make this happen. Each of their more than 95,000 employees receives "four buckets" of instruction, including required e-learning modules, training specific to their business unit, education central to their job roles, and additional guidance related to their career paths.[4]

In countries around the world, training has become increasingly important to prepare workers for new jobs. For example, in Japan with the increasing numbers of women entering traditionally male factory jobs, more training is needed to help them learn the necessary skills. At Toyota Motor Corp., women have been given more training in everything from sexual harassment policies to skills for working on assembly lines.[5] In the United Kingdom, there is a sense of urgency about upskilling the workforce based on a 2006 report concluding that drastic measures must be taken to keep the UK workforce competitive. As a result, there has been a stronger alignment between universities, business, and government in training the population.[6]

Employee skill-level at top priority

Many employers throughout the world view the skill level of their workforce as the top priority for planning. A 2006 report found that employers are very concerned about the skill levels of new entrants to the workforce, and feel that many are deficient in their skills and work readiness. They worry that increasing technology is "de-skilling" the population. Their suggestion is continual training for employees. They also noted that the skills expected to increase in importance for the future included: critical thinking/problem solving, information technology application, teamwork and collaboration, creativity/innovation, diversity, leadership, oral communication, professionalism/work ethic, ethics/social responsibility, written communications, and foreign languages.[7] More recently, a 2008 survey of

HR professionals found that 94 percent did not feel that their workforce was adequately prepared to meet the future goals of their firm. The number one driver behind this concern was the need to retain skilled staff, followed by finding top talent and developing future leaders.[8]

Training and Fortune's "Best Companies"

Organizations with exceptional training opportunities and programs often make *Fortune* magazine's list of the **"Best Companies to Work For,"** an honor that also translates into financial success. One study found that companies that made *Fortune*'s list had 50 percent less turnover than their peers and returned about three times more money for stockholders.[9] To become a leading-edge company, a firm will need to be more concerned with the types of programs they use to improve workplace learning and performance, not simply how much money they spend on training. A transformation of a firm's training efforts and other practices and systems that support training may be needed. For example, successful firms align their training with high-performance work practices (e.g., self-directed work teams, access to business information), innovative compensation practices (profit sharing, group-based pay), and innovative training practices (e.g., mentoring or coaching programs, training information systems).

U.S. workers not competing well

Not only must firms invest in the continual learning of workers in order to be competitive, but many companies are providing training to workers who are new to the workforce. Many companies also include an assessment of workforce trainability as part of their analysis for expansion and plant openings. Unfortunately, recent evidence indicates that many U.S. workers are not competing well on the trainability criterion. In 2005, Toyota selected Ontario, Canada, over the United States as the place for a new plant for its mini-SUVs. They chose Canada over several U.S. states offering substantial financial incentives based to some extent on the relative trainability of Ontario's workforce. The president of the Automotive Parts Manufacturers' Association stated that the educational level in parts of the United States was so low that trainers for Japanese plants have to use "pictorials" to teach some illiterate workers how to use high-tech equipment. Other reports support the contention that auto companies with plants in parts of the United States are disappointed in the trainability of the U.S. workforce.[10]

Many firms provide life training in addition to skills training. When Marriott Hotels hires new workers, it enrolls them in a six-week training course with classes on hotel duties and self-esteem and stress. At Burger King, basic training for starting restaurant jobs also includes Life 101 (e.g., teaching employees how to balance a checkbook, the importance of getting to work on time). Ecolab established partnerships with welfare-to-work community groups and started a training program at a Wisconsin plant to teach entry-level employees math, basic physics, and blueprint-reading skills.[11] This chapter provides an overview of employee training. We will discuss the importance of training in the context of the organization's competitive strategy and the need to link training needs with the mission and goals of the organization. You will learn how to design and evaluate a training program and to tailor the training to particular situations.

DEFINING TRAINING AND DEVELOPMENT

Training defined

Training is defined as any attempt to improve employee performance on a currently held job or one related to it. This usually means changes in specific knowledge, skills, attitudes, or behaviors. To be effective, training should involve a learning experience, be a planned organizational activity, and be designed in response to identified needs. Ideally, training also should be designed to meet the goals of the organization while simultaneously meeting the goals of individual employees. The term *training* is often confused with the term *development*. **Development** refers to learning opportunities designed to help employees grow. Such opportunities do not have to be limited to improving employees' performance on their current jobs. At Ford, for example, a new systems analyst is required to take a course on Ford standards for user manuals. The content of this training is needed to perform the systems analyst job at Ford. The systems analyst, however, also may enroll in a

Development defined

course entitled "Self-Awareness," the content of which is not required on the current job. This situation illustrates the difference between "training" and "development." The focus of "development" is on the long term to help employees prepare for future work demands, while "training" often focuses on the immediate period to help fix any current deficits in employees' skills.

Training should be aligned with strategy

The most effective companies look at training and career development as an integral part of a human resources development (HRD) program carefully aligned with corporate business strategies. In the UK, HR professionals and managers noted that the status of the HRD/training function has increased in the past five years and is seen as more strategic. They also said that demonstrating stronger links between the role of HRD and performance improvement and having stronger partnerships with managers would enhance the importance of the HRD/training field even more.[12] **The American Society for Training and Development** (ASTD) Award winners for the Best Firms are those that strike a balance between training and other types of learning efforts (e.g., performance analysis, organizational development, talent management, process improvement). In 2008, the top ten winners included firms from all around the world in diverse industries, such as Janus Capital Group, BB&T, American Infrastructure, LQ Management LLC, Ohio Health, Sisters of Charity Providence Hospitals, Perkins & Will, Robert W. Baird & Co. Scottrade, and Wake Med Health & Hospitals.[13]

EXTENT OF TRAINING AND DEVELOPMENT

ASTD's BEST organizations

U.S. organizations with more than 100 employees spent $109 billion on employee learning and development in 2007 with nearly $80 billion spent on the internal learning function and the remainder ($29 billion) spent on external services.[14] ASTD's BEST organizations spent an average of $1,531 per employee on learning and an average of 44 hours a year in training. The BEST award winners were defined as those organizations honored for their exceptional efforts to foster, support, and leverage enterprisewide learning for business results. Common characteristics of BEST winning organizations were:

- Evidence that learning has value in the organization's culture (by learning opportunities, C-level involvement, and learning for growth).

- Evidence of a link between learning and performance (by alignment with the business, strategy, measurement, effectiveness, efficiency, and nonlearning solutions).

- Evidence that the firm has leveraged technology in learning.

- Evidence of investment in learning and performance initiatives.[15]

In 2007, the ASTD BEST Award winner Mercedes-Benz built a $30 million training center, called the Mercedes-Benz Institute, in its new $300 million plant in Alabama. The 100,000-square-foot center houses labs for teaching basic skills in welding, hydraulics, pneumatics, computer-aided design, measurement, and robotics. They set aside $60 million to send new workers to Germany for training.[16] Motorola mandates 40 hours of training per employee per year and has invested over $170 million in training.[17] Training has been viewed positively among employees. Approximately two-thirds of employees, regardless of age or gender, view the training they have received from their employers to be useful in helping them perform their current job duties. They were less enthusiastic about how well it has prepared them for higher-level jobs (about half were satisfied). They also viewed the training their employer provided as critical for determining whether or not they would stay with their current firm.[18]

Corporations are offering a variety of training programs to meet their organizational needs. These include content on IT and systems; processes, procedures, and business practices; industry-specific training; managerial or supervisory training; interpersonal skills; compliance; sales; executive development; basic skills; new employee orientation; customer service; and quality.[19] Figure 8-2 lists the most frequent types of training offered in 2003. The importance of training is likely to continue in the future given recent trends in the

Figure 8-2
Most Frequent Types of Training Offered

Type of Training	Percentage of Firms Offering
Computer systems/applications	96%
New hire orientation	96
Management development, nonexecutive	91
Technical training	90
Communication skills	89
Sexual harassment	88
Supervisory skills	88
Leadership	85
New equipment operation	85
Performance management/appraisal	85
Team building	82
Customer service	81
Product knowledge	79
Executive development	78
Safety	77
Computer programming	76
Personal growth	76
Managing change	75
Problem solving/decision making	75
Time management	74
Train-the-trainer	74
Diversity/cultural awareness	72
Hiring/interviewing	71
Strategic planning	69
Customer education	68
Quality/process improvement	65
Public speaking/presentation skills	62
Basic life/work skills	61
Ethics	61
Sales	55
Wellness	54

Source: "2003 Industry Report," *Training* 40(9) (2003), pp. 21–38. Respondents were asked the extent to which they used these methods via classroom, via technology, via a blended approach, or "do not provide." The figures shown here are for those who reported using any of the three means of providing training.

workforce. As the United States shifts from manufacturing to service jobs, more workers are needed in service-based industries. In addition, increasing technology demands that current employees enhance their skills and technical sophistication. For example, U.S. Steel (USX) invested money in training for workers so that they would be able to use the new technology they implemented in its production processes. Similarly, Xerox spent about $7 million on its training center to assist its sales staff in gaining additional training to better meet customers' needs for handling documents.[20] Employees at RJR Nabisco who have been confronted with new technology in their jobs are given the option of receiving retraining or early retirement.[21] Employees themselves are asking for additional training in using new technology.[22]

A SYSTEMS VIEW OF TRAINING

Needs assessment

The basic process of training is illustrated in Figure 8-3. Three major steps are involved: assessment, development, and evaluation. The goal of the **assessment** phase is to collect information to determine if training is needed in the organization. If it is needed, it is then important to determine where in the organization it is needed, what kind of training is needed, and what specific knowledge, abilities, skills, or other characteristics (KASOCs) should be taught. This information is collected by conducting three types of analyses: at the

**Figure 8-3
A Systems Model of
Training**

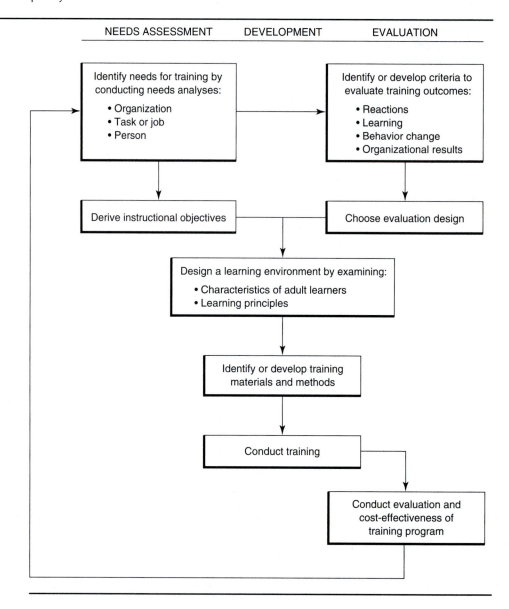

NEEDS ASSESSMENT   DEVELOPMENT   EVALUATION

Identify needs for training by
conducting needs analyses:

- Organization
- Task or job
- Person

Identify or develop criteria to
evaluate training outcomes:

- Reactions
- Learning
- Behavior change
- Organizational results

Derive instructional objectives

Choose evaluation design

Design a learning environment by examining:

- Characteristics of adult learners
- Learning principles

Identify or develop training
materials and methods

Conduct training

Conduct evaluation and
cost-effectiveness of
training program

Development phase

Evaluation phase

organizational, job, and individual level of analysis. After the information is compiled, objectives for the training program can be derived. The goal of the **development** phase of training is to design the training environment necessary to achieve the objectives. This means trainers must review relevant learning issues, including characteristics of adult learners and learning principles as they apply to the particular training and potential trainees under consideration. Also, trainers must identify or develop training materials and techniques to use in the program. Finally, after the appropriate learning environment is designed or selected, the training is conducted. The goal of the **evaluation** phase is to examine whether the training program has been effective in meeting the stated objectives. The evaluation phase requires the identification and development of criteria, which should include participants' reactions to the training, assessments of what they learned in the training program, measures of their behavior after the training, indicators of organizational results (e.g., changes in productivity data, sales figures, employee turnover, accident rates), and return on investments (ROI) or, as discussed in Chapter 6, utility analysis. An experimental design is chosen to assess the effectiveness of training. The choices of the criteria and the design are both made *before* training is conducted in order to ensure that training will be properly evaluated. After the training is completed, the program is then evaluated using the criteria and design selected.

Discrepancies between Research and Practice

Research in training is needed now more than ever before as the demand for training increases in organizations.[23] In addition, since much of the literature on training comes from a variety of scientific fields (e.g., industrial and organizational psychology, human resource development, cognitive psychology, anthropology, education, human factors, computer science), it is increasingly important to integrate the findings across those disciplines. Various fields in psychology even define training differently.[24]

Compared to other areas of HRM, practitioners have a fairly strong knowledge of some areas of training research.[25] A recent survey of training processes used in corporate America revealed some discrepancies between the academic recommendations regarding training program development and evaluation and the current state of the practice.[26] While larger companies were more likely to have done **formal needs assessments,** written specific instructional objectives, and evaluated the training with something other than a simple, post-training reaction questionnaire, the majority of all classes of respondents did none of these things. Small businesses rarely did any of these things as part of their training. Over 60 percent of all surveyed companies, regardless of company size, relied only on trainee reactions to assess the training, taken upon completion of the training, and had no systematic follow-up to further evaluate the training. Less than 10 percent of companies used any form of control group to evaluate the effects of the training. Over 50 percent of companies admitted that managerial training programs were first tried because some other company had been using them. As one training director put it, "A lot of companies buy off-the-shelf training programs just because they had heard or knew that a competitor was using the same training. Shouldn't we expect more data to determine training needs?"

Majority of U.S. companies do not do formal needs assessment

Research findings often ignored

Other scholars also have noted the gaps between research and practice in the training field. Practitioners[27] point out that research findings are often ignored and faddish programs are adopted with little proven utility. In addition, training needs assessments and evaluations are often rare despite their importance, and most training is informal even though this is not the best approach to use.

In order to address some of the gaps between research and practice, the **American Society for Training and Development** has initiated and published their ASTD 2006 Research-to-Practice conference proceedings. In this extensive report, they have included almost 20 articles examining a variety of training issues such as evaluation efforts, learning transfer, and Web-based and classroom instruction. The intent of the proceedings is to share knowledge that will affect practice in the field.[28]

NEEDS ASSESSMENT

The first step in training is to determine that a need for training actually exists. An organization should commit its resources to a training activity only if the training can be expected to achieve some organizational goal. The decision to conduct training must be based on the best available data, which are collected by conducting a needs assessment. This needs analysis ideally should be conducted in the context of a **human resource planning (HRP)** program and timely and valid performance data. Companies that implement training programs without conducting a needs assessment may be making errors or spending money unnecessarily. For example, a needs assessment might reveal that less-costly interventions (e.g., personnel selection, a new compensation system, job redesign) could be used in lieu of training. Despite the importance of conducting needs assessments, few employers conduct such an analysis in the context of their strategic plans or any form of strength, weakness, opportunity, or threat analysis (SWOT analysis).

Three primary types of analysis

A **needs assessment** is a systematic, objective determination of training needs that involves conducting three primary types of analyses. These analyses are used to derive objectives for the training program. The three analyses consist of an **organizational analysis,** a **job analysis,** and a **person analysis.**[29] After compiling the results, objectives for the training program can be derived.

Many trainers suggest that a training need is any discrepancy between what is desired and what exists. Thus, one of the goals of the needs assessment is to note any discrepancies. For example, the World Bank recently determined through a needs assessment that

Performance discrepancies

many of its constituents from eastern Europe required training in transforming state-owned businesses into self-sustaining businesses. The organization contracted with a number of universities to develop and provide the necessary training. Comparisons between the expected level of performance specified(from the job analysis) and the current level of performance exhibited (evident in the person analysis) may indicate performance discrepancies. The Sheraton Corporation, for example, specified that all hotel managers must be familiar with the implications of the 1990 Americans with Disabilities Act (ADA) for hotel operations (see Chapter 3). A test on the law was administered, and scores on the test were used as a basis for identifying those managers who needed training on the implications of the law. Performance discrepancies, however, should not be automatically interpreted as a need for training. The analyst must determine whether the discrepancy is a skill or knowledge deficiency, thus requiring training. If, however, the required skill is present and performance is still lacking, then the problem may be motivational in nature and thus require some other type of organizational intervention (e.g., new reward or discipline system). One study noted that organizations that conducted needs analyses were better able to use the results in the design and evaluation phases than organizations that did not.[30]

Organizational Analysis

Where emphasis should be placed

An organizational analysis tries to answer the question of *where* the training emphasis should be placed in the company and what factors may affect training. To do this, an examination should be made of the organizational goals, personnel inventories, performance data, and climate and efficiency indices. This examination should ideally be conducted in the context of the labor supply forecast and gap analysis. Organization system constraints that may hamper the training process also should be explored. Training does not exist in a vacuum, and the context in which it occurs has an impact on whether individuals will learn.[31] Many companies rely on very detailed surveys of the workforce to determine training needs as part of the planning effort. Motorola and IBM, for example, conduct annual surveys that assess particular training needs in the context of the company's short- and long-term goals.

The review of short- and long-term goals of the organization and any trends that may affect these goals is done to channel the training towards specific issues of importance to the firm (e.g., international expansion, improved customer satisfaction, increased productivity). For example, after Merrill Lynch pleaded guilty to a number of fraudulent business practices, the new chief executive officer (CEO) ordered training in business ethics for all employees. To reduce layoffs, IBM retrained hundreds of employees to be sales representatives. Not only was IBM able to minimize layoffs, but the larger sales staff was able to attack another corporate goal: to improve customer satisfaction.

Data from a human resource information system (HRIS) can reveal projected employee mobility, retirements, and turnover. The more sophisticated inventories also can indicate the number of employees in each KASOC or competency group, which can then be compared to what is needed based on the gap analysis of the HR planning process. For example, the Ford Manufacturing Systems Division decided to change to a new programming language for future support work. The first step it took was to determine the extent to which current staff was sufficiently skilled in the new language. The HRIS quickly revealed how many of the staff had at least basic knowledge of and experience with the new language.

A review of climate and performance efficiency data is important to identify problems that could be alleviated with training.[32] Climate indices are quality-of-work-life indicators and include records on turnover, grievances, absenteeism, productivity, accidents, attitude surveys, employee suggestions, and labor–management data (e.g., strikes, lockouts). Job satisfaction indexes provide data on employee attitudes toward the work itself, supervision, and co-workers. Performance data should be the specific record of important outcomes over a specific period of time. A record of competency assessment could be useful data as well. Multirater data should be maintained here also. Efficiency indexes consist of costs of labor, materials, and distribution; the quality of the product; downtime; waste; late deliveries; repairs; and equipment utilization. These data are examined to find any discrepancies between desired and actual performance.

It is also important to identify any organization system constraints on training efforts. For example, if the benefits of training are not clear to top management, they may not plan and budget appropriately for training. Consequently, the training program may not be properly designed or implemented. Omni Hotels requires senior executives to attend training programs to ensure that they are supportive of the training that lower-level managers receive. In addition, the training staff makes sure that the training is tailored to Omni so that trainees can more readily see the value of the training.[33]

Organizational analysis test hypotheses regarding training needs

Organizational analysis should test hypotheses about training needs. You're testing theories related to strategy execution. For example, a retail marketing manager received a complaint from a vendor that the sales staff did not understand the advantages of a particular product. The manager then "mined" the customer survey and complaint database to determine the extent to which product knowledge of the sales staff was a problem. (He was able to determine that the complaint may have been an isolated event.)

Job Analysis

What should be taught in training

A job analysis tries to answer the question of *what* should be taught in training so that the trainee can perform the job satisfactorily. As discussed in Chapter 4, a job analysis should document the tasks or duties involved in the job as well as the KASOCs (or competencies) needed to carry out the duties. When conducting a job analysis to determine training needs, both a *worker-oriented* approach, which focuses on identifying behaviors and KASOCs, and a *task-oriented* approach, which describes the work activities performed, should be used. The **critical incident technique (CIT)** is particularly valuable because it provides considerable detail on the job and the consequences of specific work behaviors. A task-oriented approach is beneficial in identifying specific training objectives that are used in curriculum development and program evaluation. Ideally more than one method of job analysis should be used to determine training needs. If interviews or questionnaires are used and discrepancies exist between what a supervisor says is an important job duty and what an employee states, these discrepancies should be resolved before any training programs are designed.[34]

Person Analysis

Who needs the training

A person analysis attempts to answer the question of *who* needs training in the firm and the specific type of training needed. To do this, the performance of individuals, groups, or units on major job functions (taken from the performance appraisal data) or assessments of KASOCs or competencies are compared to the desired levels. Many companies use self-assessments in this process. For example, Ford determined the training needs for a new computer language based on a self-assessment questionnaire distributed to the staff. At the managerial level, many organizations (e.g., IBM, AT&T, Federal Express, the World Bank, and the Federal Aviation Administration) use peers and subordinates to provide performance information about their managers. Knight-Ridder uses a 360-degree appraisal system to determine training needs. Managers receive "competency" ratings from customers, peers, subordinates, and their managers. At Ford, each supervisor is responsible for completing an individual training plan for each subordinate. The plan is developed jointly by the supervisor and the subordinate. The two decide on the courses that should be taken and the time frame for completion. The goal is for each employee to reach a certain level of proficiency considered necessary for current and future tasks. Many organizations in the service sector rely on customers for information about sales personnel. Bloomingdale's, for example, uses "paid" customers to assess the sales techniques of probationary employees. The data are then used to determine the appropriate managerial intervention to take with the employee (e.g., training, discipline, new compensation).

Identify performance discrepancies

Performance discrepancies are used to indicate areas needing attention. It is important to determine whether any discrepancies are due to a lack of KASOCs, which KASOCs are missing, and whether they can be developed in employees through training. Individuals may lack the necessary skills or perceive themselves as lacking the skills (i.e., they may lack confidence in their abilities). In these cases, training may be needed. In other situations, employees may have the skills yet lack the needed motivation to perform, and other action may be called upon (e.g., changes in the reward system, discipline). Employees also can be

Figure 8-4 **Data Sources Used in Training Needs Assessment**

Organizational Analysis	Job/Task Analysis	Person Analysis
Organizational goals and objectives	Job descriptions	Performance appraisal data
HRIS data	Job specifications or task analysis	Work sampling
Skills/competency inventories	Performance standards	Interviews
Organizational climate indexes	Performing the job	Questionnaires
Efficiency indexes/performance data	Work sampling	Tests (KASOCs)
Changes in systems or subsystems (e.g., equipment)	Reviewing literature on the job	Attitude surveys
	Asking questions about the job	Training progress charts/checklists
Management requests	Training committees/conferences	Assessment centers
Exit interviews	Analysis of operating problems	Critical incidents
Management-by-objectives or work planning systems	O'NET data	Self-efficacy measures

Source: Academy of Management Review by M.L. Moore and P. Dutton. Copyright 1978 by Academy of Management (NY). Reproduced with permission of Academy of Management (NY) in the format Textbook via Copyright Clearance Centre.

tested on the desired behaviors using a performance test such as those discussed in Chapter 6. If they can perform the duties satisfactorily, the organization will know that skills training is not required. The U.S. Navy, for example, uses miniature training and testing in order to determine skill level prior to comprehensive training. Pratt & Whitney and Office Depot are among the many companies that use an assessment center to measure supervisory skills judged to be critical based on its goals. Person analysis can also be used to assess trainability—whether the individual is capable of benefiting from the training and who, among candidates, might benefit the most. We discuss *trainability* later in the chapter. Research is clear that individual difference variables such as cognitive ability and motivation to learn are related to trainability and the extent to which someone will learn.[35]

Techniques for Collecting Needs Assessment Data

A variety of techniques have been suggested for conducting a needs assessment and for collecting data to use in the organizational, job, and person analyses. Figure 8-4 lists these techniques. Some techniques (e.g., work sampling) can be used for more than one type of analysis. Thus, efforts to coordinate and integrate results are recommended.

Deriving Instructional Objectives

After completing the three types of analyses in the needs assessment, the training professional should begin to develop instructional or learning objectives for the performance discrepancies identified. Instructional objectives describe the performance you want trainees to be able to exhibit. Well-written learning objectives should contain observable actions (e.g., time on target; error rate for things that can be identified, ordered, or charted), measurable criteria (e.g., percentage correct), and the conditions of performance (e.g., specification as to when the behavior should occur). Some sample learning objectives for a training program with sales employees are:

■ After training, the employee will be able to smile at all customers even when exhausted or ill, unless the customer is irate.

■ After training, the employee will be able to calculate markdowns on all sales merchandise (e.g., 30 percent markdown) correctly 100 percent of the time.

Advantages of deriving objectives

Although training programs can be developed without deriving learning objectives, there are several advantages to developing them. First, the process of defining learning objectives helps the trainer identify criteria for evaluating training programs. For example, specifying an instructional objective of a 20 percent reduction in waste reveals that measures of waste may be important indicators of program effectiveness. Second, learning objectives direct trainers to the specific issues and content to focus on. This ensures that trainers are addressing important topics that have been identified through strategic planning. Also, learning objectives guide trainees by specifying what is expected of them at the end of training. Finally, specifying objectives makes the training department more accountable and more clearly linked to other human resource activities, which may make the training program easier to sell to line managers.

DEVELOPMENT OF THE TRAINING PROGRAM

After a needs analysis has been conducted and the staff is confident that training is needed to address the performance problem or to advance the firm's strategic mission, the training program is developed. This can be done by an in-house training staff or by outside consultants. Many firms now even design and manage their own corporate training centers. Some of the companies that have their own corporate universities include Toyota, BB&T, Ford, Disney, GE, Union Carbide, IBM, Home Depot, Xerox, Motorola, Phillips Petroleum, McDonald's, Black & Decker, Aetna Life & Casualty, Kodak, and Goodyear Tire & Rubber.[36] To develop the program, the trainer should design a training environment conducive to learning. This can be done by setting up preconditions for learning and arranging the training environment to ensure learning. Following this, the trainer should examine various training methods and techniques to choose the combination most beneficial for accomplishment of the instructional objectives of the training program.

Designing a Learning Environment for Training

To design a training program in which learning will be facilitated, trainers should review the basic principles of how individuals learn. Learning principles should be reviewed and integrated into the design of the training program and materials. Also, issues of how to maximize transfer of new behaviors back to the job should be addressed. Finally, trainers should design their programs to meet the needs of adults as learners, which means understanding how adults best learn. For example, adult learners want to set their own goals for training since they see themselves as capable of self-direction. In addition, they often enjoy experiential learning techniques and self-directed learning more than conventional informational techniques. They are problem-centered and are more receptive to training that enables them to solve problems of particular interest to their situation. They want to be able to apply the training they receive to their day-to-day work experiences and are less interested in the program if they cannot see a direct application to their work situation.[37]

Preconditions of Learning

Trainees must be ready to learn before they are placed in any training program. To ensure this, trainers should determine whether trainees are **trainable** (i.e., whether they have the ability to learn and are motivated to learn). In addition, trainers should try to gain the support of trainees and their supervisors prior to actually implementing the program. This is particularly important for training in sensitive areas such as diversity and gender and race discrimination.

Trainability

Ability and motivation to learn

Before the learner can benefit from any formal training, he or she must be trainable or ready to learn. This means the trainee must have both the ability and the motivation to learn. To have the ability, the trainee must possess the skills and knowledge prerequisite to mastering the material. One way to determine this is to give trainees a performance test or work sample (i.e., an example of the types of skills to be performed on the job) and measure how quickly they are able to learn the material or how well they are able to perform the skills. Assessing trainees' ability to learn is of increasing concern to corporate America. In view of the increasing technological knowledge required in most jobs, many Americans are not being educated at a level compatible with the requirements of most entry-level jobs. This situation appears to be getting worse in the United States since the entry-level jobs of the future are being "up- skilled" while the pool of qualified workers is shrinking.

It has been estimated that over 30 million workers in the United States are functionally illiterate, meaning that they cannot read or write well enough to perform their job duties.

Sun Oil, Campbell Soup, and Digital Equipment work with state and local governments in partnership programs to help address literacy issues among the workforce.[38] Research clearly shows that employees with higher cognitive ability and basic math and reading skills are more trainable.[39]

Learning and individual characteristics

It's not enough that trainees have the ability to learn the skills; they must also have the desire or motivation to learn. Research also finds that employees who are more conscientious, more oriented toward learning, less anxious, and younger are more trainable.[40] One way to assess motivation to learn is to examine how involved they are in their own jobs and career planning. The assumption is that those individuals who are more highly involved will have higher motivation to learn.[41] It is also important to assess the attitudes and expectations of trainees regarding training since their views will most likely affect their reactions to the program and the amount they learn.[42] For example, employees who choose to attend training learn more than those who are required to attend.[43] Some companies link successful completion of training programs and acquired skills with compensation. At Ford, employees must select 40 hours of training from a list of options. An employee must fulfill the 40 hours to qualify for merit pay.

E-learning Readiness

Given the increasing use of distance learning formats, it is also important to assess learners' readiness to participate in online learning. The readiness of learners to enter into distance learning environments may play a critical role in increasing their course-completion and program-retention rates. Thus, a tool, the **E-learning Readiness Self-Assessment,** has been designed to provide a quick, yet comprehensive analysis of preparedness for success in an online training program. It addresses questions about the learner's access to technology, online skills, motivation, online audio, Internet skills, and views about training success.[44]

Gaining the Support of Trainees and Others

If trainees do not see the value of training, they will be unlikely to learn new behaviors or use them on their jobs. Trainees should be informed in advance about the benefits that will result from training. If they see some incentives for training, it may strengthen their motivation to learn the behaviors, practice them, and remember them. To gain the support of trainees for the training program, the trainer must point out the intrinsic (e.g., personal growth) and extrinsic (e.g., promotion) benefits of attending training. At Saturn, employees are strongly encouraged to receive skills training. In fact, 5 percent of their yearly compensation is based on the amount of training they receive.

Supervisory support is critical

In addition to garnering the support of trainees for training, the support of their supervisors, co-workers, and subordinates should be sought. For example, if the trainees' supervisors are not supportive of training, then they may not facilitate the learning process (e.g., allow employees time off for training, reward them for using new skills). Likewise, if their peers or subordinates ridicule them for attending training, they may not be motivated to attend training programs or to learn.[45] Trainers can improve the likelihood of acquiring others' support for training by getting their opinions on the content of training, the location, and the times. At Patapsco Valley Veterinary Hospital located in Ellicott City, Maryland, staff members are consistently asked for their opinions on the most convenient times to hold training sessions. In addition, the owners of the practice set a positive example by attending the training sessions themselves and by rewarding employees for participating in training and using their new skills on the job.

Conditions of the Learning Environment

After ensuring that the preconditions for learning are met, trainers should build a training environment in which learning is maximized. To do this, trainers need to decide how to best arrange the training environment by addressing the issues below.

Whole versus Part Learning

Research has shown that when a complex task is to be learned, it should be broken down into its parts if this can be done. Trainees should learn each part separately, starting with the simplest and going on to the most difficult. However, **part learning** should be combined with **whole learning;** that is, trainees should be shown the whole performance so that they know what their final goal is. The training content should be broken down into integrated parts, and each part should be learned until it can be performed accurately. Then a trainee should be allowed to put all the parts together and practice the whole task. One method that combines part and whole learning is called progressive part learning. In this approach, the trainees learn one part, then learn and practice that first part along with a second part, then learn and practice the first and second parts along with a third part, and so on. This might be used if the topics to be taught are somewhat interdependent (e.g., a communications course that involved sessions on active listening, being assertive, using nonverbals).

Massed versus Spaced Practice

Spaced practice generally more effective

Practice is important for trainees to learn a new skill or behavior. Trainers can observe the practice sessions and provide feedback to the trainees to correct their mistakes. **Spaced** practice (i.e., practicing the new behavior and taking rest periods in between) is more effective than **massed** practice (practicing the new behavior without breaks), especially for motor skills. For example, it would be easier for you to learn how to play golf by having a lesson on putting and then going out to practice putting, rather than learning how to do all of the possible golf shots (e.g., putting, chipping, pitching, driving, etc.) and then going out to play. If a learner has to concentrate for long periods of time without some rest, learning and retention may suffer. It's a little like cramming for an examination: rapid forgetting sets in very soon. Consequently, spaced practice seems to be more productive for long-term retention and for transfer of learning to the work setting. Of course, it takes longer for spaced practice than for massed practice, so trainees may resist it (e.g., they may be less receptive to attending four half-day workshops than two full-day sessions). On the other hand, tasks that are difficult and complex seem to be mastered and then performed better when massed practice is provided first, followed by briefer (spaced) sessions with more frequent rest periods.[46]

Overlearning

Recommended when task not immediately practiced

Overlearning (i.e., practicing far beyond the point of performing the task successfully) can be critical in both acquisition and transfer of knowledge and skills. Generally, overlearning increases retention over time, makes the behavior or skill more automatic, increases the quality of the performance during stress, and helps trainees transfer what they have learned back to the job setting.[47] Overlearning is desirable in a program when the task to be learned is not likely to be immediately practiced in the work situation and when performance must be maintained during periods of emergency and stress. For example, overlearning skills for driving or flying may be important so that in a crisis situation the individual will be able to quickly remember what actions should be taken. Pat Head Summitt, rated as the top coach (most wins among both men and women coaches) in collegiate basketball, believes in the importance of overlearning, which she calls "discipline." She has her nationally ranked team, the Tennessee Lady Volunteers, practice their plays over and over again in preparation for critical games.[48] This might be one reason why the Lady Vols have won eight National Basketball Championships! Figure 8-5 presents a summary of the research on the trainee characteristics and work environment variables shown to be related to training success and training transfer.

**Figure 8-5
Predictors and Correlates of Trainability**

TRAINEE CHARACTERISTICS RELATED TO GREATER TRAINING SUCCESS
High cognitive ability
High basic reading and math skills
Oriented toward learning
Less anxious
High conscientiousness (from the Five-Factor Model—see Chapter 6)
High achievement motivation
Self-efficacy/confidence in success
High motivation to learn
Perceive training as relevant to job/career
Value outcomes (learning)

WORK ENVIRONMENT CORRELATES OF TRANSFER
Opportunity to perform trained tasks
Positive climate for learning
Reinforce importance of continuous learning
Time and opportunity for training and practice

Source: Adapted from W. Arthur, W. Bennett, Jr., P. Edens, and S. Bell, "Effectiveness of Training in Organizations: A Meta-analysis of Design and Evaluation Features," *Journal of Applied Psychology* 88 (2003), pp. 234–245.

Goal Setting

19 percent increase in productivity

Goal setting can help employees improve their performance by directing their attention to specific behaviors that need to be changed. If employees set specific, challenging goals, they can reach higher levels of performance. For example, research has shown that goal setting has led to an average productivity increase of 19 percent.[49] Goal setting improves performance because it affects four mechanisms: (a) it directs and focuses a person's behavior, (b) it increases an individual's effort toward attaining the goal, (c) it encourages an individual to persist toward the goal or work harder and faster to attain it, and (d) it enables an individual to set specific strategies for attaining the goal.[50] Training programs should include specific, yet challenging goals so trainees can reach higher levels of performance or greater mastery of the training material. Trainees should be encouraged to set public goals and to record their accomplishments to ensure greater transfer of their training skills.

Knowledge of Results

For trainees to improve performance, they need to receive timely and specific feedback or **knowledge of results.** Feedback serves informational and motivational purposes. It shows trainees any gap between their performance and the desired performance and what particular skills or behaviors they need to correct. Also, it can motivate them to meet their performance goals once they see that they are coming close to accomplishing them. Trainers should build into the training environment opportunities for providing feedback to trainees. For example, the trainer could give pop quizzes to trainees during the session and call out the correct answers. Trainees could then quickly score their work to see how well they are doing in the session and where they need additional learning or practice. Sometimes trainees can provide feedback to one another (e.g., observers can be used in role-plays to provide feedback to role-players).

Attention

Attention to objectives

Trainers should try to design training programs and materials to ensure that trainees devote attention to them. They can do this by choosing a training environment that is comfortable to trainees (e.g., that has good temperature, lighting, seats, plenty of room, snacks) and free from distractions (phone calls, interruptions from colleagues). This is becoming increasingly more critical and challenging as trainees bring more and more technology (Blackberries, cell phones, laptops) into the classroom. No matter how motivated trainees are, if the environment is not comfortable to work in, trainees will have difficulty learning. Trainers also should make sure that trainees are familiar with and have accepted the learning objectives. They can do this by asking trainees to describe how accomplishing the objectives will resolve problems on the job. If trainees are able to translate learning objectives into relevant job issues, they may pay more attention to the training sessions.

Retention

Rehearsal helps

The ability to retain what is learned is obviously relevant to the effectiveness of a training program. Many factors have been found to increase retention. If the material presented is meaningful to trainees, they should have an easier time understanding and remembering it. Trainers can make the content meaningful by (1) presenting trainees with an overview of what is to be learned so that they will be able to see the overall picture, (2) using examples, concepts, and terms familiar to the trainees (e.g., use medical terms and examples when training doctors and nurses), and (3) organizing the material from simple to complex (teach someone how to serve the ball before you teach him/her strategies in tennis). Retention also can be enhanced by rehearsal or requiring trainees to periodically recall what they have learned through tests.

Using Learning Principles to Develop Training Materials

The learning principles described above should be considered not only when designing the training environment but also when developing training materials. Any materials used with trainees should be able to stimulate them into learning and remembering the information. To ensure that this occurs, trainers need to make sure that the learning principles are built into their training materials. For example, the materials should provide illustrations and relevant examples to stimulate trainees. In addition, the objectives of the material should be clearly stated and a summary should be provided.[51]

Transfer of Training

The ultimate goal of a training program is that the learning that occurs during training be transferred back to the job. Research strongly supports the view that the posttraining climate will affect whether training influences behaviors or results on the job. To maximize transfer, the following suggestions have been offered.[52] These include ideas for before the training is conducted, during the training session itself, and once the employee has returned to the job:

Before Training

1. Align the training program with the organization's needs using competency modeling.
2. Involve supervisors and trainees in the project team.
3. Use sound instructional design theory.
4. Develop application-oriented objectives based on the competency.

During Training

1. Maximize the similarity between the training context and the job context. That is, the training should resemble the job as closely as possible. At GE, for example, the "action-learning" process focuses on real business problems.
2. Require practice of the new behaviors and overlearning in training.
3. Provide realistic work-related tasks.
4. Provide extra spaces in training books to note ideas during training.
5. Include a variety of stimulus situations in the practice so trainees will learn to generalize their knowledge and skills. Coach Pat Summitt sets up grueling basketball game schedules with top-ranked teams so that the Lady Vols will play in a variety of situations and be ready for the NCAA playoffs each year.
6. Label or identify the important features of the content to be learned to distinguish the major steps involved.
7. Develop, and have available on the job, job aids to remind employees of the key action steps necessary on the job. For example, Alcoa uses job aids in many of its manufacturing jobs.
8. Make sure that the general principles underlying the specific content are understood in training.
9. Provide opportunity (time) to synthesize material or plan for application. At Lockheed Martin, trainers from the Robert H. Smith School of Business leading the Executive Leadership Strategies Program give executives time at the end of each day to synthesize their learning for the day. They also have them present their synthesis for the week-long training at the end of the week, along with an action plan for how they will apply the skills.
10. Build the trainee's **self-efficacy** for learning and using the new skills. Self-efficacy is a feeling of control and accomplishment, the sense that you can control your own destiny. Self-efficacy is related to motivation to learn, which is subsequently related to motivation to transfer the skills. Trainers can use verbal persuasion as one tactic to convince trainees that they can learn the tasks. Self-efficacy has been shown to be related to learning using a sample of Navy warfare officers in midlevel managerial positions. In addition, encourage trainees to develop an action plan including specific measurable goals.[53]

After Training

1. Encourage trainees to practice skills on their jobs in between training sessions. For example, the executive education programs conducted by the Robert H. Smith School of Business for some of its corporate clients (e.g., Entergy, Lockheed Martin) often require "homework assignments" such as customer-value projects, organizational systems projects, and individual leadership development plans in between attendance at sessions. The assignments encourage trainees to apply their new skills in the workplace, using an **action learning model**.

Action learning model

2. Ensure that there is a supportive climate for learning and for transferring new behaviors. This can be done by building managerial support (emotional and financial) for training, providing trainees with the freedom to set personal performance goals, and encouraging risk taking among trainees. One study used 505 supermarket managers from 52 stores and found that the work environment, measured by training climate and learning culture, was directly related to the transfer of trained behaviors.[54] It is also important to encourage peer support since this type of support has been shown to influence transfer of training skills.[55]

3. Have trainees present their new learning to co-workers once they return.

4. Once back on the job, employees should be given opportunities to demonstrate that they can use the new skills. For example, one study of plane mechanics from the Air Force found that after training they were given opportunities to perform only about half of the tasks they learned in training.[56] Likewise, in a study of university employees, it was found that situational constraints (e.g., adequate resources, time) limited the amount that trainees could transfer new skills to the work environment.[57]

5. Encourage continual learning by employees. They should realize that one-time training in an area is not sufficient to maintain effective skills. Retraining also may be needed to update skills.

Relapse Prevention

Sometimes, despite trainers' best efforts to get individuals to transfer what they have learned back to the job, it is difficult for trainees to maintain new behaviors or skills over a long period. They encounter high-risk situations and revert back to their old habits. Most people experience relapses after learning new behaviors. Think about all the times you or someone you know went on a diet or started an exercise program. Perhaps you were quite successful sticking to the plan after attending a training program (e.g., Weight Watchers). Then, one weekend you go on a trip with friends. Next thing you know you are eating lots of snacks and ignoring your exercise plan. This is a relapse. The same thing often happens to employees after they have attended a training program. For example, a manager learns how to control his temper in training, yet the first time returning back to the job he encounters an irate employee and he screams at the person. **Relapse prevention** is needed to assist trainees.[58] This model emphasizes the learning of a set of self-control and coping strategies when the trainee is faced with high-risk situations.[59]

Employees should be made aware of the relapse process itself by informing them there are some situations that make it difficult for trainees to use their new behaviors. For example, they may be faced with peers or supervisors who are not supportive of their new skills.[60] They should learn to identify and anticipate high-risk situations they will face when returning from training. They should be instructed on how to cope in these situations. Teaching these issues should increase trainees' **self-efficacy** so that they can effectively use their new training skills back on the job.

Choosing Methods for the Training Program

Training methods can be divided into two categories:

1. Methods that are primarily *informational* or transmittal in nature; that is, they use primarily one-way communication in which information is transmitted to the learners.

2. Methods that are *experiential* in nature; that is, the learner interacts with the instructor, a computer/simulator, customers, or other trainees to practice the skill.

Some of the major methods, including their uses, benefits, and limitations, are described below and in Figures 8-6 and 8-7. Electronic learning or e-learning can be both an informational and an experiential method of training.

Figure 8-6   **Informational Training Methods**

Uses	Benefits	Limitations
LECTURE Gaining new knowledge To present introductory material	Equally good as programmed instruction and television Low cost Reaches a large audience at one time Audience is often comfortable with it	Learners are passive Poor transfer Depends on the lecturer's ability Is not tailored to individual trainees
AUDIOVISUALS Gaining new knowledge Gaining attention	Can reach a large audience at one time Allows for replays Versatility Can reduce trainer, travel, and facility costs	Is not tailored to individual trainees Must be updated Passive learners
INDEPENDENT STUDY Gaining new knowledge Completing degree requirements Continuous education	Allows trainees to go at their own pace Minimizes trainers' time Minimizes costs of development	Expensive to develop a library of materials Materials must be designed to adjust to varying reading levels Performance depends on trainee's motivation Is not applicable for all jobs
E-LEARNING Gaining new knowledge Pretraining preparation to ensure that all trainees have similar backgrounds	Convenient Allows trainees to go at their own pace Can guarantee mastery at a specified level Encourages active trainee involvement Provides immediate feedback to trainees	Expensive to develop Is not easily applicable for all tasks (e.g., cognitive tasks, verbal, psychomotor) Does not lead to higher performance than lectures

Most training programs utilize several training techniques since no one approach is best suited for every purpose. In fact, there has been increased interest in the use of blended training approaches in organizations. This often means the integration of classroom and e-learning training approaches.[61] Microsoft relies on a balanced portfolio of blended learning for its more than 70,000 employees that includes formal classroom sessions, lab workshops with mentors, brief expert- and leader-driven talks, online community discussions, think-tank sessions, networking events, and online knowledge-management databases made available on the firm's intranet. Key content includes information about innovative technologies and what Microsoft calls "deep-dive" topics that emphasize the need for soft-skills development.[62] IBM's international sales training program includes both classroom and **on-the-job training (OJT),** which is given over one year. AMC Theatres uses videotapes, detailed training manuals, and OJT programs to train ushers and concession personnel. To determine which combination of methods to select for a particular training program, a developer should first clearly define the purpose of and the audience for the training. In addition, an assessment of the resources available to conduct the training is necessary. This will mean examining the staff, materials, and budget to assess sufficiencies for handling training demands. It is also important to consider whether the focus will be on skill acquisition, maintenance, or generalization of the skill to other areas. One recent study found that trainees rated as more effective those methods that involved them more. They also preferred more individualized training methods, like one-on-one instruction, and technology-based methods such as computer simulations, multimedia presentations, and computer-assisted programmed instruction.[63]

Experiential methods favored by trainees

At a minimum, the training methods selected should (1) motivate the trainee to learn the new skill, (2) illustrate the desired skills to be learned, (3) be consistent with the content (e.g., use an interactive approach to teach interpersonal skills), (4) allow for active participation by the trainees to fit with the adult learning model, (5) provide opportunities for practice and overlearning, (6) provide feedback on performance during training, (7) be structured from simple to complex, (8) encourage positive transfer from the training to the job, and (9) be cost effective. In many cases, trainers will use several

Figure 8-7   Experiential Training Methods

Uses	Benefits	Limitations
ON-THE-JOB TRAINING		
Learning job skills	Good transfer	Depends on the trainers' skills and willingness
Apprenticeship training	Limited trainer costs	May be costly due to lost production and mistakes
Job rotation	High trainee motivation	May have frequent interruptions on the job
		Often is haphazardly done
		Trainees may learn bad habits
E-LEARNING		
Gaining new knowledge	Self-paced	Trainees may have difficulties with computers
Drill and practice	Standardization over time	Limited interactions for trainees
Individualized training	Feedback given	Less useful for training interpersonal skills or psychomotor tasks
	Convenient	
	Can reduce costs	
EQUIPMENT SIMULATORS		
To reproduce real-world conditions	Effective for learning and transfer	Costly to develop
For physical and cognitive skills	Can practice most of the job skills	Requires good fidelity
For team training		
GAMES AND SIMULATIONS		
Decision-making skills	Resembles the job tasks	Highly competitive
Management training	Provides feedback	Time-consuming
Interpersonal skills	Presents realistic challenges	May stifle creativity
CASE STUDY OR ANALYSIS		
Decision-making skills	Decision-making practice	Must be updated
Analytical skills	Real-world training materials	Trainers often dominate discussions
Communication skills	Active learning	
To illustrate diversity of solutions	Problem-solving practice	
ROLE-PLAYING		
For changing attitudes	Gains experience of other roles	Initial resistance of trainees
To practice skills	Active learning	May not take it seriously
To analyze interpersonal problems	Close to reality	
BEHAVIORAL MODELING		
To teach interpersonal skills	Allows practice	Time-consuming
To teach cognitive skills	Provides feedback	May be costly to develop
To teach training/teaching skills	Retention is improved	
	Strong research evidence	
SENSITIVITY TRAINING		
To enhance self-awareness	Can improve self-concept	May be threatening
To allow trainees to see how others see them	Can reduce prejudice	May have limited generalizability
	Can change interpersonal behaviors	

Use multiple methods different techniques. For example, teaching supervisors how to give performance feedback may first begin with a lecture or overview of the performance appraisal process, followed by small-group discussions or videotapes depicting effective coaching, and then role-plays to have supervisors practice their feedback skills. In addition to using multiple methods for training employees, employers should also have numerous ways for employees to enhance their learning. At ASTD's BEST firms, a diverse set of learning opportunities exist for employees. Almost all employees had access to on-the-job learning (98%), formal training (97%), job aids (93%), knowledge bases (91%), tuition reimbursement (84%), electronic performance support (83%), and mentoring and coaching (71%). They also had access to job rotation (49%), financial support for memberships in professional associations (54%), and support for attending conferences (55%).[64]

Informational Methods

Informational methods are used primarily to teach factual material, skills, or attitudes. Generally, they do not require the trainee to actually experience or practice the material taught during the training session. Some of the more commonly used informational techniques include lectures, audio and video media, and self-directed learning (SDL) methods. E-learning is one of the most popular approaches today.

Lectures

The lecture method is the most commonly used technique for training employees and teaching students. A 2004 survey found that 85 percent of firms offer or still use a classroom with an instructor for some training.[65] The method is often supplemented with group discussions, audiovisual aids, motion pictures, or television. The approach can also vary in the degree to which discussion is permitted, since some lectures involve all one-way communication, while others may allow trainees to participate by asking questions or providing comments. Despite the criticism of this method, recent research shows lecture-based training is quite an effective way to facilitate the transfer of theories, concepts, procedures, and other factual material.[66] In addition, a meta-analysis of the effects of lecture, modeling, and active participation on the performance of older trainees found that all three methods had positive effects on learning and skill measures.[67]

Audio and Video Media

A variety of audiovisuals are available to trainers, including films, videos, slides, overheads, audiotapes, flip charts, and chalkboards. Videoconferencing has gained in popularity as costs have become more affordable for employers and different systems have become more compatible. The staff of Greenberg Traurig, an international law firm, set up a videoconference system that is used almost constantly to share information and multimedia presentations in the 375-attorney firm.[68] FedEx Kinko's has videoconferencing facilities available at over 150 U.S. locations, with costs of about $225 per hour.[69] Other firms using videoconferencing include JCPenney, IBM, AT&T, and Texas Instruments. Often, these multimedia approaches are used to supplement other training techniques, including lectures and self-directed learning methods. They can address a variety of topics such as motivational techniques, EEO issues, performance appraisal interviews, leadership skills, and teamwork.

Podcasting is another popular method to reinforce and promote training to its target audience. It involves recording a portion of audio or video content that is punchy and useful and posting it online or on the firm's intranet site and providing a link to download the recording. The use of podcasting has shown some benefits for the training function, including reduced training costs, increased participation, and greater learner engagement. One organization reported being able to deliver their training for $30,000 instead of $125,000 since it reduced the number of training sessions by 50 percent. Another firm was able to get 70 percent participation instead of the usual 40 percent participation by using podcasts for training. Two helpful sites for creating podcasts are: www.freeconference.com and www.audioacrobat.com. Use the first Web site to get participants' permission to be recorded, and the second site to publish your podcast. **Audio Acrobat** generates the appropriate HTML codes for the Web site, the e-mails, and the downloads. There are both audio and video podcasts that can be used. Podcasts will not replace live, in-person training, but they are making it easier for trainees to engage in training on their own schedule, with some of the latest technology, and at a reasonable price.[70]

Two good websites for creating podcasts

Self-Directed Learning (SDL) Methods

Several informational methods for training are considered to be SDL approaches because the trainee takes responsibility for learning the necessary knowledge and skills at his or her own pace. A wide range of decisions can be given to the trainee, including the topic of study, objectives, resources, schedule, learning strategy, type and sequence of activities, and media. In most cases, trainees work without direct supervision, set their own pace, and are allowed to choose their own activities, resources, and learning environments. Generally, the training department's role is to provide assistance by establishing learning centers with available materials and by having trained facilitators on hand for questions. Larger companies such as Motorola, Sunoco, and Office Depot have been successful in setting up such centers and encouraging self-directed learning by employees. In these centers, trainees can be given self-assessment tools or instruments.

Advantages of SDL

The advantages of SDL include (1) reduced training time, as compared to more conventional methods (e.g., lecture); (2) more favorable attitudes by trainees compared to conventional techniques; (3) more consistency with an adult learning approach; (4) minimal reliance on instructors or trainers; (5) mobility (i.e., a variety of places can be used for training); (6) flexibility (trainees can learn at their own pace); (7) consistency of the information taught to all trainees; and (8) cost savings. There are also several disadvantages, including (1) high developmental time for course materials and extensive planning requirements, (2) difficulties in revising and updating materials, and (3) limited interactions with peers and trainers.

SDLRS and outcomes

Research indicates that employees with high levels of readiness for SDL as measured by the **Self-Directed Learning Readiness Scale (SDLRS)** were more likely to be higher-level managers, to be outstanding performers,[71] to possess greater creativity,[72] and to have a higher degree of life satisfaction.[73] Also, employees who were outstanding performers in jobs requiring high levels of creativity or problem solving or involving high levels of change were more likely to have high SDLRS scores. In addition, employees with higher SDLRS scores were successful in relatively unstructured learning situations in which more responsibility rests on the learners.[74] A variety of SDL approaches are available. Two of the more commonly used techniques include independent study and various forms of e-learning. **Independent study** requires a trainee to read, synthesize, and remember the contents of written material, audio or videotapes, or other sources of information. The training or personnel department can develop a library of materials for trainees to use in teaching themselves at their own pace various skills or knowledges. Companies such as Coors, Digital Equipment Corporation, Kraft, and U.S. Gypsum utilize extensive self-study materials for their sales employees. Trainees can also design their own training curriculum by opting for correspondence courses or enrolling in independent study courses at local schools or on the Web. Generally, in these programs, trainees are required to master the content on their own without direct supervision. Sanofi-aventis is one of the largest pharmaceutical firms and a winner of the 2007 ASTD BEST firms. In addition to classroom training, they have an extensive self-directed learning program consisting of more than 700 courses offered via CD-ROM, textbook, audio CD, DVD, and online. Every employee is encouraged to create an individual development plan, and employees are required to earn continuing professional education hours annually. Trainers have used Brainshark Rapid Learning, an asynchronous development tool, to create online learning objects and to track learners' progress.[75]

E-learning

E-learning is typically (although not always) an individualized learning method that allows for study of material online. With the proliferation of e-learning, podcasts, and webinars, the control of learning is shifting from the trainer to the learner. UBS uses an e-based program to train new stockbrokers. Best Buy uses e-learning for technical training such as installing car stereos. Caterpillar has an extensive e-learning program. In 2006, employees participated in more than 562,000 e-learning sessions.[76] Most programs build in the important learning principles by (1) specifying what is to be learned (i.e., the behavioral objectives); (2) breaking down the learning topic into small, discrete steps; (3) presenting each step to the trainee and requiring him or her to respond to each step of the learning process (by reading each part); (4) testing the trainees' learning at each step (by responding to questions); (5) providing immediate feedback to the trainee on whether his or her response was correct or incorrect; and (6) testing the level of skill or knowledge acquired at the end of the training module. **E-learning** has replaced "programmed instruction" in training classification but is based on the same principles. One recent study found that Web-based

More effective for training "declarative" knowledge

instruction was more effective than classroom instruction for teaching declarative knowledge, and was equally effective in teaching procedural knowledge, and trainees were equally satisfied with both methods. Generally, Web-based trainees learned more when they were practicing the training material, when they received feedback during training, and in long courses.[77]

Online courses rely on a self-directed learning approach and are gaining in popularity with the rise of podcasts, teleconferences, and instant messaging. Online training is a viable alternative to classroom training and is used to teach almost everything. Despite the numerous benefits of online courses, HR professionals should exercise caution when using a Web-based format to teach "soft skills." Participants need opportunities to interact and practice to truly learn them. If online courses will be used to teach softer skills, trainers should use a variety of exercises, videos, audios, and graphics so that trainees enjoy the training and are more likely to practice the skills. Trainers should also make sure the online courses are designed to show how learning will promote success on the job, use peers to support the training, break the skills into concrete learning modules, provide feedback throughout the course, and create opportunities to practice the skills.[78]

Experiential Methods

Experiential methods are often used to teach physical and cognitive skills and abilities. These techniques include OJT, computer-based training (CBT), equipment simulations, games and other simulations, case analyses, role-playing, and behavior modeling. In addition, a variety of electronic training-delivery media and distance learning techniques have become popular as instructional/experiential methods.

On-the-Job Training

Much industrial training is conducted on the job (e.g., at the work site and in the context of the job). Often, it is informal, as when an experienced worker shows a trainee how to perform the job tasks. The trainer may watch over the trainee to provide guidance during practice or learning. For example, sales employees use coaching calls where a senior sales person coaches a new sales employee. Five steps are utilized:[79]

1. Observation of the new employee.
2. Feedback obtained by the new employee.
3. Consensus (i.e., the coach and the new employee arrive at an agreement as to the strengths and weaknesses of the sales call).
4. Rehearsal of a new sales call.
5. Review of the employee's performance.

In 2006, Ruby Tuesday's restaurants introduced a "master's" program. Company leaders attended training and were certified as "burger masters." They then went back to their restaurants to teach their staff to ensure consistency among restaurants. They also opened a culinary arts center, which is dedicated to building a hands-on training experience for all employees from hourly to senior managers. Within the first year, they were able to retain more highly trained staff and turnover was decreased by 20 percent from the previous year.[80]

Although OJT is often associated with the development of new employees, it can also be used to update or broaden the skills of existing employees when new procedures or work methods are introduced. In some cases, the trainer may be a retired employee. For instance, at Corning Glass Works, new employees are paired with retirees for a brief on-the-job introduction regarding the company culture and market data. Following this, they are exposed to formal classroom and field training.[81] Many companies combine OJT with formal classroom training. At McDonald's, after a three-hour induction, new employees are partnered with a buddy who is a member of the training squad.[82] Dow Chemical alternates sales employees between classroom training at corporate headquarters and OJT experiences in the field for a year. Similarly, Wang Laboratories spends up to nine months alternating salespeople from company headquarters and field offices. Restaurant employees at the Hard Rock Café are trained by OJT and the use of job aids (i.e. training materials). Workers view this approach very favorably.[83]

Conditions when OJT is best

OJT is best used when one-on-one training is necessary, only a small number (usually fewer than five) employees need to be trained, classroom instruction is not appropriate, work in progress cannot be interrupted, a certain level of proficiency on a task is needed for certification, and equipment or safety restrictions make other training techniques inappropriate. The training should emphasize equipment or instruments that are to be used, as well as safety issues or dangerous processes.

Apprenticeship programs often are considered OJT programs because they involve a substantial amount of OJT, even though they do consist of some off-the-job training. Typically, the trainee follows a prescribed order of coursework and hands-on experience. The Department of Labor regulates apprenticeship programs, and many require a minimum of 144 hours of classroom instruction each year, as well as OJT with a skilled employee.[84]

Many professions (e.g., medicine) or trades require some type of apprenticeship program that may last anywhere from two to five years. Some of the most common occupations to offer apprenticeship programs include electricians, carpenters, plumbers, pipe fitters, sheet-metal workers, machinists, tool-and-die makers, roofers, firefighters, bricklayers, cooks, structural-steel workers, painters, operating engineers, correction officers, and mechanics.[85] In Europe, apprenticeships are still one of the most likely ways for individuals to gain entry into skilled jobs, while in the United States only 2 percent of high school graduates enter apprenticeship programs.[86] This is a problem for the U.S. workforce since the pool of qualified skilled labor for future jobs has been shrinking. In France in one apprenticeship program alone, there are currently 4,200 apprentices with the Association des Compagnons du Devoir (elite artisans responsible for restoring historical sites such as Notre Dame Cathedral and Arc de Triomphe). Restricted to men, they begin as young as 15 and undertake up to nine years of lessons, community chores, and hands-on training with 6,500 companies that have contracts with them. They train for an additional two years and have to complete a personal building project. Only one in 10 typically survives the apprenticeship period and is allowed to join the ranks of Compagnons.[87]

Another commonly used technique for OJT training is **job rotation,** which involves moving employees from one job to another to broaden their experience. Many U.S. companies are showing greater interest in having their employees be able to perform several job functions so that their workforce is more flexible and interchangeable. For example, in the automobile industry today, it is fairly common to see employees being trained on two or more tasks (e.g., painting and welding). This is done at GM's Saturn plant in order to relieve employees' boredom as well as make the company less dependent on specialized workers. GE requires all managerial trainees to participate in an extensive job rotation program in which the trainees must perform all jobs they will eventually supervise. This helps managers develop the broader background required for future managerial positions. At Lockheed Martin, a leadership development program was established for new HR college recruits. They are rotated to a variety of HR departments (recruiting, selection, compensation) to gain broader experiences as HR professionals. Black and Decker provides a three-year job rotation program for its new MBA employees entering into its financial development program.

Computer-Based Training (CBT)/E-Learning

The latest workplace forecast conducted by the **Society of Human Resource Management** ranked e-learning as the second most important science and technology trend that will affect the workplace.[88] The survey found that when used effectively, e-learning has been able to deliver training for large numbers of employees at reduced costs and that there was an increased usage of e-learning during an economic downturn. Another recent study found that Web-based instruction was more effective than classroom instruction for teaching declarative knowledge and procedural knowledge. Interestingly, the researchers also noted that trainees were more satisfied with Web-based classes that had higher levels of human interaction than lower levels. When trainees were not given the opportunity to interact with others during Web-based courses, they preferred classroom instruction.[89] One leading provider of CBT software, CBT Group, has training deals with Cisco Systems, IBM, Informix, Microsoft, Netscape Communications, Novell, Oracle, PeopleSoft, SAP, and Sybase, among others.

Effective computer skill training is vital to organizational productivity. One recent study demonstrated that the behavior modeling approach to computer skill training could be improved by incorporating **symbolic mental rehearsal** (SMR). SMR is a specific form of mental rehearsal that establishes a cognitive link between visual images and symbolic memory codes. The authors recommend that practitioners use SMR for improving the effectiveness of computer skill training.[90]

Symbolic mental rehearsal (SMR)

Chunking refers to chopping computer-based training into its smallest parts and sending them through a network so that learners receive just the instruction they need when they need it. Spring Corporation chunks CBT on the corporate intranet and is one of the leaders in using training over an intranet.[91] The most popular processing software packages (e.g., Microsoft Word) use CBT to introduce learners to the use of the software. The U.S. Armed Forces use CBT extensively for training many of their technicians. In fact, the military and NASA have numerous advanced technologies such as intelligent tutoring systems and virtual reality that are used for training purposes.[92] In some CBT programs, trainees interact directly with computers to actually learn and practice new skills. This is done similarly to the PI system and is called computer-assisted instruction (CAI). For example, Dialect Interactive Lectures (DIALECT) are university lectures that have been converted into multimedia-based digital learning material. DIALECT use animation, computer simulations, and hyperlink facilities to guide students through lectures.[93] CBT has the advantage of being self-paced, standardized, self-sufficient, easily available, and flexible. This is particularly important in today's fast-paced environment, where organizations cannot afford for employees to be away from the job for large amounts of time. In fact, many employees view it as a proven way to save time and money while delivering consistent content.

Electronic training-delivery media involve some of the fastest-growing instructional methods. The latest round of CBT-oriented software offers revolutionary ways in which interactive training is developed and delivered. Multimedia training programs often feature text, graphics, sound, pictures, videos, simulations, and hyper-text links that enable trainees to structure their own learning experiences.[94] In 2005, it was reported that over $500 million had been spent on Web conferencing with the figure expected to top $3 billion by 2011. At The Home Depot, they deliver training on their more than 40,000 products to employees via the company's Web-based training model, a video-driven e-learning experience that consists of 15 minutes of video and synchronized test, followed by an assessment.[95] Most CBT systems support links to the Internet and to corporate intranets. Internet-based e-learning has emerged as a cost- and time-efficient way to address many companies' training needs. The recent SHRM survey found very positive results in terms of user reactions and efficiencies. Given these trends, it is clear that traditional training methods will continue to decline as electronic delivery techniques increase in usage. This is particularly true of more innovative firms that use a greater variety of learning technologies for training.[96]

Distance Learning Programs

Online education is the fastest growing sector of the training market. Online learners have gone from 3 million in 2001 to more than 6 million by 2006.[97] Many resources now exist for designing and implementing distance learning programs.[98] In addition, a comprehensive list of vendors is provided by the Distance Education Clearinghouse Web site (http://www.uwex.edu/disted).

Banco National de Mexico, one of the oldest and largest banks in Mexico, graduated its first class of 11 executives from a global MBA program from San Diego–based National University, which is a distance learning program. The company found that enabling managers to complete the coursework without having to leave their work or homes was beneficial.[99] The Schwan Food Company expanded the educational opportunities it offered to its employees. They contracted with three accredited institutions to create seven-week online modules that help students earn bachelor's degrees in three years or less. They also created an associate's degree and an MBA. The material in the programs is beneficial to employees in that it addresses specific company issues as well as topics in general.[100]

Research on the effectiveness of distance education programs has only begun.[101] In general, offering training or educational programs over the Internet enables employees to access high-quality education at their own pace. They have access to class material, conduct research without traveling, and have dialogs with professors and classmates via e-mail, bulletin boards, and chat rooms. Some programs use videoconferencing or transmit lectures via satellite. In this regard, students may have an easier time juggling careers and families.[102] Numerous organizations have successfully used distance learning programs for their employees, including Ford, AT&T, EDS, MCI Communications, the U.S. Department of Defense, the Tennessee Valley Authority, United Technologies Corporation, Lockheed Martin, and Lucent Technologies.[103] Organizations have reported the following

Benefits of distance learning   benefits from distance learning programs:[104]

- A fast, effective way to train global employees.
- Increased the impact and productivity of dollars invested in training and education programs.
- Reduced travel costs and made time formerly spent traveling available for more productive uses.

- Allowed for the training of more people, more often, in sessions that are easier to schedule and coordinate.

- Offered the ability to add students and instructors as needed without incurring significant additional expenses.

- Delivered a consistent message that can be disseminated quickly companywide.

- Provided real-time updates and just-in-time information access.

- Delivered to both work and home sites that are convenient for trainees.

- Offered live interactive programs delivered to multiple networked sites for group learning.

- Is learner-centered and enabled students to have more control over the pacing and sequencing of the learning experience.

- Offered easy access to learning resources.

One recent article provides a set of research-based principles for "learner control" training in the e-learning environment. "Learner control generally refers to 'a mode of instruction in which one or more key instructional decisions are delegated to the learner.'" Simply put, trainees have greater control over their training, such as pace, materials covered, and sequence.[105] Figure 8-8 presents guidelines for such more effective e-learning.

Equipment Simulations

Some training may involve machines or equipment designed to reproduce physiological and psychological conditions of the real world that are necessary in order for learning and transfer to occur. For example, driving simulators or flight simulators are often used to train employees in driving or flying skills. Another example of a simulation is the FireArms Training System (FATS), which is used by more than 300 law enforcement agencies in the United States.[106] In this simulation, officers are confronted with a number of everyday work situations (e.g., fleeing felons) on a video screen. The military uses virtual reality simulators for training involving war game demonstrations. One exercise, called the Synthetic Theater of War, links tactics, techniques, and processes of modern systems to illustrate battles.[107] Equipment simulators also are relied on in training for space missions (astronaut training). While many of these simulations are extremely costly, some have become more affordable. In addition, using simulators for training incurs only a fraction of the cost of using the real equipment to train employees.

Games, Simulations, and Outdoor Experiential Programs

Some training programs rely on a variety of games, nonequipment simulations, or outdoor experiential programs. In fact, these instructional techniques appear to be gaining in popularity, with hundreds of different types of games available for teaching technical, managerial, professional, and other business-related skills. At Scottrade, a retail brokerage firm, they use a customer service simulation training module. For example, trainees might communicate with a "customer" who holds accounts with a competitor. Trainees from different departments submit their "best customer call" for consideration into a competition among departments.[108] Some of the more common games include in-baskets and business games. Most games are used to teach skills such as decision making as well as analytical, strategic, or interpersonal skills. **Business games** typically require trainees to assume various roles in a company (e.g., president, marketing vice president) where they are given several years' worth of information on the company's products, technology, and human resources and asked to deal with the information in a compressed period of time (several weeks or months). They make decisions regarding production volumes, inventory levels, and prices in an environment in which other trainees are running competitor companies. The most successful business games keep the focus on specific corporate objectives or problems such as profits, customer service, or labor costs.

At Wachovia, one of the most innovative learning firms, an initiative was developed for employees in the audit division. The *Welcome to the Jungle!* program uses a visual learning map that combines metaphors, activities, games, hands-on skills practice, and participants' own experiences to teach and reinforce audit concepts. Department leaders team with participants to embark on a journey "through the jungle" that includes games, quizzes, and role-plays in a highly interactive learning experience.[109]

Figure 8-8　　　　　　　　Guidelines for Learner Controlled Training in e-Learning

PREPARING TRAINEES FOR LEARNER-LED INSTRUCTION
Guideline #1: Understanding Learner Control Is Half the Battle
- Instruct employees about areas they can control and how this increased control can increase learning.
- The perception of control can increase learning.

Guideline #2: Give It Time
- Typical learner-controlled training tasks last from 30 to 60 minutes.
- "Provide trainees with enough time to learn how to use learner control and with suggested completion times for each section of the training task."
- 10 or more separate training sessions are recommended as users become more familiar with the system as time progresses.

Guideline #3: Calibrate Expectations
Ensure trainees understand the training will be challenging. Adult users often perceive learning as an easy process and when confronted with the challenge of training they may become frustrated.

DESIGNING LEARNER-CONTROLLED TRAINING
Guideline #4: Offer Help
- Offer self-tests and feedback so trainees can self-regulate the number of examples to view and the amount of practice items to complete.

Guideline #5: What's Good for One Trainee May Not Be Good for Another
- "Trainees who are high in ability, prior experience, and motivation may benefit the most from learner control."
- "Create programs that provide trainees high in learning ability [also known as 'g'] and prior experience with more learner control options than trainees low in ability and prior experience."
- Motivation: "When trainees are made aware of the organizational objectives of the training they are often more motivated to successfully complete the training program."

Guideline #6: More Isn't Necessarily Better
- Match learner control to the amount of control needed for effective instruction and training objectives.
- Structure training tasks based on trainees' learning preferences.

Guideline #7: "Skipping" Is Better than "Adding"
For optional/additional training material, use the word "skip" additional instruction rather than "add" additional material.

Guideline #8: Keep It Real
Increase meaningfulness of training by using familiar contexts and examples.

Guideline #9: Footprints Help ("You Are Here")
Provide trainees with a "map" to track their training progress.

Guideline #10: Keep Each Instructional Segment Self-Contained
- Each section should be short and concise.
- Trainees should not have to revisit a previous section to complete the current section.

Guideline #11: Share Design Control
- Obtain user preferences from trainees prior to training; for instance, does the user prefer having multiple windows open during the training session?
- "Allow the trainees to stop, pause, or restart the program where they wish."

Guideline #12: Be Consistent
- "Keep the font size and color as well as the background color consistent from one instructional segment to another."

Guideline #13: Create Smooth Transitions
Have clear relationships between training segments.

CREATING WORKPLACE CONDITIONS THAT FACILITATE SUCCESSFUL LEARNER-LED INSTRUCTION
Guideline #14: Promote It
Supervisors can improve learner-controlled effectiveness by setting difficult but attainable goals regarding the level of skill mastery and encouraging the trainees to use their newly obtained skills on the job.

Guideline #15: Make It Matter
Ensure that trainees judge the goal of participating in training is not only attainable but also valuable.

Guideline #16: Organizational Climate Matters
Organizations with climates that encourage employee participation, empowerment, and autonomy may find it easier to implement learner-controlled training programs.

Source: Adapted from Renée E. DeRouin, Barbara A. Fritzsche, and Eduardo Salas, "Optimizing E-Learning: Research-Based Guidelines for Learner-Controlled Training," *Human Resource Management 43* (2004), pp. 147–162. Reprinted by permission of John Wiley & Sons.

One very popular cross-functional simulation is **The Marketplace Business Simulation.** Working in teams, trainees must assume various roles in the start-up of a firm in the microcomputer industry. The teams work over a compressed period of time to play 2 to 3 years in the game. Performance is measured on a number of short- and long-term metrics (e.g., financial, marketing, human resource) comprising a **Balanced Scorecard.** Numerous levels and variations of the game are available depending on the expertise and backgrounds of the trainees. The simulation has been used all over the world as a capstone, integrative experience to an EMBA, MBA, or undergraduate program as well as by organizations (Nextel, Hughes Communications).[110]

In-baskets, as discussed in Chapter 6, are used to train managerial candidates in decision-making skills by requiring them to act on a variety of memos, reports, and other correspondence that are typically found in a manager's in-basket. Participants must prioritize items and respond to them in a limited time period. In-baskets are often included in assessment centers. For example, the method is used as one component of the week-long executive development program at the Center for Creative Leadership.

Outdoor experiential programs have gained in popularity as training methods for teams. In 2004, 20 percent of firms often or always used experiential programs, and it is estimated over $100 million is spent annually on them.[111] Firms and programs such as **Outward Bound** and **Higher Pursuits** have developed a variety of outdoor activities and challenge courses (rope courses, canoeing trips, hiking trips) that can be used to help employers build stronger teams. By placing a work unit in a challenge course or physical activity, the coaches or counselors can observe how the unit works together and can debrief them and provide feedback on issues of communication, conflict, and trust. In the Executive Leadership Strategies Program conducted at Lockheed Martin Corporation, senior leaders learn about their own personalities and issues of trust and teamwork as they participate in a set of outdoor ropes challenges delivered by The University of Maryland Campus Recreation center.

Case Analyses

Most business students are very familiar with case analysis, a training method often used in management training to improve analytical skills. Trainees are asked to read a case report that describes the organizational, social, and technical aspects of some organizational problem (e.g., poor leadership, intergroup conflict). Each trainee prepares a report in which he or she describes the problems and offers solutions (including potential risks and benefits). Working in a group, trainees may then be asked to justify the problems they have identified and their recommendations. The trainer's role is to facilitate the group's learning and to help the trainees see the underlying management concepts in the case. One variation to the traditional case method is called a **living case.** This has trainees analyze a problem that their organization or another realfirm is currently facing.[112]

Role-Playing

In a role-playing exercise, trainees act out roles and attempt to perform the behaviors required in those roles. Role-plays are commonly used in training to teach skills such as oral communication, interpersonal styles, leadership styles, performance feedback reviews, and interviewing techniques. In the popular MBA course, "Executive Power and Negotiations," at The University of Maryland's Robert H. Smith School of Business, students participate in role-plays every class period to enhance their negotiating skills across a variety of situations (e.g., receiving jobs, raises and promotions, international deals, ethical dilemmas). Similarly, in the EMBA course "Leadership and Human Capital," executives are videotaped while role-playing and given feedback on their skills. Checkfree Services, Inc., uses role-plays to teach managers skills for setting expectations, handling conflict situations, and using behavioral-based interviewing.[113] At the *Chicago Tribune,* trainees are assigned the role of a supervisor giving performance appraisal feedback to a subordinate, while other trainees play the role of the subordinate. Xerox uses role-plays in some of its training programs to teach managers how to develop a culturally diverse workforce. Role-plays are very common components of sexual harassment training programs.

Behavior Modeling

Bandura's theory

Behavior modeling is quickly growing as a technique for training managers on interpersonal and supervisory skills. Many large companies such as Exxon, Westinghouse, and Union Carbide use this approach. Based on Bandura's **theory of social learning,**[114] the method consists of four consecutive components: (1) *attention* (watching someone perform a behavior usually through videotapes), (2) *retention* (processes to help the trainee retain what was observed), (3) *motor reproduction* or behavioral rehearsal (using role-plays to practice new behaviors), and (4) *motivation* or feedback/reinforcement (receiving feedback on the behaviors performed). The success of this approach to training is based on the notion that many of us learn by observing others. For example, suppose you have just taken a job as a sales representative. You may spend some time watching the techniques used by other reps to get ideas for how to perform the job. If you practice the behaviors you have observed and get feedback from the "models" or others, your learning should be enhanced. Generally, trainees should observe predominately positive examples of the behaviors if the goal is to get them to reproduce the behaviors. At the U.S. Naval Construction Battalion at Gulfport, Mississippi, the use of behavior modeling resulted in superior retention of knowledge, transfer of learning, and end-user satisfaction.[115]

Modeling very effective for educators

Behavioral modeling is an excellent approach for training trainers and educators where a "master" teacher can serve as the model for the future trainer or teacher or someone who is having difficulties in the classroom. For example, many graduate programs assign a new grad student to a "star" professor who is teaching a course that the grad student will teach in the near future.

EVALUATION

Evaluation involves the collection of information on whether trainees were satisfied with the program, learned the material, and were able to apply the skills back on the job. It may be important to determine whether trainees are capable of exhibiting the appropriate level of a skill (e.g., do new supervisors know all of the organization's policies and procedures?). It may be important to know whether or not trainees have changed their behavior and if the change was due to training (e.g., do supervisors complete the necessary paperwork for disciplining an employee more after the training than before it was conducted?). Further, it may be critical to know that if the organization places a new group of supervisors in the same training program they will also improve their learning or behaviors. Evaluation efforts can be designed to answer these various questions or address these issues.[116]

Evaluation ensures that programs are accountable and are meeting the particular needs of employees in a cost-effective manner. This is especially important today, as organizations attempt to cut costs and improve quality. Without evaluation, it is very difficult to show that training was the reason for any improvements, and as a result management may reduce training budgets or staffs in times of financial hardship. While most companies recognize the importance of evaluation, few actually evaluate their training programs.[117] Many successful firms that emphasize training do so almost as a matter of faith and because of their belief in the connection between people and profits.[118] Some firms, such as GE, believe that new ways must be used to evaluate training programs. They use surveys to realign training as needed and examine returns in the form of tangible and intangible business results, increased consumer satisfaction, and career development for GE workers.[119] The BEST organizations (as rated by ASTD) incorporate a wide variety of criteria to maximize the link between learning and performance. As a result, they have been able to show a wide range of benefits from their learning programs such as fewer work-related injuries, decreased errors, cost savings, improved productivity, larger market share, and better collaboration among work groups.[120] As an example, Caterpillar makes sure that every major program is graded by a performance scorecard and a reporting process that examines business impact. Reaction, application, and ROI data are reviewed monthly and reported to the board of governors quarterly. Over the past six years, the firm completed 11 studies to show how its corporate university program improved business performance.[121]

Types of Criteria

5 types of data

In a survey of learning executives (e.g., HR executive, CEO, Chief Learning Officers) 67 percent stated that their most pressing issue was establishing a link between learning and organizational performance. A secondary concern reported by 49 percent was establishing ROI or value for learning.[122] Thus, trainers should try to collect five types of data when evaluating training programs: measures of reactions, learning, behavior change, organizational results, and return on investment (ROI) utility. The first four of these criteria are widely used to evaluate corporate training programs, and the last, ROI,[123] has been added as another important source of evaluation data.[124]

- *Reactions*—trainees' attitudes toward the training program, instructor, facilities, and so forth.

- *Learning*—changes in knowledge by trainees or level of knowledge reached after training.

- *Behavior*—changes in job performance or level of job performance reached after training.

- *Results*—changes in organizational measures (e.g., productivity, turnover, absences) due to training.

- *ROI*—monetary value of the results (benefits of training minus costs of training; expressed as a percentage).

Although most organizations rely on reactive measures as the sole basis for evaluating their training, scores on reactive measures say very little about the more important criteria. As one recent review put it, "There is very little reason to believe that how trainees feel about or whether they like a training program tells researchers much, if anything, about (a) how much they learned from the program (*learning criteria*), (b) changes in their job-related behaviors or performance (*behavioral criteria*), or (c) the utility of the program to the organization (*results criteria*). This is supported by the lack of relationship between reaction criteria and the other three criteria." Yet, reaction measures are the most widely used evaluation criteria in applied settings. There is, however, some good news. In a comprehensive meta-analysis of 162 training evaluation studies, it was found that the average or mean effect sizes for training interventions (across all topics and methods used) were fairly large. This reveals that reactions, learning, behavior, and results criteria should lead to meaningful positive changes in the organizations.[125]

Reactions

Reaction measures are designed to assess trainees' opinions regarding the training program. Using a questionnaire, trainees are asked at the end of training to indicate the degree to which they were satisfied with the trainer, subject matter and content, the materials (books, pamphlets, handouts), and the environment (room, breaks, meals, temperature). It is important to assess trainees' satisfaction with multiple aspects of a training program and not just their overall satisfaction.[126] Also, they may be asked to indicate the aspects of the program they considered to be most valuable and least useful to them. You have probably been asked to complete a reaction form or course evaluation instrument for some of your classes.

Little correlation between reaction and other criteria

Favorable reactions to a program do not guarantee that learning has occurred or that appropriate behaviors have been adopted. In fact, there is little correlation between *reactions* and *other criteria*. However, it is important to collect reaction data for several reasons: (1) to find out how satisfied trainees were with the program, (2) to make any needed revisions in the program, and (3) to ensure that other trainees will be receptive to attending the program. Trainees should be given ample time at the end of the session to complete the reaction form. Also, trainers should assess trainees' reactions several months after the program to determine how relevant trainees felt the training was to their jobs. An example of a reaction form is presented in Figure 8-9.

Learning

Learning measures assess the degree to which trainees have mastered the concepts, knowledge, and skills of the training. Typically, learning is measured by paper-and-pencil tests (e.g., essay-type questions, multiple choice), performance tests, and simulation exercises. These measures should be designed to sample the content of the training program. Trainees should be tested on their level of understanding before and after training to determine the effect of training on their knowledge. Figure 8-10 presents two examples of performance tests used to assess learning. Figure 8-11 presents a more commonly used type of learning measure. Regarding learning criteria, trainee learning appears to be a necessary but insufficient prerequisite for changes in behavior, improvements in actual on-the-job performance, and "bottom-line" results.

Figure 8-9 An Example of a Trainee Reaction Questionnaire

Evaluation Questionnaire

(Please return this form *unsigned* to the Training and Development Group)

1. Considering everything, how would you rate this program? (Check one)

Unsatisfactory _____ Satisfactory _____ Good _____ Outstanding _____

Please explain briefly the reasons for the rating you have given:

2. Were your expectations: exceeded _____ matched _____ fallen below _____? (Check one)

3. Are you going to recommend this training program to other members of your department?

Yes _____ No _____ If you checked "yes," please describe the job titles held by the people to whom you would recommend this program.

_____

_____

4. Please rate the relative value (1 = very valuable; 2 = worthwhile; 3 = negligible) of the following components of the training program to you:

Videos _____ Role-playing exercises _____
Workbooks _____ Small group exercises _____
Small group discussions _____ Lectures _____
Cases _____ Readings, articles _____

5. Please rate the main lecturer's presentation (1 = not effective; 2 = somewhat effective; 3 = very effective) in terms of:

Ability to communicate _____
Emphasis on key points _____
Visual aids _____
Handout materials _____

6. Please rate the following cases, readings, and videos by placing a checkmark in the appropriate column:

	Excell.	Good	Fair	Poor
Overcoming Resistance to Change				
Reviewing Performance Goals				
Setting Performance Goals				
Handling Employee Complaints				
Improving Employee Performance				
Slade Co.				
Superior Slate Quarry				
McGregor's Theory X and Y				
Henry Manufacturing				
First Federal Savings				
Claremont Industries				

7. Was the ratio of lectures to cases (check one): High _____ OK _____ Low _____?

8. Were the videos pertinent to your work? (check one)
To most of my work? _____
To some of my work? _____
To none of my work? _____

9. To help the training director and the staff provide further improvements in future programs, please give us your frank opinion of each case discussion leader's contribution to your learning. (Place your checkmarks in the appropriate boxes.)

	Excellent	Above Average	Average	Below Average	Poor
DAVIS					
GLEASON					
LAIRD					
MARTIN					
PONTELLO					
SHALL					
SOMMERS					
WILSON					
ZIMMER					

10. How would you evaluate your participation in the program? (check)
Overall workload: Too heavy _____ Just right _____ Too light _____
Case preparation: Too heavy _____ Just right _____ Too light _____
Homework assignments: Too heavy _____ Just right _____ Too light _____

11. What suggestions do you have for improving the program?

_____

_____

Source: Wexley, Kenneth N.; Latham, Gary P.; *Developing and Training Human Resources in Organizations*, 2nd Edition, © 1991. Reprinted by permission of Pearson Education, Inc. Upper Saddle River, NJ.

Figure 8-10
Examples of Learning
Performance Tests

MECHANICS

"You have in front of you a gear reducer, a line shaft, bearings, and coupling. I want you to assemble and adjust the proper alignment so that the finished assembly is a right-hand (or left-hand) driven assembly. Set the coupling gap 1/8 inch apart. You do not have to put the grid member in place or fasten the coupling covers. After you are finished, I will ask you where and how the grid member should go in. You will have 45 minutes to complete this job."

PAINTERS

"I want you to boost yourself up about 10 feet off the floor using this boatsman chair, and then tie yourself off so that you don't fall. After that, I would like you to hook this spraygun to the air supply, set the regulator to the correct pressure, and then spray this wall."

Source: Kenneth N. Wexley and Gary P. Latham, *Developing and Training Human Resources in Organizations*, 2nd ed., © 1991. Reprinted by permission of Pearson Education, Inc., Upper Saddle River, NJ.

Behaviors/Performance

**Learning and actual
performance not highly
correlated**

Behavioral criteria are measures of actual on-the-job performance and can be used to identify the effects of training on actual work performance. Issues pertaining to the transfer of training are also relevant here. Behavioral criteria are typically operationalized by using supervisor ratings or objective indicators of performance. Although learning and behavioral criteria are conceptually linked, researchers have had limited success in empirically demonstrating this relationship. This is because behavioral criteria are susceptible to environmental variables that can influence the transfer or use of trained skills or capabilities on the job. For example, the posttraining environment may not provide opportunities for the learned material or skills to be applied or performed. Behaviors of trainees before and after training should be compared to assess the degree to which training has changed their performance. This is important because one of the goals of training is to modify the on-the-job behavior or performance of trainees. Behaviors can be measured by relying on the performance evaluation system to collect ratings of trainees both before and after training. For example, trainees of the Federal Aviation Administration must submit subordinate evaluations of their supervisory behavior prior to attending the national training center in Florida. Subordinates also submit evaluations of the same supervisors' behavior six months after the training. To determine whether or not the supervisors' skills have improved due to training, the performance evaluations they received from their subordinates before and

Figure 8-11
Sample Learning Measure

SAMPLE ITEMS FROM A MGIC TEST TO EVALUATE SUPERVISOR KNOWLEDGE

1. T or F   When preparing a truth-in-lending disclosure with a financed single premium, mortgage insurance should always be disclosed for the life of the loan.

2. T or F   GE and MGIC have the same refund policy for refundable single premiums.

3. T or F   MGIC, GE, and PMI are the only mortgage insurers offering a nonrefundable single premium.

4. _____   Which one of the following is not a category in the loan progress reports?

     a. Loans approved

     b. Loans-in-suspense

     c. Loans denied

     d. Loans received

5. _____   Which of the following do not affect the MGIC Plus buying decision?

     a. Consumer

     b. Realtor

     c. MGIC underwriter

     d. Secondary market manager

     e. Servicing manager

6. _____   The new risk-based capital regulations for savings and loans have caused many of them to:

     a. Convert whole loans into securities

     b. Begin originating home equity loans

     c. Put MI on their uninsured 90s

Source: Reprinted with permission of the publisher. From *Evaluating Training Programs: The Four Levels.* Copyright © 1996 by Kirkpatrick, Barrett-Koehler, Inc., San Francisco, CA. All rights reserved. www.bkconnection.com.

Figure 8-12
Sample Survey Behavioral Measure

Instructions: The purpose of this questionnaire is to determine the extent to which those who attended the recent leadership program have applied the principles and techniques that they learned back on the job. The survey results will help us to assess the effectiveness of the program. Please circle the appropriate response for each question.

5 = Much more   4 = Some more   3 = The same   2 = Some less   1 = Much less

	Time and Energy Spent after the Program Compared to Time and Energy Spent before the Program				
Understanding and Motivating					
1. Getting to know my employees	5	4	3	2	1
2. Listening to my subordinates	5	4	3	2	1
3. Praising good work	5	4	3	2	1
4. Talking with employees about their families and interests	5	4	3	2	1
5. Asking subordinates for their ideas	5	4	3	2	1
6. Managing by walking around	5	4	3	2	1
Orienting and Training					
7. Asking new employees about their past experiences, etc.	5	4	3	2	1
8. Taking new employees on a tour of the department and facilities	5	4	3	2	1
9. Introducing new employees to their co-workers	5	4	3	2	1
10. Being patient with employees	5	4	3	2	1

Source: Reprinted with permission of the publisher. From *Evaluating Training Programs: The Four Levels.* Copyright © 1996 by Kirkpatrick, Barrett-Koehler, Inc., San Francisco, CA. All rights reserved. www.bkconnection.com.

after completion of training are compared. A variety of performance appraisal measures can be used to assess behavioral changes of trainees. These were described in detail in Chapter 7. Figure 8-12 presents a sample behavioral measure.

Organizational Results

The purpose of collecting **organizational results** is to examine the impact of training on the work group or entire company. Data may be collected before and after training on criteria such as productivity, turnover, absenteeism, formal complaints/lawsuits, accidents, grievances, quality improvements, scrap, sales, and customer satisfaction. The trainer will try to show that the training program was responsible for any changes noted in these criteria. This may be difficult to do without a careful design and data collection strategy, since many other factors could explain the changes detected. For example, changes in dollar sales could be due to a new pay system rather than to a sales training program. An evaluation using a results measure (pharmacy sales) was conducted for a training program designed for pharmacy technicians at 2,000 Walgreen stores. Sales for pharmacies where technicians had received 20 hours of classroom training and 20 hours of OJT were $9,500 greater annually than those for pharmacies where technicians received only OJT. Results criteria (e.g., productivity, sales, company profits) are the most distal and macro criteria used to evaluate the effectiveness of training.

Results criteria are frequently operationalized by using **utility analysis estimates.** As discussed in Chapter 6, utility analysis provides a methodology to assess the dollar value gained by engaging in specified personnel interventions including training.

The Effectiveness of Organizational Training

As noted earlier, a recent meta-analysis determined the effectiveness of organizational training.[127] While the effects differed as a function of the type of criteria used to evaluate the training, the overall effect of the training was comparable to (or larger than) those reported for other organizational interventions, such as the effects for performance appraisal and feedback, management by objectives, and goal setting on productivity.

Testing for the effect of skill or task characteristics was intended to shed light on the "trainability" of particular skills and tasks. For both learning and behavioral criteria, the largest effects were obtained for training that included both cognitive and interpersonal skills, followed by psychomotor skills. Where results criteria were used in the study, the largest effect was obtained for interpersonal skills and the smallest for psychomotor skills. A medium effect was obtained for cognitive skills or tasks.

The study also examined the effectiveness of training delivery methods as a function of the skill or task being trained. The magnitude of the effect sizes was generally favorable and ranged from medium to large regardless of delivery methods or skill type. As an example of this, even the findings for the lecture method were positive. Findings were generally favorable for lectures across all skill or task types and evaluation criteria. The results suggest that organizational training is generally effective. Furthermore, the authors also suggest that the effectiveness of training appears to vary as a function of the specified training delivery method, the skill or task being trained, and the criterion used to operationalize effectiveness.[128]

Big decrease in effect sizes from learning measures to performance data

Comparisons of the effect sizes for learning criteria versus behavioral and results criteria showed a substantial decrease in effect sizes from learning to the other criteria. The authors concluded that the effect may have been due to the fact that the manifestation of training learning outcomes in job behaviors and organizational results may be a consequence of the favorability of the posttraining environment for the performance of the learned skills. "Environmental favorability" is defined as the extent to which the transfer or work environment is supportive of the application of new skills and behaviors learned or acquired in training. Thus, learned skills will not be demonstrated as behaviors or performance if workers are denied the opportunity to perform them; the social context and favorability of the posttraining environment play a critical role in determining whether the trained skills are transferred to the job.

Assessing the Costs and Benefits of Training

A variety of methods can be used to assess the dollar value of training. We have mentioned calculations of **ROI and utility analysis.** No matter which approach is used, costs and benefits associated with training must be estimated. Some **costs** that should be measured for a training program include (1) one-time costs such as needs assessment costs, salaries and benefits of training designers, purchase of equipment and media (computers, videos, handouts, distance learning techniques), program development costs, evaluation costs for the first offering of the program; (2) costs associated with each training session such as trainers' costs (salaries and benefits, travel, lodging, meals) and facilities rental; and (3) costs associated with trainees including trainee wages during training, travel, lodging, meals for trainees during training, and nonreusable training materials.

It is important to compare the **benefits** of the training program with its costs. One benefit that should be estimated is the dollar payback associated with the improvement in trainees' performance after receiving training. This is often difficult to approximate. Since the results of the experimental design will indicate any differences in behavior between those trained versus those untrained, the trainer can then estimate for that particular group of employees (e.g., managers, engineers) what this difference is worth in terms of the salaries of those employees. Often, the amount gained per trainee per year is multiplied by the number of persons trained. Another factor that should be considered when estimating the benefits of training is the duration of the training's impact, that is, the length of time during which the improved performance will be maintained. While probably no programs will show benefits forever, those that do produce longer-term improved performance will have greater value to the organization.

Return on Investment (ROI)

Given the increasing amount of money that firms budget for training, it is imperative that companies be able to estimate the **return on investment (ROI)** that training provides them. To do this, firms should assess the costs and benefits associated with their programs. However, one study noted that **ROI** metrics were used by only 20 percent of respondents. This may be because a lot of training is targeted to leadership and other soft skills that are difficult to track in terms of concrete measurements.[129] In one study that did examine ROI with several training programs at a pharmaceutical firm, it was found that the managerial training programs had an average **ROI** of 45 percent, while the sales and technical training programs had an average **ROI** of 156 percent. At Ford, all training programs are evaluated against the criterion of product line profitability. A tracking system shows costs and revenue for training facilities and individual courses.[130] The basic **ROI** formula is as follows:

$$\text{ROI (\%)} = \frac{\text{Net program benefits}}{\text{Program costs}} \times 100$$

For example, at an 18-week literacy program for entry-level electrical and mechanical assemblers at Magnavox Electronics Systems Company, the results were impressive. The benefits (productivity and quality) were $321,600 while the costs were only $38,233. Thus, the **ROI** is calculated as 741 percent. This means that for each dollar invested, Magnavox received $7.41 over the cost of the program.[131]

$$\text{ROI} = \frac{\$321,600 - \$38,233}{\$38,233} \times 100 = 741\%$$

When making **ROI** calculations, it is important to use reliable and credible sources and to be conservative when estimating benefits and costs for training. It is also important to involve management when deciding on what is an acceptable **ROI** as a target goal for the training. For example, British Airways has utilized training to become one of the most profitable airlines in the world. Before training begins, a tangible value for the training investment is set, reflecting how much improvement in customer satisfaction is to be expected if training is successful.[132] At Caterpillar, they have their own university which delivers competency courses to dealers via e-learning in eight different languages that address specific needs that arise from a needs assessment. In 2007, they reported that 4,500 dealers were engaged and that early performance metrics indicated nearly 400 percent return on investment for dealers.[133]

Utility Analysis

Another approach that can be used when calculating the value of training is a utility model. (See Chapter 6 for a review of utility.) This is difficult but may be important for showing top management the value of training for the organization. Utility is a function of the duration of a training program's effect on employees, the number of employees trained, the validity of the training program, the value of the job for which training was provided, and the total cost of the program. **Utility analysis** measures the economic contribution of a program according to how effective it was in identifying and modifying behavior.[134] Because the calculations involved in a utility analysis are based on subjective estimations, this model has not yet gained widespread acceptance by trainers as a practical tool for evaluating return on training investments.[135]

Designs for Evaluating Training

Answers two primary questions

Control groups

After determining the criteria to use in evaluating the training program, the trainer should choose an experimental design. The design is used to answer two primary questions: (1) whether or not a change has occurred in the criteria (e.g., learning, behavior, organizational results) and (2) whether or not the change can be attributed to the training program. Designs employ two possible strategies to answer these questions. The first is to compare the trainee's performance before and after participation in training. This is done to see what changes may have occurred in learning, behavior, or organizational results. While this is important for answering the question of whether change has taken place, it is deficient in answering the question of whether the change can be attributed to the training program since the criteria may have changed for a number of reasons. Answering the second question requires a design comparing the changes that occurred in the trainees with changes that occurred in another group of employees who did not receive the training (e.g., a **control group**), yet are similar to the training group in important ways (e.g., similar job titles, rank, geographical location). The most effective experimental designs use both strategies (i.e., before–after measures and a control group) and are better able to answer both questions. Some of the more commonly used designs for training evaluation are described below.[136]

One-Shot Posttest-Only Design

In many organizations, training is designed and conducted without prior thought given to evaluation. For example, a plant manager may decide to put all the employees in a safety training course. After the course is completed the manager decides to evaluate it. At this point, the design would look like the one below:

$$\text{TRAINING} \longrightarrow \text{MEASURE}$$

Any of the four types of criteria (reactions, learning, behavior, organizational results) could be used as the "after" measures. It would be difficult, however, to know what, if any, changes occurred since no "before" measure (pretest) was made. In addition, because the results may not be compared with those of another group who did not receive training, it would not be possible to say whether any change was due to the training. If, however, the primary goal was to make sure that the trainees reached a certain mastery level, then the design might still be appropriate (e.g., the trainees reached a 95 percent safety goal).

One-Group Pretest–Posttest Design

Another design for evaluating the training group on the criteria is to measure the group before and after the training. This design is as follows:

$$\text{MEASURE} \longrightarrow \text{TRAINING} \longrightarrow \text{MEASURE}$$

This design can assess whether a change has occurred for the training group in the criteria (e.g., learning, behavior) that is useful. Unfortunately, it is not able to tell for sure whether or not the change is due to training, since there is no control group. A change that is detected could have been caused by the introduction of new equipment, a new manager, or revised pay systems, or occurred for a number of other reasons. If the trainer is going to use this design, it is important to document other events that have occurred during the measurement period to determine the most likely explanations for any detected changes.

Posttest-Only Control Group Design

A much stronger design for assessing the effectiveness of a training program is shown here:

$$\text{GROUP 1: R: TRAINING} \longrightarrow \text{MEASURE}$$
$$\text{GROUP 2: R: NO TRAINING} \longrightarrow \text{MEASURE}$$

In this design, two groups are used and individuals are **randomly assigned** (R) to either group (i.e., an individual has an equal chance of being put in either group 1, the training group, or group 2, the **control group**). The use of random assignment helps to initially equalize the two groups. This is important to ensure that any differences between the two groups after training are not simply caused by differences in ability, motivation, or experience. The **posttest-only control group** design is useful when it is difficult to collect criteria measures on individuals prior to offering them the training. For example, the trainer may believe that giving individuals a pretest, such as a learning test, may overly influence their scores on the posttest, which might be the same learning measure. Another trainer may not have time to give pre-measures. Individuals are randomly assigned to the two groups, and their scores on the posttest are compared. Any differences on the posttest can be attributed to the training program since we can assume the two groups were somewhat equal before training. It would be beneficial to make sure the employees from the control group are placed in a training program later so that they have similar opportunities.

Pretest–Posttest Control Group Design

Another powerful design that is recommended for use in training evaluation is as follows:

$$\text{GROUP 1: R: MEASURE} \longrightarrow \text{TRAINING} \longrightarrow \text{MEASURE}$$
$$\text{GROUP 2: R: MEASURE} \longrightarrow \text{NO TRAINING} \longrightarrow \text{MEASURE}$$

Individuals are randomly assigned to the two groups. Criteria measures are collected on both groups before and after the training program is offered, yet only one group actually receives the training (group 2 is the control group). Comparisons are made of the changes detected in both groups. If the change in group 1 is significantly different from the change in group 2, we can be somewhat certain that it was caused by the training. The two features that make this a stronger design are the ***randomization*** of people into the groups and the use of a *control group*. These aspects enable us to determine (1) if a change occurred and (2) whether the change was due to training. Since many organizations will want all of the employees in both groups to receive the training, the training can be offered to group 2 at a later time.

Multiple Time-Series Design

Another design recommended for use in training evaluation is shown below:

GROUP 1: R: MEASURE → MEASURE → MEASURE → TRAINING → MEASURE → MEASURE → MEASURE

GROUP 2: R: MEASURE → MEASURE → MEASURE → NO TRAINING → MEASURE → MEASURE → MEASURE

In this design, individuals are randomly assigned to either of two groups, and the criteria measures (learning, behavior, results) are collected at several times before and after the training has been offered. This design allows us to observe any changes between the two groups over time or any trends in performance. If the effects of training held up over several months, this design would offer stronger support for the program. Of course, this design might be more costly or difficult to implement since it requires taking measurements of individuals multiple times.

Benchmarking Training Efforts

To conduct a thorough evaluation of a training program, training departments can benchmark their practices against the best in the industry. They can compare their training department to leading-edge companies in terms of (1) training activities (e.g., percent of payroll spent on training, average training hours per employee, training dollars spent per employee, percent of employees trained per year, training staff per 1,000 employees), (2) training results (e.g., average percent of positive trainee ratings per year, average percent of satisfied trainees, average percent gain in learning per course, average percent of improvement in job performance, cost savings as a ratio of training expenses, revenues per employee per year, profits per employee per year), and (3) training efficiency (e.g., training costs per student hour, time on task). **The American Society for Training and Development (ASTD)** provides conferences and sessions each year where HR and training professionals can learn strategies from the ASTD BEST award winners. See www.astd.org for more information.

PLANNING FOR TRAINING EFFECTIVENESS IN ORGANIZATIONS

One recent review on training concludes: "We must do a better job of linking training outcomes to organizational and business outcomes, and do so while involving organizational decision makers."[137] Four guidelines are offered for training professionals on planning "collaborative" interventions that are more likely to affect business objectives. Figure 8-13 presents these guidelines.

**Figure 8-13
Collaborative Planning for Training**

Guideline: Develop a theory of impact

Goal:	Link evaluation and measurement to unique capabilities and/or strategic initiatives of the organization.
Strategies:	• Identify business results that matter to the organization.
	• Link training outcomes to measures of organizational effectiveness.
	• Link measures of organizational effectiveness to job-level knowledge and skills.
Tools:	• Scan internal and external environment to determine organization-level strategic initiatives.
	• Develop logic models or causal models linking training to organizational impact.
	• Involve decision makers in long-term planning for training.

Guideline: Reframe the point of evaluation from proof to evidence

Goal:	Establish reasonable expectations from decision makers about the type of evidence that will demonstrate training success.

continued

Strategies:
- Distinguish between proof and evidence in the minds of decision makers.
- Identify required levels of evidence to show training success.
- Frame expectations for evaluation outcomes in the minds of decision makers.

Tools:
- Clarify the purpose for evaluation or intended use of information.
- Clarify costs of evaluation as a function of evaluation rigor.
- Involve decision makers in planning for training evaluation.

Guideline: Isolate the effects of training

Goal: Eliminate or reduce counterarguments to claims that training is effective.

Strategies:
- Demonstrate linkage between training and organizational effectiveness.
- Choose appropriate research designs.

Tools:
- Use control groups and pretests whenever possible.
- Use trend lines or staggered start dates for training when more sophisticated research designs are unavailable.
- Use the internal referencing strategy when other research designs are unavailable.

Guideline: Establish accountability for training

Goal: Improve the impact of training on individual and organizational effectiveness by involving all organizational members in the planning of training.

Strategies:
- Increase motivation to train in trainees.
- Increase support by peers and supervisors on the job.
- Increase organizational support for training.

Tools:
- Use evidence of past training success to enhance motivation of future trainees.
- Clarify the relationship between training and organizational effectiveness and train supervisors in posttraining support behaviors.
- Involve decision makers in planning for training.

Source: K. Kraiger and W. J. Casper, "Collaborative Training for Training Impact", *Human Resource Management* 43 (2004), p. 343. Reprinted with permission from John Wiley & Sons.

SPECIAL TRAINING PROGRAMS

Training for Generational Transitions

Competition for talent is a worldwide phenomenon. By 2010, Baby Boomers (those born between 1946 and 1964) will be retiring in droves, and there are not as many individuals in the following generation (X) to fill that void. There are only 43 million Gen Xers to fill the shoes of 76 million boomers. Thus, a skills shortage will be facing many employers, particularly in the financial and IT areas. Many CFOs and CIOs note that finding talent is one of their biggest concerns.[138] Not only is the private sector in U.S. firms facing a labor shortage, but the public sector is probably facing an even greater workforce deficit. With nearly half of all supervisors and nearly 40 percent of current federal employees expected to retire by 2016, federal agencies are racing against the clock to find top talent. Chief Human Capital Officers (CHCOs) are charged with the job of addressing generational transitions and leadership development issues. Agencies may also receive help from the U.S. Congress. The *Federal Supervisor Training Act* was a bill introduced in 2007 which updates and improves mandatory supervisor training programs.[139]

Baby-Boomer training

Some training has now been targeted toward Baby Boomers to retain them in the workforce or to rehire them. Baby Boomers are the "institutional memory" of a firm. Consequently, they should be valued and retained so that they maintain their loyalty to the firm or they may take their market tips, trade secrets, and fellow employees to competitors. To protect their investment, employers can use their experienced workers in a number of ways: as subject matter experts for new hires; to write work manuals for older equipment, processes, and business functions; to form innovative intergenerational teams; and to launch phased retirement, age-related sabbaticals, and rehired-retiree programs.[140]

In addition to focusing on training Baby Boomers, employers should also examine how their training enhances the learning and performance of their other generations of workers (Generation X and Y employees). Generation X and Y employees are currently in the workforce and are already participating in many training programs in organizations. Some firms have already discovered that they will need to provide a different type of training for these newer employees. For example, after experiencing much higher than normal turnover rates among Gen Y drivers, UPS had to change the way it viewed and delivered training. Instead of lowering its standards and the expectations for drivers, it changed the way it prepared them to hit the road. After 20 months of analysis and design, UPS opened Integrad in 2007 in Landover, Maryland. The $5.5 million 11,500-square-foot learning facility has revolutionized how UPS trains its drivers. The Integrad learning lab offers many different delivery methods including online learning, 3-D models, podcasts, videos, hands-on learning, and classroom methods. Aspiring UPS drivers must complete a 21-hour precourse before attending the 46-hour learning lab in MD. The program is so successful in terms of quality, production, safety, and business development that UPS has already had phone calls from other organizations that want to come and benchmark them.[141]

In Europe, employers are also recognizing that they need to prepare the next generation of workers for employment as well as try to keep some of the older workers from leaving. Still, the latest research finds many organizations failing to prepare for the wave of departing workers and their less-experienced replacements. Lifelong learning initiatives such as workplace training, technical skills transfer, and training outside the office were rated as highest in Britain compared to France, Spain, Germany, and Italy. In India, "finishing schools" are gaining in popularity as a way to help new college graduates learn workplace fundamentals (e.g., arriving on time, dressing appropriately, learning listening skills).[142]

Employee Orientation Programs and Onboarding

Most firms provide some type of employee orientation where new employees are informed about their roles and responsibilities (i.e., what is expected of them) in an effort to ease their transition to the firm. The trend seems to be continuing as more firms have been placing their new employees in orientation programs to familiarize them with their supervisors and co-workers, the company policies and procedures, the requirements of their jobs, and the organizational culture. The intent is to increase an employee's job satisfaction and to reduce turnover. Unfortunately, most of these programs are not properly planned, implemented, or evaluated. All too often new employees are given a brief introduction to the company and are then left to learn the ropes by themselves. Often this leads to feelings of confusion, frustration, stress, and uncertainty among new employees. In fact, job satisfaction is often related to an employee's orientation. If employee dissatisfaction leads to turnover, this can be quite costly for the firm. For example, at Merck & Company, turnover costs have been estimated to range from 1.5 to 2.5 times the annual salary paid for a job.[143]

Three objectives for orientation

Generally, the objectives of an employee orientation program are threefold: (1) to assist the new employee in adjusting to the organization and feeling comfortable and positive about the new job; (2) to clarify the job requirements, demands, and performance expectations; and (3) to get the employee to understand the organization's culture and quickly adopt the organization's goals, values, and behaviors. A Realistic Orientation Program for New Employee Stress (ROPES) has been suggested as the model. Employees would be given realistic information about the job and the organization, general support and reassurance from managers, and help in identifying and coping with the stresses of the job. This should reduce turnover of new employees, resulting in savings for the company.[144]

Three stages

Most orientation programs consist of three stages: (1) a general introduction to the organization, often given by the HR department; (2) a specific orientation to the department and the job typically given by the employee's immediate supervisor; and (3) a follow-up meeting to verify that the important issues have been addressed and employee questions have been answered. This follow-up meeting usually takes place between a new employee and his or her supervisor a week or so after the employee has begun working. A follow-up meeting is very important because often new employees may feel uncomfortable seeking out a supervisor regarding any questions they face. A supervisor or a human resources representative should meet with the employee to be sure that he or she is effectively "learning the ropes" of the organization. The orientation program used by the Disney Corporation for employees of Walt Disney World in Orlando, Florida, follows this multiple-stage format in most respects. Individuals begin their employment by attending a one-day program, "Disney Traditions II," which describes the history of the organization and the values of the culture. On this first day, employees are also taken on a tour of the facilities. On the second day, they are provided with descriptions of the policies and procedures. The third day, OJT begins with an assigned buddy who is an experienced co-worker. Buddies spend anywhere from two days to two weeks showing new employees their job duties and providing feedback as they attempt to perform the tasks. As a result of participating in the orientation program, employees express less confusion with their new jobs.[145]

The training department should be actively involved in planning, conducting, and evaluating orientation programs. They also should enlist the support of other employees to serve as mentors to new employees. Also, supervisors should be called on to help orient new employees to the workforce and should receive training on how to do this. In the follow-up meeting, supervisors should be required to complete a checklist, indicating that they have discussed with new employees the major issues of concern. Employees should sign the checklist to confirm that they have received the orientation information. Evaluation of the orientation program is the responsibility of the human resource department. At The Home Depot, the learning organization developed a learning map which new associates receive on their first day of orientation. It illustrates customers' shopping journeys in the store by putting associates in customers' shoes. Trainees interact with each other to form responses to hypothetical customer questions. In 2006, more than 100,000 new hires went through the orientation.[146] American Express recently launched a number of initiatives to address attrition and to increase employees' engagement in the firm. "Connections" is a program that educates new employees about the firm's values, vision, and customers.[147]

Well-developed orientation programs are rare

Well-developed orientation programs are effective in preparing a new employee for a firm, yet these are more the exception than the norm. With today's "war for talent" faced by employers, it is critical for firms not only to hire new employees, but to retain them. *Onboarding* might be one answer to this concern. **Onboarding** is a systematic process to establish a positive trajectory early in a person's career.[148] It includes cultivating key relationships and access to information, phased implementation, and defining multiple roles. Often it is used for new managers. Onboarding provides information and tools to new managers when they are ready to use them and is best implemented throughout a period of weeks or months. Four phases are often commonly used (prearrival, orientation, assimilation, integration). For the *prearrival* of the new manager, it is important to make sure that direct reports and key constituents know about his/her start date and relevant background information. During the *orientation/introduction* phase, provide the essential tools so the new manager can be effective (e.g., computer passwords, office equipment, knowledge of office layout, administration codes, access to company e-mail and intranet). For the *assimilation* phase, deliver essential background information about the company strategy, expected contribution, short-term goals, and key working relationships. In the *integration/contribution* phase, define long-term results and make sure that early contributions by the person are visible.[149]

More and more firms are recognizing that onboarding can be an important part of the talent management process by ensuring that the early entry period is successful for new managers. At Avon, the goal of onboarding is to help newcomers become educated about the cultural norms and part of the family at Avon. With over 320,000 employees worldwide, Citigroup recognizes the importance of newcomers feeling a sense of belonging to the firm. Introducing its 37 networks (e.g., Hispanic, Pride, Working Parents affinity groups) to new employees on the first day enables them to start to feel connected to the firm. At Pepsi Bottling Group, onboarding is taken very seriously by investing a lot to give new managers what they need to do the job effectively.[150]

Differences between orientation and onboarding

The differences between orientation programs and onboarding are primarily in terms of timing, focus, delivery, and responsibility. While orientation is often a single event (day) and focuses on HR policies and procedures, onboarding is usually a phased approach and has a broader focus on success factors and company culture. Orientation is often classroom-led while onboarding uses multiple approaches such as Web-based and classroom methods and CD-ROMs. Perhaps most important, orientation is often seen as the responsibility of only the HR department, while the responsibility for onboarding is shared among HR, the new boss, a peer coach, and the process owner.[151]

Training for Teams

Training techniques can be chosen for individual-level training or for training that is conducted for work teams. With the increasing popularity of teams in organizations,[152] it is common for employers to send their teams to training sessions. For example, Hewlett-Packard started its team members on a two-week training and orientation program to familiarize everyone with the existing processes and the needs of the business.[153] Likewise, Allied Signal sent their maintenance teams from the Garrett Engine Division to a two-day course in team building. Cummins Engine Company places improvement teams through a five-day training program that is based on an action learning model (classroom and OJT training).[154] GE sends entire teams to participate in business games, all of which deal with real GE strengths, weaknesses, opportunities, and threats (SWOT) analysis.

Trust building important

Team training often focuses on teaching members how to work more effectively or efficiently in teams. Some topics include team building, problem solving, running effective meetings, managing stress, managing productivity, appraising team members' performance, and managing conflict. **Trust building** is also an important component of the training.[155] Employers offer training in problem solving, meeting skills, communication skills, handling conflict, roles and responsibilities, quality tools and concepts, and evaluating team performance.[156] In general, trainers use a variety of training techniques when conducting team training such as information-based, demonstration-based (videos) and practice-based (role-plays) methods.[157] In some cases, "ropes" or challenge courses are used to build stronger, more cohesive teams.[158] At Patapsco Valley Veterinary Hospital, employees participate in team-building training sessions, including outdoor challenge activities, to further enhance communication, trust, and collaboration among the team of veterinarians, vet technicians, and receptionists. They also cross-train their team of technicians and receptionists to provide greater flexibility in staffing for the firm.

Cross-functional teams

Often, teams are formed with individuals from various functional areas (e.g., marketing, finance, sales, production). These **cross-functional teams** may require training in other disciplines to help them understand what is involved in other functional areas (called multiskilling or cross-training). This has been used in the military,[159] in high-technology firms,[160] and in assembly plants.[161] Generally, job rotation may be used or individuals may receive training from their peers on other disciplines. For example, peer trainers have been used at T. J. Maxx, a national retail chain, and at Xerox.[162] In fact, sometimes unstructured or informal learning from peers is more effective than structured classroom training.[163] Peers are helpful in socializing new employees, reducing stress, and helping newcomers establish satisfying social relationships.[164] The benefits of cross-training are that it may provide employees with more skill variety or interesting tasks, allow for more flexibility in getting the work done when teammates are absent, and help workers to better understand the entire work process.[165] It may be important to clarify expectations of cross-training during an employee's orientation to the firm in order to set a realistic preview of the job.

Diversity Awareness Training

Managing diversity effectively is one of the greatest challenges for organizations over the next century.[166] Many firms throughout the world face discrimination claims from immigrants, women, older workers, gays, lesbians, various racial and ethnic groups, those with physical disabilities, and those of varying religious affiliations. In addition, different values, attitudes, and behaviors of generations (e.g., Baby Boomers, Generation Y) or types of workers (blue collar vs. white collar) have implications for the management and training necessary to use with these groups.[167] Some employers have been proactive about hiring more diverse employees to mirror the population or have trained their employees to better reach a diverse client base. BB&T has expanded its services to Spanish-speaking communities by training employees to interact with Spanish-speaking clients (using DVDs, CDs, workbooks). Upon completion of the self-study guide, employees call into a telephone testing service to measure their proficiency.[168]

Other firms, however, have minimized diversity issues, and subsequently have faced discrimination suits (e.g., State Farm Insurance with gender bias; Denny's Restaurant with racial bias).[169] Research on diversity issues has increased.[170] In addition, training for increasing awareness of the diverse workforce has become more prevalent in organizations, and a variety of different programs exist.[171]

Diversity awareness programs have been developed for a variety of reasons, including improving the productivity and competitiveness of the firm, changing attitudes and stereotypes, reducing conflict, improving communication and work relationships, enhancing creativity, and improving the progress and satisfaction of women, minorities, and others into upper management positions.[172] When Texaco settled a race discrimination lawsuit, it agreed to put its 29,000 employees through a two-day workshop on race, gender, and culture. Texaco has tripled the number of workshops it offers each month and hired an additional 27 consultants. The workshops focus on four broad areas: creating a diverse workforce, managing a diverse workforce, creating an environment that values a diverse workforce, and leveraging diversity into a competitive business advantage.[173] Deloitte and Touche USA employs more than 40,000 people in 90 American cities. One of their most innovative learning initiatives is the Cultural Navigator, a package of tools and resources that presents a wide range of easy-to-use learning, consulting, and assessment solutions. It enables individuals to compare their personal profiles with those of other cultures and identify areas of commonality and differences. A cultural simulator tests and reinforces awareness and learning by creating online simulations around a variety of management topics pertaining to a specific country or region.[174] AT&T boasts one of the nation's most progressive diversity programs.[175] Chase offers a comprehensive diversity program for all its employees, including awareness training and skill building. Similarly, ExxonMobil has a training program called Internal Resource Education that is an intense team-based course conducted in three one-week segments.[176] American Express created a program called Diversity Learning Labs for training.[177]

To assist in the placement and advancement of employees with disabilities, the EEOC has written material and a video on hiring and developing individuals with disabilities. In recent years, researchers have offered suggestions for assisting employees with disabilities to become more effectively socialized in organizations.[178] Sears became a model by benchmarking the practices of other firms and then adopting them to their own workplace.[179] Some firms (e.g., Xerox, American Express, Disney) have offered diversity training programs to reduce discrimination due to disability.

Flaws with diversity programs

Despite all the new training initiatives for diversity awareness, some recent studies have found a number of flaws with the programs, including not addressing development or advancement issues, not providing tools to reinforce the training, no metrics for evaluating effectiveness of training, clear objectives not established, material too U.S. focused, concerns of line managers not dealt with, trite content, little thought leadership shown, poor facilitation skills, and employers' policies and practices not addressed.[180] Diversity training programs will only be successful if they have top management support and participation. They also need the input of middle management and line managers to know the kinds of issues faced by employees on a daily basis.[181]

American Express formed a high-level diversity council to guide and drive the company's diversity efforts. Likewise, at Hewlett-Packard, the diversity initiatives are driven by the Diversity Leadership Council, which is comprised of senior executives. Along with top managers, immediate supervisors and peers must support and reinforce diversity programs. In addition, trainees should be rewarded for positive changes in their behaviors.[182]

Other factors determining whether or not a company adopts a diversity training program include whether the firm is large, has a high strategic priority of diversity relative to other competing objectives, has the presence of a diversity manager, and has in place a large number of other diversity-supportive policies.[183] Other research has shown the perceived success of diversity training programs to be related to mandatory attendance for all managers, long-term evaluation of training results, managerial rewards for increasing diversity, and a broad definition of diversity in the organization.[184] Apple South's president, S. Kirk

Programs must be fully integrated

Kinsell, states that diversity management can be successful only when it is "integrated fully—that is, made a part of all customer, vendor and employee programs."[185] In addition, as firms continue to become more global, it is important for their training programs to address diversity issues around the world (not just in the United States).

Sexual Harassment Training

Most large firms now offer training on sexual harassment issues. In California, training on sexual harassment is mandatory for all supervisors. All different types of organizations have been accused of sexual harassment, from manufacturing (e.g., Mitsubishi Motor Manufacturing of America) to pharmaceuticals (e.g., Astra Pharmaceuticals) to the military

(Navy Tailhook incident), where suits were filed, and managers were subsequently fired or reassigned.[186] Training on sexual harassment issues has increased dramatically. The Federal Aviation Administration introduced a training program to respond to women's complaints of harassment.[187] Training has increased in organizations in part due to two 1998 Supreme Court cases. As discussed in Chapter 3, these cases left employers even more vulnerable to sexual harassment lawsuits, and the Court clarified what employers could do to protect themselves against liability. In **Faragher v. City of Boca Raton** (1998), the Court sent a message to employers that they must be proactive about sexual harassment by developing a policy and by training employees on it. The city of Boca Raton had a policy on sexual harassment, but did little to communicate it to employees. In **Burlington Industries Inc. v. Ellerth** (1998), the Supreme Court emphasized that employees with sexual harassment claims should communicate them through existing channels in the company before filing suit. Kimberly Ellerth had not done this. This case pointed out the importance of training employees on the sexual harassment policies and procedures that should be followed when making claims. Most larger firms (over 100 employees) have policies on sexual harassment, but they often do not clearly communicate to or train their employees regarding these policies. Companies such as Texas Instruments and Motorola, however, have provided sexual harassment training classes for a number of years.[188] Some firms have hired outside consultants to conduct the training, while others rely on their own training staffs to develop and deliver the courses.

Faragher v. City of Boca Raton

Burlington v. Ellerth

Description of policy critical

Training on sexual harassment should include a description of the firm's policy, including[189]

- A statement indicating the firm's strong opposition to sexual harassment.

- Definitions of sexual harassment, using examples relevant to employees' jobs. Enough detail should be given so employees understand what "quid-pro-quo" harassment is as well as what constitutes a "hostile environment."

- The procedure for reporting harassment (e.g., reporting to the HR director, installing an anonymous hot line).

- The procedure that will be used to investigate claims and that protects whistleblowers.

- Descriptions of punishments for offenders, regardless of their level in the organization.

Many organizations now use e-learning for their sexual harassment training.

Cross-Cultural Training and Training for International Assignments

With increasing globalization of business, cross-cultural training should not be considered a one-shot program but rather a life long endeavor to learn about other cultures. Companies will have to invest more heavily in such training programs.[190] Tata Consultancy Services Limited, an information technology firm with over 93,000 employees based in India, invests heavily in cross-cultural and cultural diversity training to help employees work in new areas. They constantly rotate people across roles and geographies since they believe that the continuing globalization of learning is one of the biggest challenges for workplace learning.[191]

As one expert stated, "The key to successfully competing in the global marketplace may be staffing key expatriate positions with accomplished/skilled leaders."[192] Thus, firms have realized that to be successful in their overseas projects, they need to better prepare individuals to work in international assignments. Studies document the high rate of U.S. expatriate failures ranging from 25 percent to 50 percent.[193] These early returns can be costly for firms with respect to goodwill, reputation, and finances. In many cases, the difficulties encountered by expatriates have been blamed on inadequate training programs. For example, Honeywell surveyed 347 managers who lived abroad or traveled regularly and found that increased training was cited as critical for executives and employees assigned overseas. **Cross-cultural training** has been found to reduce the severity of culture shock and reduce the time necessary for managers to adjust to the culture, reach a level of cultural proficiency, and become effective and productive in their assignments.[194] Training and orientation for international assignments are more common today. It is estimated that 50 percent of companies that send employees overseas are conducting pretraining and orientation.[195] Other countries such as Japan are more committed to the importance of

Reduces severity of culture shock

training for international assignments. This may explain the low (less than 10 percent) failure rate cited for most of Japan's multinational corporations. In Japanese firms, overseas training is typically conducted over a one-year period where international assignees are taught about the culture, customs, and business techniques of the host country.[196]

Outsourcing expatriate training

A growing number of U.S. firms have shown a strong commitment to international training and orientation[197] although increasingly more companies are outsourcing expatriate training.[198] Federal Express sends future expatriates and their families on "familiarization" trips, which also serve as "realistic job previews." Over 70 percent of companies now pay for similar trips. Gillette is a leader in this area with international assignments as a part of its junior trainee program. The objective of the program is to build careers with a global perspective.[199] American Express provides U.S. business school students summer jobs in a foreign location. Colgate-Palmolive trains recent graduates for multiple overseas assignments. Many large international companies have also established health care policies for traveling executives. One new topic for discussion in recent training programs has been safety issues due to increased violence experienced by businesspeople working in foreign countries.[200]

Skills Needed by International Assignees

To design effective training programs to better prepare U.S. managers and employees for assignments overseas, it is important to understand the kinds of skills they will need for international assignments. As we discussed in Chapter 6, in addition to good technical skills, individuals who will be working overseas need to be adaptable and have skills in languages and an understanding of social customs, cultural values, codes of conduct, and motivation and reward systems in the host country.[201] For Middle Eastern assignments, for example, Bechtel places great emphasis on the importance of religion in the culture. Also, expatriates need assistance in the practical aspects of foreign assignments (e.g., housing, schools, currency, and health issues). Visits to the country can aid in reassuring employees and their families about their home, hospitals, dentists, and schools. Training programs should include expatriates and their families, particularly in cultures where women are excluded culturally from doing a variety of things during the day. For instance, in Saudi Arabia, women have many restrictions about dress and proper behaviors.

Five training dimensions

Cross-cultural training programs aim to heighten awareness and understanding along several dimensions, including.[202]

1. *Communication*—Expatriates will need to understand and communicate directly and through nonverbal means in order to listen to the concerns and motives of others.
2. *Decision making*—They will have to develop conclusions and take actions on the basis of inadequate, unreliable, and conflicting information, and to trust their feelings, impressions, and facts.
3. *Commitment*—They will need to become involved in relationships and inspire confidence in others.
4. *Ideals*—They will have to value the causes and objectives of others from a radically different social environment.
5. *Problem solving*—They will have to make decisions needed to achieve common goals.

"Cultural intelligence"

Role of self-efficacy

Understanding cultural influences at the individual level is the key to understanding cultural influences in the workplace. **Cultural self-knowledge** is critical for this understanding.[203] A three-level construct called "cultural intelligence" has been proposed where a person's self-efficacy through social interaction in cross-cultural settings plays a key role in the subsequent effectiveness of such interactions. High self-efficacy results in the initiation of cross-cultural interactions which persist in the face of early failures. In addition, individuals with high self-efficacy engage in problem solving in order to master required skills.[204]

There are several examples of cross-cultural training programs used by organizations. For instance, ARAMCO, a Saudi Arabian corporation, uses an extensive orientation program for employees and their families. The program includes practical housekeeping information such as local transportation, shopping, day-to-day finances, and comparisons of the beliefs and customs of the Saudi and American people. The International Development Agency's prede-parture program for overseas volunteers has several objectives, including the following: communicate respect, be nonjudgmental, display empathy, practice role flexibility, and tolerate ambiguity. Research on cross-cultural training indicates expatriates perform better and are more satisfied with their assignments after such training.[205]

Training Techniques

To teach and acquire the skills necessary to be successful in an international assignment, a variety of training techniques can be used. Procter and Gamble uses several methods to refine language skills and to improve intercultural awareness among international assignees.[206] Their "P&G College" for new and mid-level managers emphasizes globalization issues. In any program developed, it is recommended that the international assignee and his or her family be actively involved in the training to ease the transition and build a supportive environment. It is further suggested that the training should be led by people who have served in the specific country and that the training should begin a year before the employee's move to that country. This is often not done, however, as many companies try to squeeze the training into the last six weeks.[207] To teach employees about area studies or the host country's environment (e.g., geography, climate, political system, customs, religion, labor force, economy, etc.) and the company's international operations, *informational* approaches such as lectures, reading material, videotapes, and movies can be effectively used. One technique, the **cultural assimilator,** was designed as a programmed learning technique to test trainees' knowledge of cultural differences and their understanding of these issues for effective functioning in a foreign culture.[208] To teach trainees about the host country's norms, values, and interpersonal styles so that they will be able to effectively understand and negotiate with host individuals, **experiential approaches** may be beneficial. These might include role-playing and simulations (simulations specific to the culture). Using both a cognitive approach to training (e.g., cultural assimilator) and an experiential approach (e.g., behavior modeling) together has been tried for cross-cultural training. With U.S. government managers, it was discovered that using both techniques together resulted in higher performance than using either technique alone.[209]

Use experiential approaches

Field experiences are recommended to provide a more in-depth view of the host country's customs, values, and behaviors. These experiences can take a variety of forms, including (1) short family trips to the host country, (2) informal meetings with other American families that have lived in the host country, (3) minicultures (i.e., the family visits a multicultural environment in the United States such as an ethnic neighborhood), and (4) host-family surrogates (i.e., a U.S. family from a background similar to the host country has the expatriate family stay with them for a period of time so they can observe the customs). The value of such experiences is to provide a realistic preview of what is to be expected in the overseas position.[210] Finally, *language skill* classes and cassettes are recommended for developing the verbal skills crucial to the interpersonal communication and day-to-day dealings of the family in the host country. In a 12-country study of 3,000 executives, respondents from many countries viewed foreign language skills as critical to a firm's competitive advantage.[211] This should include not only verbal communication skills, but also nonverbal messages and meanings.

Training for Inpatriates

In addition to providing training for expatriates, U.S. firms are increasingly providing training for foreign nationals who are coming to the United States to work. For example, SC Johnson Wax has been bringing employees into the United States for the past 10 years. Eli Lilly and Company brings in about 20 people a year, typically in the fields of science, finance, and marketing. Their training needs are very similar to those of expatriates. To help them adjust, the following tips are offered:[212]

1. Make sure the spouse and children are content with the new location.
2. Make the necessary arrangements to process Social Security numbers in order to help them get a driver's license, a bank account, and credit cards.
3. Provide training with U.S. managers on dealing with people from the other culture.

4. Help them establish credit in the new country.

5. Use relocation counselors to help them with real estate, schools, stores, community activities, and whatever else may be needed to help them get settled.

6. Provide assistance to accompanying spouses (e.g., jobs, educational reimbursements, career guidance, etc.).

7. Provide cross-cultural training to inpatriates and U.S. employees.

8. Offer competitive compensation.

9. Provide language training for employees and their spouses and children.

SUMMARY

Over the years, training has become increasingly popular as a tool for increasing employee and managerial performance in organizations. Most organizations and governmental agencies provide some formal training, and spend millions of dollars doing so. Successful training depends upon a systematic approach involving a careful needs assessment, solid program design, and thorough evaluation of results. Training programs should not be designed as quick fixes for every organizational problem, nor should they rely on faddish techniques. Instead, training should be designed to meet the particular needs of the organization and its employees. It should be viewed as a *continual learning* endeavor by employees and managers to stay current and to anticipate future needs. As greater demands are placed on organizations to remain competitive, firms must ensure that their workforces are motivated and able to take on these challenges. An emphasis on continual training and development is one way this can be done. Employees who receive training not only will be more valuable to their firms, but also will earn 30 percent more than those who don't receive such training.[213] Some employers have established their own corporate universities to conduct their own employee continual learning and education. These firms' educational endeavors (e.g., Motorola University, Disney University, Intel University, BB&T University, Sprint's University of Excellence, Tennessee Valley Authority's University, Job Boss University, Sun Microsystems University) are based on the "Corporate Quality University" model for conveying the corporate value of perpetual learning.[214] This model is a guiding philosophy that argues for involving all employees as well as primary customers and suppliers in continual learning to improve overall productivity. Other goals associated with this philosophy are to link training to the strategic directions of the company, to provide an infrastructure for the organization's training initiatives that minimizes duplication, and to form collaborative alliances with employees, suppliers, customers, and academic institutions.[215] The virtual university created by Air Products and Chemicals is another such example that is now available in 40 countries and connects 18,000 people.[216] Figure 8-14 illustrates how some of the training initiatives we have discussed in this chapter can be aligned with the organization's strategy.

Most successful training programs are those that have strong support from top management. Top-level executives (C-level) have been increasingly showing their support for training in several ways (i.e., making public statements in support of learning, participating as a speaker or instructor in sessions, including the learning objectives as part of individuals' performance goals). For example, Bob Stevens, CEO of Lockheed Martin, kicks off many training programs for his managers by speaking at their programs, and many of his other senior-level executives also participate as speakers. Also, successful firms elevate the importance of the training function by having it run by a senior-level officer of the firm. For example, 95 percent of the ASTD BEST firms reported having a C-level officer responsible for learning. This was significantly different from three years prior when 70 percent of BEST firms had a C-level person responsible for learning.[217]

Generally, if a firm uses its own managers to actually lead some of the training sessions, it results in much higher acceptance and subsequent application of the training.[218] Satyam Computer Services, rated as one of ASTD's BEST firms, had 60 senior leaders volunteer their time to deliver the "Satyam Way" learning program to 28,000 associates in

Continual learning

Corporate universities

Figure 8-14 **Strategic Training and Development Initiatives and Their Implications**

Strategic Training and Development Initiatives	Implications
Diversify the Learning Portfolio	Use new technology such as the Internet for training
	Facilitate informal learning
	Provide more personalized learning opportunities
Expand Who Is Trained	Train customers, suppliers, and employees
	Offer more learning opportunities to nonmanagerial employees
Accelerate the Pace of Employee Learning	Quickly identify needs and provide a high-quality learning solution
	Reduce the time to develop training programs
	Facilitate access to learning resources on an as-needed basis
Improve Customer Service	Ensure that employees have product and service knowledge
	Ensure that employees have skills needed to interact with customers
	Ensure that employees understand their roles and decision-making authority
Provide Development Opportunities and Communicate to Employees	Ensure that employees have opportunities to develop
	Ensure that employees understand career opportunities and personal growth opportunities
	Ensure that training and development addresses employees' needs in current job as well as growth opportunities
Capture and Share Knowledge	Capture insight and information from knowledgeable employees
	Logically organize and store information
	Provide methods to make information available (e.g., resource guides, Web sites)
Align Training and Development with the Company's Strategic Direction	Identify needed knowledge, skills, abilities, or competencies
	Ensure that current training and development programs support the company's strategic needs
Ensure that the Work Environment Supports Learning and Transfer of Training	Remove constraints to learning, such as lack of time, resources, and equipment
	Dedicate physical space to encourage teamwork, collaboration, creativity, and knowledge sharing
	Ensure that employees understand the importance of learning
	Ensure that managers and peers are supportive of training, development, and learning

Source: Based on S. Tannenbaum, "A Strategic View of Organizational Training and Learning," in *Creating, Implementing and Managing Effective Training and Development,* ed. K. Kraiger (San Francisco: Jossey-Bass, 2002), pp. 10–52.

just 75 days.[219] Managers also make a commitment to invest the necessary resources to provide sufficient money and time for training. For example, training is considered a part of the corporate culture and aligned with the strategy of the firm. As ASTD revealed in their State of the Industry report, the BEST firms had clearly defined processes to link learning strategies and initiatives to increases in both individual and organizational performance. Almost all of them reported improvements from training in employee and customer satisfaction, quality of products and services, cycle time, productivity, retention, revenue, and overall profitability.[220]

Integrate training with career development programs

Many of the most successful U.S. companies have also integrated their training programs with their employee career development programs. In the past, training programs have emphasized employer needs for training in the context of the firm's strategic plan. Career development programs tend to emphasize the employee's perspective. Ideally, training and career planning should be well integrated with a focus on the strategic plan of the organization and customer requirements. Chapter 9 elaborates on these issues.

Discussion Questions

1. Why should a training (or HRD) department develop a mission and goals? Why should these goals be tied to the organization's strategic objectives? How would you ensure that this occurs?

2. Why is e-learning so popular today?

3. How would you set up a study to evaluate the effects of an online training program versus a lecture-based approach?

4. Why is it important to understand a systems model of training (needs assessment, development, evaluation)? Which aspects are employers most likely to skip when developing training programs? Why is this a problem?

5. Suppose you are instructed to determine whether a training curriculum is needed to address literacy issues in the workplace. How would you conduct the needs assessment? Be specific about the techniques you would use to conduct an organizational, task, and person analysis.

6. You have been contracted to deliver a training program for employees on generational differences in the workplace. You ask the CEO for the results of the needs assessment indicating that this training is needed. You are informed that no needs assessment was performed. How would you respond to this? If you decide to convince the CEO that a needs assessment must be performed, what would you say? If you decide to design the training program, how would you proceed?

7. Results from a preliminary company needs assessment indicate that managers have a negative opinion of the training offered by the firm, think the training is a waste of time, and are resistant to attending future training by the training staff. What additional information would you want to collect from the managers before sending them to a training program? What methods would you use to collect the information? What recommendations would you offer to the firm to ensure that managers still receive future training?

8. Some people say that employees already understand racial and sexual harassment and that we no longer need training for managers. What do you think? Why is this training needed or not needed? Defend your view. If you were to design a program, what would be the major features of a training program designed to make employees and managers aware of racial and sexual harassment issues in the workplace? Whom would you select to attend such a training program and how would you evaluate the effects of the training? Would such training be effective? Explain your answer.

9. Suppose you are designing a training program for waitresses/waiters at a restaurant. Write several instructional objectives for the training program. Why is it important to prepare objectives before developing and conducting training?

10. Suppose you were going to design a training program for newly hired sales associates for a retail chain. Results from the needs assessment indicate they would need training on company policies and procedures, selling clothing to customers, and handling customer complaints and returns. What learning principles would you build into the program? What training methods would you choose for your training program? Explain your choices.

11. A group of 60 consultants in a large firm has just completed SAP and PeopleSoft training. You have been called in to evaluate the training. What might you do to evaluate the effectiveness of the training at this point (you were not able to collect any pre-measures with this group)? You did hear that another group of 60 consultants will be attending the same training in two months.

12. Describe a number of ideas for building the motivation of trainees *before* and *during* a program. What suggestions would you offer for ensuring that trainees are motivated to transfer their skills *after* they leave the training and are back at their jobs?

13. Why is it important that trainees receive support from others for attending training and applying their training skills? Do you think they often receive the necessary support? Why or why not?

14. Distance learning is becoming the fastest-growing technique for training employees and students. Describe the benefits and drawbacks for distance learning for employees in the workforce. What would be the advantages and disadvantages

of a distance education graduate degree program in human resource management or an MBA?

15. What ideas do you have for training employees who are going on an international assignment? What about for those employees coming back to an organization after an international assignment? What issues would you discuss and what techniques would you recommend for both programs?

16. Why is it important to assess the costs and benefits of training?

17. Why is it important to collect multiple criteria to assess the effectiveness of a training program? What if a company insisted that only reactions needed to be collected? How might you convince them of the importance of also collecting learning, behavioral, and results measures?

18. What do you see as the future trends for the field of training?

Chapter 9

Career Development*

OVERVIEW

The workplace has changed. The business environment is highly turbulent and complex, resulting in ambiguous and contradictory career signals. Individuals, perhaps in self-defense, are altering some of their career-related attitudes and behaviors and becoming ambivalent about their desires and plans for career development. The traditional psychological contract in which an employee entered a firm, worked hard, performed well, was loyal and committed, and thus received ever-greater rewards and job security has been replaced by a new contract based on continual learning and identity change. In short, the organizational career is dead, while the protean career or boundaryless career is alive and flourishing.[1]

Not that long ago, individuals believed that there was *only one* occupation for which each person was best suited, that the best career decision would be made when a person was *young,* and that once a field was chosen, the choice was *irreversible.* They also believed that *interests* were more important in determining career choices than were skills and aptitudes, and that individuals who were successful in a career only moved *upward.*[2] Today, fewer people subscribe to these assumptions about careers. The career as we once knew

*Contributed by Joyce E. A. Russell.

293

it—as a series of upward moves, with steadily increasing income, power, status, and security—has died. Nevertheless, people will always have work lives that unfold over time, offering challenge, growth, and learning. So, if we think of the career as a series of lifelong work-related experiences and personal learnings, it will never die.[3] The career of the 21st century is measured by continual learning and identity changes rather than by chronological age and life stages. With downsizings, delayerings, right-sizings, restructurings, and layoffs, the covenant employees used to believe in between the employer and the employee seems null. Jack Welch, former CEO of General Electric, said there is a one-day contract between employer and employee, in which all that counts is the current value that each party contributes to the relationship. Of course, Jack Welch also strongly believed in providing opportunities at GE for developing and challenging employees.[4]

Interestingly, in a 2005 online survey, 44 percent of senior HR executives predicted that as many as half of their employees would be looking for jobs once the economy improves. Similarly, in the SHRM 2004 U.S. Job Recovery and Retention Poll,[5] they noted that 75 percent of those who were currently employed were either actively or passively job searching. Employees with less than 5 years of work experience and those with 11–20 years of experience were the most likely to be searching for jobs. These findings are of great concern to HR professionals since the defections at their firms could lead to difficulties in serving customers and achieving organizational goals. In addition, given the existence of multiple generations in the workplace (Traditionalists, Baby Boomers, Generation X, and Generation Y), it has become increasingly more challenging to meet the differing needs of employees. Thus, there is ever greater interest in career development, and trainers have never before faced so many challenges in meeting the needs of individual employees and organizations in designing career systems.

To cope in today's turbulent times, it has become increasingly important for both organizations and employees to better address career needs. This chapter describes some current career-related issues of relevance to practicing managers. We begin by describing what individuals and organizations can do to address some of the changing career forces. We then define some of the key career concepts and models, and describe some of the issues involved in designing career development systems in organizations. We describe the various components of career systems and how career systems can be coordinated with other programs in organizations. Finally, we review career issues for a number of targeted groups of employees.

DEFINITIONS

Career means advancement

While most people think the term **career** means "advancement" in an organization, a broader view of career defines it as an "individually perceived sequence of attitudes and behaviors associated with work-related activities and experiences over the span of a person's life."[6] In other words, the term *career* has an *internal* focus and refers to the way an individual views his or her career and has an *external* or objective focus and refers to the actual series of job positions held by the individual.[7] Understanding career development in an organization requires an examination of two processes: how individuals plan and implement their own career goals (career planning) and how organizations design and implement their career development programs (career management). These processes are illustrated in

Career planning

Figure 9-1. As noted, **career planning** is a deliberate attempt by an *individual* to become more aware of his or her own skills, interests, values, opportunities, constraints, choices, and consequences. It involves identifying career-related goals and establishing plans for

Career management

achieving those goals.[8] **Career management** is the *organizational* process of preparing, implementing, and monitoring career plans undertaken by individuals alone or within the organization's career systems.[9]

Career development system

A **career development system** is a formal, organized, planned effort to achieve a balance between individual career needs and organizational workforce requirements.[10] For example, the organization has certain needs for staffing, and employees have needs to effectively utilize their personal skills. A development system is a mechanism for meeting the present and

Figure 9-1 A Model of Organizational Career Development

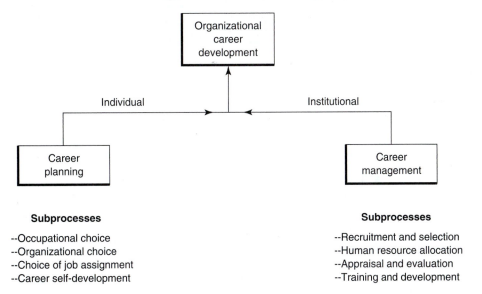

Subprocesses

--Occupational choice
--Organizational choice
--Choice of job assignment
--Career self-development

Subprocesses

--Recruitment and selection
--Human resource allocation
--Appraisal and evaluation
--Training and development

Career: The sequence of a person's work-related activities and behaviors and associated attitudes, values, and aspirations over the span of one's life.

Organizational career development: The outcomes emanating from the interaction of individual career planning and institutional career management processes.

Career planning: A deliberate process for (1) becoming aware of self, opportunities, constraints, choices, and consequences; (2) identifying career-related goals; and (3) programming of work, education, and related developmental experiences to provide the direction, timing, and sequence of steps to attain a specific career goal.

Career management: An ongoing process of preparing, implementing, and monitoring career plans undertaken by the individual alone or in concert with the organization's career system.

Source: T. G. Gutteridge, "Organizational Career Development Systems: The State of the Practice," in *Career Development in Organizations,* D. T. Hall and associates. Copyright © John Wiley & Sons Inc., 1986. Reprinted with permission of John Wiley & Sons, Inc.

future human resource needs of the organization. Stanford Professor Jeffrey Pfeffer looks at formal systems of career development as a key to competitive advantage. Says Pfeffer, "Career systems that emphasize promotions from within not only promote advantages in terms of managing the employment relationship but also make it more likely that strategies for achieving competitive advantage through people will be understood and pursued."[11] A career planning system coordinated with an organization's staffing system will foster a well-integrated system.

Development practices   **Career development** practices have been shown to enhance the career satisfaction of employees and to improve organizational effectiveness.[12] It may be difficult, however, to completely integrate individual and organizational career efforts because the rate at which an individual grows and develops may not parallel an organization's needs. For example, many of the Baby Boomers in the workforce are interested in advancing in their present positions, yet are finding those positions to be scarce given the thinning out of management jobs in organizations due to downsizings. As a result, Baby Boomers held an average of 10.2 jobs from age 18 to age 38.[13] With all the recent changes in organizations (downsizings, mergers, divestitures), it has become even more important to try to integrate the needs of employers with those of employees.

This chapter emphasizes the importance of understanding career development in organizations by examining the interaction of individual and organizational career processes. Of particular value is an understanding of the role HR managers must play to design career development systems. One model focuses on a dynamic interaction of the individual and the **The "matching" process**   organization over time through a **"matching" process.** If the matching process works well, the organization and the individual will benefit. The organization may experience increased productivity, higher organizational commitment, and long-range effectiveness, and the employee may have greater satisfaction, security, and personal development.[14]

IMPLICATIONS OF WORKPLACE CHANGES FOR INDIVIDUALS AND ORGANIZATIONS

What Should Individuals Do?

Predictors of future salary

Given the changing views of careers in organizations, what should individuals do to be prepared for future jobs, and why is this important? Assuming salary is a good measure of career advancement, one recent review provides some helpful guidelines for predicting future success.[15] In terms of what an individual can control, the most important predictors of future salary are (in order of importance): (1) education level; (2) political knowledge and skills; (3) work experience; (4) hours worked; and (5) sponsorship by a colleague. The following tips are offered for individuals regarding their careers.

- The focus today should be on an individual's *employability.* Individuals should not worry about holding on to a specific job, but rather should make sure they have developed the competitive skills needed in the marketplace. They need to have *portable competencies.*[16]

- Employees need to *take more control of their careers* than they ever have before and look out for their own best career interests. Not all employees, however, have typically done this, especially those outside the United States. For example, in Iceland individuals generally do not engage in career self-management to any great extent.[17]

- Employees must develop new and better personal skills of *self-assessment and career planning,* especially because organizations do not have the resources to completely plan individuals' careers.[18] The protean or boundaryless career is one that is driven by the person, not the organization. Pursuing this new career model requires a high level of self-awareness and personal responsibility.

- Individuals need to *set career goals and clearly define* what they are interested in (e.g., talents, preferences).

- Especially during the early career period, employees need to maintain a *technical specialty.* They must also be careful not to become obsolete or too narrow in their functional expertise.

- Individuals must invest in *reputation building* or image enhancement to illustrate success and suitability for jobs.[19]

- Individuals will need to develop their *collaboration skills* because the use of project teams in organizations will continue to increase.[20]

- Employees will need to develop multiple *networking and peer learning* relationships. This will also help them to find new jobs during difficult economic times.

- The new career will be a continual learning process and necessitate that the individual develop self-knowledge, *adaptability, and flexibility.* Individuals will need to be adaptable to changing job requirements.[21]

- Employees will need to periodically *solicit feedback* to appraise how they are doing relative to their career goals.

- Individuals now need to commit to *lifelong learning* to keep their skills relevant, whether by additional schooling or taking on new assignments.

What Should Organizations Do?

Organizations likewise need to become more active in implementing career development programs. Companies are designing career programs in an effort to decrease employee turnover, prevent job burnout and obsolescence, and improve the quality of employees' work lives. Child care, concierge services, and other employee support programs will increase as employers compete to attract and keep qualified employees in what is predicted to be the most severe shortage of skilled labor in history. The top concerns among employees today are: burnout, lack of career growth, feeling disconnected from the firm, and a general distrust or lack of confidence in leadership's ability to drive the organization forward.[22] A number of organizations such as Chevron, CIGNA, Sears Information Services, Texaco, Turner Broadcasting, the Internal Revenue Service, and Marriott International participated

Recommendations for creating a career-resilient workforce

in a conference specifically to share their strategies for creating a career-resilient workforce.[23] A few recommendations for organizations are provided below:[24]

- It is the employee's responsibility to manage his or her own career, yet it is the employer's responsibility to provide employees with the *tools and opportunities* to enhance their skills. The end result should be a career-resilient workforce, one that has self-reliant workers who are capable of reinventing themselves to keep up with the fast pace of organizational changes.[25]

- Create an *environment for continual learning* by supporting and rewarding employee development and learning (e.g., professional associations, training, schooling). Some organizations such as Motorola, Ford, and Intel are especially effective at this.[26]

- Provide *opportunities for self-assessment.* Have career counselors and career resource centers available.

- Provide opportunities for additional *training,* including orientation, core training, and computer-based training.[27]

- Have managers trained as *coaches and mentors* to assist employees.

- Encourage employees to create individual development plans that meet their personal career needs and the firm's strategic goals. Employees at Checkfree Services, Inc., create and implement their Individual Development Plans after attending an intense week-long training program called the Customer Solutions University.[28] Similarly, all bank employees at BB&T have a personal development plan that oulines objectives, strengths, and opportunities for growth.[29]

- Assist employees with striking *balances between their work and nonwork* lives (e.g., child care, elder care, flexible work arrangements leisure pursuits).

- Use *reward systems* that support the organization's career development strategy.

- Make sure the career programs are *integrated with other human resource programs* (e.g., training, performance appraisal, selection).

- Before outsourcing employees try to *redeploy* the current workforce to teach them the new skills needed.

IMPORTANCE OF UNDERSTANDING CAREER DEVELOPMENT

Initiatives that could have undesired consequences

Today's competitive business environment has forced organizations to restructure and downsize, resulting in fewer hierarchical levels and traditional promotional opportunities for employees. At the same time, there is increased pressure to improve productivity or risk falling prey to larger corporations. The creation of new technologies has required that individuals update their skills or else become outdated. A number of organizational change initiatives could have unintended and undesired consequences for individuals. These include the following:

- **Downsizing**—jobs are cut from the organization.
- **Delayering**—jobs are reclassified more broadly, yet old reporting lines exist to maintain managerial control.
- **Decentralizing**—responsibilities are reassigned from the corporate centralized function to functions in each location or at lower levels.
- **Reorganization**—companies may be refocusing around core competencies.
- **Cost-reduction strategies**—the same work is done with fewer resources.
- **IT innovations**—how the work is done is altered due to advances in information technology.
- **Competency remeasurement**—skill sets required of employees are redefined or measured in different ways.
- **Performance-related pay**—pay is linked to performance and used as a motivator.

Figure 9-2

Organizational Change Initiatives and Their Effects on Careers and Individuals

Organizational Change Form	Effects on Jobs and Careers	Psychological Impact on Individuals	Remedial and Mitigating Strategies
Downsizing	Job security	Anxiety	Openness and involvement
Delayering	Plateauing	Lowered self-esteem	Delegation and self-management
Decentralization	Segmentation and fragmentation	Competitive behaviors	Team building and mobility
Reorganization	Displacement	Frustration	Self-appraisal and pathfinding
Cost-reduction	Work intensification	Stress	Time and task management
IT innovation	Deskilling	Lowered self-efficacy	Reskilling
Competency remeasurement	Obsolescence	Self-defense	Coaching and mentoring
Performance-related pay	Individualism and politics	Low trust behaviors	Team-based objectives and feedback

Source: N. Nicholson, "Career Systems in Crisis: Change and Opportunity in the Information Age," *Academy of Management Executive* 10, no. 4 (1996), p. 43.

Figure 9-2 depicts some of the organizational change initiatives, their effects on jobs and careers, their psychological impact on individuals, and the necessary strategies to remedy or mitigate the negative effects.

Understanding career development is also important today due to the changing workforce. Current labor force changes have included a greater proportion of working mothers and members of multiple generations (e.g., Traditionalists, Baby Boomers, Gen X, Gen Y) who are competing for a limited number of jobs. In addition, employees have changed their values such that now they want more self-fulfillment in work and to be in charge of managing their own career planning. They want opportunities for growth in their careers and to expand their knowledge and skills. They also demand well-balanced lives in which comparable value is placed on work, family, and leisure. Generation X employees seem less interested in climbing the corporate ladder, acquiring fancy titles, or spending their careers in one type of work or job. Rather, they want to explore and do different kinds of jobs where they can express their own individual values.[30] Similarly, Generation Y employees have their own perspectives and views about work (i.e., they want to engage in meaningful work that will have an impact on society).

EEO law and career development programs

Social and generational changes are increasing societal pressures on organizations to be more creative and responsible. Corporations are now more likely to offer child care programs, flexible work scheduling, and parental leave time. As discussed in Chapter 3, increased litigation as a consequence of new laws such as the Age Discrimination in Employment Act, the Americans with Disabilities Act, the Civil Rights Act, and the Equal Pay Act is forcing companies to take care to avoid discrimination in their career development programs.

A greater emphasis will be placed on designing and implementing relevant *career development systems* in organizations. Organizations will have to find more creative ways to help people develop since employees will not be able to rely on organizational growth to provide them new career opportunities and promotions. Line managers will need to provide career counseling to employees, and HR managers must offer training for managers in career coaching skills.[31] For example, the Coca-Cola and Ford career systems require training for all managers in how to conduct career development discussions with employees in the context of performance appraisal. The intention is to make managers more accountable for the development of their employees.[32]

Figure 9-3   **Twenty Questions: A Career Development Culture Index**

Instructions: If your answer is yes to a question, make a check mark in the space to the left of the number of that item. See the scoring instructions at the end of the exercise.

—————— 1. Does senior management use work assignments and work relationships to develop employees?

—————— 2. Do they do it consciously or intentionally for developing people (as opposed to doing it only for business purposes)?

—————— 3. Are these career development activities part of the business plan for the employee's unit?

—————— 4. Is the organization's purpose expressed in human terms with which employees can identify?

—————— 5. Does top management value employee development?

—————— 6. Is career development owned by senior line management (as opposed to being seen as owned by HR)?

—————— 7. Is diversity actively promoted by senior line management?

—————— 8. Is employee development done by senior line management for the explicit purpose of supporting the business strategy?

—————— 9. Are new forms of employee mobility being used (such as cross-functional, cross-business teams)?

—————— 10. Is personal development or self-knowledge (for example, 360-degree feedback) promoted?

—————— 11. Is career development part of the overall corporate strategy?

—————— 12. Is there a strong succession planning process, which puts emphasis on development as well as identification?

—————— 13. Do employees have significant input to plans for their future development and assignments?

—————— 14. Does career development include opportunities for risk and learning (adaptability)?

—————— 15. Does career development include personal (identity) learning as well as task learning?

—————— 16. Do most people believe that career development should also take family and personal balance needs into account?

—————— 17. Is there general agreement in management about whether historical career development approaches are appropriate for the future?

—————— 18. Is it relatively easy for employees to access information about other job opportunities in the company?

—————— 19. Are employees encouraged to be empowered and self-directed in their careers?

—————— 20. (The acid test): Are individual employees aware of your organization's career development activities?

Scoring:

Add up the number of checks (symbolizing "yes" to the item).

Key: 17 or more checks . . . . Outstanding

         10–16 . . . . Good

         6–9 . . . . Fair

         <5 . . . . Work needed!

Source: Z. B. Leibowitz, C. Farren, and B. L. Kaye, *Designing Career Development Systems.* Copyright © John Wiley & Sons 1986. Reprinted with permission of John Wiley & Sons, Inc.

DESIGNING CAREER DEVELOPMENT SYSTEMS

An effective **career development system** integrates *individual career planning* endeavors and *organizational career management* activities. Today, corporations' career development programs (Lincoln Electric, Wal-Mart, IBM, Bell Atlantic, Xerox) involve career assessment by employees with the manager serving as a facilitator and the organization providing a supportive environment. HR specialists can help organizations determine if their firm has a culture that supports career development by administering the Career Development Culture Index shown in Figure 9-3. Low scores reflect ineffective (or nonexistent) career development systems. High scores reflect an effective system likely to correlate with lower voluntary turnover rates.

Benefits of Career Development Systems

Some of the benefits of a career development system for employees, managers, and the organization are presented in Figure 9-4. Managers can benefit from career development programs by being better able to communicate with and develop their staff. Employees may benefit from a career development system by acquiring a deepened appreciation of their own skills and career possibilities and assuming a greater responsibility for managing their own careers. The organization may gain from a career development system by increased employee loyalty, improved communication throughout the organization, lower turnover rates, and strengthened human resource systems. For example, the Federal National Mortgage Association reduced turnover of its sales force by 50 percent after instituting a supervisory training program on career planning.

Figure 9-4   **Benefits of a Career Development System**

Managers/Supervisors	Employees	Organization
Increased skill in managing own careers	Helpful assistance with career decisions	Better use of employee skills
Greater retention of valued employees	Enrichment of present job and increased job satisfaction	Dissemination of information at all organization levels
Better communication between manager and employee	Better communication between employee and manager	Better communication within organization as a whole
More realistic staff and development planning	More realistic goals and expectations	Greater retention of valued employees
Productive performance-appraisal discussions	Better feedback on performance	Expanded public image as a people developer
Greater understanding of the organization	Current information on the firm and the future	Increased effectiveness of personnel systems
Enhanced reputation as a people developer	Greater personal responsibility for career	Clarification of goals of the organization

Source: Z. B. Leibowitz, C. Farren, and B. L. Kaye, *Designing Career Development Systems.* Copyright © John Wiley & Sons 1986. Reprinted with permission of John Wiley & Sons, Inc.

To maintain the career development program, it is essential to integrate it into the organization's ongoing employee training and development strategy. The program should be evaluated as needed to determine revisions and to keep the continued support of top management. Figure 9-5 shows some of the criteria that may be used to evaluate the program that may indicate success. Success can be measured by individual and organizational goal attainment, the actions that are completed (e.g., use of career tools), and changes in performance measures and attitudes.

Figure 9-5   **Indicators of Career Program Effectiveness**

Goal attainment

Achievement of prespecified individual and organizational objectives on qualitative as well as quantitative dimensions

Individual	Organizational
Exercise greater self-determination	Improve career communications between employees and supervisors
Achieve greater self-awareness	Improve individual/organizational career match
Acquire necessary organizational career information	Enhance organization's image
Enhance personal growth and development	Respond to EEO and affirmative action pressures
Improve goal-setting capability	Identify pool of management talent

Actions or events completed

1. Employee use of career tools (participation in career workshops, enrollment in training courses)
2. Career decisions conducted
3. Employee career plans implemented
4. Career actions taken (promotions, cross-functional moves)
5. Management successors identified

Changes in performance indexes

1. Reduced turnover rates
2. Lower employee absenteeism
3. Improved employee morale
4. Improved employee performance ratings
5. Reduced time to fill job openings
6. Increased promotion from within

Attitudes/perceptions

1. Evaluation of career tools and practices (participant's reaction to career workshop, supervisor's evaluation of job-posting system)
2. Perceived benefits of career system
3. Employees' expression of career feelings (responses to career attitude survey)
4. Evaluation of employee career planning skills
5. Adequacy of organizational career information

Source: T. G. Gutteridge, "Organizational Career Development Systems: The State of the Practice," in *Career Development in Organizations*, D. T. Hall and associates. Copyright © John Wiley & Sons Inc., 1986. Reprinted with permission of John Wiley & Sons, Inc.

Limited research in effects of career development programs

Research on the effectiveness of career development programs is sparse, yet promising. One study found that 44 percent of administrators of career development programs for Fortune 500 companies regarded them as "very helpful."[33] IBM evaluated the effectiveness of its career development workshop and found improvements in the participants' abilities and responsibilities for their own career planning. They also discovered that employee perceptions of better job opportunities (defined as opportunities to use new and different skills) had increased substantially.[34] Pratt & Whitney reported that its turnover rate for new engineers had decreased by 25 percent after instituting a career development program.

Of course, measures of program success may vary depending on whom you are asking in the organization. Employees, managers, organizations, and the HR staff may differ in the specific factors they view as indicative of program success. For example, employees may say that a career program is effective if it organizes a way for them to plan and manage their career interests or offers them opportunities to discuss their career decisions with their supervisors. Managers may view a career program as successful if it offers them staffing flexibility or helps them to identify pools of qualified employees to meet forecasted openings. Organizations may find a program to be useful if it increases the attractiveness of the organization to potential employees (recruits) or raises the motivation and productivity of current employees or enhances retention of employees. Finally, the HR staff may determine that a program is successful if it has credibility or enhances the reputation of the career or training department with line managers.[35]

COMPONENTS OF CAREER DEVELOPMENT SYSTEMS

Most effective programs use both individual planning and organizational career management

A variety of career development components (i.e., activities and tools) exist for use in organizations. HR managers should be familiar with these components, since they often serve as internal or external consultants responsible for designing the career development system. Some of the activities and tools are for *individual career planning,* and others are commonly used for *organizational career management.*[36] The most effective career development programs use both types.

Some of the more popular career development activities are listed in Figure 9-6. These programs were cited as having the greatest positive impact on employees' job satisfaction, communication, retention, work motivation, views or image of the firm, and commitment to the firm.[37] No matter which tools are used for career development, what is important is that employees develop their own individualized career development plans. Raychem, for example, requires every employee to have a learning or development plan.[38]

Development programs are retention tools

Career development programs are effective *retention* tools and are quickly becoming an employee expectation. Larger corporations began to develop CD programs in the late 1980s and early 1990s, and they are beginning to appear in smaller firms. Organizations recognize that they can link their career programs to specific business objectives while developing their employees to meet their goals. At the same time, employees are kept abreast of changing technology and are developing career-related skills. Career development programs tell employees that the organization values and respects them by investing in their future career growth.[39]

Self-Assessment Tools

Self-assessments are usually among the first techniques implemented by organizations in their career development efforts. Thus, it is important for managers to become familiar with the different self-assessment and career exploration instruments available. Typically, individuals completing self-assessment exercises for career-planning purposes go through a process where they think through their life roles, interests, skills, and work attitudes and preferences. They try to plan their short- and long-term goals, develop action plans to meet those goals, and identify any obstacles and opportunities that might be associated with them.[40] Hewlett-Packard employees at the Colorado Springs Division complete a variety of

Figure 9-6

Types of Organizational Career Development Interventions

Self-assessment tools
    Career planning workshops
    Career workbooks
Individual counseling
Information services
    Job-posting systems
    Skills inventories
    Career ladders and paths
    Career resource centers
Organizational assessment programs
    Assessment centers
    Psychological testing
    Promotability forecasts
    Succession planning
Developmental programs
    Assessment centers
    Job rotation programs
    Tuition refund plans
    Internal training programs
    External training seminars
    Formal mentoring programs
Career programs for special target groups
    Fast-track or high-potential employees
    Terminated employees (outplacement programs)
    Supervisors and managers
    Senior-level executives
    Professional employees
    Technical employees
    Women
    Minorities
    Employees with disabilities
New employees (early-career issues)
    Employee orientation programs
    Anticipatory socialization programs
    Realistic recruitment
Middle-career and older-career issues
    Programs to combat obsolescence or plateauing
    Workshops on older-worker issues
    Preretirement programs
    Incentives for early retirement
Programs to assist employed spouses and parents
    Policies on hiring couples
    Work–family programs
    Part-time work
    Job-sharing programs
    Relaxed policies on transfers and travel
    Flexible work arrangements
    Paid maternity/paternity leave
    Child-care services
    Adoption benefits

self-assessment exercises, including a written self-assessment, vocational interest tests (e.g., Strong Interest Inventory), and 24-hour diaries before meeting with their managers for career counseling.[41] Six months after the course, 40 percent of the participants had planned internal career moves and 37 percent had already advanced to new positions in the firm. Of those, 74 percent stated that the career-development program played a critical part in their job change. Two tools often used to assist individuals in their self-assessments include career-planning workshops and career workbooks.

Career-Planning Workshops

After individuals complete their self-assessments, they may share their findings with other individuals in career workshops. For example, General Electric provides career training to its engineering staff followed by periodic meetings to share results.[42] In general, most workshops use experiential exercises in a structured, participative group format to educate individuals on how to prepare and follow through on their career strategies. A group format allows participants to receive feedback from others so they can check the reality of their plans and consider other alternatives. In addition, workshops are beneficial in helping employees gain greater self-awareness and insight and learn more about career opportunities in the organization. TVA offered career planning workshops to many of its employees, and employees found them to be helpful in better understanding their career needs and insights.[43] At NASA Goddard Space Flight Center, career awareness workshops are conducted to educate employees about alternative career paths and to provide counseling to them. Eli Lilly and Company in Indianapolis uses workshops with executives and managers to give them feedback on their own career concepts and motives, as well as advice on how to provide career counseling to their subordinates.[44]

Career Workbooks

Career workbooks consist of questions and exercises designed to guide individuals to figure out their strengths and weaknesses, job and career opportunities, and necessary steps for reaching their goals. One popular example of a generic career workbook is the annual book "What Color Is Your Parachute?"[45] Individuals use this manual to learn about their career possibilities since it provides suggestions for job hunting and making career changes. Many workbooks are tailor-made for a particular company and can be completed in several sessions. If "homegrown" workbooks are used, they should contain a statement of the organization's career policy, a description of the career options in the organization, and the strategies available for obtaining career information. The workbooks should also illustrate the organization's structure, career paths, and job qualifications for jobs along the career ladders.[46] Check out the self-assessment tool available through **O*NET**. In Chapter 4, we discussed the model that was the basis for the **O*NET** development (go to www.onetcenter.org). There are also other Internet-based career services available for free, often through university and corporate career centers (e.g., Career Leader). These are useful for finding jobs, posting résumés, networking, and learning about careers. For example, the **Talent Alliance** is an Internet-based resource cosponsored by member companies that provides support for the self-initiated, self-paced career exploration. Personal inventory tools prompt self-discovery of leadership style, motivation, technical skills, and work context.[47]

Individual Counseling

One common career development activity is career counseling. Individual career counseling helps employees understand their career goals in one-on-one counseling sessions using workbooks and other self-assessment exercises [48] and through discussions of the employees' interests, goals, current job activities and performance, and career objectives. Because the counseling sessions often are conducted on a one-on-one basis, they may be very time-consuming and not as cost-effective as other career development methods.

Generally, career counseling is provided by the human resource, training, or career department, although some organizations hire professional counselors and others use line managers as career counselors. PricewaterhouseCoopers assigns all employees, including partners, coaches to assist them in job-related and career concerns.

If supervisors are used in career-counseling sessions, they should be given clearly defined roles and training in career issues, performance evaluation, and listening and communication skills. In addition, they should be required to meet with their subordinates on a consistent basis to review career goals and plans and to assist employees in developing their career objectives. Supervisors should be told that part of their job is to help employees develop. They should be rewarded for their efforts as career coaches to encourage them to devote the necessary time to this role. For example, at Federal National Mortgage Association and at Baxter Health Care Corporation, managers' bonuses are directly linked to the career development programs for women and minorities. Both companies identify key females and minorities early in their careers and develop specific plans for them for acquiring the necessary skills in advancement. In general, supervisors can be valuable sources of career information for employees. Some tips for helping managers be more effective as coaches include:[49]

■ Practice active listening and paraphrasing to make sure you truly understand what the employee is saying.

■ Support the employee's learning by asking him or her about the actions he or she has taken and how successful they were.

■ Help the employee work on easier career goals first, then more difficult ones.

■ Help the employee write out scripts and role-play possible scenarios (e.g., interviewing for jobs).

■ Provide positive feedback as employees take relevant career actions (e.g., attending career workshops).

Information Services

Internal communication systems are often used by organizations to alert employees to employment opportunities at all levels, including upward, downward, and lateral moves. They may also be used to keep ongoing records of employees' skills, knowledge, and work experiences and preferences. These records are valuable for pointing out possible candidates for job openings in the company. Several systems commonly used for compiling and communicating career-related information include job-posting systems, skills inventories, career ladders and paths, and career resource centers.

Job-Posting Systems

Job-posting systems are commonly used by companies to inform employees about openings in the organization using Web sites, bulletin boards, newsletters, computer systems (e-mail), and other company publications. While they serve an informational purpose, postings also may be useful as a motivational tool. They imply that the organization is more interested in selecting employees from within the company than from outside the organization. This is a sound strategy since one of the **"High-Performance Work Characteristics"** is a policy of promoting managers from within the organization. Guidelines for effective job-posting systems include:

Promoting from within is an HPWC

■ Posting all permanent promotion and transfer opportunities for at least one week before recruiting outside the organization.

■ Outlining minimum requirements for the position (including specific training courses).

■ Describing decision rules that will be used.

■ Making application forms available.

■ Informing all applicants how and when the job was filled.

It is also important that all employees have access to the job postings. At Ford, a training matrix is available for each job family in which specific courses are linked as optional or recommended for a particular job classification. Raychem has created an internal network, called the Internal Information Interview Network, of more than 360 people within the firm who are willing to talk with any employees who want to learn more about their jobs.[50] Company intranets can be useful for ensuring all employees have access to job postings. Employees can simply log in to the site, view positions by job title and location, and apply for the position immediately. The use of an intranet can be particularly useful when a collective bargaining agreement requires job openings be made available to employees before hiring outside the organization. If the firm's Web site is used to list jobs, it is important that employees can find those jobs on the Web site and that the application process is easy to use.

Skills Inventories

Skills inventories are company files of data on employees' skills, abilities, experiences, and education that are often computerized. They may contain comprehensive records of employees' work histories, qualifications, education degrees and major fields of study, accomplishments, training completed, skill and knowledge ratings, career objectives, geographical preferences, and anticipated retirement dates.[51] Skills inventories are created to help organizations know the characteristics of their workforce so they can effectively utilize employees' skills. They also reveal shortages of critical skills, which is useful for indicating training needs. AT&T has a department, Resource Link, that operates as an internal temporary services unit to meet the variable workforce needs of the company's business units and divisions.[52]

Career Ladders and Career Paths

Organizations usually map out steps (job positions) that employees might follow over time. These steps are used to document possible patterns of job movement, including vertical or upward moves and lateral or cross-functional moves. Illustrations of career paths and ladders are helpful for answering employees' questions about career progression and future job opportunities in the organization. For example, General Motors groups jobs by job families such as HR, engineering, clerical, systems professional, and so forth, to show employees the career possibilities in each of the various job fields. ARCO (Atlantic Richfield Company) has a lot of lateral movement for positions. They make special arrangements for employees who want to shift career paths.[53]

Typically, the description of a career path or ladder illustrates a career plan complete with the final goal, intermediate steps, and timetables for reaching the goal. In addition, the qualifications necessary to proceed to the next position are specified as is any minimum time required prior to advancing. For example, in an academic position, the path may look like Instructor → Assistant Professor → Associate Professor → Professor. At a consulting firm, the path may look like Consultant → Senior Consultant → Manager → Partner. An employee may be required to spend a minimum amount of time in each level and gain increasing responsibilities before moving to the next higher level.

"Fast-track" employees

Common in many organizations is the development of career paths for "fast-track" employees that outline the series of career moves that will prepare them for upper management. In recent years, many companies have developed multiple or dual career paths.[54] This is becoming more common in firms hiring professional employees (e.g., scientists, engineers). Previously, if an engineer wanted to advance in a firm, he or she had to eventually move into a management position to move up the corporate ladder. Today, many organizations (e.g., National Security Agency) offer dual career ladders so that technical employees and professionals can advance through either a management track or a scientist track. This enables them to remain in a technical, professional field yet still be able to advance in the firm to a higher status and higher-paying position.

Career Resource Center and Other Communication Formats

One of the least expensive approaches for providing career information is setting up a career resource center. A center consists of a small library set up to distribute career development materials such as reference books, learning guides, videos, and self-study tapes. Universities are well known for having career centers where students can obtain company brochures and videos and career books and gain access to computers to research firms on the Internet. Kodak has three internal career services, "Kodak Career Services," which consist of a career library of tapes, books, and career counselors.[55] Other methods for communicating organizational career information and programs may include the use of flyers, brochures, newsletters, and manuals. Today, with the increasing use of computers, many firms are placing career resource information on their company's intranet. The program at PricewaterhouseCoopers, called MYC or Managing Your Career, enables employees to directly ask questions about career issues. Sun Microsystems, Apple Computer, and Raychem have centers set up with career specialists where employees can work on self-assessments, receive counseling, check on internal and external job openings, and attend seminars on networking or interviewing. Their centers are highly visible and easily accessible, which conveys to employees that the firms want their career centers to be used. Other companies have formed partnerships to enable their employees to receive career assistance.

Organizational Assessment Programs

Assessment programs consist of methods for evaluating employees' potential for growth and development in the organization. For example, Johnson & Johnson has used career assessment to facilitate the staffing and development of special "tiger teams," which are formed to speed up the development of high-priority new products.[56] Some of the more popular assessment programs include assessment centers, psychological testing, 360-degree appraisal (described in Chapter 7), promotability forecasts, and succession planning.

Assessment Centers

In addition to their use as decision-making tools, assessment centers are popular as developmental tools. One survey found that 43 percent of surveyed firms used assessment centers as part of their career development programs.[57] AT&T, JCPenney, Sears Roebuck & Co., IBM, GE, TVA, Bendix, and Pratt & Whitney are among the companies using assessment centers for development as well as employee decision making.[58] "Assessment centers are particularly predictive of advancement criteria such as career progress, salary advancement, long-term promotion, and potential development." As described in Chapter 6, participants in an assessment center engage in a variety of situational exercises, including tests, interviews, in-baskets, leaderless group discussions, and business games. Their performance on these exercises is evaluated by a panel of trained raters (usually middle- to upper-level managers), and they are given in-depth developmental feedback on their strengths and weaknesses. This feedback is often very useful for improving their own insights about their skills and for helping them outline realistic future career goals and plans.

Psychological Assessment

Diagnostic tests and other inventories may be used for self-assessment or with career counseling. They consist of written tests and questionnaires that help individuals determine their vocational interests, personality types, work attitudes, and other personal characteristics that may reveal their career needs and preferences. In addition to **O*NET,** useful tools are the Strong Vocational Interest Inventory, the Myers-Briggs Type Indicator, various measures of the Big-Five personality factors, and the Kuder Preference Schedule, which assesses preferences for certain jobs and job characteristics.

Promotability Forecasts

Forecasts are used by the organization to make early identifications of individuals with exceptionally high career potential. Once individuals are identified, they are given relevant developmental experiences (e.g., attending conferences, training) to groom them for higher positions. Several companies now have such programs for women and minorities in an effort to get greater female and minority representation at higher managerial levels. Others, such as AT&T, track the progress of high-potential managers and provide them with developmental assignments.[59] It is important that promotability forecasts do not

Audit for possible EEO problems

exclude employees based upon factors protected under Title VII, such as age, sex, or race. HR must be diligent in ensuring that all employees are treated fairly and equally. The 80 percent rule discussed in Chapter 3 is a good internal auditing measure for assessing potential legal trouble with forecasting.

Succession Planning

Succession planning involves having senior executives periodically review their top executives and those in the next-lower level to determine several backups for each senior position. This is important because it often takes years of grooming to develop effective senior managers and there is a critical shortage in companies of middle and top leaders for the next five years, especially as Baby Boomers retire. Organizations will need to create pools of candidates with high leadership potential. A number of firms are concerned and proactive about developing their "talent pipeline." For example, Lockheed Martin and Microsoft are recruiting top talent and aggressively promoting "high-potential" employees; matching leaders with positions; providing challenging cross-function experiences; and rewarding employees who bring the greatest value to the organization.[60]

In addition to executive level succession planning, organizations can use succession planning for mid- to upper-level management positions. Management succession can create a career ladder for employees and can be a planning reprieve for the anticipated brain drain as the Baby Boomers retire. At Lawrence Livermore National Laboratory, they made some recent changes to the succession pool program. A greater emphasis was placed on coaching, challenging assignments, and learning options at every level to help develop emerging and existing managers for current and future leadership roles.[61]

Succession planning critical for small business

Succession planning can be informal or formal. For informal succession planning, the individual manager identifies and grooms his or her own replacement. This is more prevalent in smaller firms. In fact, one survey of 800 small business owners found that only 25 percent have a succession plan and that only 50 percent of them have even written it down.[62] Succession planning for family businesses seems to be especially important for the firm to remain successful.[63] Formal succession planning involves an examination of strategic (long-range) plans and HR forecasts and a review of the data on all potential candidates. The objective is to identify employees with potential and increase managerial depth as well as to promote from within the company. In addition, it includes determining and clarifying the requirements of the managerial position and developing plans for how future managerial requirements will be met. It involves behavioral profile matching between the individual managers' skills, behavioral flexibility, and adaptability and the organization's future needs as depicted by the organization's strategic plan.[64] In one study of Fortune 500 firms with succession plans, components used in the plans included identification of high-potential employees, updated lists of possible replacements, performance appraisals of all employees, and individual development plans and management development programs. The factors rated as most important in selecting specific candidates for grooming included past job performance, past positions or prior employment, perceived credibility, area of expertise and career path, and values and attitudes.[65]

There are many benefits of having a formal succession planning system. In a survey of Fortune 500 firms, succession planning programs were perceived to have a positive impact on an organization's profitability, organizational culture, and organizational efficiency.[66] Organizations also benefit from increased employee commitment, increased retention, and higher corporate performance. Some of the general benefits of a succession planning program are listed in Figure 9-7.

Programs needs top management support

Regardless of what type of succession planning program is used (formal or informal), most successful programs obtain the support and commitment of top managers.[67] For example, Schwan Foods, one of the recipients of ASTD's BEST Awards, credits its success in building future leaders to the CEO who expresses a strong commitment to employee training and leadership development.[68] Usually, committees of top managers work together to

Figure 9-7
Benefits of Formal Succession Planning

- Provides a specific connection to business and strategic planning.
- Provides a more systematic basis to judge the risks of making particular succession and development moves.
- Assists in developing systematized succession plans that fit with a distinct trend to codify, wherever possible, more general and comprehensive corporate planning actions.
- Reduces randomness of managerial development movements.
- Helps to anticipate problems before they get started—and thereby avoids awkward or dysfunctional situations.
- Increases managerial depth, which can be called on as needed.
- Provides a logical approach for locking succession planning into the process of human resource planning—connecting formats (data, timing) with process (judgments, discussions, analyses).
- Facilitates integration of the many components of human resource planning after having done many of these separately in the past.
- Improves the identification of high-potential and future leaders.
- Exploits the use of computer power or capabilities to improve succession planning formats and processes further.
- Broadens the use of cross-functional development techniques to improve competencies and quality of decision making.
- Stimulates inquiry into the fit of succession planning with the philosophy of the organization.
- Improves internal promotion opportunities.
- Overcomes the limitations of reactive management approaches and goes to planned management of managerial positions.
- Establishes a logical basis for choices among qualified candidates.
- Improves fulfillment of EEO objectives.
- Makes informal but critical criteria (e.g., "fit") more explicit.

Source: E. H. Burack, *Creative Human Resource Planning and Applications: A Strategic Approach*, 1988, p. 167. Reprinted with permission.

identify high-potential candidates and then outline developmental activities for them. They may include a formal assessment of the performance and potential of candidates and written individual developmental plans for candidates. Of course, with the current turbulent times in organizations (i.e., with downsizings, layoffs, mergers), some argue that it is foolish to spend a lot of time on succession planning efforts or identifying candidates for jobs that may not even exist in the future.[69] In addition, the firm's strategic goals may change, making some candidates, previously groomed for top positions, no longer the right choice.[70] For example, AT&T and IBM relied on succession-planning procedures that resulted in having the right kinds of leaders for the wrong times.[71] The individual's own aspirations for moving into senior management positions have only recently been considered when making succession plans, despite the obvious importance of this.[72] It is clear that each organization has to weigh the pros and cons of providing a succession-planning system. In general, in most organizations, a succession-planning system seems to be highly beneficial.[73]

Developmental Programs

Developmental programs consist of **skills assessment** and training programs that organizations may use to develop their employees for future positions. Development programs can be internal and run by the human resource staff, or be offered externally in the form of seminars and workshops. DuPont offers in-house seminars on various job functions and hands out a list of employee contacts with whom individuals can follow up to find out more about various job functions.[74] Other corporations have three- to four-year training programs at lower levels to groom employees for subsequent managerial positions.[75] One survey of 12 leading companies found that they agreed on the criteria for a successful executive development process: (1) extensive CEO involvement, (2) a clearly stated development policy, (3) CEO development linked to the business strategy, (4) an annual succession-planning process and on-the-job developmental assignments, and (5) line management responsibility for the program.[76]

Common programs

Some commonly used programs for development include assessment centers, job rotation programs, in-house training programs, and tuition-refund or assistance plans. Xerox and 3M use many of these programs to develop their employees.[77] In some cases, organizations (e.g., Pacific Bell) provide college credit to an employee when he or she has completed courses offered by the firm (e.g., training or human resource courses).[78] In addition to assessment centers, discussed earlier, 360-degree feedback systems are useful for helping employees better understand their strengths and weaknesses for managerial jobs. Many companies (e.g., GE, Lockheed Martin) also use **job rotation** programs that enable employees to develop a broader base of skills (cross-functional training) as part of the managerial training program. Other firms provide **stretch assignments** to help employees revitalize stagnant careers or to advance their careers. Stretch assignments provide real, high-stakes work experience in a safe environment. The global chief learning officer at Deloitte Touche Tohmatsu in Amsterdam says that "stretch assignments can help people leverage their talents to develop new skills or connect with new stakeholders."[79] For stretch assignments to work, employees should have mentors to help them develop learning goals, and they should be engaged in assignments that are challenging and will bring them some exposure. The Professional Development Institute at Duke University and Health System has wholeheartedly embraced stretch assignments for their supervisors. The supervisor and his/her manager design the stretch assignment to be a learning opportunity in a function beyond the person's current role.[80]

Job sampling

Apple Computer lets people sample jobs by filling in for employees who are on sabbaticals. Some firms, such as Xerox, American Express, and Wells Fargo & Co., use sabbaticals to enable employees to get paid while working for charitable organizations. In this way, employees come back to their jobs refreshed and possessing new skills.[81] Most Fortune 500 companies cover expenses for job-related and career-oriented courses taken at colleges. They also offer internal programs on a variety of topics, including technical training and interpersonal skills. For example, Highmark, an independent licensee of the Blue Cross Blue Shield Association, encourages all 11,000 employees to take advantage of a variety of learning opportunities (e.g., on-the-job learning sessions, job aids, formal courses, online courses, tuition reimbursement programs).[82]

Mentoring

Another developmental program continuing to gain in popularity is mentoring. In fact, research with senior executives has shown that having a mentor is more important than ever before.[83] Mentoring consists of establishing formal relationships between junior and senior colleagues or peers.[84] These relationships contribute to career functions (e.g., sponsorship, coaching, and protection of the colleague; exposure to important contacts and resources; assignment of challenging work) and to psychosocial functions (e.g., role modeling, counseling, acceptance and confirmation of the colleague, friendship). Employees who receive mentoring feel they are getting social support which is then related to their job satisfaction.[85]

Meta-analyses results support mentoring

Some recent meta-analyses of the effects of mentoring on objective (e.g., promotions, compensation) and subjective (career satisfaction) outcomes have supported claims associated with the benefits of mentoring, particularly for career satisfaction, but also revealed that the magnitude of the effects associated with objective career outcomes was quite small. The researchers also found that objective career success indicators, such as compensation and promotion, were more highly related to career mentoring than to psychosocial mentoring. Career mentoring behaviors such as sponsorship, exposure and visibility, coaching, and protection are more related to the enhancement of the task-based elements of work that are more strongly related to promotions and salary. The authors argue that the degree of mentoring provided does not play as large a role in objective career success as does the presence of a mentor, while the degree of mentoring is more strongly related to career satisfaction.[86]

In addition to benefits for protégés, mentoring also has positive outcomes for mentors. In a recent review of research in this area, it was found that serving as a mentor was related to the mentor's salary, promotion rate, and subjective career success. Those with experience as mentors reported greater job satisfaction, greater affective organizational commitment, and fewer intentions to change jobs than did those with no experience as mentors. Serving as a mentor has been shown to help prevent career plateauing. In addition, mentors are viewed as good organizational citizens and as better performers by their bosses.[87]

Formal mentoring programs began in the United States in the late 1980s and early 1990s. Some of the companies with formal mentoring programs include Federal Express, Merrill Lynch, and The Jewel Companies.[88] Bank of America's program uses "quad squads" that consist of a mentor and three new hires (a male, a female, and a racial minority group member). Infosys Technologies Limited, a global IT and consulting services provider, provides employees with personalized coaching and mentoring. Some organizations institutionalize **like-to-like mentoring** relationships (e.g., Hispanic mentors with Hispanic protégés) to better assist individuals in assimilating to the organization's culture.[89]

Like-to-like mentoring

In addition to creating their own mentoring programs there are firms that now specialize in assisting organizations in setting up their mentoring programs. For example, MENTTIUM Corporation was founded in 1990 by Gayle Holmes to help women reach senior-level positions in Fortune-ranked companies. The firm provides three primary mentoring programs: MENTTIUM 100, which helps pair up high-potential mid-level women from client organizations with senior executives from other organizations; MENTTOR, which matches a protégé and mentor in the same organization; and *circles,* which is a group mentoring model that matches senior leaders with multiple protégés within a given firm.[90] Despite the benefits of mentoring programs for both mentors and protégés, they are still not used in many law firms or consulting agencies.

E-mentoring

Mentoring traditionally occurs in face-to-face meetings. However, with the advent of technology, increasingly more mentoring is being provided in electronic forms. E-mentoring has also been called online mentoring, virtual mentoring, or telementoring. Generally e-mentoring refers to a mutually beneficial relationship between a mentor and protégé which occurs primarily through electronic means (e-mail, instant messaging, chat rooms, social networking spaces). It can occur as part of a formal mentoring program or informally. One example is **MentorNet,** which is an e-mentoring program that pairs graduate and undergraduate students in technical fields with industry professionals.[91]

MentorNet

Firms such as Dow Chemical have used a Web-based mentoring program called "open mentoring" to initially pair up protégés and mentors over the Internet. Similarly, at IBM, since employees are geographically dispersed, much mentoring is done by electronic means. The U.S Office of Personnel Management also uses e-mentoring to pair up federal workers with subject matter experts in their fields. In some firms, such as Disney/ABC, mentoring is done using both face-to-face methods and e-mentoring.[92]

Advantages of E-mentoring

E-mentoring has numerous advantages, including: (1) greater access to mentors, (2) reduced costs of administering the mentoring program, conducting training, and reproducing materials; (3) equalization of the status of the mentor and protégé or at least fewer status differences apparent; (4) decreased emphasis on demographics (race, age, physical characteristics); (5) a record of interactions; (6) helps some less assertive (or more shy) protégés feel more comfortable getting mentoring; and (7) enhances networking throughout the organization. Of course, there are also potential problems with e-mentoring such as: (1) increased likelihood of miscommunication; (2) slower development of relationships compared to face-to-face mentoring; (3) reliance on varying degrees of competency in technical communication skills; (4) computer problems; and (5) increased concerns over privacy and confidentiality.[93]

E-mentoring yields same benefits

Recently, researchers have been examining the relative effectiveness of face-to-face vs. electronic mentoring. There has been some evidence that those engaged in e-mentoring relationships receive many of the same benefits as those in face-to-face mentoring relationships (support, guidance, professional friendships, career development, new perspectives, networking skills, and personal development). Another study, however, found that electronic chat resulted in less psychosocial and career support for those with male peer mentors than female peer mentors. This was due to the fact that male mentors condensed their language to a greater extent than did female mentors.[94] Obviously, as technology continues to advance, more research on the use of e-mentoring will be needed. Organizations will also want to examine whether e-mentoring continues to serve as an efficient and cost-effective way of orienting and socializing new employees and developing their talent pipeline.[95]

CAREER PROGRAMS FOR SPECIAL TARGET GROUPS

Career development programs are often put into effect to meet the unique needs of particular employees. Although many different groups and issues may be targeted for career development, some of the more common programs are those that focus on fast-track employees, outplacement issues, entrenched employees, supervisors, executives, women and minorities, new employees, late-career employees, and employed spouses and parents.

Fast-Track Employees

Assessment centers for early identification of "stars"

Organizations often identify "stars," or individuals with high career potential, and place them on a fast track for upward moves in the company. AT&T, for example, uses assessment centers for the early identification of managerial talent. These specially recruited and selected employees are given rapid and intensive developmental opportunities in the company.[96] The identification and development of these employees requires organizations to exert extra recruitment efforts and to monitor the career progress of these employees frequently. Organizations must provide considerable feedback, training, and counseling, as well as offer quicker job changes and more challenging job assignments, particularly during the employees' first few years on the job. Managers who are responsible for identifying and developing fast-track employees should be recognized for their efforts if they are to take their responsibilities seriously. For example, Baxter Health Care links managers' bonuses to the early identification and development of promising female employees. At Eli Lilly, managers assess their employees and make decisions about their career potential and offer them opportunities for development. Northern Telecom has a program that identifies fast trackers and helps them to develop a variety of skills that go beyond their own technical expertise.[97]

Outplacement Programs

Outplacement programs assist terminated employees in making the transition to new employment. Generally, outplacement programs involve individual counseling sessions with external or internal counselors where individuals are able to share their feelings about being let go. The programs may also contain financial counseling. Workshops may be used to show individuals how to become successful job seekers by teaching them how to identify their skills and abilities, develop résumés, and interview with prospective employers. Outplacement programs stressing the importance of self-confidence and individual career planning may be particularly beneficial for middle- or late-career employees who have been laid off. This is because many older people have been forced into involuntary retirement, often with insufficient skills and financial assets.[98] The programs should help laid-off employees deal with their anger, depression, stress, grief, or loss of self-esteem associated with the job loss. During economic downtimes (e.g. financial crisis in 2008), outplacement programs are especially important. Many terminated employees suffer changes in their mental health. The programs also should encourage them to develop support networks. If an organization is going to use downsizing, the following recommendations can make it less traumatic and more fair:[99]

Recommendations for downsizing

- Be fair in implementing layoffs; spread them throughout the organizational ranks, not just among lower-level employees.
- Allow employees to leave with dignity; if possible, allow them to leave of their own accord.
- Help those displaced find new jobs.
- Avoid belittling laid-off employees.
- Be cautious when hiring outside executives; educate them on the internal morale.
- Keep employees informed about the company's goals and expectations.
- Set realistic expectations.
- Use ceremonies to reduce anger and confusion and convey to employees what is going on.

Outplacement programs have been shown to benefit employees by helping them cope with the shock and stress associated with losing a job and by helping them find jobs faster than they could on their own. This also may lower the likelihood that they will take legal action against the firm for laying them off. A firm that offers outplacement programs may be viewed more positively by the **"survivors,"** which may help maintain their morale and reduce job insecurity. In some cases, employees are given the option of "job sharing" or reduced workweeks, enabling them to keep their jobs, although with fewer hours and less pay. The organization also benefits since it helps reduce labor costs and overtime while retaining valuable expertise and knowledge about the company. AT&T developed an innovative program, called Resource Link, that consists of an internal contingent of displaced managers and professionals who can be assigned to temporary projects of 3 to 12 months' duration. This gives project managers the assistance they need without hiring permanent staff. The program has been so popular that some employees have volunteered to be assigned to the unit to gain exposure to different parts of the business. One recent study looked at almost 2,000 managers and executives using an outplacement company. Controlling for past salary, severance, and demographics, results demonstrated that displaced managers and executives participating in programs that demonstrated higher levels of outplacement support had a greater likelihood of reemployment and had higher salaries in new jobs than individuals participating in programs with lower levels of outplacement support.[100]

Provide assistance for "survivors"

It is important to provide some assistance to survivors. Their attitudes will be influenced in large part by how fairly they thought the layoffs were conducted. Often the morale of those remaining hits an all-time low, confidence is shaken, and communication and trust are fragmented. In many cases, survivors will have increased workloads and job responsibilities due to the loss of personnel. They may experience work overload and stress, and could benefit from counseling and realistic information about the firm's future and their future role with the company.[101] It is critical that a firm address the needs of the remaining employees if it is to be competitive.

**Figure 9-8
Roles for Executives and
Managers to Foster the
Successful Redeployment of
Displaced Workers**

To build career resilience
- Enhance and maintain value of current employees (continuous learning environment).
- Foster a culture of entrepreneurship internal to the organization by rewarding creative new ideas and self-management.
- Assign people to teams and work processes rather than to single, unifunctional jobs.
- Adopt continuous improvement programs based on employee participation.
- Partner with regional universities and colleges and government and community agencies to develop support systems for displaced workers.
- Train people in areas that create or add value through problem solving and support.
- Form new initiatives and joint ventures.

To build career insight
- Offer assessment and feedback processes to help people better understand their strengths and weaknesses.
- Provide problem-focused (in addition to symptom-focused) training to teach the unemployed job search skills, entrepreneurship, and realistic expectations.
- Conduct human resource forecasting to inform and direct organizational initiatives. This entails conducting job analyses for positions that do not yet exist and communicating the results as input to individual and organizational planning. Moreover, scenarios of likely environmental trends and organizational strategies can be constructed as ways to envision different sorts of change and its implications.
- Assist federal and state programs for reemployment and coping that recognize individual (e.g., age, profession, malleability) and regional economic factors.

To build career identity
- Fund and implement outside redeployment efforts stemming from restructuring (outplacement).
- Support the professional development of all functional specialities; develop job families and career paths within speciality areas.
- Train employees in multiple skills and use these different skills in role assignments.
- Join with other organizations and agencies in the community to create new economic opportunities (e.g., participate in job fairs).

Source: *Academy of Management Executive* by M. London. Copyright 1996 by Academy of Management (NY). Reproduced with permission of Academy of Management (NY) in the format Textbook via Copyright Clearance Center.

A number of recommendations have been offered for fostering the successful redeployment of displaced workers due to restructurings and downsizings. Figure 9-8 lists some of these suggestions.

Entrenched Employees

Steps to take to eliminate effects of entrenchment

Due to the large number of organizational restructurings and downsizings, many employees stay with their organization to keep their jobs, but do not stay as committed or attached to them as their employers would like. In fact, Gallup reported that one of every three workers would choose a different career if given the chance to start over. These employees have become entrenched in their careers. They stay in the job because of their investments, psychological preservation, and a perception that there are few career opportunities. To eliminate the potentially adverse consequences of **entrenchment,** organizations can take some of the following steps:[102]

- Offer generous severance pay packages to fund employees' explorations into new careers.

- Encourage portability of benefits such as pension funds and accrued time off.

- Provide ongoing career counseling and outplacement assistance to attend classes while still employed.

- Offer tuition reimbursement and time off for employees to attend classes.

- Implement staged retirement programs.

- Give employees time to rotate to other positions in the organization to explore other career options.

- Allow employees to phase out of jobs and not automatically eliminate them.

- Emphasize the importance of learning and development throughout the organization.

- Encourage employees to think about career-planning issues.

- Extend portability of medical coverage and other insurances for 18–24 months.

Supervisors and Career Counseling

Supervisors are increasingly being called upon to play a greater role in managing the career progress of their employees. They may serve as coach, advisor, performance appraiser, and referral agent. In a profile of the superior CEO, working with people (coaching, growing and developing people, leading teams) was listed as one of the top eight qualities needed.[103] To be effective in these roles, they should be trained as career coaches and mentors to help subordinates develop and implement their career plans in one-on-one counseling sessions. Further, they should be instructed on how to integrate counseling into their performance appraisal and selection activities. AT&T has one such program in place for training supervisors in career counseling, performance-appraisal skills, and mutual goal setting with subordinates. American Express recently created an initiative called Coaching to Extraordinary Customer Care, which focused on developing the coaching skills of frontline supervisors to help them offer better instruction to employees and thus improve customer satisfaction. Those leaders are now better equipped to review employees' performance, talk about their aspirations, and coach them to excel. Since beginning the program, American Express has achieved a 7 percent increase in customer satisfaction scores.[104]

Executive Coaching

Use of 360-degree appraisal

Executive coaching has recently arisen as a popular method for career and leadership development of managers.[105] See the Web site of the International Coach Federation (www.coachfederation.org). Executive coaching is described as a practical, goal-focused form of personal one-to-one learning for executives.[106] An executive meets with a coach who may be an internal career counselor or an external consultant. In the coaching session, the coach and executive typically discuss the results of a 360-degree assessment of the executive (see Chapter 7) or some other performance review, which describes his or her strengths and areas for improvement. The coach works individually with the leader to improve performance, develop or refine behaviors, and devise strategies for enhancing his or her career and preventing derailment. Meetings are held to establish career development plans and to follow up and assist executives on their career progress.

Coaching has become popular because it provides individualized, targeted, flexible, just-in-time development for executives. In addition, because executives may change jobs, a coach can help them in better managing their careers.[107] At the Robert H. Smith School of Business at the University of Maryland, an executive coaching program was created by the author to help Executive MBA students refine their leadership, interpersonal, and negotiation skills. Over the course of their 18 months in the EMBA program, each executive meets with a highly trained coach multiple times to review various leadership assessment tools they have completed (e.g., personality tests, assessment center data, peer feedback, organizational 360-degree feedback) and to develop and measure progress on an Individual Leadership Development Plan. Executives have found the program to be particularly beneficial in enabling them to advance to higher-level jobs.[108]

Texas Commerce Bank uses coaches for its senior 25 executives. Deloitte & Touche USA implemented an organizationwide coaching initiative that offers every employee the opportunity to coach and be coached and strives to make informal two-way coaching an everyday occurrence. They offer numerous workshops to teach coaching. In addition, their Coaching for Critical Talent services provide confidential individual coaching to support the acceleration of professional development for managers and executives.[109]

Limited research but quite positive

Since executive coaching is so new, few studies evaluating its effectiveness currently exist. One study revealed that participants in an executive coaching program viewed it as very valuable and that they had changed their behaviors. In another study, most executives rated their executive coaching experience as very satisfactory. Most leaders like coaching because they receive direct one-on-one assistance from a respected person, they don't have to leave their offices, it fits within their time frames, and they can see fast results if they are dedicated to it.[110] Novations, a Boston-based consulting firm, noted that 48 percent of firms are relying on coaching at the same rate as in the past, 19 percent are increasingly relying on coaching, and 33 percent of U.S. firms are relying less on coaching than they have in the past. The decrease in reliance may be due to what they call "commodity coaching" whereby a coaching firm provides so many days of coaching to multiple leaders in the organization, which is really just training hours, not executive-level coaching.[111]

313

Programs for Women, Minorities, and Employees with Disabilities

With the increasing numbers of women, immigrants, minorities, and people with disabilities entering the workplace, employers have recognized the importance of assisting these employees with their career needs. The primary issues facing employers are recruiting and selecting diverse employees, promoting them, and retaining them in the organization. To adhere to EEO or affirmative action guidelines, some organizations are supporting minority recruitment, selection, and training efforts (see Chapter 5). They are also providing additional feedback, educational opportunities, counseling, and career management seminars to meet the unique needs of these groups.[112] These practices are designed to help these employees compete for management positions. For example, top managers at Xerox and Kodak encourage the development of networks and support groups for women and minority groups (e.g., African-Americans, Hispanics). *Working Mother* magazine rates the Best Companies for Multicultural Women. They note that it takes more than having strong diversity programs in place to be a Best Company. A firm also has to have resources and top-level commitment—and perhaps most important, accountability on the part of managers for the advancement of multicultural women. Those top 20 firms that met these criteria in 2008 included: Allstate, American Electric Power, American Express, Chubb & Son, Citi, Colgate-Palmolive, Credit Suisse Securities, Deloitte, Ernst & Young, General Mills, IBM, JP Morgan Chase, Kraft Foods, MetLife, Pepsico, PricewaterhouseCoopers, Procter and Gamble, TAP Pharmaceutical Products, Verizon Communications, and Wal-Mart Stores.[113]

Best Companies for women and minorities

Tenneco established a women's advisory council to help identify the barriers that kept women from advancing into management. As a result, more women were able to move into Tenneco's upper management ranks. Other companies, including Dow Chemical Company, Honeywell, Polaroid, and GE Silicone, also have solicited assistance and advice from women's groups in the recruitment, mentoring, and advancement of women.[114]

Catalyst

Catalyst is one of the most prominent nonprofit organizations called upon to assist firms in their efforts to capitalize on the talents of their female employees and maximize opportunities for women in management positions. This is critical because women often see many barriers to senior-level management positions.[115] Recently, Catalyst published a book on creating women's networks in organizations. They document the successful networking efforts by companies such as Dow Chemical, Bausch & Lomb, Kodak, and Kimberly-Clark.[116] Networks are an effective system for assisting employees with career issues and addressing their unique concerns (e.g., social isolation, discrimination, glass ceiling). The benefits of these networks include serving as advisors to senior management and human resource staff regarding issues for the particular population, such as women and minorities, providing support, providing career development assistance, and helping the organization to change.

Healthiest companies for women

Some firms have focused on trying to retain their female employees. One way that some have tried to do this is by showing a commitment to the health of their female employees. Each year, *Working Woman* magazine rates the healthiest companies for women. The best firms have implemented practices such as increasing insurance coverage to help women affected by depression and providing employee assistance services; prenatal services; health resource centers; work-exercise programs; in vitro treatments; screenings for blood pressure, cholesterol, breast cancer, and osteoporosis; medical libraries; stress prevention programs; and counseling. These companies have lowered their insurance costs because they have prevented more serious illnesses from developing.

"Opt-out" revolution

The so-called **"opt-out" revolution** is receiving a great deal of media attention. This is a term that describes the trend of highly trained and educated women, mostly mothers, choosing to drop out of the job market to devote more attention to the family. A recent review examines this trend and presents a "kaleidoscope" career model that fits concerns for life balance and challenge with the demands of parenting. "Like a kaleidoscope that produces changing patterns when the tube is rotated and its glass chips fall into new arrangements, women shift the pattern of their careers by rotating different aspects in their lives to arrange their roles and relationships in new ways."[117] The review also presents guidelines on how women can increase career success and how organizations can improve the workplace so as to attract and retain valuable women. Similarly, other researchers note that the term "opting out" may be inappropriate and argue instead that women are enacting an updated "we are self-employed" model to reflect the new types of activities they are engaged in.[118]

Programs for New Employees (Early-Career Issues)

When an employee begins working in a company, he or she generally has been exposed to some type of recruitment effort and company orientation. Or if the employee has worked part-time for a company or served in an internship program, he or she has been socialized regarding the unique characteristics of the job and organization. These initial employment programs may be valuable mechanisms to familiarize the employee with the career policies and procedures of the organization.

Employee Orientation Programs

Orientation programs for new employees help reduce anxieties since they provide information on organizational policies, procedures, rules, work requirements, and sources of other information. Orientation programs may also be used to educate employees about any career programs, career paths, and opportunities for advancement. For example, Texas Instruments has developed an orientation program to address the unique concerns of new employees regarding career options.[119] The program includes a realistic job preview, an introduction to the formal mentoring program, a bibliography of readings relevant to career planning, and a guideline for career planning based on a study of Texas Instrument employees. The American Express Learning Network, a team of learning and development professionals, recently launched Connections, an orientation program that educates new employees about the firm's values, vision, and customers. A specially trained facilitator developed a customized curriculum for each group of new employees, based on their pre-hire screening assessments. At Wakemed Health & Hospitals, a private health care system based in Raleigh, North Carolina, nursing fellows attend orientations and ongoing educational programs throughout the year, and during their first months on the job they participate in a personalized clinical orientation on their units. This thorough training and support enhances their patient-care skills and professional development.[120]

Anticipatory Socialization Programs

Socialization programs (internships, cooperative education programs) are beneficial for individuals to develop accurate, realistic expectations about their chosen career field and about the world of work. Socialization through peer support in organizations and universities is also beneficial for reducing stress.[121] By working for an organization part-time or for several months, individuals may learn how well they are suited to the particular job or organization. This knowledge may help them gain a better sense of responsibility, maturity, and self-confidence about work. At Wipro Technologies, an India-based technology company, students enrolled in schools use a portal called Campus2Career to receive training on Open Source standards technology and development methods. They are assigned to work units and are paired with mentors from the organization to whom they report their progress. This project work has helped the students meet mandatory requirements for their school degrees and has cut down on the training they would need at Wipro once working there (from 10 weeks to 3 weeks). In addition, the program has contributed revenue to the firm's bottom line.[122]

Frito-Lay, IBM, Procter and Gamble, BB&T, GE, Campbells, Johnson & Johnson and Saturn are some of the many companies that hire interns and then make permanent offers if those internships are successful experiences. At Scottrade, a retail brokerage firm, the training department created a 20-week intern learning map, which is an online program that resembles a college campus. Each week interns learn about topics such as customer service, corporate culture, and account funding. Within six months of the introduction of the new program, 64 interns had been hired as associates and were on the pathway to leadership in the company.[123]

Realistic Recruitment

As discussed in Chapter 5, when job applicants are given a realistic, balanced, accurate view of the organization and the job (i.e., provided with positive *and* negative information), they experience less reality shock, dissatisfaction, and turnover.[124] This is true for new employees as well as current employees who are transferring to new jobs in the organization. To meet career development needs, job applicants should be informed in realistic job previews about the skills required of various positions in the organization and their own readiness and aptitude for those positions. 360-degree performance feedback can provide them with information about their own skills relative to other jobs in the firm. Such data should assist them in developing their future career goals and action plans.

Programs for Late Career and Retirement

In recent years, the number of older workers has increased because of the aging of the Baby-Boom generation. With increasing corporate restructurings, and economic difficulties, many of these older employees have lost their jobs. Some firms have opted to use early retirement for their older employees rather than retraining and redeploying them. And more employees have been choosing to retire early.[125] As a result, late-career and retirement issues have become increasingly important to organizations.[126]

Some organizations offer programs to help supervisors increase their awareness of issues facing late-career employees. It is critical that employers handle retirement issues effectively since they affect not only the retirees, but also the morale of the remaining staff.

Supervisory training important

Generally, supervisors are instructed on the changing demographics of the workforce, laws regarding older employees, stereotypes and realities of the aging process, and strategies for dealing with the loss of older employees who retire (i.e., the loss in their departments of expertise and skills). Supervisors also may be taught to develop action plans for enhancing the performance of their older workers. These plans involve giving older workers more concrete feedback, allowing them to serve as mentors, and providing them with training and cross-training opportunities. It is important that managers help employees deal with career plateaus so they can continue to be challenged and productive. Just offering one or two workshops is not enough. In some cases, providing ongoing coaching and opportunities for personal and professional development is needed. This will be particularly important for those older workers who take on intra-organizational job changes or international assignments.[127]

It is critical that older employees are aided in their transition to retirement. To do this, many companies have instituted retirement planning programs. The focus of preretirement workshops is to help preretirees understand the life and career concerns they may face as they prepare for retirement. Topics that may be discussed include health, finances, making the transition from work to retirement status, safety, housing and location, legal affairs, time utilization, Social Security, second careers, use of leisure time, and problems of aging. Often, individual counseling and group workshops are used, and efforts are made to tailor the programs to the needs of the participants and their spouses. Another type of assistance given to preretirees may be for education such as the Retirement Education Assistance Plan available to potential retirees at IBM.

Flexible work schedules

It is also important to offer flexible work schedules for late-career employees. Some do not want to quit their jobs but want to cut back the number of hours they work so they can enjoy their hobbies, go back to school, travel, or spend more time with their families. Polaroid gave its older employees the option to share jobs rather than be laid off. Many companies, such as McDonald's, Home Shopping Network, Aetna, Prudential, GEICO, Wal-Mart, and Monsanto, have hired older employees to work part-time or for temporary jobs. This has been beneficial due to the critical shortage of young people to hire. In fact, a study by the Society for Human Resource Management found that over 80 percent of firms that aggressively recruited and hired older employees found them to be more amenable than younger individuals to working part-time.[128] As employees age, it is going to be imperative for organizations in the United States, and in other parts of the world, to make good use of the expertise and talent residing in their older employees if they are to remain competitive. To do this, firms will need to make sure that their older workers feel valued in the workplace. Ageism and indulging in stereotypes toward older workers can reduce the effectiveness of all employees.[129]

Programs to Improve Work–Family Balance

Society has seen increasing numbers of working mothers and two-income households. Recent reports have indicated that 90 percent of working adults expressed a concern about not spending enough time with their family. In addition the total number of hours worked by employees has increased continuously over the last 20 years.[130] In recent years, organizations have been much more interested in developing family-responsive policies and programs designed to alleviate individuals' conflicts between work and family. Several such organizational trends in these practices include:

■ Increasing use of flexible work schedules and training for managers in implementing the schedules.

- More openings of on-site child-care centers.

- A greater number of companies (e.g., Xerox, Motorola) setting aside monies employees can use for paying child-care costs or buying a first home.

- Greater use of paid leaves for fathers and adoptive parents.

- More programs that set goals for advancing women into senior management positions and increasing numbers of companies holding managers accountable for meeting these goals.

- Continued support and funding for American Business Collaboration for Quality Dependent Care, which is a $100 million, six-year commitment that participating companies have made to improve and expand child and elder care in their communities.

In recent years, organizations have become more interested in helping individuals balance demands from their work and family roles. Employers are beginning to realize that individuals may experience role conflict and difficulties dealing with travel, child care, household tasks, job transfers, and relocations, and may have trouble determining priorities for their various roles and responsibilities. This may be especially true for dual-career couples since each partner has a high level of commitment to his or her career. *Working Mother* magazine routinely rates the best companies for working mothers. The top 10 *rated* in 2007 were Baptist Health South Florida, Booz Allen Hamilton, Ernst & Young, General Mills, IBM, KPMG, The McGraw-Hill Companies, PricewaterhouseCoopers, UBS, and Wachovia.[131]

Best companies for working mothers

Policies on Hiring Couples and Relocation Assistance

Many employees, particularly members of **dual-career couples,** have expressed less willingness to accept relocation offers from their employers. In a large-scale study of U.S. firms, spouse willingness to relocate was shown to be the most important factor related to employee willingness to relocate.[132] It is not surprising then that some organizations have begun offering relocation assistance to the spouses of their employees. Companies vary in the amount and type of assistance provided to employees and spouses considering relocations. Assistance ranges from none at all to locating jobs for spouses. One study found that 50 percent of U.S. firms provide job-related assistance to a **"trailing spouse."** Unisys pays up to $500 to a spouse to help with résumé writing and job hunting.[133] Motorola provides assistance to dual-career couples by finding jobs for spouses of employees who take international assignments. Both the spouse and the expatriate were found to view the policy positively.[134] Johnson & Johnson offers personal counseling and job search information to relocating families. Some companies (ConAgra, Burlington Northern Santa Fe Railway) have hired relocation consultants and firms to assist them in planning the relocation of large numbers of employees. They also involved employees throughout the planning process.[135]

Assistance for "trailing spouse"

Some firms have altered their policy on **"nepotism"** to allow hiring both spouses. They may still keep the rule that an employee cannot work under the direct supervision of his or her spouse. There are a number of benefits to hiring both spouses, including lower recruiting and relocation costs for the employer, and the practice encourages employees to remain with the firm or to accept intraorganizational moves or transfers. It also helps employers who are trying to hire for branches in remote geographical areas. Of course, one downside is that if one of the spouses wants to leave the firm, the other may also leave.

Work–Family Programs

Organizations are becoming more involved in designing programs to help employees manage their work–family role conflict by providing a place and procedure for discussing conflicts and coping strategies.[136] For example, in 2007 KPMG launched Web-based training for employees and managers to help them have more productive conversations about career development and introduced an interactive Web site to help staffers identify steps for building satisfying careers. Organizations are changing their practices for recruitment, travel, transfers, promotions, scheduling hours, and benefits to meet the needs of the larger numbers of dual-career couples. For example, General Electric and Procter and Gamble require fewer geographic moves in order to advance. Booz Allen Hamilton has created new part-time career models. DuPont has been very active in providing assistance to their more than 3,500 dual-career couples and has developed more flexible employment plans to accommodate the family demands of both male and female employees. DuPont also trains its supervisors to be more sensitive to family issues, allows longer parental leave for fathers and mothers, and has instituted adjustable work schedules. Mobil Oil provides flexible work schedules, a part-time option, childbirth and other leaves, and a national network of child care information. General Mills created new time-off options to help staffers maintain balance, including flex vacation and sabbaticals. IBM offers a range of programs from flexible work schedules and meeting-free Fridays to online resources that identify job and learning opportunities.

Flexible Work Arrangements and Telecommuting

Employers have been adopting a number of flexible work arrangements in order to assist employees. Some of these include flextime, job sharing, part-time work, compressed workweeks, temporary work, and work at home (telecommuting). These programs enable employees to address their work and family concerns and reduce their potential stress or conflict between their various life roles. Of the 100 firms rated the best for working mothers, 54 have established training programs to educate managers on how to implement alternative work arrangements, including Aetna, TRW, Texas Instruments, SAS Institute, Sara Lee Corporation, and Prudential.

Telecommuting growing in popularity in U.S.

Telecommuting is growing in popularity, although only 55 percent of U.S. companies surveyed offer fully supported flexible working environments compared with much higher adoption rates in other regions such as France (75 percent) and Switzerland (73 percent). In a telecommuting survey, U.S. employees cited upper management's lack of trust in employees and concerns regarding reduced productivity as the major reasons why they were not allowed to telecommute. On the other hand, companies across Europe and in Australia cited "increasing employee productivity" as the key driver behind the adoption of a flexible work arrangement. American firms cited "employee retention" as their top reason for using telecommuting.[137]

In another survey, a third of U.S. companies surveyed offered employees the option of working at home, and many gave them computers linking them to the office. Home-based work is found primarily in firms in industries such as education, professional services, consulting, small business, repair, and social-service occupations. Gandalf Technologies, a computer networking company, allows employees to telecommute from home several days a week. AT&T lets many of its employees telecommute at least part of the week from home via computer. Many U.S. companies now have call-center operations that are handled by part-time employees working at home.[138]

Some difficulties with telecommuting are communication problems with other employees, limited access to necessary supplies and equipment, and family interruptions. Another issue is how to supervise such workers.

Many benefits for telecommuting

There are a number of benefits to telecommuting. IBM has saved considerable money on office space by going mobile through telecommuting, "hoteling" (being assigned to a desk via a reservations system), and "hot desking" (several people using the same desk at different times). About 10,000 employees share offices with four people on average. Many studies show that people's strategic planning skills go up when they telecommute since they have uninterrupted time to think clearly. In fact, it has been estimated that people who work at home are 5 to 20 percent more productive because they have fewer distractions.[139] It may be important to provide orientation or training to educate employees and managers on the rules of telecommuting. It will be important to see how different generations of workers feel about telecommuting.

Maternity and Paternity Leave

With the passage in 1993 of the **Family and Medical Leave Act (FMLA),** employers with more than 50 employees are required to allow 12 weeks of unpaid leave from work for either parent following the birth, adoption, or severe illness of a child. By 1996, more companies were offering financial aid for adoption. Two-thirds of the top-rated 100 companies for working mothers provided this benefit (e.g., Eli Lilly offers up to $10,000). The McGraw-Hill Companies, rated as one of the 2007 top 10 places to work for working mothers, provides adoption assistance in addition to parental leave. Many of the top-rated firms for working mothers include additional benefits for leave time. For example, in 2007 Ernst & Young enhanced their parental leave policy to include six weeks of fully paid leave for primary caregivers and six weeks of fully paid short-term disability for birthmothers. They also introduced the Working Mothers Network to help women make the transition back to work following parental leave. Also, PricewaterhouseCoopers began giving mothers an extra three weeks of fully paid maternity leave to be used at any time up to one year following a child's birth or adoption.[140]

Unresolved issues for pregnant women

Despite these advances, some unresolved issues and obstacles facing pregnant employees still exist. With pressures at work, they may be rushed by their bosses through maternity leave or denied comparable jobs or promotions when they return to their jobs.[141] The workplace culture may emphasize overtime work to such a degree that employees are discouraged from taking advantage of maternity or paternity leave policies. Employees may be reluctant to take time off out of fear of losing their jobs in this era of downsizings. Mothers, in particular, may be concerned about being passed over for promotions, which researchers have found does happen.[142]

Job pressures are related to increased risks for pregnant women. One study found that women lawyers who worked more than 45 hours a week were three times more likely to experience a miscarriage in the first trimester of pregnancy than were women who worked less than 35 hours a week. Pregnant employees may face stereotypes among their colleagues who believe they will lose interest in their jobs or quit. A study of 140 bank employees found that their performance actually increased during pregnancy. In addition, it was noted that 80 percent of women return to work after maternity leave. Cigna HealthCare in Hartford, Connecticut, developed a training program to debunk stereotypes about pregnant women and to help managers be supportive in dealing with pregnant employees. A few tips follow:[143]

- Discuss and reach agreement with a pregnant employee on how her work will be covered during her leave.
- Discuss with co-workers worries they have about covering for a woman on leave. Make sure the work is distributed fairly.
- Be patient with new mothers' efforts to balance their expanded responsibilities.
- Weigh short-term scheduling hassles against the long-term benefits of retaining an employee.

Child Care and Elder Care Services

Today, employees must concern themselves with both child care and elder care. Elder care may be of great concern to employees, particularly if their parents suffer from health problems. Firms providing elder care as a benefit to employees include Gannett Co., First Union Corporation, General Motors Corporation, Eddie Bauer, The DuPont Merck Pharmaceutical Company, Corning, The McGraw-Hill Companies, Baptist Health South Florida, and Deloitte & Touche LLP.[144]

Very positive effects for child care

Generally, employers find it beneficial to provide child care assistance to employees, which results in higher morale, easier recruitment of parents as employees, lower turnover, and tax savings. When employers assisted employees with child care or elder care concerns, it was found that these employees did not have to use company time to make phone calls, visit doctors, and so on. DuPont reported savings of $6.78 for every dollar spent on resource and referral, and Aetna reported $3.59 in savings per dollar spent.[145] Marriott reported savings in reduced turnover with its "Associate Resource Line," a toll-free hot line with bilingual social workers who provide advice on child care and elder care issues, among other things.

Some employers (e.g., Bankers Trust New York Corporation, Merrill Lynch & Co.) have opened backup centers to help employees who run into problems with their child care arrangements. First Tennessee Bank opened a center for mildly sick children to cut down on employee absences when parents had to stay home with sick children. The center has saved the company considerable money.

Effectiveness of Programs

Businesses that offer flexible schedules, part-time or alternative work options, work–family conflict seminars, and telecommuting are not just being nice to their employees. These programs have an impact on the bottom line. They have been shown to increase employees' loyalty, thereby reducing turnover and absenteeism and increasing organizational productivity.[146] One survey of 2,376 pregnant women in 80 communities across the United States found that those in the most accommodating companies in terms of health insurance, sick days, job-protected leave, flexible scheduling, and supervisor understanding were more satisfied with their jobs, took fewer sick days, worked more on their own time, worked later into their pregnancies, and were more likely to return to work.[147]

Higher job satisfacting fewer sick days, positive effects

One survey of 75 large corporations with these programs found increased commitment to the job, higher morale, higher productivity, superior job performance, and reduced absenteeism.[148] Flextime, job sharing, and part-time work seem to be the most effective and least costly programs in terms of keeping employees and increasing productivity. Neuville Industries, a 575-employee sock manufacturer in North Carolina, found that with its work–family programs (on-site day care center, flextime, emergency backup child care) turnover was half (45 percent a year) the industry average (80 to 100 percent at other plants). At Aetna Health Plans, telecommuting has increased productivity of claims processed by 29 percent. The firm is also saving $12,000 per year in office space. Deloitte & Touche allowed reduced hours for partners, provided the opportunity for employees to be made partner while working part-time, and made more women partners, decreaing turnover 8 percent between 1993 and 1995.

Repatriates

One recent article on the **"boundaryless"** trend examined the perceived impact of an international assignment on career advancement and the effectiveness of expatriate career management systems. The majority of expatriates viewed their international assignment as an opportunity for professional development and career advancement yet expressed skepticism that the assignment would be helpful for advancement within their own companies. In fact, individuals and organizations have different views on why employees take international assignments in the first place. Employers often underestimate the importance of career, work–life balance, and development considerations and overestimate the financial reasons for why individuals take the assignments.[149]

As we discussed in Chapter 8, more organizations have been offering training for expatriates to prepare them for overseas assignments. While this is important, it is also critical to offer some developmental opportunities for repatriates to prepare them for their return back to the firm after an overseas assignment. It has been estimated that 15 to 40 percent of *repatriates* leave the company within 12 to 18 months of their return from overseas assignments. Many organizations find themselves losing valuable, highly skilled employees simply because the repatriation process was handled poorly.[150] Commonplace in Japanese and European firms, repatriation programs often do not exist in U.S. firms. One survey revealed that only 30 percent of U.S. companies reported any type of repatriation program for managers reentering the domestic organization. This may explain why U.S. managers who are repatriates have more difficulties adjusting than do their Japanese and European counterparts.[151]

High turnover rates for repatriates

Adjustment problems for repatriates

Often the difficulties associated with reentry are not anticipated by an employee, his or her family, or the organization. Most U.S. repatriates experience considerable adjustment problems and "reentry shock" upon their return to their firm. They report having difficulty getting back to high levels of productivity. If they have been abroad for a long time, they may be technologically obsolete.[152] Problems often occur because the organization does not realize that the repatriate needs assistance in readapting to work-related and non-work-related routines. Because the person is coming "home," issues such as reverse culture shock often are not addressed.[153] Yet foreign experience may have changed the employee's attitudes and beliefs in a profound way. The changes may have occurred so subtly that the employee does not initially recognize these internal changes. Repatriates often are not given enough time to become reacclimated to life in the United States. Some experts state that it may take as long as 18 months for them to readjust. Repatriates often report feeling disoriented in their communities and among co-workers.

Repatriates report frustration with their organizations' limited attempts to place them back in permanent assignments. Many complain that they are penalized for taking international assignments because they are placed in lower-level positions than their peers when they return. They may find that they have been passed over for promotion opportunities.

In one survey of 56 U.S.-based multinational firms, 56 percent said a foreign assignment was detrimental or immaterial in one's career, 47 percent said the repatriates are not guaranteed jobs with the organization upon completion of the assignment, and 65 percent reported that the foreign assignment was not integrated into their overall career planning. In addition, only 20 percent considered the organization's repatriation policies adequate to meet repatriates' needs.[154] In a more recent survey, expatriates reported low satisfaction with and serious concerns about their company's repatriation program and policies. They experienced major setbacks in their careers upon their return home. This is not surprising since most organizations do not fully utilize the new skills and experiences that repatriates bring back to their firms. Managers often are not sure how to establish career paths or ladders for those who have taken an international assignment.[155]

Problems for repatriates

The following is a list of problems repatriates may face within their companies:[156]

- Feeling out of place in the corporate culture of the home office.
- Receiving little, if any, guidance regarding the career opportunities available upon their return.
- Being passed over for promotions that go to co-workers who did not go abroad.
- Receiving lower salaries than while they were on the international assignment.
- Not being able to effectively utilize the new skills that were acquired while abroad; not receiving support for using those skills.
- Not receiving recognition for the work that was completed during the international assignment.
- Losing the social status as a key employee at the foreign office.

For a repatriation program to be effective, it must be part of an overall organizational philosophy that values continued productive employment of international employees. The organization must be committed to addressing all phases of international assessments beginning with a pretraining program to prepare employees before they leave on their assignments to a reentry program when they return. The career or training staff must be willing to take on the role of a **"repatriation advocate."** They should track international assignments and reasons employees leave assignments early or leave the company early. Many companies have set up permanent offices in other countries. Career staff should collect information that addresses cultural, communication, and job-related issues faced by most employees assigned to regions of the world. Linkages between the region or foreign country, the type of assignment held, and the difficulties experienced with returning to the home office should be documented. By using this information, the career staff can more accurately determine the specific career needs of repatriates and advocate for them.

Organization should have repatriation "advocates"

For repatriates' transitions to be successful, several career development practices are recommended:[157]

Recommended practices should reduce stress

- A year before they return they should begin a repatriation program.
- Once back to the firm, retraining and reorientation should be provided to help them learn of any new changes in their job, department, corporate culture, or organization.
- Repatriates should be given opportunities to use the experiences and skills they gained from their international assignments.
- They should be given definite assignments, and these assignments should be clearly linked to their career paths.
- Mentors should be provided to repatriates to help them cope with their transition.
- Ongoing career management should be provided to them.
- Assistance in housing and compensation should be provided to ease their transition.

Taken together, these practices should reduce the stress and disorientation experienced by repatriates as well as improve their performance. Repatriates if assisted in these ways may become more committed to the firm and opt to remain there.

SUMMARY

Career programs should be integrated with other HR programs

Career development programs must be integrated with and supported by the existing HR programs in the organization if they are to be successful. Career programs and HR programs need to be linked to meet individuals' growth needs and the organization's staffing needs. 3M has established a career resources department to better integrate its career programs, performance appraisal process, and HR planning systems. Boeing's development program called CAREERS is linked with its other HR programs.[158]

Individuals should have access to performance appraisal information and maps of organizational career paths to help them in career planning. This information may help employees evaluate their strengths and weaknesses in order to set goals based on possible career alternatives. Supervisors should be able to use performance appraisal data to assist employees in developing realistic career plans. In Coca-Cola's career program, managers are given training to provide such guidance.[159]

Career or job changes by employees should be based on an overall understanding of organizations' job descriptions, job posting systems, and selection policies. The continued development of employees and rewards for their performance should be founded on strategic organizational training and development systems and compensation plans. Organizational career information and planning systems should be developed to be consistent with the organization's strategic plans and existing forecasting systems, skills inventories, and succession plans. Coordinated, integrated efforts of the career staff, managers, and employees themselves are the key to success in an organization's career development program.

Focus should be organizational and individual effectiveness

Career development programs must be concerned with organizational and individual effectiveness over the short and long run. It is the responsibility of the career staff to work with management to ensure that career programs are integrated with the HR functions and are routinely evaluated. It is, however, the responsibility of management to view career development as necessary to an effective HR system. Managers must be willing to work with career professionals to formulate new strategies for career development and to provide support to them as they design and implement new career development programs.[160] Finally, it is the responsibility of the individual to create his or her own career opportunities. The following quote provides some advice for individuals as they attempt to navigate their way through their careers:

> Careers in today's world are what you make them. The apparent boundaries in a department are also your platforms for further opportunity. Organize your employment around your professional and social networks. . . . Don't wait for formal training, but make sure the colleagues you surround yourself with sustain new learning for you, and try to reciprocate for them. Look after yourself, but don't be afraid to trust and to build trust around you. Remember that who you are and what you achieve will always be embedded in your relationships with others.[161]

Discussion Questions

1. Should organizations adopt formal career development policies and programs? How do these programs affect their ability to be flexible in terms of staffing? How do they influence their ability to recruit employees?

2. What would you say to those who argue that establishing attractive career programs for employees will only enhance their own marketability and enable them to leave the firm faster?

3. What is the role of EEO in career development? What is the role of the training or career staff in designing and implementing career development programs?

4. Recently, the role of managers has changed and today more are being called to be career "coaches" for their employees. What suggestions would you give to managers about what that new role involves? What if they say they don't have time to be a career coach. How would you convince them that this role is critical today for retaining today's workers, especially Gen Y workers?

5. Describe several career development programs that would be useful for individuals planning on making a career or job change. Suppose they have worked in one field for 7–10 years (e.g., engineering) and have decided to switch jobs (e.g., to consulting). How should they prepare for this change?

6. What is the value of self-assessment for individual career planning and organizational career management? Why should employees seek feedback from others regarding their job performance and career plans? How could performance appraisal information (360-degree appraisal) be used to assist individuals in career development?

7. Why is it important to integrate career development programs with other programs in organizations (e.g., performance appraisal, training, selection, compensation)? Offer some suggestions for how this can be done.

8. Should organizations make special efforts to deal with career–family issues through part-time work, job sharing, flextime, relocation assistance, and other programs? Should they also have special programs in place for employees who are not married nor parents?

9. With the increasing number of organizations experiencing downsizings and layoffs, it has become critical that they have career programs in place to assist outplaced employees. What suggestions would you offer for the types of assistance that are needed in outplacement programs?

10. Companies are increasingly expecting their employees to take international assignments, and yet they are not providing much career development for them while they are away and when they return. Why is this important to do? What recommendations would you offer?

11. How can companies use career programs to retain their most talented employees? How might these differ for the various generations at the workplace (e.g., Gen Y, Gen X, Baby Boomers, Traditionalists)? What career programs would keep you employed at a particular firm?

12. During troubled economic times (e.g., financial crisis), what advice would you give to today's workers so that they could continue to thrive in their careers?

Part 4 | Compensating and Managing Human Resources

Chapter 10

Compensation: Base Pay and Fringe Benefits*

OBJECTIVES

After reading this chapter, you should be able to

1. Understand the traditional model for base pay programs.
2. Describe the basic approaches to job evaluation.
3. Describe the contemporary trends in compensation.
4. Explain the role of government in compensation.
5. Know the various forms of fringe compensation, including the government-mandated programs.
6. Define the different types of pension plans.
7. Understand the complexities of international compensation.

OVERVIEW

The Tribune Company developed a new performance management system, closely following the prescriptions provided in Chapter 7. At an orientation session in which the new system was introduced to management, the first several questions had to do with the relationship between the new system and pay. Pay is very important to people and very important to organizations. Research on high-performance work systems indicates that characteristics of a firm's compensation system are strongly related to corporate financial performance.[1]

Compensation

The term **compensation refers to all forms of financial returns and tangible benefits that employees receive as part of an employment relationship.** As the business environment becomes increasingly complex and global, the challenge to create and maintain effective compensation programs, given cost constraints, also requires greater professional expertise, organizational understanding, creativity, and vision than ever before.

Three trends

During the last decade, three key trends in compensation have occurred. First, there has been a dramatic increase in the diversity of compensation strategies and practices. Not too long ago, employees received a base salary (which the organization probably described as being "competitive") and a set of preestablished benefits (which the organization probably described as being "comprehensive"). Today, firms are providing

Diversity in strategies

*Contributed by Christine M. Hagan.

327

variable pay, hiring bonuses, lump-sum recognition bonuses, group incentive plans, broad-based success-sharing programs, plus a broader and more flexible selection of employee benefits.

Rise in inequity

The second noteworthy trend has been a significant rise in pay inequity. In the last decade, chief executives' average compensation has more than tripled. The average corporate chieftain now earns in a single day almost what the typical U.S. worker earns in a year. A new book entitled *The Big Squeeze* by *New York Times* writer Steven Greenhouse documents this inequity. "A profound shift has left a broad swath of the American workforce on a lower plane than in decades past, with health coverage, pension benefits, job security, workloads, stress levels, and often wages growing worse for millions of workers." [2] Greenhouse writes that at a time when executive pay is soaring and employee productivity has risen more than 15 percent since 2001, the average wage for the typical American worker has increased by 1 percent.

According to one expert, "U.S. CEOs are far and away the highest paid CEOs in the world. Yet, from a long-term perspective, and compared to CEOs in other countries, they cannot be considered the very best performers." [3] According to management guru Rosabeth Moss Kanter, in 1982 the CEO of a large American corporation earned an estimated 42 times what the average worker earned. By 1990, that figure had increased to 120 times; by 1997 that figure had increased to 280 times; by 2000 the gap peaked at 531 to 1. Since then, it has fallen back to about the 1997 level of 280 to 1, where it has remained. Compare this with the ongoing, steady ratios in Europe and Japan of less than 40 to 1. [4] Of course, this increase in U.S. CEO pay has far exceeded the average growth in corporate revenues, growth in value, or the cost of living. In fact, a study of 1,500 U.S. companies found that, between 1992 and 2002, every 1 percent increase in total compensation for each of the top five executives predicted a .22 percent decrease in shareholder return over the next year, and a .12 percent decline over the coming three years. [5] This chapter was written during the economic turmoil of 2008. The implications for executive pay, regulatory and otherwise, have yet to be determined. Greater regulation of executive pay, by governments and corporate boards, is likely.

Pay programs to communicate change

A third trend is that pay programs are increasingly being used to communicate major change and realignment in organizations, particularly during and after major downsizing and reengineering efforts. As IBM began to rebuild itself in the late 1990s, one of the key tools for change was a complete redesign of the pay system. It scrapped its traditional approach to evaluating work and its pay grade structure. It reduced the number of different jobs from 5,000 to fewer than 1,200. It significantly increased the percentage of an individual's pay that was directly related to performance and created pay-at-risk programs at all levels in the organization (a big first for IBM!). [6] Although HR and compensation experts continued to design and develop the framework of the pay program, significant day-to-day administration of the program was transferred to line managers, making compensation more of a management tool than an HR program. Compensation experts have traditionally argued the importance of directly aligning business strategies and compensation programs. This past decade, however, has seen a rethinking of the role that compensation programs play in supporting, communicating, and even leading the way to new organizational values and performance norms.

A state of transition

As a result, compensation programs are in a state of transition. Organizations are experimenting with different types of structures; they are allocating money differently to programs; they are questioning the traditional (rather rigid) approach to compensation program design; they are looking for innovative ways to "get more" for their investment in compensation; and they are putting more of a focus on long-term success criteria.

Does pay matter?

Does pay matter? Research suggests that reward systems can influence a company's success (or failure) in three ways. [7] First, the amount of pay and the way it is packaged and delivered to employees can motivate, energize, and direct behavior. IBM's compensation program redesign (described above) was directly targeted at changing the way IBMers thought about their work, focused their energies, and directed their performance. Second, compensation plays an important role in an organization's ability to attract and retain qualified, high-performance workers. Unless applicants find job offers to be appropriate in terms of the amount and type of compensation, they may not consider employment with a particular firm. Compensation strategies and practices can clearly shape the composition of a workforce. This is especially important for firms operating in tight, high-expertise labor markets. Microsoft, for example, sets out to hire a certain percentage of the top technical talent that graduates each year. In addition to investing heavily in recruiting and selection activities, they offer job candidates a generous sign-on bonus, a competitive base salary, stock options, and a flexible benefits program, which allows individuals to select the benefits and coverage that they both need and value most.

Finally, the cost of compensation can influence firm success. On average, the overall cost of labor is estimated to be 70 percent of a firm's total costs.[8] Within the United States, firms that wish to pursue a strategy based on cost leadership must find ways to reduce those costs without sacrificing quality. Organizations that compete in global marketplaces have greater cost-competitor pressures. The average hourly wage for a U.S. production worker in 2006 was $23.82, which ranked 16th highest among the 29 industrialized countries of the world. In Europe, the average cost of a production worker in 2006 was $28.76 (in U.S. dollars). In Mexico, the average in 2006 was $2.76.[9] In summary, then, the strategy and structure of compensation programs have important implications for businesses and their ability to create and sustain competitive advantage. They can also cause big trouble as evidenced by the failures of numerous corporations in 2008.

Does compensation matter to individual workers? Recent discussions suggest that money motivates people on two basic dimensions. The instrumental meaning of money relates directly to what money buys: better houses, better educations for children, better vacations, clothes, and cars. The symbolic meaning of money concerns how wealth is viewed by ourselves and within our society in general. In the United States, "rich" is usually equated with "successful," "intelligent," "diligent," and "highly motivated," while "poor" tends to be equated with "failure," "unmotivated," "uneducated," perhaps "lazy" and "slovenly." One recent discussion of the issue pointed to all the money-oriented slang expressions used in our culture as an indication of the value of material possessions: "put your money where your mouth is," "crime doesn't pay," "paying the piper," "hitting pay dirt," "you get what you pay for," and "there is no free lunch."[10]

In job situations, money motivates behavior when it rewards people in relation to their performance or contributions, when it is perceived as being fair and equitable, and when it provides rewards that employees truly value.[11] Recent research supports the belief that **U.S. workers prefer pay that is based on their own performance**—not the performance of the team, group, or company. In one particular study, employees reporting the strongest preference for individualized rewards were also the highest-performing employees.[12] Research also indicates that employee satisfaction with pay is correlated with organizational commitment and trust in management, while it is inversely related to absenteeism and lateness, seeking alternative employment opportunities, terminating employment with the organization, pro-union voting, and incidents of theft.[13] It is also interesting to note that the particular components of pay have different value to different people. Research indicates that younger people tend to focus predominantly on cash compensation. As people age, however, their preference tends to shift to benefits and workplace flexibility.[14] It should be no surprise that life stage, career stage, and individual circumstances create differences in compensation preferences.

What makes an employee satisfied with pay? First of all, research indicates that individuals differ in the way in which they conceptualize pay satisfaction.[15] According to **equity theory,** pay satisfaction is a function of the comparisons of an individual's input–outcome ratio with his or her perceptions about the input–outcome ratios of referent others. In other words, people compare themselves to others, focusing on two variables: inputs and outcomes. Inputs refer to individuals' characteristics (e.g., education, previous work experience, special licenses), effort (e.g., how long they persist in seeking a solution to a problem), and performance (e.g., number of units produced). Outcomes are what people get out of their jobs (e.g., pay, promotion, recognition). It's important to note that these comparisons are based on perceptions, rather than on any objective, or quantifiable, measures of actual inputs and outcomes. Also important is that these judgments are made in terms of ratios—that is, relationships of "equal to," "greater than," or "less than." Pay satisfaction

U.S. workers prefer individual pay-for-performance

Equity theory

occurs when people perceive that they are paid appropriately in relation to others. When employees feel underpaid, they are dissatisfied and may withhold effort or engage in negative or counterproductive behaviors. What happens when these comparisons suggest that a worker is overpaid? Originally, researchers hypothesized that individuals would feel guilty and would work harder or smarter in order to close the gap. More recent evidence suggests that employees whose comparisons and perceptions indicate that they are overpaid tend to rethink their comparisons in order to find (or rationalize) a more equitable balance.

Does compensation matter at the societal level?

Does compensation matter at the societal level? Over the course of history, societies that produced more also enjoyed higher standards of living. This means that their citizens enjoyed higher qualities of life, including better transportation systems, higher levels of education, more luxuries, better health care, and more time off.[16] In addition, governments tend to use higher standards of living as platforms for social change. Legislation such as the Fair Labor Standards Act (which includes the minimum wage and child labor rules), the Employee Retirement Income Security Act (ERISA), the Equal Pay Act (EPA), the Pregnancy Discrimination Act, and the Age Discrimination in Employment Act (ADEA) are aimed at ensuring that people are treated justly and that the poorer and less powerful members of society are protected from flagrant abuse. Former President Bill Clinton championed legislation to limit the tax deductibility of excessive executive compensation. Remember that organizations deduct the compensation they pay to employees as a "business expense" when they calculate their taxes. Excessive compensation to high-level employees, then, actually reduces the amount of taxes paid by a corporation. Who makes up the shortfall? Clinton's law limited an organization's deduction to $1 million for the compensation it paid to any individual in any year unless the pay was specifically and explicitly based on performance. Considering the continued escalation of executive compensation up until 2008 and the failures of numerous major financial institutions in 2008, proposed legislation such as the "Say on Pay" Act and other legislative and regulatory actions could already be in place.[17]

At the same time, some argue that the relatively high cost of U.S. labor, in general, is the principal reason that the United States has trouble competing globally in certain industries. Some assert that industry setbacks can be traced to product price increases necessitated by the unreasonable wage and benefits demands of its workers. Two-tier pay systems are becoming more common in some industries (e.g., automotive, airlines) where newly hired employees are paid at a significantly lower rate (and with fewer benefits) than other employees doing the same work.

Five Objectives for Effective Compensation

An effective compensation system typically has the following five objectives:

1. It enables an organization to attract and retain qualified, competent workers.

2. It motivates employees' performance, fosters a feeling of equity, and provides direction to their efforts.

3. It supports, communicates, and reinforces an organization's culture, values, and competitive strategy, especially long-term strategy.

4. Its cost structure reflects the organization's ability to pay.

5. It complies with all government laws and regulations.

Attract and retain employees

Motivate employees

Compatible with long-term strategy

Ability to pay

As organizations ponder changes to their compensation systems, they should consider all five of these objectives. The ability to attract highly qualified individuals can be determined by **selection ratios** and vacancy rates. The ability to retain can be ascertained by looking at voluntary termination rates, perhaps in combination with performance appraisal data (high turnover rates among the highest performers would be a sign that the compensation system should be changed). The ability to motivate and compatibility with corporate culture or strategy can be determined by looking at employee surveys performance appraisal data and other performance indicators. And the cost structure should be assessed relative to the compensation packages for competitors paying for the same type of work. Employees are very sensitive to changes in their compensation. Major changes to their compensation can have a profound effect on these objectives, for better or for worse.

Numerous federal, state and local laws and regulations

Of course, all these considerations exist in the context of the numerous laws and regulations that affect compensation. The last objective is quite a challenge and perhaps more so since 2008. Although some federal laws (e.g., the National Labor Relations Act discussed in Chapter 13 and the Employee Retirement Income Security Act) preempt state laws, employers could be subject to state and local laws and regulations in addition to the major federal laws described in this chapter. Many states increased their minimum wage in 2008 and 2009 above the new federal standards, and several states passed protections for military families and those claiming sexual orientation discrimination which may affect employee benefits. States also passed laws in 2008 related to child labor, prevailing wages, time off, and the timing and method of wage payment. Three states (Washington, New Jersey, and California) currently require paid family leave, and others may have already passed similar legislation by the time you read this. Over 120 cities and counties also have **living wage laws** as of 2008 with a required hourly pay rate well above the minimum wage.

Cash compensation

Fringe compensation

Compensation is divided up into two parts. **Cash compensation** is the direct pay provided by employers for work performed. Cash compensation has two elements: base pay (e.g., hourly or weekly wages plus overtime pay, shift differential, uniform allowances) and pay contingent on performance (e.g., merit increases, incentive pay, bonuses, gain sharing). **Fringe compensation** refers to employee benefits programs. Fringe compensation also has two dimensions: legally required programs (e.g., Social Security, workers' compensation) and discretionary programs (e.g., health benefits, pension plans, paid time off, tuition reimbursement). This chapter covers *base pay* programs and *fringe* benefits. Pay that is contingent on measures of performance will be covered in Chapter 11.

As indicated earlier, compensation systems are in a state of transition. Traditional designs focus primarily on attracting and retaining qualified workers and complying with government regulations. Newer pay models balance these concerns with increased attention to motivating and directing performance and to aligning pay with achieving important firm effectiveness goals.

CASH COMPENSATION: BASE PAY

The traditional model for structuring base pay programs has existed in its relatively unchanged form for more than 50 years.[18] In the 1800s business owners knew their employees, their performance, and their financial needs, and individual pay was established on that basis. As businesses grew, bureaucracies were created to provide structure, organization, and direction. Professional managers replaced business owners, while rapidly growing hierarchies distanced them from most workers. Efficiency and effectiveness became the most important business objectives. In the late 1800s, Frederick Taylor designed a formal, systematic way of assigning pay to jobs while helping a steel company identify methods for improving productivity. His methodology came to be called *job evaluation.*

In the following sections, we will describe the traditional approach to base pay administration, examine some recent trends in base pay program design, and discuss the government's role in shaping employer practices in cash compensation. Figure 10-1 depicts and summarizes the steps involved in creating and installing a traditional compensation plan.

THE TRADITIONAL APPROACH TO COMPENSATION

What Is Internal Equity?

Job evaluation is defined as the process of assessing the value of each job in relation to other jobs in an organization. Traditional compensation programs use job evaluation to create internal equity among jobs. Internal equity means that individual employees perceive that their position is treated fairly within a pay program in relation to other jobs in the organization.

Figure 10-1   The Traditional Approach to Compensation

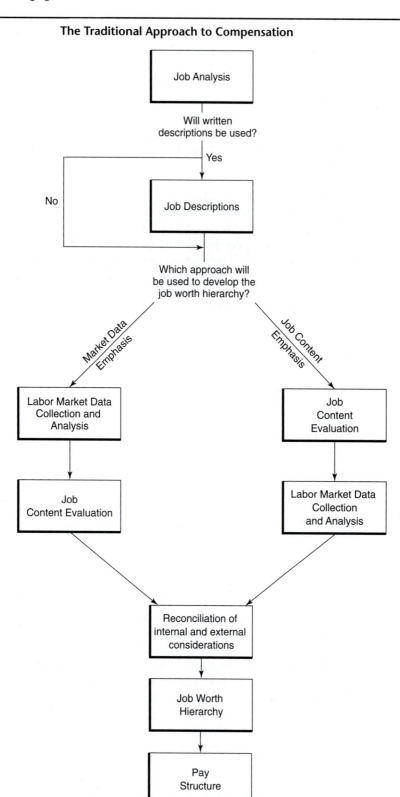

Job evaluation focuses on the duties and responsibilities assigned to a job. It's important to note that traditional job evaluation does not directly consider the credentials or characteristics of the person who occupies the job, or the quality or quantity of the individual's performance. Traditional job evaluation is described as an objective procedure that measures the complexity of the work, the amount of responsibility, and the level of effort required of each position in relation to other positions in the organization. Traditional job evaluation typically results in a hierarchy of jobs ranked in order of their relative value to the firm.

Three steps to job evaluation

Traditional **job evaluation** typically involves three steps. During step one, job analysis is conducted. You will recall from the discussion in Chapter 4 that job analysis is the process of collecting and evaluating relevant information about jobs. During this step, job descriptions are usually drafted (or updated) and job specifications (KASOCs) are identified. See Chapter 4 for a full discussion of the methods and techniques for collecting information through job analysis. Step two involves actually rating the job. Once again, you may recall from Chapter 4 that some standardized approaches to job analysis, particularly O*NET and the Position Analysis Questionnaire, provide information relating to compensation. However, most organizations use some form of job evaluation specifically developed for use in determining pay. Step three involves carefully reviewing the job evaluation results. This is typically done by arranging jobs in hierarchical order using the job evaluation results. At this point, it is important to study the evaluations in relation to one another. Consider this something of a "sore thumbing" process that looks at the final results of the job evaluation and identifies positions that don't appear to fit best where the job evaluation plan has placed them. This is also the stage in which evaluators should try to identify judgmental biases that may have crept into the evaluation process.

Job Evaluation Methods

Three basic job evaluation approaches are most common: job ranking, job classification, and point-factor plans. Each of these methods is described and explained below. A summary of the approaches is provided in Figure 10-2.

Job ranking

The oldest, fastest, and simplest method of job evaluation, **job ranking** involves placing jobs in order from most valuable (or most important or most difficult) to least valuable (or least important or least difficult) using a single factor such as job complexity or the importance of the job to the firm's competitive advantage. This method typically looks at each job as a whole and does not examine the tasks that make up the job. Although it is the simplest method, ranking is seldom the recommended approach.[19] Typically, the ranking factor is not well-defined so that the resulting hierarchy is very difficult to explain to employees. In addition, since the approach focuses on the total job, often the highest-level duty becomes the basis for the evaluation. Finally, the ranking approach provides no information concerning how much more valuable one job is in relation to another, or how the KASOCs of one job relate to those of another. This could be a key drawback for an organization that is committed to employee development, internal mobility, cross-training programs, and career ladders.

Figure 10-2	Summary of Three Traditional Job Evaluation Methods		
Method	**Procedure**	**Advantages**	**Disadvantages**
Ranking	Rank order whole jobs for worth or compare pairs of jobs	Simplest method; inexpensive, easy to understand	Only general rating of "worth"—not very reliable; doesn't measure differences between jobs
Classification	Compare job descriptions to preestablished grade descriptors	Simple, easy to use for large numbers of jobs; one rating scale	Ambiguous, overlapping grade descriptors
Point factor	Reduce general factors to subfactors; give each factor weights and points; "score jobs"; use points to determine grades	More specific and larger numbers of factors; off-the-shelf plans available (e.g., Hay plan); more precise measurements	Time-consuming process; more difficult to understand; greater opportunity to disagree

Figure 10-3   Grade Descriptors for Federal Job Classification System Serving as a Yardstick in Job Rating

Grade GS-1
Includes all classes of positions the duties of which are to perform, under immediate supervision, with little or no latitude for the exercise of independent judgment, the following: (1) the simplest routine work in office, business, or fiscal operations; or (2) elementary work of a subordinate technical character in a professional, scientific, or technical field.

Grade GS-18
Includes all classes of positions the duties of which are: (1) To serve as the head of a bureau. This position, considering the kind and extent of the authorities and responsibilities vested in it, and the scope, complexity, and degree of difficulty of the activities carried on, is exceptional and outstanding among the whole group of positions of heads of bureaus. (2) To plan and direct, or to plan and execute, new or innovative projects.

Job classification

The **job classification** method was originally developed, and continues to be used, by the federal government. Here, each job is measured against a preexisting set of job classes that have been designed to cover the full range of work that would be performed by federal government employees. In other words, broad descriptions are designed in advance to reflect the characteristics of the jobs that would be placed at each level in that system. Job classification, then, involves comparing a specific position to these generic descriptors and deciding which level fits best. Figure 10-3 presents the generic descriptors for two job levels within the federal job classification system. The classification system is relatively inexpensive and easy to administer.[20] But as the number and diversity of positions grow, it is increasingly difficult to write level descriptors in advance that will cover the full range of jobs. When specific level descriptors don't exist, the classification method becomes unclear and difficult to communicate to workers. In addition, like the ranking method, it is difficult to know how much difference exists between job levels. Finally, in any whole job rating system, one must be cautious about the same type of rater errors that can creep into job evaluation and performance appraisal (see Chapter 7). For example, a halo-type error might be committed when a rater is overwhelmed by one particular element of a job.

Point-factor plans

Under a **point-factor plan,** a variety of factors are the basis for determining relative worth. Point-factor plans are the most widely used approach to job evaluation in the United States and in Europe. In choosing factors, the organization decides: "What particular job components do we value? What job characteristics will we pay for?" Companies should choose factors for a job evaluation plan that are based on the organization's strategy, that reflect the type of work performed, and that are generally acceptable to its stakeholders. Skill, effort, responsibility, and working conditions are the most common factors found in point-factor plans.[21] Figure 10-4 presents a summary of the three major factors within the **Hay plan,** which is the most popular point-factor plan.

After the factors are identified and described, they are usually weighted because all factors are probably not equally important to an organization. For example, factors such

Figure 10-4   Major Factors of the Hay Plan

Know-How	Problem Solving	Accountability
Sum total of every kind of skill, however acquired, required for acceptable job performance. Know-how has three subfactors:	Original "self-starting" thinking required by the job for analyzing, evaluating, creating, and reasoning. Problem solving has two subfactors:	Answerability for action and for the consequences of the action; the measured effect of the job. Accountability has three subfactors:
1. Practical procedures, specialized techniques.	1. The thinking environment in which problems are solved.	1. Freedom to act (personal control).
2. Ability to integrate and harmonize the diversified functions of management.	2. The thinking challenge of the actual problems typically encountered by the position.	2. The impact of the job on end results (direct versus indirect).
3. Interpersonal skills.		3. Magnitude—the general dollar size of areas most affected by this job.

Figure 10-5 **Example of Degree Statements for the Factor "Physical Requirements"**

FACTOR: PHYSICAL REQUIREMENTS
This factor appraises the physical effort required by a job, including its intensity and degree of continuity. Analysis of this factor may be incorrect unless a sufficiently broad view of the work is considered.

Degree
1. Light work involving a minimum of physical effort. Requires only intermittent sitting, standing, and walking. (10 Points)
2. Repetitive work of a mechanical nature. Small amount of lifting and carrying. Occasional difficult working positions. Almost continuous sitting or considerable moving around. (20 Points)
3. Continuous standing or walking, or difficult working positions. Working with average-weight or heavy materials and supplies. Fast manipulative skill in almost continuous use of machine or office equipment on paced work. (30 Points)

   A higher degree rating for a job translates into a greater number of job evaluation points.

as responsibility, decision making, and mental effort tend to be more heavily weighted than physical effort or working conditions. Next, *degree statements* must be constructed. Sometimes called *factor scales*, these are statements of the extent to which the factor is present in any given job. Figure 10-5 illustrates a typical degree statement for the factor "Physical Requirements." When a position's evaluation is complete, the point scores on each factor are totaled. The more valuable a job is, the higher its total point score.

Unlike job ranking, point-factor plans do not rank jobs in an organization purely based on a comparison of one against another, and they do not rely on a rater's perception of the whole job. Instead, each job is examined concerning the degree to which each factor is present. In this way, the point-factor plan is similar to the classification approach in that it uses an external standard, evaluating each job in relation to that standard. Unlike the classification system, however, the point-factor approach breaks jobs down into component parts and assigns point values for various characteristics. In a point-factor plan, a job's relative worth is the sum of the numerical values for each degree within each factor. A job hierarchy is derived by ranking jobs by their total point score.

Point-factor plans have a number of advantages.[22] The written evaluation enables an organization to trace, analyze, and document differences among jobs. Such differences can be the foundation for training, development, and career progression programs. The fact that jobs are broken down into parts and evaluated using the same criteria over and over again limits the opportunity for rater bias to enter the process. Finally, when explaining job evaluation to employees, point-factor plans tend to have a high level of integrity. On the other hand, point-factor plans are expensive to design or buy and they are time-consuming to install and maintain. Some consultants assert that point-factor plans should be administered by evaluation committees consisting of line operating managers.[23] The time and cost of such commitments must be considered.

Job families   Point-factor job evaluation is typically conducted within a *job family* in order to establish internal equity among similar types of work. While definitions differ a little, a **job family** is essentially a group of jobs having the same basic nature of work but requiring different levels of skill, effort, responsibility, or working conditions (e.g., entry versus senior level). For example, an Accounting job family might include Accounting Clerks, Accounting Assistants, Junior Accountants, Accountants, Senior Accountants, Accounting Supervisors, Assistant Controllers, and so on. A point-factor plan enables an organization to document the precise distinctions among the levels of work within a job family. Use of job families can also facilitate comparisons to the external marketplace.

Pay equity policies   Point-factor job evaluation is also used as part of **pay equity or comparable worth policies** with the point comparisons made across job families. For example, the definition in the Minnesota Local Government Pay Equity Act for "equitable compensation" states that ". . . compensation for female dominated classes is not consistently below the compensation for male-dominated classes of comparable value. . . ." *Comparable value* compares points across

335

different (male vs. female dominated) job families; go to http://www.doer.state.mn.us /lr-peqty/resource.htm for the details of the program.

In summary, an organization chooses a job evaluation approach that it believes will best meet its needs and systematically evaluates each job within or against that standard. Within a traditional compensation plan, the goal involves creating not only an internally equitable program, but also one that is externally competitive. The next group of activities focuses on considering pay practices in the marketplace so that the organization may effectively compete for qualified workers.

What Is External Equity?

The process of pricing jobs involves identifying the compensation provided by other organizations for jobs similar to yours. When your pay practices are similar to the practices of other organizations competing for the same talent, then your program is said to be competitive, or **externally equitable.** When we concern ourselves with external equity, we shift our focus from an administrative value system to an economic one. Thus, one should not expect the results of job surveying and the results of job evaluation to match one another.[24] In fact, some small companies bypass the time and expense of job evaluation and go straight to the marketplace to find the wage information they need in order to set pay. This

Market pricing

is called a **market pricing approach.** Some authors say the use of this approach is one of the fastest-growing trends in U.S. industry today.[25] Others assert that it is not an effective method for two reasons. First, most companies have some unique jobs or job responsibilities that are more effectively priced in relation to other jobs (and responsibilities) within an organization than they are to similar jobs in the external marketplace. Second, the strategic importance of jobs within a particular company may be misstated if compared only with the external labor market. See Critical Thinking Application 10-A for further consideration of this issue in reference to executive pay.

Pay surveys

The principal tool for establishing external equity is **salary surveys.** Most organizations utilize some sort of survey information in order to approximate the prevalent pay practices in their particular marketplace. Within a traditional compensation program, comparing an organization's practices to those of the marketplace typically involves three steps: (1) planning the data collection activities, (2) collecting the survey information, and (3) analyzing the information.

Benchmarks jobs

Planning to survey involves choosing which jobs will be surveyed. Typically, organizations survey benchmark positions. **Benchmarks** are well-known jobs, with many incumbents, that are strategically important and are structured in such a way that one would expect to find them in the general marketplace. Next, the organization should decide what sources it will use for gathering market data. The least expensive and the quickest approach is to obtain data from public sources, such as local chambers of commerce, the U.S. Department of Labor (e.g., the O*NET), and various other state and local agencies. Another alternative is to purchase a survey from a consulting firm. These are more expensive than local or government surveys, but they are usually of higher quality. An organization can also conduct its own survey or can contract with an outside firm to conduct such a survey on its behalf. This is the most expensive option, but it typically provides the highest quality of information, since the company sponsoring the survey decides who will be invited to participate, which jobs will be covered, and the extent of the information that will be gath-

O*NET for salary data

ered. Check out salary.com, SalaryExpert.com, careerjournal.com, or the **Occupational Outlook Handbook** at stats.bls.gov for information related to benchmarking. Try http://online.onetcenter.org to get recent salary information for particular jobs in particular regions of the U.S.

The activities involved in actually collecting survey data depend on whether the organization decides to purchase survey information or to sponsor its own survey. During this phase, it is important to make certain that job content is carefully matched to survey descriptions and that the information gathered is of the highest quality possible. If an organization is buying an existing survey, it must make certain that the data represent the

Relevant job market

relevant market. As discussed in Chapter 5, the geographical pool is expanding for many jobs. Internet recruiting and other improvements in technology now make it possible to consider regional, national, and global labor marketplaces in order to locate the best job candidates and/or the most cost-effective candidates. Effective surveys tend to go beyond base pay and provide information concerning all elements of compensation (e.g., eligibility for incentive pay and bonuses, time-off provisions, benefits provided). Good surveys provide information in addition to practices relating to existing workers and will include salary ranges, hiring ranges, recent actual pay increases, and other similar information.

Finally, when it comes to analyzing market data, practices vary widely among organizations.[26] Some organizations look at competitor pay data only very generally, using average salaries or median starting salaries, or some other index that it believes to be meaningful, to guide its decision making about its own pay policies. Other organizations invest considerable time, effort, and money analyzing data using least-squares regression analysis to aggregate data across jobs and across companies. An organization should choose the type and the depth of the analysis based on its own individual needs, the complexity of its marketplace, the amount of time the organization can afford to allocate to the project, the professional expertise that is available within the organization, and the resources that it is able and willing to spend for outside advice and assistance.[27]

Tie pay levels to market average for most jobs

In general, organizations tie their pay practices for most positions to the market average, although there are situations when organizations choose to pay above or below average based on their strategy or goals. For example, Merck, the highly successful pharmaceutical company, pays its research and development division above market for researchers with particular specialties that are compatible with Merck's strategic goals. One very interesting

Paying above market

experiment in above-market compensation involves a New York City charter school that as of 2009 pays its teachers $125,000, plus a potential bonus based on schoolwide performance (about twice as much as the average New York City public school teacher earns). The school's founder is abiding by what research in education indicates: teacher quality is the key to student academic performance. Too early to tell how this unique approach to compensation in education will work out. Organizations that are willing to train new employees may find that they can pay below market for such positions with the assumption that there is a learning curve.

Developing the Pay Structure

How an organization structures its base salary program is primarily a matter of organizational philosophy, although marketplace practices are often important to consider in highly competitive situations. In structuring a program, several options are available. First, an organization can use a single rate structure in which all employees performing the same work receive the same pay rate. Second, an organization can use a tenure-based approach that focuses on how long an individual has been employed in a particular job. Third, some organizations use a combination of a tenure-based plan and a merit-based plan. For example, employees begin at a fixed rate, progress to higher rates during their first year based on time in the job, then any additional pay increase is awarded solely on the basis of performance. Yet another option would be a pay system based on productivity. An individual who is paid only a sales commission is an example of this. A fifth and increasingly popular option could be some form of base pay with an incentive opportunity, either based on individual, team, unit, or company performance. As will be dicussed in Chapter 11, a dominant trend is to separate the pay-for-performance component of

Separate pay-for-performance from base pay

compensation from the base pay component so that total compensation is more closely linked to recent performance indicators. Finally, many organizations combine elements of these approaches to create their own formal program. The most common traditional pay structure involves grouping similar jobs into pay grades and assigning a salary range, with a minimum, midpoint, and maximum.[28] The use of pay grades simplifies program administration. Rather than hundreds (or thousands) of unique pay rates, grouping jobs into grades typically means 10 to 25 pay grades (depending on company type and size). Pay ranges, as opposed to pay rates, provide increased flexibility that enables managers to consider particular job-related characteristics of individual employees or job candidates. In traditional programs, employees typically progress through pay ranges based on a combination of tenure and merit.

In summary, then, this traditional pay model focuses on internal equity (through job evaluation), external equity (through market surveying), and some reconciliation of these to arrive at a final pay structure that fits well with the organization's strategy and goals and that will enable the organization to attract and retain qualified employees. As indicated earlier, this general approach has dominated compensation practice for the past 50 years.

Assessing the Traditional Approach to Pay

Over the past decade or two, new forms of pay programs have evolved. They represent a considerable break from the traditional approach. Before describing these trends, it is useful to look at why organizations are interested in experimenting with new approaches.[29]

Nature of work is changing

First, the basic nature of work is changing. Globalization, competitive pressures, the unpredictable business environment, the shift from a manufacturing to a service economy, and the drive toward quality have influenced the way work is structured, performed, and supervised. Today, key issues are worker empowerment, team-based processes, and a coaching style of supervision. Jobs are more fluid and more broadly defined. Traditionally described tasks are being replaced by more general worker roles. When IBM reduced the number of different jobs it utilized from more than 5,000 to fewer than 1,200, it was responding to these same pressures by "generalizing" and broadening work. Traditional job evaluation is built on a different work philosophy. Many traditional job evaluation programs place great value on specialty knowledge and the dollar value of areas managed. Few, if any, traditional job evaluation plans explicitly consider customer service challenges, responsibility for quality, or working successfully within and across teams as valuable dimensions of jobs. Thus, some argue that traditional job evaluation plans reward the wrong things.

Second, the traditional approach assumes that paying competitively is a primary goal of a compensation system. To this end, compensation experts within organizations tend to be "outwardly focused," monitoring competitor practices, adopting those that appear to be successful, and using surveys to identify appropriate levels of pay. As discussed in Chapter 1, this element of compensation management may actually encourage "trendy, faddish thinking." In contrast to this traditional mindset, successful companies today are trying to differentiate themselves from others in the marketplace. Critics of the traditional approach urge compensation experts to "focus inwardly" on what will motivate, direct, and energize performance given the strategy and goals of the individual organization.

Successful companies trying to differentiate

"Entitlement mindsets"

Third, critics argue that traditional plans create **"entitlement mindsets"** on the part of employees. Annual base salary increases and similar pay scale adjustments foster an expectation among employees that pay moves only in one (upward) direction. Organizations in highly competitive situations may not be able to absorb these continuous increases in fixed costs. One strength of the traditional approach is that it conveys a sense of orderliness, rationality, fairness, and objectivity to the process of ranking job value within an organization. Job evaluation plans, especially point-factor plans, identify the particular factors that are valued in an organization. Despite this systematic foundation, the traditional compensation process provides numerous opportunities for bias, rater errors, and other forms of distortion and controversy.[30] Many have argued, for example, that traditional compensation programs have been biased against jobs historically held by women. Referred to as the comparable worth dilemma, traditional plans have been criticized for measuring internal job worth and then relying on market survey information to establish actual pay. The net result is that some jobs could be rated quite high in terms of their job content using a job evaluation plan, but paid comparatively low if the market undervalues their contribution. Comparable worth supporters argue that this occurs frequently because the marketplace is discriminatory. The prestigious National Academy of Sciences drew this conclusion in 1981.[31] Proponents of comparable worth legislation argue that waiting for an economic market adjustment is too slow and that it ignores a basic inequity in our society. We will discuss the comparable worth equity issue in the section on government compliance later in this chapter.

In summary, there are a variety of reasons the traditional internal equity/external competitive approach to compensation has been called into question. In the next section, we will describe some of the noteworthy efforts in this direction. Figure 10-6 illustrates the characteristics of three contemporary pay approaches that are described and discussed below.

Figure 10-6   **A Comparison of Three Contemporary Approaches to Pay**

Approach	Description	Advantages	Disadvantages
Broadbanding	Replaces traditional narrow salary ranges (40–60 percent spread) with fewer, wider bands (200–300 percent spread)	More consistent with downsized, flatter organizational structures Breaks down previous structural pay barriers among jobs to facilitate empowerment, teamwork, etc. Greater flexibility; more useful managerial tool	Traditional cost control in pay structure is lost Job pricing may be more difficult May be more difficult to communicate to employees
Pay for knowledge	Employees paid on basis of either (1) degree of specific knowledge they posses or (2) an inventory of skills	Encourages workforce flexibility and enhanced competence Fewer supervisors needed as employees improve knowledge and skill Fosters sense of individual empowerment about pay	Pay costs may get out of control Unused skills may get rusty Creating and maintaining skill and competency menus take time and effort Do we pay for inputs or outcomes?
Team pay	Any form of compensation contingent on group membership or team results	Reinforces concepts of teams, empowerment May better communicate and support organization's culture and goals	May demotivate top individual performance Few existing plans; beginning to emerge

Current Trends in Salary Administration

Broadbanding

Broadbanding is an approach to base pay that is receiving considerable attention in the business press.[32] In theory, it is considered to be more consistent with the broader, downsized, flatter organizations that exist today. Broadbanding involves consolidating existing pay grades and ranges into fewer, wider bands. While a traditional pay range might be $30,000–$45,000 (i.e., 50 percent spread from minimum to maximum), a job band could be $25,000–$75,000 (i.e., 300 percent spread). Broadbanding provides greater flexibility in setting pay rates, and it provides considerably more latitude in defining work and in moving people around within an organization. Northern Telecom clustered more than 34 pay grades into 10 bands and replaced 19,000 job titles with approximately 200 generic job titles. General Electric collapsed 30 pay grades covering administrative, executive, and professional employees into five broad bands.

Hewitt Associates studied the experience of 106 organizations that replaced traditional pay grades with broad bands by conducting focus groups that included affected employees, the managers responsible for administering the new plans, and top organizational executives.[33] Employee groups asserted that broadbanding encourages developmental and lateral career moves and facilitates cross-functional teams because differences in titles, levels, and salaries are minimized. Managers agreed with these observations and added that they liked the greater flexibility the approach provided in setting and managing pay. Executives viewed bands as a mechanism that could be molded to support a business's organizational style, strategy, and vision. An American Compensation Association study of broadband organizations found that 78 percent considered the approach to be effective.[34]

Insufficient research has been conducted to date to indicate whether broadbanding is a long-term, effective pay model.[35] Traditionally, narrow pay grades and ranges place upper limits on an individual's earnings. Some experts argue that broadbanding could increase payroll costs without specifically fostering corresponding increases in worker productivity. Some argue that broadbanding is appropriate for higher-level positions only.

Pay for Knowledge, Competencies, or Skills

In these types of plans, employees are paid on the basis of either the degree of specific, technical knowledge they hold or an inventory of knowledge and/or skills that they possess.[36] These plans are based on the assumption that knowledge, skill, or competence will be translated into improved employee performance and, ultimately, superior organizational effectiveness. Advocates assert that such plans can increase worker productivity and product quality, while decreasing absenteeism, turnover, and accident rates. One estimate of the popularity of the approach is that as many as 40 percent of large organizations use this approach, but only for a very small percentage of their workforce. **Paying for knowledge** has long been a viable pay strategy in scientific, technical, and professional disciplines in which expertise and innovation were sources of competitive, albeit intangible, advantage. Business schools, for example, typically pay considerably more for an assistant professor with a Ph.D. than for an instructor with an MBA. Similarly, unionized professions, such as teachers and nurses, have strongly favored pay based on education and experience. These plans are based on the assumption that professional competence increases with training and longevity. As technology continues to move forward at its rapid pace, such plans are increasing in popularity.

The most modern application of this thinking can be found in organizations designing and implementing **skills-based pay.** Originally found in new, nonunion manufacturing organizations, interest in this approach has grown considerably. Although it is not used as widely as its publicity might indicate (only 5 percent of U.S. organizations are believed to have implemented some version of the approach), its influence has been felt in some industries, such as pharmaceuticals and telecommunications. In a typical *skills-based* pay plan, the array of knowledges or skills that the organization values becomes like a pay menu. Employees begin at an entry-level rate. Incremental pay increases are awarded as employees demonstrate knowledge, or mastery, of specific, additional skills. Three types of potentially useful skill enhancements have been identified: (1) skill depth is increased when employees learn more about specialized areas, enhancing their ability to solve difficult problems and moving along a career track to becoming an expert, or master; (2) skill breadth is improved when employees learn more and different tasks, or jobs, in the organization; (3) self-management skills are increased when employees improve their abilities to organize and schedule work, to supervise work quality, and to perform other administrative tasks.

Supporters argue its merits: (1) the cross-training and acquisition of knowledge can create a flexible, empowered workforce; (2) fewer supervisors are needed; and (3) programs encourage employees to take responsibility for and control over their own development and their own compensation growth. Opponents assert that, first, potentially higher individual pay costs may be uneconomical unless they are offset by higher worker productivity. Second, unless skills are used regularly, they become rusty, although the pay for the skill may continue indefinitely. Third, depending on the growth and direction of the organization, employees can still reach the top of the skills-based pay scale, resulting in the same frustration that these plans are designed to remedy. Fourth, one very controversial issue is whether organizations should pay for inputs (e.g., individual credentials) or outcomes (performance). Skills-based pay represents paying for inputs. In contrast, some organizations believe that the best response to rising costs in uncertain environments is to put increasing amounts of pay at risk, that is, paying for outcomes, for the attainment of real individual, group, or organizational goals. Paying for knowledge, competence, or skills suggests that credentials hold potential performance value. When organizations pay on this basis, they should do so understanding that they are assuming the risk that these credentials will ultimately improve performance.

Team Pay Plans

With the wide growth in the use of teams within organizations has come discussion concerning how team members should be compensated. There appears to be a general consensus that teams require a different compensation approach than for work that is organized for and performed by individuals. However, there currently appear to be more questions than answers.[37] In one study of 230 large U.S. organizations, Hay Associates reported that 80 percent were satisfied with their use of teams, but that only 40 percent were satisfied with the related pay program.

One group of experts argues that it is important to distinguish between behaviors that a company values (as in teamwork) versus a true organizational form (as in teams). In addition, at least five types of teams have been identified: management teams, work teams, quality circles, virtual teams, and problem-solving teams. In sorting through the

5 percent of U.S. corporations use skill-based pay

Pros and cons of skills-based pay

Five types of teams

Figure 10-7   Summary of Federal Laws Affecting Direct Compensation

Laws	Provisions
Fair Labor Standards Act (FLSA) of 1938	Sets minimum wage ($6.55 per hour in July 2008), overtime pay requirements, and rules governing child labor (states can increase rate)
Equal Pay Act (EPA) of 1963	Men and women must be paid the same when they hold "substantially equal" jobs in terms of skill, effort, responsibility, and working conditions (some exceptions apply)
Davis-Bacon Act of 1931	Workers employed in construction industry must be paid at the prevailing local pay rate when working on government contracts.
Walsh-Healey Act of 1936	Workers employed in organizations providing goods to federal offices and projects must be paid the prevailing local rate for such work
Services Contract Act of 1965	Workers providing services to government offices and projects must be paid the prevailing local rate for such work

types and uses of teams, three criteria have been suggested as a basis for determining whether a team is a candidate for some kind of customized form of pay: (1) the team is the ongoing, relatively permanent form of work organization in use; (2) the work is truly interdependent; and (3) the team shares responsibility for its own decision making concerning its work.

Use broadbanding with profit-sharing for teams

Some experts recommend that team units use broadbanding in combination with incentive profit-sharing plans based on team results (see the next chapter). Depending on the environment, a division and/or organizational component may be added to the incentive plan as well. Some organizations report the use of pay for knowledge systems, particularly skills-based pay, as a compensation approach for teams.

Government Influence on Compensation Issues

In Chapter 3, you read about equal employment opportunity regulations that were enacted by the federal government to positively influence social change. The government also provides a legal framework about direct compensation within which organizations must operate. These rules ensure that minimum operating standards of fairness and humanity are applied to compensation matters in the employer–employee relationship.[38] Figure 10-7 summarizes the principal provisions of the most important federal regulations governing pay. Of course, as with most HRM activities, the reader should be aware that state, county, and local laws also may regulate pay policies.

The Fair Labor Standards Act (FLSA)

The broadest, most comprehensive legislation that affects base pay programs is the **Fair Labor Standards Act (FLSA).** Enacted in 1938, the law focuses on three main areas: minimum wage, overtime pay, and child labor rules. In 1963, the **Equal Pay Act (EPA)** amended the FLSA to include a prohibition against pay differentials based on gender. The Act also requires that employers maintain detailed records of time worked and pay received by each employee. The record-keeping requirement is used to determine whether or not an organization has complied with the law.

Many lawsuits regarding overtime

The number of lawsuits filed against employers alleging violations of the FLSA has risen from 1,854 (filed in 1991) to 4,389 (filed in 2006). The Employer Policy Foundation (an employer-supported think tank) estimated that full compliance with the FLSA would cost employers an additional $19 billion per year.[39] Since 2001, courts have ruled against such organizations as Starbucks ($18 million), Perdue Farms ($10 million), T-Mobile ($4.8 million), and Bank of America ($4.1 million). As of late 2008, Wal-Mart Stores remained mired in about 80 wage and hour suits filed since 2006 with one jury award of $172 million to workers in California and $78.5 million in Pennsylvania. As in the Wal-Mart cases, the larger awards focus on violations of overtime provisions.

Minimum wage is higher in certain states

The **minimum wage law** places a bottom limit on what an employer may pay. When the law was passed in 1938, the minimum wage was $.25. As of July 2008, the federal minimum wage for covered nonexempt employees is $6.55 per hour but will rise to $7.25 in July, 2009. In addition, many states (and some cities) also have minimum wage laws, some of which are indexed. For example, in Florida the minimum wage was set at $6.79 in 2008, with an annual adjustment based on the consumer price index.

Where an employee is subject to both the state (or city) and federal minimum wage laws, the employee is entitled to the higher of the two minimum wages. An employer of a tipped employee is required to pay only $2.13 an hour in direct wages if that amount plus the tips received equals at least the federal minimum wage, the employee retains all tips, and the employee customarily and regularly receives more than $30 a month in tips. Some states also have minimum wage laws specific to tipped employees. Visit the Department of Labor Web site (www.dol.gov) for a state-by-state breakdown of minimum wage law. A minimum wage of $4.25 per hour applies to workers under the age of 20 during their first 90 days of employment as long as their work does not displace other workers. After 90 days of employment, the employee must receive a minimum wage stipulated in the FLSA.

There has been much discussion about whether minimum wage laws represent too much government involvement in the private sector and whether a minimum wage is healthy for an economy. Those in favor of the regulation argue that a minimum wage is necessary to ensure that employers do not take unfair advantage of workers. Opponents argue that the law actually puts people out of work because employers tend to eliminate jobs as the cost of doing business rises.

Overtime pay

The FLSA's **overtime** provisions establish 40 hours as the standard workweek and require that employers pay workers at least 1.5 times their regular hourly rate for all work in excess of 40 hours in any workweek (hence the expression, time-and-one-half).

Under the 2004 Department of Labor "FairPay" rules, workers earning less than $23,660 per year—or $455 per week—are guaranteed overtime protection. The flood of class-action lawsuits related to overtime eligibility appears to center on the actual work performed by exempt employees designated as "executives, professionals or supervisors." In order to qualify for the executive employee exemption, all of the following tests must be met:

"Fair Pay" rules

- The employee must be compensated on a salary basis (as defined in the regulations) at a rate not less than $455 per week.

- The employee's primary duty must be managing the enterprise, or managing a customarily recognized department or subdivision of the enterprise.

- The employee must customarily and regularly direct the work of at least two or more other full-time employees or their equivalent.

- The employee must have the authority to hire or fire other employees, or the employee's suggestions and recommendations as to the hiring, firing, advancement, promotion, or any other change of status of other employees must be given particular weight.

The revised rules haven't helped stem the tide of litigation, which appears to center on the term "primary duty." In addition to the Wal-Mart cases, the biggest recent settlements have been on behalf of stockbrokers working for Citigroup ($98 million) and $87 million against UBS Financial Services. More recent cases now target computer technicians, pharmaceutical sales reps, and accounting firm personnel.[40]

Child labor laws

The **child labor** provisions restrict the employment of children by organizations. Employees must be at least 18 years old to perform any kind of hazardous work; at least 16 years old to work in manufacturing, mining, and transportation positions; and at least 14 years old to perform work in most other jobs. Special work hour limitations apply to 14- and 15-year-olds. In spite of these clear regulations, an Associated Press investigation (1997–1998) followed 165 children working illegally in 16 states, from New Mexican chili fields to a sweatshop in New York City. The investigation found that the work products of these children ended up in such places as JCPenney, Pillsbury, Wal-Mart, ConAgra, Campbell Soup, and Newman's Own. (Most of these companies launched major investigations when told that their suppliers illegally employed children.) One labor economist estimates that 290,200 children were employed unlawfully in the United States in 1998; 59,600 of these children were believed to be below the age of 14.[41]

The Equal Pay Act (EPA)

The FLSA was amended in 1963 to include the **Equal Pay Act (EPA).** This provision requires that men and women be paid the same when they hold "substantially equal" jobs in terms of skill, effort, and responsibility that are performed under the same working

Few EPA claims

conditions. The jobs need not be identical, but they must be substantially equal. It is job content, not job titles, that determines whether jobs are substantially equal. The EPA seems to have worked. Only 818 EPA claims were filed with the EEOC in 2007.

EPA exceptions

The EPA provides for a few exceptions where pay differences are allowed. The EPA allows pay differences for the same job based on differences in job tenure, quality or quantity of performance, individual differences in education or experience, or some other factor other than gender. In correcting a pay differential, no employee's pay may be reduced. Instead, the pay of the lower-paid employee(s) must be increased.

One typical contemporary example is setting a pay rate for the same job that pays more than the pay for an incumbent with years of experience. Some departments within colleges of business now hire newly minted Ph.D.s at a salary above the pay of a senior professor who teaches the same classes. The fact that the senior professor is a female and the newly hired, inexperienced assistant professor is a male does not mean the EPA has been violated. The market is a "reasonable factor other than gender." These exceptions are known as "affirmative defenses," and it is the employer's burden to prove that they apply. Thus, in this university example, should an EPA lawsuit be filed, the college of business would probably have to produce data showing that the competitive market requires the higher starting salary for new assistant professors.

Title VII can be used for pay discrimination claims

The filing of a claim under the EPA does not preclude pursuing a claim under Title VII. This can be important because the Civil Rights Act contains no provision stipulating job similarity. Plaintiffs who can establish that they have been paid a lower rate due to gender, race, religion, or national origin are eligible for judicial relief under Title VII, regardless of the job's similarity to other work. (See Critical Thinking Application 10-B.) Figure 10-8 presents a summary of the EPA and other forms of compensation discrimination.

Fair Pay Act

Many employers keep salaries and raises confidential. Such was the case at the Goodyear Tire and Rubber Company plant in Alabama when Lilly Ledbetter discovered that over many years she had received smaller raises than men in comparable supervisory positions. The Supreme Court ruled in 2008 that Ms. Ledbetter had not filed a timely claim (within the 180-day deadline) under Title VII. A proposed piece of legislation called the Ledbetter Fair Pay Act (HR 2831) passed the House of Representatives in 2008 stipulating that the 180-day clock would restart with each "discriminatory" pay check as long as some part of the paycheck reflects the discrimination. The Ledbetter Fair Pay Act could now be the law.

Figure 10-8   **Equal Pay and Compensation Discrimination**

EQUAL PAY ACT

The Equal Pay Act requires that men and women be given equal pay for equal work in the same establishment. The jobs need not be identical, but they must be substantially equal.

It is job content, not job titles, that determines whether jobs are substantially equal. Specifically, the EPA provides:

Employers may not pay unequal wages to men and women who perform jobs that require substantially equal skill, effort, and responsibility, and that are performed under similar working conditions, within the same establishment. Each of these factors is summarized below:

Skill—Measured by factors such as the experience, ability, education, and training required to perform the job. The key issue is what skills are required for the job, not what skills the individual employees may have.

Effort—The amount of physical or mental exertion needed to perform the job.

Responsibility—The degree of accountability required in performing the job.

Working Conditions—These encompass two factors: (1) physical surroundings like temperature, fumes, and ventilation; and (2) hazards.

Establishment—The prohibition against compensation discrimination under the EPA applies only to jobs within an establishment. An establishment is a distinct physical place of business rather than an entire business or enterprise consisting of several places of business.

Pay differentials are permitted when they are based on seniority, merit, quantity, or quality of production, or a factor other than sex. These are known as "**affirmative defenses**," and it is the employer's burden to prove that they apply. In correcting a pay differential, no employee's pay may be reduced. Instead, the pay of the lower-paid employee(s) must be increased.

TITLE VII, ADEA, and ADA

Title VII, the ADEA, and the ADA prohibit compensation discrimination on the basis of race, color, religion, sex, national origin, age, or disability. Unlike the EPA, there is no requirement under Title VII, the ADEA, or the ADA that the claimant's job be substantially equal to that of a higher-paid person outside the claimant's protected class, nor do these statutes require the claimant to work in the same establishment as a comparator.

Prevailing Wage Laws

Davis-Bacon Act

Walsh-Healey Act

Services Contract Act

Several federal laws have been designed to make certain that workers employed on government contracts receive fair wages relative to other local workers. The three most important laws are the **Davis-Bacon Act** of 1931, the **Walsh-Healey Act** of 1936, and the **Services Contract Act** of 1965, and they cover federal contracts for construction, goods, and services, respectively. Typically, prevailing wage levels have been equal to union wage levels, which, in effect, creates a higher minimum wage for federally funded projects. At the same time, these regulations ensure that large federal projects, awarded on the basis of competitive bids, do not create a decline in an area's wage rates.

Pay Equity or Comparable Worth Policy

Proposed to eliminate bias

One contemporary pay topic concerns the policy of **comparable worth** or **pay equity** introduced earlier in the chapter. First enunciated in 1934 and adopted as policy in 1951 by over 100 nations (not the United States), a comparable worth or pay equity policy requires a pay structure that is based on an internal assessment of job worth (i.e., a job evaluation process). It has been proposed as a means of eliminating gender and (occasionally) racial discrimination in the wage-setting process.

Should an electrician earn more than a first-grade teacher, or a custodian more than a librarian? These questions are almost always resolved by the labor market and the forces of supply and demand. Advocates for comparable worth or pay equity policies argue that occupations dominated by female workers are paid less than "comparable" male-dominated jobs because of systematic discrimination against women in the labor market. Thus, to rely on the market is to merely continue with the systemic discrimination. A pay equity or comparable worth policy would require employers to establish wages that reflect similarities and differences in the "worth" of jobs for the particular organization, with "worth" derived from an internal study that typically uses a point-factor job evaluation method but then links points (which define the "worth") to wages *across* job families and then mandates comparable pay based on comparable points. Thus, market forces for any particular job are not the primary basis for setting rates.

Pay equity studies use point-factor job evaluation

Pay equity assumes that the traditional method of achieving equity within, but not between, job families is inherently unfair. The theory of "within but not between" assumes, for example, that clerical jobs are compared to each other, that skilled trades jobs are compared to each other, and that professional jobs are compared to each other. The problem with this assumption is that jobs are typically not compared across job families. Thus, a skilled trade job evaluated at 400 points on a point-factor plan might be paid 20 percent higher than a clerical job receiving the same number of points, due to different labor market rates. In Washington State, for example, the average wages of women were 20 percent lower than those of men for jobs found to have the same number of job evaluation points. Thus, jobs in the clerical families may have shared equitable pay, but they were systematically lower than wages paid to men in traditionally male-dominated jobs, such as skilled trades. Advocates of comparable worth maintain that the labor market undervalues the economic worth of jobs performed predominantly by women and minorities.

Comparisons *across* families to determine equity

Traditionally, the lower-paid job families included many women's jobs. For a number of reasons, job families with a large proportion of "female-dominated" jobs (defined in most comparable worth studies as jobs where more than 70 percent of the incumbents are women) have been compensated at a lower rate than have job families with many "male-dominated" jobs. According to the Bureau of Labor Statistics, in fact, 80 percent of U.S. female workers are employed in occupations in which at least 70 percent of all employees are women.[42]

Arguments against pay equity

Opponents to comparable worth pay policies present three arguments against the idea. First, they argue that, for most situations, there is no legal mandate to pay comparable worth salaries. Second, they argue that a comparable worth approach would mean inflating salaries relative to the external market and that most companies could not afford to do this and stay in business. In the State of Washington, for example, it was estimated in 1986 that providing a pay plan based on a comparable worth policy carried an annual cost of $400 million. Third, opponents argue that if women really want to advance in terms of salary, they can do so by preparing themselves to enter traditionally male-dominated jobs where they will enjoy the same pay—a right that is protected legally. This argument relies on an assumption that, over time, as women migrate away from lower-paid jobs because they can obtain more lucrative pay in other careers, the pay for such traditionally female work will rise to reflect the worker shortage.

Male vs. female wage differences reduced under pay equity policy

There is little question that differences between male and female wages are reduced under a pay equity policy. Women in Sweden, for example, earn 92 percent of what men earn under a long-standing pay equity program. The United Kingdom, Ireland, Switzerland, and Australia provide additional examples of wage gap decreases after pay equity programs were implemented. No country in the world pays women as much as men. (Sri Lanka, just southeast of India, leads the world in this regard, paying women, on average, 96 percent of what men earn.)

Paycheck Fairness Act

Various forms of federal pay equity legislation are pending before Congress. For example, the **Paycheck Fairness Act** was reintroduced by Senator Tom Harkin of Iowa in 2008 (it's been around since 1999). An amendment to the EPA, the law would establish "equal pay for equivalent work." For example, within individual companies, employers could not pay jobs that are held predominately by women less than jobs held predominately by men if those jobs are equivalent in value to the employer. The bill also protects workers on the basis of race or national origin. Like the EPA, the Paycheck Fairness Act makes exceptions for different wage rates based on seniority, merit, or quantity or quality of work. Other versions of "fair" pay legislation are also before Congress. Some form of amendment to the FLSA is now likely. The influence of unions and legislative successes at the state and local levels will keep the issue politically viable.

As of 2009, according to the **National Committee on Pay Equity,** 20 states have some form of pay equity policy for segments of the workforce. Seven states have comprehensive pay equity policies for all or almost all employees who work for those states. Bills have been introduced in over 25 state legislatures since 2000. However, as of January 2009, no major pieces of state legislation had passed since 2002. Check out www.pay-equity.org for recent activity.

Policy capturing

As has been typical to justify legislative action, advocates of a pay equity policy for employees of the State of Florida conducted a pay equity study to document what they regarded as "systemic" discrimination against women and minorities in the manner in which the state had been paying its employees. Known as **"policy capturing,"** the study derived the predictive dollar value for the factors of the "point-factor" system in order to "capture" the historical policy linking job factors to the actual pay of state employees.

Thus, an equation was derived that best explained the relationship between factor ratings from the job evaluation and the actual pay of the thousands of jobs under study. This equation was then used to study the "fairness" of the Florida pay system with the assumption that regardless of the job family under study, the application of the predictive equation using the particular factor ratings for any family would result in a prediction that approximated the actual pay for every job family. As is typical, however, that is not what was found. When the equation derived across all job families was used to predict the "female-dominated" job salary ("dominated" means over 70 percent of the occupants of the family are female), the predicted salary of the female-dominated job families was significantly higher than their actual salaries. The reverse effect was found for the male-dominated jobs such that their predicted salaries were significantly lower than their actual salaries. A study reporting these findings was presented to the Florida legislature for their action. Unlike other states that have implemented pay equity policies, the legislature took no action.

The Wage Gap

At the Wage Equity Day festivities in 2008, several speakers made reference to the "wage gap" between men and women. Despite over 40 years of the Equal Pay Act, the National Committee on Pay Equity reported in June 2008 that women earned 77 cents for every dollar earned by men, African-American women earned 72 cents on the dollar, and Hispanic women earned 59 cents per male dollar. Says Connecticut Congresswoman Rosa DeLauro, one of the co-authors of the **Paycheck Fairness Act,** "No matter how hard women work or whatever they achieve in terms of advancement in their own profession and degree, they will not be compensated equitably." But a new book disputes the arguments attributing the wage gap to discrimination. Says Warren Farrell, author of *Why Men*

Earn More, the wage gap exists primarily because of the type of work women choose and the number of hours worked.[43]

Farrell compared the starting salaries of men and women with Bachelor's Degrees in 26 categories of employment, from investment bankers to dieticians. Women are paid equally in one category; in every other category, their starting salaries exceed men's. A female investment banker's starting salary is 116 percent of a man's. A female dietician's is 130 percent, that is, $23,160 compared to $17,680.

Another argument Farrell makes is that women often prefer jobs with shorter and more flexible hours in order to accommodate family responsibilities. For example, women generally favor jobs that involve good social skills and no travel. These jobs generally pay less. Another reason men earn more is that they work more hours per week. According to the Bureau of Labor Statistics, full-time men work about 45 hours a week versus 42 for women. Women choose to avoid particularly dangerous jobs that pay well. Over 92 percent of occupational deaths are men. Of course, women have a legal right to enter dangerous professions, the most dangerous of which are over 95 percent male.

Other Compliance Issues

As indicated earlier, many states and localities have their own regulations that cover workers in addition to the federal legislation. Human resource professionals must stay educated on these matters and be prepared to ensure that their organization complies with such laws. Often legislation covers areas with which business management would rather not concern itself. Such issues as maintaining records that document compliance with the overtime provisions of the FLSA or documenting the basis for a particular position's exemption from coverage under the overtime provisions of FLSA are not issues that are foremost in the minds of most CEOs. However, the cost of noncompliance can be extremely high and can include back pay awards, penalties, and interest. One method that has been recommended

Compliance audit

to assist HR professionals is the **compliance audit.** This is an analysis of employee records and organizational policies, communications, and practices to ensure that both the letter and the spirit of the laws are being followed. This audit is an abbreviated form of the audit that would be conducted by a federal compliance officer if the organization were under review. The audit pinpoints problem areas so they can be proactively addressed.

In this section, we have examined the general methods and processes used by organizations to establish pay programs. We discussed the traditional approach, which may still be very effective in some organizations, and noted some recent trends. In addition, we briefly looked at the way the government involves itself in pay issues. In the next section, the emphasis is shifted away from wage and salary payments to the area of employee benefits.

FRINGE COMPENSATION: EMPLOYEE BENEFITS

Employee benefits focus on maintaining (or improving) the quality of life for employees and providing a level of protection and financial security for workers and for their family members. Like base pay plans, organizations use fringe compensation programs to attract, retain, and motivate qualified, competent employees.

Research supports the importance of the benefits package in applicants' job selection process.[44] Recent research, for example, shows that women are particularly attracted to a company with a strong pro-family fringe compensation package. These packages become relatively more important when the unemployment rate is low and the competition for qualified workers is high. However, employees tend to underestimate the cost of benefits to the

Employees underestimate the cost of benefits

organization. For example, one study found that current employees estimated the cost of benefits to the organization was 12 percent of payroll when the actual cost was 31 percent.[45] Organizations are now working harder to better explain the cost of the benefit package to employees.

Benefit trends

Three important trends characterize employee benefit plans as they exist in organizations today.[46] First, over the past several decades, the popularity of employee benefits has increased significantly. In 1929, benefits offered to employees averaged 3 percent of payroll; by 1950, the figure had risen to 16 percent; by 2004, the cost of benefits was about 29 percent of payroll.[47] Second, while benefit plans initially were quite uniform, recent years have seen considerable variation in the type of benefits offered. The third trend is the increased flexibility employees have these days in selecting their own benefit coverages.

The rise in the popularity of employee benefit programs is attributable to a variety of forces. During World War II, the War Labor Board (WLB) excluded employee benefit improvements from wage stabilization controls because such benefits were "on the fringe of wages," so benefit program improvements were not expected to be inflationary. Since then, benefits have grown largely due to favorable federal tax policies.[48]

Tax advantages

Three general types of tax advantages relate to employee benefit programs, provided that the plans comply with certain rules. First, employers are allowed **tax deductions** for the costs of benefit programs. In this way, the cost of benefits is treated in the same way as direct payroll costs. Second, employees receive many benefit plans, as well as some plan payouts, on a **tax-free** basis. For example, when an employer offers a health care plan, three things typically occur: (1) the organization deducts the cost of the plan from its earnings for tax purposes; (2) employees are not taxed on the cost of the plan that the employer has provided to them; (3) employees are not taxed on the reimbursement they receive under the terms of the plan for covered services. Particularly when individual tax rates are rising significantly, these tax advantages make employee benefit programs attractive alternatives to direct pay for many employees. The third tax advantage is that some benefits are **tax-deferred.** For example, when an employer sets aside pension money for an individual, taxes are not paid on that money (or the investment earnings on the money) until the money is actually withdrawn by the employee, presumably during retirement. Similarly, when an employee makes certain types of contributions to a company 401(k) program, those contributions are typically made on a pretax basis. Employer contributions are not taxable for the individual, nor is any interest accumulation taxable until the employee begins actually withdrawing the money. Liberal loan provisions and rollover options permit the delay of taxes even longer. Thus, favorable tax treatment has made employee benefits a worthwhile investment both for organizations and for individual workers.

Great differences in benefit programs

While employee benefit programs were at one time quite uniform, there is now considerable variance. Benefit programs vary as a consequence of the organization's human resource philosophy, its size, its location, the type of business, the industry, and the type of job that an individual holds.[49] Some companies such as Stride Rite, Johnson Wax, Procter and Gamble, and Merck have a strong pro-family orientation to their benefit package with options such as family care leave, child and elder care support, dependent care accounts, adoption benefits, alternative work schedules, and on-site day care. In general, larger companies offer a wider array of benefits.[50] Across large, medium, and small organizations, benefit programs for professional and technical employees tend to be the most comprehensive, followed by those for clerical and sales employees, and then for blue-collar and service employees.[51]

In 2008, serious consideration was being given in Congress to legislation that would require employers, health plan sponsors, and insurers to offer mental health coverage that is equal to other benefits provided under health care plans. Past attempts to pass a mental health parity bill have been strongly opposed by employer groups which claim such a measure would sharply increase the cost of health insurance and probably force businesses to trim or eliminate health care benefits.

Flexible benefits

A growing number of U.S. companies now offer flexible, or cafeteria-style, benefit plans.[52] With the increasing diversity of the workforce, cafeteria plans are particularly valued by the two-income family because duplicate coverage can be replaced with other valuable benefits, such as increased time off or child care allowances. Cafeteria plans are not new. Decades ago, organizations were reluctant to implement them for two reasons: (1) the increased administrative complexity created by managing a large variety of possible benefit combinations across an entire workforce and (2) the concern that benefit costs might rise dramatically when employees are allowed to opt out of coverages that they would be unlikely to use and replace those programs with benefits that they might use extensively. Over the past decade, however, the increased sophistication in user-friendly computer software and consulting firms that have built considerable track records assisting companies with these plans have supported the rapid growth of cafeteria plans, and this growth is expected to continue for the foreseeable future.

Categories of Employee Benefits

As we said earlier, fringe benefits may be divided into legally required programs and discretionary benefits. Discretionary benefits include (1) employee welfare programs; (2) long-term capital accumulation programs; (3) time-off plans; and (4) employee services.

Legally Required Programs

Figure 10-9 summarizes the principal provisions concerning legally required benefits. Five benefits programs are required by federal law. Social Security, unemployment insurance, and workers' compensation are basic income continuity programs. In other words, they provide payments when an individual is not working. The **Consolidated Omnibus Budget Reconciliation Act (COBRA)** and the **Family and Medical Leave Act (FMLA)** focus primarily on employees' right to maintain their health care benefits. The FMLA allows workers to take job-protected, unpaid time off to care for themselves or a family member. According to the Department of Labor, almost 17 percent of U.S. workers reported having used the FMLA over 18 months.

Social security

Social Security: Under the Social Security program, eligible individuals are covered by a comprehensive program of retirement, survivor, disability, and health benefits. Individuals are eligible for Social Security retirement benefits in the form of monthly payments when they reach the stipulated age under the program, and provided they have worked long enough to qualify for benefits.

Disability

Disability Social Security benefits are comparable to retirement benefits and are provided only when a disability is expected to endure for at least one year, or is expected to result in death. In addition, individuals must be disabled for six months before they qualify for payments. Survivor benefits may be available to a worker's beneficiaries, depending on their length (and recency) of employment.

Medicare

The Medicare program provides health care benefits to nearly all United States citizens aged 65 or older regardless of whether or not they have worked. Medicare is also available to individuals receiving Social Security disability benefits after a specified period of time. Medicare Part A covers hospital costs. Part B is a voluntary and contributory supplement covering medical expenses. Part C (passed in 1997) provides new health care coverage options to Medicare recipients, including managed care plans, medical savings accounts, and Medigap protection to fill the unpaid gaps in Medicare Parts A and B. Medicare Part D (passed in 2003; implemented in 2006) covers some prescription drug costs.

Figure 10-9 **Summary of Federal Laws Affecting Indirect Compensation**

Law	Provisions
Social Security Act of 1935	Requires that companies cover employees under comprehensive program of retirement, survivor, disability, and health benefits (OASDHI).
Workers' Compensation Laws	Requires that employers finance variety of benefits (i.e., lost wages, medical benefits, survivor benefits, and rehabilitation services) for employees with work-related illnesses or injuries on "no-fault" basis.
Federal Unemployment Tax Act (FUTA)	Requires that employers pay taxes to cover laid-off employees for up to 39 weeks (additional extensions possible).
Consolidated Omnibus Budget Reconciliation Act (COBRA)	Requires employers to provide access to health care coverage in particular instances when coverage would otherwise be terminated. Cost of coverage may be completely passed on to worker. Administrative record-keeping fee also may be charged.
Family and Medical Leave Act of 1993 (FMLA)	Requires employers to continue providing health care coverage to employees who are on FMLA leave (up to 12 weeks per year for specified family emergencies) on same basis as it was provided before the leave.

Employers and employees share equally the cost of providing Social Security coverage to individuals. The tax paid by employers and employees is based on the Federal Insurance Contributions Act (FICA). In 2008, the tax for the retirement, survivor, and disability portion of the Social Security program was 12.4 percent of the first $102,000 earned by an employee. Half this amount (6.2 percent) was paid by the employer; the other half was paid by the employee through payroll deduction. The Medicare portion of the Social Security program cost 2.9 percent on all earnings (with the same employer–employee split).

When the program was established in 1938, there were 39 workers for each retiree. In 1950, there were 16 workers paying in for each retiree. Today, there are about 3.5 workers for each Social Security beneficiary. Unless major action is taken and soon, there is big fiscal trouble ahead for the federal government. Social Security, Medicare, and Medicaid represented over 40 percent of the federal budget in 2008. Assuming no major changes to these programs, it is estimated that by 2030 the three programs will consume about 70 percent of the federal budget. Without growing and huge deficits, tax increases of around 40 percent would be necessary unless there were major cuts in other federal programs (including defense). Unfortunately, young workers and families, not retirees, would bear the brunt of either the necessary higher taxes or degraded public services.

Unemployment insurance

Unemployment Insurance: The unemployment insurance program in the United States is jointly managed by the federal government and the states. The program is designed to encourage employers to stabilize their workforces, and it provides emergency income for workers when they are unemployed.[53] The federal unemployment tax is 6.2 percent on the first $7,000 of wages. However, in the majority of states, an employer's tax rate is higher than this federal guideline and is based on general pay trends in the state. In addition, most states allocate taxes to individual organizations using an "experience rating" approach which imposes higher tax rates on companies that create the unemployment.

In terms of payouts under the unemployment program, the individual states decide how much to pay, how long to pay, and on what basis they will pay. In general, employees who are covered under FUTA (the Federal Unemployment Tax Act), and whose employment is terminated, are eligible to receive unemployment payments for up to 26 weeks. A 1970 amendment permitted an extension of these benefits, usually for an additional 13 weeks. Such Supplemental Unemployment Benefits (SUBs) are usually triggered when a state's unemployment rate exceeds a particular level. Since late 2001, when the economy weakened, additional 13-week extensions have been approved, permitting unemployment recipients up to 65 weeks of benefits such extensions were in effect in 2009.

To be eligible to receive benefits, the worker must have been employed previously in an occupation covered by the insurance, must have been dismissed by the organization (but not for misconduct), must be actively seeking work, and (in all states but Rhode Island and New York) may not be unemployed due to a labor dispute.

Workers' compensation

Workers' Compensation Insurance: Unlike unemployment compensation insurance, workers' compensation (WC) programs are managed solely by the states with no direct federal involvement or mandatory standards. Typically, workers' compensation provides for medical expenses and pay due to lost work time in cases where the illness or injury is work-related. The primary purpose of workers' compensation programs is to provide for benefits to injured or ill workers on a no-fault basis and thus to eliminate the costly lawsuits that would otherwise clog the legal system and disrupt employer–employee relations.[54]

The first laws for handling occupational disabilities and death were enacted in 1910, and they have existed in all states since 1948. Employers are fully responsible for the cost of the coverage, and they may not require any employee contributions. To facilitate the consideration of claims, most states have established workers' compensation boards or commissions. In most states, employers are free to select their own carriers to insure the risk (or to self-insure the risk), investigate claims, and process payments. More will be said about workers' compensation programs in Chapter 14.

COBRA

Consolidated Omnibus Budget Reconciliation Act of 1985 (COBRA): This law was enacted in order to provide current and former employees, and their eligible dependents, with a temporary extension of employer-provided group health insurance when coverage would otherwise be lost. When it is the employee whose coverage is lost (e.g., layoff or other form of termination), the individual has the right to continue medical coverage for up to 18 months. When a dependent's coverage is lost (e.g., due to the death of the worker, divorce, or reaching the maximum age for a dependent child), the covered individual is entitled to continue the coverage for a maximum of 36 months. In all cases, the individual pays the full cost of the coverage and organizations have the option of adding a 2 percent surcharge to cover administrative costs.

FMLA

Family and Medical Leave Act of 1993 (FMLA): FMLA entitles all eligible employees to receive unpaid leave for up to 12 weeks per year for specified family and medical emergencies relating to self, spouse, parents, and children. When the employee returns to work, the act requires the employer to place the individual in the same or an equivalent job, with the same pay, benefits, and conditions of employment. During the leave, the employer is required to continue to provide coverage under the health care program on the same basis as it was provided before the leave. In other words, if the cost of the insurance was shared between the employer and employee, the employer can continue to require such cost contributions. If an employee on a leave fails to live up to his or her financial obligations to the plan (e.g., payment within 30 days), the employer may drop the employee after giving at least 15 days' notice. Supervisors may have personal liability for violations of the FMLA.

In 2008, FMLA was revised to provide up to 26 weeks of leave per 12-month period to an eligible employee who is the spouse, son, daughter, parent, or next of kin to care for a wounded member of the U.S. Armed Forces (the latter term in this revision specifically includes National Guard and Reserves). New Jersey recently became the third state (with California and Washington) to provide paid family leave for workers to care for newborns, newly adopted children, or seriously ill family members.

Discretionary Plans: Employee Welfare Programs

The benefits of greatest concern to both employees and employers in this category are health care plans. Also included in this category are survivor benefits, which include all types of life insurance.

Health care

Health Care Plans: In 2007, 71 percent of workers had access to employer-provided health care benefits and 52 percent actually participated in such plans. On average, employers paid 81 percent of the cost of premiums for single coverage, and 71 percent of the cost for family coverage. Actual employee contributions towards health care premiums averaged $81.37 per month for single coverage and $312.78 per month for family coverage.[55]

A disturbing contemporary trend is the dropping of health care benefits for workers and retirees. Can an employer drop health care benefits for workers who are under the age of 50 while maintaining them for retirees? The Supreme Court recently ruled in *General Dynamics Land Systems v. Cline* that the Age Discrimination in Employment Act does not prohibit an employer from practicing "reverse age discrimination" where older workers are favored over younger workers who are over 39.

Health Care Management Tools: Four other health care management tools are increasingly popular: (1) wellness programs, (2) personal responsibility clauses, (3) periodic health care plan audits, and (4) managed care plans. **Wellness programs** are typically used in two ways: (1) to educate employees to make informed decisions about their lifestyles and their health care and (2) to challenge employees' belief that employers are responsible for their health and for paying all their medical care costs. One survey found that 76 percent of respondents had wellness plans in place.[56] Wellness programs will be discussed further in Chapter 14.

Wellness programs

Personal responsibility clauses

Personal responsibility clauses are based on the principle that if employees or their dependents take personal risks, then they should bear additional responsibility for the costs arising from resulting illness or injury. The two most targeted behaviors for plan incentive or disincentive strategies are smoking and seat belt use but other activities (e.g., extreme sports) may also apply.

Health plan audits

Health care plan audits focus on carefully tracking plan utilization and costs in order to determine whether the organization's health care spending is generally effective.[57] Audits include examining claims to ensure that benefits are paid accurately and within acceptable time frames, conducting employee surveys about health care and lifestyle issues, tracking which providers are widely used (for the purpose of possibly negotiating volume discounts), and making certain that when more than one insurance plan is in effect (e.g., coverage under a spouse's plan), benefit payments are correctly coordinated.

Managed care

Managed care continues to grow. Popular approaches include **health maintenance organizations (HMOs)** and **preferred provider organizations (PPOs).** HMOs are organizations comprised of health care professionals who provide services on a prepaid basis. PPOs are usually hospitals and health care professionals that offer reduced rates based on a contractual arrangement with the organization.

Government Regulation of Health Care Programs: The **Employee Retirement Income Security Act of 1974 (ERISA)** is the most comprehensive piece of employee benefits legislation ever enacted in the United States.[58] It was passed because many retiring workers were not getting the benefits that had been promised to them over their working lifetimes.[59] Earlier in this chapter, we described the tax advantages enjoyed by company-sponsored benefit plans. In order to qualify for this favorable treatment, however, an employee benefit plan must be "qualified"; that is, the plan must be in full compliance with all provisions of ERISA.

ERISA

HIPAA

Under ERISA, health care plans must be set forth in written documents that clearly describe the terms of the plan. Employees are entitled to detailed information concerning their health care plan and the state of its financing. Each year, organizations are required to submit annual reports concerning the state of the plan and to send a summary of the annual report to all plan participants. In 1996, ERISA was revised to include the **Health Insurance Portability and Accountability Act (HIPAA).** This act, which applies to all employers offering group health plans, significantly reduced an employer's ability to deny or limit coverage for preexisting conditions, or to require higher premiums based on an individual's medical condition. Effective in 2003, health care privacy rules were implemented that require health care entities (plans, providers, etc.) to obtain a patient's written consent before releasing any health care information. In order to obtain consent, the act requires full disclosure about how and for what purpose such medical information will be used.

ADEA

Pregnancy Discrimination Act

Under the **Age Discrimination in Employment Act (ADEA),** employer health plans must offer the same benefits to employees aged 65 and older (and their spouses, if applicable) as the plan provides to younger employees. (Traditionally, organizations moved employees at age 65 onto Medicare and provided a Medicare Supplement policy. This practice has been outlawed under these ADEA provisions.) The **Pregnancy Discrimination Act of 1978** requires that pregnancy and pregnancy-related disabilities be treated the same as other illnesses or disabilities. Employers who offer health care plans, temporary disability plans, and sick leave are now legally required to include pregnancy as a covered condition. As mentioned earlier, both **COBRA** and **FMLA** are primarily aimed at preserving health care benefits for individuals.

Life insurance

Life Insurance: One of the oldest and most common forms of employee benefit is group life insurance. In 2004, 60 percent of full-time workers in the United States were covered under company-provided life insurance programs. More than half of those programs based benefits on a fixed multiple of earnings. The most common multiple is 1.0 times earnings (59 percent of plans), followed by 2.0 times earnings (25 percent of plans).[60] Group life insurance typically provides coverage to all employees of an organization without physical examinations, with premiums typically based on the group characteristics.[61]

Discretionary Plans: Long-Term Capital Accumulation Plans

A **pension is** a payment to a retired employee based on the extent and level of employment with the organization. The term *long-term capital accumulation plan* is the generic name for any program that seeks to systematically set aside money during one's working lifetime, primarily for use during one's retirement. This category includes not only pensions, but also 401(k) programs, thrift and other savings programs, traditional profit-sharing plans, and a large variety of similar arrangements.

Pension plans

The Major Pension Plans: In 2007, 61 percent of workers were employed in companies that offered pension plans. Fifty-one percent actually participated in such plans.[62] There are two types of plans: **defined benefit plans** and **defined contribution plans.** A defined benefit plan (DB) guarantees a specific retirement payment based on a percentage of preretirement income. Typically, the amount is based on years of service, average earnings during a specified time period (e.g., last five years), and age at time of retirement. The typical target benefit in a defined benefit plan is to replace approximately 50 percent of an individual's

Defined benefit plans

final average pay.[63] A small but growing percentage of defined benefit plans (approximately 5 percent) are indexed to adjust pensions for inflation.[64] In a defined benefit plan, the employer funds employees' pensions over their working lifetimes. An employer's commitment to an employee is for a particular payout, at a particular time, based on a formula specified by the plan. Defined benefit programs typically involve significant administrative fees, particularly for actuarial services, to ensure that the plan is financed appropriately under ERISA requirements. In addition, defined benefit plans are required to purchase insurance with the Pension Benefit Guarantee Corporation (PBGC), which acts like the FDIC by insuring pension moneys in the event that the company goes bankrupt (or is otherwise unable to meet its promised obligation).

Pension Guaranty Benefit Corporation (PGBC)

In 2005, United Airlines, under bankruptcy protection, was granted permission to terminate its employee pension plans that would have obligated United to pay $3.2 billion in pension payouts over five years. The **Pension Guaranty Benefit Corporation** assumed responsibility for the 134,000 people who were part of the pension plans. The result of the takeover significantly lowered pension checks for United retirees with obligations to the PGBC of around $10 billion. Experts worry that other companies will opt to dump their pension obligations on the already deeply indebted PGBC.

Many large companies cut their pensions from 2005 through 2008 according to Watson Wyatt Worldwide, a compensation consulting firm. Eleven percent of these firms either discontinued their pension plans altogether or froze benefits to workers. It is estimated that defined benefit plans fell about $500 billion into arrears in 2008. How did this happen? Companies lobbied for and received lax regulations on how to calculate pension obligations, estimating returns on pension investments twice as high as they actually returned. Companies do this so they can use more revenue to report as earnings. They of course have the PBGC to fall back on to bail them out if they cannot meet real pension obligations. Unfortunately, at the end of 2008, the PBGC had a $20 billion deficit, mainly because of the pension obligations they've already assumed and because companies do not pay sufficient premiums to adequately fund this federal insurance agency.

Most public employers (e.g., state and local government) have defined benefit programs. Police and fire departments, school systems, universities, and park budgets will have to cover benefits for a growing number of retired and near retired public employees. States have promised about $2.7 trillion in pension benefits, health care and other benefits for their retired workers in the next 30 years. Unfortunately, only about $2 trillion has been set aside, so the balance will have to come from annual state and local budgets.

Defined contribution plans

In a **defined contribution (DC)** plan, an employer provides a specific dollar amount (typically a percent of base salary) that is paid into an individual's account each period. The most common DC plan is the 401(k) plan, which is named after the section of the Internal Revenue Code which regulates these plans. In a typical 401(k) plan, employees defer a percent of pay (subject to certain limitations) that is fully or partially matched by the company. Employees choose among investment options and, typically, may take the vested portion of the account with them if they leave employment before they are eligible to retire (vesting refers to the point in time when pension monies set aside by a company become the actual property of that individual).

In a 401(k) plan, the employer makes no promise to an employee about a pension amount: an individual's pension is the account balance at the time of retirement. As a result, administrative costs are lower under 401(k) programs (and other DC plans) than they are under traditional DB plans, and plan communication is simplified. DB plans have been more common historically than DC plans, but recent concerns about cost uncertainties pushed many companies to replace their DB plans with the simpler, less expensive DC plans. IBM froze pension benefits for its American employees beginning in 2008 and now offer 401(k) plans. Among the many companies that have recently frozen pension plans for employees are Verizon, Hewlett-Packard, Motorola, and Sears. In 1990, similar numbers of employees were covered under DB plans (35 percent) and DC plans (35 percent). By 2009, the percent of employees covered under DB plans declined to under 20 percent while the number of employees covered under DC plans was about 40 percent. In fact, the number of employees participating in 401(k) plans since 1995 has more than doubled.

Figure 10-10   **Retirement Plan Trends**

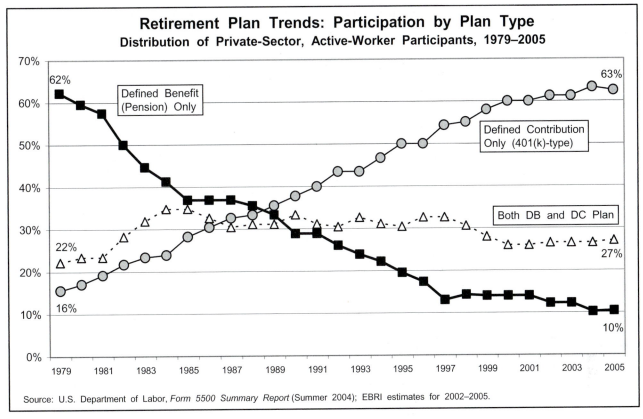

Source: U.S. Department of Labor, *Form 5500 Summary Report* (Summer 2004); EBRI estimates for 2002–2005.

Employee Stock Ownership Plan (ESOP)

Figure 10-10 presents the trends for the private sector. Another popular form of DC plan is the Employee Stock Ownership Plan (ESOP). In an ESOP, the company contributes stock, rather than cash, to employee accounts. Individual allocations are typically based on a person's level of earnings. At the time of retirement, an employee participating in an ESOP receives cash that is directly based on the value of the underlying stock at that time. Some 401(k) plans include company stock as one of the possible investment choices. When this occurs, employees who choose to invest their account balance heavily in the company's stock are, in effect, converting their 401(k) plan into an ESOP. Enron's 401(k) program provides a good example. Because of the enormous success of Enron in its heyday, many employees bypassed 19 other investment options, choosing instead to invest their 401(k) account balances in Enron stock. When the company crashed and burned, employee 401(k) balances were wiped out. Critics have since argued that organizations should limit the amount of 401(k) money that can be directly invested in the company's stock (unless, of course, the plan is specifically designed to be an ESOP). Other forms of DC plans include traditional profit-sharing plans, thrift and savings plans, Section 403(b) tax-deferred annuity plans (for education institutions and/or private tax-exempt organizations), and Section 457 plans (for government employees).

Government Role in Pension Plans: As mentioned earlier, the **Employee Retirement Income Security Act (ERISA)** regulates employee pension plans. The requirement that defined benefit plans purchase insurance through the PBGC is an ERISA rule. Since establishment of this rule, more than 1,500 pension plans have resorted to the PBGC in order to meet their pension commitments.[65] ERISA has passed extensive rules concerning the way pension funds may be invested (in general, using a "prudent man" rule focusing on capital preservation), has broadened participation rules (people at all levels in the organization typically enter a plan after only one year of employment), and liberalized vesting rules (after two to three years, at least a portion of the company contribution belongs to the employee). Before ERISA, many pension plans had no vesting provisions; if you weren't working for the company the day you retired, you were not entitled to any benefit.

ERISA

Other nonbenefits legislation has significantly influenced pension plan provisions. The **Civil Rights Act of 1964** and subsequent amendments, which prohibit discrimination on the basis of gender, outlawed pension differences between men and women even if such distinctions were based on real life expectancy differences. Today, most plans use unisex tables that combine the life expectancy rates of men and women.[66] Amendments to the **Age Discrimination in Employment Act (ADEA)** outlawed mandatory retirement ages and required that individuals who worked beyond the firm's "normal" retirement age must continue to accumulate retirement credits on the same basis as any other eligible employee.[67]

Discretionary Plans: Time-Off Programs

The cost of paid time off represents one of the highest benefit costs for employers today.[68] In March 2004, the cost of paid time off amounted to 6.7 percent of total hourly compensation. According to the United States Bureau of Labor Statistics (BLS), 77 percent of full-time workers receive paid vacation (average 9 days per year); 76 percent receive paid holidays (average 8 days per year); 57 percent receive paid sick leave; 77 percent receive pay for jury duty; and 54 percent receive military leave.[69] Of course, multinationals must comply with the laws of the host country for its citizens.

Long-term disability (LTD) coverage typically provides for the replacement of at least some income in the event that an individual contracts a long-term illness or sustains an injury that prevents him/her from working. In small organizations, 20 percent of organizations cover full-time workers with some form of protection. In medium and large organizations, 43 percent of organizations report covering full-time workers in LTD programs.[70]

Discretionary Plans: Employee Services

Although there are a variety of programs, the most common employee services are education programs, employee assistance programs, employee recognition programs, and child care. We will briefly discuss each of these below.

Education Programs: Many organizations have educational programs for their employees that range from literacy programs to tuition refunds for college or graduate school. According to BLS, 72 percent of medium and large U.S. firms offer job-related tuition plans and 36 percent of small organizations offer job-related tuition assistance.[71] In addition, some companies are helping their workers cope with educating their kids. Aluminum Co. of America, for example, hands out over 200 scholarships a year to employees' children.

Employee Assistance Programs (EAPs)

Employee Assistance Programs and Mental Health Care: Employee assistance programs (EAPs) typically provide counseling, diagnosis, and treatment for substance abuse, family and marital problems, depression, and financial and other personal difficulties. EAPs are used by about 70 percent of Fortune 500 companies with about one-third of U.S. employees having access to the programs. Other companies simply cover treatment for mental disorders within their health care programs. EAPs tend to be cheaper and more effective than simple reimbursement.[72] We will discuss EAPs in more detail in Chapter 14.

Employee Recognition Programs: A growing number of organizations offer awards to employees for extended service, work-related achievements, and suggestions for improving organizational effectiveness. Awards are often in the form of gifts and travel rather than cash. Suggestion systems offer incentives to employees who submit ideas that result in greater efficiency or profitability for the company. According to the National Association of Suggestion Systems, employees were awarded almost $128 million for suggestions in one year.

Child care

Child Care: A growing number of companies are also offering various forms of child care benefits. There is evidence that this benefit can reduce employee absences, improve recruitment, and help retain valuable employees.[73] In 2007, BLS reported that 15 percent of U.S. workers had access to employer assistance for child care, most typically as a feature in a cafeteria benefits program. A small but growing number of companies offer on-site centers. Dominion Bankshares in Roanoke, Virginia, reported decreased absences among its 950 employees since its on-site day care center was established. With a variety of government financial incentives now available, and considerable political activity on the subject, there is every reason to believe that child care will become quite common as an employee benefit in years to come.

There is a growing recognition that illness among employees' children can be costly to the company in terms of absenteeism, tardiness, and work stress. AT&T invested in sick bays through hospitals and child care centers. Hoffman-LaRoche and Hughes Aircraft offer sick child care to employees' children through convenient medical centers. The 3M Company covers up to 78 percent of the fees for home health care for kids.

COMMUNICATING THE BENEFITS PROGRAM

As we indicated earlier in the chapter, most employees have little understanding of the costs involved in a benefits program. While ERISA requires that plan and cost information be routinely distributed to benefit participants, most employees know very little about how to value such programs, particularly relative to the programs offered by others. Yet, if an organization's benefits are supposed to be a key tool for attracting and retaining competent workers, this type of understanding would seem to be of paramount importance.

Over the past decade or so, companies have focused attention on improving the information they provide to employees about their benefits. The goals in benefits communication should be to clearly explain the coverages that are available under the plan and to present the value of the benefit package to current and future employees. Today, many employers provide counseling for employees to enhance their understanding of the benefits program and have stepped up their investment in benefits-related recruitment literature. One very popular tool is the **Benefits Statement,** which is a periodic report customized for and distributed to each individual employee identifying his/her coverages and providing very specific cost information on each such program. Other methods used to explain benefits include paycheck inserts, employee publications, posters, and audio/video recorded messages.

Benefit statements

When organizations implement flexible, or cafeteria, benefits, they typically find that they must step up their investment in employee benefits education. When employees are given choices about which coverages to select and which to decline, organizations should feel comfortable that employees are making these selections based on an educated understanding of each benefit option. At Citicorp, for example, employees are exposed to software, videos, seminars, and several other teaching tools that explain their flexible benefit program. Each Citicorp employee receives a printout of benefits compared to the previous year, a computer disk, and a workbook that explains how to determine the tax and "out-of-pocket" implications of the benefit options. Each year, the University of Miami holds a two-day, on-campus benefits fair in which every benefits provider stands ready to give whatever information employees need in order to make their benefit selections for the coming year. Providers include claims processors, representatives from each health care provider (every HMO sends a team of representatives to explain their programs to individuals), and each of the five firms that invest pension funds. The university takes the opportunity to combine the benefits fair with a health fair and provides free flu shots, tests cholesterol levels, and provides other information relating to wellness issues. In addition, at the end of the year, the university sends every employee a personalized benefits statement itemizing and describing an individual's coverages and their costs to the university.

Benefit fairs

INTERNATIONAL COMPENSATION

With over 100,000 U.S. companies now involved in some type of global venture, it is estimated that over 60 million workers are employed overseas by U.S. companies. More than 75 percent of the employees of Gillette work outside the United States and more than 70 percent of profits come from overseas sales. Chapter 2 discussed the HR strategies that companies use to help guide an organization's expansion overseas (i.e., ethnocentric, polycenric, geocentric, regiocentric). The three types of workers were also discussed (parent-country nationals, host-country nationals, and third-country nationals). McDonald's now has over 10,000 restaurants in over 100 countries, and the vast majority of the employees are host-country nationals. The expansion of retail giants such as Wal-Mart, Home Depot, and Office Depot into foreign markets has followed this same pattern.

While the discussion here focuses on executive and professional compensation for multinational corporations, there is no question that labor costs (both cash compensation and benefits) play a major role in corporate decisions regarding plant and operations openings, closings, and locations. Virtually no teddy bears are made on U.S. soil today because they can be produced at a fraction of the cost in a developing country such as Haiti or Honduras. The costs of total compensation plus ancillary regulation are the main reasons manufacturing and even some service organizations have moved from the United States.

To fully realize their growth potential, U.S. companies must staff their international operations with personnel who are technically competent, culturally proficient, and cost-effective. In the early stages of globalization, when managers were needed for overseas operations, companies often chose successful managers from company headquarters and enticed them to spend time establishing and building such operations. The main HR goal was ensuring that these managers were "kept financially whole" through a series of complex allowances plus special incentives and benefits.

Trends in global management

As organizations have become more proficient in effectively managing global overseas operations, two trends have emerged. First, the availability of well-trained, competent host-country nationals prepared to manage businesses within their borders has increased. As organizations have achieved access to larger, broader markets by globalizing, many host countries have increased the number of jobs in their economy, improved their standards of living, and benefited from transfers of technology. One form of technological transfer has involved the improved ability on the part of host-country nationals to direct and manage enterprises. In addition, in almost all cases, it's cheaper to employ host-country nationals than to use expatriates, particularly if the reference point for expatriate compensation is the United States, Germany, or a similar country that has both high management salaries and a strong currency.[74] AT&T estimates that expatriate managers cost three times as much as host-country nationals. And yet, the assignment failure rate among expatriates is considerably higher than the failure rate for host-country nationals.[75] AT&T, like so many other American companies, has seen its overseas business increasing, but it has reduced the number of expatriates, replacing them with host-country nationals.

Host-country national more likely to be available

The second trend involves the growing recognition that managing global operations involves a particular expertise that is different from traditional U.S. managerial technology. No longer is an international "tour of duty" simply an assignment. No longer is sending over an American manager in order to supervise operations and resolve problems based on the "American way" considered to be an effective solution. Instead, organizations are increasingly committed to developing management teams that are globally focused. In some organizations, considerable global experience is recognized as a major strategic imperative. At General Electric, for example, an individual will not advance beyond a particular level without significant experience managing overseas operations. Each of the final candidates in the search for Jack Welch's replacement had spent considerable time working outside the United States during the past decade or so. *The Wall Street Journal* reports that 28 percent of executive-level searches required individuals with significant overseas management experience.[76] According to management guru Rosabeth Moss Kanter, global management skills are becoming a major core competence for future business leaders. Such leaders will be globally skilled as (1) integrators, who will see beyond obvious cultural country and cultural differences; (2) diplomats, who can resolve conflicts and influence locals to accept world standards or commonalities; and (3) cross-fertilizers, who recognize the best from various places and adapt it for utilization elsewhere.[77]

Developing globally-focused teams

Global management skills

The result is that international compensation programs, like base pay programs, are in a state of transition as their emphasis shifts. Typical questions asked these days include: "When should we utilize a host-country national versus someone from someplace else?" "How much can we afford to spend in order to provide developmental opportunities for high-potential employees?" "How should we integrate third-country and host-country nationals with parent-country nationals in order to develop a world-class, global workforce?" The answers to these questions have strong implications for compensation practices. Yet, little formal research is available to guide compensation policy and practice in global settings.[78]

Going-rate approach

Two traditional approaches exist in the area of international compensation: (1) the **going-rate approach** and (2) the **balance sheet approach.**[79] In the going-rate, or market-rate, approach, pay is linked to the prevailing pay in the local area. Burger King, for example, uses a standardized job evaluation instrument (translated into eight languages) and a standard pay structure for its restaurants. However, personnel in different countries receive different pay based on market surveys conducted within each country. In general, this approach is very similar to the general compensation model described earlier in this chapter (i.e., conduct job evaluation, review pay surveys, create a final structure). However, the going rate also can be used for expatriates. When using the approach, however, the organization must carefully consider its relevant market and the reference points it will use. For example, a Japanese bank operating in New York City, using a management team from Japan, would need to decide whether its reference point would be local U.S. salaries, other Japanese competitors in New York, all foreign banks operating in the area, or other Japanese expatriates in the region.

Balance sheet

The traditional approach used by U.S. companies for compensating expatriates is the **balance sheet approach,** in which the goal is "to keep the expatriate whole." This usually means that pay equity focuses on other home-country colleagues and compensating the individual for the additional costs of an international assignment. What happens to third-country nationals? Traditionally, companies headquartered in the United States used U.S. pay practices as the reference point for U.S. expatriates and home-country practices as the reference points for third-country nationals. This most certainly saves money, but it can create serious pay inequities when expatriates from different home countries work together.[80]

International pay scales

A newer, emerging approach resolves this dichotomy by developing an international pay scale that ties all expatriate pay to some common reference point. This approach means that pay remains relatively equivalent regardless of the location of a particular assignment, or the home country of a particular expatriate. This approach further standardizes international compensation and moves it away from an individual, case-by-case focus.[81]

Three factors typically influence an organization's approach to international pay design, particularly when expatriates are used.[82] First, the expected length of the assignment influences the type and amount of special benefits and allowances. Assignments lasting less than one year, typically, do not require major modifications to domestic pay practices. Second, the degree of mobility expected of the expatriate influences practices. Assignments that require the employee to move from one foreign location to another will probably require greater incentives to offset family disruptions. Third, the desired reference point to be used for pay equity purposes makes a difference in pay program design. Some companies are beginning to use host-country pay levels (i.e., the going-rate approach described above) for expatriates on long-term assignments, because they believe that it facilitates an individual's integration into foreign countries and avoids obvious pay inequities within local work groups.

Compensation for international assignments typically has four components, each of which is explained below: (1) base salary, (2) foreign service premiums, (3) allowances, and (4) benefits.

Base Salary

In international compensation, base salary represents the amount of cash compensation that will be provided to an individual each pay period, plus it often serves as a reference point for calculating other allowances. Base salary may be paid in parent- or host-country currency. If parent-country currency is used, the organization must monitor fluctuations in the exchange rate (since the expatriate will be required to exchange the money in order to make local purchases). If host-country currency is used, the organization must monitor the country's inflation rate and changes in the cost of living (to ensure that the expatriate's purchasing power does not inappropriately erode).

Foreign Service Premiums

Foreign service premiums are monetary payments above and beyond base salary that companies offer in order to encourage employees to accept expatriate assignments. Such premiums typically apply to assignments that extend beyond a year. Foreign service premiums tend to range between 5 and 40 percent of base pay.[83] Companies typically disburse premiums

357

Figure 10-11
U.S. Department of State Indices of Hardship Differentials and Danger Pay—January 2008

City, Country	Hardship Differential	Danger Pay
Kabul, Afghanistan	35%	35%
Minsk, Belarus	25	—
Beijing, China	10	—
Bogota, Colombia	5	15
Santo Domingo, Dominican Republic	20	—
Tallinn, Estonia	10	—
Athens, Greece	0	—
Port-au-Prince, Haiti	25	20
Bombay, India	20	—
Jerusalem	0	20
Antananarivo, Madagascar	25	—
Mexico City, Mexico	15	—
Islamabad, Pakistan	20	25
Lima, Peru	15	—
Warsaw, Poland	0	—
Moscow, Russia	15	—
Riyadh, Saudi Arabia	20	25
Freetown, Sierra Leone	30	—
Ankara, Turkey	10	—
Caracas, Venezuela	20	—

Source: www. http://aoprals.state.gov/content/Documents/Jan08quar.doc. Accessed July 25, 2008.

to expatriates through periodic lump-sum payments in order to remind the individual that the payment is directly tied to the international assignment.[84]

Hardship pay

Hardship premiums are used to compensate expatriates for exceptionally hard living and working conditions in some foreign locations. Many organizations refer to the U.S. Department of State schedule that uses three criteria in identifying hardship: (1) difficult living conditions due to inadequate housing, isolation, inadequate transportation facilities, and lack of food or consumer services; (2) physical hardship relating to extreme climates, high altitudes, and the presence of dangerous conditions that might affect physical and mental well-being; and (3) unhealthy conditions, such as diseases and epidemics, lack of public sanitation, and inadequate health facilities. In the late 1990s, the State Department identified 150 places as hardship locations. Hardship allowances range from 5 to 25 percent of base salary. Like foreign service premiums, organizations tend to provide them in periodic lump-sum payments. **Danger pay** compensates employees for their willingness to work in politically unstable places. Figure 10-11 shows a sample of some hardship and dangerous locations and the percent differential paid for working in these areas.[85]

Danger pay

Allowances

There is great variation in the types of allowances that are used in international compensation. Changes in **purchasing power** due to inflation and **exchange rate** fluctuations (both mentioned earlier) are typically handled with cash allowances. Most organizations provide some type of **housing allowance** in order to provide a level of comfort to the international worker. Depending on the company and the country, housing allowances range from company-provided housing (mandatory or optional), to a fixed-dollar cash bonus, to a cash allowance calculated as a percentage of base salary. **Educational allowances** provide for a variety of needs and are mainly focused toward the expatriates' children. Possible allowances include the cost of private or boarding schools, language class tuition, books and supplies, room and board, and uniforms. **Relocation allowances** typically cover moving, shipping, and storage charges; temporary living expenses; subsidies for major appliance or car purchases; and lease-related charges. Increasingly, organizations are providing special **spouse assistance** to help offset income lost by an expatriate's spouse as a result of relocating abroad. Allowances include cash payments equivalent to the spouse's former wages, assistance in locating suitable employment in the new location (e.g., paying search fees), and continuing supplements if the spouse's income is less than previously earned. Many companies also offer **home leave allowances** in order to encourage the maintenance of ties with family and friends. Such allowances usually cover all expenses relating to visits back to the home country (usually, two trips per year).

Expatriate Benefits

In many ways, expatriate benefits are a bigger problem in international compensation than pay. Employee benefits and the related tax issues vary considerably from country to country. Key questions that an organization needs to ask itself when dealing with the benefits of expatriates include: "Should we keep expatriates in parent-country programs, even if we do not get a tax deduction for it?" "Can we legally enroll the individual in the host-country benefits and make up the differences in actual coverage?" "What should we do about Social Security issues?" Within the European Union, Social Security is portable. It is not in most other places in the world.

Most U.S. expatriates remain under their parent-country's benefit plan. In countries where employees may not opt out of Social Security (or other mandatory pension) coverage, the firm will typically cover this expense.

Taxation issues

One particularly challenging international compensation problem involves taxation.[86] For U.S. expatriates, an assignment overseas often means that they will be double-taxed—both in the country of assignment and in the United States. Most organizations choose between two strategies for managing taxes on behalf of their expatriates. In the **tax equalization approach,** firms withhold taxes based on the home-country tax obligation and pay all taxes in the host country. The **tax protection approach** involves the employee paying all taxes up to the amount he or she would pay in the home country. Under this approach, considering the tax credit for foreign earned income provided by the United States, if taxes in the foreign country are less than those that would have been paid in the United States, the international employee gets to keep the windfall.

SUMMARY

Because of the importance that compensation holds for their lifestyle and self-esteem, individuals are very concerned that they be paid a fair and competitive wage. Organizations are concerned with pay, not only because of its importance as a cost of doing business, but also because it motivates important decisions of employees about taking a job, leaving a job, and performance on the job.

Base pay

When designing **base salary** compensation plans, it is important that an organization choose an approach that is in alignment with its organizational philosophy and that supports its organizational goals. In some cases, the traditional approach to pay still provides the best answer. This approach involves the use of a job evaluation plan (to measure internal job worth and to foster internal equity), the review of market salary data (to identify externally competitive practices), and the reconciliation of these two in the form of a final pay structure. Due to the basic changes in organizations today and the new global challenges and opportunities, there is a growing search for new compensation approaches in the hope that they will better focus employees on achieving organizational goals. Such new approaches to pay include broadbanding, pay for knowledge (or skills-based pay), and team pay plans. To date, however, the relative effectiveness of these new approaches remains to be tested.

Employee benefits

Employee benefits programs are also the subject of considerable evaluation with many variations in the benefits that are offered by organizations. Benefits mainly have been directed at assisting employees in maintaining a particular lifestyle and providing for their long-term welfare and security. The rise of flexible (or cafeteria) benefit plans suggests the importance of considering individual preferences, the increasing diversity of the workforce, and lifestyle realities when structuring an employee benefits program.

The government's goal concerning its regulation of pay and benefits is to ensure that discrimination does not exist and that certain minimum levels of fairness are maintained in compensation programs. A number of federal, state, and local laws already regulate compensation, and new laws are likely.

Base pay programs and fringe benefit programs must be assessed for the extent to which they attract, retain, and motivate the workforce relative to major competitors. The cost of labor is critical to corporate performance and must be constantly monitored to determine whether costs can be reduced with no loss in fulfilling the organization's strategy. By the same token, when required skills for competitive advantage are in great demand, companies that do not respond with competitive pay packages will lose out. While America's most admired companies such as Coca-Cola, Mirage Resorts, United Parcel Service, and Microsoft all take steps to control and (at times) reduce their labor costs, they also make certain that their compensation packages attract, retain, and motivate their key personnel.

Regardless of which particular compensation program is chosen, organizations need the capacity to measure individual or group results so that such performance may be reflected in pay. The next chapter will look at the methods that are used to reward employees for their contributions to an organization. These decisions are by no means easy, but when combined with other components of compensation, an effective pay-for-performance program can be a powerful tool with which to attract, retain, and motivate a high-quality workforce.

It is estimated that 47 percent of private-sector employees in the United States have had at least part of their compensation tied to their company's profitability or stock price. According to one review, if you include stock options, deferred stock, profit sharing, and cash bonuses that are linked to a company's performance, almost 50 percent of the 114 million employees of private-sector companies had some form of stock or profit-related pay.[87]

It is now clear that many of these pay-for-performance programs were deeply flawed and contributed to the unfortunate economic events that began in 2007. Bankers, traders and lenders were encouraged to take short-term risks with little responsibility for their actions. Managers at publicly traded institutions, among them, Lehman Brothers, Washington Mutual, Countrywide Financial, Bear Sterns, Morgan Stanley, and Citigroup, encouraged their traders and lenders to do larger and riskier deals. When things were going well, these employees, their managers, the firms' executives and the stockholders all prospered (especially the executives). Money was made by simply doing a lot of business deals with no apparent consideration of the long-term risk and implications.

The new leadership in Washington may soon take significant action to regulate corporate compensation programs. As one expert on the subject of Wall Street compensation put it, "after nearly 18 months spent doing triage on one of the worst financial crises in our nation's history, there is now a shred of hope that those who are in a position to do something about the root cause of the problem—Wall Street's bloated and ineffective compensation system—just might act."[88]

Discussion Questions

1. Research CEO pay on the Internet (try www.aflcio.org/paywatch and Graef Crystal's columns at www.bloomberg.com/columns). Identify persons you believe to be the most overpaid and underpaid and explain why. Determine if any new legislation or regulation could affect executive pay.

2. It has been proposed that HR managers should be more involved with compensation committees charged with determining executive pay packages. How should HR be involved?

3. What is more important for organizational effectiveness—internal equity or external equity? Explain your answer.

4. Pay expert Ed Lawler says pay the person, not the job. Explain what you think he means and how that would work.

5. What is broadbanding and what does the latest research say about its effects?

6. The Paycheck Fairness Act has been proposed to promote pay equity. Research this legislation and determine its status and/or effects.

7. A constant political debate is whether or not the minimum wage should be increased. Research this topic and justify your position on the topic.

8. Workers' compensation programs and the FMLA have proven to be problematic laws for employers. Research these laws to determine the recent controversies and proposed solutions. Why are there so many lawsuits regarding overtime?

9. Research the current trends in defined contribution versus defined benefit programs. From the employer's perspective, what program is preferable and why? Now, consider the employee's perspective.

10. What is the most typical pay policy for expatriate assignments? How would you determine the entire pay package?

Chapter 11

Rewarding Performance

OBJECTIVES

After reading this chapter, you should be able to

1. Understand the determinants of effective reward systems.
2. Identify the critical variables related to the selection of the most appropriate reward systems.
3. Describe the evidence on the effectiveness of different types of reward systems.
4. Know the relative advantages and disadvantages of the various reward systems.

OVERVIEW

As Harvard professor Rosabeth Moss Kanter put it, "America is . . . already well on its way to transforming the meaning of the paycheck . . . the most important trend in pay determination has actually been the loosening relationship between job assignment and pay level."[1]

Professor Kanter's remarks were prophetic for 21st century compensation. As discussed in Chapter 10, a strong trend in compensation administration over the last 15 years has been the installation of various forms of reward systems for employee performance, often called "pay-for-performance" (PFP) or performance incentive systems. The term *pay-for-performance* is a little misleading since many performance-based incentive systems now award something other than pay for desired performance. Luxury cruises, golf outings, and trips to Las Vegas are common parts of such incentive programs. The terms "pay-for-performance," *reward,* or *incentive* systems will be used interchangeably in this chapter. In general, these incentive pay systems put more employee pay at risk compared to the more traditional pay systems and do indeed loosen the relationship between assignments and pay levels. This loosening at least theoretically provides more flexibility for organizations.

What better way to motivate employees to be more focused on meeting (or exceeding) customer requirements and increasing productivity than to establish a closer connection between meeting such requirements and compensation? Research has found certain characteristics of such reward systems to be major elements of **"high-performance work systems"** (HPWS) and linked such systems to bottom-line firm performance, particularly when what employees are rewarded for is closely aligned with the company's strategic objectives and a high percentage of employees participate in the plan.[2] Controlling labor costs and increasing productivity through clearer linkages between pay and performance are key human resource management (HRM) components of competitive advantage.

But many firms jump on the PFP bandwagon without thoroughly understanding the potential difficulties and limitations of PFP systems. The most recent review of the vast literature concluded that "the evidence on PFP is generally positive. To be sure, there are some very important caveats: pay is not the only important motivator in organizations, and PFP programs can yield serious, unintended negative results."[3] There are clear guidelines to follow, and failure to follow them can doom a PFP system.[4]

And there are many classic failures. Harvard Professor Kevin Murphy summarized the research on PFP nicely: "Business history is littered with firms that got what they paid for."[5] Sears had a very clear PFP system in which mechanics were paid bonuses as a percentage of repair receipts. Receivables went up, mechanics got higher pay, and 41 states indicted Sears for fraud. Columbia Hospitals is probably another example of getting what you pay for in a PFP system. When you can increase your profits by "gaming" a government entitlement system like Medicare, the government just might think the "gaming" constitutes fraud. Paying teachers for higher student test scores invites "teaching to the test" or worse unless proper safeguards are put in place. New York State discovered internal e-mails blasting companies that Merrill Lynch analysts were pushing as "strong buys." Merrill settled a lawsuit for $100 million. Morgan-Stanley lost a similar lawsuit when a Florida jury determined that they were fraudulently pushing Sunbeam stock with full knowledge the stock was overpriced. They were assessed $1 billion in punitive damages.

More recent examples of classic PFP failures are the dissolved investment bank Bear Stearns, which provided lucrative incentive packages for its sales force to sell very risky bundled mortgage notes, and the bankrupt Countrywide Financial, which provided great incentives for the approval and writing of highly risky and ultimately defaulted home mortgages that destroyed the company. In both these cases, individuals cashed in based on their sales incentive system while leaving the company in shambles with deals that went very bad. Says pay consultant Alan Johnson, "Wall Street is a sales business—they sell bonds, securities, transactions, ideas. . . . They're not paid to be long-term, philosophical, reflective. The pressure is to do the next merger, sell more stocks and bonds, do more trading—whatever boosts current profits and bonuses, the long-term consequences be damned."

In the best-seller *Freakonomics,* authors Stephen Dubner and Steven Levitt put it this way: "For every clever person who goes to the trouble of creating an incentive scheme, there is an army of people, clever and otherwise, who will inevitably spend even more time trying to beat it. Cheating may or may not be human nature, but it is certainly a prominent feature in just about every human endeavor. Cheating is a primordial economic act: getting more for less. So it isn't just the boldface names—inside-trading CEOs and pill-popping ballplayers and perk-abusing politicians—who cheat. It is the waitress who pockets her tips instead of pooling them. It is the Wal-Mart payroll manager who goes into the computer and shaves his employees' hours to make his own performance look better. It is the third-grader who, worried about not making it to the fourth grade, copies test answers from the kid sitting next to him."[6]

One of the primary causes of the subprime mortgage and home foreclosure crisis was the combination of mortgage loan applicants who exaggerated their incomes on their loan applications and the mortgage brokers, paid primarily contingent on the number of loans that were approved (not paid off), who had little or no incentive to verify these incomes. Needless to say, organizations need to be very careful about setting up the performance measures used for their PFP systems. Indeed, some experts maintain that flawed compensation systems in the form of incentive systems with short-term performance measures and no consideration of long-term effects were at the heart of the economic crisis of 2008.

PFP systems are very common for executives, often in the form of stock options and stock grants. Stock options become valuable when a company's stock price rises above a level set in the option. Options are supposed to provide an incentive to improve a

Evidence on PFP is positive but many caveats

Classic PFP failures

"Cheating is a primordial economic act"

Option backdating

company's stock performance. However, it turns out many times options are backdated to a date when the stock price was low to allow executives to exercise an unwarranted option. **Backdated options** are set at a low stock price to make them immediately valuable. In a classic case of "take the money and run," Countrywide Financial's chief executive, Angelo R. Mozilo, realized $121.5 million from exercising stock options and was awarded $22.1 million of compensation in 2007, a year in which Countrywide lost $704 million, and its shares declined 79 percent. On the edge of bankrupcy in 2008, Countrywide was purchased by the Bank of America at firesale prices. Over 15,000 Countrywide employees lost their jobs.

Over 200 companies have been the subject of government investigations into whether option dates were chosen to ensure maximum profit, a process that is illegal if not properly accounted for on company books. Brocade Communication's former chief executive, Gregory L. Reyes, was convicted of criminal charges over backdating. He was sentenced to 21 months in prison and fined $15 million. Brocade's former personnel director was also sentenced to prison for backdating options.

There are few objective defenders of the obscenely exorbitant pay for U.S. CEOs these days. Since 1990, when U.S. CEO pay was already substantially higher than European and Japanese CEO pay, U.S. CEO compensation has risen over 600 percent while the average American worker's pay increased 38 percent.[7] Most of the increase in CEO pay is due to the so-called PFP components of the pay package and, in particular, stock options. Compensation that is overloaded with stock options drives affected executives to focus on stock price and drive the stock price up using whatever chicanery is available.

PFP can be a key to success

Many of our most successful companies have endeavored to establish a stronger connection between employee pay and strategic goals. Federal Express, for example, won the prestigious Malcolm Baldridge Award and credited the clear linkage it had established between worker pay and customer satisfaction data. Stanford Professor Jeffrey Pfeffer, whose research was discussed in Chapter 1, has identified a successful PFP system as a key to the success of some of the most profitable companies in the United States.[8] Lincoln Electric Welding is one such company. Pfeffer attributes Lincoln Electric's success to its incentive management program (go to lincolnelectric.com for details on the program). But he also emphasizes that Lincoln's PFP system could only be pulled off in the context of a management system based on great trust between workers and management.

One survey of the largest United States companies found that 90 percent connect at least part of some employees' pay to performance.[9] Among the many companies that have implemented some form of PFP system for nonmanagerial employees in recent years are General Motors (GM), the Tribune Company, Blockbuster Video, Coca-Cola, Burger King, Office Depot, Mirage Resorts, United Parcel Service (UPS), Grumman, and Wal-Mart. One of the strongest trends in services is the formal use of customer data in reward systems for individuals, work units, and stores. Office Depot, for example, has a number of bonus systems based on assessments conducted by "mystery shoppers" (see Chapter 7). One survey of 2,719 midsize companies found that 30 percent of companies paid lump-sum bonuses averaging 3.5 percent of annual salary.[10]

The purpose of this chapter is to review the major types of PFP systems and to discuss their relative advantages and disadvantages. The determinants of effective PFP systems are described first, followed by an exploration of questions of fairness and practicality regarding PFP. Next, the major problems associated with PFP will be reviewed.

Reward systems come in all shapes and sizes. One of the most important considerations is the **level-of-performance measurement.** The most common type of PFP is to tie pay to individual performance in a merit pay system. However, in an effort to promote teamwork, a growing number of companies now tie pay to unit or group performance, and others tie pay to organizational or company performance.[11] Within each of these three general categories, however, there are numerous approaches. As discussed in Chapter 7, the accurate measurement of performance and the linkage of the performance measures to the strategic long-term goals of the organization are the keys to successful PFP efforts.

DOES PFP WORK?

Experts in the area of PFP have concluded, "the usefulness of money as well as its many symbolic meanings suggests that, far from being a mere low order motivator, pay can assist in obtaining any level on Maslow's motivational hierarchy, including social esteem and self-actualization."[12] A study of **"high-performance work systems"** found certain types of PFP systems and characteristics were correlated with stronger firm performance.[13]

What is being rewarded?

It's clear that PFP systems work. It's also clear that PFP has the potential to cause all kinds of trouble. It all kind of depends on what is being rewarded, what is not being rewarded, and what really matters to the organization.

Organizations need to be careful what they wish for. Employees of pure investment banks such as Goldman Sachs and Lehman Brothers took home an average of 60 percent of the revenue of the firms in one year. The prospect of huge bonuses encouraged excessive borrowing and high risk investment that came back to haunt these companies in 2008 after the bonus money had been dispersed. Numerous corporate executives and their sales forces got very rich, but the companies and their stockholders were far worse off in the long run. Lehman and another investment bank, Bear Stearns, did not even survive. Obviously, **what is measured and what is rewarded are critical factors in the success or failure of PFP systems.** Organizations must insure that short-term performance measures are correlated with more important long-term strategic goals and outcomes.

Short-term measures must correlate with long-term measures

A great deal of the economic crisis of 2008 can be explained by incentives and the "gaming" of incentive systems. A lot of what Countrywide Financial, Lehman Brothers, and Bear Stearns did was sell "paper." They sold mortgages (albeit really risky ones), bonds, securities, and "credit swaps" (all linked to those risky loans), and they were paid essentially at the point of transaction. Their incentives were to sell more stuff that would boost the "bottom line" and make executives and shareholders happy. With the exception of the top management team, the CEO and the board, all of whom were apparently asleep at the switch, these employees weren't paid to consider or incorporate into their selling strategies the long-term consequences of their actions. So they didn't.

Contingency factors

Experts provide a number of important **"contingencies"** or conditions which are related to the relative effectiveness of reward systems. Figure 11-1 presents a summary of the most important contingencies. You will note that the characteristics of the employee matter. Effective systems are particularly important for attracting and keeping top talent. High performers are more receptive to and also more critical of PFP systems. The characteristics of the reward system are critical as well. For example, changes to pay systems, particularly without employee input, can have a significant negative impact. One study found over a 100 percent increase in employee theft after the company cut pay by 15 percent with no explanation.[14] Also, while pay will have little effect where people receive similar pay increases

---

Figure 11-1   **Examples of Contingency Factors Affecting Pay Importance**

Individual Difference Contingencies

1. Pay is more important to extroverts than to introverts.
2. Receiving performance-based pay is more important to high academic achievers than to others.
3. High-performance employees appear to be particularly sensitive to whether their higher performance is rewarded with above-average pay increases, while low performers prefer low-contingency pay systems.
4. Pay appears to be more important to men than to women.
5. People with high need for achievement and higher feelings of self-efficacy prefer pay systems that more closely link pay to performance.

Situational Contingencies

1. Pay is more important in job choice when pay varies widely across employers than when pay is relatively more uniform.
2. There is a declining marginal utility to additional increments of pay.
3. The salience or "importance" of pay is likely to rise after *changes* are made to pay systems. Employees are particularly sensitive to pay *cuts*.
4. Employee reactions to changes in pay depend heavily on communication of the *reasons* for pay policies and changes.
5. Pay is probably more important in job choice than in decisions to quit.
6. Pay will do little to motivate performance in systems where people receive similar pay increases regardless of individual or firm performance. However, dramatic changes in performance can occur when pay is made more contingent on performance.

Source: Adapted from S. L. Rynes, B. Gerhart, and K. A. Minette, "The Importance of Pay in Employee Motivation: Discrepancies between What People Say and What They Do," *Human Resource Management* 43 (2004), pp. 381–394.

Marginal utility

despite large differences in performance, dramatic changes in performance can occur when pay is made more contingent on performance. Regarding marginal utility, there is evidence that being "under market" has a stronger motivational impact than does the positive effect of being "above market." Job candidates often reject offers simply because of the pay. Pay is probably relatively more critical in terms of job choice than in decisions to quit because pay is one of the few characteristics people can know with certainty before taking a job. Once you've had a job for a while, other factors like the quality of supervision will have a strong impact on decisions to stay or leave.

The bottom-line on reward systems

The bottom line on the effects of reward systems is that such systems can be very effective if they are tailored to particular work situations and strategies and enhance the connection between worker effort and desired rewards. Above all, they are effective if they reward performance in those areas most important for the long-term success of the organization.

Domino's Pizza claimed an increase in sales in excess of 20 percent after implementing a complicated PFP system. International Business Machines (IBM) attributes a 200 percent increase over 10 years in productivity in manufacturing to its PFP system. One survey reported improved output from two out of three companies using some form of PFP when incentives were provided for meeting specific performance targets.[15] The evidence is strong that PFP systems are effective when what an organization is actually rewarding is highly compatible with its long-term strategic objectives and execution.[16]

Compatibility with long-term objectives is the key to success

The events of 2008, particularly irresponsible lending practices, underscore the need for this compatibility. Countrywide Financial has been called the "poster child" for the subprime mortgage crisis. A $500 billion home loan machine, most of Countrywide's sales staff and lenders, its managers, and its executives made huge sums of money in 2006 and 2007 through highly risky subprime lending. Borrowers with questionable credit histories, who probably should not have been granted home loans in the first place, were unable to make their mortgage payments and defaulted on their loans. By late 2007, the company had lost over $700 billion, the stock price fell 79% and over 11,000 employees had lost their jobs. In 2008, a securities fraud case was initiated by the FBI. Unfortunately, there are many other stories like Countrywide's where bad incentive systems rewarded highly risky behavior that ultimately doomed companies.

WHAT ARE THE DETERMINANTS OF EFFECTIVE REWARD SYSTEMS?

Although pay is generally regarded as a motivator, organizations are often confronted with unique sets of issues and problems related to PFP and therefore must develop strategies to deal with them. The most important determinants of effective PFP are summarized in Figure 11-2.

Expectancy/instrumentality theory (see Figure 11-3), particularly when combined with **goal-setting,** has a great deal of predictive power in understanding PFP systems. Expectancy/instrumentality theory explains why more pay often leads to higher performance and why in other cases the connection is often not all that strong.

**Figure 11-2
Determinants of Effective
PFP Systems**

1. Worker values outcomes (money, prizes).
2. Outcome is valued relative to other rewards.
3. Desired performance must be measurable.
4. Worker must be able to control rate of output or quality.
5. Worker must be capable of increasing output or quality.
6. Worker must believe that capability to increase exists.
7. Worker must believe that increased output will result in receiving a reward.
8. Size of reward must be sufficient to stimulate increased effort.
9. Performance measures must be compatible with strategic goals for short and long term.

**Figure 11-3
Expectancy/Instrumentality
Theory**

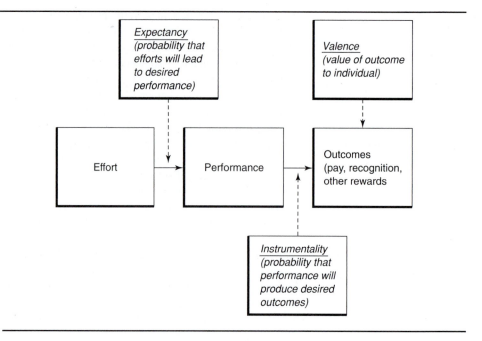

Motivation is a function of the perception a worker has about the likelihood or probability that working harder will lead to higher performance and the probability that higher performance will lead to valued outcomes like more money. Of course, performance is also a function of a worker's (or student's) knowledge, skills, and abilities. A worker's perception of the critical effort-to-performance relationship is to some extent a consequence of that worker's self-assessment of his or her KASOCs as related to the work. In addition, if workers believe that situational constraints beyond their control have more to do with performance than their own effort or competencies, their perception of the probability that effort will lead to higher performance will be very low (see points 4–6 in Figure 11-2). While the determinants presented in Figure 11-2 can increase the likelihood of an effective PFP system, all are not required for an effective PFP system. Figure 11-3 presents a model of the critical role of workers' perceptions of the probabilities of outcomes in determining the success or failure of any PFP system.

Increases in pay as a reward for increases in performance must be valued by the specific employee or work unit for which the PFP plan is intended—and must be valued highly relative to other rewards. Occasionally group norms or cultural values deemphasize money as a reward for performance, or oppose differential rewards for differential outputs. Unions, for example, have traditionally opposed pay systems based on individual output, such as piece-rate incentive systems. Some unions (e.g., the United Auto Workers, the Communication Workers of America, and the Teamsters) have become more receptive to PFP systems in

Unions and PFP

recent years when trust is established between the union and management. The Teamsters have supported a profit-sharing plan for UPS workers in their latest collective bargaining agreement. At GM's Saturn plant, UAW members work for a salary (about $53,000 per year), with 20 percent of the amount fluctuating up or down since it is tied to assessments of car quality, productivity, and company profits.

These examples are certainly exceptions rather than the rule. In general, unions strongly favor organization-wide or plant-based PFP systems and not individual PFP systems, which the unions maintain will inevitably pit worker against worker. Unions typically resist reward systems that are linked to individual performance. When the state of Florida mandated an individual merit pay system for teachers, the American Federation of Teachers (AFT) worked diligently to promote regulations regarding the merit pay process which ultimately led to the demise of the system. Within two years, the state had rescinded the individual PFP program.

Some companies also regard individual PFP systems as contrary to their team-oriented philosophy of management and organizational culture. United Technologies is one example.

Its PFP reward system uses only aggregated methods of rewards in which unit and company-wide performance measures are the basis of the awards.

The organization must identify those measures of performance (e.g., customer data, outputs, products, services, behaviors, cost reductions) that are most compatible with their short and long-term strategic goals and their execution. For example, increased output may be desirable only in situations in which there is customer demand for more of the product. Needless to say, the organization should tie pay only to those aspects of value that are critical for the organization. You may recall from Chapter 7 that six aspects of value in the measurement of performance were identified. While most organizations place equal weight on the quality and the quantity of performance, some companies have a clear preference for one of these aspects over the other.

Quantity and quality are aspects of value

The PFP system should establish a reward system for those aspects of value that are compatible with the short-term and long-term strategic goals of the *organization.* For example, retailers often offer incentives for the sale of certain merchandise that is overstocked. Inventory control and sales projections drive the time range for the incentive system. Marriott's strategic goal was to be the "hotel of choice" for business travelers. It established a telephone survey of their patrons' experience and then tied the customer satisfaction data to bonuses. Home Depot outsources all of its home installations, and it does a follow-up survey of customers of the recommended installers in order to determine whether they were pleased with the service. A favorable review gets the vendor a small bonus while an unfavorable review could doom the vendor.

The reward criteria are critical

The proper emphasis on criteria can be tricky but can make or break a reward system. Inspectors working for the Federal Emergency Management Agency were paid per inspection after a hurricane in Florida. The result was a whole lot of fraudulent inspections leading to over $10 million in awards for damages that didn't occur. In 2008, some divisions of the Association of Community Organizations for Reform Now, or ACORN, paid canvassers for each voter registration form submitted. Among the prospective "voters" who submitted registration forms were Mickey Mouse and Donald Duck. Only when ACORN adjusted its "piece-rate" incentive system to pay for validated registration forms did these rather suspicious forms cease to be a problem. We've already discussed the bad home loan applications processed by loan agents who were paid for loan approvals, not for the loans actually being paid. The national economic crisis partly caused by this dubious practice dominates the news at the time of this writing.

Perhaps because of the Exxon *Valdez* oil spill off the Alaska coast, Conoco made environmental issues a major strategic priority. Environmental criteria became a component of its incentive system for top managers. Xerox Corporation places great emphasis on customer service and now uses customer survey data as a criterion in its bonus system. According to Xerox's president, it is possible that an executive of a profitable unit would not get a bonus at all if the customer survey data indicated poor performance. The Aluminum Company of America now emphasizes improvements in safety records as a part of its managerial bonus system. Workers at a Monsanto Corporation chemical plant in Louisiana can earn bonuses for meeting goals that include reducing injuries and preventing emissions from escaping into the environment. As a part of the settlement of a class-action racial discrimination lawsuit, Texaco places considerable weight on diversity issues in its PFP plans for executives. Executives are evaluated and paid based on their ability to keep and develop minorities and women. Wal-Mart installed a similar program in the context of their ongoing huge class-action, sex discrimination lawsuit.

Successful PFP systems recognize that all of the determinants presented in Figure 11-2 are intimately related. For example, to determine the nature of a reward that should be offered for an increased level of effort, a firm must know the relative importance of money to its typical worker, the increased value to the firm of any given performance increase, and the worker's perception of the increased effort required and the likelihood of receiving the reward. Money fails to motivate if the required level of extra effort results in unacceptable fatigue to the worker or prevents the worker from enjoying a valued social life. Success is more likely with more worker involvement in the development of the PFP system. Employee participation in the development will enhance acceptance of the plan. As discussed above, high performers are likely to seek out other employment if they do not feel they have been recognized with the financial rewards they feel they deserve.[17]

Worker involvement in PFP design is important

WHAT ARE THE MAIN
PROBLEMS WITH PFP PROGRAMS?

There are many potential problems with PFP systems. Figure 11-4 presents a summary of the problems judged by experts to be most responsible for the failure of such systems. PFP systems can be expensive to develop and maintain. In addition to the initial cost of establishing standards and rates, changes in procedures, equipment, and product may require revision of any existing standards and reward structures. In many cases a revision of the compensation system will be viewed with suspicion. Historically, some short-sighted firms have taken advantage of changes in the production process to reduce the amount of reward for any given level of effort. General Motors established what it thought were challenging production targets for a Michigan plant and let workers go home when the targets were achieved. GM then increased the targets when it found workers were able to go home early. Such actions had a long-term negative effect on worker responses to other GM PFP systems. Again, the more worker involvement in pay plan changes, the greater the acceptance of the changes.

More worker involvement fosters acceptance of changes

Many problems can arise in a PFP system that relies on performance appraisals. One frequent problem is that workers do not feel that their rewards are closely linked to their performance, a critical component of expectancy/instrumentality theory. This low probability often occurs when employees believe that the performance *measure* does not accurately reflect their performance. However, as discussed in Chapter 7, employees often have inflated ideas about their performance levels, which translate into unrealistic expectations about rewards as well. One study found that the majority of workers who were rated even slightly less than the highest level (e.g., 8 on a 9-point scale) were more dissatisfied than satisfied with the rating. Those with larger discrepancies between their self-assessments and their supervisor's ratings were more dissatisfied with their merit pay increase.[18]

Problems with performance appraisals

Given their beliefs about their own performances, a large portion of the workforce may receive performance ratings below their expectations, and thus rewards will likely fall short of their expectations. As discussed in Chapter 7, there can be a perception of bias in the process even if such bias does not exist. To the extent that workers perceive that the performance measurement component of the PFP system is biased or invalid, the perceived connection between pay and performance will be undermined and the PFP system will be less effective. This is a common problem when performance is measured by supervisory ratings. Some experts on PFP go so far as to say that if performance must be measured by supervisory ratings, PFP is not worth the trouble. One such expert concluded that when ratings must be used, "the approach is so flawed that it is hard to imagine a set of conditions which would make it effective."[19] While this conclusion may be overly pessimistic, there is no denying that PFP systems based on single-source ratings of performance can be problematic. In one of the largest Title VII class-action lawsuits to date, it was alleged that Coca-Cola discriminated against African-Americans in the manner in which it evaluated personnel and awarded merit increases. (See also the discussion of the problems with Ford's rating system in Critical Thinking Application 7-C.) Companies should not contemplate PFP until they have great confidence in the accuracy and fairness of their performance measurement system. If ratings are to be the primary basis for the rewards, the use of multiple sources of raters, including customers if possible, is a preferable strategy over the typical "top-down" supervisory ratings.

Use multiple rating sources if possible

**Figure 11-4
Reasons for the Failures
of PFP Systems**

1. Poor perceived connection between performance and pay.
2. The level of performance-based pay is too low relative to base pay. The cost of more highly motivating programs may be prohibitive.
3. Lack of objective, countable results for most jobs, requiring the use of performance ratings.
4. Faulty performance appraisal systems, with poor cooperation from managers, leniency bias in the appraisals, and resistance to change.
5. Union resistance to such systems and to change in general.
6. Poor (or negative) relationship between rewarded outcomes and long-term performance measures and objectives.

Rewarded outcomes must be tied to long-term success

Misaligned pay strategies can be costly

Constraints on performance

10–15 percent of base is recommendation

Many PFP plans fail because the performance outcomes that were rewarded were not related to the performance objectives of the entire organization as a whole and to those aspects of performance that were most important to the long-term success of organization. A PFP system may put inordinate emphasis on the quantity of output when the organizational emphasis should be on quality improvement or cost effectiveness. As one expert in compensation put it, "Misaligned pay strategy not only fails to add value, it produces high costs . . . as well as inappropriate and misdirected behavior."[20] The organization must constantly ensure that the aspects of value that are emphasized in the PFP system are the same ones that are the priority of the organization and **compatible with the long-term strategic goals of the organization.** The events of 2008 underscore this critical need.

Recall from the discussion of performance appraisal in Chapter 7 that it is possible to weight performance dimensions (which are combinations of job functions with aspects of value: quantity, quality, timeliness, need for supervision, effects on constituents, and cost). This weighting process should reflect the strategic plan of the unit and the organization. Unfortunately, the typical measurement process for PFP systems that does involve quantity and output or sales is far more haphazard than this. In fact, one survey found that the majority of workers who were paid on a PFP system had little understanding of the criteria for performance measurement.[21]

The organization also should ensure that workers are *capable* of increasing their performance. You may recall the discussion in Chapter 7 regarding **constraints on performance.** An employee working on an assembly line or operating a machine with a preset speed may not have the opportunity to increase the quantity of performance. For higher pay to result in higher performance, workers must believe in (and be capable of) higher levels of performance. When workers believe that performance standards exceed their capabilities, they will not expend extra effort.

Finally, one of the most common problems with PFP systems is that an insufficient amount of money is available to reward meritorious performance.[22] Truly deserving performers often judge the system to be unfair and inequitable. (The truly deserving performers may in fact be paid seriously under-market and thus be more likely to leave the organization.)[23] Regarding the performance-based component, the lowest level recommended for a PFP system is between 10 and 15 percent of the base salary in order for the money to be considered significant and for the PFP system to be effective.[24] However, many companies disperse various rewards at rates far below these recommendations. At Bank of America, an employee earning $5,000 per month who achieved the very highest performance appraisal was eligible for the highest PFP award of 5 percent. This increased her or his earnings $250 per month (before taxes). Most employees who were surveyed about this PFP system didn't think the amount of money involved was worth what they regarded as the extra effort. Many of the highest-rated employees indicated that, despite their "maxed-out" merit increase, they would look for employment elsewhere. When performance ratings are used as the basis for the rewards, pay is rarely seen as sufficiently differentiated, especially among the highest performers.

WHAT ARE THE LEGAL IMPLICATIONS OF PFP?

As discussed in Chapter 10, all decisions regarding compensation, including all that are derived from PFP systems, are subject to complaints using the same sources of redress discussed throughout the book. PFP systems have been challenged for more subtle forms of alleged discrimination. For example, as discussed here and in Chapter 7, situational constraints on performance can affect the basic fairness and equity of the PFP system and have been the basis of Title VII actions. An office furniture retailer terminated a female employee for failure to meet a sales quota in a difficult territory. She argued that her opportunity to meet the quota was severely restricted by situational constraints that were beyond her control and that men were not so constrained. She also argued that benefits such as providing sample products that were made available to the male sales personnel were deliberately denied her. Her complaint resulted in a large out-of-court settlement. The Wal-Mart class-action sex discrimination case alleged similar discrimination in the pay system, as did the Ford case discussed earlier (see Critical Thinking Applications 5-C and 7-C).

"Disparate impact" and PFP results

The "disparate impact" theory can be used in lawsuits involving reward systems alleging race, gender, or age bias. The company may have to explain why a lower percentage of women or minorities or older workers received merit increases when the PFP system was based on merit ratings, particularly when most raters are white, male supervisors. The statistical finding of "adverse impact" itself puts the employers in a difficult situation which may require them to defend their performance measurement system. Organizations should always monitor their incentive decisions for possible "disparate impact" evidence.

HOW DO YOU SELECT A PFP SYSTEM?

In designing a PFP system, while there are numerous questions that need answers, three major questions should be asked and answered first:

1. Who should be included in the PFP system?
2. How will performance be measured?
3. Which rewards or incentives will be used?

The process for developing the characteristics of a performance measurement system apply to the first two questions, which were discussed in Chapter 7.

Who Should Be Included in a PFP System?

In general, all employee groups should be included in a PFP system, with one critical condition: the PFP system should be developed with specific groups and conditions in mind. The "devil" is in the details of PFP systems, so production workers, middle management, salespeople, engineers, professionals, and senior executives and top management should probably have different systems. Many companies use very different PFP systems for different jobs. For example, McDonald's has eight different PFP systems for various classes of employees. IBM has six different systems. Many companies have different PFP systems as a function of their organizational and unit-level strategies, with some form of market share measurement for a start-up product or service, and cost cutting for a more established product or service line. Some companies use a variety of different PFP systems for the same job families. For example, AMOCO has an individual merit pay system, a unit-level PFP component called gainsharing, and an employee stock ownership program (ESOP) for the same employees.

American workers prefer individual PFP systems

Other companies have reward systems that are compatible with an egalitarian culture that attempts to minimize the distance between people at different levels in the organizational hierarchy. In general, however, American workers prefer individual PFP systems where they can control their own destinies. Great deference should be given to this preference unless a compelling argument can be made that individual PFP systems will foster competition among employees that will ultimately interfere with meeting company or unit-level strategic objectives. Companies can also use combinations of individual and unit-based performance measures based on the particular outcome measures that are selected for rewards.

Tailored systems to situation

So the bottom line is that you should try to involve as many workers in a PFP system as possible, but each system should be tailored to particular work situations. Organizations should avoid PFP systems that promote individual competition among workers that interferes with meeting major corporate or unit-level objectives.

How Will Performance Be Measured?

The answer to this question will of course vary with the particular workers and work units. Above all, the criteria selected must be compatible with both the short-term and, more importantly, the long-term strategic objectives of the organization. Performance should be measured to maximize the reliability and the validity of the performance measures, with validity being defined as the extent to which the measure used to define performance is correlated with some ultimate criterion of organizational performance.

What Are the Rewards in an Incentive System?

Cash payments, percentage increases in base pay, and numerous noncash prizes are still the most common rewards for performance. While these incentives are flexible and well suited to short-run objectives, stock awards and stock options are an approach for meeting long-run objectives. Stock options are becoming more common for lower-level employees and are a bigger percentage of the raise for lower-level managers. In addition to quarterly bonuses based on "mystery shopper" data, Wendy's also awards stock to employees for performance and time on the job.

Stock ownership plans

Another company with an employee stock ownership plan is Publix Super Markets. This highly successful privately held company has made *Fortune*'s list of "Great Companies to work for" for many years. Its stockholders are its 135,000 workers. If you work more than 1,000 hours per year at Publix and work more than one year, you get Publix stock. Publix "associates" clearly have a sense of ownership in the company. Says Publix spokesperson, Anne Hendricks, "Put yourself in the place of a Publix associate: If you see areas where you can eliminate waste, you're going to do it, because you're going to see it in your next dividend check."

Stock options

Many companies award stock options to the top management team and sometimes other employees. Options are typically additions to upper-management pay that also include a cash bonus. Although there are several types of stock options, the most popular today are incentive options that give an executive the right to purchase stock at a specified price within a designated time period. If the company does well and the stock price goes up, everyone is happy. Actually, some CEOs have made out all right even if the stock price went down as corporate boards awarded new options and lowered exercise prices. As discussed above, options have developed a bad reputation lately due to the numerous examples of corporate executives making millions exercising options just before a stock headed south and accusations of **backdating stock option** awards to increase the value of the options. Executives and HR managers have gone to jail for backdating.

Many highly successful companies also offer options to lower-level employees. Some experts argue that Federal Express has low turnover among its drivers and maintains a union-free environment at least to some extent because these employees own a part of the company and are granted options.[25]

Options must be expensed

One reason for the past popularity of stock options was that companies were not required to report stock options as an expense. However, a new accounting rule now requires that stock options be reported as an expense. As a result, many companies have reduced their stock option grants. The National Center for Employee Ownership reports that 34 percent of publicly traded companies have discontinued their programs.[26]

A Discrepancy between Research and Practice

With regard to actual *pay* for performance, another strong trend today is a **bonus-based** PFP system in which the performance-based pay is not permanently tied to an employee's base pay. In fact, experts have been recommending this approach for years, mainly because the size of the bonus that can be offered can be greater and the cost to the organization in the long run is far less (a bonus that results in an increase in your base salary will be in your base salary forever).[27] Compensation experts maintain that base pay should be tied to expected levels of work and that PFP should be tied to performance that exceeds that level. Workers are more likely to exceed that level if the performance–outcome connection is stronger and the reward is greater. This connection is typically stronger with bonus-based systems. A growing number of companies now pay lump sums based on corporate or division profits, and the lump sum does not increase an employee's base salary (base pay is typically adjusted based on cost-of-living figures and surveys of competitors' pay). GM's Saturn plant operates on a 20 percent rate of "risk" for all salaried workers, based on Saturn's profits, with no tie-in to future base salaries. Champion International pays managers based on growth in earnings per share of stock relative to the stock of the 10 major competitors. The bonus awarded to senior managers is not tied to the managers' base pay.

Recommendation: Use bonus-based PFP not tied to base pay

Behavioral encouragement plans

Many organizations use bonuses as part of a **"behavioral encouragement plan"** where employees get payments for specific accomplishments such as safety compliance or attendance. Taco Bell gives biannual bonuses based on an assessment of customer service by a market research company. Other bonuses are granted to store managers for store sales and target profit levels.

Federal Express managers have "small spot" awards of $100 that are available for unusual achievement. For example, one "small spot" award was given to a driver who went well beyond the call of duty to deliver a package when the weather would have been a justifiable excuse. Home Depot has a holiday, bonus-based system available to all employees and awards deep discounts on Home Depot products.

The long-term costs of PFP systems that are tied into base pay can be enormous. For example, the State of Florida awarded $5,000 increases to the base pay of 797 faculty based on the quality and quantity of undergraduate teaching they had performed up to three years earlier. The conservative amortized cost of the 797 $5,000 awards was $148.2 million over 20 years. Remember this was for work already performed. No evidence has ever been presented that the program actually increased either the quality or the quantity of undergraduate teaching. Many of these outstanding professors no longer teach at all but still get over $5,000 per year for great teaching they did 10 (or more) years earlier! ***Bottom line: PFP should be bonus-based and not tied to base pay.***

Should You Use Individual, Group, or Company-Level PFP?

Organizations use incentive pay to reward individuals, units, teams, or departments of workers, or the entire organization. As discussed in Chapter 7, among the major issues in performance measurement are the extent to which output is controlled at the group or individual level, whether individual contributions can be measured, and the extent to which important teamwork among unit members would be affected by the PFP system.

At Champion International, for example, earnings are compared only to the company's major competitors so as to control for factors beyond the influence of the managers, such as inflation, interest rates, and general state of the economy. Managers perceive this relative comparison to be fairer than comparisons to absolute earnings, which are more susceptible to changes in the general state of the economy. (Recall the discussion above of constraints on performance and the importance of perceived constraints on the critical probability statements in expectancy/instrumentality theory: If I believe factors beyond my control have more to do with performance outcomes than do my own efforts, my motivation to try harder will diminish.) In general, **PFP systems are more effective when specific worker contributions can be clearly measured.** If individual contributions cannot be measured reliably, then the smallest number of workers whose performance is determined to be important (e.g., related to strategic objectives) and, of course, measurable would constitute the incentive group or unit.

Measure and reward individual performance if possible

But, individual PFP can reduce teamwork

An organization may choose to use a group plan even when it is possible to measure output on an individual basis. Individual PFP plans can increase competition among workers and may reduce cooperation and teamwork. As two experts put it, "when companies change the dynamics of work from structure-driven—organized around individual role and functions—to process-driven—often organized around teams—they should change the reward system to support those new dynamics."[28] Workers will be less likely to assist their co-workers if such an effort will adversely affect their own production rate or potential rewards. **If teamwork and cooperation are important, but team members are competing for a set number or amount of awards, a group or unit-based system is preferable.** At the GM Saturn plant in Tennessee, while individual measurement was possible on a number of important outcome measures, an individual PFP system was thought to be contrary to the company's team-oriented approach to production. Thus, Saturn's UAW-endorsed PFP system is based strictly on unit-level and company-wide measures of performance. One health care products manufacturer designed its work teams around project teams for 50 product development employees. But they maintained their old compensation system with job classes, individual performance appraisal, and merit pay. The compensation system turned out to be dysfunctional for the new project-based job structure.

When Should Team-Based PFP Be Used?

A growing number of organizations now use some form of team bonus. One survey of Fortune 1,000 companies found that 70 percent of companies now use some form of team bonus, with 17 percent of these organizations applying bonuses to at least 40 percent of their employees.[29]

Team-based pay as part of team-based model

Team-based PFP is a better approach when it is part of a comprehensive team-based model of HRM and compensation. For starters, the job evaluation process would place more emphasis on the work products of the team with less emphasis on individual job descriptions. The focus of the pay structure in general is on objectives and results *of the team*. The performance appraisal and career development systems also focus on team performance and contributing to team performance by new skill acquisition. The performance appraisal system usually includes peer assessment, and great weight is given to the extent to which employees contribute to team performance. (These individual assessments, however, are usually used only as developmental tools and not directly tied to pay.) All forms of reward and recognition programs place emphasis on the team. Company-wide recognition programs focus on team performance and team contribution to the company's strategic goals. Reactions to team-based approaches depend on individual team-member characteristics. One study found that people who are more collectivist in their orientation (high on the "Agreeableness" factor of the Big Five, for example) tend to prefer team-based rewards.[30]

Some individuals prefer team-based pay

There are many examples of individually based PFP systems even where teamwork is critical. Great professional athletes are always paid a premium for their greatness despite the need for teamwork. Remember, the critical issues regarding the level of aggregation of the performance measures (individual, group, organization) are identifying and measuring performance criteria that the organization seeks to increase or improve in its strategic plan and then linking pay to performance on those measurements. When the pool of award or merit money is not fixed or set among team members, combining individual and group systems may be the most motivating. One review summed it up this way: "Both individual and group-based pay plans have potential limitations. Individual-based plans may generate too little cooperation when work is highly interdependent and may be seen as unfair when system factors rather than individual effort and ability determine performance. In contrast, group-based plans can weaken incentive effects via **'free-rider'** problems, which generally increase with group size. 'Free riders' are workers who benefit from group-based pay but who don't do their share of the work. Group-based plans can also result in detrimental sorting effects if high achievers go elsewhere to have their individual contributions recognized and rewarded."[31]

"Free-rider" issues with team PFP

Now that the major factors have been introduced that should be considered in designing a PFP system, let's look at the individual, group, and company-based systems in some detail.

INDIVIDUAL PFP PLANS: MERIT PAY AND INCENTIVE SYSTEMS

Individual PFP systems can be divided into merit pay systems and incentive systems specifically tied to production rates. **Merit pay plans** are the most common and perhaps the most troublesome of PFP systems because performance is typically measured by ratings done by supervisors. **Incentive plans** rely on some countable results to be used as a basis for setting the PFP rate. These are also known as *piece-rate* systems. **Sales incentive plans** set certain commissions for sales of specified products or services. Each of these methods will be examined next.

What Are Merit Pay Plans?

Merit pay plans call for a distribution of pay based on an appraisal of a worker's performance. The merit pay is usually folded into the base pay of the recipient and is usually granted as a percentage of a worker's base pay. At the Tribune Company, for example, 4 percent merit money was distributed to individual units (e.g., TV and radio stations and newspapers owned by Tribune). Unit heads then distributed 4 percent to department heads, who had a total pool of 4 percent of their payroll to distribute among the workers. Obviously, the bigger the pool of meritorious workers, the smaller the average percentage that could be granted.

Surveys indicate that workers prefer merit pay plans that link individual performance with desired outcomes. At least compared to straight pay with no tie-in to performance, workers in general prefer merit pay plans even after they've been granted what they regarded as less than satisfactory raises based on the plan. But many studies have found little relationship between merit pay plans that rely on performance appraisals by supervisors to measure performance and important organizational outcomes, such as productivity increases or cost reductions.

Review again the reasons for failure of PFP systems in Figure 11-4, and you will see that many of these reasons are unfortunately characteristic of merit pay systems. The most serious problem is the failure to create a clear linkage between employee performance and pay. The performance appraisal system and the evaluators of performance are mainly responsible for this problem. There are several factors related to the appraisal system that contribute to this breakdown in the linkage between pay and performance. The fundamental problem is with *measuring* performance, a problem compounded in service industries in which individual performance is more difficult to measure.

Fundamental merit pay problem: measuring performance

An important cause of the measurement problem is the lack of skill of those who do the appraisals. As discussed in Chapter 7, this lack of skill is often manifested in *leniency* bias in the ratings. Leniency causes ratings to be so bunched at the high end of the rating scale that very little distinction can be made between superior and other performances.

Leniency bias

Rater characteristics

Research has established that rater characteristics, including their personality traits, can predict the average rating raters give across all people whom they rate. Rater "discomfort," defined as the extent to which a person feels uncomfortable giving negative feedback and measured by the **Performance Appraisal Discomfort Scale (PADS),** has been shown to be correlated with the average rating level given by the rater (i.e., higher discomfort is related to more lenient ratings). Also, a rater with a low "Conscientiousness" score (from the Five-Factor Model discussed in Chapter 6) combined with a high "Agreeableness" score will tend to inflate ratings. Recent research shows incremental validity for the prediction of rater leniency using all three rater characteristics (low rater Conscientiousness + high rater Agreeableness + high rater Discomfort = highest Leniency levels). The good news is that raters can be trained to reduce their levels of discomfort, which does then reduce leniency.

Raters can be trained to be more accurate

Even raters who do not fit the personality profile above will inflate ratings over time if they feel the merit money is being distributed to work units as a consequence of the rater's average ratings (higher ratings by the supervisor get the supervisor more merit money to distribute). The results of this systemwide rating inflation are twofold: (1) a merit pay system in which the amount of the merit pay is relatively trivial because so many individuals are judged to be eligible and (2) a system in which the best performers perceive their merit pay as a gross inequity because the system is supposed to be based on merit.

High turnover among best performers

Research shows high turnover among the best performers when these performers can clearly discern real performance differences (because of actual true differences in countable results) but they nevertheless receive only token merit increases because of chronic rating leniency in supervisory ratings. The implication of this research is clear. If there is an important countable outcome, develop a PFP system that establishes rewards based on *outcome* differences, not ratings. Otherwise, the best performers will seek out an organization that provides abundant rewards for high levels of performance.

Use countable outcomes if possible

One popular approach to dealing with leniency is to impose a **forced-distribution rating,** or ranking system in which the number of people rated at the highest level is controlled. Raters tend to dislike these approaches, however. Microsoft dropped their forced-distribution system in 2008 after numerous complaints by managers who were "forced" to comply with the rating level distributions. Also, the workers felt the system promoted unhealthy competition within work units that relied on collaboration and teamwork to function most effectively. One study conducted by pay guru Ed Lawler found negative results for forced-distribution systems. Among his theories for the results was "when employees in a work area compete with each other for ratings, knowing there is always a percentage at the bottom who will be forced out, it creates fear and selfishness. People are much less likely to help each other, train each other, share information, and operate as an effective team. In today's flatter, knowledge work–driven, more team-based organizations, excessive internal competition can take a significant toll on organizational performance."[32]

Avoid forced-distribution

**Figure 11-5
Recommendations for Merit
Pay Plans**

1. Use a bonus system in which merit pay is not tied to the base salary.
2. Maintain a bonus range from 0 to 20 percent for lower pay levels and from 0 to 40 percent for higher levels.
3. Pay attention to the process issues of the merit pay plan. Involve workers in decision making and maintain an open communication policy.
4. Take performance appraisal seriously. Hold raters accountable for their appraisals, and provide training.
5. Focus on key organizational factors that affect the pay system. Information systems and job designs must be compatible with the performance measurement system.
6. Include group and team performance in evaluation. Evaluate team performance where appropriate, and base part of individual merit pay on the team evaluation. Use multiple rates if possible.
7. Consider special awards separately from an annual merit allocation that recognizes major accomplishments.

Source: Adapted from E. E. Lawler, "Recommendations for Merit Pay Plans," *Strategic Pay,* San Francisco, CA. Copyright © 1990. Reprinted by permission of John Wiley & Sons Inc.

Many quality improvement experts maintain that pay should not be linked to performance, particularly at the individual level. Deming, the most highly regarded of the quality gurus before he died in 1995, believed that performance appraisal fosters competition among individual workers and diverts attention away from the *systems* related to the quality of the product or service.

Despite Deming's comments, most individuals prefer to be paid on the basis of some measure of their own performance. The problem is creating the linkage when the criteria are ambiguous. The merit pay principle is easy when criteria are available that are countable (not rated by supervisors) and important (linked to the strategic plan of the organization or unit or to specific customer requirements). Although most jobs do not easily provide objective criteria, and firms thus rely on ratings, alternatives to supervisory ratings are available. As discussed in Chapter 7, ratings by internal and external customers on the extent to which their expectations are met could be a preferable alternative to supervisory ratings. Studies have found that including some measure of customer satisfaction as one of the outcome measures has a positive effect on sales, profits, and subsequent customer satisfaction.[33] Federal Express conducts customer-related performance reviews every six months.

Use customer appraisal data where possible

Although they have problems, merit pay systems are still widely used. In addition to the recommendations presented in Chapter 7 for sound performance appraisal systems, Figure 11-5 presents a set of recommendations for the use of individual merit pay systems. Organizations should strive to follow these prescriptions.

What Is Incentive Pay?

Piece-rate pay

Incentive pay is based on units produced and provides the closest connection between individual effort or performance and individual pay. There are two types of individual incentive systems based on nonrated output: the **piece-rate system** and the **standard hourly rate.** Many variations of piece work have been used over the years, but most share common characteristics. A firm using the piece-rate system will determine an appropriate amount of work to be accomplished in a set period of time (e.g., an hour) and then define this as the standard. (Recall from the discussion in Chapter 4 that job analysis methods can be used to establish work standards.) Then, using either internal or external measures, a fair rate is set for this period of time. The piece rate is then calculated by dividing the base wage by the standard. Today, to comply with regulations such as the minimum wage, piece-rate plans should include an hourly wage and a piece-rate incentive.

The basic piece rate is the oldest and most common wage incentive plan. The oldest approach, popular in textile and apparel mills, is called *straight piece work.* With this approach, a worker is paid per unit of production with no base pay. Used in early American times when work was done at home, the straight piece-rate approach is still popular, particularly with the increased use of electronic monitoring of performance. Data processing personnel, customer service representatives, and some clerks, for example, are paid based on a specific formula tied to the finished product or the number of customers served or processed. In general, if individual performance can be accurately measured and teamwork or worker collaboration is not important for the desired performance outcomes, a piece-rate approach is the recommended approach. However, a stable, base hourly wage is recommended along with the piece-rate incentives.

International Piece-Rate Pay

Minimum wage of the host country

The piece-rate pay method is also very common in factories around the world, particularly in textile factories where (typically) young women are paid by the piece of clothing produced. Nike, Ralph Lauren, Liz Claiborne, and Tommy Hilfiger maintain that the hourly rate they pay with the piece-rate system complies with the minimum wage laws of the host country. For example, in 2008 Nike paid the following wages in *full compliance with the minimum wage requirements of the respective countries:* 20 cents an hour in Vietnam; 30 cents an hour in Haiti; and 50 cents an hour in Indonesia. According to Medea Benjamin of Global Exchange, a San Francisco world labor watchdog group, these hourly rates do not even get the employees three decent meals a day. Nike, Liz Claiborne, Reebok, and numerous other companies signed on to a "Code of Conduct" of the Fair Labor Association that put some controls on the pay and treatment of international workers. With regard to wages, however, compliance with the minimum wage laws of the host country is all that is stipulated.

Production variability

Differential rate

The basic piece rate provides a production incentive based on paying only for what is actually produced. A simple piece-rate approach often results in production variability that can disrupt the flow of product to customers. **Production variability** occurs because employees may be willing to forgo extra effort on some days when they are tired, bored, or ill, but will work especially hard on other days when they need some extra money. Frederick Taylor developed the **differential rate** as a response to the variation potential in piece-rate systems.[34] Taylor's differential rate had two piece rates: one for performing below standard and a higher rate for meeting or exceeding the standard, thus encouraging workers to at least meet the standard. One major advantage of piece-rate systems is that they are easy to understand. They are useful in labor-intensive industries such as textiles or agriculture, where individual production can be reliably measured. Migrant workers who harvest fruit and vegetables are often paid by unit of production.

Lincoln Electric, a Fortune 500 Ohio company, is cited as *the* success story regarding piece-rate pay. In fact, Stanford's Jeff Pfeffer considers Lincoln to be one of corporate America's greatest success stories, citing Lincoln's piece-rate system as a primary reason for their success.

When does piece-rate work best?

Except for some industries like textiles, individual piece-rate systems are less popular now than they were 20 years ago as a growing number of jobs are team-based or are in areas such as the service sector, which often precludes the establishment of a clear standard for determining the rate of production and the piece rate. Piece-rate incentive systems in their various forms tend to work better when the situation is repetitive, the pace is under the direct control of individual workers, there is little or no interaction or cooperation required among workers, and the results can be easily measured or counted. But even for companies in which incentive systems would seem to work, there can be trouble. The major problem with incentive systems is that an adversarial relationship can develop between workers and management. Workers make every effort to maximize their financial gains by attempting to manipulate the system of setting rates, setting informal production norms, and filing grievances regarding rate adjustments. Lincoln Electric, for example, had great difficulty implementing a piece-rate system in some of its international plants when they expanded in the 1990s. Plants in Germany and Brazil were ultimately shut down. The highly acclaimed management system apparently does not automatically transfer across the world.

There are numerous examples of worker attempts to sabotage piece-rate incentive systems. One expert on pay systems tells the story of how a sales force selling baby foods in South Florida kept secret their highly successful efforts at selling the food to senior citizens because they feared that their method would be rejected by management.[35]

Unfortunately, many jobs outside of sales and straight assembly work do not have a reliable measure of production or performance. Another problem is that adjustments in the standard are required whenever there is a significant change in the machinery or production methods. Finally, work group norms can develop that will restrict the productivity of any one individual. Employees may worry that high earnings under the PFP system will result in an adjustment of the standard. Also, some workers may worry that high productivity may translate into terminations if inventories get too large.

Some banks have piece-rate systems for data entry jobs in which individuals entering check amounts have virtually no interaction with co-workers. Workers control the rate of data entry, and the computer tallies the rate of production. One bank reported a 30 percent increase in production after installing a piece-rate system for data entry personnel.[36] Many customer service reps, whose performance is closely monitored by computer, are also paid by piece rate.

Potential problems

The adversarial relationship that can develop between workers and management regarding a piece-rate system can be reduced or eliminated if workers participate in the rate-setting process through task forces. Says one expert, "If they do not involve employees, there is a good chance that the employees will find a way to get involved—for example, by organizing a union."[37] Despite these cautionary notes, piece-rate incentive systems can be very effective when there is good trust between workers and managers.

Standard Hourly Rates

Standard hourly rates differ from piece-rate systems in that the production standard is expressed in time units. Using job analysis, the standard time for a given task is established and the organization then sets a fair hourly wage rate. The standard rate for any task is the wage rate times the standard. For example, if the standard time for a task is four hours and the fair hourly wage is $10, the standard rate is $40. The worker receives the $40 standard rate of pay regardless of the length of time it takes to complete the task. A common example is auto body repair. A customer is given an estimate based on a standards book listing the time required to repair various parts of a car and the hourly wage rate. Insurance companies use a similar book to check the accuracy of the estimate.

Halsey plan

In some standard hourly plans, the rate varies with output. For example, the **Halsey plan,**[38] developed in 1891 by Frederick Halsey, divided between employer and worker the savings realized from performing a task in less than the standard time. Halsey believed that sharing the rewards with management would reduce the likelihood that management would increase the standard as worker output increased. Although Halsey proposed a one-third worker and two-thirds organization split, today his plan is more commonly known as the **"Halsey 50-50 plan,"** because savings are equally divided.

Bottom-Line on Incentive System

When managers are considering an incentive system, they must take into account the firm's organizational strategy, culture, and position in the marketplace. Incentive plans in manufacturing are advisable if there are (1) high labor costs, (2) a high level of cost competition in the marketplace, (3) relatively slow advances in technology, (4) a high level of trust and cooperation between labor and management, and (5) individuals can control or affect the rate of production.[39]

The loss of U.S. jobs conducive to individual incentive systems, particularly in manufacturing, combined with the trend toward more team-based work systems, indicates that the decline in individual incentive systems in the United States based on rates of production will continue.

What Are Sales Incentive Plans?

Performance-based sales incentive plans have been found to increase sales over time.[40] Sales incentive plans share many of the characteristics of individual incentive plans, but there are also unique requirements. Both the determinants of employee control over output and measurability of performance have added dimensions for sales. Because an output measure can be easily established as the level of sales, in dollars or units, a common assumption is that salespeople are paid strictly on the volume of product sold. In many cases, however, employers expect salespeople to perform duties beyond strictly sales. Like any PFP system for a job with many important performance dimensions, if sales duties include customer training, market analysis, and credit checks, then the PFP system should involve complex measures of performance that include these dimensions along with sales data. Thus, a critical first step for a sales incentive program, as for all other incentive programs, is to determine what aspects of performance are most important to the firm. The next step is to decide on the methods of measurement and the appropriate levels of compensation. To motivate employees to increase customer satisfaction, many companies now incorporate client- or customer-based survey results into their sales compensation systems to underscore the need for nurturing customer relations as well as selling products and services.[41]

Commission-based pay

Approximately 75 percent of salespeople are on a commission-based, incentive plan.[42] **Commission plans** pay the salesperson directly on sales data. Although simple in concept, commissions can become complex. Ordinarily, commissions are a percentage of the dollar value of sales. However, the percentage can increase, decrease, or be constant in relation to changes in sales volume, depending on the nature of the product and its market. Commissions should provide sufficient incentive to the salesperson without adding too much to product cost. Because commissions can be highly variable over time, some firms protect salespeople from low sales periods by using a **draw-plus commission system.** At JCPenney, for example, a salesperson can draw against an account up to a predetermined limit during slack periods. During periods of higher commissions, the draw account is repaid from commissions in excess of the draw limit. A draw is essentially an interest-free loan to the salesperson, repayable when commissions exceed the draw limit. Another common sales incentive plan uses commissions in conjunction with a base salary. The base salary serves as a guaranteed minimum wage, and the commissions are an incentive to sell. Inclusion of salary as part of compensation is useful when the firm requires the salesperson to perform activities other than sales.

Draw-plus

Many variations of sales compensation exist. Bonuses for a specific product and bonuses for sales levels are common. In each case, the reward should be tied to a specific performance criterion that is of value to the firm and that justies the additional expense. Sales incentive programs may have equity problems that differ from a manufacturing situation. Operators of similar machines face the same workplace challenge, but salespeople with different territories may experience different levels of opportunity and challenge.

Most companies now have databases that enable them to establish and sustain a fair sales incentive program through the maintenance of the sales history of particular territories. For example, Steelcase offers greater incentives for new business in low-volume territories where their analysis indicates greater competition. Information systems now provide more sophisticated incentive systems that can promote equity among the sales force.

Stockbrokers often receive a large percentage of their pay based on commissions from stocks. This situation is considered the underlying cause of litigation by brokers' customers who claim this conflict of interest led to brokers pushing poor stocks that paid high commissions. As discussed earlier, the national mortgage crisis can also be partly blamed on a flawed commission-based incentive system for mortgage brokers.

Alternatives to cash

Many companies now offer rewards other than money as recognition for sales performance. Trips and prizes, which can be purchased by the company at a price considerably less than the cost of cash-only incentive programs, are quite common as a form of sales commission today, particularly in insurance, real estate, and the tourism industry. JM Family Enterprises provides trips to the Bahamas on the company yacht, haircuts, and massages as part of their awards system for top performers. Employees tend to overestimate the costs & such programs for the employer.

What Are Bonuses?

Bonuses more effective than base-pay adjustments

Bonuses are one-time payments based on performance. They have the advantage of not adding permanently to the base wage and can be given based on either rated or nonrated output measures. Bonuses also can be based on individual or group-based measures. Some workers prefer them to merit pay plans because they get the money all at once and it looks like a larger sum. Fifty dollars every two weeks does not have the same impact as a single payment of $1,300. In general, bonuses are more effective because they allow for larger one-time awards without the amortized effect of tying pay for performance into base pay.

WHAT ARE GROUP INCENTIVE PLANS?

There are three major types of group-based incentive plans: **profit sharing, gain sharing, and employee stock option plans.** Profit sharing distributes a portion of corporate profits among designated employees. Gain sharing divides a portion of cost reductions or productivity increases between groups covered by the plan. Stock option plans distribute stocks and stock options to employees based on corporate performance measures such as return on equity.

All three types are designed to establish a link between pay and performance, but performance is measured at the group, unit, or company level. Many PFP systems combine individual PFP systems with some form of group incentives. Recall the discussion of Lincoln Electric, where the piece-rate method is combined with profit sharing for all employees. In general, as **expectancy/instrumentality theory** would predict, (see **figure 11-3**) group-based systems are at least theoretically less motivating because individual employees typically do not perceive a strong connection between their efforts and performance. The use of all three of the group plans have increased in the last few years, and the majority of gain sharing plans in the United States were introduced in the past 25 years. Manufacturing organizations are more likely to adopt group plans than are service-oriented firms. Group plans are generally preferable to individual plans under the popular team-based approaches to production or service, although, as discussed in Chapter 7, this depends principally on the ability (or inability) to sort out individual contributions to important outcomes.

Group plans are best when cooperation and teamwork are essential

Successful group incentive plans require the same determinants as individual plans. The measures differ in that a group plan must be based on a measure of group performance or productivity. The use of group plans is particularly effective when cooperation and teamwork are essential and when a goal of the system is to enhance the feeling of participation. Group plans are most useful when tasks are so interrelated that it is difficult (or impossible) to identify a measure of individual output. The size of the "group" can range from two people to plantwide or companywide. The smaller the group, the more a worker will identify individual effort as affecting group performance.

FLSA compliance

Group PFP plans require special considerations. First, because of the "free-rider" effect, there is potential for conflict when all group members receive the same reward regardless of individual input. Second, strong group norms that control output can inhibit group efforts. Third, the variable compensation distribution formula must meet the **Fair Labor Standards Act** requirements for calculating for wages and overtime pay.[43] While these three issues can complicate matters, there is nonetheless strong evidence that group incentives can increase productivity.[44]

What Is Profit Sharing?

Controlling turnover

Group size should be small

Profit sharing is designed to motivate cost savings by allowing workers to share in benefits of increased profits. As discussed in Chapter 10, retirement income for employees is frequently linked to a profit-sharing plan. Rewards can be periodic cash disbursements or deposits to an employee account. Either a predetermined percentage of profit or a percentage above a certain threshold is allocated to a pool (e.g., 10 to 25 percent). This pool is disbursed to employees on the basis of some ratio, usually related to their wage. Many companies now have options from which the employee may select a particular profit-sharing plan compatible with his or her long-range plans. Profit sharing has been criticized as being remote and perceptually unrelated to individual performance, but research indicates that it produces generally positive results.

Many firms also use profit sharing as a tool to control employee turnover. At Johnson & Johnson, the allocation is distributed in equal increments over a period of years, and an employee sacrifices the remaining distributions by leaving the firm before the period is up. Obviously, some of the incentive value of profit sharing for higher performance is lost when it is used in this fashion. In general, profit sharing works best as an incentive when the group size is small enough that employees believe they have some impact on group profitability.

The typical profit-sharing plan uses profits to fund retirement plans and is thus advantageous for tax purposes. However, some companies pay annual bonuses based on company profits. Anderson Windows, for example, has a profit-sharing pool that has paid employees up to 84 percent of their annual salary. This approach gives Anderson greater flexibility during hard times since company costs go down when company performance goes down. Given the relatively lower base pay for its employees, Anderson was able to retain most of its employees in 2008 despite a significant downturn in business.

While employees generally approve of profit sharing, they get testy when their base pay is affected in a negative way by profit-sharing provisions. When DuPont Corporation announced that there would be 4 percent cuts in the base pay of all its 20,000 employees due to poor sales in the fibers division, worker dissatisfaction was so high that the profit-sharing plan was scrapped. If the company was profitable, workers would have earned an additional 12 percent above their base pay under the plan. The major reason for the dissatisfaction with the system was the lack of perceived connection between worker performance and company profits. UAW workers at Caterpillar struck the company partially because they wanted an increase in base salary and a decrease in the risk of the profit-sharing plan. One UAW contract for 2007 Saturn workers scaled back the profit-sharing component of the innovative wage accord. Poor sales at Saturn had a great deal to do with the union's position.

Profit sharing can be seen as a way to align the goals of management and employees. When employees perceive profit sharing favorably, commitment to the organization and trust in management tend to increase, thus "encouraging employees to exert maximum effort, share information, and invest in firm-specific training that may not be valued outside the firm."[45] Studies have reported increases in productivity between 7 and 9 percent. However, workers' beliefs that they have sufficient control to contribute to the profitability of the organization are critical to the success of profit-sharing programs.

Productivity increases between 7 and 9 percent

One study concluded that "when profit sharing is perceived as both an opportunity for individual input to the organization's success and a reflection of the organization's desire to treat employees fairly, higher levels of commitment follow. Structuring profit-sharing systems to enhance perceptions of input (e.g., some portion of the profit sharing based on individual contribution to performance) and reciprocity (e.g., some portion based on years of service) appears to be advantageous."[46]

Profit-sharing for performance and seniority

What Is Gain Sharing?

Gain sharing is a group incentive system that gives participating employees an incentive allocation based on improved performance. Performance can be defined by increased productivity, lower costs, improved safety measures, or customer satisfaction indices. Gain sharing bonuses are typically given on a monthly basis, and the range in bonus pay is between 5 and 10 percent of base pay. Effective gain sharing programs are based on a formula derived with worker input and which workers perceive as fair.

Worker involvement is critical

Gain sharing is a popular approach to motivate higher levels of group productivity. While there are subtle differences among various PFP programs classified as "gain sharing," all of them essentially involve worker involvement and the process of sharing in the financial benefits of reducing costs or increasing productivity. One survey found that gain sharing is the second most important compensation topic among human resource managers.[47]

More gain sharing plans were instituted in the mid-1980s than in the previous 50 years,[48] and almost 40 percent of Fortune 1000 manufacturing firms rely on some form of gain sharing.[49] Gain sharing plans either try to reduce the amount of labor required for a given level of output (cost saving) or increase the output for a given amount of labor (productivity increase) (or both). The method for determining the standard production rate and the incentive rate must be clearly defined. Gain sharing plans generally are based on the assumption

Cooperation and trust are critical

that better cooperation among workers and between workers and managers will result in greater effectiveness. Successful plans require an **organizational climate** characterized by trust across organizational levels, worker participation, and cooperative unions. An organized

Employee suggestion systems

employee suggestion system is also characteristic of almost all gain sharing plans. To maximize cost saving and productivity increases, there must be employee involvement in the plan development and execution. A successful gain sharing plan requires workers and management to work toward a common goal. Gain sharing encounters difficulty when management downgrades employee input or unions adopt a strong adversarial position. Like profit sharing, instrumentality can be low since employees may not perceive a strong connection between their performance and desired outcomes.

Financial measures parallel firm performance

Gain sharing plans can get complicated. Measures of productivity are usually adapted to particular situations. For example, one firm uses both the labor/sales ratio and the cost-of-quality/sales ratio as financial measures. Another firm uses savings on warranty costs as a measure for its engineers and designers. As one expert puts it, "The financial measures of performance have great educational value in spurring employee understanding of business fundamentals . . . financial measures tend to closely parallel overall firm performance."[50]

Most types of gain sharing plans use a productivity ratio to capture labor's contribution to value added. The differences among the plans concern how labor's cost is calculated for the numerator and how organizational output is measured for the denominator.

Gain sharing plans are different from profit sharing in two major ways:

1. Gain sharing is based on a measure of productivity, not profit.

2. Gain sharing rewards are given out frequently, whereas profit sharing is annual and often tied to a retirement plan as deferred payment.

What Are the Four Approaches to Gain Sharing?

There are four basic approaches to gain sharing, although there is considerable variation within them. The four approaches are the **Scanlon plan,** the **Rucker plan,** the **IMPROSHARE plan,** and **Winsharing.** In addition to the productivity ratio, other issues influence the selection of a gain sharing plan. One of the most important aspects of a PFP system, strength of reinforcement, is roughly equal for the four methods. A summary of the issues to be considered in selecting a plan is provided in Figure 11-6.

Scanlon plan

The **Scanlon plan,** the most common gain sharing plan, measures the relationship between the sales value of production and labor costs. Like all gain sharing options, employee participation is an important component of this approach. Screening committees are used to evaluate cost-saving suggestions from employees with labor cost savings serving as the incentive. Savings are measured by a monthly calculation of the ratio of payroll to sales value of production compared to baseline data.

The Scanlon plan is the oldest form of gain sharing.[51] Developed by Joseph Scanlon, a steelworker, a union official, and later a professor at the Massachusetts Institute of Technology, the plan was originally devised to keep the La Pointe Steel Company from going bankrupt. The plan received wide public attention because of a *Life* magazine article published in 1946. At the time, its unique aspects were (1) rewarding the group for suggestions by individuals in the group; (2) joint labor–management committees designed to propose and evaluate labor-saving suggestions; and (3) a worker reward share based on reduced costs, not increased profits.

**Figure 11-6
Factors to Consider in Designing a Gain Sharing Program**

1. **Performance and financial measures.** The bonus formula must be perceived as reasonable, accurate, and equitable.
2. **Plant or facility size.** Plants with fewer than 500 employees are ideally suited to gain sharing, while plants with over 2,000 employees are not.
3. **Types of production.** Plants with highly mixed types of production will find it difficult to introduce gain sharing because the measurement process is so complicated.
4. **Workforce interdependence.** Highly integrated work units are ideal for gain sharing.
5. **Workforce composition.** Some workforces may not be as motivated by financial incentives.
6. **Potential to absorb additional output.** Initial increase in productivity must be useful to the organization and must not entail negative consequences for the workforce (e.g., layoffs).
7. **Potential for employee efforts.** Can employee efforts actually affect productivity to a significant extent, or does automation (or other factors) impede worker effects?
8. **Present organizational climate.** An initial level of trust is required.
9. **Union–management relations.** Union should be an active partner in program development.
10. **Capital investment plans.** Don't install gain sharing if large capital investments are planned.
11. **Organized employee suggestion system.** Do not downgrade or ignore employee input.

Source: Reprinted from "Gain Sharing: Do It Right the First Time" by M. Schuster, M.I.T., *Sloan Management Review,* Winter 1987, pp. 17–25, by permission of publisher. Copyright © 2006 by Massachusetts Institute of Technology. All rights reserved.

Scanlon plans require a considerable commitment by workers and management to cooperate in the development and maintenance of the program. While the track record for Scanlon plans is mixed, there are some great success stories. One paint manufacturer in Texas reported a 78 percent increase in production over its 17-year history of using a Scanlon plan.[52] The keys seem to be employee trust, understanding, and contributions to improvements. For example, one expert attributed the Scanlon plan's success this way: "A formal method for having all organizational members contribute ingenuity and brainpower to the improvement of organizational performance . . . and improvement of relations across functional groups and levels of the organizational hierarchy."[53]

Rucker plan

The **Rucker plan** is another successful group incentive system. While similar to Scanlon, the Rucker formula includes the value of all supplies, materials, and services. The result is a bonus formula based on the value added to the product per labor dollar. Thus, an incentive is created to save on all inputs, including materials and supplies. The advantage of Rucker over Scanlon is the linkage of rewards to savings other than labor savings, plus greater flexibility. The disadvantage is that concepts such as value added and the adjustments for inflation make the Rucker plan more difficult to understand and explain compared to the Scanlon plan.

IMPROSHARE

A third category of gain sharing is **IMPROSHARE,** which stands for "improved productivity through sharing."[54] IMPROSHARE is similar to Scanlon except that the IMPROSHARE ratio uses standard hours rather than labor costs. Engineering studies or past performance data are used to specify the standard number of hours required to produce a base production level. Savings in hours result in reward allocation to workers. IMPROSHARE "rewards all covered employees equally whenever the actual number of labor hours used to produce output in the current week or month is less than the estimated number it would have taken to produce the current level of output in the base period."[55] IMPROSHARE is easy to administer, and employees have no difficulty understanding the formula.

Winsharing

Winsharing combines gain sharing with profit sharing.[56] Winsharing is based on the rational proposition that if your PFP system results in more product being produced than cannot be sold, your PFP system needs some alterations. Winsharing takes market demand into consideration. Winsharing payouts are based on whether group performance is achieved relative to business goals. Financial performance in excess of the goals is split evenly between workers and the company. Winsharing differs from profit sharing because group performance measures are used that are independent of profit measures.

What's the Bottom Line on Gain Sharing?

Research has found numerous benefits from gain sharing plans, including improved productivity and quality.[57] The strong trend is to use some form of gain sharing with other approaches to improving productivity and performance.[58] Kendall-Futuro, a health care products company, improved their "just-in-time" performance with gain sharing. At Timken's Faircrest Steel Plant in Canton, Ohio, employees participated in the design of a gain sharing plan that has generated average payouts of over $6,000 a year per worker.

Union teamwork and cooperation is essential

The teamwork and cooperation between union workers and management is an essential component of the success of the program.[59] The company reports strong success so far. Other major companies offering gain sharing plans include Georgia Pacific, Huffy Bicycle, Inland Container, Eaton Corp., TRW, and General Electric.[60] Gain sharing is evolving from a simple productivity concept into a family of measures all designed to improve performance.[61] Whirlpool instituted such a family that featured gain sharing. The board of directors receives stock options when targets are met. Senior managers can receive up to 100 percent of base salary as annual stock options. Whirlpool eliminated profit sharing and instituted **winsharing** which increased worker performance as well as knowledge about shareholder value.[62]

Success of gain sharing plans in general depends on significant involvement and support by high-level management, actual employee participation and understanding, and realistic employee and (if applicable) union expectations.[63]

Group size and results

Companies that are reluctant to involve unions in strategic planning will have difficulty with gain sharing programs. There is also considerable evidence that group size affects gain-sharing results. For example, doubling the number of employees covered from 200 to 400 was associated with a 50 percent drop in the average productivity gain.[64]

One review of Scanlon, Rucker, and IMPROSHARE plans concluded that:

1. IMPROSHARE is easier for workers to comprehend.
2. With IMPROSHARE workers have more control over physical productivity.
3. IMPROSHARE does not require management to reveal sensitive corporate financial information.

The advantages of Scanlon and Rucker plans over IMPROSHARE are that:

1. Workers actually share in the financial risks of the company (appealing to management).
2. The Scanlon plan typically allows for more integration with problem-solving processes.

Support for IMPROSHARE

A well-controlled study of IMPROSHARE found that productivity continues to rise sharply after the initial introduction of the plan for at least three years. After three years, few gains occur and productivity begins to plateau at the higher level (likely because slack has been eliminated and further changes may require dramatic production process changes).[65]

What Are Employee Stock Option Plans?

As discussed earlier, many companies use employee stock option plans to compensate, retain, and attract employees. These plans are contracts between a company and its employees that give employees the right to buy a specific number of the company's shares at a fixed price within a certain period of time (usually more than five years). Employees who are granted stock options hope to profit by exercising their options at a higher price than when they were granted.

Employee stock option plans should not be confused with the term *"ESOPs," or Employee Stock Ownership Plans,* which are retirement plans (discussed in Ch.10). An employee stock ownership plan (ESOP) is a retirement plan in which the company contributes its stock to the plan for the benefit of the company's employees. With an ESOP, employees do not buy or hold the stock directly.

The Securities and Exchange Commission presents the following example of a stock option plan on its Web site: An employee is granted the option to purchase 1,000 shares of the company's stock at the current market price of $5 per share (the "grant" price). The employee can exercise the option at $5 per share—typically the exercise price will be equal to the price when the options are granted. Plans allow employees to exercise their options after a certain number of years or when the company's stock reaches a certain price. If the price of the stock increases to $20 per share, for example, the employee may exercise his or her option to buy 1,000 shares at $5 and then sell the stock at the current market price of $20.

Companies sometimes revalue the price at which the options can be exercised. This may happen, for example, when a company's stock price has fallen below the original exercise price. Companies revalue the exercise price as a way to retain their employees. Many of our nation's largest companies have such option plans for non-managerial employees (e.g., Lockheed, JCPenney, Texaco, Procter and Gamble, Avis).[66]

Also, as discussed earlier, many U.S. companies have been accused of "backdating" the dates when options were granted for executives. If the stock price goes up, "backdating" can increase compensation. It can also be illegal.[67]

Options work best with extensive employee involvement

In principle, options sound like a terrific idea: Companies sell stock to workers in order to give them a financial stake in the company. Stock allocations are made to the employee's account based on relative base pay. Research results on the effects of stock options are unclear, however, one review concluded that "few of the studies have found strong and significant effects."[68] Options tend to work better when combined with extensive employee involvement and problem solving.

A popular method designed to replace fixed compensation costs with variable wages and benefits, options give the organization greater flexibility in response to a competitive environment. Santa Fe Railway reduced employee pay for the first time in the company's 122-year history. The pay cuts were replaced with stock options that resulted in bonus checks for all 2,400 salaried employees. Some employees received checks in excess of $100,000. Needless to say, Santa Fe employees are now very happy with the new incentive system. Behlen Manufacturing has had great success in using a blend of base pay, gain sharing, profit sharing, and options to support its organizational goals. There are also some sad stories indicating options are no panacea. At Burlington Industries, employees bought out the company only to watch the stock plummet to less than half its purchase value.

Effects of stock options

One review drew the following conclusions and implications for options.[69]

1. Since stock options are distributed differentially in proportion to performance or contribution, they may be perceived as more equitable than profit or gain sharing, particularly by employees seeking some sense of control or ownership in the company.

2. Options might generate weaker levels of work motivation and subsequent performance than other incentive systems as their ultimate value is determined, at least in part, by market forces over which the employee has no control (e.g., the 2008 stock market).

3. Consequently, the eventual value (or even anticipated ownership component) of stock options may turn out to be less proportionate to actual employee contributions or performance than expected. The result can be relatively stronger perceptions of inequity and lower instrumentality.

MANAGERIAL AND EXECUTIVE INCENTIVE PAY

In a 2006 editorial, the *New York Times* concluded that "there is no shortage of numbers and studies detailing the widening gap between what American companies pay workers and the millions of dollars those same companies pay top executives."[70] While correlational research generally supports the use of long-term reward systems for executives, which are directly tied to the long-term strategic goals of the firm, the absolute value of these awards is regarded by just about all experts on the subject as ridiculously high.[71] In general, executive incentive plans are linked either to net income, some measure of return on investment, or total dividends paid. These incentives are paid in the form of bonuses, not permanently tied to base pay, and the awarding of stock options. Even *The Wall Street Journal* concedes

Pay for no performance

that things are out of control. In a lengthy exposé entitled "Pay for No Performance," a *WSJ* article documents the loss in linkage between pay and performance.[72] Nicholas Kristof of the *New York Times* asks, "Are you capable of taking a perfectly good 158-year-old company and turning it into dust? If so, then you may not be earning up to your full potential. You should be raking it in like Richard Fuld, the longtime chief of Lehman Brothers."[73] Fuld took home almost a half a billion dollars in total compensation between 1993 and 2007. He "earned" $45 million or $17,000 an hour in 2007 just before the company went bankrupt.

CEO pay rose again in 2007 despite the fact that for years now only CEOs themselves and the occasional compensation consultant (who benefits directly from larger pay packages) are actually defending the packages. One of the highest-paid CEOs of late is George David of United Technology, one of the largest military contractors. The wars in Iraq and Afghanistan are the most probable reasons for UT's strong performance, not anything this man has done. He earned over $75 million in 2007 and over $60 million in 2006. The expected total direct compensation (TDC is the sum of base salary, annual bonus, and the grant value of stock options, restricted stock, and other long-term incentives) increased over 20 percent since the wars began. Another obscene example of war profiteering is David Brooks, CEO of DHB Industries, a bulletproof vest manufacturer. Mr. Brooks has earned over $250 million since the Iraq and Afghanistan wars began.

One trend is the movement away from stock options and toward other long-term awards. Executive pay is a hot political issue. Even Warren Buffett has called it "obscene." "It's just way off the charts," says portfolio manager Jennifer Ladd, who is fighting for lower executive pay.[74] Management guru Peter Drucker argued that no CEO should earn more than 20 times the company's lowest-paid employee. He reasoned that if the CEO took too large a share of the rewards, "it would make a mockery of the contributions of all the other employees in a successful organization." Several pieces of legislation, aimed at regulating or controlling executive pay, were pending before Congress in 2009.

Unintended consequence of executive PFP: earnings restatements

A large portion of executive compensation is now tied to meeting earnings goals. According to a *Forbes* magazine editorial, "Accepted accounting principles are an art, not a science. Give a smart boss the incentive to do it, and he can push the earnings envelope to the limit—or beyond." Delphi, OfficeMax, Qwest, and WorldCom are companies that heaped big performance-based bonuses on their bosses but subsequently had to restate earnings lower after accounting shenanigans were discovered. Paying for performance "has vastly increased the number of accounting disasters," says Paul Hodgson, a senior research associate at the Corporate Library, a corporate-governance research firm in Portland, Maine. According to a study by the comptroller of New York State, between 1995 and 2002, when companies were increasingly tying bonuses to earnings, the number of earnings restatements increased from 44 to 240.[75]

Are There Documented Negative Consequences to Widening Pay Dispersion?

While there has been considerable commentary about the negative consequences of the widening dispersion between CEO pay and the pay of others, little research has shown a relationship between this gap and subsequent performance decrements or higher turnover. The problem of pay dispersion may be more acute in more technologically intensive industries where executives are encouraged to be entrepeneurially aggressive and they often are compensated very well based on their performance. However, intensive teamwork and coordination are often required for the development of high-tech products or services, thus indicating the need for a PFP system with more of a team or corporate-level orientation. One study found that pay dispersion in high-tech firms is predictive of subsequent performance decrements.[76] A recent study found that the discrepancy between the CEO's pay and that of the "top management team" increased the likelihood that members of the team would leave the organization.[77] Pay dispersion tends to diminish communication, increase status gaps, and foster aggressive competition for advancement to lucrative top posts within a company. One recent survey of pay satisfaction in a retail environment found significant decreases in pay satisfaction among the rank and file workers after the top management team's pay was made public. Employees also indicated higher rates of intentions to leave the organization, stronger interests in joining a union, and lower levels of organizational commitment and trust. The extent to which the CEO was thought to be overpaid was a strong predictor of these negative outcomes.

Pay dispersion can result in turnover of key personnel and lower pay satisfaction

Should You Use Short- or Long-Term Measures of Performance?

A principal distinction between managerial and executive incentives is the time horizon of the performance measure that is the basis of the incentive. Although many lower-level managers are being awarded stock options, they often have incentives based on short-term measures. As discussed earlier, these short-term incentives must be compatible with the long-term strategic goals of the firm.

Top executives have both short- and long-term performance incentives. Managers and executives have a wider area of discretion in making decisions that affect the firm. As a consequence, the PFP system is designed to reinforce a sense of commitment to the organization. Most managers receive bonuses related to profit. The amount is usually awarded as a percentage of their base pay, although there is a trend toward awarding lump sums not tied to the base pay. As higher profitability thresholds are attained, the manager receives bigger bonuses. The bonus structure for any given manager often depends on the relative contributions of all managers, with the assessment of relative contribution made at a higher level. This method suffers from the drawbacks discussed previously regarding profit sharing for individuals. Many managers might feel that they have a negligible impact on organization profits. As the link between performance and pay becomes weaker, the reward loses incentive value. The link can be strengthened by clearly defining performance standards, while basing the amount of the reward on corporate profitability.

Executives and their boards should be concerned with the long-term viability of the firm. There are many situations in which a decision option can have a conflicting impact on a firm's short- and long-run profitability. Investing in research and development (R&D) will depress short-term profit but should ultimately improve a competitive position. Cuts in services may add to short-run profits but ultimately damage market share.

A stock option plan gives an executive the right to purchase a stock, over a specified period, at a fixed price. The theory is that if the executive is prudent and hard working, the stock price will go up. If the stock price does increase, the executive can purchase it at the lower fixed price, effectively receiving as a bonus the difference between the fixed purchase price and the higher market price. Congress periodically revises legislation controlling the awarding of stock options.[78]

Problems with options

Although take-home pay wasn't too shabby without them, CEO salaries went through the roof through abuse of stock options. Numerous experts endorsed the use of options on the assumption that executives would profit when shareholders profited. This is often not the case. As one expert concluded, "shareholders lost their shirts, but executives went right on raking in the dough."[79] Many companies awarded huge option grants despite terrible corporate performance by any reputable measure. Many companies simply adjusted performance goals for no particular reason. According to a stinging *BusinessWeek* exposé, almost 200 companies swapped or repriced stock options "to enrich members of a corporate elite who already were among the world's wealthiest people. When CEOs can clear $1 billion during their tenures, executive pay is clearly too high. Worse still, the system is not providing an incentive for outstanding performance."[80] Although there are many excellent Web sites, pay expert Graef Crystal's columns at www.bloomberg.com provide the most objective treatment of executive pay.

SARs

Restricted plans

Performance share plans

There are many variations on stock options. *Stock appreciation rights (SARs),* for example, do not involve buying stock. Having been awarded rights to a stock at a fixed price for a specified period, the executive can call the option and receive the difference between the fixed and market prices in cash. *Restricted stock plans* give shares as a bonus, but with restrictions.[81] The restrictions may be that the executive cannot leave the company or sell the stock for a specified time. *Performance share plans* award units based on both short- and long-term measures. These units are later translated into stock awards. Other incentive stock option plans are part of retirement packages. These may include profit-sharing and stock bonus plans. In both cases, employers pay into a retirement fund based on corporate profits. Recent evidence suggests that stock incentives may not be effective.[82]

Executive incentives of the future are more likely to be tied to long-term corporate performance, which may involve qualitative assessment of performance along with corporate financial performance. New products and service lines, environmental impact assessments, and new territorial penetration are some of the long-range measures that may be used to assess executive performance. For example, McDonald's, Burger King, and General Electric (GE) place considerable weight on their long-term growth in the European sector as a basis for compensating senior management. The trend in executive compensation is against heavy reliance on stock prices as a basis for compensating executives, since such reliance would promote short-term perspectives to the detriment of the long-term strategic plan of the organization. So-called

"Claw-back" provisions

"claw-back" provisions in executive contracts are more likely where boards can demand cash returns by executives if information reveals performance decrements.

What about the Corporate Board Room?

Corporate boards have been called "America's last dirty little secret."[83] They have very lucrative and comprehensive compensation packages that are rarely linked to corporate performance. One study found companies with outside directors who owned substantial stock holdings were less likely to overpay their CEO and, more importantly, presided over superior corporate performance.[84]

One major flaw of corporate governance is that boards of directors in the U.S. provide little oversight and have been called "ornamental." As Warren Buffett has said, "in judging whether corporate America is serious about reforming itself, CEO pay remains the acid test." So far, corporate America is failing the test.

Lake Wobegon effect

"Boards pay CEOs after negotiations that are often more like pillow talk. Relationships are incestuous, and compensation consultants provide only a thin veneer of respectability by finding some 'peer group' of companies so moribund that anybody shines in comparison."[85] The result is the so-called **"Lake Wobegon effect,"** where all CEOs are judged to be above average. One study of 1,500 companies found that over two-thirds claimed to be outperforming their respective peer groups. More shareholders' power may be the answer. Britain and Australia give shareholders more rights than in the U.S. As stated earlier, relevant legislation such as the Shareholder Vote on Executive Compensation Act (**"Say on Pay Act"**) could ultimately affect executive pay if such legislation becomes law.

"Say on Pay Act"

HOW DO COMPANIES KEEP ENTREPRENEURS AND PROMOTE INTRAPRENEURS?

In the current climate of competitive pressures and great opportunity for launching new businesses, many companies are attempting to retain entrepreneurial mavericks within the corporate umbrella and promote intrapreneurial thinking. Many high-tech firms are funding employee ventures by using innovative compensation schemes. At IBM, employees can submit business plans for IBM risk capital. Employees can negotiate a share of the profits from an idea that they might have otherwise pursued on the outside.[86] The basic principle of entrepreneurial pay is that the employee places a major portion of salary at risk, with the percentage of employee ownership of the venture determined by the portion of salary at risk.

Funding employee ventures

The potential for large returns replaces many of the standard perks expected by employees. Payoffs may have a variety of bases, from profits produced by the venture to increases in parent company stock value. Although such payoffs may be less than if the venture were truly independent, the risk for the employee is also more limited. In addition, there is the support and expertise available from the parent. American Telephone and Telegraph (AT&T), for example, wanted to increase the risk its people were willing to take in entrepreneurial efforts. Three venture approaches were offered, corresponding to the levels of risk the venture employee was willing to take.

Many companies have adopted special award programs for major entrepreneurial accomplishments. Microsoft, Merck, IBM, Amoco, Xerox, and AT&T, for example, have programs in which the awards can exceed $100,000 for research discoveries that lead to product development. These special programs are independent of any other PFP systems within the companies.

WHAT ARE THE MANAGERIAL CHALLENGES FOR PFP PROGRAMS?

A well-designed PFP system should lead to lower costs, higher profits, and a higher degree of individual or group motivation. Introduction of a well-designed PFP system can provide a more accurate estimate of labor costs as well as prompt workers to make more effective use of their time, supplies, and equipment. Using a mix of plans often has the best results. These same general principles also apply to small business. Research has clearly established that involving employees in the process of developing or changing a PFP system will ultimately lead to more effective results. Figure 11-7 presents three strategic positions to make PFP systems more effective. Once again, sound measurement is the key.

Use a mix of PFP plans

Sound measurement is key

PFP systems are more complicated than lock-step, straight compensation. There are numerous challenges that must be met. Emphasizing one measure can lead to reduced performance levels in other measures. A strong focus on output or quantity can reduce quality, which could lead to increased costs in quality control. In addition, a focus on output could jeopardize safety.

**Figure 11-7
Three Strategic Positions for
Pay Systems**

1. **Pay the person.** People should be paid according to their individual market value—both internal and external. Pricing a job (not the individual) is not good enough. Need to measure knowledge, skills, and competencies of individuals against the external market.
2. **Pay-for-performance approach needs to translate business strategy into measures that can be used for reward system.** Individual, team-based, and business-based PFP systems all should have a place in any single organization for any single person.
3. **Individualize the reward system.** Individualize the system to fit characteristics of persons the organization wants to attract and retain. Avoid one-size-fits-all PFP systems.

Source: Ferris, Gerald R; Buckley, M. Ronald; Fedor, Donald B., *Human Resource Management: Perspectives, Context, Functions, and Outcomes,* 4th ed, Pearson Education. Reprinted with permission of the authors.

**Reward all important work
dimensions**

Remember the discussion in Chapter 7 about the definition of performance and the various aspects of value. A PFP system should reward all important dimensions of performance. An overemphasis on one dimension or one aspect of value such as quantity will result in a deemphasis on other aspects such as quality.

Increased overhead

A second challenge is the increased overhead expense of installing and maintaining the PFP system. Unless the production process is very stable, maintenance costs for PFP systems can be substantial, and consultants in this area are very expensive. A third challenge is the difficulty in setting standards that accurately reflect task requirements and are perceived as fair. This problem can be greater when a system adds new processes or equipment, as workers will be suspicious of new standards. A fourth challenge is that there will be resistance to any change involving employee compensation, particularly when base pay is affected. Unions have been born out of attempts to radically alter compensation systems. In addition to the typical fear of anything new, workers may oppose change to avoid being victimized by new rates and standards. The final challenge is that PFP systems are more likely to be subject to legal actions for possible discrimination.

Difficulty setting standards

Resistance to change

Possible legal action

Management may resist change because of the expense of revising the pay system, the time required to do more valid performance measurement, and the difficulties that develop in defending PFP decisions. Finally, variations in pay due to performance differences may lead to conflict, a potential problem in a team or process-oriented work setting focused on the external customer. When measures are explicit and objective, some conflict will occur. When methods are subjective or ambiguous, as with the typical performance appraisal system, significant reward differences may not be perceived as justified, resulting in even greater conflict. Let's not forget the warning from the authors of *Freakonomics*. Incentive systems invite cheating and "gaming" of the system. Close monitoring is required. Over 200 companies have been the subject of recent government investigations into whether they "backdated" their executives' stock options to maximize the value of the options, an illegal practice if the company does not take a charge for the value of the granted options. Executives and HR directors have gone to jail for this (apparently) common practice.

**More measurement ambiguity
will result in more conflict**

Close monitoring is required

SUMMARY

**PFP system must be
compatible with long-term
success**

The PFP system must support the long-term competitive strategy and viability of the organization. If the strategy emphasizes entrepreneurial activity and independent effort, individualized PFP systems become increasingly important and effective. Incentive systems must also be compatible with organizational values. Closed, secretive cultures do not mix well with performance incentives. Openness and trust are necessary if employees are to accept the standards and believe in the equity of the rewards. Lincoln Electric's much touted piece-rate system would probably not be successful without the other elements of the Lincoln management system which is based on mutual trust and a fair distribution of the products of hard work. Organizational culture clearly affects the nature of incentives selected and, in the end, the effectiveness of the system. Individual PFP plans are preferable when individuals contribute important criteria or attain certain outcomes that can be clearly measured and teamwork is not seriously undermined by the process of individual performance measurement and rewards. Highly interdependent jobs or groups will dictate group or organizational-based PFP plans.

Money is clearly a motivator

As one expert on the subject has put it, "Paying for performance will not solve all of the motivational problems associated with the new workforce and strong national competition. However, it can be an important part of a total performance management system that is designed to create a highly motivating work environment."[87] There is no question that money *is* a motivator. A key question is, Motivation for what? Following the measurement principles presented in Chapter 7 for defining performance is a critical step in linking the performance appraisal, performance management, and pay-for-performance systems. At Countrywide, mortgage lenders were paid when the mortgage contract was signed and "up-front" fees were paid, not if and when the mortgage was paid off.

There is probably no clearer example of incentive pay gone bad than the well-documented troubles in investment banking and insurance in 2008. Bankers got huge rewards when their high-risk investments did well. If those same strategies went sour down the line, they probably lost a bonus the next year. Many bankers even lost their jobs. But they almost never have to give back even a dime of the millions they made off their previous "bets" that ultimately put their company in jeopardy or out of business completely (think Lehman Brothers here). Just maybe pay for performance should include a provision about **"give-backs,"** or the release of money over time and subject to a longer-term assessment of the original investment or incentive scheme. There is a trend toward including "give-back" or "claw-back" provisions as a part of executive compensation systems.

Pay consultant Alan Johnson may have captured the connection between compensation and the economic woes of 2008. "Wall Street is a sales business—they sell bonds, securities, transactions, ideas. . . . They're not paid to be long-term, philosophical, reflective. The pressure is to do the next merger, sell more stocks and bonds, do more trading—whatever boosts current profits and bonuses, the long-term consequences be damned."[88] Obviously, the long-term consequences should be the ultimate criterion in evaluating any incentive system, and the compatibility between this selling behavior and the long-term consequences are absolutely critical.

Long-term consequences should be the ultimate criterion

Bottom-line on PFP systems

The bottom line remains that for any PFP system to work, rewards valued by the worker must be clearly linked to outcomes valued by internal and, most important, external customers and stockholders. Virtually all of the research on "high-performance work systems" supports the view that proper PFP systems can help to create and sustain a competitive advantage. The evidence supports the value of carefully designed PFP systems with a focus on long-term success measures. When the focus is on organizations that follow academic guidelines for development and maintenance, PFP systems look like a winner. A recent review of the vast literature provided a great "bottom-line" summary: "Every pay program has its advantages and disadvantages. Programs differ in their sorting and incentive effects, their incentive intensity and risk, their use of behaviors versus results, and their emphasis on individual versus group measures of performance. Because of the limitations of any single pay program, organizations often elect to use a portfolio of programs, which may provide a means of reducing the risks of particular pay strategies while garnering most of their benefits. For example, using only an individual incentive program could result in unacceptably high levels of competitive behavior and focus on overly narrow objectives. On the other hand, relying exclusively on gain sharing could result in the underrewarding of high individual performers, thus risking their attraction, motivation, and retention. However, offering a mix of these different programs offers the possibility that the advantages of each can be captured, while minimizing the disadvantages."[89] All of these programs should be developed, administered and evaluated in the context of the long-term success of the organization.

Offer a mix of tailored programs

Chapter 12 will turn to other HRM systems and characteristics that can contribute to the productivity, competitive advantage, and long-term success of organizations.

Discussion Questions

1. Deming and others think PFP is a bad idea. What do you think?

2. Why is trust so important for PFP systems?

3. When is a group-based PFP system better than an individual system?

4. Some experts argue that a corporation's board of directors should be paid only with stock options. What do you think?

5. How would you go about combining individual and group-based PFP systems?

6. Some experts believe that if you have to use performance appraisals as the main source of data for a PFP system, you shouldn't bother with the PFP system. What do you think?

7. Under what conditions (if any) should a company install a forced-distribution rating system for PFP?

8. Conduct research on executive compensation contracts. Determine to what extent "claw-back" or "give-back" provisions are part of the contract. Describe such a program and how the "claw-back" works.

Chapter 12

Managing the Employment Relationship*

*Contributed by Jennifer Robin.

OBJECTIVES

After reading this chapter, you should be able to

1. Explain the concept of organizational justice and how it relates to all aspects of relationship building with employees.

2. Understand how actions taken at organizational entry help to build the employment relationship.

3. Know the major laws and legal doctrines governing the employment relationship.

4. Show familiarity with the complexities of employee handbooks, some current issues, and ways to avoid lawsuits.

5. Understand policies and procedures associated with discipline and grievances.

6. Explain the various ways that an employee can exit an organization and the measures organizations can take to make this parting of ways a more positive experience for all involved.

OVERVIEW

An employee handbook was presented to an employee after he had been working at an organization for several months. From the employee's perspective, two sections of the handbook implied an employment contract. The first section outlined the job security of individuals in the industry, although it made no mention of job security within this particular organization. The second section was the organization's disciplinary policy, which outlined specific circumstances and behaviors that were subject to discipline, up to and including termination. Upon his termination, the employee sued the organization, claiming that these two sections of the handbook constituted an **implicit contract.** The employee won the suit on the basis of the disciplinary policy published in the employee handbook. Because he was terminated for an act that was not explicitly outlined in the disciplinary policy, the court ruled that the employer violated an implicit contract. The court ruled that employee handbooks represent choices for the organization to implement contracts or modify existing contracts with every employee.[1]

*Contributed by Jennifer Robin.

This case relates to several issues relevant to the subject of this chapter, an organization's attempts to create and manage its relationships with employees. The situation described above illustrates an instance of the internal and external forces by which an employment relationship is formed, namely, organizational policies and procedures on the one hand and employment law on the other. Specifically, this case illustrates the challenges associated with organizational entry and exit—the beginnings and endings of an employment relationship. We touched on various aspects of the employment relationship in Chapter 3 when the major employment laws were described, in Chapter 5 when we discussed recruitment, in Chapter 6 on selection processes, in Chapter 7 on performance management, and even in Chapter 10 on compensation theory and practice. Chapter 12 provides a more complete description of the elements of the employment relationship that affect specific HR activities.

You may recall the discussion of SAS, the highly successful North Carolina computer software company. SAS has never had a losing year and has never laid off a single employee. SAS founder Jim Goodnight puts it simply: "If employees are happy, they make the customers happy. If they make the customers happy, they make me happy." SAS has a voluntary turnover rate that is substantially below their competitors (3 percent per year versus 20 percent for the industry). Jeff Chambers, Director of HR, estimates that SAS saves between $60 and $70 million annually because of this 17 percent advantage.

Numerous studies now document that there is a reliable causal relationship between employee attitudes in the form of their commitment to the organization, their satisfaction with the job, their perceived engagement with and trust in the firm, and their perceptions of fairness and justice at work and vital customer outcomes such as satisfaction and repeat business translating into better financial performance. One study showed that positive

Employee relations as a competitive advantage

employee relations served as an "intangible and enduring asset and . . . a source of sustained competitive advantage at the firm level."[2] Another study found that "employee satisfaction and engagement are related to meaningful business outcomes." Of course, good employee attitudes evolve from good personnel policy. One excellent study found that the level of employees' satisfaction regarding working conditions, the recognition and encouragement they receive for their good work, the opportunities provided to help them perform well, and the commitment to product or service quality all contributed to the business units' "bottom line." Business units with more progressive HR policies had higher monthly revenue.[3]

Thus, concern for perceptions of organizational justice or measuring job satisfaction should be of interest even to the "hard liners" focused on the bottom line. Having engaged, committed, and satisfied employees can certainly help you get there. The HR policies described on the pages to follow can facilitate more positive employee attitudes.

INTRODUCTION

HR professionals are managers by virtue of their directing many critical projects and ongoing efforts in organizations. Perhaps the most important thing an HR professional helps to "manage" is the relationship the organization has with each employee. While many of the elements of this relationship are established through policies, procedures, and processes common to every employee, contingencies also must be established to accommodate each unique relationship an individual develops.

This chapter discusses the actions organizations take to establish and maintain positive associations with their employees, starting with the mechanisms associated with organizational entry, then the ways of maintaining an ongoing relationship, and, lastly, how to effectively accomplish organizational exit. Each of these establishes expectations and responsibilities for the employee's performance while making the employee aware of his or her rights as a member of the organization. The fundamental basis for this exchange of rights and responsibilities is **"organizational justice."**

Organizational Justice

Justice, or fairness, is thought to exist when people receive those things they believe they deserve based upon their contributions. While there are obvious moral imperatives to treat employees in a fair and just manner, there are more instrumental reasons as well. Research has shown that perceptions of justice impact organizational outcomes such as productivity, absences and turnover, accident rates and health costs, and theft from the organization.[4] It is clear that fairness and justice should be the bedrock of any relationship an organization establishes with an employee.

That being said, it is important to recognize that justice is a *perception* on the part of an individual. No matter how much time and effort practitioners and leaders in organizations spend in an attempt to create perceptions of justice, these perceptions are ultimately impossible to manipulate fully. In other words, one will likely never create a situation in which everyone enjoys the satisfaction of perceived justice. Illustrative of this is a study in which individuals were asked how a lump sum of money should be distributed within the organization. The lowest level of employees believed the money should be divided *equally* among all employees, while managers thought this money should be divided *based upon departmental inputs*.[5] This study shows that differences in justice perceptions exist between distinct employee groups such as managers and employees; imagine the differences in perceptions of justice that undoubtedly exist among all individual employees! There are four types of organizational justice that affect the employment relationship and predict a number of important work outcomes, including performance and turnover.

Distributive justice

Distributive justice requires equity in the allocation of rewards or penalties given by the organization. In other words, a relationship that is "distributively just" is one in which the ratio of inputs to outcomes for one individual is equitable to that of another. Typically we hear of distributive justice with regard to pay, which is one obvious component of the organization–employee relationship. But distributive justice pertains to other policies as well. For instance, employees in organizations are often awarded varying amounts of paid vacation. An employee with only two weeks of paid vacation may resent his or her colleague's receipt of three weeks of paid vacation, particularly when both employees work equally hard. Because the perceived ratio of inputs to outcomes is not equal (in this case, the inputs are equal while the outcomes are not), perceptions of distributive *injustice* result for this individual.

Procedural justice

Although distributive justice is an important concept, procedural justice is even more basic to the establishment of relationships with employees. **Procedural justice** results from a perception of fair rules, laws, or policies that allocate valued rewards and punishments. This type of justice refers to the underlying manner in which policy was established and its fair execution. To continue with our example, the number of paid vacation days may be awarded to each employee on the basis of his or her tenure. Perhaps three weeks' paid vacation is awarded to an employee for 15 years of continuous service, while those with 5 to 10 years of service receive two weeks of paid leave. If an employee felt deserving of three weeks' paid leave after only 5 years of service, he or she would perceive procedural *and* distributive injustice. In other words, this individual is dissatisfied with the way in which his or her number of vacation days is calculated as well as with the ultimate number of vacation days received.

Conversely, the individual may be unhappy that he or she receives only two weeks' vacation but still respects and understands the organization's policy. He or she may be unhappy with the *amount* of paid leave received (i.e., distributive injustice) but feels as though the amount of paid leave was arrived at by an appropriate procedure (i.e., procedural justice). In this situation, the individual still may have overall feelings of fairness. Said another way, "perceived procedural fairness may help mitigate the effects of perceived unjust outcomes."[6] Given this, one can see why procedural justice is crucial to the efficient operation of the organization. Some suggest that an employee's repeated interpretation of policies and procedures as fair builds trust in the organization, which subsequently allows more leeway in terms of employee reactions to its more negative distributive decisions (e.g., low pay increases).[7] There is strong evidence that procedural and distributive justice are related. Employees will react more favorably to negative outcomes if they perceive the procedures to be fair.

Interpersonal and informational justice

The other two types of organizational justice are interpersonal and informational justice. **Interpersonal justice** is associated with the treatment an employee receives from a supervisor or manager as decisions are being made, and **informational justice** is the

**Figure 12-1
Some Examples of
Questionnaire Items
Measuring Justice
Dimensions**

Distributive justice—regarding the results of work:
1. Did the result reflect the effort you put into the work?
2. Is the outcome appropriate for the work you did?
3. Is the outcome justified given your performance level?

Procedural justice—regarding those procedures used to obtain an outcome or result:
1. Did you get an opportunity to express your opinions during the procedures?
2. Were the procedures free of bias?
3. Were the procedures applied consistently?
4. Were the procedures based on accurate information?

Interpersonal justice—regarding the authority figure who enacted the procedure. Were you . . .
1. Treated in a polite manner?
2. Treated with respect?
3. Treated with dignity?

Informational justice—regarding the authority figure who enacted the procedure. Has your supervisor/manager . . .
1. Been candid in communications with you?
2. Explained the procedure thoroughly?
3. Provided details of the procedure in a timely manner?

adequacy of the explanations that were provided by supervisors or managers. Research on these two additional factors underlying perceptions of justice has shown that all four justice factors contribute to the prediction of many important criteria, including performance evaluations, employee rule compliance, organizational commitment, and helping others, or organizational citizenship behavior. Figure 12-1 presents some examples of questionnaire items that have been used in research relating the four justice dimensions to important organizational outcomes.

Perceived justice is related to performance measures

Research shows that perceived fair treatment has significant effects not only on worker attitudes (e.g., job satisfaction and commitment to the organization), but on specific individual behaviors, including absenteeism and citizenship behavior. In addition, research has demonstrated associations between perceived justice and individual work performance. One study in the hotel industry illustrated the strengths of these relationships. The authors concluded that the "results of this study show that fair policies and treatment of employees in organizations may increase an organization's capability to address the needs of its customer base. Fair treatment of employees appears to translate into both employee retention and enhanced customer service, as employees are more committed to the organization and its goals, and both employee retention and customer service satisfaction affect profitability. Interventions aimed at the fairness climate thus seem likely to improve organizational performance. Research supports a trickle-down model of organizational justice in which employee perceptions of fairness are related to their organizational commitment, which influences customer reactions to employees."[8]

Ethics Programs

An interesting twist on the notion of justice and fairness is formalized ethics programs. As a complement to an employer's specific attempts to be fair, formalized **ethics programs** are designed primarily to ensure honest, fair, and responsible actions *on the part of employees*. Ethical thinking programs usually emphasize four elements:

1. Respect the customs/rituals of others.

2. Think of yourself and the organization as a part of the larger society.

3. Try to evaluate a situation objectively and evaluate the anticipated and unintended consequences of each possible action.

4. Consider the welfare of others as much as is feasible.

Why ethics programs? you may ask. While organizational policy or legal obligation binds employees to specific behavior in most instances, these programs attempt to ensure that employees will *always* act in a manner that is ethical and fair to the organization. Accordingly, benefits of formalized ethics programs are reduced employee misconduct and added protection against lawsuits brought against the organization. Relevant to the latter benefit, the Federal Sentencing Guidelines of 1991 include steeper consequences for federal criminal misconduct if an organization does not have formalized ethics programs in place.[9]

Some elements of ethics programs appear to be working overall. In a 2003 National Business Ethics Survey, the Ethics Resource Center notes that employees are reporting violations more than ever. In 1994, 48 percent of employees responded that they reported violations; in 2003, that percentage rose to 65 percent. The likelihood of reporting is directly related to the nature of the program. Programs with the highest likelihood of reporting were those that included a written statement, training, advice lines, and reporting systems.[10]

Most important component is managerial support

The most important component of the ethics program may be managerial support and role modeling. It seems that a formalized ethics program in and of itself is not enough to ensure that employees behave in an ethical manner. At any rate, the trend shows that organizations are feeling at liberty to demand fair and ethical employee behavior, just as the organization attempts to provide the same through its policies, procedures, and practices.

Some ethics programs are innovative in communicating expectations about employee relationships. Lockheed Martin uses an ethics game in which employees test their ethics knowledge and problem-solving skills through 34 scenarios. Dilbert™ and Dogbert™, popular characters created by Scott Adams, serve as the subjects in the scenarios, creating a sense of play that is hard to replicate in instructor-led presentations of ethics information. Lockheed Martin distributes a self-paced, interactive CD recapitulating the ethics information, as well as a calendar and a computer screensaver outlining the company's "twelve building blocks of trust." As another example, Texas Instruments uses formal training and a 14-page booklet to communicate its expectations for ethical behavior. At the back of the booklet is a tear-out, wallet-sized card that includes tips for diagnosing the ethical implications of situations. The card contains the following:

- Is the action legal?
- Does it comply with our values?
- If you do it, will you feel bad?
- How will it look in the newspaper?
- If you know it's wrong, don't do it!
- If you're not sure, ask.
- Keep asking until you get an answer.[11]

In sum, justice, fairness, and ethics, on the part of both the organization and the employee, are fundamental to the employment relationship. We now turn to specific organizational actions that help to build and foster this relationship. Those actions that are common at the outset of the relationship, or at the stage known as "organizational entry," are discussed first.

ORGANIZATIONAL ENTRY

The employment relationship likely begins when an individual enters the selection process for a position or contract with an organization. It is here that individuals begin to form expectations as to how they will be treated. The most fundamental questions at this early stage are the individual's employment status and work arrangement.

Employment Status

As discussed in Chapter 5, there is a strong trend in the United States toward the use of contingent workers, including part-time, temporary, contract, and leased workers. The temporary help industry provides in excess of 3 million workers today, a 300 percent

Independent contractors

increase since 1991. But should a temporary worker be considered an employee or an independent contractor? The distinction between these two classifications is not always clear, while the implications may be crucial to the establishment of a healthy employment relationship. Organizations can avoid large tax liabilities by classifying workers as contractors rather than employees, and many costly benefits of employment (e.g., health insurance, retirement plans, stock options) are made available only to employees of the organization. Undoubtedly, it affords clear financial advantage to classify employees as contractors. However, the mere labeling of employees as contractors is not sufficient; several facets of the employment relationship need to be considered in making this distinction.

Right to control

In determining if the worker should be considered an employee or a contractor, a full assessment of the circumstances of the working relationship is needed, although the focus is often on a few key areas. Specifically, it is important to assess the worker's **"right to control."** The right to control is simply the extent of the employer's supervision over the manner and means of doing the work. If the worker has complete control over the manner and means of accomplishing the end result, he or she is likely in a contract relationship. Alternatively, if a supervisor can dictate the means by which the worker accomplishes tasks, the worker should be classified as an employee. The extent to which the worker must follow established HR policies and practices, including disciplinary and grievance programs, is also important. If the worker must strictly adhere to these policies and procedures, the worker is likely to be considered an employee rather than a contractor. Other important issues in determining the fundamental nature of the worker's status include length of employment, tax treatment, method of payment, level of the worker's economic dependency on the employer, whether the employer trains the worker, who controls the work schedule, and whether benefits are paid.

Two cases illustrate the complexity of this seemingly simple question. Microsoft arranged a contract agreement with its computer programmers, as did Time-Warner with its freelance writers. In both cases, the courts ruled that the companies had misclassified the workers as independent contractors, thus precluding the employees from participating in benefits and stock option plans. While the courts concluded that the misclassification was not intentionally illegal, the courts ordered immediate participation of all misclassified workers in these programs. It is clear that misclassification in order to avoid tax liability and paying benefits can result in big penalties, unnecessary legal fees, and time-consuming litigation.

Misclassification can result in big fines

Flexible Work Arrangements

Another crucial question at this early stage is that of the work arrangement. Specifically, will the new employee work a traditional schedule (i.e., eight hours per day, five days per week, 50 weeks per year), or one that is less rigid? One survey of 521 of the nation's largest firms indicated that more than 90 percent offered alternative work schedules ranging from flextime to job sharing to summers off.[12] These programs are designed to help employees balance their work and nonwork lives by allowing workers to adopt more flexible work schedules. Some of the more popular programs include telecommuting, flextime, permanent part-time work, job sharing, and compressed workweeks.

Telecommuting

As discussed in Chapter 5, telecommuting is a work arrangement that has been growing in popularity due to the cost of driving to work and improvements in technology. Telecommuting continues to grow in the American workforce. By 2009, there could be more than 65 million traditional telecommuters who work mostly from home. Through the help of wireless technologies, there may be millions more additional telecommuters such as salespeople who spend most of their time out of the office. **Telecommuting** enables employees to work at home using computers, video displays, and phones to transmit letters and completed work back to the office. At Pacific Bell, 70 percent of the employees working at home reported higher job satisfaction. Research on telecommuting has been very strong. Research indicates worker morale tends to be high, voluntary turnover is low, and performance appears to be unaffected by this very worker-friendly approach to work.[13]

Strong support for telecommuting

Flextime	Nearly 30 percent of U.S. firms now offer some version of flextime. **Flextime** means that the employee can choose his or her work schedule within some limits. Generally, most employees are required to be at work during some "core" period of time, often in the middle of the day. In most instances, the core period is between 10 a.m. and 2 p.m. About 15 percent of employers make 9 a.m. to 3 p.m. their core period, while another 28 percent make 9 a.m. to 4 p.m. their core period.
Effective in relieving work–family conflicts	**Flextime** has been shown to be effective in relieving work–family conflict among private-sector employees.[14] In addition, the federal government's survey of 325,000 employees who participated in a flextime program demonstrated that 90 percent of them believed the program was at least somewhat important for resolving their work–family conflicts.[15] Flextime has been shown to be related to less tardiness, absenteeism, and sick leave taken by employees and to increases in productivity and quality of work.[16]
	One disadvantage associated with flextime is the difficulty in scheduling meetings and trying to locate employees. Also, it may require the use of time clocks, which are often perceived by employees as a managerial control mechanism. Moreover, flextime may not be appropriate for all jobs. Where tasks are highly interdependent, such as on a manufacturing assembly line, it may be more difficult to administer.
	Today, some firms are expanding on the idea behind flextime. For instance, Barrios Technology offers flexible work hours and flexible workplaces (flexplace). Flexplace offers employees the option of working at home or in a satellite office closer to home.
Permanent Part-Time Work	Another relatively recent work arrangement is the use of **permanent part-time work.**[17] While part-time work has always been available on a temporary basis for some jobs, it has only recently been applied on a permanent basis to professional jobs. Among the companies offering permanent part-time work are AT&T, Barrios Technology, IBM, DuPont, UPS, and Herman Miller. While little research is available on the effectiveness of these changes, research in some firms has shown that part-timers were more productive than full-timers and had lower absenteeism.[18] Moreover, a Catalyst study of 2,000 managers (both full-time and part-time) showed that 78 percent of full-time professionals and 98 percent of part-time professionals agreed that offering part-time work encourages employee retention.[19]
Job Sharing	**Job sharing** is when two people divide the responsibilities for a regular, full-time job. For example, one person may work mornings, while the other person works in the evenings. Job sharing provides the organization with more staffing flexibility and enables the firm to attract and keep good employees. In addition, one early study found that each person does closer to 80 percent of the work of a full-time employee, rather than the expected 50 percent.[20] Employees also favor job-sharing programs because it allows them to reduce their work hours while still keeping their professional skills up to date.[21] Check out www. jobsharing.com for an online job sharing service.
Compressed Workweeks	Yet another innovative arrangement allows employees to work fewer days during the week, with longer hours per day worked. For example, employees could work four 10-hour days instead of five 8-hour days. This type of work schedule has been an option for years for some occupations such as firefighters, police officers, nurses, hair stylists, and technicians. Today, it is being used in other occupations and firms, including tellers at Citibank and operators at US Sprint.[22] Using **compressed workweeks** has a number of benefits for both employees and employers. This arrangement, like other flexible arrangements, allows employees to better accommodate their other life demands so they are not forced to leave the firm. Employee morale and productivity are higher, and tardiness and absenteeism are lower.[23] In addition, the organization can make better use of its equipment and resources. There are some drawbacks, though. Understaffing, scheduling meetings, and coordinating team projects are three common problems. One of the most serious concerns is the increased employee fatigue brought on by working longer hours in one given day.
	Once a worker's employment status and work arrangement are clear, the organizational entry time period is crucial for companies to establish the underpinnings of a positive and productive relationship. Next, we discuss two ways in which organizations do this: realistic job previews and socialization/orientation programs.

Realistic Job Previews

Establishing a relationship with employees may begin before the individual is actually hired by the organization. As discussed in Chapter 5, an organization may choose to provide **realistic job previews** (RJPs), which are presentations of relevant, balanced, and unbiased information about the organization, the job, and the conditions under which the job candidate will work.[24] More traditional recruitment would focus solely on the positive aspects of the job, often overoptimistically describing the conditions of employment. This has been called the "flypaper approach" because its goal is to attract as many candidates as possible. The flypaper approach is less desirable because, while some candidates ultimately will enjoy and accept the working conditions, others will not and will most probably leave the organization.[25]

Can reduce turnover 5–10 percent

Early employee turnover is often the result of misinformation about the job's requirements; thus, informing applicants of the realities of the job is necessary. Research has shown that RJPs can reduce the voluntary turnover in an organization 5 to 10 percent.[26] Four mechanisms are hypothesized to be at work here.[27] First, RJPs lower expectations to appropriate levels. It is commonly known that high expectations are often met with disappointment and dissatisfaction. By lowering expectations, RJPs guard against this disillusionment on the part of new employees. Second, RJPs can help the employee create coping mechanisms for the stressful aspects of the job. If these stressful conditions are anticipated, it is more likely that they will be adequately handled. Third, RJPs convey honesty on the part of the organization; the candidate with negative as well as positive information is less likely to feel he/she was seduced into a job by way of dishonesty on the part of organizational agents. Finally, RJPs allow for candidates to withdraw from the process voluntarily if the job doesn't meet their standards or fulfill their specific career goals.

30 percent use RJPs

Thirty percent of organizations surveyed by SHRM reported using RJPs as a selection technique for nonmanagerial jobs.[28] There are several ways to conduct realistic job previews. Information provided by recruiters and interviewers, videotapes, job samples, and candid conversations with job incumbents are some of the methods used. By conducting RJPs, the organization takes advantage of an opportunity to communicate the relevant employee rights and responsibilities before the candidate is actually hired. Although more specific information and detailed instructions will surface over the course of the candidate's actual employment with the organization, RJPs afford the candidate a first insight into relevant organizational policies and procedures.

Of course, the downside of RJPs is that the organization may have to recruit a larger number of job candidates. The process of self-selection facilitated by RJPs usually eliminates some highly qualified candidates who ultimately may have thrived in the position. Indeed, the most qualified candidates are probably the ones with the most job opportunities as well. By virtue of the negative aspects of the job presented in the RJP, these high-potential applicants may narrow the number of employment options they have. Also, including the negative aspects of a job in an RJP does not give the organization license to ignore these aspects. If there are stressful or otherwise unpleasant elements of a job, the organization should endeavor to reduce these such that the RJP can be more positive and thus attract more candidates to stay in the applicant pool.

Socialization and Orientation

Socialization is the process by which an individual comes to appreciate the values, abilities, expected behaviors, and social knowledge essential for assuming an organizational role and for participating as an organization member. Accordingly, socialization is commonly thought of as a learning process. Individuals learn how to operate within the explicitly (i.e., policies and procedures) and implicitly (i.e., cultural) expressed environments. Moreover, socialization takes place over time; it is not a discrete event. It may take months, even years, for employees to become fully adjusted to the organization's working environment.

Orientation is a term used for the organizationally sponsored, formalized activities associated with an employee's socialization into the organization. While realistic job previews may be employed primarily to reduce involuntary turnover and only indirectly inform employees of their rights and responsibilities, orientation activities have the specific purpose of doing so. Orientation programs often include informational training sessions on topics relevant to the newcomer (e.g., key policies and procedures, corporate vision and mission, and compensation and benefits), site tours, and interactions with various organizational members. Orientation programs also may include the assignment of the individual to a mentor, a practice that has been shown to provide the most access to organizational (i.e., systemwide) information, more than that provided by co-workers, supervisors, and objective referents such as policy manuals.[29] Sears Roebuck and Company recently reduced their turnover rate by more than half, from approximately 17.5 percent to 7.5 percent. Mentoring was cited as a chief reason for that decline.[30]

Institutionalized socialization

Individualized socialization

Organizationally sponsored orientation programs are part of what is called **institutionalized socialization.** This type of socialization is formal; that is, each member of the organization receives the same, sequential, fixed information upon organizational entry. On the other hand, **individualized socialization** is tailored to each individual employee; one employee's induction into his or her organizational role may be very different from that of his or her peers if organizationally sponsored programs are not provided. Most often, an employee is socialized with some of both tactics. The degree to which the organization uses either institutionalized or individualized tactics depends upon many factors. For instance, the number of employees hired is likely to affect the time and effort placed upon an institutionalized program. If the organization is very small, it may be more efficient to rely primarily upon individualized socialization.

More formalized programs more successful

Use formal and informal socialization

Research has shown that the more formalized the program, the more success in reducing role ambiguity, role conflict, and intentions to quit.[31] Corning Glass Works found that new hires were 69 percent more likely to be with the company after three years when they completed a formalized orientation program rather than being left on their own to sort out the job.[32] It seems that these types of orientation programs most successfully communicate knowledge about the organization and the individual's role within the larger system. Individualized tactics, however, have been shown to be related to innovation and would obviously provide more immediately relevant (i.e., just-in-time) information.[33] Moreover, this informal socialization may be used to complement and solidify what is learned in formal training.[34] Ultimately, it is best to rely upon both types of socialization tactics, using orientation programs and other formalized actions to assure that individuals have requisite general knowledge, while using more individualized tactics to communicate details and encourage creativity and process improvement on the job. Renaissance Worldwide, a Massachusetts-based consulting firm, does just this. New hires spend time in a corporate orientation program sponsored by the Human Resources department. Here, general information on such things as benefits and paid leave are provided. Then, the new hire spends time with his or her manager, learning group strategies and goals, the relationships among all group members, and other job-specific information.[35]

As with RJPs, some unique employee orientation techniques have been utilized by organizations. Southwest Airlines uses some of its employee orientation time to complete necessary paperwork, but Southwest also asks employees to complete a form listing their hobbies and clothing sizes. This information is then used to celebrate employees' birthdays and anniversaries with tailor-made presents.[36] At the end of their orientation program, Ernst & Young employees receive a customized employee handbook, likened to the "triptik" provided by some travel organizations. This customized guidebook tells employees what they're responsible for learning and where they're responsible for learning it over the subsequent six to nine months.[37] Finally, one software company takes action to begin socializing employees before they arrive for their first day. Specifically, a four-step program is used by this company and recommended to others in order to make new employees feel at home:

1. Mail a personal note of welcome to new employees.

2. Send employee handbooks, information on benefits, maps, and other information on the area, company programs, and a résumé of work projects being accomplished by department personnel.

3. Personally call the new employee to answer any questions he or she may have regarding the materials already sent.

4. Call the new employee the night before the first workday.[38]

As with any HR intervention, care must be taken to design a program that reaps the benefits described above without causing further confusion, helplessness, or information overload, which may inadvertently create disenchantment with the organization. One expert cautions against the following:

- Using too much valuable orientation time to complete paperwork.
- Giving too much information too quickly.
- Giving information that is irrelevant to adjusting to the position and the organization.
- Scaring the employee by spending an inordinate amount of time discussing the negative aspects of the job.
- Using lectures and videos rather than methods that allow for two-way communication.
- Limiting orientation to the first day at work.
- Selling the organization.[39]

Promissory estoppel

The last point, selling the organization, can be a serious problem if the sales pitch includes false or misleading information. One New York lawyer won a lawsuit against her former law firm after they laid her off less than three months after recruiting her with a plethora of inflated financial information about the firm (this is known as **promissory estoppel**).

Once an employee has completed the initial stages of socialization, he or she begins to perform the roles associated with the position he or she fills in the organizational structure. The next section discusses the tactics organizations can use to form an ongoing, productive, and positive relationship with each of its employees.

THE ONGOING RELATIONSHIP

Consider for a moment all of the personal relationships you maintain. To some people, you are a family member—child, parent, grandchild, grandparent, and so on. To others, you are a friend, confidant, tennis partner, neighbor, or acquaintance. Perhaps you are also a significant other, a spouse, or a life partner. Consider now all of the ways in which you sustain these relationships. You may have some general rules when it comes to the important people in your life; you may always send cards for birthdays, for instance. But you also must be prepared to relate differently to others depending upon the role you fill in their lives and changes that occur over time.

Now consider the employment relationship. The employee is related to an *entity,* not a person, which presents some obvious differences. However, we are still calling this association a *relationship*. As with your personal relationships, the organization must have mechanisms in place to handle both the portions of the relationship that are common to all employees (e.g., most policies and procedures) and those that deal with each employee's unique situation. As you can imagine, such things as an employee's tenure, health, and violation of rules and regulations may require an organization to alter the relationship. For instance, an employee with five years' tenure may receive two weeks' paid vacation, while the employee receives three weeks of paid leave when he or she reaches 15 years of tenure. Each organization will establish its own policies, procedures, and contingencies. We provide a brief overview of the ways in which the ongoing employment relationship can be managed.

Internal forces influencing the working relationship are the employees themselves (through participation programs) and organizationally established policy and procedure. Also in this section, employee discipline and grievance procedures are discussed. First, though, one of the most important influences upon the ongoing relationship is not determined by the organization at all: the external legal environment.

External Forces: Law

The external forces governing the employment relationship are employment laws. Not only is it a good business practice to ensure fair dealing with employees, but organizations are legally bound to do so in some cases. Labor and equal employment laws are discussed in

Chapters 3 and 13, but four types of legal doctrine and legislation are particularly relevant to the established employment relationship.

Employment-at-Will

The **employment-at-will** doctrine is a common-law standard that states that a *private* institution has the right to terminate its employees, with or without just cause, in the absence of a written contract. Proponents of the employment-at-will doctrine argue that individuals often exercise this right; they may resign from the organization at any time without providing reasons or a rationale for doing so. An organization having the ability to terminate employees at will simply introduces mutuality into this facet of the relationship. It is important to note that employment-at-will does not exist when there is either a contract (implied or explicit) or a collective bargaining agreement or the employee works for a public agency. The major exceptions to the "at-will" employment doctrine are found in labor and antidiscrimination statutes enacted by federal and state legislatures. Employment-at-will could not be invoked when the true underlying reason for the employment action was discriminatory. For instance, as we learned in Chapter 3, an organization may not terminate an employee because of race, sex, disability, age, pregnancy, or religion. Employees are also protected from retaliation related to EEO laws as well. In addition, as discussed in the next chapter, employees have strong protection for union activity, mainly through the National Labor Relations Act.

EEO and labor are exceptions

There are three additional major exceptions to the employment-at-will doctrine that are recognized by states. However, it should be recognized that the adoption of these exceptions, and indeed the strength of adoption of the doctrine itself, differs from state to state. For instance, one study concluded that six states have adopted all three of the exceptions discussed below, while four states have not adopted any.[40] Although not a universal statute, the "at-will" doctrine and the exceptions listed below provide legal guidance for much of the relationship between employers and employees, as is noted below and throughout this chapter. The three common exceptions to employment-at-will are

Public policy exception

1. *Public policy:* An employer cannot terminate an employee for engaging in activities that are deemed to be beneficial to the public welfare, for example, opposing an employer's illegal activities. In general, the courts have encouraged employees to oppose an employer's potential unlawful conduct. As to whether public policy overrides the "at-will" doctrine, the focus is on the degree of an employer's interference with the public welfare. The "public policy" must be defined by a statute, a regulation, a constitutional provision, a "professional code of ethics," or some other "tangible foundation" rather than on an individual employee's sensibilities. The public policy exception covers four categories:

- Refusing to commit illegal or unethical acts.
- Performing a legal duty (military service or jury duty).
- Exercising legal rights (filing for workers' compensation).
- Whistleblowing (reporting employers for safety, health, or statutory violations).

Implied contracts exception

2. *Implied contracts:* A minority of state courts recognize "implied-in-fact" contracts and infer a contractual obligation prohibiting employers from firing at-will employees. Implied contracts could be (1) an employer's written discharge procedure or promise of termination only for "just cause" contained in a company document; (2) contracts created by the employer's oral representations of job security; (3) a covenant of "good faith and fair dealing" that a minority of state courts read into employment agreements prohibiting employers from terminating their employees in bad faith or with malice; and (4) known as "promissory estoppel," a promise of employment or continued employment in unambiguous terms where the employer can expect and foresee the employee's reliance on the promise, an employee relies on the promise, and the employee has relied on the promise to his injury. There are many examples where an individual quits one job and, after relying on the offer of new or continued employment, is never given the opportunity to start work or is discharged shortly after beginning work. This could constitute promissory estoppel. One study concluded that courts in 34 states have

Oral statements can create an enforceable contract

held that an employer's oral statements can create an enforceable contract for employment. Thus, a hiring official's statement to a prospective employee that employment will continue as long as the employee's performance is adequate or satisfactory or as long as the employee does the job has been held to create a contract.[41]

Tort theories

3. *Tort theories:* The weakest of the exceptions includes the intentional infliction of emotional distress and defamation. The tort of intentional infliction of emotional distress compensates individuals who are victims of conduct deemed by society as extreme and outrageous. The employee must assert that the employer harassed him or her or acted in some other extraordinary or outrageous manner, causing the employee emotional distress. The **defamation** exception stipulates that an employer cannot publish an untrue statement about an employee to a third party. Here, the employer might have to prove that the statement is either true or protected by an "absolute or qualified privilege."

Wrongful termination

Because **"wrongful termination"** suits are quite common, HR professionals should be aware of the common law governing employment in their state. Further, to avoid such wrongful termination lawsuits, organizations should take steps to ensure that terminations are substantiated by documentation and that they follow a standard procedure. Moreover, some suggest that organizations should actually take responsibility for educating employees as to the meaning of employment-at-will. When surveyed on this issue, a full 83 percent of respondents thought that a satisfactory employee could not lawfully be fired in order for the organization to replace her with someone at a lower wage.[42] Of course, abiding by employment-at-will principles, this practice is probably acceptable. It seems that most employees have little understanding of their employment rights provided under law. As discussed later in the chapter, most experts recommend that at the very least, employee handbooks include a clear stipulation that the employer is an "employment-at-will" organization.

Whistleblowing

One practice protected by various federal, state, and local laws is **whistleblowing,** or reporting misconduct to persons who have the power to take action.[43] By definition, whistleblowing can be internal (e.g., to the supervisor or HR department) or external (e.g., to the media, legislators, or professional organizations) reporting of wrongdoing. However, those cases that represent "whistleblowing" to most people are those in which the whistleblower reports information externally. "Whistleblower" statutes and the courts protect whistleblowers from retaliation for informing authorities about the practices of the employer. Whistleblower laws have been enacted and applied to encourage employees to come forward with such information while protecting them from employer reprisals.

One famous recent example is that of Dr. Jeffrey Wigand, former vice president for research and development for the tobacco company Brown and Williamson (B&W), who discovered that a flavoring used in B&W tobacco was a serious carcinogen. After reporting this discovery to the president of the firm, Dr. Wigand was fired. Dr. Wigand then spoke to investigators at the Food and Drug Administration, testified in several state lawsuits against the tobacco industry, and was interviewed for the CBS program *60 Minutes*. The whistleblowing incident was dramatized in the 1999 movie *The Insider* starring Russell Crowe as Dr. Wigand. Dr. Wigand claimed he experienced retaliation in several forms: He was fired, physically threatened, and received negative publicity after his public reports.[44] While most instances of whistleblowing are not this extreme, it is important to recognize the legal obligations of organizations when faced with reports of internal wrongdoing.

Unfortunately, those legal obligations are complex and vary from state to state. Employees are not uniformly protected against retaliation from whistleblowing; however, many constitutional, federal, and state laws can protect employees based upon the nature of their actions. The First (i.e., Freedom of Speech) and Fourteenth (i.e., Due Process) Amendments prohibit government officials from retaliating, as do federal laws such as the Clean Air Act, the Occupational Safety and Health Act (OSHA), the Civil Service Reform Act, and the False Claims Act. Moreover, 44 states have a clear "public policy" exception to

42 states have whistleblowing protection for public employees

their employment-at-will doctrine, 42 states have specific whistleblowing protection for public employees, and 19 states have whistleblowing protection for private employees.[45] At any rate, organizations should be aware of the specific laws protecting their employees, and they should take measures to promote internal reporting. These measures help the organization to avoid costly litigation and public relations problems. Anonymous reporting policies and established lines of communication for reports of misconduct may encourage employees to report misconduct internally so that it can be handled internally.

It is important to realize that certain employee obligations may restrict divulging information which is in no way whistleblowing and thus not protected as such. For instance, employees have a duty to protect confidential information. This is called a **covenant of**

Covenant of nondisclosure

nondisclosure, and the formal policy regarding such conduct often appears in the employee handbook. In 2005, the Supreme Court of Missouri held that "an employee and a new employer may be liable for damages to a former employer if the employee engages in direct competition while still employed." Nondisclosure agreements protect trade secrets and other information privileged by the organization.

Organizations also can mandate a certain degree of employee loyalty through **noncom-**

Noncompete agreements

pete agreements. These agreements are contractual arrangements with employees that restrict their acceptance of employment with an industry competitor upon voluntarily leaving the current organization. Courts are not always receptive to these agreements, and most states have statutes that govern their enforceability. In general, these statutes ask whether there is a legitimate business interest in the enforcement of the noncompete agreement and whether the agreement is not excessive in terms of the restrictions on the employee, the time limit of the agreement, and its geographic scope.[46] For example, the New Hampshire Supreme Court recently deemed too broad to be enforced provisions in employment contracts that for three years after the end of their employment employees could not solicit business from any company that had ever been a customer of the employer. While there is a trend toward more restrictive contracts, such covenants are not favored and are more carefully scrutinized in the courts when a person's abilities to earn a living and better himself or herself appear to be restricted.

Privacy

There has been a great deal of legal activity related to privacy since 2002. Before this date, the federal Privacy Act of 1974 established protection against the use of employment records for purposes other than business functioning. Applying only to federal organizations, this statute allows employees to review, amend, and bring civil suit for misuse of their employment records. Many states have similar laws for private-sector employees, covering both personnel files and any information about an employee's medical condition. It is important to recognize, though, that the enforcement and stringency of privacy law varies from jurisdiction to jurisdiction. However, records such as performance appraisals, disciplinary actions, and formal complaints are typically deemed confidential in the courts. In many states, an employer may be liable for invasion of privacy if the employer publicly discloses a private fact that is objectionable to a reasonable person and is not a legitimate public concern. Some states (e.g., New York, California) have clear restrictions on the business use of information concerning off-duty conduct such as political or union activities, including revealing these activities to prospective employers. The Electronic Privacy Information Center at www.epic.org provides a summary of privacy laws for each state.

In the case of medical information, HR departments may have a surprising amount of documentation. For instance, records may include results from physicals, **Family and Medical Leave Act** information, documentation of accommodations required under the **Americans with Disabilities Act,** information related to genetic testing (protected under the 2008 **Genetic Information Nondiscrimination Act** or GINA), and records from Employee

HIPAA

Assistance Programs. The **Health Insurance Portability and Accountability Act** (HIPAA) of 2005 is the most complex of the legal restrictions on use of employee medical information. Employer-sponsored group health plans, not the employer, are covered by these rules. The health plan must limit access to employees' protected health information (PHI) and ensure it is not used in employment-related decisions. Because of the highly sensitive nature of the information, it is recommended that medical records be kept separate from the personnel files and that access to their contents be highly restricted.[47]

Particularly relevant to the issue of privacy is the use of HR information systems (HRIS). While computerized storage of data aids the HR professional, it also allows for easy access to sensitive information by unwanted individuals. Moreover, information in HRIS is often keyed from written documents, making the databases susceptible to errors. It is recommended that organizations enact procedures to periodically confirm the accuracy of information. Moreover, organizations should remind employees to update key information in order to capture relevant information changes such as marriage or an increase or decrease in the number of dependents reported. Likewise, supervisors should be reminded to update records with disciplinary actions, complaints, and terminations.[48] Finally, anyone with access to sensitive information, be it in a file or an HRIS, should be warned that the information is confidential and that breach of the confidentiality is a serious offense that may result in termination.[49]

PATRIOT Act

Records that may be relevant to terrorism investigations are the exception to this rule. The Providing Appropriate Tools Required to Intercept and Obstruct Terrorism (PATRIOT) Act allows government officials access to business records and transactions. In some cases, officials are allowed to conduct surveillance in the workplace. While the constitutionality of this law is still being tested in the courts, it appears that organizations are now to be held simultaneously responsible for balancing employee privacy concerns and governmental requests for information.

It is obvious that employers are now faced with a serious predicament. Aside from the legal obligation to do so, organizations should be concerned for the basic respect of an employee's privacy by limiting the amount of information gathered to that which is needed to carry out the business function. However, this respect for privacy must now be balanced with a desire (and obligation) to cooperate with the government in its antiterrorism efforts. Antiterrorism efforts aside, methods by which information is gathered, stored, utilized, and distributed should be considerate of employee privacy.

A controversial issue is the extent to which employers should monitor their employees and their equipment for the unauthorized use of computers and the Internet. Employers try to strike a balance of respecting their employees' privacy while maintaining their security and protecting the organization's culpability from unauthorized (and perhaps) illegal use of technology Shanti Atkins of Employment Law Learning Technology describes the dilemma this way: "Corporations are really in a bind. They can be sued for violating an employee's privacy by exercising too much control over electronic communication or Internet use, but also for not exercising enough control and allowing workers to be subjected to harassment." No policy clearly makes the employer liable for the inappropriate use of company e-mail and other systems (e.g., text-based sexual harassment). Michael Overly, author of *E-Policy: How to Develop Computer, E-Policy and Internet Guidelines to Protect Your Company and Its Assets*, concludes that the courts have said that if a company has a written policy notifying employees of computer and Internet use monitoring, the expectation of employee privacy is removed.

Investigative consumer reports

FCRA

Privacy and the Job Applicant: Employers often request consumer reports or more detailed "investigative consumer reports" (ICRs) from a consumer credit service as a part of the background check. If this is so, employers need to be aware of **The Fair Credit Reporting Act** (FCRA), amended in 2005, a federal law that regulates how such agencies provide information about consumers. Under the FCRA, employers must receive approval from an applicant that any consumer document can be secured and must provide such an approval in writing to the consumer credit agency. If the employer decides to reject the applicant based to some extent on the report, the applicant must be provided a copy of the report before the employer takes any formal action regarding the applicant.

The FCRA may also apply to internal investigations of suspected employee misconduct. Under 2005 amendments, employers do not have to give advance notice of an investigation to employees. However, employers do have to provide a summary of the nature of the information provided that led to any adverse action such as a termination.

Off-duty behavior

Privacy versus Employer Rights: Can an employer impose rules regarding the off-duty behavior of employees? While there are exceptions, the general answer to this question is yes. "If you test positive for tobacco, you can't work here." So says Howard Weyers, CEO of WEYCO, Inc., a Michigan health care company. Mr. Weyers's policy applies to all smoking regardless of when, where, or how often you do it. His rationale is quite simple. He says smokers cost him too much money. According to the Centers for Disease Control, a smoker will cost a company an average of $3,400 in lost productivity and health care cost every year. While 28 states and the District of Columbia have passed laws protecting smokers, in general, Mr. Weyers has the legal right to impose such a rule on his employees. But Lewis Maltby of the National Workrights Institute says the no smoking rule is the "first step on a slippery slope. . . . If you smoke, or you drink, if you eat too much junk food, you're promiscuous. What comes next?"

Military Rights

With the United States involved in protracted wars in Iraq and Afghanistan, more reserve and National Guard units are being called to active duty. Today, nearly half of U.S. military members are reservists. Many reservists may be on active duty for six months or longer and are unsure of their rights concerning their job and benefits.

USERRA

The federal **Uniformed Services Employment and Reemployment Rights Act (USERRA)** establishes the rights of reservists and members of the National Guard to return to work at the end of their service. The **USERRA** applies to all employers regardless of their size and protects those serving in the U.S. reserve forces of the Army, Navy, Marine Corps, Air Force, Coast Guard, Public Health Service Commissioned Corps, and the National Guard. While on active duty, employees must receive all benefits available to other employees on comparable leaves of absence. Employees also may use accrued vacation while on leave but cannot be forced to do so. While the law does not require employers to pay a worker on active duty, many employers pay the difference between a worker's regular salary and his or her military pay.

The **Family and Medical Leave Act** was amended in 2008. Businesses are now required to offer up to 26 weeks of unpaid leave to employees who provide care to wounded U.S. military personnel. Employers also must provide 12 weeks of FMLA leave to immediate family members (spouses, children, or parents) of soldiers, reservists, and members of the National Guard who have a "qualifying exigency." With the continuing demands on the military reserve and National Guard, several states had already passed family military leave acts giving soldiers' family members limited unpaid leave entitlements.

Worker Adjustment and Retraining Notification Act (WARN)

As discussed in Chapter 5, the **Worker Adjustment and Retraining Notification Act (WARN)** requires organizations to give affected employees 60 days' written notice when a plant will close or when mass layoffs are expected. **WARN** covers employers with more than 100 full-time employees, and its compliance is required when there will be an employment loss of six months or more. Go to www.doleta.gov for the details of WARN.

Evidence shows that the overall time frame of notification before plant closings has slightly increased as a result of this law.[50] However, in many individual instances, the WARN Act does not protect workers with a 60-day notice. Particularly in the case of unforeseen circumstances, many cases have been filed in which courts have ruled on the side of employers. For instance, when a General Dynamics contract with the U.S. Navy was suddenly canceled, the courts ruled that the 17-day notice the company provided to its workers was adequate.[51] Similarly, a court ruled that the owners of the Atlantis Casino in New Jersey did not violate the WARN Act when the New Jersey Casino Control Commission unexpectedly ordered the casino's closing.[52] Figure 12-2 presents a legally acceptable notice that complies with WARN.

Internal Forces: Employee Surveys

Beyond the external legal forces that govern the ongoing working relationship to some extent, there are two major internal forces that must be considered. The first of these is the influence of the employees themselves. Particularly in cases where formalized participation and involvement programs exist, the employees may have the power to make suggestions, become involved in management decision making, and provide feedback to the organization and its leaders. Generally, it is believed that involving employees in decision making will result in improved job attitudes and cooperation and reduced turnover, absenteeism, and grievances. In practice, organizations involve their employees in actual

Figure 12-2 **A Legally Acceptable Notice That Complies with WARN**

NOTICE OF LAYOFF TO AFFECTED EMPLOYEES PURSUANT TO THE WORKER ADJUSTMENT AND RETRAINING NOTIFICATION (WARN) ACT

To: ——————————— Name of Employee ——————— Position ————————— Date ——————

As has been previously announced, ABC Company will experience a reduction in its workforce, and a number of employees of ABC Company will experience layoffs, as a result of a significant downturn in business and a resulting corporate-wide reorganization. This notice, which is issued in compliance with the Worker Adjustment and Retraining Notification (WARN) Act, is to inform you that you are likely to be laid off due to the loss of business revenue and related reorganization. The purpose of this notice is to provide you with the answers to some questions that you may have regarding your layoff so that you can prepare to locate other employment. The information provided below represents the best information available to the company at the time this notice was issued.

1. *Is my layoff going to be permanent or can I expect to be recalled to employment at some time in the future?* At this time, you should consider your layoff to be permanent. As part of the corporate reorganization, ABC Company will attempt to continue operation of its manufacturing facilities by obtaining additional contracts or new business. If these efforts are successful, some employees may be maintained or recalled to work. However, because the success of such efforts is entirely unknown at this time, no ABC Company employee who is being laid off should count on being recalled to employment with the Company.

2. *When will the layoffs begin and when am I likely to be laid off?* ABC Company expects layoffs to begin around _____. The layoffs may come in stages, depending upon the need for workers as the joint venture moves towards dissolution. Your employment is likely to end around _____ but your layoff may be sooner or later, again depending upon the business need to maintain workers as the full impact of the business downturn and the resulting corporate reorganization becomes known.

3. *Do I have any right to "bump" other employees from their jobs based on my seniority with the company?* ABC Company does not recognize strict seniority rights, but may take seniority into consideration as a factor in determining which employees to lay off and the timing of each employee's layoff. Seniority also will be considered as a factor in recalling employees, should ABC Company be successful in maintaining operation of the facilities. However, seniority will be just one factor in these decisions, and other factors, such as business necessity, expertise, and past performance, also will be taken into account in making these decisions.

4. *Will the company be providing any severance benefits to employees who are laid off?* The company has established a Reduction in Force Policy and a Severance Pay Plan to provide employees with further information regarding their employee benefits and to assist employees during this difficult time. If you have not received a copy of either the Reduction in Force Policy or the Severance Pay Plan summary plan description, you may obtain copies by contacting _____ at (703) ___-____.

5. *Whom can I contact for further information?* If you have further questions or need additional information, you may contact _____ at (___) ___-____.

---

decision making to varying degrees; many use such tactics as quality circles, autonomous work teams, and high-involvement initiatives to engage employees and include them in decision making. Fundamental to these initiatives, however, is the solicitation of employee feedback. Virtually all organizations gather feedback from their employees, and most often this is accomplished through employee survey systems.

Employee feedback programs

A growing body of research shows that employee feedback programs are effective in increasing an organization's productivity and product and service quality. In the case of the human resource function, organizational productivity and quality are influenced indirectly through the satisfaction and support that the HR programs give to each employee. Feedback provided by employees, then, can help the human resource function evaluate its programs and take corrective action where needed—either through initiating programs to address shortcomings or discontinuing programs that are not well received.

Survey results reveal an organization's strengths and weaknesses and provide a means for comparing results against norms established by data from other organizations as well as against internal norms established in other departments. An example of a typical employee survey and definitions of the factors that are assessed are shown in Figures 12-3 and 12-4.

On-line employee surveys

Go to www.employeesurveys.com for online tailored employee surveys.

In addition to their evaluation purpose, employee surveys also may be used to facilitate planned organization change and team building based on feedback and discussion of the survey data, thus improving the employment relationship over time. Companies often begin the review of survey data by comparing the organization's data against outside or internal norms to establish an initial benchmark. If the same survey is repeated in subsequent years, it becomes especially valuable to compare data in a given year with the data from previous years. Analyzing the trend of data over several years is a particularly powerful tool for understanding what is going on in the organization. Many companies combine attitude surveys with 360-degree appraisals (see Chapter 7) for a more comprehensive perspective.

Many organizations also find it useful to compare the data (and trends) for different units across the organization to pinpoint specific parts of the organization where particular issues or concerns may be arising. This approach facilitates the development of action strategies specific to individual parts of the organization as well as other action strategies relevant for the entire organization. Survey data also promote the early identification of

Figure 12-3   **Example of an Employee Opinion Survey**

HUMAN RESOURCES INDEX

The objective of this survey is to determine how members of this organization feel about the effectiveness with which the organization's human resources are managed. The survey provides you an opportunity to express your opinions in a way that is constructive. Your views will be valuable in assisting the organization to evaluate and improve its performance.

    The survey is to be done anonymously. Please **do not put your name** on the response sheet or identify your responses in any way. Responses can in no way be traced to any individual. The frank and free expression of your own opinions will be most helpful to the organization.

    Listed below are a series of statements. After you have read each statement, please decide the extent to which the statement describes your own situation and your own feelings, using the following scale:

A) almost never

B) not often

C) sometimes (i.e., about half the time)

D) often

E) almost always

Then, using a No. 2 pencil, darken the appropriate box on the response sheet. For example, if you believe that the statement is true "sometimes," darken block C on the answer sheet next to the number corresponding to the indicated statement.

    Questions 65 and 66 should be answered in **pencil** on the back of the **response sheet.**

    When you have completed the survey, please return the response sheet and this survey form in accordance with the directions in the cover letter.

IN THIS ORGANIZATION:

1. There is sufficient communication and sharing of information between groups.
2. The skills and abilities of employees are fully and effectively utilized.
3. Objectives of the total organization and my work unit are valid and challenging.
4. The activities of my job are satisfying and rewarding.
5. I have received the amount and kind of training that I need and desire to do my job well.
6. Leadership in this organization is achieved through ability.
7. Rewards are fairly and equitably distributed.
8. First-level supervision is of a high quality.
9. Management has a high concern for production and effectively communicates this concern.
10. My job provides ample opportunity for a sense of individual responsibility.
11. There is a sense of loyalty and belonging among members of this organization.

- •
- •
- •

63. By and large, most members of this organization are sensitive, perceptive, and helpful to one another.
64. In general, complete and accurate information is available for making organizational decisions.

65. The things I like best about this organization are:_____

66. The things I would most like to change are:_____

Source: Fred E. Schuster, Professor of Management, Florida Atlantic University, Boca Raton, FL 33431. Copyright © 1977. Reprinted with permission.

difficulties and permit timely response before minor concerns become major issues. In this way, feedback from employees changes the ongoing employment relationship. It is hoped that these changes are iterative improvements to the association between the organization and its employees.

    Attitude surveys are used most effectively as part of a comprehensive assessment and intervention strategy. The focus is often on the business unit and the manager or supervisor of the unit. Companies use the same survey questions in order to establish interpretive and predictive data. For example, researchers at the Gallup Organization conducted focus groups across several industries to determine the characteristics of successful employees and managers. They focused on the importance of the managers' influence over the **"engagement level"** of employees and their job satisfaction with their companies. They found that the specific facet of job satisfaction most related to job performance was satisfaction with the supervisor. "Engagement" in the Gallup research refers to a worker's involvement, satisfaction, and enthusiasm for work. Gallup uses a set of 12 key questions and maintains a huge database from hundreds of companies. For example, workers are asked to indicate how satisfied they are with their company in terms of encouraging their development and providing opportunities and the necessary information and equipment to do the job. One excellent study focused on these "engagement" scores and profit data of business units and found a difference of

Engagement and unit profit

Figure 12-4   **Factor Definitions from an Employee Survey**

1. **Reward system** (RWD): compensation, benefits, perquisites, and other (tangible and intangible) rewards.
2. **Communication** (COM): flow of information downward, upward, and across the organization.
3. **Organization effectiveness** (OE): level of confidence in the overall abilities and success of the organization; how well the organization achieves its objectives.
4. **Concern for people** (PLP): the degree to which the organization is perceived as caring for the individuals who work for it.
5. **Organization objectives** (OO): the extent to which individuals perceive the organization to have objectives that they can understand, feel proud of, and identify with.
6. **Cooperation** (COP): the ability of people throughout the organization to work effectively together to achieve shared goals.
7. **Intrinsic satisfaction** (IS): rewards that people receive from the work itself (sense of achievement, pride in a job well done, growth and development, feeling of competence).
8. **Structure** (STC): rules and regulations, operating policies and procedures, management practices and systems, the formal organization structure and reporting relationships.
9. **Relationships** (REL): feelings that people have about others in the organization.
10. **Climate** (CLM): the atmosphere of the organization, the extent to which people see it as a comfortable, supportive, pleasant place to work.
11. **Participation** (PAR): opportunity to contribute one's ideas, to be consulted, to be informed, and to play a part in decision making.
12. **Work group** (WG): feelings about the immediate group of people with whom one works on a daily basis.
13. **Intergroup competence** (ITG): the ability of separate work groups to work smoothly and effectively together to accomplish shared objectives.
14. **First-level supervision** (FLM): confidence that members of the organization have in the competence and integrity of first-line supervisors.
15. **Quality of management** (QM): confidence that members of the organization have in the competence and integrity of middle and higher management.

Source: Fred E. Schuster, Professor of Management, Florida Atlantic University, Boca Raton, FL 33431. Copyright © 1977. Reprinted with permission.

approximately 1 to 4 percentage points in profitability for high engagement units and from $80,000 to $120,000 higher monthly revenue or sales (and for one organization, the difference was more than $300,000). The authors concluded that "employee satisfaction and engagement are related to meaningful business outcomes at a magnitude that is important to many organizations and that these correlations generalize across companies."[53]

Wal-Mart's "Grass Roots" survey

Since 1994, Wal-Mart has surveyed its associates annually as part of the "Grass Roots survey program." Like the Gallup survey, the purpose of the Grass Roots program is to assess employees' perceptions of work-related issues. Results are calculated by store, and the top three concerns are posted at each store. Store managers are expected to meet with their employees to discuss concerns and to develop action plans to address them. Responses are also used to calculate an "**Unresolved People Index**" (which was originally called the Union Potential Index) to identify stores at risk of union organizing activity. Stores scoring high on the index are targeted for intervention by company management with expertise in avoiding union organizing. The stores are then surveyed again subsequently to assess whether there was any improvement after the intervention. The survey process was actually used against Wal-Mart in the recent sex discrimination lawsuit. An expert witness testified that while the survey is "an efficient mechanism for assessing employees' perceptions about barriers to equal opportunity associated with gender . . . [it] has never been used to assess employees' perceptions on issues such as whether they have been treated unfairly due to gender (or race) or the firm's commitment to diversity. Nor have the results of Grass Roots Surveys ever been analyzed by gender or race in order to assess perceived discriminatory barriers."

Internal Forces: Employee Handbooks

An organization's published policies and procedures (i.e., employee handbooks) are the second of the two major internal forces governing the employment relationship. Generally stated, the purpose of policies and procedures is to establish the guidelines by which the organization and the employee contribute to the mutual relationship. Many companies end up in court because of their handbooks. Others survive in court for the same reason.

Thus, the creation and distribution of an employee handbook should not be taken lightly; however, there is often disagreement about what purposes a handbook should serve. Lawyers often will recommend that the handbook be filled with legal disclaimers, many of which can alienate or confuse the employee or candidate. Employee relations specialists may recommend that the handbook include warm and cuddly human relations statements that may end up implying more job security than the employer intended. Neither extreme is desirable, and bad employee handbooks may be worse than no handbook at all. It is important to carefully consider each and every aspect of content in an employee handbook. Go to www.HR-Guide.com for online help on developing employee handbooks.

In their handbook on handbooks, *Inc.* magazine notes that employee handbooks should be used to communicate company policies and procedures, establish the mutual agreements between the employee and the organization while avoiding contractual language, explain the company's philosophy, excite and motivate the employees about their jobs, and convey a broader sense of the company mission and vision.[54] Guidelines for writing a handbook and what to include in it are presented in Figure 12-5. One key guideline regarding

Figure 12-5 **Guidelines for Writing a Handbook**

- Prepare a list of all the policies you think your company needs. Review the list with your management group and with supervisors who will be using these policies.
- Pull out all the policies you now have and review them, bringing them up to date and discarding those that aren't needed.
- When writing policies, be brief and eliminate trite and verbose language. Keep them short and concise.
- Because some courts have ruled that employee handbooks and policy manuals can be considered employment contracts, it is important to insert a clause that states the handbook or manual should not be considered an employment contract and that employment is a strictly "at-will" relationship. You may wish to obtain more specific language from an attorney.
- Keep the language simple. If it is too technical, people won't read it.
- Don't undercut your supervisors' or managers' authority. You are paying them to manage, so give them the opportunity to do so.
- Write policies that are realistic for your size and type of business.
- Avoid redundancy—don't cover the same ground in two policies.
- Be sure your policies conform to local, state, and federal laws.
- Leave the lengthy details of benefit programs to a benefit handbook; don't include them in the policies.
- Be careful not to sound "preachy" by using condescending or patronizing language.
- Do not use sexist language.

WHAT TO INCLUDE IN AN EMPLOYEE HANDBOOK

• Accidents/injuries	• Garnishments	• Rest areas
• Alcohol or drug use	• Grievance procedure/rights	• Right to amend handbook
• At-will statement	• Holidays	• Safety administration
• Benefits	• Jury duty time off	• Safety/OSHA issues
• COBRA issues	• Layoffs	• Separation pay
• Company rules	• Leaves	• Service awards
• Complaint/ADR procedures	• Lockers/personal property	• Sexual harassment/other harassment
• Confidentiality agreement	• Maternity leave of absence	• Smoking
• Dating policy	• Military leave of absence	• Solicitation
• Demotion	• Nepotism policy	• Suggestions
• Disciplinary action and warning notices	• Noncompete agreements	• Support of recreational activities
• Dress codes, protective clothing	• Nondisclosure covenants	• Telephone/cell phone/e-mail/Internet/ intranet use
• Drug testing	• Open door policy	• Temporary employees/status/I-9 forms
• Educational assistance	• Organizational bulletins	• Terminations
• Emergency procedures	• Orientation sessions	• Testing
• Employee assistance	• Overtime	• Time cards
• Employee suggestions	• Ownership of patents, inventions, royalties	• Training programs
• Employer/employee rights	• Pay days	• Transfers
• Employment procedures	• Performance appraisal	• Unemployment compensation
• Equal Employment Opportunity	• Personal leave of absence	• Vacation
• Ethical statements/policy	• Personal time off	• Violence policy
• Exit interviews	• Pre-employment physical exam	• Visitors
• External communication	• Pregnancy	• Voting
• Falsification of records	• Professional memberships	• Warning system
• Flexible time off	• Promotions/job postings	• Whistleblowing policy
• Flextime	• References	• Worker's compensation
• FMLA	• Relocation	• Work week
• Funeral time off		

Source: Adapted and updated from M. F. Cook, "Personnel Policies and Employee Communications: Handling New Issues in Today's Work Environment," *New Directions in Human Resources: A Handbook* (Englewood Cliffs, NJ: Prentice Hall, 1987).

handbooks is that they should be evaluated regularly for possible revision. Most handbooks that have not been revised in the last few years may have failed to address numerous federal, state, and local laws, regulations, and executive orders that may be directly relevant to the employment relationship. Among the more pressing issues that organizations now face in the way of establishing policy are sexual harassment, Internet and computer usage, dispute resolution programs, performance monitoring, trade secrets and noncompete clauses, smoking in the workplace, cell phone policy, personal appearance, nepotism, employee dating, and conflicts of interest. The Web site for the Society of Human Resource Management (shrm.org) provides model policies for most of these issues and several online articles about good and bad employee handbooks.

Many organizations now maintain their handbooks on the company intranet. This affords easy accessibility for all parties and allows for efficient changes and immediate notice of such changes through e-mail. In addition, the contents of employee handbooks often differ depending on the particular classification or status of the worker and the location of the workers. Remember our discussion earlier regarding employment status and work arrangements. Therefore, electronic copies offer a much more efficient means of providing such tailored information.

Handbooks should also reflect the conditions of employment for particular states or countries. Furthermore, it may be necessary to provide a copy of the handbook in languages other than English. Regardless of the format of the handbook (e.g., hard copy, intranet only), there should always be a provision for an acknowledgment of the receipt of the handbook. We will discuss this issue later since it is so important. Two specific policies of importance are those addressing sexual harassment and technology usage.

Sexual Harassment Policies

Like other issues that have been covered in this chapter, addressing sexual and other forms of harassment in the workplace makes both conceptual and legal sense for organizations. Because sexual harassment is one of the most extreme examples of employee disrespect, perceptions of injustice and emotional reactions to harassment undermine work performance and organizational efficiency. As discussed in Chapter 3, the Supreme Court has ruled that formally stated policies could protect organizations from lawsuits even when a supervisor sexually harassed an employee unbeknownst to the organization.[55] In short, one of the first actions an HR professional should take upon entering a new organization is to verify the presence of a sexual harassment policy. If one does not exist, create one! In California, both a policy and mandatory training are the law for all employers. The policy must be published in the handbook.

A sexual harassment policy should demonstrate management's understanding of the issue and express commitment to eliminating it. Likewise, the construction of the policy should encourage employees to come forward with complaints. A good sexual harassment policy should include information on the purpose of the policy, the legal and behavioral definitions of sexual harassment, the importance of the problem, reporting procedures and organizational actions such as investigations and discipline, and names and phone numbers for individuals to report complaints.[56]

Technology Usage Policies

Just as employers regulate such things as usage of the telephone, office supplies and equipment, and other company property, some are finding it increasingly necessary to regulate Internet use and e-mail. A 2008 survey found that 96 percent of organizations had restricted Internet access for employees and 50 percent of companies monitor internet use.[57] As you may expect, concerns of privacy and confidentiality are at issue. It is important that employers ask themselves if a reasonable expectation of privacy exists with the usage of the Internet and e-mail at their workplace. If so, courts may determine that monitoring of e-mail and Internet usage is a violation of privacy.

In general, employers can monitor e-mail and Internet activity when these activities are conducted with the employer's equipment, particularly when a specific policy is in place concerning the proper usage of the technology. Excessive personal use of the Internet and e-mail is obviously counterproductive and may be of particular concern when it infringes upon the organization's morals and values. For example, one recent study found that 20 percent of male U.S. workers access at least one pornographic site per week while at work. Employers are allowed to monitor and stop such behavior.

Employee handbooks should present technology usage policies in such a way that employees are very clear about their rights and responsibilities when creating, accessing, and disseminating information from the work environment.[58] Relatedly, handbooks should include a policy on cell phone use at work, including both personal and company-provided phones. Employers can be judged culpable for the reckless behavior of employees who talk on their cell phones while driving or performing other potentially dangerous tasks. Such culpability can be reduced if an employee handbook clearly prohibits such behavior.

Employee Handbooks as Implied Contracts

One of the most important components of any employee handbook is a statement that makes clear the fact that the contents of the employee handbook should not be construed as evidence of an implicit or explicit employment contract.[59] In the context of an employee handbook, an implicit contract could mean that an employee's failure to engage in specified behaviors under certain circumstances outlined in the discipline and termination policies serves as an unwritten guarantee of job security. Most organizations ask that employees sign a document stating that they have read the policy and procedure handbook and that they accept that its contents are not legally binding. As in the court case mentioned in this chapter's "Overview," employers can be sued for wrongful termination on the basis of the contents of an employee handbook.

In fact, any management employee's verbal comments to employees about the duration of employment also may serve as an implicit contract.[60] For instance, managers should not state that employment will continue as long as the employee abides by the policies and procedures contained in the employee handbook. Courts in about 30 states have adopted the "implied contract" exception to the employment-at-will doctrine. Consequently, courts could very well rule for the employee in any case in which it is determined that an implied contract of employment is in effect.

Simply put, handbooks should introduce the concept of **employment-at-will**. However, whether this statement has any legal significance depends upon many factors, including other statements made by the employer that are relevant to the allegation and the state court's interpretation of the employment-at-will doctrine. A sample statement that attempts to release the handbook from interpretation as a contract is presented below.

Sample disclaimer regarding "at-will"

SAMPLE DISCLAIMER

This manual is not to be construed as a contract. Employees of Company X are employed on an at-will basis, meaning that either the employee or Company X may terminate the employment relationship at any time, with or without notice. Nothing contained in this manual is intended to provide or guarantee employment for a specific period of time, nor does this manual create any type of employment contract. Within the limits allowed by law, Company X reserves the right to amend, modify, or cancel this manual, as well as any and all of the various policies, procedures, guidelines, standards, benefits, and programs outlined within, whenever it deems appropriate.

Wrongful terminations

Interestingly, while organizations must take care to avoid certain language for fear of wrongful termination lawsuits, other handbook language can actually protect organizations in court. That is, if the court finds that a handbook is considered to be an implied contract, then its contents are binding for both employers *and* employees. For instance, a Continental Airlines employee contested his termination on the grounds that the airline had incorrectly counted his absences in violation of the implied contract, or the handbook. The U.S. Court of Appeals reversed a $200,000 verdict against Continental when it ruled that there are both benefits and responsibilities associated with a handbook that creates an implied contract. The handbook stipulated that the employee must use a formal internal appeals process to contest personnel actions, an action that the terminated employee did not take. Thus, employees can have certain "implied" obligations under a handbook as well.

Violations of Policy/Discipline

As the adage goes, "Rules were made to be broken." While you, in the role of an officer of the organization, may not want employees to live by this creed, undoubtedly there will be violations of the policies set forth for appropriate conduct. It is for this reason that discipline policies and guidelines must be enacted. Many differences exist in the actions that organizations deem necessary as recourse for violations of policy, some of them being very fundamental differences. Specifically, while some may choose a discipline approach, others may focus more upon punishment for the misconduct.[61] **Punishment** is the provision of a negative consequence following a behavior. It is focused upon the past and penalizes undesirable behavior. On the other hand, **discipline** is more future oriented; its goal is to point the way to more positive and productive behavior rather than to penalize the person for his or her mistakes. Although different organizational cultures will undoubtedly support different blends of punishment and discipline, the goal of these policies should be to improve productivity. Therefore, a discipline approach is ultimately more desirable.

Before any discipline takes place, organizational members should attempt to diagnose the problem to be sure that the employee is to blame for the incident. In courts of law, organizations are held responsible for a thorough investigation. Individuals have won large judgments against their former employers when they failed to conduct such investigations prior to termination. Particular attention should be paid to allegations of serious misconduct such as sexual harassment.

Even when the employee is to blame, a causal analysis should be done to determine the best tactics for preventing the misconduct in the future. Briefly, one should determine if the problem resulted from misunderstanding, lack of knowledge, or motivation. If an employee does not *understand* why his or her behavior was inappropriate, communicate with the employee. If the employee does not *know how* to perform properly, train the employee. Finally, if the employee is not *motivated* to perform correctly, look for systems/issues that can be changed. Ultimately, motivation issues may be the hardest to address, but cases of misconduct are a good opportunity to examine motivational factors in the workplace.

While the investigation and/or the causal analysis may uncover information that lessens the need to hold the employee fully accountable, discipline is the appropriate action in most cases. For discipline, the guiding principles are generally the same as the bases for selection decisions:

Guiding principles for discipline

1. Decisions should be based on job-related criteria; that is, behavior that is being disciplined should have a direct impact upon job or organizational performance.

2. Employees should be treated consistently.

3. Company policy should be followed; any deviation from company policy due to mitigating circumstances should be clearly documented and rationalized.

4. Communication to all involved should be accurate and honest, but confidentiality should be maintained when appropriate.

If possible, a legal expert (e.g., an HR specialist or lawyer) should be consulted before an actual decision is made.

Of course, if employees continue to violate policy, discipline should become more and more severe, a practice often called **progressive discipline.** Organizations often respond to misconduct first with some minimal warning, followed by more severe punishments up to and including termination or discharge. An example of a progressive disciplinary program is:

Progressive discipline

- Verbal warning.
- Written warning copied to supervisor's file.
- Written warning copied to HR file.
- Suspension or demotion.
- Termination.

The severity of the misconduct should be taken into account when an organization determines the appropriate disciplinary actions along the progressive discipline continuum. If it is found that an employee has stolen large amounts of money from the operating budget, the organization is likely to exercise termination and even press criminal charges. This situation should not be handled merely with a verbal warning. Lateness, on the other hand, lends itself more readily to a multiple-step, progressive discipline approach. Specific actions that result in deviations from strict progressive discipline should be outlined in an employee handbook. However, the wording of these policies should not be exclusive. In other words, the specific actions leading directly to termination should be provided as examples, not a definitive listing of reasons one may be terminated. The latter approach makes the discipline policy susceptible to charges of an implicit contract, putting the organization at risk for a wrongful termination suit.

While setting limits is important, enforcement is paramount. Obviously, ignoring cases of misconduct allows problem employees to perform at a level of decreased productivity and efficiency. Failing to use established discipline policies may also have other indirect effects. First, management may lose credibility in the eyes of other employees if it does not carry out policies that have been explicitly set forth. Furthermore, the morale of other employees may be diminished by their having to make up for poor productivity on the part of one underperforming employee. Much of the literature on sound management and talent retention discusses the sensitivity of employees to these issues. As one source put it: "Many good employees leave because they don't see recurring labor problems handled by their managers."[62]

Exceptions to progressive discipline

Of course, a discipline policy should allow for exceptions to progressive discipline given certain offenses. In particular, employees should be given an opportunity to disclose a medical reason for the problem. If such disclosures are made, a lawyer or HR specialist should be consulted to determine the Americans with Disabilities Act or Family Medical Leave Act implications of the matter. Remember our discussion of reasonable accommodation regarding the ADA (see Chapter 3). The ADA is particularly relevant for drug and alcohol use policies. Recovering alcoholics and recovering drug users are protected by the law; thus, employees who are participating in legitimate rehabilitation programs are covered. The ADA does not protect active or illegal users.

Grievances

As astute as an organization may be in establishing policies and practices that allocate rewards and distribute punishments fairly, employees may have cause to challenge decisions made on the part of the organization. Most typically, this is executed by way of a formally established grievance procedure. A *grievance* can be defined in many ways; an organization establishing a grievance policy should define the term succinctly. Some organizations limit grievances to treatment by a supervisor, while others state that a grievance may be filed against the administration or interpretation of a company policy, but not against the policy itself.[63] The simplest way to define a **grievance** may be to say that it is a formal, written complaint about the way in which the employment relationship is being carried out.

Most decisions resulting from formal grievances are specific to the individual filing the complaint, but grievances can be made on behalf of a group of affected employees. At any rate, *grievance procedures* are important because of the seriousness of claims of unfair treatment, but also because they increase acceptance of an organization's policies and procedures. Thibaut and Walker have noted that employees evaluate policies as more fair and just when they believe that they have control over the process of implementing and administering organizational decisions.[64]

In unionized organizations (see Chapter 13), the grievance procedure is usually elaborate, drawing on stewards and other union leaders to argue the grievance if it is not rectified through written procedures. In nonunionized organizations, the extensiveness of the grievance procedure varies, although there is a trend toward detailed procedures in large organizations. Among the most informal procedures are general open-door policies and commitment on the part of supervisors and managers to promote fair dealing with employees. The problem with these generalized mechanisms to handle employee grievances is that virtually all executives say that they adopt an open-door policy. Moreover, they are more popular with professional employees; manufacturing employees may prefer a more explicit system.[65]

Peer review process

More formalized grievance procedures in nonunionized organizations often include some sort of peer review process.[66] Peer reviews are typically done by a group of organizational members using a process described in the employee handbook. The procedure for submitting a grievance and processing a grievance and the degree to which the peer decision is binding must be established. Research has found that peer review systems are generally well accepted by managers and executives and that they actually motivate supervisors to perform better so as to avoid a peer review.[67]

Mediation and arbitration

Finally, nonunion grievance procedures may provide for formal **mediation and arbitration** as final steps, much as in the procedures in unionized organizations. In this case, complaints are often first heard by an external mediator who attempts to settle the dispute. If the mediation fails, binding arbitration may follow. With **binding arbitration**, the complaint is heard by

Binding arbitration

arbitrators (usually from one to three arbitrators), and decisions are then legally binding. Most companies rely on organizations such as the **American Arbitration Association** (see AAA.org), which can handle both the mediation and the arbitration process. In general, research that has examined arbitration as a dispute resolution tactic is positive from both the employer and the employee perspectives. The most recent evidence indicates that employees are more likely to prevail in arbitration than in fully litigated cases. Moreover, employees typically do not abuse the system with frivolous disputes, and employers can further assure this by limiting in the employee handbook the issues available for arbitration. Arbitration typically reviews the execution of an established company policy, not the policy itself.[68]

Despite generally positive reviews, arbitration agreements and stipulations can be complex in practice. As this is an area of heavy legal activity, the laws in this area are changing rapidly. In one court case, an employee of Y-3 Holdings in California signed an

Figure 12-6   **Sample Dispute Resolution Program**

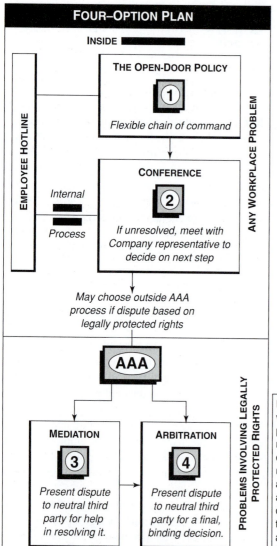

FOUR–OPTION PLAN

INSIDE ▌▬▬▬▬▬

THE OPEN-DOOR POLICY

(1)

Flexible chain of command

EMPLOYEE HOTLINE

ANY WORKPLACE PROBLEM

Internal ▬▬▬
Process ▬▬▬

CONFERENCE

(2)

If unresolved, meet with Company representative to decide on next step

May choose outside AAA process if dispute based on legally protected rights

AAA

PROBLEMS INVOLVING LEGALLY PROTECTED RIGHTS

MEDIATION

(3)

Present dispute to neutral third party for help in resolving it.

ARBITRATION

(4)

Present dispute to neutral third party for a final, binding decision.

OUTSIDE ▌▬▬▬▬

INTRODUCTION

The new ▬▬▬▬ Dispute Resolution Program is a four-option plan for resolving problems that happen at work. It encourages open communication, protects your work relationships, and helps keep costs and tempers under control. For serious legal disputes, it also makes available the experience and objectivity of the American Arbitration Association (AAA).

Founded in 1926, the American Arbitration Association (AAA) helps businesses, associations, and all levels of government resolve over 60,000 cases each year.

EMPLOYEE HOTLINE
CALL (800)▬▬▬▬▬

Effective ▬▬▬ ▬▬▬ will adopt this four-option program as the exclusive means of resolving workplace disputes for legally protected rights. That means if you accept or continue your job at ▬▬▬▬ after that date, you will agree to resolve all legal claims against ▬▬▬▬ through this process instead of through the court system.

Figure 12-6 *(Continued)*

FOUR OPTIONS— AN OVERVIEW

Option One—The Open-Door Policy helps you solve your problem early through the **Chain of Command.** Discuss it with Business Unit Personnel or Corporate Employee Relations. An **Employee Hotline,** (800) ███████, puts you in touch with a confidential Adviser who can also help you. If you think your problem is serious enough, you may want to request a **Legal Consultation.** If approved, ███████████ will pay for most of it.

Option Two—The Conference is the next step if your problem is still unresolved. You can sit down with a Company representative and the Program Administrator to decide what process you would like to use to settle your dispute. If both parties agree, an in-house resolution process can be arranged. If your dispute involves a legally protected right, such as protection from discrimination or harassment, you may prefer to go to mediation or arbitration through AAA.

Option Three—Mediation lets you and the Company discuss your legal dispute with a neutral third party, AAA. The neutral party or mediator can listen to both sides of the story and help you work it out together. To use AAA, you pay a processing fee of $50. *Mediation is only for disputes involving legally protected rights.*

Option Four—Arbitration lets you present your legal dispute to a neutral third party, AAA, for a final decision. The arbitrator will decide your case after hearing arguments from both sides. AAA can make an award just like a judge in the court system. To use AAA, you pay a fee of $50, unless you have already paid it for mediation. *Arbitration is only for disputes involving legally protected rights.*

QUESTIONS AND ANSWERS

 How does the new Open-Door Policy differ from the old one?

For the first time in the history of the Company, the Open-Door Policy has been put into writing. Both old and new Open-Door Policies call for resolving workplace disputes through the Chain of Command. Improvements to the Policy include an Employee Hotline, the opportunity to talk with an Adviser, and, if approved, a legal consultation for serious legal disputes. ███████████ will be training all of its managers and supervisors in how to use the new program.

 What do I do if the supervisor I approach ignores the Open-Door Policy?

If the first person you approach under the Open-Door Policy doesn't help you, proceed immediately to another level of supervision in the Chain of Command. You may also want to call the Employee Hotline at (800) ███████ or call your Business Unit Personnel Manager or Employee Relations.

 What happens if my supervisor starts to make things difficult for me after I complain?

Take your problem to a higher level in the Chain of Command, or to an Adviser through the Employee Hotline. The Adviser will help you decide on a strategy for handling your problem or refer you to someone in the Chain of Command.

 Can I use the ███████ Dispute Resolution Program to solve any problem that happens at work?

You may use Options One, the Open-Door Policy, and Two, the Conference, to address any workplace dispute.

Options Three and Four, the AAA process, can be used to resolve only those problems or disputes involving legally protected rights, such as discrimination for age, sex, or religion; on-the-job harassment; or being asked to commit unlawful acts.

 How does arbitration differ from a court trial?

With arbitration, the decision is final; except under rare circumstances, it may not be reversed by subsequent proceedings. With a court trial decision, an appeal may be filed, causing endless delays. Also, an arbitration proceeding is usually much more informal than a case in court. The biggest difference, however, lies in the reasonable cost of arbitration. Because arbitration is faster and less formal, it ends up costing much less to prepare the case for both the employee and the employer.

6 **If I don't like the arbitrator's decision, can I appeal it through the court system?**

Arbitration awards are final, binding, and may be enforced under the law, with only limited appeals allowed through the courts.

Document understanding of policy

acknowledgment form that she had received, understood, and agreed to the terms in the company handbook that included a description of the binding arbitration agreement. The California Appeals Court ruled that the employee's signature on the acknowledgment form did not necessarily pertain to the arbitration agreement. Bottom line: Employers should obtain specific documentation of the employee's understanding and agreement regarding the arbitration policy itself and not just an acknowledgment of the contents of the handbook. Figure 12-6 presents an outline of a comprehensive (and successful) dispute resolution program. There are many options to dispute resolution.

As can be seen, there are many mechanisms that an organization may use to maintain the employment relationship. In fact, there are many other programs that also help to keep the working relationship healthy (i.e., work–family programs, award programs, employee suggestion programs) that were not discussed due to space constraints. Next, an inevitable event in the employment relationship is discussed: organizational exit. As with those practices that maintain the employment relationship, organizational exit should be conducted in a way that is fair, productive, and satisfactory to all involved.

ORGANIZATIONAL EXIT

Organizational exit can take many forms. Simply defined, **organizational exit** is the dissolution of the employment relationship. Four distinct forms of exit are discussed here.

Sometimes the organization originates an individual's exit, as in *termination;* at other times, the individual does so, as in *resignation* (or voluntary turnover) and *retirement.* Still other times, the organization institutes large-scale organizational exit by engaging in downsizing and *layoffs.* In all instances, this marks the end of the formalized employee–employer relationship; however, measures should be taken to make the separation as amicable as possible while maintaining productivity, learning from the experience, and perhaps making changes to organizational policies, procedures, and practices as a result.

Termination

Termination is the dissolution of the employment relationship that is originated by the organization. While we know that termination can happen for any reason as provided by the employment-at-will doctrine, it occurs most often for poor performance and misconduct. In general, termination for poor performance occurs when an employee consistently fails to meet a minimum standard or fails to meet a specific goal, objective, standard, or quota. Consistent unauthorized absences and tardiness are also common reasons for termination. Failure to follow organization policy or procedure is yet another reason for termination. More broadly, the reasons for termination often vary according to the level the employee occupies within an organization. Lower-level employees are most often terminated due to job performance, insubordination, or failure to comply with written policies and procedures. Managers and other higher-level employees are often fired when there is a lack of fit or a personality characteristic that has resulted in negative organizational outcomes.[69]

Consistency is a driving force of employee acceptance of dismissal practices. Termination should not be used for vague or unsubstantiated reasons, and documentation (e.g., discipline records, performance appraisals) should inform the decision to terminate an employee.[70] It is of the utmost importance that employers make every attempt to apply rules consistently. Recall the discussion of the legal prescriptions for performance appraisals in Chapter 7. One of the best predictors of the outcomes of cases favorable to the employer is consistent application of the policy. Consistency also helps to establish the perception of *procedural justice,* which we have discussed. These perceptions of fairness at termination are extremely important. If employees feel as if they were treated fairly, they are less likely to file wrongful termination claims. Moreover, adequate notice on the part of the employer and the provision of aid in finding a new job have been shown to increase feelings of justice at termination.[71] Although we have spoken periodically about the separate legal and psychological reasons for maintaining a fair employment relationship, here one can see that the two are clearly linked.

Although retaining an ineffective employee often undermines the performance of the work group and the organization, termination often is cited as one of the most troubling aspects of a manager's job. The HR department is often heavily involved when an employee is to be terminated. In some cases, HR managers handle all of the details involved when terminating an employee. In other cases, it is incumbent upon the employee's direct supervisor to carry out the termination; however, it is typically not without support from the HR department and (oftentimes) legal clearance. At the very least, HR may provide coaching and training on how to effectively handle termination meetings. Undoubtedly, when

**Figure 12-7
Guidelines for Conducting
Termination**

Before the meeting:

- If you have doubts about terminating the employee, consult corporate counsel.
- Document each level of progressive discipline.
- Investigate serious misconduct before terminating the employee.
- Prepare severance packages and the final paycheck.
- Recognize that the task before you is not an easy one, but that the actions you take can minimize potential negative consequences.
- Consider the timing of the termination, taking care to schedule the meeting at the best time of day for the employee.
- Give the employee a chance to disclose a medical reason.
- Have HR review the situation to make certain termination abides by law, company policy, and collective bargaining agreement.
- If this is a group layoff, review compliance with WARN and ADEA.

During the meeting:

- Consider having a witness present if anger and mistrust surround the termination.
- Maintain full control of the meeting. Don't allow the employee to blame others or report the misconduct of co-workers at this time.
- Get to the point quickly:
  —The employee has been fired.
  —Outline severance, ongoing benefits, and noncompete agreements.
  —Develop a consistent story to be relayed to other employees and agree upon the contents of any future recommendation letters.
  —Tell the employee that he or she is no longer responsible for duties at the organization. Rather, he or she should focus on new job search.
- Do not end the meeting with an apology. Rather, shake the employee's hand and wish him/her well in the future.

After the meeting:

- Update personnel files.
- Document any agreements.
- Arrange for exit services such as outplacement, benefits, or severance.
- Review job descriptions and discipline policies. Could the termination have been prevented if either were more clear or descriptive? If so, consider making those revisions.
- Shut down access to premises and equipment.

managers talk about the difficulty of terminations, they are often referring to the termination meeting itself, the face-to-face interaction with the employee to be terminated. Compiling recommendations from trade magazines in several industries,[72] the best practices for before, during, and after this meeting appear in Figure 12-7 above.

Resignation/Voluntary Turnover

Ask an HR manager what his/her organization's turnover rate is, and you are likely to be answered first with a groan or a sigh. It seems the turnover statistic (i.e., the rate at which employees voluntarily resign from their position within the organization) is never at a level that is acceptable given the operating environment and the organization's goals and growth strategies. In a recent survey, 52 percent of managers said that they had a problem retaining high-performing employees.[73]

Though it seems counterintuitive, some degree of resignation and turnover is probably beneficial, as it allows the organization to renew itself and invites its practices to be critically examined from another point of view. However, too much turnover is problematic and predictive of corporate financial problems. The high-performance work systems research we have alluded to so often throughout the book presents data showing superior corporate financial performance for organizations with relatively lower turnover. One reason for the negative financial impact may be the high cost of replacing employees. The U.S. Department of Labor estimates that it costs approximately one-third of a new employee's salary to replace the employee, and some say that this figure is more like one-half.[74] Consider that the time consumed in exiting the employee while recruiting and hiring another is substantial. And any efficiencies gained by way of intact internal and external customer relationships are undermined when an employee voluntarily resigns.[75] For these reasons, organizations typically take action to investigate the reasons for employee turnover and ultimately attempt to

Figure 12-8   **Cycle of Failure in Service Company**

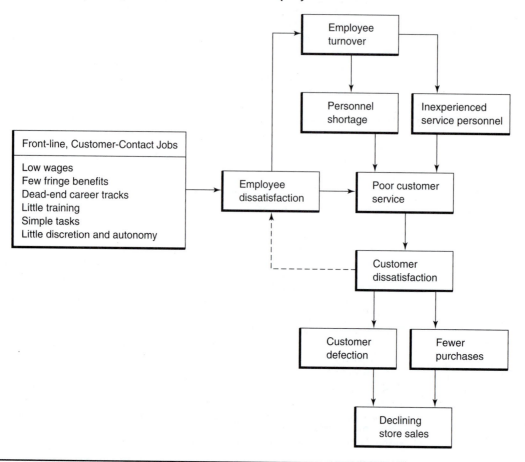

Source: P. W. Hom and R. W. Griffeth, *Employee Turnover.* Cincinnati, OH: SouthWestern, 1992, p. 24. Reprinted with permission from the author.

minimize its occurrence. Figure 12-8 presents the cycle of failure for a service company due to the connection between high turnover and quality of service. Figure 12-9 presents a model that illustrates the determinants of voluntary turnover.

Throughout this book several ways to minimize unnecessary employee turnover have been suggested. The use of more valid selection procedures covered in Chapter 6 is one approach. Creating and sustaining fair relationships with employees that are considerate of procedural and distributive justice issues will help build commitment to the organization. Giving employees **realistic job previews** and ensuring that they are socialized appropriately will facilitate appropriate expectations. Policies and procedures that produce productive, efficient, and positive relationships with employees are also critical. Other recommendations from various experts include:

■ Provide a safe and secure work environment in which the employee does not feel threatened.

■ Provide feedback to employees.

■ Ensure that employees are managed properly by providing management training and feedback.

■ Provide pay and benefits commensurate with other organizations in your industry.

■ Provide flexible working hours and family-friendly policies.

■ Provide opportunities for growth and development, and, where possible, advancement.

■ Involve employees in business matters and keep them abreast of company happenings.

■ Don't send the message that employees are expendable.[76]

Figure 12-9　　　　　　　　**Integrative Model of Turnover Determinants**

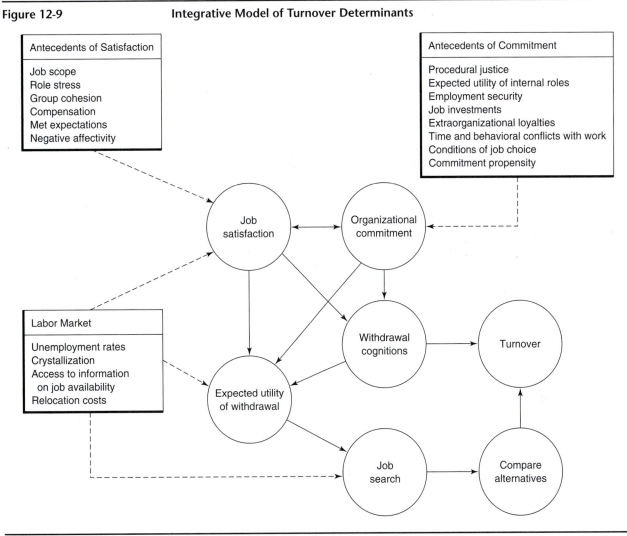

Source: P. W. Hom and R. W. Griffeth, *Employee Turnover.* Cincinnati, OH: SouthWestern, 1992, p. 108. Reprinted with permission from the author.

Exit interviews

When employees do leave, organizations often conduct **exit interviews** or distribute **postemployment surveys** in order to assess the reasons for voluntary turnover. Using either the face-to-face or survey technique, individuals in the organization attempt to uncover the reasons for the employee's departure. The content of exit interviews and surveys is quite varied across companies. They may cover any of the following: reasons for leaving, satisfaction with the job, the quality of management, perceived opportunities for advancement, and the adequacy of pay, training, and performance appraisals.[77] Much like employee surveys, this information allows organizations to assess how well their retention strategies are working, update benefits and other programs, and discontinue programs that are not well-accepted by employees. Moreover, it may send a message to employees that their opinions are valued, even as they leave the organization.[78] It is often recommended that exit interviews be conducted by someone who was only indirectly related to the employee while he or she was working in the organization, perhaps even an external consulting firm. Assuring confidentiality by using such measures while also building trust in the interview likely will produce more candid responses.[79] One study has shown that both fear of blame and concern that responses will not be held confidential are reasons that employees are not truthful in exit interviews.[80]

Many organizations do not conduct exit interviews. At the very least, though, most organizations keep tabs on the rate of turnover. One way to calculate a turnover rate is to consider it as a percentage of the total number of employees. In other words, the turnover rate is the number of turnovers divided by the average total number of workers. Other firms calculate the mean or median length of tenure of employees. In some industries, such as retail and food service, turnover is stunningly high. One study commissioned by Coca-Cola showed that the median tenure of employees working in supermarkets was only 148 days.[81] On the other hand, the SAS Institute (ranked #29th in *Fortune*'s 2008 best places to work)[82] has a turnover rate of only 3 percent.[83] (Go to www.fortune.com for its current standing.)

Downsizing and Layoffs

Downsizing and layoffs were discussed in Chapter 5 under HR planning. We focus here on the impact upon the employment relationship of these activities. While a **layoff** refers to the *tactical,* physical action of eliminating redundant skills in the organization, **downsizing** is the name given to the overall organizational *strategy* to which the layoff may contribute. These terms (as well as various others) are often interpreted in a similar manner: "downsizing" is often used to refer to the elimination of jobs associated with the overall strategy. The term *rightsizing,* having a meaning similar to downsizing, appeared in many popular press articles during the 1990s. The expression does not enjoy widespread use, likely because it is a thinly veiled euphemism for massive job loss. The term *layoff* typically is reserved for manufacturing employees, but is formally defined as above, which would pertain to an employee at any level. At any rate, we focus here on the effects such events have upon individual employees and the associated organizational actions regardless of the terminology one prefers. Because of its popularity in current HR publications, the term *downsizing* is used here.

The Causes and Effects of Downsizing and Layoffs

In some cases, downsizing is undertaken to reduce labor costs and streamline organizational operations. In other cases, downsizing results from mergers and acquisitions in which the resulting company is plagued with redundant functions. At any rate, organizations are often not realizing all of the cost benefits they hoped to receive from downsizing because they must replace functions, either by hiring consultants or training those that remain on the job. Moreover, productivity gains are short-lived; in fact, they are more a reflection of the reduction in operating expenses than they are true output advances. Finally, motivation and morale are damaged, which can have indirect effects upon both the productivity and the economic consequences discussed above.[84]

Effect on "survivors"

Indeed, downsizing can have devastating effects upon individual employees, both those that have been downsized and those that haven't, who are called **survivors.** Specifically, downsized employees probably face many emotions. Their initial response may be shock, anger, confusion, relief, or a degree of escapism. Eventually, these employees need to confront the task of becoming reemployed without succumbing to frustration and self-doubt.[85] Organizational actions, discussed in the next section, can help employees avoid such emotions by preparing them for the transition to a new job, a new organization, or a new career.

Even for those employees that do not lose their jobs as a result of downsizing, there may be serious psychological consequences. David Noer, who has written several books on the topic, notes that the emotional reactions of the survivors are much like those of the individuals who were downsized.[86] Indeed, a content analysis of those that survived a downsizing showed that experienced emotions included anger, anxiety, cynicism, resentment of upper management, and resignation, mixed with some hope.[87] There are tangible consequences in the workplace that survivors must deal with as well. Many times, organizations cut the staff positions they need to devise a new "leaner" strategy and vision, so expected benefits from such drastic actions are never realized.[88] Also, energies are drained and stress levels of survivors are acute, given that the survivors are now expected to accomplish the additional work of those who have been released from the organization.

It should be noted that there are some instances of positive individual outcomes as a result of downsizing. Due to relief from surviving the cuts or the heightened awareness of performance that a downsizing brings, individual effort after a downsizing may actually increase.[89] The degree to which overall outcomes are positive or negative, however, depends upon organizational measures taken to optimally execute the downsizing efforts.

Organizational Measures

Organizational actions and policy for dealing with downsizing should be geared toward maintaining goodwill to those directly affected by the downsizing and toward reassuring and maximizing productivity among the survivors. It has been shown in several studies that the manner in which an organization executes the reduction in employees affects levels of bitterness and dissatisfaction felt by both layoff victims and survivors.[90] For instance, advanced notice of the downsizing has been shown to reduce negative feelings.[91] Indeed, there is agreement on this among many authors' recommendations for successful downsizing.[92]

Outplacement programs

Additionally, some form of outplacement assistance for downsized workers is quite common and recommended to amicably end the employment relationship. **Outplacement programs** are simply those that help discharged employees find new jobs. Outplacement efforts may include the provision of information to affected employees concerning continuation of benefits and compensation, announcements to other employers via personal contact or broader-scale advertising concerning availability of skilled workers, career and job-seeking counseling, and training on the development of résumés and interview skills. While these efforts obviously help the employee through the downsizing experience, they benefit organizations by reducing legal risks, reducing severance pay and unemployment compensation, preserving morale among survivors, and maintaining a positive public image.[93] The oldest (and largest) of outplacement firms is Challenger, Gray & Christmas (www.challengergray.com), which claims a median placement time of 3.2 months versus an average of 5 months for the industry.

In sum, organizations must take actions to alleviate the discomfort for both downsized employees and survivors. But must a large number of employees be laid off during times of economic need? If an organization considers other alternatives before downsizing its employees, employees may perceive the layoffs as more of a business necessity, thus harboring less bitterness and dissatisfaction as a result. One alternative to layoffs is **work-sharing programs,** in which employees voluntarily reduce the number of hours or days per week they work in order to cut labor costs while maintaining their gainful employment. Organizations also could limit the availability of vacation and overtime and redistribute workers to needed areas through transfers.[94] The disadvantage of these alternatives is that it decreases costs associated with wages alone, not health or other benefits. However, these costs could provide some degree of immediate financial gain.

Work-sharing

Early retirement programs

Other alternatives would decrease the size of the workforce, but less disruptively. For instance, organizations could limit the inflow of employees, often called a **hiring freeze.** Also, organizations sometimes offer **early retirement packages** as a tactic to reduce the number of employees in the workforce. These packages often include incentives for retiring such as bonuses, full benefits before they are earned through tenure, or supplemental income until the employee is able to receive full Social Security benefits.[95] Ford had a very successful early retirement program in 2001 and 2002 probably due to the extra incentives offered to those who took the early retirement plan. Again, though, these measures are not without disadvantages. Hiring freezes and early retirement packages are very blunt cutting tools when it comes to downsizing. In other words, organizations utilizing these measures could be left with a number of vacancies in key areas while having a surplus of workers in functions and jobs considered redundant.

Retirement

Retirement has been defined as an exit from an organizational position or career path of considerable duration taken by individuals after middle age and taken with the intention of reduced psychological commitment to work thereafter.[96] After the **Age Discrimination in Employment Act** repealed mandatory retirement, retirement became a voluntary decision for nearly all Americans—at least those living and working within the United States. Organizations headquartered in the United States that employ workers overseas may be subject to different laws and regulations. For example, a U.S. company does not violate the ADEA if an American worker is forced to retire at the age of 65 under a German collective bargaining agreement that stipulates mandatory retirement.

While some liken retirement to turnover because of its willfulness, the two concepts have been clearly distinguished.[97] Where retirement signals a decreased involvement in work, turnover does not. Because of its unique nature, it is worthwhile to consider the reasons for which individuals decide to retire. Retirement is influenced by both personal characteristics and economic concerns. Specifically, government policies, individual and family characteristics, and the organization's policies all affect an individual's decision to retire.[98] Figure 12-10 presents a model of the influences upon this decision.[99] At any rate, the organization has an influential part in the retirement decision. We turn now to those organizational actions that help maintain a positive relationship with retiring employees.

Organizational Actions

Flexible plans

While many adjustments to retirement are incumbent upon the employee, organizations are adopting more and more practices to facilitate the transition to non- or reduced-working life. Specifically, more flexible retirement plans allow employees to phase into retirement more slowly, preventing the shock that often comes with the end of work. Examples include part-time work, longer vacation periods or sabbaticals, altering the content of the job, accepting a demotion, and second-career assistance. It stands to reason that more flexible retirement plans (i.e., those that offer a variety of alternatives for reducing the amount of time that is worked) may help employees successfully adjust to the change. When employees are allowed to choose the path to retirement that is most workable given some unique combination of these considerations, a more successful transition can be expected.

Some organizations are transitioning employees to retirement by using them as volunteers and ambassadors for their own social programs. Corporations such as American Express Financial Services, Amoco Corporation, The Gillette Company, and H. J. Heinz Company are doing so.[100] Specifically, these retired employees participate in volunteer activities in the name of their former employer, providing a win-win situation for all involved.

Figure 12-10   **Influences on the Retirement Decision**

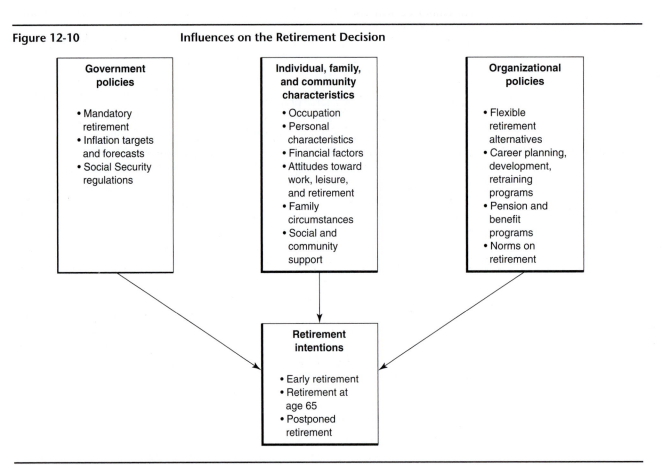

Source: B. Rosen and T. H. Jerdee, *Older Employees: New Roles for Valued Resources,* 1985, p. 143. Reprinted with permission.

The retiree benefits from continued interaction with others in a helping role, continued affiliation with the organization, and contact with the larger community. The organization reaps obvious public relations and visibility benefits.

Typically, even if organizations do not provide flexible retirement options and/or other creative transition programs, they offer some sort of informational programs intended to ease the transition into retirement. These programs may include information on both the economic and social concerns facing retiring workers. It is recommended that these programs be conducted in small groups to build social networks around the retirement decision.[101] In fact, spouse participation is encouraged.[102] Finally, it is recommended by many that the transition to retirement begin years before the actual date of departure from the organization. One recommendation is that attendance at retirement programs should begin at least five years prior to retirement and should continue for some time after.[103] These types of transition programs should be the very least that organizations consider offering in addition to the monetary benefits associated with retirement.

Spouse participation is encouraged

SUMMARY

Managing the employment relationship is a little-talked-about function of the HR department. While this may be the case, it is not because the employment relationship is less important than selection, training, or performance appraisal. Rather, *all* human resource functions are crucial to maintaining the employment relationship; it is a broad function that permeates the entirety of the HR professional's job. In other words, perceptions of fairness and justice are not limited to the organizational actions discussed in this chapter. An employee will consider his or her entire employment experience when forming perceptions of fairness.

That being said, some functions of the HR department are carried out for the sole purpose of building and maintaining the employment relationship. Realistic job previews and socialization programs provide employees with information needed to begin forming a relationship with their employer. Next, the maintenance of the relationship is governed by the external force of employment law and internal forces such as employee handbooks. Legal issues are employment-at-will, whistleblowing, privacy, the Worker Adjustment Relocation Notification Act, and many more. HR professionals must help to create an operating environment perceived as fair and just while always considering and integrating the legal environment. The HR department must create, maintain, and review employee handbooks, discipline policies, and grievance systems. At present, privacy issues concerning employee records must be balanced against government antiterrorism requirements. Finally, employers must manage the exit of their employees, be it voluntary or involuntary, a single case or a mass layoff.

Delicate balancing act

In sum, managing employee relationships is a delicate balancing act: Organizational concerns for productivity must balance individual concerns for justice, legal doctrine must balance internal procedure, and the uniqueness of each employee must balance the efficiencies gained when establishing overall policy. Any actions that an organization takes to create and maintain relationships with its employees must consider each of these competing forces. This is not an easy task at any given moment, let alone in the tumultuous time we entered in 2008. However, keeping the employment relationship in balance will undoubtedly lead to productivity and efficiencies that would not be gained otherwise.

Discussion Questions

1. A CEO once told an HR consultant that organizational justice is a "touchy feely concept not related to anything important." If you were the HR consultant, what would you say to that?

2. Should realistic job previews be applied to overseas assignments? If so, how would you go about constructing a realistic job preview for such an assignment? Pick one country and do a draft of an RJP for an assignment there.

3. The "covenant of good faith and fair dealing" as related to employment-at-will implies that excellent performance over an extended period of time grants the performer a right to be terminated only for "just cause." But only 11 states have adopted this exception to employment-at-will. Research your state and take a position on whether your state should join the 11 or drop the exception.

4. Should companies have the right to monitor all Internet "surfing" at work? How would you react if a company stipulated that no personal surfing is allowed and, if discovered, could result in termination?

5. How does a binding arbitration agreement work? Should companies be allowed to adopt a binding arbitration requirement for their current employees in which employees surrender their right to litigate employment disputes through the court system? Explain your answer. What is the current state of the law regarding arbitration?

6. Should companies purchase software that shuts down all access terminated employees have to company equipment, credit cards, website access and premises as soon as the termination takes effect? Why would a company need to purchase such software?

7. To what extent would you be attracted to an organization that offered a variety of work arrangements such as flextime, telecommuting, four-day workweeks, and job sharing?

Chapter
13

Labor Relations and Collective Bargaining*

OBJECTIVES

After reading this chapter, you should be able to

1. Understand why people join unions.
2. Know the basic elements of labor law.
3. Understand collective bargaining as a tool for labor negotiation.
4. Identify the bases of power in collective bargaining related to both unions and management.
5. Describe current trends and issues in labor relations.
6. Describe the state of labor relations in other countries.

OVERVIEW

Issues related to organizational justice and practices related to employee discipline and grievances are major factors in the employment relationship and have a great deal to do with why employees join unions. Unions are organizations that represent employees' interests to management on almost all critical HR issues. The topics covered in Chapters 10 and 11 have to do with increasing productivity and performance through compensation practices. Unions generally resist such efforts and prefer greater stability and equality in workers' paychecks. This resistance may have something to do with the negative attitudes business students have toward unions and certainly contributes to the antipathy that management has toward organized labor.

Although 2008 showed some areas of optimism for organized labor, things clearly have not been going well for unions and union organizing. Union membership in the United States, about 20 million in 1980, was under 16 million in 2008 although employment over that same period rose from 87.5 million to 134 million. A *New York Times* editorial in 2008 opined that "the future of organized labor is not cause for great optimism. Employers have become more aggressive about keeping unions out. Competitive pressures from globalization, deregulation and technological change have resulted in the loss of many union jobs."[1]

Although some believe that unions have become an institution of the past, there is evidence that attitudes toward unions are improving and some data indicating that union organizing is gaining ground in certain areas. *The New York Times* editorial from 2008 did note the slight uptick in union membership from 12.0 percent of the workforce in 2006 to

*Nancy Brown Johnson wrote a previous version of this chapter.

427

12.1 percent in 2007. One of the keys to recent union organizing success is clearly related to outsourcing. In general, occupations recently organized such as janitors, health care workers, hotel and restaurant workers, supermarket workers, truckers and warehouse operators all have low to no potential for offshore relocation.

American support unions

The American public is generally supportive of unions. Responses to a Gallup Poll question that has been used for many years on the approval or disapproval of unions have consistently favored labor by almost a 2:1 margin or better. Also, surveys of nonunion workers since the late 1970s report that a sizable, and increasing, proportion of nonunion workers would vote for union representation if they were given the chance.[2] There is also evidence that unions are now more supportive of innovative pay-for-performance systems and productivity enhancement programs such as quality circles and work team designs.

Management students today often learn the "ideal" way to manage firms' human resources, making it difficult for them to comprehend the adverse working environments that led to (and still lead to) unionization. People in the early part of the 20th century often worked under conditions many of us cannot fathom: "dark, satanic mills," with workweeks of at least 60 hours and with no provisions for safety, illness, vacations, or retirement.[3] The union's role in improving these conditions is clear. While the goal of unions today in the United States is still to improve working conditions and increase workers' economic status, the need and effects are more subtle than they were during the early years of unions.

Nonunion workers are protected by laws unions helped pass

The United States has legislation governing wages and hours, equal employment opportunity (EEO), family and medical leave, pensions, mergers, Social Security, and health and safety. Almost all U.S. workers benefit from this legislation, which probably would not be law were it not for the past political successes of labor unions. But this legislative success also fosters a feeling among American workers that unions may not be needed. The relatively clean (and safe) service industries, not yesterday's harsh factories and coal mines, provide for a substantial proportion of present-day U.S. employment. Most workers today face mental rather than physical strains, which makes the need for unions less clear. Nonetheless, service work often pays low wages with few benefits and is (some argue) in need of union protection.

2007 was first year union membership increased in over 25 years

The number of U.S. workers belonging to a union grew by 311,000 to 15.7 million in 2007. Union membership thus increased by .1 percent from the previous year to 12.1 percent of the workforce. This is the first increase in union representation since the 1970s when about 25 percent of U.S. workers belonged to a union and was likely to be wiped out in the aftermath of the 2008 economic crisis and recession.

Figure 13-1 presents a summary of union members in 2007, membership by industry and occupations, demographic characteristics, earnings, and membership rates across the states (it was 35 percent in 1945 and 25 percent in 1973).[4] Unions are nonetheless an important influence upon workers and firms—both union and nonunion. The AFL-CIO, which represents over 9 million workers, has 53 national and international union affiliates in the United States.[5] Go to www.aflcio.org for links to all affiliated unions. The largest

Largest union is the National Education Association

union is the National Education Association with over 2,500,000 members. As discussed in Chapter 2, increased globalization also may necessitate stronger consideration of international labor relations. Although Starbucks in the United States has almost no union representation for its U.S. employees, when Starbucks expanded to Italy and Sweden, management had to be well informed about labor relations in those countries, where many of its workers are unionized.[6] The online Georgetown University law library (www.ll.georgetown.edu) is an excellent source for international labor relations.

Worker–management relationships are strongly affected by the presence of unions. HR decisions, such as compensation, promotion, discipline, demotion, and termination, require union involvement. In general, management must handle personnel matters with the union rather than with each individual employee. As discussed in Chapters 10 and 11, unions have a great influence over pay structure and the compensation system in general. Nonunion firms also concern themselves with union activities because they usually desire to maintain their nonunion status. To do so, firms must be aware of unions and their history, their goals, their influences upon firms, and the legal issues binding both sides. Obviously, the working conditions, wages, and terms of employment of unionized firms have an effect on the way in which nonunion employers manage their HR in order to maintain nonunion status.

Figure 13-1 **Union Members in 2007**

Compared to 1997, the typical 2007 union member was more likely to be a female, a professional or a manager, or a public sector worker, and less likely to work in manufacturing. In 2007, the number of workers belonging to a union rose by 311,000 to 15.7 million. Union members accounted for 12.1% of employed wage and salary workers.

- Workers in the public sector had a union membership rate nearly five times that of private sector employees.
- Education, training, and library occupations had the highest unionization rate among all occupations, at 37.2%, followed closely by protective service occupations at 35.2%.
- Among demographic groups, the union membership rate was highest for black men and lowest for Hispanic women.
- Wage and salary workers ages 45 to 54 (15.7%) and ages 55 to 64 (16.1%) were more likely to be union members than were workers ages 16 to 24 (4.8%).

Membership by Industry and Occupation

- The union membership rate for public sector workers (35.9%) was substantially higher than for private industry workers (7.5%).
- Within the public sector, local government workers had the highest union membership rate, 41.8%. This group includes many workers in several heavily unionized occupations, such as teachers, police officers, and fire fighters.
- Private sector industries with high unionization rates include transportation and utilities (22.1%), telecommunications (19.7%), and construction (13.9%).
- Unionization rates were relatively low in agriculture and related industries (1.5%) and in financial activities (2.0%).
- Farming, fishing, and forestry occupations (2.7%) and sales and related occupations (3.3%) had the lowest unionization rates.

Demographic Characteristics of Union Members

- In 2007, the union membership rate was higher for men (13.0%) than for women (11.1%). The gap between their rates has narrowed considerably since 1983, when the rate for men was about 10% higher than the rate for women. The rates for both men and women declined between 1983 and 2007, but the rate for men declined much more rapidly.
- Black workers were more likely to be union members (14.3%) than were whites (11.8%), Asians (10.9%), or Hispanics (9.8%). Within these major groups, black men had the highest union membership rate (15.8%) while Hispanic women had the lowest rate (9.6%).

Union Representation of Nonmembers

About 1.6 million wage and salary workers were represented by a union on their main job in 2007, while not being union members themselves. Slightly more than half of these workers were employed in government.

Earnings

In 2007, among full-time wage and salary workers, union members had median usual weekly earnings of $863 while those who were not represented by unions had median weekly earnings of $663.

Union Membership by State

- In 2007, 30 states and the District of Columbia had union membership rates below that of the U.S. average, 12.1%, while 20 states had higher rates. All states in the Middle Atlantic and Pacific divisions reported union membership rates above the national average and all states in the East South Central and West South Central divisions had rates below it.
- Among the five states reporting union membership rates below 5.0% in 2007, North Carolina posted the lowest rate (3.0%). The next lowest rates were recorded in Virginia (3.7%), South Carolina (4.1%), Georgia (4.4%), and Texas (4.7%).
- Four states had union membership rates over 20.0% in 2007—New York (25.2%), Alaska (23.8%), Hawaii (23.4%), and Washington (20.2%).
- The largest numbers of union members lived in California (2.5 million) and New York (2.1 million). Nearly half (7.8 million) of the 15.7 million union members in the U.S. live in 6 states.

Source: Bureau of Labor Statistics (www.bls.gov).

This chapter will begin with a discussion of what factors affect employee decisions to join unions followed by a review of the major legislation affecting the labor movement and management today. The factors and procedures related to union organizing also will be covered. An overview of collective bargaining will then be presented with a description of the methods that unions and organizations employ to achieve their goals. The chapter will close with a discussion of the contemporary labor movement in the context of increased globalization.

Most business students today hold a negative view of the American labor movement. Unions are often viewed as antimanagement, striving to control or even reduce productivity, while demanding higher wages and ironclad protection for workers regardless of their performance. Indeed, the law requires management to meet and confer with union representatives when formulating policy and making decisions regarding virtually all important elements of HRM. The presence of a union or efforts to organize workers require HR expertise in labor relations. A lot can go wrong when managers have limited knowledge of labor law and organizing strategy. Management also should use HR specialists to negotiate and renegotiate labor contracts. But there is no question that some knowledge of labor law and collective bargaining

Most business students have a negative view of unions

is critical in any work environment where union organizing efforts are serious. Management also should understand why workers would contemplate giving up part of their paycheck to be represented by a union. Let's turn to that issue first.

WHY DO WORKERS JOIN UNIONS?

Understanding unions and why people organize is important for managers whether or not their organization is unionized. As discussed in Chapter 12, perceptions of organizational justice, job satisfaction, and perceptions of fair pay likely deter union organizing drives. There are three general reasons why workers join unions: (1) dissatisfaction with the work environment, including working conditions, compensation, and supervision; (2) a desire to have more influence in effecting change in the work environment; and (3) employee beliefs regarding the potential benefit of unions. Figure 13-2 presents a summary of the major determinants.

Workers' dissatisfaction with their jobs and, in particular, dissatisfaction with their wages, benefits, and supervision are most related to the tendency to vote for a union.[7] One surprising finding is that the work itself does not seem to be strongly related to union voting. The best predictors in several studies are satisfaction with pay, working conditions, and supervision rather than the work itself. Satisfaction with first-line supervision appears to be particularly important as well as concerns regarding job security.

Best predictors of union voting

A second general reason for joining unions is a belief that there are no other options for either gaining more influence at the workplace or finding employment elsewhere. In general, to the extent that management has mechanisms for employees to voice their concerns about HRM policy, there is less tendency on the part of workers to favor unionization. A formal grievance procedure as discussed in Chapter 12, for example, which has been used successfully by employees, can deter union activity since workers perceive that there are alternatives to unions as an approach to correcting problems at work. Workers are much more likely to join a union if they perceive that they have little or no influence on important matters at work. But U.S. workers today in general do feel they have influence at work.

Design to have more influence

Figure 13-2   **Determinants of Propensity to Join Unions**

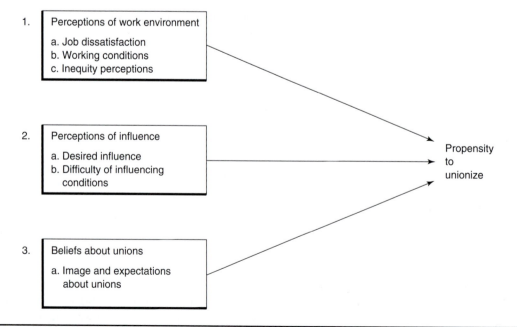

Source: T. Kochan, *Collective Bargaining and Industrial Relations*, Homewood, IL: Richard D. Irwin, 1980, p. 144. Copyright © The McGraw-Hill Companies.

Progressive human resource policies and increased government protection are often cited as the major reasons for the decline in employee demand for union representation.

The third critical reason for joining unions is that employees believe that unions can actually improve conditions and, in particular, can have an impact at their own workplace. In general, this belief is driven by the extent to which unions represent workers in any particular industry or occupation. A worker who perceives that unions are more likely to help solve problems in the workplace is more likely to vote for unionization.

Belief that unions can foster change

Companies attempt to influence employees' beliefs about unions. Campaign tactics by management include written communications, meetings, threats, and actions against union supporters. These can negatively affect workers' votes for unionization. Companies often use consultants who specialize in refuting the claims of union organizers and presenting horrendous scenarios if the union should prevail. It is estimated that there are over 1,000 such firms and an additional 1,500 private consultants in the union prevention or "busting" business (check out www.tbqlabor.com for one example of such a firm). Union tactics, although less often examined, also influence workers' willingness to join unions. One study found that unions that conducted a rank-and-file organizing strategy were more likely to win certification.[8] Such a strategy involves reliance on a slow underground person-to-person campaign that involves using employees themselves to organize the campaign.

Employer resistance

While most Americans believe unions can improve things at work, many are generally hostile to unions. They think unions protect ineffective workers, abuse their power through strikes, are corrupt, and impede productivity improvement programs. One study found that knowing an employee's general opinion about unions in these areas was a strong predictor of how an employee would vote for union representation.[9] Most business students aspire to management positions. There is no question that management prefers a nonunion environment. The focus of unions on the so-called bread-and-butter issues such as wages, benefits, and job security is viewed by management as constraining.

Management strongly prefers a non-union environment

THE LEGAL ENVIRONMENT OF LABOR RELATIONS

Figure 13-3 highlights the two major federal laws affecting labor relations in the United States. The **National Labor Relations Act,** also known as the Wagner Act, was designed to protect private-sector workers' rights to organize and join unions. The **Taft-Hartley Act** was designed to place limits on some of the powers of unions. In addition, state laws can also play a role in union organizing efforts. For example, states can pass **"right-to-work"** laws, which allow workers to work in an establishment under a collective bargaining agreement without having to join a union. Since passage of the NLRA, 41 states have passed similar legislation governing employees of state and local government. Executive order 10988 extended similar rights to federal employees in 1962.

National Labor Relations Act (NLRA)

The **National Labor Relations Act (NLRA)**, also known as the **Wagner Act,** became law during the great depression of 1935. The NLRA formally recognized private-sector workers' rights to organize and bargain collectively with representatives of their own choosing. To enforce that right, the NLRA described what constituted unfair labor practices by employers. Prohibited activities included forbidding employers from (1) interfering with employee representation and collective bargaining rights; (2) dominating or interfering with the affairs of unions; (3) discriminating in regard to hiring, retention, or any employment condition against workers who engage in union activity or who file unfair labor practice charges; and (4) not bargaining in good faith with employee representatives. Further, the NLRA established the **National Labor Relations Board** (NLRB) to enforce the Wagner Act and to conduct representation elections. Essentially, the goal of the NLRB is to regulate the *processes* of organizing and collective bargaining, not necessarily the *outcomes*. As an independent federal agency (see www.nlrb. gov), the two primary functions of the NLRB are (1) to prevent and correct unfair labor practices and (2) to administer certification and decertification elections to determine whether workers choose to be represented.

Two functions of the NLRB

431

Figure 13-3   **Major Implications of NLRA and Taft-Hartley Act**

NLRA (Private-sector employees only)

MANAGEMENT CANNOT:

Interfere with, restrain, or coerce employees in the exercise of their rights to organize, bargain collectively, and engage in other activities for their mutual aid or protection (e.g., threaten employees with the loss of a job if they vote for the union).

Dominate or interfere with the formation or administration of any labor organization or contribute financial or other support to it.

Encourage or discourage membership in any labor organization by discrimination with regard to hiring or tenure or conditions of employment, subject to an exception for valid union-security agreements. Discharge or otherwise discriminate against an employee because he or she has filed charges or given testimony under the Wagner Act.

Refuse to bargain collectively with representatives of the employees; that is, bargain in good faith.

41 States have similar legislation governing government employees

Executive order 10988 extended similar rights to federal employees

Taft-Hartley

UNIONS CANNOT:

Restrain or coerce employees in the exercise of their right to join or not join a union.

Restrain or coerce an employer in the selection of his or her bargaining or grievance representative.

Cause or attempt to cause an employer to discriminate against an employee due to membership or nonmembership in a union, subject to an exception for valid union-shop agreements.

Refuse to bargain collectively (in good faith) with an employer if the union has been designated as a bargaining agent by a majority of the employees.

Induce or encourage employees to stop work in order to force an employer or self-employed person to join a union or to force an employer or other person to stop doing business with any other person (secondary boycott).

Induce or encourage employees to stop work in order to force an employer to recognize and bargain with the union where another union has been certified as a bargaining agent (strike against a certification).

Induce or encourage employees to stop work in order to force an employer to assign particular work to members of the union instead of to members of another union (jurisdictional strike).

Charge an excessive or discriminatory membership fee as a condition to becoming a member of the union.

Cause or attempt to cause an employer to pay for services that are not performed or not to be performed (featherbedding).

Source: Adapted with permission from J. J. Kenny and L. G. Kahn, *Primer of Labor Relations*, Washington, DC: Bureau of National Affairs, 1989, pp. 1–3. Reprinted with permission from BNA Books.

Unfair labor practices (ULP)

NLRB rules on appeals

NLRB decisions subject to review by U.S. Court of Appeals

Recent NLRB rulings

Chamber of Commerce v. Brown

When an **unfair labor practice (ULP)** charge is filed, a field office conducts an investigation to determine whether there is reasonable cause to believe the NLRA was violated. If the Regional Director determines that the charge lacks merit, it is dismissed. A dismissal may be appealed to the General Counsel's office of the NLRB. If the Regional Director finds reasonable cause to believe a violation of the law has been committed, that office of the NLRB seeks a voluntary settlement to remedy the alleged violations. If the settlement efforts fail, a formal complaint is issued and the case goes to a hearing before an NLRB judge. The judge issues a written decision that may be appealed to the five-member NLR Board in Washington for a final agency determination. The Board's decision is subject to review in a U.S. Court of Appeals.

About 30,000 ULPs are filed each year, and about one-third are found to have merit. Over 90 percent are settled. The NLRA also empowers the NLRB to petition a federal district court for an injunction to temporarily prevent unfair labor practices by employers or unions and to restore the status quo, pending the full review of the case by the Board. The NLRA also *requires* the Board to seek a temporary federal court injunction against certain forms of union misconduct, principally involving "secondary boycotts" and certain forms of picketing.

Some academic experts maintain that many of the most recent NLRB rulings are contrary to the goals of the NLRA. For example, the NLRB overturned a Clinton-era ruling that gave nonunion employees the right to have a colleague accompany them to an investigative or disciplinary ruling involving a colleague (known as the **Weingarten rule**). The NLRB reversed a 1990s ruling granting graduate students the right to unionize. The NLRB also ruled that a company claiming "financial distress" did not have to share financial information with the union during contract negotiations and that unions did not have the right to use company e-mail for union organizing.

There is no question that the NLRA has been interpreted at least to some extent based on the political leanings of the decision makers, either NLRB members or judges. A classic example may be the 2008 Supreme Court ruling in *Chamber of Commerce v. Brown*. The democratic-leaning California legislature passed a pro-union law prohibiting companies receiving more than $10,000 of state funds from using those funds to "assist, promote or deter union organizing." The U.S. Supreme Court found the California law to be in violation of the NLRA and rejected the law. It is possible that a future pro-union piece of federal legislature could amend the NLRA to make such state laws in compliance.

President Obama supports a major piece of labor legislation that could have a big impact on union organizing. Unions strongly support an amendment to the NLRA called **the Employee Free Choice Act (EFCA),** which has three important provisions: (1) The EFCA would allow certification of a union as the bargaining representative of a unit of employees if the NLRB found that a majority of those employees have signed authorization cards designating the union as its bargaining representative. A company has the legal ability to allow its workers to have union representation (without going through the NLRB) if a majority of potential members support unionization. The EFCA would make this recognition mandatory, taking away a company's ability to force a majority of potential members to go through the NLRB election process. (2) The EFCA would declare that if an employer and a union are engaged in bargaining for their first contract and are unable to reach an agreement within 90 days, either party may refer the dispute to the **Federal Mediation and Conciliation Service (FMCS)** for mediation. If the FMCS was then unable to bring the parties to agreement after 30 days of mediation, the dispute would be referred to arbitration, and the results of the arbitration would be binding on the parties for two years. (3) Violations of the National Labor Relations Act would now face civil fines of up to $20,000 per violation against employers found to have willfully or repeatedly violated employees' rights during an organizing campaign or first-contract drive, and the amount an employer is required to pay when an employee is discharged or discriminated against during an organizing campaign or first-contract drive would increase to "three times back pay." The EFCA, with perhaps some changes from the description above, may already be the law of the land as you read this.

The Employee Free Choice Act–proposed legislation

The Taft-Hartley Act

Limited power of unions

The Taft-Hartley Act of 1947, an amendment to the NLRA, was designed to limit the power of unions by regulating labor activities allowed under the NLRA. Labor called this amendment to the NLRA the "slave labor bill." Taft-Hartley amended the NLRA by describing what constituted unfair labor practices by unions and (1) restricted use of the strike, including granting the president of the United States the power to issue an injunction against a strike; (2) restricted unions from interfering with workers' right to organize; and (3) prohibited union discrimination against workers who did not want to participate in union activities, including strikes.

22 states have right-to-work laws

The Taft-Hartley Act provided states with the option of enacting right-to-work legislation. **Right-to-work** laws declare that union security agreements that require membership as a condition of employment are illegal. As of 2009, 22 states have enacted right-to-work laws.[10] To aid in the peaceful settlement of contractual disputes, the Federal Mediation and Conciliation Service (FMCS) was established and provided emergency dispute provisions for the settlement of strikes affecting national health and safety (see www.fmcs.gov). Thus, the Taft-Hartley Act further restricted union activity. One purpose of the FMCS is to provide trained representatives to assist in labor negotiations (see www.fmcs.gov).

Other Important Labor Laws

The Landrum-Griffin Act

A "bill-of-rights" for union members

In the late 1950s, the U.S. Senate held hearings investigating and exposing union corruption that ultimately resulted in the 1959 Landrum-Griffin Act. Designed to protect workers from their unions, Landrum-Griffin, also an amendment to the NLRA, provided for the employee "bill of rights," union filing of annual financial statements with the Department of Labor, and the requirement that unions hold national and local officer elections every five years and three years, respectively. The main purpose of Landrum-Griffin was to allow for the monitoring of the internal activity of unions. Union officials were now accountable for union spending, union elections, and other activities.

The Railway Labor Act of 1926

The Railway Labor Act was jointly crafted by both labor and management in the railroad industry. Airline workers became covered in 1935. The focus of the law is upon avoiding prolonged strikes whenever possible. In recent years, negotiations in the airline industry have been quite protracted, spanning over several years. On the other hand, strikes have been averted for the most part. The President does have the right to intervene to preclude a strike.

The Civil Service Reform Act (CSRA) of 1978

Prohibits strikes by federal employees

While similar to the NLRA in its provisions but applicable only to federal employees, the CSRA prohibits wage negotiations (they're set by Congress) and strikes. The CSRA also established the Federal Labor Relations Authority (FLRA) as an independent agency within the executive branch of the government. The FLRA has authority similar to the NLRB. (See www.flra.gov.) The FLRA regulates the conduct of collection bargaining related to the federal government.

HOW DO WORKERS FORM UNIONS?

The process of organizing workers can be lengthy although the proposed **EFCA** could expedite this process. Typically, and following the NLRA, the steps are as follows:

1. Either union membership is solicited by the employees who contact a union or a union might conduct an organizing drive.
2. At least 30 percent of employees must sign **authorization cards** that stipulate that a particular union should be their representative in negotiating with the employer (see Figure 13-4 for an example).
3. The NLRB is petitioned to conduct an election.
4. Assuming the authorization cards are in order, the NLRB sets a date for the election.
5. A secret ballot representative certification (RC) election is held, which requires that a majority of eligible voting workers accept the union.

NLRB ruling in Oakwood Healthcare

The process of gathering authorizing cards and the eligibility of those who sign them can be challenged (and often is). For example, the NLRB made a controversial ruling in *Oakwood Healthcare* that "charge" nurses are "supervisors" based on their interpretation that employers can label workers as supervisors if these workers assign another employee

**Figure 13-4
Sample Union
Authorization Card**

Date . . . . 20 . . . .

STRICTLY CONFIDENTIAL

Office & Professional Employees International Union, Local 153, AFL-CIO
265 West 14th Street, New York, NY 10011

I hereby authorize Office & Professional Employees International Union, Local 153, AFL-CIO, to represent me and to petition the National Labor Relations Board to conduct a secret ballot election among the staff.

Name . . . . Tel. No. . . . .
(Please print)

Address . . . .
(Zip Code)

Present Employer . . . .

Present Employer's Address . . . .

Position . . . . Dept. . . . .

Signature . . . .

CONFIDENTIAL

Source: Office & Professional Employees Union, New York, NY.

to another location to work at a certain time or to perform a significant task. These supervisors are thus not eligible to be represented by a union of registered nurses under NLRA. The ruling will probably be challenged all the way to the Supreme Court.

Goal of NLRB is an uncoerced vote

The goal of the NLRB is to maintain an environment in which workers can make an uncoerced decision regarding the certification election. Figure 13-5 presents an example of an NLRB election notice.

Figure 13-5   NLRB Election Notice

NOTICE TO EMPLOYEES
FROM THE
National Labor Relations Board

A PETITION has been filed with this Federal agency seeking an election to determine whether certain employees want to be represented by a union.

The case is being investigated and NO DETERMINATION HAS BEEN MADE AT THIS TIME by the National Labor Relations Board. IF an election is held Notices of Election will be posted giving complete details for voting.

It was suggested that your employer post this notice so the National Labor Relations Board could inform you of your basic rights under the National Labor Relations Act.

YOU HAVE THE RIGHT under Federal Law

- To self-organization
- To form, join, or assist labor organizations
- To bargain collectively through representatives of your own choosing
- To act together for the purposes of collective bargaining or other mutual aid or protection
- To refuse to do any or all of these things unless the union and employer, in a state where such agreements are permitted, enter into a lawful union-security agreement requiring employees to pay periodic dues and initiation fees. Nonmembers who inform the union that they object to the use of their payments for nonrepresentational purposes may be required to pay only their share of the union's costs of representational activities (such as collective bargaining, contract administration, and grievance adjustments).

It is possible that some of you will be voting in an employee representation election as a result of the request for an election having been filed. While NO DETERMINATION HAS BEEN MADE AT THIS TIME, in the event an election is held, the NATIONAL LABOR RELATIONS BOARD wants all eligible voters to be familiar with their rights under the law IF it holds an election.

The Board applies rules that are intended to keep its elections fair and honest and that result in a free choice. If agents of either unions or employers act in such a way as to interfere with your right to a free election, the election can be set aside by the Board. Where appropriate the Board provides other remedies, such as reinstatement for employees fired for exercising their rights, including backpay from the party responsible for their discharge.

NOTE:

The following are examples of conduct that interfere with the rights of employees and may result in the setting aside of the election.

- Threatening loss of jobs or benefits by an employer or a union
- Promising or granting promotions, pay raises, or other benefits to influence an employee's vote by a party capable of carrying out such promises
- An employer firing employees to discourage or encourage union activity or a union causing them to be fired to encourage union activity
- Making campaign speeches to assembled groups of employees on company time within the 24-hour period before the election
- Incitement by either an employer or a union of racial or religious prejudice by inflammatory appeals
- Threatening physical force or violence to employees by a union or an employer to influence their votes

Please be assured that IF AN ELECTION IS HELD every effort will be made to protect your right to a free choice under the law. Improper conduct will not be permitted. All parties are expected to cooperate fully with this Agency in maintaining basic principles of a fair election as required by law. The National Labor Relations Board, as an agency of the United States Government, does not endorse any choice in the election.

NATIONAL LABOR RELATIONS BOARD
an agency of the
UNITED STATES GOVERNMENT

THIS IS AN OFFICIAL GOVERNMENT NOTICE AND MUST NOT BE DEFACED BY ANYONE

FORM NLRB-666 (5-90)   ☆U.S. GOVERNMENT PRINTING OFFICE: 1941-312-471751356

Source: National Labor Relations Board.

E-mail for organizing

Many unions now use the Internet to conduct the authorization step (for an example, try walmartworkerslv.com/authorization) although an NLRB ruling allows an employer to bar employees from using company e-mail for organizing efforts. In general, an employer may lawfully maintain a rule banning all nonwork-related solicitations—including messages about unionization—from its computer system as long as it does not enforce the rule in a discriminatory manner.

Many employers do not get very involved in union prevention activities until step 2 because they are often not aware of the union organizing efforts until this step has been reached. Regardless, managers should have a thorough understanding as to what behaviors are lawful and unlawful under the NLRA.

If a majority vote is received for the union, the NLRB certifies the union and the union is then recognized as the exclusive bargaining unit for the workers. The union then enters negotiations with the employer. If a majority do not accept the union, another certification election cannot be held for 12 months. Even after a union is certified negotiations often break down. A high percentage of certified unions never obtain a contract.

Decertification elections

Employers also get involved after a union vote and may work toward a **representation decertification (RD)**, which also is conducted by the NLRB at least 12 months after a certification vote. While the petition for an RD must be made by the rank-and-file workers, management also is allowed, in the rare case of union misconduct, to initiate a decertification drive. Usually, decertification elections are specifically barred when a labor contract is in effect. The number of NLRB elections declined in 2007 to 1,502 and lower than the rate in 2006. Unions won over 60 percent of the votes in 2007. There were 329 decertification elections in 2007. Unions prevailed in 37 percent of them.

Traditionally, unions organize workers through campaigns. Bottom-up campaigns begin when workers become dissatisfied with some aspect of their work and contact a union to request organization. Top-down campaigns are initiated by the union as part of a strategy to increase their representation in the area or industry. In order to gain worker support unions employ a variety of tactics, including worker-to-worker campaigns, increasing internal pressure tactics, and community involvement.[11] Their goal is to help build a sense of injustice and a belief that the union can effectively remedy the wrong. As a part of their organizing strategy, union organizers often use **"salting"** where union sympathizers gain employment in nonunion firms for the purpose of organizing. While employers have argued that "salts" obtained employment under false pretenses, the Supreme Court held in **Town & Country Electric v. NLRB** that as long as the "salts" did the work for which they were hired, employers violated the NLRA if they took actiond against them.[12]

Town & Country Electric v. NLRB allows "salts"

Management typically counters the union campaigns with a campaign of their own. They can communicate with the workers citing the harmful effects of unions and hold "captive audience meetings" where workers must listen to management discuss their reasons for not wanting a union. In regulating the campaign process, the goal of the NLRB is to promote an environment in which workers feel free to vote their conscience whether or not it is for or against unions. By law, workers should not be subject to threats or intimidation from either the union or management. Management violations include promising wages or firing workers for union activity. In recent years, management has often employed consultants who specialize in refuting the claims of union organizers as well as more aggressive management tactics. Often the result is management violating the NLRA and engaging in such tactics as illegally firing workers for union activity. Despite the illegality of these actions, there is evidence that many companies engage in these activities as the penalties for these actions are weak.[13]

Weak penalties for violating NLRA

While the NLRB-supervised route is still the typical method of organizing, it is not the only way. Many unions feel that they do not have a level "playing field" in union organizing drives and the regulation of election conduct. Thus, they will avoid elections where possible and may have already succeeded in passing the EFCA that would preclude elections. Some unions had been successful at obtaining what are known as **neutrality agreements** from management. These agreements often contain provisions in which management agrees to recognize the union if a majority of the workers sign authorization cards and they

Neutrality agreements

waive their rights to wage a countercampaign. Management will typically agree to a neutrality clause when the union and management have a preexisting relationship such as a collective bargaining agreement at another location.

Alternative approach to typical election model

An alternative and growing trend in the U.S. is non-NLRB organizing or a "corporate" or "pressure" campaign. By rejecting the typical election model, unions have more freedom to take advantage of particular issues related to the targeted company. Particularly effective at non-NLRB organizing is the 1.5 million member **Service Employees International Union** (SEIU) in recently organizing janitors, health care and hotel workers, and immigrant workers. While the goal is the same as an NLRB-supervised effort, that is, to secure a collective bargaining agreement but without the election, the strategies vary from civil disobedience to boycotts to news coverage of employer indiscretions. Some recent examples involve farm workers where adverse publicity has been directed at Taco Bell, McDonald's, and Burger King to pressure growers to increase the pay of tomato pickers. Some unions have established new programs for developing and implementing strike-alternative, pressure-campaign strategies and tactics.

Non-NLRB organizing more successful

A 2008 study found that the non-NLRB election approach to organizing was more successful for the union than the traditional approach. From 1990 to 2001, unions were more likely to win a non-NLRB organizing drive than an NLRB-supervised election and despite a 9:1 ratio of NLRB to non-NLRB organizing, the difference in the number of workers actually organized each approach was small.[14]

THE EFFECTS OF UNIONS

Workers join unions to improve their wages, working conditions, and job security. This section presents opinions regarding whether or not unions actually do provide these improvements and what these effects mean for firm performance. Estimates of union and nonunion wage differentials range from 3 percent (utilities) to 52 percent (construction). On average, the differential in pay was between 15 and 20 percent in 2008 while the "fringe benefit" (e.g., health care, pensions) differential is higher.[15] Unions also have a positive fringe benefit effect. In general, those who are usually paid the least tend to benefit the most from unionization. Studies show that younger workers, nonwhites, people living in the South and the West, and blue-collar workers seem to gain the most from unionization. Interestingly, little apparent difference exists between the wage gains from unionization for males and females. Research on public-sector unions shows a 24 percent pay differential for public-sector employees represented by unions versus public-sector employees not represented. In 2007, full-time wage and salary union workers had median weekly earnings of $863, compared with a median of $663 for workers not represented by unions.[16]

Pay differential between 15 and 20 percent in 2008

Fringe benefit differential even higher

Those paid the least benefit the most from unions

Variations in union wage effects across industries partially occur due to the union's ability to take "wages out of competition." Wages can be taken out of competition in several ways. First, labor demand may be relatively insensitive to wage changes (inelastic). That is, consumers will absorb the increased labor costs without offsetting employment effects. The extent of union organization in a particular market also can affect union power. More unionized markets have greater union/nonunion wage differentials because of less nonunion wage competition. The extent of bargaining coverage further augments this effect. This coverage can take several forms. For example, one union may bargain for the entire market—so that all union firms in the industry have virtually identical contracts. In the auto industry, the UAW bargains with one of the big automakers and then uses this contract as a pattern for remaining settlements. This strategy has become less effective as nonunionized automakers have gained market share. A union negotiating simultaneously with numerous employers, such as in steel and coal, provides another example of extensive industry coverage. A union that bargains at the plant level has much less power than those that negotiate on a broader basis.

Union advocates maintain that the **"collective voice"** of unions reduces worker quit rates, thereby leading to retention of experienced workers, lowering a firm's training costs, and raising its productivity. Another side benefit is that management is forced to become more efficient when faced with the necessity of providing higher wages to unionized employees.

Why does management resist unions?

This suggests that unions may actually have positive effects on management. If so, why does management strenuously resist unions? Are they behaving rationally? Or do they resist unions only because unions threaten their decision-making autonomy? Two theories exist regarding the unions' effects upon firms' productivity. On one hand, productivity is predicted to decrease in unionized firms because unions create resource misallocation and demand restrictive work rules. In contrast, the collective voice view predicts that productivity gains may occur because the union wage effect causes firms to manage better, employ better-quality labor, substitute capital for labor, and reduce voluntary turnover, leading to the development of a more experienced and better-trained labor force.

Evidence mixed on productivity-zero to mildly negative effects

The evidence is mixed regarding the effects of unions on organizational productivity. Unions tend to have a negative effect on productivity when there is relatively greater conflict between the union and management. Florida State professor Jack Fiorito summed up the confusing evidence on unions and productivity this way: "There is indeed considerable variation by industry; overall union productivity effects are probably in the zero to mildly negative range."[17] Positive productivity effects generally tend to be found in competitive industries with higher union wage effects (i.e., where firm survival apparently depends upon offsetting the higher wage costs with increased productivity).[18] Research indicates that when unions and management are working for a **"bigger pie"** as well as fighting over their relative share, the result is higher productivity. Under conditions of poor labor–management relations, where the focus is on taking a bigger share of the same size pie, the result is usually lower productivity.

Unionization affects profits

What of the argument that unions raise wages to noncompetitive levels and have thus seriously affected the ability of some U.S. industries to compete? One surprising study of 134 industries concluded that "heavily unionized industries are not found to have lost any more to imports nor gained any more in exports than comparable U.S. industries . . . industrial concentration appears to be a significant disadvantage."[19] This means that U.S. industries facing a more globally competitive environment after less domestic competition tended to have more difficulty competing *regardless of union status.*

Studies show that unionization negatively affects accounting profits and shareholder wealth. For example, shareholder wealth decreases during union organizing campaigns and strikes and increases during concession bargaining. Unions do not seem to change the overall firm value, but they do redistribute the firm's economic profits from the stockholders to the workers. Research on **"high-performance work systems"** establishes a relationship between the absence of labor unions and corporate financial performance.[20]

Unions and HPWS characterstics

Unions can also influence firms through unilateral management responses (in anticipation of union pressure) and can influence nonunion firms through spillover and threat effects (i.e., adoption of "unionlike" practices through imitation or to prevent unionization). The recent improvements in the compensation and benefits of Wal-Mart employees are probably one example of these **"spillover" effects.** However, such effects could erode in the future due to competitive pressures and declining unionization.

Spillover effects

Unions and Quality of Worklife Issues

As discussed in Chapter 12, quality of worklife (QWL) issues came to the forefront in the 1980s and play an important role in the labor–management relationship. QWL programs such as job redesign efforts, upward communication, team-based work configurations, and quality circles (QCs) have elicited a variety of union responses. Overt hostility and resistance characterize some unions' reactions to QWL programs. A significant faction of the UAW membership at the Saturn plant, for example, opposed the negotiated worker involvement programs. These members fear that management intends to use these programs to circumvent the union and the collective bargaining relationship. Other members cautiously indicate that they prefer the collective bargaining process to QWL programs but will support QWL programs if there is no attempt to bust the union or interfere with the collective bargaining process.

The labor–management partnership between GM's Saturn Corporation and the United Auto Workers (UAW) was an innovative approach to labor relations. This partnership includes the union as a partner in decisions regarding the product itself, technology, suppliers, business planning, training, quality control systems, job design, and manufacturing systems. Local management and union leadership have established a system of co-management in which bargaining unit members occupy 50 percent of the operations management positions. The main goal of the partnership was to improve and sustain the quality of Saturn vehicles. The partnership seems to have worked. According to J.D. Power and Associates, Saturn had led domestic car lines in consumer ratings based on vehicle quality.[21]

Union support important for QWL success

Many have argued that union support remains critical for successful implementation of QWL programs. One study cited management neglect in inviting union participation early enough, or not at all, as a contributing factor to many failures of QWL programs.[22] Generally, in union settings, management is seen as more careful in evaluating the decision to implement a QWL program than in firms where a union is not present. One study found that the presence of "high-involvement" management practices was rare in union settings in the United States compared German union settings.[23]

Union leaders assert that workers have everything to gain by demanding that employees work to achieve the highest possible product and service quality. This means that QWL programs are important as well as training, up-to-date equipment, and quality materials and resources. These will enable employees to achieve first-rate quality in goods and services.[24]

Mixed results on QWL programs in union settings

There is limited research and mixed results on the effects of QWL efforts in union settings. Two studies found that QWL programs did not have any effect upon the firm's economic performance.[25] However, more recent research has found that unionized firms had more gains from employee participation than did nonunion firms.[26] Other research has shown that QWL programs can improve the firm's industrial relations.[27] One study found that participants in employee involvement programs felt that these programs were better at resolving differences than collective bargaining.[28]

Firms must be cautious in their implementation of **nonunion work teams** because of legal concerns regarding violations of the NLRA prohibition regarding company unions. The NLRA states that it is unlawful for an employer "to dominate or interfere with the formation or administration of any labor organization or contribute financial or other support to it." In the 1994 ***Electromation v. NLRB*** case, the U.S. Court of Appeals upheld the NLRB's ruling that management committees addressing employee dissatisfaction with absenteeism and attendance bonuses represented illegal employer domination.[29] However, the facts of this case suggest that management had established these committees to avoid unionization.

Electromation v. NLRB

Republicans proposed but failed to pass the **Teamwork for Employees and Managers or (TEAM) Act** to make it easier for workers and management to arrange various types of worker involvement or employee "voice" organizations. In general, the NLRB and the courts have restricted the use of alternative "voice" such as quality circles unless employer control is ceded to these self-governing bodies.[30]

Union Effects on Worker Satisfaction

Union workers report more dissatisfaction with supervision and job content than do non-union workers. Only pay provides more union satisfaction.[31] This finding may reflect unions encouraging members to voice their dissatisfaction rather than to quit. Voluntary turnover rates are substantially lower under unions. Alternatively, union workers may feel compelled to stay because of the **"golden handcuffs"** of better wages, health insurance, and working conditions. They may feel that they cannot afford to quit when they are dissatisfied. The most recent research indicates that union membership has no effect on either general job satisfaction or intention to quit.[32]

"Golden handcuffs"

Unions and HRM

There can be no question that with a union HRM decisions are more constrained. In unionized organizations, the union itself gives employees a voice in the development of work rules. Termination is generally for cause only. Total compensation is almost always higher. Staffing and performance management activities are often subject to collective bargaining. Management must justify the reason for the termination or discipline of union workers.

Termination for cause only

COLLECTIVE BARGAINING*

Collective bargaining occurs when representatives of a labor union meet with management representatives to determine employees' wages and benefits, to create or revise work rules, and to resolve disputes or violations of the labor contract. For almost 16 million workers, collective bargaining represents the primary process for determining their wages, benefits, and working conditions. Despite the decline in unions and their membership in recent years, it is unlikely that either unions or collective bargaining will ever disappear. In fact, there is recent evidence that union activity is surging in some occupations (e.g., nursing) and developing in others (physicians).

Labor relations tied to HR planning

Organizations and unions need to maintain knowledge of bargaining strategies and guidelines in order to successfully represent their respective interests. Knowledge of labor relations and collective bargaining is important for HRM specialists and general managers. In fact, it is difficult to separate labor relations as a human resource (HR) function from the many other HR functions. For example, labor relations is closely tied to HR planning since the labor contract generally stipulates policies and procedures related to promotions, transfers, job security, and layoffs. The area of HR where a knowledge of collective bargaining is probably most critical is compensation and benefits, since almost all aspects of wages and benefits are subject to negotiation.

Collective bargaining should be viewed by both the union and management as a two-way street. This means that the basic interests of management must be protected as well as the rights of employees. Both sides have a responsibility to each other. For example, unions should not expect management to concede on issues that ultimately would impair the company's ability to stay in business. Likewise, management must recognize the rights of employees to form unions to argue for improved wages and working conditions.

The Labor Contract

A **labor contract** is a formal agreement between a union and management that specifies the conditions of employment and the union–management relationship over a mutually agreed upon period of time (typically two to three years, but up to five years). The labor contract specifies what the two parties have agreed upon regarding issues such as wages, benefits, and working conditions. The process involved in reaching this agreement is a complex and difficult job requiring a willingness from both sides to reconcile their differences and compromise their interests. This process is also bound to certain "good-faith" guidelines that must be upheld by both parties.

Taft-Hartley Act

The **Taft-Hartley Act** of 1947 (section 8d) states: "to bargain collectively is [to recognize] . . . the mutual obligation of the employer and representative of the employees to meet at reasonable times and confer in good faith with respect to wages, hours, and other terms and conditions of employment, . . . or the negotiation of an agreement, or any question arising thereunder, and the execution of a written contract incorporating any agreement reached if requested by either party, . . . such obligation does not compel either party to agree to a proposal or require the making of a concession." Thus, the law requires that the employer negotiate with the union once the union has been recognized as the employees' representative. Good-faith bargaining is characterized by the following events:

- Meetings for purposes of negotiating the contract are scheduled and conducted with the union at reasonable times and places.
- Realistic proposals are submitted.
- Reasonable counterproposals are offered.
- Each party signs the agreement once it has been completed.

Good-faith bargaining

Good-faith bargaining does not mean that either party is required to agree to a final proposal or to make concessions.

* This section was written by Roger L. Cole and Joseph G. Clark, Jr.

The National Labor Relations Board further defines the **"duty to bargain"** as covering bargaining on all matters concerning rates of pay, wages, hours of employment, and other conditions of employment. **"Mandatory"** issues for bargaining include wages, benefits, hours of work, incentive pay, overtime, seniority, safety, layoff and recall procedures, grievance procedures, and job security. **"Permissive"** or "nonmandatory" issues have no direct relationship to wages, hours, or working conditions. These might include changes in benefits for retired employees, performance bonds for unions or management, and union input into prices of the firm's products. **Permissive** issues can be introduced into the discussion by either party; however, neither party is obligated to discuss them or include them in the labor contract.

Issues in Collective Bargaining

The major issues discussed in collective bargaining fall under the following four categories:

1. **Wage-related issues.** These include such topics as how basic wage rates are determined, cost-of-living adjustments (COLAs), wage differentials, overtime rates, wage adjustments, and two-tier wage systems.
2. **Supplementary economic benefits.** These include such issues as pension plans, paid vacations, paid holidays, health insurance plans, dismissal pay, reporting pay, and supplementary unemployment benefits (SUB).
3. **Institutional issues.** These consist of the rights and duties of employers, employees, and unions, including union security (i.e., union membership as a condition of employment), check-off procedures (i.e., when the employer collects dues by deduction from employees' paychecks), employee stock ownership plans (ESOPs), and quality-of-worklife (QWL) programs.
4. **Administrative issues.** These include such issues as seniority, employee discipline and discharge procedures, employee health and safety, technological changes, work rules, job security, and training.

While the last two categories contain important issues, the wage and benefit issues are the ones that receive the greatest amount of attention at the bargaining table. In recent years, however, issues of job security have become increasingly important as bargaining items.[33] In addition, the unions have adapted to a variety of workplace changes and have played an important role in defining public policies. For example, they have been active in negotiating family-friendly contract provisions such as child care, elder care, domestic partnership benefits, and paternity leaves and in promoting health and safety protections for their members.[34]

Types of Bargaining

Distributive is zero-sum negotiation

Bargaining between labor and management can take several different forms. Three of the most common are distributive, integrative, and concessionary bargaining. *Distributive* bargaining is the most common type of bargaining and involves zero-sum negotiation. In other words, one side wins and the other side loses. Union employees may try to convince management that they will strike if they don't get the wages or working conditions they desire. Management, in turn, may be willing to try to ride the strike out, especially if they have cross-trained other workers or have external replacements to fill in for those on strike. In distributive bargaining, unions and management have initial offers or demands, target points (e.g., desired wage level), resistance points (unacceptable wage level), and settlement ranges (acceptable wage level).

Integrative bargaining is a win-win approach

Integrative bargaining is similar to problem-solving sessions in which both sides are trying to reach a mutually beneficial alternative or a win-win solution. Both the employers and the union try to resolve the conflict to the benefit of both parties. One example might consist of providing retraining opportunities to employees to avoid having to lay off workers. Plant safety and incentive pay systems are other programs that involve collaborative efforts between management and employees. Another name for this type of bargaining has been

Interest-based bargaining

"interest-based bargaining." The objective is for both parties to find the common ground between them, to build relationships, and to eliminate the adversarial elements of traditional bargaining. This was used when a public electric and water utility, Salt River Project, located in Phoenix, Arizona, was experiencing tension with the International Brotherhood of Electrical Workers (IBEW) Local 266. To resolve an impasse in communications, they tried using a new approach, interest-based bargaining. Both sides shared information about their interests and concerns and they created a list of possible solutions to best meet everyone's needs.

The early 21st century has seen an increased sensitivity on the part of unions and employers to the "shrinking or disappearing pie" phenomenon with more and more international competition. This apparently led to greater interest in "integrative bargaining" approaches and a decreasing rate of strike activity. Among these approaches is "mutual gains bargaining." "While some companies have openly challenged the bargaining role of unions and unilaterally introduced changed work practices, others have sought to move toward *'mutual gains bargaining.'* "[35] Some research supports the notion that collective bargaining can achieve performance advantages through cooperative programs compared to both nonintegrative bargaining approaches but also compared to nonunion firms, including those with high employee involvement.[36]

Mutual gains bargaining

Concessionary bargaining involves a union's giving back to management some of what it has gained in previous bargaining. Why would labor be willing to give back what it worked so hard to obtain? Usually such a move is prompted by labor leaders who recognize the need to assist employers in reducing operating costs in order to prevent layoffs, plant closings, or even bankrupcy. Thus, it is often economic adversity that motivates concessionary bargaining.[37] A good example is the agreement between GM and the International Union of Electric Workers that granted GM around-the-clock operations, wage and benefit concessions for new hires, and a two-week mass vacation. The concessions were made to save over 3,000 jobs at a plant in Ohio. In some cases, despite a financial crisis, the union may not be willing to concede. This may be because the union does not view management's arguments as credible. Thus, the degree of trust between management and the union may influence the extent to which concessionary bargaining occurs. The UAW and the "Big Three" American auto companies were negotiated major concessions to their 2007 contracts in an effort to help save the suffering and near bankrupt U.S. automakers.

Concessions

Two-tiered pay structures

What kinds of concessions are sought by employers? Often they relate to wages and benefits (e.g., health insurance and pensions), for example, putting a cap on increases in compensation or installing a two-tiered pay structure. For example, in return for wage concessions, the union may receive a gain sharing plan that links compensation with performance data, or some form of profit-sharing or stock ownership. Other demands made by unions in return for concessions include restrictions on work rules, transfers of work, subcontracting, and plant closures; getting advance notice of shutdowns and severance pay; and transfer rights for displaced employees.

Conducting Labor Contract Negotiations

Preparing for Negotiations

Because of the complexity of the issues and the broad range of topics discussed during negotiating sessions, a substantial amount of preparation time is required. To prepare for negotiations, one must have a planning strategy. Negotiating teams typically begin data gathering for the next negotiation session immediately after a contract is signed. Preparation includes reviewing and diagnosing the mistakes and weaknesses from previous negotiations and gathering information on recent contract settlements in the local area and industrywide (e.g., comparative industry and occupational wage rates and fringe benefits). Preparation also includes gathering data on economic conditions, studying consumer price indices, determining cost-of-living trends, and looking at projections regarding the short-term and long-term financial outlook. Internal to the firm, data such as minimum and maximum pay by job classification, shift work data, cost and duration of breaks, an analysis of grievances, and overtime data are almost always of interest to both sides. Often unions and large corporations have research departments that collect necessary data for negotiations. Management is likely to come armed with data regarding grievances and arbitration, disciplinary actions, transfers, promotions, layoffs, overtime worked, individual performance measures, and wage payments.

Employers develop written plan

During the preparation phase of contract negotiations, employers develop a written plan covering their bargaining strategy. The plan takes into account what the employer considers the union's goals to be and the degree to which it is willing to concede on various issues. Such a plan is useful to the negotiators because it helps them to identify the relative importance of each issue in the proposal.

Both the union and management send their negotiating teams to the bargaining table. The union's negotiating team generally consists of local union officials, union stewards, and one or more specialists from the national union staff. Management's negotiating team usually consists of one or more production or operations managers, a labor lawyer, a compensation specialist, a benefits specialist, and a chief labor relations specialist, who heads the team.

Meetings in Contract Negotiations

One of the most important objectives of early bargaining meetings is to establish a climate for negotiations, in other words, determining whether the tone of the negotiations is going to be one of mutual trust with "nothing up our sleeves," one of suspicion with a lot of distortion and misrepresentation, or one of hostility with a lot of name calling and accusations. Also, early meetings are used to establish the bargaining authority of each party and determine rules and procedures that will be used throughout the negotiation process. Both parties try to avoid disclosing the relative importance they attach to each proposal so that they will not have to pay a higher price than is necessary to have the proposal accepted. Generally, each side tries to determine how far the other is willing to go in terms of concessions, and the minimum levels each is willing to accept. It is best not to establish a position that is too extreme, or one that is too inflexible. For instance, **"take it or leave it"** proposals are typically ineffective. One of the best examples of a "take it or leave it" philosophy of bargaining was at General Electric from the 1940s to the 1970s. During this period, GE's policy was that management initially brought to the bargaining table its final proposal. The unions obviously viewed this as

General Electric v. NLRB

unethical and illegal (lack of good-faith bargaining). A 1964 NLRB and Appeals Court case supported the unions and found them guilty of bad-faith bargaining based upon their "take-it-or-leave-it" policy combined with other tactics designed to circumvent the union. Thus, GE eventually relinquished this policy.

Successful negotiations are contingent upon each side remaining flexible. It is hoped that the end result will be a "package" representing the maximum and minimum levels acceptable to each of the parties. The bargaining zone, which is illustrated in Figure 13-6, is the area bounded by the limits of what the union and employer are willing to concede. If neither the union nor management is willing to change its demands enough to bring them within the inside boundaries of the bargaining zone, or if neither is willing to extend the limits to accommodate the other's demands, then negotiations reach impasse.

Figure 13-6
Desires, Expectations, and Tolerance Limits That Determine the Bargaining Zone

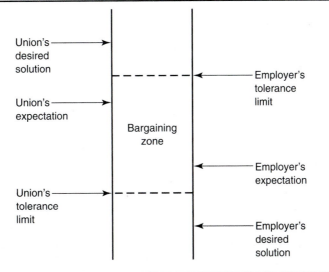

Source: From Stagner/Rosen. *Psychology of Union—Management Relations,* 1E. © 1966 Wadsworth, a part of Cengage Learning, Inc. Reproduced by permission. www.cengage.com/permissions.

The union team is first to present its initial proposals. Usually, the original union proposal demands more than it expects to end up with (i.e., excessive demands in terms of changes in, additions to, and deletions from the previous contract), which will allow leverage for trading off for management concessions. The management negotiating team then states the management case, often presenting unrealistic counterproposals and data supporting the view that union workers are treated well. The early meetings are often characterized by both parties remaining far apart on the issues; however, as negotiations proceed, there is generally movement toward a pattern of agreement. As topics are discussed and considered, mutual concessions are offered, counterproposals are made, and eventually a tentative agreement is reached.

When a tentative agreement is reached, in most cases, the union members vote on the contract. If it is approved, the contract is ratified; if it is voted down, more negotiating takes place. The next step involves the actual drafting of a formal document, attempting to keep it in simple, clear, and concise terms. In fact, however, most contracts are difficult to read and some sections are virtually incomprehensible for the rank and file (e.g., most often sections on seniority and grievance procedures). The last step is the actual signing of the agreement by the representatives of the union and management. The typical labor agreement defines the responsibilities and authority of unions and management and stipulates what management activities are not subject to union authority (e.g., purchasing and hiring).

Resolving Bargaining Deadlocks and Impasse Resolution

If neither the organization nor the union is willing to remain flexible and make concessions, then negotiations reach a deadlock or **impasse** that can eventually result in a strike on the part of the union or a lockout on the part of management. So how can these breakdowns in negotiations be avoided? One way is to delay consideration of the more difficult issues until the latter stages of bargaining and, for the time being, to simply agree to disagree on the tougher decisions. The easier questions can be considered in the beginning, thus giving both sides a feeling of making progress. Another way to avoid breakdowns in negotiations is for each side to be prepared to offer propositions and to accept alternative solutions to some of the more controversial issues.

If the two parties are unable to compromise and resolve a deadlock, then they have the option of calling in a **mediator,** a neutral third party who reviews the dispute between the two parties and attempts to open up communication channels by suggesting compromise solutions and concessions. Mediation is based upon the principle of voluntary acceptance. This means that mediators act as go-betweens between the parties to help clarify the issues but that they have no conclusive power or authority to impose or recommend a solution. In fact, either party may accept or reject the mediator's recommendations. The **Federal Mediation and Conciliation Service (FMCS)** was established by the Taft-Hartley Act. Mediators perform their services for free and mediate an average of about 15,000 labor disagreements per year.[38]

Sometimes government intervention is necessary to resolve deadlocks. This is generally in cases where a work stoppage would threaten the national security or the public welfare. For example, one of the provisions of the Taft-Hartley Act is a national emergency strike provision that gives the president of the United States the power to stop a strike if it imperils national health or safety.

The Union's Economic Power in Collective Bargaining

The basis for the union's power in collective bargaining is economic and generally takes one of three forms: striking the employer, picketing the employer, or boycotting the employer.[39]

Striking the Employer

One tool a labor union can use to motivate an employer to reach an agreement is to call a strike. A **strike** is simply a refusal on the part of employees to perform their jobs. Strikes occur when the union is unable to obtain an offer from management that is acceptable to its members. Strikes are rare these days. From 1981 to 1990, the average annual number of major work stoppages (involving 1,000 or more workers) was 72 while the average was 27 for 1996–2005. According the Bureau of Labor Statistics, there were 21 major work stoppages during 2007, 12 from the private sector and nine involving state or local

21 major work stoppages in 2007

governments. The largest major work stoppage in total days idle was between the Alliance of Motion Picture and Television Producers and the Writers Guild of America East and West, with 10,500 workers accounting for 409,500 lost workdays. The mean length of a work stoppage in 2007 was 10.5 days, down from 26.5 days in 2006. Numerous work stoppages in 2007 were short in duration, with six work stoppages lasting two days or less.[40]

Before a union goes on strike, it must first assess the consequences of a strike and its members' willingness to make the sacrifices and endure the hardships (e.g., lost pay) that are part of striking. Even when the union perceives the strike as necessary, employees may not be willing to strike. Factors such as loyalty to the organization and commitment to the job have been shown to differentiate workers who are willing to strike and those who are not.[41] Another part of this assessment also involves determining whether or not the employer can continue operating by using supervisory and nonstriking employees.

There are a number of risks to the union and its members in striking. For one, replacement employees can vote the union out in an NLRB-conducted decertification election. Also, a strike can result in a loss of union members. The public also may withdraw its support from union members and often does.

The power of the strike to pressure management has been seriously diminished during the past decades. Automation, recent court rulings, and a growing number of unemployed workers willing to serve as replacements have helped management. After Congress passed the Wagner Act in 1935, workers' rights to organize and to strike were guaranteed. However, the 1938 Supreme Court ruling in *NLRB v. Mackay Radio & Telegraph*[42] weakened this right by permitting the permanent replacement of economic strikers by management.[43] The use of replacement workers seriously undermines the economic pressure that strikes once had. Even though this court decision was made in 1938, it was not until the 1980s that the ruling was frequently applied. One example is the 2006 Northwest Airlines strike by its machinists. Northwest had replacement workers ready to go the very first day of the strike action by the Aircraft Mechanics Federal Association. Many workers who went on strike never got their jobs back.[44]

Employers can hire permanent replacement workers

Since President Reagan hired nonunion workers to replace air-traffic controllers in 1981, management's hiring of nonunion members has been a regular and successful strikebreaking weapon. The Reagan and two Bush administrations have fostered a climate that has made strikes risky for unions. Employers are now emboldened to use or threaten a union with permanent striker replacements. As stated in one review, "In many situations, the strike has actually become the strongest weapon in the employer's arsenal. If an employer is intent upon busting a union, the strike becomes an integral part of this effort. Union-busters commonly advise employers to create strike situations as a means of creating a 'union free environment.'"[45]

While the diminished power of the strike certainly reflects a power shift to employers, with more international competition, there are ever more mutual employer-union incentives to reduce conflict and to avoid strikes.

Alternative strategies to the strike

As with organizing efforts, unions have developed alternative strategies to the strike. Some recent examples involve farm workers, where adverse publicity has been directed at Taco Bell, McDonald's, and Burger King to pressure growers to increase the pay of tomato pickers. Some unions have established new programs for developing and implementing strike-alternative, pressure-campaign strategies and tactics. These so-called **corporate campaigns** are designed to exert pressure on employers by using demonstrations, advertisements, stockholder pressure, and other negative publicity for employers that can lead to pressure on employers from consumers.

Strike activity likely to decline

Strike activity will probably continue to decline for the foreseeable future. The main reasons are declining union density, a decrease in the perceived and real effectiveness of strikes as a bargaining weapon, and growing mutual concern about the costs of a protracted strike. Because of this decline in strike effectiveness, unions are now looking at alternatives to the strike, including in-plant strategies and corporate campaigns. In addition, strike cost concerns have encouraged management and labor to explore more cooperative approaches to collective bargaining.

Picketing the Employer

Another union tactic is the **picket.** The picket is used by employees on strike to advertise their dispute with management and to discourage others from entering or leaving the premises. Picketing usually takes place at the plant or company entrances. It can result in severe financial losses for a firm and eventually can lead to a shutdown of the plant if enough employees refuse to cross the picket line. Picket lines can become very emotional at times, especially when employees or replacements attempt to cross them. These people may become the target of verbal insults and, although rarely, even physical violence. Companies hire security firms to protect nonstriking and replacement workers.

Boycotting the Employer

Boycotting encourages refusing to patronize an employer, refusing to buy or use the employer's products or services. As an incentive to employees to honor the boycott, heavy fines may be levied against union members if they are caught patronizing an employer who is the subject of a union boycott. The union hopes that the general public also will join the boycott to put additional pressure on the employer.

Primary and secondary boycotts

Generally, there are two types of boycotts: the primary boycott and the secondary boycott. The primary boycott involves the refusal of the union to allow members to patronize a business where there is a labor dispute. In most cases, these types of boycotts are legal. A secondary boycott refers to the union trying to induce third parties, such as suppliers and customers, to refrain from any business dealings with an employer with whom it has a dispute. This type of boycott is illegal under the **Taft-Hartley Act.**

Secondary boycotts illegal

The Employer's Power in Collective Bargaining

Employers may come to the bargaining table with their own base of power. Foremost is their ability to determine how to use capital within the organization. This enables them to decide whether and when to close down the company, the plant, or certain operations within the plant; to transfer operations to another location; or to subcontract out certain jobs. All these decisions must be made in accordance with the law. This means that management must be sure that its actions are not interpreted by the National Labor Relations Board (NLRB) as attempting to avoid bargaining with the union.

If an employer is confronted with a strike by one or more of its unions, then the firm must weigh the costs associated with enduring the strike against the costs of agreeing to the union's demands. There are a number of considerations the employer must take into account: (1) how the employer's actions will affect future negotiations with the union, (2) how long the firm and the union can endure a strike, and (3) whether business can continue during the strike. Today, employers are more able to endure strikes than they were in the past. This is because the permanent hiring of replacements has greatly weakened the power of the strike. Research finds that the use of replacement workers usually prolongs strikes.[46]

Use of replacement workers prolongs a strike

In general, union members themselves are less willing to support a strike, and without strike unity, the power of the strike is negligible. Also, technological advances have increased some employers' ability to operate during a strike with a substantially reduced staff. Strikes in the public sector are illegal in most states, although walkouts have occurred in some states where strikes are illegal. Federal employees cannot strike pursuant to the 1978 Civil Service Reform Act.

Lockouts

The lockout is another source of power for the employer. A **lockout** is basically a shutting down of operations, usually in anticipation of a strike. The lockout can also be used to fight union slow-downs, damage to property, or violence within the plant. Generally, lockouts are not used very often because they lead to revenue losses for the firm. Many states allow employees to draw unemployment benefits, thus weakening the power of the lockout.

Administration of the Labor Contract

The earlier part of this chapter dealt with the negotiation of the labor contract. In this part of the chapter, we will address the application and interpretation of the labor agreement. Despite the incredible amount of time and effort that goes into negotiating and carefully writing the contract, most are written in such broad, ambiguous terms that a great deal of interpretation is required in order to put the contract to work. Most rank-and-file union workers do not clearly understand the labor contract.

Most of the problems associated with the interpretation or application of the labor contract are resolved at the lower levels of the **grievance** procedure (i.e., between the supervisor and the union steward). Grievance procedures and the time limits associated with them are generally spelled out in the contract for the purpose of reaching quick, fair, and equitable solutions to contract problems. Unresolved grievances proceed progressively to higher and higher levels of management and union representation. If the grievance procedure fails (i.e., the grievance reaches a deadlock or stalemate), most contracts stipulate that the final step will be binding **arbitration.** Arbitration involves bringing in a third party, an impartial outsider mutually agreed upon by both parties, to decide the controversy. In the following section, both the grievance procedure and the arbitration process will be reviewed. Figure 13-7 illustrates what these processes look like.

Grievance Procedure

Grievance is a formal complaint

When an employee believes that the labor agreement has been violated, the employee files a grievance. A **grievance** is a formal complaint regarding the event, action, or practice that violated the contract. The grievance procedure serves a number of purposes. The primary purpose is to determine whether the labor contract has been violated. Also, the grievance procedure is designed to settle alleged contract violations in as friendly and orderly a fashion as possible, before they become major issues. Other purposes of the grievance procedure include preventing future grievances from arising, improving communication and cooperation between labor and management, and helping to obtain a better climate of labor relations. The grievance procedure also helps to clarify what often is not clear in the contract (e.g., defining lawful or unlawful conduct). Grievance procedures generally establish

Figure 13-7   **A Grievance Procedure**

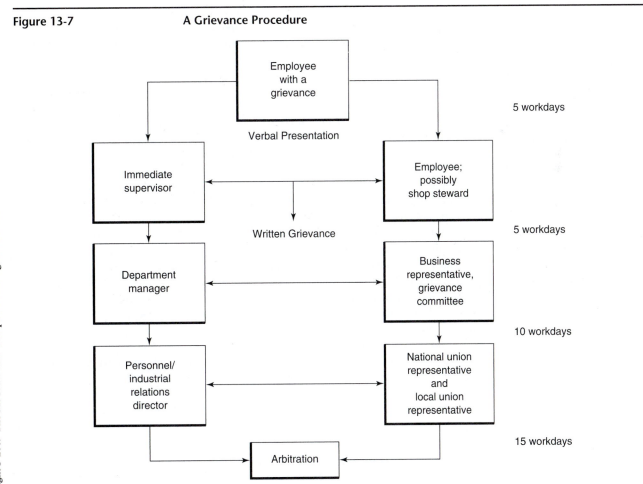

Source: R. E. Allen and T. J. Keaveny, "A Grievance Procedure," *Contemporary Labor Relations*, 2nd ed., p. 530. Reprinted with permission of the author.

the following: (1) how the grievance will be initiated, (2) the number of steps in the process, (3) who will represent each party, and (4) the specified number of working days within which the grievance must be taken to the next step in the hearing. Failure to comply with time limits may result in forfeiture of the grievance.[47]

Resolution of Grievances

In most cases the labor contract stipulates that the employee's grievance be expressed orally or in writing to the employee's immediate supervisor. One advantage of expressing the grievance in written form is that it reduces the chance that differing versions of the grievance will be circulated. It also forces the employee to approach the grievance in a comparatively rational manner, thus helping to eliminate or reduce the likelihood of trivial complaints or feelings of hostility. Generally, the grievance is processed through the union steward, who will discuss it with the employee's supervisor.

Most grievances are settled early in the process. Settlement generally occurs after an employee has either presented his or her grievance in writing to the supervisor or appealed to the next higher level. An early settlement is contingent, however, on each side being willing to listen to the other side and discuss the problem in a rational and objective manner. Settlement can be hampered if both sides enter the procedure with an attitude of "win-lose" as opposed to "win-win."

When a grievance does not get settled in the first or second step, it goes to a higher level, often to company representatives (e.g., a general superintendent) and union representatives (e.g., a grievance committee). These representatives meet to further discuss the grievance and try to reach a solution agreeable to all. In most cases, the burden of proof in a grievance proceeding is on the union. Sometimes a mediator will be brought in to help resolve the grievance. The mediator's role in a grievance resolution is much the same as in contract mediation (i.e., to get the two parties to communicate and to offer compromise solutions). The mediator's role is not to establish which side is right or wrong. His or her recommendations and suggestions can be accepted or rejected by either party. The role of the mediator, as will be seen later, is much different from that played by the arbitrator, whose decisions are final and binding.

Mediator's role

Arbitration Process

While there is no law that forces parties to include arbitration in their labor agreements (either party can refuse to incorporate any arbitration provisions), almost all labor agreements in the United States do provide for arbitration as the final step in the grievance procedure. In the majority of grievances filed, arbitration is not necessary since resolutions are usually made during lower-level discussions. In fact, arbitration should be the last resort after all other options in the grievance process have failed. Since both parties share the cost of arbitration, there is a financial disincentive to rely upon it. Arbitration involves bringing in an impartial third party (referred to as the *arbitrator* or *adjudicator*), who is mutually agreed upon by both parties to break the deadlock between the union and management. Unlike the mediator's role of providing *recommended* solutions, the arbitrator's role is to make a ruling that is "final and binding upon both parties."

Arbitration should be last resort and is usually binding

Major League baseball and NHL hockey use **binding arbitration** in salary determination. In this form of negotiation, the player and the team each put in an offer for what they consider to be an acceptable salary. If no agreement is reached, the arbitrator hears arguments from both sides and chooses one of the figures. The decision reached then becomes binding on both the player and the team.

Arbitration is generally not used as a method of breaking a deadlock in negotiating a new labor contract in the private sector. This is because both labor and management would prefer to make their own decisions regarding conditions of employment rather than have these decisions made by a third-party arbitrator. However, because most public-sector workers do not have the right to strike, arbitration is often used as a substitute for the strike in the public sector. Of course, arbitration will take on a much more important role if the *Employee Free Choice Act* becomes law.

The Decision to Arbitrate: The decision as to whether or not to take a grievance to arbitration depends upon a number of factors and circumstances. At least two things might happen before arbitration becomes necessary: (1) the union could withdraw the grievance or (2) the employer could give in. If neither of these happens, then both sides must decide whether or not the case is important enough to justify the costs in terms of time, money, and effort. They also should determine what the chances are for a favorable ruling.

Duty of fair representation

According to the *duty of fair representation doctrine,* unions cannot ignore their legal obligation to provide assistance to their members who are pursuing a grievance. Even if the union knows that an employee's case is weak, it often pursues the case to demonstrate its commitment to its members. In addition, management cannot refuse to arbitrate unresolved grievances if the labor contract contains an arbitration clause.

Selection of the Arbitrator: Most labor agreements state that union and management will select an arbitrator from a panel of names submitted by either the **FMCS** or the **American Arbitration Association (AAA).** Neither party is obligated to use either service. Either of these organizations will provide the two parties with a list of names (usually seven) from their roster of arbitrators. The two parties will then agree upon an arbitrator through a process of elimination or some other mutually acceptable procedure. Many labor contracts stipulate a procedure for appointing an arbitrator. In some cases, a *permanent* arbitrator may be appointed under the terms of the labor agreement. The advantages of using a permanent arbitrator are that it saves time in the selection process, the arbitrator is already familiar with the contract and the current state of labor relations in the company, and there is a greater likelihood of uniformity in decisions because there tends to be more consistency in the interpretation of the contract. The other option for selecting an arbitrator is what is known as the "ad hoc method," which simply calls for a different arbitrator for each case. Despite the fact that the selection process takes longer, the ad hoc method is more popular precisely because the parties are not stuck with the same arbitrator for every case.

The Arbitration Process: While arbitration hearings are considered quasi-judicial, they are less formal than court proceedings. The arbitration hearing begins with a submission agreement, either oral or written, that describes the issues to be resolved through arbitration. Once the issues are presented, it is up to each of the parties to educate the arbitrator about relevant issues, facts, evidence, and arguments. The arbitrator does not play the role of fact finder; however, he or she does have the right to question witnesses or to request additional facts. Interestingly, union complaints of employers' failures to disclose information for collective bargaining purposes have increased.

Arbitrators are not bound by formal rules of evidence like those used in a court of law. For example, hearsay evidence may be introduced as long as it is identified as such. Throughout the arbitration proceedings, a court recorder may be present to prepare a transcript of the hearing.

Basis for the Arbitrator's Decision and Award

After hearing all of the evidence, the arbitrator writes his or her opinion supporting the decision and award. This includes providing a written rationale for the decision (i.e., an explanation for why the decision was made the way it was). The written opinion of the arbitrator presents the basic issues of the case, the pertinent facts, the position and arguments of each party, the merits of each position, and the reasons for the case. As a rule of thumb, the arbitrator has 30 days in which to consider the evidence and to prepare a decision.

Contract is the final authority

A fair decision and award must be based strictly upon the contract if relevant contract language exists. Also, the decision should be based upon an accurate assessment and interpretation of the contractual clauses of the labor agreement. The contract is the final authority. That is why the contract language is so important; it should be as clear-cut and precise as possible. Unfortunately, contractual language usually is unclear and ambiguous and has many different meanings. When contract language is silent, such factors as past practice, negotiation history, and other relevant laws play an important role in the arbitrator's decision.

Due process

In reaching a decision, an arbitrator must decide if the employee was accorded due process. The arbitrator must also determine whether the employer had just cause for any actions taken against the complainant. One final consideration for the arbitrator is to make sure that his or her decision is not based upon precedents established in previous cases, but rather on the facts of the current case. The arbitrator's awards should be clear and to the point. If the union receives the award, the arbitrator should state explicitly what actions the employer must take to comply with the provisions of the contract.

Criticisms of the Arbitration Process

Probably the criticisms heard most often about arbitration relate to costs and delays. Arbitration can be both expensive and time-consuming. However, supporters of arbitration will counter that argument with the fact that the costs associated with strikes and lockouts are even greater. The average fee for an arbitrator exceeds $2,000 per day, plus expenses. These costs include all the arbitrator's expenses such as hotel, travel, and meals; his or her time to analyze and write up the case and opinion; and other miscellaneous costs such as those associated with lawyers and stenographers.

Strategies to decrease costs

A few strategies have been found to reduce the costs of arbitration. These include developing a system to ensure that only grievances of high importance to the union and employer end up in arbitration, using arbitrators from the local area, consolidating grievances into one hearing, and having the arbitrator issue an award without providing a detailed written opinion.

The arbitration process is also frequently criticized for being too time-consuming. Cases often become backlogged due to arbitrators' busy schedules. Also, the actual hearings get drawn out because of the need to read lengthy transcripts or briefs. Finally, the writing of the opinion is very time-consuming. Several things can be done to cut down on this excessive time. These include using new arbitrators with smaller case loads, creating a permanent panel of arbitrators from which to choose, and cutting out transcripts and posthearing briefs (i.e., having the arbitrator take his or her own notes).

Miniarbitration

Some employers try to reduce arbitration time and costs by using a form of expedited arbitration sometimes referred to as ***miniarbitration.*** Miniarbitration requires that a hearing be held within 10 days after an appeal is made. Also, arbitration hearings are completed in one day, the arbitrator's decision must be made within 48 hours after the close of the hearing, there are no transcripts or briefs, and the fee is paid for only the hearing day. Miniarbitration is not always appropriate, but it generally works well with simple, routine cases. Another alternative is a process called *grievance mediation,* which combines aspects of both mediation and arbitration. It is much less formal than arbitration, with no briefs or cross-examinations of witnesses.

CURRENT AND FUTURE U.S. TRENDS IN LABOR RELATIONS

Union Membership

The future of unions in the United States is unclear. There can be no question that political power at the state and federal levels has diminished. As of 2009, some of that political clout may have already returned. Legislation dealing with how unions can spend members' dues will be on many state legislative agendas. Republicans tend to support "paycheck protection" ballot initiatives that give union members more say in how their money is spent. With the unions suffering from declining membership and unfavorable legislation, a new movement has begun within the union leadership to place greater emphasis on union organizing.

Change to win coalition

Five of the largest **AFL-CIO** affiliates formed a separate coalition in 2005 in order to focus on organizing. The **Change to Win Coalition** is composed of unions that were very unhappy with the leadership of AFL-CIO President John Sweeney, who was reelected in 2005. The new coalition is made up of the **Service Employees International Union,** the **United Food and Commercial Workers Union, Unite Here,** the **Laborers' International Union,** and the **International Brotherhood of Teamsters.** The coalition maintains that the AFL-CIO has spent too much money on politics and not nearly enough to organize new members. The five unions represent 5 million workers. The Coalition pledges to devote 75 percent of its income to organizing.

Unions continue to challenge team-based productivity improvement programs as violations of the NLRA. They have also successfully blocked the Republican-supported Teamwork for Employees and Management (TEAM) Act. A ruling by the NLRB upheld a claim by the union at DuPont's largest chemical plant that the company's quality circles (QCs) constituted an employer-dominated labor organization and thus violated NLRA as an unfair labor practice. A similar ruling also affected Electromation, Inc.

These rulings make the environment unclear as to the continued formation of employee committees and have left many organizations wary of testing empowerment programs in a union environment. Of course, QCs are still legal if first agreed to as part of a collective bargaining contract.

UAW concessions

There are challenging times ahead for the United Auto Workers (UAW). The union has been offering major concessions in an effort to help the "Big Three" American automakers (Ford, GM and Chrysler) get financial help from the federal government in 2008. In that year, UAW labor costs averaged $73.12 per hour in wages and benefits at "Big Three." (this figure includes retiree costs). Auto workers at Japanese plants in the U.S., all non-union, averaged $44.17 per hour. It is estimated that there is an additional $1,500 in labor costs in a GM car compared to a Toyota. Among the proposed concessions were an end to a "jobs bank" that paid 3,500 laid off UAW workers 95% of their salaries when they were not working. None of the Japanese plants have a "jobs bank." The UAW also negotiated **a two-tiered wage structure** in 2007 that should be very beneficial to the "Big Three" down the road if they can survive the 2009 recession. Under this new structure, salaries for newly hired workers are lower than the structure for current workers.[48]

Unions gaining support among women, minorities, and immigrants

Unions are gaining support among women, minorities, and immigrants.[49] Since the rate of women and minorities entering the workforce is higher than the rate for white males, this represents a bright spot for the future of unions. In fact, one highlight for unions in the early part of the 21st century is the increase in the number of women who joined unions and the growth of unionism among nurses, a fast-growing occupation with critical real (and projected) shortages. Most experts predict that if union representation is to increase, the focus of organizing must be on jobs that can't be moved overseas. In many of these jobs, women represent the majority of workers.

Successful union targets

A prime and successful target of late has been nursing home employees who toil at very difficult and physically taxing jobs at slightly more than the minimum wage. The Service Employees International Union won the right to represent 75,000 home care workers in Los Angeles County. This is the single largest gain for unions anywhere since the first auto contracts were signed over 75 years ago. Unions even won 25 of 37 elections in the South for health care workers and over 75 percent of elections across the country in the late 90s.[50]

Many physicians are unionizing against health maintenance organizations due to low fees, excessive patient loads, and increased interference in what physicians believe to be their decision making regarding medical treatment.[51] The Federation of Physicians and Dentists claims over 42,000 members as of 2007.[52]

There are a few recent and successful union organizing efforts. Hollywood casting directors (the people who pick the actors) recently voted to become Teamsters. Says Gary Zuckerbroad, a casting director and organizer who weeds out auditioning actors, "Every other major craft in the entertainment industry is unionized. Casting directors get no residuals—writers do." But a key question in this case is whether casting directors, given the nature of their jobs and as independent contractors, are even protected by the NLRA. Are they management since they participate in hiring the actors?

Recent court and NLRB rulings not favorable to unions

Recent court rulings and NLRB decisions are certainly not favorable for unions. "The cumulative effect is to decrease the capability of unions to organize," says Theodore St. Antoine, former Dean of University of Michigan Law School and professor of labor law. These rulings and the growing conservatism of the federal judiciary should make labor organizing more difficult, and, given the decline in unions in most sectors of the U.S. economy, things have apparently gone from bad to worse in terms of union organizing. The elections of 2008 have clearly improved the political situation for unions in Washington.

As of 2009, no American Wal-Mart worker belonged to a union. Wal-Mart's prices are about 14 percent lower than its competitors for lots of reasons (e.g., economies of scale, price control pressures on suppliers, technology on products bought and sold, cheaper imports). Low wages are certainly another factor. Sales clerks in some areas of the United States earn less at Wal-Mart than unionized workers doing essentially the same work for competitors. Health care benefits are estimated to be 30 percent less than coverage for

451

workers within the same industry. There is no doubt that Wal-Mart will continue to be a high-priority target for union organizing. Recent success organizing Wal-Mart workers in Canada will encourage this effort.

There is a lot at stake for managers too. Research shows that managers who preside over a successful union organizing effort are much more likely to be fired and not promoted. Many former Wal-Mart managers, for example, have reported that they were warned they would be fired if any part of their workforce even authorized an election.

Public-Sector Union Membership

While private-sector union membership has been dropping, public-sector, or government employees' unionization has been on the increase. Public-sector employees generally have less bargaining power than private-sector employees. This is because unions often have to negotiate or bargain with more than one person or group. Also, many governmental entities prohibit striking. Colorado and Florida, for example, forbid striking by any state employee, including teachers. However, many state employees in midwestern states have maintained the right to strike. Visit the website of the **National Education Association** (nea.org) for a study of teacher salaries as a function of the right to strike.

Public-sector unionization on the increase—40 percent in 2007

The most sophisticated (and successful) of the service sector unions has been the **American Federation of State, County, and Municipal Employees (AFSME)**, which emphasizes workplace dignity and safety, pay equity programs (comparable worth), resistance to performance and electronic monitoring, and career development. AFSME, an affiliate of the AFL-CIO, has 1.3 million members. According to the *Philadelphia Inquirer,* "AFSME seems to represent labor's future. A majority of its members are women, nearly a quarter of them are minorities, and more than half are younger than 40."[53]

Mergers and Acquisitions

A common occurrence today is for a new company to buy a failing (or failed) business. What then are the legal obligations of the new company with regard to active collective bargaining agreements? Federal labor law addresses the duties of the new employer to recognize and bargain with the predecessor's union. In the 1987 case *Fall River Dyeing & Finishing Corp. v. NLRB,* the U.S. Supreme Court established that when (1) a successor employer shows "substantial continuity" in business operations, (2) the bargaining unit is appropriate (performing essentially the same jobs under the same working conditions), and (3) the predecessor employed a majority of the new employer's workers, then the successor employer is required to recognize and bargain with the predecessor union.[54] However, there is no duty imposed on the successor employer to hire the predecessor's workers unless the failure to hire them was based upon their union status. Also, the successor is not legally required to adopt an old collective bargaining agreement that was made with the predecessor.

Fall River Dyeing v. NLRB

Union lobbyists have been successful in passing legislation regulating mergers and acquisitions. According to the Investor Responsibility Research Center, 39 states now have some form of antitakeover statute. This legislation typically requires a lengthy waiting period for completion of a takeover or the approval by the corporation's board of directors. Legislation enacted in Massachusetts is considered the most favorable for unions. Hostile takeovers in Massachusetts require approval by the board of directors, and a long waiting period is stipulated for the takeover. Workers laid off within two years of the takeover get severance pay, and new management must recognize all existing collective bargaining agreements.

Antitakeover statutes

Retraining Provisions

Mergers and acquisitions, downsizing, and deregulation have all imposed great threats to job security, particularly for union workers. One of the key ways that unions have begun to deal with this threat is through retraining provisions in collective bargaining agreements. For example, job security has become a prime concern of unions in the deregulated and technologically changing telecommunications industry.

Some unions have cooperated with management to enhance employee development in order to limit downsizings and maintain jobs. Model programs have been initiated in the past by the United Auto Workers with Ford and GM and the Communications Workers of America with AT&T. These programs were jointly funded by management and the union. They were designed to help employees prepare for reemployment in the face of layoffs or to help workers gain more marketable skills that could be used within or outside the firm.[55]

Employee Benefits

With declining membership and the need to attract women, unions have emphasized health care and family-oriented benefits in recent years.[56] For example, unions such as the American Federation of Teachers (AFT), the Amalgamated Clothing and Textile Workers Union, the International Ladies Garment Workers Union, the Communication Workers of America, and the National Union of Hospital and Health Care Employees have taken active roles in child care and family-leave issues. These and other unions were instrumental in the passage of the Family and Medical Leave Act discussed in Chapter 10. In some cases the union lobbies for child care funds from the state legislature, and in some cases the union is directly involved in supporting child care centers.[57] The UAW and Ford jointly operate child care resource and referral centers in many locations.

A Proposal to Reinvent U.S. Trade Unionism

Experts on U.S. unionism drafted a proposal in 2005 with the goal of revitalizing the union movement.[58] They prefaced their list of recommendations with the following context: "The economic and political changes over the last thirty years both in the United States as well as globally have resulted in a far more hostile environment for labor unions specifically and for working people generally. In this context, contrary to the spirit of A. Philip Randolph's notion that the essence of trade unionism is social uplift, the trade union movement is rarely looked to today as a voice of progress and innovation, or a consistent ally of progressive social movements."[59]

After much discussion, this consortium of experts concluded: "The current situation necessitates a new approach to strategy, tactics, and fundamentally, the vision of trade unionism. This is more than the production of new mission statements, but instead rests on the necessity to rethink the relationship of the union to its members, to the employer(s), to government, to U.S. society as a whole, and to the larger *global village*. Can the union . . . rise to the challenge of being a means to confront injustice, or is the union condemned to be solely an institutional mechanism to lessen the pain of contemporary capitalism on those fortunate to be members of organized labor?" Figure 13-8 presents a summary of their strategy for reinventing trade unionism in the United States. They have an uphill battle. The Democratic Party dominance in Washington will certainly help.

Figure 13-8　　　　　**A Strategy for Reinventing Trade Unionism in the 21st Century**

1. **There is a need for a vision that includes, but is not limited to, organizing the unorganized:** There must be massive organizing of the unorganized.

2. **The union movement must be unapologetically pro-public sector and pro-public service.**

3. **The union movement must stand for the expansion of democracy:** Organized labor must stand AND fight for an expansion of democracy beyond the limits of formal legality.

4. **We must have a U.S. union movement structure suited to advancing organizing of the unorganized workers:** The question of the shape and structure of the U.S. union movement cannot be driven by a concern about jobs for the officers and staffs of the current unions.

5. **The union movement must reshape its political program to focus on the needs of the working class:** The union movement has made the repeated mistake of assuming that it can tell its members how to vote, and that the Democratic Party structure will automatically represent their interest.

6. **The union movement must organize in the South and Southwest:** There is a direct (though not exclusive) relationship between union membership and one's tending to vote in one's own economic interests.

7. **State federations and central labor councils must be democratic, inclusive, young and audacious:** Too many central labor councils and state federations are disconnected from the realities that their members face and most of the working class.

8. **The union movement needs real membership education:** It is presumptuous to think that either organized or unorganized workers will blindly follow or adhere to a certain point-of-view without providing them with a coherent and up-to-scale mechanism by which they can access information.

9. **The U.S. union movement must build both global union partnerships and solidarity with others fighting global injustice.**

Source: Adapted from K. Bronfenbrenner, D. DeWitt, B. Fletche, et al., "Futurer of Organized Labor in the U.S.: Reinventing Trade Unionism for the 21st Century," *Monthly Review Online*, February 2005.

INTERNATIONAL ISSUES

There are several unique characteristics of the U.S. labor relations system relative to systems in most other countries. Among the most significant are the following:

1. In the United States, unions have **exclusive representation** (i.e., there is representation by only one union for any given job in the United States). In Europe, more than one union, often with religious and political affiliations, may represent the same workers.

2. In the United States, the government plays a **passive role** in labor relations and dispute resolution, characterized by regulating the process, not the outcomes. In Western and Eastern European countries, Australia, Canada, and Latin America, the role of the government is much more active.

3. In the United States, there is generally an **adversarial relationship** between the union and management, while in most other countries the relationship is much more conciliatory and cooperative.

4. Collective bargaining in the United States is more **decentralized** (i.e., agreements are negotiated primarily at the local level). Unions in Europe, Japan, and Canada rely primarily on macro-negotiation by industry.

5. In the United States, unions place a high **emphasis on economic issues** such as wages, benefits, and job security, while in other countries (e.g., France), the unions emphasize political issues to a greater degree. Swedish unions emphasize both economic and political issues. For example, the Swedish model is considered humane since their goal is to replace unemployment benefits by a guarantee of work or training for long-term unemployed people. In China, unions have very little political or economic power and great difficulty in organizing workers.

Codetermination

In several countries, trade unions influence firm economic and financial decisions by including worker representatives as members on the supervisory boards. In Germany, workers are represented at the plant level in work councils and at the corporate level through **codetermination.** Work councils are committees that have representatives from both employees and managers. They have responsibility for the governance of the workplace, including hiring and firing workers, training issues, and overtime.[60] Codetermination is usually associated with Germany because, there, a **full-parity system** was established in the steel and coal industry. Labor and management are equally represented on the supervisory or corporate boards of these companies. Some form of codetermination also can be found in other industries in Germany. Since 1976, German law has required companies with over 2,000 employees to have the same numbers of management and worker representatives on the supervisory board (usually 11 members including the chair, who is chosen by the other 10 members). The decisive vote is cast by the "neutral" chair in tie situations. AEG-Telefunken, a German appliance and machinery company, provides a good example of the codetermination principle: AEG was in deep financial trouble in the early 1980s. Surprisingly, the chair cast the deciding vote in favor of the labor representatives' proposal to persuade the government to provide more aid.[61]

When making union comparisons across countries, it is important to recognize that even within a country there may be marked differences among unions. In Germany today, two of the biggest unions are IG Metall with over 2 million members representing cars and electronics and IG Chemie with over 1 million members representing chemicals. Their approaches to union issues are quite different even though both were established in 1890–1891. The main goal of IG Metall is to fight for better benefits, wages, and hours even if it means losing members as companies lay off workers. On the other hand, IG Chemie recently signed an agreement that allows employers who are in trouble to cut wages by up to 10 percent in return for job security. IG Metall has a similar agreement.[62]

The head of the works council at the Hamburg factory of Daimler Benz Aerospace (DASA), Hans-Gunter Eidtner, was able to persuade the IG Metall union to eliminate overtime pay so that employees would not lose their jobs. German workers seem more eager to compromise given the large number of people out of work. In fact, as in the United States, employers are increasingly making deals with workers that improve productivity and flexibility. Most of the companies negotiate concessions with the works councils at individual factories, then gain approval (often reluctantly) from national unions. Companies in eastern Germany have an easier time making deals and cutting labor costs since the unions are less powerful than in western Germany. Some of the agreements reached in Germany are similar to those reached in the United States where employees are expected to make some concessions in order to help out struggling companies.[63] Some of these are listed below:

- At Bayer, the chemical union agreed to reduce bonuses, eliminate an employee share-purchase program, and introduce flexible work hours over three years.
- At Volkswagen, the union agreed to a two-tier wage system and temporary employees will earn 10 percent less than current employees.
- Workers at the Hanover tire plant for Continental will increase their workweek by 75 minutes and make other concessions worth about $20 million.
- At Deutz, a machinery maker, employees will accept a second year of pay cuts and will receive up to $11 million in Deutz stock.

U.S. Managers and Unions

Antiunion orientation a problem for U.S. expatriates

A lack of understanding of union structure and the underlying social dimension is often cited as a major cause of difficulties for expatriate American managers of multinational corporations. While American managers tend to have an antiunion orientation in their management style, unions carry considerably more clout in other countries. This attitude often can result in serious (and quick) trouble. For example, Johnson & Johnson's joint venture with a German pharmaceutical company ran into difficulties at the start because Johnson & Johnson managers apparently did not recognize the importance of the work councils at German plants and the practical implications of codetermination for the manufacturing process. Codetermination also stipulates that a labor director be treated as a manager who is charged with attending to worker concerns. Labor directors have great influence in Germany and often participate in corporate strategic planning. The management board is elected by the supervisory board and must include a labor director who is approved by labor representatives. Johnson & Johnson's expatriate managers did not recognize the significance of the labor director in the daily operation of the joint venture plants. Consequently, the firm experienced problems on matters related to work rules, productivity measures, and job responsibilities.

Similar cases of difficulties for expatriate managers have been noted in Japan, where joint consultation systems are very common yet very alien to American managers. Over 75 percent of Japan's largest employers have a joint consultation system in which employee groups meet monthly with management to discuss policy, production, personnel issues, and even financial matters. Although not as common as in large companies, consultation systems and participative management systems are becoming more common for small and medium-sized Japanese companies as well. Japan has **enterprise unions** in which most firms have a single union with virtually all job families in the same union. For instance, in large firms such as Toyota, Toshiba, and Hitachi, workers in each company are organized into a union. This ensures that the union's loyalty will not be divided among different companies. There is no clear distinction between labor and management. In fact, many Japanese executives started their careers as union members, were promoted to leadership positions in the union, and then moved into management jobs in the same company. Thus, they have an appreciation for the perspective of labor and management. There is considerable trust between labor and management. Bargaining is done by the central organization during the "spring offensive" with details negotiated at the individual company.

Enterprise unions

Figure 13-9 presents the percentage of employees who are unionized around the world as of 2007. Union membership was lower in the United States (13 percent) than in many countries. For example, union participation was highest in Sweden (81 percent). While many Central and South American countries have a higher percentage of workforce union

**Figure 13-9
Unionization around
the World**

	Percent
United States	12%
Australia	28
Canada	30
France	31
Germany	26
Ireland	44
Italy	34
Japan	22
Korea	12
Mexico	32
Netherlands	29
Spain	11
Sweden	81
United Kingdom	30

Source: http://www.ilr.cornell.edu/library/research/QuestionOfTheMonth/archive/laborUnionsAcrossTheWorld.html. Accessed October 26, 2008.

membership (e.g., Mexico, Argentina, Brazil), there is no guaranteed right to collective bargaining. Unions in Central and South America are generally very political.

Union membership is decreasing in many European countries. In Great Britain, for example, membership has dropped about 15 percent in the last 15 years. Unions there are closely tied to the Labour Party and can be militant. Wildcat strikes, for example, are illegal in the United States, but are a more common form of protest in Britain.[64]

Termination for cause only in Europe

The effect of unions and labor law on MNCs varies widely with European unions taking tough stands regarding wages, employment-at-will, and the ability to globally integrate operations and in that in many developing countries labor unions and labor laws provide very little protection of workers and their rights.[65] Ford plants in Germany can be closed only after an extended period of consultation with affected parties. Many European countries impose stiff fines for terminating employees, even if the layoffs are temporary.

Another problem for MNCs is the inability to integrate optimal manufacturing operations across borders because powerful labor unions exert strong political pressure. The result of this suboptimization is higher manufacturing costs. The influence of the German Metal Workers' union on GM operations is often cited as a case in point.

Guidelines for MNC

The pro-labor Organization for Economic Cooperation and Development in Paris has issued **"Guidelines for MNCs"** that attempt to guarantee the same basic social and labor relations rights for all workers. However, union attempts to develop uniform standards for MNCs have not proven very fruitful to date. As noted earlier, the National Labor Relations Board created in the United States in 1935 was designed to enable workers to exert pressure on companies to achieve fair wages and address poor working conditions. In most cases, the NLRA has been applied to U.S. firms located in the States.[66] It has not been extended to U.S. firms located in other countries, despite the fact that some argue that this would be advantageous for employers and unions. Some of the possible benefits would include providing some stability for corporations and unions dealing in the global labor market, discouraging multinational firms from establishing facilities in foreign countries that have poor working conditions and weak labor standards, and allowing unions to use legal means to exert economic pressure on firms without worrying about whether they will flee to underdeveloped countries.[67]

National Labor Committee

The **National Labor Committee,** a coalition formed in 1983 of 25 of the member unions of the AFL-CIO to monitor conditions in Central America, has alleged that some companies have contracted with offshore manufacturers that use child labor, maintain sweatshops, and severely underpay their employees. It also contends that U.S. firms have a duty to monitor their offshore contractors to ensure that they are not acting unethically or illegally. This means that U.S. firms should perform self-checks, adopt a code of conduct for their offshore operations, communicate the code and monitor compliance with it, and train managers to ensure that they understand the code and enforce it.[68]

Global Collective Bargaining and Productivity

Effects of unions world-wide

A 2005 World Bank study entitled "Unions and Collective Bargaining: Economic Effects in a Global Environment" concluded that union members, and other workers covered by collective agreements in industrial as well as in developing countries, get significantly higher average wages than workers who are not affiliated with a trade union.[69] The wage differential was larger in the United States (15 percent) than in most other industrial countries (5 to 10 percent). The report, which reviewed more than a thousand studies on the effects of unions and collective bargaining, found that bargaining coordination between workers' and employers' organizations in wage setting and other aspects of employment (for example, working conditions) was an influential determinant of a country's economic performance.

Union membership reduced wage differences between skilled and unskilled workers and also between men and women. In some countries such as Germany, Japan, Mexico, South Africa, and the United Kingdom, unionized women workers have a greater pay advantage over their nonunionized counterparts than unionized men. In the United States and the United Kingdom, unionized nonwhite workers tend to get a higher wage markup than white workers. In Mexico and Canada, unions have been found to reduce the discrimination against indigenous people.

What should be clear from this brief discussion of international labor relations is that we can make very few generalizations about labor relations across borders. The role of government, social agendas, religious affiliation, and underlying political and economic issues must be understood before one can thoroughly understand the diversity of international labor relations.

SUMMARY

As a result of the changes taking place in the size and composition of the workforce, the advances in technology, and the increased competition from foreign businesses, the future of unions and the collective bargaining system in the U.S. is uncertain. There is little doubt that unions must be willing to be flexible and to adapt to the changes taking place. Unions must find a way to attract the new entrants into the labor force such as women, minorities, and immigrants—if they are to survive.

What does the future hold for unions and collective bargaining? The fate of the **Employee Free Choice Act** discussed earlier could have a significant effect on union organizing in the future. Some critics of conventional collective bargaining say that the current system cannot survive because it is inefficient, ineffective, excessively time-consuming, and characterized by exaggerated opening demands and inflated counterproposals.

Politics have played a major role in the current state of labor unions. As one expert put it, "Federal administrations under Reagan and both Bush presidencies launched various anti-union initiatives, always under the guise of a more positive public policy goal. Privatization was touted as making government services more efficient, but it also meant shifting workers to coverage under private-sector labor relations laws that seem less effective in protecting worker and union rights. In the name of efficient government contracting, federal governments sought to weaken 'prevailing wage' laws and projectwide union recognition agreements that help to limit incentives for private contractors to oppose unions in federally funded work (particularly on construction projects)."[70] The political environment improved significantly for unions in 2009.

NLRB interpretive decisions tend to track with the political party in power. The NLRB was controlled by Democrats during the eight years of the Clinton administration (1992–2000) and the decisions tended to be pro-union. Decisions under George W. Bush tended to be more pro-business. The NLR Board has five seats. The President appoints members to five-year terms; Republicans have held the majority of seats most recently, but this may have already changed under President Obama. While all NLRB interpretative decisions are subject to federal judicial interpretation of the NLRA, the federal judiciary has gotten more conservative and pro-business as well.[71] Managers in nonunion environments must be aware that many of the rights provided to union workers also extend to nonunion workers under the National Labor Relations Act.

Cooperation and collaboration are the watchwords being used to describe contract negotiations today. This is true in the United States and in other countries. Collaboration can take many forms. For example, management can create committees on which employees are represented (e.g., shop committees, department committees, quality circles [QCs]). Also, there has been a movement toward greater cooperation in handling disciplinary problems and resolving grievances.

Unions and collective bargaining will continue to play an important role in the lives of American workers as long as they are able to help workers overcome dissatisfaction with management and meet their economic needs. Greater cooperation between labor and management is needed to make organizations more effective and competitive. In some industries, that cooperation may be necessary in order to survive in these difficult times.

Change to win coalition

A major recent labor development was the formation of the Change to Win Coalition which broke from the AFL-CIO in 2005. The two major unions of the new Coalition are the Teamsters and the Service Employees International Union (SEIU). Over 4 million workers left the 13-million-strong AFL-CIO to join the Coalition. Other members of the Change to Win Coalition are the Laborers' International Union of North America, the United Farm Workers, and the United Brotherhood of Carpenters and Joiners of America, which is not in the AFL-CIO.

The breakup may do even more damage to unions by reducing the AFL-CIO's clout. Says Robert Reich, Secretary of Labor under former President Bill Clinton, "It's very bad news in the short term . . . a fundamental principle in the union movement is that in unity there's strength. The reverse is also true. In disunity there's weakness." But Anna Burger, the first chairperson of the Coalition, says labor will reverse its long slide as a social and political force by focusing on the nation's lowest-paid workers. Certainly, SEIU has been very successful organizing such groups as home health care and child care workers, building service workers, and private security workers, all heavily female and minority. The jury is still out as to whether the Coalition can take advantage of the SEIU's successful organizing techniques and apply them to other unions.

Time will tell about the comeback of unions in the 21st century. Some experts are now predicting a resurgence with new, aggressive leadership and a more sympathetic ear from middle-class workers, women, and minorities. As one prominent academic put it, "There is little room to doubt that unions are 'down.' Whether they are 'out' is another matter. Despite abundant gloomy indicators on union vitality, there are signs of life and sources of hope for the future of U.S. unions."[72] The most recent elections have clearly established a more positive political atmosphere in Washington.

Discussion Questions

1. Should public employees be allowed to strike?
2. What are the major effects of unions on compensation?
3. Why do unions sometimes have a positive impact on productivity?
4. If unions are to survive, what do you think they will have to do to attract and maintain members?
5. Should companies be allowed to hire workers based on their attitudes toward unions?
6. Why is it advantageous for both the union and management to remain flexible during collective bargaining negotiations?
7. Describe the sources of power brought to the bargaining table by both the union and management.
8. Describe how the union and management might prepare for labor negotiations. How are their preparations similar and different?
9. Should the government be allowed to intervene in strikes that are not a threat to national security or public welfare in order to expedite their resolution? Why or why not?
10. How might a multinational corporation better prepare itself for dealing with the differing union environments in other countries?
11. Compare and contrast unions in the United States, Germany, and Japan. How are they similar and different? What can they learn from one another?
12. What became of the Employee Free Choice Act? If it became law, any effects to date?

Chapter
14

Employee Health and Safety*

OBJECTIVES

After reading this chapter, you should be able to

1. Understand the extent and costs of employee accidents, illnesses, and deaths on the job.

2. Discuss the role of workers' compensation programs for job-related injuries and illnesses.

3. Describe legal issues related to health and safety.

4. Explain the functions of OSHA and review research on the effectiveness of OSHA and related regulations.

5. Discuss recent approaches that have been used to improve workplace safety and health.

6. Review contemporary issues and programs that seek to improve worker health and safety, including drug testing, antismoking policies, threat management teams, stress management interventions, employee assistance programs, and employee wellness programs.

OVERVIEW

Employers, unions, employees, and government agencies have a great and growing interest in health and safety issues related to the workplace. With the number of work-related injuries, illnesses, and deaths, it is no surprise! According to the **National Safety Council,** each workday a fatality occurs every two hours and a debilitating injury occurs every two seconds. Industrial accidents cost the U.S. economy an estimated $121 billion per year. However, there is some indication that injury and illness statistics look more favorable in recent years. For example, while 5,488 fatal work injuries in the United States were recorded in 2007, this figure is 6% less than the previous year. Fatal injuries among Hispanic and Latino workers also fell compared to 2000 data. There were 4 million recorded cases of nonfatal incidents of occupational injury or illness in 2007 compared to almost 6 million in 2000.[1] These indications of improvements should be interpreted with caution. First of all, the government changed its criteria for reporting nonfatal injuries. Second, studies indicate that reported accidents represent only about half of all accidents.[2] There is

Industrial accidents cost the U.S. economy $121 billion per year

*Susan M. Stewart, and Harriette McCall contributed to an early version of this chapter.

evidence that illegal immigrants are doing more of our most dangerous work and many deaths and injuries are not reported.

Examples of the costs to individual employers are immense as well. General Motors (GM) was fined $1.94 million for safety violations by the **Occupational Safety and Health Administration (OSHA)**. One of the largest meatpackers, John Morrell and Co. of Sioux Falls, South Dakota, was cited by OSHA and assessed a $4.33 million fine for safety violations. According to the federal agency, more than 800 of the 2,000 employees at the plant sustained "serious and sometimes disabling injuries." The rate of injuries at the plant was 652 times more than the rate of injuries for businesses in general. USX, the giant steel company, was fined $7.3 million for numerous violations of safety, health, and recordkeeping, including 58 "willful" hazards. Criminal charges and convictions against management for willful neglect of worker health and safety can happen, but they're rare. One investigation reported that from 1982 to 2002, 2,197 workers were killed on the job nationwide because employers "willfully" violated safety laws. In 93 percent of the 1,242 cases investigated by OSHA, according to David Uhlmann, former chief of the Justice Department's environmental crimes section, an average of less than two prosecutions per year has been brought by OSHA.[3] Criminal manslaughter prosecutions for intentional safety violations are more common at the state or local level.

Despite these disturbing statistics, safety issues have not been a priority to students or researchers in management. Since 2000, many safety experts have argued that worker health and safety issues have not been a high priority of the federal government. According to public health experts, from 2000 through 2008, OSHA issued the fewest significant standards in its history. Only one significant health standard was issued during this period but only as ordered by a federal court. During the same period, OSHA squelched many existing and proposed regulations. There were several high-profile and tragic crane accidents in 2008. According to government figures, 72 workers died in such accidents in 2006, the most recent year for which data are available. Yet, according to an OSHA consultant, the Agency took no regulatory action for years on revised crane standards despite an OSHA assessment that the new standards could prevent 48 worker deaths per year.[4]

This chapter will review the costs of employee injuries, illnesses, and deaths and the regulatory environment that seeks to improve work safety and health. Human resource professionals should understand these issues so they can take a proactive stance in managing employee health and safety. Considerable attention will be given to the role of the **Occupational Safety and Health Administration Act of 1970** and the federal regulations that have been issued regarding this law. OSHA is responsible for establishing and enforcing occupational health and safety standards and for inspecting and issuing citations to organizations that violate these standards. OSHA is without question one of the greatest legislative accomplishments of organized labor, and research on its effectiveness will be reviewed in this chapter. The final portion of the chapter will cover contemporary issues related to employee health and safety and will discuss some of the controversial steps organizations are taking to improve their employee health, safety, and performance records (e.g., drug testing, antismoking policies, threat management teams, employee assistance, and wellness programs).

Ferguson-Hall Co. Inc., an excavation contractor, really felt the costs of a workplace accident in 2006. One of its employees died after the bank of an unprotected 8 1/2-foot deep water line excavation collapsed on him. The U.S. Labor Department's Occupational Safety and Health Administration (OSHA) sought the maximum fine after an inspection found that the excavation had no cave-in protection. OSHA cited Ferguson-Hall for an alleged willful violation of safety standards that require collapse protection.

State prosecutors have argued successfully for the criminal prosecution of managers who cause injury or illness to employees.[5] For example, three senior managers of Film Recovery Systems in Illinois received 25-year sentences for recklessly exposing their employees to toxic cyanide fumes. Five senior executives of Chicago Magnet Wire Company were prosecuted for causing illnesses by allowing workers to be exposed to hazardous chemicals. A supervisor at Jackson Enterprises in Michigan was convicted of involuntary manslaughter for an employee's death.[6]

Criminal charges against management

Recent examples of employer costs

The death and accident figures presented above vary substantially as a function of the industry, occupation, and organization size. Moderate-sized organizations (50 to 100 employees) have higher accident rates than smaller or larger companies. This may be because moderate firms cannot offer extensive safety programs or cannot closely supervise their employees. According to the **Bureau of Labor Statistics (BLS),** the jobs with the highest number of fatalities in 2007 were fishing, pilots/flight engineers, loggers, iron workers, refuse collectors, power-line workers, and roofers. The chance of the average American worker sustaining a fatal work injury was 3.8 per 100,000 workers. Needless to say, the odds aren't nearly as good in mining, construction, and agriculture.

Unions were instrumental in improving working conditions

While the current statistics are disturbing, they do not compare to the early days of industrial growth in the United States. The Industrial Revolution was born with little concern for employee health or safety. Working conditions were often so unbearable and serious injuries were so pervasive that employees began to demand that management implement safeguards. Union activity emphasized improving employee working conditions. Today, many older Americans suffer because of the conditions to which they were exposed at work decades ago. For example, 49 workers from a foundry in Michigan got tuberculosis because of their exposure to silica at the foundry in the 1940s (silica is a glassy material found in sand). There are thousands of other examples.

U.S. safety standards superior to developing countries and on a par with Europe

Despite the work-related injuries, illnesses, and deaths that occur each year in this country, U.S. health and safety standards are superior to those in most developing parts of the world. In most other countries that maintain reliable data on the subject, injury and illness figures are even more alarming than those in the United States. Most developing countries have very basic safety laws and few resources for safety enforcement. In addition, they have antiquated equipment and limited training available to employees about safety issues. These developing countries are often so in need of economic development that they accept any industry, even those that have the potential for significant harm. This presents serious ethical questions for firms operating in the developing nations. However, in many European countries with strong national unions, safety law enforcement mechanisms are often ranked higher than those in the United States. The rankings are as follows: Sweden, Finland, United Kingdom, and the United States. In countries such as the Netherlands, France, Belgium, Denmark, and Luxembourg, legally mandated employee safety committees give workers more control over workplace safety issues.[7]

Without question, the American workplace is safer today than it was 60 years ago, but there is still considerable room for improvement. One modern-day issue being addressed includes the use of **chemical hazards.** More than 30 million workers are potentially exposed to one or more chemical hazards per year. There are an estimated 650,000 existing hazardous chemical products, and hundreds of new ones are introduced annually. Most have never been tested for toxicity, and no regulatory restraints affect their use. New materials, composed of exotic combinations of plastics, carbons, and other substances, are introduced into the workplace at an alarming rate, with little knowledge of their interactive effects on worker health.

Some health experts argue that the government and OSHA has been slow to act on such hazards in recent years. In 2000, a Missouri doctor found a pattern at a microwave popcorn plant where nine workers came down with a rare lung disease. Scientists at the **National Institute for Occupational Safety and Health (NIOSH),** a division of OSHA, studied the science behind the chemical, examined patients, and inspected the factory. A NIOSH report concluded that the workers became ill because of exposure to diacetyl, a popular food-flavoring agent. NIOSH recommended regulatory action. But no action was taken by OSHA, and the head of OSHA described the science related to the effects of diacetyl as "murky."[8]

Repetitive Strain Injury

Another growing problem is **repetitive strain injury** (RSI), the so-called disease of the new millennium. Since 1990, cases of RSI have increased by 80 percent. RSI is an umbrella term for a number of overuse injuries affecting the soft tissues (muscles, tendons, and nerves) of the neck, upper and lower back, chest, shoulders, arms, and hands. **RSI** is an occupational injury that occurs from continuous and repetitive physical movements, such as assembly-line work or data entry. Typically arising as aches and pains, these injuries can progress to become crippling disorders that prevent sufferers from working or leading normal lives. The most frequently hit area with this disorder is in the wrist and is called carpal tunnel syndrome. Carpal tunnel syndrome accounts for one-third of workplace injuries in the United States and costs about $20 billion yearly. In 2007, the median days away from work were highest for cases of carpal tunnel syndrome. Median days away from work—the key measure of severity for occupational injuries and illnesses—designates the point at which half the cases involved more days and half involved fewer days. For carpal tunnel syndrome, the median was 27 days. The average worker's compensation claim for carpal tunnel syndrome is about $17,000.

Job burnout

Workers today also suffer more subtle forms of health problems at work. Research concludes that workplace stress, for example, has reached alarming proportions due to company restructuring, increased work demands, layoffs, downsizing, conflicts with family obligations, and the strain of the continuing wars and the state of the economy.[9] Chronic and long-term stress is commonly referred to as **job burnout.** Job burnout is a particular type of stress that tends to be experienced by workers in specific areas such as police work, customer service centers, health care, education, and the airline industry. Job burnout is costing U.S. industry billions of dollars. One estimate revealed that almost $90 billion is lost each year due to burnout and its related implications (i.e., emotional exhaustion, poor performance, absenteeism). Prolonged stress, along with fatigue, sleep loss, drugs, exposure to harmful chemicals, and disorders, can result in worker errors that are the cause of most workplace accidents.[10]

In addition to the obvious effects of pain, suffering, and a decreased quality of life, the impact of injuries and illnesses on productivity is enormous. In 2007, there were approximately 1 million cases of injuries or illnesses related to work that involved days away from work. Wage and productivity losses, medical expenses, and administrative expenses amounted to over $100 billion, with approximately 2 percent of payroll used for disability payments through workers' compensation. Indirect costs to the employer, including the monetary value of time lost by workers, replacing workers, damage to company equipment or property, and the cost of time required to investigate incidents (i.e., written reports), amounted to over $10 billion.[11] The bottom line work-injury cost is in excess of $201 billion per year. One study reported that employees who had suffered accidents were unsatisfied with their jobs and had higher levels of job tension and lower organizational commitment and faith in management.[12] Given these facts, the interest in health and safety issues by employees, employers, unions, and government agencies is understandable.

COMMON WORKPLACE INJURIES AND DISEASES

Employees are subjected to a number of on-the-job injuries each day. The most costly lost-time workers' compensation claims by cause of injury are for those resulting from motor-vehicle accidents, followed by injuries from a fall or slip. Injuries are usually caused by overexertion such as picking up heavy objects, falling, being struck by objects, or hyperextending a limb. Back problems are very common. Lower back disability (LBD) accounts for almost 25 percent of all lost workdays at a cost of almost $30 billion per year. LBD is even common among white-collar workers. Merrill Lynch is one company that has moved aggressively with a comprehensive program directed at LBD. They purchased new office equipment for their 60,000 white-collar workers designed to reduce workplace back injuries and RSI. Workers can request an audit of their workspace to determine its ergonomic soundness. The comprehensive program seems to be working.

Lower back disability accounts for 25 percent of lost workdays

It can be difficult for employers to detect the cause of certain diseases. For example, an individual may suffer a hearing loss due to working in a plant with an extremely high noise level or for other reasons not related to the workplace. In fact, more and more supervisors are beginning to worry about the effects of noise on employee health, morale, and productivity. Some adverse effects caused by persistent loud noise include constriction of blood vessels to the brain and other key organs, damage to the nervous system, and triggering of seizures among epileptics. One study of typical open-office noise found elevated urinary

Workplace noise

epinephrine levels and motivational deficits related to typical open-office noise.[13] OSHA's prescribed standard for acceptable noise levels in the workplace is 85 decibels. Unfortunately, many work settings today have daily noise levels well over the OSHA standard. Workers who are most at risk of noise pollution include factory workers, jackhammer operators, and printing-press operators. For effective noise management, supervisors should take worker complaints about noise seriously and act on them and rotate workers so that no one worker has lengthy exposure to loud noises. In addition, to avoid litigation, employers must introduce and enforce safety regulations in the workplace.

Food poisoning

Many employee illnesses also are caused by food poisoning. A likely source of infections is the plant or office lunchroom, where improperly handled food can contaminate tabletops and work surfaces. Another threat is from food that employees bring from home. In the workplace, it is important to provide employees with refrigerated food storage and disposable utensils, plus a sink and paper towels for cleanup. Housekeeping personnel should make sure to use germicides or disinfectants rather than liquid soap.[14]

Sleep deprivation

A major cause of accidents and injuries at work (and at home) is sleep deprivation. Most adults need between 7 and 8 hours of sleep per night. Deprivation is caused by a number of factors, some of which are related to work (and preventable). Some people, perhaps due to workload, simply do not allocate the necessary 7 or 8 hours for sleep. Travel and night work often cause great difficulty. Sleep disorders and a myriad of other personal issues are often the cause of deprivation.

Strong and cumulative effects from sleep loss

The impact of deprivation is clear, and the effects are quick and dramatic. Motor vehicle accidents and work accidents are more likely along with decreased productivity. Sleep deprivation can also cause difficulties with social relationships at work and at home and contribute to major medical problems. According to Dr. David Dinges, a scientist in charge of a University of Pennsylvania study on deprivation, "the first finding, and it stunned us, was there's a cumulative impairment that develops in your ability to think fast, to react quickly, to remember things. And it starts right away . . . a single night at four hours or five hours or even six, can in most people, begin to show effects in your attention and your memory and the speed with which you think. A second night it gets worse. A third night worse. Each day adds an additional burden or deficit to your cognitive ability."[15] Employers can be held liable if they contributed to the sleep deprivation of their employees and the deprivation is linked to an injury or an accident.

LEGAL ISSUES RELATED TO HEALTH AND SAFETY

Many state and local laws are designed to protect workers from illness and injury in addition to the federal OSHA. The Michigan foundry referred to earlier now must abide by strict OSHA standards regarding silica emissions. As evidenced by the fines against GM, John Morrell and Company, USX, and others discussed above, penalties are imposed for violating these laws and regulations. Under OSHA rules, employees now have a "right to know" about hazards to which they may be exposed at work. Companies are now required to issue a **hazard communication** to their workers when they may be exposed to certain hazardous chemicals. Under OSHA, employees can refuse to work and be supported by the law when certain unsafe conditions exist. Employers need to keep equipment, machinery, and the workplace in good, safe working order.

"Right to know" about hazards

In some states, if a fatality occurs from a willful violation of safety rules, company officials can serve time in prison and pay substantial fines. In addition, as one state attorney general said, "The workplace offers no refuge from criminal laws."[16] Prosecutors are now charging employers and supervisory personnel with involuntary manslaughter for negligence regarding workplace safety. This type of criminal prosecution can involve much heavier penalties.

In addition to this legal pressure, many employers seek a safe working environment because they wish to foster a high quality of work life (QWL) for their employees. Other employers recognize the costliness of accidents, illnesses, and injuries and endeavor to reduce these costs as much as possible through a variety of health and safety programs.

The major legislation related to health and safety, the steps that organizations have taken to reduce accidents and injuries, and the major contemporary issues that affect employee health and safety are reviewed below. Following this, the major controversies of the day such as AIDS policies, drug testing, antismoking policies, and responses to workplace violence are examined.

Workers' Compensation

Liability without fault

As discussed in Chapter 10, **workers' compensation** is a federally mandated insurance program developed on the theory that work-related accidents and illnesses are costs of doing business that should be paid for by the employer and passed on to the consumer. The direct cost of claims to U.S. businesses has been around $70 billion annually. Workers' compensation is based on the concept of **liability without fault,** which provides that workers who are victims of work-related injury or illness are granted benefits regardless of who is responsible for the accident, injury, or illness. This means that if an organization participates in the workers' compensation system, a worker may not sue the employer for negligence, even if the injury was clearly the employer's fault. On the other hand, even careless or accident-prone workers are generally covered by workers' compensation, and injuries that are the result of co-workers' negligence also are covered. Most state laws, however, deny benefits if the worker was under the influence of alcohol or controlled substances (illegal drugs) when the injury occurred.

What Employers Need Workers' Compensation Coverage and What Are the Costs?

Employer must pay premium

While workers' compensation laws differ across the states, the basics are about the same. Figure 14-1 presents the highlights of the law as they apply to employers and employees. Keep in mind that state law stipulates the detail. Thus, for example, whether a worker can make a claim for psychological stress at work depends on the state (in most states, the worker cannot). Employers, including governments, with a small number of full-time or part-time employees (four is the average) are required to carry workers' compensation insurance. Employers typically purchase an insurance policy from an agent representing a company approved by a state regulatory agency. These premiums can be pricey, and the rates differ across the states (and the industry). Some employers pay in access of $4 per $100 of payroll. The rate is partially determined by the firm's health and safety record. Across the United States, it is the employer's responsibility to pay the entire premium for this coverage.

While the law differs across the states, employers typically do not have to pay for the first few days of disability (usually 7), but if time of the disability extends to over a set

---

Figure 14-1   **Highlights of Workers' Compensation Law**

Employers' Responsibilities

Employers with a small number of full-time or part-time employees (4 is the average) must carry insurance.

Must report the injury to the carrier within about 7 days after their knowledge.

Typically pay 100% of the policy from a company approved by a state regulatory agency.

Covers all accidental injuries and occupational diseases related employment.

Although there are exceptions, workers' compensation does not pay for mental stress or "pain and suffering" from such a condition.

Compensation is not paid if the injury was caused by the employee' s willful intention to injure or kill himself- or herself or another or if the injury was caused primarily because the employee was intoxicated or under the influence of drugs.

Compensation must still be paid when an employee refuses to obey safety rules.

Employees' Issues

Must report injury or illness as soon as possible (usually not later than 30 days).

Can report the injury to the insurance company if the employer doesn't comply.

Must typically choose a doctor from a list provided by the insurance company.

The employer is generally not required to hold a job open for a victim.

It is unlawful to fire someone for filing or a claim.

Reemployment services are available to help employees return to work. Services include vocational counseling, transferable skills analysis, job-seeking skills, job placement, on-the-job training, and formal retraining.

If a claim is denied, an employee can get an attorney or work with a state agency. A petition for benefits must usually be filed within two years of the original decision.

number of days (usually 21), the employer would be obligated to pay for the first 7 days as well. In terms of lost work, the benefit check is paid at about two-thirds of the average weekly wage.

What Injuries or Diseases Are Covered?

The law covers all accidental injuries and occupational diseases arising out of and in the course and scope of employment. This includes diseases or infections resulting from such injuries. Visit the Web site of the **National Council on Compensation Insurance (NCCI)** for more detail. State laws differ on what conditions are not covered. In general, the law does not provide compensation for any of the following conditions: (1) a mental or nervous injury due to stress; (2) a work-related condition that causes an employee to have fear or dislike for another individual because of the individual's race, color, religion, sex, national origin, age, or handicap; and (3) "pain and suffering" from the condition.

An employer cannot sue an injured worker for causing the accident nor can an injured worker sue the employer for an injury. This trade-off makes it possible for injured workers to receive immediate medical care, at no cost to the injured worker, without any consideration for who was at fault, the employer or the employee. In civil law, negligence must be established through litigation before any compensation is awarded. In general, compensation is not paid if the injury is caused by the employee's willful intention to injure or kill himself or herself or another or if the injury is caused primarily because the employee is intoxicated or under the influence of drugs. If an injured worker refuses to submit to a test for drugs or alcohol, the employee may forfeit eligibility for benefits.

Partial payment

Compensation must still be paid, although in a reduced amount (e.g., 25 percent) even when the employee refuses to use safety equipment like a hard hat or safety goggles or refuses to obey a safety rule. Compensation will still be paid, but partial wage replacement may be reduced, if the employee knew about the safety rule prior to the accident and failed to observe the rule, or if the employee knowingly chose not to use safety equipment where the employer had directed the use. There is great variability in payouts for injuries; even today, injuries to body parts are worth different amounts in different states.

When a worker is injured on the job or develops a disabling occupational disease, the worker must file a claim, either with the company or with its insurance carrier (or in some states, with a state agency), to request workers' compensation benefits. In most states, benefits begin after a short waiting period (two to 14 days) and include a wage replacement payment (a percentage of the worker's salary) and a reimbursement of medical costs. The employer (or its insurance carrier) may require the injured worker to be treated by a doctor selected by the company.

Employers can challenge claims

Employers may contest a worker's compensation claim if they believe (1) the injury (or illness) is not a result of the work, (2) the employee is capable of performing the job despite the injury or illness, or (3) the employee has made a fraudulent claim. Other issues that may involve a challenge to a worker's compensation claim include heart attacks, strokes, or other stress-related problems. In some states, the law places the burden on the employee to prove that the disabling condition was a result of work effort or work-related stress and would not have occurred otherwise.

Fraudulent claims

There is no question that there is considerable fraud related to workers' compensation. Employers can (and do) challenge a workers' compensation claim if it is suspected the employee is not injured or is exaggerating the extent of injury. *The Wall Street Journal* reported that the "Fake Bad Scale" is growing in use as "proponents hail the true-or-false test as a valid way to identify people feigning pain, psychological symptoms or other ills to collect a payout. In hundreds of cases, expert witnesses have testified that the test provided evidence that plaintiffs were lying about their injuries, just as suggested by the test's colorful name: the Fake Bad Scale." *The Journal* reported that use of the scale surged in 2007 after publishers of the Minnesota Multiphasic Personality Inventory (discussed in Chapter 6) incorporated the Fake Bad Scale as a scored subset of the MMPI. According to a survey by St. Louis University, the Fake Bad Scale has been used by 75 percent of neuropsychologists, who regularly appear in court as expert witnesses. In 2008, a panel representing the American Psychological Association concluded that "there appeared to be a lack of good research supporting the test."[17]

"Fake Bad Scale" for fraud cases has limited research support

Disputes related to workers' compensation are common. Many states have established dispute resolution agencies in an attempt to resolve the dispute more quickly. For example, the state of Florida established the **Employee Assistance and Ombudsman Office (EAO),** which requires injured workers, employers, and medical providers to file a request for assistance with this agency for mandatory dispute resolution. Some employees are challenging the no-fault assumptions of the workers' compensation system, arguing that an employer who knowingly exposes workers to hazardous substances or dangerous working conditions should not be protected from negligence lawsuits. In most instances, the courts have ruled that all employer conduct short of an "intentional wrong" will fall under the rubric of workers' compensation. However, there are some exceptions to this general rule. One state court ruled that a company that withholds information from employees regarding the development of a serious occupational disease could be sued for negligence and fraud.[18]

No fault provisions

The fact that a company may have violated an **OSHA standard** will not necessarily remove the protection of workers' compensation. The no-fault provisions of the system (with the above-noted exception) make irrelevant the issue of whether the employer or the worker was to blame. The worker gets medical treatment and a portion of his or her wages; the employer is insulated from litigation in return for paying the workers' compensation benefits.

If a worker becomes disabled due to a job-related accident or illness, the employer may be obligated under the 1990 Americans with Disabilities Act (ADA) to provide "reasonable accommodations" for that worker, assuming the disability qualifies as a disability under the ADA. This accommodation might include job restructuring or reassignment. However, the injury must qualify as a disability under the ADA.

Workers' comp laws encourage safety

While provisions of workers' compensation laws, such as the premium imposed, encouraged employers' efforts to improve their health and safety records, the effects of such provisions were not very impressive. Many states took matters into their own hands to do more in this area. Between 1911 and 1948, each state passed a workers' compensation law. This created a myriad of rules and regulations, which resulted in a lack of uniformity in policies and regulations across the states. This prompted political pressure from numerous constituencies, particularly unions, for a federal law aimed primarily at the reduction and prevention of occupational fatalities, injuries, and illness. The result of the pressure was passage of the Occupational Safety and Health Act in 1970.

The Occupational Safety and Health Administration Act

The **Occupational Safety and Health Administration (OSHA)** was created in 1970 within the U.S. Department of Labor. It was designed to reduce occupational diseases and on-the-job injuries. The Occupational Safety and Health Administration aims to ensure employee safety and health in the United States by working with employers and employees to create better working environments. According to its Web site, since its inception in 1971, OSHA has helped to cut workplace fatalities by more than 60 percent and occupational injury and illness rates by 40 percent. At the same time, U.S. employment has increased from 56 million employees at 3.5 million worksites to more than 135 million employees at 8.9 million sites. In Fiscal Year 2007, OSHA had 2,150 employees, including 1,100 inspectors. The agency's appropriation is $486.9 million (go to OSHA.gov for revised information). Figure 14-2 presents a summary of the various agencies and functions that derive from OSHA.

1,100 OSHA inspectors in 2007

Based on the latest available data, occupational injury and illness rates declined again to 4.6 cases per 100 employees, with 4.2 million injuries and illnesses among private-sector firms. Approximately 33 percent of work-related injuries occurred in goods-producing industries and 67 percent in services.

There were 5,703 employee deaths in 2006, a slight decrease from the 2005 total of 5,734. The fatality rate of 3.9 deaths per 100,000 employees was down slightly from a rate of 4.0 in 2005. Fatalities related to highway incidents and homicides increased, while deaths related to falls decreased.

There were 5,488 worker deaths in 2007, a slight decrease from 2006. The fatality rate of 4.0 deaths per 100,000 workers remained the same from 2007 to 2008. Fatalities related to highway incidents, falls, and electrocutions declined while homicides and deaths related to fires and explosions and contact with objects or equipment increased (go to www.osha.gov for the latest figures). According to the **National Safety Council** (www.nsc.org), between 1912 and 2007, unintentional work deaths (per 100,000 workers) were reduced from 21 to 13.

Figure 14-2   **The Basics of OSHA and Worker Safety**

Agencies under the Occupational Safety and Act of 1970

Occupational Safety & Health Administration

Occupational Safety & Health Review Commission (OSHRC)

National Institute for Occupational Safety and Health (NIOSH)

State Agencies (22 states) (Arizona, California, Hawaii, Indiana, Iowa, Kentucky, Maryland, Michigan, Minnesota, Nevada, New Mexico, New Jersey, New York, North Carolina, Oregon, South Carolina, Tennessee, Utah, Vermont, Virginia, Washington and Wyoming)

Health Agency Actions

Issue standards; conduct inspections, citations, variances

Review citations; abatement

Render decision on contested citations

Conduct research

Standards; enforcement

Train Compliance Safety and Health officers (COSHOs)

The NSC proclaimed 2005 to be the start of a "promising trend" in the adoption of safety as a "core corporate value" among an increasing number of corporate leaders.

Specifically, the purpose of OSHA is to accomplish the following:

1. Encourage employers and employees to reduce workplace hazards and to implement new or improve existing safety and health programs.

2. Provide for research in occupational safety and health to develop innovative ways of dealing with occupational safety and health problems.

3. Establish "separate but dependent responsibilities and rights" for employers and employees to achieve better safety and health conditions.

4. Maintain a reporting and recordkeeping system to monitor job-related injuries and illnesses.

5. Establish training programs to increase the number and competence of occupational safety and health personnel.

6. Develop mandatory job safety and health standards and enforce them effectively.

7. Provide for the development, analysis, evaluation, and approval of state occupational safety and health programs.

OSHA applies to all U.S. employers

Coverage of the OSHA Act of 1970, which includes virtually all employers and their employees in the United States, is provided either directly by federal OSHA or through an OSHA-approved state program. OSHA seeks to assist the majority of employers who want to do the right thing while focusing its enforcement resources on sites in more hazardous industries—especially those with high injury and illness rates. Less than 1 percent of inspections—about 467 (2006 data)—came under the agency's **Enhanced Enforcement Program,** designed to address employers who repeatedly and willfully violate the law. Strong enforcement has helped to increase alleged violations by more than 10 percent over the past 10 years. At the same time, injuries and illnesses continue to decline significantly.

Enhanced enforcement program

State Health and Safety Plans

OSHA encourages states to create their own safety and health programs for workers, thus largely superseding enforcement, compliance, and outreach through federal OSHA, although the federal agency has responsibility for approving and monitoring state plans. In return, the law allows states to receive up to 50 percent of their plan's operating costs in grant form from the agency. Twenty-two states have chosen to develop and operate their own occupational safety and health compliance programs for private- and public-sector employees (see Figure 14-2 for a list of the states). Four others operate programs that cover public employees only. OSHA has responsibility for approving and monitoring state plans. State plans must set job safety and health standards that are "at least as effective as" comparable federal standards. State plans must adhere to stringent guidelines, such as conducting inspections to enforce standards, covering public employees, and running safety training and education programs. Says one expert, "State plans give the states flexibility to build occupational safety and health

22 state programs monitored by OSHA

467

programs around a state's geographic, economic, political and cultural peculiarities. Loggers in Oregon, for instance, are faced with struck-by hazards because the trees are pulled off slopes. In North Carolina, tree felling is the biggest hazard to workers."[19]

Three strategies

OSHA has focused on three strategies in recent years: (1) strong, fair and effective enforcement; (2) outreach, education, and compliance assistance; and (3) partnerships and cooperative programs. It should be noted that OSHA devoted considerable time and expense at "ground zero" of the World Trade Center tragedy. Nearly 400 OSHA staffers monitored conditions at the work site to monitor health and safety issues for all workers in the area. OSHA conducted over 100 air samples in the area and found that all samples fell below the OSHA standard for asbestos. They also tested the area for dioxin, metals, volatile organic compounds, carbon monoxide, silica, and freon. They provided respirators and other personal protection equipment. During that same time period, OSHA issued an Anthrax Matrix that provided guidelines for equipment and workspaces and assessed risk for anthrax exposure. OSHA's role continues to be assistance and consultation.

Standards

OSHA has two major functions: to impose enforceable standards and to conduct workplace inspections to ensure that employers are complying with the standards and providing a safe and healthful workplace.

OSHA standards are practices, means, methods, or processes reasonably necessary to protect workers on the job. The noise and asbestos standards are two examples. It is the responsibility of employers to become familiar with standards applicable to their work-places, to eliminate hazardous conditions to the extent possible, and to comply with the standards. Compliance may include ensuring that employees have and use personal protective equipment when required for safety or health.

"General duty clause"

Even in areas where OSHA has not established a standard that addresses a specific work hazard, employers are responsible for complying with the OSH Act's "general duty" clause. The **general duty clause of** the OSH Act [Section 5(a) (1)] states that each employer "shall furnish . . . a place of employment which is free from recognized hazards that are causing or are likely to cause death or serious physical harm to his employees."

The 22 states with OSHA-approved job safety and health programs must set standards that are at least as effective as the equivalent federal standard. Most of the state-plan states adopt standards identical to the federal ones (two states, New York and Connecticut, have plans which cover only public sector employees).

OSHA has expanded its role in protecting workers from hazardous materials. Maximum exposure limits were set for 164 substances, and limits were tightened for 212 others. The limits cover the maximum amount of time a worker can be exposed to specific substances during an eight-hour workday. Among the substances regulated for the first time were cotton dust, wood dust, grain dust, gasoline, acrylic acid, tungsten, and welding fumes. OSHA also cut maximum exposure limits for carbon monoxide, chloroform, and hydrogen. In addition to exposure to hazardous materials, it is also important to examine the protective clothing worn by employees. Choosing the appropriate protection level and material of personal protective apparel is critical.

Variances—four types

Employers may ask for a temporary (up to one year) **variance** from a standard when they cannot comply with a new standard by its effective date. OSHA may grant a permanent variance from a standard when an employer can demonstrate that it has alternatives in place that protect employees as effectively as compliance with the standard would.

Generally, a variance is an exception to compliance with some part of a safety and health standard granted by OSHA to an employer. For example, sometimes employers may not be able to comply fully and on time with a new safety or health standard because of a shortage of personnel, materials, or equipment. Or employers may prefer to use methods, equipment, or facilities that they believe protect employees as well as or better than OSHA standards. In situations like these, employers may apply to OSHA for a variance. There are four types of variances: *temporary, permanent, experimental*, and *national defense*.

Recordkeeping and Reporting

Before OSHA became effective, no centralized and systematic method existed for monitoring occupational safety and health problems. Statistics on job injuries and illnesses were collected by some states and by some private organizations. With OSHA came the first basis for consistent, nationwide procedures—a vital requirement for gauging safety problems and solving them.

Employers with 11 or more employees must maintain records

Employers with 11 or more employees must maintain records of occupational injuries and illnesses as they occur. The records permit the **Bureau of Labor Statistics** to compile data, to help define high-hazard industries, and to inform employees of the status of their employers' record. OSHA provides a free 24-hour hot line for reporting workplace safety or health emergencies.

Forms 300/301

Recordkeeping forms must be maintained for five years at the establishment and must be available for inspection by representatives of OSHA. The Injury and Incident Report **(Form 301)** must be completed within seven days once a recordable work-related injury or illness has occurred. The Log of Work Related Injuries and Illnesses **(Form 300)** is used to classify work-related injuries and illnesses and to note the severity of each case. The Summary **(Form 300A)** provides the totals for the year in each category. Figure 14-3 presents a summary of employer obligations as outlined by the U.S. Department of Labor.

Keeping records of accidents is important not only to meet compliance issues, but also for identifying ergonomic problems in the workplace. Records should be kept not only for visible traumas, but also for musculoskeletal injuries such as strained backs, pulled limbs, and RSIs. Analyzing these records can identify areas where poor manual handling or ergonomics causes work-related injuries. Statistics on absences are also valuable and enable organizations to draw comparisons between their firm and others. Unfortunately, many firms do not keep very detailed absence records, if they keep any.

Defining Occupational Injury or Illness

An **occupational injury** is any injury, such as a cut, fracture, sprain, or amputation, that results from a work-related accident or from exposure involving a single incident in the work environment. An **occupational illness** is any abnormal condition or disorder, other than one resulting from an occupational injury, caused by exposure to environmental factors associated with employment. Included are acute and chronic illnesses or diseases that may be caused by inhalation, absorption, or ingestion of or direct contact with toxic substances or harmful agents. Alcoholism has even been considered an occupational illness in a case involving an employee who developed an alcohol-related problem as a result of the socializing responsibilities associated with his job.

All occupational illnesses must be recorded, regardless of severity. All occupational injuries must be recorded if they result in the following:

When are they recorded?

- Death (must be recorded regardless of the length of time between the injury and death).
- One or more lost workdays.
- Restriction of work or motion.
- Loss of consciousness.
- Transfer to another job.
- Medical treatment (other than first-aid).

Workplace Inspection

COSHOs

To enforce its standards, OSHA is authorized under the act to conduct workplace inspections. Every establishment covered by the act is subject to inspection by OSHA **compliance safety and health officers (COSHOs),** who are chosen for their knowledge and experience in the occupational safety and health field, and who are trained in OSHA standards and in recognition of safety and health hazards.

Under the act, "upon presenting appropriate credentials to the owner, operator, or agent in charge," a COSHO is authorized to carry out the following:

- "Enter without delay and at reasonable times any factory, plant, establishment, construction site or other areas, workplace, or environment where work is performed by an employee of an employer."
- "Inspect and investigate during regular working hours, and at other reasonable times, and within reasonable limits and in a reasonable manner, any such place of employment and all pertinent conditions, structures, machines, apparatus, devices, equipment and materials therein, and to question privately any such employer, owner, operator, agent, or employee."

Priorities for inspections

OSHA's highest priorities for inspections are to first go to imminent danger situations and actual fatal accident sites. Next, it inspects workplaces with valid employee complaints or target industries (those with high rates of accidents). Finally, it performs random inspections and reinspections of various work sites. OSHA conducted 38,579 inspections in 2006, most of which were directed at hazardous works sites and to investigate complaints or serious injuries or fatalities.[20] Over 59 percent of inspections are directed at the construction industry.

With very few exceptions, inspections are conducted without advance notice. In fact, alerting an employer in advance of an OSHA inspection can bring a fine of up to $1,000 and/or a six-month jail term. If an employer refuses to grant admittance to the COSHO, or if an employer attempts to interfere with the inspection, the Act permits appropriate legal action.

***Marshall v. Barlow's* on warrants**

Based on a 1978 U.S. Supreme Court ruling in ***Marshall v. Barlow's Inc.,***[21] **OSHA may not conduct warrantless inspections without an employer's consent**. It may, however, inspect after acquiring a judicially authorized search warrant based on administrative probable cause or on evidence of a violation. Employers are not required to allow inspectors to observe all work areas, nor are they required to provide all requested documents. Warrants and administrative subpoenas may be necessary but are routinely granted.

If employees are represented by a recognized bargaining representative, the union ordinarily will designate an employee representative to accompany the compliance officer. Similarly, if there is a plant safety committee, the employee members of that committee will designate the employee representative. OSHA requires that employees—whether represented by a union or not—have a right to select a representative for the inspection. OSHA regulations require that the inspector consult with a "reasonable number of employees" if no representative is designated.

Inspection Tour: After the opening conference in which the scope of the inspection is stipulated, the COSHO and accompanying representatives proceed through the establishment and inspect work areas for compliance with OSHA standards. The route and duration of the inspection are determined by the compliance officer. If an employer is concerned about an apparent expansion of the inspection from what was said at the opening conference, another opening conference may be requested to discuss the expansion. At that point, the employer can demand a warrant. While talking with employees, the compliance officer makes every effort to minimize work interruptions. The compliance officer observes conditions, consults with employees, takes instrument readings, examines records, and may even take photos or videotape (this is for recordkeeping purposes, and employers may request that confidentiality be maintained).

Employees are consulted during the inspection tour. The compliance officer may stop and question workers, in private if they so desire, about safety and health conditions and practices in their workplaces. All employees are protected, under the act, from discrimination from their employer for exercising their safety and health rights.

Records and postings are checked

Records and postings are checked. The compliance officer inspects records of injuries, illnesses, and deaths that the employer is required to keep. He or she checks to see that a copy of the totals from the last page of OSHA Form 300 have been posted.

Closing Conference: After the inspection tour, a closing conference is held between the compliance officer and the employer or the employer's representative. This is the time for free discussion of problems and needs—a time for frank questions and answers.

The compliance officer discusses with the employer all unsafe conditions observed on the inspection and indicates all apparent violations for which a citation may be issued or recommended: (1) a description of the violation; (2) the proposed financial penalty, if any; and (3) the date by which the hazard must be corrected. The employer is then

Appeal rights

informed of appeal rights. The **OSHA Appeals Commission** hears appeals regarding citations. That judgment also can be appealed to the **U.S. Court of Appeals** for that geographical area.

Most frequent violations

While OSHA looks for violations of all types, they rely on their extensive data to look for certain violations. In 2007, the most frequently found violations concerned scaffolding, fall protection, and hazard communications.[22]

Figure 14-3   Summary of Employer Obligations

U.S. Department of Labor
Occupational Safety and Health Administration

An Overview:
Recording Work-Related Injuries and Illnesses

The Occupational Safety and Health (OSH) Act of 1970 requires certain employers to prepare and maintain records of work-related injuries and illnesses. Use these definitions when you classify cases on the Log. OSHA's recordkeeping regulation (see 29 CFR Part 1904) provides more information about the definitions below.

The *Log of Work-Related Injuries and Illnesses* (Form 300) is used to classify work-related injuries and illnesses and to note the extent and severity of each case. When an incident occurs, use the *Log* to record specific details about what happened and how it happened. The *Summary* — a separate form (Form 300A) — shows the totals for the year in each category. At the end of the year, post the *Summary* in a visible location so that your employees are aware of the injuries and illnesses occurring in their workplace.

Employers must keep a *Log* for each establishment or site. If you have more than one establishment, you must keep a separate *Log* and *Summary* for each physical location that is expected to be in operation for one year or longer.

Note that your employees have the right to review your injury and illness records. For more information, see 29 Code of Federal Regulations Part 1904.35, *Employee Involvement*.

Cases listed on the *Log of Work-Related Injuries and Illnesses* are not necessarily eligible for workers' compensation or other insurance benefits. Listing a case on the *Log* does not mean that the employer or worker was at fault or that an OSHA standard was violated.

When is an injury or illness considered work-related?

An injury or illness is considered work-related if an event or exposure in the work environment caused or contributed to the condition or significantly aggravated a preexisting condition. Work-relatedness is presumed for injuries and illnesses resulting from events or exposures occurring in the workplace, unless an exception specifically applies. See 29 CFR Part 1904.5(b)(2) for the exceptions. The work environment includes the establishment and other locations where one or more employees are working or are present as a condition of their employment. See 29 CFR Part 1904.5(b)(1).

Which work-related injuries and illnesses should you record?

Record those work-related injuries and illnesses that result in:

▶ death,

▶ loss of consciousness,

▶ days away from work,

▶ restricted work activity or job transfer, or

▶ medical treatment beyond first aid.

You must also record work-related injuries and illnesses that are significant (as defined below) or meet any of the additional criteria listed below.

You must record any significant work-related injury or illness that is diagnosed by a physician or other licensed health care professional. You must record any work-related case involving cancer, chronic irreversible disease, a fractured or cracked bone, or a punctured eardrum. See 29 CFR 1904.7.

What are the additional criteria?

You must record the following conditions when they are work-related:

▶ any needlestick injury or cut from a sharp object that is contaminated with another person's blood or other potentially infectious material;

▶ any case requiring an employee to be medically removed under the requirements of an OSHA health standard;

▶ tuberculosis infection as evidenced by a positive skin test or diagnosis by a physician or other licensed health care professional after exposure to a known case of active tuberculosis.

What is medical treatment?

Medical treatment includes managing and caring for a patient for the purpose of combating disease or disorder. The following are not considered medical treatments and are NOT recordable:

▶ visits to a doctor or health care professional solely for observation or counseling;

▶ diagnostic procedures, including administering prescription medications that are used solely for diagnostic purposes; and

▶ any procedure that can be labeled first aid. (*See below for more information about first aid.*)

What do you need to do?

1. Within 7 calendar days after you receive information about a case, decide if the case is recordable under the OSHA recordkeeping requirements.

2. Determine whether the incident is a new case or a recurrence of an existing one.

3. Establish whether the case was work-related.

4. If the case is recordable, decide which form you will fill out as the injury and illness incident report.

   You may use *OSHA's 301: Injury and Illness Incident Report* or an equivalent form. Some state workers compensation, insurance, or other reports may be acceptable substitutes, as long as they provide the same information as the OSHA 301.

How to work with the Log

1. Identify the employee involved unless it is a privacy concern case as described below.

2. Identify when and where the case occurred.

3. Describe the case, as specifically as you can.

4. Classify the seriousness of the case by recording the **most serious outcome** associated with the case, with column J (Other recordable cases) being the least serious and column G (Death) being the most serious.

5. Identify whether the case is an injury or illness. If the case is an injury, check the injury category. If the case is an illness, check the appropriate illness category.

471

Abatement period

OSHA provides an **abatement period,** which is the amount of time the employer has to fix the problem. Employers are rarely given more than 30 days to make the stipulated improvements. However, longer periods may be granted if the employer must make major changes or order new equipment or parts that will not arrive within 30 days. Requests for extensions can be made to the area OSHA representative.

The compliance officer explains that OSHA area offices are full-service resource centers that provide a number of services such as training speakers and technical materials on safety and health matters. The compliance officer also explains the requirements of the Hazard Communications Standard, which requires employers to establish a written, comprehensive hazard communication program that includes provisions for container labeling, material safety data sheets, and an employee training program. (Employers have been cited for over 60,000 violations of the Hazard Communications Standard since 1985.) Employers are required to certify to OSHA that they have corrected workplace hazards cited by the agency.[23]

Hazard communications standard

Citations and Penalties

After the compliance officer reports his or her findings, the area director determines what citations, if any will be issued, and what penalties, if any, will be proposed. Citations inform the employer and employees of the regulations and standards alleged to have been violated and of the proposed length of time set for their abatement. The employer will receive citations and notices of proposed penalties by certified mail. The employer must post a copy of each citation at or near the place a violation occurred for three days or until the violation is abated, whichever is longer. Figure 14-4 presents a summary of the penalty options OSHA will consider.

Types of violation

These are the types of violations that may be cited and the penalties that may be proposed:

- *Other than Serious Violation*—A violation that has a direct relationship to job safety and health, but probably would not cause death or serious physical harm. A proposed penalty of up to $7,000 for each violation is discretionary.

- *Serious Violation*—A violation where there is substantial probability that death or serious physical harm could result and that the employer knew, or should have known, of the hazard. A mandatory penalty of up to $7,000 for each violation is proposed. A penalty for a serious violation may be adjusted downward, based on the employer's good faith, history of previous violations, the gravity of the alleged violation, and size of business.

- *Willful Violation*—A violation that the employer knowingly commits or commits with plain indifference to the law. The employer either knows that what he or she is doing constitutes a violation, or is aware that a hazardous condition existed and made no reasonable effort to eliminate it. Penalties of up to $70,000 may be proposed for each willful violation, with a minimum penalty of $5,000 for each violation. A proposed penalty for a willful violation may be adjusted downward, depending on the size of the business and its history of previous violations. Usually, no credit is given for good faith.

Figure 14-4   **Employer Penalties for OSHA Violations**

Violation	Description	Penalty
Other than serious violation	Violation not capable of causing death or serious injury	Fine up to $7,000 per violation (discretionary)
Serious violation	Substantial probability that death or serious physical harm could result and that the employer knew, or should have known, of the hazard	Fine up to $7,000 per violation (mandatory)
Willful violation	Intentional (knowing) violation	Possible criminal penalties; fines up to $10,000 per violation
Repeat violation and or failure to correct the violation	Finding of similar violation; failure to correct violation	Fine up to $70,000 per violation; up to $7,000 per day if violation continues

If an employer is convicted of a willful violation of a standard that has resulted in the death of an employee, the offense is punishable by a court-imposed fine or by imprisonment for up to six months, or both. A fine of up to $250,000 for an individual, or $500,000 for a corporation, may be imposed for a criminal conviction.

■ *Repeated Violation*—A violation of any standard, regulation, rule, or order where, upon reinspection, a substantially similar violation can bring a fine of up to $70,000 for each such violation. To be the basis of a repeated citation, the original citation must be final; a citation under contest may not serve as the basis for a subsequent repeated citation.

■ *Failure to Abate Prior Violation*—Failure to abate a prior violation may bring a civil penalty of up to $7,000 for each day the violation continues beyond the prescribed abatement date.

Additional penalties

Additional violations for which citations and proposed penalties may be issued upon conviction are:

■ Falsifying records, reports, or applications can bring a fine of $10,000 or up to six months in jail, or both.

■ Violations of posting requirements can bring a civil penalty of up to $7,000.

■ Assaulting a compliance officer, or otherwise resisting, opposing, intimidating, or interfering with a compliance officer while they are engaged in the performance of their duties is a criminal offense, subject to a fine of not more than $5,000 and imprisonment for not more than three years.

Citation and penalty procedures may differ somewhat in states with their own occupational safety and health programs. Employees may request an informal conference with OSHA to discuss any issues raised by an inspection, citation, notice of proposed penalty, or employer's notice of intention to contest.

Top five OSHA violations

In 2006, the "top five" violations of OSHA standards were related to (in order of the number of violations): (1) scaffolding; (2) hazard communication; (3) fall protection; (4) lockout/control of hazardous energy respiratory protection; and (5) electrical wiring. The top "willful violations" in addition to these five were: protection systems—excavation, noise exposure, permit violations for confined spaces, and machine guarding.

Services Available

Consultation Assistance: Free consultation assistance is available to employers who want help establishing and maintaining a safe and healthful workplace. Largely funded by OSHA, the service is provided at no cost to the employer. As part of this service, no citations are issued, no penalties are imposed, and information is kept confidential. Besides helping employers to identify and correct specific hazards, consultation can include assistance in developing and implementing effective workplace safety and health programs with emphasis on the prevention of worker injuries and illnesses. Training and education services also can be provided.

Voluntary Protection Programs

Voluntary Protection Programs: Voluntary protection programs (VPPs) represent a major component of OSHA's effort to extend worker protection beyond the minimum required by OSHA standards. When combined with an effective enforcement program, VPPs, expanded on-site consultation services, and full-service area offices can expand worker protection to help meet the goals of the OSHA. VPP participants establish and maintain excellent safety records and programs that are recognized by OSHA as models for their industries. The cooperative interaction with OSHA gives companies the opportunity to provide OSHA with valuable input on health and safety issues and to provide the industry with effective models of excellence in health and safety.

Unlike other companies, VPP participants are not subject to routine OSHA inspections. Establishing and maintaining OSHA-endorsed programs following the VPP model are reflected in significantly lower injury rates for participating companies. For example, the average VPP worksite has a days-away-from-work rate of 52 percent below the average for its industry. These sites typically do not start out with such low rates. Reductions in injuries and illnesses begin when the site commits to the VPP approach to safety and health management and the challenging VPP application process. Among the members of the VPP programs is the New Holland, Michigan, Ford Motor Company plant. Ford reported a

13 percent increase in productivity since joining the VPP program and a 16 percent drop in scrapped product that had to be reworked. According to the OSHA Web site, VPP worksites "save millions each year because their injury and illness rates are more than 50 percent below the averages for their industries."

The VPP program was revised in 2000 to allow previously ineligible employers, especially small businesses, to raise the health and safety achievement levels expected of participants. OSHA expects VPP sites to participate in outreach programs that assist other workplaces and help OSHA accomplish its goals. Visit OSHA's outstanding Web site for more details on this program.

Star, merit, and demonstration VPPs

The three VPPs—Star, Merit, and Demonstration—are designed to perform the following functions:

■ Recognize outstanding achievement of those who have successfully incorporated comprehensive safety and health programs into their total management systems.

■ Motivate other companies to achieve excellent safety and health results in the same outstanding way.

■ Establish a relationship between employers, employees, and OSHA that is based on cooperation rather than coercion.

The **Star** program, OSHA's most demanding and the most prestigious VPP, is open to an employer in any industry who has successfully managed a comprehensive safety and health program to reduce injury rates below the industry's national average. Specific requirements for the program include systems for management commitment and responsibility; hazard assessment and control; and safety planning, rules, work procedures, and training that are in place and operating effectively.[24]

The **Merit** program, also open to any industry, is primarily a stepping stone to Star program participation. A company with a basic safety and health program that is committed to improvement and has the resources to do so within a specified time period may work with OSHA to meet merit qualifications.[25]

The **Star** Demonstration program is designed for worksites with Star-level quality safety and health protection to test alternatives to current Star eligibility and performance requirements. Promising and successful projects are considered for changes to Star requirements.

Training and Education: OSHA's area offices are full-service centers offering a variety of informational services such as speakers, publications, audiovisual aids on workplace hazards, and technical advice. The OSHA Training Institute in Arlington Heights, Illinois, provides basic and advanced training and education in safety and health for federal and state compliance officers; state consultants; other federal agency personnel; and private-sector employers, employees, and their representatives. Institute courses are also offered to the public and cover areas such as electrical hazards, machine guarding, ventilation, and ergonomics.

Employer Responsibilities under OSHA

As an employer, you must abide by these OSHA guidelines:

■ Meet your **general duty responsibility** to provide a workplace free from recognized hazards that are causing or are likely to cause death or serious physical harm to employees and comply with standards, rules, and regulations issued under the act.

■ Familiarize yourself and employees with mandatory OSHA standards and make copies available to employees for review upon request.

■ Examine workplace conditions to ensure they conform to applicable standards.

■ Minimize or reduce safety and health hazards.

■ Ensure that employees have and use safe tools and equipment (including appropriate personal protective equipment) and that such equipment is properly maintained.

■ Employ color codes, posters, labels, or signs in several languages to warn employees of potential hazards.

■ Establish or update operating procedures and communicate them so that employees follow safety and health requirements.

- Provide medical examinations when required by OSHA standards.
- Report to the nearest OSHA office within 48 hours of any fatal accident or one that results in the hospitalization of five or more employees.
- Keep OSHA-required records of work-related injuries and illnesses and post a copy of the totals from the last page of OSHA Form 300 during the entire month of February each year.
- Post, at a prominent location within the workplace, an OSHA poster informing employees of their rights and responsibilities.
- Provide employees, former employees, and their representatives access to the Log and Summary of Occupational Injuries and Illnesses (OSHA Form 300) at a reasonable time and in a reasonable manner.
- Cooperate with the OSHA compliance officer by furnishing names of authorized employee representatives who may be asked to accompany the compliance officer during an inspection.
- Refrain from discriminating against employees who properly exercise their rights under the act.
- Post OSHA citations at or near the work site involved. Each citation, or citation copy thereof, must remain posted until the violation has been abated or for three working days, whichever is longer.

Although OSHA does not cite employees for violations of their responsibilities, each employee "shall comply with all occupational safety and health standards and rules, regulations, and orders issued under the act" that are applicable.

Employee Rights under OSHA

Employees have a right to seek a safe workplace without fear of punishment. That right is spelled out in Section 11(c) of the act. All employees are covered except workers who are self-employed and public employees in state and local government.

The law says employers shall not punish or discriminate against workers for exercising the following rights:

Protection from retaliation

- Complaining to an employer, union, OSHA, or any other government agency about job safety and health hazards.
- Filing safety or health grievances.
- Participating on a workplace safety and health committee or in union activities concerning job safety and health.
- Participating in OSHA inspections, conferences, hearings, or other OSHA-related activities.

If an employee is exercising these or other OSHA rights, the employer is not allowed to discriminate against that worker in any way, such as through firing, demotion, transferring the worker to an undesirable job or shift, or threatening or harassing the worker.

Whirlpool v. Marshall

In *Whirlpool v. Marshall,* the Supreme Court ruled in 1981 that although there is no specific language in the law about walking off a job, employees who have a reasonable apprehension of death or serious injury may refuse to work until that safety hazard is corrected. The employer may not discipline or discharge a worker who exercises this right, although the employer is not required to pay the worker for the hours not worked.[26]

Workers believing they have been punished for exercising safety and health rights must contact the nearest OSHA office within 30 days of the time they learn of the alleged discrimination. A union representative can file the complaint for the worker. The worker does not have to complete any form. Any OSHA staff member will complete the forms after asking what happened and who was involved.

Following a complaint, OSHA investigates the organization. If an employee has been illegally punished for exercising safety and health rights, OSHA asks the employer to restore that worker's job earnings and benefits. If necessary, and if it can prove discrimination, OSHA takes the employer to court. In such cases, the worker does not pay any legal fees.

If a state agency has an OSHA-approved state program, employees may file their complaint with either federal OSHA or the state agency under its laws.

Additional employee rights

Employees also have these additional rights under OSHA:

- Review copies of appropriate OSHA standards, rules, regulations, and requirements that the employer should have available at the workplace.

- Request information from your employer on safety and health hazards in the area, on precautions that may be taken, and on procedures to be followed if an employee is involved in an accident or is exposed to toxic substances.

- Request the OSHA area director to conduct an inspection if you believe hazardous conditions or violations of standards exist in your workplace.

- Have your name withheld from your employer, upon request to OSHA, if you file a written and signed complaint.

- Learn about OSHA actions regarding your complaint and have an informal review, if requested, of any decision not to inspect or to issue a citation.

- Have your authorized employee representative accompany the OSHA compliance officer during the inspection tour.

- Respond to questions from the OSHA compliance officer, particularly if there is no authorized employee representative accompanying the compliance officer.

- Observe any monitoring or measuring of hazardous materials and have the right to see these records, as specified under the act.

- Have your authorized representative, or yourself, review the Log and Summary of Occupational Injuries (OSHA Form 300) at a reasonable time and in a reasonable manner.

- Request a closing discussion with the compliance officer following an inspection.

- Submit a written request to the **National Institute for Occupational Safety and Health (NIOSH)** for information on whether any substance in your workplace has potentially toxic effects in the concentration being used, and have your name withheld from your employer, if you so request.

Notice on variances

- Receive notification from your employer if he or she applies for a variance from an OSHA standard, testify at a variance hearing, and appeal the final decision.

- Submit information or comment to OSHA on the issuance, modification, or revocation of OSHA standards and request a public hearing.

The Effects of OSHA

OSHA has had a profound impact on employer actions regarding health and safety issues. The establishment of formal safety committees, improved equipment and machinery, improved medical facilities and staff, and, in general, greater emphasis on safety and prevention are among the major changes that are the direct result of OSHA.

OSHA has been used as the "poster child" for excessive governmental regulation since Ronald Reagan attacked the agency when he ran for president. Republicans in particular who attack "big government" argue that OSHA regulations seriously hinder productivity and increase costs. Critics argue that OSHA is often meddling in areas where there is enough protection for workers at the state level through workers' compensation and by companies on their own because it's in their best interest to keep workers safe and healthy. The cartoon in Figure 14-5 illustrates this anti-OSHA attitude. President George W. Bush signed legislation in 2001 repealing an **ergonomics standard,** designed to reduce injuries to workers from repetitive motions and lifting. Business groups, including the Chamber of Commerce, claimed the standard would cost $100 billion to implement. One of the most active lobbyists advocating the repeal of the standard was Edwin Foulke, who was appointed the director of OSHA. Needless to say, Mr. Foulke is not a fan of government regulation or OSHA. Since he took control, OSHA has withdrawn numerous proposed regulations and, as of 2008, had issued no major new standards under his direction.

Says ABC network's John Stossel, OSHA is made up of "a bunch of clueless busybodies trying to micromanage everybody's life." James Knott, owner of a Massachusetts manufacturing facility, is not a big fan of OSHA either. He says OSHA has never been helpful

Figure 14-5
Newspaper Carrier after OSHA

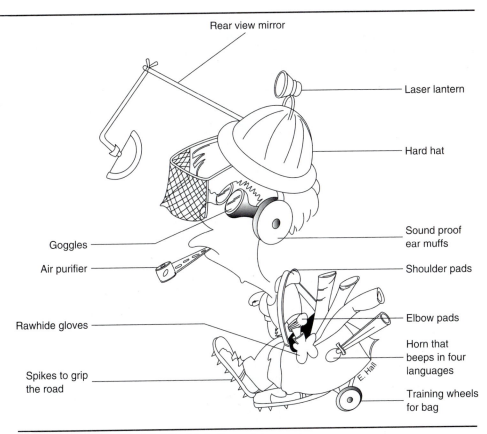

Rear view mirror

Laser lantern

Hard hat

Sound proof ear muffs

Shoulder pads

Elbow pads

Horn that beeps in four languages

Training wheels for bag

Goggles

Air purifier

Rawhide gloves

Spikes to grip the road

Source: Copyright (c) 2006 by E. Hall. Reprinted with permission.

about anything. "They send their inspectors around who invent complaints and then they would like you to pay them money; they're extortionists."[27] But what most critics of OSHA ignore is that while OSHA and its inspectors have made mistakes along the way in issuing regulations and citations, companies have appeal processes. For example, Mr. Knott had particular problems regarding an OSHA inspector's recommendation under the **"General Duty Clause"** that he extend the height of a fence. Mr. Knott could have appealed this recommendation to the Occupational Safety and Health Review Commission (OSHRC) or requested a variance. If Mr. Knott lost at the OSHRC level, he could also contest the citation to the U.S. Court of Appeals. There are many options for organizations against OSHA "complaint inventions" and imposed fines and orders.

It is very difficult to evaluate the effects of OSHA using data on injuries, accidents, and fatalities. Recall the recent changes to the reporting rules for injuries in 2002. These new definitions of course resulted in changes in occupational injury and illness statistics provided by the **Bureau of Labor Statistics.** Using the new definitions, the BLS reported that there were 4.4 million nonfatal injuries and illnesses in private-industry workplaces in 2002, resulting in a rate of 5.5 cases per 100 equivalent full-time workers. While these data follow the trend of declining cases and rates seen throughout the past decade, because of the change in definition they cannot be compared with data from prior years.

Workers' compensation claims down

Some may also cite the decline in construction injuries as an illustration of OSHA's positive effects. Workers' compensation claims dropped more than 10 percent in 2007. (See Figure 14-6.) Construction is a high priority industry for OSHA because of their reported injury rate. OSHA did more inspections in this industry than any other in those same two years.

There's another possible explanation for the decline in reported injuries. Fewer injuries were reported. Why would that be? Down in Florida after five hurricanes in 2004, roofers were in high demand. As one contractor put it, "I couldn't staff my jobs without illegal immigrants; and I probably couldn't get any bids given what my competition is up to." Illegal immigrants who fall off the roof tend not to make workers' compensation claims.

**Figure 14-6
Construction Injuries**

Although construction is one of the most dangerous industries to work, the number of workers' compensation claims has dropped more than 15 percent in the past two years.

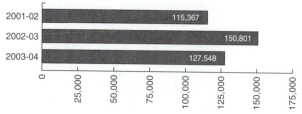

Workers' compensation petitions

2001-02	115,367
2002-03	150,801
2003-04	127,548

NONFATAL INJURIES

Of the 4.1 million nonfatal injuries in the workplace in 2003, construction ranks fourth in occupational injuries.

Workplace injuries, by industry
Ranked by percent

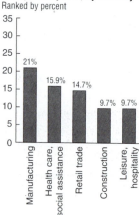

Manufacturing 21%
Health care, social assistance 15.9%
Retail trade 14.7%
Construction 9.7%
Leisure, hospitality 9.7%

FATAL INJURIES

In 2003, construction had the most fatalities with 1,126, but still ranked only fourth among industry fatality rates.

Top five industry fatality rates
Per 100,000 employees

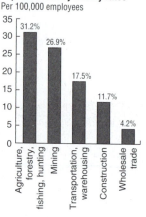

Agriculture, forestry, fishing, hunting 31.2%
Mining 26.9%
Transportation, warehousing 17.5%
Construction 11.7%
Wholesale trade 4.2%

Sources: Bureau of Labor Statistics, Office of the Judges of Compensation.

Suspicious injury data

Their bosses tend not to submit the injury data to OSHA. The poultry industry also reports surprisingly good injury data to OSHA for jobs that most experts would regard as highly likely to cause hand and wrist injuries or repetitive strain injuries. Yet, many poultry plants reported a perfect record of no such injuries over several recent years. The injury logs within this industry are particularly impressive. And highly suspicious. Statistics always need to be interpreted in context!

OSHA also has come under fire from safety experts for trivial fines—at times, only in the hundreds of dollars. Two months before the horrendous Phillips Petroleum explosion, OSHA neglected to conduct a complete inspection of the plant after an accident killed one worker. OSHA does have some power to ask the Justice Department to prosecute employers who intentionally or negligently injure their employees, but critics of OSHA have maintained that state prosecutions are necessary because few employers have been charged under federal law. Fines for violations that led to a fatality are quite small. For example, in one state, less than 20 percent of fines for death-related citations exceeded $10,000.

Subsequent to September 11, 2001, OSHA devoted considerable (and valuable) resources to the World Trade Center site. As a result and with no additional funding, many of their other activities were reduced in scope and magnitude. OSHA under President George W. Bush had more limited goals and fewer claimed accomplishments. There were fewer inspections and fines under Bush than his predecessor. In an editorial, the *New York Times* opined that OSHA "has shirked its responsibility to upgrade workplace safety. In seven years, it has issued but one major rule change protecting workers against a chemical toxin—and that was forced on it by court order."[28] Things will change beginning in 2009.

OSHA can use its subpoena powers to have employees testify under oath about safety violations. Business executives can face jail terms for their behavior and policies regarding the health and safety of their workers. State Supreme Courts in New York, Illinois, and Michigan have already ruled that employers can face criminal charges and prison. As one expert put it, "For the first time, the cost of ignoring OSHA has become greater than the cost of complying."[29] Initiatives such as special emphasis programs on silica and nursing homes have enabled OSHA to do a better job of getting to the most hazardous workplaces.[30]

Fatality data

The key question, however, is whether having OSHA in place has reduced workplace deaths, accidents, or injuries. The data regarding fatalities are clear. Workplace deaths went from 21 per 100,000 in 1912 to only 4 per 100,000 in 2006.[31] However, while this trend has been steady, the same trend line of reduced fatalities existed even before OSHA was passed in 1970. There has been a decrease in the rate of injuries and illnesses involving lost work days from 1984 to 2006. But there has been an increase in total injuries and illnesses since 1984, mainly due to reports of RSI.[32] Nearly two-thirds of all workplace injuries are some form of RSI, with over 300,000 cases reported in 2006.

Most workplace injuries are RSI

Little attention to worker behavior

Another criticism of OSHA is that its focus is almost exclusively on unsafe working conditions and managerial responsibility; however, virtually no attention is given to employee behavior and responsibility. Because of this lack of attention, most experts agree that the impact of OSHA on accident rates will be moderate. Experts generally agree that more attention must be paid to behaviors and attitudes.[33] GM, for example, reported that in 1976 it was spending $15 per car to comply with OSHA regulations, but there had been no positive impact on accident rates as a function of the regulations. GM claimed that many accidents were a consequence of improper behavior by employees.[34] Other experts maintain that the long-term impact of OSHA will be overwhelmingly positive because of the increased knowledge of hazardous substances discovered through OSHA activities. For example, critical information about a great number of carcinogens such as PCBs, cotton dust, asbestos, and vinyl chloride can be directly linked to OSHA research. The banning of asbestos in 1989 would probably not have occurred had it not been for OSHA research.

Right-to-know

The **right-to-know** provisions of OSHA have had a positive impact on company health and safety records. These provisions specify the employees' right to know if they are working with unsafe substances, how to work with them safely, and how to administer first aid if workers come in contact with toxic chemicals. These provisions also require that a "material safety data sheet" be provided with each chemical used. This form provides all necessary information about the substance, what precautions to take, and how to treat any injury associated with its use.

Unions take a much more positive position on the effects of OSHA and have been at the forefront in advocating many of the preventative provisions of OSHA. For example, over 20,000 workers are trained annually in the recognition and control of work hazards. Still, unions favor more aggressive enforcement that is more uniform across the country and a faster process for the development of new standards. Unions have worked very hard on behalf of their members to control RSI.[35]

PROGRAMS TO REDUCE ACCIDENTS AT WORK

Four general strategies

Organizations have tried a variety of strategies directed at reducing or eliminating unsafe behaviors at work. These programs can be classified into four general areas: personnel selection, employee training, incentive programs, and safety rules and regulations. Health and safety guru E. Scott Geller has 50 key principles to a total safety culture, a subset of which is presented in Figure 14-7. All four general areas are covered by these principles.[36] Views by top management toward safety are very important and vary across cultures. In general, plants are safer in the United States, Japan, and the European Union.[37] The Worker Rights Consortium, a student "watchdog" group that evaluates working conditions at facilities all over the world, evaluates non-U.S. manufacturing facilities using OSHA standards

Figure 14-7
Some Key Principles of a
Total Safety Culture

1. Safety should be internally, not externally, driven.
2. Culture changes require people to understand the principles and how to use them.
3. A total safety culture requires continuous attention to factors in three domains: environment, behavior, and person.
4. Don't count on common sense for safety improvement.
5. Safety incentive programs should focus on process rather than outcomes.
6. People view behavior as correct to the degree they see others doing it.
7. On-the-job observation and interpersonal feedback are key to total safety culture.
8. Behavior is directed by activators and motivated by consequences.
9. People compensate for increases in perceived safety by taking more risks.
10. Stressors lead to positive stress or negative distress, depending on appraisal of personal control.
11. When people feel empowered, their safe behavior spreads to other situations.
12. Numbers from program evaluations should be meaningful to all participants.

Source: Adapted from E. S. Geller, *Working Safe: How to Help People Actively Care for Health and Safety.* Radnor, PA: Chilton Book Company, 1996. (Dr. Geller has 50 principles.)

and regulations. Good communication is vital to successful safety and health programs and to business in general. Employee participation and involvement in safety issues and programs are critical for successful programs.[38] In addition, research has shown that management's demonstration of concern after an employee's injury creates a "halo effect" that can aid the worker's recovery and speed return to work. Also, workers who experienced the halo effect expressed more satisfaction with their treatment from the firm and were less likely to seek a lawyer.[39]

With the growth of at-home workers, OSHA took an interest in health and safety conditions in the home, but this interest passed with the change in administration in 2000. The 1992 Management of Health and Safety at Work Regulations require that employers carry out a risk assessment of home workers.[40]

HPWS and safety

One excellent study focused on **high-performance work systems** (HPWS) and applied the "commitment" and "high involvement" principles of HPWS to improving workplace safety.[41] They argue that safety should be considered a performance variable much like production, profits, sales, quality control, or customer complaints. They found strong support for the hypothesis that a high-performance work system will improve workplace safety by increasing employee trust in management and perceived safety climate. A company achieves this level through selective hiring, extensive training, and team-based structures and decision making. Specifically, they found individual safety knowledge, safety motivation, safety compliance, and safety initiatives were all related to safety incidents (i.e., injuries requiring first-aid and near misses). The research confirmed the importance of organizational factors in ensuring worker safety.

Selective Hiring

Selective exclusion

Selective hiring focuses on the fit between employees and their work environment. This is achieved through the **"selective exclusion"** of high-risk employees. High-risk applicants are defined as those who have histories of drug addiction or alcoholism, and those with low levels of emotional maturity and trustworthiness. Researchers in this area argue, "Organizations committed to occupational safety will attend closely to how they hire new personnel and will incorporate the value of occupational safety into their employee-selection processes to achieve a better fit." They also called for the use of work teams in the selection of future members which could also improve safety levels—"requiring applicants to go through several rounds of interviews in which the organization's values are conveyed could also enhance occupational safety."[42] Although research examining the relationship between selection practices and occupational safety is sparse, research shows that companies with more safety-focused selection procedures had lower injury rates.

Can you predict accident proneness?

We describe **"accident-prone"** people as those who inadvertently hurt themselves or destroy something at work. Is it possible to predict accident proneness? If so, we might change our personnel decisions to select those people who are less likely to be in accidents. Organizations such as Domino's Pizza, Greyhound, and every police department in the nation would love to be able to avoid employing individuals with a knack for traffic mishaps.

Three findings on accident proneness

Unfortunately, while there have been numerous attempts to identify careless, accident-prone people, the evidence really boils down to three general findings: (1) older employees are safer than younger ones (regardless of job tenure); (2) physical characteristics, such as hearing and vision, are related to accident rates when they are critical aspects of a job; and (3) a record of accidents or driving citations does predict similar activity in the future. Chapter 6 described some tests that have potential for the prediction and prevention of employee accidents. Related tests should identify applicants who don't use drugs and are honest, value-driven, customer-oriented, respectful, and responsive to authority—in short, "safe" employees. More research is needed in this area. Employers also need to understand their potential liabilities related to *negligent hiring* and negligent retention. We discuss these terms later.

Safety Training

Formal systems more effective

In some organizations, there exist only informal safety training procedures. In these situations, a new employee may be given a brief orientation to company policy, including safety issues; spend a day or two with a supervisor or lead person; and is then expected to work safely. Research indicates that a formal system of safety training is much more effective. In addition, because safety programs are so costly, it is important to be able to show that the programs save the firm money.

Research clearly shows that workers who receive more safety training suffer fewer work-related injuries than others. The most effective training "allows employees to acquire greater competencies to control their work, leading them to perform their jobs more safely. To be maximally effective, training must extend beyond the mere provision of knowledge related to how to do one's job safely. Employees must also be empowered to use new skills following training."[43]

Supervisory safety practices important

Companies that place more emphasis on worker safety have seen benefits from their actions. One study found that climate perceptions in the form of supervisory safety practices significantly predicted injuries requiring medical attention.[44] When managers pay more attention to safety issues and reward employees for safety-related behaviors, accidents are reduced. Another study suggests that interactive approaches to training may be the best way to get employees to really understand safety issues. At TrueTime Inc., the safety staff gives a brief review of the company's safety procedures to the employees each year at the company meeting. Each employee is then given a custom, randomly generated quiz. Employees have to seek answers to the questions by checking source materials and glossaries, studying the policies, and examining reports. This encourages employees to take an active learning approach to learning about the firm's safety procedures.

OSHA has issued **"voluntary training guidelines"** for employers that provide a framework for the development, administration, and evaluation of training programs. These guidelines are especially helpful for organizations that have no expertise in formal training development and evaluation. One study supported the use of accident simulations as a training method.[45] In addition, providing training sessions in several languages increases the chance of compliance by the millions of workers for whom English is a second language. The message on safe work practices and job hazards needs to get through to everyone.

OSHA standard regarding training

An OSHA standard requires training for employees who operate powered industrial trucks. The training rule covers nearly 1.2 million employees who drive trucks in general industry and for maritime employers. There are over 800,000 powered industrial trucks operating in the workplace. As of 2006, statistics indicate that about 500 workers are killed each year in incidents related to industrial truck operations and nearly 50,000 suffer injuries that result in lost workdays. Approximately 20 to 25 percent of those incidents are partly due to inadequate training. The cost for employers to comply with the rule is estimated to be approximately $35 million in the first year and $20 million annually each year thereafter. Compliance will ultimately save employers between $8 million and $42 million annually in property damage and $770,000 paid as a result of lawsuits involving workers injured in forklift accidents that could be attributed to deficiencies in training.[46]

Training programs are typical in industries with serious accident problems. For example, the construction industry employs only 5 percent of the workforce yet has the highest lost-time injury rate of any major industry (it accounts for 20 percent of all occupational fatalities). As a result, some contractors include the cost of supplying safety equipment and employee training in their bids.[47] Training programs also exist in public safety arenas. For example, in the restaurant industry, training is used to educate restaurant employees about food illnesses. This is critical because as many as 9,000 people die annually in the United States and an estimated nine million become sick from illnesses transmitted by restaurant food.[48]

Food illnesses

Most training programs generally focus on hazards at work, safety rules and regulations, and safe and unsafe work behaviors. For example, one study describes a bakery that developed a detailed behavior observation code of safe and unsafe behaviors.[49] Participants in the safety program were then shown slides of the unsafe and safe behaviors. Goals were set for increasing the percentage of safe behaviors, and a feedback chart was set up for monitoring group performance. Supervisors also were trained in giving positive reinforcement for safe work behaviors. The training and monitoring increased the percentage of safe behaviors more than 20 percent.

An aging workforce

Today, when developing training programs, human resource professionals should recognize the aging of the workforce and be sure that training addresses changes in workers' strength, size, flexibility, and stamina. The National Institute on Aging's Gerontology Research Center recommends that employers use routine medical checkups to determine employee health initially and then track positive or negative changes in work ability.[50] Training should be adjusted to fit the needs of the aging workforce. In addition, with the increasing numbers of corporate downsizings, it is important to be sure that a core set of employees (who will be with the company for some time) are trained in safety procedures. In high-turnover facilities, long-term training for all employees is impractical. However, it is possible to find long-term employees who are interested in worker safety and health. These employees can be the core group who are able to train new employees as they enter the organization.[51]

Many manufacturers use a peer review process to improve safety records. The objective is to shape behavior with immediate and constant feedback and positive reinforcement. At Alcoa, all workers must submit safety suggestions and are rewarded for good ones. Production-line workers can stop the line at any time if they spot a safety problem. Other companies employ industrial psychologists and engineers to study the worker–machine interface. At DuPont Corporation, engineers observe workers and then redesign valves and install key locks to reduce accidents. At Monsanto's Pensacola, Florida, plant, psychologists used the critical incident technique (CIT) of job analysis. Experts drew **"cause trees"** to identify the root causes of the less-than-obvious problems. If a worker slipped on oil, for example, the root cause was not oil but the failure of maintenance to attend to an oil leak. A safety scorecard also was prepared, and workers reviewed processes to check for "shortcuts and deviations," which ultimately predict trouble. Safe workers win recognition at weekly safety meetings, and free lunches and promotions have been tied to safety records. As a result of this comprehensive approach to safety, Monsanto's record improved from 6.5 to 1.6 lost-time injuries per hundred workers in the five years of the program.

Cause trees

Supervisory support is critical

Safety training is important not only for employees, but also for supervisors. Workplace health and safety efforts cannot succeed without the support and efforts of supervisors. In general, supervisors must know (1) about any hazards in their area of supervision and any hazards that may affect their subordinates when traveling outside their area of supervision; (2) what safety procedures and devices are needed to safely carry out the jobs in their departments; (3) about safety rules, policies, procedures, and programs that have been developed; and (4) what is required under all applicable occupational health and safety legislation.[52] Supervisors also should be aware of safety rules associated with contractors. For example, companies that hire contractors who fall short on safety procedures may find themselves jointly liable when workers are injured. A key factor in determining contractor status and employer liability is who supervises outside employees working under a specific contract. Management should assume that the company could have some liability for anything that occurs on the property. Thus, a firm would be wise to make a contractor's health and safety record a factor in the selection process when contractors are hired.[53]

What supervisors must know

Liability for contractors

Teamwork, Supervision, and Decentralized Decision Making

Sense of "team" important

Teamwork and decentralized decision making should benefit employee performance and safety performance by fostering higher group cohesion. The quality of supervisor–employee relationships as well as cohesion with the work group are the best predictors of the tendency to comply with safety rules. Working in teams also causes workers to feel more responsible for their own and each other's safety. One study found that a sense of belongingness to a group and personal control was related to the propensity to actively care for co-worker safety. Teamwork and decentralized decision making should also provide workers who are more familiar with the work situation greater opportunities for control. Research in chemical plants and with manufacturing teams supports this view. It is also argued that teams should enhance occupational safety when they promote the sharing of ideas that result in better solutions. Flight crews performed more effectively as groups in dangerous situations than when they were formed in a hierarchical structure with the captain at the top of the chain of command.

Incentive Systems

Today, safety incentives are a hotly competitive and growing segment of the highly profitable corporate incentive industry. Even small incentives can change employees' attitudes.[54] As discussed in Chapter 11, many employers use safety contests where company units compete with one another for cash or prizes. Other contests are set up so that each unit competes with its own safety record. If a lower number of accidents occurs over a period of time, an award is given. At DuPont, directors give safety awards and workers win cash prizes if their units remain accident-free for six months. These prizes are only one part of their safety philosophy. As part of an overall safety management that focuses on injury prevention and a goal of zero accidents and injuries, DuPont has used many forms of recognition to increase awareness of safety excellence.[55] At Kodak, volunteer observers take turns supervising peers and providing token awards (e.g., free soft drinks). Summer construction workers at Colorado State University started driving more safely when the city began offering the incentive of small coolers for carrying meals.[56] At Hunter Industries, a sprinkler manufacturer, the safety and health coordinator created a three-level safety incentive program. Level one involves mandatory safety activities; level two includes wellness and self-enrichment activities; and level three includes community involvement. Based on the program, the company has met total regulatory compliance for the past three years and has reported improved work habits and cost savings.[57]

Research supports value of safety programs

There has been some research on incentive systems for accident reduction. This research suggests that safety programs that include incentives, help offset the high cost of health insurance benefits, workers' compensation claims, and lost-time injuries.[58] Bulova Corporation of Woodside, New York, has a guide for setting up a successful safety incentive program.[59]

When awards are substantial, failure to report accidents is a possibility. For example, offering safety prizes of significant worth (e.g., new car, tropical vacation) may provide employees with an incentive not to report injuries.[60] To decrease occupational accidents, safety programs must be run and promoted effectively. First, it is necessary to determine what types of behaviors are to be controlled. Next, the human resource professional must prioritize the behaviors and then develop a plan and the appropriate rewards. For example, one common program used by many firms is safety bingo. Monthly drawings and quarterly drawings are also popular, as are special contests.[61]

Safety Rules

Detailed handbooks most effective

Most companies now publish employee handbooks with formal rules and regulations that stipulate what employees can and cannot do in the workplace. Unfortunately, many of these rules and regulations are too general to be effective. The most effective employee safety handbooks are those that carefully describe the steps to be taken on the job to ensure maximum safety. For each step, potential dangers are identified to alert the worker. In addition to specificity in the rules, it is also critical to get workers to read and comprehend safety handbooks. Some companies require that employees pass a test about safety-related issues before they begin work and during their employment as well.

No matter how thorough the training, safety rules will be meaningless if they are not enforced. There are, unfortunately, numerous cases where a worker ignored a safety rule and

Consistent enforcement is key

was injured, or when a supervisor ordered workers to ignore a safety rule. Consistent enforcement of safety rules, with discipline for infractions, will benefit management in several ways. First, it will send a clear message to employees that the company takes safety seriously. Second, it should reduce injuries. Third, a company may be able to avoid an OSHA citation if it can demonstrate that it complied with relevant OSHA standards (or the general duty clause), that it trained its workers properly, and that the injury was the result of a worker's intentional refusal to adhere to work rules. Documentation of consistent discipline for work rule violations would be necessary for a company to avoid OSHA liability. Safety committees comprised of management and nonmanagement employees can be used to enforce safety rules. Committee members can identify safety hazards and devise solutions to safety problems. In addition, they can organize safety training courses or workshops to increase employees' awareness of safety issues.

CONTEMPORARY ISSUES RELATED TO HEALTH AND SAFETY

AIDS and the Workplace

As human immunodeficiency virus (HIV) and acquired immune deficiency syndrome (AIDS) continue to plague millions of Americans, numerous organizations are becoming more vulnerable to the tremendous loss exposure associated with the increasing presence of these diseases in the workplace.[62] According to the Centers for Disease Control (CDC), two or three employees in all U.S. companies with a workforce of at least 300 people suffer from AIDS or have dependents, spouses, significant others, or friends with the disease. AIDS is now one of the leading causes of death for people between the ages of 25 and 44, with the majority of the U.S. workforce in this age group. The CDC reported that over 16,000 Americans died of the disease in 2006. The virus has spread to over 40 million people worldwide, with most of those people in their prime working years. AIDS has become a critical health care issue for employers and employees alike, with corporations incurring increasing costs related to the growing number of AIDS cases. Overall, AIDS-related corporate expenses include the patient's health insurance, disability benefits, employee life insurance, and pension costs. They also include the costs of hiring and training replacements and the costs of any lawsuits. The cumulative costs of treating AIDS exceeded $20 billion in 2008. The estimated losses in productivity were over $70 billion.

AIDS victims are now protected by a variety of state and local laws that prohibit discrimination against disabled people. As discussed in Chapter 3, AIDS has typically been defined as a legal disability under the Rehabilitation Act of 1973, which prohibits discrimination against the disabled by federal contractors, and is covered by the 1990 **Americans with Disabilities Act (ADA) and the 2008 ADA Amendment Act.** The ADA protects the jobs of people with AIDS-related disabilities and helps keep them in the workforce. Few jobs exist where having HIV or AIDS prohibits an employee from performing essential job functions. However, should such a situation occur, employers must make **reasonable accommodations** for the employee under the ADA (e.g., equipment changes, workstation modifications, flexible work schedules). With appropriate and reasonable accommodations, there is no reason people with HIV and AIDS cannot continue to work for many years.

The ADA and 2008 ADA Amendment Act

Businesses must be careful to abide by the ADA when hiring. They cannot ask job candidates about their HIV or AIDS status, nor can they require HIV testing on a preemployment or pre-offer basis. Upon the extension of an offer, however, employers may require an HIV test or pose questions concerning the prospective employee's HIV status, as long as all applicants in a particular job category are treated similarly. Of course, test results must be treated confidentially. A positive HIV test result cannot prompt a job revocation unless the employer can demonstrate that the individual poses a direct health threat to co-workers or customers that cannot be eliminated through reasonable accommodations. Such arguments are extremely difficult to make and customer or potential co-worker preference data cannot be used to justify such a position. Overall, management should be very familiar with the organization's AIDS policy and training should be provided to ensure that all employees understand the policy and its implications. OSHA has excellent guidelines on its Web site for formulating a policy and training personnel.

Managers and human resource professionals should understand the legal implications of HIV and AIDS in the workplace because many claims of AIDS-related discrimination cases have been filed. In a typical case, the Florida Commission of Human Relations ruled that a teacher who was fired because he had AIDS was a victim of disability discrimination. The teacher was awarded almost $200,000. Another example was when an HIV-positive physician sued Philadelphia's Mercy Health Corporation for discrimination when he was barred from performing invasive medical procedures unless his patients signed a consent form that disclosed his HIV status. The doctor sued (and won) under Section I of the ADA, which prohibits discrimination in employment, and Section III, which prohibits public facilities from discriminating against people with disabilities.

In July 1992, OSHA imposed the **Bloodborne Pathogen Standards,** which state that all workplaces with employees that could be "reasonably anticipated" to contact blood or body fluids must comply. Under these guidelines, OSHA takes the position that there is no such thing as a risk-free population. According to these OSHA standards, employers must write an "exposure control plan," which details the procedure for identifying individuals at risk and how the organization will comply with the standards; "universal precautions," which detail how blood and body fluids are handled; and "cleaning protocols," which detail the location of cleaning supplies and the handling of cleaning wastes. Furthermore, employers must provide "personal protective equipment" such as gloves, masks, mouth guards, and smocks for workers who might come in contact with blood and other bodily fluids; "communicate the presence of hazards," which places warning labels and signs for restricted areas; educate and train employees of OSHA standards; and keep records as evidence that companies are complying. Employers who violate the regulations are subject to OSHA penalties.

Comprehensive HIV/AIDS policy

OSHA mandates that businesses have a comprehensive HIV/AIDS policy and communicate the plan throughout the workplace. One survey found that only one-third of large and mid-size companies have formal HIV/AIDS policies.[63] The **CDC AIDS Clearinghouse** provides businesses with information on policy formation, employee education, manager and supervisor training, volunteerism, and family education in a kit titled "Business Response to AIDS." This kit helps companies develop specific policies and programs to deal with AIDS-related work issues. Most major companies take the position that AIDS-afflicted employees should be treated the same as other employees as long as they can perform their jobs. The Bank of America allows co-workers to transfer from departments where there are AIDS victims, but there has not been a single request to date. This is undoubtedly because the bank has provided a great deal of information about the disease to its employees and about the very low risk of transmission in the workplace. Through 2008, the CDC has not found a single case of AIDS transmission based on casual contact at work. The CDC believes that AIDS-afflicted employees do not have to be isolated or restricted from any work area, although there is much debate about possible restrictions in hospitals, food service, and dental settings. Caution is suggested for health care workers and patients or clients who may be exposed to blood, mucous membranes, or lesions.

Levi Strauss and IBM have been at the forefront in the development of a comprehensive AIDS-awareness program. The educational component of the Levi Strauss program includes informative brochures, a manager's guide to treating AIDS-afflicted employees, a policy manual, and a guidebook for policy makers. The company also provides an opportunity for employees to meet with medical professionals to discuss HIV/AIDS issues in more detail.[64] Since the enactment of the program, Levi Strauss has not incurred any lawsuits, employees refusing to work with AIDS-afflicted employees, or requests for reassignment. The IBM policy is to encourage AIDS-afflicted employees to work as long as they are capable and to ensure their privacy.

Drugs in the Workplace

It is not necessary to remind students that the abuse of controlled substances is a serious social problem—one that plagues employers as well as law enforcement agencies. The **Substance Abuse and Mental Health Services Administration** estimated that drug abuse costs U.S. businesses $102 billion annually in lost productivity, accidents, absenteeism, turnover, medical claims, and thefts.[65] Other reported consequences of drug abuse include increased on-the-job violence, workforce irritability, fistfights, and job mistakes. Employees using drugs are 3.6 times more likely to be involved in on-the-job accidents than other employees, and more liability insurance–covered accidents are caused by drug-impaired employees. This may be because today's drug users are relying more on amphetamines (e.g., crystal methedrine), which accelerates their systems, turning them from "recreational users" into "volatile abusers." Previously, employees had relied more on depressants such as alcohol and marijuana.[66] Of course, alcohol abuse still leads to a number of workplace symptoms, including unexcused and frequent absences, tardiness and early departures, fights with employees, on-the-job accidents, and poor judgments.

As discussed in Chapter 6, many companies have responded to the drug crisis with a drug testing program. In one such company, personal injuries reportedly dropped from 15.5 per year before random urine testing to 5.8 per year five years after initiating the program.

The Drug Free Workplace Act

The Drug Free Workplace Act of 1988 requires federal contractors to provide a drug-free workplace. Under the law, employers must educate employees about the risks of drug use and establish penalties for substance abuse. Furthermore, organizations must have specific policies on substance abuse, establish awareness programs, and notify employees and applicants that a drug-free state is a condition of employment. In response, U.S. companies have increasingly turned to drug testing both as a screening device for job applicants and as a means of evaluating current employees.

An American Management Association (AMA) survey found that 78 percent of all companies test at least some employees and applicants for drug abuse.[67] The firms that participated in the survey stated the rise in drug testing was due to the following factors:

- Department of Transportation (DOT) and Department of Defense (DoD) regulations that, with local and state legislation, mandated testing in certain job categories.

- The practical effects of the Drug Free Workplace Act of 1988.

- Court decisions that recognize an employer's right to test both employees and job applicants in the private sector.

- Action by insurance carriers to reduce accident liability and control health costs.

- Corporate requirements that vendors and contractors certify that theirs is a drug-free workplace.

Random drug testing

According to the AMA survey, over 70 percent of companies conduct random drug testing of current employees. Motorola, for example, recently ordered all of its U.S. employees to undergo random drug testing at least once every three years, with more frequent testing for employees with positive test results. A Kansas City manufacturer of food processing equipment used a private undercover drug agent to monitor drug use. In a drug "sweep," she found that two dozen workers were either using or dealing drugs. The icing on the cake was the internal theft of a $16,000 piece of equipment. The agent found that an employee had sold it for $800 to buy drugs. Investigators are doing the same thing at a number of other companies that are suffering financial and behavioral consequences from employee drug abuse.[68]

Before a company initiates drug testing, the following questions should be addressed: Why do we want this program? Do we have a problem with drugs in our company? What will we do with the results of drug tests? Can our current discipline policy handle violations of this policy? How much will the program cost? Can we afford it? Will it affect morale? Should it be a punitive or rehabilitative program? Only after these questions are answered satisfactorily should a company consider implementing drug testing.

Five approaches to drug testing

Some companies use five approaches to drug testing: preemployment screening, random testing of current employees, "reasonable cause" testing in response to performance problems, return-to-duty testing after drug treatment or suspension, and postaccident testing. Science makes it possible to ascertain if a person has ingested a controlled substance, and more and more companies are joining the ranks of those who at least test applicants for the presence of drugs. The AMA survey found that 77 percent of the companies that responded test all new hires for drugs in preemployment physical examinations. Surprisingly, workers are quite tolerant of testing. The aforementioned survey found 60 percent of those questioned supported random drug testing of current employees with no probable cause.[69]

Two questions that science has not yet been able to answer, however, are exactly how much of a controlled substance an individual must ingest to be impaired and just what impaired means. For example, most states have set a 0.10 percent blood alcohol level to establish impairment by alcohol; a similar standard does not exist for controlled substances. While some employers declare that a drug test result showing any amount of a controlled substance will be grounds for rejecting an applicant or discharging a worker, other employers have set some level as the threshold for an assumption that the employee is impaired. Computerized tests are now available to help employers determine whether workers in safety-related jobs are impaired. One test operates like a video game and takes less than a minute to determine eye–hand coordination and reaction time. Old Town Trolley Tours of San Diego, California, uses the test to assess drivers.

Legal challenges to personnel actions based on drug testing

Because of the lack of a standard for impairment, combined with the manner in which the presence of drugs is usually ascertained, many employment decisions made on the basis of positive drug test results have been legally challenged. The latest analysis indicates that urine is the most widely used specimen in the detection of drugs and offers about a 1–3 day window of detection. Hair analysis offers the largest window of detection (from 7 to 100+ days) while saliva analysis may be useful in determining very recent drug use (1–36 hours). Sweat analysis is another option that could be useful for the continuous monitoring of drug use (1–14 days). Drug testing has become a fast, convenient process with the development of point-of-collection drug testing devices.[70]

Drug testing reduces drug use

So does workplace drug testing reduce drug use? One recent large-scale study says yes, it does. Drug testing programs are clearly achieving one of the desired effects: deterring drug use.[71]

Although there are no federal laws regulating drug testing, drug testing programs have been challenged using a number of legal theories. Private-sector employers generally have been able to successfully defend their drug testing programs in court, but there are a number of exceptions. In California, for example, the court ruled that Southern Pacific wrongfully fired a computer programmer when she refused to provide a random-test urine specimen. Another California court ruled that Kerr-McGee Chemical Corporation violated a worker's privacy by requiring her to submit to a drug test. However, other California decisions have supported drug testing. Lower courts in Michigan and Texas have sided with employers on random urinalysis, while a court in New Jersey found for the plaintiff. Utah is the only state that clearly permits drug testing of employees and applicants and authorizes firing employees who refuse to be tested. Maine explicitly allows testing for "probable cause," but limits random testing to safety-sensitive jobs.

Fourth amendment protection

Public employers are bound by the Fourth Amendment of the U.S. Constitution, which forbids "unreasonable" searches and seizures. However, even characterizing a urine test as either a search (of the urine) or a seizure (of body fluids) has not legally established that drug testing by public employers is unconstitutional. Supreme Court decisions now permit public employers to use drug testing for employees engaged in jobs where public safety is an issue, such as railroad engineers, U.S. Customs agents, and nuclear power plant workers. Private-sector employers, however, are not bound by the Fourth Amendment, and challenges must be based on contract claims or "public policy" grounds.

Components of a sound policy

This does not mean, however, that a company should establish a drug testing program without concern for potential legal consequences. Unionized employers must bargain with the union about the procedures to be used, according to the National Labor Relations Board (NLRB). Nonunionized employers must consider that not all positive drug results indicate that the employee is presently impaired or has even ingested a controlled substance, as the ingestion of innocuous substances (poppy seeds, quinine water) may result in a positive test result. At a minimum, the company should make sure its program includes the following components:

■ Notice to employees (or applicants) that drug testing will be conducted and the procedures to be used.

■ An opportunity for the individual to disclose which prescription or over-the-counter drugs he or she is currently taking as well as other information that might skew the test results.

- A careful chain of custody to ensure that samples are not lost, mixed up, or switched.
- A dignified but secure method of collecting samples.
- Confirmation of all positive drug results with more sensitive tests.
- The opportunity for the individual to have the sample retested at his or her own expense.
- Confidentiality of test results.

In developing a drug testing policy, a company must determine what, if any, substances are permissible. For example, will a positive reading for marijuana be treated the same way as a positive reading for heroin? If testing is performed on current employees, will it be done only "for cause" (for example, after an accident or if a supervisor determines that an employee appears impaired) or randomly without cause?

Potential legal claims to drug testing in the public sector include Fourth Amendment challenges to the testing. This occurs if there was no reasonable cause to conclude that the employee had ingested controlled substances or if the drug testing represented a violation of the employee's constitutional due process rights. This may occur if the employee is discharged without being given an opportunity to challenge the test results. All employers may face charges of defamation (if test results become known to anyone but those who need the information); contract claims (for currently employed workers); and claims of discrimination against workers with disabilities (e.g., if the employee is a recovering drug abuser).

Human resource managers are well advised to consult with legal counsel before developing a drug testing program. Model programs that have withstood litigation are available, and an attorney can advise managers of any state laws that may affect the way the program is designed or administered.

Smoking and the Workplace

Effects of second-hand smoke

One of the most volatile issues for human resource professionals today is a company's position on smoking. Growing information about the adverse effects of secondhand smoke has led to a call for a ban on smoking in the workplace. The U.S. Environmental Protection Agency reported that secondhand smoke causes 3,800 lung cancer deaths per year and classified it as a "class A" life-threatening carcinogen, a rating used only for substances (i.e., asbestos, radon, benzene) proven to cause cancer in humans. The Centers for Disease Control and Prevention estimated that $75 billion is spent annually on medical expenses attributed to smoking. Businesses lose $82 billion in lost productivity from smokers.[72] And smokers take about 6.5 more sick days a year than nonsmokers. About one in five Americans—or 46 million people—smoke. The costs of property fires ($500 million per year) and additional cleaning required because of smoking ($4 billion per year) are also significant. The American Heart Association reported that passive smoking is the third greatest preventable cause of death in the United States.

Nonsmoking employees can file workers' compensation and disability claims and legal suits against companies where smoking is not restricted. For example, the Wisconsin Labor and Industry Review Commission awarded an employee $23,400 in workers' compensation benefits because her eight-year exposure to secondhand smoke resulted in a permanent disability. The California Compensation Insurance Fund paid $85,000 in damages to an employee who suffered a heart attack from her exposure to smoke at work. In addition, a federal hearings examiner awarded a widower $21,500 a year for life to compensate for his wife's death due to lung cancer believed to be caused by her job as a Veterans Administration nurse on a hospital ward where heavy smoking was common.

Guide to workplace smoking policies

The U.S. Environmental Protection Agency's **"Guide to Workplace Smoking Policies"** recommends that employers create ventilated smoking lounges to separate smokers from nonsmokers. One study found that smokers in a nonsmoking organization reduced the number of cigarettes smoked per work shift and decreased levels of nicotine and carbon monoxide. Thus, worksite smoking restrictions may promote meaningful reductions in tobacco exposure and consequent health risks.

Can employers prohibit employees from smoking on and off the job?

A growing number of companies are banning smoking for employees both on and off the job. Weyco, a Michigan-based health care company, told their current employees who smoked that they had 15 months to quit. Weyco offered free cessation classes and even paid for treatments such as hypnotism and acupuncture. They then banned all smoking from their property, banned all smokers from new positions, and conducted breath tests to determine if employees smoked. If employees tested positive, they were charged $50 a month if they weren't enrolled in a cessation program. When they tested everyone again, four employees refused to be tested and were terminated. The company stated that the no-smoking policy was part of Weyco's goal for healthy lifestyles. Critics are concerned about the "slippery slope" regarding lifestyle. Weyco employs a health consultant to help workers with their diet. What comes next; a no Big-Mac policy?

The "slippery slope"

Section 654(a) of OSHA states that the "general duty" of an employer is to provide places of employment "free of recognized hazards that are causing or likely to cause death or serious physical harm to his/her employees." OSHA has never successfully developed regulations regarding indoor air quality that include tobacco smoke. Yet, given that the Surgeon General's report now documents the effects of sidestream smoke and the EPA places tobacco smoke in the top tier of known carcinogens, the OSHA obligation to take action seems obvious. Many states and municipalities have enacted antismoking laws.[73]

Smokers' rights laws

The Michigan company that banned all smoking could not impose such a rule in most of the 29 states with "smokers' rights laws." A New Jersey state law, for example, prohibits discrimination in hiring, pay, and working conditions against smokers "unless the employer has a rational basis for doing so." Unfortunately, it is now up to employers to determine what constitutes a "rational basis." Are higher health care costs a rational basis? The state of New York has one of the most sweeping laws regarding protections for non-smokers. Employers must adopt and post a written policy on smoking that must include smoke-free work and eating areas.

Employees who smoke are more expensive

Growing evidence that health care costs more for smokers than nonsmokers is prompting some companies to levy additional charges on smokers and offer incentives for quitting. Provident Indemnity Life Insurance Co. offers nonsmokers 33 percent discounts on health and life insurance. At Mahoning Culvert in Youngstown, Ohio, smokers who are attempting to quit contribute 50 cents a day to a pool that accumulates for one year. To that pool of $182.50, the company adds $817.50 to reward each smoker who manages to quit for a year. An additional $500 is given the second year. Other companies have drawings for prizes and other incentives to encourage employees to quit smoking. Some companies have taken the punitive route. Lutheran Health Systems, a Fargo, North Dakota, hospital and nursing home chain, charges smokers a 10 percent premium on their health insurance. U-Haul International deducts $5 every other week from the paychecks of smokers. Several fire departments have imposed deadlines by which smoking firefighters must quit or be terminated. Particularly in hazardous work environments where the risks of cancer are great (e.g., daily exposure to chemical fumes), companies are more likely to impose no-smoking rules. While insurance premiums and increased health care costs are major reasons for employers' move toward a smoke-free workplace, pressure by nonsmokers has also contributed to the development of formal no-smoking policies at many organizations. One survey found that 85 percent of organizations surveyed indicated they had prohibited or restricted workplace smoking.[74]

A seven-step plan for plan development

A seven-step plan has been proposed for the development of a smoking policy:[75]

1. Top management should make a commitment to the development of a smoking policy.

2. Pertinent state and local laws should be reviewed.

3. Unions should be involved (if applicable).

4. The smoking policy should be tailored to particular work situations or stations.

5. A committee of smokers and nonsmokers from a cross-section of the workforce should be formed.

6. The workforce should be surveyed to determine attitudes toward smoking and toward possible smoking policies.

7. A proposed policy should be circulated throughout the workplace. Enforcement of policy violations on a consistent basis will encourage employee compliance.

Violence in the Workplace

The workplace appears to be no safe haven from the threat or reality of violence, and research suggests that both the frequency and severity of work-related violence are increasing. Estimates indicate that more than 1.9 million violent workplace crimes occur each year with half of these infractions caused by employees or former employees. About 10 percent of these violent workplace crimes involve offenders armed with handguns. An American Management Association survey of 311 organizations found that almost 25 percent indicated at least one employee had been attacked or killed on the job since 1990.[76] A Society for Human Resource Management (SHRM) survey found that of more than 1,000 employers, 48 percent had experienced at least one violent incident in the last year.[77]

Homicide is second leading cause of death at work

Homicide is the second leading cause of fatal occupational injury in the United States. Homicides are surpassed only by motor vehicle crashes as a cause of job-related deaths.[78] In 2007, the number of work-related homicides increased by 13 percent from 2006. The statistics on extreme cases of workplace violence (e.g., murder, rape) are disturbing. The trend may get worse because now over 40 states have legalized the possession of concealed weapons.[79] Employers, however, can ban concealed weapons in the workplace. The company parking lot is another matter. If employers do ban guns, there should be a written policy that is communicated to all employees and is contained in an employee handbook or in the policies and procedures manual. Florida was among a growing number of states that now make it illegal for an employer to prohibit employees from possessing any legally owned firearm that is lawfully possessed and locked inside or locked to a private motor vehicle in the employer's parking lot. Some critics of the law, including the Chamber of Commerce, claim that the new law unconstitutionally violates private property rights and conflicts with the "general duty" clause of the OSH Act. A 2008 lawsuit claims that the Florida law conflicts with this obligation because it creates a workplace hazard that is likely to cause death or serious physical harm to employees. Similar legislation in Oklahoma was overturned on this basis in 2007 by a federal judge. The effects of such legislation on workplace violence remain to be seen.

Negligent hiring

Employers do have an obligation to protect workers from violence under the **"general duty clause"** of OSHA. OSHA can (and has) issued citations for preventable violence in the workplace. In addition, a legal cause of action for **negligent hiring** or retention may be determined if the employer hires or retains an employee with a history of violence or who acts in a negligent manner. The European Commission's definition of workplace violence includes "incidents where persons are abused, threatened, or assaulted in circumstances relating to their work, involving an explicit challenge to their safety, well-being, or health." The Manufacturing, Science, and Finance Union has outlawed workplace bullying. According to the law, if an employer fails to adequately address a complaint from an employee about bullying, the employer could be subject to civil proceedings. In general, as awareness of the problem increases, employers are installing various security systems and training employees to avoid or defuse incidents.[80]

Human resource professionals must be aware of the many forms of less severe violence (see Figure 14-8) that are occurring and must be taken seriously.[81] Although no method exists that can perfectly predict a violent employee, the growing number of workplace homicides has made it possible to construct a profile of the typical perpetrator (see Figure 14-9). While violent employees may not have all the profile characteristics, most have a majority of them.

OSHA guidelines

OSHA issued the first federal guidelines regarding workplace violence on March 14, 1996. The guidelines, which are not mandatory, recommend that social service and health care employees carefully assess security issues that may result in workplace violence. About 66 percent of all those assaulted in the workplace are health care and social service employees. While OSHA's initial guidelines focus on these industries, another set of guidelines is being prepared to protect workers in the night retail industry, which also is disproportionately victimized by violence. In general, OSHA's guidelines state that a workplace violence prevention program should include the elements of any good safety and health program, which are management commitment, employee involvement, work-site analysis, hazard prevention and control, and training and education.[82]

Consequences

It is clear that employee violence costs companies dearly. There is the immediate cost of human suffering, pain, and possibly the precious loss of life. The effect of workplace

**Figure 14-8
Levels of Workplace
Violence**

MODERATELY INJURIOUS

- Property damage, vandalism
- Sabotage
- Pushing, fistfights
- Major violations of company policy
- Frequent arguments with customers, co-workers, or supervisors
- Theft

HIGHLY INJURIOUS

- Physical attacks and assaults
- Psychological trauma
- Anger-related accidents
- Rape
- Arson
- Murder

Source: S. M. Burroughs and J. W. Jones, "Managing Violence: Looking Out for Trouble," *Occupational Health and Safety,* April 1995, pp. 34-37.

violence on traumatized employees, families of employees, and coworkers is difficult to put into exact financial terms. Beyond human losses, the organization itself becomes a victim of workplace violence. The **National Safe Workplace Institute** estimates that workplace violence costs employers approximately $4 billion a year.[83] Rising health care costs, higher workers' compensation fees, and increased legal expenditures are a few of the significant consequences. For example, insurers paid $12 million to settle lawsuits by the parents of four teenage girls who were murdered during a robbery at an Austin, Texas, "I Can't Believe It's Yogurt" store where the girls worked. In the aftermath of a violent incident, the organization usually pays for medical and post-trauma stress treatments, lost wages due to increased absences, increased security and property damage, and investigations, which may include the use of outside experts such as management consultants. Another cost component is the loss of employee productivity. Revenue losses from disruption in work progress, turnover, and the diminished public image of the organization may result in reduced sales potential and lower stock value.

**Figure 14-9
Violent Employee Profile**

PRIMARY CHARACTERISTICS

- White middle-aged male
- Holds a white- or blue-collar position
- History of violence towards others
- Abuses illicit drugs
- Weapon owner and/or served in the military
- Extremely withdrawn, a "loner"
- Few interests outside of work
- Constantly disgruntled, a "troublemaker"
- Perceives unfairness, injustice, or malice in others

SECONDARY CHARACTERISTICS

- Overreacts to corporate changes
- Suffers from interpersonal conflict
- Recently fired or laid off, or perceives soon will be
- Argumentative/uncooperative
- Extremist opinions and attitudes
- Makes sexual comments or threats of physical assault
- Disobeys company policies and procedures/has difficulty accepting authority
- May sabotage equipment and/or property
- Steals

Note: Most individuals prone to violence will possess a majority of these traits.

Source: S. M. Burroughs and J. W. Jones, "Managing Violence: Looking Out for Trouble," *Occupational Health and Safety,* April 1995, pp. 34-37.

Violence Prevention Programs

Taking specific actions to prevent workplace violence can create a security-conscious organizational culture, thereby potentially reducing a company's exposure to violent employee crime. These prevention programs involve screening potential employees, communicating your company's commitment to nonviolence through policies and procedures, training and educating supervisors and workers, building a threat management team with the aid of employee assistance programs, and implementing security measures.

Preemployment Screening: Human resource professionals can reduce the potential for violent incidents and negligent hiring claims by using comprehensive preemployment screening procedures. Such procedures can usually detect service-oriented employees with strong interpersonal skills, as opposed to excessively violent and aggressive workers. Scientifically based paper-and-pencil or computerized tests can serve as a baseline assessment for measuring future changes in an employee's behavior. Such tests typically measure the likelihood that an applicant is prone to abusive, argumentative, or hostile workplace behavior. To obtain credible information about a high-risk applicant, a valid measure of violence potential that complies with professional guidelines should be chosen. Research shows that well-validated instruments can detect applicants who possess a history of violent behavior who, once hired, may become counterproductive employees.

Predictive instruments are available

The optimum preemployment screening program will combine testing with employment verification (if there's a gap in work history, find out why), reference checks, criminal record checks, drug testing, and structured interviews. Interviewers should be educated to ask questions that may elicit responses indicating a candidate's likelihood for future violent outbursts. It is useful to design a standard assessment form to ensure candidates are compared consistently. Examples of structured interview questions include the following:

Background checks

- Tell me about a time at work when you were so angry that you yelled at a supervisor or fellow employee.
- Were you ever angered to the point where you felt like yelling at someone, even though you didn't?
- Did you ever actually push or hit someone who made you really angry?
- Did you ever yell at or hit an obnoxious customer?
- Would any of your past supervisors or co-workers remember a situation where you yelled at or hit anybody?

To avoid potential litigation, have the preemployment screening process, including structured interview questions, reviewed by an expert in human rights legislation. This will ensure that the department keeps within any legal restrictions. Furthermore, such processes may provide necessary information about the candidate should that person become violent after being hired and file a discrimination suit under the ADA, which protects people with mental impairments. There is a strong overlap between violent behavior and mental illness. The evidence gathered about the individual at the front end may help the charged organization to show that it tried to avert preventable violence to maintain a safe work environment. One or two hours of legal advice in advance could make a world of difference. A small employer could easily spend $100,000 on litigation related to claims of **negligent hiring.**

Negligent hiring occurs when an employee who actually caused the death or injury had a clear history or reputation indicating a propensity to behave in a certain way and this record would have been discoverable by the employer through appropriate due diligence. For example, a victim of sexual harassment could have a cause of action against an employer based on this theory if the victim could show that the employer was aware or should have been aware that the harasser had been terminated for sexual harassment. What if an employee had a great driving record when he was hired but was convicted of reckless and drunk driving off the job but while he was employed? Could the employer be sued for negligent retention if there was a car accident while that employee was working? The short answer to this question is yes. **Negligent retention** occurs where an employer failed to remove an employee from a position of responsibility after it became apparent or should have been apparent that the employee should not have had this responsibility. Employers have to

Negligent retention

practice due diligence for their current employees as well and be aware if there are issues away from work as well.

What if a job applicant had a known history of violence using a gun? Could an employer decide not to hire this individual? What if an employee made a threat to a co-worker? Could the employee be terminated because the employee had mentioned that he held a concealed weapons permit and he kept his gun in his car? The answers depend on the state but in Florida are both probably no. The 2008 Florida law prohibits terminating or otherwise discriminating against an employee for exercising the right to keep and bear arms or for exercising the right to self-defense as long as the firearm is not exhibited on company property for any reason other than lawful defensive purposes.

Policies and Procedures: By sending a strong message about the company's commitment to workplace safety, employees will feel more secure about reporting statements or behaviors that they perceive as threatening. One way to encourage such reports is to require employees to read and sign a **"Zero Tolerance for Violence Policy"** prohibiting the use of (and, where lawful, possession of) weapons, engaging in harassment, and making verbal or physical threats on the job. Under this policy, employees will feel obligated to notify the human resource or security department regarding threats or violent encounters. A survey by SHRM revealed that 73 percent of respondents had a written policy addressing rules and regulations about weapons in the workplace, 59 percent said they have a written policy addressing violent acts in the workplace, and 39 percent do not have a written policy. Some companies offer a confidential hot line or Web site through which reports can be made. A zero-tolerance policy will be effective only if the human resource and security departments have the reputation for promptly handling matters seriously and with concern for all employees involved. As part of this policy, security procedures (e.g., visitors should wear ID badges) and planned escape routes should be identified and emergency phone numbers should be published. This way employees can refer to these important policies and procedures to know exactly what is expected of them.

Training and Education: Most employees do not become violent without displaying some early warning signs or symptoms. Therefore, employees and supervisors should learn to recognize and respond to highly stressed individuals and violent incidents and use non-confrontational response techniques to defuse potential problems. Supervisors must learn to recognize workers who display signs of extreme stress and whose work deteriorates significantly. Employees who begin to display irresponsible and inappropriate behaviors such as chronic absenteeism and lateness, grievances and complaints, and overt anger and resentment also should be monitored. Too many tragic situations occur because warning signs go unnoticed, suspicious acts never get reported, or reported information is ignored. It is in these cases that a situation explodes and workers shake their heads and wonder how they could have missed such obvious signs.

Management can help ease a frustrating work environment by giving employees an outlet to air their grievances without fear of reprisal. When possible, managers should take action to resolve the complaints. Establishing trust, cooperation, creativity, and internal teamwork will encourage mutual respect and allow for the development of team problem-solving skills. Basic interpersonal skills such as listening, giving positive encouragement, and learning to be prepared for change should be part of any program.

Employee assistance programs

Employee assistance programs (EAPs) provide specific programs designed to help employees with personal problems. EAPs are a resource to intervene with violent employees, but they are only one way in which human resource departments can help. Training and education programs should incorporate stress management, active coping techniques, and drug abuse awareness. Employers can make educational materials available to employees and their families to help them identify and handle harassment, domestic abuse, substance abuse, and other emotional problems. Companies can even provide voluntary self-defense training and classes in personal safety and security to teach employees how to reduce their chances of being victimized.

Companies where violence has previously occurred need to be especially aware of situations that could lead to employee anger or frustration because that workplace is already perceived by employees as unsafe. Workplace violence should be an ongoing topic of company meetings, workshops, newsletters, and new-hire orientation classes.

Handling layoffs and terminations is a highly sensitive area that requires special training because certain employees may become hostile after a dismissal. A person charged with this responsibility needs to remain neutral when disciplining or terminating employees. In return, employees should have the opportunity to submit written grievances or appeals about their termination or any other pertinent issues. Consideration should be made as to how the dismissal is conducted. Some managers recommend using only one room during the process. The affected individual should remain in the room while meeting with the manager, human resource representative, and outplacement counselor. This prevents the person from moving around the building and possibly causing a scene.

After a dismissal, confidential psychological counseling should be offered as well as outplacement services such as vocational counseling and job search or résumé-writing assistance. It is critical that keys, identification badges, and access cards are collected. Following up with an employee after termination is a good idea because violent acts typically occur within one week after an ex-employee has threatened to retaliate. This follow-up may be in the form of a structured exit interview where the former employee can vent his or her feelings or a simple phone call to find out how the person is doing.

Threat management teams

Threat Management Teams: Most experts agree that in addition to formal policies and procedures, companies need to form a threat management team. A **threat management team** is responsible for translating workplace violence policies into action, with particular emphasis on prevention. Typically this team is staffed with individuals from both inside and outside the company including a human resource professional, a psychologist, a lawyer, a security guard, and a key front-line manager who is capable of supervising a tense situation. A strong negotiator also can be part of the team.

The first task of the team is to conduct an initial risk assessment to determine if a threat is serious enough to justify deployment of the team and its resources. Risk assessment involves collecting personnel data to identify past and present problems with the employee posing the threat. Based on such assessment, the team then develops an initial action plan. This phase involves mobilizing the resources needed to intervene in the situation and planning additional steps.

The team should outline the scope of activities and operations that it will cover and set criteria for convening and reporting incidents to law enforcement and the media. Before extreme violence hits, the team must establish a relationship with local police and designate a spokesperson to deal with press reports. A formal procedure for investigating threats also must be defined. Some companies bring in an expert to evaluate the threat objectively and to guide action after the investigation.

Threat management teams also plan escape routes, coordinate medical and psychological care of injured victims, train employees to administer emergency aid to victims, and organize transportation for employees who are in no condition to drive following an incident. Employees and their families must be kept informed during the crisis and immediately thereafter. Therefore, a team member will be responsible for telephoning families to provide updates of victims' conditions, answering payroll or use-of-sick-leave questions, and other necessary matters. Primary and refresher training criteria should be set for all team members. It is recommended that a company develop crisis scenarios against which the threat management team can practice its response. The team also can prepare news releases and potential question-and-answer lists before a crisis occurs.

Security: Workplace violence can be prevented in some cases by employing security measures. Often these are used to protect employees and employers from violent people outside the organization (e.g., former employees). In this area, much can be accomplished at little cost. For example, a threat management team member can arrange regular police checkups and rearrange offices and furniture to provide escape routes that are accessible to employees who, because of their positions, may be obvious targets of disgruntled persons. Limited and controlled access, security awareness briefings, surveillance cameras, and silent alarms all can help reduce employee vulnerability. Making high-risk areas visible to more people and installing good external lighting are two more strategies. In short, the company should make it difficult for anyone to engage in violence.

As stated earlier, the goal of the OSHA Act of 1970 is "to ensure, so far as possible, every working man and woman in the nation safe and healthful working conditions." By law it is every organization's responsibility to prevent workplace violence from occurring and to be prepared to handle it should a situation arise. If a violent incident occurs on a company's premises, and inquiries show an absence of reasonable preventive efforts, the company could be held liable. While it is unrealistic to believe that a company can eliminate the threat of workplace violence, proper precautions can increase employee protection.

Video Display Terminals

Over 30 million Americans now work with video display terminals (VDTs). Many workers who spend considerable time in front of VDTs complain of eye fatigue and irritation, blurred vision, headaches, dizziness, and various muscular and wrist problems. Some VDT users have reported complicated or failed pregnancies. While one California study found that pregnant women who worked at VDTs for 20 hours or more a week had twice the risk of miscarriage as other clerical workers, a larger, more recent study sponsored by the federal government found no relationship between long exposure to VDTs and miscarriage.[84] Unions such as the American Federation of State and Municipal Employees (AFSME) are now demanding that pregnant women be allowed to switch to jobs not involving VDTs. Although there is no denying that electric and magnetic fields can influence biological processes, the critical question related to VDTs is the extent to which exposure is harmful. More research is urgently needed on this topic.

Employees should be properly trained in using ergonomic work methods and equipment to reduce the visual and muscular problems associated with VDTs. Visual problems can be minimized by correcting seat levels and angles, by using monitors that control contrast and brightness or have antiglare screens, and by lowering light levels in places where VDTs are used. People who work as little as two hours a day in front of a computer monitor can develop "computer vision syndrome," the symptoms of which include eye strain, blurred vision, headaches, and dry, irritated eyes. Specially designed glasses are available to reduce this syndrome. Muscular and wrist problems can be reduced by using adjustable chairs, keyboard support equipment, and physical therapy for the eyes, hands, wrists, shoulders, and back. The World Health Organization (WHO) has adopted a standard that states workers should sit at least three feet away from the back of a terminal (where the radiation is generated).

VDT workstation checklist

OSHA issued a VDT workstation checklist (see Figure 14-10) in 2000 designed to help workers and employers identify, analyze, and control hazards related to VDT tasks. The checklist is a very useful guideline for companies with potential VDT injuries such as repetitive strain injuries.

While evidence on the physical effects of VDTs has been questioned, the psychological stress related to work with VDTs is well documented, because workers are concerned that increased usage could affect their health or offspring. It seems that the speed with which technology has evolved has not been matched by the dissemination of knowledge about health and safety issues related to its use.[85]

Repetitive Strain Injuries (RSI)

It is estimated that over one million people are afflicted by ergonomic injuries each year at an annual cost of at least $50 billion with workers' compensation claims of $20 billion. Repetitive strain injuries (RSIs) such as carpal tunnel syndrome are now a very common workers' compensation claim in jobs involving essentially the same movements over and over again. Digital Equipment lost a large class action lawsuit in 1996 for RSI injuries a jury concluded had been caused by the design of their VDT keyboards. Similar lawsuits against several manufacturers are now pending.

Ergonomics

Ergonomics is the science of designing work space and equipment to be as compatible as possible with the physical and psychological limits of people. OSHA put an ergonomics standard in place in 2000 that they estimated would prevent 4.6 million RSI injuries in the first 10 years. The standard was repealed by Congress under George W. Bush's administration. Business groups such as the Chamber of Commerce strongly oppose an ergonomics standard, claiming OSHA had seriously underestimated the cost of compliance. OSHA has since provided voluntary guidelines for certain industries. They issued a

Figure 14-10 **VDT Workstation Checklist**

Instructions: Evaluate the workstation by answering yes or no to the following statements related to working conditions, the chair, keyboard/input device, monitor, work area, and accessories.

WORKING CONDITIONS Y N

The workstation is designed or arranged for doing VDT tasks so it allows the employee's . . .

A. **Head** and **neck** to be about upright (not bent down/back).
B. **Head, neck,** and **trunk** to face forward (not twisted). ___ ___
C. **Trunk** to be about perpendicular to floor (not leaning forward/backward). ___ ___
D. **Shoulders** and **upper arms** to be about perpendicular to floor (not stretched forward) and relaxed (not elevated). ___ ___
E. **Upper arms** and **elbows** to be close to body (not extended outward). ___ ___
F. **Forearms, wrists,** and **hands** to be straight and parallel to floor (not pointing up/down). ___ ___
G. **Wrists** and **hands** to be straight (not bent up/down or sideways toward little finger). ___ ___
H. **Thighs** to be about parallel to floor and **lower legs** to be about perpendicular to floor. ___ ___
I. **Feet** to rest flat on floor or be supported by a stable footrest. ___ ___
J. **VDT tasks** to be organized in a way that allows employee to vary VDT tasks with other work activities, or to take micro-breaks or recovery pauses while at the VDT workstation. ___ ___

SEATING Y N

The chair . . .

1. **Backrest** provides support for employee's lower back (lumbar area). ___ ___
2. **Seat width** and **depth** accommodate specific employee (seatpan not too big/small). ___ ___
3. **Seat front** does not press against the back of employee's knees and lower legs (seatpan not too long). ___ ___
4. **Seat** has cushioning and is rounded/has "waterfall" front (no sharp edge). ___ ___
5. **Armrests** support both forearms while employee performs VDT tasks and do not interfere with movement. ___ ___

KEYBOARD/INPUT DEVICE Y N

The keyboard/input device is designed or arranged for doing VDT tasks so that . . .

6. **Keyboard/input device platform(s)** is stable and large enough to hold keyboard and input device. ___ ___
7. **Input device** (mouse or trackball) is located right next to keyboard so it can be operated without reaching. ___ ___
8. **Input device** is easy to activate and shape/size fits hand of specific employee (not too big/small). ___ ___
9. **Wrists** and **hands** do not rest on sharp or hard edge. ___ ___

MONITOR Y N

The monitor is designed or arranged for VDT tasks so that . . .

10. **Top line** of screen is at or below eye level so employee is able to read it without bending head or neck down/back. (For employees with bifocals/trifocals, see next item.) ___ ___
11. **Employee with bifocals/trifocals** is able to read screen without bending head or neck backward. ___ ___
12. **Monitor distance** allows employee to read screen without leaning head, neck, or trunk forward/backward. ___ ___
13. **Monitor position** is directly in front of employee so employee does not have to twist head or neck. ___ ___
14. **No glare** (e.g., from windows, lights) is present on the screen that might cause employee to assume an awkward posture to read screen. ___ ___

WORK AREA Y N

The work area is designed or arranged for doing VDT tasks so that . . .

15. **Thighs** have clearance space between chair and VDT table/keyboard platform (thighs not trapped). ___ ___
16. **Legs** and **feet** have clearance space under VDT table so employee is able to get close enough to keyboard/input device. ___ ___

ACCESSORIES Y N

17. **Document holder,** if provided, is stable and large enough to hold documents that are used. ___ ___
18. **Document holder,** if provided, is placed at about the same height and distance as monitor screen so there is little head movement when employee looks from document to screen. ___ ___
19. **Wrist rest,** if provided, is padded and free of sharp and square edges. ___ ___
20. **Wrist rest,** if provided, allows employee to keep forearms, wrists, and hands straight and parallel to ground when using keyboard/input device. ___ ___
21. **Telephone** can be used with head upright (not bent) and shoulders relaxed (not elevated) if employee does VDT tasks at the same time. ___ ___

GENERAL Y N

22. Workstation and equipment have sufficient adjustability so that the employee is able to be in a safe working posture and to make occasional changes in posture while performing VDT tasks. ___ ___
23. VDT workstation, equipment, and accessories are maintained in serviceable condition and function properly. ___ ___

PASSING SCORE = "YES" answer on all "working postures" items (A–J) and no more than two "NO" answers on remainder of checklist (1–23).

standard for the meatpacking industry in 1990, and many companies from other industries have adopted the guidelines.

OSHA can use the "general duty clause" for ergonomic problems

OSHA can cite employers for hazards that may cause RSIs. Although a specific OSHA rule may never be implemented, OSHA can use the **general duty clause** of the law. Pepperidge Farm has been fined $310,000 based on an inspection of a Pennsylvania plant. In the appeal of the fine, a judge ruled that OSHA could use the general duty clause for the reported RSI. But OSHA has a limited number of inspectors, and ergonomics-related investigations are very labor intensive. There was some OSHA activity related to RSI in 2005 under the general duty clause of OSHA.

State regulations on ergonomics

California is the only state with its own safety standards designed to protect workers from repetitive motion injuries such as carpal tunnel syndrome. These regulations require improved working conditions if employees suffer nerve, muscle, or joint injuries as a consequence of repetitive motion. Workers also can demand that employers at least consider wrist guards, adjustable tables, increased breaks, and job rotation as ways of combating the injuries. The workstation checklist in Figure 14-10 would be an excellent diagnostic tool.

While there is no ergonomics standard, OSHA has done considerable research that focused on musculoskeletal injury. One recent study investigated a test of the "best practices" musculoskeletal injury prevention program designed by OSHA to safely lift physically dependent nursing home residents. The results were quite impressive with significant reductions in resident handling injury incidence, workers' compensation costs, and lost workday injuries after the intervention. The "best practices" prevention program significantly reduced injuries for full-time and part-time nurses in all age groups and all lengths of experience in all study sites.[86]

Occupational Stress

The shock of seeing a highly regarded National League umpire collapse and die on the field at Cincinnati's Riverfront Stadium on opening day of the baseball season turned the sports world's attention to questions about wellness and stress on the job. An autopsy established that Jerry McSherry, 51, died of severe coronary artery disease. He had an enlarged heart and a reccurring weight problem. Richie Phillips, the head of the umpires' union, reported that Jerry brought "a lot of stress onto himself."

The description sounds both familiar and universal. Rising stress levels have been blamed on work stressors such as the threat of terrorism, the information age, widespread layoffs, global competition, as well as violent crime, immigration, or any other modern threat Americans zero in on. The stress levels on our soldiers and civilians were extremely high in 2007 and 2008 with numerous ill effects, including violence among our own troops. Soldiers returning from the Iraq War and Afghanistan are showing a number of difficulties,

Post traumatic stress disorder

including PTSD, alcohol and drug use, and depression. A 2008 study in the journal *Military Medicine* reported that 6 percent of returning vets had PTSD and 27 percent indicated excessive alcohol use. The study also reported that 62 percent of service members reported receiving some kind of mental health care since returning home from Iraq or Afghanistan.

The new initiatives to make organizations more competitive and productive also have great potential to increase stress in workers. What is the main culprit of stress? According to a survey conducted in 2000, over 50 percent of respondents blamed their stress levels on "having to work more than 12 hours a day to get the job done."[87] This is a pervasive national problem. A 2007 study found that Americans work more hours than any other industrialized nation.

Effects of stress

Stress is making workers sick, increasing the potential for violence at work, and affecting productivity and accident rates. One in 10 workers reports that workers have come to blows because of work stress. Forty-two percent report verbal abuse at the office. Twenty-three percent say they have been driven to tears at work. Fourteen percent report that they work with equipment damaged from workplace rage. One in eight workers says he/she has called in sick because of stress, and 20 percent have quit a job because of stress. Job stress also can lead to alcohol and drug use and is a frequently cited problem in workers' compensation claims. Problem drinkers file five times more compensation claims and use three times more accident benefits than nonabusers.[88] Job stress costs corporate America an estimated $200 billion annually in absenteeism, lost productivity, accidents, and medical insurance. High levels of stress at work or at home could also be linked to premature aging. One recent study found that chronic stress hastened the shriveling of the tips of the bundles of genes inside cells, which shortens their life span and speeds the body's deterioration. Worse, stress is contributing to the deaths of hundreds of workers every year. The highest concentration of deaths occurred among operators, fabricators, laborers, and service workers.

Definition of job stress

Job stress has been defined as a "situation wherein job-related factors interact with a worker to change his or her psychological and/or physiological condition such that the person is forced to deviate from normal functioning."[89] Stress is considered to be a major problem for workers in today's turbulent and highly competitive environment, with its emphasis on cost control, reduced labor expense, and higher productivity. Stress should be distinguished from a **stressor,** which is the object or event that causes the stress. For example, the speculation that work with VDTs may be hazardous could be considered a stressor that may cause stress in some employees. Exposure to secondhand smoke, which may cause cancer, now serves as a stressor for many nonsmoking workers. Figure 14-11 presents a model of the antecedents, outcomes, and consequences of stress. Stressors

Stressors

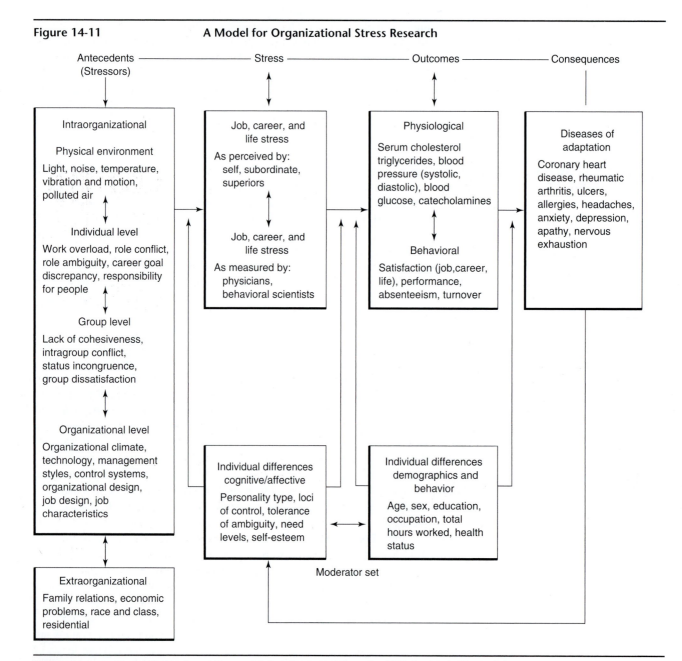

Figure 14-11   **A Model for Organizational Stress Research**

Source: J. M. Ivancevich and M. T. Matteson, *Stress and Work: A Management Perspective,* 1980. Reprinted with permission.

can be found in the physical environment due to lighting or noise problems, temperature, or polluted air. We know that these potential stressors can have an interactive effect such that, for example, temperature combined with a noisy environment may cause even greater stress than the two sources independently. Sleep loss has particular interactive potency.

Job demands

Role overload
Role conflict

Prolonged exposure to certain job demands has been linked to several measures of mental and physical stress as well as productivity problems and absenteeism. **Job demands** have been defined as psychological stressors, such as working too hard or too fast, having too much to do (**role overload**), or having conflicting demands from several sources (**role conflict**).[90] An individual may perceive **role conflict** when pressures from two or more sources are exerted such that complying with one source creates greater problems regarding another source. For example, workers may try to maintain a high quality standard while simultaneously trying to meet a very difficult quantity standard, or managers may attempt to hit a quota for production while reducing labor costs. Also, employees in matrix organizational structures may experience role conflict if they have two bosses: one in charge of their "line" job and one in charge of the "project" job or team they have been assigned to.

Role ambiguity

Another source of stress is **role ambiguity,** in which workers simply do not understand what is expected on the job or where what is expected is contrary to what they think should be done. An example of role ambiguity occurs when a boss is vague about an employee's responsibilities or the time frame in which the employee has to complete specific tasks. Research on role ambiguity and conflict is plentiful. As in other areas related to stress, the reactions to the stressors tend to vary widely depending on an individual's characteristics. For example, people with **Type A** personalities suffer more stress and experience a greater number of health problems than do Type B people. Type A people tend to do just about everything quickly (walk, talk, eat) and have little tolerance for people who go at a more

Proactive personalities more
effective in stressful situations

moderate pace.[91] Research also shows that people with more **"proactive"** personalities are more able to control stressful situations and handle job demands.[92] A "proactive" personality exhibits a tendency to initiate and maintain actions that can alter the surrounding environment.

Family conflicts

Other sources of individual stress include conflicts between job and family obligations. Women in particular tend to experience this conflict. "Family responsibilities can place tremendous pressure on women. When both husband and wife have careers, the wife is often expected to keep her housekeeping role in addition to her work role. . . . More and more Superwomen are now questioning their multiple roles. With this uncertainty comes more conflict and stress."[93] As discussed in Chapter 9, many corporations are aware of this extra burden on women and are providing employment options designed to reduce this source of stress. Companies such as DuPont, Merck, and General Mills offer family leave, flexible work schedules, telecommuting, and on-site day care.

Telecommuting

One review of 80 studies found reduced turnover, absenteeism, and increased productivity in companies that help employees balance work with family obligations.[94] For example, Xerox, Tandem Computers, and Corning Inc. enabled their employees working in teams to develop their own schedules that would meet their personal needs while addressing their work demands. They found a decrease in absenteeism and the teams became more effective, self-directed, and independent.[95] Studies show telecommuting in particular is an effective strategy for reducing stress at work (not to mention the cost of getting to and from work). Concern for their personal safety is an additional significant stressor for women. Some companies now provide coping-skills training, including self-defense programs. Research shows that such training increases women's perceived self-efficacy regarding the ability to exercise self-defense.[96]

Role of manager critical

The role of the manager in alleviating stress appears to be critical. Recent research documents that stress levels are on the rise and that the primary sources of stress are work–family conflicts. Organizations that help employees cope with these roles report less stress and reductions in workers' compensation claims, medical expenses, and voluntary termination. Ensuring that work–family policies are created in a just manner through employee surveys can help create procedures that are representative of all groups' concerns and are consistent across persons and time. However, "the leader who enacts those procedures must be supportive—even the best parental leave procedure cannot overcome supervisors who forbid their employees from using it."[97]

The work group, unit, or organization can be a stressor as well, aside from the issues of role ambiguity and conflict. Particularly in this era of downsizing many U.S. corporations are feeling the crunch by reducing payroll costs. Supervisors and managers are being asked to make hard personnel decisions regarding cutbacks. As a result, employees worry more now that their jobs may be on the line. Jobs affected by recent major changes are generally stressful. If a company was purchased, has gone through a layoff or downsizing, has imposed mandatory overtime, or has undergone a major reorganization, the employees, regardless of rank, are likely to have high levels of stress.

Some jobs are more likely to cause stress than others. Air traffic controllers, for example, report higher rates of ulcers, chest pains, and headaches than other workers and after only three years of work! Nurses and teachers also report high and increasing levels of stress. While high-level executives lament their stressful responsibilities, the evidence regarding stress-related illnesses does not support the belief that higher-level management jobs are more stressful than other jobs. In fact, one large-scale study found that rates of coronary heart disease were greater at lower management levels.[98] Researchers have found that stress is a function of high job demands in combination with low control at work. So when an individual has little authority to make decisions in a highly demanding job, the most negative aspects of stress should be expected.[99] There is also evidence that coping responses to stressors and control differ as a function of culture.[100]

Role of low job control

Job performance exams

Because stress and fatigue cannot be measured by biochemical testing, some employers have turned to testing an employee's ability to perform a safety-sensitive job. These job performance exams are generally computer-based and check an employee's visual acuity, coordination, and reaction time. Even though such exams were developed nearly 40 years ago by NASA to check the performance skills of astronauts, the technology was first made available to the general public just a few years ago. An example of a test is one that measures responses while the test subject tries to keep a diamond-shaped cursor aligned with the center of the computer screen. The cursor moves randomly and quickly, so the subject's responses must be fast and accurate. This test takes 30 seconds to complete, and employees have eight chances to match or beat their baseline score. If they fail, then the employer can reassign them for the day or request that they take the day off.

Burnout

A relatively new term for one type of stress is **burnout,** which is a reflection of emotional exhaustion, depersonalization, and reduced personal accomplishment. While originally meant to reflect an emotional reaction in people who often work closely with people, burnout can be found both within as well as outside human-services occupations. Burnout is common among police officers, teachers, social workers, and nurses. People experiencing burnout may develop cynical attitudes toward their jobs and clients and may feel emotional exhaustion, depersonalization, and a sense of low personal accomplishment or control.[101] However, burnout is not inevitable in these jobs. A stress reduction program for public school teachers found that the effects of burnout could be reduced using positive feedback about teacher competencies.[102]

Job design

Recent research also shows that attempts to decrease job demands and increase job control should be directed at specific job situations and not occupational groupings. Interventions tailored to redesigning particular jobs have proven effective. Interventions will be most successful if they are "tailor-made to address the most important job demands and job resources in specific working environments."[103]

To address stress-related issues and other employee concerns in the United Kingdom, the Working Time Directive became effective in November 1996. This directive contains specific rules relating to all workers, additional rules for those working at night, and general rules on health and safety. The time that an employee spends at work is restricted to 48 hours a week, averaged over a period of up to four months.[104]

As noted in Figure 14-11, there are psychological, physiological, and behavioral consequences of stress. However, reactions to the same stressors vary greatly with the individual. Although individual reactions are difficult to predict, it is known that some people can handle tremendous amounts of stressors without any manifest stressful reactions. For example, people with more proactive personalities are less susceptible to stress under demanding work conditions. Other people fall apart, become violent, or turn to drugs or alcohol. Psychological stress may be manifested in anxiety, depression, irritability, and hostility and also may have physiological consequences such as high blood pressure, numbness, fatigue, and heart problems. Of course, the stress also may affect work performance, work attendance, and accident rates. These consequences can have profound (and costly) organizational consequences, including union organizing, workers' compensation, poor work products, and legal problems. McDonald's Corporation, for example, was held liable for a fatal crash caused by a 19-year-old who had worked a double shift. More recently, a social worker was paid damages after a legal battle to prove that his job caused him to have two nervous breakdowns, brought on by stress and his "impossible workload."

Types of stress

There are different types of stress. While most people assume that stress is always bad for workers and that organizations should always find methods for preventing or reducing it, some research actually shows the opposite effect—that stress can have desirable consequences. Some dimensions of stress are associated with *positive* work outcomes. One study of executives found that stress related to the challenging or rewarding aspects of work was related to positive outcomes while stress which associated with hindering or constraining job experiences was negative. Challenge-related stress was correlated with job satisfaction and less job search, and hindrance-related stress was associated with more job search and less job satisfaction.[105] A more recent study found similar effects but also that both types of stress were positively related to psychological strain.[106]

Challenge-related stress can be good

Three intervention targets

Figure 14-12 provides a framework of specific intervention programs and the stress outcomes that they may be directed toward. The three intervention targets in the figure correspond to (1) changing the degree of stress potential in a situation by reducing the intensity or number of stressors present, (2) helping employees to modify their appraisal of potentially stressful situations, and (3) helping employees to cope more effectively with the consequences of stress. Stress management and reduction programs are common in industry today. At Motorola, for example, programs emphasize exercise, nutrition, relaxation techniques, time management, and self-awareness. Cigna Corporation provides employees with breaks during which they can relax with new age music, meditation, and stretches or increase their energy level by listening to a tape of empowering thoughts or getting up and moving to upbeat music. Cigna even has a massage therapist who will come to an employee's desk to soothe tense neck muscles. Other organizations have attempted to reduce physical stressors by redesigning the workplace. One survey found that 12 percent of Americans indicate that they work in a cubicle "like the cartoon character Dilbert." Work space is another important variable related to stress.

Work space

Role ambiguity and **role conflict** often can be reduced by interventions following a job analysis and survey research. Studies point to immediate supervisors as a primary source of stress among workers. Survey data may help to pinpoint unit-level problems before they result in serious organizational difficulties such as termination, absences, and disabilities. Many organizations incorporate their stress reduction programs into comprehensive employment assistance programs. We will examine these programs next. Figure 14-13 presents a summary of well-documented stress producers and stress reducers.

Employee Assistance Programs

EAPs are effective

EAPs are programs designed to assist employees with performance problems. EAPs are a growing form of employee benefit that provides help to millions of U.S. employees for a variety of problems related to performance. Although cost estimates of EAPs exceed $750 million, most organizations report the programs to be very cost effective. For example, executives at Banc One Financial Services receive in-office counseling. Lucent Technologies also set up its own internal counseling divisions to coach difficult workers. In San Francisco, companies pay NoonTime University $8,000 for six three-hour lunchtime training sessions for 20 to 24 employees. There are over 10,000 organizations with formal EAPs treating job stress, alcoholism and other forms of drug abuse, marital and emotional difficulties, and financial problems. One survey found that EAPs are available to employees working for companies with 1,000 or more workers, but only 45 percent of all workers utilize their services.[107] One poll of *Employee Benefit Plan Review* subscribers revealed that 32 percent of employees turned to EAPs because of corporate restructurings and

Figure 14-12   **Stress Management Interventions: Targets, Types, and Outcomes**

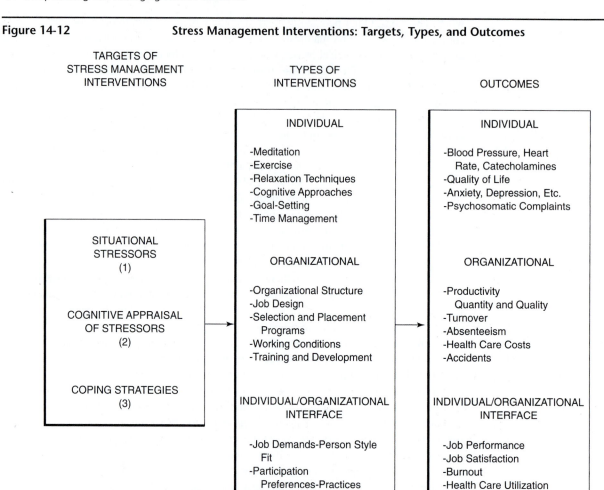

TARGETS OF STRESS MANAGEMENT INTERVENTIONS

SITUATIONAL STRESSORS
(1)

COGNITIVE APPRAISAL OF STRESSORS
(2)

COPING STRATEGIES
(3)

TYPES OF INTERVENTIONS

INDIVIDUAL

-Meditation
-Exercise
-Relaxation Techniques
-Cognitive Approaches
-Goal-Setting
-Time Management

ORGANIZATIONAL

-Organizational Structure
-Job Design
-Selection and Placement Programs
-Working Conditions
-Training and Development

INDIVIDUAL/ORGANIZATIONAL INTERFACE

-Job Demands-Person Style Fit
-Participation Preferences-Practices
-Autonomy Preferences-Practices
-Co-Worker Relationships

OUTCOMES

INDIVIDUAL

-Blood Pressure, Heart Rate, Catecholamines
-Quality of Life
-Anxiety, Depression, Etc.
-Psychosomatic Complaints

ORGANIZATIONAL

-Productivity Quantity and Quality
-Turnover
-Absenteeism
-Health Care Costs
-Accidents

INDIVIDUAL/ORGANIZATIONAL INTERFACE

-Job Performance
-Job Satisfaction
-Burnout
-Health Care Utilization

Source: J. M. Ivancevich, M. T. Matteson, S. M. Freedman, and J. S. Phillips, "Worksite Stress Management Interventions," *American Psychologist*, February 1990, pp. 252–261. Reprinted with permission.

downsizings. The number of EAPs has increased because the thousands of companies with federal contracts must adopt formal antidrug policies under the provisions of the 1988 **Drug Free Workplace Act.** Many EAPs also are equipped to handle problems related to AIDS and workplace violence. In addition, EAPs can be designed to provide physical help with controlling blood pressure, weight, and smoking.

General goal of EAP   The general goal of an EAP is to provide treatment for employees who are having problems so they can return to normal, productive functioning on the job. While the vast majority of EAPs are in large organizations, even small businesses are getting involved with EAPs through consortiums with other small businesses. Most EAP referrals are based on an assessment of job performance and referrals by supervisors, although many employees also volunteer to attend EAPs. EAP staff often provide training for managers and supervisors on making "constructive confrontations" with their employees regarding work-related deficiencies. Supervisors are thus exempted from trying to diagnose the causes of a problem. Getting at the cause of the performance problem is left to professionals (e.g., people with graduate degrees in psychology and social work), who are trained to make such diagnoses and treat people accordingly. Most EAPs are based on the principle of voluntary participation. Labor unions generally support drug counseling and EAPs but oppose coercion to participate in such programs as a condition of employment, as well as opposing drug testing of any kind.[108]

An EAP is typically run by an outside health service organization, with an average cost of about $35 per employee per year. The research data on the effects of EAPs are quite

Figure 14-13 **Stress Producers and Reducers**

Stress Producers

Highly stressful situations at work

The company where I work was recently purchased by another company.

Layoffs have occurred in the past year; more are being contemplated.

My work unit is reorganizing.

I expect that the company will be sold or relocated.

My pay and/or benefits were cut recently.

Mandatory overtime is frequently required.

I have little control over how I do my work.

Consequences of making a mistake on my job are severe.

My workload varies greatly.

My job is fast-paced.

I have to react quickly and accurately to rapidly changing conditions.

I have many personal conflicts on the job.

My supervisor is incompetent

I often have work–family conflicts

My work often deprives me of a good night's sleep.

Stressful situations at work

I have little or no opportunity for advancement.

I have to deal with lots of red tape to get things done.

Staffing, money, or technology is inadequate for my job.

My pay is below the market rate for my skills and knowledge.

My sick and vacation time are inadequate.

My work schedule is rotated among shifts.

New machinery, equipment, or ways of working have been introduced recently.

Noise or vibration levels are high.

Room temperatures are either too high or too low.

I am generally isolated from my co-workers.

Performance of work units generally is below average.

I get docked if I'm late for work.

Somewhat stressful situations

There are few or no windows or natural lighting on my job.

I have little or no privacy at work.

Meal breaks are unpredictable.

Work is sedentary.

Work is physically exhausting.

Stress Reducers

Role clarity greatly reduces stress

I have clear, planned goals and objectives for my job.

I know what my responsibilities are.

I know what is expected of me.

I feel certain about how much authority I have on the job.

Explanations are clear of what has to be done.

Highly effective stress reducers

Management takes significant action to reduce stress.

Mental health benefits are provided in health insurance coverage.

My employer has a formal EAP.

I am given information regularly on how to cope with stress.

I have a current and clear job description.

Management and employees talk openly with each other.

Employees are free to talk with one another.

Employer offers exercise and other stress-reduction classes.

Employees are recognized and rewarded for their contributions.

Adequate resources are provided to get the job done.

Effective stress reducers

Work rules are published and are the same for everyone.

Child care programs are available.

Employees can work flexible hours.

I can telecommute if I want.

Perks are granted fairly, based on a person's level in the organization.

Employees have access to the technology they need.

Employees receive training when assigned new tasks.

My employer encourages personal-support groups.

I have a place and time to relax during the workday.

I really like my boss.

Somewhat effective stress reducers

An employee assistance program is available.

Employees' work spaces are not crowded.

Employees can put up personal items in their work areas.

Management appreciates humor in the workplace.

Elder care programs are available.

positive. EAP advocates estimate that for every dollar spent, organizations recover from three to five dollars because of increased productivity, decreased insurance costs, and reduced workers' compensation claims and sick leave. Adolph Coors Company reported savings of $6 for every $1 spent on the EAP. AT&T reported a savings of almost $600,000 as a result of its EAP activities. In one study of 110 employees, 85 percent of poor performers were judged to be no longer poor after the EAP. The rate of improvement for all participants was 86 percent. There was a significant decrease in the number of accidents in which these individuals were involved. Absenteeism also went down, as did visits to the medical department. In short, at least for this sample of AT&T workers, the EAP was a great success.[109] United Airlines estimates that for every $1 spent for its EAP, it realizes savings of $16.35 through reduction in employee absences.[110]

GM reports that about 10 percent of its 600,000-employee workforce is experiencing alcohol or other drug-related problems, so GM emphasizes substance abuse in its EAP programs. As stated earlier, many other organizations have responded to problems of substance abuse by implementing drug testing programs, which may involve entry-level screening for drug usage as well as random drug testing of current employees. Such policies are controversial but, in most circumstances, legal. Under the doctrine of employment at will, employers may dismiss employees for any reason other than those covered by statute (e.g., race, sex, religion, age, national origin, disability). Firing a nonunion employee who fails a drug test is legal in almost every state and has been done thousands of times. However, most human resource management experts take the position that termination should be a last resort after an attempt at intervention through an EAP, which should be prompted by unacceptable performance.

Employee Wellness or Fitness Programs

Designed to prevent health problems

Programs include smoking cessation, fitness training, screening, stress management

Due to the staggering health care costs described in Chapter 10, many companies have set up wellness, fitness, or health management programs for employees. While EAPS are designed to treat employee problems, wellness programs are designed to prevent problems. One survey found that 75 percent of large employers participated in wellness programs. Unions also have been increasingly involved in promoting health and safety protections for their members.[111]

Wellness is defined as a "freely chosen lifestyle aimed at achieving and maintaining an individual's good health."[112] Companies have discovered that the best way to reduce health care costs is to keep employees healthy. In general, healthy employees are more productive than unhealthy ones. Research shows that employees who set specific, obtainable goals related to improving their health often increase their perceived control and confidence to overcome barriers to performing healthy behaviors.[113] As long as goals are reasonable and employees experience success in their first few attempts at reaching their goals, a motivational change is brought about by this mastery. This motivational change involves increasingly higher levels of control and confidence, especially over work-related barriers (i.e., work piling up while the employee uses release time to exercise).

One problem with wellness programs is that healthy people tend to take advantage of the programs while those most in need stay away. Incentive programs can help encourage those most needy employees. One survey found that 39 percent of employers offer incentives to participate in wellness programs. Workers get rewarded for meeting health-related wellness criteria. Most large U.S. corporations offer some form of formal wellness programs involving health assessment, exercise planning, counseling or support groups, stress management, weight control, and smoking cessation. Some insurance companies offer reduced rates for organizations with organized wellness programs.[114]

At New York Telephone, the wellness program focuses on the following major areas of health: smoking cessation, cholesterol reduction, alcohol abuse control, fitness training, stress management, and cancer screening. New York Telephone reported a savings of almost $3 million in reduced absences and medical treatment because of its wellness program. Kimberly-Clark offers a variety of health-related programs, including an exercise routine available at the fitness center on the premises, weight control consultation, blood pressure analysis and treatment, and nutritional advice. These programs are available to the company's entire workforce, and 88 percent of employees are enrolled in one or more of the programs. While the cost is high (about $435 per employee per year), the director of the program is certain the bottom line will support its effectiveness. There are many other success stories. IBM, Johnson & Johnson, Tenneco, Campbell Soup, and Xerox all report success with their fitness and wellness programs. One Xerox work location provides a soccer field, an Olympic-size pool, two gyms, tennis courts, a weight room, and over 2,000 acres of running space. Johnson & Johnson reports savings of $378 per employee as a result of its comprehensive wellness program, which it now also administers for 60 other companies. The goals of the program are basic: stop smoking, eat fruit and fewer fatty foods, get some exercise, and buckle up.[115]

The effectiveness of Pacific Bell's FitWorks health promotion program was assessed in four of its construction sites. The results of the one-year study found that employees who had access to physical training equipment had lower heart rates after step tests, greater lower-body muscular endurance, and greater flexibility than those who did not work out.[116] John Alden Financial has found that corporate wellness programs boost productivity, lower health care costs, and help firms attract and retain top-quality employees.[117] This organization's wellness activities include a health fair, an employee-published cookbook of nutritious recipes, numerous sports clubs, substance abuse prevention campaigns, an in-house fitness center, and many health-related seminars and workshops. Provided below are some tips for launching wellness programs based on the experience of John Alden Financial and other corporate members.[118]

Tips for starting a wellness program

- *Start small:* Launch simple programs such as blood pressure and cholesterol screening or distribute information about nutrition to employees.

- *Delegate responsibility:* Let employees plan and implement activities and conduct a survey to assess employees' health and recreational interests.

- *Schedule activities around the workday:* Schedule events before work, during lunch, or after work so the activities do not take employees away from their regular duties.

- *Learn from other companies:* Find out what other firms in the area or industry have done and learn from their experiences.

- *Take advantage of community services:* Many local health agencies and nonprofit organizations provide health screenings and information for free.

SUMMARY

The active role of management

Top management is taking a more active role in improving the health and safety of workers. Figure 14-14 summarizes the managerial steps for improving the work environment as recommended by one expert.[119]

The first step (affirming management commitment) means that management must make resources available for health and safety issues. Research shows that plants with superior health and safety records spend more money on health and safety. In addition to management commitment to safety, it is also crucial to have employee participation. This can be done by empowering employees to take ownership in the safety of the organization.[120] The second step for improving the work environment calls for a clearly established policy and results-oriented set of objectives for health and safety. Third, managers should perform planned and unplanned inspections of work sites to assess compliance. Fourth, as the safety manager at DuPont states, "When plant managers begin to audit people and their actions, dramatic changes occur . . . audits foster fewer unsafe acts." Managers also should establish an atmosphere in which employees feel comfortable reporting unsafe working conditions so that all potential hazards can be identified. Managers must form a partnership designed to maximize employee safety and health and acknowledge that a trained, safe workforce is the most productive workforce an employer can have.[121] The fifth step is to identify particular employees at risk so that appropriate training and policies can be developed. The development of an employee database or the use of a comprehensive personnel inventory (see Chapter 5) could assist with this effort. The sixth step for enhancing managerial attention is to make corrections in the work environment based on the research and employee data analysis. This may include a number of preventive measures. With the proliferation of complaints regarding carpal tunnel syndrome and related stress symptoms, this step may include ergonomics or work station redesign. Where the

**Figure 14-14
Eight Essential Steps in Improving the Work Environment**

1. Affirm management's commitment to a safe and healthy environment.
2. Review current safety objectives and policies.
3. Conduct periodic evaluations and inspections of the workplace.
4. Identify potential and existing work hazards in the areas of safety and health.
5. Identify the employees at risk.
6. Make the necessary improvements in the workplace.
7. Prepare and conduct preventive programs.
8. Monitor the feedback results and evaluate costs.

Source: S. Greenfield, "Management's Safety and Health Imperative: Eight Essential Steps to Improving the Work Environment." *Minerva Occasional Paper Series (2.9).* Cincinnati, OH: Xavier University, 1989.

job situation contributes to an unsafe environment, management should take the appropriate action. The seventh step calls on management to prepare and conduct preventive programs. Aggressive antidrug policies, EAPs, threat management teams, and wellness programs are examples. The final step is for management to evaluate actions and feed the results back to employees. An assessment of the monetary value of health and safety programs is one necessary component of this step. Many companies report considerable savings from such programs.

Savings from health and safety programs

Gillette saved over $1.2 million from its health and safety programs. Procter & Gamble reported direct cost savings in excess of $1.5 million. A. M. Castle & Company in Franklin Park, Illinois, started a safety program in 1980. Since then it has reported fewer injuries and reduced lost time, as well as significant cost savings for the company. In addition, employees are involved in the program, which covers a wide range of health and safety issues, including alcohol and drug abuse, fleet safety, and equipment maintenance.[122] Exeter Healthcare, Inc., implemented a program called PEPS—Patient/Resident, Employee, Plant Safety. It took place in four phases: program development, implementation, outcome analysis, and program enhancements. Within the first eight months of the program, patient/resident falls were reduced 40 percent in one quarter, with further reductions in following quarters. Exeter's work-related costs were far below what was ever anticipated, and work injuries and related costs showed an 85 percent drop in one year.[123] Milliken & Company's emphasis on employee participation in safety has elevated the textile firm to unrivaled status in American industry. Of Milliken's 55 U.S. facilities, 30 have been judged good enough for inclusion in OSHA's elite voluntary protection program. The basic belief of the programs is that all incidents can be prevented. Star status is awarded to those sites that excel in these areas: management commitment and planning, hazard assessment, hazard correction and control, safety and health training, association awareness/ownership participation, and safety and health process assessments. One of the most recent Star designees is Milliken's New Holland Plant in Gainesville, Georgia.[124]

More companies are developing formal health and safety policies, and management is now more likely to be held accountable for accident rates and other health-related measures. In the next century, even greater interest in the subject and more programs that focus on employee behavior are likely. Drug testing, antismoking programs, threat management teams, EAPs, and wellness programs hold promise as methods that can contribute to a more productive and healthy workforce.[125]

International programs

Employee health and safety are issues of importance not simply in the United States. Most other countries have some policies on these issues, and their rules are changing to reflect greater concerns among employees for injuries and illnesses. For example, in Ireland, in 1989 the Safety, Health, and Welfare Work Act was enacted. This set out provisions for establishment of the National Authority for Occupational Safety and Health to promote, encourage, and foster the prevention of accidents and injury to health at work. Under the act, the employer's duties are to provide (1) a safe place at work, (2) safe equipment, and (3) personal protective equipment. These efforts initially cost the companies money, but over the long term have reduced premiums, absenteeism, and claims against the firms.[126] In Britain, an important case occurred in 1994: *Walker v. Northumberland County Council* extended the common-law duty of an employer to provide a safe system of work for employees in terms of mental as well as physical health.[127] In Canada, the city of Toronto recently began a new program for its workforce of approximately 7,000. The goal of the new initiative is the successful return to work for employees with psychological disabilities (e.g., suffering from work-related stress). Toronto now provides a wide range of rehabilitation services for injured and ill employees.[128]

For U.S. human resource professionals, a key element of human resource management in a foreign country is employee morale. Companies operating in harsh and high-threat locations can maintain good morale and prevent unnecessary turnover by providing safe working and living conditions as well as basic comforts. Human resource professionals can prepare their employees if they have analyzed the working conditions in the other country and have developed plans to deal with potential illnesses or injuries.[129]

Discussion Questions

1. Why is a 20-year-old with three years of experience more likely to be involved in an accident than a 30-year-old with three years of experience? After you develop your theory for this fact, explain how companies can intervene to reduce (or wipe out) the effect.

2. How could you as a manager develop a strategy for increasing employees' motivation to work more safely?

3. Devise a training program and a policy directed at increasing the physical fitness of your employees. Take a position on smoking, alcohol use, and other health-related matters and state whether you would make the programs mandatory.

4. Do you think managers should be held criminally liable for health and safety violations? Should they go to jail for such violations? If so, under what conditions? If not, why not?

5. Do you support a policy of random drug testing for all employees? Explain. Would you be less attracted to an organization that required random drug testing with no probable cause?

6. Should a company be allowed to prohibit smoking or drinking alcohol on or off the job for its employees? Explain your answer.

7. Given the accumulated evidence on the effects of smoking, why hasn't OSHA taken steps to regulate smoking and second-hand smoke in the workplace?

8. What kinds of work-related factors affect employees' stress levels? What recommendations would you offer a company to manage the stress of its employees?

9. Compare and contrast employee assistance and wellness programs. What is the value of each for an organization?

10. Why has violence in the workplace become a larger problem for organizations? What recommendations would you offer to a company to ensure that it does not experience violence? Be specific.

RECOMMENDED INTERNET SITES

AFL-CIO	http://www.aflcio.org/home.htm
Bureau of Labor Statistics	http://www.bls.gov/
Centers for Disease Control and Prevention	http://www.cdc.gov/
Department of Labor	http://www.dol.gov/
Employment and Training Administration	http://www.doleta.gov/
Environmental Protection Agency	http://www.epa.gov/
Equal Employment Opportunity Commission	http://www.eeoc.gov/
FedWorld	http://www.fedworld.gov/
National Institute for Occupational Safety & Health	http://www.cdc.gov/niosh/homepage.html
National Safety Council	http://www.nsc.org/
Occupational Safety and Health Administration	http://www.osha.gov/
Occupational Safety and Health Resources	http://www.osh.net/
Office of Personnel Management	http://www.opm.gov/
Worker Rights Consortium	http://www.wrc.org

APPENDIX A
Critical Thinking Applications

CRITICAL THINKING APPLICATION 1-A

What Do You Know about HRM?[1]

To access this exercise, go to the "Test Your Knowledge" section of the book's Web site (www.mhhe.com/bernardin5e). Follow the directions for completing "What do you know about HRM?" and then print the feedback page (to be handed in at the discretion of your instructor). After you complete the online portion of the CTA, answer the following questions:

1. Why is there such a discrepancy between what academic research finds (and recommends) and what is actually practiced? How could this gap be closed more quickly?
2. Pick at least one question where you were (and perhaps still are) surprised by the correct answer. Do a search of some of the research that was cited to justify the correct answer and make a determination if more recent research either corroborates the correct answer or disputes it. Write a short summary of this research and make sure you record the entire citation for the research (see the endnotes for examples of complete citations).

[1]Rynes, S. Colbert, A. and Brown, K. (2002). HR professionals' beliefs about effective human resource management practices: Correspondence between research and practice. *Human Resource Management, 41*, 149–174. Reprinted with permission of John Wiley & Sons.

CRITICAL THINKING APPLICATION 1-B*

Corporate Social Responsibility and Human Resource Management

It seemingly took the recent spate of financial accounting scandals to more strongly deliver the message of Corporate Social Responsibility (CSR) to both business leaders and the general public. Recent surveys conducted in the United States suggest that managers no longer treat CSR as a "necessary evil," but are now more inclined to believe that effective CSR management can lead to improved financial performance.[1]

CEOs are now increasingly looking for ways in which social performance and reputation can directly benefit the organization financially, through either lowered costs and/or increased sales revenue. For example, firms are using their rankings on lists like *Forbes*'s annual "100 Best Companies to Work For" to attract the most qualified and loyal employees. CSR has also become a marketing tool for many businesses eager to sell themselves to a socially conscious public which rewards good ethics, employee relations, and environmental management with increased purchasing and brand loyalty. Buoyed by recent evidence that suggests effective Corporate Social Performance leads to financial growth, firms are attempting to leverage the value of social responsibility by creating CSR strategies that target all operations and functions of the organization, including human resources management (HRM).[2]

With specific respect to HRM, both managers and academics are seeking to tie CSR to personnel selection and employee retention. Since both functions are critical elements in HRM, the ability of CSR to promote them adds to the strategic value of HRM to the firm. For example, firms which are deemed to be socially responsible are potentially more attractive to potential applicants because of their enhanced reputation and social desirability. Increased interest and desire to work at the company give the organization not only a greater pool of applicants from which to choose but perhaps a criterion on which to select its employees: compatibility with the corporate culture of social responsibility. For CSR strategies to be implemented effectively, employees must relate to the CSR values of the firm which promote the management of multiple stakeholder relationships and a commitment to goals beyond the financial bottom line. Once employees are hired, CSR also helps to facilitate and sustain the employee–firm relationship. Most CSR firms recognize their employees as primary stakeholders, and therefore commit themselves to the preservation of mutually beneficial relationships.[3] Also, because of similarity between personal and organizational values, employees of firms that practice superior CSR are expected to identify more closely and strongly with the goals of these firms, thereby leading to decreased voluntary turnover. Therefore, a commitment to CSR leads to a commitment to employee well-being, which benefits the firm through cost reduction, skill development, and the retention of valuable employees.

While the benefits of CSR to HRM seem feasible, most organizations do not formally use CSR to match applicants' attitudes or dispositions regarding salient issues as a hiring tool. The lack of research in this area may be caused by the lack of measurement tools that assess the compatibility of applicants' attitudes or preferences regarding CSR and the corporate positions on the same CSR issues. Since CSR is normally treated as a business-level issue, there has been little effort to formally gauge employee attitudes toward stakeholder commitment, environmental protection, and social concern. However, because of the inherent need for qualified and committed employees to effectively implement strategy, it seems the onus is on those firms which are undertaking or plan to undertake CSR strategies to find ways of more formally incorporating CSR into personnel decision making.

To access this exercise, go to the "Self-Assessments" section of the book's Web site (www.mhhe.com/bernardin5e). Follow the directions for completing "Corporate Social Responsibility and Human Resource Management" and then print the feedback page (to be handed in at the discretion of your instructor). After you complete the online portion of the CTA, answer the following questions:

1. Most people regard corporate social responsibility in the straight business sense; that is, CSR must be linked to the "bottom line" or corporate financial performance. Do you agree with this position? Explain your answer.
2. Conduct research related to CSR and corporate performance since Orlitzky, Schmidt, and Rynes (2003). Does the new research support the conclusions of their meta-analysis?
3. Did your responses to the questionnaire approximate the mean data from other students? If there were significant differences (about 2 points higher or lower), in what areas were these differences? Do you have any theories as to why you were higher or lower in these areas?

*Contributed by Richard Peters.
[1]Hill, R. P., Ainscough, Shank, T., and Manullang, D. (2006). Corporate social responsible investing: A global perspective. *Journal of Business Ethics, 70,* 165–174; Simms, J. (2002). Business: Corporate social responsibility—You know it makes sense. *Accountancy,* p. 1311.
[2]This evidence comes from a meta-analysis which shows a positive correlation between CSR and firm financial performance. See Orlitzky, M., Schmidt, F. L., and Rynes S. L. (2003). Corporate social and financial performance: A meta-analysis. *Organization Studies, 24*(3), 403–410; see also Van der Laan, G., Van Ees, H., and Vantteloostuijn, A. (2008). Corporate social and financial performance: An extended stakeholder theory and empirical test with accounting measures. *Journal of Business Ethics, 79,* 299–310.
[3]Waddock, S. A., Bodwell, C., and Graves, S. B. (2002). Responsibility: The new business imperative. *Academy of Management Executive, 16*(2), 132–148.

CRITICAL THINKING APPLICATION 1-C

Resolution: Close Down the Human Resources Department

A great deal of research indicates that it is line management that will determine whether or not human resources can create and sustain a competitive advantage for organizations. While HR staff develop, purchase, and administer HR activities, the proper use of these activities by line management has the most to do with their effectiveness. *Fortune* magazine's

Thomas Stewart argues that outsourcing those HR functions that can be outsourced will ultimately save the company money and thus facilitate a competitive advantage through reducing costs.[1] This cost reduction could then increase profits and/or help the company compete on price.

Some HR departments are already responding by outsourcing many functions traditionally done by full-time employees. Compensation and executive recruiting are two of a growing number of areas that are more likely to be outsourced. Stewart argues that an "in-house" HR department will probably cost the company much more money and since it's line management (not the HR staff) that really determines HR effectiveness, the use of outsourced personnel to perform certain HR activities should have little impact on effectiveness. For example, instead of using full-time HR staff to develop and implement a new performance management system, the company could contract with a company to do this work.

Stewart refers the reader to the Washington, D.C. based Corporate Leadership Council, which concluded that indirect compensation (benefits), personnel recordkeeping, and employee services such as outplacement and retirement counseling, and health and safety issues (drug testing, wellness programs, workers' compensation) could all be outsourced to save money.

Stewart goes beyond the Council's recommendation. He argues that many HR functions can now be purchased from vendors with considerable savings and no loss in quality. For example, recruiting can be done through "head-hunters" now for even low-level jobs. Personnel testing, performance management, and pay-for-performance systems can be purchased from consulting firms with impressive expertise in these areas. He cites Nucor Steel, which has an HR staff of four for its 6,000-person operation. Nucor farms out most of its HR work.

Stewart is not the only one critical of HR. Says Keith Hammonds, deputy editor of *Fast Company,* in a 2005 article diplomatically entitled "Why We Hate HR," "After close to 20 years of hopeful rhetoric about becoming 'strategic partners' with a 'seat at the table' where the business decisions that matter are made, most human-resources professionals aren't nearly there. They have no seat, and the table is locked inside a conference room to which they have no key. HR people are, for most practical purposes, neither strategic nor leaders."[2]

Hammonds asks, "Why are annual performance appraisals so time-consuming—and so routinely useless? Why is HR so often a henchman for the chief financial officer, finding ever-more ingenious ways to cut benefits and hack at payroll? Why do its communications—when we can understand them at all—so often flout reality? Why are so many people processes duplicative and wasteful, creating a forest of paperwork for every minor transaction?"

Mr. Hammonds pointed to a 2005 survey which found that only 40 percent of employees thought their companies were effective at retaining high-quality workers. Only 41 percent thought performance evaluations were fair and 58 percent rated their job training as favorable.

Most respondents said they had little opportunity for advancement—and that they didn't know how to move up in their organization. Hammond also recommends serious downsizing and outsourcing of HR functions.

Assignment

Generate a list of reasons why there may be another side to this story. What key questions would you want to ask Mr. Stewart and Mr. Hammonds regarding outsourcing? Compile a list of advantages and disadvantages to outsourcing that could help a company make thoughtful decisions regarding HR.

[1]Stewart, T. A. (January 15, 1996). Taking on the last bureaucracy. *Fortune,* pp. 105–108.
[2]Hammonds, K. H. (2005, August) Why we hate HR. *Fast Company, 97,* 40–43.

CRITICAL THINKING APPLICATION 2-A

What Is the Origin of Your University Apparel?[1]

Chapter 2 discusses the issues, problems, and advantages related to the use of offshore facilities for manufacturing. We've probably all heard Jay Leno take a crack at Nike about working conditions in the overseas "sweatshops" where Nike products are made. You may be wearing a shirt or hat right now with your university logo on it. Do you have any idea where the apparel was manufactured and under what conditions?

On March 25, 2002, 12 students at Florida State University were arrested by FSU campus police for demonstrating in an area not designated for free speech. These students were members of United Students Against Sweatshops (USAS) and were protesting a decision by then University President Sandy D'Alemberte to not join the Worker Rights Consortium (WRC), an organization initiated by the USAS that monitors factories worldwide to ensure humane working conditions.[2]

The USAS is an international student movement that fights for sweatshop-free working conditions in factories around the world. Students from more than 30 schools started the organization in 1998. These students wanted to increase awareness of workers' rights issues and coordinate efforts between campuses to address workers' rights as a greater force. A part of the plan was to develop an organization that monitors production facilities. That plan resulted in the Worker Rights Consortium.[3]

The Worker Rights Consortium was started in October 1999 by the USAS.[4] Its purpose is to "assist in the enforcement of manufacturing Codes of Conduct adopted by colleges and universities . . . to ensure that factories producing clothing and other goods bearing college and university names respect the basic rights of workers." The organization is supported by affiliation fees from each member school in the amount of 1 percent of the previous year's gross licensing revenues (with a minimum of $1,000 and a maximum of $50,000).[5]

Since its inception, the WRC has had success both domestically and abroad. At Mexmode, a textile factory in Atlixco, Mexico, the WRC and the USAS pressed Nike to allow the workers to form an independent labor union with voluntary membership.[6] Additionally, the WRC issued a negative report regarding New Era Cap Co. near Buffalo, New York. The report resulted in some schools canceling contracts with New Era and others pushing for the company to resolve its struggle with its employees.[7] This pressure resulted in a resolution between the workers and New Era.[8]

As of November 2008, there were 183 colleges and universities affiliated with the WRC. Princeton was the latest to join as of 2008. Essentially, these schools joined the Consortium out of concern for the conditions under which their school paraphernalia (hats, sweats, shirts, etc.) are produced. The USAS initiated the WRC as a response to the inadequacy of the Fair Labor Association (FLA).[9]

The Fair Labor Association was established after a Clinton administration initiative in response to growing public concern about inhumane working conditions, especially in Third World countries. The FLA is a partnership of manufacturers, educational institutions, consumer groups, and human rights organizations started in 1996 that monitors production factories and enforces humane standards. Its purpose is to improve factory working conditions in the United States and abroad. The FLA monitors the factories of participating companies and makes decisions about how to rectify existing problems.[10]

The FLA has been successful in its attempts to improve working conditions. For example, at the BJ&B/Yupoong facility in Villa Altagracia, Dominican Republic, the FLA resolved a dispute issued on behalf of 20 workers dismissed for supporting the organization of a union. The day after the complaint was filed, FLA reps arrived at the plant for inspection. The issue was resolved with the dismissed workers being rehired.[11]

However, the USAS and other parties believe the FLA's system has problems. In a report to the Faculty Senate Steering Committee, the Committee on Apparel Licensing stated that the FLA monitoring system is "fundamentally flawed." Among these flaws are that a small percentage of facilities are monitored, the participating companies choose their monitors and the factories to be monitored, monitors are restricted by confidentiality, the process is slow, and the FLA voting structure favors the manufacturers over the workers.[12]

Dara O'Rourke, a professor of environmental and labor policy at M.I.T., is displeased with the FLA's choice of monitoring companies, particularly Pricewaterhouse-Coopers. Professor O'Rourke has inspected over 100 factories for various international organizations and claimed: "PwC's monitoring efforts are significantly flawed." O'Rourke adds, "PwC's audit reports glossed over problems of freedom of association and collective bargaining, overlooked serious violations of health and safety standards, and failed to report common problems in wages and hours." PwC's Randy Rankin commented, "I think we do very good work in this field, and we're contributing to improving conditions on behalf of our clients."[13]

511

On April 9, 2002, the FLA board approved changes to the FLA monitoring system, perhaps in response to the numerous critiques. The FLA now randomly selects which factories will be monitored and also will choose the monitoring company. Additionally, the visits are unannounced and reports are posted on the FLA Web site. The FLA believes these changes will improve its system.[14] However, all of this changes little since almost half of the FLA board are company representatives and the voting structure still favors the manufacturers.

This is the situation that the leadership at Florida State walked into. The FSU Faculty Senate Steering Committee formed a committee in spring 2000 to study the issue of apparel licensing for FSU paraphernalia. After researching the issue, the committee submitted a report recommending the university join the WRC.[15] The FSU student government also passed a resolution supporting WRC membership. Nonetheless, the FSU president rejected the proposal.[16] Since FSU is already a member of the FLA (one of the 17 original universities to join), D'Alemberte is apprehensive about spending 1 percent of the university's licensing revenues ($17,000–$21,000 annually) on a redundant measure. Additionally, he believes that if FSU were to support human rights organizations financially, there are other organizations such as the Lawyers Committee for Human Rights and Amnesty International that might be more deserving.[17] However, FSU would have much more influence on manufacturer behavior through the WRC. It would not be merely financial support, but the power to cancel licensing contracts. With a championship athletics program, FSU's business is important to any manufacturer. That is the support the WRC wants from FSU. This would be quite different from supporting most other human rights organizations.

The issue of worker rights abroad is growing to the point of rivaling worker rights issues in the United States. As the economy becomes more global, conditions in workplaces around the world become more transparent. The FLA was one of the first responses to the opposition people brought against manufacturers for unfair treatment of employees. However, the USAS was not satisfied with the FLA's approach to rectifying workplace problems and created the WRC. Colleges and universities are now faced with choosing between the FLA and WRC (though membership in both is permitted).[18]

Assignment

Take a position on whether FSU should have joined the WRC. Conduct a Web search to determine the current state of the controversy. Assuming your instructor doesn't provide the information, conduct research on your campus to find out where most of your campus paraphernalia is produced and what companies have the licensing agreements. Find out whether the supplier is cleared by the FLA and/or the WRC. Is your school affiliated with either the FLA or the WRC? Is there a USAS chapter active on your campus? Go to the Web sites of the USAS and the WRC and review their mission statements and past accomplishments. What is your opinion about the intervention of such organizations as the FLA, WRC, and USAS? Would you consider joining the USAS? Do you think your university should join the WRC if it doesn't belong already?

Relevant organizations with Web addresses: USAS, www.usasnet.org; WRC, www.workersrights.org; FLA, www.fairlabor.org; Global Exchange, www.globalexchange.org; Human Rights Watch, www.hrw.org; International Labour Organization, www.ilo.org; Sweatshop Watch, www.sweatshopwatch.org; Verité, www.verite.org.

[1]Contributed by Mike Ryan.
[2]Twelve Florida State students arrested in protest. (2002, March 26). Sun-Sentinel.com (http://www.sun-sentinel.com/news/ local/florida/sfl-0326fsu_protest.story), accessed June 11, 2002.
[3]United Students Against Sweatshops Web site (http://www.usasnet.org/who/history.shtml), accessed June 6, 2002.
[4]Marklein, M. B. (1999, October 20). Sweatshop foes form alliance of universities. *USA Today* (http://www.usasnet.org/resources/articles/NLC/USAToday 10-20-99.html), accessed June 10, 2002.
[5]Worker Rights Consortium Web site (http://www. workersrights.org), accessed June 13, 2002.
[6]Thompson, G. (2001, October 8). Mexican labor protest gets results. *New York Times.*
[7]Hats Off: A U.S. cap company gets a hard look from universities. *The Wall Street Journal Online* (http://www. workersrights.org/wsj.pdf), accessed June 13, 2002.
[8]Williams, F. (2002, June 6). New Era cap, union reach deal to end strike. *The Buffalo News* (http://www.workersrights.org/ buffalo_news_6.5.02.pdf), accessed June 13, 2002.
[9]A renewed analysis of the Fair Labor Association. (2002). USAS Web site (http://usasnet.org/old/oldsite/organizing/info/flacritique.pdf), accessed June 10.
[10]Fair Labor Association Web site (http://www. fairlabor.org/html/summary.html), accessed June 13, 2002.
[11]FLA facilitates key agreement to re-hire workers under third party complaint process. (2002, January 28). Fair Labor Association Web site (http://www.fairlabor.org/html/press.html#Press012902), accessed June 13, 2002.
[12]Committee report on apparel licensing to FSU Faculty Senate Steering Committee, March 28, 2001.
[13]Greenhouse, S. (2000, September 28). Report says global accounting firm overlooks factory abuses. *New York Times* (http://www.hartford-hwp.com/archives/26/073.html), accessed June 11, 2002.
[14]Changes to the FLA: A comparison of the old and new system. Fair Labor Association Web site (http://www.fairlabor.org/ html/new_fla_comparison.html), accessed June 13, 2002.
[15]Committee report on apparel licensing to FSU Faculty Senate.
[16]Twelve Florida State students arrested.
[17]Yeager, M. (2002, March 4). Sweatshop campaign by students comes to head. *Tallahassee Democrat* (http://www.tallahassee.com/ mld/democrat/news/local/2786363.htm), accessed June 12, 2002.
[18]Worker Rights Consortium Web site.

CRITICAL THINKING APPLICATION 2-B

International HR: How about a Cuppa?[1]

Starbucks (www.starbucks.com) opened its first location in 1971 in Seattle's Pike Place Market. By 1987, with the backing of local investors, Starbucks Corporation had 17 locations. One year later, Starbucks introduced a mail-order catalog with service to all 50 states and expanded to 33 locations. Starbucks built a new roasting plant in 1990 and opened its 84th location. In 1991, Starbucks became the first U.S. privately owned company to offer a stock option program that included part-time employees and started offering coffee in airport locations. 1992 saw Starbucks complete its initial public offering trading on the Nasdaq under the symbol "SBUX."

By 1995, Starbucks had formed an alliance with Canadian bookstore Chapters Inc. and Starbucks Coffee International formed a joint venture with SAZABY Inc. to develop

Starbucks coffeehouses in Japan. Its 676 locations began selling compact discs. One year later, Starbucks Coffee International opened locations in Japan, Hawaii, and Singapore. In just five years, Starbucks opened its 300th Japanese location. Also in 1996, Starbucks Coffee Japan introduced a stock option program for its full- and part-time partners and successfully implemented an IPO.

Starbucks locations in 2008 total 5,240 (after closing 600 stores). As of 2008, Starbucks had over 4,500 coffeehouses in 47 countries, including China, Argentina, Brazil, Chile, Colombia, Peru, Venezuela, and Australia. Starbucks currently has existing partnerships in numerous markets, including Austria, Bahrain, Canada, Germany, Greece, Hong Kong, Israel, Japan, Kuwait, Lebanon, Malaysia, Mexico, New Zealand, Oman, Philippines, Qatar, Saudi Arabia, Singapore, South Korea, Spain, Switzerland, Taiwan, Thailand, United Arab Emirates, and the United Kingdom.

Starbucks does not sell individual franchises or subfranchises. Starbucks Coffee Company either will operate its coffeehouses directly (or through a local subsidiary) or will enter into a business agreement with a company or group of individuals. This company or group is granted the right to develop and operate coffeehouses throughout a defined region. Their development strategy adapts to different markets addressing local needs and requirements.

Starbucks currently uses three business strategies: joint ventures, licenses, and company-owned operations. Starbucks' global success would not be possible without their international partners, who share in their values and commitment to bringing the Starbucks experience to customers worldwide.

They choose their partners based on:

Shared values and corporate culture

Strong multiunit retail/restaurant experience

Dedicated human resources

Commitment to customer service

Quality image

Creative ability, local knowledge, and brand-building skills

Strong financial resources

Assignment

So what are the critical HR issues with regard to Starbucks' international goals? What are the key questions that must be asked once research has determined the market is going to be profitable in a particular country? In terms of the HR domains discussed in Chapter 1, what answers are required before getting too far along in plans to open another location? Write down what you regard as the top five most important questions for which you need answers. Select a country that you believe would be a good opportunity for a Starbucks location. Then think about the variables you considered in selecting that country. Write down those variables.

¹Contributed by Mary E. Wilson.

CRITICAL THINKING APPLICATION 3-A

Are Dreadlocks Protected under Title VII?

Christopher Polk was a delivery employee for FedEx when he watched to a Lord Jamal music video rapping about Rastafarian beliefs in the sanctity of dreadlocks. Such dreadlocks, permanently interlocked strands of hair, were worn by African chieftains 6,000 years ago. Polk became a Rastafarian and grew shoulder-length locks to symbolize his new religious path. Dreadlocks are now quite fashionable and worn by many who do not practice Rastafarianism.

But Polk's new hair style violated FedEx grooming policy of a "reasonable style." After several internal rounds of problem solving, FedEx ordered Polk to cut his hair or be assigned to a job with no direct customer contact and lower pay. He refused and was terminated. He sued under Title VII, claiming religious discrimination. Six other FedEx employees lost their jobs for the same reason. These are not isolated cases. Police departments, prison authorities, retailers, and schools have also been sued after refusing to allow dreadlocks that are not covered at work.

In general, courts have allowed employers to impose their own grooming standards providing that such standards are applied uniformly or fairly. For example, when Afros were all the rage, an employer could be accused of not applying a grooming policy fairly if Afros were banned but long hair or ponytails were allowed for men. But there was no religious basis to these hairstyle cases. Although limited, the legal track record for hair styles based on religion versus grooming policy is more favorable to plaintiffs like Mr. Polk. For example, Sikh men have won lawsuits based on their religion that requires them to wear their beards.

Assignment

Should Mr. Polk and others be allowed to violate a grooming policy on the basis of a religious proclamation on the sanctity of dreadlocks? Why or why not? If you answer "yes," is there any point where you would draw the line in terms of company policy regarding appearance and the religious implications of dress? Does FedEx have a right to impose a reasonable grooming policy based on customer reactions to personnel appearances?

CRITICAL THINKING APPLICATION 3-B

Allegations of Religious Discrimination

In 2008, the Equal Employment Opportunity Commission (www.eeoc.gov) received 2,745 charges of religious discrimination, resolved 2,341 religious discrimination charges, and recovered over $7 million in monetary benefits for charging parties and other aggrieved individuals (not including monetary benefits obtained through litigation). Title VII of the Civil Rights Act of 1964 prohibits employers from discriminating against individuals because of their religion in hiring, firing, and other terms and conditions of employment. Title VII covers employers with 15 or more employees, including state and local governments. It also applies to employment agencies and to labor organizations, as well as to the federal government.

Under Title VII:

Employers may not treat employees or applicants less—or more—favorably because of their religious beliefs or practices. For example, an employer may not refuse to hire individuals of a certain religion, may not impose stricter promotion requirements for persons of a certain religion, and may not impose more or different work requirements on an employee because of that employee's religious beliefs or practices.

Employees cannot be forced to participate—or not participate—in a religious activity as a condition of employment.

Employers must reasonably accommodate employees' sincerely held religious beliefs or practices unless doing so would impose an undue hardship on the employer. A reasonable religious accommodation is any adjustment to the work environment that will allow the employee to practice his or her religion. Flexible scheduling, voluntary substitutions or swaps, job reassignments and lateral transfer, and modifying workplace practices, policies and/or procedures are examples of how an employer might accommodate an employee's religious beliefs. An employer is not required to accommodate an employee's religious beliefs and practices if doing so would impose an undue hardship on the employer's legitimate business interests. An employer can show undue hardship if accommodating an employee's religious practices requires more than ordinary administrative costs, diminishes efficiency in other jobs, infringes on other employees' job rights or benefits, impairs workplace safety, causes co-workers to carry the accommodated employee's share of potentially hazardous or burdensome work, or if the proposed accommodation conflicts with another law or regulation.

Employers must permit employees to engage in religious expression if employees are permitted to engage in other personal expression at work, unless the religious expression would impose an undue hardship on the employer. Therefore, an employer may not place more restrictions on religious expression than on other forms of expression that have a comparable effect on workplace efficiency.

Employers must take steps to prevent religious harassment of their employees. An employer can reduce the chance that employees will engage unlawful religious harassment by implementing an anti-harassment policy and having an effective procedure for reporting, investigating, and correcting harassing conduct.

It is also unlawful to retaliate against an individual for opposing employment practices that discriminate based on religion or for filing a discrimination charge, testifying, or participating in any way in an investigation, proceeding, or litigation under Title VII.

Assignment

Consider each of the four scenarios below and answer the questions after each one.

1. Muhammad, who is Arab American, works for XYZ Motors, a large used car business. Muhammad meets with his manager and complains that Bill, one of his co-workers, regularly calls him names like "camel jockey," "the local terrorist," and "the ayatollah," and has intentionally embarrassed him in front of customers by claiming that he is incompetent. How should the superior respond?

2. Three of the 10 Muslim employees in XYZ's 30-person template design division approach their supervisor and ask that they be allowed to use a conference room in an adjacent building for prayer. Until making the request, those employees prayed at their workstations. What should XYZ do?

3. Susan is an experienced clerical worker who wears a hijab (head scarf) in conformance with her Muslim beliefs. XYZ Temps places Susan in a long-term assignment with one of its clients. The client contacts XYZ and requests that it notify Susan that she must remove her hijab while working at the front desk, or that XYZ assign another person to Susan's position. According to the client, Susan's religious attire violates its dress code and presents the "wrong image." Should XYZ comply with its client's request?

4. Anwar, who was born in Egypt, applies for a position as a security guard with XYZ Corp., which contracts to provide security services at a government office building. Can XYZ require Muhammad to undergo a background investigation before he is hired?

CRITICAL THINKING APPLICATION 4-A

Can PAS Defend Its Test in Court?

Personnel Assessment Systems was asked to develop a job-related and valid screening test to hire armed and unarmed security guards for a large corporation. The job analysis method is described below. Supervisors were asked to complete the following form.

Required Abilities and Characteristics Rating Form

Personnel Assessment Systems is studying security officer jobs in several companies to develop a valid battery of tests for hiring decisions. As part of our research, we are asking you for some information about the kinds of abilities and other characteristics required for effective performance in the entry-level security job with which you are most familiar. In the space below please write in the job title of the security job under study. Then fill in the information requested below on your experience performing and supervising this particular job.

Take a minute to think about the duties performed by security officers in this position and the kinds of abilities and characteristics they should have. On the following pages, we have listed a number of abilities and characteristics that may be necessary for performing as a security officer. Please read each one and decide how important you feel this ability or characteristic is to perform the *essential functions* of the security officer job. Use the following scale to make your ratings:

0—Neither useful nor necessary to perform one or more of the essential functions of the job at a minimally acceptable level

1—Useful but not necessary to perform one or more of the essential functions of the job at a minimally acceptable level

2—Necessary to perform one or more of the essential functions of the job at a minimally acceptable level

All of the following abilities and characteristics were assessed as "essential functions" (2s) by 75 percent or more of supervisors who were asked to complete the job analysis form.

Ability or Characteristic

Color vision: ability to distinguish red, yellow, blue, and green colors

Normal peripheral visual field (150°–180°)

Visual acuity: ability to distinguish small details from a complex background; ability to read indicator numbers from a normal viewing distance

Depth perception

Auditory acuity: ability to hear changes in pitch or loudness of equipment noises; ability to distinguish spoken language from a noisy background

Tactual acuity: ability to feel heat or vibrations in equipment

Sense of smell

Ability to read and comprehend blueprints, schematics, diagrams, or structures

Ability to respond appropriately under stress

Emotional stability

Analytical ability: ability to reason way through problems; detect trends, plan actions in a logical, orderly manner

System comprehension: ability to comprehend entire systems and how they function; ability to foresee system implications of malfunctions or of own actions; ability to *anticipate* required future conditions in numerous interacting systems

Ability to retain and recall information

Attention to detail: ability to perceive and interpret small details

Conscientiousness in checking and caring for equipment

Ability to add, subtract, multiply, and divide whole numbers, decimals, fractions

Ability to comprehend, use, and/or compute logs, powers, trigonometry, scientific notation

Ability to follow complex sequence of activities

Ability to control one's temper

Ability to remain calm in difficult situations

Ability to stay alert for possible unlawful activities

Ability to follow directions carefully

Ability to reason with multiple concepts and operations

Ability to identify clerical errors quickly

Ability to detect rule violations

Based on these job analysis results, PAS developed a test, a portion of which is presented below, that would be administered to job applicants. PAS then developed a "suitability" scoring procedure for the test, including the following:

Suitability for *responding to stressful aspects* of the job such as reacting quickly in dangerous situations, always controlling one's temper, remaining emotionally in control under difficult circumstances and dealing with difficult individuals.

The applicant's responses indicate (below average, average, above average) likelihood that the applicant will react appropriately and effectively in stressful situations.

Suitability for *interacting with clients, customers, and others* such as being friendly with customers/clients; always being courteous, treating all people the same regardless of their race, gender, age, national origin or disability, and being able to effectively communicate with different types of clients and customers.

Portion of Security Officer Test

Format: Job applicants must indicate whether each statement is TRUE OR FALSE about them:

1. Most of the time, I feel life has let me down.
2. I used to steal a lot when I was young.
3. I'm almost always angry to some extent.
4. I would like to be a police officer.
5. People from different races are more different than the same.
6. I like to jump from job to job.
7. I have trouble understanding written material.
8. I often feel things are out of my control.
9. Almost everyone I know is luckier than I.
10. I drink liquor or beer almost every day.
11. At times, I just want to punch someone.
12. Kids who are bad deserve to be spanked.
13. I dislike most of the people I know.
14. Things are out of my control most of the time.
15. I often lose my self-control.
16. I have a little problem with alcohol.
17. Everybody should be allowed to carry a handgun.
18. I cannot tolerate others' mistakes.
19. I'm almost always happy.
20. Stealing from an employer is acceptable if the employer cheats you.

21. I skipped over 20 days of school in my last year of high school.
22. I tend to get quite irritable when I'm tired.
23. I have great difficulty sleeping.
24. I enjoy watching a good fight.
25. Police officers deserve respect.
26. If I got this job, I'd probably keep it for about six months.
27. I've gotten into more than 15 physical fights in my life.
28. Success in life is mainly due to luck.
29. I've been drunk more than five times in my life.
30. I can tolerate a great deal before I get upset.
31. If I am hired for this job, I'll almost certainly keep it for over a year.
32. I almost always reach personal goals I set for myself.
33. If I am in charge, things have to be done my way or I'll quit.
34. I tend to get angry when I am criticized in a group.
35. When a person gets annoyed with me, I quickly get annoyed back.
36. I fear big government.
37. I don't believe in gay marriage.
38. I get depressed often.
39. Sometimes I am not in the mood to see anyone.
40. I get angry often.
41. I have fewer friends than most people.
42. Most people think I am too emotional.
43. I often get angry too quickly with people.
44. Daring and foolish things are fun to do.
45. I feel I am an outgoing, social person and fun to be with.
46. Marijuana should be legalized.

Assignment

Based on your understanding of the law and the job analysis results, can the company use this test to screen applicants? Are there specific test items that are (or may be) legally problematic? What (if any) other information do you need about the job analysis, the test, or anything else to be able to take a definitive position on whether the company should use the test? Do you regard any of these questions as an invasion of privacy? If so, which items?

CRITICAL THINKING APPLICATION 4-B

What to Do with Job Diagnostic Survey Results

To access this exercise, go to the "Self-Assessments" section of the book's Web site (www.mhhe.com/bernardin5e). Follow the directions for completing the "Job Diagnostic Survey" and then print the feedback page (to be handed in at the discretion of your instructor). After you complete the online portion of the CTA, answer the following questions:

1. Conduct research on the Job Diagnostic Survey and the Job Characteristics Model and after receiving information on how to interpret your score, make some predictions about the implications of your score for important work outcomes for you.
2. Play the role of an HRM consultant. Explain how you would use JDS results from a work unit to facilitate changes in the design of work. What steps would you take to ensure you are receiving accurate information?
3. If you were assigned to consider redesigning jobs within your organization, would you use the JDS to gather data or use some other approach to job analysis? Explain your answer.

CRITICAL THINKING APPLICATION 5-A

Recruiting on the Internet[1]

iLogos Research *Global 500 Web site Recruiting: 2003 Survey* found 94 percent of firms are using corporate career Web sites. iLogos estimates in 2008–2009 the Global 500 career Web site adoption rate will reach nearly 100 percent since the current late-adopters will catch up with technology.[2]

A 2002 iLogos study, *Where the Jobs Are: Fortune 500 Job Postings on Careers Web Sites and Major Job Boards,* found that 81 percent of Fortune 500 companies are posting job openings on their own career Web sites (e.g., www.starbucks.com/aboutus/hotjobs.asp) compared with 51 percent for Monster (www.monster.com), 43 percent for HotJobs (www.hotjobs), and 22 percent for CareerBuilder (www.careerbuilder.com). The study stated the total number of available positions on Fortune 500 corporate career Web sites was found to be approximately 75,000 compared with roughly 25,500 for Monster, 13,200 for Career-Builder, and 7,800 for HotJobs (the numbers for 2008 are much higher for all three sites).[3]

As discussed in Chapter 5, recruiters complain that the Web has increased the number of résumés they must now sift through. Despite the additional work it creates, many recruiters prefer online recruiting due to the cost savings. One study of 45 Fortune 500 companies by iLogos Research revealed that the hiring cycle was shortened by 9 percent by posting jobs online. If the company took only online applications or résumés, it saved the average company another 12 percent, and when those applications or résumés were screened electronically, the company saved another 9 percent for an overall savings of 30 percent.[4] This is impressive considering speed is essential when it comes to winning top talent. As Peter Cappeli said in his article "On-Line Recruiting" in the *Harvard Business Review,* "the first company to make contact often gains a huge advantage."[5]

Some companies may experience even higher returns. Dow Chemical (http://www.dow.com/careers/index.htm) actually saved 62 percent in the time it takes to fill a job by accepting applicants only online. It also saved 26 percent on its costs-per-hire average and reduced recruiting staff by 40 percent worldwide.[6]

With the decreased revenues seen at Monster/TMP (18.4 percent), Webhire (25 percent), and Dice.com (15 percent)[7] organizations are looking outside traditional online recruiting methods. The U.S. Army uses electronic gaming to attract recruits; for example, Army Target Practice, Patriot Missile System, and Blackhawk Challenge and organizations are exploring environments such as Second Life, a customizable virtual world, as another channel to attract young recruits. Furthermore, an organization can manage its image and what people are saying about the organization by being actively involved in social networking sites such as Facebook and MySpace.[8] Adaptive Path, a tightly held LLC, used blogging and the professional social networking site LinkedIn to recruit its first CEO. The process took just 3 months from start to finish![9]

With HRM becoming a more strategic and integral component of the competitive advantage equation, the adage "first to market" can now be considered "first to talent." One of the ways a company can find its talent faster is in an efficient sorting tool. A hiring management system (HMS) tends to automate the process by standardizing the application in order to screen and track the candidate quickly. Although standardizing limits the applicant to the choice on the pull-down boxes, it can help companies track the application. Tracking can calculate how long it takes to fill a job or how long it takes for that new hire to become productive, giving the manager essential feedback on which employees are more productive based on the standardized information from the application.

In addition to the time, the average cost per hire through online recruiting is $152 compared with $1,383 using traditional methods like temporary agencies, according to a report by Thomas Weisel Partners.[10] Some experts argue that the practice of online recruiting using the best methods delivers better candidates, lowers hiring costs, and gives companies a competitive advantage. In fact, at companies such as Sun Microsystems (www.sun.com/corp_emp/), Microsoft (http://www.microsoft.com/careers/ default. mspx), and Unisys (http://www.unisys.com/about_unisys/ careers/ index.htm), online recruiting is second in securing new hires. Employee referral programs are still more efficient.[11]

As you probably know by going into your own college or university's Web site, schools at all levels are recruiting online. Even the federal government recruits online (www.usajobs.opm.gov/). So it is highly probable that you will be filling out an online application or submitting your résumés online. In addition to completing an online application, you may be asked to do a Net interview. The typical Net interview may use digital conferencing equipment.

Some recruiters are now using video résumés. "I think it's a great idea. I can get a better feel for communication skills and the type of role people are looking for," says Jean Moss, HR manager for Symagery Microsystems (www.symagery.com).[12] The applicant has a one- to two-minute faux interview for the video résumé. The video file is then attached to the résumé file and e-mailed or posted on the job board. The interviews "help tell if the candidates are people you could work with and how they carry themselves in an interactive situation," says Kirsten Watson, president and CEO of HireTopTalent (www.hiretoptalent.

com/videohandshake/index.html.[13] YouTube may even be ahead of the curve by allowing users to post a video résumé free of charge. As of November 2008 there were over 1,500 résumés on the site, and many job boards are following suit and plan to launch a video résumé service.[14]

Assignment

1. Would you be more or less attracted to an organization that used online recruiting only? Explain your answer.
2. How do you feel being limited to "what's in the box" (see www.dow.com/careers/index.htm as an example) on a standardized application?
3. Are there any methods described in Chapter 5 that could be adapted for online screening?
4. What are the legal implications for using a standardized application?
5. Would you be more or less attracted to an organization that required a video résumé? Explain your answer.
6. What are the legal implications for requiring a video résumé?

[1]Contributed by Mary Wilson. Updated 2008, by Renee Bartlett.
[2]iLogos Research (2003). *Global 500 Web site recruiting: 2003 survey.*
[3]iLogos Research (2002). *Where the jobs are: Fortune 500 job postings on career Web sites and major job boards—summary,* p. 5.
[4]iLogos Research (1998). *Achieving results with Internet recruiting,* pp. 10–11.
[5]Cappeli, P. (2001). On-line recruiting. *Harvard Business Review, 79*(3), 139–147.
[6]Gill, J. (2001). *Now hiring. Apply online.* www.businessweek.com/careers/content/ju12011/ca20010718_003.htm.
[7]Industry Trends. (2002, May). *Online Recruiting Strategist.* http://www.huntscanlon.com/newsarchives/orsarchives/2002/may.htm#6.
[8]Cheese, P. (2008). *Netting the Net Generation.* http://www.businessweek.com/managing/content/mar2008/ca20080313_241443.htm.
[9] Merholz, P/ (July 17, 2008). *Blogging: A New Approach to Exec Recruiting.* http://www.businessweek.com/managing/content/jul2008/ca20080717_160041.htm.
[10]JobTipLotto.com. *Editorial—new & unique method of finding a job.* http://www.alamedajtl.com/html/news/editorial.html.
[11]McCool, J. D. (2002). *Adventures in online recruiting.* www.thestandard.com/article/0.1902.15665.00.html?body_page 2.
[12]www.hiretoptalent.com/videohandshake/index.shtml.
[13]Click here for sneak preview. (2002). *Profit, 21*(1), 69.
[14]Cullen, Lisa (2007, February 22). *It's a wrap. You're hired!* http://www.time.com/time/magazine/article/0,9171,1592860,00.html.

CRITICAL THINKING APPLICATION 5-B

Hi, I'm in Bangalore (but I Can't Say So)

In a *New York Times* article entitled "Hi, I'm in Bangalore (but I Can't Say So)," Mark Landler describes the training for customer service center workers in India.[1] "Hi, my name is Susan Sanders, and I'm from Chicago," said C. R. Suman, who is actually from India and is sitting in Bangalore as she talks with an American caller regarding a service offered by a U.S. telecommunications company. Part of Ms. Suman's training at Customer Asset, the Indian call center, is to "fake it" as an American. She not only receives considerable dialect training so callers think they are speaking with a midwesterner, she also is given instructions to lie to the caller about where she is from and where she is at the time of the call. "Susan's" parents are Bob and Ann, she has a brother Mark, and she attended the University of Illinois. Ms. Suman's training included an episode of *Friends* in which she was supposed to learn the "in" phrases. Defenders of this practice maintain that customers are troubled if they find out that the company representative with whom they are dealing is over 8,000 miles away. Ms. Suman earns about $3,500 per year for full-time work with Customer Asset.

Assignment

1. What do you see as the major advantages and disadvantages of contracting with an overseas customer call center?
2. What do you see as the advantages and disadvantages of allowing this outsourced organization to lie to your customers about who they are and where they are?
3. Is it unethical to contract with such an organization?
4. What if Customer Asset presented data showing American callers are more satisfied with the call service they receive from the "fake" Americans than from call center associates who admit they are Indians sitting in India?
5. Would you be more accepting of this practice if data showed customers feel more secure about transactions if they feel they are interacting with an American?
6. Do a Net search to determine what the salary would be of a customer service representative working in the United States.

[1]Landler, M. (2001, March 21). Hi, I'm in Bangalore (but I can't say so). *New York Times* (http://NYTimes.qpass.com/qpass-archives/).

CRITICAL THINKING APPLICATION 5-C

Is Wal-Mart Guilty of Gender Discrimination?

Wal-Mart is the largest private employer in the United States and the world's largest retailer. Through its Wal-Mart and Sam's Club divisions, it operates over 3,000 stores across the country in every state of the U.S. There are so many Wal-Mart locations in the United States that, according to Wal-Mart, the average store is within 30 miles of the next Wal-Mart store. In the United States, Wal-Mart employs nearly 1 million "associates," Wal-Mart's term for its hourly employees. In its last fiscal year, it had sales exceeding $200 billion. Wal-Mart claims that it has 100 million customers each week. In 2000, Betty Dukes filed a sex discrimination claim against Wal-Mart. Dukes claimed that after six years of hard work and excellent performance reviews, she was denied the training Wal-Mart required to enable her to advance to a higher, salaried position. The lawsuit, *Dukes vs. Wal-Mart Stores, Inc.* (see www.walmartclass.com), was eventually expanded to represent 1.5 million women, comprising both current and former employees. As of January 2009, the lawsuit was the largest EEO class-action suit in history.

The plaintiffs charge Wal-Mart with discriminating against women in promotions, pay, and job assignments, in violation of Title VII of the 1964 Civil Rights Act. In a new book, *Selling Women Short: The Landmark Battle for Workers' Rights at Wal-Mart*, journalist Liza Featherstone reviews

the lawsuit. As described in Salon.com, Ms. Featherstone "paints a picture of Wal-Mart as a hypocritical, falsely pious, exceptionally greedy corporation that creates a massive sinkhole for working women."[1] Female employees from many stores across the United States claim they were repeatedly passed over for promotions, made to endure sexist comments from male co-workers, and paid significantly lower salaries for doing the same amount of work (or more).

The plaintiffs made the following claims:

1. Through its Wal-Mart and Sam's Club divisions, it is the industry leader not only in size, but also in its failure to advance its female employees. There are two workforces at Wal-Mart. By far the largest workforce is female, which comprises over 72 percent of the hourly sales employees, yet only one-third of management positions. This workforce is predominantly assigned to the lowest-paying positions with the least chance of advancement. The other workforce is male. This workforce is the reverse image of the female workforce—it comprises less than 28 percent of the hourly sales workers, yet holds two-thirds of all store management positions and over 90 percent of the top Store Manager positions. This disparate distribution of the genders is the result of purposeful discrimination and of practices that serve no reasonable business purpose yet have a disproportionate impact on women.

2. The class-action lawsuit was brought by present and former Wal-Mart employees on behalf of themselves and all other similarly situated women who have been subjected to Wal-Mart's continuing policies and practices of gender discrimination. Plaintiffs, and the class that they represent, charge that Wal-Mart discriminates against its female employees by advancing male employees more quickly than female employees, by denying female employees equal job assignments, promotions, training, and compensation, and by retaliating against those who oppose its unlawful practices.

3. Wal-Mart employs uniform employment and personnel policies throughout the United States. All of its stores are linked by state-of-the-art electronic and video communications, through which all stores regularly report payroll, labor, and other employment data. Regardless of division, there are uniform policies for employees, uniform "orientation" procedures, uniform salary, assignment, pay, training, and promotion policies. All stores are regularly audited for compliance with these uniform, companywide policies and procedures.

4. The vast majority of Wal-Mart store employees are hourly paid sales associates, who report to department heads. Each store has a number of assistant managers who have different functional responsibilities, one or more "co-managers," and a store manager. District and regional managers supervise the stores.

5. Few objective requirements or qualifications for specific store assignments, promotions, or raises exist. Salaries are supposed to conform to general company guidelines, but store management has substantial discretion in setting salary levels within salary ranges for each employee. Salaries are also adjusted based on performance reviews, which are largely based on subjective judgments of performance. Plaintiffs are informed and believe that Wal-Mart policy prohibits employees from exchanging information about their salary levels.

6. The hourly sales workforce at Wal-Mart is predominantly female, representing over 72 percent of all hourly employees. Yet, male and female employees are not evenly distributed among the departments in the store. In some departments and positions, such as furniture, garden, electronics, hardware, sporting goods, guns, produce, and stocking, males are disproportionately assigned. In other departments, such as front-end cashier, customer service, health and beauty aids, cosmetics, housewares, stationery, toys, layaway, fabrics, and clothes, women are disproportionately assigned. Plaintiffs are informed and believe that the male-dominated departments and jobs are better paid and offer greater opportunities for advancement than the female-dominated positions and departments.

7. Male employees are more likely than female employees to obtain "cross-training" in other departments or to receive training and support to enter into departments that would aid their advancement.

8. Plaintiffs are informed and believe that female employees are paid less than male employees who perform substantially similar work, with similar or lesser skills and experience. Plaintiffs are further informed and believe that segregated assignment patterns exacerbate such unequal pay, because men are more likely to be assigned to departments that pay better than departments to which women are assigned.

9. Although women comprise the substantial majority of all hourly employees, the source from which most managers are drawn, their representation in management is the polar opposite. Women hold only about one-third of the positions that Wal-Mart identifies as management. However, even this figure overstates the proportion of female managers in true management positions. Thus, the "one-third" of management positions held by women includes traditionally "female" positions, such as assistant managers whose primary responsibility is supervising cashiers, and the lowest level of managers. Plaintiffs are informed and believe that women comprise less than 10 percent of all Store Managers and approximately 4 percent of all District Managers. There are few, if any, female Regional Managers. There is only one woman among the 20 executive officers of the company. Plaintiffs are informed and believe that even when women are promoted, on average they are advanced later, and then more slowly, than similarly situated male employees.

10. The workforce profile of Wal-Mart does not reflect the industry or the profile of its largest competitors. In fact, although it is the largest discount retailer in the country, it lags far behind its competitors in the promotion of women. Thus, while Wal-Mart's store management is only about one-third female, among its 20 top competitors, women comprise over 56 percent of management, even though the proportion of hourly workers that are female at these companies is comparable to Wal-Mart. These differences are consistently found around the country. Moreover, these differences are longstanding. In fact, female representation among managers at Wal-Mart is at a substantially lower level today than the level of representation among Wal-Mart's competitors in 1975.

11. This pattern of unequal assignments, pay, training, and advancement opportunities is not the result of random or nondiscriminatory factors. Rather, it is the result of an ongoing and continuous pattern and practice of intentional sex discrimination in assignments, pay, training and promotions, and reliance on policies and practices that have an adverse impact on female employees that cannot be justified by business necessity, and for which alternative policies and practices with less discriminatory impact could be utilized that equally serve any asserted justification. These policies and practices include, without limitation:

    a. Failure to consistently post job and promotional openings to ensure that all employees have notice of and an opportunity to seek advancement or more desirable assignments and training.

    b. Reliance upon unweighted, arbitrary, and subjective criteria utilized by a nearly all-male managerial workforce in making assignments, training, pay, performance review, and promotional decisions. Even where Wal-Mart policy states objective requirements, these requirements are often applied in an inconsistent manner and ignored at the discretion of management.

    c. Reliance on gender stereotypes in making employment decisions such as assignments, promotions, pay, and training.

    d. Pre-selection and "grooming" of male employees for advancement, favorable assignments, and training.

    e. Maintenance of largely sex-segregated job categories and departments.

    f. Deterrence and discouragement of female employees from seeking advancement, training, and favorable assignments and pay.

    g. Paying female employees lower compensation than similarly situated men.

h. Assigning women to lower paying positions, and positions with lesser advancement potential than those given to men, and advancing women more slowly than similarly situated male employees.

i. Providing less training and support to female employees and managers than that given to male employees and managers.

j. Harassing female employees interested in advancement and subjecting them to a hostile work environment.

k. Requiring, as a condition of promotion to management jobs, that employees be willing to relocate, often to significantly distant stores, and applying this policy to require frequent and substantial relocations of its managers without any reasonable business justification. Plaintiffs are further informed and believe that the relocation policy is applied disparately between male and female employees, to the disadvantage of female employees.

l. Retaliating against female employees who have complained either internally or externally about Wal-Mart's treatment of its female employees. Wal-Mart maintains a companywide, toll-free telephone number, which it encourages employees to use if they have a problem or complaint in their store or with store management. Plaintiffs are informed and believe that Wal-Mart retaliates against women who use this number to report discrimination, sexual harassment, or other unfair working conditions.

Assignment

Conduct research on the *Dukes et al. v. Wal-Mart* case and determine the present status. What arguments and/or evidence did Wal-Mart present to argue against the gender discrimination claims. Based on what you have reviewed, was Wal-Mart guilty of gender discrimination as alleged? Try to take a definitive position and then justify that position with specific evidence or arguments. If you are unsure, what specific information do you need to be able to render a verdict in this case? Setting aside the alleged illegalities, what specific HR practices could Wal-Mart improve to make their HR more effective and (perhaps) to lower the likelihood of such Title VII lawsuits in the future?

[1]Pikul, C. (2004, November 22). Women vs. Wal-Mart. Salon.com

CRITICAL THINKING APPLICATION 6-A

What Privacy Do We Have in the Workplace?[1]

Currently debated privacy issues have included drug testing, medical information kept on employees and family members, credit history, and certain questions on personality tests. Employers have maintained records on employees since the employer/employee relationship was first established. Research on personnel recordkeeping has revealed that as the employer/employee relationship changed, the level and amount of information collected on employees also changed. Employers had personal knowledge of employees in the 1800s, could vouch for the employees' integrity, and could observe the personal patterns of behaviors (going to church, etc.). The amount of information kept in files was not as important because of the face-to-face interaction.[2]

In order to hire the right person, limit negligent hiring claims, and provide employee benefits, companies need to keep extensive dossiers on employees. The management (sharing and disclosing) of those dossiers was the subject of a report by the U.S. Privacy Protection Commission investigation established by the Privacy Act of 1974. Survey data was collected in 2005 to determine corporate privacy policies.[3]

The Commission recommended the following as fair information practices:

- Acquire only relevant information.
- Consider pretext interviews unacceptable methods of gathering information.
- Use no polygraph or lie detector tests in employment.
- Allow and encourage employees to see and copy records pertaining to them.
- Keep no secret records.
- Establish a procedure for challenging and correcting erroneous reports.
- Use information only for the purpose for which it was originally acquired.
- Transfer no information without the subjects' authorization or knowledge.
- Destroy data after their purpose has been served.[4]

The results of the survey revealed that the majority of companies still do not have formal policies that follow the Commission's guidelines in regard to disclosure and access. Informing and evaluating the recordkeeping system are being done by most companies. However, many companies surveyed are still shy of following the Commission's recommendations. The survey results are listed below:

Policy to inform employees of routine disclosure?	56%
Personal access to records?	34%
Policy of evaluating record system?	65%
Inform employees on types of records maintained?	82%
Inform employees of how information is used?	58%
Inform individual of collecting information?	66%[5]

Are you entitled to your privacy regarding your political proclivities? Can a company ask and use such information in its personnel decisions? What about government entities? Discrimination based on one's political affilations or positions is not allowed for career service positions in the federal government and under many state and local civil service rules. According to an internal report from the Inspector General for the U.S. Department of Justice, in 2008, aides to former Attorney General Alberto R. Gonzales broke Civil Service laws by using politics to guide their hiring decisions, picking less-qualified applicants for important nonpolitical positions, and slowing the hiring process at critical times. The U.S. Department of Justice policy on nondiscrimination is contained in the Code of Federal Regulations, Section 42.1(a) of 28 C.F.R. Part 42, Subpart A, which states: "It is the policy of the Department of Justice to seek to eliminate discrimination on the basis of race, color, religion, sex, sexual orientation, national origin, marital status, political affiliation, age, or physical or mental handicap in employment within the Department and to assure equal employment opportunity for all employees and applicants for employment." It is thus a violation of civil service rules to ask political questions of job candidates and to use political information to make decisions for nonpolitical positions within the Department of Justice.

Suppose that you have just come from a job interview in which you were asked the following questions in a personality screening test for a homeland security position. The security company has assured you that your answers will be strictly confidential and that emotional stability (which this test claims to test) is essential for the job. Based on the information provided by the U.S. Privacy Protection Commission listed above and subsequent surveys as well as information from Chapter 3 on job relatedness, evaluate and justify your reaction to the following questions. You realize that this position is a high-stress and safety-sensitive job.

1. I enjoy social gatherings just to be with people.
2. The only interesting part of the newspaper is the "funnies."
3. Our thinking would be a lot better off if we would just forget about words like "probably," "approximately," and "perhaps."
4. I usually go to the movies more than once a week.
5. I looked up to my father as an ideal man.
6. I liked *Alice in Wonderland* by Lewis Carroll.
7. When a person "pads" his income tax report so as to get out of some of his taxes, it is just as bad as stealing money from the government.
8. Women should not be allowed to drink in cocktail bars.
9. I think Lincoln was greater than Washington.
10. I feel sure there is only one true religion.
11. I am embarrassed by dirty stories.
12. Maybe some minorities get rough treatment, but it is no business of mine.
13. I fall in and out of love rather easily.
14. I wish I were not bothered by thoughts about sex.
15. My home life was always happy.
16. Only a fool would ever vote to increase his own taxes.

17. When a man is with a woman, he is usually thinking about things related to her sex.
18. I hardly ever feel pain in the back of my neck.
19. I have no difficulty starting or holding my urine.
20. My sex life is satisfactory.
21. I am very strongly attracted to members of my own sex.
22. I used to like "drop-the-handkerchief."
23. I've often wished I were a girl (or if you are a girl) I've never been sorry that I am a girl.
24. I go to church almost every week.
25. I believe in the second coming of Christ.
26. I believe in life hereafter.
27. I've never indulged in any unusual sex practices.
28. I believe my sins are unpardonable.[6]
29. I donated money to the Obama for President campaign.
30. I donated money to the McCain for President campaign.

Assignment

Should the company be allowed to ask such questions? Think of all issues that you considered in taking your position or if you aren't sure what your position on this is, what additional information do you need? How would the company prove the "job relatedness" of such a test? (Review Chapter 3 material or go to www.eeoc.gov for discussion of this term.) When must the company prove the "job relatedness" of the test? In your home state, can a company use political information to make decisions about people? (Search for the answer to this question.)

[1]Contributed by Mary E. Wilson.
[2]Linowes, D. F., and Spencer, R. C. (1996). Privacy in the workplace in perspective. *Human Resource Management Review, 6* (3), 165–182.
[3]Benardin, H. J. (2005). *Privacy in the workplace.* Unpublished survey.
[4]Ibid., pp.177–178.
[5]Ibid.
[6]Taken from Psychscreen, a screening tool used by Target stores based on the Minnesota Multiphasic Personality Inventory (MMPI) and the California Personality Inventory (CPI). Source: Alderman, E., and Kennedy, C. (1995). *The right to privacy.* New York: Alfred A. Knopf.

CRITICAL THINKING APPLICATION 6-B

The Measurement of Personality Traits[1]

Overview

Research supports the proposition that stable personality characteristics are related not only to success in particular occupations but also to job and life satisfaction. The purpose of this exercise is to provide a profile of your personality based on valid measures of personality.

As discussed in Chapter 6, the "Big Five" factor structure has gained widespread acceptance by personality researchers and has greatly influenced the research into individual differences. There is also strong evidence that personality measures have utility in providing vocational and career guidance. It is clear that certain Big Five factors and their combinations are correlated with career choice, success, performance, and satisfaction. More recent research also supports the validity of core self-evaluations. Unless specified otherwise by your instructor, this CTA has two online assignments, one for the Five-Factor Model or "Big Five" self-inventory and one for the "Core Self-Evaluations Scale."

Part A. The Five-Factor Model of Personality

To access this exercise, go to the "Self-Assessments" section of the book's Web site (www.mhhe. com/bernardin5e). Follow the directions for completing "A Profile of your Personality Based on the Five Factor Model" and then print the feedback page (to be handed in at the discretion of your instructor). After you complete the online portion of the CTA, answer the following questions:

Discussion Questions for Part A:

1. What does research say about the use of the Five-Factor Model (FFM) for predicting success as a manager?
2. What does research say about the use of the Five-Factor Model for predicting success in sales?
3. How does the validity of personality tests compare to the validity of general mental (or cognitive) ability tests? Explain this in correlational terms.
4. Doesn't faking on tests like the one you took completely undermine the usefulness of such tests for actual personnel selection? Wouldn't the "fakers" get the job and those who answered honestly not be hired (or promoted)? Justify your answer with research.
5. Are there any other methods besides self-report inventories that would provide for an assessment of personality traits that might improve the validity in the assessment of these traits?
6. What is incremental validity? Does this term apply to the assessment of personality traits?

Part B. The Core Self-Evaluations Scale[2]

To access this exercise, go to the "Self-Assessments" section of the book's Web site (www.mhhe.com/bernardin5e). Follow the directions for completing the "Core Self Evaluations Scale" and then print the feedback page (to be handed in at the discretion of your instructor). After you complete the online portion of this CTA, answer the following questions:

Discussion Questions for Part B:

1. What does research say about the relationship between the FFM and the Core-Self Evaluations Scale?
2. If you were going to use a self-report inventory to select sales personnel, would you use a Big-Five measure, the CSES, neither, or both? Explain your answer and cite any relevant research.

[1]Contributed by Kathleen Bernardin.
[2] Judge, T. A., Erez, A., Bono, J. E., and Thoresen, C. J. (2003). The core self-evaluations scale: Development of a measure. *Personnel Psychology, 56,* 303–331.

CRITICAL THINKING APPLICATION 7-A

Should We Measure Competencies in Performance Appraisal?

One strong trend in performance appraisal is the assessment of so-called competencies. Competencies have been defined as bundles of knowledges, skills, or abilities. Many of these "competencies" look a lot like the old traits that have been condemned in a plethora of articles on appraisal. As an illustration, the managerial competencies used by the American Management Association include self-confidence, positive regard, self-control, spontaneity, stamina, and adaptability.[1]

Many experts argue that performance appraisal should first focus on *the record of outcomes* that the person (or persons) actually achieved on the job, that is, a focus on actual performance first. Diagnostics (or causal theories) can come later. There is nothing wrong with assessing what qualities a person possesses, but that should not be confused with measuring performance.[2] We can assess the extent to which a person possesses certain technical skills through ratings by those familiar with a person's skills (although it would probably be better to use some form of test). It is the manifestation of those skills on the job in the form of outcomes that constitutes performance.

Great performance data are available online for all major sports. We can assess Shaquille O'Neal's psychomotor skills, his height, his hand size, his anxiety level, all of which may be predictors or correlates of his performance. But his foul shooting in the 2007–2008 season was 51 percent and that is one measure of his performance. Since seven-foot six-inch Yao Ming led all centers at 86 percent, we can probably rule out height as a simple diagnostic. (Go to NBA.com.)

Many companies use a software program that gives ratings on a competency labeled "integrity." Some appraisal experts suggest that an elimination of such "competency" labels would help focus the managers' attention on actual behaviors and the outcomes that result from the behaviors. Another popular software package calls for evaluations of managers on their "personal maturity." Needless to say, store managers often disagree with ratings indicating they need work on their "personal maturity."

Assignment

Whenever, is it appropriate to measure competencies? Describe an appraisal system in which the purposes for the appraisal system were accomplished when the system called for assessments of personal competencies as opposed to a record of performance outcomes.

[1]Parry, S. B. (1996, July). The quest for competencies. *Training,* pp. 48–53.
[2]Hagan, C. H., Konopaske, R., Bernardin, H. J., and Tyler, C. L. (2006). Predicting assessment center performance with 360-degree, top-down, and customer-based competency assessments. *Human Resource Management, 45,* 357–390.

CRITICAL THINKING APPLICATION 7-B

The Role of Mystery Shoppers in Performance Appraisal[1]

The retail industry has made noteworthy efforts in soliciting customer feedback through its use of "mystery shopping." Typically, this involves contracting with an organization to provide anonymous individuals who periodically shop the store, evaluating and reporting about the experience from a customer's viewpoint. Mystery shoppers usually review a predetermined menu of variables for each store they shop, based on criteria established by the retail organization. At The Limited and The Gap, for example, mystery shoppers follow a script to test the extent to which store employees adhere to their training regarding customer interactions.

The use of mystery shopping has become very popular.[2] Many organizations, including Burger King, Neiman Marcus, Hyatt Hotels, Hertz Auto Rentals, Barneys New York, and Revco Drug Stores, have had extensive experience using mystery shoppers to obtain customer-based information. The method is now being used in the public sector to determine if liquor is being sold to minors and to assess nonprofit service.

Office Depot converts its mystery shopping data into a customer satisfaction index, which also includes customer complaints. The index is reported to each store manager once a month. The data, aggregated across the year, become a key determinant of each manager's annual appraisal, bonus, base salary increase, and objectives for the next appraisal cycle.

One survey[3] reported that a high percentage of retail and service companies use customer data for decision making, and 71 percent reported supplementing customer surveys with mystery shoppers. While recent case studies describe the value of mystery shopping,[4] little research has examined the validity or reliability of mystery shopping data. One study found that mystery shopper data was correlated with assessment center performance and overall store performance among retail managers.[5] Since efficiency data are easiest to identify and contract out, mystery shoppers may be focusing on issues such as determining the length of time it takes an associate to approach them, or how long they await final service delivery, or the number of times the telephone rings before it is answered, or the number of different individuals that become involved when a customer request strays from the norm. These measures are effective customer measures *only* when they capture information that real customers value highly. In other words, if an organization's source of competitive advantages is price, or convenience, or uniqueness of service features, or value in relation to competitors, then the above efficiency measures may create an inaccurate, or a mixed, signal to employees about the performance efforts that are really valued.

Assignment

Pick a job in which "mystery shoppers" might provide helpful and unique data or, if you have first-hand contact with customers, write up an assessment as to why this concept would not work in your setting. If you think such a method would be useful, describe how you would develop the system and incorporate data from this system into the performance-appraisal system. Also, could your university use "mystery shoppers"? If you think it could, what would

the "shoppers" look for? Are "mystery students" really necessary given the opportunity available to collect other presumably valid data?

[1]Contributed by Christine M. Hagan.
[2]Luria, G., and Yagil, D. (2008). Procedural justice, ethical climate and service outcomes in restaurants. *International Journal of Hospitality Management*, 27, 276–283; see also Helliker, K. (1994, November 30). Smile: That cranky shopper may be a store spy. *The Wall Street Journal*, p. B1.
[3]Wilson, A. M. (2002). Attitudes towards customer satisfaction measurement in the retail sector. *International Journal of Market Research*, 44, 213–222.
[4]Hagan, C., and Bernardin, H. J. (2003). Customer feedback as a critical performance dimension. In C. R. Schriesheim and L. L. Neider (Eds.), *New directions in human resource management*, Greenwich, CT: Information Age Publishing (pp. 1–27)
[5]Hagan, C. H., Konopaske, R., Bernardin, H. J., and Tyler, C. L. (2006). Predicting assessment center performance with 360-degree, top-down, and customer-based competency assessments. *Human Resource Management*, 45, 357–390.

CRITICAL THINKING APPLICATION 7-C

Allegations of Age and Race Discrimination against Ford Motor Company

Nine white-collar workers at Ford Motor Company filed a multimillion-dollar age discrimination lawsuit against the automaker, a challenge to the company's controversial employee evaluation process.

In addition, another group of salaried Ford employees filed a Title VII class action age and reverse discrimination suit against the Dearborn-based company in federal district court. The claims came as some Ford employees complained that President Jacques Nasser was attempting to sweep out older workers. Nasser had said he wanted to build a younger, more diverse management that would embrace new technology in rapid change while better reflecting Ford's customer base.

At issue in both cases was Ford's forced-distribution appraisal system for its top 18,000 managers and executives. Under Ford's new policy, instituted to replace the old appraisal system, 10 percent of employees had to receive A grades, 80 percent had to get Bs, and 10 percent received Cs.

Those who received Cs were not eligible for a raise or bonus, and a C grade for two consecutive years was grounds for demotion or termination. Lawyers for the nine employees who filed suit claimed Ford was using the grading scale to systematically weed out older workers. They asked the court to prohibit further use of this system. "We believe Ford is using this system to get rid of older workers," said Morgan Bonanny, a lawyer for the plaintiffs. "Our hope is to stop this program before anyone else gets hurt."

Ford spokesman Edward Miller said the grading system—referred to internally as the "performance management process"—does not take an employee's age into account. "It's designed to be fair to everybody," he said. "We want all our people to contribute at higher levels, but the age of a worker shouldn't be a consideration." While Ford is not the only major company using a forced-distribution system, the automaker has been among the most vocal in promoting and defending the approach.

Some within Ford maintain that the grading system struck a nerve at Ford because its conservative corporate culture traditionally favored the promotion of long-time, loyal managers—often white males. The new system has meant that many veteran white-collar workers were being passed over for promotion by younger managers.

The lawsuit claimed that the plaintiffs unfairly received poor evaluations that led to economic loss, embarrassment, and mental anguish. The workers sought several million dollars in damages.

One of the plaintiffs in the case said he had a history of good reviews in his 23-year career as a Ford engineer. He was chosen to participate in the Ford six sigma quality improvement program. Ford had said the six sigma program was intended only for top employees.

But then he was informed he would receive a C grade and was not eligible for a raise or bonus. He claims his supervisor could not tell him specifically where his performance came up short. He said he first noticed that the culture had changed for older workers after he returned from a six-year Ford assignment in Germany. "There was this pervasive fear," he said. "At our age it was reality—you don't get promoted."

A separate Title VII class-action lawsuit also was filed against Ford on behalf of several current employees. The plaintiffs in this case, all white, claimed they were unfairly given C ratings in the last year on annual performance report reviews. In addition, each of the men is between 40 and 50 and is considered at a leadership level at Ford. The lead attorney planned to cite several diversity programs at Ford as well as public comments made by the CEO and other company executives as proof that the automaker is making personnel decisions based on race, age and gender.

Ford has increasingly made diversity a top priority for managers in recent years. At the same time, it has become a hot-button issue among employees. The top 300 managers were asked to outline a plan to increase the diversity in their organization. Part of the executives' bonuses hinged on how well they accomplished these goals. During the same period that Ford had installed the forced-distribution system, *Fortune* magazine rated Ford one of the country's best companies for minorities. No other automaker made the top 50. "Increasing diversity is a major goal," Ford's Miller said. "We want to be inclusive. But the evaluations are based totally on job performance."

Assignment

How would you test the theories of discrimination in these complaints? Play the role of consultant to Ford and write a one-page memo recommending specific data and documentation that should be analyzed. Your memo should also include an evaluation of the forced-distribution rating system and refer to research on its effects. Ford would also like your opinion as to whether the plaintiffs in the ADEA (age) case can use a "disparate impact" theory to define "prima facie" discrimination. Provide an example of how statistics could be used to show "prima facie" discrimination in decisions related to retention or terminations. Who would have the burden of proof if such evidence was presented?

CRITICAL THINKING APPLICATION 7-D

Performance Appraisal Characteristics Questionnaire

To access this exercise, go to the "Self-Assessments" section of the book's Web site (www.mhhe.com/bernardin5e). Follow the directions for completing the assignment and then print the feedback page (to be handed in at the discretion of your instructor). After you complete the online portion of the CTA, answer the following questions:

1. Prepare an example of an "80 percent rule" violation showing prima facie evidence of "disparate impact" against olders workers. Use any type of personnel decision (e.g., terminations/retentions, promotions) that would involve performance appraisal data.
2. Should a forced-distribution system be installed to eliminate problems with personnel decisions? Explain your answer based on research.
3. Assuming the company has violated the "80 percent rule" in its decision making, what should the company do next?

CRITICAL THINKING APPLICATION 8-A

Workplace Diversity Training[1]

What is workplace diversity? The answer to this question may be the first step in initiating diversity training in the workplace. Whether to include only the protected groups under Title VII or to broaden the definition to include the "invisible" minorities, such as individuals with mental disabilities, older workers, substance abuse conditions, or various sexual orientations, may be a factor specific to the organization or the company's location.

Once diversity has been defined, the next question to address is: What is it about workplace diversity that is important for the organization? One major purpose is to facilitate the meeting of diversity hiring and promoting goals. Other organizations that have looked to diversity training to "sensitize" employees to the differences of cultures and biases have been greeted with multimillion-dollar settlements from the "sensitizing." Lucky Stores supermarket chain in California was ordered to pay $90 million in damages to over 20,000 women after airing sex and racial stereotypes in a workshop designed to increase sensitivity.[2] Jeffrey Mello asserts that a "best practice" workplace diversity initiative relates that program with the overall strategy of the organization, "such as meeting the changing needs of customers and/or expanding markets both domestically and abroad."[3] A strong argument is made that a "solid business case increases the likelihood of obtaining the leadership commitment and resources needed to successfully implement diversity initiatives."[4]

It may be that what is important to an organization is capital conservation. Organizations like Mazda North America Inc., Archer Daniels Midland Co., Arkansas Human Services Department, Texaco, JCPenney, and Baker and McKenzie were all ordered to pay in the millions of dollars that some say a "best practice workplace diversity" program would have avoided.[5] According to EEOC, there were over 27,000 new harassment claims made in 2007 alone with total monetary benefits in fiscal year 2007 alone at over $65 million.[6]

The next question is what is to be trained? The damages in court cases are awarded based on behavior and instances of illegal conduct. San Diego Gas & Electric Company and Wal-Mart were ordered to pay $3 million and $5 million, respectively, to employees who were subjected to illegal conduct. At the power company, a black former employee had been called "nigger," "coon," and "boy" and was threatened by a co-worker in the presence of a manager to "beat his black ass." He also had racial and sexual graffiti written about him on the men's room walls. SDG&E did not stop or discipline the transgressions. A woman stockroom clerk was subject to comments concerning her anatomy and unwelcome attempts to kiss her by her supervisor at Wal-Mart. Wal-Mart was ordered to pay even though the company has a strong sexual harrasement policy because the store manager did nothing to stop the harassment after the employee complained.[7]

How is the training going to be done? Careful planning and designing will prevent problems such as poor attendance and nonownership of diversity management. A division executive of a major insurance firm declined to send his managers to the company's diversity training. His response was a blunt "if there's a problem, just tell us what you want us to do. Don't waste our time with this diversity stuff."[8]

Finally, how will the diversity training be evaluated? Accounting for the benefits, which may include increased productivity due to incident-free workdays (much like accident-free workdays promoted by OSHA), enhanced public opinion about the organization, or recruitment and retention of valued diverse employees, is crucial to an effective workplace diversity program. A recent study supports the view that diversity training may not be effective as a vehicle for facilitating more effective diversity hiring. The study found that diversity training had very little effect on the racial and gender mix of a company's top ranks. Assigning a diversity point person or task force had the best record of success although that wasn't too effective either.[9]

Assignment

You have been asked to design a diversity training program for incoming freshmen at your school. Try to answer the questions presented above in this context. Develop a method for the training program. Do a Web search to identify online diversity programs and find one program that reports at least one evaluative criterion to support use of their program. Using Kirkpatrick's model (discussed in Chapter 8), give one example of each of the four types of data for evaluation that you would use to evaluate either your own new program or a ready-made online program.

[1]Contributed by Mary E. Wilson.
[2]Murray, K. (1993, August 1). The unfortunate side effects of "diversity training." *New York Times,* p. F5.
[3]Mello, J. A. (1996). The strategic management of workplace diversity initiatives: Public sector implications. *International Journal of Public Administration, 19*(3), 425–447.
[4]Robinson, G., and Dechart, K. (1997). Building a business case for diversity. *Academy of Management Executive, 11,* 21–31.
[5]DB Pargman Diversity Training Web site, www.dbpargman.com/lawdiversity.htm, accessed July 23, 2002.
[6]The U.S. Equal Employment Opportunity Commission. (2008). *EEOC Litgation Statistics, FY 2007,* eeoc.gov/stats/litigation.html, accessed July 29, 2008.
[7]Paskoff, S. A. (1996, August). Ending the workplace diversity wars. *Training, 33*(8), 42–47.
[8]Ibid., p. 43.
[9]Cullen, L. T. (2007, April 26). Employee diversity training doesn't work. *Time* online, http://www.time.com/time/magazine/article/0,9171,1615183,00.html.

CRITICAL THINKING APPLICATION 8-B

Sexual Harassment Training[1]

Sexual harassment is a form of sex discrimination that violates Title VII of the Civil Rights Act of 1964. Title VII applies to employers with 15 or more employees, including state and local governments. It also applies to employment agencies and labor organizations. Unwelcome sexual advances, requests for sexual favors, and other verbal or physical conduct of a sexual nature constitutes sexual harassment when this conduct explicitly or implicitly affects an individual's employment, unreasonably interferes with an individual's work performance, or creates an intimidating, hostile, or offensive work environment.

Sexual harassment can occur in a variety of circumstances, including, but not limited to, the following:

> The victim as well as the harasser may be a woman or a man. The victim does not have to be of the opposite sex.
>
> The harasser can be the victim's supervisor, an agent of the employer, a supervisor in another area, a co-worker, or a nonemployee.
>
> The victim does not have to be the person harassed but could be anyone affected by the offensive conduct.
>
> Unlawful sexual harassment may occur without economic injury to or discharge of the victim.
>
> The harasser's conduct must be unwelcome.

It is helpful for the victim to inform the harasser directly that the conduct is unwelcome and must stop. The victim should use any employer complaint mechanism or grievance system available.

When investigating allegations of sexual harassment, The Equal Employment Opportunity Commission (EEOC) looks at the whole record: the circumstances, such as the nature of the sexual advances, and the context in which the alleged incidents occurred. A determination on the allegations is made from the facts on a case-by-case basis.

Prevention is the best tool to eliminate sexual harassment in the workplace. Employers are encouraged to take steps necessary to prevent sexual harassment from occurring. They should clearly communicate to employees that sexual harassment will not be tolerated by providing sexual harassment training to their employees and by establishing an effective complaint or grievance process and taking immediate and appropriate action when an employee complains.

It is also unlawful to retaliate against an individual for opposing employment practices that discriminate based on sex or for filing a discrimination charge, testifying, or participating in any way in an investigation, prodeeding, or litigation under Title VII. As of 2008, employers operating in California must comply with state law AB 1825, mandating sexual harassment prevention training for supervisors. If an employer has 50 or more employees, including independent contractors and temps, they must abide by the law. A "Supervisor" is "any individual having the authority . . . to hire, transfer, suspend, lay off, recall, promote, discharge, assign, reward, or discipline other employees, or the responsibility to direct them, or to adjust their grievances, or effectively to recommend that action, if, in connection with the foregoing, the exercise of that authority is not of a merely routine or clerical nature, but requires the use of independent judgment." Thus, even employees who merely have input into personnel decisions, but who are not themselves final decision makers, may be considered "supervisors" who must receive training. The law mandates two hours of sexual harassment prevention training to supervisory employees every two years. The format can be interactive, computer-based training.

An employer's compliance with AB 1825 does not automatically provide protection from liability for sexual harassment of any current or former employee or applicant. A claim that training did not take place does not automatically result in the liability of an employer for harassment. Plaintiffs may argue, however, that the failure to meet the new training mandates is partial evidence of an employer's failure to take all reasonable steps to prevent harassment.

Advocates of the new law claim that the training will change behavior and reduce sexual harassment in the workplace. Some experts claim the EEOC stipulates that employers should periodically train employees. Under *Farragher v. Boca Raton,* if employers do train employees and an employee makes a claim, using an "affirmative defense" argument, the employer may be able to avoid liability even if the alleged bad conduct occurred. In 2003, California's Supreme Court adopted a slight variation of the affirmative defense for lawsuits brought under the state Fair Employment and Housing Act (FEHA). Under the FEHA, an employer is strictly liable for a harassing manager. However, a company may still avoid financial responsibility if it has effectively trained employees on its antiharassment policy. Finally, in 1999, the U.S. Supreme Court (followed by California) stated that if employees win a claim for harassment or discrimination, employers can avoid punitive damages if they show a good faith effort to comply with the law by

training employees. Some experts maintain that policy statements and handbook subject matter are not enough.

Under AB 1825, the training must include information and practical guidance regarding federal and state laws that prohibit sexual harassment, including prevention and correction of harassment, and remedies available to victims. The statute specifically requires employers to use practical examples aimed at instructing supervisors in the prevention of harassment, discrimination, and retaliation.

Assignment

To access this exercise, go to the "Self-Assessments" section of the book's Web site (www.mhhe.com/bernardin5e). Follow the directions for completing the assignment and then print the feedback page (to be handed in at the discretion of your instructor). After you complete the online portion of the CTA, answer the following questions:

1. What reactive, learning, behavioral, and results/outcome measures do you propose to assess the effects of this training program? Write at least one specific example of each type of evaluative criteria.
2. How does this type of training compare to alternative training approaches that could have been used to comply with the law? What specific approaches would be more effective? Is this training in compliance with AB 1825?
3. What type of evaluative measure is the test you just completed online? Is it a reactive, learning, behavioral, or results measure? What is your opinion of the quality of this measure?
4. What organizational analysis do you suppose the state of California conducted in order to justify this legislation? You may either provide some possible data or find information online to track the history of the legislation.
5. If you were hired as a consultant to the state of California charged with evaluating the effects of state law AB 1825 legislation, what specific evaluative criteria would you use?

[1]Contributed by Jennifer Collins.

CRITICAL THINKING APPLICATION 9-A

Careers and Corporate Social Responsibility[1]

Research shows that your perceptions and opinions about the importance of corporate social responsibility can affect your attitudes toward potential and current employers. Conduct an Internet search on *corporate social responsibility* and social performance. Look for definitions of the term and choose a definition most compatible with your philosophy. Identify examples of firms that appear to be displaying socially responsible behavior based on this definition and other companies that seem to be illustrating irresponsible behaviors.

Assignment

Your research should attempt to identify the following:

1. The types of behavior that are indicative of socially responsible and irresponsible actions.
2. The real and potential difficulties faced by organizations in their attempts to manage social responsibility.
3. Provide suggestions for how organizations can evaluate their corporate social performance.
4. Outline a general plan for how an organization should conduct a corporate social audit.

Provide an explanation for why the behavior is indicative of socially responsible or irresponsible performance. In addition, describe the consequences of the behavior for the employee workforce and for any clients or customers or the general public. Consider the extent to which you would weigh corporate social responsibility in your career planning and job choice. Which of the socially responsible actions identified do you think would be most resisted by management? Why? How could this resistance be addressed?

[1]Contributed by Joyce E. A. Russell and Lillian T. Eby.

CRITICAL THINKING APPLICATION 9-B

O*NET Skills Search

O*NET is the Occupational Information Network and is available to all users free of charge. O*NET is a primary source of occupational information and can facilitate career counseling, education, employment, and training activities by governments and organizations. The database contains information about knowledges, skills, abilities (KSA), interests, general work activities (GWA), and work context. O*NET data and structure also link related occupational, educational, and labor market information databases to the system. Among many other things, O*NET can accomplish the following:

1. Facilitate employee training and development initiatives.
2. Develop and supplement assessment tools to identify worker attributes.
3. Create skills-match profiles.
4. Explore career options that capitalize on individual knowledge, skill, and ability profiles.
5. Improve vocational and career counseling efforts.

The Skills Search function is designed to help people use their skill set to identify occupations for exploration. You select a set of skills from six broad groups of skills to create a customized skill list. You begin by selecting Skills from one or more of the six skill groups identified: Basic Skills, Complex Problem Solving Skills, Resource Management Skills, Social Skills, Systems Skills, and Technical Skills. Below is what you will see when you have the appropriate page of the O*NET Web site to start your skills search:

Source: O*NET OnLine

Skills Search

Select skills from one or more of the six skill groups below. Start by selecting as many skills as you have or plan to acquire. (See *Skills Search* for more details.)

Basic Skills | Complex Problem Solving Skills | Resource Management Skills | Social Skills | Systems Skills | Technical Skills

Basic Skills

Developed capacities that facilitate learning or the more rapid acquisition of knowledge:

- Active Learning—Understanding the implications of new information for both current and future problem solving and decision making.
- Active Listening—Giving full attention to what other people are saying, taking time to understand the points being made, asking questions as appropriate, and not interrupting at inappropriate times.
- Critical Thinking—Using logic and reasoning to identify the strengths and weaknesses of alternative solutions, conclusions or approaches to problems.
- Learning Strategies—Selecting and using training/instructional methods and procedures appropriate for the situation when learning or teaching new things.
- Mathematics—Using mathematics to solve problems.
- Monitoring—Monitoring/assessing performance of yourself, other individuals, or organizations to make improvements or take corrective action.
- Reading Comprehension—Understanding written sentences and paragraphs in work-related documents.
- Science—Using scientific rules and methods to solve problems.
- Speaking—Talking to others to convey information effectively.
- Writing—Communicating effectively in writing as appropriate for the needs of the audience.

Complex Problem Solving Skills

Developed capacities used to solve novel, ill-defined problems in complex, real-world settings:

- Complex Problem Solving—Identifying complex problems and reviewing related information to develop and evaluate options and implement solutions.

Resource Management Skills

Developed capacities used to allocate resources efficiently:

- Management of Financial Resources—Determining how money will be spent to get the work done, and accounting for these expenditures.
- Management of Material Resources—Obtaining and seeing to the appropriate use of equipment, facilities, and materials needed to do certain work.

- Management of Personnel Resources—Motivating, developing, and directing people as they work, identifying the best people for the job.
- Time Management—Managing one's own time and the time of others.

Social Skills

Developed capacities used to work with people to achieve goals:

- Coordination—Adjusting actions in relation to others' actions.
- Instruction—Teaching others how to do something.
- Negotiation—Bringing others together and trying to reconcile differences.
- Persuasion—Persuading others to change their minds or behavior.
- Service Orientation—Actively looking for ways to help people.
- Social Perceptiveness—Being aware of others' reactions and understanding why they react as they do.

Systems Skills

Developed capacities used to understand, monitor, and improve sociotechnical systems:

- Judgment and Decision Making—Considering the relative costs and benefits of potential actions to choose the most appropriate one.
- Systems Analysis—Determining how a system should work and how changes in conditions, operations, and the environment will affect outcomes.
- Systems Evaluation—Identifying measures or indicators of system performance and the actions needed to improve or correct performance, relative to the goals of the system.

Technical Skills

Developed capacities used to design, set up, operate, and correct malfunctions involving applications of machines or technological systems:

- Equipment Maintenance—Performing routine maintenance on equipment and determining when and what kind of maintenance is needed.
- Equipment Selection—Determining the kind of tools and equipment needed to do a job.
- Installation—Installing equipment, machines, wiring, or programs to meet specifications.
- Operation and Control—Controlling operations of equipment or systems.
- Operation Monitoring—Watching gauges, dials, or other indicators to make sure a machine is working properly.
- Operations Analysis—Analyzing needs and product requirements to create a design.
- Programming—Writing computer programs for various purposes.
- Quality Control Analysis—Conducting tests and inspections of products, services, or processes to evaluate quality or performance.

- Repairing—Repairing machines or systems using the needed tools.
- Technology Design—Generating or adapting equipment and technology to serve user needs.
- Troubleshooting—Determining causes of operating errors and deciding what to do about it.

Assignment

Assignment: Go to http://online.onetcenter.org/skills/ and complete the online skills match using all six skills groups. Retrieve your O*NET feedback, printing the summary report for those jobs with the highest skills match. Bring this to class. In addition, investigate the O*NET Web site and find answers to the following questions:

1. What is an O*NET-SOC code? Explain what a standard occupational classification is.
2. Explain the process that was used to match your skills to a particular job? How does the system do the match?
3. What is an SVP rating?
4. What is a job zone?
5. Could an employer use the skills match to make hiring decisions or develop hiring criteria? For example, should an employer require all applicants to do the skills match and then determine whether the job the employer is trying to fill appears in the skills match feedback?
6. Were the jobs identified for you as compatible with your skills search really compatible with your interests and aspirations? Explain your answer.
7. Are there any other options in the O*NET Web site that could provide useful vocational advice? Could you use the "find occupations" option at http://online.onetcenter.org/?

CRITICAL THINKING APPLICATION 10-A*

Defending Corporate Executive Pay

According to Graef Crystal, named the "foremost authority on executive compensation" by *Fortune* magazine, "The modern American CEO is a cross between an ancient pharaoh and Louis XIV—an imperial personage who almost never sees what the little people do, who is served by bootlicking lackeys, who rules from posh offices, who travels in the modern equivalent of Cleopatra's barge, the corporate jet, and who is paid so much more than the ordinary worker that he hasn't the slightest clue as to how the other 99.9 percent of the country lives."[1]

According to The Corporate Library, CEOs of a Standard & Poor's 500 company made an average of $14.2 million in total compensation for 2007 and a median compensation package of $8.8 million.[2] In addition, huge severance packages were given to CEOs of companies at the center of the mortgage and banking crisis. Washington Mutual paid its CEO Kerry Killinger over $54 million from 2002–07 and planned to pay him $14.4 million in

2007. In return, he led the 120-year-old firm into the biggest bank failure in U.S. history. Alan Fishman, who replaced Killinger just a few weeks before the bank's demise in 2008, was entitled to $11.6 million in cash severance and will probably keep his $7.5 million signing bonus.

The International Monetary Fund estimates that the financial turmoil set off by the collapse of the mortgage market will exceed $1 trillion. CEOs of the firms most responsible for causing this crisis made hundreds of millions of dollars in pay in the years immediately prior to the trouble.

There are also numerous examples of what could be called "war profiteering." George David, CEO of United Technology, one of the largest military contractors, earned over $100 million from 2003 through 2005 alone while his company was being sued for providing malfunctioning equipment for the military.

According to a *Wall Street Journal* study, executive compensation grew much faster than did corporate earnings in 2007. A study of randomly selected public companies found that CEO compensation increased over 20 percent from 2006, but revenues grew at only 2.8 percent. The study also found that, as of February 2008, the average top executive received overall compensation of almost $18 million. During the same time period, the median pay for workers rose 3.5 percent to $36,140 in 2007. Says former Secretary of Labor Robert Reich, "Not since the era of the robber barons of the late 19th century has income and wealth been so concentrated as it is in 21st century America."

Take the Money and Run

During the boom years for five investment banks (Morgan Stanley, Bear Stearns, Merrill Lynch, Citigroup, and Lehman Brothers), their CEOs were reported to have earned $60 million in cash compensation in 2006 alone when things were going great for the mortgage industry. The direct effect of the risky and, some would say, incompetent management in that and previous years was (and is) devastating losses for all of these firms and their shareholders. In 2008 alone, these five firms lost a combined $330 billion in stock market capitalization. Former Bear Stearns CEO James Cayne's compensation peaked in 2006 when he received a $17 million bonus, $14.8 million in restricted stock, $1.7 million in stock options, and more than $6.1 million in other compensation. He realized another $10.3 million right before the collapse of the company. He resigned in 2008 before the government bailout of the company.

A growing but still small number of companies adopted provisions (called clawbacks) allowing the companies to recover executive pay that they find to have been based on incorrect financial statements. In a typical example, GE requires that its board determine that an executive has engaged in fraud or intentional misconduct before the company can recover performance-based pay. A rare "clawback" policy specifies that a company will move to recover stock awards if financial statements are restated as a result of errors, omission, or fraud.

Defenders of CEO pay argue that executive pay is set based on studies of the pay of CEOs in the industry and that pay is approved by the corporate board. As one board member put it, "if we don't pay him what the market pays, we'd lose him and then watch what happens to our stock price." Another line of argument is that CEO pay is not really out of line relative to star athletes or entertainers. There were numerous articles critical of executive pay long before the economic crises that started in 2008. The corporate failures, government bailouts, and other disasters of that year could validate the argument that companies should not pay their top people so much money and then invoke the "market" to justify the salaries. Many experts argue that the market was (and is) corrupted by decision makers, all of whom were (and are) the direct beneficiaries of the inflated salaries. The most common response from those who defend huge compensation packages is that the "market" for this elite and very limited supply of executives dictates these competitive salaries. Others now argue that the events of 2008 clearly show that (apparently) this "elite" core is hardly elite and that the supply of executives who could do a whole lot better than those who were in charge and who commanded (and received) these salaries is much larger than pay consultants and corporate boards would have us believe.

Investors are now pushing for more shareholder involvement in executive pay with "say on pay" in proxy statements. Another problem that has been cited for exorbitant packages has to do with the compensation consultants who recommend packages to the board. When the board uses the same firm for compensation and other much more lucrative HR services, there is the obvious risk that relatively more "generous" packages will be recommended in order to stay on the good side of a CEO who has a lot a do with awarding the other contracts. A possible remedy for this problem: Require companies to document (in their proxy statements) all fees paid to consultants they hire, for compensation design and all other services.

Assignment

1. Should the government put more regulatory constraints on executive pay? Explain your answer. Do a search to determine if there is any new or pending legislation or regulation that would regulate executive pay.
2. Do you agree with the argument that executive pay is based on an external market analysis (the principle of external equity) and is thus fair?
3. Do you think "clawbacks" should be mandatory and, if so, what should they stipulate? Conduct an on-line search to get an idea of how many companies are requiring "clawbacks" in their proxy statements.
4. Should "say on pay" be mandatory for all executive pay packages? Should corporate boards alone continue to make decisions with respect to executive pay packages or should consent of a majority of

shareholders be required? Suggest one or two advantage and disadvantages.

5. Do you agree with the recommendation to require full disclosure regarding pay consultants? Explain your answer.

6. What about the argument that CEO pay is no more out of line than the compensation of movie stars or star athletes?

*Contributed by Harry Schwartz and John Bernardin.
[1]Crystal, G. (1991). *In search of excess*. New York: Norton, p. 3.
[2]Data from The Corporate Library is based on 211 proxy statements filed through April 9, 2008.

CRITICAL THINKING APPLICATION 10-B

Illegal Pay Discrimination, Bad Pay Policy, or Both?

The following letter was written by Ms. Julia Kate, a female associate, and addressed to the director of the clinical counseling center.

> Dear Dr. Boseman:
>
> The purpose of this letter is to request an assessment of my salary in the context of my performance and responsibilities and the salary levels that have been set for three staff members recently hired by the Counseling Center. In the past year, the Center hired one male Ph.D. at $10,000 more than I earn and two unlicensed counselors at almost my identical salary rate.
>
> I believe my salary is extremely low given the following facts: (1) My job performance has been rated at the highest level for all six years I have been on staff; (2) the recently hired Ph.D., a male, had no experience and performs the identical work I perform; (3) the recently hired M.Ed., a male, who is paid at the same level as I, had no experience in counseling. As you know, with the exception of the referrals to which I refer below, assignments of clients to staff members are based strictly on space available and not the possession of a particular staff member's credentials.
>
> While I recognize that credentials do translate into higher salaries for persons performing identical work, so too do other credentials such as the possession of an applicable license and qualifications and experience in supervising graduate student interns. I receive no additional compensation for this license despite the fact that it enables me to supervise interns while the two Master's level associates hired do not possess such a license and thus cannot (and do not) supervise students. I have supervised graduate students since 1997. In addition, I have a Master's in Social Work (MSW), a terminal degree that, as a credential, has far more external marketability than the degrees possessed by the two new hires.
>
> I am also the designated specialist who receives all referrals from the county regarding sexual assault and rape. I have had to use my expertise in this highly sensitive area on several occasions.
>
> Rational (and legal) compensation systems set and adjust pay levels based on a number of factors, including the credentials, experience, supervisory responsibilities, and, of course, the job performance of the incumbents.

> Based on these factors, my salary is difficult to explain, especially when compared to the new staff of the Counseling Center.
>
> Thank you for considering these issues. I look forward to your response. Ms. Julia Kate

Assignment

Write a one-page position paper. Is this a violation of the EPA? Would there be a violation of the "Paycheck Fairness Act" if this legislation has amended the FLSA? What about a Title VII violation? Does Ms. Kate have a case? If Dr. Boseman feels Ms. Kate has an EPA case, can he reduce the pay of the newly hired Ph.D. to match Ms. Kate's salary to erase the problem? Does it matter that the Counseling Center hired the male Ph.D. eight months ago? If so, how is this relevant in a Title VII claim? If you cannot take a position on the allegations, stipulate what specific additional information you need to reach a conclusion. The legal implications aside, what should Dr. Boseman do?

CRITICAL THINKING APPLICATION 10-C

Legal or Illegal Compensation Plan?[1]

The city of Tampa, Florida, approved a revised pay plan granting raises to all city employees in the Police and Fire Departments. The stated purpose of the plan was to "attract and retain qualified people, provide incentives for performance, maintain competitiveness with other public sector agencies and ensure equitable compensation to all employees regardless of age, sex, race and/or disability."

A revision of the plan, which was motivated, at least in part, by the City's desire to bring the starting salaries of police officers up to the regional average, granted raises to all police officers and police dispatchers. Under the provisions of the plan, officers and dispatchers with fewer than five years' tenure received proportionately greater raises than employees who had more than five years' tenure. Although some officers over the age of 40 had less than five years of service, most of the older officers had more.

Within the police department there were five basic jobs included: police officer, master police officer, police sergeant, police lieutenant, and deputy police chief. The police officer is the entry level, or lowest ranked position in the hierarchy. Each of these positions was divided into a series of steps and half-steps. The salary for each job was based on a compensation survey conducted in comparable communities in the Southeast. As is typical in most organizations, the majority of personnel were in the three lowest ranks, and in each of the ranks there were officers both under and over the age of 40. Each employee was assigned to a position within the range that was equal to the lowest step that would give him or her a minimum 2 percent raise. The few officers in the two highest ranks were all over 40.

All of the officers received increases in their pay. Criteria for granting increases were applied consistently and without regard to the age of the employee. The officers in the two highest ranked jobs received raises that were higher in dollar amount than the more junior positions. However, because the base salaries for these positions were higher, the relative percentage increase was smaller.

Thirty police officers and public safety dispatchers over the age of 40 filed suit pursuant to the Age Discrimination in Employment Act (ADEA). They were members of the class complaining of the "disparate impact" of the award.

The plaintiffs' evidence established two principal facts: First, almost two-thirds (66.2 percent) of the officers under 40 received raises of more than 10 percent while less than half (45.3 percent) of those over 40 did. Second, the average percentage increase for the entire class of officers with less than five years of tenure was higher than the percentage for those with more seniority. Because older officers tended to occupy more senior positions, on average they received statistically significant, smaller increases when measured as a percentage of their salary. The City's explanation for the differential was the need to raise the salaries of junior officers to make them competitive with comparable positions in the market.

Assignment

Can the older workers use "disparate impact" theory in their age discrimination claim? Justify your answer. Based on the facts above, is the City of Tampa guilty of unlawful discrimination against older workers? Explain your answer. If "disparate impact" theory is allowed in ADEA cases, who has the burden of proof once "prima facie" evidence is presented and what is that burden? What case law backs up your position? What is your view of the methods they used to adjust pay rates?

[1]Contributed by Karen Preston.

CRITICAL THINKING APPLICATION 11-A

The Case for and against Pay-for-Performance Systems

If you want employees to perform at a higher level, you can motivate them to excel by tying their compensation to a particular performance index. After all, the way to influence employees is through the wallet, right? According to Alfie Kohn, author of four books and professional business lecturer, this is not the case.[1] Drawing from Frederick Herzberg's motivation theory, Kohn claims that financial incentives cannot motivate employees to improve their performance; however, the absence of financial incentives can create employee dissatisfaction or demotivation. For example, if your salary was cut, you would become frustrated and might seek another source of employment, but if you received a raise, you wouldn't improve your performance over the long haul. Sure, you might become exceptionally productive right before your evaluation for your yearly bonus or right after you received a raise, but not when looking at the big picture. At best, pay-for-performance (PFP) incentives motivate employees to

temporarily alter their behavior; they do not encourage any lasting changed behavior. In fact, once the reward is taken away, employees will revert back to their old patterns of behavior.

So, according to this argument, PFP incentives are generally ineffective, temporary employee bribes. "Jump through these hoops and you'll get this" is the inevitable philosophy behind reward systems. Employees are reduced to mere objects controlled by the wiles of manipulative bosses. Surprisingly enough, a rewarding system is not much different from a punishing system; not receiving a reward has a similar effect to being punished. For every employee who "wins" (receives an award), there is an employee who "loses" (does not receive an award). With increased emphasis on self-managed work teams and quality work circles, competition and hostility among workers over who secured the largest reward is the last thing a U.S. firm needs. Employees will abandon risk taking, innovation, and creativity—the key ingredients for competitive advantage—in an attempt to minimize challenges and maximize their personal wealth. In the worst-case scenario, employees will engage in unethical or illegal behavior just to finesse a greater payoff. Therefore, the emphasis shifts from employees excelling at their jobs to excelling at the incentive-winning game. Recent examples include Washington Mutual, Countrywide Mortgage, Lehman Brothers, and Bear Stearns. PFP incentives, Kohn argues, do not motivate employees to improve their performance; "they motivate [them] to get rewards."

Charles M. Cummings, senior compensation consultant at William M. Mercer, Inc., has refuted Kohn's "blanket condemnation of incentive plans," citing that properly constructed pay-for-performance systems can be successful.[2] Cummings finds fault with Kohn's premise that PFP systems reduce employees to simple objects trying to take a bite off the golden carrot dangling in front of their noses. Such manipulative and highly ineffective systems are found only in "hierarchical, traditional organizations" and are not representative of the way PFP systems should be designed nor of the way these systems are now being built. Furthermore, in such a traditional organization, employees are largely performing specialized tasks that do not directly affect the firm's bottom line. Rather, they have to rely on their supervisors to integrate their tasks into a meaningful, profitable whole. Without a feeling of worth to the organization, it is little wonder that employees will lack *intrinsic* (inner) motivation and have to be "bribed" by their bosses to perform their meaningless jobs. Cummings suggests that more firms today are shifting to *team-based PFP plans* (e.g., profit sharing, gain sharing) rather than *individualistic plans* (e.g., the ill-fated merit pay), which Kohn describes in his argument. Team-based PFP plans not only help employees comprehend their significance to the organization as a whole but also provide the intrinsic motivation necessary for optimum job performance. (Participants in quality work circles, self-managed work teams, and the like will experience this intrinsic motivation because they can see the fruits of their labors with results that hit the bottom line.)

Contrary to Alfie Kohn's assumption, Cummings believes that "most people have a need to have their achievements acknowledged by others." Because employees are being respected for their accomplishments with a properly designed and implemented PFP system, they will generate "goodwill and commitment" toward the organization. These feelings are much different from the feelings of ill will that Kohn describes. A proper PFP system can be very successful in an organization and can attain a competitive advantage through loyal and motivated workers.

Assignment

Consider the arguments above and take a position. Do you agree with Kohn or Cummings? Are there situations in which the opposing position would ever apply? What does the latest research indicate regarding this question? Think of a real-life example to support the position you have taken. Kohn says employees will abandon risk taking with PFP. Is that necessarily true? What are some examples of high risk taking under a PFP system that was clearly not a good thing for the company in the long run?

[1]Kohn, A. (1993, September–October). Why incentive plans cannot work. *Harvard Business Review*, pp. 54–63.
[2]Cummings, C. M. (1994, May–June). Incentives that really do motivate. *Compensation and Benefits Review*, pp. 38–40.

CRITICAL THINKING APPLICATION 11-B

The Prediction of Rating Error

Research has established that rater characteristics, including their personality traits, can predict the average rating raters give across all people they rate.[1] Rater characteristics can thus predict leniency, a chronic problem with merit pay systems. Rater "discomfort," defined as the extent to which a person feels uncomfortable giving negative feedback and measured by the Performance Appraisal Discomfort Scale (PADS), has been shown to be correlated with the average rating level given by a rater. The purpose of this exercise is to have you complete the PADS to determine your rating tendencies.[2]

To access this instrument, go to the "Self-Assessments" section of the book's Web site (www.mhhe.com/bernardin5e). Follow the directions for completing the assignment and then print the feedback page (to be handed in at the discretion of your instructor). After you complete the online portion of the CTA, answer the following questions:

1. What other personality characateristics have been linked to rating tendencies such as leniency?
2. If a person scores at a high discomfort level on the PADS, does this mean he or she will be a lenient rater?

3. What steps that could be taken to alleviate rating leniency in an appraisal system?
4. Some experts recommend the use of a forced-distribution rating system to control leniency. Do you agree with this recommendation?

[1]Kane, J. S., Bernardin, H. J., Villanova, P., and Peyrefitte, J. (1995). The stability of rater leniency: Three studies. *Academy of Management Journal, 38,* 1036–1051.
[2]Villanova, P., Bernardin, H. J., Dahmus, S., and Sims, R. (1993). Rater leniency and performance appraisal discomfort. *Educational and Psychological Measurement, 53,* 789–799.

CRITICAL THINKING APPLICATION 11-C

Can We (and Should We) Apply the Lincoln Electric Method?

The sign on the front door at Lincoln Electric in Cleveland, Ohio, says it all: "No admittance prior to 30 minutes before the start of work." That's right. Lincoln Electric, a highly successful maker of welding machinery, has to keep workers from starting early! How does it motivate workers?

Although some unionists compare it to "sweatshops," this Fortune 500 company pays its 3,000 employees according to the piece-rate system. Workers are simply paid for what they produce. Except for a two-week vacation and a pension, workers earn only what they produce according to a piece-rate formula. According to former CEO Don Hastings, the average Lincoln worker earns over $72,000 based on the piece-rate system, a rate he claims is the highest salary for a factory worker in the world.

Some other company policies are also unusual. First, Lincoln still maintains a lifetime employment policy. It has never laid off a worker, even during the 2008 recessionary times, when it had a 40 percent reduction in sales volume. Second, it distributes substantial bonuses to workers based on company performance; some workers earned over $40,000 in bonuses in 2007. Third, the base pay of the CEO is only about seven times that of the average annual wage of a factory worker (former CEO Hastings argues that trust is critical for this process to work and that obscene executive salaries ruin trust). His bonus is a direct function of company profits and fluctuates just like the workers' bonuses do. Hastings credits this trust with the incredible cooperation Lincoln got from its Cleveland plant when international ventures turned sour in the early 90s. Workers stepped up production and exceeded all targets during difficult times with factories in Brazil and Germany.

Lincoln gained controlling interest in three welding businesses in China in 2004, giving them the dominant share of this huge and growing market. John M. Stropki was named president and CEO in 2005.

Chapter 7 discussed different aspects of value in performance. If the piece rate pays a worker for a quantity produced, what happens to quality? At Lincoln, workers are paid only for pieces that meet carefully defined specifications. If there is a quality problem with a piece, workers are responsible for the correction. And what about teamwork? Lincoln also uses performance appraisals that reveal a letter grade for each worker's dependability, quality, output, and cooperation. The straight A workers get the highest bonuses.

The executives and factory workers at Lincoln agree that management is overhead. Their philosophy is "every worker must be a manager, and every manager must be a worker . . . in self-management is found the true meaning of efficiency, because nothing increases overhead as quickly and nonproductively as extra layers of management."[1] The workers are also heavy stockholders; over 80 percent of the workers own stock and the stock is closely held by the Lincoln family, the workers, and several foundations. The year-end profit sharing probably breaks the record for distribution. An average of over 40 percent of Lincoln's pre-tax income goes to the employees.[2]

Assignment

Does the Lincoln system generalize to many other work situations? Think of one work setting in which you think the piece-rate method might work. Generate a list of the key contingencies that may be related to the success of a piece-rate system in that setting.

Also, in addition to the piece-rate method, to what extent are the other characteristics of the Lincoln compensation and management systems critical for Lincoln's success? (Even in 2008, a terrible year for machinery, Lincoln had still maintained its lifetime employment record.) Do you think a CEO's pay relative to that of the producers of the goods and services is critical for establishing and maintaining employee trust? Do you think trust is important? Expectancy theory says nothing about trust. Or does it? Also, is this a work setting for so-called workaholics only? Explain your answer.

[1] Handlin, H. C. (1992). The company built upon the golden rule: Lincoln Electric. In B. L. Hopkins and T. C. Mawhinney (Eds.), *Pay for performance: History, controversy, and evidence.* New York: Haworth Press, p. 156.
[2] Chilton, K. W. (1994, November/December). Lincoln Electric's incentive system: A reservoir of trust. *Compensation & Benefits Review,* pp. 29–34.

CRITICAL THINKING APPLICATION 11-D

Should Teacher Pay Be Tied to Student Test Scores?

Former Massachusetts Governor Mitt Romney proposed large increases in state spending on education that took effect in 2006 and included provisions for merit pay tied to the classroom performance for public school teachers in his state. The merit pay could add $5,000 or more to a teacher's annual salary. "The ability to close the achievement gap is the civil rights issue of our generation," Mr. Romney said in an interview, noting his concern over student test scores.[1]

As of 2008, Arizona, Florida, Iowa, New Mexico, and North Carolina had various forms of merit pay for teachers

that reward classroom performance. Other states are moving in that direction although there is considerable resistance from teacher unions, which almost always fight merit pay proposals and programs. Minnesota has also proposed an extra $2,000 per year for teachers based on their students' achievement. Some cities have also pursued merit pay for their teachers. A Denver, Colorado, ballot initiative was approved in 2005 that raised property taxes $25 million a year to be used for a teacher pay initiative that included performance-based bonuses and salary increases. The common thread behind these initiatives and programs is the tie-in between classroom performance and teacher pay. The American Board for Certification of Teacher Excellence (www.abcte.org) has been working on a model merit pay plan for all states.

Among the criticisms of teacher merit pay are the criteria for eligibility. Some programs restrict eligibility to only those who teach certain classes (e.g., science and math) and those who are at the top as measured by student classroom test score improvement. In Massachusetts, there was great resistance to the proposals. Arranging deck chairs on the *Titanic* is how one scholar has described merit pay for teachers. Catherine A. Boudreau, president of the Massachusetts Teachers Association (www.massteacher. org), a branch of the National Education Association, called Governor Romney's proposals "short on substance, long on politics." She describes merit pay plans as "inequitable, divisive and ineffective." Kathleen A. Kelley, president of the Massachusetts Federation of Teachers (www.mfteducator.org), said that Mr. Romney's plan was developed with no input from the education community. In response to this criticism. Mr. Romney said, "You know, I would just love it if you could just throw out all the special interests from education."

Assignment

Conduct research on teacher merit pay. What does research say about the subject? What has happened to teacher merit pay in Massachusetts since Governor Romney left office? What do teacher unions say about the subject? How have teachers been paid in the past and what has been the role of actual classroom performance? Generate a list of potential problems with teacher merit pay tied to classroom performance and then possible solutions to those problems. Why not just tie student performance to teacher pay directly? Where is your state on this subject?

[1] Janofsky, M. (2005, October 4). Teacher merit pay tied to education gains. (www.NYtimes.com).

CRITICAL THINKING APPLICATION 12-A

Employment-at-Will[1]

Chapter 12 discussed the employment-at-will doctrine and its impact upon organizational initiatives and practices (i.e., employee handbooks, termination). The chapter also discussed the circumstances under which an employee may file a lawsuit in some states. This exercise affords you the opportunity to research perceptions of this doctrine and your own state's laws. Kim[2] asserts that workers appear to systematically overestimate protections provided to them by the law, particularly with regard to employment-at-will. Defenders of the "at-will" doctrine argue that workers have full information to enter into an "at-will" contract with their employers, while critics of the doctrine suggest that workers do not have such information.

Furthermore, the critics note, employers are in a powerful position when it comes to negotiating an (implicit or explicit) employment contract as organizations essentially support the livelihood of individual workers.

In a study investigating how well workers understand the employment-at-will doctrine, Kim found that, on the whole, many individuals erroneously deemed terminations for no "good reason" as unlawful, when in fact they were legal based upon the employment-at-will doctrine. For instance, 89 percent of workers surveyed believed that an employee cannot be lawfully terminated for simple reasons of personal dislike. This is in fact lawful as long as EEO laws are not violated.

No matter what your stance is on the issue, it is an interesting question as to whether workers tend to correctly estimate their job security under employment-at-will. The following exercise guides you through a replication of Kim's study and requests that you conduct research on employment-at-will in your state.

Assignment

A study was discussed in which individuals were asked their perceptions of employment-at-will. Specifically, they were asked to define the concept and they were presented with a scenario in which they were to determine if a termination was lawful. Do a similar "study" by asking five people the following questions.

1. Define employment-at-will.
2. Can an employer legally fire someone who was performing satisfactorily merely to replace her with someone at a lower wage?
3. Can an employer legally fire someone who refuses to participate in illegal billing practices?
4. Can an employer legally fire someone who has been accused of stealing, even if the employee can prove that he or she is not the culprit?

The results from the entire class will then be compiled.

1. How many individuals correctly defined employment-at-will?
2. How many people correctly answered "yes" to the scenario presented in question 2? (In Kim's study, only 17.8 percent of the individuals surveyed correctly answered "yes.")
3. How many people answered "no" to the scenario presented in question 3? (In Kim's study, 87.2 percent correctly answered "no.")

4. How many people correctly answered "yes" to the scenario presented in question 4? (In Kim's study, 10.4 percent of respondents correctly answered "yes.")
5. What are some alternative explanations for your results? That is, are there reasons other than familiarity with employment-at-will (or lack thereof) that could have produced your results?
6. If your results are markedly different from those reported by Kim, what alternative explanations could there be?
7. Can an employer invoke the employment-at-will doctrine and fire an employee who is trying to form a union in the company?

What are the exceptions to employment-at-will in your state? What relevant statutes and common-law decisions can you find using the library at your campus, legal resources, and the Internet? Does your state have "whistleblowing" laws that protect such activity? How are such laws related to "whistleblowing?"

[1]Contributed by Jennifer R. D. Robin.
[2]Research based on Kim, P. (1997). Bargaining with imperfect information: A study of worker perceptions of legal protection in an at-will world. *Cornell Law Review, 83*, 105.

CRITICAL THINKING APPLICATION 12-B

Developing Organizational Policy and a Code of Ethics[1]

Most large companies have developed codes of ethics and strict policy stipulations regarding employee behavior. The calamities at Countrywide Mortgage, Enron, Merrill Lynch, Tyco, WorldCom, Morgan Stanley, HealthSouth, and many others have stirred even more activity in this area. The information on policy and ethics is typically disseminated to employees during orientation when they join the firm and is included in the company handbook. It may be provided in the form of rules of conduct regarding professional demeanor, dress, working hours, and statements on EEO and affirmative action. Guidelines for whistleblowing or reporting problems with conduct, health, safety, sexual harassment, discrimination, use of drugs or alcohol on the job, theft, fraud, Internet usage, or other grievances also may be included. While the information in the company policies manual often serves as a firm's ethics code, it may not be labeled as such.

Assignment

Do research to identify a company you are familiar with and from which you can borrow the firm's policies and procedures handbook or retrieve it through the Internet. Write a brief description of the company you have chosen. Identify the code of ethics for employee behavior and what (if any) policy exists regarding ethics and employee behavior. What issues are addressed? How confident do you feel in the company's code of ethics? What, if any, changes would you make in the organization's code of ethics? Why? Outline the changes you would make.

1. Identify the important components of the organizational code of ethics.
2. Design a plan for implementing an ethical code in a company.
3. Provide suggestions for how an organization can monitor compliance with its code of ethics.
4. Provide an outline of what the code of ethics should look like.
5. How does the company monitor the system to be sure that the policy and code of ethics were being adhered to? What suggestions would you make to the firm if supervisors were not enforcing the ethical codes (e.g., allowing unsafe behaviors to go unreported)?

Does the employee handbook deal with the following issues? Should it?

1. A strict no-smoking policy for all employees on or off the job and a requirement that employees should report breaches of this policy to HR.
2. Absolute proscriptions against any Internet surfing that is not business-related.
3. A warning that computer usage will be monitored for surfing violations and performance measurement. The company warns new hires up front that electronic performance monitoring is routine and should be expected.
4. A strict prohibition against the use of personal cell phones. Only emergency calls are allowed during work hours. A warning also is included in the handbook about the possibility of telephone monitoring by management.
5. A strong statement from the CEO that employees are expected to participate in the United Way program and that the goal is 100 percent participation.
6. A statement that all employment disputes will be resolved through a mediation and arbitration process and that this requirement is a condition of employment and continued employment.
7. A strict statement that the employer and employee have an "at-will" relationship and that no matter what anyone working for the company may have said, the "at-will" condition still stands.
8. A strict statement prohibiting any relatives of employees from working for the company.

Would you be comfortable working for an organization with the policies and procedures handbook you reviewed? Generate a list of the advantages and disadvantages. How would you feel if a firm for which you worked implemented the other policies described?

[1]Contributed by Joyce E. A. Russell and Lillian T. Eby.

CRITICAL THINKING APPLICATION 13-A

Unionizing FedEx[1]

In a world of more competition and higher profits and shareholders' return on investment, unionizing does not seem to make sense. Or does it? Some employees at Federal Express have been trying to unionize since 1991. The pilots were successful in 1993. The ground employees have sought unionization at various sites for the six years it took for the National Labor Relations Board to rule that Federal Express continues to be covered under the Railway Labor Act. Legislation could amend this decision. This NLRB ruling prevented the local sites from unionizing because the election to unionize has to be conducted at all sites within a given job category simultaneously (under the Railway Labor Act). As of January 2009, FedEx ground employees were not unionized.

As of 2009, The International Brotherhood of Teamsters has not emphasized organizing FedEx workers because of the difficulty created by the ruling regarding the Railway Labor Act. The U.S. Department of Labor continues to consider Federal Express to be a cargo airline and, at the time of that DOL ruling, almost all of FedEx's freight was carried at some point by an aircraft. The RLA requires that a union organize on a companywide basis. The IBT has an active Airline Division and represents workers at a lot of RLA regulated airlines (e.g., Northwest and Airborne Express). Over 25 percent of surveyed Teamster members in 2005 believed that organizing FedEx should be a priority for the Teamsters.

FedEx pilots, about 4,000 strong, are now covered under the Air Line Pilots Association (ALPA). ALPA represents approximately 66,000 pilots in collective bargaining agreements.

Despite the fact that FedEx employees earn less than their unionized counterparts at UPS, FedEx continues to be cited as one of the best places to work by several publications and organizations. FedEx is also a *Fortune* Globally Admired Company.

FedEx continues its aggressive policy of no unionization. When employees in their Antigua location went on strike on August 23, 1999, the company terminated all its employees and closed the office two days later on August 25 after over 12 years.[2] They had contracted with Parcel Plus to continue FedEx servicing customers. FedEx still hires independent contractors. Approximately 31 percent of FedEx's total employment is direct. The majority of employment is indirect (i.e., independent contractors).[3] Some question the classification of those employees as independent contractors. Independent contractors have control over their work and the way they conduct that work. FedEx is very specific on what is required to be one of their independent contractors down to how you and your truck need to look.

A UPS strike cited part-time and subcontract work as grievances so that the Teamsters' negotiation of UPS contracts included a "no shift of package delivery work to part-timers" clause and a "no subcontracting of feeder work except during peak season, and then only if local union agrees" clause. Teamsters' organizers and FedEx employees who are pro-union believe that those issues and wage differential are the reasons for unionizing.

The 2008 efforts by the Teamsters are mainly directed at the mechanics. FedEx cut pension benefits and raised health insurance rates in 2008. Says Teamsters President James Hoffa, "[FedEx mechanics] are really talking about how they are disillusioned with FedEx, and they are seeing their life go backward instead of forward." Authorization cards for the mechanics were being collected as of January 2009. Says one FedEx rep, "the Teamsters will say and do anything to organize, despite FedEx's record of winning multiple awards for being one of the best places to work around the globe. Over the years, our employees have repeatedly re-jected third-party representation." The Teamsters Union was also targeting FedEx Ground delivery drivers in 2008. Bloomberg reports that FedEx's current system provides a 30 percent cost advantage over UPS that has helped stretch their market share lead over UPS by 9 percent since 2002.[4]

Assignment

Conduct online research to derive compensation data com-paring UPS with FedEx driver pay. Suppose you are a newly hired FedEx employee. Based on what you know about FedEx and its competitors, would you sign a card to certify a union at FedEx? If yes, explain what information weighed the heaviest in your decision. If no, is there addi-tional information you need to help you make your deci-sion? Compile a list of questions you believe to be vital for your decision? If no, and you request no further informa-tion, explain what information weighed the heaviest in that decision. Why is it beneficial for FedEx to have so many drivers classified as "independent contractors?"

[1]Contributed by Mary E. Wilson.
[2]*The Daily Observer*. (1999, August 26). FedEx quits Antigua, all workers fired. Also see http://members.aol.com/BobKutchko/UnionPride2/ page6.html, accessed July 2002.
[3]SRI (2001). Global impact of FedEx on the new economy. http://www.fedex.com/ us/about/download/economy/sri_exec_summary.pdf?link4,30, accessed July 2002.
[4]Heath, T. (2008, July 11). Teamsters' attempts to organize airline mechanics not likely, FedEx says. *Memphis Business Journal* online.

CRITICAL THINKING APPLICATION 13-B

Do You Support the Employee Free Choice Act (EFCA)?

Unions strongly support an amendment to the NLRA called the Employee Free Choice Act (EFCA). As of January 2009, the legislation had passed the U.S. House of Representatives but not the U.S. Senate. President Obama supports the EFCA. There are three important provisions to the EFCA as it was written in 2008.

1. The law would allow certification of a union as the bargaining representative of a unit of employees if the NLRB found that a majority of those employees

have signed authorization cards designating the union as its bargaining representative. Even before passage of the EFCA a company has the legal ability to allow its workers to have union representation (without going through the NLRB) if a majority of potential members support unionization. The EFCA would make this recognition mandatory, taking away a company's ability to force a majority of potential members to go through the NLRB election process.

2. The EFCA would declare that if an employer and a union are engaged in bargaining for their first contract and are unable to reach an agreement within 90 days, either party may refer the dispute to the Federal Mediation and Conciliation Service (FMCS) for mediation. If the FMCS was then unable to bring the parties to agreement after 30 days of mediation, the dispute would be referred to arbitration, and the results of the arbitration would be binding on the parties for two years.

3. The EFCA would stipulate that violations of the National Labor Relations Act could result in civil fines of up to $20,000 per violation against employers found to have willfully or repeatedly violated employees' rights during an organizing campaign or first-contract drive and an increase in the amount an employer is required to pay when an employee is discharged or discriminated against during an organizing campaign or first-contract drive to "three times back pay."

Advocates of the EFCA make these arguments:[1]

1. A recent survey found that 58 percent of American workers would join a union if they could while private sector union membership was at 7.4 percent.

According to a National Labor Relations Board (NLRB) annual report,[2] 31,358 people were disciplined or fired for legal union activity. That's one worker every 17 minutes. This "chilling effect" seriously inhibits union or-ganizing. According to *Fortune* magazine, "workers are routinely fired or discriminated against for supporting unions, most employers hire anti-union consultants to block organizing drives, and some go so far as to close down work sites when employees vote for a union."[3]

The NLRB now sets a secret-ballot election one or two months following the verification and approval of the authorization card process (although in many cases there are legal challenges to the authorization step that have delayed the election for months or years). During the period between the authorization and the election, the company retains over-whelming power to influence the outcome of the vote.

According to Professor Harley Shaiken, "The NLRB-supervised elections often take place in highly coercive environments. As a result, they approximate plebiscites in a dictatorship rather than a functioning democracy. The votes may be counted honestly, but the outcome ratifies the inequitable atmosphere in which the vote occurs."[4]

2. Numerous writers and scholars have expressed concern that the historical link between a thriving economy and a thriving middle class is now broken. In a 2006 speech before the U.S. economic crisis, Henry Paulson, former Treasury Secretary under President Bush, stated that "amid this country's strong economic expansion, many Americans simply aren't feeling the benefits."[5] Nobel prize winner Paul Krugman concurred, stating, "All indicators of the economic status of ordinary Americans—poverty rates, family incomes, the number of people without health insurance—show that most of us were worse off in 2005 than we were in 2000, and there's little reason to think that 2006 was much better."[6] A 2008 book by Steven Greenhouse concludes: "Since 1979, hourly earnings for 80 percent of American workers (those in private-sector, nonsupervisory jobs) have risen by just 1 percent, after inflation. The average was $17.71 at the end of 2007. For male workers, the average hourly wage actually slid by 5 percent since 1979. Worker productivity, meanwhile, climbed 60 percent. If wages had kept pace with productivity, the average full-time worker would be earning $58,000 a year; $36,000 was the average in 2007. The nation's economic pie is growing, but corporations by and large have not given their workers a bigger piece."[7] On the economic front, things have only gotten worse since 2006. Many experts argue that a major cause of the growing inequity is due to the decline of unions. Greenhouse and others argue that this decline is to some extent a consequence of the power and fear tactics of employers to prevent union organizing.

While worker pay is stagnant (or worse), benefits and working conditions have declined. According to Mr. Greenhouse, the typical American worker puts in 1,804 hours of work a year—135 hours more per year than the typical British worker, 240 hours more than the average French worker, and 370 hours (or nine full-time weeks) more than the average German worker. No one in the world's advanced economies works more.[8] Of course, a much higher percentage of British, French, and German workers are unionized.

3. Unions can reverse this growing inequity trend. According to the Bureau of Labor Statistics, the American union wage advantage is 28.1 percent for wages and 43.7 percent for total compensation—wages and benefits.[9] Other analysis controlling for education, experience, industry, and region indicates about a 15 percent union advantage with larger differences for African Americans, Hispanics, and Asians.

According to a *BusinessWeek* story, "Because unions boost workers' bargaining power and help them win a greater share of productivity gains, any resurgence would give low-wage workers more clout to deal with the effects of factors such as globalization, immigration, and technology."[10]

Washington Post columnist Steven Pearlstein summed up the need for the EFCA this way: "Over the years, [the right to form unions and bargain collectively] has been whittled away by legislation, poked with holes by appeals courts and reduced to irrelevancy by a well-meaning bureaucracy that has let itself be intimidated by political and legal thuggery . . . and for those workers who happen to win a union, any company willing to use intimidation and delaying tactics will never have to sign a first contract with a union, even if employees really want one."[11]

In his testimony before Congress, Professor Shaiken concluded: "At issue is the right to make a choice free of coercion for 'representatives of one's own choosing.' To restore this right to millions of American workers, one has to go back to the future: reform the current dysfunctional labor relations system to achieve the spirit of the Wagner Act in a 21st century setting. The Employee Free Choice Act represents an important approach to redressing the lack of balance today through three main provisions: restoring the union recognition procedure that the Wagner Act initially provided; stiffening penalties to deter employer misconduct; and instituting first contract mediation/arbitration to thwart bad faith bargaining."[12]

Those opposed to the EFCA argue that Congress should do the following in direct opposition to the EFCA.[13]

1. Protect workers' privacy during organizing drives and guarantee every worker the right to vote in a private-ballot election.
2. Ensure that workers hear from both sides during an organizing drive and have time to reflect on their choice so they can make an informed and considered decision.
3. Protect the right of workers and employers to bargain collectively without having government officials unilaterally impose employment contracts on them.

Assignment

Conduct research on the EFCA and determine its present legislative status and content. Review the advocates' arguments above and also conduct online research to identify and consider arguments opposed to the law (see endnote 13 below for starters). Write a two-page typed position paper stating your support of or opposition to the law. This paper should state precisely what the NLRA procedures are for recognizing a union *prior to passage of the EFCA* and what the penalties are for employer violations of the NLRA. If by the time you are reading this the EFCA is now the law, conduct research on its effects to date.

[1] Shaiken, H. (2007, February 8). Strengthening America's middle class through the Employee Free Choice Act. Testimony before the U.S. House of Representatives Subcommittee on Health, Employment, Labor, and Pensions.
[2] According to 1993–2003 *NLRB Annual Reports*, an average of 22,633 workers per year received back pay from their employer. The NLRB orders employers to award back pay to workers they illegally fired, demoted, laid off, suspended without pay, or denied work as a result of their union activity.
[3] Gunther, M. (2007, June 7). Cingular bucks anti-union trend. *Fortune* online.
[4] Shaiken, Strengthening America's middle class.
[5] Paulson, H. (2006, August 1). Speech at Columbia University. http://www.ustreas.gov/press/releases/hp41.htm.

[6] Krugman, P. (2006, February 27). Graduates versus oligarchs. *The New York Times* online.
[7] Greenhouse, S. (2008). *The big squeeze: Tough times for the American worker.* New York: Borzoi Books.
[8] Ibid.
[9] Mishel, Lawrence, Bernstein, Jared, and Allegretto, Sylvia (2007). *The state of working America 2006/2007.* Ithaca, NY: ILR Press.
[10] Conlin, M., and Bernstein, A. (2004, May 31). Working and poor. *BusinessWeek* online.
[11] Pearlstein, S. (2004, February 24). Workers' rights are being rolled back. *Washington Post* online.
[12] Shaiken, Strengthening America's middle class.
[13] Sherk, J., and Kersey, P. (2007, April 23). How the Employee Free Choice Act takes away workers' rights. The Heritage Foundation online, http://www.heritage.org/research/Labor/bg2027.cfm.

CRITICAL THINKING APPLICATION 14-A

Can Health and Safety Behavior Be Predicted?

Companies are very interested in assessing job applicants' tendencies to behave (and misbehave) at work. The purpose of this CTA is to introduce some approaches for assessing the potential for certain behaviors or outcomes.

To access this exercise, go to the "Self-Assessments" section of the book's Web site (www.mhhe.com/ bernardin5e). Follow the directions for completing "Can Health and Safety be Predicted?" and then print the feedback page (to be handed in at the discretion of your instructor). After you complete the online portion of the CTA, answer the following questions:

1. What does research conclude regarding Type A personality, proactive personality, and work outcomes? Which personality type is more effective in a stressful work situation?
2. Can you predict an individual's tendency to be violent? What does research conclude?
3. Why is it so important to screen certain employees for their potential driving behavior? What is the best approach to this assessment?
4. Do you think these types of questions are useless for actual decision making because answers can be faked?
5. What would be your reaction if you were told you were not hired based on your responses to this questionnaire?

CRITICAL THINKING APPLICATION 14-B

The Measurement of Stress at Work

There are many causes of stress at work; some issues or situations are more stressful than others. The purpose of this CTA is to give you some insights into the relative potency of work situations for causing stress at work.

Assignment

To access this exercise, go to the "Self-Assessments" section of the book's Web site (www.mhhe.com/bernardin5e). Follow the directions for completing "The Measurement of Stress at work" and then print the feedback page (to be handed in at the discretion of your instructor). After you complete the online portion of the CTA or exercise, answer the following questions:

1. Some work situations are considered more stressful than others. How does research make that determination?
2. Are some individuals more prone to react well (or poorly) to stressful situations? What types of personalities are more likely to handle stress well?
3. What are the overall effects of a stressful work situation? What actions can a company take to reduce the stress.
4. What actions could an organization take to reduce role conflict and role ambiguity? Why would that be an important thing to do?
5. What does research say about the effects of a highly demanding work situation in which the worker has little or no control of the situation?

APPENDIX B
Chapter Exercises

Note: *Exercise 1.1, An Interview with an HRM Specialist, is available online at www.mhhe.com/bernardin5e.*

EXERCISE 1.2: AN ASSESSMENT OF CUSTOMER SATISFACTION AND THE RELATIONSHIP TO HRM ACTIVITIES

Overview

Chapter 1 described a variety of new challenges and trends confronting organizations today, many of which include concerns about productivity, product service and quality, and customer satisfaction.

As a practicing manager or an HRM specialist, you are likely to be asked to meet the human resource challenges related to productivity and/or customer satisfaction. Nine out of every 10 jobs are predicted to be in the services sector in the next 20 years. Productivity figures reflect a generally slow rate of productivity growth for many services industries. Assessments of product and service quality are also unfavorable, and customer service indexes are low in many segments of the services sector, although they have improved in recent years.

Chapter 1 presents an argument and cites research that shows human resource activities have the potential to enhance customer satisfaction, increase productivity, and improve product and service quality. We emphasized that the most effective HRM programs are those in which the focus is always on the ultimate criterion of customer satisfaction. This exercise will focus on those HRM efforts that are customer oriented and will generate discussion about steps that can be taken to improve customer satisfaction.

Learning Objectives

After completing this exercise, you should be able to

1. Identify some specific examples of how HRM can affect customer satisfaction.
2. View customer satisfaction from an HRM perspective, such as the impact of employee attitudes, the diversity of worker characteristics, and the job skills gap, and how you as a manager or HRM specialist could improve customer satisfaction through HRM activities.
3. Identify HRM activities that may be useful for tackling problems related to customer satisfaction.

Procedure

Part A: Individual Analysis

Think back over an experience you have had with any product or service. It could even be experiences related to your interaction with the university. Write two examples of what you regard as high customer satisfaction and two you regard as poor customer satisfaction regarding those products or services. Write the negative examples on Form 1.2.1 and the positive examples on Form 1.2.2. After describing each experience, review the HRM activities discussed in Chapter 1 and form hypotheses as to what particular domains or activities may have been primarily responsible for the excellent or poor customer satisfaction. Generate a list of the possible causes. Be creative in your hypotheses and attempt to go beyond simple theories such as a "training" problem as the cause. Bring the completed forms to class for discussion.

On Form 1.2.3, write what you regard as your absolute favorite product or service that you have actually purchased in any area. This can be any product, large or small, cheap or expensive. In the space provided, write a short explanation of why you regard this particular product or service as your favorite. Bring Form 1.2.3 to class.

Part B: Group Analysis

Approximately six people should be designated to discuss responses on Form 1.2.1 while the same number of students are designated as observers of the group. If possible, each observer should be assigned to observe the group performance of only one group participant. The observer should review the participant's Form 1.2.1 before group discussion. Each observer should use Form 1.2.4 as the context for observing group participation of the participant to whom he or she has been assigned. *Observers should review the directions for observation before the observation period. Form 1.2.4 should be completed by the observer immediately after group discussion is completed while the participant is completing Form 1.2.5 (self-assessment).*

All members of the first discussion group should also read each other's Form 1.2.1 and attempt to discern trends in the incidents. For example, was the dissatisfaction mainly caused for poor product or service quality? Was the product or service representative incompetent and not knowledgeable about the product or service? After identifying any trends in the dissatisfaction, discuss the HRM activities proposed as the major causes of the poor customer service. Generate a list of the most important HRM activities the group believes to be directly or indirectly responsible for the customer service problems. The group should attempt to reach consensus on the top three HRM activities that could be directed at correcting the customer service problems.

After about 15 minutes of discussion, each observer should evaluate the participant's performance in the group and each participant should complete the self-assessment on Form 1.2.5. The pairs should then switch roles, and the new discussion group should discuss the responses on Form 1.2.2, also attempting to identify the major HRM

activities thought to be the causes of the excellent customer services that were provided and the extent to which HRM was responsible relative to other organizational functions. The second group can use the first group's analysis as a starting point. Again, the group should attempt to reach consensus on the top three HRM activities thought to be responsible for the positive customer satisfaction.

Part C: Self- and Observer Assessment and Feedback Session

After completing the second group exercise, participants should make a self-assessment using the rating scale on Form 1.2.5 while the observer is completing Form 1.2.4. After Forms 1.2.5 and 1.2.4 are completed, students should pair off and take turns reviewing their respective self- and observer assessments. Discussion should then center on each individual's performance in the group, the written responses, areas of strength or weakness, and the rationale of their respective positions regarding HRM activities.

Name _____ Group _____

FORM 1.2.1

Think of two situations in which you felt very dissatisfied with a product or the customer service you received. Describe each circumstance in some detail and consider the causes of the dissatisfaction in terms of possible HRM activities. What were you expecting and what did you receive? Answer the questions below for each situation:

1. Describe the organization (e.g., fast food, department store, university setting).
   Situation 1

   Situation 2

2. Describe the experience and the poor product or service in some detail.
   Situation 1

   Situation 2

3. What do you regard as the major causes for your dissatisfaction? To what extent do you believe HRM activities were related to the dissatisfaction? Specifically, which activities are most related to the customer dissatisfaction and how could HRM improve the service?
   Situation 1

   Situation 2

FORM 1.2.2

Think of two situations in which you felt very satisfied with a product or the customer service you received. Describe each circumstance in some detail and consider the causes of the service in terms of possible HRM activities. What were you expecting and what did you receive?

1. Describe the organization (e.g., fast food, department store, university setting).

   Situation 1

   Situation 2

2. Describe the experience and the good service or product quality in some detail.

   Situation 1

   Situation 2

3. What do you regard as the major causes of your satisfaction? To what extent do you believe HRM activities were related to your satisfaction? Specifically, which activities do you believe to be most related to the customer service you have received?

   Situation 1

   Situation 2

Name _____

FORM 1.2.3 WHAT ARE YOUR FAVORITE PRODUCTS OR SERVICES?

1. What do you regard as the most favorite product or service you have ever purchased? Explain why you regard this product or service so highly (be specific).

    What (if any) role did human resources have in making this product or service so good?

2. What do you regard as the least favorite product or service you have ever purchased? Explain why you regard this product/service so poorly (be specific).

    Do you think human resources had anything to do with the lack of regard you have for this product/service?

Observer's name _____ Discussant's name _____ Group _____

FORM 1.2.4 OBSERVER ASSESSMENT FORM

Directions for observation: Get familiar with the 10 behaviors or activities listed below. Observe your designated discussant on the extent to which he or she exhibited these behaviors. *Rate the extent to which the participant exhibited the behaviors described below. Make your ratings in the space provided. Use the following scale to make your ratings:*

1. Not at all

2. To a little extent

3. To some extent

4. To a great extent

5. To a very great extent

x. Does not apply

To what extent did the participant

_____ 1. Help establish a clear course of action to complete the work?

_____ 2. Speak effectively in the group?

_____ 3. Argue persuasively for a point of view?

_____ 4. Present a point of view concisely?

_____ 5. Write clearly and concisely?

_____ 6. Show sensitivity to other group members?

_____ 7. Stimulate and guide group members toward resolution of the assignment?

_____ 8. Listen carefully to other opinions and suggestions?

_____ 9. Analyze all pertinent information carefully before taking a position?

_____ 10. Display a willingness to state a position in a complex situation?

Name _____

FORM 1.2.5 SELF-ASSESSMENT FORM

Rate the extent to which you exhibited the behaviors described below in the group. Make your ratings in the space provided. Use the following scale to make your ratings:

1. Not at all

2. To a little extent

3. To some extent

4. To a great extent

5. To a very great extent

x. Does not apply

To what extent did you

_____ 1. Help establish a clear course of action to complete the work?

_____ 2. Speak effectively in the group?

_____ 3. Argue persuasively for a point of view?

_____ 4. Present your point of view concisely?

_____ 5. Write clearly and concisely?

_____ 6. Show sensitivity to other group members?

_____ 7. Stimulate and guide group members toward resolution of the assignment?

_____ 8. Listen carefully to other opinions and suggestions?

_____ 9. Analyze all pertinent information carefully before taking a position?

_____ 10. Display a willingness to state a position in a complex situation?

EXERCISE 1.2 ASSESSMENT QUESTIONS

1. Describe the experience you had in providing feedback on your designated discussant's performance. To what extent did you feel comfortable in that role?

2. How might that role be improved with better directions, better assessment devices, etc.?

3. How did you feel about receiving feedback on your group performance? To what extent did you find the feedback helpful? How might that process be improved?

4. Did this exercise give you a better understanding of the relationship between HRM-related activities and customer satisfaction? Explain your answer.

EXERCISE 1.3: HUMAN RESOURCE ISSUES AT VALLEY NATIONAL BANK*

Overview

Chapter 1 introduced you to the human resource issues that HRM professionals and general managers must deal with if they are to assist the organization in becoming competitive and in meeting its goals. This exercise enables you to further develop your analytical skills as you assess the human resource issues affecting competitiveness at Valley National Bank.

Learning Objectives

After completing this exercise, you should be able to

1. Identify human resource issues that may affect organizational effectiveness and competitiveness.
2. Develop strategies for dealing with human resource concerns.

Procedure

Part A: Individual Analysis

Step 1. Read Chapter 1, paying particular attention to the discussion of the human resource domains as they relate to competitive advantage.

Step 2. Read the background information on Valley National Bank provided in Exhibits 1.3.1 and 1.3.2. Identify the human resource issues facing the vice president's department and under which of the HR domains (e.g., Organizational Design, Staffing, Performance Management and Appraisal) each issue belongs. Outline some strategies for dealing with these issues. Develop a rank-ordered *chronological* priority list of the first three issues that require your attention. Provide a written justification for your recommendations. Enter your rank orderings and justifications in the space provided on Form 1.3.1. **Answer the assessment questions** on pages 561 and 562 *before class* as well.

Part B: Group Discussions

Step 1. In groups, identify what you believe to be the potential competitive advantage(s) of the accounting department. Review Form 1.3.1 and the Assessment Questions for this Exercise and determine the human resource issues or activities of greatest concern to the accounting department. Reach a consensus on the chronology of the top three issues that require attention. Discuss why these issues must be resolved if the department is to assist the Bank in becoming more competitive. Identify the benefits and drawbacks to each recommendation. Reach consensus on the assessment questions as well.

Step 2. A representative from each group will then present the consensus recommendations and rationale to the rest of the class.

Part C: (Optional)

Students should complete the self- and peer assessment instrument.

*Contributed by Dave Ulrich.

Exhibit 1.3.1   **Background Information For Valley National Bank**

Recent Bank History

Valley National Bank is a relatively young financial institution with close to $10 billion in assets, although it shortly will acquire another bank to bring its size up to about $12 billion in assets. As a whole, there is a wealth of technical talent in the company, yet most of the experiences have been developed within the confines of $1 and $2 billion institutions. The managers and employees have not had much collective experience managing a $12 billion company. Senior managers currently recognize they must make some critical strategic decisions regarding the future of the bank if they are to remain competitive in the next decade.

Accounting Department

The vice president of accounting reports directly to the senior vice president of management accounting, who in turn reports to the controller of the company (see the condensed organizational chart in Exhibit 1.3.2). The vice president, **Suzanne Roberts,** was promoted into her current position to manage a department that the previous manager had let get out of control. Her job is to provide managerial accounting software to line and staff management throughout the organization so that managers might be able to make better decisions in the daily operations of their respective departments. The software, although difficult to implement, has proved to be very useful in institutions with postures of high growth. The information provided by the programs is financial in nature and, for the most part, is the type of information that VNB bankers are not used to receiving. Therefore, two key goals are: to educate the company in the use of the new software so that the bank ultimately benefits in terms of bottom-line results and to use the software to identify those sectors of business in which the bank does exceptionally well so that better and more focused strategic decisions can be made.

As challenging as her stated primary job responsibilities are, Ms. Roberts believes that another issue she currently faces is getting the right people in the right places in her department so that they can accomplish their goals. When she came into the department, she quickly concluded that some of the best contributors in the department were also the lowest-paid employees.

Bob Phillips was the former manager of the department. Through a merger, he came to Valley National Bank to manage the department, having had experience supervising two people at his previous position. In his role as vice president of accounting, he was asked to supervise about 10 people. Over two years, things got so out of hand that his employees reported that they were not clear what they were supposed to do, except in emergency situations, which seemed to be happening every day. Performance reviews of employees were late by up to six months. Naturally, employee morale was very low and attitudes toward the company became hardened. Good people quit the bank or transferred to other departments. Finding replacements for these individuals was done poorly; often the first person who walked in for the interview was hired. Today, there are several people working for the department who probably should never have been hired. Unfortunately, their options are such that it probably pays for them to stay rather than voluntarily leave.

Bob lacked the organizational and planning skills needed to effectively manage his people. In addition, his weak interpersonal skills have created hard feelings among some of the employees in the department. He usually can arrive at a very good financial/accounting solution to a problem and has an extensive knowledge of all major software programs. However, he has a difficult time working with other people to implement his solutions. Needless to say, some employees resent that Bob is still

paid a good salary and given a good title to go with his reduced responsibilities. **Mr. Sterrett,** the VP of HR, believes the company should sever its ties with Bob, but other external factors make this choice difficult. For example, Bob has faced some very severe personal and health problems since transferring to Valley National Bank.

Carla Goodman previously worked for Bob for about 15 years. When the accounting department at Valley National was established, she was placed in charge of several people and given a promotion of two pay-grade levels. This decision proved to be disastrous because she could not (or would not) accept the responsibility of supervising and reviewing people. She was quickly relieved of these duties, but her salary grade level remained intact so that today she is overpaid for her overall responsibilities. Her title is such that it implies a lower pay level in the company, but it fools no one. She is average as a technical worker and understands the flow of transactions well. Currently, Ms. Roberts often has Carla working by herself because she doesn't make very good impressions with people. She tends to openly criticize the company, which draws concerns from other employees in the department. In fact, on occasion, she and Bob have resorted to shouting matches to get their respective points across to each other. Ms. Roberts also received an anonymous note reporting possible sexual harassment issues between Carla and another employee.

Greg Williams has been with the company about eight years and has worked for Ms. Roberts for about 2.5 years in various capacities. He has progressed in a very normal fashion in the bank. However, he has seen younger people such as Ms. Roberts move ahead of him on the organizational ladder. He expresses concern that his career may be leveling off unless something dramatic happens. He is not the quickest person to catch on to things in a technical sense, and he has a difficult time interacting effectively with people. This reduces his chances for a promotion. In general, he is a conscientious, mild-mannered employee who doesn't normally complain about things. He is good at taking orders but not very good at handing them out.

Kathy Lewis is the most promising employee in the department today in terms of future potential within the company. She is technically sharp, with considerable knowledge of the new information systems, and has shown some promise in the effective management of people. She has been an employee of the company for a number of years and worked for Bob at the previous bank before the merger. She understands his odd nature. Her skills allow her to get more done than most people, and she is willing to put in extra hours to get things done. She did announce her resignation from the company at one time because of the mounting problems with the department, but a senior vice president talked her into staying by implying changes would be made sometime. Kathy is probably worth more to the bank than her current salary indicates, especially in light of the salaries of Bob and Carla. The normal guidelines should allow her to catch up in the next one to two years. She probably could also gain from receiving experience in other departments, but Ms. Roberts recognizes that she could not afford to let Kathy go because of the lack of depth with the other employees.

Overall, things are probably not as bad as they may appear to be. Ms. Roberts, however, does get concerned from time to time about the general lack of depth in the department as Mr. Jack Richter, Valley National Bank president, looks to the department to help the bank become more competitive. Ms. Roberts has met with Mr. Sterrett of the HRM Department, who has recommended that Bob be terminated immediately but that Carla should be retained because she could file a sex discrimination lawsuit. Sterrett also recommends that Carla's pay should be cut immediately.

**Exhibit 1.3.2
Organizational Chart**

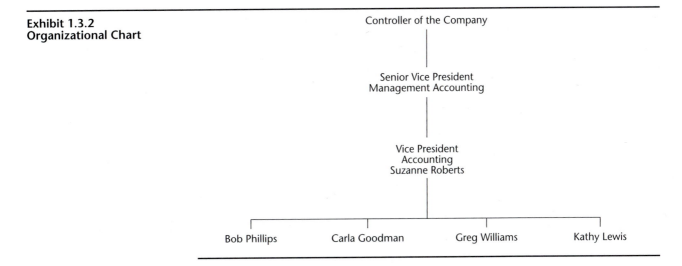

Name _____   Group _____

FORM 1.3.1 PRIORITY LIST OF HRM ISSUES

First issue in need of attention:

    Justification:

    Action to be taken:

    What is the HR domain (e.g., Organizational Design, Staffing, etc.) for this issue?

Second issue in need of attention:

    Justification:

    Action to be taken:

    What is the HR domain?

Third issue in need of attention:

    Justification:

    Action to be taken:

    What is the HR domain?

FORM 1.3.1 (*Continued*)

Name _____ Group _____

List the potential internal strengths at Valley National.

List the potential internal weaknesses at Valley National.

FORM 1.3.1 (*Continued*)

Name ———————————————————— Group ————————————————————

List the potential external opportunities at Valley National.

List the potential external threats at Valley National.

EXERCISE 1.3 ASSESSMENT QUESTIONS

1. Do you agree or disagree with the recommendations of Mr. Sterrett? Explain your position. Is it lawful to cut employees' pay as Mr. Sterrett recommends?

2. What other information would be helpful in preparation for recommending action to be taken?

Name _____ Group _____

3. What steps would you take to determine the legality of your action?

4. What is potentially "unique" about VNB, and how could the "uniqueness" give the bank a competitive advantage?

5. Among the five domains of HRM (see Figure 1-3 in Chapter 1 of the text), what domain usually drives other HR domains when significant organizational change is necessary?

EXERCISE 2.1: INTERNATIONAL HR STRATEGIES: THE DERIVATION OF POLICY*

Overview

Chapter 2 discusses the issue how to staff various forms of overseas operations. Review the discussion in the chapter on the issues affecting decisions about the use of expatriates, the upfront training costs, the cultural orientation costs, and the high level of assignment failure. Consider the information provided in the case and take positions on each question posed.

Learning Objectives

After completing this exercise, you should be able to

1. Understand some of the complexities of international HRM.
2. Provide recommendations for decisions related to staffing and compensating international operations.

3. Outline the key issues that should be considered in dealing with expatriates and repatriates.

Procedure

Part A: Individual Analysis

Step 1. Read the attached background material on LeBert Graphics provided in Exhibit 2.1.1.

Step 2. Assume the role of consultant to the vice president of HR and respond to the issues he has raised. Prepare concise, written responses for each issue and point out any contingencies that should be considered. Answer the questions presented on Form 2.1.1.

*Contributed by Brenda E. Richey, Associate Professor, Department of Management, International Business and Entrepreneurship, Florida Atlantic University.

Exhibit 2.1.1

William O'Dell, vice president for human resources at LeBert Graphics (LG), a fast-growing software development firm headquartered in Boston's Route 128 technology belt, was visiting the firm's first overseas subsidiary, LeBert Graphics Bangalore, Ltd. (LGB). The visit had been going well, but a recent lunch with his good friend Ashok Rao had left him troubled. Rao was one of many Indian expatriates who had migrated to the United States in the 1980s. He had been with LG for a number of years and had recently accepted an assignment to return to his hometown to head up the firm's new development lab. O'Dell was thankful to have him there—not just because of his development skills, but because he hoped he would serve as a cultural broker between headquarters and local employees.

During lunch, Rao noted how the city had changed. He had decided not to return to Bangalore after college in the United States because of the lack of opportunities. Now the city was booming, and computer software was the driving force. Neighbors in the technology park where LG had located included Siemens Components and Hitachi Asia.[1] The nature of the industry had changed too. Initially, foreign firms had employed Indian workers for basic programming. Although cheap, these employees did not always have the training or skill levels seen in their American counterparts. No longer. There were still large pools of these competent but not exceptional employees. Recruiting for the new operations, however, he found many of the applicants had technical skills that would equal those of any of their Boston staff.[2] These were the employees they needed for the software development operations.

The market had changed in other ways too. Today, the best of these software engineers had more options. Because of a worldwide shortage, there were a host of firms looking for skilled engineers. An engineer could work for the local operations of a foreign firm, on temporary assignment basis in the United States or Europe, or could find a place in one of the many local, start-up firms.[3] Some had great success starting their own software firms in the United States. While the same range of opportunities might not exist for those with more basic skills, the growth in foreign investment and start-ups in Bangalore also gave these employees many attractive options locally.

At first, the conversation appeared casual, the reminiscences of an old friend. However, Rao also had mentioned a conversation he had overheard in which one of the brightest engineers in the development unit had complained to a coworker that although

he was a principal engineer on a joint Boston–Bangalore project, his American counterpart was receiving over four times his salary. On reflection, O'Dell was convinced that Rao had been attempting to draw his attention to an issue that was important to some of the Indian staff.

O'Dell's initial reaction had been, "Of course, that's why we located in Bangalore in the first place." Technology skills were abundant, and pay rates for software engineers were a fraction of those in Boston. Moreover, the pay levels reflected the fact that productivity in the programming unit was not always up to U.S. standards. On reflection, he realized that the issue was much more complex.

On one hand were the economics. Cost savings not achieved now might be lost forever. Manufacturing firms that had moved operations to low-cost, offshore sites often had found that the benefits were partly illusory. Wages were low, but at times so was productivity. Employees were often willing, and with appropriate training, supervision, and equipment, productivity levels would rise. However, as these employees became more productive, they also became more attractive to other employers. Moreover, as the economy in these regions developed, there was often a shift in the exchange rate. Salaries rose locally, but because of exchange rate effects, they rose even more in U.S. dollars. Firms using contractors might shift to another, lower-cost site. Such shifts could be disruptive, however, and were even more difficult when the firm had invested directly in the overseas location.

It would be simpler, O'Dell thought, if the firm were in Bangalore for the short term. LG's interests in Bangalore had changed dramatically over the past year, however. LG had been using an Indian subcontractor to outsource basic programming for years. Individual pay levels had not concerned them directly. The Indian firm handled all issues related to recruitment, performance evaluation, and compensation. Recently, LG had decided both to bring the programming in-house (by acquiring the Indian firm) and to open a software development lab.

The decision to move the operation in-house reflected a desire for greater control. It would allow greater emphasis on quality, especially after they trained the programmers to more closely meet the company's special needs. The decision to open the software development lab represented an even more dramatic shift. The new lab operation could take advantage of the rapidly developing skills of the Indian engineers, particularly in "hot jobs" for which there was a worldwide shortage. Moreover, the fast-growing Asian markets held real potential for LG. This required the development of programs that met the special needs of their Asian customers. At first the technology would originate in Boston, but substantial local adaptation was required. Later, the lab should stand alone in developing programs for the region and possibly the world market. These efforts required day-to-day interaction and teamwork between engineers at both locations. Soon the projects would require short-term transfers of personnel between facilities.

[1]Ristelhueber, R. (April 1997). Bangalore builds a high-tech future. *Electronic Business Today, 23*(4), 20.

[2]Stremlau, J. (November 1996). Bangalore: India's Silicon City. *Monthly Labor Review, 119*(11), 50–51.

[3]Leung, J. (June 1996). Brains fuel technology: Boom town. *Asian Business, 32*(6), 28–34.

Exhibit 2.1.1 (*Continued*)

The discussion reminded him of a project he had left on his desk before the trip: developing a compensation plan for the revamped India operations. The project had not focused on compensation levels, but it had raised related questions. What type of compensation package was appropriate? Should they follow local custom as to vacations and leave? Should the generous stock option and pension plans, available to employees in Boston, be extended to these operations?

Custom and government regulation varied substantially from one nation to the next. In some nations, pensions were part of a government social security system; in others, they were provided by firms. In some nations they were not required at all. Even something as simple as "monthly pay" differed: In Singapore a typical compensation package paid the employee by the month for 13, instead of 12, months.[4] These were just a few of the differences O'Dell had run across in research for the project. The list could go on forever. No wonder compensation systems, like other aspects of human resource management, traditionally had been one of the most "local" aspects of a multinational's operations. Local wage scales were used, and the firms tended to follow local custom in regard to vacations, pensions, and other aspects of the compensation package. But with engineers

of similar skill levels working together on a daily basis, how long would these distinctions be possible? Might some of these engineers be hired in the United States? Would LG offer different packages based on the facility they were assigned to? How would that affect recruiting? And what about the engineers transferred to Boston for six months: should they receive a different package while on tour? For the programmers doing more routine work, the issues might not be as complex but were still important. Considering the cost of the training planned for the Bangalore staff, it was vital to keep these employees on board and motivated despite the many opportunities open to them.

While the focus was on India for now, the firm also had considered opening subsidiary operations in Russia and Brazil. His project was the first step in an effort to decide the extent to which the firm's performance review and compensation plans should be integrated globally. The issue did not just concern the employees abroad. At home, some concern had been expressed about the long-term outlook. Software engineers were hot now, but in 10 years would the salaries reflect a lower, global scale? And would all the jobs be overseas? The opportunities abroad were exciting but had brought their share of headaches.

---

[4]Learning to manage host-country nationals. (March 1995). *Personnel Journal, 74*(3), 60–67

FORM 2.1.1

1. How does culture affect the role of pay as a motivating force for workers? Would this issue be raised differently in the United States?

2. What would be the advantages and disadvantages of using the existing LG compensation package in India? How might it differ from a more typical Indian package? What additional information would O'Dell need to make this decision?

3. What other human resource issues might O'Dell need to be concerned about? Prepare a list and explain how they might interact.

4. How do these issues relate to the strategic choices that the firm has made? Does the analogy to a manufacturing firm seem appropriate?

EXERCISE 2.2: GOING GLOBAL WITH MARRIOTT CORPORATION*

Overview

Marriott International has about 3,000 lodging properties in the United States and 67 other countries and territories. The company operates and franchises hotels under the *Marriott, JW Marriott, The Ritz-Carlton, Renaissance, Residence Inn, Courtyard, TownePlace Suites, Fairfield Inn, SpringHill Suites, and Bulgari* brand names; develops and operates vacation ownership resorts under the *Marriott Vacation Club, Horizons by Marriott Vacation Club, The Ritz-Carlton Club,* and *Grand Residences by Marriott* brands; operates *Marriott Executive Apartments;* provides furnished corporate housing through its *Marriott Execu-Stay* division; and operates conference centers. The company is headquartered in Bethesda, Md., and had approximately 151,000 employees at 2007 year-end. It has been ranked as the lodging industry's most admired company and one of the best companies to work for by *Fortune®*, and was recognized by the U.S. Environmental Protection Agency (EPA) with the 2007 Sustained Excellence Award and Partner of the Year in 2004. In fiscal year 2007, Marriott International reported sales from continuing operations of $13 billion. A key to Marriott's success in each of their lines of business came from Marriott's deserved reputation of providing outstanding service to guests and customers. As a result of their excellent service, the Marriott Corporation was considered by customers around the world as the "preferred provider" or the provider customers thought of first when making lodging or food choices.

Marriott's goal for the first decade of the 21st century was a major emphasis on global expansion. Along with being the "provider of choice," Marriott needed to become the "employer of choice" for international assignments. It was felt that if Marriott could not continue to attract, retain, and manage their employees in their overseas operations, then their rapid growth would slow down. Managing employees and becoming the international employer of choice was not an option; it was seen as central to business success and should be directly linked to the "provider of choice" emphasis. For example, one of Marriott Corporation's central challenges has been to ensure that all overseas operations are staffed with the most qualified and cost-effective employees who will join and stay in the business. In the past, Marriott had some problems with expatriate attrition and performance and difficulties in repatriation as well.

Learning Objectives

After completing this exercise, you should be able to

1. Identify a number of specific HRM practices that can be pursued by Marriott to create and sustain its goal to be the international "employer of choice."

2. Understand the connection between the goal to be the international "employer of choice" and the "provider of choice."

Procedure

Individual Analysis

1. Before class, generate a list of four actions the organization can take that will directly contribute to their goals regarding making Marriott the international employer of choice in the most efficient manner. Bear in mind that competitive advantage does entail labor costs, so your recommendations must be made in the context of estimated relative costs for the various actions the organization could take. Rank order the four actions.

2. Try to think of international opportunities and policies to which you would be attracted as a recent college graduate. How could Marriott gather information to meet its objectives in the context of cost control, the "provider of choice" emphasis, competitive advantage, and total customer satisfaction in their overseas operations? If your instructor has not assigned a country or region, identify one country where Marriott has a hotel and develop an HRM strategy for attracting and retaining the most qualified staff. Prepare your list of four key HRM actions on Form 2.2.1 and provide a concise written justification for your rank ordering of actions. What competitive-advantage principles did you consider in compiling your priority list? Explain how you would go about researching the problems with expatriate attrition, performance, and difficulties in repatriation as well.

Group Exercise

1. In groups of about six people, exchange your priority lists so that all group members have had an opportunity to review each one. Attempt to reach consensus on a rank-ordered list of four specific actions the Marriott Corporation should take to contribute to its goal of becoming the international "employer of choice" in the context of the "provider of choice" emphasis. How could the HRM systems contribute to the "employer of choice"?

2. A group leader will be designated who will present the consensus view of the group. Discussion should focus on the extent to which the various groups agree on the priority list of Marriott activities.

3. Students should complete the Assessment Questions after group discussion (Form 2.2.2).

*Contributed by Dave Ulrich.

FORM 2.2.1 PRIORITY LIST FOR MARRIOTT'S GLOBAL GOALS

Priority #1:
    Justification:

Priority #2:
    Justification:

Priority #3:
    Justification:

Priority #4:
    Justification:

Explain how you would go about researching the problems with expatriate attrition, performance, and difficulties in repatriation.

1. To what extent do the recommendations made by your group generalize to organizations other than Marriott? If they do not generalize, why not?

2. To what extent are the recommendations unique to international expansions and international operations?

EXERCISE 2.3: INTERNATIONAL ASSIGNMENT PROBLEMS AT XYZ CORPORATION*

Overview

As noted in Chapter 2, international human resource managers encounter a number of selection, retention, and compensation challenges when managing their global workforces. This exercise focuses on some of the personal and organizational factors behind the turnover of expatriates while abroad and upon repatriation. Students are encouraged to critically evaluate some of the options organizations have when developing training, career development, and repatriation programs for international assignees.

Learning Objectives

After completing this exercise, you should be able to

1. Understand some of the basic challenges that international human resource managers encounter when sending executives abroad on long-term international assignments.
2. Understand some of the basic challenges associated with the repatriation of executives from long-term international assignments.
3. Evaluate ways international human resource managers can effectively manage these challenges to reduce turnover.

Procedure

Part A: Individual Analysis

Prior to class, students should read the background information on XYZ Corporation and answer the questions at the end of the case.

Part B: Group Analysis and Class Discussion

1. Students should work in groups of 3 to 4 members to discuss the challenges presented to Sheila Carlson.
2. Students should compare answers to the questions at the end of the case and develop a consensus on a strategy to reduce turnover at XYZ Corporation.
3. A group leader should share the consensus-driven strategy with the class.

Scenario

Sheila Carlson recently took over the position as director of international human resources at XYZ Corporation. XYZ is a large multinational corporation based in the United States with subsidiaries in 20 countries. They sell a wide range of high-end consumer goods and have historically employed an innovative strategy, selling highly innovative products at a premium. They also pay above the market rate and provide an extensive benefit package to attract highly qualified and innovative workers. They employ over 30,000 expatriates currently and recently expanded their operations into the emerging markets of Dubai, China, Russia, and Brazil.

The previous director, John Fleming, had extensive duties managing the international assignment program for XYZ. XYZ sent expatriate managers from the U.S. to foreign subsidiaries for a number of reasons, including filling a skills gap, launching new endeavors, and transferring the company's corporate culture to the local facility. Expatriates were generally sent over for two or three years, but some were sent over for shorter periods when locals could be used to fill the positions and the corporate culture had been transferred to the subsidiaries successfully. Around 20 percent of the assignments ended prematurely, as some expatriates chose to return to the United States before completing their assignments. The majority of the time they stated that their spouses' inability to adjust to the new culture was the primary reason for their early return to the United States.

For three years, John Fleming handled the recruitment, selection, training, development, and compensation of expatriates. To recruit candidates, XYZ typically looked internally first, identifying promising employees with solid job performance records and technical expertise and, of course, a willingness to relocate internationally. About 85 percent of the expatriate population was male, 60 percent married, and 50 percent accompanied on assignments by their children. The female expatriate population was small when compared to the company's large pool of promising female candidates. Females who accepted international assignments were usually divorced, single, and/or without children. Those who declined were often married with working spouses. Once promising employees were identified, John offered them the position along with a generous compensation package, utilizing the balance sheet approach. Typically, potential expatriate managers were offered a base salary of around $250,000 annually, along with the following benefits: cross-cultural and language training, company cars, chauffeurs, housing differentials, cost of living allowances, domestic help, country club memberships, tuition for the international schooling of children, foreign-service premiums in hazardous locations, extended vacation time to learn local customs, and tax equalization. Once the assignment was complete, these additional benefits were necessarily dropped. Cross-cultural and language training were not offered to the spouses, domestic partners, or family of the expatriate managers, as they were deemed unnecessary expenses.

Despite the provision of an extensive benefit package for expatriates, many voiced concerns and some dissatisfaction. Some said that they felt "out of sight, out of mind" while on assignment. This feeling was exacerbated on their return to the United States, when they noted that their workplaces had changed dramatically—different managers, new subordinates and colleagues, new workplace

*Contributed by Stephanie Thomason.

policies. They wished they had maintained more contact with the home office during their assignments. Others complained about the lack of support for trailing spouses in securing visas, finding employment, and funding training and education.

A formal repatriation program had not been established at XYZ, and tracking the career paths of expatriate executives following repatriation had not been formally executed under John's tenure. Over the past year, however, John had received word that a large number of key managers had chosen to leave XYZ soon after they repatriated. In exit interviews, many stated that XYZ's repatriation program was inadequate, as they were placed in lateral positions and the company paid little attention to the international experience they had accumulated on assignment. Some experienced a "reverse culture shock," as their lifestyle in the United States was quite different from the lifestyle to which they had grown accustomed while abroad. A loss of benefits, extended vacation time, and shorter work weeks were difficult to handle for many. A few added that their spouses and children had a difficult time finding friends with similar cross-cultural experience.

When Sheila took over the position, she was told that the international assignments program suffered from some additional flaws. For one, locals in some host countries were complaining that the pay of U.S. expatriate managers was exorbitant, given their own pay. Local managers in India and China were averaging around $9,000 a year, while expatriate managers were averaging $250,000. In many cases, locals felt equally qualified and questioned the policy of sending expatriates for extended periods of time. To resolve this issue, Sheila thought about making compensation changes and/or reducing the lengths of the assignments, but what compensation changes would be appealing to expatriates and locals? XYZ placed great value on its workforce, particularly its expatriate managers, so Sheila didn't want to rock the boat too much.

She also knew she needed to reduce turnover in the expatriate workforce, both during and after the international assignment. She wondered whether XYZ was choosing the right people. Should we only recruit single executives to reduce the family issues? Should we more actively recruit promising female candidates? She had many questions. Sheila knew she would be extremely busy over the next few months and was anxious to get to work.

Name _____ Group _____

1. Why were expatriate managers returning early from their international assignments? What could Sheila do to remedy this situation?

2. What steps should Sheila take to establish a repatriation program?

3. XYZ is currently using a balance sheet approach to compensation. Should the company consider other alternatives, such as localization or cafeteria-style benefits?

Name _____ Group _____

4. What country-level factors should Sheila consider when developing an international compensation plan?

5. Should Sheila consider phasing out the extended benefits over time following repatriation to the United States? If so, how much time?

6. What can Sheila do to reduce the "out of sight, out of mind" perceptions of expatriate managers?

FORM 2.3.1 (*Continued*)

Name _____ Group _____

7. What can Sheila do to reduce the "reverse culture shock" of expatriates and their families?

8. What can Sheila do to address the concerns of locals who feel that expatriates' pay is excessive, given their own pay?

9. What can Sheila do to more actively recruit promising female expatriate candidates?

Sources: Global Relocation Trends Survey, GMAC, 2008. Hofstede, G. (2001). Culture's consequences: *Comparing values, behaviors, institutions;* Thousand Oaks, CA: Sage Publications. Tung, R. (1982) Selection and training procedures of U.S., European, and Japanese multinationals: A model for U.S. firms? *California Management Review,* 25(1), 57–71.

EXERCISE 3.1: *ZIMPFER V. PALM BEACH COUNTY*

Overview

Chapter 3 presented you with a variety of laws affecting HRM. One of those laws was the Age Discrimination in Employment Act (ADEA). The following case requires you to apply your understanding of the ADEA to provide some recommendations for Palm Beach County.

Learning Objectives

After completing this exercise, you should be able to

1. Identify the critical issues associated with age discrimination cases.
2. Provide recommendations for a plaintiff filing an age discrimination case and for the employer in defending EEO practices.
3. Outline policies that organizations should adopt to reduce the probability of age discrimination or claims of age discrimination.

Procedure

Part A: Individual Analysis

Step 1. Read the background material on Palm Beach County provided in Exhibit 3.1.1.

Step 2. Assume the role of the HR director and respond to the issues described below. Answer each question on Form 3.1.1.

Part B: Group Analysis

Step 1. In groups, attempt to reach consensus on the five questions. Each student should review each other student's Form 3.1.1 before the discussion.

Step 2. The instructor will designate one or more representatives to present each group's consensus position.

Exhibit 3.1.1　　　　　**Background Material For Palm Beach County**

Palm Beach County has requested your opinion regarding an alleged violation of the Age Discrimination in Employment Act. Mr. **Bryce Zimpfer,** age 52, has been an employee of the county for 16 years in the employee relations area. The Department of Human Resources posted a job vacancy for employee relations manager (see Exhibit 3.1.2), and Mr. Zimpfer applied for the position. The department filled the position with Mr. **Brad Merriman,** age 33, an outside applicant with less experience in employee relations than Mr. Zimpfer.

After filing a timely complaint with the EEOC, Mr. Zimpfer retained Ms. Lynn Szymoniak, an attorney who is now attempting to reach a settlement with the division's legal staff. In preparation for these negotiations, the attorney asked an industrial psychologist, Dr. **Marcy Josephs,** to examine the résumés of the job applicants and submit a report as to whether Mr. Zimpfer was more qualified for the position than Mr. Merriman. Dr. Josephs submitted a report and concluded that on the basis of her résumé analysis, Mr. Zimpfer was more qualified for the position than Mr. Merriman (see Exhibit 3.1.3).

Exhibit 3.1.2   **Job Vacancy**

Position Description: Employee Relations Manager

NATURE OF WORK

This is professional personnel and labor relations work developing and managing programs and activities to enhance relationships between management and employees; to promote employee satisfaction, well-being, and quality of work life; to develop greater productivity in the workforce; and to achieve sound labor/management working relationships. Work is of a highly responsible nature, requiring considerable independent judgment and decision making. Work is performed under the direction of the Director, Employee Relations and Personnel, and is reviewed through conferences, reports, and results achieved.

EXAMPLES OF WORK

Initiates and manages programs that aim to improve communication and participation. These may be employee orientation meetings, committees, attitude surveys, suggestion boxes, awards programs, newsletters, newspapers, handbooks, benefits brochures, and other media such as posters or payroll stuffers that communicate policies and practices to employees.

Develops programs that monitor and detect employees' dissatisfactions with policies or working conditions. These include adequate complaint and grievance procedures, communication of these to employees, and adequate follow-up with management to resolve problems.

Initiates procedures for reviewing adverse actions taken by supervisors to ensure that such actions are fair. Investigates the facts of the case and determines whether any disciplinary action is appropriate. Directs and trains supervisors in discipline and discharge procedures.

Develops and monitors performance review systems, employee assistance programs, incentive/awards programs, quality circles, and others whose purpose is to motivate workers toward greater productivity.

Initiates programs to improve the quality of supervision, primarily training programs to improve knowledge of effective supervisory practices. May develop and present training programs for supervisors. May write and disseminate supervisors' handbooks or manuals.

Assists the Director in interpreting the provisions of labor contracts to supervisors. May conduct supervisory training sessions in contract administration. Reviews and recommends policy and benefit changes to the Director that are needed to enhance employee/management relations.

Audits and approves personnel actions when applicable to ensure compliance with policies.

May supervise counselors or specialists in carrying out these employee relations activities.

Performs related work as required.

REQUIRED KNOWLEDGE, SKILLS, AND ABILITIES

- Thorough working knowledge of federal and state laws affecting public personnel administration and labor relations.
- Thorough knowledge of merit system principles and policies.
- Knowledge of organization and functions.
- Knowledge of the principles of management and supervision.
- Ability to organize work and supervise professional staff.
- Ability to write and interpret correspondence and reports.
- Ability to speak to a wide variety of groups and present ideas effectively.
- Ability to deal tactfully and persuasively with staff, employees, supervisors, administrators, and union officials.
- Ability to conduct personal and investigative interviews.
- Ability to interpret complex legal cases and documents.
- Ability to conduct independent research and analysis.

MINIMUM ENTRANCE REQUIREMENTS

Graduation from an accredited college or university with major course work in Human Resources Management, Industrial Relations, or Labor Relations, or closely related field; considerable progressively responsible experience in employee or labor relations; or any equivalent combination of related training and experience.

Exhibit 3.1.3

CULLEN & SZYMONIAK, P.A.

ATTORNEYS-AT-LAW

1030 Lake Avenue

Lake Worth, Florida 33460

(561) 585-4666

MARK A. CULLEN   October 25   LYNN E. SZYMONIAK

Marcy M. Josephs, Ph.D.

10475 Northwest Michigan Avenue

Birmingham, Michigan 48275

Dear Dr. Josephs:

I am very pleased that you are available to assist us with the Bryce Zimpfer case. Please find enclosed the following documents:

1. The job announcement, announcing the position of Employee Relations Manager;
2. A job description for the position of Employee Relations Manager;
3. Copies of the newspaper ads announcing this position;
4. A Referral List listing the candidates chosen for an interview for the position of Employee Relations Manager;
5. The resumes, cover letters, and applications of the applicants listed on the referral list; and
6. The application and resume of Bryce Zimpfer.

Based on your review of the above documents, please advise me:

1. Whether Mr. Zimpfer's qualifications equalled or exceeded the qualifications of the applicants selected for an interview; and
2. In particular, whether Bryce Zimpfer's qualifications equalled or exceeded the qualifications of J. Brad Merriman—the candidate ultimately selected for the position. The experts' reports are to be exchanged on this case on November 12. Thank you again for your assistance.

Yours truly,

LYNN E. SZYMONIAK, ESQ.
Enclosures

Exhibit 3.1.4

MARCY MILLER JOSEPHS, PH.D.

INDUSTRIAL PSYCHOLOGIST

10475 NORTHWEST MICHIGAN AVENUE

BIRMINGHAM, MICHIGAN 48275

November 13

Lynn E. Szymoniak, Esq.

Cullen & Szymoniak, P.A.

1030 Lake Avenue

Lake Worth, FL 33460

Dear Ms. Szymoniak:

The purpose of this letter is to respond to your request for expert opinion in matters related to Bryce Zimpfer. In your letter of October 25, you requested that I render an opinion regarding the following:

1. Whether Mr. Zimpfer's qualifications equalled or exceeded the qualifications of the applicants selected for an interview; and

2. In particular, whether Bryce Zimpfer's qualifications equalled or exceeded the qualifications of J. Brad Merriman—the candidate ultimately selected for the position.

In rendering my opinion, I have reviewed the following documents:

1. The job announcement from Palm Beach County announcing the position of Employee Relations Manager;

2. A job description for the position of Employee Relations Manager;

3. Copies of the newspaper ads announcing this position;

4. A Referral List prepared, listing the candidates chosen for an interview for the position of Employee Relations Manager;

5. The resumes, cover letters, and applications of the applicants listed on the referral list; and

6. The application and resume of Bryce Zimpfer.

Based on my review of the aforementioned documents, I have the following opinions:

1. Mr. Zimpfer's qualifications equalled or exceeded the qualifications of several of the applicants selected for an interview; and

2. Mr. Zimpfer's qualifications exceeded the qualifications of Mr. J. Brad Merriman.

Exhibit 3.1.4 (*Continued*)

The following is a description of the procedure I followed to arrive at these opinions:

1. Based on a reading of the job announcement, the job description and the newspaper ad, I constructed three applicant/work requirement matrices for purposes of assessing applicant qualifications with regard to program/activities, work examples, and required knowledge, skills, and abilities (KSAs). See Figures 1, 2, and 3. The first column of each matrix represents the critical work requirements of the job as reflected in the job announcement, and job description.

2. I read each resume and recorded those work requirements with which each applicant had experience or requisite KSAs. I performed this task on three occasions (for the three matrices), each time evaluating the resumes in random order.

3. I performed the identical task described in Step 2 five days later with no reference to the completed matrices from Step 2. Thus, I made two independent evaluations of each of the three work requirement matrices.

4. I examined the discrepancies in the applicant/requirement cells of each matrix from the Step 2 and Step 3 evaluations and reviewed the resumes for purposes of reconciling the disagreements.

   The totals in the last row of Figures 1, 2, and 3 reflect the final evaluations I have made of each candidate after reconciling the few discrepancies between the Step 2 and Step 3 evaluations.

5. The opinions rendered above with regard to Mr. Zimpfer are based on the final evaluations of the three matrices.

The matrix analysis on which I have based my opinions represents a content-valid and objective approach to the evaluation of applicant resumes. It is far superior in terms of validity and reliability to a nonquantitative evaluation procedure which calls for a global evaluation of the applicants in terms of suitability for a multifaceted job.

Sincerely,

Marcy M. Josephs, Ph.D.
MMJ:im

Exhibit 3.1.4 (*Continued*)

FIGURE 1

PROGRAMS AND ACTIVITIES ANALYSIS

Programs/Activities	Zimpfer (52)	Atkinson (28)	Bender (40)	Bledsoe	Merriman (33)	Schwab
Performance appraisals	X	X		X	X	
Employee assistance	X		X			X
Employee benefits	X	X	X	X	X	
Employee publications	X		X			X
Counseling and discipline	X				X	
Grievance procedures	X		X	X	X	
Attendance and leave policy	X			X		
Layoff policy	X				X	
Unemployment compensation						
Contract administration	X	X	X	X	X	
Totals	9	3	5	5	6	2

Ages (where available) are in parentheses.

FIGURE 2

WORK SAMPLE ANALYSIS

Examples of Work	Zimpfer	Atkinson	Bender	Bledsoe	Merriman	Schwab
Employee orientation	X		X			X
Attitude surveys	X		X			
Suggestion boxes					X	
Awards program			X			
Newsletters	X		X			
Handbooks						
Benefits brochure	X	X				
Grievance procedures	X		X	X		
Disciplinary action			X	X		X
Supervisory training	X	X	X	X		X
Interpreting labor contracts	X	X			X	X
Policy and benefits	X	X	X	X	X	X
Audits and approves personal actions				X		
Totals	8	4	8	5	3	5

FIGURE 3

KNOWLEDGE, SKILLS, AND ABILITIES ANALYSIS

	Zimpfer	Atkinson	Bender	Bledsoe	Merriman	Schwab
State and federal law	X	X	X	X	X	X
Ability to speak to variety of groups		X	X	X		X
Conduct interviews	X	X	X		X	X
Interpret complex legal cases and documents						X
Conduct independent research	X		X			X
Totals	3	3	4	2	2	5

FORM 3.1.1

1. Was Mr. Zimpfer a victim of illegal age discrimination according to the ADEA and case law? Explain your position. Cite relevant court cases to justify your position. If you are undecided, explain why.

2. What (if any) further evidence should be ascertained before the county fully understands the legal implications of its actions?

FORM 3.1.1 (*Continued*)

3. Who has the ultimate burden in proving age discrimination in this case and what is that burden?

4. What policies should the county adopt to reduce the possibility of age discrimination suits in the future?

5. Could Palm Beach County be vulnerable to a future ADEA lawsuit using a "disparate impact" theory? If so, who would have the ultimate burden in such a case and what would the burden be? What critical Supreme Court rulings are relevant to these questions?

EXERCISE 3.2: *Goebel et al. v. Frank Clothiers*

Overview

Many Title VII cases involve the presentation of statistical evidence that is alleged to indicate illegal discrimination. The purpose of this exercise is to review the statistical evidence presented and to assess the implications of the data for the organization.

Learning Objectives

After completing this exercise, you should be able to

1. Calculate adverse impact for a selection procedure.
2. Provide recommendations for a plaintiff filing a race discrimination case and for the employer in defending EEO practices.
3. Understand the burden of proof issues related to Title VII cases.

Procedure

Part A: Individual Analysis

Step 1. Read the attached background material on *Goebel et al. v. Frank Clothiers* provided in Exhibit 3.2.1.

Step 2. Assume the role of the HR director and respond to the issues described below. Please prepare concise, written responses for the legal division of Frank Clothiers. Answer the questions presented on Form 3.2.1.

Part B: Group Analysis

Step 3. In groups of about six, members should attempt to reach consensus on issue #1. A rationale for the position should be developed that includes relevant court citations.

Step 4. The instructor will designate one member from each group to present the group position and rationale.

Exhibit 3.2.1   **Goebel et al. vs. Frank Clothiers**

A division of Frank Clothiers had 36 openings for assistant store manager last year (see Exhibit 3.2.2 for the job description). As part of their voluntary affirmative action program, Frank Clothiers filled the vacancies with 16 Black/African Americans, 10 Hispanic/Latinos, and 10 Whites. The selection process was a multiple-hurdle approach that began with an application form and a test of basic verbal and math skills called the **Wonderlic Personnel Test** (WPT; For sample items from the test, go to: http://espn.go.com/page2/s/closer/020228test.html; for more information, go to www.wonderlic.com).

    Applicants who scored 25 (out of 50) or higher on the test were then given an interview by the store managers. Based on the interview performances, the vacancies were filled. The race/ethnicity of those who took the Wonderlic were as follows:

	Black or African American	Hispanic or Latino	White
Test Scores			
Number scoring 25 or higher	25	28	74
Number scoring less than 25	26	20	29
Totals	51	48	103

    Dennis Goebel, one of the African-American applicants who scored 19 on the test, filed suit on behalf of all Black/African-American applicants who scored less than 25. Mr. Goebel claimed race discrimination based on Title VII of the Civil Rights Act of 1964. Frank Clothiers has argued that more African-Americans (i.e., 16) were actually hired than any other racial/ethnic category. Thus, the company asserts, there is obviously no racial discrimination in the selection process.

Exhibit 3.2.2   **Assistant Manager Job Description (Frank Clothiers)**

SUMMARY

Under general direction from the store manager, provides some administrative and functional supervision of a store unit, including inventory control, sales and returns, vendor relations, cash management, and related reporting. May supervise regular and/or temporary customer service and stock management staff.

Duties and Responsibilities:

1. Assists in managing the operation of a store unit, including purchasing of supplies and books, special orders, receiving and shipping, and return of overstocked or defective merchandise.
2. Supervises personnel, which typically includes recommendations for hiring, firing, performance evaluation, training, work allocation, and problem resolution.
3. Prepares drafts of purchase requisitions and related paperwork, including annual budgets and accounts payable; monitors expenditures and revenue; makes periodic scheduled and ad hoc reports of store activity.
4. Through the store manager, helps to develop and control department budgets; researches and compiles administrative reports for personnel, payroll, and trade organization surveys for cost estimation and budget review.
5. Helps to coordinate some department marketing activities.
6. Assists in year-end inventory, utilizing computer to check for theft and shrinkage.
7. May oversee or manage the operation of auxiliary services such as vending machines or student service areas.
8. Uses systems and processes to establish and maintain records for the operating unit.
9. Assists with the implementation of policies and procedures consistent with those of the organization to ensure efficient and safe operation of the unit.
10. Performs miscellaneous job-related duties as assigned.

Minimum Job Requirements:
High school diploma or GED.

Knowledge, Skills, and Abilities Required:

- Ability to gather data, compile information, and prepare reports.
- Skill in the use of personal computers and related software applications.
- Ability to prepare routine administrative paperwork.
- Ability to communicate effectively, both orally and in writing.
- Ability to supervise and train employees, to include organizing, prioritizing, and scheduling work assignments.
- Skill in examining and re-engineering operations and procedures, formulating policy, and developing and implementing new strategies and procedures.
- Ability to receive, stock, and/or deliver goods.
- Employee development and performance management skills.
- Skill in the use of computers, preferably in a PC, Windows-based operating environment.
- Skill in budget preparation and fiscal management.
- Ability to foster a cooperative work environment.
- Knowledge of procurement rules and regulations.
- Knowledge of retail advertising, sales promotion, and/or visual merchandising techniques.
- Strong interpersonal and communication skills and the ability to work effectively with a wide range of constituencies in a diverse community.
- Ability to develop and maintain recordkeeping systems and procedures.
- Knowledge of retail floor merchandising and stock control procedures.

Working Conditions and Physical Effort:

- Work is normally performed in a typical interior/office work environment.
- No or very limited physical effort required.
- No or very limited exposure to physical risk.

FORM 3.2.1

1. Were Mr. Goebel and other African-American applicants victims of racial discrimination because of the hiring policies of Frank Clothiers? Explain your position and cite all relevant **Supreme Court** decisions. If you cannot take a definitive position, explain what specific information you require to be able to take a position.

2. Is there evidence of disparate impact against African Americans in the decisions that were made? On what basis did you arrive at this position? Illustrate how the "80 percent rule" can be used with the data in Exhibit 3.2.1 and whether there was a violation of this rule.

3. If disparate impact is evident, what steps should the defendant take next? Provide specific recommendations.

Name _____   Group _____

4. An associate of the Personnel Department proposes that Frank should continue to use the Wonderlic but that the test scores should be interpreted by the racial/ethnic classification of the test taker. For example, raw scores on the Wonderlic would be converted to percentages *within ethnic classification*. With such a procedure, African-Americans taking the test who receive the exact raw score as whites would receive a higher percentage score on the exam because of the "within-ethnic" interpretation. He argues that this procedure would enable Frank to continue using a valid and useful test while avoiding adverse impact. (Mr. Goebel would have advanced to the interview with this approach.) Take a position on this recommendation.

5. Gordon Howe, a white male, scored 48 on the WPT and was interviewed but not selected. Does Mr. Howe have a possible Title VII lawsuit? Could whites who were interviewed but not hired file a Title VII class-action lawsuit?

6. Can "disparate impact" theory be used in cases involving subjective selection processes like interviews? What Supreme Court case supports your position?

EXERCISE 3.3: A CASE OF ILLEGAL SEXUAL HARASSMENT?*

Overview

It is critical that employers and employees be very familiar with how sexual harassment is defined in the courts and what situations constitute illegal behavior. This exercise challenges you to think about some of these issues.

Learning Objectives

After completing this exercise, you should be able to

1. Define what is meant by illegal sexual harassment.
2. Understand the key provisions of a sexual harassment policy.
3. Outline the policies the organization should adopt to prevent charges of sexual harassment in the future.

Procedure

Part A: Individual Analysis

Step 1. Read the attached background material in Exhibits 3.3.1 and 3.3.2. You have been hired as a consultant to render opinions on the legal standing of Bowman, Idaho, and of Putnam County. Read each exhibit carefully.

Step 2. Answer the questions that apply to each case. Answer each question on Form 3.3.1. Questions 3 and 4 apply to both cases.

Part B: Group Analysis

Step 1. In groups of about six people, students shall attempt to reach consensus on the four questions. Each student should review each other student's Form 3.3.1 prior to the discussion.

Step 2. The instructor will designate one or more representatives to present each group and consensus position.

Exhibit 3.3.1   **Complaint of Ms. Smith**

Ms. **Kathleen Smith** first worked part-time as a park recreation counselor for the city of Bowman, Idaho. Her immediate supervisor was **Jack McKenna**. She has brought an action against Mr. McKenna and the city alleging that the city and Mr. McKenna created a "hostile working atmosphere" by subjecting Ms. Smith to repeated and uninvited requests for dates and (later) lewd remarks and offensive speech. Ms. Smith had never met or spoken with the superintendent of recreation for the city.

Ms. Smith never complained about her treatment to higher management while employed and did not file a formal complaint under the city's sexual harassment policy guidelines because she feared retaliation. She did complain to a co-worker who also witnessed some of the incidents. The co-worker informed Mr. **Al Kaline**, the Bowman HR manager. However, no action was taken by the city since, Mr. Kaline argues, pursuant to the city's sexual harassment guidelines, no formal complaint was made.

The city included the antidiscrimination/harassment policy in its employee handbook, which was given to all employees. Each employee signed a document that the handbook was received. In addition, each employee was required to complete an online sexual harassment course as a condition of employment.

The guidelines were clear on the procedure to follow if one felt that he or she had been a victim of discrimination and/or sexual harassment. The guidelines stipulated that all formal claims of harassment must be submitted to the employee's immediate supervisor with Mr. Kaline informed at the same time. The complaint must be filed within six months of the alleged events.

Ms. Smith claimed that Mr. McKenna had asked her out on dates on numerous occasions. The propositions were made in the employee lounge while they were alone and, on other occasions, in front of other Bowman employees. Mr. McKenna also liked to tell "off color" jokes to his subordinates. He would later maintain that Ms. Smith dressed in a "provocative" manner and she should therefore expect "to be asked out."

In the period in which the alleged sexual harassment took place, the following personnel actions were taken in the recreational unit:

Percent Salary Increases for the Year

All counselors 5.8% (average)
Ms. Smith 8.5%

Christmas Bonuses

All counselors $250 (average)
Ms. Smith $500

Promotions to Head Counselor

Total: 4 (including Ms. Smith)

When questioned about his knowledge of events, Mr. Kaline stated that "there was clearly no evidence that refusal to submit to sexual advances was related to any negative action against Ms. Smith. She is a good employee and is recognized as such through merit increases, bonuses, and promotions. Also, Ms. Smith did not follow the city's policy on filing harassment complaints. Thus, no further action should (or could) be taken."

---

*Contributed by Jenrifer Collins.

Exhibit 3.3.2

Mr. **Joseph Nixon** worked as an aide to Putnam County Commissioner **Diane Richards**. Mr. Nixon reported directly to Commissioner Richards. Mr. Nixon, along with another commissioner's aide, **Michael Whitman**, filed a claim of sexual harassment against Commissioner Richards and the Putnam County Board of County Commissioners.

According to Mr. Nixon and Mr. Whitman, Commissioner Richards pressured them into sexual relations, threatening to have them fired if they did not agree. Over a period of 18 months, Mr. Nixon and Mr. Whitman on separate occasions engaged in sexual activities with Commissioner Richards. During this period, Mr. Nixon traveled with Commissioner Richards to several commission-related meetings. Mr. Nixon alleges that Commissioner Richards insisted that they share hotel accommodations while on these trips. Hotel documentation substantiates this claim. Additionally, Mr. Nixon alleges that Commissioner Richards invited him to her home several times while her husband and family were absent.

Furthermore, Mr. Nixon and Mr. Whitman were involved in a romantic relationship with each other. Mr. Nixon alleges that Commissioner Richards demanded that he end his relationship with Mr. Whitman or he would be fired. According to Mr. Nixon, when he refused to end the relationship, Commissioner Richards terminated him. It is the policy of Putnam County Board of County Commission that commission aides serve at the pleasure of the appointing commissioner. Commissioner Richards claims that Mr. Nixon was terminated because of poor job performance and leaving the work area for hours without permission.

It should also be noted that prior to Mr. Nixon's tenure with the Putnam County Board of County Commissioners, Mr. Nixon and Commissioner Richards were involved in a romantic relationship. Initially, Commissioner Richards denied having any sexual relationship with either of the plaintiffs. However, six months after the charges were filed Commissioner Richards admitted having a romantic relationship with Mr. Nixon before he was hired and during his tenure as a commission aide. She also admitted having a sexual relationship with Mr. Whitman. However, Commissioner Richards claims that in both instances, the relationships were agreed to by the men.

Mr. Nixon and Mr. Whitman further allege that the county administrator and other commission employees were aware of the relationships. While the county has a sexual harassment policy, there is no formal training provided to commission employees or commissioners. The policy is included in the New Employee Handbook which is given to every new employee.

FORM 3.3.1

1. Does the alleged sexual harassment in Bowman constitute a violation of Title VII? Explain your answer. If you are not ready to take a definitive position, explain what information you require. What court cases are relevant here?

2. Do the alleged charges brought against Putnam County constitute a violation of Title VII? Is the County liable? Explain your answer. What changes, if any, should the County make to their sexual harassment policy?

3. Do Nixon and Whitman have legitimate discrimination claims? Explain your answer.

4. For both cases: Could (or should) the organizations institute a no-dating policy that would explicitly prohibit dating between supervisors and subordinates? Is such a policy legal?

5. In both cases, what if the plaintiffs were contingent or leased employees? Would the City and County still be liable for Title VII violations?

EXERCISE 3.4: REVERSE DISCRIMINATION OR LEGAL AFFIRMATIVE ACTION?

Overview

Chapter 3 presents considerable detail on Title VII of the Civil Rights Act and the evolution of affirmative action programs. The purpose of this exercise is to introduce some of the complexities and ramifications of affirmative action programs. Two real cases are described that involve allegations of reverse discrimination.

Objective

After completing the exercise, you should be able to

1. Understand the variables that must be considered when determining the legality of affirmative action programs.
2. Know the conditions under which the sex (or race) of an employee may be taken into consideration for personnel decisions.

Procedure

Part A: Individual Analysis

Each student should study the cases presented in Exhibits 3.4.1 and 3.4.2 and take positions as required. First, read Exhibit 3.4.1. Then complete the assessment questions presented on Form 3.4.1. Next, read Exhibit 3.4.2 and complete Form 3.4.2.

Part B: Group Analysis

Step 1. In groups of no more than six, students should review each student's completed forms and then attempt to reach consensus on a position. Once the consensus is reached, each group should adopt a group position. One group member will be asked to present the group's position to the rest of the class.

Step 2. After completing step 1, each student should complete a self- and peer evaluation form for all group members.

Exhibit 3.4.1 Jones v. Purple Cabs

After four tough years working on the road for the Purple Cabs, **Diane Harrison** applied for a less-strenuous desk job as a road dispatcher. At that time not one of the California company's 238 skilled positions was held by a woman. Harrison knew, however, that two years earlier, the company had enacted a voluntary affirmative-action policy designed to correct that imbalance.

Harrison has 18 years' clerical experience and four years as a road maintenance worker. Another candidate for the position, **Edward Jones**, had 11 years as a road yard clerk (clerical position) and four years as a road maintenance worker. He also had previous experience as a dispatcher in private employment.

The position of road dispatcher required four years of dispatcher or road maintenance work experience with the county. Twelve employees applied for the job. Nine were judged to be minimally qualified and interviewed by a two-person board. Seven of the applicants scored about 70 and were certified as eligible for selection. Jones scored 77, and Harrison ranked next with 73. At a second interview, three supervisors recommended that Jones be promoted. At the second interview, one male panel member described Harrison as a rabble-rousing, "skirt-wearing" troublemaker.

The local supervisor picked Jones, but the company's affirmative-action coordinator recommended Harrison. When she got the job, Jones got a lawyer. Jones claimed he was a victim of reverse discrimination and filed suit under Title VII of the 1964 Civil Rights Act.

POSITIONS

A. The Purple Cab plan is consistent with Title VII's purpose of eliminating the effects of past employment discrimination. Given the obvious imbalance in the skilled craft division and given the commitment to eliminating such imbalances, it was appropriate to consider as one fact the sex of Ms. Harrison in making its decision. Thus, the Court should decide in favor of Purple Cabs.

B. To decide against Mr. Jones to complete the process of converting Title VII from a guarantee that race or sex will not be the basis for employment determinations, to a guarantee that it often will. Ever so subtly, we effectively replace the goal of a discrimination-free society with the quite incompatible goal of proportionate representation by race and by sex in the workplace. Thus, the court should decide in favor of Mr. Jones.

FORM 3.4.1

1. What position do you support (A or B)? What is the basis for your answer (e.g., a court decision, the language of Title VII, EEOC Guidelines)? Be specific.

2. Given the actual wording in section 703j of Title VII (see Figure 3-3 in Chapter 3 of the text), which seems to explicitly prohibit preferential treatment, how can an organization show preference to women as in this case? Doesn't position B seem more compatible with Section 703j?

3. To what extent did you take into consideration the great disparity in the number of male and female dispatchers? What conditions are necessary for an organization to show preferential treatment based on a protected class characteristic?

4. To what extent did you consider the qualifications of the candidates in taking your position? Did they have to be equally qualified? What if Jones had an interview score that was 10 points higher than Harrison?

5. Would you have a different opinion in this case if the defendant was a public agency in the state of California? Could the Michigan State Police take race or gender into consideration after defining a pool of qualified candidates as a part of their voluntary affirmative action programs? Explain your answers.

Exhibit 3.4.2   **Taxman v. Piscataway Township**

The Board of Education of the Township of Piscataway, New Jersey, developed an affirmative action policy applicable to employment decisions. The board's affirmative action program, (AAP) a 52-page document, was originally adopted in response to a regulation promulgated by the New Jersey State Board of Education. That regulation directed local school boards to adopt "affirmative action programs" to address employment as well as school and classroom practices and to ensure equal opportunity to all persons regardless of race, color, creed, religion, sex, or national origin. The board also adopted a one-page "policy" entitled "Affirmative Action–Employment Practices." It is not clear from the record whether the policy superseded or simply added to the program, nor does it matter for purposes of this appeal.

The AAP document states that the purpose of the program is "to provide equal educational opportunity for students and equal employment opportunity for employees and prospective employees" and "to make a concentrated effort to attract… minority personnel for all positions so that their qualifications can be evaluated along with other candidates." The "policy" document states that its purpose is to "ensure [ ] equal employment opportunity… and prohibit [ ] discrimination in employment because of [, inter alia,] race…"

The operative language regarding the means by which affirmative action goals are to be furthered is identical in the two documents. "In all cases, the most qualified candidate will be recommended for appointment. However, when candidates appear to be of equal qualification, candidates meeting the criteria of the affirmative action program will be recommended." The phrase "candidates meeting the criteria of the affirmative action program" refers to members of racial, national origin, or gender groups identified as minorities for statistical reporting purposes by the New Jersey State Department of Education, including African Americans. The "policy" document also clarifies that the affirmative action program applies to "every aspect of employment including… layoffs…"

The board's affirmative action policy did not have "any remedial purpose"; it was not adopted "with the intention of remedying the results of any prior discrimination or identified underrepresentation of minorities within the Piscataway Public School System." At all relevant times, African-American teachers were neither "underrepresented" nor "underutilized" in the Piscataway School District workforce. Indeed, statistics showed that the percentage of African-American employees in the job category that included teachers exceeded the percentage of African-Americans in the available workforce.

The board accepted a recommendation from the superintendent of schools to reduce the teaching staff in the Business Department at Piscataway High School by one. At that time, two of the teachers in the department were of equal seniority, both having begun their employment with the board on the same day nine years earlier. One of those teachers was plaintiff Sharon Taxman, who is white, and the other was Debra Williams, who is African-American. Williams was the only minority teacher among the faculty of the Business Department.

Decisions regarding layoffs by New Jersey school boards are highly circumscribed by state law; nontenured faculty must be laid off first, and layoffs among tenured teachers in the affected subject area or grade level must proceed in reverse order of seniority. Seniority for this purpose is calculated according to specific guidelines set by state law. Thus, local boards lack discretion to choose between employees for layoff, except in the rare instance of a tie in seniority between the two or more employees eligible to fill the last remaining position.

The board determined that it was facing just such a rare circumstance in deciding between Taxman and Williams. In prior decisions involving the layoff of employees with equal seniority, the Board has broken the tie through "a random process which included drawing numbers out of a container, drawing lots, or having a lottery." In none of those instances, however, had the employees involved been of different races.

In light of the unique posture of the layoff decision, Superintendent of Schools Burton Edelchick recommended to the board that the affirmative action plan be invoked in order to determine which teacher to retain. Superintendent Edelchick made this recommendation "because he believed Ms. Williams and Ms. Taxman were tied in seniority, were equally qualified, and because Ms. Williams was the only African-American teacher in the Business Education Department."

While the Board recognized that it was not bound to apply the affirmative action policy, it made a discretionary decision to invoke the policy to break the tie between Williams and Taxman.

As a result, the Board "voted to terminate the employment of Sharon Taxman, effective June 30…"

At her deposition, Paula Van Riper, the board's vice president at the time of the layoff, described the board's decision-making process. According to Van Riper, after the board recognized that Taxman and Williams were of equal seniority, it assessed their classroom performance, evaluations, volunteerism, and certifications and determined that they were "two teachers of equal ability" and "equal qualifications."

At his deposition Theodore H. Kruse, the board's president, explained his vote to apply the affirmative action policy as follows:

A. Basically I think because I had been aware that the student body and the community which is our responsibility, the schools of the community, is really quite diverse and there—I have a general feeling during my tenure on the board that it was valuable for the students to see in the various employment roles a wide range of background, and that it was also valuable to the workforce and in particular to the teaching staff that they have—they see that in each other.

Asked to articulate the "educational objective" served by retaining Williams rather than Taxman, Kruse stated:

A. In my own personal perspective I believe by retaining Ms. Williams it was sending a very clear message that we feel that our staff should be culturally diverse, our student population is culturally diverse and there is a distinct advantage to students, to all students, to be made—come into contact with people of different cultures, different background, so that they are more aware, more tolerant, more accepting, more understanding of people of all background.

Q. What do you mean by the phrase you used, culturally diverse?

A. Someone other than—different than yourself. And we have, our student population and our community has people of all different background, ethnic background, religious background, cultural background, and it's important that our school district encourage awareness and acceptance and tolerance and, therefore, I personally think it's important that our staff reflect that too.

Following the board's decision, Taxman filed a charge of employment discrimination with the Equal Employment Opportunity Commission. Attempts at conciliation were unsuccessful, and the United States filed suit under Title VII against the board in the United States District Court for the District of New Jersey. Taxman intervened, asserting claims under both Title VII and the New Jersey Law Against Discrimination.

Following discovery, the board moved for summary judgment and the United States and Taxman cross-moved for partial summary judgment only as to liability. The district court denied the board's motion and granted partial summary judgment to the United States and Taxman, holding the board liable under both statutes for discrimination on the basis of race. *United States v. Board of Educ. of Township Piscataway* 832 F.Supp. 836, 851 (D.N.J.1993).

A trial proceeded on the issue of damages. By this time, Taxman had been rehired by the board and thus her reinstatement was not an issue. The court awarded Taxman damages in the amount of $134,014.62 for back pay, fringe benefits, and prejudgment interest under Title VII. A jury awarded an additional $10,000 for emotional suffering under the NJLAD. The district court denied the United States' request for a broadly worded injunction against future discrimination, finding that there was no likelihood that the conduct at issue would recur, but it did order the board to give Taxman full seniority reflecting continuous employment. Additionally, the court dismissed Taxman's claim for punitive damages under the NJLAD.

Title VII makes it unlawful for an employer "to discriminate against any individual with respect to his compensation, terms, conditions, or privileges of employment" or "to limit, segregate, or classify his employees… in any way which would deprive or tend to deprive any individual of employment opportunities or otherwise affect his status as an employee" on the basis of "race, color, religion, sex, or national origin." [FN6] 42 U.S.C. 2000e-2(a). For a time, the Supreme Court construed this language as absolutely prohibiting discrimination in employment, neither requiring nor permitting any preference for any group.

The Supreme Court interpreted the statute's "antidiscriminatory strategy" in a "fundamentally different way," holding in the seminal case of ***United Steelworkers v. Weber***, 443 U.S. 193, 99 S.Ct. 2721

Exhibit 3.4.2 (*Continued***)**

that Title VII's prohibition against racial discrimination does not condemn all voluntary race-conscious affirmative action plans. In *Weber,* the court considered a plan implemented by Kaiser Aluminum & Chemical Corporation. Prior to 1974, Kaiser hired as craftworkers only those with prior craft experience. Because they had long been excluded from craft unions, African-Americans were unable to present the credentials required for craft positions. Moreover, Kaiser's hiring practices, although not admittedly discriminatory with regard to minorities, were questionable. As a consequence, while the local labor force was about 39 percent African-American, Kaiser's labor force was less than 15 percent African-American and its crafts workforce was less than 2 percent African-American. In 1974, Kaiser entered into a collective bargaining agreement that contained an affirmative action plan. The plan reserved 50 percent of the openings in an in-plant craft-training program for African-American employees until the percentage of African-American craft-workers in the plant reached a level commensurate with the percentage of African-Americans in the local labor force. During the first year of the plan's operation, 13 craft-trainees were selected, seven of whom were African-American and six of whom were white.

Thereafter, Brian Weber, a white production worker, filed a class-action suit, alleging that the plan unlawfully discriminated against white employees under Title VII. The plaintiffs argued that it necessarily followed that the Kaiser plan, which resulted in junior African-American employees receiving craft training in preference to senior white employees, violated Title VII. The district court agreed and entered a judgment in favor of the plaintiffs; the Court of Appeals for the Fifth Circuit affirmed.

The Supreme Court, however, reversed, noting initially that although the plaintiffs' argument was not "without force," it disregarded "the significance of the fact that the Kaiser-USWA plan was an affirmative action plan voluntarily adopted by private parties to eliminate traditional patterns of racial segregation." The Court then embarked upon an exhaustive review of Title VII's legislative history and identified Congress's concerns in enacting Title VII's prohibition against discrimination—the deplorable status of African-Americans in the nation's economy, racial injustice, and the need to open employment opportunities for African-Americans in traditionally closed occupations. Against this background, the court concluded that Congress could not have intended to prohibit private employers from implementing programs directed toward the very goal of Title VII—the eradication of discrimination and its effects from the workplace:

It would be ironic indeed if a law triggered by a nation's concern over centuries of racial injustice and intended to

improve the lot of those who had "been excluded from the American dream for so long," 110 Cong. Rec. 6552 (1964) (remarks of Minnesota Senator Hubert Humphrey), constituted the first legislative prohibition of all voluntary, private, race-conscious efforts to abolish traditional patterns of racial segregation and hierarchy.

The court found support for its conclusion in the language and legislative history of section 2000e-2(j) of Title VII, which expressly provides that nothing in the act requires employers to grant racial preferences. According to the Court, the opponents of Title VII had raised two arguments: the act would be construed to impose obligations upon employers to integrate their workforces through preferential treatment of minorities, and even without being obligated to do so, employers with racially imbalanced workforces would grant racial preferences. Since Congress addressed only the first objection and did not specifically prohibit affirmative action efforts, the Court inferred that Congress did not intend that Title VII forbid all voluntary race-conscious preferences. The court further reasoned that since Congress also intended "to avoid undue federal regulation of private businesses," a prohibition against all voluntary affirmative action would disserve this end by "augment[ing] the power of the Federal Government and diminish[ing] traditional management prerogatives…"

The court then turned to the Kaiser plan in order to determine whether it fell on the "permissible" side of the "line of demarcation between permissible and impermissible affirmative action plans." The Court upheld the Kaiser plan because its purpose "mirror[ed] those of the statute" and it did not "unnecessarily trammel the interests of the [nonminority] employees":

The purposes of the plan mirror those of the statute. Both were designed to break down old patterns of racial segregation and hierarchy. Both were structured to "open employment opportunities for Negroes in occupations which have been traditionally closed to them." 110 Cong. Rec. 6548 (1964) (remarks of Sen. Humphrey).

At the same time, the plan does not "unnecessarily trammel" the interests of the white employees. The plan does not require the discharge of white workers and their replacement with new black hires. Nor does the plan create an absolute bar to the advancement of white employees; half of those trained in the program will be white. Moreover, the plan is a temporary measure; it is not intended to maintain racial balance, but simply to eliminate a manifest racial imbalance.

FORM 3.4.2

1. Was Ms. Taxman a victim of illegal discrimination under Title VII? Explain your answer, citing pertinent cases and discussion.

2. What does the term "manifest imbalance" mean to you? Is there "manifest imbalance" in this case?

3. What is the most important Supreme Court case that justifies your position?

4. If you decided for Ms. Taxman, what do you propose as the remedy? If Ms. Taxman had been awarded the job, would Ms. Williams have had redress through Title VII? Explain your answer, citing any applicable case law.

5. Should universities be allowed to take race into consideration in admissions decisions in order to foster a more diverse student body? What is the current state of the law regarding this issue?

EXERCISE 3.5: *JOSEPH GARCIA V. HOOTERS, CAMERON V. LAVEILLE MAISON*

Overview

What is allowable as a BFOQ? The Supreme Court has said that BFOQs are allowable if they are "reasonably necessary to the normal operation of that particular business." What if a business has a competitive strategy that appeals to a particular segment of the population that has certain strong preferences for services to be provided by the establishment? (Recall the Chapter 3 discussion of the *Pan Am v. Diaz* Supreme Court case.) The 1991 decision in *UAW v. Johnson Controls* stated that the exception to Title VII in the form of BFOQs applies only to policies that involve the "essence of the business." The purpose of this exercise is to present two cases with characteristics that are hardly unique for the industry. We will ask you to take a position as to the legality of a company policy that the company claims falls under the "business essence" or BFOQ exception to Title VII.

Learning Objectives

After completing this exercise, the student should be able to

1. Understand the conditions under which a BFOQ or an "essence of the business" argument is a legal defense.

2. Know the role of customer preference in Title VII cases.

3. Consider the implications of the cases for related policies.

Procedure

Step 1. Prior to class, read the case histories in Exhibit 3.5.1 and answer the questions on Form 3.5.1.

Step 2. In groups of about six people, each student should review the other group members' responses and then attempt to reach group consensus on each of the questions. One person should be designated as the group spokesperson, and the group position should be presented.

Exhibit 3.5.1

JOSEPH GARCIA V. HOOTERS

Hooters Restaurants had a competitive strategy of appealing to the young, affluent male population through a number of features. Large-screen television for sports events, happy hours, sports celebrity events, and very attractive waitresses were part of their strategy. Joseph Garcia was a waiter from Chicago who had worked at similar restaurants for over 10 years. He heard from a friend that Hooters was hiring. However, he was told he would have to apply in person. When he showed up at one of the establishments, he was told that they in fact were not hiring. He learned a few weeks later that an attractive female had been hired at the same restaurant. He filed a timely claim with the EEOC.

CAROL CAMERON V. LAVEILLE MAISON

LaVeille Maison is a five-star restaurant in East Cupcake, Michigan. Carol Cameron, a waitress with over 10 years' experience in "upscale" restaurants and an esoteric knowledge of wine, applied for a job at LaVeille Maison at a period when the restaurant was hiring waiters in preparation for the heavy winter season. The restaurant only employs waiters and makes the argument that five-star French restaurants traditionally employ only waiters. After learning that LaVeille Maison had hired three new waiters, Ms. Cameron filed a timely Title VII lawsuit against the restaurant.

FORM 3.5.1

1. Was Mr. Garcia a victim of illegal sex discrimination? Explain your answer in some detail based on your understanding of BFOQs.

2. Was Ms. Cameron a victim of sex discrimination?

FORM 3.5.1 (*Continued*)

3. In principle, do you see these cases as the same in terms of your interpretation of legal BFOQs, business necessity, "essence of the business," or "job relatedness"?

4. What if, in doing a background check on Ms. Cameron, it is discovered that Ms. Cameron had quit a previous employer complaining that she had developed carpal tunnel syndrome. Could management use this information and reject Ms. Cameron on this basis?

EXERCISE 3.6: HIRING A BANK TELLER*

Overview

Chapter 3 discusses the numerous laws that can affect the process of selecting employees. The purpose of Exercise 3.6 is to consider these laws in the context of a hiring situation.

Learning Objectives

After completing the exercise, you should be able to

1. Recognize the relevance of particular laws for specific situations.
2. Consider the major provisions and key concepts of those laws as they apply to a specific situation.

Procedure

Part A: Individual Analysis

Prior to class, read Chapter 3 and the scenario below and complete Form 3.6.1.

Part B: Group Analysis and Class Discussion

In groups of about six, students should review each member's Form 3.6.1 and then attempt to reach consensus on key questions from the form as designated by the instructor. Class discussion will focus on key laws and provisions.

Scenario

Applicant Background

Anna has multiple sclerosis. Up until 10 months ago she was able to walk with the aid of a cane. Now she uses a wheelchair to get about, but she can stand, unassisted, for very short periods of time. She has recent work experience as a cashier in a local cafeteria, which went out of business a few weeks ago. She worked part time at the cafeteria for six years and was highly regarded by the manager and staff as a pleasant, hard-working person. Anna left when the establishment closed. Before that, she worked part time as a concierge in a local hotel for five years. She speaks fluent English and Spanish. Her credit rating and background are impeccable, and she has excellent references.

Anna answered the following advertisement in her local newspaper for the position of bank teller with a very large, well-known bank in the southeast:

TELLER (P/T)

The ideal candidate must be available to work a flexible schedule. Good communication skills, positive customer service attitude, and professional manner a must. Qualified candidates must have min. 1 year recent cash handling experience; 6 months teller experience preferred. Bilingual (Eng/Span) preferred. We offer a pleasant working environment, competitive salary. Call Monday after 9:00 A.M.

*Contributed by Lori Spina.

Anna called and, after answering a few basic questions about her previous work experience, spoke with Dave, the location manager. He asked her some additional questions about money handling. Dave asked her to come in for an interview.

Bank Background

This bank is a small branch office in a community of 25,000 people. The manager likes to maintain a pool of five tellers, and Dave attempts to schedule them around peak times to best serve the customers. Competition is fierce with five other banks to serve the community. High customer service is a driving force in the organization. The bank's success depends on quality service delivery. The manager prides himself on leading the competition in customer service. Tellers perform a variety of tasks at their stations and also cover the drive-thru window. The drive-thru window station is two steps below the rest of the floor. Historically, the manager has had difficulty finding qualified people who are bilingual to fill this vacancy.

The Interview

Anna arrives for her appointment 15 minutes early. She is anxious to make a good impression and needs to get back into the workforce. She has many ideas and thoughts about how to perform the job.

Dave is under pressure to fill this slot. He has not been impressed by the previous applicants. He is impressed with Anna's résumé and her references. Her work experience appears to be more than adequate. Dave does not know that Anna uses a wheelchair, and he has never interviewed a disabled person. Dave's secretary escorts Anna into Dave's office.

Dave: So, you must be Anna. I'm Dave, the branch manager. Come on in.

Anna: Thank you. I hope I'm not too early.

Dave: No, not at all. Let's begin the interview, shall we? You indicated on the phone that your previous job was that of a cashier in a cafeteria, correct?

Anna: Yes, that's right. I usually worked the peak shift from 8:00 A.M. until 2:00 P.M. on my designated days. In addition to the usual register duties, such as keeping track of my cash balance, I also was responsible for the writing and placement of the daily specials menu boards, iced beverage stock count, and the general care and cleanliness of the condiments/register area.

Dave: Tell me, Anna, how did you manage to work at a register for six hours?

Anna: Well, I usually took a break after the coffee break crowd left but before the lunch crowd arrived. I have multiple sclerosis, but I have no fatigue issues.

Dave: That's not exactly what I meant. I don't know much about multiple sclerosis. Does it run in your family? (Anna looks surprised but does not respond to the question.) I mean, well, let's talk about the job here as teller. All tellers here have to work their own stations and share the drive-thru station. They don't only sit or stand at their stations. They also have to run for signature cards and research items. When a customer arrives at the drive-thru, whichever teller is free first automatically moves to that station. During peak times it gets pretty hectic behind the counter. It's hard to imagine your being able to keep up with all of this. We cannot afford to slow the pace.

Anna: If you are asking me how I would be able to perform under the situation you described, I have some ideas about how I can work both stations. I thought about this after we scheduled the interview, and I think that there are some practical ways to work it.

Dave: I'm glad that you've thought about this ahead of time. That is quite commendable. But on to another demand of the job. We are very proud of our customer service record. In fact, we enjoy the best customer service reputation in the community. We deliver quality work in a timely manner. We know that our customers don't want to waste time waiting in line. So we strive to meet their needs. And we deliver what they have come to expect, great service. That's why we schedule for peak times, even though the hours are somewhat irregular for employees. How do you see yourself fitting into our environment?

Anna: I understand the flexible schedule and don't mind working that way. In fact, after we spoke on the phone to set up this interview, I spoke with a teller at my bank so as to understand what you meant in the ad by a flexible schedule. Also, I don't believe that there was ever a complaint about the quality of my work or my not being able to keep up with the work flow when I worked at the cafeteria. I am very quick with transactions, and I enjoy meeting the customers. I got to know most of the regulars pretty well at the cafeteria.

Dave: Well, I think this about wraps up the questions that I have. Is there anything else that I can answer for you before we finish up?

Anna: Do you want to know about my ideas for doing the job?

Dave: I think that might be a bit premature. We can talk about that if you are one of the finalists for the job. Anything else?

Anna: No, I think I am about finished here. Thanks for the appointment.

Dave: Certainly, we will let you know of our decision soon. Good-bye.

Anna: Good-bye.

Dave is in a quandary. He realizes that Anna is qualified for the position but he does not know how to approach the issue of her using a wheelchair. No other candidate to date is as experienced with money handling and has the language skills as she. The main office wants Dave to make a decision within the next two to three days. The prospects for the remaining interviews do not look promising. Dave decides to interview everyone who has applied before making a decision.

Over the next two days Dave talks to two of his best friends. They are professionals in their fields and are managers as well. Dave still has not interviewed anyone as highly qualified as Anna but has reservations about hiring her. Dave's friend Ben is in real estate and owns a small firm. Ben advises Dave to follow his gut feeling and not take the risk. Carl, an insurance actuary, advises Dave that Anna's MS could get much worse. Carl's main point is that the adjustments to the work environment could be costly and affect customers down the road.

Dave decides to hire another person, Nancy. Even though Nancy does not speak Spanish fluently, Dave decides that she can get by and, if necessary, use another teller to handle intricate transactions in Spanish. Dave feels that he has made the right decision and secretly hopes that he does not lose another teller in the near future.

Anna receives a letter of thanks from Dave, who states that she is not going to get the job. Anna feels that she did not have the opportunity to explain her ideas about performing the job. She wrestles with the thought of legal action. Anna is well versed in the subject of the **Americans with Disabilities Act (ADA).** She is also aware of the new **Genetic Information Nondiscrimination Act (GINA)** but is unsure as to what employers can or cannot ask or require. After a few days she contacts an attorney to discuss the incident. The attorney recommends that they file suit against Dave and the bank.

FORM 3.6.1

1. Does Anna have a case here? What are the critical variables?

2. Under the ADA, who is a qualified individual with a disability? If Anna filed a lawsuit, who would have the burden of proving that Anna was (or was not) a qualified employee with a disability? Is it Anna or the Bank?

3. What critical terms related to the ADA must be considered in considering the legal implications of Dave's decision? How do they apply in this case?

Name _____ Group _____

4. Can expense or cost be a variable when considering "reasonable accommodation"?

5. What about Carl's point that multiple sclerosis is a progressive disease and that Anna will almost certainly get worse, thus creating potential problems of absenteeism and health care costs. Can Dave consider this issue in his decision?

6. Could Dave ask Anna about the nature or severity of her disability? Could he ask her about ability to perform certain job functions?

7. Based on Carl's comments regarding the probability of Anna's MS worsening, could Dave require Anna to submit to and share genetic testing results as a condition of employment? Could Dave use such information?

EXERCISE 4.1: Writing a Position Description

Overview

This exercise shows you how to write a position description (PD) that describes either a job you have, have had, or, if you have never worked, the job of someone else. As stated in Chapter 4, job or position descriptions are used for a number of personnel decisions. Many organizations start with job descriptions when they do restructuring and job design. Job descriptions are routinely used to set and adjust wage rates. The information also can be used to assist in recruitment efforts or develop selection devices, work teams, or performance-appraisal systems. To serve HR purposes most effectively, the PD must be current and accurate and it must be consistent with the goals and objectives of the organization, particularly in terms of customer requirements.

Learning Objectives

After completing this exercise, you should be able to

1. Identify the key components of job descriptions.
2. Prepare a position description report, including data on position objectives, tasks and duties, supervision and guidance, contacts, services and products provided to critical customers, and job qualifications or specifications.
3. Understand the purposes to be served by the position description.

Procedure

Part A: Individual Assignment: Completion of the Position Description

Before class, read the general guidelines for completing the position description (Exhibit 4.1.1). Then complete Form 4.1.1, the position description. Prior to class, students should also complete the Assessment Questions.

Part B: Peer Review

Students should bring their completed Form 4.1.1 to class. Students should be paired off and first review their respective position descriptions. Each student should serve as an examiner to try to interpret the PD of the other person. The examiner should try to sum up what is involved in the job and whether clear task statements have been written. The incumbent should clear up any confusion about job duties, requirements, and job specifications. Any needed changes to the PD should be made directly on Form 4.1.1. The discussion also should focus on any job specifications for the job, particularly those that may cause adverse impact. The examiner also should focus on the identification of the customers with whom the incumbent has contact for products or services that derive from this position and determine whether certain tasks on which the incumbent spends considerable time may be unnecessary in terms of the needs of the internal and external customers. The examiner should continue to seek clarification until he or she is confident the position description is as good as it can be. The examiner should then sign Form 4.1.1 in the space provided.

Exhibit 4.1.1   **General Guidelines for Completing the Position Description**

The position description should be written in your own words—it should not be written in technical "classified language." Basically the position description should be a collection of the tasks that add up to the total work assignment. All major work activities that are performed in the job should be described. The tools and equipment used should be mentioned. Also include the decisions made in performing the job, the outcomes, the products or services, and the relevant customers for each.

Samples of completed position descriptions for the jobs of public health nurse, mechanic helper, and human resources manager are also provided in Exhibits 4.1.2, 4.1.3, and 4.1.4. Review these samples as you read these instructions. Note the various sections to the position description (see Form 4.1.1).

PART I: COMPILING ORGANIZATIONAL INFORMATION

Step 1. Following the items listed in Part I (Organizational Information) state the name of the incumbent, the date, and the official job title. In item 5, you should state the working title if this title is different from the official title. Often, employees are given working titles for use. For example, a supervisor on a road crew may officially be a highway maintenance engineer.

Step 2. If possible, ask a supervisor or a personnel officer to complete the information requested from the other items listed in Part I.

Step 3. After reviewing the instructions, complete the items of Form 4.1.1, Part II: Position Information. This is the most important part of the position description because it provides information on the position's duties.

PART II: POSITION INFORMATION

Item 11—Objective

Item 11 asks you to state the chief objective of the position. This statement should be no more than two to three sentences. It should state why it is important that the tasks and duties that make up the job are performed. In writing item 11, it may help you to think of this statement as a definition of the position, or perhaps the essential aspect of the job. For example, the objective of a *child welfare supervisor* may be: "To orientate new caseworkers located in local courts, detention homes, and children's institutions by planning and teaching classes and seminars on social casework principles." This example of a position's main objective was used because: (1) it was *brief* (has no more than several lines); (2) it was *descriptive* (states the main tasks and duties of the position without giving detailed information); (3) it gives the reader an *overview* (what to expect in the more detailed listing of tasks); and (4) it states the *main purpose* for why the position exists.

Exhibit 4.1.1 (*Continued*)

Item 12—Tasks and Duties

In this section, you are to identify the tasks and duties that are performed in the job. Read the instructions for item 12 on Form 4.1.1 and write down the tasks on a separate sheet of paper. After you have completed this, arrange the tasks in order of the most important task first and finish with the least important task of the position. When these tasks are listed, decide the percent that each task requires of the total working time. Be sure these percentages total to 100. Writing all the tasks and duties of the position is difficult. Outlined below are some guidelines that should help. Following these are some examples of good and poor task statements.

1. Use action verbs to start each task statement, such as compiles, enters, totals, balances, writes, answers, telephones, or interviews. Avoid nondescriptive verbs such as prepares,

conducts, coordinates, processes, or assists—these verbs do not tell the reader what you are really doing.

2. Use task statements to explain: What is done? What actions are you performing? To what or to whom? What is the purpose of this task? What references, resources, tools, equipment, or work aids are you using? Do you write reports? Do you train and supervise employees?

3. Try to group closely related tasks together. This grouping of tasks will help you more clearly define and explain to the reader what you are responsible for in your position.

4. It is important to include all the major tasks and duties of your position. It is not necessary to include minor things such as "sits in chair, pulls open drawer, takes out a pen from desk, begins to write."

EXAMPLES OF GOOD AND POOR TASK STATEMENTS

Poor	Good
Ensures that all daily cash is accounted for.	Balances cash in register by comparing it with the total on the register tape; locates and corrects errors in order to account for all cash receipts; writes totals on cash report for approval by head cashier.
Assists with the inspection of construction projects.	Inspects construction operations (erosion control, asphaltic concrete paving, painting, fencing, sign placement); compares visual observations with the construction specifications and plans.
Trains subordinate employees.	Instructs employees under his/her supervision in company policies, office procedures, applicable state and federal laws, and firm report preparation to facilitate improved job performance; distributes firm reading materials, schedules work assignments, and leads staff meetings.

Item 13—Supervision and Guidance

Item 13 asks you to state what work actions and/or decisions are made *without* first getting a supervisor's approval. This decision making is an important element in the evaluation of the job. In answering this question, consider the following examples:

1. If you are a clerk typist, you may edit a memorandum that was drafted by your supervisor in order to make it more grammatically correct.

2. If you are a clerk, you may set up your own filing procedures and reorganize your section's files.

You also may want to list any procedural manuals, laws, and/or standards that are used as guides in the work.

Item 14—Contacts

In many positions, contact with other people is a necessary part of the job. Item 14 requests that you list any contacts you have with individuals, customers, or organizations. Also state the purpose of these contacts, how often they occur (e.g., daily, weekly), and whether they are inside or outside the organization.

Item 15—Most Important Service or Product/Internal and External Customers

Item 15 requests a listing of the most important services or products that are expected from this position and an identification of the internal and external customers who receive them (not by

name, just category). Note that managers or supervisors should not be considered customers and their demands may require tasks to be performed that detract from your attention to more important customers (e.g., external customers). Demands from managers should be linked to other internal or external customers.

Item 16—Entry Requirements/Job Specifications

Item 16 asks for information on the KASOCs that an employee must possess on the *first* day of the job. This information will be used in recruiting new employees. There are four sections to be answered.

1. *Knowledge, abilities, skills, and other personal characteristics:* State the KASOCs that a new employee must bring to the position. Use the definitions provided in Chapter 4.

2. *Special licenses, registration, or certification:* Identify occupational certifications or licenses, if any, that an applicant must hold to comply with laws or regulations.

3. *Education or training:* State the educational background or area of study that would provide the knowledge required for entry into the position.

4. *Experience:* State the level and type of experience an applicant should have to be qualified to fill the position. Examples might include "journey level carpentry with experience in remodeling interiors" or "supervisory experience."

Exhibit 4.1.2   **Public Health Nurse Position Description**

PART I: ORGANIZATIONAL INFORMATION

1. Name (last, first, middle): Black, Sandy C.

2. Date: Nov. 12

3. Job title: Public Health Nurse

4. Position number: 123456

5. Working title if different:

6. Agency:

7. Work location (county or city) and location code:

8. Agency code:

9. Title and position number of immediate supervisor:

10. Organizational unit:

PART II: POSITION INFORMATION

11. Objective of the position: To ensure that state employees are in good health by providing public health services.

12. Tasks and duties:

Percent of Total Working Time	Work Tasks and Duties
25%	Evaluates employees' or potential employees' physical condition by taking medical histories and examining the employee using diagnostic tools, such as stethoscope and otoscope, and interprets the results of laboratory tests.
25%	Treats work-related injuries to reduce absenteeism by administering medication and vaccines under the clinical guidance of a physician.
15%	Meets routinely with staff to review existing clinical services in order to improve them.
20%	Reviews accident reports to identify health and safety hazards. Analyzes causes of accidents and makes recommendations to management for eliminating hazards.
5%	Develops programs to educate employees on health-related issues. Uses self-prepared or programmed lesson plans, films, and other audiovisual materials.
5%	Orders supplies to maintain an adequate inventory. Completes requisition forms and sends them to the planning or supply room.
5%	Answers requests for medical status of employees from insurance companies or personnel staff by discussing results of examinations and current medical status over the telephone or by completing medical forms.
100%	

13. Describe work actions and/or decisions you make *without* prior approval and the extent of advice and guidance received from your supervisor: I decide how to treat minor injuries—giving first aid. I determine if a laboratory test is within acceptable limits. I plan educational programs.

Exhibit 4.1.2 (*Continued*)

14. Contacts:

Contacts	Purpose	How Often	Inside/Outside Organization
Employees	Perform physicals, treat injuries, and obtain information on the workplace	Daily	Inside
Insurance companies	Provide medical claim information	Weekly	Outside
Benefits staff (DPT)	Provide information for worker's compensation claims	Monthly	Inside

15. The most important service or product provided:
    Contact with and treatment of employees.

16. Qualifications for entry into the position:
    A. KASOCs:

    Ability to obtain personal information from people and to determine if they are being truthful. Knowledge of nursing services in the employment setting.

    B. Special licenses, registration, or certification:
       RN

    C. Education or training (cite major area of study):
       Nursing

    D. Level and type of experience:
       Experience in providing nursing services to a wide variety of people.

17. I understand the above statements, and they are complete to the best of my knowledge.

Sandy C. Black   *Nov. 12*
_____   _____
Employee's Signature   Date

Connie Brown   *November 13*
_____   _____
Examiner's Signature   Date

Exhibit 4.1.3   **Mechanic Helper Position Description**

PART I: ORGANIZATIONAL INFORMATION

1. Name (last, first, middle): Green, Chris M.

2. Date:

3. Job title: Mechanic Helper

4. Position number:

5. Working title if different:

6. Organization:

7. Work location (county or city) and location code:

8. Agency code:

9. Title and position number of immediate supervisor:

10. Organizational unit:

Exhibit 4.1.3 (*Continued*)

PART II: POSITION INFORMATION

11. Objective of the position:

   To maintain highway construction equipment in good operating condition by inspecting and repairing equipment, when necessary.

12. Tasks and duties:

Percent of Total Working Time	Work Tasks and Duties
25%	Inspects highway equipment to identify any operating problems by visually checking and listening to the equipment.
25%	Repairs highway equipment, cars, dump trucks, and small engines needed to perform road maintenance work by overhauling motor transmissions and differentials, replacing axles, springs, and wheel bearings using small motorized shop equipment, hand tools, and shop repair manuals.
20%	Maintains equipment to prevent breakdowns by installing spark plugs, starters, distributor caps; changing oil; and greasing equipment using standard mechanic tools.
15%	Tunes up and analyzes gasoline engines to locate minor problems and provide for optimum engine performance by using the Peerless Engine Analyzer.
15%	Helps other mechanics by gathering tools and parts, purchasing, and picking up parts at local suppliers and moving equipment from one place to another as directed by the foreman.
100%	

13. Describe work actions and/or decisions you make *without* prior approval and the extent of advice and guidance you receive from your supervisor: I decide how to repair the equipment. If the work is going to take more hours than planned, I tell my supervisor.

14. Contacts:

Contacts	Purpose	How Often	Inside/Outside Organization
Supply stores	Pick up parts or supplies.	Weekly	Outside

15. The most important services or products provided and the customers:
   Perform repair work as assigned. Customer is car owner.

16. Qualifications for entry into the position:

   A. KASOCs:
      Knowledge of gasoline-powered engines.
      Ability to drive equipment.
      Ability to read and follow instructions in repair manual.
   B. Special licenses, registration, or certification:
      Apprentice license for mechanic
   C. Education or training (cite major area of study):
      Heavy equipment mechanics
   D. Level and type of experience:

17. I understand the above statements, and they are complete to the best of my knowledge.

Chris M. Green
_____
Employee's Signature

April 19
_____
Date

Bobby Drangela
_____
Supervisor's Signature

4-20
_____
Date

Exhibit 4.1.4   **Human Resources Manager**

SUMMARY REPORT FOR

11-3040.00 - Human Resources Managers
Plan, direct, and coordinate human resource management activities of an organization to maximize the strategic use of human resources and maintain functions such as employee compensation, recruitment, personnel policies, and regulatory compliance.

Sample of reported job titles: Human Resources Manager, Director of Human Resources, HR Director (Human Resources Director), Employee Benefits Manager, Employee Relations Manager

View report:	Summary	Details	Custom

Tasks | Knowledge | Skills | Abilities | Work Activities | Work Context | Job Zone | Interests | Work Styles | Work Values | Related Occupations | Wages & Employment

Tasks

- Administer compensation, benefits and performance management systems, and safety and recreation programs.
- Identify staff vacancies and recruit, interview and select applicants.
- Allocate human resources, ensuring appropriate matches between personnel.
- Provide current and prospective employees with information about policies, job duties, working conditions, wages, opportunities for promotion and employee benefits.
- Perform difficult staffing duties, including dealing with understaffing, refereeing disputes, firing employees, and administering disciplinary procedures.
- Advise managers on organizational policy matters such as equal employment opportunity and sexual harassment, and recommend needed changes.
- Analyze and modify compensation and benefits policies to establish competitive programs and ensure compliance with legal requirements.
- Plan and conduct new employee orientation to foster positive attitude toward organizational objectives.
- Serve as a link between management and employees by handling questions, interpreting and administering contracts and helping resolve work-related problems.
- Plan, direct, supervise, and coordinate work activities of subordinates and staff relating to employment, compensation, labor relations, and employee relations.

Knowledge

Personnel and Human Resources—Knowledge of principles and procedures for personnel recruitment, selection, training, compensation and benefits, labor relations and negotiation, and personnel information systems.

English Language—Knowledge of the structure and content of the English language including the meaning and spelling of words, rules of composition, and grammar.

Customer and Personal Service—Knowledge of principles and processes for providing customer and personal services. This includes customer needs assessment, meeting quality standards for services, and evaluation of customer satisfaction.

Administration and Management—Knowledge of business and management principles involved in strategic planning, resource allocation, human resources modeling, leadership technique, production methods, and coordination of people and resources.

Law and Government—Knowledge of laws, legal codes, court procedures, precedents, government regulations, executive orders, agency rules, and the democratic political process.

Clerical—Knowledge of administrative and clerical procedures and systems such as word processing, managing files and records, stenography and transcription, designing forms, and other office procedures and terminology.

Education and Training—Knowledge of principles and methods for curriculum and training design, teaching and instruction for individuals and groups, and the measurement of training effects.

Economics and Accounting—Knowledge of economic and accounting principles and practices, the financial markets, banking and the analysis and reporting of financial data.

Psychology—Knowledge of human behavior and performance; individual differences in ability, personality, and interests; learning and motivation; psychological research methods; and the assessment and treatment of behavioral and affective disorders.

Mathematics—Knowledge of arithmetic, algebra, geometry, calculus, statistics, and their applications.

Exhibit 4.1.4 (*Continued*)

Skills

Active Listening—Giving full attention to what other people are saying, taking time to understand the points being made, asking questions as appropriate, and not interrupting at inappropriate times.

Management of Personnel Resources—Motivating, developing, and directing people as they work, identifying the best people for the job.

Reading Comprehension—Understanding written sentences and paragraphs in work related documents.

Writing—Communicating effectively in writing as appropriate for the needs of the audience.

Speaking—Talking to others to convey information effectively.

Negotiation—Bringing others together and trying to reconcile differences.

Time Management—Managing one's own time and the time of others.

Social Perceptiveness—Being aware of others' reactions and understanding why they react as they do.

Critical Thinking—Using logic and reasoning to identify the strengths and weaknesses of alternative solutions, conclusions, or approaches to problems.

Instructing—Teaching others how to do something.

Abilities

Oral Comprehension—The ability to listen to and understand information and ideas presented through spoken words and sentences.

Oral Expression—The ability to communicate information and ideas in speaking so others will understand.

Speech Clarity—The ability to speak clearly so others can understand you.

Speech Recognition—The ability to identify and understand the speech of another person.

Written Comprehension—The ability to read and understand information and ideas presented in writing.

Written Expression—The ability to communicate information and ideas in writing so others will understand.

Deductive Reasoning—The ability to apply general rules to specific problems to produce answers that make sense.

Problem Sensitivity—The ability to tell when something is wrong or is likely to go wrong. It does not involve solving the problem, only recognizing there is a problem.

Inductive Reasoning—The ability to combine pieces of information to form general rules or conclusions (includes finding a relationship among seemingly unrelated events).

Near Vision—The ability to see details at close range (within a few feet of the observer).

Work Activities

Establishing and Maintaining Interpersonal Relationships—Developing constructive and cooperative working relationships with others, and maintaining them over time.

Communicating with Supervisors, Peers, or Subordinates—Providing information to supervisors, co-workers, and subordinates by telephone, in written form, e-mail, or in person.

Making Decisions and Solving Problems—Analyzing information and evaluating results to choose the best solution and solve problems.

Staffing Organizational Units—Recruiting, interviewing, selecting, hiring, and promoting employees in an organization.

Getting Information—Observing, receiving, and otherwise obtaining information from all relevant sources.

Judging the Qualities of Things, Services, or People—Assessing the value, importance, or quality of things or people.

Guiding, Directing, and Motivating Subordinates—Providing guidance and direction to subordinates, including setting performance standards and monitoring performance.

Resolving Conflicts and Negotiating with Others—Handling complaints, settling disputes, and resolving grievances and conflicts, or otherwise negotiating with others.

Evaluating Information to Determine Compliance with Standards—Using relevant information and individual judgment to determine whether events or processes comply with laws, regulations, or standards.

Coaching and Developing Others—Identifying the developmental needs of others and coaching, mentoring, or otherwise helping others to improve their knowledge or skills.

Work Context

Telephone—How often do you have telephone conversations in this job?

Indoors, Environmentally Controlled—How often does this job require working indoors in environmentally controlled conditions?

Structured versus Unstructured Work—To what extent is this job structured for the worker, rather than allowing the worker to determine tasks, priorities, and goals?

Contact with Others—How much does this job require the worker to be in contact with others (face-to-face, by telephone, or otherwise) in order to perform it?

Electronic Mail—How often do you use electronic mail in this job?

Spend Time Sitting—How much does this job require sitting?

Freedom to Make Decisions—How much decision making freedom, without supervision, does the job offer?

Importance of Being Exact or Accurate—How important is being very exact or highly accurate in performing this?

Face-to-Face Discussions—How often do you have to have face-to-face discussions with individuals or teams in this job?

Letters and Memos—How often does the job require written letters and memos?

Exhibit 4.1.4 (*Continued*)

Job Zone

Title:	Job Zone Four: Considerable Preparation Needed
Overall Experience:	A minimum of two to four years of work-related skill, knowledge, or experience is needed for these occupations. For example, an accountant must complete four years of college and work for several years in accounting to be considered qualified.
Job Training:	Employees in these occupations usually need several years of work-related experience, on-the-job training, and/or vocational training.
Job Zone Examples:	Many of these occupations involve coordinating, supervising, managing, or training others. Examples include accountants, human resource managers, computer programmers, teachers, chemists, and police detectives.
SVP Range:	(7.0 to < 8.0)
Education:	Most of these occupations require a four-year bachelor's degree, but some do not.

Interests

Enterprising—Enterprising occupations frequently involve starting up and carrying out projects. These occupations can involve leading people and making many decisions. Sometimes they require risk taking and often deal with business.

Social—Social occupations frequently involve working with, communicating with, and teaching people. These occupations often involve helping or providing service to others.

Conventional—Conventional occupations frequently involve following set procedures and routines. These occupations can include working with data and details more than with ideas. Usually there is a clear line of authority to follow.

Work Styles

Attention to Detail—Job requires being careful about detail and thorough in completing work tasks.

Concern for Others—Job requires being sensitive to others' needs and feelings and being understanding and helpful on the job.

Integrity—Job requires being honest and ethical.

Independence—Job requires developing one's own ways of doing things, guiding oneself with little or no supervision, and depending on oneself to get things done.

Initiative—Job requires a willingness to take on responsibilities and challenges.

Dependability—Job requires being reliable, responsible, and dependable, and fulfilling obligations.

Persistence—Job requires persistence in the face of obstacles.

Stress Tolerance—Job requires accepting criticism and dealing calmly and effectively with high stress situations.

FORM 4.1.1 THE POSITION DESCRIPTION

PART I: ORGANIZATIONAL INFORMATION

1. Name (last, first, middle):

2. Date:

3. Job title:

4. How many people in organization have this title?

5. Working title if different:

6. Organization:

7. Work location (county or city)

8. Division within organization:

9. Title of immediate supervisor:

10. Organizational unit:

PART II: POSITION INFORMATION

11. State the chief *objective* of the position in a brief statement:

12. Before filling out the next section, think about the *tasks and duties* performed in the position. Consider the time spent on the tasks and duties, how important they are to achieving the objective of the position, and the processes or ways in which these tasks and duties are performed. After considering these aspects of the position, state the tasks and duties that are performed in the position.

- State the *most important* duty first and finish with the *least important* duty of the position.
- Calculate the percent that each duty requires of the total working time. Be sure these percentages total 100.
- Include *all* tasks, duties, and functions that are performed *except* those that occupy 2 percent or less time, unless they are considered very important.

Percent of Total Working Time   **Work Tasks and Duties**

FORM 4.1.1 (*Continued*)

13. What work actions and/or decisions are made *without* prior approval? To what extent are the advice and guidance from a supervisor received? State examples of the type of supervisory advice and guidance that are received as well as actions or decisions made without prior approval.

14. List and explain the *contacts,* if any, both within and outside the organization, that are a routine function of the work. Do not list contacts with supervisors, co-workers, and subordinates.

Contacts	Purpose	How Often	Inside/Outside Organization

15. What are the most *important* services or products expected from an incumbent in the position described and who are the customers with these expectations?

Most Important Service/Product: Customer:

Second Most Important:

Third Most Important:

Fourth Most Important:

FORM 4.1.1 (*Continued*)

16. What are the *qualifications for entry* into this position:

    A. What KASOCs should a new employee bring to this position?

    B. Special licenses, registration, or certification:

    C. Education or training (cite major area of study):

    D. Level and type of experience:

17. I understand the above statements, and they are complete to the best of my knowledge.

_____	_____
Employee's Signature	Date
_____	_____
Supervisor's Signature (optional)	Date
_____	_____
Examiner's Signature	Date

EXERCISE 4.1 ASSESSMENT QUESTIONS

1. Could you use this job analysis to determine essential functions on the job? How could this be done?

2. When preparing the job description, why is it important to list the critical customers for the products or services and the major tasks and duties of the job? Are there tasks that could be excluded with little or no effect on critical customers?

3. How often should a position description form be updated? Explain your response.

4. Explain how your job description could be used to evaluate your performance or to develop methods for hiring people for the position. Do you think having a highly detailed job description is actually counterproductive for certain jobs? Explain your answer.

5. How could the O*NET be used for developing job descriptions?

6. You are assigned the task of writing a position description for a personnel recruiter. How would you proceed?

Note: *Exercise 4.2, The Use of the Critical Incident Technique to Analyze the Job of University Professor, is available online at www.mhhe.com/ bernardin5e.*

EXERCISE 4.3: JOB ANALYSIS AT COMPTECH

Overview

Chapter 4 discusses the purposes of job analysis and the derivation of the job description and job specifications as critical products. This exercise explores the methods that could be used to assess job specifications, to solve HR problems, and to consider the implications of the actions recommended.

Learning Objectives

After completing this exercise, you should be able to

1. Evaluate the processes that could be followed to assess job specifications.
2. Consider the legal and practical implications of the job specifications based on the methods you have recommended and the particular specifications you recommend.
3. Evaluate the best methods for developing training programs based on job analysis information.
4. Explore the use of job analysis to identify problems of high employee turnover.

Procedure

Part A: Individual Analysis

Before class, read the scenario presented below and answer the questions on Form 4.3.1. In the space provided, write down any questions for which you need answers in order to take a definitive position on any of the issues.

Part B: Group Analysis

In groups, students should review each member's Form 4.3.1 and then attempt to reach consensus on the requested positions. You are allowed to ask the professor only three questions, so decide what additional information is most important in order for you to address the most critical issues. A designated group spokesperson will present the positions of the group. Class discussion will focus on the positions taken.

Scenario

CompTech is a large retailer of computer products. With 442 stores in the United States and a plan for 70 more stores within two years, CompTech is the fastest growing computer retailer in the United States. The company's most important strategic objective is to meet customer requirements and expand the customer base into small-business workstations in order to build a long-term relationship. You have been retained to develop a plan for a "CompTech University" that will provide training for all store managers before taking over a store. In addition, you have been asked to evaluate the hiring process for store managers, to assess problems, and to suggest solutions. CompTech, in competition with the other retailers, has had some difficulty recruiting store managers, and the problem appears to have worsened in recent years. In addition, its turnover rate of store associates is higher than the average in retail although it is offering competitive pay packages. Exhibit 4.3.1 presents the breakdown of management vacancies at CompTech, plus an ethnic and gender breakdown. The retailer's orientation in the past has been to hire experienced store managers from outside the company (approximately 60 percent of store managers are hired from outside the company). However, district managers, responsible for from 8 to 13 stores in a geographical area, are given great discretion in the methods and criteria they use to hire store managers (including job specifications). Historically, based on data from their comprehensive human resource information system (HRIS), the company has, over the years, hired 139 store managers who had MBAs when they were hired and another 178 who had at least three years' experience as store managers with another company. The company has had to employ a costly employment agency to locate managerial candidates along with an expensive advertising/recruiting campaign, with frequent ads in *The Wall Street Journal* and the *New York Times*. The problem has become more acute in areas with an abundance of retail outlets where retail store managers are in great and increasing demand.

Jamie Carlyle, the vice president of human resources, has specific requests and would like you to consider these issues in particular:

1. Many district managers have required (and now require) an MBA or at least three years' experience as a store manager as a condition of employment to be hired as a store manager for that district. Carlyle would like you to devise a method for evaluating the validity, cost, and usefulness of these job specifications in particular. What method (or methods) of analysis do you recommend?
2. Carlyle wants to include training modules for store manager at CompTech University. How would you conduct a job analysis of the store manager job to determine what specific KASOCs are essential or critical for the job?
3. Carlyle is interested in a more "job-related" approach to selecting managers. How do we proceed with this objective?

Exhibit 4.3.1   Comptech Manager Demographics

	Assistant Manager	Associate Manager	Store Manager	District Manager
WM*	612	405	282	25
WF	292	164	56	8
BM	135	85	31	2
BF	115	41	15	0
HM	93	42	19	3
HF	41	20	10	0
Vacancies	20	12	30	3

*W, B, H, M, F represent White, Black, Hispanic, Male, and Female.

4. Carlyle has the job description for Store Manager that is copied in Exhibit 4.3.2. There is apparently no job description for the assistant and associate positions. How should she proceed?

5. The ability to fill store manager positions and the vacancy time is to some extent a function of geographical area. Carlyle is not sure the standard annual salary that CompTech pays the store manager is competitive. How could she proceed with a study of salary for store manager and its relationship to recruitment, vacancies, and turnover?

Carlyle is not certain how to go about addressing the most important HRM issues as they relate to CompTech's strategic plan and would like your advice on this issue as well. Finally, Carlyle welcomes any opinions regarding the manner in which CompTech is filling managerial positions and any issues related to HRM problems and CompTech's objectives. Use Form 4.3.1 to respond to these issues.

Exhibit 4.3.2   Job Description for Store Manager at Comptech

Plans and directs store operations. Major responsibilities are carrying out policy, managing daily operations and all human resources. Reports to District Manager.

Major Duties

- Direct and coordinate activities of all departments.
- Manage staff, prepare schedules, assign duties.
- Review financial statements, sales and activity reports, and other performance data to measure store performance.
- Impose departmental policies and convey store objectives.
- Determine staff requirements. Oversee interviewing, hiring and training of new employees.
- Monitor store's budget activities with maximum efficiency.
- Coordinate all activities with outside vendors.
- Manage the movement of goods into and out of store.

Annual pay: $90,000 plus possible 10% performance-based bonus

FORM 4.3.1

1. What are the current **job specifications** for the store manager job? Based on the information you have (or could have), how would you assess the validity of these specifications? What approaches or methods would you use? (You can propose particular statistical analysis, particular job analysis methods, or both; be specific.)

2. What hypotheses or proposals do you have so far regarding CompTech's strategic position? What do you regard as the critical strengths and weaknesses based on the data you have?

3. Carlyle is giving strong consideration to hiring a full-time Training and Development Manager for CompTech (CompTech has never employed such a specialist). How should she proceed as she considers this action? Could O*NET be helpful?

4. If CompTech decides to drop the MBA requirement, what possible effects could such a change in policy have on other human resource activities? What possible advantages do you see by keeping the MBA?

5. Carlyle is partial to the use of the PAQ to set job specifications. What is your position on the use of the PAQ for this purpose relative to other job analysis methods?

6. Given Carlyle's interest in the training program and the "job-related" selection tests, what job analysis method should be used for the development of these HR products?

FORM 4.3.1 (*Continued*)

7. Could Carlyle use the O*NET to address any issues? If so, what could she learn?

8. Do you see any potential EEO issues that should be considered at CompTech? Explain your answer and conduct any analyses you believe to be related to these issues.

EXERCISE 5.1: A TURNOVER PROBLEM AT THE *FORT LAUDERDALE HERALD**

Overview

The chapter discusses the importance of using data for better human resource planning and recruitment. The employee "matching" model is described. This exercise presents data from a newspaper that document the problems the company is having recruiting and retaining personnel. Your job is to use the data and the research discussed in Chapter 5 as a basis for making recommendations for action directed at their problems.

Objectives

After completing this exercise, you should be able to

1. Know how to calculate and use yield ratios for planning.
2. Know how an HR problem (e.g., turnover) can be solved most efficiently and effectively using various approaches to HR planning, recruitment, and related HR actions.
3. Evaluate HR problems in the context of the organization's strategic objectives.

Procedure

Part A: Individual Analysis

Prior to class, read the background data on the *Fort Lauderdale Herald* below. Using Chapter 5 material and the information that is provided on the newspaper and its problems and issues, consider changes to HR systems that could improve the situation that is described. Then, answer the questions on Form 5.1.1 citing specific information from the case or the chapter that supports your answers (provide Chapter 5 page numbers where applicable).

Part B: Group Analysis

In groups, members should review each other's responses and then attempt to reach consensus on the recommendations to go forward to the director. Analyze those recommendations in the context of the problems, the data presented, research regarding planning, recruitment and personnel retention, the potential effects on other HR programs, and the cost of implementation. Justify any specific recommendations with relevant research. A group spokesperson will then be designated to present the group consensus recommendations.

Scenario

The *Fort Lauderdale Herald* is located in southern Florida, one of the fastest-growing regions in the United States. Because of the increased migration and despite the generally terrible state of the newspaper industry, subscriptions to the *Herald* have been holding steady in some areas and increasing in others. This increased circulation has created a need for more customer service. In addition, competition in the area has increased with two new papers

*Contributed by Renee Bartlett and Joan E. Pynes.

and the expansion of a Miami paper into the metropolitan area. The strategic goal of the paper is to expand the customer base in Palm Beach, Broward and Dode County. The advertisement the *Herald* has used in the past for **Customer Service Representatives** states the following:

The job specifications and major responsibilities are:

- knowledge of MS Word and some Excel expertise;
- typing 35 WPM;
- filing;
- experience in customer contact and answering telephones;
- referring customer calls to supervisor;
- some selling of additional services; and
- calls for nonpayment of bills.

The starting salary for Customer Service Reps is $9.25 an hour for a 30-hour workweek. Customer Service Reps work six days per week in 5-hour shifts. The reps do not receive any fringe benefits.

Customer Service Reps spend a majority of the workday talking on the telephone with subscribers or potential subscribers regarding new accounts and account problems, renewing and expanding subscriptions, plus delivery and other problems with the newspaper.

Billing errors consume approximately 30 percent of the rep's time. Problems with newspaper delivery and billing errors are up in the past six months and, because of that, the volume of calls has spiked in recent months. The reps spend the remainder of their time responding to customer complaints, such as late, unacceptable (e.g., wet papers), or nondelivery of the paper, and soliciting new business through cold calls or calling subscribers for up-selling purposes. The most common complaints center on delivery or non-delivery of the paper such as: "the newspaper was supposed to be delivered at 7:00 AM, but did not arrive until 9:00"; "the paper was thrown in a puddle and can't be read"; "the paper was thrown in my neighbor's yard"; and so forth. Most of the subscribers who call are not friendly when registering their complaints. A 2008 study determined that automating the complaint process related to the delivery of the paper was likely to foster nonpayment of subscription service and more cancellations.

While the newspaper has successfully recruited new Customer Service Reps, turnover in the position is very high. The Director of Human Resources has prepared the recruitment data shown in Exhibit 5.1.1. The data show that the company screened 633 applicants to produce 78 people who accepted a job offer. Within six months, 51 percent of new hires resigned from the newspaper.

Exit interviews with departing Customer Service Reps revealed many reasons why they were dissatisfied with the job (see Exhibit 5.1.2).

Exhibit 5.1.1 **Data on Recruitment Sources for Customer Service Representatives, Last 3 Years**

Recruitment Sources	Total # Applicants	Potentially Qualified	Interview	Qualified & Offered Job	Accepted Job	6-Month Survival	Recruitment Cost (Total)
Corporate Web site	150	12	9	8	5	3	$200
Job board	300	20	11	9	6	2	$690
Newspaper	115	78	64	56	53	24	$465
Walk-in	31	20	14	9	7	3	$295
Public employment agency	37	19	7	7	7	6	$250
Total	633[a]	149[b]	105	89[c]	78	38	$1,900

[a] 341 Whites, 177 Blacks, and 115 Hispanic/Latino
[b] 91 Whites, 43 Blacks, and 15 Hispanic/Latino
[c] 64 Whites, 20 Blacks, and 5 Hispanic/Latino

Exhibit 5.1.2 **Most Frequently Given Explanations for Customer Service Rep Turnover (Last 3 Years)**

- All customer service reps are required to work on Saturday and Sunday from 7:00 A.M. to 1:00 A.M.
- Seventy-five percent of calling customers are irate at things over which the customer service reps have no control.
- Customer service reps must sit for long periods of time, talking with customers on the phone. Physical movement is restricted.
- Customer service reps have little contact with coworkers.
- The work environment is noisy and hectic.
- Customer service reps have not been properly trained to respond to billing complaints.
- Cold calls for subscriptions result in 78 percent hang-ups.
- Reps receive no additional remuneration for solicitation successes.
- Supervisors monitor a sample of calls taken each day and often contradict what the customer service reps say to customers.
- Customer service reps don't like cold calls.
- Customer service reps don't like calling people at dinner time.

FORM 5.1.1

Ms. Adalyn Saline, the Director of Human Resources, has asked you to analyze the recruitment and selection process and the related data and to make specific recommendations. While she requests answers to the four questions below, she encourages you to think of the "big picture" when you respond to Question #4. Use this form to record your answers and be sure to document your answers with specific references (give chapter page numbers) or data presented.

1. What are the yield ratios for each step in the recruitment and selection process across all recruitment sources? What are the implications of these ratios for future hiring? Could you also calculate a yield ratio for a particular recruitment source? Why would that be helpful to do? (Note: a great answer would provide an actual example from Exhibit 5.1.1.)

2. What are the advantages and disadvantages of the various recruiting methods used by the *Fort Lauderdale Herald?* (Use the data in Exhibit 5.1.1 and Chapter 5 discussion.) Where should they focus their recruitment efforts in the future?

FORM 5.1.1 (*Continued*)

Name _____ Group _____

3. Recommend at least three HR planning/recruitment/selection/retention strategies designed to do any of the following:

   a. Improve customer satisfaction.
   b. Increase the efficiency of the customer service function (Ms. Saline encourages you to be as creative in your thinking as possible).
   c. Increase the tenure of the Customer Service Reps (or decrease the need for them).

4. What additional studies or data are necessary given the data presented in Exhibit 5.1.1 and the problems described in the case? (Ms. Saline is interested in potential legal issues and strongly encourages any creative and cost-effective approaches to problem solving; she encourages you to keep in focus the goal of retaining and expanding the customer base.)

Note: *Exercise 5.2, Permalco's Recruiting Challenge, is available online at www.mhhe.com/bernardin5e.*

EXERCISE 5.3: RECRUITING AT JULIA RICHTER'S "DRESSED FOR SUCCESS"*

Overview

A proper recruiting plan is more than putting a résumé online. As an HR professional, you must think through the entire recruiting process. This exercise presents a typical company expansion with a need for staffing a new location.

Learning Objectives

After completing this exercise, you should be able to

1. Identify the essential steps in recruitment planning.
2. Suggest logical and efficient recruiting solutions.
3. Identify recruiting methods that promote diversity.

Procedure

Part A: Individual Analysis

Prior to class, read the background information on *Dressed for Success* in the Scenario below. Think about the implications of this information for a current recruitment plan. Then answer the questions at the end of the exercise.

Part B: Group Analysis

In groups, members should review each other's recruitment plan, recruitment tools, and diversity recruitment tools. Reach a consensus on the best plan and tools for each question. Justify your recruitment tools with relevant research.

Scenario

Dressed for Success is a chain of clothing boutiques located throughout the southeastern U.S.A. The chain has been in operation for 15 years and has seven stores. The stores sell a variety of women's designer clothes, shoes, and accessories. The owner has recently decided to expand operations into the Miami South Beach area. The new store will require a Store Manager and a minimum of five Sales Associates.

You have just been hired as the new Manager of Human Resources, responsible for (among many other things) ensuring adequate staffing levels at all store locations. The Fort Lauderdale store will open in four months. The Store Manager will need 30 days to train, staff, and prepare the store for opening day.

The owner, Ms. Julia Richter, has given you the following KASOCs for each position:

Store Manager: 4-year college degree; 5 years' retail sales experience; minimum of 2 years' management experience.

Sales Associate: Minimum of 1 year sales experience (retail preferred); experience in upscale retail sales; and knowledge of designer apparel. Ms. Richter emphasizes that these KASOCs "seemed to work in the other stores."

The Store Manager will oversee all daily operations of the store. The position duties include sales, preparation of daily sales and deposit report, maintaining store displays, inventory management, customer service, and also hiring, training, retaining, and supervising store employees. The Store Manager will receive a base salary of about $50,000 per year plus profit sharing.

The Sales Associates will be the front-line sales staff. The position duties include sales, customer service, restocking merchandise, and helping track inventory supplies. Associates will receive about $9.50 per hour plus 5 percent commission on individual sales.

Assignment

Develop a recruitment plan for both the Store Manager and Sales Associate positions. Provide a specific chronology of events. Address the following: (1) What three recruiting/advertising methods do you recommend for *Dressed for Success?* Ms. Richter specifically requests information about the costs and benefits of online recruiting and/or the use of a "headhunter" for the Store Manager job. She requests that you do research on this issue and take a firm position. Does the Internet provide any information about the compensation being considered for these jobs? (2) Ms. Richter is also concerned about diversity. What recruitment methods should be implemented to help increase diversity in the organization? (3) Ms. Richter wants your opinion of the salary levels she has set. Conduct Internet research to determine if what she is recommending is appropriate. She also wants to know if formal job descriptions should be written for the store manager job and the human resources manager. Write Ms. Richter a memo that addresses these issues.

*Developed by Renee Bartlett.

EXERCISE 5.4: HR Planning at COMPTECH*

Overview

How does a company plan and respond to its human resource needs? What are the steps necessary to ensure that the company will have the right people in the right jobs? As stated in Chapter 5, HR planning is the forecasting of human resource needs in accordance with the company's strategic business planning. Proactive HR planning can be used to more effectively implement business strategies and react more swiftly to threats and challenges that may be encountered. For this exercise you will create such a plan for the profiled company, COMPTECH, INC.

Learning Objectives

After completing this exercise, you should be familiar with the process of HR planning, including

1. Using an environmental scan to identify internal and external strengths, weaknesses, opportunities, and threats.
2. Conducting labor supply forecasts, labor demand forecasts, gap analysis, action planning, and controlling and evaluating the HR plan as it unfolds.
3. Tying all aspects of the HR plan together so that they work seamlessly with the business at hand.

Procedure

Part A: Individual Analysis

Before class, read the COMPTECH, INC., scenario and answer the questions on Form 5.4.1.

Part B: Group Analysis

The class should break into groups and then formulate an HR plan for COMPTECH.

1. Each group should take one of the five steps in HR planning: environmental scanning, labor demand forecasting, labor supply forecasting, gap analysis, and action planning.
2. Each group should meet and determine issues relevant to their assignment, and possible strategies for facing those issues.
3. After meeting separately, groups will then collaborate to complete an HR plan for COMPTECH, INC.

Scenario

Background

Founded in 1980 by two "downsized" IBM software engineers, Maryland-based COMPTECH is credited by many analysts as being the inventor of the personal computer superstore concept. COMPTECH is the leader in the discount computer retail sales industry and America's largest personal computer retail outlet. The company operates over 350 stores in the United States and Canada and employs over 10,000 full-time associates.

History

When Jordan Green and Kyle Brown lost their positions at IBM in 1980, the wave of corporate downsizings in the United States had just begun. Green and Brown received generous severance packages from IBM and decided to go it on their own rather than begin second careers in another corporate environment. Working out of Green's home, they marketed themselves as "computer odd jobbers," primarily through word of mouth among friends and associates. Their first contract was to handle the weekend relocation of a small architectural firm owned by one of Jordan's tennis partners.

The partners set to work on a Friday afternoon, confident that neither would miss his Sunday morning tea time. Unfortunately, the job proved to be more complicated than it would have been inside IBM's corporate headquarters. Reconfiguring the client's network in the new location required several additional port hubs and LAN adapters. The nearest retail outlet was 60 miles away and would not open until Monday at 10:00 A.M. Green and Brown recognized a need for a retail personal computer outlet to cater to small businesses and self-employed professionals. That weekend, COMPTECH was born.

The first COMPTECH retail store was opened in Somers, New York, in 1981 in leased warehouse space. The concept was promoted as a one-stop-shopping center for personal computer needs. The store carried personal computer equipment of all kinds and also offered installation, maintenance, training, and specialized technical services. Within six months, Green and Brown had a staff of eight and were looking for space to open a second location.

After opening their fifth store in the Northeast, the partners decided to expand nationwide. With financial backing from a venture capital group, they moved into every region of the United States. During the next 12 years, COMPTECH experienced an average growth rate of 27 new stores per year. In 1990, the company acquired a chain of computer stores in Canada. By 2009, COMPTECH employed over 10,000 personnel across the United States and Canada.

COMPTECH went public in 1990 at $2.00 a share—by 1994, the stock was selling at $27.00 per share. In 2009, COMPTECH realized gross annual sales in excess of $10 billion. Exhibit 5.4.1 shows the company's domestic market share lead among its top competitors.

*Contributed by David Herst.

Exhibit 5.4.1 2009 U.S. Personal Computer Retail Sales

Competitor	Gross Sales ($ billions)
Dell.com	$15
COMPTECH	10
Manufacturer direct sales	8
Warehouse chains	7
Mail order companies	5
Retail chains	3
Small computer stores	2
Total	$50

The COMPTECH Retail Operation

Because COMPTECH strives to maintain uniformity in each of the retail stores, layout and appearance are very similar from store to store and region to region. Corporate headquarters is responsible for planning and choosing models for store presentation; retail managers have little discretion in terms of merchandising approaches. Monthly floor plans for the stores are developed by corporate merchandising and distributed through the district managers. The stores, which range in size from 15,000–20,000 square feet, are brightly lit and project a high-tech efficiency look. The product line includes a wide variety of personal computers, peripherals, printers, and software. In 2009, the average COMPTECH retail store stocked about 3,500 kinds of computers, and computer-related items. Sales were divided among product categories as follows:

Product Group	Percent of 2009 Revenues
Stationary personal computers	30%
Portable personal computers	22
Printers	18
Software	12
Peripherals	10
Technical services	8

While the company's meteoric rise was sparked by the growth in the work-at-home market and decreasing prices for personal computers, the unique strategy of combining a warehouse atmosphere with the highest levels of customer service must be credited as well. The company continues to build on that winning strategy.

In 2000, COMPTECH introduced its Newcomer's Club for customers buying their first computers. For a flat fee of $75, the customer receives installation service and a one-hour in-home orientation training session. The Newcomer's Club helped boost personal computer sales by 5 percent nationwide during the holiday season. Last year, the company announced its trade-in program for personal computers. Customers will receive a credit of $250 toward the purchase of a new COMPTECH computer package when they trade in their old computer—no matter what make, year, or type. The computer packages consist of a computer, monitor, printer, and plus scanner, a small digital camera. COMPTECH is considering the possibility of developing warehouse-type outlets for sales of the used computer components.

Shrinking margins on computer hardware and the success of the Newcomer's Club have prompted COMPTECH to expand into consumer services. This year the company plans to offer a service to install wireless home networking. A deal with the local cable and telephone companies to resell broadband Internet access has been in the works. COMPTECH plans on bundling the network installation with the reselling of broadband services. Management is also considering a comprehensive program aimed at the fast-growing telecommuting market. In addition, COMPTECH is pushing the high-margin printer cartridge business but is finding it hard to compete with online stores such as Dell.com, which has an advantage in overhead.

COMPTECH continues to expand geographically, with plans to enter the South American, Eastern European, and perhaps Chinese markets in the next three years. COMPTECH plans to sell some of the used computers collected through the trade-in program in these emerging markets, as well as offer state-of-the art equipment for the upscale buyer. The company has also developed a state-of-the-art Web site. Of the 150 million American households with computers, 120 million are equipped with modems and connected to the Internet. Of these, 40 million have high speed, or broadband, Internet access. Because of low overhead associated with online sales, COMPTECH contintues to push its Web-based store. The assistance and online computer training for small businesses are additional opportunities that the company is considering.

Human Resources

The organization structure that evolved at COMPTECH is very similar to most other large retail operations in the United States. CEO Jordan Green is supported by seven Senior Vice Presidents (SVPs) in various functional areas as well as Vice Presidents (VPs) for Human Resources and Legal Services. The five Regional Vice Presidents (RVPs) are responsible for the Northeast, Southeast, Midwest, Northwest, and Southwest. Under the Regional Vice

Exhibit 5.4.2

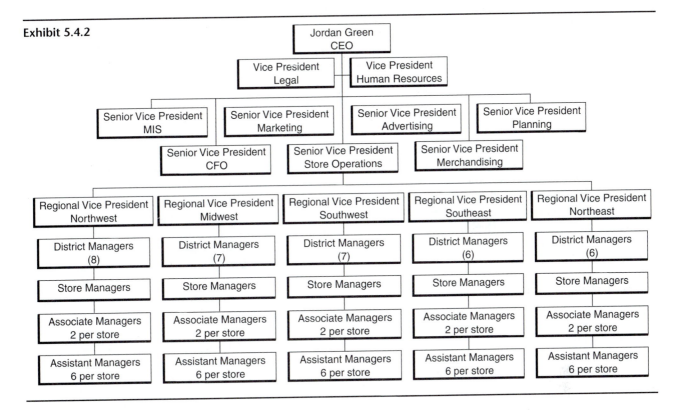

Presidents are the District Managers (DMs). There are approximately 35 district managers. Each district manager is responsible for approximately 10 stores. Exhibit 5.4.2 shows COMPTECH's organizational structure for its U.S. operations.

The Vice Presidents

Vice presidents provide expert advice and strategic input to the president according to their functional area. They make sure that COMPTECH's information systems, marketing, store operations, advertising, merchandising, planning, and financing are all considered when developing and maintaining the business plan. They are directly responsible for providing expert knowledge within each functional area to the CEO on COMPTECH's strengths, weaknesses, opportunities, and threats. They are a vital part of both creating and implementing COMPTECH's business strategy.

The Regional Vice Presidents

Regional vice presidents (RVPs) are responsible for developing strategies and goals for the region and helping the district managers develop implementation plans and schedules. They work closely with the vice presidents to determine overall business strategy and to implement the strategy once it has been created. Regional vice presidents are directly responsible for all stores in their geographic area. They are also given some decision authority to pursue strategies tailored to their region.

The District Manager Job

The job of the district manager is to participate in the development of the regional and district strategy, communicate corporate directives, and supervise and monitor store operations. DMs and regional vice presidents work together to develop implementation plans for marketing, budgeting, and purchasing. The DM has full responsibility for ensuring that the plans are implemented at the store level by communicating directives and monitoring progress of store management.

DMs screen, select, and evaluate all store managers and associate managers and conduct regular inspections of all the stores within the district. The DM is responsible for following up on monthly store performance reports to identify problem areas and develop plans and final solutions. The DMs' oversight function is carried out primarily through conducting regular on-site visits, or "DM Audits," at each of the stores, which are an important component of the store managers' annual evaluations. The district manager is also responsible for selecting and evaluating the performance of all other management level personnel in the district.

The Store Manager Job

The store manager (SM) provides the administrative and functional supervision of a store unit, including inventory control, sales and returns, vendor relations, cash management, and related reporting. The SM supervises all regular and/or temporary customer service and stock management staff. In addition, the SM manages the operation of a store unit, including purchasing of all supplies, special orders, receiving and shipping, and return of overstocked or defective merchandise. Finally, the store manager supervises personnel, which typically includes recommendations for hiring, firing, performance evaluation, training, work allocation, and problem resolution.

Associate Managers

Associate managers (AMs) typically work as a second-in-charge to the store manager. They assist in the day-to-day running of the store by monitoring departments, conducting hiring interviews, evaluating sales associates, supervising assistant managers, conducting training, and scheduling employee shifts. They are also responsible for monitoring inventory levels and implementing sales initiatives.

Assistant Managers

Assistant managers run different departments within each store. They may be in charge of portable computers, software, networking, corporate sales, or customer service. Their primary functions include providing service to customers within their specialized area, monitoring trends, and advising the store manager on day-to-day operations within the store.

Sales Associates

Sales associates are the first-line customer service and sales representatives for COMPTECH. They greet customers, assist them in making purchasing decisions, and advise them on their computer needs.

The company is known for its progressive human resource practices and emphasis on employee training. All COMPTECH sales associates receive a minimum of three weeks' intensive training on COMPTECH's entire product line before joining the floor sales staff. Sales associates receive a base salary as well as incentive pay based on their sales performance. COMPTECH employees earn 10 percent more than their peers in similar organizations. Approximately 90 percent of the workforce at COMPTECH are full-time employees. Turnover in new

stores averages about 40–50 percent for the first few months and then generally averages out to about 30 percent per year. A breakdown of employee trends since 2000 is presented in Table 5.4.1.

Industry Challenges

Personal computer hardware has been the mainstay of COMPTECH's product line. The PC equipment market has matured, however, and further growth from that segment is not expected. Purchases of personal computers have begun to level off in the United States, and growth is tied primarily to replacement sales. Many imitators have entered COMPTECH's market. BESTPRICE, a national retail chain offering computers and other electronic products as well as appliances, has been threatening COMPTECH's position in several key markets for some time. Other warehouse chains and even large retail department stores are expanding their personal computer departments. This is to say nothing of online direct sales companies such as Dell.com, which dominates the PC market in the United States. Finally, new technological developments, including access to rented disk time through telecommunications providers, are slowing the growth of the personal computer market.

Increasing competition and reduced revenues and profits have led to intense rivalry and price competition among computer retailers in the United States, and competition is increasing abroad as domestic companies begin to look beyond their home markets for new opportunities. The U.S. price wars that began in 1991 continue unabated, with suppliers forced to slash list prices, cut dealer margins, and introduce lower-cost lines aimed at the home-user market.

Another trend that has had a negative impact on COMPTECH's business is the increasing tendency of computer manufacturers to use alternative channels for distribution of their product. Mail order catalogues, television home shopping channels, direct customer sales through third-party (e.g., Dell.com) manufacturer Web sites, and telemarketing operations are becoming common distribution mechanisms for PCs.

The decline in growth of the personal computer equipment business has serious implications for COMPTECH.

Table 5.4.1	**Employee Staffing Trends 2000–2009**						
Position	Staffing Levels	Sales Associate	Assistant Manager	Associate Manager	Store Manager	District Manager	Organizational Exit
Sales Associate	10,000	7,162	58				2,780
Assistant Manager	1,300		1,005	123			172
Associate Manager	780[a]		16	686	24		54[i]
Store Manager	450[b]			9	408	7	26[ii]
District Manager	42[c]				3	35	2[iii]

[a]580 whites, 110 blacks, 90 Hispanics.
[b]360 whites, 40 blacks, 50 Hispanics.
[c]32 whites, 6 blacks, 4 Hispanics (2 DMs became RVPs).
[i]10 whites, 32 blacks, 12 Hispanics.
[ii]4 whites, 6 blacks, 16 Hispanics.
[iii]0 whites, 1 black, 1 Hispanic.

Meeting the challenge of competing in this environment means that every store must carefully monitor and match the price points of its competitors. The evolving multimedia technologies must be fully supported at each store, which could require significant employee retraining. The retail stores must generate growth through sales of peripherals, providing consumer and small business computer services, and perhaps most importantly, maintaining their customer base by providing a flawless level of customer service. Attracting and retaining qualified technical personnel is vital to COMPTECH's success.

The challenge for COMPTECH is to find a way to sustain its growth without sacrificing its record of excellence in service. COMPTECH's corporate goal is to achieve 4–5 percent same-store gains in sales during each of the next five fiscal years. In the United States, small business sales/support and technical services are expected to be an important component of that growth.

FORM 5.4.1

1. What are the major SWOTs at COMPTECH? Use information from the chapter to determine the internal issues that will need attention. Review recent business trends in the retail computer sales sector and in the labor market in general (both domestic and foreign) to help you complete the environmental scan.

2. Determine the external labor supply available this year in five different states by using statistics from the Bureau of Labor Statistics Web site (www.bls.gov) or some other source. Employment statistics can be found at the State and Local Employment link under the Employment and Unemployment section. *Hint*: After clicking on the link, scroll down until you see the link for Create Customized Tables. These will help you find the applicable statistics.

3. What type, or types, of HR planning analysis do you propose for the data presented in Table 5.4.1? How do you propose to assess the internal trends in employee movement? Indicate what positions will require more training/retention efforts and what positions will require greater recruitment/selection efforts.

Name _____   Group _____

4. How would you use gap analysis for dealing with immediate HR issues and for HR planning?

5. COMPTECH executives set the goal of increasing the diversity of COMPTECH, but there was no specificity to the goal. They have requested that you provide a game plan for achieving this goal. Provide a chronological outline of your strategy.

6. Given all of the data presented in the case, what is your chronological HR action plan for COMPTECH, INC.?

EXERCISE 6.1: SHOULD TENNECO USE THE WONDERLIC TEST?

Overview

Although general mental or cognitive ability tests have been shown to be valid, they are likely to result in adverse impact against minorities because of test score differences. Recall the discussion in the text regarding the Wonderlic Personnel Test. The purpose of this exercise is to have the student consider the options available for dealing with the problem of a test that will probably cause adverse impact.

Learning Objectives

After completing this exercise, you should have a better understanding of the implications of the use of cognitive ability tests and should be capable of developing and articulating a rationale for the use of specific methods of selection.

Procedure

Part A: Individual Analysis

Before class, read the scenario presented below regarding the Tenneco Corporation and answer the questions on Form 6.1.1. Be prepared to defend your position in group discussion.

Part B: Group Analysis

In groups, each student should review the written responses of other members to the questions on Form 6.1.1. The group should then attempt to reach consensus on each of the questions. A written group response should be developed for each of the questions, and a group spokesperson should be designated to present the group's positions on the use of the test.

Scenario

Tenneco Corporation has decided to use of the *Wonderlic Personnel Test* (see www.wonderlic.com/products) as part of its selection process for assistant store managers. Each assistant store manager has management responsibilities for one convenience store. Responsibilities include complete supervision of at least 15 employees, including hiring, firing, and scheduling; budgetary matters; inventory; vendor deliveries; and customer issues. Tenneco hopes to maintain a policy of promotion from within and has administered the Wonderlic to 400 store employees. A consultant from the Wonderlic Company recommends a particular minimum score of 24 for the assistant manager job. With this recommended passing score, the rate of passing (scoring at the minimum or higher) based on the ethnicity race of the job candidates was as follows: Whites: 75 percent passed; Blacks: 51 percent passed; Hispanics: 58 percent passed; Asian or Pacific Islander: 83 percent passed; American Indian/Alaskan Native: 70 percent passed. The five-week training program at Tenneco headquarters has room for only 40 managerial trainees. The training is required for promotion to assistant store manager. As a new HRM personnel specialist, you have been asked to recommend a specific policy for the use of the Wonderlic results and other possible selection procedures. Answer each of the questions on Form 6.1.1.

FORM 6.1.1

1. Is there evidence of adverse impact against minorities if the Wonderlic Personnel Test is used as the sole basis for entry into the training? Explain your answer.

2. Given your response to Question 1, what are the policy options for this situation? What policy do you recommend that Tenneco adopt for the use of the Wonderlic? Defend your response by considering the job situation, the need for further research, legal and social implications, and alternative methods of selection. Provide a detailed recommendation and rationale for action. If you take a position to drop the use of the Wonderlic, how do you propose to identify the 40 candidates?

3. What if you conducted a PAQ analysis that indicated that the Wonderlic was a valid test to use for this job? Do you believe that this result establishes the legality of the Wonderlic? Given that the Wonderlic consultant recommended the particular passing score, is Tenneco on safe legal ground if candidates are selected based on that Wonderlic passing score?

FORM 6.1.1 (*Continued*)

4. Could Tenneco convert each raw score on the Wonderlic to a percentile based on the ethnicity of the test taker? How might such a policy affect adverse impact? Is it legal?

5. Tenneco is also considering an interviewing process as the final hurdle for selecting trainees. What is your view of this option? If interviews are to be conducted, are there any recommendations for the interview content, process, or procedure? What do you recommend?

6. Another suggestion is to review the *Wonderlic* test and to remove all culturally biased questions to eliminate the adverse impact. Do you agree with this suggestion? Explain your answer.

EXERCISE 6.2: HIRING A PLANT MANAGER AT DYNAMO INDUSTRIES*

Overview

Personnel selection decisions are typically made based on a collection of information from several sources. An organization may have test scores, previous performance appraisals, interview ratings, biographical information, and other data on the candidates. This exercise gives the student a feel for making a final recommendation based on such a collection of data. In addition, through the group interaction, students should gain an understanding of the process involved in a leaderless group discussion.

Your assignment is to review candidate credentials for the plant manager positions at Dynamo Industries in Pittsburgh.

Learning Objectives

After completing this exercise, you should be able to

1. Distinguish candidate information that is valuable and should be considered in the decision from that which should be ignored.
2. Articulate your rationale for decisions.
3. Suggest ways in which the selection process could be improved.
4. Understand the dynamics of a leaderless group discussion.

Procedure

Part A: Individual Analysis

Before class, review the material presented in the scenario below. Assume the following: You are the vice president of personnel. You are to write a report (a two-page executive summary followed by *no more* than two pages of supporting information) that includes the following:

a. A rank ordering of your top three choices for the Pittsburgh job based on the information you have now.
b. An *in-depth* discussion of how this rank ordering was reached (a rationale for some candidates being ranked higher than others and for others not being ranked). As part of this analysis, comment on the recommendation by the Ad Hoc committee on Diversity that Mr. Jackson should be hired since he meets the minimum qualifications and Dynamo has an affirmative action program.
c. A detailed discussion of how the selection process for hiring a plant manager should be changed in the future in order to make the process more effective. (e.g., additional selection devices to use, additional information to gather, sources to drop or change, methods for deriving a recommendation). Be specific in your recommendations.
d. A request for whatever additional information you would like to have regarding the process or the

candidates or issues that should be considered that could affect your rank orderings. Your instructor may stipulate that requests for additional information may be e-mailed prior to the class meeting.

This report will be sent to the vice president of production and to the president of Dynamo Industries. Bring this report to class.

Part B: Group Analysis

Groups should be charged with reaching a consensus on the rank ordering of the top three candidates. Each member should be given an opportunity to review the others' written reports. The instructor will designate the time to be allotted to this process and will provide additional information on request. In addition, each group should reach consensus on the changes to be made for hiring the plant manager in the future.

Scenario

Dynamo Industries is a medium-sized manufacturer of small electrical motors headquartered in St. Paul, Minnesota. The firm employs 9,800 people. Dynamo Industries has plants in St. Paul; Columbus, Ohio; Atlanta; San Diego; Pittsburgh; Providence, Rhode Island; and Little Rock, Arkansas. All these plants are unionized, although the power of the respective unions varies greatly.

Recently, the company has been trying to hire a new plant manager (see job description in Exhibit 6.2.1) for the Pittsburgh plant (plant managers report directly to the vice president of production). Although Dynamo Industries has experienced slightly above-average growth and profit compared to its competitors, the Pittsburgh plant has been a trouble spot. Over the past three years, production costs there have been extremely high and there has been labor strife (e.g., numerous work slowdowns, an excessive number of grievances filed). The most recent Pittsburgh plant manager was terminated, although by mutual agreement, the company stated he left for a better job with another company. Because of the importance of the plant manager position, Dynamo Industries has used several expensive selection devices. These devices are detailed below. After a thorough recruitment effort (both within and outside the company) and some initial screening, the list of job candidates has been reduced to eight names. Exhibit 6.2.2 contains extensive information on each of the eight candidates.

Dynamo Industries does not have an established philosophy for filling job openings. In the past, it has favored promotion from within the company. However, the vice president of production was hired externally. Dynamo has no policy on lateral transfers. In the recent past, such transfers have been rare. The key issue seems to be whether the company benefits from the transfer.

*Contributed by James A. Breaugh.

Exhibit 6.2.1   **Plant Manager Job Description**

(Written by the vice president of production)

The plant manager (PM) is ultimately responsible for the operating efficiency of the entire plant. In fulfilling his/her responsibilities, the PM regularly consults with subordinate supervisory personnel (the PM frequently delegates duties). A plant manager must be somewhat knowledgeable of production methods and the capabilities of equipment. Some of the activities the plant manager is directly or indirectly involved in include

1. Procuring materials.
2. Maintaining the plant.
3. Controlling quality.
4. Using manpower.
5. Establishing budgets.
6. Revising production schedules because of equipment failure or operation problems.
7. Consulting with engineering personnel concerning the modification of machinery to improve production quantity, the quality of products, and employee safety.
8. Conducting hearings to resolve employee grievances.
9. Participating in union–management contract negotiations.
10. Ensuring safety.
11. Establishing community relations.

Exhibit 6.2.2   **Background Information on the Candidates**

---

1. *George Martin*—age 44. Education: B.A., University of Wisconsin; M.A. (Industrial Relations), Cornell University. He is a plant manager of a relatively small (580 nonunion employees) plant (located in Cleveland) of one of Dynamo's competitors. Martin has held that job for the past six years. He has been with that company for 14 years. No reference information was gathered because Martin was concerned about his present employer's reaction.

2. *Tony Caciopo*—age 59. Education: high school graduate. He is an assistant plant manager (Providence). Caciopo has been with Dynamo for 24 years. He has been assistant plant manager in Providence for the past 10 years. He had a severe heart attack four years ago but appears to have recovered. Ten years ago, he was offered a job as plant manager by Dynamo but turned it down because of health problems his wife was having.

3. *Kathy Joyce*—age 36. Education: B.A., Indiana University. She is currently plant manager of the Little Rock plant. She desires a lateral transfer because it would enhance job opportunities for her husband. Joyce has been with Dynamo for five years. She has been plant manager at Little Rock for two years.

4. *Barry Fein*—age 49. Education: associate degree (2 years) from Morehead State University. Until two months ago, Fein was plant manager at a large, unionized textile plant. Two months ago, the company Fein worked for discontinued this product line and he was let go. Fein had been with his former company for 20 years and was plant manager for 5 years. His letters of reference were excellent.

5. *Ron Jackson*—age 33. Education: B.A., Howard University; M.B.A., Northwestern. He is currently an assistant plant manager at the Pittsburgh plant. He has been with the company for four years; he has been assistant plant manager for two years. He has served as acting plant manager at Pittsburgh for the past two months.

6. *Jay Davis*—age 46. Education: B.A., Harvard; M.B.A., Harvard. He is currently assistant plant manager (Atlanta). Davis has been with Dynamo for 10 years; the past 7 years he has been assistant plant manager (6 years in St. Paul, the past year in Atlanta).

7. *Frank Hall*—age 58. Education: B.S. (chemistry), Duke University. He is currently vice president for production for one of Dynamo's major competitors. He says he seeks a demotion so that he is required to travel less. He has been vice president of production for six years. Before that, he was a plant manager for 12 years. The plant was organized. No reference information is available. However, he has received outstanding reviews in trade publications for his performance as vice president.

8. *Tom Doyle*—age 36. Education: B.A., Williams College; M.B.A., University of Chicago. For the past two years, Tom has worked as a special assistant to the vice president of production. Before this he was an assistant PM for two years and a PM (Little Rock) for three years. Tom was the youngest PM ever appointed at Dynamo. He was very ineffective as a PM and after three years was removed from this position.

**Exhibit 6.2.3
Personality Profile**

Each of the eight candidates was examined by a psychiatrist. In addition to interviewing each candidate, the psychiatrist utilized personality tests (e.g., 16PF, the Myers-Briggs Type Indicator, and the Thematic Apperception Test) in drawing the following conclusions.

CANDIDATES' RATINGS

	High	Medium	Low
Ability to handle stress	Martin Caciopo Davis	Joyce Jackson Fein Doyle	Hall
Ability to resolve conflict	Joyce Davis Caciopo	Martin Doyle Hall	Fein Jackson
Interpersonal skills	Martin Joyce	Hall Jackson Caciopo	Davis Fein Doyle
Most likely to succeed as a plant manager	Martin Caciopo	Joyce Doyle Hall Jackson	Fein Davis

Exhibit 6.2.4

Interviewers' Ratings

	Vice President Production	Vice President Personnel	Columbus Plant Manager	Atlanta Plant Manager
George Martin	6.5	6	5.5	4
Tony Caciopo	5	5.5	4.5	6
Kathy Joyce	6	6.5	5	5.5
Barry Fein	4	4	3	4
Ron Jackson	5	5.5	4.5	5
Jay Davis	4.5	5	3.5	6.5
Frank Hall	6.5	7	Interviewer on vacation day of interview	4
Tom Doyle	5.5	6	4.5	6

Note: Each of the interviewers went through a one-day interview training program. The vice president of production's interviews averaged three hours in length. The other interviews averaged 60 minutes in length. Interview ratings were made on a seven-point scale (1 = poor candidate. . . 7 = excellent candidate). All interviews were semistructured.

**Exhibit 6.2.5
General Mental Ability
(GMA) Test And
Handwriting Analyses**

Candidate	GMA Test	Handwriting Rating
George Martin	119	5
Tony Caciopo	116	2
Kathy Joyce	141	0
Barry Fein	122	1
Ron Jackson	114	5
Jay Davis	148	4
Frank Hall	112	3
Tom Doyle	125	5

Note: The intelligence test (Wechsler Adult Intelligence Scale) given by Dynamo Industries is commonly used for selecting candidates for management. Individuals scoring below 115 tend not to do well in managerial jobs. Standard error equals 3.5. The handwriting analyst rated the plant manager candidates in terms of their likelihood of success as the Pittsburgh plant manager (0 = very poor prospect . . . 5 = very strong prospect).

Exhibit 6.2.6   **Promotability Ratings, Performance Ratings, and Work Sample Scores**

Candidate	Promotability	Performance	Work Sample Score
George Martin	Not available	NA	19.5
Tony Caciopo	6	5	15.5
Kathy Joyce	5	6	18.5
Barry Fein	NA	NA	18.5
Ron Jackson	5.5	6	18
Jay Davis	7	7	16.5
Frank Hall	NA	NA	19
Tom Doyle	5.5	6	17.5

Note: A promotability rating was made as part of the annual performance review (7 = ready for immediate promotion . . . 1 = should not be promoted). The performance rating ranges from 1 = poor performance . . . 7 = exceptional performance. As part of the selection process, all applicants went through a series of work sample tests (i.e., in-basket, leaderless group discussion, and production planning exercise). Scoring was done by trained raters from the personnel department (20 = highest possible score). Exhibit presents the average rating across the work sample tests.

EXERCISE 6.3: What Questions Can You (and Should You) Ask in an Interview?*

Overview

Case law has established the potential legal liability inherent in the employment interview. Given the subjective nature of the process and the discretion interviewers typically exercise in employment interviews, there is great opportunity for biases that could be interpreted as violations of any number of state, federal, or local laws on equal opportunity. Take note that the Supreme Court ruled in *Watson v. Ft. Worth Bank & Trust* that "disparate impact" theory may be used in cases involving "subjective employment practices" such as interviews and performance appraisals. Research also has established that there are optimal approaches to conducting the employment interview. Employment interviews can have high validity if certain guidelines are followed.

This exercise explores the potential legal implications of a number of questions often posed by interviewers. In addition, interview questions will be examined to determine their potential for contributing to a valid interview.

Learning Objectives

After completing this exercise, you should be able to

1. Identify those interview questions that are of questionable legality.
2. Know the major laws that may affect the interview process.
3. Know the recommended approach to conducting interviews.

Go to http://www.mhhe.com/business/management/buildyourmanagementskills/menu.html and locate the "online" file for the exercise entitled "What questions can you (and should you) ask in an interview?" Follow the directions for completing the assignment and then print the feedback page to be handed in at the discretion of your instructor. After you complete the online portion of the exercise, answer the questions on Form 6.3.1.

*Developed by M. Ronald Buckley and Robert Eder.

FORM 6.3.1 ASSESSMENT QUESTIONS

1. How would you design a training program so that future interviewers would understand what can and cannot be asked in an employment interview?

2. If your organizational research had clearly established (with data) that women with children under the age of five are more likely to be absent from work than others, could the company then use this information to make decisions?

3. How would you design a structured, situational, or behavioral interview for an overseas assignment? Based on the evidence, is the situational or the behavioral interview more valid?

4. Discuss the ethical and legal implications of asking applicants about the health history of family members. Setting aside the possible legal issues, should a company take family health into consideration when evaluating an applicant?

5. Relative to alternative methods of selection, what role should an interview play in the selection of retail assistant managers? If you use more than one method, how would you go about weighing the information?

6. A colleague suggests that you do not have to develop a structured, behavioral interview as long as you get at least three colleagues to do independent, unstructured interviews and then evaluate candidates. Do you agree with the colleague? Justify your answer.

EXERCISE 7.1: Performance-Appraisal Feedback: A Role-Play Exercise*

Overview

As described in Chapter 7, the performance-appraisal process is a key human resource management function. The face-to-face performance feedback session can be an important part of this process because it allows the rater and ratee to thoroughly discuss the appraisal ratings. It also enables them to derive some developmental suggestions to improve the ratee's performance. This exercise provides an opportunity to role-play a face-to-face performance feedback session.

Learning Objectives

After completing this exercise, you should be able to

1. Understand and apply general guidelines for providing performance feedback.
2. Understand and apply guidelines for the observation of behavior.
3. Evaluate the effectiveness of a performance-appraisal feedback session.

Procedure

Part A: Analysis

Step 1.   Each student should read Exhibits 7.1.1, 7.1.2, and 7.1.3 before class. Based on the discussion in Chapter 7, write a one-page critique on the performance form and the extent to which it will help with the feedback process.

Step 2.   In class, the instructor will set up teams of three individuals. You will be assigned one of three roles: feedback giver, recipient, and observer of the feedback giver. If you have been assigned the role of feedback giver (Chris Williams), then carefully review Exhibit 7.1.1 and make notes about the content and message of the feedback you will give to one of your subordinates, Jesse Anderson. Also, review Exhibit 7.1.2, the guidelines for providing feedback. If you have been assigned the role of feedback recipient, then you are Jesse Anderson, the subordinate. Your supervisor, Chris Williams, will be setting up a meeting to discuss your performance. If you have been assigned the role of observer, you should review Exhibits 7.1.2 and 7.1.3 so you can accurately observe and take notes on the feedback giver's behavior in the appraisal session.

Part B: Role-Play

The person assuming the role of Chris Williams, the supervisor, will call Jesse Anderson, the subordinate, into Chris's office and provide the feedback to Jesse in about 15 minutes. The observer will take notes during the feedback session.

Part C: Feedback

After the role-play has been completed, the observer should share his or her observations with the feedback giver. The intent is to give some constructive and positive information to the feedback giver to enhance that person's appraisal skills in the future. Feedback recipients also may want to offer their own perspectives on how comfortable they felt with the feedback session and whether or not they felt motivated to improve their performance after receiving the feedback.

Part D: Class Discussion

The class as a whole should discuss the types of behaviors they observed that were characteristic of effective and ineffective appraisal sessions. The instructor could chart their responses.

*Contributed by Sharon L. Wagner, Richard G. Moffett III, and Catherine M. Westberry.

Exhibit 7.1.1 **Performance-Appraisal Form**

SOUTHEAST BANK AND TRUST (CONFIDENTIAL)

Name of Employee:	*Jesse Anderson*	Date:	12/5
Name of Supervisor:	*Chris Williams*	Dept:	S-2

Directions: Please rate each factor based on observed behaviors. Answer as honestly and accurately as you can. Provide comments for especially poor or outstanding performance.

Job knowledge: Technical knowledge required to perform the job; skills in implementing policies and procedures; effectively using resources and equipment.

1	2	3	4	5
Unsatisfactory	(Marginal)	Acceptable	Above average	Outstanding

Comments: Has occasionally used the wrong equipment, seems to be uninformed about some of the company's procedures.

Interpersonal skills: Works well with others; displays helpfulness and cooperation with internal and external customers; effectively handles conflict of interests and difficult customers.

1	2	3	4	5
Unsatisfactory	Marginal	Acceptable	(Above average)	Outstanding

Comments: Coworkers and customers have consistently commented on how Jesse gets along with most everyone. A number of situations have arisen in the department that Jesse was instrumental in resolving.

Work quality: The quality of the work including aspects of completeness and thoroughness; adherence to company and organizational standards.

1	2	3	4	5
(Unsatisfactory)	Marginal	Acceptable	Above average	Outstanding

Comments: Has turned in several projects that needed considerable revisions and rework.

Reliability: Can be counted on to attend meetings punctually; turn in assignments when due; and volunteer to assist others in projects.

1	2	3	4	5
(Unsatisfactory)	Marginal	Acceptable	Above average	Outstanding

Comments: Has missed most departmental meetings; has consistently come to work late in the past few months; is difficult to find when help is needed on projects.

Quantity of work: Meets company and departmental standards for production.

1	2	3	4	5
Unsatisfactory	Marginal	(Acceptable)	Above average	Outstanding

Comments: Productivity has been acceptable.

Exhibit 7.1.2   **Guidelines for Providing Performance-Appraisal Feedback**

1. Inform the employee about the purpose of the meeting. Describe the procedure that you will be following. Attempt to establish rapport with the ratee. You may want to inform the ratee that you may be taking some notes (i.e., ask if that is OK).
2. Focus on describing the ratee's behaviors. Avoid evaluating or blaming the ratee.
3. Be sure to indicate effective behaviors (i.e., praise the employee's strengths) as well as ineffective behaviors. Probe for specific causes of the employee's problem areas (e.g., why s/he believes s/he has a particular performance problem).
4. Be sure to make specific references to the appraisal form and ratings.
5. Discuss specific plans of action for improving the employee's deficiencies.
6. Jointly set developmental goals for the employee. Make sure you reach agreement with the employee regarding performance expectations and goals.
7. Strive to make your nonverbal behavior match your verbal message (i.e., maintain eye contact, maintain good posture, avoid use of uhs and uhms).
8. Provide feedback on each behavioral dimension, giving clear behavioral examples of performance to support the ratings.
9. Periodically check the ratee's understanding of the feedback you provide.
10. Answer any questions fully and politely. Remember that the only useful feedback is high-quality feedback.
11. Summarize the content of the feedback session.
12. Set a date for a future meeting to assess progress toward the goals.
13. Keep in mind that feedback directed at the *person* and away from the *task* will *decrease* the effectiveness of the feedback.
14. Feedback designed to be demoralizing is most likely to have detrimental effects.
15. Negative feedback focused on the *task* (not the *person*) can have positive effects a performance.

Exhibit 7.1.3   **Guidelines for Observing Behavior**

1. Focus on observing the behavior of the rater, and, secondarily, the behavior of the ratee (i.e., how he/she responds to the rater).
2. Record the behaviors you observe (i.e., things that the role-players do and say). Don't make judgments about the behaviors. For example, write "sat back in his chair with his arms folded" rather than "acted uninterested."
3. Try to record verbatim statements from the role-player whenever possible, particularly statements that indicate exceptionally good or poor performance.
4. In addition to recording statements made by the role-players, be sure to observe and record nonverbal behavior, tone of voice, eye contact, body posture (e.g., leaning forward to show interest).

Note: *Exercise 7.2, The Heartland Greeting Cards Consulting Problem, Exercise 7.3, Price Waterhouse v. Hopkins, and Exercise 7.5, The Development of a Performance Appraisal System for Instructors, are available online at www.mhhe.com/bernardin5e.*

EXERCISE 7.4: PERFORMANCE APPRAISAL AT DARBY GAS & LIGHT*

Overview

HR professionals are often asked to critique current systems and modify them to meet the changing needs and objectives of the organization. Often, they also are asked to design programs to train raters on using the appraisal systems. This exercise enables you to critique an appraisal system and offer your suggestions for how it should be changed. It also allows you to consider all aspects of an appraisal system.

Learning Objectives

After completing this exercise, you should be able to

1. Critique an appraisal system and offer suggestions for revisions.
2. Interpret the findings from a needs assessment report.

Procedure

Part A: Individual Analysis

Step 1. Before class, read the background information on the firm presented in Exhibit 7.4.1. Review the appraisal form currently being used by the firm as illustrated in Exhibit 7.4.2.

Step 2. A survey was administered to managers and to employees at Darby Gas & Light. They were asked to indicate the types of rater training for supervisors that would be most beneficial. Results from the survey are reported in Exhibit 7.4.3. Review these findings. Respond to the questions listed in Form 7.4.1.

Part B: Group Analysis

In class, your group will be asked to revise the Darby form and performance-appraisal system.

**Exhibit 7.4.1
Background Information
for Darby Gas & Light**

Steve Shakely is the CEO of a moderately sized public utility, Darby Gas & Light. Darby employs about 250 professionals (e.g., engineers, systems analysts) and support staff, including 25 managers. The firm recently started using a new appraisal system that consists of yearly formal reviews by managers of their subordinates using the rating form illustrated in Exhibit 7.4.2. All employees are rated by their immediate supervisor once a year, and these ratings are used to make administrative decisions (e.g., promotions, merit increases, transfers, terminations, demotions). Mr. Shakely has hired you as an external consultant to review the appraisal form and offer your recommendations for the form and the entire appraisal system. The 25 managers are not formally evaluated.

Mr. Shakely also is interested in your plans for a rater training program. The managers have never received any formal training in conducting appraisal interviews with their subordinates. The firm's HR director, Linda James, recently surveyed the managers and 100 of the employees to assess the areas in which supervisors needed training for doing appraisals and for conducting feedback sessions. A summary of her findings is presented in Exhibit 7.4.3. The numbers indicate the percentages of managers and employees who agreed that supervisors needed training in those areas.

*Contributed by Joyce E. A. Russell.

Exhibit 7.4.2

EMPLOYEE EVALUATION FORM
DARBY GAS & LIGHT

Employee's name _____ SSN _____

Supervisor's name _____ SSN _____

Date of review: _____ Date of feedback: _____

Instructions:
This appraisal form is to be used with all employees of Darby Gas & Light, including supervisors. Raters should circle one number on the scales below to indicate the employee's level of performance on the dimension and should provide comments about the employee's performance on that dimension. Dimensions marked with an asterisk must be evaluated for all supervisory employees. After completing the ratings for the employee, be sure to schedule a feedback session with the employee to review the ratings.

1. JOB KNOWLEDGE	1 low	2	3 average	4	5 high

Comments: _____

_____

2. DECISION MAKING	1 Low	2	3 average	4	5 high

Comments: _____

_____

3. *MOTIVATING OTHERS	1 low	2	3 average	4	5 high

Comments: _____

_____

4. DEPENDABILITY	1 low	2	3 average	4	5 high

Comments: _____

_____

5. *LEADERSHIP	1 low	2	3 average	4	5 high

Comments: _____

_____

6. PROBLEM SOLVING	1 low	2	3 average	4	5 high

Comments: _____

_____

7. COMMUNICATION	1 low	2	3 average	4	5 high

Comments: _____

_____

8. *PLANNING AND ORGANIZING	1 low	2	3 average	4	5 high

Comments: _____

_____

9. TEAMWORK/COOPERATION	1 low	2	3 average	4	5 high

Comments: _____

_____

Exhibit 7.4.2 (*Continued*)

| 10. *EMPLOYEE DEVELOPMENT | 1
low | 2 | 3
average | 4 | 5
high |

Comments: _____

_____

| 11. PROFESSIONAL DEVELOPMENT | 1
low | 2 | 3
average | 4 | 5
high |

Comments: _____

_____

| 12. APPEARANCE AND WORK HABITS | 1
low | 2 | 3
average | 4 | 5
high |

Comments: _____

_____

Exhibit 7.4.3

Survey Results About Supervisor Appraisal Training Needs

Area for Training	Percent Who Agreed Training for Supervisors Was Needed	
	Managers	Subordinates
	(N = 20)	(N = 100)
Giving specific, constructive criticism to employees	50%	35%
Giving specific, positive feedback to employees	10	50
Identifying available training opportunities for employees	40	40
Identifying employees' skills	40	45
Conducting a career development session with employees	15	30
Eliminating bias in employees' performance appraisals	10	50
Setting goals for employees' future performance	10	15
Understanding situational constraints on subordinates' performance	15	75
Administering rewards for good performance	15	55
Administering discipline for poor performance	45	15
Dealing effectively with employees who get upset in the feedback session	60	50
Providing timely feedback on performance	15	60
Identifying career paths for employees	40	50
Providing more precise criteria for appraising performance	55	70

FORM 7.4.1

1. After reviewing Exhibit 7.4.2, list what you regard as the major problems with the Darby appraisal system. Make specific recommendations about changing the system and cover what you regard as all aspects of the appraisal system.

2. What revisions to the rating form would you suggest? What particular methods (formats) discussed in Chapter 7 do you recommend? Do you recommend the same methods for all Darby jobs?

3. Suppose the firm wants to use the current form for employee feedback (i.e., to provide feedback to employees on their strengths and weaknesses). Do you think the instrument will be useful for this purpose? Why or why not? What, if any, revisions would you suggest so that the form can be used for employee development?

FORM 7.4.1 (*Continued*)

Name _____ Group _____

4. Suppose Darby has used this form to both promote people and make merit pay adjustments. Suppose also that Darby has been informed that six African-Americans have claimed discrimination based on promotion and pay policies. What (if any) advice can you give the company? What specific data should Darby evaluate in the context of these claims?

5. Based on the survey data and what you know about performance appraisal, what areas are most important for a rater training program? Any particular rating errors or biases clearly in need of attention based on the survey data?

6. Self-ratings with this form average almost two points higher than supervisory appraisals. Should supervisors review self-appraisals before they evaluate performance? Explain your answer based on possible rating errors.

FORM 7.4.1 (*Continued*)

Name _____ Group _____

7. Steve just read a Jack Welch book (former CEO of GE), and Jack likes "forced distribution." What should you tell Steve about this rating method? How does it work and what is the "track" record?

8. Should the managers be formally evaluated? If so, describe the system you recommend.

9. A performance appraisal "guru" said to use ratings of "relative frequency." What does this mean? Give an example.

EXERCISE 8.1: CONDUCTING A NEEDS ASSESSMENT*

Overview

To determine whether training is needed to address a particular area of concern in an organization (e.g., performance problem), it is first necessary to conduct a needs assessment. As stated in Chapter 8, a thorough needs assessment consists of an organizational analysis, a job or task analysis, and a person analysis. This exercise gives the student practice in conducting a needs assessment.

Learning Objectives

After completing this exercise, you should be able to

1. Understand the various components of a needs assessment.
2. Develop items to conduct an organizational analysis, task analysis, and person analysis.
3. Interpret the results from a needs assessment, describing the implications for designing a training program.

Procedure

Step 1. Before coming to class, each person should review Chapter 8, paying particular attention to the section on needs assessment. Choose a job with which you are very familiar. Collect and review job analysis data (see Chapter 4). From this material, generate a list of "possible training topics" for an individual in that job (i.e., what are the different types of training that might be beneficial for performing that job). For example, if the job is a patrol officer, possible training topics might include handling firearms, dealing with domestic issues, arrest procedure, teamwork, stress management, legal issues, and investigation. You should generate as long a list as possible (e.g., 40 to 50 topics).

Step 2. Using Form 8.1.1, interview employees (at least two) in the job you have chosen. Try to choose a representative sample of employees for the interviews. You may interview them individually or in a group.

Step 3. Summarize your findings from the needs assessment in a one-page report to the vice president of human resources. Offer *specific* recommendations regarding training for the job.

Step 4. Students will be paired. Form 8.1.1 should be exchanged and critiqued. Reviewers should evaluate the extent to which the responses to Form 8.1.1 provide guidelines for improving the training functions for this job.

*Contributed by Jeffrey D. Kudisch, Stephanie D. Myers, and Joyce E. A. Russell.

Job: _____   Organization: _____

Interviewer(s): _____   Date: _____

PART A: BACKGROUND INFORMATION OF INTERVIEWEE

Years in the job: _____   Years in the company: _____

Highest level of education completed: _____

PART B: ORGANIZATIONAL ANALYSIS (ATTITUDES AND CLIMATE FOR TRAINING)
From your perspective, what are the purposes of training?

How successful are current training programs in your firm for achieving these purposes?

If you asked a fellow worker to give his or her opinion regarding training in this firm, what would his or her response likely be?

Do you think trainees are motivated to attend training? Explain your response.

Do you think employees in your job experience resistance toward attending training? Do you have any suggestions for minimizing this resistance?

FORM 8.1.1 (*Continued*)

What positive consequences are associated with successful completion of training (e.g., increased pay, greater promotional opportunities, recognition)? Are there any negative consequences associated with attending training (e.g., loss of production, loss of status among peers)?

Do you think it is difficult for trainees to apply the skills they learned in training once they return back to the job? Why or why not?

For training programs you have attended, are you asked to provide your reactions to the programs? Are you given learning tests before and after training to assess a change in your learning?

PART C: TASK AND PERSON ANALYSIS

Describe the major duties of your job. Rank these in terms of importance.

Take a moment to think about an individual who is especially effective at your job. What knowledges, abilities, or skills does this person possess? Can these skills be enhanced through training?

Looking ahead over the next five years, do you foresee any additional job demands being added to the current responsibilities in your job? If so, what additional skills or abilities will be needed to meet these demands?

Note to the interviewer: Hand the list of "possible training topics" to the interviewee(s). Provide the following instructions:

Step 1. After looking over the list, circle those 10 areas that are most critical to successful performance in your job.

Step 2. Of the 10 items you identified, check those areas in which training would be beneficial to your job performance.

Reviewer's Name_____

Comment on the extent to which this needs assessment provides guidelines for meeting training needs.

EXERCISE 8.2: RAINYDAY INSURANCE ADJUSTERS COMPANY*

Overview

Often in organizations, new equipment may be installed without designing or offering the appropriate amount or type of training. As a result, productivity and job satisfaction of employees may decline, causing business losses for a firm. In some cases, the training problems also may be related to other problems in the organization (e.g., communication, management issues). It is the HR professional's job to diagnose the nature of the problems and offer realistic, timely recommendations. This exercise provides the student with some case information and has the student diagnose the problems with the company and offer recommendations for addressing those problems.

Learning Objectives

After completing this exercise, you should be able to

1. Understand how to interpret partial needs assessment information to determine the next steps that must be taken in collecting additional information.
2. Use needs assessment information to develop plans for designing or implementing training.

Procedure

Part A: Individual Analysis

Step 1. Read the background material presented in Exhibit 8.2.1. Note that you have been hired by the CEO to help the company interpret its problems and to draft some recommendations. In the first few days, you have collected some information, which is contained in the exhibit.

Step 2. Complete the questions found in Form 8.2.1.

Part B: Group Analysis

Step 1. In groups, discuss your responses to Form 8.2.1.

Step 2. As a group, reach consensus on what the company's problems are. Then outline a short-term plan (within the month) and a longer-term plan (over the next six months) to address those problems. Make sure your group includes the timeline for when each recommendation should be implemented and what the benefits and drawbacks are to each suggestion.

*Contributed by Steven M. Barnard and Joyce E. A. Russell.

Exhibit 8.2.1   **Background Information on Rainyday Insurance Adjusters Company**

Based in south Florida, Rainyday Insurance Adjusters is a medium-sized company with 135 employees and seven managers. They process the claims of policy holders who have experienced various misfortunes (e.g., hurricanes, floods). Their primary job is to determine the amount to be paid out and process the paperwork for some of the smaller insurance agencies in the area so that final payments can be issued. Although the company is only eight years old, it has done quite well and has seen a large increase in business. It has a reputation for quality work and quick turnaround on claims. Because customers are often eager to move on after misfortunes strike, Rainyday has built a loyal following among the insurance agencies that depend on it. Delayed claims often cost these companies time and money when they have to interact with continuous customer complaints.

To accommodate the increase in customers, six months ago, Rainyday expanded its office in the current building and upgraded all its equipment to make the company more efficient and to allow workers to process claims more quickly. In particular, computers were upgraded to facilitate speedier turnaround and higher capacity from claims processors. The new computers represent a large investment the company cannot afford to underutilize. Since installation of the computers, Rainyday has experienced a number of problems with voluntary turnover among claims processors as well as decreased productivity and increased errors.

Recently, the CEO of Rainyday, Rebecca Stephens, hired you as a consultant to help determine what, if any, training needs the claims processors have. There are 85 processors in the claims department. On your first day, you talked with several employees in the claims department. Fran, one of the more senior claims processors, has been with the company since it started eight years ago. He has become increasingly dissatisfied since the new computers arrived. As he remarked to you, "The managers told us the new computers would make our jobs easier, but they have been nothing but trouble. We spend half of our time printing out the forms and then we have to go back and correct errors on them. Also, some of the newer claims processors have been bugging me to show them how to fill out the forms. I don't have time for that, and besides, they should have learned it themselves in all those hotshot computer classes they have taken. On top of all that, my manager, Paula, stops by every day and tells us we all need to work faster because we are getting behind. I'm telling you, I have had it. I'm about to join the others and quit."

After your conversation with Fran, you decide that before you start drafting an action plan for the training program, you had better meet with Fran's manager to get her perspective. Paula seems friendly enough and is very open about what she thinks are the reasons for the problems. "Ever since we got the new computers, we have been having problems. Errors have increased, productivity has gone down, and we have had a lot of employees quit. At first, I thought it was just the new computers, but I also noticed a lot of bickering among the claims processors. It seems the more senior processors have resented the new hires, perhaps because some of their buddies quit the firm." After further inquiry, Paula mentioned that when the new computers arrived, she offered to send everyone to the local high school to take a computer class that would teach them how to use the computers and the software. The class was offered early in the morning (6:30 A.M. to 8:00 A.M.) so employees could take the class and still make it to work only one hour later than they normally arrived. They could get to work by 8:30 A.M., which was one hour after their normal start time. Paula also told employees they would be paid for the hour of work they missed. As she noted to you, "I was surprised that the employees did not seem more excited about the idea of the training. In fact, a number of employees told me that they did not want to be going to school with a bunch of teenagers and said they would just train themselves."

After talking with Paula, you asked her to point you in the direction of one of the newer employees who had been experiencing conflicts with the more senior employees. You reserved a conference room and met with Malcolm. He was very talkative and had a lot to complain about, especially regarding the older employees. "I'm having a pretty tough time here. After I took those computer classes at the high school, the computers have been really easy to work with, but I'm still having trouble filling out the claims forms. One of the senior employees, Randall, is supposed to help me, but he seems too busy. I think that he and the other old-timers are just jealous that some of the newer employees know the shortcuts on the computer. It's kind of funny watching them try to format their claims; they get so frustrated because they don't have a clue how to work the computers. I told a few of them I would show them, but they said they didn't need help from 'a youngster.' Fine by me; I have plenty to do."

After meeting with Malcolm, you realize that things don't sound too good. Because of the delays in the work by the claims processors, customers have been complaining to the insurance companies. Consequently, the firms are threatening to drop Rainyday. With all of their expansion efforts, Rainyday needs customers now more than ever. The CEO said to you as you were leaving for the day, "If things don't improve soon, we may be out of business." She encouraged you to develop a training program or whatever you think would help to improve the productivity of the claims department.

FORM 8.2.1 BASED ON THE INFORMATION YOU REVIEWED IN EXHIBIT 8.2.1, RESPOND TO THE FOLLOWING QUESTIONS

1. What do you see as the major problems at Rainyday Insurance Adjusters Company?

2. What are the causes of those problems?

3. What steps should be taken to better understand the performance problems at Rainyday? That is, what would you do to conduct a more thorough needs assessment to better pinpoint the problems?

4. Provide several suggestions for addressing the problems in the claims department at Rainyday.

Note: *Exercise 8.3, Backwoods Mail Order Company, is available online at www.mhhe.com/bernardin5e.*

EXERCISE 8.4: The Development and Evaluation of a Training Program for Graduate Student Instructors

Overview

A common practice, particularly in larger, research-oriented universities, is to give graduate students, who have limited (or no) training in teaching, complete responsibility for teaching an undergraduate class. Thus, while graduate students may possess adequate knowledge to cover the subject matter, many have had little (or no) training in organizing a class, teaching techniques, testing, grading, and so on. The objective of this exercise is to develop a training program for graduate student instructors and to propose a design for evaluating the training.

Learning Objectives

After completing this exercise, you should be able to

1. Outline the steps to be followed in the conceptualization, development, and evaluation of a training program.
2. Discuss the advantages and disadvantages of the various training techniques and the evaluation of design options.
3. Develop an approach to determine who should receive the training.

Procedure

Part A: Individual Preparation

Step 1. Before class, review the memo in Exhibit 8.4.1 and respond to the requests from the Associate Dean.

Step 2. On Form 8.4.1, write a chronology of the steps you will follow to complete the assignment. Pay close attention to what Dr. Richter has requested in the memo.

Part B: Group Analysis

Step 1. In groups of four to six students, each member should review each other member's response on Form 8.4.1.

Step 2. The group should attempt to reach consensus on the chronology of events and the position to be taken on the issues raised by Dr. Richter. One group member should take careful notes to represent the consensus and all aspects of the training program, the design of evaluation, and the criteria to be used as a part of the evaluation process.

Part C: Class Discussion

One member of each group should present the group's recommendations for the steps to be followed for the training program. Class discussion will follow on the areas where the groups agree and disagree. An attempt should be made to reach consensus on all major points that must be addressed by the task force.

Part D: Self- and Peer Evaluation

Complete a self- and a peer evaluation form based *only* on the performance in the exercise.

Exhibit 8.4.1 **Dr. Richter's Memo Requesting Your Recommendations**

TO: Training Task Force Members
FROM: Jack Richter, Associate Dean, and Eminent Scholar, College of Business
SUBJECT: Charge to the Training Task Force

Congratulations on your appointment to the Training Task Force. You were selected to join this group based on your expertise in training and development. As you may know, there have been a number of concerns raised about the quality of undergraduate teaching, with more concern expressed about graduate students for the College of Business (COB). While the graduate students appear to be highly motivated to teach, most of our grad students have received little or no training prior to their assignment to teach an undergraduate classes. My office receives a significant number of complaints regarding teaching quality although we're not clear as to the specific nature or extent of the problem. Your job as a member of the task force is as follows: (1) Determine if there really is a need for some form of required training for some (or all) COB graduate student instructors and perhaps other instructors; (2) Assuming there is a clear need for training, prepare a detailed outline stating the objectives of and the content of the training; (3) State who among the COB future instructors should receive the training (i.e., all future instructors or only those who fail to meet some imposed standard); (4) Identify the specific techniques that should be used for the training (e.g., lecture, role-plays) and write at least two objectives for such training; and (5) Provide a plan for evaluating the effects of the training. Specify the criteria and experimental design that should be used for evaluation. Keep in mind that I am very familiar with training methodology and research and prefer *detailed* suggestions on a strategy. (I know in general what organizational, task/job and person analysis is so I need more detail than this.) Also, please keep costs in mind but consider whether the program should be expanded to other instructors/professors in addition to graduate students. In general, what should we examine as we consider whether we need to train, what we should train, and who should be trained? Keep in mind that the College of Business has a great deal of archival data that could be used to refine the analysis of the problem.

Prior to the group meeting, take a position on each of the issues I have raised (and any others you can think of) and provide a *detailed* chronology using Form 8.4.1. Also, answer the four questions on Form 8.4.1.

I look forward to our meeting.

FORM 8.4.1 CHRONOLOGY OF STEPS FOR TRAINING PROGRAM DEVELOPMENT & EVALUATION

Assignment   **Detailed and Chronological Description of Action to be Taken**

    Step   1.

              2.

              3.

              4.

              5.

Name _____ Group _____

Critical Questions Related to the Assignment:

1. What data should we examine (or collect) to determine whether any training is really needed and who should be trained?

2. If we do training, what specific experimental design do you recommend and what evaluative criteria should we use?

3. A colleague has recommended using the *Self-Directed Learning Readiness Scale.* Why would we do this? What does this scale measure and what does it predict?

4. What specific types of training should be used? *Be specific.* A colleague has stated that a lecture-based approach to training is ineffective. Please comment on this contention. (Note: Give the page number, of relevant Chapter 8 material.)

EXERCISE 8.5: SELF-DIRECTED LEARNING ASSESSMENT*

Overview

The concern with developing self-direction in learning is ubiquitous throughout higher education and workplace human resource development efforts, reflecting the increasing understanding that the unprecedented growth in information and technology, accompanied by rapid social, political, and economic change, demands continuous learning and problem solving by each individual in order to maintain individual and organizational competency. In response to this whitewater of change, it seems logical that our educational institutions and our workplace human resource development efforts must transition from deliverers of content to developers of self-directed lifelong learners who have a strong information base from which to grow.

Objectives

The purpose of this questionnaire is to have students complete a short version of the Self-Directed Learning Readiness Scale (SDLRS), also called the Learning Preference Assessment (LPA). Upon completion, students will be given a score interpretation based on the research related to the SDLRS.

Learning Objectives

After completing this exercise, you should be able to

1. Estimate your own learning preferences.
2. Describe ways of incorporating SDL into the training process.

Procedure

Part A: Indivdual Analysis

Go to http://www.mhhe.com/business/management/buildyourmanagementskills/menu.html and locate the "online" file for the exercise entitled "Self-Directed Learning Assessment." Follow the directions for completing the assignment and then print the feedback page (to be handed in at the discretion of your instructor). After you complete the online portion of the exercise, answer the questions on Form 8.5.1.

Part B: Group Analysis

Step 1. In groups of five or six, discuss your views on the validity and usefulness of the SDL measure. Reach consensus on how a company could use the SDLRS as a part of its training or selection program.

Step 2. Provide some ideas for increasing the level of readiness among employees for SDL. Assume that you are a manager and you want to encourage SDL among your employees. Describe several strategies you might use to get them to manage their own learning.

Part C: Class Discussion

As a class, discuss the importance of using SDL approaches for the continuing training of employees. Explain the relative advantages and disadvantages of these approaches over other, more conventional training techniques (e.g., lecture, films).

*Contributed byPaul Guglielmino and Lucy Guglielmino.

FORM 8.5.1

1. What does the SDLRS predict? Do you feel the interpretation of your score reflected your disposition on self-directed learning? Explain your answer.

2. It is important to note that the online instrument you completed represents only a sample of the complete SDLRS. The validity and reliability studies discussed in Chapter 8 have been done on the full instrument. To access more information about the SDLRS and a bibliography of studies, students should go to www.guglielmino734.com. To take the full assessment, go to www.lpasdlrs.com. What effect could the shorter form have on the reliability and validity of the self-directed learning scores?

FORM 8.5.1 (*Continued*)

3. Could a company use scores on the SDL or the SDLRS to make staffing decisions, to select particular people for training, or as a basis for recommending particular training methods or techniques? Explain your answers.

EXERCISE 9.2: CAREER DEVELOPMENT SELF-ASSESSMENT EXERCISE

Overview

Most career development programs in organizations use self-assessment exercises. In fact, these exercises may be the first activities employees participate in that help them to better understand their personal career interests and goals. Self-appraisal is important for enhancing self-awareness. It generally requires the collection of data about yourself, such as your values, interests, and skills, and the determination of goals and action plans for life and career planning. As an employee you might want to engage in a self-assessment exercise for career planning purposes. As an HR professional, you might be asked to develop a self-assessment exercise to use with employees for career planning purposes. Examples of some of the possible activities that may be included in a self-assessment exercise are included in this exercise.

Learning Objectives

After completing this exercise, you should be able to

1. Understand your values, skills, interests, experiences, and life and career preferences.
2. Be able to describe your immediate goals, the associated benefits and risks, and the skills you may need to develop to meet your goals.
3. Understand some of your own work attitudes and preferences and the issues associated with making career decisions and changes.
4. Be able to describe some of the activities used in a self-assessment exercise.

Procedure

Part A: Individual Analysis

Step 1. Complete the self-assessment exercise in Form 9.2.1 before coming to class. Be as candid as possible in your responses.
Step 2. Each individual should answer the assessment questions listed in Form 9.2.2.

Part B: Group Analysis

As a class, address the following issues:

A. Discuss the importance of using a self-assessment as a career planning tool. Describe how a self-assessment may be beneficial for individual growth and development as well as for organizational HR purposes (e.g., staffing, training).
B. Explain how you might use a self-assessment tool as part of a career development system you design for an organization.

FORM 9.2.1 CAREER SELF-ASSESSMENT INSTRUMENT

PART A: VALUES AND EXPERIENCES

1. Describe the roles in your life that are important to you. Examples might include your work or career, family life, leisure, religious life, community life, and volunteer activities. Explain why these roles are important to you. Indicate how important each role is to your total life satisfaction. Assign a percent to each role (0 to 100 percent) so that the total adds up to 100 percent.

2. Describe your background and experiences, including
    a. *Education.* List the names of technical schools or colleges you have attended. List degrees earned or to be earned and your major or minor.

    b. *Work experience.* List any jobs you have held, including part- and full-time jobs, voluntary jobs, internships, cooperative education (co-ops).

    c. *Skills.* Describe any skills that you possess that you feel would be valued in the workplace.

    d. *Extracurricular activities.* Describe any nonwork activities that you engage in for personal development or recreational pursuits.

    e. *Accomplishments.* Summarize any recognition you have received that is related to your education, work experience, skills, or extracurricular activities.

3. Read the following list of skills. Put a + next to those you feel you are particularly strong in and *circle* those you would like to develop more thoroughly in the future.

    Communication (written or oral communication, listening skills)

    Management skills (supervising, persuading others, planning, organizing, delegating, motivating others)

    Interpersonal skills (working effectively with others)

    Team building (working effectively with groups or teams)

    Creativity (innovativeness, generating ideas)

    Training skills (ability to teach skills and knowledges to others)

    Mathematical skills (computation ability, budgeting, accounting proficiency)

    Sales/promotion (ability to persuade, negotiate, influence)

    Scientific skills (investigative abilities, researching, analyzing)

    Service skills (handling complaints, customer relations)

    Office skills (word processing, filing, bookkeeping, recordkeeping)

4. Rate yourself on each of the following personal qualities or work characteristics. Write one response for each characteristic, using the following scale: 1 = very low; 2 = low; 3 = average; 4 = high; 5 = very high.

_____ Emotional maturity

_____ Initiative/independence

_____ Punctuality

_____ Ability to handle conflict

_____ Ability to plan, organize, and determine work priorities

_____ Ability to work with others

_____ Willingness to do more than is expected (to go above and beyond requirements)

_____ Tolerance for changes in assignments or team members

_____ Dependability in completing work

_____ Flexibility and open-mindedness

_____ Perseverance/willingness to work

_____ Ability to set and achieve goals

_____ Tolerance for ambiguous, unusual, or different ideas or situations

_____ Ability to lead projects

_____ Integrity in work (honesty)

_____ Ability and interest in coaching others as needed

_____ Ability and interest in supporting or recognizing others' contributions

PART B: WORK ATTITUDES AND PREFERENCES

1. Describe an ideal job for you. What would it be like? Describe the activities, people, rewards, and other features that would be a part of your job experience.

2. Think about the ideal job you described above. Rank the following values or attributes in terms of how important they are for you in your work (1 = most important; 12 = least important). *No ties allowed.*

Values/Conditions	Rank
Independence or autonomy	_____
Financial reward or affluence	_____
Sense of achievement or accomplishment	_____
Helping others	_____
Creating something	_____
Equality, fairness	_____
Loyalty	_____
Job security	_____
Pleasant working conditions	_____
Friendships at work	_____
Variety of tasks	_____
Opportunities for promotions	_____

FORM 9.2.1 (*Continued*)

3. What talents do you wish to use in your work?

4. What type of working relationship with other people do you prefer? That is, do you prefer working alone or with other people? Do you enjoy working with a few people you know well or helping people you don't know?

5. What type of physical work setting is desirable to you (e.g., office, outdoors, plant facility, working at home)?

6. How much freedom and independence do you want in your work? For example, do you want to set your own hours? Determine your own projects? How much guidance or structure by others do you need in your work (i.e., do you need others to outline the scope of your projects and provide deadlines)?

7. Think of one time when you felt like a real professional. What were you doing or what had you just done? Why was this achievement meaningful?

PART C: GOALS AND ACTION PLANNING

1. Describe your career goals for the next several years.

2. What specific things will you need to do to meet your goals?

3. What internal and external obstacles might you encounter along the way toward achievement of your goals?

4. Describe any skills or assistance you will need to meet your goals.

5. How much commitment do you have to your goals? Explain.

FORM 9.2.2 ASSESSMENT QUESTIONS

1. What did you learn about yourself that you did not realize before?

2. How important are your career and work in your total life? Why is this important for you to realize?

FORM 9.2.2 (*Continued*)

3. How can completing a self-assessment assist you in preparing a résumé or interviewing for a job?

4. What will you do to follow up on this self-assessment?

EXERCISE: 10.1: PROBLEMS IN THE PAY SYSTEM*

Overview

Chapter 10 discusses the importance of internal and external equity in structuring an effective pay program. This exercise describes a situation in which perceived inequities exist and the organization is already realizing the effects of these perceptions.

Learning Objectives

After completing the exercise, you should be able to

1. Determine the critical variables that must be considered in assessing the fairness of a pay system.
2. Assess the weights to be given to data related to internal and external equity.
3. Develop a system that can more closely monitor the effects of pay on critical personnel data.

Procedure

Part A: Individual Analysis

After reading the chapter and before class, read the scenario below and all exhibits and then answer the questions on Form 10.1.1.

Part B: Group Analysis

In groups of about six, students should first review all of their respective Forms 10.1.1 and then attempt to reach consensus on the questions. The group should prepare a concise written response to each of the questions on Form 10.1.1.

Scenario

Denise Nance is the director of the Computer Center/User Assistance (CCUA) department of a large manufacturing company in the rural Southeast. Last year's revenue was $23.5 million. Profit was in line with expectations.

Recently, a serious problem has developed in her division. A growing percentage of her employees have left the company in the past year, which has affected unit productivity and costs. While turnover in her department has always been a problem, things appear to have gotten out of hand. Until now, turnover had run around 20 percent per year for lower division staff personnel and 15 percent per year for middle division employees.

However, in the past three months, CCUA has lost five data processors (50 percent of the total) and six (75 percent) computer analysts. Previously, Ms. Nance had no policy regarding exit interviews or turnover control, but informal discussions with the individuals who have left have led to the hypothesis that many employees leave because they feel they are underpaid.

To complicate matters, Ms. Nance's supervisor, Julie Linquist, the vice president in charge of technical services, is becoming increasingly concerned about the costs associated with the human resource function at CCUA. Exhibit 10.1.1 presents a recent memo from Ms. Linquist to Ms. Nance concerning the problem.

Following Ms. Linquist's orders, Ms. Nance conducted phone interviews with 12 former employees (the only ones available) and distributed questionnaires to her current workforce.

The survey results indicated a number of interesting findings, which are summarized in Exhibit 10.1.2. The dominant reason for individuals leaving CCUA was pay. The current workforce also indicated strong dissatisfaction with current pay levels. Although the survey was not limited to data processing IIs and computer analyst Is, both Ms. Nance and Ms. Linquist believe that these two positions are of particular concern. Responses from both current and past employees from both job classifications were similar to those of the entire sample.

The data processor II position currently carries a salary range of $11.00 to $12.70 per hour. The average actual pay of the seven incumbents is $12 per hour ($24,960 per year based on their 40-hour workweek). In addition, employees receive 40 hours of paid leave for the first year with an increase of 5 hours every 1,000 hours of service. Health insurance plus basic life insurance is provided by the company at a cost of $950 per year per employee. CCUA usually employs 10 DP IIs, but the current level is only 7.

The computer analyst I position currently carries a salary range of $25,500 to $32,500. The average actual salary paid to the eight incumbents is $31,500. Paid leave for CA IIs is 9 days for the first year of service, increasing by 2 days for every following year with a limit of 21 days of paid leave. Health and life insurance coverage costs the company $950 per year per employee.

Recruitment costs average $450 for each data processor IIs and $850 for computer analyst Is. Costs are low for the DP IIs because they have been obtained, primarily, from the local marketplace. Entry-level individuals are hired 75 percent of the time, and the organization spends considerable resources to train them. By contrast, the computer analysts are recruited from the regional market. Prime candidates typically possess either considerable experience in a similar position or a college degree in information systems management with light, but related, part-time (or summer) work experience.

Ms. Nance budgets $255,490 for data processing IIs and $293,984 for computer analysts. The company is in the sixth month of its fiscal year. During this fiscal year, the CCUA department has been using a 3.5 percent salary increase budget to reward its performers and to keep pace with the marketplace.

*Contributed by James R. Harris and Lee P. Stepina.

Ms. Nance obtained a pay survey conducted by Decision Sciences, Inc., a reputable information-systems consulting firm. The data are depicted in Exhibit 10.1.3. A compensation analyst at DSI has suggested that, based on the verbal descriptions provided by Ms. Nance, the data processor II position would probably most closely match the survey's "data processor" position, while CCUA's computer analyst I job is most comparable with the survey's "junior analyst and programmer" position.

Exhibit 10.1.1

```
To: Denise Nance, Director of CCUA

From: Julie Linquist, Vice President Technical Services

Re: Personnel Problems


I don't know what's going on down there but Jon Anderson of placement services just informed me that
you requested another listing for a data processing person and another computer analyst. According to
my records, that's the fifth DP person and the sixth computer analyst you have lost this year! It
costs a lot of money to hire new people. This is obviously not the pattern that I want to see from
your department. I want you to investigate this immediately.

I want you to contact the individuals who you lost and find out why they left. I also want you to talk
to the employees who are still there and find what, if anything, could potentially be causing the
problem. Let's get this problem cleared up now.
```

Exhibit 10.1.2   **Survey Results**
All items scaled 1 (satisfied) to 5 (dissatisfied).

Current Employees	Mean	SD
Supervision	2.1	1.6
Working conditions	1.9	1.8
Task characteristics	3.0	2.1
Pay	4.2	0.5
Benefits	4.3	1.1
Work hours	3.1	.9
Physical conditions	1.4	1.5
General satisfaction	3.9	0.7

Employees Who Left	Mean	SD
Supervision	1.9	1.5
Working conditions	2.4	1.7
Task characteristics	3.7	2.0
Pay	4.8	1.1
Benefits	4.5	0.6
Work hours	3.0	2.0
Physical conditions	1.7	0.5
General satisfaction	4.2	1.2

Reasons for leaving:

Not enough money	83.3%
Spouse left area	8.3%
Child care problems	8.3%

Exhibit 10.1.3 **Excerpt From Decision Sciences**

Title	Average Weighted Salary	Mfg/ Consumer	Mfg/ Industrial	Banking	Other Financial Services	DP Services	Wholesale Distribution
IS Management							
1 CIO/VP	106,864	128,611	100,741	124,318	109,130	157,500	130,000
2 Manager/supervisor	65,811	83,333	74,821	76,500	67,143	60,000	57,143
End-User Support							
3 Manager end-user computing	56,808	74,167	62,667	57,500	58,500	55,000	48,750
4 Information center manager	54,346	56,667	60,833	56,818	53,500	63,333	49,000
5 PC specialist support	38,058	40,000	48,077	39,211	36,250	37,000	38,636
6 LAN manager	45,880	55,000	52,857	46,000	46,000	52,000	52,000
7 WP supervisor	36,538	55,000	42,500	32,600	34,000	40,000	34,000
Systems Analysis/Programming							
8 **Manager**	65,357	83,182	63,913	68,611	64,286	66,364	72,000
9 Senior systems analyst and programmer	50,345	50,714	53,333	52,143	51,471	56,250	52,000
10 Systems analyst and programmer	43,220	44,000	43,462	45,250	42,647	48,750	60,455
11 Intermediate analyst and programmer	37,517	40,000	38,571	37,750	38,000	38,125	40,000
12 Junior analyst and programmer	35,156	33,750	40,714	35,000	32,143	37,500	32,875
13 **Application/Operating Systems Programming Manager**	64,481	79,000	67,667	68,529	71,765	68,750	66,667
14 Senior applications/operating sys. prog.	52,434	55,000	55,938	52,353	56,000	55,000	53,125
15 Applications/operating sys. prog.	44,419	48,571	46,250	46,176	46,563	46,429	40,000
16 Intermediate applications/operating sys. prog.	37,150	42,500	40,000	35,000	38,636	35,000	37,500
17 Junior applications/operating sys. prog.	29,709	30,000	32,500	29,615	30,455	30,000	28,750
Data Com/Telecom/Connectivity							
18 Network manager (LAN-WAN)	57,546	63,750	59,643	59,643	72,500	57,222	58,333
19 Telecommunications manager	57,136	58,750	66,111	59,231	67,500	63,125	60,000
20 Communications specialist	42,276	37,000	43,000	41,667	46,818	40,000	43,750
21 Database manager/administrator	61,077	71,000	60,500	64,643	70,385	52,500	62,000
22 Database analyst	48,194	52,000	55,000	46,000	51,250	42,500	47,500
23 Microcomputer/workstation manager	44,500	35,000	55,000	46,818	43,750	47,500	43,750
24 Data processor	27,500	26,000	29,000	28,000	26,500	26,000	27,000

Exhibit 10.1.3 (*Continued*)

	Government	Medical/ Legal	Trans./ Utilities	Education	Construction/ Mining	Other	Average Salary by Company Revenue ($ Million)				
							Less than $200	$200– $499	$500– $4,999	$5,000– $19,999	$20,000+
1	71,731	64,500	114,167	103,571	76,667	101,600	82,292	84,697	104,844	128,780	129,700
2	51,739	42,500	66,667	51,250	52,000	65,104	50,204	61,094	68,534	75,811	73,269
3	53,750	—	63,462	49,000	43,750	54,310	47,200	46,667	58,871	62,593	60,857
4	47,500	40,000	61,364	46,000	—	51,500	43,529	46,250	56,957	60,741	56,071
5	30,455	27,143	41,071	31,429	30,000	38,250	36,053	31,600	39,405	40,429	40,833
6	42,500	40,000	44,500	34,000	40,000	45,833	42,368	46,667	48,519	46,250	46,172
7	36,667	40,000	40,000	25,000	25,000	38,846	32,500	40,000	36,667	38,235	37,000
8	55,294	40,000	67,105	50,000	62,500	65,814	58,958	53,421	65,288	71,216	68,261
9	45,926	40,000	52,750	40,000	46,000	49,375	46,935	46,250	49,500	53,784	52,843
10	38,571	35,000	42,727	32,500	40,000	41,667	45,000	39,464	42,750	43,663	44,692
11	31,316	25,000	39,000	32,500	40,000	38,448	35,000	38,333	38,256	36,250	38,500
12	32,500	30,000	40,313	30,000	30,000	33,913	37,500	36,000	33,529	33,750	36,667
13	53,333	47,500	66,875	47,500	62,500	62,027	51,667	51,250	66,395	70,789	68,889
14	47,105	—	56,875	45,000	47,500	50,286	43,947	46,667	52,391	55,429	57,206
15	37,500	40,000	47,000	36,000	55,000	43,500	41,500	37,273	44,390	45,571	46,562
16	33,571	—	38,846	32,500	—	36,250	40,000	30,455	38,448	35,556	39,444
17	23,125	—	37,273	25,000	26,000	26,875	30,000	26,875	30,192	29,038	31,176
18	49,231	47,500	68,750	40,000	55,000	60,000	46,154	61,667	54,630	80,000	64,500
19	46,429	—	54,231	43,750	55,000	55,556	41,538	48,333	57,000	82,258	61,852
20	36,786	—	49,000	36,250	55,000	41,071	39,000	33,182	39,189	45,825	47,857
21	51,786	—	69,000	55,033	70,000	55,962	47,778	51,364	60,000	66,818	66,765
22	42,143	—	50,000	40,000	55,000	46,136	46,000	46,429	46,207	48,500	50,781
23	43,000	40,000	47,600	40,000	—	38,848	35,714	43,750	45,000	44,412	47,941
24	25,000	28,000	25,500	25,000	—	28,000	25,000	27,000	28,000	28,500	29,000

FORM 10.1.1

You have been retained as a consultant to evaluate the situation and make recommendations for action. Ms. Nance wants your positions on the following:

1. Are the CCUA department's current pay practices concerning data processor IIs and computer analyst Is externally equitable (i.e., competitive)? Explain your answer.

2. What specific action, if any, do you recommend be taken now? Be specific and justify your recommendations as fully as possible.

3. What specific strategy(ies) do you recommend for the future so that these types of problems can be anticipated and (it is hoped) avoided.

4. As is often the case in business, we typically find that we must make decisions, or recommendations, on the basis of incomplete, imperfect information. What additional information in this situation would have enabled you to improve the quality of your recommendations?

5. Conduct a Web search (O*NET?) to determine how accurate the data are in Exhibit 10.1.3 for the systems analyst/programmer job title. Summarize your findings below, citing the relevant Web site(s) and the methods of the pay survey. What are the outsourcing options for the data processing and computer analyst jobs? Locate pay data for outsourcing options.

Note: *Exercise 10.3, Developing an Employee Benefits Program, is available online at www.mhhe.com/bernardin5e.*

EXERCISE 10.2: SHOULD THE STATE ADOPT A PAY EQUITY POLICY?

Overview

The chapter discusses the controversial issue of pay equity or comparable worth. Many U.S. states and municipalities and over 100 countries have adopted some form of pay equity policy for government workers. In 2009, Congress debated the **Paycheck Fairness Act,** a bill supported by President Obama that included pay equity provisions. Ontario, Canada, has mandated pay equity for all public and private employers. Many collective bargaining writs now place great emphasis on pay equity adjustments based on studies that find evidence of gender or race-based inequities in the pay system. This exercise examines the issues and implications of pay equity for public and private employers. Students will review the summary of a pay equity study.

Learning Objectives

After completing the exercise, you should be able to

1. Understand the major components of a pay equity study.
2. Anticipate some of the advantages and disadvantages of a pay equity policy.
3. Discuss the implications of pay equity adjustments on market rates and private-sector employment.

Procedure

Part A: Individual Analysis

Congratulations! You have been appointed to the State University Task Force on Compensation. Your assignment is to review the report (Exhibit 10.2.1) submitted by a consulting firm under contract to an ad hoc committee of the state legislature. After reviewing state compensation information and conducting a pay equity study, the consulting firm made specific recommendations to the legislature. As a member of the task force, your job is to take a position on each of the recommendations. On Form 10.2.1, state your position and provide a justification in the space provided. Answer all of the questions on Form 10.2.1.

Part B: Group Analysis

In groups, students should attempt to reach consensus on the recommendations. Each group should prepare concise justifications for its recommendations.

Exhibit 10.2.1   **Executive Summary of Pay Equity Study**

The underlying theory of pay equity is that the wages for female-dominated occupations are artificially depressed due to historical bias against the value of "women's work." The goal of pay equity studies is to use objectively measured criteria to examine the relative value of all jobs to an employer in an effort to correct for any gender-based under-valuation.

Crucial to pay equity policy is the recognition that jobs that require equivalent or *comparable* skill, effort, knowledge, responsibility, and working conditions should be compensated equally. Once implemented, pay equity policy assures that an employer's classification and compensation systems are administered and maintained objectively and fairly.

Pay equity studies are typically conducted using point-factor job evaluations but, unlike the typical point-factor study where pay rates for jobs are set within a particular job family only and no comparisons are made *across* families, a pay equity study makes comparisons *across* job families. In a common approach for assessing pay equity, known as "policy-capturing," benchmark jobs for major job families under study are evaluated using a point-factor job evaluation method and current salaries are then statistically related to (i.e., regressed onto) the compensable factor ratings for each benchmark job. A statistical equation emerges that derives the predictive weights for the factors rated in the study which best predicts the actual salary for all benchmark jobs under study (based on the job factor ratings). For example, the predictive weight for "prerequisite knowledge" might be three times as great as the weight for "supervisory responsibilities," which in turn may be twice as predictive as "budget authority." These weights are then converted to dollar values so that the overall equation can be used to predict salaries based on the historical "policy." This equation is derived from the study of how factor ratings are correlated with salary across all major job families. Next, the female-dominated job families (families with 70 percent or more women) are identified and the overall equation is used to "predict" the salaries for the female-dominated families.

A perfectly fair (and equitable) system would find that when the overall equation is used to "predict" the salary for any given family, the predicted salary for that family would approximate the actual salary. Thus, in an equitable system, when we attempt to predict the salaries for the female-dominated jobs, the predictions would closely match the actual salaries these jobs are paid. But what typically happens in pay equity studies is that when the compensable points applied to the female-dominated job families are inserted into the overall predictive pay equation, the result is an estimate of salary for the female-dominated jobs that is substantially higher than the salary the female-dominated job families are actually earning. Females in the female-dominated jobs are thus "underpaid" when their real pay is compared to their "predicted" pay based on the overall pay "policy." The same process is followed for male-dominated jobs where policy-capturing studies tend to show that the male-dominated families are overpaid. A pay equity policy would then use the predictive equation from all job families and adjust the female-dominated jobs to match the salaries that are predicted. This would be considered pay equity.

To accomplish the above objective, we examined a representative sample of 300 families in the career service system. This served as the basis of our analysis in determining objectively what job content characteristics the state apparently valued when setting pay. The question that guided this study is, in setting pay rates, does the state value work differently (and perhaps in a biased manner) for male-dominated jobs as opposed to female- and minority-dominated jobs? In other words, is there a difference in monetary return for jobs with similar characteristics and requirements?

The state utilizes a position classification system whereby positions are consolidated into job families and these families are assigned to pay grades. For some job families, the pay grades within the family were determined by a point-factor job evaluation system. Jobs from other families were determined by comparisons to the external market for the same jobs. The present study was designed to provide a model of "equitable compensation" for the state that is derived from the data resulting from its current pay policy. Using this model, the analysis shows which families are underpaid and which families are "overpaid." The recommendations, if adopted, will bring female- and minority-dominated classes in line with equitable compensation.

As is typical in pay equity studies, the approach utilized for this study is called *policy capturing*. Through policy capturing, one form of "relative worth" is derived for all jobs under study. As described above, a compensation model was developed in which specific job content features, such as the number of persons supervised, the level of education, the level of analytic reasoning, and the years of prerequisite experience, were grouped into compensable factors. Each of the 300 job families was then evaluated in terms of relevance of each factor. Exhibit 10.2.2 presents a portion of the "point-factor" methodology used to evaluate compensable factors. As described above, weights for these factors were then derived to determine the "predictive" dollar value for each factor rated for the 300 families. Thus, the weights for each compensable factor are derived from a statistical model that makes explicit what is currently (and historically) valued implicitly within the organization across all job families and jobs. The relationship between compensable factors and pay is thus determined. The ability of each compensable factor to predict salary level is then derived through policy capturing. Pay equity adjustments are indicated when this statistical relationship is violated simply because the jobs are performed by a high percentage of females. This methodology was selected because it does not impose outside standards for fair compensation on the state. Rather, it looks at the current compensation policy and, if enacted, simply adjusts the existing pay rates in instances where its own standards are not met. Policy capturing techniques thus allow the state to adjust its salary grades to eliminate any influence of gender or race bias without radically altering its basic philosophy of compensation.

Findings

As a result of the above analysis, it was determined there is substantial undervaluation of female-dominated classes in the Career Service System. A model of equitable compensation has been developed to adjust for the resulting pay inequities.

Another objective of this study was to assess the cost of correcting gender-based pay inequities for the purpose of budget planning by the legislature. The total cost to the state for making pay equity adjustments to the female-dominated classes is estimated to be $75,552,000. An implementation model is recommended that suggests an appropriations schedule of $9,552,000 for the first year and $16,500,000 for the next four years to adjust base-pay rates for families found to be "underpaid."

The wage-setting process in the state is not structured in a way that facilitates the maintenance of internal equity. This is primarily because there is no quantitative job evaluation system tied to a unified wage structure that would keep future inequities from occurring. Women and minorities are underrepresented in job classes at the upper end of the wage structure. It is also recommended that the point-factor system used in the study should be adopted for use by the state for all job families.

Exhibit 10.2.2   **Part of Point Factor Job Evaluation Method**

1. Prerequisite knowledge
   11 Doctorate, law, medical, or other degree beyond master's
   10 Master's
    9 Some graduate education, but no degree
    8 B.A. or B.S.
    7 Two- or three-year college degree
    6 Some business or vocational school courses (such as typing, nursing, or drafting), *after* finishing high school or G.E.D.
    5 Some college
    4 High school or G.E.D.
    3 Some business or vocational courses (such as typing, nursing, plumbing, or drafting) but no G.E.D. or high school degree
    2 Some high school
    1 Elementary school
    0 None

2. Experience
    5 5 years or equivalent
    4 4 years
    3 3 years
    2 2 years
    1 1 year
    0 None

3. Supervision
    4 Major program or department
    3 Second-line supervision—supervises supervisors
    2 First-line supervision—hire, fire, discipline, promote
    1 Does not supervise, but coordinates, plans, and schedules, may be team leader or occasional supervisor
    0 Does not supervise

4. Mathematics
    3 Complex mathematics (statistics, advanced trig, and algebra)
    2 Basic math
    1 Basic arithmetic
    0 None

5. Special certification or license
    1 Yes
    0 No

6. Writing
   10 Technical, legal, scholarly, or policy analysis of length and creativity
    9 Formal reports or manual, technical reports/manual, more routine
    8 Monthly or annual reports, programs or work plans, technical specs, reports for others to review
    7 News releases, speeches
    6 Case histories
    5 Editing writing of others
    4 Writing original letters or memos
    3 Taking or writing minutes, dictation
    2 Writing (including patient records)
    1 Simple recording, tallying
    0 None

7. Information gathering
    6 Deciding what information should be gathered (policy decisions)
    5 Deciding how information should be gathered (design and planning decisions)
    4 Conducting complex information gathering—not routine
    3 Conducting data analysis under other's supervision—including lab tests
    2 Cataloging or classifying information
    1 Collecting or tallying information
    0 None

Exhibit 10.2.2 (*Continued*)

8. Recordkeeping
    4   Maintains records and files where confidentiality is required
    3   Maintains detailed client, patient, or inmate records, weekly or monthly
    2   Prepares and maintains files and records such as personnel, technical, financial
    1   Prepares and maintains daily records such as logs, supply inventory, medical charts, daily calendar
    0   None

9. Organize/prioritize work
    5   Set work objectives for agency
    4   Responsible for organizing and prioritizing work in unit
    3   Responsible for organizing and prioritizing work of projects
    2   Organize and prioritize own work and schedule appointments for others (not limited to coworkers)
    1   Organize own work only
    0   No responsibility for organizing work

10. Training/teaching (integral part of job)
    5   Developing and implementing educational programs at the state level for employees at educational agencies
    4   Other employees
    3   Clients, inmates, patients
    2   Students
    1   Training/teaching on occasion
    0   None

11. Budget authority
    5   Determine budget priorities for major department
    4   Set budget for division within major department
    3   Propose or prepare budget or financial projection for unit
    2   Propose or prepare budget or financial projection for individual projects (includes assembling data)
    1   Authority to spend budgeted money
    0   No budget authority

12. Laws, policies, regulations, administrative codes
    5   Develop agency position and defend laws or administrative codes
    4   Draft laws or administrative codes for agency use
    3   Ensure compliance with law, regulation, or administrative codes with public
    2   Ensure compliance within or across agencies
    1   Interpret administrative codes and regulations in order to carry out job
        responsibilities (i.e., determining eligibility or safety compliance)
    0   No responsibility related to laws, etc.

FORM 10.2.1

1. The state legislature should appropriate $75,552,000 to cover the costs of the pay equity adjustments indicated by this study.
   Agree _____ Disagree _____ Unsure _____ . If you are unsure, what specific additional information do you require before you take a position?

   Justification:

2. The policy-capturing analysis established that there is a violation of the Equal Pay Act.
   True _____ False _____

   Explain your answer:

3. The results of the "policy capturing" study established that there is a clear violation of Title VII.
   True _____ False _____

   Explain your answer:

4. If the state follows the recommendations, what impact could the policy have on private-sector compensation in the state?

5. To create internal equity faster and more cheaply, the consultants could have recommended reducing the pay of "overpaid" jobs or workers. What are the implications of this action based on research? Could you do this if there is an Equal Pay Act violation?

6. Explain exactly how the pay equity study determined that female-dominated jobs were "underpaid" and that some male-dominated jobs were found to be "overpaid." What does the term *policy capturing* mean in terms of this pay equity study?

7. Conduct research on the status of the "Paycheck Fairness Act." If this legislation is or were to become law, do the findings reported in this study indicate illegal discrimination under this legislation?

EXERCISE 11.1: THE DESIGN OF A PFP SYSTEM FOR MEGA MANUFACTURING*

Overview

This exercise evaluates the feasibility of different approaches to PFP given the strategic plan of the organization. As discussed in the chapter, the effectiveness of the PFP system depends on a number of factors. This exercise will give the student the opportunity to consider some of these factors in proposing an ideal PFP system.

Learning Objectives

After completing this exercise, you should be able to

1. Identify the key organizational variables that should be considered in the development and/or revision of a PFP system.
2. Understand the role and importance of other HRM activities (e.g., job analysis, performance appraisal) in the development of a PFP system.

Procedure

Part A: Individual Analysis

Step 1. Before class, read the scenario below.
Step 2. You have been retained as a consultant who must report to Ellen Lennett, director of incentive program development at Mega Manufacturing corporate headquarters. You will be working with the Kanto division. You have been asked to address the five issues raised on Form 11.1.1. Respond to each of the issues and recommend a specific program that supports both Mega's incentive policy and Kanto's situation. Your recommendation should consider *at least* the five points. Also, prior to class, complete the Assessment Questions form.

The two memos in Exhibits 11.1.1 and 11.1.2 may be relevant to the recommendations you will make. Ellen Lennett has received the notes, one from Don Walker, vice president, compensation and benefits, and the other from Bill Idrey, a compensation specialist she sent to help the Kanto personnel department.

Part B: Group Analysis

Step 1. In groups, each member should review the individual reports and take notes on the most important points. Each member also should devise his or her own strategy for identifying the best group response to make for each of the five questions presented in Form 11.1.1 plus any additional issues the group considers to be relevant. The group also should devise a list of key questions that must be answered by

management before a firm position can be taken on the elements of the PFP system.

Step 2. One group member should be designated to make a five-minute presentation of the group's position before the rest of the class. A "free for all" discussion should then focus on the various recommended plans.

Scenarios

Mega Manufacturing International is a large diversified company with its corporate headquarters in Boston and manufacturing plants, research and development facilities, and distribution and marketing centers in the United States and around the world. Mega Manufacturing is pursuing a long-range strategy of producing high-technology products for three markets: military, industrial, and retail consumer. Because of the intense competitive pressures in its chosen arenas, Mega Manufacturing believes it must obtain the maximum effort from its personnel. In support of this belief, Mega Manufacturing has adopted a policy of paying for performance (PFP). Typically, many of its divisions have incentives comprising a substantial portion of executive pay (40 percent to 150 percent of base pay possible in various types of incentives) and a significant portion of supervisory and employee compensation (5 percent to 25 percent possible).

To expand its capabilities in the new electronic surface-mount technology, Mega Manufacturing acquired GW Industries, which had several plants producing high-quality surface-mount electronic parts. The Kanto assembly plant was part of GW Industries; however, it was an older plant producing electronic parts for an industrial process rapidly approaching obsolescence. Although the products were produced on an assembly line, individual workers had relatively little contact with each other, and the skills required were relatively low. Kanto had been a profitable operation for GW, but Mega Manufacturing has to switch Kanto to a different product and process or close the plant.

Kanto has a reputation for paying average to below-market wages, but it was viewed as a dependable and stable employer with a good benefits package. As a consequence, Kanto has had a stable and loyal workforce; but with the buyout of GW and the consequent uncertainty surrounding Kanto's future, there has been talk of unionizing and some of the more skilled employees are known to be seeking other jobs.

Mega has decided to offer Kanto the opportunity to manufacture an extremely complex switching device for a military contract. Although the total manufacturing process is complex, it can be broken into steps, with each step consisting of individual skills that can be learned relatively quickly. Groups of individuals, each with a specific skill, will have to work closely together to achieve the required

*Contributed by E. Brian Peach and M. Ronald Buckley.

quality levels for each step in the switching device assembly. The nature of the process is such that each individual will have to take an active interest in the success of the assembly or the device will be unsatisfactory.

The two memos in Exhibits 11.1.1 and 11.1.2 may be relevant to the recommendations you will make. Ellen Lennett has just received the following notes, one (Exhibit 11.1.1) from Don Walker, vice president, compensation and benefits, and the other (Exhibit 11.1.2) from Bill Idrey, a compensation specialist whom Ms. Lennett sent to help the Kanto personnel department.

Exhibit 11.1.1

```
TO:        Ellen Lennett
SUBJECT:   Kanto incentive program
FROM:      Don Walker
```

Ellen,

We need to give Kanto some more help on setting up its incentives to adequately support the new switching assembly process. We cannot allow the conversion process to delay our completing switching assemblies as there is a large late delivery penalty. Also, Bids and Contracting apparently goofed and bid too low on the contract to maintain our usual margins. It appears we have to make up 3% somewhere.

Exhibit 11.1.2

```
TO:        Ellen Lennett
SUBJECT:   Kanto Incentive Program
FROM:      Bill Idrey
```

Just a quick note to advise you of some early problems I'm encountering.

1. The employees are learning the new skills, but the supervisors are having trouble (resisting?) learning the necessary composite skills.
2. The parts we're getting from our Indonesian plant will sometimes test OK individually, but not work in the final assembly. It apparently is not feasible to test the intermediate assembly steps.
3. Although job analysis says the steps and tasks are essentially equal, two of the assembly steps are perceived as being more important and thus as having higher status by the workers.
4. Robert Horne, the plant manager, is complaining that the new final quality check supervisor, Beatrice Inggold, is too strict and will slow down production.
5. Engineers from Design & Fabrication come in and watch, occasionally making suggestions, but I'm darned if I can see what they are contributing.

FORM 11.1.1

1. Is an incentive program appropriate? Explain your position.

2. If so, should there be one, two, or several plans?

3. Who should be included?

4. What should be the basis for incentive payments?

5. What kinds of incentives should be included?

1. What were the key variables you considered in your selection of an individual- or group-based PFP system?

2. What changes in organizational characteristics would seriously affect your recommendations?

3. What circumstances would lead you to conclude that a PFP system would not be in the best interests of the organization?

EXERCISE 11.2: PAY FOR PERFORMANCE AT DEE'S PERSONALIZED BASKETS

Overview

This exercise provides an opportunity for the student to develop a framework for a PFP system, training for the program, and a framework for the evaluation of the system. The problem is common to many organizations. As discussed in Chapter 11, while pay for performance is the preferred method of compensation for most jobs, there are many problems with such systems, including the apparent inability on the part of evaluators to be critical in their evaluations. Many experts on PFP systems maintain that this is the major problem with most PFP systems in operation today that use ratings as the basis for measurement. This exercise is designed to allow the student to construct a PFP system that would minimize such problems.

Learning Objectives

After completing this exercise, you should be able to

1. Consider different PFP options for different jobs.
2. Evaluate the relative advantages and disadvantages of the different approaches to PFP.
3. Consider the various issues related to training for PFP, including transfer, relapse, and cost.
4. Develop an evaluation design that can assess the effects of the PFP system.

Procedure

Part A: Individual Analysis

Before class, read the background material on Dee's Personalized Baskets presented in Exhibit 11.2.1. Answer the questions on Form 11.2.1.

Part B: Group Analysis

Step 1. Assume the role of a team of HR consultants to consider the development of a PFP system. In addition, you have been asked to develop a managerial training program to prepare managers for the new PFP system. You also have been asked to evaluate the effectiveness of the PFP system.

Step 2. Among the critical issues that your team should address are those listed on Form 11.2.1. Review each consultant's responses on Form 11.2.1. Discuss each response and prepare a plan to deal with each.

Step 3. Prepare a short presentation for the vice president that covers your team's ideas regarding the design of the PFP system. Remember that management will weigh heavily both your recommendations as well as your plan for implementation.

Exhibit 11.2.1   **Background Material for Dee's Personalized Baskets**

Nancy Harrison, HRM vice president of Dee's Personalized Baskets in Orlando, Florida, is disturbed by lagging productivity figures and problems of product quality and high turnover. She is intrigued by the results of a recent attitude survey of her employees. She has decided to experiment with some form of PFP system of compensation. The company's current system of compensation pays either straight hourly rates to nonsupervisory personnel or straight salary to all supervisory/managerial/sales personnel with a year-end bonus that is a percentage of base pay as determined by the board. The attitude survey results indicated employees believed that they would work harder if they perceived a stronger tie between their level of effort and their pay. Most of the 200 employees who would be part of the new pay system prepare individual baskets of gifts (perfumes, fancy soaps, fancy foods, wine, etc.), which are ordered by customers for clients and potential clients.

There are two distinct elements of the business. The largest and most reliable part of the business is partnerships with several of the largest hotels in the area to provide high-volume baskets for hotel rooms usually commensurate with the start of a convention. The convention contracts average around 300 baskets and have a profit margin of about 8 percent (the baskets retail for an average of $9.50). These high-volume baskets are produced by most of the assemblers who work around the supplies of goodies that typically go into the baskets (snacks, fruit, candy, hotel amenities). A growing and more profitable part of the business is much larger and more expensive baskets that retail for an average of $94 with a profit margin averaging 16 percent. The baskets are usually thematic and tailored to the particular situation or proclivities of the recipient. This part of the business represents about 20 percent of the business, but a goal is to expand in this area. Design and assembly of these baskets requires some artistic talent. There is a sales staff of three who currently work on straight salary.

Few respondents to the survey felt that they were recognized in any significant way for working harder than others. People most disturbed by the failure to recognize greater effort were the same people who indicated they were more likely to seek other employment. The turnover rate has increased for three straight years, and Dee's has lost some good people. The organization has a performance-appraisal system, but the ratings are generally very high. For the last performance-appraisal period, the average rating of effectiveness made by the 20 supervisors was 7.5 on a 9-point rating scale (with 9 representing "highly effective" performance).

FORM 11.2.1

1. What type(s) (if any) of PFP system(s) do you recommend for Dee's? Be as specific as possible and consider all jobs. What (if any) additional information would help you develop the most effective PFP system? (You may take a position against all PFP systems but make sure you explain why.)

2. Describe the chronology of steps for implementing the PFP system or explain why you are opposed to a PFP system for this situation.

3. Jessica Harrison, Dee's president, read an airline magazine article about gain sharing and was very impressed. She thinks it's a perfect approach for motivating the basket assemblers. How does gain sharing work, what conditions are necessary for maximum effectiveness, and what does the research say about its effects? Ms.Harrison wants your research-based, "bottom-line" opinion as to whether gain sharing is (or is not) a good PFP approach for Dee's.

FORM 11.2.1 (*Continued*)

4. What is measured using the PADS? What role (if any) should this score play in the PFP system or training raters for the system?

5. How would you address the high turnover rate? Could this problem be related to compensation?

EXERCISE 12.1: AN APPROACH TO DOWNSIZING

Overview

Chapter 12 discusses the role of the corporate restructuring and downsizing that have occurred in the United States in recent years. Many management experts maintain that overhead reduction and downsizing are required in order for U.S. corporations to remain competitive. The purpose of this exercise is to assess the effectiveness of downsizing strategies used by a phosphate company and a pharmaceutical company.

Learning Objectives

After completing this exercise, you should have

1. A better understanding of different approaches to downsizing and the advantages and disadvantages of each.
2. Knowledge of the potential problems that can develop with downsizing programs.

Procedure

Part A: Individual Analysis

Step 1. Prior to class, review the two scenarios below and the notes related to the downsizing/restructuring processes. Complete Forms 12.1.1 and 12.1.2 prior to class. The phosphate company notes were taken by Rosemary Richter, the company president's secretary, who attended the management meeting in which the president (Abbott) announced the need to downsize (Exhibit 12.1.1). Answer the relevant questions on Form 12.1.1.

Step 2. You also have been asked to review the documents that were prepared pursuant to a downsizing/restructuring program by Brooks Pharmaceutical (Exhibit 12.1.2). While Brooks had to reduce its workforce, management was very interested in retaining those personnel with the best performance records and also those who had been hired as a part of their diversity program. Study these documents and prepare questions of clarification so as to help you understand the entire process of restructuring. On Form 12.1.2, comment on the effectiveness of this restructuring process and point out any potential restructuring scenarios that could pose difficulties for Brooks.

Part B: Group Analysis

Step 1. In groups of about six people, attempt to reach consensus on the Form 12.1.1 answers. Organize a group response to items 2 and 3. The instructor will designate one presenter.

Step 2. The group also should generate a list of questions regarding the downsizing and restructuring at Brooks. Attempt to reach consensus on Question 3 of Form 12.1.2 (p. 723).

Exhibit 12.1.1   **Notes from Downsizing Meeting**[1]

CONFIDENTIAL STAFF MEETING NOTES

Meeting called by company president Jarold Abbott. All unit managers attended.

The purpose of the meeting was to provide an assessment of the financial situation and the need to take immediate action. We should make preparations for a full **unit manpower review** (UMR) and "show and tell" that will reduce our manpower by about one-half. We will use UMR, a performance appraisal of each employee, to "clean house." New organization charts are to be drawn up as if we are running all out and then taking every bit of the "fat" out. "Show and tell" will be a reduction in force from half rate to one-third rate. (In preparing the organization charts for the UMR and the "show and tell," early retirement is an area to look at. I will distribute a list of employees who would be eligible for a program we are considering.) This is a snapshot look at the company. Concern has been expressed regarding the seniority system that we have used in past reductions in force. This time, we need to make decisions based on future needs and potential. If a less senior person has more potential, that person should be retained. This applies to all employees, not just management. Possible transfers should be considered based on a skills match.

We presently have some 30 people in the hourly ranks between 60 and 65 and some 22 people on salary 55 and up. We want to reduce hourly by 200 people and salary by 60. People 55 and up will probably be eligible for the early program being considered.

ADMINISTRATIVE

Presently there are three people in the Traffic area. Smith states that at present rates, this is one person too many. This department can function with the supervisor and one clerk, with possibly one-half person from another area in accounting assisting when workload is high.

The purchasing supervisor's position is a training slot. He handles most of the contracts and fills in as a buyer for vacation relief for purchasing agents and storekeeper. He spends a great deal of time supervising the warehouse to improve purchasing and warehousing. Jones stated the warehouse is where we should "stash" maintenance supervisors as storekeepers and storage superintendents. Three people could be used here assuming no warehouse coverage on third shift.

Cost Accounting

Messenger can go. Records retention—part of that function could possibly be shared by inventory clerk, data processing clerk, or property control clerk.

Laboratory

Laboratory will be reorganized with a reduction of seven people.

Projects

Herz supervises project engineers and handles special projects. He, with Andrews, will head up the wet rock grinding study. Three senior project engineers: Valk is handling the absorbing tower and pump tank project. Naberhaus is working on rock wetting project and special projects for production. Wischmeyer is an electrical engineer.

Plant Engineering

Konopnicki supervises plant engineers with heavy emphasis on vibration analysis and mechanical failures.

One senior plant engineer (Lamb).

Two plant engineers I (Broussard and Martin). Martin learning vibration analysis and working with Konopnicki. Broussard expert on rubber lining materials.

Three development engineers (Stanton, Neff, and Chamberlin). Neff will be transferred to Projects Group and Stanton reassigned to Maintenance. Consider eliminating chief plant engineer position and returning Konopnicki to senior plant engineer.

Process

Andrews supervises process engineers and makes sure that environmental government regulations in force. Andrews will also be working on wet rock grinding study.

One chemist I (Riddle). Does all forms on governmental regulations, pond water balances, and any special DAP projects.

Two process engineers I (Marrone and Katzaras). Marrone will temporarily fill in for Andrews. Katzaras working on cogeneration project.

One engineer II (Stone). DAP projects.

Environmental Engineering

One supervisor and three technicians who keep track of governmental sampling. Ken to draw up organization chart that reflects number of people he needs with no capital projects and operating at one-third rates (interface with Production and Maintenance). Possibly eliminate chief plant engineer and move to Maintenance. Project can cover both areas.

PRODUCTION

Presently the Production department is structured with four production superintendents and four area superintendents. At one-third rates, Persons would like to restructure to combine Areas I and IV and Areas II and III. This would eliminate two superintendents, keeping four area superintendents. Possibly eliminating area superintendent in Area IV (Price), who will be interviewing for position at Hardee County. Four shift supervisors can be eliminated at one-third rates who will become guards under Industrial Relations. Some early retirement may be offered.

MAINTENANCE

The department is now staffed by two general superintendents and one superintendent over planning and coordination. The area superintendent position in Area III could be eliminated (Garcia is retirement age) and the planner (Card) could be moved over to pick up contractors. One maintenance clerk also can be eliminated. At one-third rates, #2 and #3 shifts in Area I. Eliminate #3 shift in Area II and possibly shift #1. McDuffie will draw up an organization chart as if Goebel, Garcia, and Lopata were to retire.

---

[1] Notes taken by Rosemary Richter.

FORM 12.1.1

1. How do you evaluate this approach to workforce reduction? What (if anything) did Abbott do right and what did he do wrong? What additional information do you need about the downsizing effort in order to fully understand the process?

2. Three months after this meeting, Garcia (age 58) and Lopata (age 55) were discharged. Based on the information provided, were Garcia and Lopata victims of age discrimination? Explain your answer. If necessary, what specific additional information do you require before you can take a position? Provide a set of "if–then" propositions (e.g., if I know "X," then "Y" follows).

FORM 12.1.1 (*Continued*)

3. Must the company adhere to the WARN Act? How do they meet this obligation?

4. How would you evaluate the fairness of this approach to downsizing? What are some examples of possible difficulties with distributive and procedural justice?

FORM 12.1.1 (*Continued*)

Name ——————————————————— Group ———————————————————

5. Is "disparate impact" theory applicable to downsizing decisions? If so, create some data that would illustrate the use of this theory of discrimination.

6. If prima facie evidence of age discrimination is found, what burden (if any) would Brooks Pharmaceutical have?

Exhibit 12.1.2   **Key Considerations in Brooks Restructuring**

- New sales structure.
- No relos for reps and DL/minimal relocations for Rls and Als.
- Key job requirements and past performance.
- Maintenance of organizational diversity.
- Role of tenure in retention process.

- Role of customer constancy.
- Role of bumping.
- Role of pooling.
- Retention of our strongest leaders.
- Retention of identified successor candidates.

To: Managers
From: Moro Hipple
Subject: The HR Diversity Challenge Process
Goal: To follow through with our operating principles. Valuing a diverse organization—by proactively considering diversity in our restructuring process.

Stages/dates in the process:

- Preliminary ratings   6/5
- Rating sheet discussion   6/6–6/7
- Management/HR review   6/22–6/24
- Adverse impact analysis/challenges   6/28
- Final ratings for decisions   7/1

Rating sheet discussions at the area offices:

- These discussions must include a representative from human resources who will challenge decisions and ensure the integrity of the process.
- HR challengers will receive a report prior to arrival at the area office that details diversity data for personnel in the area.

Management/HR Review:

- HR challengers will review retention decisions with respect to diversity. HR challenger will ensure the integrity/objectivity/documentation of the process.

Impact analysis: The final structure will be assessed against the predownsizing structure to test for adverse impact (80 percent rule).

- A report will be generated by HR indicating predownsizing (current) diversity data assessed by area and position for comparison to the new organization.

The result of this analysis may lead to a possible further challenge.

To: All Employees
From: David Brooks, CEO
Subject: Equal Employment Opportunity
Date: February

On behalf of the management of Brooks Pharmaceuticals Division, I wish to reaffirm our commitment to equal employment opportunity. It is Brooks' policy to provide equal employment opportunity to all individuals without regard to race, color, religion, age, sex, national origin, Vietnam Era veteran, or disability status. This priority covers all phases of employment, including but not limited to recruiting, hiring, training, promoting, placement, demotion, or transfer; layoff, termination, or recall; rates of pay or other forms of compensation, fringe benefits; the use of all facilities; and participation in all Company-sponsored employee activities. We impose only valid requirements to ensure that employment and promotional decisions are made in accordance with equal employment opportunity.

I have appointed Moro Hipple, senior vice president of Human Resources, to coordinate, implement, monitor, and report on the effectiveness of the Pharmaceuticals Division's Affirmative Action Program. All managers and supervisors are charged with the responsibility of ensuring that any discrimination in employment is avoided. All employees are expected to recognize this policy and cooperate with its implementation.

Our affirmative action plans and programs have been developed to help us achieve full utilization of our human resources. We have made substantial progress in equal opportunity in recent years and with your continued support we will continue to move forward.

FORM 12.1.2

1. Based on what you know so far, evaluate the Brooks approach to workforce reduction. What did Brooks do right and what did they do wrong?

2. What additional information do you need about the downsizing effort at Brooks in order to fully understand the legal implications of its restructuring?

3. One month after the restructuring, Brooks is informed by the EEOC that, thus far, four complaints have been filed against Brooks for age discrimination in the process. What data should you examine in order to determine the possibility of discrimination? Should Brooks be concerned about an ADEA claim based on the disparate impact theory?

EXERCISE 12.2: COMPUDUDES CONSIDERS ARBITRATION OPTIONS FOR EMPLOYEE DISPUTES

Overview

As discussed in Chapter 12, there has been a rapid "privatization" of the employment dispute resolution process in the American workplace. Supreme Court rulings have allowed employers to move away from costly, time-consuming litigation by adopting alternative dispute resolution (ADR) procedures for both existing employees and new hires. The American Arbitration Association reports that it currently provides ADR services for over 500 employers with five million employees. In 2001, the Supreme Court in *Circuit City v. Adams* determined that an employer can insist on the submission of an employment dispute to binding arbitration as a condition of employment.

One critical issue is the choice of appropriate ADR program characteristics and the effects of such characteristics on employees' attitudes. ADR programs vary from traditional mediation and arbitration to more unusual techniques such as "mock trials." There are two crucial issues for employers. The first issue is the choice between mediation, arbitration, or some combination. With mediation, the disputing parties attempt to resolve the issue themselves with the assistance of a neutral third party. Arbitration requires the parties to present their case to a neutral third party who then will make a determination on the issues. Many companies use some combination of the two for their ADR procedure.

The second issue is whether ADR procedures should be voluntary or mandatory. Voluntary ADR programs give the parties the option to select ADR, generally after the dispute has arisen; mandatory programs stipulate in advance that all disputes that arise in the course of employment will be referred to mediation and/or arbitration. Employer-imposed ADR programs may provide for any combination of these characteristics.

Learning Objectives

After completing this exercise, you should have

1. An understanding of different approaches to ADR.
2. Knowledge of the differences in attitudes toward the ADR options and the implications of those attitudes.

Procedure

Part A: Individual Analysis

Prior to class, review the four ADR options presented in Exhibit 12.2.1 in the context of the scenario presented. Complete your ratings for each of the options on Form 12.2.1. In the space provided, make any comments regarding the options.

Part B: Group Analysis

In groups of about six people, calculate ratings for each option and then, representing the interests of Compududes, attempt to reach consensus on the policy to adopt or decide that none of the options should be adopted. If you reject all options, derive an alternative program. The group also should generate a list of questions regarding the ADR program options, their implementation, and the AAA.

Exhibit 12.2.1

You are a recent college graduate who has just started a paid internship with Compududes, a computer retailer. You receive the following e-mail from the HR department:

> Compududes is considering four new policies for resolving problems that happen at work and that cannot be resolved through the "open door policy," which allows any employee to discuss any work-related problem with the manager of the department. Each proposed new policy encourages open communication, protects your work relationships, and helps keep costs and tempers under control. For serious, legal disputes, the new policy makes available the experience and objectivity of the American Arbitration Association (AAA). The AAA helps businesses, associations, and all levels of government resolve disputes. Thus, for any labor dispute such as sexual harassment or possible discrimination claims, we would like to involve the AAA.

We would like your opinion about the four options we are considering. Make your ratings of the four options on Form 12.2.1.

Option #1: The **voluntary mediation** ADR program: If you fail to resolve your disputes through the "open door policy," you may voluntarily elect to involve the AAA in resolving the dispute. This neutral body or mediator can listen to both sides of the story and help you work it out together. To use AAA, you will pay a $50 processing fee.

Option #2: The **mandatory mediation** option: If you fail to resolve your dispute through the "open door policy," the AAA will then be asked to attempt to resolve the dispute. This neutral body or mediator can listen to both sides of the story and help you work it out together. For the use of AAA, you will pay a $50 processing fee.

Option #3: The **voluntary mediation plus voluntary binding arbitration** option: If you fail to resolve your dispute through the "open door policy," you may voluntarily elect to involve the AAA. This neutral body or mediator can listen to both sides of the story and help you work it out together. To use AAA, you will pay a $50 processing fee.

If you fail to resolve the dispute to *your satisfaction* through mediation, you may elect to present your dispute to AAA for binding arbitration. The arbitrator will decide your case after hearing arguments from both sides. With arbitration, the decision is final, binding, and enforced under the law, with only limited appeals allowed through the courts. The decision to go to arbitration is voluntary.

Option #4: The **mandatory mediation plus binding arbitration** option: If you fail to resolve your dispute through the "open door policy," the AAA will then attempt to resolve the dispute through mediation. This neutral body or mediator can listen to both sides of the story and help you work it out together. For the use of AAA, you will pay a $50 processing fee.

If you fail to resolve the dispute through mediation, your dispute will then be automatically presented to the AAA for binding arbitration. The AAA arbitration will decide your case after hearing arguments from both sides. With arbitration, the decision is final, binding, and enforced under the law, with only limited appeals allowed through the courts.

FORM 12.2.1

Review the four ADR options the company is considering. Rate the extent to which you agree or disagree with each policy using the following scale: Strongly disagree = 1; Disagree = 2; Undecided = 3; Agree = 4; and Strongly agree = 5

Options

1   2   3   4   5

__ __ __ __ __   1. The procedure described is fair to all.

__ __ __ __ __   2. The procedure is advantageous to management.

__ __ __ __ __   3. I trust management at this organization.

__ __ __ __ __   4. This option makes me more motivated to work here.

__ __ __ __ __   5. The outcomes from this option should favor the employees.

__ __ __ __ __   6. This option is fair for any labor dispute, including union-organizing issues.

__ __ __ __ __   7. I would have no problem accepting a job offer from Compududes if this option was in place.

Conduct a Web search and learn what you can about the American Arbitration Association and ADR. From the employee's and employer's perspectives, what are the critical issues that should be considered? What changes would you make to any of the options to increase their fairness to all parties? Does the plaintiff have any other options after losing a binding arbitration case? How does such a policy relate to the "employment-at-will" doctrine?

EXERCISE 12.3: HANDLING AN EMPLOYEE'S TERMINATION*

Overview

Chapter 12 discussed employee discipline and termination. Several issues are involved when an employee is performing below standards to the point where it is necessary to terminate the employment relationship. This exercise puts you in the role of HR professional and asks that you go through several steps leading up to the termination of an employee.

Learning Objectives

After completing this exercise, you should be able to

1. Experience the process by which HR professionals handle requests for termination by line managers and supervisors in the organization.
2. Make decisions on crucial issues involved in the termination process.
3. Develop an understanding of the sensitivity and gravity of the termination process.

Procedure

Part A: Individual Analysis

Step 1. Read the scenario below and the accompanying exhibits associated with the termination of a customer service representative. Then follow these steps to ensure that the termination is carried out appropriately:

1. The first step is to investigate the situation to make sure the supervisor's claims are true. Whom will you contact? What questions will you ask? What precautions should you take to assure that your investigation is confidential and legally appropriate?
2. Ensure that the necessary documentation is in place based upon the discipline policy and your expertise as an HR manager.

*Contributed by Jennifer Robin.

3. Assume that the termination is in fact warranted. Managers typically hold termination meetings at *The Daily Register,* but it is not unheard of for the HR department to conduct this meeting. Given the available information, who should conduct the meeting? What steps will you take to prepare the manager and/or yourself for this meeting? Prepare an agenda for the termination meeting.
4. *The Daily Register* has some guidelines for severance packages, benefits, and outplacement services, but they are very informal and typically decided upon on a case-by-case basis. In this situation, what would you recommend for Jeanette?

Step 2. Write a one-page memo in which you take a position on each question raised in step 1.

Part B: Group Analysis

Step 1. In groups, each member should review the memos of all other members. Each group should attempt to reach consensus an each question.

Scenario

You've been working at *The Daily Register,* a regional newspaper, for the last 12 months in the HR department. Your supervisor, the HR manager, is leaving for vacation tomorrow. With impeccable timing, one of the sales managers, Paul White, has submitted the paperwork for terminating one of his employees. The sales department is responsible for soliciting and securing advertisers for the newspaper. Paul maintains that Jeanette Landis has failed to reach sales goals for the last six months despite numerous attempts at discipline. Furthermore, Jeanette has threatened to file a lawsuit if *The Daily Register* terminates her employment. The HR manager delegates the handling of the termination to you. The documents sent by Paul, documents that you've received in HR, Jeanette's job description, and the company's discipline policy appear in Exhibits 12.3.1 through 12.3.6.

Exhibit 12.3.1

Return-path:	pwhite@ourcompany.com
Content-return:	allowed
Date:	Wed, 11 Apr 15:45:01–0400
From:	"Paul White" pwhite@ourcompany.com
Subject:	Termination
To:	you@ourcompany.com

HR Staff:

I have sent the necessary materials to your office to fire one of my customer service reps, Jeanette Landis. I've been pulling my hair out trying to get her to sell something for the past 6 months, but she can't do it! She repeatedly misses her sales goals by a huge margin due to her laziness and stupidity. I need to be rid of her as soon as possible so I can get an employee in here that can do the job. I could suspend her next, but I doubt it will help. Can you give me the go-ahead so I can show her the door? I know I was reluctant to fire my old high school buddy last year, but I will *gladly* hold this termination meeting.

Paul

Exhibit 12.3.2

From Paul's file:

Performance Appraisal
Name: Jeanette R. Landis
Position: Customer Service Representative
Last Review: **Review Period:** 12.6 to 6.6
Job knowledge: Employee's ability to understand the required duties, responsibilities, skills, and procedures.

Rating: Exceeds Requirements
Comments: Jeanette has an excellent understanding of the requirements of her job. She has been instrumental in training new staff members this period.

Quality of Work: The degree to which the employee's work is accurate, complete, and conforms to *The Daily Register* and supervisor requirements.

Rating: Meets Requirements

Comments: The sales Jeanette makes are processed appropriately. She reports them to me in an acceptable fashion, and she maintains customer accounts adequately.

Productivity: Employee produces a large volume of work, is timely, and meets all deadlines.

Rating: Unsatisfactory

Comments: Jeanette does not make new sales. Rather, she maintains customer orders for the same ad, run on the same day, for the same cost. She does not make attempts to win new customers or grow current accounts. This area needs severe improvement. It is recommended that Jeanette repeat sales training.

Organizational Skills: Employee uses time effectively, sets priorities, and demonstrates initiative on projects.
Rating: Needs Improvement

Comments: Jeanette should be using time to increase her customer base. Despite discussions this quarter, no evidence of this is present. She is not a high initiative person.

Communication Skills: The employee's ability to convey ideas and information effectively and appropriately to others.

Rating: Exceeds Expectations

Comments: Jeanette is extremely articulate. Other Customer Service Representatives solicit her opinion on ad content on a regular basis.

Overall Rating: Needs Improvement **Recommended Performance Raise:** N/A (Commission sales)

Supervisor Signature: _____   Date: _____

Employee Signature: _____   Date: _____

Exhibit 12.3.3

From Paul's file:

Record of Disciplinary Action
Name: Jeanette Landis
Position: Customer Service Representative
Date: 10.2

Reason for Action: Jeanette has failed to meet sales goals for the second month in a row. We have discussed the reasons for her performance, and she has assured me that she will meet them next month. At this time, no further training is needed.
Disciplinary Action Taken: Documented verbal warning

Supervisor Signature: _____   Date: _____

Employee Signature: _____   Date: _____

HR Signature (if necessary): _____   Date: _____

Exhibit 12.3.4

From your files (copies also provided from Paul):

Record of Disciplinary Action
Name: Jeanette Landis
Position: Customer Service Representative
Date: 3.3
Reason for Action: Jeanette has again failed to reach sales goals. In December, it was recommended that she attend sales training. She has failed to schedule this training and has not made improvements in her sales as established last month. If she fails to schedule training within the next 30 days, she understands that further steps will be taken.
Disciplinary Action Taken: Written warning copied to HR.

Supervisor Signature: _____

Employee Signature: _____

HR Signature (if necessary): _____

Exhibit 12.3.5

The Daily Register

Disciplinary Policy: *The Daily Register* attempts to provide the resources, training, and information required for individuals to perform their jobs successfully. If for any reason performance is not up to the standards set by the employee handbook, job description, or direct supervisor, the employee shall be disciplined as follows.

If an employee has committed a minor infraction, the following steps will be taken:

1. A verbal warning will be given and will be documented, signed by the employee, and placed in the supervisor's file.
2. A written warning will be documented, signed by the employee and filed with the supervisor.
3. A written warning will be documented as in step two, but also copied to the HR manager. This warning becomes a permanent part of the employee's file.
4. A third offense is grounds for suspension.
5. Upon the fourth offense, the individual may be terminated.

Minor Infractions:

Excessive personal telephone calls and long distance calls without approval, misuse of office supplies or equipment, excessive and unapproved absences and/or tardiness, misuse of leave time, failure to reach performance standards.

A major infraction will be examined on an individual basis and may be grounds for immediate termination and/or legal action. Examples of infractions include the following:

Major Infractions:

Breach of confidentiality, falsifying records, embezzlement, violation of Drug Free Workplace or firearms policies, sexual harassment.

Exhibit 12.3.6

The Daily Register
Job Description
Job Title: Customer Service Representative
Department: Sales
Purpose and Scope: The Customer Service Representative is responsible for selling advertising space in *The Daily Register*. He or she is crucial to the profitability of the organization, securing revenue from one of three stakeholders (i.e., advertisers, subscribers, and other readers).
Responsibilities: The Customer Service Representative is responsible for selling advertising space in the newspaper to both established accounts and new customers. Once advertising orders are placed, he or she is responsible for communicating to the creative services department as to the size, content, and design of the ad. Finally, the Customer Service Representative handles questions and concerns about the presentation of the advertisement.
Organization Relationships: The Customer Service Representative reports to the Sales Manager.
Job Requirements: The Customer Service Representative is required to have training in the following areas:

- 4-year degree
- Minimum of 2 years of work experience, preferably in sales
- Knowledge and understanding of sales
- Knowledge of sales techniques such as cold calls, market research, and presentation.

  Fulfillment of experience and training requirements upon hire is at the discretion of the Sales Manager.

Approval:
Dept. Manager/Supervisor: _____**Paul White**_____
Date: _____**2/3**_____
Human Resources Department: _____*Shirley Tyler*_____
Date: _____**15 Feb**_____

EXERCISE 13.1: ORGANIZING A UNION*

Overview

Research shows that management often neither anticipates nor understands the motivation of employees to organize into unions. This exercise explores an organizing effort from the perspectives of labor and of management.

Learning Objectives

After completing this exercise, you should be able to

1. Understand the process of starting a union organizing effort.
2. Know the steps involved in the certification process.
3. Be able to consider employee and employer reactions to a union organizing effort.
4. Know the laws and regulations that govern the process of union organizing from management's perspective.

Procedure

Part A: Individual Analysis

Step 1. Before class, read the scenario below and follow the directions of the assignment.

Step 2. Each student will be assigned to either the union organizer role or the general manager role. Each role requires you to write a letter to be used in your arguments. These arguments are described in Exhibit 13.1.1.

Step 3. Also before class, answer the questions on Form 13.1.1.

Part B: Group Analysis

Step 1. Form small groups in which members are grouped by like assignment (e.g., all union organizers together and all general managers together). The members should first review one another's letters and outlines. One letter should be selected as the most effective, then edited and submitted as the group response. Each group also should derive a chronology of steps to be taken by the union organizer to Mr. Cameron. Review

individual answers to Form 13.1.1 and reach a consensus position on each question.

Step 2. A representative from each group should write the chronological steps on a blackboard or flip chart so that comparisons across groups can be made. The writer of the most effective letter from each group should then read the letter to the class. Discussion should center on the most important elements for each side and the legal implications of various strategies proposed.

Scenario

You are a customer service representative for American Rental Car (ARC), a national rental car company. Recently, the employees at the three installations in the southeastern United States, which are managed by the general manager, Scott Cameron, have experienced significant dissatisfaction with their jobs. No raises have been given in over a year; employee benefits are sparse; employees' preferences have not been considered in the assignment of work schedules or installations; and an automated employee monitoring system has been implemented.

Many of the 100 full-time employees have been talking about unionization, although many have yet to be convinced that unionization provides the best answer. The average age of the 100 employees is 29; there are 58 females and 41 minorities. Some employees strongly believe that a union can address some of the workers' concerns. Consequently, they have contacted the Customer Service Reps of America (CSRA) for help in organizing the southeastern region of ARC. Despite numerous attempts, the CSRA has been successful in organizing only three other ARC installations nationwide because the firm engages in a very tough (and often questionably legal) campaign to stop any union organizing efforts. Before the CSRA will send an organizer to your location, it wants to be persuaded that enough employees back the union to merit the expense. Thus, it has suggested that as a first step someone write a letter to the workers convincing them of the benefits of unionization and enlisting their support.

*Contributed by Nancy Brown Johnson.

Exhibit 13.1.1

UNION ORGANIZER ROLE

Write a letter to your co-workers about the factors involved in the case. You remember from the chapter why people join unions and the benefits of membership, and you want to be sure to include these factors in your letter. Yet you know that your fellow workers will still wonder why the possible costs of unionization (e.g., union dues, getting fired, being permanently assigned to the midnight shift, and being harassed by their supervisor) are worth the benefits. From your speech class you know the importance of providing answers to counterarguments if you wish to effectively persuade your co-workers to support the union.

Prepare a chronological outline for the union organizing effort covering what steps or procedures are to be followed, what data you should gather, what to look for in management's reaction, and what to do if management does not respond fairly. Also, prepare a chronological outline of what you anticipate to be management's reaction to the union organizing effort (i.e., the steps that management will take through the course of the organizing effort).

GENERAL MANAGER ROLE

Assume the role of Scott Cameron and draft a letter to your three supervisors and six assistant supervisors stipulating what can and cannot be done regarding the union organizing effort. For example, you were just informed that one of the supervisors, Meredith Sterrett, has already begun to establish a "paper trail" on one union sympathizer so he can be terminated for poor performance if "things get out of hand." She also told an employee that if a CSRA representative showed up at her installation, she would "call the cops and have him arrested for trespassing." She recently refused to hire a black female applicant because both of the applicant's parents were members of a union. She also fired an employee because she found out he was a paid union organizer. You will need to respond to Ms. Sterrett's actions. You should also prepare an outline of a meeting to be held regarding the union organizing effort and what the firm should do regarding worker concerns. Also, prepare a chronology of steps management should take in response to the organizing effort.

FORM 13.1.1

1. A colleague informs you that under the Employee Free Choice Amendment (EFCA), a union could be recognized after authorization cards are signed. Conduct online research and determine the status of the EFCA and whether the colleague is correct. Explain how the NLRA would change under the EFCA. Under current law, can an employer recognize a collective bargaining unit after authorization cards are signed (card-check option)?

2. A manager seems to assign employees more difficult work tasks based on a belief that these particular employees are trying to organize workers. Is this a violation of the law? If yes, what law is it and what recourse do these workers have?

FORM 13.1.1 (*Continued*)

3. You are told you are in a "right-to-work" state. What does this mean? Is the state in which you reside and/or work a right-to-work state? How could this affect you personally?

4. What if your job description required you to assign other employees to various work tasks or activities? Could you join a union? Explain your answer.

Note: *Exercise 13.3, The Baseball Strike: An Example of Collective Bargaining, is available online at www.mhhe.com/bernardin5e.*

EXERCISE 13.2: UNIONS, LABOR LAW, AND MANAGERIAL PREROGATIVES*

Overview

Research indicates that general attitudes toward unions are strongly correlated with a number of workplace behaviors. These attitudes, sometimes based on limited facts about unions and their effects, can have a profound effect on a number of reactions in the workplace. Research also shows that expectancies regarding union behavior and activities can affect subsequent negotiations and managerial behaviors toward union activity. From the workers' perspective, attitudes also can affect reactions to union organizing efforts, perceptions of the extent to which unions can affect workers' pay and working conditions, and job attractiveness.

This exercise assesses attitudes toward unions in general and the extent to which these attitudes are grounded in fact. Discussion will center on the implications of the attitudes for union–management relations.

Learning Objectives

After completing this exercise, you should be able to

1. Understand the implications of preconceived attitudes toward union–management relations and managerial behavior.
2. Know some of the myths and truths about the effects of unions.
3. Adopt a more objective perspective on the subject of unions.
4. Understand the implications of the National Labor Relations Act (NLRA) for management in both union and non-union environments.

Procedure

Part A: Individual Analysis

Before reading Chapter 13 and before class, go to: http://www.mhhe.com/business/management/buildyour-managementskills/menu.html and locate the "online" file for the exercise entitled "Attitudes toward Unions." Follow the directions for completing the assignment and then print the feedback page (to be handed in at the discretion of your instructor). After you complete the online portion of the exercise, read Chapter 13 and locate the discussion that supports the answers you were given in the "online" feedback. For example, find discussion pertinent to the relationship between unions and productivity. Your instructor may also request that you locate new research that either supports or contests the "correct" answers provided in the feedback.

Part B: Individual Analysis

Go to http://www.mhhe.com/business/management/build-yourmanagementskills/menu.html and locate the "online" file for the exercise entitled "Managerial Options and Constraints under the NLRA." Follow the directions for completing the assignment and then print the feedback page (to be handed in at the discretion of your instructor).

Part C: Individual Analysis

After you have completed one or both of the "on-line" exercises, answer the following two questions: 1. Wal-Mart surveys its employees annually as part of its "grass roots" program. The survey is designed to assess employees' views regarding work-related issues. Results are tabulated by store and the top three concerns are posted at each store. Write a scenario is which you believe the use of the survey results would violate the NLRA. Explain what the violation is; 2. Freeman and Medoff (1984) concluded a comprehensive review of U.S. labor relations (prior to 1984) with this conclusion: "Our most far-reaching conclusion is that, in addition to well-advertised effects on wages, unions alter nearly every other measurable aspect of the operation of workplaces and enterprises, from turnover to productivity to profitability to the composition of pay packages. The behavior of workers and firms and the outcomes of their interactions differ substantially between the organized and unorganized sectors. On balance, unionization appears to improve rather than to harm the social and economic system" (p. 19). Do you agree or disagree that this statement still applies today? Explain your answer.

SOURCE: Freeman, Richard B. and James L. Medoff. *What do unions do?* New York: Basic Books, 1984.

*Contributed by Dr. Barry Axe

EXERCISE 14.1: THE DEVELOPMENT OF A COMPANY SMOKING POLICY

Overview

One of the most controversial health issues is smoking in the workplace. Smoking had been taken for granted in many work settings for years. Little consideration had been given to either (1) the effects of the smoking on the health of both smokers and nonsmokers or (2) the potential cost to the organization. This was so even though smoking is a known cause of cancer, heart disease, and generally bad health. As discussed in Chapter 14, many states now have legislation mandating smoke-free work environments, while some states have taken steps to protect smokers' rights.

Learning Objectives

After completing this exercise, you should be able to

1. Understand the interpersonal dynamics of policy development, particularly policy that significantly affects (and changes) the work environment.
2. Use negotiating skills in relation to your positions on a controversial matter that has no "correct answer."
3. Use your writing skills in an attempt to assuage readers who may not be easily persuaded to agree with your position.

Procedure

Part A: Individual Analysis

Before class, read the scenario below and respond as directed. Conduct a Web search to determine the current state of the law and pending legislation related to smokers' and nonsmokers' rights.

Part B: Group Analysis

Step 1. Assemble in groups and compare your developmental strategies. Attempt to reach consensus on the correct approach to take in the formulation of the policy. List all the variables that should be considered and all questions of clarification that must be answered.
Step 2. Either students will be paired off or each student should review all the group members' reports and provide constructive suggestions for improving them. The critiques should focus on the drafts

rather than starting from scratch. The feedback from the students should then be used in preparing a second letter. Each student group should select one edited letter considered to be the best.
Step 3. The consensus-derived strategy should then be presented to the rest of the class, and the selected letter should be read. Subsequent discussion should focus on the likely reactions of the major constituencies of the law firm and the overall impact of the new policy.

Scenario

You have been appointed to a committee charged with the development of a smoking policy for the clerical staff of a law firm. Several of the younger secretaries and some attorneys have complained about smoke in the work area, which is a large room (2,000 square feet with average ventilation) housing 30 secretaries. Many of the law partners prefer to hire only nonsmokers in the future, and some take the position that current employees who smoke should be told they must quit within six months or they will be terminated. Ten of the secretaries smoke, seven of whom have worked for the firm for over 10 years. Two of the seven have disabilities and have some difficulty getting around. Up to now, all employees have been free to smoke any time and any place they choose.

You have been asked to develop a policy. What steps should you follow in formulating a policy? Review the options, which range from taking no action to imposing a strict ban on smoking for all employees either on or off the job. You also have been asked to take a position on a possible policy specifying that new employees must be nonsmokers and that current employees must stop smoking within six months. What procedures should be followed before establishing a firm policy? What (if any) additional information do you need to make a specific recommendation? Is it legal to impose an absolute prohibition against smoking (both on and off the job)? Also, take a position on the so-called "slippery-slope" theory that an outright ban on employee smoking could be the first step toward a ban on other legal activities that may be unhealthy or dangerous (e.g., drinking, fatty foods, sleep deprivation, extreme sports).

EXERCISE 14.2: THE DEVELOPMENT OF AN ANTIDRUG POLICY*

Overview

As a result of the Drug Free Workplace Act, which went into effect in 1989, all federal contractors are required to provide their employees with a drug-free workplace. The Act includes the following guidelines:

1. Furnish a policy statement prohibiting controlled substances in the workplace.
2. Notify employees (regular and contract) of the prohibition and the expected penalties for violating the policy.
3. Establish a drug-free awareness program.
4. Notify employees that conformance to the drug-free policy is a condition of employment.
5. Employees must notify the employer within five days if they are convicted of violating a criminal drug statute while in the workplace.
6. Contractors must notify the contracting agency of any such convictions.
7. For all employees convicted, the contractor must impose a sanction or require the completion of a substance-abuse treatment program.
8. Continue to make a good-faith effort to maintain a drug-free workplace.

Learning Objectives

After completing this exercise, you should be able to

1. Consider implications of different policies regarding drug testing.
2. Understand the options available for deterrence and enforcement of drug abuse and enforcement of an antidrug policy.

Procedure

Part A: Individual Analysis

Before class, read the scenario below and respond as directed.

Part B: Group Analysis

In groups, each member should review the memos of all other members. Each group should attempt to reach consensus on the recommendation to the board. The recommendation must deal with all the issues raised above. Take a definitive position on random testing for all employees and on what specific steps should be taken if an employee tests positive.

Scenario

You are the manager of the HR department of a major federal contractor. Your responsibilities include implementing the drug-free workplace program mandated by the federal government. Your organization is responsible for conducting very costly and sensitive research. The machinery used in the research is complex and could be dangerous if not used properly. Some of the experiments being conducted are risky and could pose a hazard to the environment or a threat to national security. However, not all employees work with the dangerous machinery or on the sensitive experiments.

As part of the drug-free workplace, the position of the security department includes the following:

- Any employee with a substance-abuse problem should be reported to the security department, regardless of whether the substance abuse was detected by management or self-reported.
- Drug testing should be conducted for all individuals filling sensitive positions and randomly for the entire organization.
- All positive test results should be reported to the security department.
- All employees testing positive on the first test should be terminated. This includes so-called performance enhancing drugs (e.g., Adderall, Provigil) unless they are prescribed.
- Any job applicant with a history of drug or alcohol abuse should not be hired.

The Employee Assistance Program (EAP) representatives have reviewed the security department's position and disagree strongly with the proposed sanctions. In the EAP, 70 percent of the employees sent to employee counseling are self-referred. If the EAP is required to report the self-referrals to the security department, the EAP representatives argue, employees will not seek help from the EAP and will go untreated. The EAP representatives also contend that the termination sanction proposed by the security department is inhumane and may violate the Rehabilitation Act of 1973, the Americans with Disabilities Act, or inalienable rights of privacy. One board member has stated that mass drug testing as proposed "makes a mockery of the presumption of innocence and strongly implies that someone who refuses to submit to a test is guilty . . . the level of expectations of privacy is diminishing, and we are slowly surrendering our dignity."

The board of directors has requested that you, as a task force member, develop a response to both the security department and the EAP representatives. Take into consideration the health and safety of the company as well as the rights of the employees. Consider the following components: the Drug Free Workplace Act, an employee's right to privacy, confidentiality of the drug-testing program, and access to the EAP. Prepare a memo to the board of directors in which you take a position on the matter (maximum of five pages). Take a definitive position on the proposed policy regarding performance-enhancing drugs. Be prepared to defend your position in group discussion.

*Contributed by Marilyn A. Perkins.

Note: *Exercise 14.4, The Development of a Threat Management Team for a Workplace Violence Incident, is available online at www.mhhe.com/ bernardin5e.*

EXERCISE 14.3: THE DEVELOPMENT OF A HEALTH AND SAFETY POLICY

Overview

Chapter 14 discusses the role of OSHA inspectors in pursuing violations of the 1970 OSHA Act. This exercise requires you to consider the implications of health and safety regulation for managerial activities.

Learning Objectives

After completing this exercise, you should be able to

1. Understand the steps that should be taken under OSHA regulation.
2. Know the rights that employers and employees have with regard to OSHA regulation.

Procedure

Part A: Individual Analysis

Read the scenario below before class. You have been retained as a consultant to implement compliance with OSHA. As a consultant, how would you approach the problem, and what kind of advice and help would you give? Complete Form 14.3.1 and bring it to class.

Part B: Group Analysis

In class, groups should review the completed Forms 14.3.1 of individual members and attempt to reach consensus on all three aspects of the report. One group member should report the consensus recommendations to the rest of the class.

Scenario

Dynamic Duo, Inc., opened its manufacturing plant several months ago. Dynamic Duo manufactures a new form of residential siding using a combination of lightweight microspheres and proprietary resins. The product will be marketed as an alternative to premium siding which weighs half of the weight of fiber cement. The company is owned and operated by two enterprising chemistry students, Nolan Cameron and Drew Saline, from Poedunk University in Poedunk, U.S.A. The company has 75 employees, most of whom work on the floor of the plant and handle the equipment needed to manufacture siding. One supervisor is in charge. Dynamic Duo, Inc., is concerned about safety, but the owners know almost nothing about OSHA.

Before you have had a chance to advise Dynamic Duo, the plant is visited by a compliance officer who simply enters the plant and conducts a tour, unaccompanied by either management or employees. At the end of the tour, the compliance officer presents Dynamic Duo with two citations. The Dynamic Duo owners call you in as a consultant and ask you what they should do next. The citations concern scaffolding and ergonomics problems.

Unfortunately for Dynamic Duo, soon after the compliance officer's visit, five employees are injured or became ill, all on the same day. One is seriously injured, having caught his hand in a conveyor. Another person fell off some scaffolding. Four others have complained of various stomach ailments. The owners call you in again and ask you whether they need to inform anybody of the accidents and the illness or to record them somehow. What else should you tell Dynamic Duo?

FORM 14.3.1

1. What steps should Dynamic Duo's owners take immediately?

2. What legal steps would you recommend that Dynamic Duo take?

3. What advice would you give the owners concerning the company's obligations under OSHA to record accidents and illnesses?

4. Visit www.OSHA.gov and determine if you can provide any additional information to help make the plant safer. "Cut and Paste" or print out information from this Web site that would be helpful.

5. How could Dynamic Duo be issued a citation for an ergonomics violation? Mr. Cameron says, "I thought they got rid of that stupid regulation." What is your response?

6. Mr. Saline fired an employee who refused to work around some of the resins after three employees complained of stomach problems while working with the resins. The employee has threatened to sue the company but Saline has invoked the "employment-at-will" doctrine. Take a position on Mr. Saline's argument.

APPENDIX C

Assessment Guidelines for Self, Peer, and Designated Assessors

Appendix C presents the material necessary for assessments of your performance in the individual and group exercises. Your instructor has elected to use either (1) the "certified assessor" approach, in which certain students are designated to serve as assessors for specific exercises, or (2) the self/peer assessments, which are completed by group members at the conclusion of an exercise.

The certification process usually entails the designated assessors' being examined on the written responses to the exercise before the day on which the exercise is to be done in class. Assessors should receive specific feedback on their written responses and have a clear understanding of appropriate responses to the exercises.

Your instructor may elect to use the self/peer approach to assessment in addition to or as an alternative to the certified assessor approach. Regardless of the approach your instructor uses, students should become familiar with the performance dimensions that are identified and defined in Figure C.2. Research has identified these as critical for success in management. The exercises in this book are designed to enhance these as you learn, integrate, and apply the HRM content of each chapter. Read the assessor job description in Figure C.1 before you begin. Your instructor may provide additional instructions regarding self and peer assessments.

PRIOR TO OBSERVATION

1. Review the materials of the assigned chapter and the exercise to which you are assigned. Get very familiar with the recommended responses/answers and the five dimensions defined in Figure C.2.
   A. Analytical thinking
   B. Leadership
   C. Oral communication; presentation
   D. Planning and organizing
   E. Written communication
2. Review the behavioral examples for each dimension to gain further understanding of each dimension and how each is exhibited in group or written responses (see Figure C.2).

INSTRUCTIONS FOR CERTIFIED ASSESSORS

After you are assigned to a group in class, review the exercise and dimensions, including the behavioral examples for each dimension. Before discussion begins, take a seat outside the circle of participants and do not discuss the exercise with group members. (You are strictly an observer/assessor.) Before discussion, quickly review each group member's individual exercise response. Make a note of the name of any group member who has not prepared a written response. Return the exercises to the participants.

3. Once discussion begins, observe the behavior of each discussant, keeping the dimensions in mind as a frame of reference.
4. Record your observations on a plain sheet of paper, being careful to note who said what during discussion. Avoid any kind of evaluation at this point. (Do not use a complete sentence format.) Be as precise and complete as possible in recording your observations. Do not try to translate your observations into the dimensions until the observation period is over. Your attention should be directed toward making accurate observations and keeping good notes.
5. At the conclusion of the discussion, collect all written responses and, if required, the group's written response. As you review your observations, assign a positive or negative value to each observation and determine what dimension each observation illustrates. Next to each observation, enter the letter of the relevant dimension, next to the + or − value.
6. Carefully review and critique each member's written responses, noting and correcting any misspellings, poor grammar, incomprehensible sentences, and so on.
7. Enter your name ("Observer") in the space provided. After reviewing the written responses and your notes on the discussion, summarize your observations in the space provided for feedback. The feedback should be constructive with (it is hoped) both positive and negative comments. Focus on the way in which the member performed in the group and completed the

Figure C.1   **Assessor Job Description**

The job of assessor will entail three major duties: observation, evaluation, and write-up. The actual tasks associated with each of these duties are listed below.

Observation

Watch participant activities and behaviors during an exercise.

Take notes on what is seen and/or heard.

Assign + or − value to each observation.

Classify notes according to predefined dimensions.

Evaluation

Assign a numerical performance rating for each dimension (based on notes taken).

Make an overall assessment.

Write-up (if assigned)

Collect all data on each student's performance for each performance dimension.

Synthesize data for each dimension.

Complete a final report, in narrative form, highlighting the participant's strengths and weaknesses.

---

exercise. Be sure to record your name and the name of the participant.

8. After recording your feedback for each participant, make a rating on each student's performance. Your instructor will provide a copy of the rating form.

To Rate Performance

Use the following scale to make your rating:

7 = Outstanding
6 = Very good
5 = Above average
4 = Satisfactory
3 = Below satisfactory
2 = Well below satisfactory
1 = Poor
NO = Not observed

A very small percentage of students should be rated at the 7 level. *This rating is reserved for only the very best performance for that dimension.* **Most ratings should be at or near the 4 level.** Usually, however, when observing a group of about six people, close to the full range of performance levels should be observed and therefore rated. Rate all participants on one dimension and then proceed to the next dimension. Using the same rating scale, make an overall assessment of each participant.

What If a Group Member Doesn't Participate?

How do you rate someone who says virtually nothing in the group exercise? The answer to this question depends on the particular dimension. Inactivity in the group would constitute a low score for *leadership* and *planning* and *organizing*. Inactivity would probably necessitate a rating of "Not observed" (NO) for the other dimensions.

SELF-ASSESSMENT WITH DESIGNATED ASSESSORS

Students who participated in a group exercise which was observed by a "certified assessor" should do a self-assessment of his or her performance on the dimensions. Self-assessments should be made *before receiving* assessment results and feedback from the assessor. After reviewing the dimensions, record your self-assessments in the assessment log and enter the exercise number on Figure C.3. Make ratings as instructed, including the overall assessment.

SELF/PEER ASSESSMENT

If you are asked to make a self/peer assessment of the group performance, review the dimensions and take notes as you review each group member's written response. As soon as possible after group discussion, make assessments of yourself and each group member on a separate self/peer assessment form and provide feedback for peers on the reverse side. Follow the procedure described above using the same scale for rating.

ASSESSMENT LOG

Students should maintain an assessment log made up of self-assessments and peer and/or assessor ratings. Enter your self-assessments in the Student Assessment Log (C3). If you get feedback from peers or more than one designated assessor on an exercise, derive an average rating for each dimension and enter the averages on C4. Make certain self-assessments are completed on an exercise prior to receiving feedback on that exercise from assessors or peers.

Figure C.2   **Critical Performance Dimensions**

Behavioral Examples

A. **ANALYTIC THINKING:**   Identifying the fundamental ideas, concepts, themes or issues that help to integrate, interpret, and/or explain underlying patterns in a set of information or data.

Examples

Effective

"Let's take turns stating our solution to the problem. We'll write down the points we agree upon and come up with a set of solutions that everyone will be happy with. How does that sound to everyone? Who wants to write them down?"

Gather everyone's ideas, key in on main concept, look for consensus or pattern of responses.

Ineffective

Everyone talks at once, or one person dominates, or no one wants to talk. Instead, socializes with group members.

"We don't know what is wrong with the problem. Let's just put anything down to get a grade," or,

"I skipped that problem because I didn't understand it."

B. **LEADERSHIP:**   Utilization of appropriate interpersonal styles to stimulate and guide individuals or groups toward goal and/or task accomplishment.

Examples

Effective

"We've got a lot of great ideas, but we haven't heard from everyone yet. Let's write down what we have and then we'll add the rest of the ideas to our list."

Ineffective

"This case is just too complicated to come up with a solution. There is no way we can find the answer."

"I want to write down the solutions for everyone; that way my ideas will be sure to be included."

C. **ORAL COMMUNICATION; PRESENTATION:**   Effective expression of ideas or viewpoints to others in individual or group situations (includes gestures, nonverbal communication, and the use of visual aids).

Examples

Effective

"I wrote down my thoughts on a solution to this problem. Let's take turns giving our ideas so that we can hear how everyone in the group feels about the problem. How does that sound to everyone? Who wants to go first?"

Ineffective

"I am not very good at speaking before a group. Let someone else who has more experience go first."

"I didn't come up with any ideas that the rest of the group hasn't already said. Take their ideas and write them down."

D. **PLANNING AND ORGANIZING:**   Establishing a course of action for self and/or others to accomplish specific goals; planning proper assignments of personnel and appropriate allocations of resources.

Examples

Effective

"Our assignment calls for three HRM objectives. Let's talk about each objective individually and reach a consensus for each one. Who will volunteer to write them down. We better hurry; we only have 20 minutes to come up with our final list."

Ineffective

"We have too many opinions to formulate a final list. There is no way that we can decide on the three objectives in 20 minutes."

E. **WRITTEN COMMUNICATION:**   Clear expression of ideas in writing and in appropriate grammatical form.

Utilized appropriate vocabulary, proper grammar, and correct spelling. Writes legibly.

Examples

Effective

No spelling errors; few (if any) grammatical errors

Ineffective

Numerous spelling and grammatical errors

Figure C.3 **Student Self-Assessment Log—Ratings**

Name _____

Exer. #	Analytical Thinking	Leadership	Oral Communication, Presentation	Planning & Organizing	Written Communication	Overall Assessment
Average						

Use the following rating scale to make your self-assessment: 7 = outstanding; 6 = very good; 5 = above average; 4 = satisfactory; 3 = below satisfactory; 2 = well below satisfactory; 1 = poor.

Figure C.4   **Student Assessment Log—Ratings from peers/assessors**

Name _____

Exer. #	Analytical Thinking	Leadership	Oral Communication, Presentation	Planning & Organizing	Written Communication	Overall Assessment
Average						

Use the following rating scale to make your self-assessment: 7 = outstanding; 6 = very good; 5 = above average; 4 = satisfactory; 3 = below satisfactory; 2 = well below satisfactory; 1 = poor.

747

Endnotes

CHAPTER 1

1. Fiore, F. (2008, May 18). Handwriting of Hillary Clinton, John McCain and Barack Obama may speak volumes. *Los Angeles Times* online.
2. Bianchi, A. (1996, February). The character-revealing handwriting analysis. *Inc. Magazine,* 77–92.
3. Joyce, A. (2004, November 8). Interview tricks can often reveal hidden truths about applicants. *The Palm Beach Post,* p. 2F.
4. Pfeffer, J. (1994). *Competitive advantage through people.* Boston: Harvard Business School Press, p. 6.
5. Kaplan, R. S., and Norton, D. P. (1996). *The balanced scorecard.* Boston: Harvard Business School Press.
6. Huselid, M. A., Becker, B. E., and Beatty, R. W. (2005). *The workforce scorecard.* Boston: Harvard Business School Press.
7. Towers Perrin. (1992). *Priorities for competitive advantage: An IBM study conducted by Towers Perrin.* See also, Caye, J. M., Dyer, A. Leicht, M. Minto, A., and Strack, R. (2008). *Creating people advantage: How to address HR challenges worldwide through 2015.* The Boston Consulting Group. Boston, MA.
8. See Pfeffer, *Competitive advantage through people,* p. 16.
9. Hammonds, K. H. (2005, August). Why we hate HR. *Fast Company,* p. 40.
10. Sun, L., Aryee, S., and Law, K. S. (2007). High-performance human resource practices, citizenship behavior, and organizational performance: A relational perspective. *Academy of Management, 50,* 558–577.
11. Rynes, S., Colbert, A., and Brown, K. (2002). HR professionals' beliefs about effective human resource management practices: Correspondence between research and practice. *Human Resource Management, 41,* 149–174.
12. Friedman, T. L. (2006). *The world is flat: A brief history of the twenty-first century.* Expanded edition. Boston: Farrar, Straus & Giroux.
13. Schram, J. (2007). *SHRM Workplace Forecast.*
14. Marler, J. H, Liang, X, and Dulebohn, J. H. (2006). Training and effective employee information technology use. *Journal of Management 32,* 721–743.
15. Cave, D. (2008, June 9). States take new tack on illegal immigration. *New York Times* online.
16. U.S. Bureau of the Census. (2005). Profile of the foreign-born population in the U.S. *Current Population Reports,* pp. 23–206 (extrapolation).
17 Ibid.
18. Lawler, E. E., Ulrich, D., and Fitz-enz, J. (2007). *Human resources business process outsourcing:. Transforming how HR gets its work done.* San Francisco: Jossey-Bass; see also Lawler, E. (1988, August). HRM: Meeting the new challenges. *Personnel,* p. 24.
19. Ibid.
20. Huselid, Becker, and Beatty, *The workforce scorecard.*
21. Harter, J. K., Schmodt, F. L., and Hayes, T. L. (2002). Business-unit level relationship between employee satisfaction, employee engagement, and business outcomes: A meta-analysis. *Journal of Applied Psychology, 87,* 268–279.
22. Lohr, S. (2005, December 5). A new game at the office: Many young workers accept fewer guarantees. *New York Times* online.
23. Becker, B. E., Huselid, M. A., and Ulrich, D. (2001). *The HR scorecard.* Boston: Harvard Business School Press.
24. White, E. (2005, February 17). To keep employees, Domino's decides it's not all about pay. *The Wall Street Journal,* pp. A1, A9.
25. Pfeffer, *Competitive advantage through people.*
26. Sheley, E. (1996, June). Share your worth: Talking numbers with the CEO. *HR Magazine,* pp. 86–95.
27. Fox, A. (2008, June). Get in the business of being green. *HR Magazine* online, www.shrm.org/hrmagazine/articles/0608/0608fox.asp.
28. Orlitzky, M., Schimidt, F. L., and Rynes, S. L. (2003). Corporate social and financial performance: A meta-analysis. *Organization Studies, 24,* 403–411.
29. Hill, R. P., et al. (2007). Corporate social responsibility and socially responsible investing: A global perspective. *Journal of Business Ethics, 70,* 165–174.
30. Fox, Get in the business of being green.
31. Fulmer, I. S., Gerhart, B., and Scott, K. S. (2003). Are the 100 best better? *Personnel Psychology, 56,* 965–993.
32. Paul, F. (2008, June 25). Apple's profit may be higher for new iPhone. UKReuter.com.

CHAPTER 2

1. Friedman, T. L. (2006). *The world is flat: A brief history of the twenty-first century.* Expanded edition. Boston: Farrar, Straus & Giroux.
2. Bradsher, K. (2008, April 8). Asian inflation begins to sting U.S. shoppers. *New York Times.*
3. Hill, C. W. (2009). *International business: Competing in the global marketplace.* New York: Irwin McGraw-Hill.

4. World Trade Organization (2007). *International Trade Statistics.*

5. World Trade Organization (2001). *International Trade Statistics.*

6. See Friedman, *The world is flat.*

7. Daniels, J. D., Radebaugh, L. H., and Sullivan, D. P. (2004). *International business: Environments and operations.* Upper Saddle River, NJ: Prentice Hall.

8. *TRW Automotive Annual Report 2007.*

9. United Nations Conference on Trade and Development (UNCTAD). (2008). *World investment report 2007.*

10. Czinkota, M. R., Ronkainen, I. A., and Moffett, M. H. (1999). *International business.* New York: Harcourt Brace.

11. Walmart Corporation. (2008). www.walmart.com.

12. See Daniels et al., *International business.*

13. Ibid.

14. UNCTAD (2003). *World investment report 2002.*

15. Coca-Cola Corporation (2008). www.coca-cola.com.

16. Konopaske, R., and Ivancevich, J. M. (2004). *Global management and organizational behavior.* Burr Ridge, IL: McGraw-Hill Irwin.

17. UNCTAD, *World investment report 2002.*

18. Honda Automotive Corporation (2008). Corporatehonda.com.

19. Nokia Corporation (2008). *Quarterly Report.*

20. UNCTAD, *World investment report 2002.*

21. Griffin, R. W., and Pustay, R. W. (1999). *International business: A managerial perspective.* Reading, MA: Addison-Wesley.

22. Hallett, J. J. (1987). *Worklife visions.* Alexandria, VA: SHRM, pp. 45–46.

23. Zellner, W., Schmidt, C. A., Ihlwan, M., and Donley, H. (2001, September 3). How well does Wal-Mart travel? *BusinessWeek,* pp. 82–84.

24. 1996 study by the National Foreign Trade Council and Windham International cited in Schell, M. S., and Solomon, C. M. (1997). *Capitalizing on the global workforce: A strategic guide to expatriate management.* Chicago, IL: Irwin, p. 174.

25. See Griffin and Pustay, *International business.*

26. Ibid.

27. Brown, C. (1996, August 12). Banana split. *Forbes, 158*(4), 94–95.

28. Under a treaty signed in April, 2001, the European Banana Wars were brought to an official close when the EU agreed to relax many of its quotas, tariffs, and restrictions. In exchange, the U.S. suspended several trade-related sanctions that it had levied in retaliation for the bananas. In addition to the banana-growing Caribbean provinces of France, colonies and provinces of EU countries in Africa and the Pacific Islands stood to gain considerable economic benefits from the tariffs and quotas on bananas imported from outside the EU. However, both Dole and Chiquita indicated that the wars had brought each of them to the brink of bankruptcy, since the majority of their growing fields were located outside the EU in South America and the Caribbean. This, in turn, was depressing regional and national economics in some areas of the western hemisphere. For further information, see Greitner, P. (2001). Europe, U.S. end banana dispute. *The Miami Herald*, April 12, p. C1.

29. Wild, J. J., Wild, K. L., and Han, J. C. Y. (2000). *International business: An integrated approach.* Upper Saddle River, NJ: Prentice Hall.

30. See Griffin and Pustay, *International business.*

31. Cited in Daniels, Radebaugh, and Sullivan, *International business.*

32. Cited in Wild, Wild, and Han, *International business.*

33. Ibid.

34. Knowlton, C. (1992, June 23). Europe cooks up a cereal war. *Fortune.*

35. Wild, Wild, and Han, *International business;* see also Gong, Y., Shenkar, O., Luo, Y., and Nyaw, M. (2001). Role conflict and ambiguity of CEOs in international joint ventures: A transaction cost perspective. *Journal of Applied Psychology, 86,* 764–773.

36. Wild, Wild, and Han, *International business.*

37. Stewart, T. A. (1993, December 13). Welcome to the revolution. *Fortune,* p. 66.

38. Zubrzycki, J. (1997, November 10). Mastering software helps India youth snag foreign jobs. *The Christian Science Monitor,* p. D1. See also Bhargava, S. W. (1993). Software from India? Yes, it's for real. *BusinessWeek,* p. 77.

39. Landler, Mark (2001, March 21). Hi, I'm in Banglore (but I can't say so). *New York Times,* pp. A1, C4.

40. Porter, M. E. (1990). *The competitive advantage of nations.* New York: Free Press, p. 53.

41. Carmell, W. A. (2001, May–June). Application of U.S. antidiscrimination laws to multinational employers. *Legal Report,* pp. 1–5; Dowling, P. J., Welch, D. E, and Schuler, R. S. (1999). *International human resource management: Managing people in a multinational context.* New York: ITP.

42. Sanyal, R. N. (2001). *International management: A strategic perspective.* Upper Saddle River, NJ: Prentice Hall.

43. Mezias, J. (2000). Do labor lawsuits represent a liability of foreignness for foreign subsidiaries operating in the United States? Paper presented at the twenty-first Academy of Management Conference, Toronto, Ontario.

44. See Dowling, Welch, and Schuler, *International human resource management.*

45. Hill, *International business*, p. 64. See also, Adair, W. L., Okumura, T., and Brett, J. M. (2001). Negotiation behavior when cultures collide: The United States and Japan. *Journal of Applied Psychology, 86,* 371–385.

46. Kraimer, M. L., Wayne, S., and Jaworski, R. A. (2001). Sources of support and expatriate performance: The mediating role of expatriate adjustment. *Personnel Psychology, 54,* 71–100; Ryan, A. M., McFarland, L., Baron, H. and Page, R. (1999). An international look at selection practices: Nation and culture as explanations for variability in practice. *Personnel Psychology, 52,* 359–392; Shaffer, M.A., and Harrison, D. A. (2001). Forgotten partners of international assignments: Development and test of a model of spouse adjustment. *Journal of Applied Psychology, 86,* 238–254.

47. Hofstede, G. (2001). *Culture's consequences: Comparing values, behaviors, institutions, and organizations across nations*, 2nd ed. Thousand Oaks, CA: Sage Publications.

48. Liberty Global International (2008). www.lgi.com.

49. Desatnick, R. L., and Bennet, M. L. (1978). *Human resource management in the multinational company*. New York: Nichols. See also Dowling, Welch, and Schuler, *International human resource management*.

50. Bird, A., Taylor, S., and Beechler, S. (1998). A typology of human resource management in Japanese multinational corporations: Organizational implications. *Human Resource Management, 37*(2), 159–172; see also Harzing, A. (2001). Who's in charge? An empirical study of executive staffing practices in foreign subsidiaries. *Human Resource Management, 40,* 139–158.

51. Overman, S. (2000). In sync. *HR Magazine, 44*(4), 93–97; see also Turban, D. B., Lua, C., Ngo, H., Chow, I. H., and Si, S. X. (2001). Organizational attractiveness of firms in the People's Republic of China: A person–organization fit perspective. *Journal of Applied Psychology, 86,* 194–206.

52. Ibid.

53. See Dowling, Welch, and Schuler, *International human resource management*.

54. For full discussion of the rationale for international business assignments, see Stroh, L. K., Black, J. S., Mendenhall, M. E., and Gregersen, H.B. (2005). *International assignments: An integration of strategy, research, and practice*. Mahwah, NJ: Erlbaum. .

55. GMAC Global Relocation Services (2004, May). Global relocation trends 2003/2004 survey report. http.www.shrm.org/hrresources/surveys; see also Garonzik, R., Brockner, J., and Siegel, P. A. (2000). Identifying international assignees at risk for premature departure: The interactive effect of outcome favorability and procedural fairness. *Journal of Applied Psychology, 85,* 13–20.

56. GMAC, Global Relocation Services (2008, May). *Global relocation trends 2008 survey report*.

57. Ibid. For full discussion of international assignment success and failure, see Black, J. S., and Gregersen, H. (1999). The right way to manage expats. *Harvard Business Review, 77*(2), 52–63.

58. Milkovich, G. T. and Newman, J. (2005) *Compensation*, 8th ed. New York: McGraw-Hill/Irwin.

59. Ibid.

60. See GMAC, *Global relocation trends 2008*.

61. Atchison, T. J., Belcher, D. W., and Thomsen, D. J. (2004). *Internet based benefits and compensation administration*. Economic Research Institute: Prentice Hall.

62. See GMAC, *Global relocation trends, 2008*.

63. Tung, R. (1982). Selection and training procedures of U.S., European, and Japanese multinationals: A model for U.S. firms? *California Management Review, 25*(1), 57–71.

64. Mendenhall, M. E., and Stahl, G. K. (2000, Summer/Fall). Expatriate training and development: Where do we go from here? *Human Resource Management, 39*(2, 3), 251–266.

65. See GMAC, *Global relocation trends 2008*.

66. See Black and Gregersen, The right way.

67. Johnson, C. (1999). Cutting down the days. *HR Magazine, 44*(4), 93–97.

68. Stroh, L. K., Gregersen, H. B., and Black, J. S. (1998). Closing the gap: Expectations versus reality among repatriates. *Journal of World Business, 33*(2), 110–124.

69. Ibid.

70. See Johnson, Cutting down the days.

71. Studies by the International Personnel Association (IPA) and Catalyst cited in Tyler, K. (2001). Don't fence her in. *HR Magazine, 46*(3), 70–77.

72. See GMAC, *Global relocation trends 2008*.

73. Bhaskar-Shrinivas, P., Harrison, D. A., Shaffer, M. A., and Luk, D. M. (2005). Input-based and time-based models of international adjustment: Meta-analytic evidence and theoretical extensions. *Academy of Management Journal, 48,* 257–281; see also Au, K. Y., and Fukuda, J. (2002). Boundary spanning behaviors of expatriates. *Journal of World Business, 37,* 285–296; and Konopaske and Ivancevich, *Global management and organizational behavior*.

74. Kanter, R. M. (1995). *World class: Thinking locally in the global economy*. New York: Simon and Schuster, p. 88.

75. Carpenter, M. A., Sanders, G., and Gregersen, H. B. (2000). International assignment experience at the top can make a bottom line difference. *Human Resource Management, 39*(2, 3), 277–285.

76. Lublin, J. S. (1996, January 29). An overseas stint can be a ticket to the top. *The Wall Street Journal*, p. B1.

77. Carpenter, M. A., Sanders, W. G., and Gregerson, H. B. (2001). Building human capability with organizational context: The impact of international assignment experience on multinational firm performance and CEO pay. *Academy of Management Journal, 44,* 493–511.

78. Csoka, L., and Hackett, B. (1998). *Transforming the HR function for global business success*. Report #1209–98-RR. New York: Conference Board.

79. Adler, N., and Bartholomew, S. (1992). Managing globally competent people. *Academy of Management Executive, 6*(3), 52–65.

80. Conner, J. (2000). Developing the global leaders of tomorrow. *Human Resource Management, 39*(2, 3), 147–158.

81. Kanter, World class: Thinking locally in the global economy, p. 88.

82. Gregerson, H. B., Morrison, A. J., and Mendenhall, M. E. (2000). Guest editors' introduction. *Human Resource Management, 39*(2, 3), 115–116.

83. Morrison, A. J. (2000). Developing a global leadership model. *Human Resource Management, 39*(2, 3), 117–132.

84. Ibid.

85. Ibid.

86. Jeannet, J. (2000). *Managing with a global mindset*. London: Pearson Education Ltd., p. 189.

CHAPTER 3

1. Joyce, A. (2005, December 9). The bias breakdown: Asians and blacks lead in perceived discrimination at work. *The Washington Post,* p. D01.

2. Dobrzynski, J. H. (1995, September 12). Women more pessimistic about work. *The New York Times,* p. C2.

3. Dipboye, R. L., and Colella, A. (Eds.) (2005). *Discrimination at work*. Mahwah, NJ: Erlbaum; See also, Heilman, M. E. and Okimoto, T. E. (2008). Motherhood: A potential source of bias in employment decisions. *Journal of Applied Psychology, 93,* 189–198.

4. Ferguson, T. W. (1996, November 4). Boss harassment. *Forbes,* pp. 150–151; see also Holmes, S. A. (1996, November 17). Bias suit harbinger. *The New York Times,* p. 12; Kahan, S. C., Brown, B. B., Zepke, B. E., and Lanzarone, M. (2008). *Legal guide to human resources*. Boston: Warren, Gorham and Lamont.

5. See www.eeoc.gov. *Summary statistics for 2005.*

6. *McDonnell-Douglas v. Green* (1973). 411 U.S. 972. See also, *Desert Palace Inc. v. Costa,* 539 U.S. 90.

7. *Texas Department of Community Affairs v. Burdine* (1981). 450 U.S. 248. (U.S. Supreme Court).

8. *Griggs v. Duke Power Company* (1971). 401 U.S. 424. (U.S. Supreme Court).

9 *Watson v. Fort Worth Bank and Trust* (1988). 487 U.S. 977 (5th Cir.); see also, Werner, J. M., and Bolino, M. C. (1997). Explaining U.S. Courts of Appeals decisions involving performance appraisal: Accuracy, fairness, and validation. *Personnel Psychology, 50,* 1–24.

10. *Albemarle Paper Co. v. Moody* (1975). 422 U.S. 405 (U.S. Supreme Court). Open to interpretation, the 1991 CRA requires that plaintiffs "demonstrate that each particular challenged employment practice causes a disparate impact, except that if the [plaintiff] can demonstrate to the court that the elements of [an employer's] decision-making process are not capable of separation for analysis, the decision-making process may be analyzed as one employment practice." Since most employers use multiple criteria to make selection, promotion, or similar decisions, disentangling the contribution of each criteron to the disparate impact is difficult.

11. *Connecticut v. Teal* (1982). 457 U.S. 440 (U.S. Supreme Court).

12. *Meritor Savings v. Vinson* (1986). 477 U.S. 57. See also Bergman, M. E. (2002). The (un)reasonableness of reporting: Antecedents and consequences of reporting sexual harassment. *Journal of Applied Psychology, 87,* 230–242; see also Segal, J. (1996). Sexual harassment: Where are we now? *HR Magazine, 41,* 68–73; for the finest writing on this and perhaps any subject, see Bernardin, L. (1994). Does the reasonable woman standard exist and does she have any place in hostile environment sexual harassment claims under Title VII after Harris? *Florida Law Review, 46,* 291–322; Lengnick-Hall, M. L. (1995). Sexual harassment research: A methodological critique. *Personnel Psychology, 48,* 841–864; Fisher, A. B. (1993, August 23). Sexual harassment: What to do. *Fortune,* pp. 84–88; Johnson, C. (1995, May 17). Court cases give firms guidance on sexual harassment. *The Wall Street Journal,* p. B2.

13. Bradshaw, D. S. (1987). Sexual harassment: Confronting the troublesome issues. *Personnel Administrator, 32*(1), 51–53; see also Hoyman, M., and Robinson, R. (1980). Interpreting the new sexual harassment guidelines. *Personnel Journal, 59*(12), 996; *Meritor Savings Bank v. Vinson* (1986). 40 FEP Cases 1822 (U.S. Supreme Court); and Thornton, T. (1986). Sexual harassment: Discouraging it in the workplace. *Personnel, 63*(8), 18–26.

14. *Harris v. Forklift Systems* (1993). 114 S. Ct. 367, 370–77. See also, Fitzgerald, L. F., Gelfand, M. J., and Drasgow, F. (1995). Measuring sexual harassment: Theoretical and psychometric advances. *Applied Social Psychology, 17*(4), 425–445; Gutek, B. A. (1995). How subjective is sexual harassment? An examination of rater effects. *Basic and Applied Social Psychology, 17*(4), 447–467; Stockdale, M. S., Vaux, A., and Cashin, F. (1995). Acknowledging sexual harassment: A test of alternative models. *Basic and Applied Social Psychology, 17*(4), 469–496; Tang, T. L., and McCollum, S. L. (1996). Sexual harassment in the workplace. *Public Personnel Management, 25*(1), 53–58.

15. Terpstra, D. E., and Baker, D. D. (1992). Outcomes of federal court decisions on sexual harassment. *Academy of Management Journal, 35,* 181–190.

16. *Burlington Industries, Inc. v. Ellerth.* (1998). 524 U.S. 742; *Faragher v. City of Boca Raton.* (1998). 524 U.S. 775.

17. Laabs, J. (1995, July). What to do when sexual harassment comes calling. *Personnel Journal,* pp. 42–53; see also Lengnick-Hall, M. L. (1995). Sexual harassment research: A methodological critique. *Personnel Psychology, 48,* 841–863; Zigarelli, M. A. (1994). *Can they do that? A Guide to your rights on the job*. New York: Lexington; see also Block, R. N., and Wolkinson, B. (1996). *Employment law*. Cambridge, MA: Blackwell; Sims, C. S., and Drasgow, F. (2002). *The effect of sexual harassment on attrition: Time dependent modeling*. Paper presented at the 17th Annual Conference of the Society for Industrial and Organizational Psychology, Inc., Ontario, Canada; Raver, J. L., and Gelfand, M. J. (2002). *Sexual harassment in work groups: An examination of group-level antecedents and consequences*. Paper presented at the 17th Annual Conference of the Society for Industrial and Organizational Psychology, Inc., Ontario, Canada; Wadlington, P. (2002). *The generalizability of a sexual harassment model across organizations*. Paper presented at the 17th Annual Conference of the

Society for Industrial and Organizational Psychology, Inc., Ontario, Canada; Ritter, B. A., and Doverspike, D. (2002). *The changing nature of sexual harassment.* Paper presented at the 17th Annual Conference of the Society for Industrial and Organizational Psychology, Inc., Ontario, Canada; Wayne, S., et al. (2001). Is all sexual harassment viewed the same? *Journal of Applied Psychology, 86,* 179–187.

18. *Oncale v. Sundowner, Offshore Services,* 523 U.S. 75 (1998).

19. *U.S. Steelworkers v. Weber* (1979) 443 U.S. 193; see also LeRoy, M. H., and Schutz, J. M. (1995). The legal context of human resource management: Conflict, confusion, and role conversion. In Ferris, G. R., Rosen, S. D., and Barnum, D. T. (Eds.). *Handbook of human resource management.* Cambridge, MA: Blackwell, pp. 143–158.

20. *Johnson v. Santa Clara Transportation Agency,* 476 U.S. 267 (March 26, 1987).

21. *Gratz v. Bollinger* (2003). 539 U.S. 244; *Grutter v. Bollinger* (2003) 539 U.S. 306.

22. *Grutter v. Bollinger* (2003). 539 U.S. 306.

23. *Meacham v. Knolls Atomic Power Laboratory* (2008). U.S. 461 (No. 06–1505). See also, *Gross* v. FBL Financial Services, Inc. (U.S. No. 08–441).

24. *Schwager v. Sun Oil Company of PA* (1979). 591 F.2d. 58 (1th Cir.).

25. *Mastie v. Great Lakes Steel Corp.* (1976). 424 F. Supp. 1299 (U.S. District Court, Michigan).

26. *Hodgson v. Greyhound Lines, Inc.* (1975). 419 U.S. 1122.

27. *Sutton v. United Airlines, Inc.* (1999). 527 U.S. 471; *Toyota Motor Manufacturing v. Ella Williams* (2002). No. 00–1089, 534 U.S. 416.

28. EEOC (2008). Notice concerning the Americans with Disabilities Act (ADA) Amendments Act of 2008 (http://www.eeoc.gov/ada/amendments_notice.html).

29. Genetic Information Nondiscrimination Act (GINA). (2008). Public Law No: 110–233.

30. Altman, Y., and Shortland, S. (2008). Women and international assignments: Taking stock—A 25-year review. *Human Resource Management, 47,* 199–216.

Chapter 4

1. Brannick, M. T., and Levine E. L. (2002). *Job analysis: Methods, research, and applications for human resource management in the new millennium.* Thousand Oaks, CA: Sage; see also Sanchez, J. I., and Levine, E. L. (1999). Is job analysis dead, misunderstood, or both? New forms of work analysis and design. In A. I. Kraut, and A. Korman (Eds.). *Evolving practices in human resources management.* San Francisco: Jossey-Bass, pp. 43–68; See also Gael, S. (Ed.) (1988). *The job analysis handbook for business, industry and government,* vols. I, II. New York: John Wiley and Sons; Peterson et al. (2000). Understanding work using the Occupational Information Network (O*NET): Implications for practice and research. *Personnel Psychology, 54,* 451–492.

2. See Sanchez and Levine, Is job analysis dead; see also Ash, R. A. (1988). Job analysis in the world of work. In S. Gael (Ed.). *The job analysis handbook for business, industry, and government,* vol. I. New York: John Wiley and Sons, pp. 3–13.

3. Harvey, R. J. (1991). Job analysis. In Dunnette, M. D., and Hough, L. M. (Eds.). *Handbook of Industrial and Organizational Psychology,* vol. 2, 2nd ed. Palo Alto, CA: Consulting Psychologists Press, pp. 71–163.

4. Ibid.

5. Thompson, D. E., and Thompson, T. A. (1982). Court standards for job analysis in test validation. *Personnel Psychology, 35,* 865–874.

6. Go to http://online.onetcenter.org.

7. McCormick, E. J. (1976). Job and task analysis. In M. D. Dunnette (Ed.). *Handbook of industrial and organizational psychology.* Chicago, IL: Rand McNally, pp. 651–696.

8. *U.S. v. State of New York.* 21, 473 F. Supp. 1103 (N.D.N.Y. 1979).

9. See Gael, *The job analysis handbook;* also see Spector, P. E., Brannick, M. T., and Coovert, M. D. (1989). Job analysis. In C. L. Cooper and I. T. Robertson (Eds.). *International review of industrial and organizational psychology.* New York: John Wiley and Sons, pp. 281–328.

10. Levine, E. L. (1983). *Everything you always wanted to know about job analysis.* Tampa, FL: Mariner Publishing.

11. McCormick, E. J., and Jeanneret, P. R. (1988). Position analysis questionnaire. In S. Gael (Ed.). *The job analysis handbook for business, industry, and government,* vol. II. New York: John Wiley and Sons, pp. 825–842.

12. McCormick, E. J., Jeanneret, P. R., and Mecham, R. C. (1972). A study of job characteristics and job dimensions as based on the Position Analysis Questionnaire (PAQ). *Journal of Applied Psychology, 56,* 347–368.

13. *Taylor v. James River Corporation* (November 16, 1989). CA-88-0818-T.C.

14. Page, R. C. (1988). Management position description questionnaire. In S. Gael (Ed.). *The job analysis handbook for business, industry, and government,* vol. II. New York: John Wiley and Sons, pp. 860–879.

15. Tornow, W. W., and Pinto, P. R. (1976). The development of a managerial job taxonomy: A system for describing, classifying, and evaluating executive positions. *Journal of Applied Psychology, 61,* 410–418.

16. Athey, T. R., and Orth, M. S. (1999). Emerging competency methods for the future. *Human Resource Management, 38,* 215–226; see also Klemp, G. O. (Ed.). (1980). *The assessment of occupational competence.* Washington, D.C.: Report to the National Institute of Education.

17. Lievens, F., Sanchez, J. I., and DeCorte, W. D. (2004). Easing the inferential leap in competency modeling: The effects of task-related information and subject matter expertise. *Personnel Psychology, 57,* 881–904; see also Lucia, A. D., and Lepsinger, R. (1999). *The art and science of competency models: Pinpointing critical success factors in organizations.* San Francisco: Jossey-Bass.

18. Schippmann, J. S. (1999). *Strategic job modeling: Working at the core of integrated human resources.* Mahwah, NJ: Erlbaum.

19. Hagan, C. M., Konopaske, R., Bernardin, H. J., and Tyler, C. L. (2006). Predicting assessment center performance with 360-degree, top-down, and customer-based competency ratings. *Human Resource Management,* 45, 357–390.

20. Jeanneret, P. R., and Strong, M. (2003). Linking O*NET job analysis information to job requirement predictors: An O*NET application. *Personnel Psychology, 56,* 465–492.

21. Flanagan, J. C. (1954). The critical incident technique. *Psychological Bulletin, 51,* 327–358.

22. Bownas, D., and Bernardin, H. J. (1988). The critical incident method. In S. Gael (Ed.). *The job analysis handbook for business, industry and government,* vol. II. New York: John Wiley and Sons, pp. 1120–1137.

23. Bernardin, H. J. (1989). Innovative approaches to personnel selection and performance appraisal. *Journal of Management Systems, 1,* 25–76; see also Bernardin, H. J. (1987). Development and validation of a forced-choice scale to measure job-related discomfort among customer service representatives. *Academy of Management Journal, 30,* 162–173.

24. Villanova, P., and Bernardin, H. J. (1990). Work behavior correlates of interviewer job compatibility. *Journal of Business and Psychology, 5,* 179–195; Villanova, P., Bernardin, H. J., Johnson, D., and Dahmus, S. (1994). The validity of a measure of job compatibility in the prediction of job performance and turnover of motion picture theater personnel. *Personnel Psychology, 47,* 73–90.

25. Humphrey, S. E., Nalirgang, J. D., and Morgeson, F. P. (2007). Integrating motivational, social, and contextual work design features: A meta-analysis of the summary and theoretical extension work design literature. *Journal of Applied Psychology, 92,* 1332–1356; see also, Hackman, J. R., and Oldham, G. R. (1976). Motivation through the design of work: Test of a theory. *Organizational Behavior and Human Performance 16,* 250–279.

26. Hackman, J. R., and Oldham, G. R. (1980). *Work redesign.* Reading, MA: Addison-Wesley.

27. Fried, Y., and Ferris, G. R. (1987). The validity of the job characteristics model: A review and meta-analysis. *Personnel Psychology 40,* 287–322.

28. Morgeson, F. P., and Humphrey, S. E. (2006). The Work Design Questionnaire (WDQ): Developing and validating a comprehensive measure for assessing job design and the nature of work. *Journal of Applied Psychology, 91,* 1321–1339.

29. Humphrey, Nalirgang, and Morgeson, Integrating motivational, social, and contextual work design features.

30. Schneider, B., and Konz, A. (1989). Strategic job analysis. *Human Resource Management, 28,* 51–63.

31. Schuring, R. (1992). Reasons for the renewed popularity of autonomous work groups. *International Journal of Operations & Production Management, 12,* 61–68.

32. Ibid.; see also Blumberg, M. (1980). Job switching in autonomous work groups: An exploratory study in a Pennsylvania coal mine. *The Academy of Management Journal, 23,* 287–306.

33. Pearson, A. L. (1992). Autonomous workgroups: An evaluation at an industrial site. *Human Relations, 45,* 905–936. The overall effects of AWGs on productivity have been mixed.

34. Morgeson, F. P., and Campion, M. A. (1997). Social and cognitive sources of potential inaccuracy in job analysis. *Journal of Applied Psychology, 82,* 627–655.

35. Treiman, D. J., and Hartmann, H. J. (Eds.) (1981). *Women, work, and wages: Equal pay for jobs of equal value.* Washington, D.C.: National Academy Press.

36. See Gael, *The job analysis handbook.*

37. Cornelius, E. T. (1988). Practical findings from job analysis research. In S. Gael (Ed.). *The job analysis handbook for business, industry, and government,* vol. I. New York: John Wiley and Sons, pp. 48–68.

38. DeNisi, A. S., Cornelius, E. T., and Blencos, A. G. (1987). Further investigation of common knowledge effects on job analysis ratings. *Journal of Applied Psychology, 72,* 262–268.

39. Ibid.

40. Friedman, L., and Harvey, R. J. (1986). Can raters with reduced job descriptive information provide accurate Position Analysis Questionnaire (PAQ) ratings? *Personnel Psychology, 39,* 779–789.

41. Conley, P. R., and Sackett, P. R. (1987). Effects of using high- versus low-performing job incumbents as sources of job analysis information. *Journal of Applied Psychology, 72,* 434–437.

42. Dierdorff, E. C., and Wilson, M. A. (2003). A meta-analysis of job analysis reliability. *Journal of Applied Psychology, 88,* 635–646.

43. Van Iddelinge, C. H., and Putka, D. J. (2005). Modeling error variance in job specification ratings: The influence of rater, job, and organization-level factors. *Journal of Applied Psychology, 90,* 323–334.

44. Levine, E. L., Ash, R. A., Hall, H., and Sistrunk, F. (1983). Evaluation of job analysis methods by experienced job analysts. *Academy of Management Journal, 26,* 339–348.

45. Hunt, S. T. (1996). Generic work behavior: An investigation into dimensions of entry-level, hourly job performance. *Personnel Psychology, 49,* 51–84.

46. Rothman, J. (2003, September 15). 11 Steps to successful outsourcing. *Computer World* online.

47. Bridges, W. (1994, September 19). The end of the job. *Fortune.*

CHAPTER 5

1. Lawrence, S. (1989, April). Voice of HR experience, *Personnel Journal, 70.*

2. Cascio, W. F. (2002). *Responsible restructuring: Creative and profitable alternatives to layoffs.* San Francisco: Berrett-Koehler.

3. Schramm, J. (2005, March). HR's tech challenges. *HR Magazine* online.

4. Friedman, T. L. (2005). *The world is flat: A brief history of the twenty-first century.* Boston: Farrar, Straus, Giroux.

5. *The Economist* (2005). Competition intensifies for global offshoring. CEO Briefing is available as a free report from www.eiu.com/CEO_Briefing2005.

6. Bass, D. D. (2000). Survey of small business. *Nation's Business,* pp. 8–9.

7. Golden, K. A., and Ramanujam, V. (1985). Between a dream and a nightmare: On the integration of human resource management and strategic business planning processes. *Human Resource Management, 34,* 429–452; Walker, J. W. (1994). Integrating the human resource function with the business. *HR Planning, 17,* 59–77.

8. Delbecq, A. L., Van de Ven, A. H., and Gustafson, D. H. (1975). *Group techniques for progress planning: A guide to nominal and Delphi processes.* Glenview, IL: Scott, Foresman.

9. Heneman, H. G., Judge, T. A., and Heneman, R. L. (2006). *Staffing organizations.* New York: McGraw-Hill.

10. See Delbecq, Van de Ven, and Gustafson, *Group techniques for progress planning.*

11. Wikstrom, W. S. (1971). *Manpower planning: Evolving systems.* New York: The Conference Board; see also Piskor, W. G., and Dudding, R. C. (1978). A computer-assisted manpower planning model. In D. T. Bryant and R. J. Niehaus (Eds.). *Manpower planning and organization design.* New York: Plenum Press, pp. 145–154; DeLuca, J. R. (1988). Strategic career management in non-growing volatile business environments. *Human Resource Planning, 11,* 49–62.

12. See Heneman, Judge, and Heneman, *Staffing organizations.*

13. Ibid.

14. Heneman, H. G. III, and Sandver, M. G. (1977). Markov analysis in human resource administration: Applications and limitations. *Academy of Management Review, 15,* 535–542.

15. Hooper, J. A., and Catelanello, R. E. (1981). Markov analysis applied to forecasting technical personnel. *Human Resource Planning, 4,* 41–47.

16. Buller, P. F., and Maki, W. R. (1981). A case history of a manpower planning model. *Human Resource Planning, 4,* 129–138.

17. Dyer, L. (1982). Human resource planning. In K. M. Rowland, and G. R. Ferris (Eds.). *Personnel management.* Boston: Allyn and Bacon.

18. Wellner, A. S. (2001, January). Focus on recruitment and hiring. *HR Magazine,* p. 87.

19. Cascio, *Responsible restructuring.*

20. Ibid.

21. Franklin, S. (1995, October 30). Downsizing realities revealed: American Management association survey tracks layoff patterns. *The News,* p. 8C.

22. Cascio, *Responsible restructuring.*

23. Hippel, C., Mangum, S. L., Greenberger, D. B., Heneman, R. L., and Skoglind, J. D. (1997). Temporary employment: Can organizations and employees both win? *Academy of Management Executive, 11*(1), 93–104.

24. Eng, S. (1995, December 11). Corporate compatibility: Having employer who shares your values is vital to job satisfaction. *The News,* pp. 10C, 11C; Krausz, M., Brandwein, T., and Fox, S. (1995, July). Work attitudes and emotional responses of permanent, voluntary, and involuntary temporary-help employees: An exploratory study. *Applied Psychology: An International Review, 44*(3), 217–232.

25. It is estimated that over 25 million workers telecommuted in 2008. Allen, D. G., and Renn, R. W. (2002). Telecommuting: Understanding and managing remote workers. In G. R. Ferris, M. R. Buckley, and D. B. Fedor (Eds.). *Human resource management: Perspectives, context, functions, and outcomes.* Upper Saddle River, NJ: Prentice Hall, pp. 145–155.

26. *60 Minutes* (2004, August). "Out of India." (www.cbsnews.com/stories).

27. Alfonsi, S. (2008, June 24). Oil price fallout: Jobs coming home? As shipping costs rise, businesses jump ship. *ABC World News.*

28. Bazerman, M. H., and Neale, M. A. (1992). *Negotiating rationally.* New York: Free Press.

29. Peter, L. J., and Hull, R. (1969). *The Peter principle.* New York: William Morrow.

30. Kleiman, L. S., and Clark, K. J. (1984). Recruitment: An effective job posting system. *Personnel Journal, 63,* 20, 22, 25. See also Taylor, M. S., and Schmidt, D. W. (1983). A process oriented investigation of recruitment source effectiveness. *Personnel Psychology, 36,* 343–354; Breaugh, J. A. (1981). Relationships between recruiting sources and employee performance, absenteeism, and work attitudes. *Academy of Management Journal, 24,* 142–147; Rynes, S. L., Heneman, H. G. III, and Schwab, D. P. (1980). Individual reactions to organizational recruiting: A review. *Personnel Psychology, 33,* 529–542; Rynes, S. L., and Miller, H. E. (1983). Recruiter and job influences on candidates for employment. *Journal of Applied Psychology, 68,* 147–154; Barber, A. E., Hollenbeck, J. R., Tower, S. L., and Phillips, J. M. (1994). The effects of interview focus on recruitment effectiveness: A field experiment. *Journal of Applied Psychology, 79*(6), 886–896; Rosse, J. G., Miller, J. L., and Stecher, M. D. (1994). A field study of job applicants' reactions to personality and cognitive ability testing. *Journal of Applied Psychology, 79*(6), 987–992; Saks, A. M., Leck, J. D., and Saunders, D. M. (1995, September). Effects of application blanks and employment equity on applicant reactions and job pursuit intentions. *Journal of Organizational Behavior, 16*(5), 415–430; Taylor, G. S. (1994). The relationship between sources of new employees and attitudes toward the job. *Journal of Social Psychology, 134*(1), 99–110.

31. See Heneman, Judge, and Heneman, *Staffing organizations;* see also Ashford, S. J., and Black, J. S. (1996). Proactivity during organizational entry: The role of desire for control. *Journal of Applied Psychology, 81*(2), 199–214.

32. *EEOC v. Detroit Edison.* (1975). 515 F.2d 301 6th Cir. See also Schenkel-Savitt, S., and Seltzer, S. P. (1987–88). Recruitment as a successful means of affirmative action. *Employee Relations Law Journal, 13*(3), 465–470; Williams, M. L., and Bauer, T. N. (1994). The effect of a managing diversity policy on organizational attractiveness. *Human Factors, 36*(2), 315–326.

33. Hodes, B. S. (1982). *The principles and practice of recruitment advertising: A guide for personnel professionals.* New York: Frederick Fell; see also Bucalo, J. P. (1983). Good advertising can be more effective than other recruitment tools. *Personnel Administrator,* pp. 73–79; Caldwell, D. F., and Spivey, W. A. (1983). The relationship between recruiting source and employee success: An analysis by race. *Personnel Psychology, 36,* 67–72; Decker, P. J., and Cornelius, E. T. (1979). A note on recruiting sources and job survival rates. *Journal of Applied Psychology, 64,* 463–464.

34. Raines, G. (1999, March 1). Online job searches take over classifieds. Reprinted from the *New York Times* in the *Boca Raton News*, p. 2B.

35. See Heneman, Judge, and Heneman, *Staffing organizations.*

36. National Research Council. (1989). *Fairness in employment testing.* Washington, DC: National Academy Press.

37. Dee, W. (1983). Evaluating a search firm. *Personnel Administrator, 28,* 41–43, 99–100.

38. Converse, P. D. and Oswald, F. L. (2004). The effects of data type on job classification and its purposes. *Psychological Science, 46,* 99–127.

39. Fowler, E. M. (1989, November 18). Recruiters refocusing techniques. *New York Times,* p. Y35; Savill, P. A. (June 1995). HR and Inova reengineer recruitment process. *Personnel Journal, 74*(6), 109–114.

40. Kristof, A. L. (1996). Person–organization fit: An integrative review of its conceptualizations, measurement, and implications. *Personnel Psychology, 49*(1), 1–49.

41. Dee, W. (1983). Evaluating a search firm. *Personnel Administrator, 28,* 41–43.

42. Fowler, *Recruiters refocusing techniques.*

43. Rynes, S. L., Orlitzky, M. O., and Bretz, R. D. (1997). Experienced hiring versus college recruiting: Practices and emerging trends. *Personnel Psychology, 50,* 309–339.

44. Lindquist, V. R., and Endicott, F. S. (2002). *Trends in the employment of college and university graduates in business and industry.* Evanston, IL: Northwestern University.

45. Hanigan, M. (1987). Campus recruiters upgrade their pitch. *Personnel Administrator,* pp. 32, 56.

46. Cappelli, P. (March 2001). Making the most of on-line recruiting. *Harvard Business Review*, pp. 139–146.

47. U.S. Merit Systems Protection Board. (1988). *Attracting quality graduates to the federal government: A view of college recruiting.* U.S. Merit Systems Protection Board, Washington, DC.

48. Tessler, J. (1999, May 27). Web surfing is fast way to go job hopping. *The Wall Street Journal,* p. B12. See also Leonard, B. (2001, February 6). Online and overwhelmed. *HR Magazine.*

49. Weddle.com (2007, September 6). "How are people finding jobs?" Weddle.com.

50. Carlson, K. D., Connerley, M. L., and Mecham, R. I. (2002). Recruitment evaluation: The case for assessing the quality of applicants attracted. *Personnel Psychology, 55,* 461–490.

51. Meyer, S. (2008). "In defense of Millennials." http://hrcafe.typepad.com/my_weblog/2008/05/millenials.html; Gannon, M. J. (1971). Source of referral and employee turnover. *Journal of Applied Psychology, 55,* 226–228; Vecchio, R. P. (1995). The impact of referral sources on employee attitudes: Evidence from a national sample. *Journal of Management, 21*(5), 953–965.

52. Barber, A. E. (1998). *Recruiting employees.* Thousand Oaks, CA: Sage.

53. Bartol, K. M., and Martin, D. C. (1988). Recruitment source as a resource: The value of pay-related information to part-time job applicants. Paper presented at the Annual Meeting of the Academy of Management. See also Taylor, M. S., and Bergmann, T. J. (1987). Organizational recruitment activities and applicants' reactions at different stages of the recruitment process. *Personnel Psychology, 40*(2), 261–285; Taylor, M. S., and Sniezek, J. A. (1984). The college recruitment interview: Topical content and applicant reactions. *Journal of Occupational Psychology, 57;* Irving, P. G., and Meyer, J. P. (1994, December). Reexamination of the met-expectations hypothesis: A longitudinal analysis. *Journal of Applied Psychology, 79*(6), 937–949.

54. Ryan, A. M., and Tippins, N. T. (2004). Attracting and selecting: What psychological research tells us. *Human Resource Management, 43,* 305–318.

55. What do Internet job hunters say? (2001, May). *HR Magazine,* p. 45.

56. Braddy, P. W., Thompson, L., Wuensch, K. L., and Grossnickle, K. L. (2005). Internet recruiting: The effects of web page design features. *Social Science Computer Review, 21,* 374–385; see also Who's using Internet recruiting? (1999, December). *Inc.,* p. 156; Lievens, F., and Harris, M. M. (2003). Research on internet recruiting and testing: Current status and future directions. In Cooper C. L., and Robertson I. T. (Eds.). *International Review of Industrial and Organizational Psychology,* vol. 16. Chicester: John Wiley & Sons, Ltd., pp. 131–165.

57. Krumwiede, J. (2003). Managing resume flow with artificial intelligence. SHRMForum, www.shrm.org/ema; see also Cober, R. T., Brown, D. J., and Levy, P. E. (2004). Form, content, and function: An evaluative methodology for corporate employment Web sites. *Human Resource Management, 43,* 201–218.

58. Highhouse, S., et al. (2000). Assessing company employment image: An example in the fast food industry. *Personnel Psychology, 52,* 151–172; Heneman, Judge, and Heneman, *Staffing organizations;* Wanous, J. P. (1980). *Organizational entry: Recruitment, selection and socialization of newcomers.* Reading, MA: Addison-Wesley.

59. Hom, P. W., Griffith, R. W., Palich, L. E., and Bracker, J. S. (2000). Revisiting met expectations as a reason why realistic job previews work. *Personnel Psychology, 52,* 97–112; Premack, S. L., and Wanous, J. P. (1985). A meta-analysis of realistic job preview experiments. *Journal of Applied Psychology, 70,* 706–719; see also Popovich, P., and Wanous, J. P. (1982). The realistic job preview as a persuasive communication. *Academy of Management Review, 7,* 570–579; Dean, R. A., and Wanous, J. P. (1984). The effects of realistic job previews on hiring bank tellers. *Journal of Applied Psychology, 69,* 61–68; Meglino, B. M., DeNisi, A. S., and Ravlin, E. C. (1996). Effects of previous job exposure and subsequent job status on the functioning of realistic job preview. *Personnel Psychology, 46*(4), 803–810.

60. McEvoy, G. M., and Cascio, W. F. (1985). Strategies for reducing employee turnover: A meta-analysis. *Journal of Applied Psychology, 70,* 342–353.

61. Bernardin, H. J. (1989). Innovative approaches to personnel selection and performance appraisal. *Journal of Management Systems, 1,* 25–36.

62. Bernardin, H. J. (1989). The development of a scale of discomfort to predict employee turnover among customer services representatives. *Academy of Management Journal, 30,* 162–173.

63. Breaugh, J. (1992). *Recruitment: Science and practice.* Cincinnati, OH: South-Western.

64. Dowling, P. J., Schuler, R. R. S., and Welch, D. E. (2000). *International dimensions of human resource management.* Boston: Wadsworth.

65. Dowling, P. J. (1989). Hot issues overseas. *Personnel Administrator, 34,* 68–72.

66. Lublin, J. S. (1996, January 29). An overseas stint can be a ticket to the top. *The Wall Street Journal,* pp. B1, B5; see also Moran, R., Stahl, H., and Steel, R. (1989). Survey of personnel managers at 56 international companies. Cited in O'Boyle, T. (1989, December 11). Grappling with the expatriate issue. *The Wall Street Journal,* pp. B1, B4.

67. Global Relocation Services (2008, May). *Global relocation trends 2008 survey report.*

68. Mendenhall, M. E., and Oddou, G. (1995). The overseas assignment: A practical look. In Mendenhall, M. E., and Oddoe, G. (Eds.). *Readings and cases in international human resource management.* Cincinnati, OH: South-Western, pp. 206–216.

69. Stroh, L. K., Gregersen, H. B., and Black, J. S. (1998). Closing the gap: Expectations versus reality among repatriates. *Journal of World Business, 33*(2), 110–124.

70. Luk, D. (2005). Input-based and time-based models of international adjustment: Meta-analytic evidence and theoretical extensions. *Academy of Management Journal 48,* 257–281.

71. Konopaske, R., and Ivancevich, J. M. (2004). *Global management and organizational behavior.* Burr Ridge, IL: McGraw-Hill Irwin.

72. Ibid.

CHAPTER 6

1. Huselid, M. A., Becker, B. E., and Beatty, R. W. (2005). *The workforce scorecard: Managing human capital to execute strategy.* Boston: Harvard Business School Press.

2. Sackett, P., and Lievens, F. (2008). Personnel selection. *Annual Review of Psychology, 59,* 419–450; see also Cascio, W. F., and Aguinis, H. (2005). *Applied psychology in human resource management.* Upper Saddle River, NJ: Prentice Hall.

3. Russell, C. J., Mattson, J., Devlin, S. E., and Atwater, D. (1990). Predictive validity of biodata items generated from retrospective life experience essays. *Journal of Applied Psychology, 75,* 569–580. See also Kluger, A., Reilly, R. R., and Russell, C. J. (1991). Faking biodata tests: Are option-keyed instruments more resistant? *Journal of Applied Psychology, 76,* 889–896; Mael, F. A., Connerley, M., and Morath, R. A. (1996). None of your business: Parameters of biodata invasiveness. *Personnel Psychology, 49,* 613–619.

4. Hough, L. M., Keyes, M. A., and Dunnette, M. D. (1983). An evaluation of three alternative selection procedures. *Personnel Psychology, 36,* 261–276.

5. Cascio and Aguinis, *Applied psychology in human resource management.*

6. Bernardin, H. J., and Beatty, R. W. (1984). *Performance appraisal: Assessing human behavior at work.* Boston: Kent-PWS.

7. Taylor, P. J., Pajo, K., Cheung, G. W., and Stringfield P. (2004). Dimensionality and validity of a structured telephone reference check procedure. *Personnel Psychology, 57,* 745–772.

8. Schmidt, F. L. and Hunter, J. E. (2004). General mental ability in the world of work: Occupational attainment and job performance. *Journal of Personality and Social Psychology, 86,* 162–173; Ones, D. S., Viswesvaran, C., and Dilchert, S. (2004). Cognitive ability in selection decisions. In O. Wilhelm and R. W. Engle (Eds.). *Handbook of understanding and measuring intelligence.* Thousand Oaks, CA: Sage, pp. 431–468; Heneman, H. H., Judge, T. A., and Heneman, R. L. (2006). *Staffing organizations.* New York: McGraw-Hill.

9. Plaschke, B., and Alomond, E. (1995, April 21). Has the NFL draft become a thinking man's game? *Los Angeles Times* online.

10. Brown, K. G., Le, H., and Schmidt, F. L. (2006). Specific aptitude theory revisited: Is there incremental validity for training performance? *International Journal of Selection and Assessment,14,* 98.

11. Roth, P. L., Bevier, C. A., Bobko, P., Switzer, F. S., and Tyler, P. (2001). Ethnic group differences in cognitive ability in employment and educational settings: A meta-analysis. *Personnel Psychology, 54,* 297–330.

12. Schmidt, F. L., and Hunter, J. E. (2004). General mental ability in the world of work: Occupational attainment and job performance. *Journal of Personality and Social Psychology, 86,* 162–173.

13. Sackett, P., and Lievens, F. (2008). Personnel selection. *Annual Review of Psychology, 59,* 419–450.

14. Aguinis, H., and Smith, M. A. (2007). Understanding the impact of test validity and bias on selection errors and adverse impact in human resource selection. *Personnel Psychology, 60,* 165–99; Berry, C. M., Gruys, M. L., and Sackett, P. R. (2006). Educational attainment as a proxy for cognitive ability in selection: Effects on levels of cognitive ability and adverse impact. *Journal of Applied Psychology, 91,* 696–705; De Corte, W., Lievens, F., and Sackett, P. R. 2006. Predicting adverse impact and multistage mean criterion performance in selection. *Journal of Applied Psychology, 91,* 523–537.

15. Aguinis, H. (Ed.). (2004). *Test-score banding in human resource selection: Legal, technical, and societal issues.* Westport, CT: Praeger; Truxillo, D. M., and Bauer, T. N. (1999). Applicant reactions to test score banding in entry-level and promotional contexts. *Journal of Applied Psychology, 84,* 322–339.

16. Barrick, M. R., Mount, M. K., and Judge, T. A. (2001). Personality and performance at the beginning of the new millennium: What do we know and where do we go next? *International Journal of Selection and Assessment, 9,* 9–30; and Salgado, J. F. (2003). Predicting job performance using FFM and non-FFM personality measures. *Journal of Occupational Organizational Psychology, 76,* 323–346.

17. Sackett and Lievens, Personnel selection, p. 438; see also Murphy, K. R., (Ed.). (2006). *A critique of emotional intelligence: What are the problems and how can they be fixed?* Mahwah, NJ: Erlbaum; Landy, F. J. (2005). Some historical and scientific issues related to research on emotional intelligence. *Journal of Organanizational Behavior, 26,* 411–424.

18. Judge, T. A., Erez, A., Bono, J. E., and Thoresen, C. J. (2003). The Core Self-Evaluations Scale (CSES): Development of a measure. *Personnel Psychology, 56,* 303–331; see also Judge, T. A., Bono, J. E., Erez, A., and Locke, E. A. (2005). Core self-evaluations and job and life satisfaction: The role of self-concordance and goal attainment. *Journal of Applied Psychology, 90,* 257–268.

19. Miner, J. B. (1985). Sentence completion measures in personnel research: The development and validation of the Miner Sentence Completion Scales. In H. J. Bernardin and D. Bownas (Eds.). *Personality testing in organizations.* New York: Praeger, pp. 145–176. See also Miner, J. B., Chen, C. C., and Yu, K. C. (1991). Testing theory under adverse conditions: Motivation to manage in the People's Republic of China. *Journal of Applied Psychology, 76,* 343–349.

20. Rafaeli, A., and Klimoski, R. J. (1983). Predicting sales success through handwriting analysis: An evaluation of the effects of training and handwriting sample content. *Journal of Applied Psychology, 68,* 212–217.

21. Sackett and Lievens, Personnel selection, pp. 419–450; Bernardin, H. J., and Bownas, D. (1985). *Personality assessment in organizations.* New York: Praeger; see also Ones, D. S., Viswesvaran, C., and Reiss, A. D. (1996). Role of social desirability in personality testing for personnel selection: The red herring. *Journal of Applied Psychology, 81*(6), 660–679.

22. Costa, P. T., and McCrae, R. R. (1992). *Revised NEO Personality Inventory (NEO-PI-R) and NEO Five-Factor (NEO-FFI) Inventory Professional Manual.* Odessa, FL: Psychological Assessment Resources.

23. Gardner, W. L., and Martinko, M. J. (1996). Using the Myers-Briggs type indicator to study managers: A literature review and research agenda. *Journal of Management, 22*(1), 45–83.

24. Miner, Sentence completion measures in personnel research. See also Miner, Chen, and Yu, Testing theory under adverse conditions.

25. Barrick, M. R., Mount, M. K., and Judge, T. A. (2001). Personality and performance at the beginning of the new millennium: What do we know and where do we go next? *International Journal of Selection and Assessment, 9,* 9–30. see also Morgeson, F. P., Reider, M. H., and Campion, M. A. (2005). Selecting individuals in team settings: The importance of social skills, personality characteristics, and teamwork knowledge. *Personnel Psychology, 58,* 583–611.

26. Judge, T., and Erez, A. (2007). Interaction and intersection: The constellation of emotional stability and extraversion in predicting performance. *Personnel Psychology, 60,* 573–596. See also, LaHuis, D. M., Martin, N. R., and Avis, J. M. (2005). Investigating nonlinear conscientiousness-job performance relations for clerical employees. *Human Performance, 18,* 199–212.

27. Bernardin, H. J., Villanova, P., and Cooke, D. (2000). Conscientiousness and agreeableness as predictors of rating elevation. *Journal of Applied Psychology, 85,* 232–237. See also Salgado, J. F. (1997). The five factor model of personality and job performance in the European community. *Journal of Applied Psychology, 82*(1), 30–43; Stewart, J. L. (1996). Reward structure as a moderator of the relationship between extraversion and sales performance. *Journal of Applied Psychology, 81*(6), 617–619.

28. Barrick, Mount, and Judge, Personality and performance at the beginning of the new millennium.

29. Dudley, N. M., Orvis, K. A., Lebiecki, J. E., and Cortina, J. M. (2006). A meta-analytic investigation of conscientiousness in the prediction of job performance: examining the intercorrelations and the incremental validity of narrow traits. *Journal of Applied Psychology, 91,* 40–57.

30. Van Iddekinge, C. H., Raymark, P. H., and Roth, P. L. (2005). Assessing personality with a structured employment interview: Construct-related validity and susceptibility to response inflation. *Journal of Applied Psychology, 90,* 536–552; Komar, S., Brown, D., Komar, J. A., and Robie, C. (2008). Faking and the validity of conscientiousness: A Monte Carlo investigation. *Journal of Applied Psychology, 93,* 140–154; Schmitt, N., and Oswald, F. L. (2006). The impact of corrections for faking on the validity of noncognitive measures in selection settings. *Journal of Applied Psychology, 91,* 613–621; Peterson, M. H., and Griffith, R. L. (2006). Faking and job performance: A multifaceted issue. In R. L. Griffith and M. H. Peterson (Eds.). *A closer examination of applicant faking behavior.* Greenwich, CT: Information Age Publishing, pp. 233–262; McFarland, L. A., and Ryan, A. M. (2000). Variance in faking across noncognitive measures. *Journal of Applied Psychology, 85,* 812–821.

31. Bing, M. N., Whanger, J. C., Davison, H. K., and VanHook, J. B. (2004). Incremental validity of the frame-of-reference effect in personality scale scores: A replication and extension. *Journal of Applied Psychology, 89,* 150–157.

32. Rotundo, M., and Sackett, P. R. (2002). The relative importance of task, citizenship, and counterproductive performance to global ratings of job performance: A policy-capturing approach. *Journal of Applied Psychology, 87,* 66–80.

33. Barrick, M. R., and Zimmerman, R. D. (2005). Reducing voluntary, avoidable turnover through selection. *Journal of Applied Psychology, 90,* 159–166.

34. Bernardin, H. J. (1989). Innovative approaches to personnel selection and performance appraisal. *Journal of Management Systems, 1,* 25–36; see also Bernardin, H. J., Hagan, C., Schubinski, M., and Johnson, D. (1997). The development and validation of the Security Officer Profile. *Security Journal, 8,* 195–200.

35. Berry, C. M., Sackett, P. R., and Wieman, S. (2007). A review of recent developments in integrity test research. *Personnel Psychology, 60,* 271–301; see also, Sackett, P. R., and Wanek, J. E. (1996). New developments in the use of measures of honesty, integrity, conscientiousness, dependability, trustworthiness, and reliability for personnel selection. *Personnel Psychology, 49*(4), 787–795.

36. Schmidt, F. L., and Hunter, J. E. (1998). The validity and utility of selection methods in personnel psychology: Practical and theoretical implications of 85 years of research findings. *Psychological Bulletin, 124,* 262–274.

37. Marcus, B., Lee, K., and Ashton, M. C. (2007). Personality dimensions explaining relationships between integrity tests and counterproductive behavior: Big five, or one in addition? *Personnel Psychology, 60,* 1–34. See also Lee, K., Ashton, M. C., Morrison, D. L., et al. (2008). Predicting integrity with the HEXACO personality model: Use of self- and observer reports. *Journal of Occupational and Organizational Psychology, 81,* 147–167.

38. Hogan, J., Hogan, R., and Busch, C. M. (1984). How to measure service orientation. *Journal of Applied Psychology, 69,* 167–173; see also Liao, H., and Subramony, M. (2008). Employee customer orientation in manufacturing organizations: Joint influences of customer

proximity and the senior leadership team. *Journal of Applied Psychology, 93,* 317–328; Homburg, C., and Stock, R. M. (2005). Exploring the conditions under which salesperson work satisfaction can lead to customer satisfaction. *Psychology & Marketing, 22,* 393–420; Grandey, A. A., Fisk, G. M., Mattila, A. S., Jansen, K. J., and Sideman, I. A. (2005). Is "service with a smile" enough? Authenticity of positive displays during service encounters. *Organizational Behavior and Human Decision Processes, 96,* 38–55.

39. Machin, M. A., and Sankey, K. S. (2008). The effects of personality and gender on risky driving behaviour and accident involvement. *Accident Analysis and Prevention, 40,* 541–547; see also Schwebel, D. C., Ball, K. K., Severson, J., Barton, B. K., Rizzo, M., and Viamonte, S. M. (2007). Individual difference factors in risky driving among older adults. *Journal of Safety Research, 38,* 501–509.

40. Deffenbacher, J. L., Oetting, E. R., and Lynch, R. S. (1994). Development of a driving anger scale, *Psychological Reports, 74,* 83–91.

41. Jones, J. W., and Wuebker, L. (1985). Development and validation of the safety locus of control scale. *Perceptual and Motor Skills, 61,* 151–161; see also Hunter, D. R. (2005). Measurement of hazardous attitudes among pilots. *International Journal of Aviation Psychology, 15,* 23–43.

42. Schwebel et al., Individual difference factors in risky driving among older adults.

43. National Survey on Drug Use and Health (2003). *Methamphetamine use in the U.S.* See also Zigarelli, M. A. (1995). Drug testing litigation: Trends and outcomes. *Human Resource Management Review, 5,* 267–288.

44. Geidt, T. (1985). Drug and alcohol abuse in the workplace: Balancing employer and employee rights. *Employer Relations Law Journal, 11,* 181–205. See also Faley, R. H., Kleiman, L. S., and Wall, J. (1988). Drug testing in public and private-sector workplace: Technical and legal issues. *Journal of Business and Psychology, 3,* 154–186; Murphy, K. R., Thornton, G. C. III, and Reynolds, D. H. (1990). College students' attitudes toward employee drug testing programs. *Personnel Psychology, 43,* 615–632; Crant, J. M., and Bateman, T. S. (1990). An experimental test of the impact of drug testing programs on potential job applicants' attitudes and intentions. *Journal of Applied Psychology, 75,* 127–131; Zigarelli, M. A. (1995). Drug testing litigation: Trends and outcomes. *Human Resource Management Review, 5*(4), 267–288.

45. Schmitt, N., and Mills, E. (2001). Traditional tests and job simulations: Minority and majority performance and test validation. *Journal of Applied Psychology, 86,* 451–458.

46. Hooper, A. C., Cullen, M. J., and Sackett, P. R. (2006). Operational threats to the use of SJTs: Faking, coaching, and retesting issues. In J. A. Weekley and R. E. Ployhart (Eds.), *Situational judgment tests: Theory, measurement, and application.* Mahwah, NJ: Lawrence Erlbaum Associates, pp. 205–232; Weekley, J. A., and Jones, C. (1999). Further studies of situational tests. *Personnel Psychology, 52,* 679–700.

47. Roth, P. L., Bobko, P., and McFarland, L. A. (2005). A meta-analysis of work sample test validity: Updating and integrating some classic literature. *Personnel Psychology, 58,* 1009–1037; see also Weekley, J. A., and Ployhart, R. E. (2005). Situational judgment: Antecedents and relationships with performance. *Human Performance, 18,* 81–104.

48. Potosky, D., and Bobko, P. (2004). Selection testing via the Internet: Practical considerations and exploratory empirical findings. *Personnel Psychology, 57,* 1003–1034; see also Ployhart, R. E., Weekley, J. A., Holtz, B. C., and Kemp, C. (2003). Web-based and paper-and-pencil testing of applicants in a proctored setting: Are personality, biodata, and situational judgment tests comparable? *Personnel Psychology, 56,* 733–752; Xiao, X., and Wang, Z. M. (2004). Use new technology to design electronic assessment centers. *International Journal of Psychology, 39,* 439; Silvester, J., and Anderson, N. (2003). Technology and discourse: A comparison of face-to-face and telephone employment interviews. *International Journal of Selection and Assessment, 11,* 206–214; Taylor, P. J., Pajo, K., Cheung, G. W., and Stringfield, P. (2004). Dimensionality and validity of a structured telephone reference check procedure. *Personnel Psychology, 57,* 745–772.

49. Thornton, G. C. III, and Byham, W. C. (1982). *Assessment centers and managerial performance.* New York: Academic Press. See also Fitzgerald, L. F., and Quaintance, M. K. (1982). Survey of assessment center in state and local government. *Journal of Assessment Center Technology, 5,* 9–19; Schneider, J. R., and Schmitt, N. (1992). An exercise design approach to understanding assessment center dimension and exercise constructs. *Journal of Applied Psychology, 77,* 32–41; Schmitt, N., Schneider, J. R., and Cohen, S. A. (1990). Factors affecting validity of a regionally administered assessment center. *Personnel Psychology, 43,* 1–12; Gaugler, B. B., and Rudolph, A. S. (1992). The influence of assessee performance variation on assessors' judgements. *Personnel Psychology, 45,* 77–98; Reilly, R. R., Henry, S., and Smither, J. W. (1990). An examination of the effects of using behavior checklists on the construct validity of assessment center dimensions. *Personnel Psychology, 43,* 71–84.

50. Kraut, A. I., and Scott, G. J. (1972). Validity of an operational management assessment program. *Journal of Applied Psychology, 56,* 124–129.

51. Bray, D. W., and Campbell, R. J. (1968). Selection of salesmen by means of an assessment center. *Journal of Applied Psychology, 52,* 36–41. See also McEvoy, G. M., Beatty, R. W., and Bernardin, H. J. (1987). Unanswered questions in assessment center research. *Journal of Business and Psychology, 2,* 97–111.

52. Pynes, J. E., and Bernardin, H. J. (1989). Predictive validity of an entry-level police officer assessment center. *Journal of Applied Psychology, 74,* 831–833.

53. Gaugler, B. B., Rosenthal, D. B., Thornton, G. C. III, and Benton, C. (1987). Meta-analysis of assessment center validity. *Journal of Applied Psychology, 72,* 493–511; Schippmann, J. S., Prien, E. P., and Katz, J. A. (1990). Reliability and validity of in-basket performance measures. *Personnel Psychology, 43,* 837–860.

54. Bowler, M. C., and Woehr, D. J. (2006). A meta-analytic evaluation of the impact of dimension and exercise factors on assessment center ratings. *Journal of Applied Psychology, 91,* 1114–1164.

55. Tyler, C., and Bernardin, H. J. (2003). Predictive validity and adverse impact: A comparison of three managerial selection methods. *Best Papers of the Academy of Management: HR,* F 1-6. Paper presented at the annual meeting of the Academy of Management, Vancouver, Canada.

56. Chen, C. C., and Chiu, S. F. (2005). Exploring boundaries of the effects of applicant impression management tactics in job interviews. *Journal of Management, 31,* 108–125; see also Lievens, F., and De Paepe, A. (2004). An empirical investigation of interviewer-related

factors that discourage the use of high structure interviews. *Journal of Organizational Behavior, 25,* 29–46; Maurer, S. D. (2002). A practitioner-based analysis of interviewer job expertise and scale format as contextual factors in situational interviews. *Personnel Psychology, 55,* 307–327; Christina, S. C., and Latham, G. P. (2004). The situational interview as a predictor of academic and team performance: A study of the mediating effects of cognitive ability and emotional intelligence. *International Journal of Selection and Assessment, 12,* 312–320.

57. Buckingham, M., and Clifton, D. (2001). *Now, discover your strengths.* New York: The Free Press.

58. Schmidt, F. L., and Rader, M. (2001). Exploring the boundary conditions for interview validity: Meta-analytic findings for a new interview type. *Personnel Psychology, 52,* 445–464.

59. Raymark, P. H., Eidson, C. E., and Attenweiler, W. J. (2004). What do structured selection interviews really measure? The construct validity of behavior description interviews. *Human Performance, 17,* 71–93; Allen, I. D., Facteau, J. D., and Facteau, C. L. (2004). Structured interviewing for OCB: Construct validity, faking, and the effects of suggestion type. *Human Performance, 17,* 1–24; see also Howard, J. L., and Ferris, G. R. (1996). The employment interview context: Social and situational influences on interviewer decisions. *Journal of Applied Social Psychology, 25*(2), 111–136; Marlowe, C. M., Schneider, S. L., and Nelson, C. E. (1996). Gender and attractiveness biases in hiring decisions: Are more experienced managers less biased? *Applied Psychology, 81*(1), 11–21; Prewett-Livingston, A. J., Feild, H. S., Veres, J. G. III, and Lewis, P. M. (1996). Effects of race on interview ratings in a situational panel interview. *Journal of Applied Psychology, 81*(2), 178–186.

60. Schmidt, F. L., and Zimmerman, R. D. (2004). A counterintuitive hypothesis about employment interview validity and some supporting evidence. *Journal of Applied Psychology, 89,* 553–561.

61. McFarland, L. A., Ryan, A. M., Sacco, J. M., and Kriska, S. D. (2004). Examination of structured interview ratings across time: The effects of applicant race, rater race, and panel composition. *Journal of Management, 30,* 435–452; see also Harris, M. M., Lievens, F., and Van Hoye, G. (2004). "I think they discriminated against me": Using prototype theory and organizational justice theory for understanding perceived discrimination in selection and promotion situations. *International Journal of Selection and Assessment, 12,* 54–65; Williamson, G., Campion, J. E., Malos, S. B., Roehling, M. V., and Campion, M. A. (1997). Employment interview on trial: Linking interview structure with litigation outcomes. *Journal of Applied Psychology, 82,* 900–912.

62. Taylor, P. J., and Small, B. (2002). Asking applicants what they would do versus what they did do: A meta-analytic comparison of situational and past behaviour employment interview questions. *Journal of Occupational and Organizational Psychology, 75,* 277–294; see also Huffcutt, A. I., Weekley, J. A., Wiesner, W. H., Degroot, T. G., and Jones, C. (2001). Comparison of situational and behavior description interview questions for higher-level positions. *Personnel Psychology, 54,* 619–644.

63. Grove, W. M., Zald, D. H., Lebow, S., Snitz, B. E., and Nelson, C. (2000). Clinical versus mechanical prediction: A meta-analysis. *Psychological Assessment, 12,* 19–30.

64. Oswald, F. L., Schmitt, N., Kim, B. H., Ramsay L. J., and Gillespie, M. A. (2004). Developing a biodata measure and situational judgment inventory as predictors of college student performance. *Journal of Applied Psychology, 89,* 187–207.

65. Highhouse, S. (2002). Assessing the candidate as a whole: A historical and critical analysis of individual psychological assessment for personnel decision making. *Personnel Psychology, 55,* 363–396.

66. Kehoe, J. F., and Olson, A. (2005). Cut scores and employment discrimination litigation. In Landy, F. J. (Ed). Employment discrimination litigation. San Francisco, CA: Jossey-Bass, pp. 410–449; see also, *Lewis v. Chicago,* 98C5596;http://www.ipmaac.org/files/lewis_v_chicago-3-22-2005.pdf.

67. Tung, R. L. (May 1987). Expatriate assignments: Enhancing success and minimizing failure. *The Academy of Management Executive,* pp. 118–125; see also Sprietzer, G. M., McCall, M. W., Jr., and Mahoney, J. D. (1977). Early identification of international executive potential. *Journal of Applied Psychology, 82*(1), 6–29.

68. Mendenhall, M., and Oddou, G. (1985). The dimensions of expatriate acculturation: A review. *Academy of Management Review, 19,* 39–47.

69. Konopaske, R., and Ivancevich, J. M. (2004). *Global management and organizational behavior.* Burr Ridge, IL: McGraw-Hill Irwin, p. 341; see also Bhaskar-Shrinivas, P., Harrison, D. A., Shaffer, M. A., and Luk, D. M. (2005). Input-based and time-based models of international adjustment: Meta-analytic evidence and theoretical extensions. *Academy of Management Journal 48,* 257–281.

70. Konopaske and Ivancevich, *Global management and organizational behavior.* See also Matsumoto, D., LeRoux, J. A., Bernhard, R., and Gray, H. (2004). Unraveling the psychological correlates of intercultural adjustment potential. *International Journal of Intercultural Relations, 28,* 281–309.

71. Konopaske and Ivancevich, *Global management and organizational behavior.*

72. Huo, Y. P., Huan, H. J., and Napier, N. K. (2002). Divergence or convergence: A cross-national comparison of personnel selection practices. *Human Resource Management, 41,* 31–44; Von Glinow, M. A., and Chung, B. J. (1990). Comparative human resource management practices in the United States, Japan, Korea, and the People's Republic of China. In A. Nedd, G. R. Ferris, and K. M. Rowland (Eds.), *Research in personnel and human resources management: International human resources management* (Suppl. 1). Greenwich, CT: JAI Press, pp. 153–171.

73. Latham, G. P., and Napier, N. K. (1990). Chinese human resource management practices in Hong Kong and Singapore: An exploratory study. In A. Nedd, G. R. Ferris, and K. M. Rowland (Eds.), *Research in personnel and human resources management: International human resources management* (Suppl. 1). Greenwich, CT: JAI Press, pp. 173–199.

74. Levy-Leboyer, C. (1994). Selection and assessment in Europe. In M. Dunnette and L. Hough (Eds.), *Handbook of industrial and organizational psychology.* Palo Alto, CA: Consulting Psychologists Press, pp. 173–190; see also Cascio, W. F., and Bailey, E. (1995). International HRM: The state of research and practice. In O. Shenkar (Ed.), *Global perspectives of human resources management.* Englewood Cliffs, NJ: Prentice Hall, pp. 15–36.

75. Huo, Y. P., Huan, H. J., and Napier, N. K. (2002). Divergence or convergence: A cross-national comparison of personnel selection practices. *Human Resource Management, 41,* 31–44; see also Shimmin, S. (1989). Selection in a European context. In P. Harriot (Ed.), *Assessment and selection in organizations.* Chichester, England: John Wiley and Sons, pp. 109–118.

76. Shackleton, V. J., and Newell, S. (1989). Selection procedures in practice. In P. Herriot (Ed.), *Assessment and selection in organizations.* Chichester, England: John Wiley and Sons, pp. 257–271.

77. Mol, S. T., Born, M. P., Willemsen, M. E., and van der Molen, H. T. (2005). Predicting expatriate job performance for selection purposes: A quantitative review. *Journal of Cross-Cultural Psychology, 36,* 590–620.

78. Ibid.

79. Gould, J. (2002). *Leader's guide for the fairness factor: How to recruit, interview, and hire to maximize effectiveness and minimize legal liability.* Carlsbad, CA: CRM Films.

80. Ibid.

CHAPTER 7

1. Bernardin, H. J., Hagan, C., Kane, J. S., and Villanova, P. (1998). Effective performance management: A focus on precision, customers, and situational constraints. In J. Smither (Ed.), *Performance appraisal: The state of the art in practice.* San Francisco: Jossey-Bass, pp. 3–45; see also Wigdor, A. K., and Green, B. F. (Eds.). (1992). *Performance assessment for the workplace,* vols. I and II: *The technical issues.* Washington, DC: National Academy Press; Moravec, M., Juliff, R., and Hesler, K. (1995, January). Partnerships help a company manage performance. *Personnel Journal,* pp. 105–108; Cardy, R. L., and Dobbins, G. H. (1994). *Performance appraisal: Alternative perspectives.* Cincinnati, OH: South-Western.

2. *The Wall Street Journal* (1996). Cited in *The Palm Beach Post* (1996, December 15), p. 3F. See also Smith, B., Hornsby, J. S., and Shirmeyer, R. (1996, Summer). Current trends in performance appraisal: An examination of managerial practice. *SAM Advanced Management Journal,* pp. 10–15; Antonioni, D. (1994). Improve the performance management process before discontinuing performance appraisals. *Compensation and Benefits Review, 26*(3), 29–32.

3. Huselid, M. A., Becker, B. E., and Beatty, R. W. (2005). *The workforce scorecard: Managing human capital to execute strategy.* Boston: Harvard Business School Press.

4. Bernardin, H. J., and Tyler, C. (2001). The legal and ethical implications of multirater appraisal systems. In A. Church et al. (Eds.), *The handbook of multisource feedback.* San Francisco, CA: Jossey-Bass, pp. 264–292; see also Austin, J. T., Villanova, P., and Bernardin, H. J. (2002). Legal requirements and technical guidelines involved in implementing performance appraisal systems. In G. R. Ferris, and M. R. Buckley (Eds.), *Human resources management: Perspectives, context, functions, and outcomes* (4th ed.). Englewood Cliffs, NJ: Prentice Hall, pp. 208–236; see also Bernardin, H. J., Hennessey, H. W., and Peyrefitte, J. (1995). Age, racial, and gender bias as a function of criterion specificity: A test of expert testimony. *Human Resource Management Review, 5,* 63–77.

5. See Bernardin et al., Effective performance management; see also Kane, J., and Kane, K. (1992). The analytic framework: The most promising approach for the advancement of performance appraisal. *Human Resource Management Review, 2,* 37–70.

6. Edwards, M. R., and Ewen, A. J. (1996). *360-degree feedback: The powerful new model for employee assessment and performance improvement.* New York: AMACOM. See also Edwards, M. R. (1990). Implementation strategies for multiple rater systems. *Personnel Journal, 69*(9), 130, 132, 134, 137, 139.

7. See Bernardin and Tyler, The legal and ethical implications of multirater appraisal systems.

8. Ableson, R. (2001, March 21). Companies turn to grades, and employees go to court. *New York Times* (www.NYTimes.com); see also Truby, M., and Garrett, C. (2001, February 14). Workers accuse Ford of age bias. *Ford Global Clipsheet* (www.clipsheet.ford.com).

9. Lawler, E. E. (2003). Reward practices and performance management system effectivesness. *Organizational Dynamics, 32,* 396–404.

10. Borman, W. C., et al. (2001). An examination of the comparative reliability, validity, and accuracy of performance ratings made using computerized adaptive rating scales. *Journal of Applied Psychology, 86,* 965–973.

11. Bernardin, H. J., and Thomason, S. (2009). Another look at forced-choice scales and perceptions of procedural justice. Paper presented at the annual meeting of the Academy of Management. Chicago, IL.

12. Bernardin, H. J., and Smith, P. C. (1981). A clarification of some issues regarding the development and use of behaviorally anchored rating scales. *Journal of Applied Psychology, 66,* 458–463.

13. Latham, G., and Wexley, K. (1977). Behavioral observation scales for performance appraisal purposes. *Personnel Psychology, 30,* 255–268.

14. Kane, J. S. (1986). Performance distribution assessment. In R. A. Berk (Ed.), *Performance assessment: Methods and applications.* Baltimore: Johns Hopkins University Press, pp. 237–273.

15. Bretz, R. D., Jr., Milkovich, G. T., and Read, W. (1992). The current state of performance appraisal research and practice: Concerns, directions, and implications. *Journal of Management, 18,* 321–352.

16. See Bernardin et al., Effective performance management.

17. Kane, J. S., Bernardin, H. J., Villanova, P., and Peyrefitte, J. (1995). The stability of rater leniency: Three studies. *Academy of Management Journal, 38,* 1036–1051.

18. Bernardin, H. J. (1989). Increasing the accuracy of performance measurement: A proposed solution to erroneous attributions. *Human Resource Planning, 12,* 239–250.

19. Peters, L. H., and O'Connor, E. J. (1980). Situational constraints and work outcomes: The influence of a frequently overlooked construct. *Academy of Management Review, 5,* 391–397; Dobbins, G. H., Cardy, R. L., Facteau, J. D., and Miller, J. S. (1993). Implications of

situational constraints on performance evaluation and performance management. *Human Resource Management Review, 3,* 105–128; Villanova, P., and Roman, M. A. (1993). A meta-analytic review of situational constraints and work-related outcomes: Alternative approaches to conceptualization. *Human Resource Management Review, 3,* 147–175.

20. See Bernardin, Increasing the accuracy of performance measurement.

21. Uggerslev, K., and Sulsky, L. M. (2008). Using frame-of-reference training to understand the implications of rater idiosyncrasy for rating accuracy. *Journal of Applied Psychology, 93,* 711–719; Bernardin, H. J., et al. (2001). Frame of reference training: A twenty year follow-up. In G. R. Ferris (Ed.), *Research in personnel and human resources management, 18,* San Francisco: CA: JAI Press (pp. 221–274). See also Bernardin, H. J., and Buckley, M. R. (1981). A consideration of strategies in rater training. *Academy of Management Review, 6,* 205–212; Bernardin, H. J., and Pence, E. C. (1980). Rater training: Creating new response sets and decreasing accuracy. *Journal of Applied Psychology, 65,* 60–66; McIntyre, R. M., Smith, D. E., and Hassett, C. E. (1984). Accuracy of performance ratings as affected by rater training and perceived purpose of rating. *Journal of Applied Psychology, 69,* 147–156; Pulakos, E. D. (1984). A comparison of rater training programs: Error training and accuracy training. *Journal of Applied Psychology, 69,* 581–588; Pulakos, E. D. (1986). The development of training programs to increase accuracy with different rating tasks. *Organizational Behavior and Human Decision Processes, 38,* 76–91; Sulsky, L. M., and Day, D. V. (1994). Effects of frame-of-reference training on rater accuracy under alternative time delays. *Journal of Applied Psychology, 79*(4), 535–543.

22. Bernardin, H. J., Cooke, D., and Villanova, P. (2000). Conscientiousness and agreeableness as predictors of rating elevation. *Journal of Applied Psychology, 85,* 232–237; see also, Bernardin, H. J., Villanova, P., and Tyler, C. (in press). Rating level and accuracy as a function of rater personality. *International Journal of Selection and Assessment.*

23. Bernardin, H. J., and Villanova, P. (2005). Research streams in rater self-efficacy. *Group & Organization Management, 30,* 61–88.

24. Hagan, C., and Bernardin, H. J. (2003). Customer feedback as a critical performance dimension: Review and exploratory empirical examination. In C. A. Schriesheim and L. L. Neider (Eds.). *New directions in human resource management* Greenwich, CT: Information Age Publishing, pp. 1–27.

25. See Bernardin and Tyler, The legal and ethical implications of multirater appraisal systems; Austin et al., Legal requirements and technical guidelines; Bernardin et al., Age, racial, and gender bias; see also Smither, J. W., London, M., Vasilopoulos, N. L., Reilly, R. R., Millsap, R. E., and Salvemini, N. (1995). An examination of the effects of an upward feedback program over time. *Personnel Psychology 48,* 1–34; Atwater, L., Roush, P., and Fischthal, A. (1995). The influence of upward feedback on self- and follower ratings of leadership. *Personnel Psychology, 48,* 35–60; London, M., and Smither, J. W. (1995). Can multi-source feedback change perceptions of goal accomplishment, self-evaluations, and performance-related outcomes? Theory-based applications and directions for research. *Personnel Psychology, 48,* 803–839; Vinson, M. N. (1996). The pros and cons of 360-degree feedback: Making it work. *Training & Development, 50*(4), 11–12.

26. Antonioni, D. (1996). Designing an effective 360-degree appraisal feedback process. *Organizational Dynamics, 25*(2), 24–38.

27. See Bernardin and Tyler, The legal and ethical implications of multirater appraisal systems; Austin et al., Legal requirements and technical guidelines; Bernardin et al., Age, racial, and gender bias.

28. See Hagan and Bernardin, Customer feedback as a critical performance dimension.

29. Finn, A., and Kayande, U. (1999). Unmasking a phantom: A psychometric assessment of mystery shopping. *Journal of Retailing, 75,* 195–217; see also Moriarty, H., McLeod, D., and Dowell, A. (2003). Mystery shopping in health service evaluation. *British Journal of General Practice, 53,* 942–946.

30. Alge, B. J., Ballinger, G. A., and Green, S. G. (2004). Remote control: Predictors of electronic monitoring intensity and secrecy. *Personnel Psychology, 57,* 377–410; see also Alge, B. J. (2001). Effects of computer surveillance on perceptions of privacy and procedural justice. *Journal of Applied Psychology, 86,* 797–804.

31. Murphy, K. R., and Cleveland, J. N. (1991). *Performance appraisal: An organizational perspective.* Boston, MA: Allyn and Bacon.

32. Becker, T. E., and Klimoski, R. J. (1989). A field study of the relationship between the organizational feedback environment and performance. *Personnel Psychology, 42,* 343–358.

33. Kluger, A. N., and DeNisi, A. (1996). The effects of feedback interventions on performance: A historical review, a meta-analysis, and a preliminary feedback intervention theory. *Psychological Bulletin, 119,* 254–284.

CHAPTER 8

1. Huselid, M. A., Becker, B. E. and Beatty, R. W. (2005). *The workforce scorecard: Managing human capital to execute strategy.* Boston: Harvard Business School Press.

2. Rivera, R. J., and Paradise, A. (2006). *State of the industry in leading enterprise.* American Society for Training and Development, p. 4.

3. Kraiger, K., McLinden, D., and Casper, W. J. (2004). Collaborative training for training impact. *Human Resource Management, 43,* 337; Goldstein, I. L., and Ford, J. K. (2002). *Training in organizations: Needs assessment, development, and evaluation* (4th ed.). Belmont, CA: Wadsworth.; see also, Noe, R. A., and Colquitt, J. A. (2002). Planning for training impact: Principle of training effectiveness. In K. Kraiger (Ed.), *Creating, implementing, and maintaining effective training and development: State-of-the-art lessons for practice,* pp. 53–79. San Francisco: Jossey-Bass.

4. ASTD's Best: Better than the rest. (2007). *Training and Development Journal, 61*(10), 71.

5. Thornton, E. (1999, April 19). Make way for women with welding guns. *BusinessWeek,* p. 54.

6. Salopek, J. (2008). Credit where it's due. *Training and Development Journal, 62*(5), 22–24.

7. Society for Human Resource Mangement. (2006). *Study: Are they really ready to work?*

8. Society for Human Resource Mangement. (2008, January). *2008 January Survey.*

9. Huselid, Becker, and Beaty, *The workforce scorecard: Managing human capital to execute strategy.*

10. Krugman, P. (2005, July 25). Toyota, moving northward. *New York Times* online.

11. Leonhardt, D., and Cohn, L. (1999, April 26). Business takes up the challenge of training its rawest recruits. *BusinessWeek,* pp. 30–32.

12. Auluck, R. K. (2006). Status matters: How does HRD shape up? In S. Carliner (Ed.), *ASTD Research-to-Practice Conference Proceedings.* ASTD, pp. 13–26.

13. ASTD's Best: Better than the rest (2007). *Training and Development Journal, 61*(10), 26–81.

14. Rivera and Paradise, *State of the industry in leading enterprise.* p. 4.

15. Ibid.

16. Stamps, D. (1997). Communities of practice. *Training, 34*(2), 34–42.

17. Pfeffer, J., and Veiga, J. F. (1999). Putting people first for organizational success. *Academy of Management Executive, 13*(2), 37–48.

18. Schaaf, D. (1998). What workers really think about training. *Training, 35*(9), 59–66.

19. Sugrue, B., and Kim, K. (2004). *State of the industry: ASTD's annual review of trends in the workplace learning and performance.* ASTD, pp. 1–24.

20. Gomez-Mejia, L. R., Balkin, D. B., and Cardy, R. L. (1995). *Managing human resources.* Englewood Cliffs, N J: Prentice Hall.

21. Thornburg, L. (1992). Training in a changing world. *HR Magazine, 37*(8), 44–47.

22. Overman, S. (1993). Retraining our work force. *HR Magazine, 38*(10), 40–44. See also Schaaf, What workers really think about training.

23. Quinones, M. A. (1996). Training and development in organizations: Now more than ever. *Psychological Science Agenda, 9*(2), 8–9.

24. Quinones, M. A., and Ehrenstein, A. (1997). Introduction: Psychological perspectives on training in organizations. In M. A. Quinones, and A. Ehrenstein (Eds.), *Training for a rapidly changing workplace: Applications of psychological research.* Washington, DC: American Psychological Association, pp. 1–10.

25. Kraiger, K., McLinden, D., and Casper, W. J. (2004). Collaborative training for training impact. *Human Resource Management, 43,* 337.

26. Bernardin, H. J. (2009). Discrepancies between research and practice: Organizational training. Unpublished manuscript.

27. Goldstein, I. L., and Ford, J. K. (2002). *Training in organizations: Needs assessment, development, and evaluation* (4th ed.). Belmont, CA: Wadsworth.

28. Carliner, S. (Ed.) (2006). *ASTD 2006 Research-to-practice conference proceedings.* ASTD.

29. Nadler, L. (1984). Human resource development. In L. Nadler (Ed.), *The handbook of human resource development.* New York: John Wiley and Sons, pp. 1–47.

30. Ribeiro, O. (2006). Developing criteria for assessing the impact of a trainer training program in a health care setting: From theory to practice. In S. Carliner (Ed.). *ASTD Research-to-Practice Conference Proceedings.* ASTD, pp. 131–142. See also Arthur, W., Bennett, W., Edens, P. S., and Bell, S. T. (2003). Effectiveness of training in organizations: A meta-analysis of design and evaluation features. *Journal of Applied Psychology, 88*(2), 234–245.

31. Quinones, M. A. (1997). Contextual influences on training effectiveness. In M. A. Quinones and A. Ehrenstein (Eds). *Training for a rapidly changing workplace: Applications of psychological research.* Washington, DC: American Psychological Association, pp. 331–356.

32. Nadler, L. (1984). Human resource development. In L. Nadler (Ed.), *The handbook of human resource development.* New York: John Wiley and Sons, pp. 1–47.

33. Joinson, C. (1995). Make your training stick. *HR Magazine, 40*(5), 55–60; Salinger, R. D. (1973). *Disincentives to effective employee training and development.* Washington, DC: U.S. Civil Service Commission Bureau of Training.

34. Goldstein, I. L. (1993). *Training in organizations,* (3rd ed.). Pacific Grove, CA: Brooks/Cole.

35. Colquitt, J. A., LePine, J. A., and Noe, R. A. (2000). Toward an integrative theory of training motivation: A meta-analytic path analysis of 20 years of research. *Journal of Applied Psychology, 85,* 678–707.

36. Blanchard, R. N., and Thacker, J. W. (1999). *Effective training: Systems, strategies, and practices.* Englewood Cliffs, NJ: Prentice Hall; Schaaf, D. (1990). Lessons from the "100 best." *Training 27*(2), 18–20.

37. Burns, R. (1995). *The adult learner at work.* Sydney, Australia: Business and Professional Publishing; Sullivan, E., and Decker, P. (1988). *Effective management in nursing* (2nd ed.). Reading, MA: Addison-Wesley.

38. Lund, L., and McGuire, E. P. (1990). *Literacy in the workforce.* New York: The Conference Board; Rosow, J. M., and Zager, R. (1992). *Job-linked literacy: Innovative strategies at work: Part II. Meeting the challenges of change: Basic skills for a competitive workforce.* Scottsdale, NY: Work in America Institute.

39. Kraiger, K., McLinden, D., and Casper, W. J. (2004). Collaborative training for training impact. *Human Resource Management, 43,* 337–351.

40. Colquitt, J. A., LePine, J. A., and Noe, R. A. (2000). Toward an integrative theory of training motivation: A meta-analytic path analysis of 20 years of research. *Journal of Applied Psychology, 85,* 678–707.

41. Noe, R. A., and Schmitt, N. (1986). The influence of trainee attitudes on training effectiveness: Test of a model. *Personnel Psychology, 39,* 497–523.

42. Baldwin, T. T., and Magjuka, R. J. (1997). Training as an organizational episode: Pretraining influences on trainee motivation. In J. K. Ford (Ed.), *Improving training effectiveness in work organizations.* Mahwah, NJ: Lawrence Erlbaum Associates, pp. 99–127; Mathieu, J. E., and Martineau, M. W. (1997). Individual and situational influences on training motivation. In J. K. Ford (Ed.), *Improving training effectiveness in work organizations.* Mahwah, NJ: Lawrence Erlbaum Associates, pp. 193–221.

43. Baldwin, T. T., Magjuka, R. J., and Loher, B. T. (1991). The perils of participation: Effects of choice of training on trainee motivation and learning. *Personnel Psychology, 44*(1), 51–66; Hicks, W. D., and Klimoski, R. J. (1987). Entry into training programs and its effects on

training outcomes: A field experiment. *Academy of Management Journal, 30*(3), 542–552. For more information on team building, outdoor education, and wilderness adventures contact: Higher Pursuits, 211 3rd Avenue, Columbia, TN 38401, JSeufert@aol.com.

44. Leigh, D., and Watkins, R. (2005). E-learner success: Validating a self-assessment of learner readiness for online training. In S. Carliner and B. Sugrue (Eds.), *ASTD 2005 Research-to-Practice Conference Proceedings.* ASTD, pp. 121–131.

45. Dobbins, G. H., Russell, J. E. A., Ladd, R. T., and Kudisch, J. D. (1995). The influence of general perceptions of the training environment on pretraining motivation and perceived training transfer. *Journal of Management, 21*(1), 1–25.

46. Allen, J. M., and Burke, K. M. (2006). Applying cognitive load theory to performance improvement. In S. Carliner (Ed.), *ASTD Research-to-Practice Conference Proceedings.* ASTD, pp. 5–10.

47. Driskell, J. E., Willis, R. P., and Copper, C. (1992). Effect of overlearning on retention. *Journal of Applied Psychology, 77,* 615–622.

48. Summitt, P. H. (1998). *Reach for the Summit: The definite dozen system for succeeding at whatever you do.* New York: Broadway Books.

49. Locke, E. A., and Latham, G. P. (1984). *Goal setting: A motivational technique that works.* Englewood Cliffs, NJ: Prentice Hall; Mealiea, L. W., and Latham, G. P. (1996). *Skills for managerial success: Theory, experience, and practice.* Chicago, IL: Irwin.

50. Latham, G. P., and Locke, E. A. (1991). Self-regulation through goal-setting. *Organizational Behavior and Human Decision Processes, 50,* 212–247.

51. Silber, K. H., and Stelnicki, M. B. (1987). Writing training materials. In R. L. Craig (Ed.), *Training and development handbook* (3rd ed.). New York: McGraw-Hill, pp. 263–285.

52. Lee, H. W., and Lim, K. Y. (2006). Ensuring the transfer of training to the workplace. In S. Carliner (Ed.), *ASTD Research-to-Practice Conference Proceedings,* ASTD, pp. 83–92. See also Baldwin, T. T., and Ford, J. K. (1988). Transfer of training: A review and directions for future research. *Personnel Psychology, 41,* 63–105; Baldwin, T. T., and Magjuka, R. J. (1991). Organizational training and signals of importance: Linking pretraining perceptions to intentions to transfer. *Human Resource Development Quarterly, 2,* 25–36; Broad, M. L., and Newstrom, J. W. (1992). *Transfer of training: Action-packed strategies to ensure high payoff from training investments.* Reading, MA: Addison-Wesley; Ellis, H. C. (1965). *The transfer of learning.* New York: Macmillan. Kozlowski, S. W., and Salas, E. (1997). A multilevel organizational systems approach for the implementation and transfer of training. In J. K. Ford (Ed.), *Improving training effectiveness in work organizations.* Mahwah, NJ: Lawrence Erlbaum; Rouiller, J. Z., and Goldstein, I. L. (1993). The relationship between organizational transfer climate and positive transfer of training. *Human Resource Development Quarterly, 4,* 377–390.

53. Chiaburu, D. S., and Day, R. (2006). Social cognitive factors influencing training motivation and training effectiveness. In S. Carliner (Ed.), *ASTD Research-to-Practice Conference Proceedings.* ASTD, pp. 27–36.

54. Tracey, J. B., Tannenbaum, S. I., and Kavanagh, M. J. (1995). Applying trained skills on the job: The importance of the work environment. *Journal of Applied Psychology, 80,* 239–252.

55. Chiaburu, D. S. (2005). Individual and contextual predictors of learning transfer: An examination using structural equation modeling. In S. Carliner, and B. Sugrue (Eds.), *ASTD 2005 Research-to-Practice Conference Proceedings.* ASTD, pp. 36–42. See also Morrison, R. F., and Branter, T. M. (1992). What enhances or inhibits a new job? A basic career issue. *Journal of Applied Psychology, 77,* 926–940; Stevens, C. K., and Gist, M. E. (1997). Effects of self-efficacy and goal orientation training on negotiation skill maintenance: What are the mechanisms? *Personnel Psychology, 50,* 955–978; Chiaburu, Individual and contextual predictors of learning transfer.

56. Ford, J. K., Quinones, M. A., Sego, D., and Sorra, J. (1992). Factors affecting the opportunity to perform trained tasks on the job. *Personnel Psychology, 45,* 511–527.

57. Mathieu, J. E., Tannenbaum, S. I., and Salas, E. (1992). Influences of individual and situational characteristics on measures of training effectiveness. *Academy of Management Journal, 35,* 828–847.

58. Marx, R. D. (1982). Relapse prevention for managerial training: A model for maintenance of behavior change. *Academy of Management Review 7,* 433–441.

59. Ibid.

60. Facteau, J. D., Dobbins, G. H., Russell, J. E. A., Ladd, R. T., and Kudisch, J. D. (1995). The influence of general perceptions of the training environment on pretraining motivation and perceived training transfer. *Journal of Management, 21*(1), 1–25. See also Chiaburu, Individual and contextual predictors of learning transfer.

61. Bersin, R. (2004). *The blended learning book: Best practices, proven methodologies, and lessons learned.* San Francisco: Pfeiffer.

62. ASTD's best: Better than the rest. (2007). *Training and Development Journal, 61*(10), 78.

63. Tejada, D. A. (2006). The relationship between corporate training methods and trainee perceived effectiveness. In S. Carliner (Ed.), *ASTD Research-to-Practice Conference Proceedings.* ASTD, pp. 183–192.

64. ASTD (2006). *ASTD State of the Industry Report.*

65. Dolezalek, H. (2004). *Training* magazine's 23rd annual comprehensive analysis of employee-sponsored training in the United States. *Training, 41*(10), 20–36.

66. Arthur, W., Bennett, W., Jr., Edens, P., and Bell, S. (2003). Effectiveness of training in organizations: A meta-analysis of design and evaluation features. *Journal of Applied Psychology, 88,* 234–245.

67. Callahan, J. S., Ki Kor, D. S. and Cross, T. (2003). Does method matter? A meta-analysis of the effects of training method on older learner training performance. *Journal of Management, 29*(5), 663–680.

68. Dolezalek, *Training* magazine's 23rd annual comprehensive analysis.

69. Jossi, F. (1998). Videoconferencing on the cheap. *Training, 35*(10), DL10–13, DL15, DL17–18, DL20.

70. *FedEx KinKo's Videoconferencing* (2005). Retrieved September 27, 2005, from http://www.fedex.com/us/customersupport/officeprint/faq/videoconf.html?link=4# topthree12. See also Mulvaney, T. (2008). Breaking the sound barrier. *Training and Development Journal, 62*(5), 26–28.

71. Guglielmino, L. M., and Guglielmino, P. J. (1991). *Expanding your readiness for self-directed learning.* King of Prussia, PA: Organizational Design and Development.

72. Torrance, E. P., and Mourad, S. (1978). Some creativity and style of learning and thinking correlates of Guglielmino's Self-Directed Learning Readiness Scale. *Psychological Reports, 43,* 1167–1171.

73. Sabbaghian, Z. (1979). *Adult self-directedness and self-concept: An exploration of relationship.* Doctoral dissertation. Ames: Iowa State University.

74. Durr, R. E. (1992). *An examination of readiness for self-directed learning and selected personnel variables at a large midwestern electronics development and manufacturing corporation.* Unpublished doctoral dissertation. Boca Raton: Florida Atlantic University; Savoie, M. (1979). *Continuing education for nurses: Predictors of success courses requiring a degree of learner self-direction.* Unpublished doctoral dissertation. Toronto, Canada: University of Toronto.

75. Sales training as dynamic as big pharma itself. (2007). *Training and Development Journal, 61*(10), 34–36. See also Schaaf, Lessons from the "100 best."

76. Laff, M. (2008). Learning parthfinder. *Training and Development Journal, 62*(4), 38–41. See also ASTD's best: Better than the rest, p. 71.

77. Sitzmann, T. M., and Wisher, R. (2006). The comparative effectiveness of web-based and classroom instruction: A meta-analysis. In S. Carliner (Ed.), *ASTD Research-to-Practice Conference Proceedings.* ASTD, pp. 161–170.

78. Smith, L. (2008). Teaching the intangibles. *Training and Development Journal, 61*(10), 23–25.

79. Monoky, J. F. (1996). Master the coaching call. *Industrial Distribution, 85*(6), 112. See also Cannell, M. (1997). Practice makes perfect. *People Management, 3*(5), 26–33.

80. ASTD's best: Better than the rest, p. 76.

81. Schaaf, Lessons from the "100 best."

82. Cannell, M. (1997). Practice makes perfect. *People Management, 3*(5), 26–33.

83. Knight, J. (2000, August). The school of hard rocks. *Training,* pp. 36–38.

84. Gitter, R. J. (1994). Apprenticeship-trained workers: United States and Great Britain, *Monthly Labor Review, 117*(4), 38–43; Reynolds, L. (1993, July). Apprenticeship program raises many questions. *HR Focus,* pp. 1, 4.

85. Apprenticeship (1991–1992, Winter). *Occupational Outlook Quarterly,* p. 29.

86. McKenna, J. F. (1992, January 20). Apprenticeships: Something old, something new, something needed. *Industry Week,* pp. 14–20.

87. Resch, I. (1998, November 30). A medieval work ethic that still works. *BusinessWeek,* p. 30J.

88. SHRM (2004, June). *Research: SHRM 2004–2005 Workplace Forecast—A Strategic Outlook SHRM.*

89. Sitzmann, T. M., and Wisher, R. (2005). The effectiveness of web-based training compared to classroom instruction: A meta-analysis. In S. Carliner, and B. Sugrue (Eds.), *ASTD 2005 Research-to-Practice Conference Proceedings.* ASTD, pp. 196–202.

90. Davis, F. D., and Yi, M. Y. (2004). Improving computer skill training: Behavior modeling, symbolic mental rehearsal, and the role of knowledge structures. *Journal of Applied Psychology, 89,* 509–523.

91. Filipczak, B. (1996). Who owns your OJT? *Training, 33*(12), 44–49.

92. Steele-Johnson, D., and Hyde, B. G. (1997). Advanced technologies in training: Intelligent tutoring systems and virtual reality. In M. A. Quinones and A. Ehrenstein (Eds.), *Training for a rapidly changing workplace: Applications of psychological research.* Washington, DC: American Psychological Association, pp. 225–248.

93. Apostolopoulos, N., Albert, G., and Zimmerman, S. (1996). DIALECT—Network-based digital interactive lectures. *Computer Networks and ISDN Systems, 28*(14), 1873–1886.

94. CFO-IT (2005). *Web conferencing: Your place and mine,* vol. 21, p. 14.

95. Walking in the customer's shoes. (2007). *Training and Development Journal, 61*(10), 58–60.

96. Bassi, L. J., and VanBuren, M. E. (1999). Sharpening the leading edge. *Training & Development, 53*(1), 23–28, 30, 32–33.

97. Abboud, S. R. (2004). Online education gets accolades; experts weigh in on distance learning. In the National Center for Education Statistics report, *Distance Education at Degree-Granting Post Secondary Institutions 2000–2001.*

98. Chute, A. G., Thompson, M. M., and Hancock, B. W. (1999). *The McGraw-Hill handbook of distance learning: An implementation guide for trainers and human resources professionals.* New York: McGraw-Hill; Harrison, N. (1999). *How to design self-directed and distance learning.* New York: McGraw-Hill; Stadtlander, L. M. (1998). Virtual instruction: Teaching an online graduate seminar. *Teaching of Psychology, 25*(2), 146–148.

99. Donoho, R. (1998). The new MBA. *Training, 35*(10), DL4–DL9.

100. ASTD's best: Better than the rest.

101. Burgess, J. R. D., and Russell, J. E. A. (2003). The effectiveness of distance learning initiatives in organizations. *Journal of Vocational Behavior, 63,* 289–303; Greengard, S. (1999). Web-based training yields maximum returns. *Workforce, 78*(2), 95; Hefner, D. (1996). The CBT revolution and the authoring engines that drive it. *CD ROM Professional, 9*(10), 46–65; Teas, D. (1996). The internet means opportunity. *Life Association News, 91*(3), 135–138.

102. Murphy, K. (1999, April 5). Welcome to the world of MBA.com. *BusinessWeek,* p. 120.

103. Lohman, J. S. (1998). Classrooms without walls: Three companies that took the plunge. *Training & Development, 52*(9), 38.

104. Burgess and Russell, *The effectiveness of distance learning initiatives;* Chute, Thompson, and Hancock, *The McGraw-Hill handbook of distance learning.*

105. DeRouin, R. E., Fritzsche, B. A., and Sales, E. (2004). Optimizing e-learning: Research-based guidelines for learner-controlled training. *Human Resource Management, 43*(3), 147–162.

106. Geber, B. (1990). Simulating reality. *Training, 27*(4), 41–46.

107. Paving the path to performance management. (2007). *Training and Development Journal, 61*(10), 55–56. See also Agres, T. (1997). VR for war games and for real. *R-and-D, 39*(2), 45–46.

108. ASTD's best: Better than the rest, p. 78.

109. Dolezalek, (2008). *Training* magazine's 23rd annual comprehensive analysis.

110. www.marketplace-simulation.com. See also Cadotte, E. R., and Bruce, H. J. (Eds.). (2003). *The management of strategy in the marketplace.* Mason, OH: South-Western.

111. Dolezalek, *Training* magazine's 23rd annual comprehensive analysis. See also Weaver, M. (1999, January/February). Beyond the ropes: Guidelines for selecting experiential training. *Corporate University Review, 7*(1), 34–37; Williams, S. D., Graham, T. S., and Baker, B. (2003). Evaluating outdoor experiential training for leadership and team building. *Journal of Management Development, 22*(1/2), 45–59.

112. Andrews, E. S., and Noel, J. L. (1986). Adding life to the case study method. *Training and Development Journal, 40*(2), 28–29.

113. ASTD's best: Better than the rest, p. 68.

114. Bandura, A. (1986). *Social foundations of thought and action: A social cognitive theory.* Englewood Cliffs, NJ: Prentice Hall.

115. Simon, S. J., Grover-Varun, T., Teng, J. T., and Whitcomb, K. (1996). The relationship of information system training methods and cognitive ability to end-user satisfaction, comprehension, and skill transfer: A longitudinal field study. *Information Systems Research, 7*(4), 466–490.

116. Sackett, P. R., and Mullen, E. J. (1993). Beyond formal experimental design: Towards an expanded view of the training evaluation process. *Personnel Psychology, 46,* 613–627.

117. Salas, E., and Kosarzycki, M. P. (2003). Why don't organizations pay attention to (and use) findings from the science of training? *Human Resource Development Quarterly, 14*(4), 487–492.

118. Pfeffer, J., and Veiga, J. F. (1999). Putting people first for organizational success, *Academy of Management Executive, 13*(2), 37–48.

119. Abernathy, D. J. (1999). Thinking outside the evaluation box. *Training & Development, 53*(2), 19–23.

120. ASTD (2006). *2006 ASTD State of the Industry Report.*

121. ASTD's best: Better than the rest, p. 71.

122. Sugrue, B., and DeViney, N. (2005). Learning outsourcing research report. *ASTD/IBM Report,* ASTD.

123. Alliger, G. M., and Janak, E. A. (1989). Kirkpatrick's levels of training criteria: Thirty years later. *Personnel Psychology, 42,* 331–342.

124. Phillips, J. J. (1997). *Handbook of training evaluation and measurement methods* (3rd ed.). Houston, TX: Gulf Publishing.

125. Arthur, W., Bennett, W., Jr., Edens, P., and Bell, S. (2003). Effectiveness of training in organizations: A meta-analysis of design and evaluation features. *Journal of Applied Psychology, 88,* 234–245.

126. Brown, K. G. (2005). An examination of the structure and nomological network of trainee reactions: A closer look at "smilesheets." *Journal of Applied Psychology, 90,* 991–1001.

127. Geber, B. (1995). Does your training make a difference? Prove it! *Training, 32*(3), 27–34.

128. Arthur et al., Effectiveness of training in organizations.

129. Laff, M. (2008). Elastic training dollars. *Training and Development Journal, 62*(5), 10–11.

130. Morrow, C. C., Jarrett, M. Q., and Rupinski, M. T. (1997). An investigation of the effect and economic utility of corporate-wide training. *Personnel Psychology, 50*(1), 91–119; Laabs, J. J. (1996). Eyeing future HR concerns. *Personnel Journal, 75*(1), 28–30, 32, 34–37; Mathieu, J. E., and Leonard, R. L. (1987). Applying utility concepts to a training program in supervisory skills: A time-based approach. *Academy of Management Journal, 30,* 316–335.

131. Ford, D. (1994). Three Rs in the workplace. In J. Phillips (Ed.), *In action: Measuring return on investment,* vol. 1, 85–104. Alexandria, VA: American Society for Training and Development; Phillips, *Handbook of training evaluation and measurement methods.*

132. Fitz-Enz, J. (1997). *The 8 practices of exceptional companies.* New York: AMACOM.

133. ASTD's best: Better than the rest, p.71. See also Parry, S. B. (1996). Measuring training's ROI. *Training & Development, 50*(5), 72–77; Jacobs, R. L. (2005). Comparing the forecasted financial benefits of blended training, classroom training, and structured on-the-job training. In. S. Carliner, and B. Sugrue (Eds.), *ASTD 2005 Research-to-Practice Conference Proceedings.* ASTD, pp. 106–111.

134. Schmidt, F. L., Hunter, J. E., and Pearlman, K. (1982). Assessing the economic impact of personnel programs on workforce productivity. *Personnel Psychology, 35,* 333–347.

135. Phillips, *Handbook of training evaluation and measurement methods.*

136. Campbell, D. T., and Stanley, J. C. (1963). *Experimental and quasi-experimental designs for research.* Boston, MA: Houghton Mifflin.

137. Kraiger, K., McLinden, D., and Casper, W. J. (2004). Collaborative training for training impact. *Human Resource Management, 43,* 337.

138. Harris, P. (2008). Calculating the skills shortage. *Training and Development Journal, 62*(4), 12–14.

139. Kaleba, K. (2008). U.S. Government seeks next generation of leaders. *Training and Development Journal, 62*(4), 14.

140. Kaye, B., and Cohen, J. (2008). Safeguarding the intellectual capital of baby boomers. *Training and Development Journal, 62*(4), 30–33. See also Byham, W. C. (2008). Flexible phase-out. *Training and Development Journal, 62*(4), 34–37.

141. Ketter, P. (2008). What can training do for Brown? *Training and Development Journal, 62*(5), 30–36.

142. Laff, M. (2008). Number crunch. *Training and Development Journal, 62*(5), 14.

143. Felon, I. A., and Pepermans, R. G. (1998). Exploring the relationship between orientation programs and current job satisfaction. *Psychological Reports, 83*(1), 367; Solomon, J. (1988, December 29). Companies try measuring cost savings from new types of corporate benefits. *The Wall Street Journal,* p. B1; Cook, M. F. (Ed). (1992). *The AMA handbook for employee recruitment and retention.* New York: AMACOM.

144. Wanous, J. P. (1992). *Organizational entry* (2nd ed.). Reading, MA: Addison-Wesley.

145. McGarrell, E. J. (1984). An orientation system that builds productivity. *Personnel Administrator, 29*(10), 75–85; Reed-Mendenhall, D., and Millard, C. W. (1980). Orientation: A training and development tool. *Personnel Administrator, 25*(8), 42–44; London, M. (1989). *Managing the training enterprise: High-quality, cost-effective employee training in organizations.* San Francisco: Jossey-Bass.

146. Walking in the customer's shoes. (2007). *Training and Development Journal, 61*(10), 58–60.

147. ASTD's best: Better than the rest, p. 80.

148. Derven, M. (2008). Management onboarding. *Training and Development Journal, 62*(4), 49–52.

149. Ibid.

150. Ibid.

151. Ibid.

152. Russell, J. E. A., and DeMatteo, J. S. (2002). Group dynamics, processes, and teamwork. In E. J. Cadotte and H. J. Bruce (Eds.), *The management of strategy in the marketplace.* Oklahoma City, OK: Southwestern Publishing, chapter 2; Russell, J. E. A., and DeMatteo, J. S. (2002). Managing the team to excellence. In Cadotte and Bruce (Eds.), *The management of strategy in the marketplace,* chapter 12.

153. Sherman, S. (1996, March 18). Secrets of HP's "muddled team." *Fortune,* pp. 116–118, 120.

154. Taylor, D, and Ramsey, R. (1993). Empowering employees to "just do it." *Training & Development, 47*(5), 71–76.

155. Banker, R. D., Field, J. M., Schroeder, G., and Sinha, K. K. (1996). Impact of work teams on manufacturing performance: A longitudinal study. *Academy of Management Journal, 39,* 867–890. See also Salas, E., Burke, C. S., Bowers, C. A., Wilson, K. A. (2001). Team training in the skies: Does crew resource management (CRM) training work? *Human Factors, 43,* 641–674; Chen, G., Thomas, B., and Wallace, J. C. (2005). A multilevel examination of the relationships among training outcomes, mediating regulatory processes, and adaptive performance. *Journal of Applied Psychology, 90*(5), 827–841.

156. Wellins, R., and George, J. (1991). The key to self-directed teams. *Training & Development, 45*(4), 26–31.

157. Cannon-Bowers, J. A., and Salas, E. (1998). Team performance and training in complex environments: Recent findings from applied research. *Current Directions in Psychological Science, 7*(3), 83–87; Salas, E., and Cannon-Bowers, J. A. (1997). Methods, tools, and strategies for team training. In M. A. Quinones and A. Ehrenstein (Eds.), *Training for a rapidly changing workplace: Applications of psychological research.* Washington, DC: American Psychological Association, pp. 249–279.

158. Ames, L. (1991, July 21). An obstacle course: Lessons in teamwork. *New York Times,* p. WC 2.

159. Cannon-Bowers, J. A., Salas, E., Blickensderfer, E., and Bowers, C. A. (1998). The impact of cross-training and workload on team functioning: A replication and extension of initial findings. *Human Factors, 40*(1), 92–101.

160. Hottenstein, M. P., and Bowman, S. A. (1998). Cross-training and worker flexibility: A review of DRC system research. *Journal of High Technology Management Research, 9*(2), 157.

161. Cottrill, M. (1997). Give your work teams time and training. *Academy of Management Executive, 11*(3), 87.

162. Filipczak, B. (1993). Frick teaches Frack. *Training, 30*(6), 30–34; Filipczak, B. (1993). Training budgets boom. *Training, 30*(10), 37–40, 42–43, 45, 47; Messmer, M. (1992). Cross-discipline training: A strategic model to do more with less. *Management Review, 81,* 26–28; Rickett, D. (1993). Peer training: Not just a low-budget answer. *Training, 30*(2), 70–72; Santora, J. E. (1992). Keep up production through cross-training. *Personnel Journal, 71*(6), 21–24.

163. Benson, G. (1997). Informal training takes off. *Training & Development, 51*(5), 93–94; Chao, G. (1997). Unstructured training and development: The role of organizational socialization. In J. K. Ford et al. (Eds.), *Improving training effectiveness in work organizations.* Mahwah, NJ: Lawrence Erlbaum Associates, pp. 129–151; Chemers, M. M., Oskamp, S., and Costanzo, M. A. (Eds.) (1995). *Diversity in organizations.* Newbury Park, CA: Sage; Leonard, B. (1998). Informal training of employees helps to boost productivity. *HR Magazine, 43*(2), 10; Stamps, D. (1997). Communities of practice. *Training, 34*(2), 34–42.

164. Allen, T. D., McManus, S. E., and Russell, J. E. A. (1999). Newcomer socialization and stress: Formal peer relationships as a source of support. *Journal of Vocational Behavior, 54,* 453–470.

165. Fisher, C. D., Schoenfeldt, L. F., and Shaw, J. B. (1999). *Human resource management* (4th ed.). Boston, MA: Houghton Mifflin; Kaeter, M. (1993). Cross-training: The tactical view. *Training, 30*(3), 35–39.

166. Plummer, D. L. (1998). Approaching diversity training in the year 2000. *Consulting Psychology Journal: Practice and Research, 50*(3), 181–189.

167. Olesen, M. (1999). The diversity issue no one talks about. *Training, 36*(5), 46–56.

168. ASTD's best: Better than the rest, p. 70.

169. Dass, P., and Parker, B. (1999). Strategies for managing human resource diversity: From resistance to learning. *Academy of Management Executive, 13*(2), 68–80.

170. Jordan, K. (1998). Diversity training in the workplace today: A status report. *Journal of Career Planning and Employment, 59*(1), 46.

171. Colombo, J. (1997, June 12). A law school's diversity checklist, *The Wall Street Journal,* p. A18. See also Owens, D. M. (2005). Multilingual workforces: How can employees help employees who speak different languages work in harmony? *HR Magazine 50*(9), 125–128.

172. Russell, J. E. A., and Eby, L. T. (1993). Career assessment strategies for women in management. *Journal of Career Assessment, 1,* 267–293; Wentling, R. M., and Palma-Rivas, N. (1998). Current status and future trends of diversity initiatives in the workplace: Diversity experts' perspective. *Human Resource Development Quarterly, 9*(3), 235–253.

173. Gadsden, E. N. (1997, June 15). Teaching diversity awareness in the workplace. *Baltimore Sun,* pp. D1, D3; Mirabella, L. (1997, June 15). Helping staff be aware of diversity. *Baltimore Sun,* p. D1.

174. A living, breathing people strategy. (2007). *Training and Development Journal, 61*(10), 42–44.

175. Dass and Parker, Strategies for managing human resource diversity; Swisher, K. (1996, July/August). Coming out in corporate America. *Working Woman Magazine,* pp. 50–53, 78, 80.

176. Diversity: America's strength. (1997, June 23). *Fortune.*

177. Dass and Parker, Strategies for managing human resource diversity.

178. Putney, D. M., Russell, J. E. A., and Colvin, C. (1996). Factors related to the effective workplace socialization of people with disabilities. *Proceedings of the Southern Management Association,* Charleston, SC; Stone, D. L., and Colella, A. (1996). A model of factors affecting the treatment of disabled individuals in organizations. *Academy of Management Review, 21*(2), 352–401; Veves, J. G., and R. R. Simms (Eds). (1995). *Human resource management and the Americans with Disabilities Act.* Westport, CT: Quorum Books.

179. Dass and Parker, Strategies for managing human resource diversity.

180. Nancherla, A. (2008). Nobody's perfect: Diversity training study finds common flaws. *Training and Development Journal, 62*(5), 20.

181. Ibid.

182. Jackson, S. E., and Ruderman, M. N. (Eds.) (1995). *Diversity in work teams: Research paradigms for a changing workplace.* Washington, DC: American Psychological Association; Russell, J. E. A. Atchley, K. P., Eby, L. T., and Fausz, A. T. (1994). Attitudes of white employees and managers towards diversity issues. In *Proceedings of the Southern Management Association,* M. Schnake (Ed.). Valdosta, GA: Valdosta State University, pp. 466–471.

183. Rynes, S., and Rosen, B. (1995). A field survey of factors affecting the adoption and perceived success of diversity training. *Personnel Psychology, 48,* 247–270.

184. Chemers, M. M., Oskamp, S., and Costanzo, M. A. (Eds.) (1995). *Diversity in organizations.* Newbury Park, CA: Sage; Fine, M. G. (1995). *Building successful multicultural organizations: Challenges and opportunities.* Westport, CT: Quorum Books; Gallos, J. V., and Ramsey, V. J. (Eds.) (1996). *Listening to the soul and speaking from the heart: The joys and complexities of teaching about workplace diversity.* San Francisco: Jossey-Bass; Hanover, J. M., and Cellar, D. F. (1998). Environmental factors and the effectiveness of workforce diversity training. *Human Resource Development Quarterly, 9*(2), 105–124; Herriot, P., and Pemberton, C. (1995). *Competitive advantage through diversity: Organizational learning from difference.* London, England: Sage; Kossek, E. E., and Lobel, S. A. (Eds.) (1996). *Human resource strategies for managing diversity.* Oxford, England: Basil Blackwell; Prasad, P., Mills, A. J., Elmes, M., and Prasad, A. (Eds.) (1996). *Managing the organizational melting pot: Dilemmas for workplace diversity.* London: Sage.

185. Hayes, J., and Prewitt, M. (1998, August 24). Operators explore diversity at 1st multicultural conference. *Nation's Restaurant News, 32*(34), 3, 127.

186. Dass and Parker, Strategies for managing human resource diversity.

187. Daniel, L. (1997, June 23). FAA offers new diversity training plan. *Federal Times, 33*(20), 6; Daniel, L. (1997). FAA tries again at diversity training. *Federal Times, 33*(21), 7.

188. Dass and Parker, Strategies for managing human resource diversity; Ganzel, R. (1998). A guide to players in distance training. *Training, 35*(10), DL4–DL22.

189. Mulligan, J., and Foy, N. (2003). Not in my company: Preventing sexual harassment. *Industrial Management, 45*(5), 26, 28–30.

190. Aycan, Z. (1997). *New approaches to employee management,* vol. 4: *Expatriate management: Theory and research.* Greenwich, CT: JAI Press; Tung, R. L. (1998). A contingency framework of selection and training of expatriates revisited. *Human Resource Management Review, 8*(1), 23–37.

191. Simple is beautiful. (2007). *Training and Development Journal, 61*(10), 62–64.

192. Harvey, H. G. (1996). Developing leaders rather than managers for the global marketplace. *Human Resource Management Review, 6,* 279–288.

193. Dowling, P. J., and Schuler, R. S. (1990). *International dimensions of human resource management.* Boston, MA: PWS-Kent. See also Jack, D. W., and Stage, V. C. (2005). Success strategies for expats. *Training and Development 59*(9), 48–52.

194. Ronen, S. (1989). Training the international assignee. In I. L. Goldstein and Associates (Eds.), *Training and development in organizations.* San Francisco: Jossey-Bass, pp. 417–453.

195. 1997 Industry Report. (1997). *Training 34*(10), 33–72.

196. Hogan, G. W., and Goodson, J. R. (1990). The key to expatriate success. *Training & Development, 44*(1), 50, 52.

197. Lubin, J. S. (1992, March 31). Younger managers learn global skills. *The Wall Street Journal,* p. B1.

198. Allerton, H. (1997). Survey says. *Training & Development, 51*(2), 7.

199. Lubin, J. S. (1996, January 29). An overseas stint can be a ticket to the top. *The Wall Street Journal,* pp. B1, B5.

200. Bensimon, H. (1998). Is it safe to work abroad? *Training & Development, 52*(8), 20–24.

201. Kemper, C. L. (1998). Global training's critical success factors. *Training & Development, 52*(2), 35.

202. Gudykunst, W. B., and Hammer, M. R. (1983). *Basic training and design: An approach to intercultural training.* In D. Landis and R. W. Brislin (Eds.), *Handbook of intercultural training,* vol. 1. Elmsford, NY: Pergamon, pp. 118–154.

203. Earley, P. C., and Erez, M. (1997). *The transplanted executive.* New York: Oxford University Press.

204. Earley, C. P. (2002). Redefining interactions across cultures and organizations: Moving forward with cultural intelligence. In B. M. Staw and R. M. Kramer (Eds.), *Research in Organizational Behavior: An Annual Series of Analytical Essays and Critical Reviews.* Kidlington, UK: Elsevier, pp. 271–99.

205. Black, J. S., and Mendenhall, M. (1990). Cross-cultural training effectiveness: A review and theoretical framework for future research. *Academy of Management Review, 15*(1), 113–136.

206. Copeland, M. J. (1987). International training. In R. L. Craig (Ed.), *Training and development handbook.* New York: McGraw-Hill, pp. 717–725.

207. McCrea, J. (1997, July). Rx for expatriates. *World Traveler,* pp. 18–20, 22, 25–27.

208. Fiedler, F. E., Mitchell, T., and Triandis, H. C. (1971). The culture assimilator: An approach to cross-cultural training. *Journal of Applied Psychology, 55,* 95–102.

209. Harrison, J. K. (1992). Individual and combined effects of behavior modeling and the cultural assimilator in cross-cultural management training. *Journal of Applied Psychology, 77,* 952–962.

210. Tung, R. L. (1998). A contingency framework of selection and training of expatriates revisited. *Human Resource Management Review, 8*(1), 23–37.

211. Ibid.

212. Solomon, C. M. (1995). HR's helping hand pulls global inpatriates onboard. *Personnel Journal, 74*(11), 40–49.

213. Galagan, P., and Wulf, K. (1996). Signs of the times. *Training & Development, 50*(2), 32–36.

214. Meister, J. C. (1998). Ten steps to creating a corporate university. *Training & Development, 52*(11), 38–43; Myers, S. D. (1997). *The role of person, outcome, environmental, and learning variables in training effectiveness.* Unpublished doctoral dissertation. Knoxville, TN: The University of Tennessee; Williams, C. P. (1999). The end of the job as we know it. *Training & Development, 53*(1), 52–54, 56, 58–60.

215. *2006 ASTD State of the Industry,* p. 17.

216. ASTD's best: Better than the rest, p. 68.

217. *2006 ASTD State of the Industry,* p. 16.

218. Maister, D. (2008). Why (most) training is useless. *Training and Development Journal, 62*(5), 52–58.

219. Managing massive change the Satyam way. *Training and Development Journal, 61*(10), 30–32.

220. *2006 ASTD State of the Industry.*

CHAPTER 9

1. Arthur, M. B., Khapova, S. N., and Wilderom, C. P. M. (2005). Career success in a boundaryless career world. *Journal of Organizational Behavior, 26,* 177–202. See also Parker P., Arthur M. B., and Inkson, K. (2004, June). Career communities: A preliminary exploration of member-defined career support structures. *Journal of Organizational Behavior, 25*(4), 489–514; Smith-Ruig, T. (2008). Making sense of careers through the lens of a path metaphor. *Career Development International, 13*(1), 20–32.

2. Osipow, S. H. (1986). Career issues through the life span. In M. S. Pallak and R. Perloff (Eds.), *Psychology and work: Productivity, change, and employment.* Washington, DC: American Psychological Association, pp. 137–168.

3. Hall, D. T., and Associates (Eds.) (1996). *The career is dead—long live the career.* San Francisco, CA: Jossey-Bass.

4. Hall D. T., and Chandler, D. E. (2005). Psychological success: When the career is a calling. *Journal of Organizational Behavior, 26,* 155–176; see also Hall, D. (2002). *Careers in and out of organizations.* Thousand Oaks, CA: Sage; Charan, R., and Colrin, R. (1999, June 21). Why CEOs fail. *Fortune 139*(12), 69–78; Welch, J. (2005). *Winning.* New York: Harper Collins.

5. Gurchiek, K. (2005). Experts predict employee exodus, urge career development. Retrieved September 29, 2005, from http://www.shrm.org/hrnewspublished/archives/CMS010953.asp. See also Burke, M. E., and Collison, J. (2004). *2004 U.S. Job Recovery and Retention Poll Findings.* SHRM.

6. Hall, D. T. (1976). *Careers in organizations.* Glenview, IL: Scott, Foresman.

7. Hall, D. T. (1987). Careers and socialization. *Journal of Management, 13,* 301–321.

8. Hall, D. T., and Associates (1986). *Career development in organizations.* San Francisco, CA: Jossey-Bass.

9. Ibid.

10. Leibowitz, Z., Farren, C., and Kaye, B. (1986). *Designing career development systems.* San Francisco: Jossey-Bass.

11. Pfeffer, J. (1994). *Competitive advantage through people.* Boston: Harvard Business School Press.

12. Barnett, B. R., and Bradley, L. (2007). The impact of organizational support for career development on career satisfaction. *Career Development International, 12*(7), 617–636.

13. Frequently Asked Questions (Online), U.S. Department of Labor, Bureau of Labor Statistics. Retrieved June 18, 2005, from http://www.bls.gov/nls/nlstaqs.htm#anch10.

14. Schein, E. H. (1978). *Career dynamics: Matching individual and organizational needs.* Reading, MA: Addison Wesley.

15. Ng, T. W. H., Eby, L. T., Sorensen, K. L., and Feldman, D. C. (2005). Predictors of objective and subjective career success: A meta-analysis. *Personnel Psychology, 58,* 367–408.

16. Managing your career: Special report. (1995, January 15). *Fortune,* pp. 34–78; Waterman, R. H., Waterman, J. A., and Collard, B. A. (1994). Toward a career-resilient workforce, *Harvard Business Review, 72*(4), 87–95; Arthur, M. B. (1994). The boundaryless career: A new perspective of organizational inquiry. *Journal of Organization Behavior, 15,* 295–309.

17. Callanan, G. A., and Greenhaus, J. H. (1999). Personal and career development: The best and worst of times. In A. Kraut and A. Korman (Eds.), *Evolving practices in human resource management: Responses to a changing world of work.* San Francisco: Jossey-Bass, pp. 146–171; Raelin, J. A. (1997). Internal career development in the age of insecurity. *Business Forum, 22*(1).

18. Sturgess, J., Conway, N., and Liefooghe, A. (2008). What's the deal? An exploration of career management behavior in Iceland. *International Journal of Human Resource Management, 19*(4), 752–768; Brousseau, K. R., Driver, M. J., Eneroth, K., and Larson, R.

(1996). Career pandemonium: Realigning organizations and individuals. *Academy of Management Executive, 10*(4), 52–66; Buckner, M., and Slavenski, L. (1994). Succession planning. In W. R. Tracey (Ed.), *Human resources management and development handbook.* New York: AMACOM, pp. 561–575.

19. Greenhaus, J. H. and Callanan, G. A. (1994). *Career management* (2nd ed.). New York: Dryden Press.

20. Allred, B. B., Snow, C. C., and Miles, R. E. (1996). Characteristics of managerial careers in the 21st century. *Academy of Management Executive, 10*(4), 17–27.

21. Callanan and Greenhaus. Personal and career development; Hall, D. T. (1996). Protean careers of the 21st century. *Academy of Management Executive, 10*(4), 8–16.

22. Gurchiek, Experts predict employee exodus; Montgomery, C. E. (1996). Organizational fit is key to job success. *HR Magazine, 41*(1), 94–96; Quinn, J. B., Anderson, P., and Finkelstein, S. (1996, March–April). Managing professional intellect: Making the most of the best. *Harvard Business Review,* pp. 71–80.

23. Linking career development with the new corporate agenda: Strategies for creating a career-resilient workforce (1997, February). Conference sponsored by the National Career Development Association, Atlanta, GA.

24. Callanan and Greenhaus. Personal and career development; Sullivan, S. E., Carden, W. A., and Martin, D. F. (1998). Careers in the next millennium: Directions for future research. *Human Resource Management Review, 8*(2), 165–185.

25. Waterman, R. H., Waterman, J. A., and Collard, B. A. (1994). Toward a career-resilient workforce, *Harvard Business Review, 72*(4), 87–95.

26. Callanan and Greenhaus. Personal and career development.

27. Weber, P. F. (1999). Getting a grip on employee growth. *Training & Development, 53*(5), 87–94.

28. ASTD's best: Better than the rest. (2007). *Training and Development Journal, 61*(10), 68.

29. Ibid., 70.

30. Lancaster, L. C., and Stillman, D. (2002). *When generations collide.* New York: Harper Business; Zemke, R., Raines, C., and Filipczak, B. (2000). *Generations at work.* New York: AMACOM.

31. Souerwine, A. H. (1981). The manager as career counselor: Some issues and approaches. In D. H. Montross and C. J. Shinkman (Eds.), *Career development in the 1980's: Theory and practice.* Springfield, IL: Charles C. Thomas, pp. 363–378. See also Gurchiek, *Experts predict employee exodus.*

32. Slavenski, L. (1987). Career development: A systems approach. *Training & Development, 41*(2), 56–60.

33. Keller J., and Piotrowski, C. (1987). Career development programs in Fortune 500 firms. *Psychological Reports, 61*(3), 920–922.

34. Bardsley, C. A. (1987). Improving employee awareness of opportunity at IBM. *Personnel, 64*(4), 58–63.

35. Leibowitz, Farren, and Kaye, *Designing career development systems.*

36. Russell, J. E. A. (1991). Career development interventions in organizations. *Journal of Vocational Behavior, 38,* 237–287; Gutteridge, T. G. (1986). Organizational career development systems: The state of the practice. In D. T. Hall and Associates (Eds.), *Career development in organizations.* San Francisco, CA: Jossey-Bass, pp. 50–94; Meier, S. T. (1991). Vocational behavior 1988–1990: Vocational choice, decision-making, career development interventions, and assessment. *Journal of Vocational Behavior, 39,* 131–181.

37. Russell, J. E. A., and Curtis, L. B. (1993, April). *Career development practices and perceived effectiveness in Fortune 500 firms.* Paper presented at the annual meeting of the Society of Industrial and Organizational Psychology, San Francisco, CA.

38. Waterman, R. H., Waterman, J. A., and Collard, B. A. (1994). Toward a career-resilient workforce, *Harvard Business Review, 72*(4), 87–95.

39. Prochaska, S. T. (2002). *Designing organizational programs for employee career development.* SHRM.

40. Martin, J. (1997, January 13). Job surfing: Move on to move. *Fortune, 135*(1), 50–54.

41. Wilhelm, W. R. (1983). Helping workers to self-manage their careers. *Personnel Administrator, 28*(8), 83–89.

42. Jackson, T., and Vitberg, A. (1987). Career development, part 2: Challenges for the organization. *Personnel, 64*(3), 68–72.

43. Curtis, L. B. (1996). *An examination of factors related to the effectiveness of a career development workshop.* Unpublished doctoral dissertation. The University of Tennessee, Knoxville, TN.

44. Brousseau, K. R., Driver, M. J., Eneroth, K., and Larson, R. (1996). Career pandemonium: Realigning organizations and individuals. *Academy of Management Executive, 10*(4), 52–66.

45. Bolles, R. N. (2005). *What color is your parachute?* Berkeley, CA: Ten Speed Press.

46. Burack, E. H., and Mathys, N. J. (1980). *Career management in organizations: A practical human resource planning approach.* Lake Forest, IL: Brace-Park.

47. London, M. (2002). Organizational assistance in career development. In D. C. Feldman (Ed.), *Work careers: A developmental perspective.* San Francisco: Jossey-Bass, pp. 323–345.

48. Brown, S. D., and Lent, R. W. (2005). *Career development and counseling: Putting theory and research to work.* New York: Wiley.

49. Peters, H. (1996). Peer coaching for executives. *Training & Development, 50*(3), 39–41; Waldroop, J., and Butler, T. (1996). The executive as coach. *Harvard Business Review, 74*(6), 111–117.

50. See also Jansen, B. J., Jansen, K. J., and Spink, A. (2005). Using the Web to look for work—Implications for online job seeking and recruiting. *Internet Research—Electronic Networking Applications and Policy, 15*(1), 49–66.

51. Russell, Career development interventions in organizations.

52. Smither, J. W. (1995). Creating an internal contingent workforce: Managing the resource link. In M. London (Ed.), *Employees, careers, and job creation: Developing growth-oriented human resource strategies and programs.* San Francisco: Jossey-Bass, pp. 142–164.

53. Brousseau, K. R., Driver, M. J., Eneroth, K., and Larson, R. (1996). Career pandemonium: Realigning organizations and individuals. *Academy of Management Executive, 10*(4), 52–66.

54. Leibowitz, Z. B., Kaye, B. L., and Farren, C. (1992). Multiple career paths. *Training & Development, 46*(10), 31–35.

55. Gutteridge, T. G., Leibowitz, Z. B., and Shore, J. E. (1993). *Organizational career development: Benchmarks for building a world-class workforce.* San Francisco, CA: Jossey-Bass.

56. Brousseau et al., Career pandemonium.

57. Gutteridge et al., *Organizational career development.*

58. Jansen, P. G., and Stoop, B. A. (2001). The dynamics of assessment center validity: Results of a 7-year study. *Journal of Applied Psychology, 86,* 741–753.

59. Rocco, J. (1991). Computers track high-potential managers. *HR Magazine, 36*(8), 66–68.

60. Gandossy, R., and Kao, T. (2004). Talent wars: Out of mind, out of practice. *Human Resource Planning, 27,* 4; ABI/INFORM Global. See also Behn, B. K., Riley, R. A., and Yang, Y. W. (2005). The value of an heir apparent in succession planning. *Corporate Governance—An International Review, 13*(2), 168–177; Biggs, E. L. (2004). CEO succession planning: An emerging challenge for boards of directors. *Academy of Management Executive, 18*(1), 105–107; Freeman, K. W. (2004). The CEO's real legacy. *Harvard Business Review, 82,* 51.

61. ASTD's best: Better than the rest, p. 75.

62. Garrett, E. M. (1994, April). Going the distance. *Small Business Reports,* pp. 22–30.

63. Greenberg, H. M., and Sidler, G. (1998, November). Succession planning: Easing the transition of your business. *Forum, 198,* 14–16.

64. Moses, J. L., and Eggebeen, S. L. (1999). Building room at the top: Selecting senior executives who can lead and succeed in the new world of work. In A. I. Kraut and A. Korman (Eds.), *Evolving practices in human resource management: Responses to a changing world of work.* San Francisco: Jossey-Bass, pp. 201–225.

65. Curtis, L. B., and Russell, J. E. A. (1993, April). *A study of succession planning programs in Fortune 500 firms.* Paper presented at the annual meeting of the Society of Industrial and Organizational Psychology, San Francisco, CA.

66. Ibid.; Who's next in line? *Strategic Direction,* May 2004, 20, 6;ABI/INFORM Global.

67. Golden, E. (1998). Nothing succeeds like succession. *Across the Board, 35*(6), 36–41.

68. Barron, T. (2004). The link between leadership development and retention. *Training & Development, 58*(4), 58–65.

69. Walker, J. W. (1998). Do we need succession planning anymore? *Human Resource Planning, 21*(3), 9–11.

70. H. Kets de Vries, M. F. R. (1995). *Life and death in the executive fast lane.* San Francisco: Jossey-Bass.

71. Mills, D. Q. (1988). *The IBM lesson: The profitable art of full employment.* New York: Random House; Schlesinger, L. A., Dyer, D., Clough, T. M., and Landau, D. (1987). *Chronicles of corporate change: Management lessons from AT&T and its offspring.* San Francisco, CA: New Lexington Press.

72. Buckner, M., and Slavenski, L. (1994). Succession planning. In W. R. Tracey (Ed.), *Human resources management and development handbook.* New York: AMACOM, pp. 561–575.

73. Beeson, J. (1998). Succession planning: Building the management corps. *Business Horizons, 41*(5), 61–66.

74. Nusbaum, H. J. (1986). The career development program at DuPont's Pioneering Research Laboratory. *Personnel, 63*(9), 68–75.

75. Gaertner, K. N. (1988). Managers' careers and organizational change. *Academy of Management Executive, 11,* 311–318.

76. Fenwick-Magrath, J. A. (1988). Executive development: Key factors for success. *Personnel, 65*(7), 68–72.

77. Georgemiller, D. (1992, Winter). Making the grades: The ABCs of educational reimbursement. *The Human Resource Professional,* pp. 16–19; Lesly, E. (1993, November 29). Sticking it out at Xerox by sticking together. *BusinessWeek,* p. 77.

78. Kurschner, D. (1996). Getting credit. *Training, 34*(6), 52–53.

79. Salopek, J. J. (2007). Stretching: Good for mind and body. *Training and Development Journal, 61*(10), 19.

80. Ibid. 18–20.

81. Dolan, K. A. (1996, November 18). When money isn't enough. *Forbes, 158*(12), 164–170.

82. ASTD's best: Better than the rest, p. 73.

83. Russell, J. E. A. (2004). *Mentoring encyclopedia of applied psychology,* vol. 2, pp. 609–616; Russell, J. E. A., and Adams, D. M. (1997). The changing nature of mentoring in organizations: An introduction to the special issue on mentoring in organizations. *Journal of Vocational Behavior, 51*(1), 1–14. Ensher, E. A., and Murphy, S. E. (2005). *Power mentoring: How mentors and protégés get the most out of their relationships.* San Francisco, CA: Jossey-Bass; Ragins, B. R., and Kram, K. E. (2007). (Eds). *The handbook of mentoring at work: Theory, research, and practice.* Thousand Oaks, CA: Sage; Kram, K. E. (1985). *Mentoring at work.* Glenwood, IL: Scott, Foresman.

84. McManus, S. E., and Russell, J. E. A. (2007). Peer mentoring relationships. In B. R. Ragins and K. E. Kram. (Eds.), *The handbook of mentoring at work: Theory, research, and practice.* Thousand Oaks, CA: Sage, pp. 273–297; Eby, L. T. (1997). Alternative forms of mentoring in changing organizational environments: A conceptual extension of the mentoring literature. *Journal of Vocational Behavior, 51*(1), 125–144.

85. Harris, J. I., Winskowski, A. M., Engdahl, B. E. (2007). Types of workplace social support in the prediction of job satisfaction. *Career Development Quarterly, 56*(2), 150–156.

86. Dougherty, T. W., and Dreher, G. F. (2007). Mentoring and career outcomes: Conceptual and methodological issues in an emerging literature. In B. R. Ragins and K. E. Kram (Eds.), *The handbook of mentoring at work: Theory, research, and practice.* Thousand Oaks, CA: Sage, pp. 51–93; Eby, L. T., Allen, T. D., Evans, S. C., Ng, T., and DuBois, D. L. (2008). Does mentoring matter? A multidisciplinary meta-analysis comparing mentored and non-mentored individuals. *Journal of Vocational Behavior, 72*(2), 254–267; Allen, T. D., Eby, L. T., Poteet, M. L., Lentz, E., and Lima L. (2004). Career benefits associated with mentoring for protégés: A meta-analysis. *Journal of Applied Psychology, 89,* 127–136.

87. Allen, T. D. (2007). Mentoring relationships from the perspective of the mentor. In B. R. Ragins and K. E. Kram (Eds.), *The handbook of mentoring at work: Theory, research, and practice.* Thousand Oaks, CA: Sage, pp. 123–147; Gentry, W. A., Weber, T. J., and Sadri, G.

(2007). Examining career-related mentoring and managerial performance across cultures: A multilevel analysis. *Journal of Vocational Behavior, 72*(2), 241–253.

88. Gunn, E. (1995). Mentoring: The democratic version. *Training, 32*(8), 64–67; Odiorne, G. S. (1985). Mentoring—An American management innovation. *Personnel Administrator, 30*(5), 63–70; Rigdon, J. E. (1993, December 1). You're not all alone if there's a mentor just a keyboard away. *The Wall Street Journal,* p. B1.

89. Dass, P., and Parker, B. (1999). Strategies for managing human resource diversity: From resistance to learning. *Academy of Management Executive, 13*(2), 68–80; ASTD's best: Better than the rest, p. 74.

90. P-Sontag, L., Vappie. K., and Wanberg, C. R. (2007). The practice of mentoring: MENTTIUM Corporation. In B. R. Ragins and K. E. Kram (Eds.), *The handbook of mentoring at work: Theory, research, and practice.* Thousand Oaks, CA: Sage, pp. 593–616.

91. MentorNet (2007). http://www.mentornet.net.

92. Ensher, E. A., and Murphy, S. E. (2007). E-mentoring: Next generation research strategies and suggestions. In B. R. Ragins and K. E. Kram (Eds.), *The handbook of mentoring at work: Theory, research, and practice.* Thousand Oaks, CA: Sage, pp. 299–322.

93. Ensher and Murphy, E-mentoring.

94. Smith-Jentsch, K. A., Scielzo, S. A., Yarbrough, C. S., and Rosopa, P. J. (2008). A comparison of face-to-face and electronic peer-mentoring: Interactions with mentor gender. *Journal of Vocational Behavior, 72*(2), 193–206.

95. Ensher and Murphy, E-mentoring.

96. Thompson, P., Kirkham, K., and Dixon, J. (1985). Warning: The fast track may be hazardous to organizational health. *Organizational Dynamics, 13,* 21–33.

97. Brousseau et al., Career pandemonium.

98. London, M. (1996). Redeployment and continuous learning in the 21st century: Hard lessons and positive examples from the downsizing era. *Academy of Management Executive, 10*(4), 67–79.

99. Tang, T., and Fuller, R. M. (1995). Corporate downsizing: What managers can do to lessen the negative effects of layoffs. *SAM Advanced Management Journal, 60*(4), 12–15, 31.

100. Butterfield, L. D., and Borgen, W. A. (2005). Outplacement counseling from the client's perspective. *Career Development Quarterly, 53,* 306–316; see also Westaby, J. D. (2004). The impact of outplacement programs on reemployment criteria: A longitudinal study of displaced managers and executives. *Journal of Employment Counseling, 41,* 19–28.

101. Brockner, J., Konovsky, M., Cooper-Schneider, R., Folger, R., Martin, C., and Bies, R. J. (1994). Interactive effects of procedural justice and outcome negativity on victims and survivors of job loss. *Academy of Management Journal, 37,* 397–409; O'Neill, H. M., and Lenn, D. J. (1995). Voices of survivors: Words that downsizing CEOs should hear. *Academy of Management Executive, 9,* 23–34.

102. Carson, K. D., and Carson, P. P. (1997). Career entrenchment: A quiet march toward occupational death? *Academy of Management Executive, 11*(1), 62–75.

103. Charan, R., and Colvin, G. (1999, June 21). Why CEOs fail. *Fortune, 139*(12), 69–78.

104. ASTD's best: Better than the rest, p. 80; Bell, C. R. (1996). *Managers as mentors: Building partnerships for learning.* San Francisco, CA: Berrett-Koehler Publishers.

105. Anderson, D., and Anderson, M. (2005). *Coaching that counts.* Boston, MA: Elsevier; Fitzgerald, C., and Berger, J. G. (2002). *Executive coaching: Practice and perspectives.* Palo Alto, CA: Davies-Black; Kilburg, R. R. (Ed.) (1996). Executive coaching. *Consulting Psychology Journal: Practice and Research, 48*(2), 57–152; Smith, L. (1993, December 27). The executive's new coach. *Fortune, 128*(16), 126–134; Witherspoon, R., and White, R. P. (1996). Executive coaching: A continuum of roles. *Consulting Psychology Journal: Practice and Research, 48*(2), 124–133.

106. Bench, M. (2003). *Career coaching: An insider's guide.* Palo Alto, CA: Davies-Black.

107. Cheramie, R. A., Sturman, M. C., and Walsh, K. (2007). Executive career management: Switching organizational and the boundaryless career. *Journal of Vocational Behavior, 71*(3), 359–374; Hollenbeck, G. P., and McCall, M. W. (1999). Leadership development: Contemporary practices. In A. I. Kraut and A. Korman (Eds.), *Evolving practices in human resource management.* San Francisco: Jossey-Bass, pp. 172–200.

108. For more information, contact the Director of Executive Coaching at jrussell@rhsmith.umd.edu.

109. A living breathing people strategy. (2007, October). *Training and Development Journal, 61*(10), 42–44.

110. Edelstein, B. C., and Armstrong, D. J. (1993). A model for executive development. *Human Resource Planning, 16*(4), 51–64; Thach, L., and Heinselman, T. (1999). Executive coaching defined. *Training & Development, 53*(3), 35–39.

111. Laff, M. (2007). Reliance on coaching may have peaked. *Training and Development Journal, 61*(10), 14.

112. Tien, H. L. S. (2007). Practice and research in career counseling and development—2006. *Career Development Quarterly, 56*(2), 98–140; Russell, J. E. A. (2005). Career counseling for women in management. In W. B. Walsh and M. Heppner (Eds.), *Handbook of Career Counseling for Women* (2nd ed.). Mahwah, NJ: Lawrence Erlbaum.

113. "2008 Best Companies for Multicultural Women," www.workingmother.com. Retrieved August 2, 2008.

114. Dass, P., and Parker, B. (1999). Strategies for managing human resource diversity: From resistance to learning. *Academy of Management Executive, 13*(2), 68–80; Deutsch, C. H. (1990, December 16). Putting women on the fast track. *New York Times,* p. F 25.

115. Litzky, B., and Greenhaus, J. (2007). The relationship between gender and aspirations to senior management. *Career Development International, 12*(7), 637–659.

116. Catalyst (1999). *Creating women's networks: A how-to-guide for women and companies.* San Francisco: Jossey-Bass; Friedman, R. A. (1999). Employee network groups: Self-help strategy for women and minorities. *Performance Improvement Quarterly, 12*(1), 148–163; Leonard, B. (1999). Linking diversity initiatives. *HR Magazine, 44*(6), 60–64.

117. Mainiero, L. A., and Sullivan, S. E. (2005). Kaleidoscope careers: An alternate explanation for the "opt-out" revolution. *Academy of Management Executive, 19*(1), 106–123.

118. Shapiro, M., Ingols, C., and Blake-Beard, S. (2008). Confronting career double binds—Implications for women, organizations, and career practitioners. *Journal of Career Development, 34*(3), 309–333.

119. Feldman, D. C. (1988). *Managing careers in organizations.* Glenview, IL: Scott, Foresman.

120. ASTD's best: Better than the rest, pp. 80–81.

121. Allen, T. D., McManus, S. E., and Russell, J. E. A. (1999). Newcomer socialization and stress: Formal peer relationships as a source of support. *Journal of Vocational Behavior, 54,* 453–470. See also Scandura, T. A. (2002). The establishment years: A dependence perspective. In D. C. Feldman (Ed.), *Work careers: A developmental perspective.* San Francisco: Jossey-Bass, pp. 159–185.

122. ASTD's best: Better than the rest, p. 81.

123. Ibid., p. 78.

124. Adkins, C. L. (1995). Previous work experience and organizational socialization: A longitudinal examination. *Academy of Management Journal, 38,* 839–862; Major, D. A., Kozlowski, S. W., Chao, G. T., and Gardner, P. D. (1995). A longitudinal investigation of newcomer expectations, early socialization outcomes, and the moderating effects of role development factors. *Journal of Applied Psychology, 80,* 418–431; Wanous, J. P. (1980). *Organizational entry: Recruitment, selection, and socialization of newcomers.* Reading, MA: Addison-Wesley.

125. Zappala, S., Depolo, M., Fraccaroli, F., Guglielmi, D., and Sarchielli, G. (2008). Postponing job retirement? Psychological influences on the preference for early or late retirement. *Career Development International, 13*(2), 150–167.

126. Van der Heijden, B. I. J. M., Schalk, R., Van Veldhoven, M. J. P. M. (2008). Aging and careers: European research on long-term career development and early retirement. *Career Development International, 13*(2), 85–94; Van Veldhoven, M., and Dorenbosch, L. (2008). Age, proactivity and career development. *Career Development International, 13*(2), 112–131.

127. Mignonac, K. (2008). Individual and contextual antecedents of older managerial employees' willingness to accept intra-organizatinal job changes. *International Journal of Human Resource Management, 19*(4), 582–599; Strenger, C., and Ruttenberg, A. (2008). The existential necessity of midlife change, *Harvard Business Review, 86*(2); Allen, T. D., Poteet, M. L., and Russell, J. E. A. (1999). Attitudes of managers who are "more or less" career plateaued. *Career Development Quarterly, 47,* 159–172; Beehr, T. A., and Bowling, N. A. (2002). Career issues facing older workers. In D. C. Feldman (Ed.), *Work careers: A developmental perspective.* San Francisco: Jossey-Bass, pp. 214–241.

128. American Association of Retired Persons. (1993). *The older workforce: Recruitment and retention.* Washington, DC: AARP..

129. Desmette, D., and Gaillard, M. (2008). When a "worker" becomes an "older worker": The effects of age-related social identity on attitudes towards retirement and work. *Career Development International, 13*(2), 168–185.

130. Lockwood, N. R. (2003). Work/life balance: Challenges and solutions. *HR Magazine, 48,* 2–10. Saltzstein, A. L., Ting, Y., and Saltzstein, G. H. (2001). Family-friendly balance and job satisfaction: The impact of family-friendly policies on attitudes of federal government employees. *Public Administration Review, 4,* 452–467; Carr, J. C., Boyar, S. L., and Gregory, B. T. (2008). The moderating effect of work-family centrality on work-family conflict, organizational attitudes, and turnover behavior. *Journal of Management, 34*(2), 244–262.

131. (2007). *Working Mother Magazine* Top 10 Places to Work. www.workingmother.com.

132. Eby, L. T. (1996). *Intra-organizational mobility: An examination of factors related to employees' willingness to relocate.* Unpublished doctoral dissertation. The University of Tennessee, Knoxville, TN; Eby, L. T., DeMatteo, J. S., and Russell, J. E. A. (1997). Employment assistance needs of accompanying spouses following relocation. *Journal of Vocational Behavior, 50,* 291–307.

133. Lublin, J. S. (1993, April 13). Husbands in limbo. *The Wall Street Journal,* pp. A1, A8.

134. Pellico, M. T., and Stroh. L. K. (1997). Spousal assistance programs: An integral component of the international assignment. In A. Zeynep (Ed.), *New approaches to employee management,* Vol. 4: *Expatriate management: Theory and research.* Greenwich, CT: JAI Press, pp. 227–243.

135. Mitchell, H. R. (1999). When a company moves: How to help employees adjust. *HR Magazine, 44*(1), 61–65.

136. "*Working Mother Magazine* Top 10 Places to Work." (2007). www.workingmother.com; see also Russell, J. E. A., and Burgess, J. R. D. (1998). Success and women's career adjustment. *Journal of Career Assessment, 6*(4), 365–387; Sutton, K. L., and Noe, R. A. (2005). Family-friendly programs and work-life integration: More myth than magic? In E. E. Kossek and S. G. Lambert (Eds.), *Work and life integration: Organizational, cultural, and individual perspectives.* Mahwah, NJ: Lawrence Erlbaum, pp. 151–169.

137. Remote worker reality check. *Training and Development Journal, 61*(10), 12; Russell, J. E. A. (2003). Introduction: Technology and Careers. *Journal of Vocational Behavior, 63*(2), 153–158.

138. Wells, S. J. (1999). Using rush hour to your advantage. *HR Magazine, 44*(3), 27–32; Wilhelm, W. R. (1983). Helping workers to self-manage their careers. *Personnel Administrator, 28*(8), 83–89.

139. Warner, M. (1997, March 3). Working at home—The right way to be a star in your bunny slippers. *Fortune, 135*(4), 165–166.

140. "*Working Mother Magazine* Top 10 Places to Work.".

141. Allen, T. D., and Russell, J. E. A. (1999). Parental leaves of absence: Some not so friendly family implications. *Journal of Applied Social Psychology, 29,* 166–191; See also Fried, M. (1998). *Taking time: Parental leave policy and corporate culture.* Philadelphia, PA: Temple University Press; Kossek, E. E., and Lambert, S. G. (Eds.) (2005). *Work and life integration: Organizational, cultural, and individual perspectives.* Mahwah, NJ: Lawrence Erlbaum.

142. Heilman, M. E., and Okimoto, T. G. (2008). Motherhood: A potential source of bias in employment decisions. *Journal of Applied Psychology, 93*(1), 189–198.

143. Shellenbarger, S. (1997, June 11). Employees, managers need to plan ahead for maternity leaves. *The Wall Street Journal,* p. B1.

144. www.workingmothers.com.

145. Goff, S. J., Mount, M. K., and Jamison, R. L. (1990). Employee supported child care, work/family conflict, and absenteeism: A field study. *Personnel Psychology, 43,* 793–810; Kossek, E. E., and Nichol, V. (1992). The effects of on-site child care on employee attitudes and performance. *Personnel Psychology, 45,* 485–509; Lawlor, J. (1996, July/August). The bottom line on work-family programs. *Working Woman Magazine,* pp. 54–56, 58, 74, 76; Dolan, K. A. (1996, November 18). When money isn't enough. *Forbes, 158*(12), 164–170.

146. Bureau of National Affairs (1993). Measuring results: Cost-benefit analyses of work and family programs. *Employee International Journal of Operations & Production Management, 24,* 1247–1268.

147. Rynes, S., and Rosen, B. (1995). A field survey of factors affecting the adoption and perceived success of diversity training. *Personnel Psychology, 48*(2), 247–270.

148. Lawlor, The bottom line on work-family programs.

149. Dickmann, M., Doherty, N., Mills, T., and Brewster, C. (2008). Why do they go? Individual and corporate perspectives on the factors influencing the decision to accept an international assignment. *International Journal of Human Resource Management, 19*(4), 731–751; Stahl, G. K., Miller, E. L., and Tung, R. L. (2002). Toward the boundaryless career: A closer look at the expatriate career concept and the perceived implications of an international assignment. *Journal of World Business, 37,* 216–227.

150. Allerton, H. E. (1997). Expatriate gaps. *Training & Development, 51*(7), 7–8; Harvey, M. G. (1989). Repatriation of corporate executives: An empirical study. *Journal of International Business Studies, 20,* 131–144; see also Allen, D., and Alvarez, S. (1998). Empowering expatriates and organizations to improve repatriation effectiveness. *Human Resource Planning, 21*(4), 29–39.

151. Allerton, Expatriate gaps; Tung, R. L. (1998). A contingency framework of selection and training of expatriates revisited. *Human Resource Management Review, 8*(1), 23–37.

152. Stroh, L. K., Gregersen, H. B., and Black, J. (1998). Closing the gap: Expectations versus reality among repatriates. *Journal of World Business, 33*(2), 111–125; Engen, J. R. (1995). Coming home. *Training, 32*(3), 37–40.

153. Black, J. S., Gregersen, H. B., and Mendenhall, M. (1992). *Global assignments: Successfully expatriating and repatriating international managers.* San Francisco: Jossey-Bass; see also Solomon C. M., Navigating your search for global talent. *Personnel Journal, 99*(1), 94–95; Feldman, D. C. (1991). Repatriate moves as career transitions. *Human Resource Management Review, 1*(3), 163–178.

154. Hegler, D. (1989, December 11). Views on the expatriate. *The Wall Street Journal,* p. B1; Napier, N., and Patterson, R. (1991). Expatriate re-entry: What do expatriates have to say? *Human Resource Planning, 14*(1), 18–28.

155. Solomon, C. M. (1995). Repatriation: Up, down, or out? *Personnel Journal, 74*(1), 28–35.

156. Finney, M. I. (1996). Global success rides on keeping top talent. *HR Magazine, 41*(4), 69–72; National Foreign Trade Council and Windham International (1995, January). *Global Relocation Trends Survey Report.*

157. Allerton, Expatriate gaps; Feldman, Repatriate moves as career transitions; Gregersen, H. B. (1992). Commitments to a parent company and a local work unit during repatriation. *Personnel Psychology, 45*(1), 29–54.

158. Greenhaus, J. H., and Callanan, G. A. (1994). *Career management* (2nd ed). New York: Dryden Press.

159. Slavenski, L. (1987). Career development: A systems approach. *Training & Development, 41*(2), 56–60.

160. Bennis, W. (1996). What lies ahead. *Training & Development, 50*(1), 75–79; Colby, A. G. (1995). Making the new career development model work. *HR Magazine, 40*(6), 150, 152; Thornburg, L. (1995). HR in the year 2010. *HR Magazine, 40*(5), 63–70.

161. Arthur, M. B., and Rousseau, D. (1996). A new career lexicon for the 21st century. *Academy of Management Executive, 10*(4), 28–39.

Chapter 10

1. Becker, B. E., Huselid, M. A., and Ulrich, D. (2001). *The HR scorecard.* Boston: Harvard Business School Press. See also, Lawler, E. E. (2002). Pay strategy: New thinking for the new millennium. In G. R. Ferris et al., *Human resource management.* Upper Saddle River, NJ: Prentice Hall, pp. 310–316; Rynes, S. L., and Bono, J. E. (2000). Psychological research on determinants of pay. In S. L. Rynes and B. Gerhart (Eds.), *Compensation in organizations: Current research and practice.* San Francisco: Jossey-Bass, pp. 3–31.

2. Greenhouse, S. (2008). *The big squeeze: Tough times for the American worker.* New York: Alfred A. Knopf.

3. Crystal, G. S., and Kay, I. T. (1997). Contrasting perspectives: CEO pay and the "efficient" marketplace. *CEO pay: A comprehensive look.* Scottsdale, AZ: American Compensation Association, p. 50.

4. Kanter, R. M. (2007). *America the principled: Six opportunities for becoming a can-do nation once again.* New York: Crown, pp. 100–101.

5. Survey conducted by Joseph R. Blasi and Douglas L. Kruse, cited in Gretchen Morgenstern (2004, April 4). Option pie: Overeating is a health hazard. *New York Times,* p. B1.

6. For full discussion of IBM, see Gerstner, L. V. (2002). *Who says elephants can't dance? Inside IBM's historic turnaround.* New York: Harper Business. See also Richter, A. S. (1998). Paying the people in black at Big Blue. *Compensation and Benefits Review, 30*(3), 51–59.

7. Gerhart, B. (2000). Compensation strategy and organizational performance. In S. L. Rynes and B. Gerhart (Eds.), *Compensation in organizations: Current research and practice.* San Francisco: Jossey-Bass, pp. 151–194.

8. Blinder, A. S. (Ed.) (1990). *Paying for productivity.* Washington, DC: Brookings Institution.

9. http://www.bls.gov/news.release/ichcc.t02.htm. Table 2. Production workers: Hourly compensation costs in U.S. dollars in manufacturing, 34 countries or areas and selected economic groups, selected years, 1975–2006.

10. Gupta, N., and Shaw, J. D. (1998). Let the evidence speak: Financial incentives are effective. *Compensation and Benefits Review, 30*(2), 28.

11. Martocchio, J. J. (2009). *Strategic compensation: A human resource management approach* (5th ed.). Upper Saddle River, NJ: Pearson Prentice Hall.

12. LeBlanc, P. V., and Mulvey, P. W. (1998). How American workers see the rewards of work. *Compensation and Benefits Review, 30*(1), 24–34.

13. For a review of the pay satisfaction literature, see Heneman, H. G. III, and Judge, T. A. (2000). Compensation attitudes. In Rynes and Gerhart, *Compensation in organizations,* pp. 61–103.

14. Barber, A. E., and Bretz, R. D. (2000). Compensation, attraction and retention. In Rynes and Gerhart, *Compensation in organizations,* pp. 32–60.

15. Carraher, S. M. and Buckley, M. R. (1996). Cognitive complexity and the perceived dimensionality of pay satisfaction. *Journal of Applied Psychology, 81,* 102–109.

16. Henderson, R. I. (2000). *Compensation management in a knowledge-based world.* Upper Saddle River, NJ: Prentice Hall, pp. 6–7.

17. Paine, T. (2000, January 4). Out-of-control CEO salaries: Should taxpayers subsidize them? *Common Sense.*

18. For a full discussion concerning the history of compensation in organizations, see Rock, M. L. (1991). Looking back on forty years of compensation programs. In M. L. Rock and L. A. Berger (Eds.), *The compensation handbook: A state of the art guide to compensation strategy and design.* New York: McGraw-Hill, pp. 3–11. See also Wallace, M. J., and Fay, C. H. (1988). *Compensation theory and practices.* Boston: PWS-Kent; DeLuca, M. J. (1993). *Handbook of compensation management.* Englewood Cliffs, NJ: Prentice Hall.

19. For a full discussion of the advantages and disadvantages of job ranking, see Bureau of National Affairs (2005). *Compensation.* Washington, DC: BNA. See also Berg, J. G. (1976). *Managing compensation.* New York: AMACOM; Sibson, R. E. (1990). *Compensation.* New York: AMACOM.

20. For a full discussion of the advantages and disadvantages of job classification, see Bureau of National Affairs, *Compensation;* Berg, *Managing compensation;* Sibson, *Compensation.*

21. For full discussion, see Martocchio, *Strategic compensation.* See also Milkovich, G. T., and Newman, J. M. (2005). *Compensation* (8th ed.). New York: McGraw-Hill/Irwin; and Sibson, *Compensation.*

22. For a full discussion of the advantages and disadvantages of point-factor job evaluation plans, see Bureau of National Affairs, *Compensation;* Berg, *Managing compensation;* Sibson, *Compensation.*

23. Kanin-Lovers, J. (1991). Job evaluation technology. In M. L. Rock and L. A. Berger (Eds.), *The compensation handbook: A state of the art guide to compensation strategy and design.* New York: McGraw-Hill, pp. 72–86. See also DeLuca, *Handbook of compensation management.*

24. Dolmat-Connell, J. (1994). Labor market definition and salary survey selection: A new look at the foundation of compensation program design. *Compensation and Benefits Review, 26*(2), 38–46. See also Lichty, D. T. (1991). Compensation surveys. In M. L. Rock and L. A. Berger (Eds.), *The compensation handbook: A state of the art guide to compensation strategy and design,* pp. 87–103. For full discussion of the economic forces in the labor market (both supply and demand sides), see Wallace and Fay, *Compensation theory and practices.*

25. For a full discussion concerning advantages and disadvantages of market pricing, see Gomez-Mejia, L. R., Balkin, D. B., and Cardy, R. L. (1995). *Managing human resources,* Englewood Cliffs, NJ: Prentice Hall. See also Brennan, J. P., and McKee, B. (1995). Structureless salary management: A successful application of a modest approach. *Compensation and Benefits Review, 27*(2), 56–62; Sibson, *Compensation.*

26. See Milkovich and Newman, *Compensation.*

27. See Lichty, Compensation surveys; DeLuca, *Handbook of compensation management;* Sibson, *Compensation.*

28. See DeLuca, *Handbook of compensation management.* See also Martocchio, *Strategic compensation.*

29. For a full discussion concerning theoretical support for new compensation approaches, see Risher, H. (1997). The end of jobs: Planning and managing rewards in the new work paradigm. *Compensation and Benefits Review, 29*(1), 13–17. See also Cappelli, P. (1997). Re-thinking the nature of work. *Compensation and Benefits Review, 29*(4), 50–59; Lissy, W. E., and Morgenstern, M. L. (1994). Currents in compensation and benefits. *Compensation and Benefits Review, 26*(5), 10–18; Schuster, J. R., and Zingheim, P. K. (1992). *The new pay: Linking employee and organizational performance.* New York: Lexington Books; Bergel, G. I. (1994). Choosing the right pay delivery system to fit banding. *Compensation and Benefits Review, 26*(4), 34–38.

30. For a full discussion of bias in compensation programs, see Arvey, R. D. (1987). Potential problems in job evaluation methods and processes. In D. B. Balkin and L. R. Gomez-Mejia (Eds.), *New perspectives on compensation.* Englewood Cliffs, NJ: Prentice Hall, pp. 20–30. See also Cook, F. W. (1994). Compensation surveys are biased. *Compensation and Benefits Review, 26*(5), 19–22; Berg, *Managing compensation;* Bureau of National Affairs, *Compensation.*

31. Treiman, D. J., and Hartmann, H. (Eds.) (1981). *Women, work and wages: Equal pay for jobs of equal value.* Washington, DC: National Academy Press. See also, Rudin, J. P. and Byrd, K. (2003). U.S. pay equity legislation: Sheep in wolves' clothing. *Employee Responsibilities and Rights Journal, 15,* 183–190; Rhoads, S. *Incomparable worth: Pay equity meets the market* (1993). Cambridge, MA: Cambridge University Press; Sorenson, E. *Comparable worth: Is it a worthy policy?* Princeton, NJ: Princeton University Press.

32. For a full discussion of broadbanding, see Martocchio, *Strategic compensation.* Also see Haslett, S. (1995). Broadbanding: A strategic tool for organizational change. *Compensation and Benefits Review, 27*(6), 40–46; Abosch, K. S. (1995). The promise of broadbanding. *Compensation and Benefits Review, 27*(1), 54–58; LeBlanc, P. V., and McInerney, M. (1994). Need a change? Jump on the banding wagon. *Personnel Journal, 73*(1), 72–82; Donnelly, K., LeBlanc, P. V., Torrence, R. D., and Lyon, M. A. (1992). Career banding. *Human Resource Management, 31*(1–2), 35–43; Lissy and Morgenstern, Currents in compensation and benefits; Bergel, Choosing the right pay delivery system; Brennan and McKee, Structureless salary management.

33. Hewitt study cited in Abosch, The promise of broadbanding.

34. ACA study cited in Lissy and Morgenstern, Currents in compensation and benefits.

35. For a discussion of broadbanding disadvantages, see Sibson, R. E. (1990). *New compensation plans: A consultant's report.* Vero Beach, FL: Sibson. See also Reissman, L. (1995). Nine common myths about broadbands. *HR Magazine, 40*(8), 79–88; Abosch, The promise of broadbanding; LeBlanc and McInerney, Need a change?

36. For a full discussion of pay-for-knowledge programs, including advantages and disadvantages, see Bennett, L. (1996). The C&BR board comments on compensation fads, custom pay plans, and team pay. *Compensation and Benefits Review, 28*(2), 67–75. See also Vogeley, E. G., and Schaeffer, L. J. (1995). Link employee pay to competencies and objectives. *HR Magazine, 40*(10), 75–81; Parent, K. I., and Weber, C. L. (1994). Case study: Does pay for knowledge pay off? *Compensation and Benefits Review, 26*(5), 44–50; Sibson, *New compensation plans;* Bergel, Choosing the right pay delivery system; Gomez-Mejia, Balkin, and Cardy, *Managing human resources.*

37. For a full discussion of teams and team-related pay, see Zingheim, P. K., and Schuster, J. R. (1995). First findings: The team pay research study. *Compensation and Benefits Review, 27*(6), 6–14. See also Cauldron. S. (1994). Tie individual pay to team success. *Personnel Journal, 73*(10), 40–47; Gross, S. E. (1995). *Compensation for teams: How to design and implement team-based reward programs.* New York: AMACOM; Dumaine, B. (September 15, 1994). The trouble with teams. *Fortune,* pp. 86–92; Lissy and Morgenstern, Currents in compensation and benefits; Bergel, Choosing the right pay delivery system.

38. See Wallace and Fay, *Compensation theory and practices.*

39. Orey, M. (2007, October 1). Wage wars: Workers from truck drivers to stockbrokers are winning huge overtime lawsuits. *BusinessWeek* online.

40. Human Resource Executive Online, http://hre.lrp.com/HRE/story,isp/storyid=15188876 (accessed 5/27/2008). For a full discussion concerning minimum wage, see Hansen, F. (1998). Labor markets and compensation. *Compensation and Benefits Review, 30*(2), 21–25. See also Dunham, S. R. (1996, July 26). We interrupt this revolution to hike the minimum wage. *BusinessWeek,* p. 47; Norton, R. (1996, May 27). The minimum wage is unfair. *Fortune,* p. 53; Prasch, R. E. (1996). In defense of the minimum wage. *Journal of Economic Issues, 30*(2), 391–397; Laabs, J. J. (1996). Maximum debate over minimum wage hike—again. *Personnel Journal, 75*(6), 12; Bernstein, A. (1996, May 20). Commentary: A minimum wage argument you haven't heard before. *BusinessWeek,* p. 42.

41. Hansen, Currents in compensation and benefits, pp. 8–9.

42. BLS statistics cited in Milkovich and Newman, *Compensation.*

43. Farrell, W. (2005). *Why men earn more: The startling truth behind the pay gap—and what women can do about it.* New York: AMACOM Books. For further information about the wage gap and the Paycheck Fairness Act, see www.nwlc.org/pdf/PaycheckFairnessFeb2002.pdf. Accessed 5/27/08.

44. Hart, D. E., and Carraher, S. M. (1995). The development of an instrument to measure attitudes toward benefits. *Educational and Psychological Measurement, 55,* 480–484; McCaffery, R. M. (1988). *Employee benefit programs: A total compensation perspective.* Boston: PWS-Kent. See also Dreher, G. F., Ash, R. A., and Bretz, R. D. (1988). Benefit coverage and employee cost: Critical factors in explaining compensation satisfaction. *Personnel Psychology, 41,* 237–254; Barber, A. E., Dunham, R. B., and Formisano, R. A. (1992). The importance of flexible benefits on employee satisfaction: A field study. *Personnel Psychology, 45,* 55–76.

45. Bernardin, H. J. (1989). A survey of state employee attitudes toward benefits. Unpublished report to the Florida legislature.

46. See Bergman and Scarpello, *Compensation decision-making;* Martocchio, *Strategic compensation;* McCaffery, *Employee benefit programs.*

47. U.S. Chamber of Commerce Annual Benefits Surveys, 2000 and 2001.

48. See Martocchio, J. J. (2006). *Employee benefits: A primer for human resource professionals* (2nd ed.). New York: McGraw-Hill/Irwin; McCaffery, *Employee benefit programs;* Steinberg, A. T. (1995). Beyond the tax code: How employee needs are driving employee benefits design. *Compensation and Benefits Review, 27*(1), 29–32; Bureau of Labor Statistics (1992, September). *Employee benefits in a changing economy: A BLS chartbook.* Washington, DC: U.S. Government Printing Office.

49. Morgenstern, M. L. (1996). Currents in compensation and benefits. *Compensation and Benefits Review, 28*(3), 10–15. See also Milkovich and Newman, *Compensation;* Martocchio, *Strategic compensation;* Bergman and Scarpello, *Compensation decision-making.*

50. Ibid.

51. Bureau of Labor Statistics (1998, April). *Employee benefits in small, private establishments, 1996.* Washington, DC: U.S. Government Printing Office. See also Bureau of Labor Statistics (1999, November). *Employee benefits in medium and large establishments, 1997.* Washington, DC: U.S. Government Printing Office.

52. Labor Letter (1990, March 27). *The Wall Street Journal,* p. 1. See also Morgenstern, Currents in compensation and benefits; Milkovich and Newman, *Compensation;* Martocchio, *Strategic compensation;* Bergman and Scarpello, *Compensation decision-making.*

53. Bureau of National Affairs. (1994). *Compensation.* Washington, DC: BNA.

54. Rosenbloom, J. S., and Hallman, G. V. (1986). *Employee benefit planning.* Englewood Cliffs, NJ: Prentice Hall.

55. See Bureau of Labor Statistics (2007, August). *National Compensation Survey: Employee benefits in private industry in the United States.* www.bls.gov and www.bls.gov/ncs/ebs/home.htm (accessed May 27, 2008).

56. For a full discussion of wellness programs, see Haltom, C. (1995). Shifting the focus from sickness to wellness. *Compensation and Benefits Review, 27*(1), 47–53. See also Povall, J. (1994). Wellness strategies: How to choose a health risk assessment appraisal. *Compensation and Benefits Review, 27*(1), 54–61.

57. For a discussion of health plan audits, see Reace, D. (1995). The collapse of health care reform—What now? *Compensation and Benefits Review, 29*(2), 69–74. See also Povall, Wellness strategies.

58. McGill, D. M., and Grubbs, D. S. (1989). *Fundamentals of private pensions.* Philadelphia, PA: University of Pennsylvania Press, p. 54.

59. For a full discussion of ERISA provisions, see Bureau of National Affairs (1994). *Compensation.*

60. See Bureau of Labor Statistics (2004, March). www.bls.gov/ncs/ebs.

61. Ibid.

62. See note 55, Bureau of Labor Statistics.

63. See McGill and Grubbs, *Fundamentals of private pensions.* See also McCaffery, *Employee benefit programs.*

64. See note 51, Bureau of Labor Statistics.

65. See Bureau of National Affairs (1994). *Compensation.*

66. Ibid.

67. Ibid.

68. See note 60, Bureau of Labor Statistics.

69. See note 55, Bureau of Labor Statistics. See also note 51, Bureau of Labor Statistics.

70. See note 51, Bureau of Labor Statistics.

71. Ibid.

72. Winslow, R. (1989, December 13). Spending to cut mental health costs. *The Wall Street Journal,* p. B1.

73. Hansen, Currents in compensation and benefits, p. 9. See also Densford, L. E. (1987, May/June). Make room for baby: The employer's role in solving the day care dilemma. *Employee Benefits News,* pp. 19–38. See also note 55, Bureau of Labor Statistics.

74. Dowling, P. J., Welch, D. E., and Schuler, R. S. (1999). *International human resource management: Managing people in a multinational context.* New York: ITP.

75. Swaak, R. A. (1995). Expatriate management: The search for best practices. *Compensation and Benefits Review, 27*(2), 21–29. Also see Martocchio, *Strategic compensation.*

76. Lublin, J. S. (1996, January 29). An overseas stint can be a ticket to the top. *The Wall Street Journal,* p. B1.

77. Kanter, R. M. (1995). *World class: Thinking locally in the global economy.* New York: Simon and Schuster, p. 88.

78. Heneman, and Judge, Compensation attitudes, p. 97.

79. See Dowling, Welch, and Schuler, *International human resource management.*

80. Ibid., p. 198.

81. See Bergman and Scarpello, *Compensation decision-making.*

82. See Martocchio, *Strategic compensation.*

83. See Dowling, Welch, and Schuler, *International human resource management.*

84. See Martocchio, *Strategic compensation.*

85. Ibid., p. 321.

86. See Dowling, Welsh, and Schuler, *International human resource management.*

87. Holland, K. (2008, April 27). When the share price is a factor in pay. *New York Times* online, www.nytimes.com/2008/04/27/jobs/27mgmt.html?pagewanted=print.

88. Cohan, W. D. (2008, November 16). Our risk, Wall Street's reward. *New York Times* online.

CHAPTER 11

1. Kanter, R. M. (1989). *When giants learn to dance.* New York: Simon and Schuster, p. 232. See also Heneman, R. (1992). *Merit pay.* Reading, MA: Addison-Wesley.

2. Huselid, M. A., Becker, B. E., and Beatty, R. W. (2005). *The workforce scorecard: Managing human capital to execute strategy.* Boston: Harvard Business School Press; Becker, B. E., Huselid, M. A., and Ulrich, D. (2001). *The HR scorecard.* Boston: Harvard Business School Press. See also Becker, B. E., Huselid, M. A., Pickus, P. S., and Spratt, M. F. (1997). HR as a source of shareholder value: Research and recommendations. *Human Resource Management, 36,* 39–47. See also McDonald, D., and Smith, A. (1995, January/February). A proven connection: Performance management and business results. *Compensation and Benefits Review,* pp. 59–64.

3. Cadsby, C.B., Song F., Tapon, F. (2007). Sorting and incentive effects of pay for performance: An experimental investigation. *Academy of Management Journal, 50,* 387–405; see also Rynes, S. L., Gerhart, B., and Parks, L. (2005). Personnel psychology: Performance evaluation and pay for performance. *Annual Review of Psychology, 56,* 571.

4. Martocchio, J. J. (2009). *Strategic compensation.* Upper Saddle River, NJ: Pearson/Prentice Hall; see also Collins, D. (1995, Summer). Death of a gain sharing plan: Power politics and participatory management. *Organizational Dynamics, 24*(1), 23–38; Lawler, E. E. III, and Cohen, S. G. (1992). Designing a pay system for teams. *American Compensation Association Journal, 1*(1), 6–19.

5. Murphy, K. (1994, June 13). Quoted in Fierman, J., The perilous new world of fair pay. *Fortune,* p. 58.

6. Levitt, S. D., and Dubner, S. J. (2005). *Freakonomics: A rogue economist explores the hidden side of everything.* New York: W. Morrow.

7. DeCarlo, S. (Ed.) (2005). Special report: CEO compensation. *Forbes,* www.Forbes.com/2005/ceoland.

8. Pfeffer, J. (1994). *HR for competitive advantage.* Boston: Harvard Business Press. See also Lawler, E. E. (1990). *Strategic pay.* San Francisco, CA: Jossey-Bass.

9. William Mercer Inc. (1996). *Compensation planning survey.* Unpublished report.

10. Anonymous (2005). The most tangible assets. *Harvard Business Review, 81,* 8.

11. Pfeffer, J. (1998). Six dangerous myths about pay. *Harvard Business Review, 76,* 108–120.

12. Rynes, S. L., Gerhart, B., and Minette, K. A. (2004). The importance of pay in employee motivation: Discrepancies between what people say and what they do. *Human Resource Management, 43,* 381–394.

13. See Becker, Huselid, and Ulrich, *The HR scorecard;* Becker et al., HR as a source of shareholder value; McDonald and Smith, A proven connection. See also Gerhart, B., and Milkovich, G. T. (1992). Employee compensation: Research and practice. In M. D. Dunnette and L. M. Hough (Eds.), *Handbook of industrial and organizational psychology* (2nd ed.), vol 3. Palo Alto, CA: Consulting Psychologists Press, pp. 431–469.

14. See note 12; see also Kahn, A. (1993, September–October). Why incentive plans cannot work. *Harvard Business Review,* pp. 54–63; Bassett, G. (1996, January/February). Merit pay increases are a mistake. *Compensation and Benefits Review,* pp. 20–22.

15. Labor Letter (1989, December 5). *The Wall Street Journal,* p. 1. See also Wright, P. (1994, May–June). Goal setting and monetary incentives: Motivational tools that can work too well. *Compensation and Benefits Review,* pp. 41–49.

16. Rynes, Gerhart, and Parks, Personnel psychology: Performance evaluation and pay for performance, pp. 571–600.

17. Ibid.

18. Bernardin, H. J. (1992). An "analytic" framework for customer-based performance content development and appraisal. *Human Resource Management Review, 2,* 81–102.

19. Lawler, E. E. (1984). Pay for performance: A motivational analysis. *University of Southern California Report,* G84–9(57), p. 12. See also Wagner, J. A. III, Rubin, P., and Callahan, T. J. (1988). Incentive payment and nonmanagerial productivity: An interrupted time series analysis of magnitude and trend. *Organizational Behavior and Human Decision Processes, 42,* 47–74.

20. Lawler, E. E. (2002). Pay strategy: New thinking for the new millennium. In G. Furtz et al. (Eds.), *Human resource management.* Upper Saddle River, NJ, Prentice Hall, pp. 308–316.

21. Bernardin, H. J., and Villanova, P. J. (1986). Performance appraisal. In E. Locke (Ed.), *Generalizing from laboratory to field research.* Boston, MA: D. C. Heath.

22. Tully, S. (1993, November 1). Your paychecks get exciting. *Fortune,* p. 83.

23. Kay, I. (1990, August 9). Quoted in Labor Letter. *The Wall Street Journal,* p. 1.

24. Kanter, R. M. (January 1987). From status to contribution implications of the changing basis for pay. *Personnel,* pp. 12–24. See also Konrad, A. M., and Pfeffer, J. (1990). Do you get what you deserve? Factors affecting the relationship between productivity and pay. *Administrative Science Quarterly, 35,* 258–285.

25. Editorial (2006, January 2). Another Marie Antoinette moment. *New York Times* online.

26. National Center for Employee Ownership, www.NCEO.org.

27. See Heneman, *Merit pay.*

28. Sauner, A. M., and Hawk, E. J. (1994, July–August). Realizing the potential of teams through team-based rewards. *Compensation and Benefits,* pp. 24–33. See also Wageman, R. (1995, March). Interdependence and group effectiveness. *Administrative Science Quarterly, 40*(1), 145–180; Wright, P. M. (1994, May/June). Goal setting and monetary incentives: Motivational tools that can work too well. *Compensation and Benefits Review,* pp. 41–49; Zingheim, P. K., and Schuster, J. R. (1995, November/December). First Findings: The team pay research study. *Compensation and Benefits Review,* pp. 6–32.

29. Ledford, G. E., Lawler, E. E., and Mohrman, S. A. (1995). Reward innovations in Fortune 1000 companies. *Compensation and Benefits Review, 27,* 76–80. See also DeMatteo, J. S., and Eby, L. T. (August 1997). Who likes team rewards? An examination of individual difference variables related to satisfaction with team-based rewards. *Best Papers Proceedings.* Boston: Academy of Management, pp. 134–138.

30. See DeMatteo and Eby, Who likes team rewards?

31. Rynes, Gerhart, and Parks. Personnel psychology: Performance evaluation and pay for performance, p. 586.

32. Lawler, E. E. (2003). Reward practices and performance management system effectiveness. *Organizational Dynamics, 32,* 403.

33. Banker, R. D., Lee, S., Potter, G., and Srinivasan, D. (1996). Contextual analysis of performance impacts of outcome-based incentive compensation. *Academy of Management Journal, 39*(4), 920–948.

34. Taylor, F. W. (1967). *Principles of scientific management.* New York: Norton. See also Taylor, F. W. (1895). A piece rate system, being a step toward partial solution of the labor problem. *American Society of Mechanical Engineers, 16,* 856–883.

35. See Collins, Death of a gain sharing plan; Lawler and Cohen, Designing a pay system for teams.

36. Halsey, F. A. (1891). The premium plan of paying for labor. Transactions. *American Society of Mechanical Engineers, 12,* 755–764.

37. See Collins, Death of a gain sharing plan; Lawler and Cohen, Designing a pay system for teams.

38. Ibid.

39. Schwinger, P. (1975). *Wage incentive systems.* New York: Halsted.

40. Banker, R. D., Lee, S., and Potter, G. (1996). A field study of the impact of a performance-based incentive plan. *Journal of Accounting and Economics, 21*(2), 195–226.

41. Hauser, J. R., Simester, D., and Wernerfelt, B. (1994). Customer satisfaction incentives. *Journal of Marketing, 13*(4), 327–350; Heneman, *Merit pay;* Bivins, J. (1989). Focus on compensation. *Stores, 71*(9), 25–30; Burns, K. C. (1992). A bonus plan that promotes customer service: Star performance—Bonus plan of Aetna Life and Casualty Co. *Compensation and Benefits Review, 24*(5), 15–20; Coopers and Lybrand. (1993). *Compensation planning for 1993.* New York: Coopers and Lybrand; Hills instills employee incentives to lure repeat business. (1993). *Discount Store News, 32*(9), 61; Kanter, R. M. (1989). The new managerial work. *Harvard Business Review, 67*(6), 85–92; Levy and Olive Garden restaurants introduce incentive plans to improve customer service (November 1992). *Restaurants and Institutions;* Schlesinger, L. A., and Heskett, J. L. (1991). The service driven service company. *Harvard Business Review, 69*(5), 71–81.

42. Henderson, R. I. (2000). *Compensation management,* 8th ed. Englewood Cliffs, NJ: Prentice Hall.

43. Mercile, K., and Lund, J. (August 1995). Variable compensation plans, overtime calculations and the Fair Labor Standards Act. *Labor Law Journal, 46*(8), 492–503.

44. Pritchard, R. D., Jones, S. D., Roth, P. L., Stuebing, K. K., and Ekeberg, S. E. (1988). Effects of group feedback, goal setting, and incentives on organizational productivity. *Journal of Applied Psychology, 73*(2), 337–358.

45. Coyle-Shapiro, J. A., Morrow, P. C., Richardson, R., and Dunn, S. R. (2002). Using profit sharing to enhance employee attitudes: A longitudinal examination of the effects on trust and commitment. *Human Resource Management, 41,* 423–439.

46. Ibid., p. 439.

47. Alexander Consulting Group. (1992). Health care costs, quality top lists of human resource concerns. *Employee Benefit Plan Review, 47*(3), 38–39; see also Welbourne, T. M., Balkin, D. B., and Gomez-Mejia, L. R. (1995, June). Gainsharing and mutual monitoring: A combined agency–organizational justice interpretation. *Academy of Management Journal, 38*(3), 881–899; Belcher, J. G., Jr. (1994, May/June). Gainsharing and variable pay: The state of the art. *Compensation and Benefits Review,* pp. 50–60.

48. Welbourne, T. M., and Gomez-Mejia, L. R. (1988, July/August). Gainsharing revisited. *Compensation and Benefits Review,* pp. 19–28.

49. Lawler and Cohen, Designing a pay system for teams.

50. Schuster, M. (1987, Winter). Gainsharing. Do it right the first time. *Sloan Management Review,* p. 23. See also Bullock, R. J., and Lawler, E. E. (1984). Gainsharing: A few questions, and fewer answers. *Human Resource Management, 23*(1), 23–40; Hatcher, L., and Ross, T. L. (1991). From individual incentives to an organization-wide gainsharing plan: Effects on teamwork and product quality. *Journal of Organizational Behavior, 12,* 169–183; Rollins, T. (1989, May/June). Productivity-based group incentive plans: Powerful, but use with caution. *Compensation and Benefits Review,* pp. 39–50.

51. Lesieur, F. (1958). *The Scanlon plan: A frontier in labor management relations.* New York: John Wiley and Sons.

52. Graham-Moore, B. (1990). 17 years of experience with the Scanlon plan: Desota revisited. In B. Graham-Moore and T. L. Ross (Eds.), *Gainsharing.* Washington, DC: Bureau of National Affairs, pp. 139–173.

53. Thigpen, P. (1994). Quoted in J. Pfeffer, *Competitive advantage through people.* Boston: Harvard Business Press, p. 62.

54. Fein, M. (1980). *An alternative to traditional managing.* Hillsdale, NJ: Mitchell Fein.

55. Kaufman, R. (1992). The effects of IMPROSHARE on productivity. *Industrial and Labor Relations Review, 45,* 311–322.

56. Schuster, J. R., and Zingheim, P. K. (1992). *The new pay: Linking employee and organizational performance.* New York: Lexington Books.

57. Wartzman, R. (1992, May 4). A Whirlpool factory raises productivity—and pay of workers. *The Wall Street Journal,* pp. A1, A4.

58. Scontrino, P. (1995, July–August). An effective productivity and quality tool. *Journal for Quality and Participation, 18*(4), 90–93. See also Reward Staff (1994, March). Sharing the gains of improved performance. *Personnel Review, 23*(2), 47–49.

59. McAninch, L. (1995, November). Gainsharing creates an environment that supports TQM. *Management Accounting, 77*(5), 38–39.

60. Imberman, W. (1995, November). Is gainsharing the wave of the future? *Management Accounting, 77*(5), 35–38.

61. Belcher, J. G., Jr. (1994, May/June). Gainsharing and variable pay: The state of the art. *Compensation and Benefits Review, 26*(3), 50–60.

62. Hewitt Associates (1995, January/February). Case studies: Whirlpool, Nike, Salomon and PSEG. *Compensation and Benefits Review,* pp. 71–76.

63. Kim, D. (1996, April). Factors influencing organizational performance in gainsharing programs. *Industrial Relations, 35*(2), 227–244.

64. Rynes, Gerhart, and Parks, Personnel psychology: Performance evaluation and pay for performance, p. 590.

65. Kaufman, The effects of IMPROSHARE on productivity, p. 311.

66. Capell, K. (1996, July 22). Options for everyone. *BusinessWeek,* pp. 80–84.

67. National Center for Employee Ownership, www.NCEO.ORL.

68. Blasi, J., Conte, M., and Kruse, D. (1996). Employee stock ownership and corporate performance among public companies. *Industrial and Labor Relations Review, 50,* 63; see also Blasi, J. (1985). *Employee ownership: Revolution not ripoff.* New York: John Wiley and Sons; Florkowski, G. W. (1991). Profit sharing and public policy: Insights for the United States. *Industrial Relations, 30,* 96–115; Florkowski, G. W. (1987). The organizational impact of profit sharing. *Academy of Management Review, 12,* 622–636; Hammer, T. H. (1988). New developments in profit sharing, gain sharing, and employee ownership. In J. P. Campbell, R. J. Campbell, and Associates (Eds.), *Productivity in organizations.* San Francisco: Jossey-Bass; Klein, K. J. (1987). Employee stock ownership and employee attitudes: A test of three models. *Journal of Applied Psychology* [monograph], *72,* 319–332; Kruse, D. L. (1991). Profit-sharing and employment variability: Microeconomic evidence on the Weitzman theory. *Industrial and Labor Relations Review, 44,* 437–453; Pierce, J. L., Rubenfeld, S., and Morgan, S. (1991). Employee ownership: A conceptual model of process and effects. *Academy of Management Review, 16,* 121–144.

69. Kraizberg, E., Tziner, A., and Weisberg, J. (2002). Employee stock options: Are they indeed superior to other incentive compensation schemes? *Journal of Business and Psychology, 16,* 212–228.

70. Editorial, Another Marie Antoinette moment.

71. Crystal, G. S. (1984). Pay for performance: It's not dead after all. *Compensation Review, 3,* 24–25.

72. Lublin, J. S. (1998, April 9). Pay for no performance. *The Wall Street Journal,* pp. R1–R18.

73. DeCarlo, S. (Ed.) (2005). Special report: CEO compensation. *Forbes,* www.Forbes.com/2005/ceoland.

74. Bebchuk, L., and Fried, J. (2004). *Pay without performance: The unfulfilled promise of executive compensation.* Boston: Harvard University Press; see also Byrne, J. A. (2002, May 6). How to fix corporate governance. *BusinessWeek,* pp. 69–78.

75. Ozanian, M. K., and MacDonald, E. (2005). Paychecks on steroids. *Forbes,* www.Forbes.com/2005/ceoland.

76. Hambrick, D. C., and Siegel, P. A. (1997). Pay dispersion within top management groups: Harmful effects on performance of high-technology firms. *Best paper proceedings.* Boston: Academy of Management, pp. 26–28.

77. Thompson, J. H., Smith, L. M., and Murray, A. F. (September/October 1986). Management performance incentives: Three critical issues. *Compensation and Benefits Review,* pp. 41–47.

78. Crystal, G. (2002, May 8). What's best when it comes to options accounting. Bloomberg.com. Congress periodically revises legislation controlling the awarding of stock options.

79. Byrne, How to fix corporate governance.

80. Ibid.

81. Edelstein, C. M. (1981). Long-term incentives for management, Part 4. Restricted stock. *Compensation Review,* pp. 31–40. See also Kerr, J., and Bettis, R. A. (1987). Board of directors, top management compensation, and shareholder returns. *Academy of Management Journal, 30,* 645–665.

82. Byrne, How to fix corporate governance.

83. Dunlap, A. (1997, August 10). Final front in crusade for corporate reform. *New York Times,* p. F13.

84. Lublin, J. (1991, June 4). Are chief executives paid too much? *The Wall Street Journal,* p. B1.

85. Balkin, D. B., and Logan, J. W. (1988, January/February). Reward policies that support entrepreneurship. *Compensation and Benefits Review,* pp. 19–32. See also Kahn, L. M., and Sherer, P. D. (1990). Contingent pay and managerial performance. *Industrial and Labor Relations Review, 43,* 107S–120S.

86. See Collins, Death of a gain sharing plan; Lawler and Cohen, Designing a pay system for teams. See also Kerr, J., and Slocum, J. W., Jr. (1987). Managing corporate culture through reward systems. *Academy of Management Executive, 1*(2), 99–108.

87. See Collins, Death of a gain sharing plan.

88. Rynes, Gerhart, and Parks, Personnel psychology: Performance evaluation and pay for performance, p. 590.

89. Ibid.

CHAPTER 12

1. Adapted from Muhl, C. J. (2001). The employment-at-will doctrine: Three major exceptions. *Monthly Labor Review, 124*(1), 3–11.

2. Huselid, M. A., Becker, B. E., and Beatty, R. W. (2005). *The workforce scorecard: Managing human capital to execute strategy.* Boston: Harvard Business School Press.

3. Harter, J. K., Schmidt, F. L., and Hayes T. L. (2002). Business-unit-level relationship between employee satisfaction, employee engagement, and business outcomes: A meta-analysis. *Journal of Applied Psychology, 87,* 268–279.

4. Greenberg, J., and Colquitt, J. A. (2006). *Handbook of organizational justice.* Mahwah, NJ: Erlbaum.

5. Lansberg, I. (1984). Hierarchy as a mediator of fairness: A contingency approach to distributive justice in organizations. *Journal of Applied Social Psychology, 14,* 124–135.

6. Sheppard, B. H., Lewicki, R. J., and Minton, J. W. (1992). *Organizational justice: The search for fairness in the workplace.* New York: Lexington Books.

7. Brockner, J. (2002). Making sense of procedural fairness: How high procedural fairness can reduce or heighten the influence of outcome favorability. *Academy of Management Review, 27,* 58–76.

8. Simons, T., and Roberson, Q. (2003). Why managers should care about fairness: The effects of aggregate justice perceptions on organizational outcomes. *Journal of Applied Psychology, 88,* 441.

9. Barrier, M. (1998). Doing the right thing. *Nation's Business, 86*(3), 32–38; Wells, S. J. (1999). Turn employees into saints? *HR Magazine, 44*(13), 48–58; Rafalko, R. J. (1994). Remaking the corporation: The 1991 U.S. sentencing guidelines. *Journal of Business Ethics, 13,* 625–636.

10. Ethics Resource Center (2003). *National business ethics survey executive summary,* http://www.ethics.org/nbes2003/ 2003nbes_summary.html.

11. Greengard, S. (1997). Lockheed Martin is game for ethics. *Workforce, 76*(10), 51; Wells, Turn employees into saints?

12. Holcomb, B. (July 1991). Time off: The benefit of the hour. *Working Mother Magazine,* pp. 31–35; Shockley, K. M. and Allen, T. D. (2007, December). When flexibility helps: Another look at the availability of flexible work arrangements and work-family conflict. *Journal of Vocational Behavior, 71*(3), 479–493.

13. Gajendran, R. S., and Harrison, D. A. (2007, November). The good, the bad, and the unknown about telecommuting: Meta-analysis of psychological mediators and individual consequences. *Journal of Applied Psychology, 92*(6), 1524–1541; see also Bailey, D. E., and Kurland, N. B. (2002). A review of telework research: Findings, new directions, and lessons for the study of modern work. *Journal of Organizational Behavior, 23,* 383–400.

14. Ford, M. T., Heinen, B. A., and Langkamer, K. L. (2007). Work and family satisfaction and conflict: A meta-analysis of cross-domain relations. *Journal of Applied Psychology, 92,* 57–80; see also Greenhaus, J. H., and Beutell, N. J. (1985). Sources of conflict between work and family roles. *Academy of Management Review, 10,* 76–88; Kush, K., and Stroh, L. (1994, September–October). Flextime: Myth or reality? *Business Horizons,* pp. 51–55; Bureau of National Affairs (1992, September 3). *Flexible work schedules.* Bulletin to Management, pp. 276–277.

15. Fernandez, J. P. (1986). *Child care and corporate productivity: Resolving family/work conflicts.* Lexington, MA: D. C. Heath and Co.; Breaugh, J. A., and Frye, N. K. (2008, June). Work-family conflict: The importance of family-friendly employment practices and family-supportive supervisors. *Journal of Business and Psychology, 22*(4), 345–353.

16. Sheppard, E. M., Clifton, T. J., and Kruse, D. (1996). Flexible work hours and productivity: Some evidence from the pharmaceutical industry. *Industrial Relations, 35,* 123–129; see also Casper, W. J., and Buffardi, L. C. (2004). The impact of work/life benefits and perceived organizational support on job pursuit intentions. *Journal of Vocational Behavior, 65,* 391–410.

17. Hornung, Severin, Rousseau, Denise M., and Glaser, Jürgen (2008, May). Creating flexible work arrangements through idiosyncratic deals. *Journal of Applied Psychology, 93*(3), 655–664; Holcomb, B. (1991, July). Time off: The benefit of the hour. *Working Mother Magazine,* pp. 31–35.

18. Fernandez, *Child care and corporate productivity.*

19. Catalyst. (2001). A new approach to flexibility: Managing the work/time equation. Available at www.catalystwomen.org/ press/factsheets/factspt.html, accessed August 24, 2001.

20. Closson, M. (1976, October 25). Company couples flourish. *BusinessWeek,* p. 112.

21. Solomon, C. M. (1994, September). Job sharing: One job, double headache? *Personnel Journal,* pp. 88–96.

22. Greengard, S. (1995, November). Discover best practices through benchmarking. *Personnel Journal,* pp. 62–73. See also Schneier, C. E., and Johnson, C. (1993, Spring/Summer). Benchmarking: A tool for improving performance management and reward systems. *American Compensation Association Journal,* pp. 14–31.

23. Holcomb, Time off; Solomon, C. M. (1991, August). 24-hour employees. *Personnel Journal,* p. 56.

24. Wanous, J. P. (1992). *Recruitment, selection, orientation, and socialization of newcomers.* Reading, MA: Addison-Wesley.

25. Schneider, B., and Schmitt, N. W. (1986). Staffing organizations (2nd ed.). Glenview, IL: Scott, Foresman.

26. McEvoy, G. M., and Cascio, W. F. (1985). Strategies for reducing employee turnover: A meta-analysis. *Journal of Applied Psychology, 70,* 342–353; Premack, S. L., and Wanous, J. P. (1985). A meta-analysis of realistic job preview experiments. *Journal of Applied Psychology, 70,* 706–719; Wanous, J. P., and Colella, A. (1989). Organizational entry research: Current status and future directions. *Research in Personnel and Human Resource Management, 7,* 59–120.

27. Greenhaus, J. H., and Callanan, G. A. (1994). *Career management.* Fort Worth, TX: Dryden Press.

28. SHRM (1997). *Survey of Human Resource Trends.* Available at www.shrm.org/press/releases/default.asp? page=hrtrend2.htm, accessed April 11, 2001.

29. Ibid.

30. Horowitz, A. (1999). Up to speed—fast. *Computerworld, 33*(7), 48.

31. Saks, A. M., and Ashforth, B. E. (1997). Organizational socialization: Making sense of the past and present as a prologue for the future. *Journal of Vocational Behavior, 51,* 234–279.

32. Ganzel, R. (1998). Putting out the welcome mat. *Training, 35*(3), 54–62.

33. Ibid.

34. Chao, G. T. (1997). Unstructured training and development: The role of organizational socialization. In J. K. Ford (Ed.), *Improving training effectiveness in work organizations.* Mahwah, NJ: Lawrence Erlbaum.

35. Ibid.

36. Ganzel, R. (1998). More than a handshake. *Training, 35*(3), 60.

37. Ganzel, Putting out the welcome mat.

38. Lindo, D. K. (1993). Orientation express. *Office Systems, 10*(11), 64–67.

39. Feldman, D. C. (1988). *Managing careers in organizations.* Glenview, IL: Scott, Foresman.

40. Muhl, C. J. (2001). The employment-at-will doctrine: Three major exceptions. *Monthly Labor Review, 124*(1), 3–11.

41. Lanza, R. and Warren, M. (2006). *United States: Employment at will prevails despite exceptions to the rule.* SHRM Whitepaper (SHRM.org); see also Walsh, D. J., and Schwarz, J. L. (1996). State common law wrongful discharge doctrines: Update, refinement, and rationales. *American Business Law Journal, 33,* 645–689.

42. Siegel, M. (1998). Yes, they can fire you. *Fortune, 138*(8), 301.

43. Miethe, T. D. (1999). *Whistleblowing at work.* Boulder, CO: Westview Press.

44. Ibid.

45. Ibid.

46. Gurchiek, K. (2005). Survey: No clear consensus on noncompete agreements. *HR Legal Reporter,* www.SHRM.org.

47. Ibid.; Flynn, G. (1995). Balance on the fine line of employee privacy. *Personnel Journal, 74*(3), 90–92.

48. Ibid.

49. Ibid.

50. Addison, J. T., and Blackburn, M. L. (1994). The Worker Adjustment and Retraining Notification Act: Effects on notice provision. *Industrial and Labor Relations Review, 47,* 650–662.

51. Hatch, D. D., and Hall, J. E. (1999). Unforeseen circumstance precludes WARN notice. *Workforce, 78*(1), 107.

52. Muhl, C. J. (1999). WARN Act. *Monthly Labor Review, 122*(4), 45.

53. Harter, Schmidt, and Hayes, Business-unit-level relationship between employee satisfaction, employee engagement, and business outcomes, p. 279.

54. Ehrenfeld, T. (1993). The (handbook) handbook. *Inc., 15*(11), 57–64.

55. *Burlington Industries, Inc. v. Ellerth,* 524 U.S. 742, 118 S. Ct. 2257, 141 L. Ed. 2d 633 (1998), aff'g 123 F. 3d 490.

56. Webb, S. (1991). *Step forward: Sexual harassment in the workplace.* Winchester, VA: Master Media.

57. Abenathy, D. J. (1998). Who's watching the net? *Training & Development, 52*(11), 18.

58. Ibid.

59. Muhl, The employment-at-will doctrine; Rasmusson, E. (March 2001). Protective measures: Put policies in place to protect your company from employee lawsuits. *Working Woman Magazine,* p. 26; Flynn, G. (2000). Take another look at the employee handbook. *Workforce, 79*(3), 132–134.

60. Muhl, The employment-at-will doctrine.

61. Arvey, R. D., and Jones, A. P. (1985). The use of discipline in organizational settings. In B. M. Staw and L. L. Cummings (Eds.), *Research in organizational behavior,* vol. 7. Greenwich, CT: JAI Press, pp. 47–82.

62. Raines, C. (1997). *Beyond generation X: A practical guide for managers.* Menlo Park, CA: Crisp Publications.

63. McCabe, D. M. (1997). Alternative dispute resolution and employee voice in nonunion employment: An ethical analysis of organizational due process procedures and mechanisms—the case of the United States. *Journal of Business Ethics, 16,* 349–356.

64. Thibaut, J., and Walker, L. (1975). *Procedural justice: A psychological analysis.* Hillsdale, NJ: Erlbaum.

65. Balfour, A. (1984). Five types of non-union grievance systems. *Personnel, 61,* 67–76.

66. McCabe, Alternative dispute resolution.

67. Tasini, J., and Houston, P. (1986, September 15). Letting workers help handle workers' gripes. *BusinessWeek,* p. 82.

68. McCabe, Alternative dispute resolution.

69. Morin, W. J., and Yorks, L. (1990). *Dismissal.* New York: Drake Beam Morin.

70. Pinder, C. C. (1988). *Work motivation in organizational behavior.* Upper Saddle River, NJ: Prentice Hall.

71. Lind, E. A., Greenberg, J., Scott, K. S., and Welchans, T. D. (2000). The winding road from employee to complainant: Situational and psychological determinants of wrongful-termination claims. *Administrative Science Quarterly, 45,* 557–590.

72. Ensman, R. G. (1998). Firing line. *Office Systems, 15*(3), 67; Garron, R. S. (2001). Take action on poor performance. *InfoWorld, 23*(7), 69; Latack, J. C., and Kaufman, H. G. (1988). Termination and outplacement strategies. In M. London and E. M. Mone (Eds.), *Career growth and human resource strategies.* New York: Quorum Books; Marchetti, M. (1997). The fine art of firing. *Sales and Marketing Management, 149*(4), 67; Opperman, M. (1997). Firing a problem employee. *Veterinary Economics, 38*(5), 34–36.

73. Middlebrook, J. F. (1999). Avoiding brain drain: How to lock in talent. *HR Focus, 76*(3), 9–10.

74. Cole, C. L. (2000). Building loyalty. *Workforce, 79*(8), 42–48; Will, M. (2001). Protecting your company from high turnover. *Women in Business, 53*(2), 30–31.

75. Middlebrook, Avoiding brain drain; Will, Protecting your company from high turnover.

76. Breuer, N. (2000). Shelf life. *Workforce, 79*(8), 28–32; Cole,. Building loyalty; Middlebrook, Avoiding brain drain; Taylor, J. (April 1999). Avoid avoidable turnover. *Workforce, Supplement, 6;* Will, Protecting your company from high turnover.

77. Giacalone, R. A., Knouse, S. B., and Montagliani, A. (1997). Motivation for and prevention of honest responding in exit interviews and surveys. *Journal of Psychology, 131,* 438–448.

78. Lilienthal, S. M. (2000). Screen and glean: What do workers really think of your company? And if they leave, what can your firm learn from their departure? *Workforce, 79*(10), 71, 80.

79. Taylor, Avoid avoidable turnover.

80. Giacalone, Knouse, and Montagliani, Motivation for and prevention of honest responding in exit interviews and surveys.

81. Breuer, Shelf life.

82. Levering, R., and Moskowitz, M. (2001). The 100 best companies to work for. *Fortune, 143*(1), 148–168.

83. Wooldridge, A. (2000, March 5). Come back, company man! *New York Times Magazine,* New York Times online.

84. Cascio, W. F. (1993). Downsizing: What do we know? What have we learned? *Academy of Management Executive, 7,* 95–104.

85. Greenhaus, J. H., and Callanan, G. A. (1994). *Career management.* Fort Worth, TX: Dryden Press.

86. Noer, D. M. (1993). *Healing the wounds.* San Francisco, CA: Jossey-Bass.

87. O'Neill, H. M., and Lenn, D. J. (1995). Voices of survivors. Words that downsizing CEOs should hear. *Academy of Management Executive, 9,* 23–34.

88. Cascio, Downsizing.

89. Brockner, J. (1988). *Self-esteem at work.* Lexington, MA: Lexington Books; Pinder, C. C. (1988). *Work motivation in organizational behavior.* Upper Saddle River, NJ: Prentice Hall.

90. Brockner, J., Konovsky, M., Cooper-Schneider, R., Folger, R., Martin, C., and Bies, R. J. (1994). Interactive effects of procedural justice and outcome negativity on victims and survivors of job loss. *Academy of Management Journal, 37,* 397–409.

91. Ibid.

92. Baker, A. M. (1988, Fall). Lessons from the Maine experience. *Human Resource Management, 3,* 315–328; Feldman, D. C., and Leana, C. R. (1989, Summer). Managing layoffs: Experiences at the Challenger disaster site and the Pittsburgh steel mills. *Organizational Dynamics, 18*(1), 52–64; Noer, *Healing the wounds;* Pinder, *Work motivation in organizational behavior;* Settles, M. F. (1988). Humane downsizing: Can it be done? *Journal of Business Ethics, 7,* 961–963.

93. Latack, J. C., and Kaufman, H. G. (1988). Termination and outplacement strategies. In M. London and E. M. Mone (Eds.), *Career growth and human resource strategies.* New York: Quorum Books.

94. Feldman, D. C. (1995). The impact of downsizing on organizational career and employee career development opportunities. *Human Resource Management Review, 5*(3), 189–221.

95. Rosen, B., and Jerdee, T. H. (1985). *Older employees: New roles for valued resources.* Homewood, IL: Dow Jones-Irwin, p. 143.

96. Feldman, D. C. (1994). The decision to retire early: A review and conceptualization. *Academy of Management Review, 19,* 285–311.

97. Adams, G. A., and Beehr, T. A. (1998). Turnover and retirement: A comparison of their similarities and differences. *Personnel Psychology, 51,* 643–665.

98. Rosen and Jerdee, *Older employees,* p. 143; Talaga, J. A., and Beehr, T. A. (1995). Are there gender differences in predicting retirement decisions? *Journal of Applied Psychology, 80,* 16–28; Brown, M. T., Fukunaga, C., Umemoto, D., and Wicker, L. (1996). Annual review, 1990–1996: Social class, work, and retirement behavior. *Journal of Vocational Behavior, 49,* 159–189.

99. Rosen and Jerdee, *Older employees,* p. 143.

100. Gerbman, R. (1999). Reach out with retirees. *HR Magazine, 44*(7), 74–80.

101. Greenhaus and Callanan, *Career management.*

102. Siegel, S. R. (1981). Preparation for retirement in commercial banking firms. *The Banker's Magazine, 164*(5), 89–93.

103. Siegel, S. R. (1989, March–April). Preretirement programs in service firms. *Compensation and Benefits Review,* pp. 47–58.

Chapter 13

1. Editorial (2008, February 7). A hopeful year for unions. *New York Times* online.

2. Fiorito, J. (2007). The state of unions in the United States. *Journal of Labor Research, 28,* 43–68; see also Peter Hart Research (June 1999). Americans' attitudes toward unions. Peter Hart and Associates (www.aflcio.org/labor).

3. Schrank, R. (1979). Are unions an anachronism? *Harvard Business Review, 57,* 107–115. See also Flynn, G. (1997). How HR has weathered the changing legal climate. *Workforce, 76*(1), 159, 162.

4. www.bls.gov.

5. See www.aflcio.org.

6. www.nasdag.com/services. "Taking the world by storm," June 12, 2002.

7. Murray, M. K. (2001). The new economy and new union organizing strategies: Union wins in healthcare. *Journal of Nursing Administration, 31,* 339–343; see also Feared, J., and Greyer, C. R. (1982). Determinants of U. S. unionism: Past research and future needs. *Industrial Relations, 21,* 1–32; Heneman, H. G. III, and Sandver, M. H. (1983). Predicting the outcome of union certification elections: A review of the literature. *Industrial and Labor Relations Review, 36,* 537–560; Curme, M. A., Hirsch, B. T., and Macpherson, D. M. (1990). Union membership and contract coverage in the United States, 1983–1988. *Industrial and Labor Relations Review, 44,* 5–33; Newton, L. A., and Shore, L. M. (1992). A model of union membership: Instrumentality, commitment, and opposition. *Academy of Management Review, 17,* 275–298; Flanagan, R. (Winter 2005). "Has Management Strangled U.S. Unions?" *Journal of Labor Research, 26,* 33–63.

8. Bronfenbrenner, K. (1997). The role of union strategies in NLRB certification elections. *Industrial and Labor Relations Review, 50*(2), 195–212.

9. Brett, J. M. (1980). Why employees want unions. *Organizational Dynamics, 8,* 47–59.

10. http://www.dol.gov/esa/programs/whd/state/righttowork.htm.

11. Bronfenbrenner, K., and Hickey, R. (2004). Changing to organize: A national assessment of union strategies. In Milkman, R., and Voss, K. (Eds.), *Rebuilding labor.* Ithaca, NY: Cornell University Press.

12. *Town and Country Electric v. NLRB, No. 94–947* (U.S. S. Ct., November 18, 1995).

13. Freeman, R. B., and Kleiner, M. M. (1990). Employer behavior in the face of union organizing drives. *Industrial & Labor Relations Review, 43,* 451–466; Morris, C. J. (1998). A tale of two statutes: Discrimination for union activity under the NLRA and RLA. *Employment Rights and Policy Journal, 18,* 327, 329–30.

14. Martin, A.W. (2008). The institutional logic of union organizing and the effectiveness of social movement repertoires. *American Journal of Sociology, 113,* 1067–1103.

15. U.S. BLS (www.bls.gov). See also Freeman, R.B. (2005). What do unions do? *Journal of Labor Research, 26,* 641–669.

16. Bureau of Labor Statistics (2008) (www.bls.gov).

17. Fiorito, J. (2007). The state of unions in the United States. *Journal of Labor Research, 28,* 51; see also, Pfeffer, J. (1994). *Competitive advantage through people.* Boston: Harvard Business School Press, p. 163. See also Hirsch, B. T. (1991). Union coverage and profitability among U.S. firms. *Review of Economics and Statistics, 73,* 69–77.

18. Freeman, What do unions do? see also Burton, J. F. (Ed.) (1985). Review symposium: What do unions do? *Industrial and Labor Relations Review, 38,* 244–263; Kramer, J. K., and Vasconcellos, G. M. (1996). The economic effect of strikes on the shareholders of nonstruck competitors. *Industrial and Labor Relations Review, 49*(2), 213–222; Beaumont, P. B., and Harris, R. I. D. (1996). Good industrial relations, joint problem solving, and HRM. *Industrial Relations Quebec, 51*(2), 391–406; GM local labor dispute spins out of control. (March 13, 1996). *The Wall Street Journal,* pp. B1, B3.

19. Hirsch, B (2004). What do unions do for economic performance? *Journal of Labor Research, 25,* p. 415; see also, Karier, T. (1991). Unions and the U.S. comparative advantage. *Industrial Relations, 30*(1) 235–272; Becker, B. E., and Olsen, C. A. (1987). Labor relations and firm performance. In M. M. Kleiner, R. N. Block, M. Roomkin, and S. W. Salsburg (Eds.), *Human resources and performance of the firm.* Madison, WI: Industrial Relations Research Association, pp. 43–86; Cutcher-Gershenfeld, J. (1991). The impact of economic performance on a transformation in workplace relations. *Industrial and Labor Relations Review, 44,* 241–260.

20. Becker, B., Huselid, M., and Ulrich, D. (2001). *The HR scorecard.* Boston, MA: Harvard Business Press.

21. Rubinstein, S. A. (2000). The impact of co-management on quality performance: The case of the Saturn Corporation. *Industrial and Labor Relations Review, 53,* 197–218. See also Ferman, L. A., Hoyman, M., Cutcher-Gershenfeld, J., and Savoie, E. J. (Eds.) (1991). *Joint training programs: A union–management approach to preparing workers for the future.* Ithaca, NY: ILR Press, School of Industrial and Labor Relations, Cornell University; Hammer, T. H., Curall, S. C., and Stern, R. N. (1991). Worker representation on board of directors: A study of competing roles. *Industrial and Labor Relations Review, 44,* 661–680.

22. Gold, C. (1986). *Labor management committees: Confrontation, cooptation, or cooperation?* Ithaca, NY: ILR Press.

23. Doellgast, V. (2008). Collective bargaining and high-involvement management in comparative perspective: Evidence from U.S. and German call centers. *Industrial Relations, 47,* 284–319; see also Goll, I., and Hochner, A. (1987). Labor–management practices as a function of environmental pressures and corporate ideology in union and nonunion settings. *Proceedings of the Fortieth Annual Meeting of the Industrial Relations Research Association,* pp. 516–524; Miller, R. L. (1996). Employee participation and contemporary labor law in the U.S. *Industrial Relations Journal, 27*(2), 166–174.

24. The UAW continues its efforts to improve quality. (1996). *Quality Progress, 29*(7), 62–63.

25. Hirsch, B. (2004). What do unions do for economic performance? *Journal of Labor Research, 25,* 415–455; Katz, H. C., Kochan, T. A., and Gobeille, K. R. (1984). Industrial relations performance, economic performance, and QWL programs: An interplant analysis. *Industrial and Labor Relations Review, 37,* 3–17. See also Katz, H. C., Kochan, T. A., and Weber, M. C. (1985). Assessing the effects of industrial relations systems and efforts to improve the quality of working life on organizational effectiveness. *Academy of Management Review, 28,* 509–526; Cooke, W. N. (1994). Employee participation programs, group-based incentives and company performance: A union–nonunion comparison. *Industrial and Labor Relations Review, 47*(4), 594–609.

26. Verma, A. (2005). What do unions do to the workplace? Union effects on management and HRM policies. *Journal of Labor Research, 26,* 417–451; see also Steel, R. P., Jennings, K. R., Mento, A. J., and Hendricks, W. H. (August 1988). Effects of institutional employee participation on industrial labor relations. Paper presented at the meeting of the Academy of Management, Anaheim, CA.

27. Leana, C. R., Ahlbrandt, R. S., and Murrell, A. J. (1992). The effects of employee involvement programs on unionized workers' attitudes, perceptions, and preferences in decision making. *Academy of Management Journal, 35*(4), 861–873.

28. Feared, J., Lowman, C., and Nelson, F. D. (1987). The impact of human resource policies on union organizing. *Industrial Relations, 26,* 113–126.

29. *Electromation, Inc. v. NLRB,* 35 F. 3d 1148 (7th Cir. 1994).

30. LeRoy, M. H. (2006). The power to create or obstruct employee voice; does U.S. public policy skew employer preference for "no voice" workplaces? *Socio–Economic Review, 4,* 311–319.

31. Hammer, T., and Avgar, A. (2005). The impact of unionism on job satisfaction, organizational commitment, and turnover. *Journal of Labor Research, 26,* 241–266.

32. Gordon, M. E., and DeNisi, A. S. (1995). A re-examination of the relationship between union membership and job satisfaction. *Industrial Relations Review, 48,* 222–236.

33. Blumenfeld, S. B., and Partridge, M. D. (Winter 1996). The long-run and short-run impacts of global competition on U.S. union wages. *Journal of Labor Research, 17*(1), 149–171.

34. Pynes, J. E. (1996). The two faces of unions. *Journal of Collective Negotiations in the Public Sector, 25,* 31–43.

35. Friedman, R. A. (2006) Bringing mutual gains bargaining to labor negotiations: The role of trust, understanding, and control. *Human Resource Management, 32,* p. 436.

36. Deery, S. J., and Iverson, R. D. (July 2005) Labor-management cooperation: Antecedents and impact on organizational performance. *Industrial and Labor Relations Review, 58,* 588.

37. Cooke, W. N. (July 2005). Exercising power in a prisoner's dilemma: Transnational collective bargaining in an era of corporate globilization. *Industrial Relations Journal, 36,* 283–302; see also Cooke, W. N. (1994). Employee participation programs, group-based incentives, and company performance: A union-nonunion comparison. *Industrial and Labor Relations Review, 47,* 594–609.

38. www.fmcs.gov.

39. Sunoo, B. P. (February 1995). Managing strikes, minimizing loss. *Personnel Journal,* 50–60; see also, Barlow, W. E., Hatch, D. D., and Murphy, B. (1996). Recent legal decisions affect you. *Personnel Journal, 75*(1), 100.

40. www.bls.gov. Work Stoppages Summary.

41. Tivendeel, J., and Watson, C. (1995). Attitudes toward unions as predictors of actual strike behavior. *Ergonomics, 38*(3), 534–538.

42. *NLRB v. Mackay Radio & Telegraph,* 304 U.S. 333 (1938).

43. AFL-CIO Committee for Workplace Fairness. (1990). Washington, DC: AFL-CIO. See also Budd, J. W. (1996). Canadian strike replacement legislation and collective bargaining: Lessons for the U.S. *Industrial Relations, 35*(2), 245–260.

44. Reuters (2006, January 16). Northwest's machinists will vote on concessions. *International Herald Tribune* online.

45. DeFusco, R. A., and Fuess, J. R. (1991). The effects of airline strikes on struck and nonstruck carriers. *Industrial and Labor Relations Review, 44*(2), p. 325.

46. Schnell, J. F., and Gramm, C. L. (1994). The empirical relations between employers' striker replacement strategies and strike duration. *Industrial and Labor Relations Review, 47*(2), 189–206.

47. Dastmalchian, A., and Ng, I. (1990). Industrial relations climate and grievance outcomes. *Industrial Relations, 45,* 311–324. See also Salipante, P. F., and Bouwen, R. (1990). Behavioral analysis of grievances: Conflict sources, complexity and transformation. *Employee Relations, 12,* 17–22.

48. Cohn, J. (2008, November 21). Debunking the myth of the $70-per-hour autoworker. *The New Republic* online. See also, "Bailout money?" *ABC World News* with Charles Gibson (December 3, 2008, broadcast); Leonhardt, D. (2008, December 10). $73 an hour: Adding it up. NYtimes online.

49. See Murray, The new economy and new union organizing strategies; Feared and Greyer, Determinants of U.S. unionism; Heneman and Sandver, Predicting the outcome of union certification elections; Curme, Hirsch, and Macpherson, Union membership and contract coverage; Newton and Shore, A model of union membership. See also Wells, M. J. (2000). Unionization and immigrant incorporation in San Francisco hotels. *Social Problems, 47,* 241–265.

50. Evans, M. (2005, February). Labor's success: Unions make strides recruiting healthcare workers. *The Week in Healthcare* (National Labor Relations Board). *Modern Healthcare.*

51. www.aflcio.org.

52. www.fpd.org.

53. Quote from www.afsme.org/about/aff.108.

54. Mace, R. F. (1988). The Supreme Court's labor law successorship doctrine after Fall River Dyeing. *Labor Law Journal, 39,* 102–109.

55. London, M. (1996). Redeployment and continuous learning in the 21st century: Hard lessons and positive examples from the downsizing era. *Academy of Management Executive, 10*(4), 67–79.

56. www.aflcio.org.

57. See Murray, The new economy and new union organizing strategies; Feared and Greyer, Determinants of U.S. unionism; Heneman and Sandver, Predicting the outcome of union certification elections; Curme, Hirsch, and Macpherson, Union membership and contract coverage; Newton and Shore, A model of union membership.

58. Bronfenbrenner, K., DeWitt, D., Fletcher, B., et al. (2005, February). Future of organized labor in the U.S.: Reinventing trade unionism for the 21st century. *Monthly Review,* online (www.MonthlyReview.org).

59. Ibid.

60. Mills, D. Q. (1994). *Labor–management relations.* New York: McGraw-Hill.

61. A Business International Research Report. (1982). *Managing manpower in Europe.* Business International Corporation. See also Hoerr, J. (1991, February). What should unions do? *Harvard Business Review,* 30–45.

62. Steinmetz, G. (1997, June 12). One union accepts reality, breaking with inflexible past. *The Wall Street Journal,* p. A14.

63. Woodruff, D. (1997, July 28). The German worker is making a sacrifice. *BusinessWeek,* pp. 46–47.

64. Consultation on new strike restrictions. (1996, December). *IRS Employment Review,* pp. 5515–5516.

65. Dowling, P. J., and Schuler, R. S. (1999). *International dimensions of human resource management.* Boston: PWS-Kent.

66. Sloan, A. A. and Whitney, F. (2007) *Labor relations.* Upper Saddle River, N.J.: Prentice Hall.

67. Hammock, B. T. (1996). The extraterritorial application of the National Labor Relations Act: A union perspective. *Syracuse Journal of International Law and Commerce, 22,* 127–154.

68. Rolnick, A. L. (1997, February 3). Muzzling the offshore watchdogs. *Bobbin, 8*(6), 72–73.

69. World Bank (2005, February). Economics perform better in coordinated labor markets (http://web.worldbank.org).

70. Fiorito, J. (2007). The state of unions in the United States. *Journal of Labor Research, 28,* 43.

71. Greenhouse, S. (2005, January 2). Labor board's critics see a bias against workers. *New York Times* online (www.NYTimes.com).

72. Fiorito, J. (2007). p. 43.

CHAPTER 14

1. Bureau of Labor Statistics. (2008). *Workplace injury and illness summary and census of fatal occupational injuries.* Washington, DC: Department of Labor.

2. Health concerns dominate construction lecture. (1997). *Occupational Safety, 15*(1), 37.

3. Frontline (2008, February 5). A dangerous business revisited. Frontline interview with David Uhlman. http://www.pbs.org/wgbh/pages/frontline/mcwane/interviews/uhlmann.html.

4. Labaton, S. (2007, April 25). OSHA leaves worker safety in hands of industry. *New York Times* online.

5. Garland, S. B. (1989, February 20). This safety ruling could be hazardous to employer's health. *BusinessWeek,* p. 34.

6. Labaton, S. (2007, April 25). OSHA leaves worker safety in hands of industry. *New York Times* online; Michigan Supreme Court rules OSH Act does not preempt state proceedings. *BNA's Employee Relations Weekly, 7,* 945.

7. *Health and Safety Statistics.* (2002). Geneva: International Labour Organization (ILO.org). See also Elling, R. H. (1986). *The struggle for workers' health: A study of six industrialized countries.* Farmingdale, NY: Baywood Publishing.

8. Labaton, S. (2007, April 25). OSHA leaves worker safety in hands of industry. *New York Times* online.

9. Bureau of Labor Statistics. (2000). *Survey of work-related health.* Washington, DC: Department of Labor.

10. Leonard, B. (1996, February). Performance testing can add an extra margin of safety. *HR Magazine,* pp. 61–64.

11. National Safety Council. (2005). *Accident facts.* National Safety Council (www.NSC.org) see also Hoskin, A. F. (1995, May). 1994 work-related deaths decline. *Safety and Health, 151*(5), 70–71; Labor Letter. (1991, June 13). *The Wall Street Journal,* p. 1; Karr, A. R. (1990, May 2). White House backs raising penalties levied by OSHA. *The Wall Street Journal,* p. A8.

12. Colburn, L. E. (1995). Defending against workers' compensation fraud. *Industrial Management, 37,* 1–2.

13. Evans, G., and Johnson, D. (2000). Stress and open office noise. *Journal of Applied Psychology, 85,* 779–783.

14. Elsberry, R. B. (1996). Food for thought on plant sanitation. *Electrical Apparatus, 49*(12), 42–43.

15. Dinges, D. (2008, June 15). Quote from *60 Minutes.* "The Science of Sleep." Transcript online.

16. Vlasic, B. (1989, July 23). Death in the workplace. *Detroit News,* p. 1.

17. Armstrong, D. (2008, March 5). Malingerer test roils personal-injury law. *The Wall Street Journal* online (http://online.wsj.com/article/SB120466776681911325.html).

18. Verespej, M. A. (1990, May 21). OSHA goes to court. *Industry Week,* pp. 91–92; see also Redeker, J. R., and Tang, D. J. (1988, April). Criminal accountability for workplace safety. *Management Review,* pp. 32–36; Glaberson, W. (1990, October 17). Court upholds prosecution of employer for job hazard. *New York Times,* p. A16.

19. Greene, M. V. (2005). State plans bring safety control home. NSC Web site (www.NSC.org).

20. OSHA (2008) Inspection reports. http://www.aflcio.org/issues/safety/memorial/upload/_21.pdf.

21. *Marshall v. Barlow's, Inc.,* 436 U.S. 307, 98 S. Ct. 1816, 56 L. Ed. 2d 305 (1978).

22. Fairfax, R. (2007, October 16). *Top 10 OSHA violations in 2007.* http://gneil.blogspot.com/2007/10/top-10-osha-violations-in-2007.html.

23. OSHA issues final rule requiring employers to certify hazard corrections. (1997). *BNAC Communicator, 15*(3), 10.

24. Occupational Safety and Health Administration. (2008). *Voluntary protection programs.* Washington, D.C.

25. Ibid.

26. *Whirlpool Corp. v. Marshall* (1981, February 26). *Daily Labor Report.* Washington, DC: Bureau of National Affairs; *Whirlpool Corp. v. Marshall,* 445 U.S. 1, 100 S. Ct. 883, 63 L. Ed. 2d 154 (1980).

27. *ABC News 20/20* (1999). John Stossel, "Give me a break.".

28. Editorial (2008, August 4). Last-minute mischief for labor. *The New York times* online.

29. See Verespej, OSHA goes to court. See also Brooks, J. (1977). *Failure to meet commitments in the Occupational Safety and Health Act.* Washington, DC: U.S. Congress, Committee on Government Operations; Uzumeri, M. V. (1997). ISO9000 and other metastandards: Principles for management practice? *Academy of Management Executive, 11*(1), 21–36.

30. OSHA doing better job of finding most hazardous workplaces, acting administrator says. (1997). *BNAC Communicator, 15*(3), 29.

31. Bureau of Labor Statistics (2003). *Workplace injury and illness summary and census of fatal occupational injuries.* Washington, DC: Department of Labor.

32. Ibid.

33. Geller, E. S. (1996). *The psychology of safety: How to improve behaviors and attitudes on the job.* Radnor, PA: Chilton Book Company; Geller, E. S. (1994). Ten principles for achieving a total safety culture. *Professional Safety, 39*(9), 18–24; Guastello, S. J. (1993). Do we really know how well our occupational accident prevention programs work? *Safety Science, 16,* 445–463.

34. Ashford, N. A. (1977). *Crisis in the workplace: Occupational disease and injury. A Report to the Ford Foundation.* Cambridge, MA: MIT Press.

35. Schwartz, R. G., and Weinstein, S. M. (1996). Getting a handle on cumulative trauma disorders. *Patient Care, 30,* 118–120; Gangemi, R. A. (1996, July). Ergonomics: Reducing workplace injuries. *Inc.,* p. 92.

36. Geller, E. S. (1996). *Working safe: How to help people actively care for health and safety.* Radnor, PA: Chilton Book Company.

37. Taylor, A. (1997). Danger: Rough road ahead. *Fortune,* pp. 114–118.

38. Pierce, F. D. (1996). 10 rules for better communication. *Occupational Hazards, 58*(5), 78–80.

39. It pays to be nice. (1997, June 12). *The Wall Street Journal,* p. A1.

40. How to get management and employees on board. (1996). *Occupational Health and Safety, 65*(1), 27.

41. Zacharatos, A., Barling, J., and Iverson, R. D. (2005). High-performance work systems and occupational safety. *Journal of Applied Psychology, 90,* 77–93.

42. Turner, N., and Parker, S. K. (2004). The effect of teamwork on safety processes and outcomes. In J. Barling and M. R. Frone (Eds.), *The psychology of workplace safety,* pp. 35–62. Washington, DC: American Psychological Association; see also Parker, S. K., Axtell, C., and Turner, N. (2001). Designing a safer workplace: Importance of job autonomy, communication quality, and supportive supervisors. *Journal of Occupational Health Psychology, 6,* 211–228.

43. Zacharatos, Barling, and Iverson, High-performance work systems and occupational safety, 78. See also Zohar, D. (2003). Safety climate: Conceptual and measurement issues. In J. C. Quick and L. E. Tetrick (Eds.), *Handbook of occupational health psychology,* pp. 123–142. Washington, DC: American Psychological Association.

44. Geller, E. S., Roberts, D. S., and Gilmore, M. R. (1996). Predicting propensity to actively care for occupational safety. *Journal of Safety Research, 27,* 1–8; see also Zohar, D. (2000). A group-level model of safety climate: Testing the effect of group climate on microaccidents in manufacturing jobs. *Journal of Applied Psychology, 85,* 587–596; Zohar, D. (2002). The effects of leadership dimensions, safety climate and assigned priorities on minor injuries in work groups. *Journal of Organizational Behavior, 23,* 75–92; Zohar, D. (2003). The influence of leadership and climate on occupational health and safety. In D. A. Hoffman and L. E. Tetrick (Eds.), *Health and safety in organizations: A multilevel perspective,* pp. 201–230. San Francisco: Wiley.

45. Dunbar, R. (1975, June). Manager's influence on subordinate's thinking about safety. *Academy of Management Journal, 18,* 364–369.

46. OSHA rule requiring forklift training becomes final in September '97. (1997). *BNAC Communicator, 15*(3), 1, 28.

47. Nwaelele, D. D. (1996). Prudent owners take proactive approach. *Professional Safety, 41*(4), 27–29.

48. Van Houten, B. (1997). In the trenches. *Restaurant Business, 96,* 25–30.

49. Komaki, J., Barwick, K. D., and Scott, L. R. (1978). A behavioral approach to occupational safety: Pinpointing and reinforcing safe performance in a food manufacturing plant. *Journal of Applied Psychology, 63,* 434–445; see also Dehaas, D. (1996). The problem with training. *OH and S Canada, 12,* 4.

50. LeBar, G. (1996). The age(ing) of ergonomics. *Occupational Hazards, 58,* 32–33.

51. Breeding, D. C. (1996). Worker empowerment: A useful tool for effective safety management. *Occupational Health and Safety, 65*(9), 16–17.

52. Strahlendorf, P. (1996). What supervisors need to know? *OH and S Canada, 12*(1), 38–40.

53. Roughton, J. E. (1996). When contractors fall short. *Security Management, 40,* 68–71.

54. Laws, J. (1996). The power of incentives. *Occupational Health and Safety, 65*(1), 24–28.

55. Wilson, J. C. (1996). Employee well-being is the real prize. *Occupational Health and Safety, 65,* 168–169.

56. See Laws, The power of incentives.

57. Minter, S. G. (1996). Putting incentives to work. *Occupational Hazards, 58*(6), S7–S9.

58. Case study in safety. (1996). *Incentive, 170*(10), P22–P23.

59. Ibid.

60. See Wilson, Employee well-being is the real prize.

61. Swearingen, M. H. (1996). Do safety incentive programs really help? *Occupational Health and Safety, 65*(10), 164–165.

62. Oswald, E. M. (1996). No employer is immune: AIDS in the workplace. *Risk Management, 43*, 18–21.

63. Smith, J. M. (March 1993). How to develop and implement an AIDS workplace policy. *HR Focus*, p. 15.

64. Feuer, D. (1987, June). AIDS at work: Fighting the fear. *Training*, pp. 61–71; see also Elliott, R. H., and Wilson, T. M. (1987). AIDS in the workplace: Public personnel management and the law. *Public Personnel Management*, pp. 209–219; Breuer, N. L. (1992, January). AIDS issues haven't gone away. *Personnel Journal, 71*, 47–49; Elkiss, H. (1991). Reasonable accommodation and unreasonable fears: An AIDS policy guide for human resource personnel. *Human Resource Planning, 14*, 183–190; Brown, D. R., and Gray, G. R. (1991, Summer). Designing an appropriate AIDS policy. *Employment Relations Today, 18*, 149–155.

65. Kedjidian, C. B. (1995, December). Say no to booze and drugs in your workplace. *Safety and Health, 152*(6), 38–41. See also Labaton, S. (1989, December 5). The cost of drug abuse: $60 billion a year. *New York Times*, pp. B1, B30; Zigarelli, M. A. (1995). Drug testing litigation: Trends and outcomes. *Human Resource Management Review, 5*(4), 267–288; Like, S. K. (1990–1991, Winter). Employee drug testing. *Small Business Reports, 16*(3), 347–358; Lehman, W. E., and Simpson, D. D. (1992). Employee substance use and on-the-job behaviors. *Journal of Applied Psychology, 77*, 309–321.

66. Drug use on the job being probed. (1996, July 5). *Baltimore Sun*, pp. 9c, 11c.

67. American Management Association. (1997). The AMA handbook for developing employee assistance and counseling programs. Washington, DC: AMA. See also Cunningham, G. (1994). *Effective employee assistance programs.* Palo Alto, CA: Sage Publications; Carroll, M. (1996). *Workplace counseling.* Palo Alto, CA: Sage Publications.

68. See Kedjidian, Say no to booze.

69. See AMA, The *AMA handbook.*

70. Dolan, K., Rouen, D., and Kimber, J. (2004). An overview of the use of urine, hair, sweat and saliva to detect drug use. *Drug and Alcohol Review, 23*, 213–217.

71. French, M. T., Roebuck, M. C., and Alexandre, P. K. (2004). To test or not to test: Do workplace drug testing programs discourage employee drug use? *Social Science Research, 33*, 45–63.

72. Schultz, M., Lee, A. and Lacy, E. (2005, January 27). Workers fume as firms ban smoking at home. *The Detroit News* online. http://www.detnews.com/2005/business/0501/27/A01-71823.htm.

73. Litvan, L. M. (1994). A smoke-free workplace? *Nation's Business, 82,* 65; see also Winslow, R. (1995, March 6). Will firms shift costs to smokers? *The Wall Street Journal*, pp. B1, B4; Rundle, R. L. (1990, January 14). U-Haul puts high price on vices of its workers. *The Wall Street Journal*, p. B10; Beck, J. (February 1994). Helping workers breathe free. *Journal of Commerce and Commercial, 399*(28163), 8A.

74. Yandrick, R. M. (1994, July). More employers prohibit smoking. *HR Magazine*, pp. 68–71.

75. Smith, L. (1993, August 9). Can smoking or bungee jumping get you canned? *Fortune, 128*(3), 92; see also Karr, A. R., and Gutfeld, R. (1992, January 16). OSHA inches toward limiting smoking. *The Wall Street Journal*, pp. B1, B7: Bureau of National Affairs. (1991). *Employment guide.* Washington, DC: Bureau of National Affairs.

76. American Management Association. (1999). *Survey of workplace violence.* Washington, DC: AMA.

77. www.shrm.org/survey on violence. See also Epstein, B. D. (1996). Preventing workplace violence. *Provider, 22,* 71–72; Bureau of National Affairs (1993, April 26). Preventing workplace violence: Legal imperatives can clash. *Employee Relations Weekly, 11*(17), 451–452.

78. National Institute for Occupational Safety and Health. (2002). *Violence: Occupational hazards in hospitals.* Washington, DC: U.S. Government Printing Office.

79. Flynn, G. (1996). What can you do about weapons in the workplace? *Personnel Journal, 75*(3), 122–125.

80. Davies, E. (1996). How violence at work can hit employees hard. *People Management, 2*(18), 50–53.

81. Burroughs, S. M., and Jones, J. W. (1995, April). Managing violence: Looking out for trouble. *Occupational Health and Safety*, pp. 34–37.

82. Stage, J. K. (1997). Attack on violence. *Industry Week, 246*(4), 15–18.

83. Kinney, J. A., and Johnson, D. L. (1993). *Breaking point: The workplace violence epidemic and what to do about it.* Chicago: National Safe Workplace Institute.

84. Stevens, W. K. (1991, March 14). Study backs safety of video terminals. *New York Times*, p. C21. See also Sullivan, J. F. (1989, November 29). New Jersey acts on video terminals. *New York Times*, p. Y13; Gettings, L., and Maddox, E. N. (1989). *Overview: When health means wealth. Human resources yearbook.* Englewood Cliffs, NJ: Prentice Hall, pp. 6.1–6.4.

85. Fine, B. (1997). Coping with computers. *Safety and Health Practitioner, 15*(3), 42–43.

86. Collins, J. W., Wolf, I., Bell, J., and Evanoff, B. (2004). An evaluation of a "best practices" musculoskeletal injury prevention program in nursing homes. *Injury Prevention, 10*, 206–211.

87. Buffa, D. (2000, November 16). Not enough hours in a day. *New York Post*, p. 3.

88. Madonia, J. F. (1984, June). Managerial responses to alcohol and drug abuse among employees. *Personnel Administrator, 8*, 134–139.

89. Beehr, T. A., and Newman, J. E. (1990). Job stress, employee health, and organizational effectiveness: A facet analysis, model and literature review. *Personnel Psychology, 31*, 665–699. See also Ivancevich, J. M., and Ganster, D. C. (1987). *Job stress: From theory to suggestion.* New York: Haworth; Schaubroeck, J., Ganster, D. C., and Fox, M. L. (1992). Dispositional affect and work-related stress. *Journal of Applied Psychology, 77*, 322–335.

90. Bruening, J. C. (1996). The ergonomics of the mind: Psychosocial issues in the office. *Managing Office Technology, 41,* 35–36.

91. Matteson, M. T., Ivancevich, J. M., and Smith, S. V. (1984). Relation of Type A behavior to performance and satisfaction among sales personnel. *Journal of Vocational Behavior, 25,* 203–214.

92. Parker, S., and Sprigg, C. A. (1999). Minimizing strain and maximizing learning: The role of job demands, job control, and proactive personality. *Journal of Applied Psychology, 84,* 925–929.

93. Loerch, K. J., Russell, J. E. A., and Rush, M. C. (1989). The relationship among family domain variables and work–family conflict for men and women. *Journal of Vocational Behavior, 35,* 288–308. See also Allen, T. D., Russell, J. E. A., and Rush, M. C. (1994). The effects of gender and leave of absence on attributions for high performance, perceived organizational commitment, and allocation of organizational rewards. *Sex Roles, 31,* 443–464; Chusmir, L., and Durand, D. (May 1987). Stress and the working woman. *Personnel,* pp. 38–43.

94. Conference Board. (1991). *Work schedules and productivity.* Atlanta: The Conference Board.

95. Azar, B. (1997). Quelling today's conflict between home and work. *APA Monitor, 28*(7), 1, 16.

96. Weitlauf, J., Smith, R. E., and Cervone, D. (2000). Generalization effects of coping-skills training: Influence of self-defense training on women's efficacy beliefs, assertiveness, and aggression. *Journal of Applied Psychology, 85,* 625–631.

97. Judge, T. A., and Colquitt, J. A. (2004). Organizational justice and stress: The mediating role of work-family conflict. *Journal of Applied Psychology, 89,* 403; see also Vermunt, R., and Steensma, H. (2001). Stress and justice in organizations: An exploration into justice processes with the aim to find mechanisms to reduce stress. In R. Cropanzano (Ed.), *Justice in the workplace: From theory to practice,* vol. 2, pp. 27–48. Mahwah, NJ: Erlbaum.

98. Ganster, D. C., and Schaubroeck, J. (1991). Work stress and employee health. *Journal of Management, 17,* 235–271; Cartwright, S., and Cooper, C. L. (1997). *Managing workplace stress.* Palo Alto, CA: Sage Publications.

99. Cooper. C. L., and Robertson, I. T., (Eds.), *International review of industrial and organizational psychology.* Chichester, England: Wiley, pp. 235–280.

100. Schaubroeck, J., Lam, S. K., and Xie, J. L. (2000). Collective efficacy versus self-efficacy in coping responses to stressors and control: A cross-cultural study. *Journal of Applied Psychology, 85,* 512–525.

101. Gordes, C. L., and Dougherty, T. (1993). A review and integration of research on burnout. *Academy of Management Journal, 18,* 621–656.

102. Russell, D. W., Altmaier, E., and Velzen, D. V. (1987). Job-related stress, social support, and burnout among classroom teachers. *Journal of Applied Psychology, 72,* 269–274; see also Cherniss, C. (1992). Long-term consequences of burnout: An exploratory study. *Journal of Organizational Behavior, 13,* 1–11; McKeown, S. (1996). Stress: No quack cures, just sensible management. *Works Management, 49*(9), 60–63.

103. Demerouti, E., Bakker, A. B., Nachreiner, F., and Schaufeli, W. B. (2001). The job demands–resources model of burnout. *Journal of Applied Psychology, 86,* 512–517; see also Ganster, D. C., Fox, M. L., and Dwyer, D. J. (2001, October). Explaining employees' health care costs: A prospective examination of stressful job demands, personal control, and physiological reactivity. *Journal of Applied Psychology, 86,* 954–959.

104. Arkin, O. (1997). Time to take account of work, rest, and play. *People Management, 3,* 47–48.

105. Cavanaugh, M. A., Boswell, W. R., Roehling, M. V., and Boudreau, J. (2000). An empirical examination of self- reported work stress among U.S. managers. *Journal of Applied Psychology, 85,* 65–74.

106. Boswell, W. R., Olson-Buchanan, J. B., and LePine, M. A. (2004). Relations between stress and work outcomes: The role of felt challenge, job control, and psychological strain. *Journal of Vocational Behavior, 64,* 165–181.

107. Feldman, S. (1991, February). Today's EAPs make the grade. *Personnel, 68,* 3. See also Spangler, J. (1992, June 29). Assistance available for those under stress. *Amoco Torch,* pp. 1–2.

108. Leonard, B. (1993, July). The tough decision to use confidential information. *HR Magazine,* pp. 72–75; see also Schultz, E. E. (1994, May 26). If you use firm's counselors, remember your secrets could be used against you. *The Wall Street Journal,* p. C1.

109. Gaeta, E., Lynn, R., and Grey, L. (1982, May). AT&T looks at program evaluation. *EAP Digest,* pp. 22–31; see also Freudenheim, M. (1989, November 13). More aid for addicts on the job. *New York Times,* pp. 27, 39.

110. See Feldman, Today's EAPs make the grade.

111. Pynes, J. E. (1996). The two faces of unions. *Journal of Collective Negotiations in the Public Sector, 25,* 31–43.

112. Health Insurance Association of America. (1983). *Your guide to wellness at the worksite.* Washington, DC: Health Insurance Association of America, p. 3.

113. Harrison, D. A., and Liska, L. Z. (1994). Promoting regular exercise in organizational fitness programs: Health-related differences in motivational building blocks. *Personnel Psychology, 47,* 47–71.

114. Wolfe, R. A., Ulrich, D. O., and Parker, D. F. (1987). Employee health management programs: Review, critique, and research agenda. *Journal of Management, 13,* 603–615; see also Erfurt, J. C., Foote, A., and Heirich, M. A. (1992). The cost-effectiveness of worksite wellness programs for hypertension control, weight loss, smoking cessation, and exercise. *Personnel Psychology, 45,* 5–27; Moore, T. L. (1991). Build wellness from an EAP base. *Personnel Journal, 70,* 104.

115. Helmer, D. C., Dunn, L. M., Eaton, K., Macedonio, C., and Lubritz, L. (1995). Implementing corporate wellness programs. *AAOHN Journal, 43,* 558–563; see also Erfurt, Foote, and Heirich. The cost-effectiveness of worksite wellness programs.

116. Petersen, C. (1996). Work-hardening program pays big dividends. *Managed Healthcare, 6*(12), 43.

117. Epes, B. (1995, August). Start an employee wellness program. *Training & Development,* pp. 12–13.

118. See Helmer et al., Implementing corporate wellness programs.

119. Greenfeld, S. (1989, July). *Management's safety and health imperative: Eight essential steps to improving the work environment.* Occasional Paper 2.9. Cincinnati, OH: Xavier University, Minerva Education Institute. See also LaBar, G. (1996). Safety gets down to business. *Occupational Hazards, 58*(8), 23–28; Geller, *The psychology of safety*; Geller, *Working safe*; Geller, Ten principles for achieving a total safety culture; Guastella, Do we really know how well our occupational accident prevention programs work?

120. Jonas, P. (1996). The missing letter in TQM. *Occupational Health and Safety, 65,* 18–19.

121. Nwaelele, O. D. (1996). Prudent owners take proactive approach. *Professional Safety, 41,* 27–29.

122. Lamb, M. R. (1996). Safety is all in a day's work at A. M. Castle. *Metal Center News, 36,* 42–50.

123. Palmer, M. (1996). Now it's safety first. *Nursing Homes, 45,* 29–36.

124. McCurry, J. W. (1996). Milliken and Co.: Textile's king of safety. *Textile World, 146,* 76–80.

125. Zacharatos et al., High-performance work systems and occupational safety.

126. Costello, A. (1996). Your health is your wealth. *Accountancy Ireland, 28,* 10–12.

127. Stress in the workplace. (1996, May/June). *British Journal of Administrative Management,* pp. 8–9.

128. Ritcy, S. (1996). Psychological job matching. *OH and S Canada, 12,* 50–56.

129. Pasquarelli, T. (1996). Dealing with discomfort and danger. *HR Magazine, 41,* 104–110.

Name Index

Pearlman, K., 766
Pearlstein, Steven, 537, 538
Pearson, A. L., 754
Pellico, M. T., 773
Pemberton, C., 768
Pence, E. C., 762
Pepermans, R. G., 766
Perkins, Marilyn A., 739
Perloff, R., 769
Perrin, Charles, 47
Peter, L. J., 755
Peters, H., 770
Peters, L. H., 761
Peters, Richard, 510
Petersen, C., 788
Petersen, M. H., 758
Peterson, N. G., 111
Peyrefitte, J., 532, 761
Pfeffer, Jeffrey, 4–5, 21, 295, 365, 378, 749, 763, 766, 769, 777, 778, 783
Phillips, J. J., 766
Phillips, J. M., 755
Phillips, J. S., 502
Pickus, P. S., 777
Pierce, F. D., 786
Pierce, J. L., 779
Pikul, C., 520
Pinder, C. C., 782
Pinto, P. R., 753
Piotrowski, C., 770
Piskor, W. G., 755
Plaschke, B., 757
Ployhar, R. E., 759
Plummer, D. L., 767
Polk, Christopher, 513
Pollin, Ellen, 202
Popovich, P., 756
Porter, Michael E., 36, 750
Poteet, M. L., 771, 773
Potosky, D., 759
Potter, G., 778
Povall, J., 776
Prasad, P., 768
Prasch, R. E., 776
Premack, S. L., 756, 781
Preston, Karen, 531
Prewett-Livingston, A. J., 760
Prewitt, M., 768
Prien, E. P., 759
Pritchard, R. D., 778
Prochaska, S. T., 770
Pulakos, E. D., 762
Pustay, R. W., 750
Putka, D. J., 754
Putney, D. M., 768
Pynes, Joan E., 631, 759, 784, 788

Q

Quaintance, M. K., 759
Quick, J. C., 786
Quinn, J. B., 770
Quinones, M. A., 763, 764, 765

R

Radebaugh, L. H., 750
Rader, M., 760
Raelin, J. A., 769
Rafaeli, A., 758
Rafalko, R. J., 780
Ragins, B. R., 771, 772
Raines, C., 17, 770, 781
Raines, G., 756
Ramanujam, V., 755

Ramsay, L. J., 760
Ramsey, R., 767
Ramsey, V. J., 768
Randolph, A. Philip, 453
Rankin, Randy, 511
Rao, Jerry, 12, 146
Rasmusson, E., 781
Raver, J. L., 752
Ravlin, E. C., 756
Raymark, P. H., 758, 760
Reace, D., 776
Read, W., 761
Reagan, Ronald, 476
Redeker, J. R., 785
Reed-Mendenhall, D., 767
Reich, Robert, 458, 529
Reider, M. H., 758
Reilly, R. R., 757, 759, 762
Reiss, A. D., 758
Reissman, L., 775
Renn, R. W., 755
Resch, J., 765
Reyes, Gregory L., 365
Reynolds, D. H., 759
Reynolds, L., 765
Ribeiro, O., 763
Richardson, R., 778
Richey, Brenda E., 563
Richter, A. S., 774
Rickett, D., 767
Rigby, Darrell, 140
Rigdon, J. E., 772
Riley, R. A., 771
Risher, H., 775
Risser, Rita, 215
Ristelhueber, R., 563
Ritcy, S., 789
Rivera, R. J., 762, 763
Rizzo, M., 759
Roberson, Q., 780
Roberts, D. S., 786
Robertson, J. T., 756
Robie, C., 758
Robin, Jennifer, 393, 534, 729
Robinson, G., 525
Robinson, R., 752
Rocco, J., 771
Rock, M. L., 775
Roebuck, M. C., 787
Roehling, M. V., 760, 788
Rollins, T., 779
Rolnick, A. L., 785
Roman, M. A., 762
Romney, Mitt, 533
Ronen, S., 210, 767
Ronkainen, I. A., 750
Roomkin, M., 783
Rosen, B., 424, 768, 774, 782
Rosen, H., 443
Rosen, S. D., 753
Rosenbloom, J. S., 776
Rosenthal, D. B., 759
Rosopa, P. J., 772
Ross, T. L., 779
Rosse, J. G., 755
Roth, P. L., 757, 758, 759, 778
Rothman, J., 754
Rotundo, M., 758
Rouen, D., 787
Roughton, J. E., 786
Rouiller, J. Z., 764
Rousch, P., 762
Rousseau, Denise M., 774, 780
Rowland, K. M., 755
Roy, Raman, 146

Rubenfeld, S., 779
Rubin, Jeff, 12, 146
Rubin, P., 778
Rubinstein, S. A., 783
Ruderman, M. N., 768
Rudolph, A. S., 759
Rundle, R. L., 787
Rupinski, M. T., 766
Rush, M. C., 788
Russell, C. J., 177, 757
Russell, D. W., 788
Russell, Joyce E. A., 245, 293, 527, 535, 661, 669, 673, 764, 765, 767, 768, 770, 771, 772, 773, 788
Russell, M. C., 788
Rust, K. G., 140
Ruttenberg, A., 773
Ryan, A. M., 163, 175, 185, 751, 756, 758, 760
Ryan, Mike, 512
Rynes, S. L., 366, 510, 749, 755, 756, 768, 774, 777, 778, 779, 780

S

Saari, Lise M., 206
Sabbaghian, Z., 765
Sacco, J. M., 760
Sackett, P. R., 754, 757, 758, 759, 766
Sadri, G., 771
Saks, A. M., 755, 781
Salas, Eduardo, 269, 764, 766, 767
Sales, E., 765
Salgado, J. F., 758
Salinger, R. D., 763
Salipante, P. F., 784
Salopek, J. J., 771
Salsburg, S. W., 783
Salsky, L. M., 762
Saltzstein, A. L., 773
Saltzstein, G. H., 773
Salvemini, N., 762
Sanchez, J. I., 753
Sanders, G., 751
Sandver, M. G., 755, 783, 784, 785
Sankey, K. S., 759
Santora, J. E., 767
Sanyal, R. N., 750
Sarchielli, G., 773
Sassi, Paul, 3
Saunders, D. M., 755
Sauner, A. M., 778
Savoie, E. J., 783
Savoie, M., 765
Scandura, T. A., 773
Scanlon, Joseph, 383
Scarpello, V. G., 64, 776, 777
Schaaf, D., 763, 765
Schaeffer, L. J., 776
Schalk, R., 773
Schaubroeck, J., 787, 788
Schaufeli, W. B., 788
Schein, E. H., 769
Schenkel-Savitt, S., 755
Schiller, Phillip, 25
Schimidt, F. L., 749
Schippmann. J. S., 753, 759
Schlageter, Diane, 153
Schlesinger, L. A., 771, 778
Schmidt, C. A., 750
Schmidt, D. W., 755
Schmidt, F. L., 510, 757, 758, 760, 766, 780, 781
Schmitt, N. W., 758, 759, 760, 763, 781
Schmodt, F. L., 749
Schneider, B., 754, 781

Company Index

Subject Index

D

Damages, 68
Danger pay, 358
Data collection methods, 97–98
Databases, privacy and, 137
Davis-Bacon Act, 344
De-skilling of the population, 246
Deadlock, in negotiations, 444
Decentralization, 135, 297, 483
Decision-making skills, 262
Defamation, 404
Defined benefit plans, 351–352
Defined contribution plans, 351–352
Degree statements, 335
Delayering, 297
Delphi technique, 135
Design, organizational, 9–10
Development; *see* Training and development
Developmental assignments, 46
Developmental programs, 308–310
Diaz v. Pan America, 62
Differential rate, 378
Dimensions, 197–198
Direct mail advertising, 154
Disabilities; *see* Americans with Disabilities
   Act (ADA)
Disability, long-term, 354
Discipline, of employees, 413–415
Discontinuities, marketplace, 48
Discretionary benefits, 348, 350–355; *see also*
   Compensation
Discrimination
   affirmative action, 70–73, 132–133,
      595–602
   age; *see* Age discrimination
   Civil Rights Act; *see* Civil Rights Act of 1964
   compensation, 530
   defined, 55–56
   disability; *see* Americans with Disabilities
      Act (ADA)
   disparate impact, 63–66, 73–74, 83, 94,
      224, 531
   downsizing and, 13
   filing a lawsuit, 62, 63
   gender, 224, 518–520
   illegal practices, 56–57
   in the interview, 202–204
   litigation involving, 14–15, 56, 58
   national origin, 56, 58
   pregnancy, 79–80, 330, 351
   race, 53–54, 56, 204, 523–524, 587–590
   religious, 513–514
   reverse, 54, 72, 74, 350, 595–602
   sex, 15, 56–59, 204
   statistics, 53–54
   in testing methods, 182
   toward women, 58–59, 518–520
Disguised-purpose attitudinal scales, 191–192
Disparate impact, 63–66, 73–74, 83, 94,
   224, 531
Displaced workers, 312
Dispositional testing, 184, 186–188
Dispute resolution, 83, 416–417, 465–466,
   725–728
Dissatisfaction, with work, 430
Distance learning, 256, 267–268
Distributive bargaining, 441
Distributive justice, 395–396
Diversification, 32
Diversity
   advertising and, 154
   changing workforce, 15–18
   downsizing and, 143
   minority hiring, 160
   programs for, 70–73

recruitment and, 132–133, 134
training for, 283–284, 524–525
Downsizing; *see also* Layoffs
   approach to, 715–724
   career development and, 297
   discrimination and, 13, 141, 143
   diversity and, 132–133, 143
   implementing, 139–141
   organizational exit, 418–425
   problems with, 141
   recommendations, 311
   strategic planning and, 10
Draw-plus commission system, 380
Drug and alcohol abuse; *see also* Employee
   health and safety
   ADA and, 75–76, 415
   employee assistance programs, 354, 493,
      501–504
   policy development, 739
   programs for, 145, 194–195
   testing for, 194–195, 485–488
Drug Free Workplace Act, 486, 502
Dual-career couples, 317, 499
Dukes v. Wal-Mart, 67, 518–520
Duty of fair representation doctrine, 449
Duty to bargain, 441

E

E-learning, 264, 266–267
E-learning Readiness Self-Assessment, 256
E-mentoring, 309–310
E-Span Interactive Employment Network, 151
E-Verify, 138–139
Early retirement, 141, 423
Economic capability, 26
Education, 7, 95–96, 354
Educational allowances, 359
EEO-1 form, 59–61
EEOC, 15, 59–62
EEOC v. Detroit Edison, 153
Effectiveness, 331
Efficiency, 331
Efficiency indices, 252, 254
Egalitarian culture, 372
80 percent rule, 65, 224
Elder care services, 319
Electronic learning, 264, 266–267
Electronic monitoring, 241–242
Electronic Privacy Information Center, 405
Electronic recruiting, 157–160
Electronic surveillance, 241
Emotional Intelligence (EI), 186
Emotional stability, 186, 189
Empirical validity, 174
Employability, 296
Employee assistance programs (EAP), 354,
   493, 501–504
Employee Benefit Plan Review, 501
Employee benefits; *see also* Compensation
   cafeteria style, 44, 347–348, 355
   child care, 319, 347, 355
   communicating the programs, 355–356
   discretionary, 348, 350–355
   elder care, 319
   employee services, 354–355
   employee welfare programs, 350–351
   401(k), 352–354
   health care, 350–351
   importance of, 346
   legally required benefits, 348–350
   mental health, 347, 354
   paternity leave, 318–319
   pension plans, 351–354
   tax advantages, 347
   time-off programs, 354

trends in, 347
unions and, 453
Employee feedback, 407–410
Employee Free Choice Act, 433, 536–537
Employee handbook, 393, 410–413
Employee health and safety, 459–507
   accidents; *see* Accidents
   AIDS, 484–485
   common injuries/diseases, 462–463
   drugs in the workplace; *see* Drug and
      alcohol abuse
   employee assistance programs, 354, 493,
      501–504
   hazardous materials, 461, 468
   impact on productivity, 462
   incentive system, 483
   job burnout, 462, 500
   legal issues, 463–479
   noise level, 463
   OSHA; *see* Occupational Safety and Health
      Administration (OSHA)
   principles of a total safety culture, 479–480
   program development, 740–742
   repetitive strain injury, 461–462, 495, 497
   right-to-know, 463
   safety rules, 483–484
   safety training, 481–482, 493–494
   smoking in the workplace, 488–489, 738
   steps to improve, 505
   stress, 462, 465, 497–501, 502, 538
   training and, 481–482, 493–494
   video display terminals, 495, 496
   violation of safety laws, 460
   violence in the workplace, 490–495
   wellness and fitness, 350, 504–505
   workers' compensation, 349, 464–466
Employee leasing, 142
Employee Polygraph Protection Act, 192
Employee recognition programs, 354–355;
   see also Reward systems
Employee referral program, 153, 191
Employee Retirement Income Security Act
   (ERISA), 15, 330, 331, 351
Employee satisfaction, 19–20, 24–25
Employee stock ownership plan (ESOP),
   353–354, 364–365, 373, 381, 385–386
Employee surveys, 407–410
Employee theft, 192–193
Employee turnover, 20–21
Employee welfare programs, 350–351
Employee wellness and fitness programs,
   504–505
Employer Policy Foundation, 341
Employment agencies, 154
Employment-at-will doctrine, 55, 403–404, 413,
   418, 533–534
Employment laws, 402–407
Employment processing outsourcing (EPO), 155
Employment relationships, 393–426
   employee handbooks, 393, 410–413
   employee surveys, 407–410
   ethics programs, 24, 396–397, 534–535
   grievances, 415–418, 447–448
   internal forces affecting, 407–413
   laws affecting, 402–407
   organizational entry, 397–402
   organizational exit, 418–425
   organizational justice, 394–396
   policy violations/discipline, 413–415
Employment screening, 178–179
Employment status, 397–398
Empowerment, 117
Engagement, 19–20
Enrichment, of jobs, 117
Enterprise resource planning systems, 105
Enterprise unions, 455